EVERYONE'S MONEY BOOK

SECOND EDITION

JORDAN E. GOODMAN

Dearborn
Financial Publishing, Inc.®

Editorial Director: Cynthia A. Zigmund
Managing Editor: Jack Kiburz
Interior Design: The Publishing Services Group
Cover Design: Design Alliance, Inc.

©1995, 1998 by Amherst Enterprises, Ltd.

Published by Dearborn Financial Publishing, Inc.®

Printed in the United States of America

98 99 00 10 9 8 7 6 5 4 3 2 1

Library of Congress Cataloging-in-Publication Data

Goodman, Jordan Elliot.
    Everyone's money book / Jordan E. Goodman. — 2nd ed.
        p.   cm.
    Includes bibliographical references and index.
    ISBN 0-7931-2869-2 (hardcover)
    1. Finance, Personal. 2. Investments. I. Title.
    HG179.G675   1998   98-12793
    332.024—dc21   CIP

Dequeuecation

Dedication

To my wife, Suzanne, whose unwavering support throughout months of unrelenting work made this book possible, and my son, Jason, who also helped his daddy complete "The Money Book" even though it was hard for him to understand why Daddy was unavailable to play with him for so long.

Acknowledgments

Everyone's Money Book would not have been possible without the generous contributions and extremely hard work of many talented people.

Foremost among these contributors are the staff of Dearborn Financial Publishing, who exhibited incredible team spirit and professionalism in making this book a reality. Editorial Director Cynthia Zigmund recognized the need to revise and update what has become a classic work in the field of personal finance, adding not only the latest resources but also the many sections on how to maximize the use of your computer to improve your personal financial management.

Managing Editor Jack Kiburz skillfully guided the second edition through the process from original manuscript to final published work.

Many other people at Dearborn were enormously important in making the concept of *Everyone's Money Book* a reality. Robert Kyle, chairman of the board, and Anita Constant, former senior vice president, provided unwavering support for all phases of the first edition. President Dennis Blitz was equally supportive of the revised and updated version. Paul Mallon, sales director, enthusiastically gave the book his full backing. Todd Sanders of the Publishing Services Group produced many well-designed renderings, which will help you understand complex concepts more clearly. Production Director Bee Svennson-Guinan helped coordinate the timely printing and binding of the book. Art Director Lucy Jenkins contributed her invaluable assistance with the color and design of the dust jacket. The staff of the dotted i worked without complaint to typeset this book under extremely tight deadlines and displayed enormous flexibility in meeting our schedules. I also appreciate the efforts of Editorial Assistant Sandra Holzbach and indexer Sharon Johnson.

Special thanks are due to copyeditor of the first edition Linda Langan, who consistently tightened up and improved my prose and whose thoughtful questions prodded me into making the book as reader-friendly as possible.

I thank *Money* magazine Managing Editor Frank Lalli, Assistant Managing Editor Frank B. Merrick and Associate Publisher Betsy Martin for their support and encouragement of this project, including their willingness to allow me to take a leave of absence to work on the book.

I also offer my heartfelt gratitude to the many people who reviewed every word of *Everyone's Money Book* for accuracy and style. Elliot R. Goodman, professor emeritus of political science at Brown University, and Norma B. Goodman, an astute investor, meticulously reviewed the entire book and suggested hundreds of helpful improvements. As my parents, their contribution extended far beyond the call of parental duty.

Each of the individual chapters was also reviewed by a highly esteemed expert in the relevant field, often an author of a Dearborn book on the subject:

- Loretta Nolan, a certified financial planner and president of Nolan Associates in Greenwich, Connecticut, who skillfully offered suggestions on Chapter 1, "Giving Yourself a Financial Checkup."

- Mark Skousen, editor of the investment newsletter, *Forecasts & Strategies,* author of *Scrooge Investing* and coauthor of *High Finance on a Low Budget,* thoroughly reviewed Chapter 2 on cash instruments.

- Gene Walden, author of *The 100 Best Stocks To Own in America,* scrutinized Chapter 3 on stocks.

- Stephen Littauer, author of *How To Buy Mutual Funds the Smart Way,* checked Chapter 4 on mutual funds for accuracy.

- Gerald Krefetz, author of the *Making the Most of Your Money Series,* offered several helpful comments on Chapter 5 about bonds.

- William F. Eng, the author and international lecturer of technical analysis and market psychology books, including *Options: Trading Strategies That Work, Trading Rules* and many other books, reviewed Chapter 6 on futures and options.

- Bart Sotnick, staff director of press and community relations for the New York Federal Reserve Bank, graciously shared his expertise on Treasury bills.

- John H. Lutley, president of The Gold Institute, in Washington, D.C., checked the accuracy of the gold section in Chapter 7, and David J. Maloney, a professional appraiser and author of *Maloney's Antiques & Collectibles Resource Directory,* provided invaluable guidance on the collectibles section in Chapter 7.

- Peter G. Miller, author of *The Common-Sense Mortgage* and several other titles and creator and host of the "Real Estate Forum" with America Online and Betty Rubin, a long-time real estate agent in Oceanside, California, both of whom ably reviewed Chapter 8 on real estate.

- Richard G. Wollack, chairman of Liquidity Fund Management Incorporated in Emeryville, California, and author of *Limited Partnerships: How To Profit in the Secondary Market,* provided his wise counsel on Chapter 9 about limited partnerships.

- John Ventura, an attorney at his Texas law firm of Ventura & Thrasher and author of *The Credit Repair Kit* and *The Bankruptcy Kit,* offered several valuable suggestions on Chapter 10 about credit.

- W. Allan Wilbur, executive director of public affairs at the National Automobile Dealers Association in McLean, Virginia, was helpful in reviewing Chapter 11 on buying a car.

- Ted Burton of the Dearborn Financial Institute provided expertise on the property and casualty section of Chapter 12 on insurance. The staff of the Insurance Information Institute in New York City reviewed the car insurance section of Chapter 12. Anne Shropshire, CLU, Insurance Division, Dearborn Financial Publishing in Chicago, commented on the disability, health and life insurance sections of Chapter 12.

- Anna Leider, president of Octameron Associates in Alexandria, Virginia, and coauthor of *Don't Miss Out: The Ambitious Student's Guide to Financial Aid* and several other books about funding college, was very helpful in her review of Chapter 13 on financing college education.

- James A. Marino, P.C., a prominent tax attorney in Chicago, was most helpful in reviewing Chapter 14 on tax planning.

- Chester H. Greenspan, a prominent estate planning lawyer and certified financial planner in Queens, New York, reviewed Chapter 16 on estate planning.

- The staff of the employee benefits consulting firm of Kwasha Lipton, in Fort Lee, New Jersey, assembled by Communications Director Ted Barna, ensured the accuracy of Chapter 17 on employee benefits.

- Several specialists in the seven fields of personal finance were consulted on Chapter 18 on finding financial advisers. One of the most helpful was Edith Lank, syndicated columnist and author of many professional real estate books, who provided valuable insights on the real estate section.

- Several experts in their respective fields, whose guidance proved beneficial, reviewed Chapter 15 on retirement and Chapter 19 on strategies for every age and situation.

In addition, I would like to thank the many organizations and publishers who gave me the permission to reprint tables, graphs and charts that are used throughout the book. These organizations are identified with a credit line under all the material they provided.

Photographer Rob Kinmouth deserves credit for taking the wonderful photographs of Jordan Goodman that appear on the cover and flap jacket.

I am also indebted to Daniel Christmas of Design Alliance, Inc., who worked long and hard to create a wonderful cover design. Cynthia Friedman, an accomplished art director for many publications and a good friend, also offered many helpful suggestions on the cover design, for which I am most grateful.

I greatly appreciate all the efforts of Pamela Irwin and Stefan Malter, who diligently checked and updated thousands of names, addresses and telephone numbers and added Web site addresses for the resources throughout this version of the book.

Many other people, some of whom wish to remain anonymous, also generously gave their time and expertise on a wide range of topics to support my efforts to create the most accurate *Everyone's Money Book* possible. I thank them all.

Although I have attempted to make the "Resources" sections as complete and accurate as possible, please forgive any errors that may have crept in or addresses and telephone numbers that may have changed since this book went to press.

In particular, the fast-changing world of the Internet means that every day there are new Web sites being created and old ones that disappear or become inactive. The financial world is one of constant dynamic change, and this book should provide you with the resources you need to maximize your financial potential.

Jordan E. Goodman
March 1, 1998

Table of Contents

List of Figures

Preface

No one will ever care about your personal financial situation as much as you do. Sure, you can hire financial advisers to help you through the thicket of complex investment decisions, tax planning, insurance programs and employee benefits. But at the end of the day, *you* will have to make the final decisions about financial matters that will affect your present and future lifestyles—as well as the financial well-being of your family.

To make those decisions intelligently, you must be armed with knowledge. If you don't understand the basics of money and personal finance, you may fall prey to some adviser who is more concerned with his or her own financial welfare than with yours. No get-rich-quick schemes really work; if they did, the schemers would not be trying to convince you to give them your money—they would be aboard their yachts in the Caribbean.

Because you are reading this book, you are clearly interested in taking charge of your finances. That is a very important first step. For some strange reason, most people work extremely hard for their money all their lives but never make the effort to maximize that money. People tend to neglect money decisions out of either fear or inertia and pay little attention to where their money is coming from or where it is going. They often live paycheck to paycheck. If you spend 99½ percent of your time earning money and less than a half of 1 percent of your time managing it, the time has come to change. By bumping up that half of 1 percent to even 5 percent or so, you can make your money work for you much more effectively and, in the process, start to realize some of your lifetime goals, which previously might have seemed unattainable. Your money can work either for you or against you; the difference depends on whether you control your money or it controls you.

This book is designed to help you gain control of your finances as easily as possible. I have spent years answering questions from people just like you on call-in radio and television shows, so I am well aware of what you need to know to get your financial act together. One of the most common questions I get is: "If I want to buy just one book that will explain this whole subject in a very understandable way, which would it be?" I surveyed the market, and despite all the personal finance books out there, none has really covered the field as comprehensively and accessibly as it could have. That's why I wrote *Everyone's Money Book* and set it up the way I did—loaded with easy-to-use worksheets, step-by-step instructions, charts, graphs, application forms and quizzes.

If you own a personal computer, you may be interested in using the software designed to complement this text. Called *Everyone's Money Software,* it allows you to enter your own numbers on all the worksheets exactly as they appear in the book. The software permits you to test various assumptions to see how the numbers work out. For example, you can calculate your monthly mortgage payment at different interest rates and with various down payments. Or you can determine how much money you will accumulate for retirement at varying levels of savings and rates of return. For more information on how to obtain this software, please call 800-553-9997.

Following each chapter is an annotated list of resources, including books, magazines, newsletters, newspapers, pamphlets and software. Many of the federal and state government agencies, trade associations and other private organizations cited offer free or low-cost publications. Taken together, the end-of-chapter resources comprise the most extensive directory of resources ever assembled in one personal finance book.

This updated version of *Everyone's Money Book* has even more resources than the original one first published in 1993. In particular, it features extensive listings of ways to use your personal computer to improve your finances. Most chapters have lists of computer programs, online services, Web sites and other computerized resources that can make your financial life more efficient, and save and make you a huge amount of money. For example, if you do your banking online, trade stocks and mutual funds through online discount brokers, and find the lowest-cost insurance policies and lowest-interest credit cards on the Web, you can make your investment in computer hardware, software and online services pay off many times over.

Solving the Mystery of Personal Finance

I know that many people and organizations in the money business have a vested interest in keeping financial knowledge as mysterious as possible, creating as much anxiety as possible, so that you pay them to explain it all and calm you down. I disagree wholeheartedly with this practice. I think that you can understand these matters well enough to feel as conversant with them as you do with your full-time work. Once you feel comfortable with the subject, you will no longer be intimidated by experts; instead, you will gain confidence to make your own decisions in your own best interest.

This book is designed to be used in many different ways at many different points in your life. Whatever your age or family situation, you will find material here to help you. You can put some information to use right away for immediate results, while other subjects might not apply to you right now. Remember, you can always return later to sections that you don't need at your present stage of life. As you become more knowledgeable about an area of personal finance, reread the corresponding chapters to learn even more, or follow up on the "Resources" sections to gain an in-depth understanding of the subject. Don't be discouraged if at first some subjects intimidate you. The world of personal finance is complicated, and you always have more to learn. I've tried to make the complex as simple and easy to understand as possible.

Maximizing Your Investment Options

The first part of the book helps you maximize your investment options. Chapter 1, "Giving Yourself a Financial Checkup," helps you determine where you stand now financially and where you want to be in the future. I help you calculate your net worth, define your financial goals, analyze your cash flow and assess your tolerance for risk, all in preparation for outlining a comprehensive personal financial plan. Then I help you set up a budget that you can stick to so you can turn your hopes into reality.

Once you've assessed your current situation and formulated a plan for the future, I explain the many tools you need to accomplish your goals. I discuss key investment alternatives, including cash instruments like CDs and money funds; stocks, mutual funds and bonds; futures and options; gold, other precious metals and collectibles; and real estate and limited partnerships.

Financing Your Present and Future Needs

In the second part of the book, I help you in financing your present and future needs. I begin by explaining the ins and outs of credit—when it makes sense to borrow and when it doesn't, both for everyday needs and for long-term uses like buying a home or car. I then guide you to the best ways to shop for and finance a new or used car. Next, I explain how to calculate how much auto, disability, health, homeowner's and life insurance you need and how to obtain the greatest coverage at the lowest cost. The following chapter discusses the complex subject of financing your children's college education—how to establish a savings plan and how to help your children apply for and win educational scholarships, grants and loans.

I continue with an overview of tax planning, offering advice on how to maximize deductions, exemptions and credits and minimize your tax liability. This chapter and the entire book are completely up to date as of the Taxpayer Relief Act of 1997, passed by Congress and signed into law by President Clinton in August 1997. This tax-planning chapter also summarizes the key provisions of the 1997 act.

The next chapter guides you through the process of planning for your retirement—a stage of life that creeps up on you much faster than you can ever imagine. I help you calculate how much you need to save and how much income you can expect from Social Security, pensions and your own investments. I then offer advice on choosing among various retirement lifestyles.

The final chapter of this second part explains what estate-planning steps you can take to pass your assets on to your heirs and minimize estate taxes.

Controlling Your Financial Destiny

The last part of the book also helps you take control of your financial future. It begins with a chapter explaining how to make the most of your employee benefits. Your company may offer many benefits you do not understand and therefore do not take advantage of. This chapter should help you get as much from your employer as possible.

I then guide you in choosing financial advisers who put their clients' interests ahead of their own. It can be quite difficult to locate accountants, bankers, financial planners, lawyers, money managers and other financial experts who put their clients ahead of their own interests. This chapter will supply the questions you need to ask potential advisers and the skills that will help you separate the worthy professionals from the incompetents.

The final chapter offers a perspective on each of the topics discussed in previous chapters, keyed to your age and family situation. I explain the special factors you should consider in all aspects of personal finance when you are in your 20s and 30s, 40s and 50s, and 60s and up. In addition, I offer customized counsel on all areas of personal finance to singles, married couples, both with and without children, and widows, widowers and divorcees.

So let's get started! All you have to lose is your fear of financial matters; all you have to gain is *control of your financial destiny.*

ANNOUNCING THE *MONEY ANSWERS CATALOG!*

To make it as easy as possible for you to save and earn thousands of dollars, I have designed the Money Answers Catalog as a service to you. I have selected many of the most helpful resources from *Everyone's Money Book,* as well as many other resources that are not found in the book, to include in a catalog that will make it much easier for you to order the products and services you need. You can find out about helpful books, newsletters, audiotapes, videotapes, software, buying services and much more through the Money Answers Catalog. Instead of having to call several phone numbers or write to many companies, you can get quick access to whatever you need with just one phone call.

Through the catalog, you can also find out about subscribing to *Everyone's Money Newsletter,* which will keep you up-to-date on the latest trends and resources in personal finance to help you save and make money. The newsletter answers your finance questions and alerts you to opportunities to cut expenses and increase investment returns. It also includes the best columns from many of the finest personal finance writers in the country on such subjects as taxes, saving, mutual funds, investing, insurance, real estate and credit.

The catalog is divided into several categories, including:

- **General reference.** Books, software, videos and other products that will help you organize your financial affairs and do effective financial planning

- **Investing.** Newsletters, books, software and online services providing the latest information on the highest-yielding CDs, best mutual funds, dividend reinvestment plans, no-load stocks, collectible trends, and much more.

- **Credit cards.** The Credit Card Optimizer that will guide you to the lowest-interest credit cards and help you improve your credit rating

- **Insurance.** Books, newsletters and services that will help you shop for the most insurance coverage at the lowest cost and give you the latest information on annuities and long-term health care coverage

- **Real estate.** Newsletters, audiotapes, videotapes and software that will help you get the best deal when buying or selling a home, rental property or commercial real estate. You will also find out about a service that will let you identify the cheapest mortgage you can qualify for anywhere in the country, and a buyer's broker location service that will help you find a broker working on your behalf when you buy a home

- **Automobiles.** Books and car-buying services that will arm you to get the best deal on a car lease or purchase

- **College financing.** Books and videotapes that will guide you through the maze of financing your children's college education, as well as services that will help you locate grants, scholarships and loans your child may qualify for

- **Retirement planning.** Newsletters, books and software that will help you plan for retirement and enjoy your golden years.

- **Estate planning.** Books and software that will help you compose a will or living trust and make other important estate planning moves

- **Money troubles.** Books and legal forms kits to help you deal with various money problems, such as bankruptcy, divorce, widowhood and a bad credit history

- **Financial advisers.** A service to help you check out financial advisers you may be thinking of working with to see if they have had any record of criminal or civil misbehavior

To get your copy of the Money Answers Catalog, send $3 by check or money order (made out to Money Answers Catalog) to:

> Money Answers Catalog
> Suite 605
> 1932 First Avenue
> Seattle, WA 98101

Please include your name and address with your request so that we can serve you better. You can also order a catalog for $3 on a credit card by calling 800-553-9997.

PART
I

*Maximizing
Your
Investment
Options*

1

Giving Yourself a
Financial Checkup

Before you can figure out how to improve your financial condition, you must take stock of where you are right now; that is, you must compute your net worth. Calculating your net worth is like weighing in before the championship fight. To find out what you weigh (financially, that is), you add up the total value of what you already own, known as your *assets,* and subtract the amount of debt you owe, known as your *liabilities.* This bottom line is known as your *net worth.* It is a snapshot in time, good only for the moment you calculate it. Consider this photo the first in a lifelong album of financial achievements. Your first statement gives you a benchmark to compare yourself against as your net worth grows over the years.

Determining Your Net Worth

By doing this exercise, you will be able to see clearly how your assets and liabilities match (or mismatch). As you find ways to control your spending, pay off your debts and increase your savings and investment assets, you can make your net worth grow, which, in turn, will permit you to reach your financial goals. If you are doing all the wrong things, like increasing your debt and depleting your savings, this will show up quickly in your net worth as well.

Calculating your net worth is also important because it lets you see at a glance whether you are accumulating enough assets to support yourself comfortably in retirement and how much money you will have to pass on to your heirs. Having a current net worth statement will also come in handy when you apply for loans, such as a mortgage, or for financial aid for your children's college education because lenders will require you to show your assets and liabilities on the application.

While you will want to compute your net worth once a year to track how you're doing, it is particularly important to do the exercise when there has been a major change in your financial situation. That might mean when you become eligible to receive an employee benefit like a pension, when you buy a home or car, when you contribute to a Keogh or an individual retirement account (IRA), or when your Aunt Sally dies and leaves you a big inheritance.

ASSETS

There are five classes of assets. What distinguishes one kind from another is how quickly you can turn it into cash or, put another way, how liquid it is. The more liquid an asset, the easier it is to put a value on it. For instance, you know exactly what the $102.55 in your checking account is worth, but you would probably have to ask a local real estate agent or appraiser to give you the current worth of your house or apartment.

Because of the different levels of liquidity of different assets, we suggest that you separate your assets into these five classes:

Current assets. Current assets are easily convertible into cash. This includes bank accounts, money-market mutual funds and Treasury securities. For each of the bank accounts, list the name of the bank where the asset is held and the current yield. Also list the yield on Treasury bills, which mature in a year or less, and U.S. savings bonds, which you can cash in any time as long as you have held them for at least six months. If you have overpaid your taxes and are due a refund from the Internal Revenue Service (IRS) or your state tax department, you should also count that as a current asset. If you are owed a bonus or commission within the next few months, that counts as current, too.

Securities. These include publicly traded stocks, bonds, mutual funds, futures contracts, warrants and options. The current market values of all such securities are available in most major newspapers, particularly *The Wall Street Journal,* as well as from your broker or from stock quotation services, such as Dow Jones News Retrieval, that you connect to by computer. For each security, list your purchase price, the number of units held (such as shares of stock), the percentage yield it pays (a dividend for a stock, interest for a bond) and when it matures (for a bond, a futures contract or an option).

Real estate. Real estate includes first and second homes, condominiums, cooperatives, rental properties and real estate limited partnerships. The current worth of all real estate should be based on appraisals from knowledgeable local experts like appraisers or real estate agents. Remember to subtract all selling costs, such as the standard 6 percent real estate broker's commission. For partnerships, list the general managing partner who is running the operation, the yield being paid to you, if any, and the year you expect the partnership to be liquidated and the proceeds to be paid out to you. Also include any mortgage loans that may be due you, such as on a house you sold on which you granted a loan.

Long-term assets. These include the cash value of life insurance policies; the worth of annuities, pensions and profit-sharing plans; IRAs and Keogh plans; any long-term loans due you; any long-term royalties due you from writing a book or having patented an invention that is still selling; and any interests you have in an ongoing business. Long-term assets are often difficult to value because you have access to their true worth only several years, or even decades, from now. Still, your life insurance company will give you the current value of policies and annuities, and your employer will tell you what your pension and profit-sharing plans would be worth if you left the company now. Valuing your interest in a closely held business is particularly tricky, but it can be done. Ask your partners what they would be willing to pay if you wanted to cash in your share. (To some extent, that depends on how actively involved in the business you are and how key it is for the business to have your services available.) You can also get some idea from a business broker who specializes in selling and buying the kind of business in which you are involved.

Personal property. Personal property such as cars, jewelry, collectibles and home furnishings should be valued at whatever you think they could be sold for now in their present condition. In valuing personal property, try to be as realistic as possible. Don't just put down what you think they are worth; this number is often inflated. You should try to get some sense of the market when you value things. For instance, check with a used-car dealer, the used-car ads in your newspaper or the *National Automobile Dealers Association Blue Book* to see what your car's model and year is now worth. Bring any rare coins or stamps into a reputable dealer for an appraisal. For antiques or other collectibles, contact a local member of the American Society of Appraisers, found in the *Yellow Pages.*

In the Assets Worksheet in Figure 1.1, you should make a detailed list of not only which assets you have but also who holds the titles to them. If you are married, you can own property jointly or separately. (See Chapter 15, "Estate Planning—Keeping Your Assets in the Family," for guidance on the best way to hold assets.) Some assets, like a securities portfolio for a child, may be held in a trust for which the parents are responsible until the child turns 18 years old. If you need more space for any category as you fill out the worksheets, copy that page and attach it to your worksheet.

LIABILITIES

Liabilities, or what you owe others, are not as much fun to add up as assets, but you've got to tote them anyway. Remember, the people and institutions to whom you owe money count your liabilities as their assets.

Liabilities should be divided into short- and long-term categories, just as assets are. That's because some debts you need to pay back very soon, like current bills

Figure 1.1   Assets Worksheet

Assets	Date Purchased	Original $ Value	Current Date	Current $ Value
1. Current Assets				
Bonuses or Commissions (due you)	_____	$ _____	_____	$ _____
Certificates of Deposit	_____	_____	_____	_____
	_____	_____	_____	_____
Checking Accounts	_____	_____	_____	_____
	_____	_____	_____	_____
Credit Union Accounts	_____	_____	_____	_____
Money-Market Accounts	_____	_____	_____	_____
	_____	_____	_____	_____
Savings Accounts	_____	_____	_____	_____
	_____	_____	_____	_____
Savings Bonds	_____	_____	_____	_____
	_____	_____	_____	_____
Tax Refunds (due you)	_____	_____	_____	_____
Treasury Bills	_____	_____	_____	_____
	_____	_____	_____	_____
TOTAL CURRENT ASSETS		$ _____		$ _____
2. Securities				
Bonds (type of bond)				
_____	_____	$ _____	_____	$ _____
_____	_____	_____	_____	_____
_____	_____	_____	_____	_____
_____	_____	_____	_____	_____
Bond Mutual Funds				
_____	_____	_____	_____	_____
_____	_____	_____	_____	_____
Individual Stocks				
_____	_____	_____	_____	_____
_____	_____	_____	_____	_____
_____	_____	_____	_____	_____
_____	_____	_____	_____	_____
_____	_____	_____	_____	_____

Figure 1.1 (continued)

Assets	Date Purchased	Original $ Value	Current Date	Current $ Value
Stock Mutual Funds		$		$
Futures				
Warrants and Options				
TOTAL SECURITIES		**$**		**$**

3. Real Estate

Mortgage Receivable (due you)		$		$
Primary Residence				
Rental Property				
Real Estate Limited Partnerships				
Second Home				
TOTAL REAL ESTATE		**$**		**$**

4. Long-Term Assets

Annuities		$		$
IRAs				
Keogh Accounts				
Life Insurance Cash Values				
Loans Receivable (due you)				
Pensions				
Private Business Interests				
Profit-Sharing Plans				
Royalties				
Salary Reduction Plans (401(k), 403(b), 457 plans)				
TOTAL LONG-TERM ASSETS		**$**		**$**

Figure 1.1   Assets Worksheet (continued)

Assets	Date Purchased	Original $ Value	Current Date	Current $ Value
5. Personal Property				
Antiques	_____	$ _____	_____	$ _____
Appliances (washing machines, dishwashers, vacuum cleaners, etc.)	_____	_____	_____	_____
Automobiles	_____	_____	_____	_____
Boats, etc.	_____	_____	_____	_____
Campers, Trailers, etc.	_____	_____	_____	_____
Clothing	_____	_____	_____	_____
Coin Collections	_____	_____	_____	_____
Computers, etc.	_____	_____	_____	_____
Furniture	_____	_____	_____	_____
Furs	_____	_____	_____	_____
Home Entertainment Equipment (CD players, stereos, televisions, VCRs, etc.)	_____	_____	_____	_____
Home Furnishings (drapes, blankets, etc.)	_____	_____	_____	_____
Jewelry	_____	_____	_____	_____
Lighting Fixtures	_____	_____	_____	_____
Motorcycles, etc.	_____	_____	_____	_____
Paintings and Sculptures	_____	_____	_____	_____
Pools, etc.	_____	_____	_____	_____
Stamp Collections	_____	_____	_____	_____
Tableware (glasses, plates, silverware, etc.)	_____	_____	_____	_____
Tools, etc.	_____	_____	_____	_____
Other	_____	_____	_____	_____
TOTAL PERSONAL PROPERTY		$ _____		$ _____
TOTAL ASSETS		$ _____		$ _____

or credit cards, while other debts, like mortgages or college loans, will take years to repay. In the Liabilities Worksheet (see Figure 1.2), you should list to whom you owe money, the interest rate you are paying, if any, when the loan comes due if there is such a maturity date and how much money you owe.

You should use the following four main categories for listing your liabilities:

Current liabilities. These are debts you must pay within the next six months. In this category would be bills from the utilities (the telephone company, the electric company, the gas company, the oil company), physicians and dentists, home repair contractors, retail stores and other short-term creditors. You should also include regular alimony or child support payments if these apply to you. If you owe money to a relative or friend who helped you out in a pinch, make sure to include that debt as well in this category.

Unpaid taxes. These taxes might be due either on April 15 or as part of your quarterly estimated tax payments to both the IRS and your state tax department. They include not only income taxes but also the capital gains taxes you owe on an asset you have sold for a profit. You should also include local property taxes, which you may have to pay directly, or which may be paid by the bank that holds your mortgage. If you owe any sales taxes on purchases you have made recently, put that down as well. Finally, if you are self-employed, you must make sure to account for Social Security self-employment taxes.

Real estate debt. This category of debt includes both first and second mortgages on your primary residence and on any second (or even third, if you should be so lucky) home you may have. It also includes any mortgages you owe on rental properties that are producing income. On a separate line, list any home equity loans outstanding on your first or second home.

Installment debt. Installment debt covers all loans you have committed to pay off over a period of time. This category includes automobile loans from either a car dealer or a bank; bank loans taken out to consolidate bills or for any other purpose, including overdraft loans attached to your checking account; education loans from your college or university; loans to pay for equipment or appliances, including computers; furniture loans; home improvement loans; life insurance loans taken against the cash value in your policies; and margin loans from a brokerage house taken against the value of your securities. If you have lost a lawsuit and there is a liability judgment against you, that should be considered part of the installment debt you owe.

Finally, if you have borrowed against your pension plan at work, which is usually some form of salary reduction plan, you normally are obligated to pay it back by payroll deduction over five years. This obligation should also be counted as installment debt. Credit card charges from MasterCard, Visa, American Express, Diners Club, Discover, as well as retail stores, on which you owe at least the minimum payment, should also be noted in this category because you control when to pay off the outstanding balance.

Figure 1.2   Liabilities Worksheet

Liabilities	To Whom	Interest Rate %	Due Date	Amount Due $
1. Current Liabilities				
Alimony	_____	_____	_____	$ _____
Bills				
Electric & Gas	_____	_____	_____	_____
Home Contractor	_____	_____	_____	_____
Oil Company	_____	_____	_____	_____
Physician & Dentist	_____	_____	_____	_____
Retail Stores	_____	_____	_____	_____
Telephone	_____	_____	_____	_____
Other	_____	_____	_____	_____
Child Support	_____	_____	_____	_____
Loans to Individuals	_____	_____	_____	_____
TOTAL CURRENT LIABILITIES				$ _____
2. Unpaid Taxes				
Income Taxes				
Federal	_____	_____	_____	$ _____
State	_____	_____	_____	_____
Capital Gains Taxes				
Federal	_____	_____	_____	_____
State	_____	_____	_____	_____
Property Taxes	_____	_____	_____	_____
Sales Taxes				
Locality	_____	_____	_____	_____
Social Security Taxes (self-employed)	_____	_____	_____	_____
TOTAL UNPAID TAXES				$ _____
3. Real Estate Liabilities				
Home # 1				
First Mortgage	_____	_____	_____	$ _____
Second Mortgage	_____	_____	_____	_____
Home Equity Loan	_____	_____	_____	_____

Figure 1.2 (continued)

Liabilities	To Whom	Interest Rate %	Due Date	Amount Due $
Home # 2				
First Mortgage	_____	_____	_____	$ _____
Second Mortgage	_____	_____	_____	_____
Home Equity Loan	_____	_____	_____	_____
Rental Property				
First Mortgage	_____	_____	_____	_____
Second Mortgage	_____	_____	_____	_____
TOTAL REAL ESTATE LIABILITIES				$ _____

4. Installment Liabilities

Liabilities	To Whom	Interest Rate %	Due Date	Amount Due $
Automobile Loans	_____	_____	_____	$ _____
Bank Loans for Bill Consolidation	_____	_____	_____	_____
Credit Cards	_____	_____	_____	_____
Education Loans	_____	_____	_____	_____
Equipment and Appliance Loans	_____	_____	_____	_____
Furniture Loans	_____	_____	_____	_____
Home Improvement Loans	_____	_____	_____	_____
Liability Judgments	_____	_____	_____	_____
Life Insurance Loans	_____	_____	_____	_____
Margin Loans Against Securities	_____	_____	_____	_____
Overdraft Bank Loans	_____	_____	_____	_____
Pension Plan Loans	_____	_____	_____	_____
TOTAL INSTALLMENT LIABILITIES				$ _____
TOTAL LIABILITIES				$ _____

Now, for the moment of truth: Take your total assets from the Assets Worksheet and subtract your total liabilities from the Liabilities Worksheet. This determines your net worth.

Total Assets	$ _____
(Minus) Total Liabilities	(_____)
Equals Positive (or Negative) Net Worth	$ _____

First, notice whether your net worth is positive or negative. If it's positive, you've been doing a good job at building assets and keeping liabilities under control. Now that you know where you stand, you are in a good position to see your net worth grow even more in coming years.

If your net worth is negative, do not despair. You have just discovered something very important about your finances. Knowing that you are under water (financially speaking) is the first step in getting out of trouble. Clearly, you have too much debt for the amount of assets you have accumulated. Remember, this is only a snapshot of your current situation. Let's hope the next time you calculate your net worth, it will be a more "positive" experience.

After you calculate your net worth each year, you should compare it to your calculations for the past five years to see how you have been progressing. Use this simple form to keep records:

Year	Net Worth	Percentage Increase/Decrease
This year	_____	_____
Last year	_____	_____
Two years ago	_____	_____
Three years ago	_____	_____
Four years ago	_____	_____
Five years ago	_____	_____

Creating Your Recordkeeping System

Filling out all the worksheets in this book will be much easier if you don't have to dig through boxes full of unopened bank and brokerage statements, life insurance records and old tax returns. Though it will take some effort at first to get organized, the time commitment will be minimal compared to the return you will earn from getting a handle on your finances. It is also invaluable to have your papers easily accessible when you are filling out your tax return or—God forbid!—you are audited and have to prove how much you paid for a stock ten years ago.

The best way to get started is to set up a filing system separate from the rest of your household files. In addition to setting up a separate file for each of the categories described in the Recordkeeping Worksheet (see Figure 1.3), it is crucial to note on the worksheet where all your important documents are located and other details such as account numbers and the names of brokers, insurance agents and other people who know about your accounts. Many a widow tells the story of how she was thrown into total financial chaos when her husband died suddenly and all the records were scattered throughout the house. Even worse, if both you and your spouse die together, it will be extremely difficult for your children or other beneficiaries to reassemble your financial records.

Figure 1.3, then, is a worksheet that consolidates all your important data in one place. You should organize your file system using the exact same categories, which are arranged alphabetically.

Defining Your Financial Goals

Now that you know where you stand financially, you must figure out where you want to go. Setting specific financial objectives and putting them in writing—listing dollar amounts and noting exactly when you will need the money—will motivate you to achieve your goals. So many people never take the time to figure out what they want because they have convinced themselves that they will never reach their targets. However, if you don't define your goals, you won't accomplish them.

This section will give you several easy-to-fill-out worksheets so you will be able to determine your highest financial priorities and how you can achieve them. You can't reach all of your goals overnight, but knowing what they are, and which ones take precedence, will help you fulfill your goals faster than if you never took the time to do this exercise. Because setting goals is really another way of defining priorities, the process helps you make sure that your limited resources and income are used most effectively to attain your highest priorities. By crystalizing your aspirations, you take charge of your life so that you control your money for the purposes you find most important.

Don't think that goal setting is too hard; you've been doing it for most of your life. When you last started a diet, you set a specific goal for how many pounds you would trim. When you were on the track team in high school, you set a goal to achieve a particular time for your event—a four-minute mile, for instance. As you went through college, you set a goal of a certain grade-point average or maybe a goal of doing well enough to enter a certain graduate school. All you are doing now is applying the same discipline to your personal finances.

Some people's financial goals differ so greatly from others' because people have been brought up with different values. For some, providing the finest education for their children is the top priority because it will allow the children to attain greater achievements than the parents could ever imagine. For others, buying

Figure 1.3   Recordkeeping Worksheet

1. Personal Information

Your Name
Address
_____
_____
_____
Home Telephone _____
Work Telephone/FAX _____
Date, Place of Birth _____
Birth Certificate Location _____
Social Security Number _____
Marital Status _____

Spouse's Name _____
Address _____
_____
Home Telephone _____
Work Telephone/FAX _____
Date, Place of Birth _____
Birth Certificate Location _____
Social Security Number _____
Marital Status _____

Child's Name _____
Spouse's Name _____
Address _____
_____
Home Telephone _____
Work Telephone/FAX _____
Date, Place of Birth _____
Birth Certificate Location _____
Social Security Number _____
Marital Status _____

Parent's Name _____
Address _____
_____
Home Telephone _____
Work Telephone/FAX _____
Date, Place of Birth _____
Birth Certificate Location _____
Social Security Number _____
Marital Status _____

Figure 1.3   (continued)

Parent's Name (Spouse)
Address

Home Telephone
Work Telephone/FAX
Date, Place of Birth
Birth Certificate Location
Social Security Number
Marital Status

Grandchild's Name
Spouse's Name
Address

Home Telephone
Work Telephone/FAX
Date, Place of Birth
Birth Certificate Location
Social Security Number
Marital Status

Grandparent's Name
Spouse's Name
Address

Home Telephone
Work Telephone/FAX
Date, Place of Birth
Birth Certificate Location
Social Security Number
Marital Status

Sibling's Name
Spouse's Name
Address

Home Telephone
Work Telephone/FAX
Date, Place of Birth
Birth Certificate Location
Social Security Number
Marital Status

Figure 1.3   Recordkeeping Worksheet (continued)

2. Professional Contacts

Accountant
Address _____
_____
Telephone/FAX _____
Assistant's Name _____

Attorney
Address _____
_____
Telephone/FAX _____
Assistant's Name _____

Banker
Address _____
_____
Telephone/FAX _____
Assistant's Name _____

Dentist
Address _____
_____
Telephone/FAX _____
Assistant's Name _____

Employee Benefits Counselor _____
Address _____
_____
Telephone/FAX _____
Assistant's Name _____

Executor of Estate
Address _____
_____
Telephone/FAX _____
Assistant's Name _____

Financial Planner
Address _____
_____
Telephone/FAX _____
Assistant's Name _____

Insurance Agent (auto)
Address _____
_____
Telephone/FAX _____
Assistant's Name _____

Figure 1.3   (continued)

Insurance Agent (health)
Address _____
_____
_____
Telephone/FAX _____
Assistant's Name _____

Insurance Agent (home)
Address _____
_____
_____
Telephone/FAX _____
Assistant's Name _____

Insurance Agent (life)
Address _____
_____
_____
Telephone/FAX _____
Assistant's Name _____

Investment Manager
Address _____
_____
_____
Telephone/FAX _____
Assistant's Name _____

Physician
Address _____
_____
_____
Telephone/FAX _____
Assistant's Name _____

Priest/Rabbi/Minister
Address _____
_____
_____
Telephone/FAX _____
Assistant's Name _____

Stockbroker
Address _____
_____
_____
Telephone/FAX _____
Assistant's Name _____

Trust Officer
Address _____
_____
_____
Telephone/FAX _____
Assistant's Name _____

Figure 1.3   Recordkeeping Worksheet (continued)

Other
Address _____
_____
_____
Telephone/FAX _____
Assistant's Name _____

Other
Address _____
_____
_____
Telephone/FAX _____
Assistant's Name _____

3. Financial Accounts

Banking Records (CDs, checking, credit union, savings)

Name of Institution	Type of Account	Account Number	Location of Documents
_____	_____	_____	_____
_____	_____	_____	_____
_____	_____	_____	_____
_____	_____	_____	_____

Bonds (corporate, municipal, Treasury bonds)

Issuer	# of Bonds	Date Bought	$ Cost	Due Date	Location of Documents
_____	_____	_____	_____	_____	_____
_____	_____	_____	_____	_____	_____
_____	_____	_____	_____	_____	_____
_____	_____	_____	_____	_____	_____

Business Ownership

Name of Business	Type of Business	% Owned	Other Partners
_____	_____	_____	_____

Childrens' Accounts

Child's Name/ Trustee	Type of Account or Trust	$ Value	Location of Funds
_____	_____	_____	_____
_____	_____	_____	_____
_____	_____	_____	_____
_____	_____	_____	_____

Figure 1.3   (continued)

Debts (auto, credit card, education, mortgage)

Type of Loan	Name of Institution	Account Number	Amount Due	Monthly Payment
_____	_____	_____	_____	_____
_____	_____	_____	_____	_____
_____	_____	_____	_____	_____
_____	_____	_____	_____	_____

Employee Benefit and Retirement Plans (401(k), IRA, Keogh plans, pension plans, profit-sharing plans, stock purchase plans)

Type of Plan	Who Is Covered	Trustee	$ Value of Plan	Beneficiary
_____	_____	_____	_____	_____
_____	_____	_____	_____	_____
_____	_____	_____	_____	_____

Insurance Policies (auto, health, home, life insurance)

Type of Policy	Insures Who or What	Name of Company	Account Number	$ Amount Insured	Location of Documents
_____	_____	_____	_____	_____	_____
_____	_____	_____	_____	_____	_____
_____	_____	_____	_____	_____	_____
_____	_____	_____	_____	_____	_____

Mutual Funds

Type of Account	Name of Company	Account Number	# of Shares	Location of Documents
_____	_____	_____	_____	_____
_____	_____	_____	_____	_____
_____	_____	_____	_____	_____

Real Estate

Type of Property	Location of Property	Date Purchased	Purchase Price	Location of Documents
_____	_____	_____	_____	_____
_____	_____	_____	_____	_____
_____	_____	_____	_____	_____

Figure 1.3　Recordkeeping Worksheet (continued)

Safe-Deposit Boxes

Depository Bank and Address	Primary and Secondary Owner of Assets	Person with Power of Attorney	Location of Contents List and Key
_____	_____	_____	_____
_____	_____		_____
_____			
_____	_____	_____	_____
_____	_____		_____
_____			

Stocks

Type of Account	Name of Company	Account Number	# of Shares	Date Bought	Purchase Price	Location of Documents
____	____	____	____	____	____	____
____	____	____	____	____	____	____
____	____	____	____	____	____	____
____	____	____	____	____	____	____
____	____	____	____	____	____	____
____	____	____	____	____	____	____

Tax Records

Persons Filing	Estimated Quarterly Payments	Location of Latest Tax Return	Location of Previous Returns
_____	____	_____	_____
_____	____	_____	_____
_____	____	_____	_____
_____	____	_____	_____
_____	____	_____	_____

Wills and Trust Documents

Family Member Covered	Attorney	Executor	Location of Documents
_____	_____	_____	_____
_____	_____	_____	_____
_____	_____	_____	_____
_____	_____	_____	_____
_____	_____	_____	_____

Figure 1.3 (continued)

4. Other Important Papers   **Location**

Appliance Instructions,
   Guarantees and Warranties   _____

Automobile Titles or Lease
   Documents   _____

Burial Plot Documentation   _____

Citizenship Papers/Passports   _____

Club Membership Records   _____

Contracts   _____

Credit Reports   _____

Divorce Decrees   _____

Educational Records and
   Diplomas   _____

Employment Records   _____

Financial Records   _____

Frequent Flier Account
   Records   _____

Health Care Proxy   _____

Health Records   _____

Home Improvement Records   _____

Inventories of Household
   Goods   _____

Jury Duty Records   _____

Living Wills   _____

Marriage Certificate   _____

Medical Insurance Forms   _____

Medicare Cards   _____

Military Discharge Papers   _____

Power of Attorney Documents   _____

Receipts for Major Purchases   _____

Rental Leases   _____

Resumes   _____

Social Security Cards and
   Earnings Records   _____

Utility Bills   _____

Other (specify)   _____

life's luxuries for immediate use is a higher goal. If you're in this group, it might be because you were brought up with a certain standard of living, and your goal is to replicate it for yourself once you are living on your own. For people who have never lived more than a bare-bones existence, a worthwhile goal may be to elevate their lifestyle by buying all the modern gadgets that make living more pleasurable.

Remember, setting goals is not only about allocating your money—it's also about allocating your time. If one of your goals is to have more free time to play with your children or do community work, that takes away from the time you can devote to advancing in your career. Nothing is wrong with that choice as long as it is one you make consciously.

If you share finances with a spouse or partner, goal setting must be done mutually. To avoid friction, you must agree, for the most part, with your spouse or significant other on which goals get the highest priority. You can avoid many financial fights by coming to terms on goals in the first place.

The goal-setting exercises in Figures 1.4–1.8, like the net worth exercise in the previous section, are not once-in-a-lifetime events. As you accomplish certain goals during your life, you must constantly be setting new ones. For example, once your children's college educations have been paid for, you may want to shift priorities in order to set aside money for a second home or for your retirement.

There are three kinds of goals: short term, medium term and long term. Within each of these three categories, you have not only goals but also priorities for those goals. Because you will probably never have enough money to achieve all your goals over the next year, you have to allocate some resources on an ongoing basis to each of the three categories so you have some chance of accomplishing the goals over time. Usually, people neglect the medium- and long-term goals in favor of the seemingly more pressing short-term goals, but that only puts off the day of reckoning. The longer you delay starting to accumulate the money for longer-term goals like buying a home or funding retirement, the more difficult the realization of those goals becomes.

This section provides a worksheet for each of the three kinds of goals. After you locate one of your goals on the worksheet, note the amount of money you will need to pay for it, how high a priority it has compared to other goals and when you would like to achieve it.

SHORT-TERM GOALS

Short-term goals are those you would like to achieve within the next year (see Figure 1.4). These might include paying off your credit cards, buying certain large items like a television, a car or furniture, or taking a long-needed vacation.

MEDIUM-TERM GOALS

Medium-term goals are items for which it takes between two and ten years to accumulate the money (see Figure 1.5). These may include building a down payment for a first or second home, creating a college fund for children older than

Figure 1.4   Short-Term Goals Worksheet

Goal	Priority	Date To Accomplish	$ Amount Needed
Build Up Emergency Reserve (worth three months' salary)	_____	_____	$ _____
Buy Adequate Insurance			
Auto	_____	_____	_____
Health	_____	_____	_____
Home	_____	_____	_____
Life	_____	_____	_____
Contribute to Charity Name _____	_____	_____	_____
Fund IRA or Keogh Account	_____	_____	_____
Increase Contribution to Company Benefit Plan	_____	_____	_____
Join a Health/Sports Club	_____	_____	_____
Make Major Home Improvements	_____	_____	_____
Make Major Purchases	_____	_____	_____
Pay Off Bills	_____	_____	_____
Pay Off Credit Cards	_____	_____	_____
Save for Christmas Gifts, Birthdays, etc.	_____	_____	_____
Take Vacation	_____	_____	_____
Other (specify)			
_____	_____	_____	_____
TOTAL $ AMOUNT NEEDED			**$ _____**

eight years or saving up to take the overseas trip of your dreams. If you have one child and plan on having another in a few years, you might want to start putting aside money for the little one now. After all, economists project that it will cost at least $250,000 to bring up a child from birth through his or her senior year in high school (assuming you are able to exert some control over the child's demands for toys in the early years and high-fashion clothes in the teen years).

LONG-TERM GOALS

Long-term goals take more than ten years to fulfill (see Figure 1.6). The most common long-term goal is a financially secure retirement, which takes a lifetime

Figure 1.5   Medium-Term Goals Worksheet

Goal	Priority	Date To Accomplish	$ Amount Needed
Create College Fund for Children			
Child 1 _____	_____	_____	$ _____
Child 2 _____	_____	_____	_____
Save Down Payment for First Home	_____	_____	_____
Save Down Payment for Second Home	_____	_____	_____
Finance Special Occasions (weddings, bar mitzvahs, etc.)	_____	_____	_____
Help Child Finance Home	_____	_____	_____
Pay Off Education Debt	_____	_____	_____
Save for Next Child	_____	_____	_____
Take Overseas Trip	_____	_____	_____
Take Time Off To Pursue an Interest	_____	_____	_____
Other (specify)			
_____	_____	_____	_____
TOTAL $ NEEDED			$ _____

of financial discipline. Other long-term goals include paying for extensive travel, starting your own business, going back to school to receive a higher degree of education, and buying a vacation home. Another long-term goal is to make sure you can afford medical attention in your later years.

TRACKING GOALS

For each goal on which you have placed a high priority, Figure 1.7 is a quick worksheet that will let you track the progress you are making toward achieving that goal.

MONTHLY SAVINGS NEEDED TO REACH GOAL

To figure out the monthly amount you need to invest to reach the goal you analyzed in the Goal-Tracking Worksheet, use the table in Figure 1.8. The left column shows the number of years you have until you need the money for your

Figure 1.6   Long-Term Goals Worksheet

Goal	Priority	Date To Accomplish	$ Amount Needed
Buy Retirement Home	_____	_____	$ _____
Buy Vacation Home	_____	_____	_____
Continue Education	_____	_____	_____
Do Community or Charity Work	_____	_____	_____
Establish Long-Term Health Care for Self and/or Spouse	_____	_____	_____
Establish Retirement Fund	_____	_____	_____
Help Older Parents	_____	_____	_____
Make a Charitable Bequest	_____	_____	_____
Pay Off Mortgage Early	_____	_____	_____
Start a Business	_____	_____	_____
Start a Second Career	_____	_____	_____
Travel Extensively	_____	_____	_____
Other (specify)			
_____			_____
TOTAL $ NEEDED			$ _____

goal. The next four columns show the divisors for four different rates of return that you can safely assume it is possible to earn, on average, over a long period of time. These rates of return assume you have adjusted for the effects of inflation and taxes, so they are known as *real after-tax yields*. The higher the rate of return, the more risk you have to take in your investment choices to achieve it. (See Chapter 3 for more on rates of return.)

To use the table, take the amount of money you will need to pay for your goal and pick an assumed rate of return. Then find the divisor for the number of years you have allocated to reach the goal. Simply divide your dollar goal by the divisor, and you have figured out the monthly amount of savings you need to reach your goal. The divisor automatically calculates the effect of compounding of interest, which becomes quite a powerful force over time.

For example, say you want to accumulate a $100,000 nest egg for your retirement in 20 years. You assume a real after-tax yield of 8 percent. When you

Figure 1.7   Goal-Tracking Worksheet

Goal   (identify)   _____

Date in the Future You Will
   Need the Money   _____

How Many Years until You
   Need the Money   _____

Amount of Money Needed
   To Accomplish This Goal   _____

Money Already Accumulated
   for This Goal   _____

Rate of Return (%) Assumed
   for Accumulated Money   _____

Money Remaining To Be
   Accumulated for This Goal   _____

Money Needed To Be Saved Each
   Year at Assumed Rate of Return   _____

Monthly Amount To Be Saved
   (previous line divided by 12)   _____

look down the 8 percent column to the 20-year line, you see the divisor of 592. Divide $100,000 by 592. You have to save $168.92 a month to meet your goal.

Here's another example for a shorter term goal: Say you need $2,000 in two years to buy furniture for your living room. Assuming a 6 percent rate of return, you divide $2,000 by the divisor of 25.4 to come up with a monthly savings target of $78.74.

With your net worth statement in hand and short-term, medium-term and long-term goals clearly defined, you should be feeling better already. But the fun is just beginning. It's now time to analyze your case flow to see where your money is coming from and where it is going on a monthly and an annual basis.

Analyzing Your Cash Flow

Now that you know how much you are worth and what your financial goals are, it's time to do a detailed analysis of where your money is coming from and where it is being spent. This is known in the financial planning world as a *cash flow analysis* because it allows you to trace your sources and uses of money.

Even though it is a simple exercise, most people never get around to it. They are left wondering, "Where did all my money go?" at the end of each month, and they anxiously wait for their next paycheck so they can pay their bills. By doing

Figure 1.8
Determining the Monthly Savings Needed To Reach a Goal

	Divisors (By Rate of Return)			
Years to Goal	2%	4%	6%	8%
1	12.1	12.2	12.3	12.4
2	24.5	24.9	25.4	25.9
3	37.1	38.2	39.3	40.6
4	49.9	51.9	54.1	56.4
5	63.1	66.2	69.8	73.6
6	76.5	81.1	86.4	92.1
7	90.2	96.6	104.1	112.3
8	104.2	112.7	122.8	134.1
9	118.4	129.5	142.7	157.7
10	133.0	146.9	163.9	183.4
11	147.8	165.1	186.3	211.1
12	163.0	184.0	210.1	241.2
13	178.5	203.6	235.4	273.7
14	194.2	224.0	262.3	309.0
15	210.4	245.3	290.8	347.3
16	226.8	267.4	321.1	388.7
17	243.6	290.4	353.2	433.6
18	260.7	314.3	387.3	482.2
19	278.2	339.2	423.6	534.9
20	296.1	365.1	462.0	592.0
21	314.2	392.1	502.9	653.8
22	332.8	420.1	546.2	720.8
23	351.8	449.3	592.2	793.4
24	371.2	479.6	641.1	872.0
25	390.9	511.2	693.0	957.2

the cash flow analysis in this section, you will never again have to be one of those people because even if you are anxious for each paycheck, you will know exactly how much income you can expect to receive as well as nearly all the expenses you plan to cover with that income. (Don't plan on any sudden windfalls, but you should expect a few surprise expenses.)

The Cash Flow Worksheet presented in this section is designed to be used on an annual basis. Some income, such as bonuses or capital gains distributions made by mutual funds, is received only at certain times of the year—for example, in December. Similarly, many expenses, such as tuition payments, fuel oil bills or quarterly tax bills, occur only during certain months of the year. By totaling all your annual income and expenses, you will get a sense of how your overall cash flow looks for the year.

It is also important to do a more short-term cash flow analysis because sometimes your expenses are due before the income arrives, causing a cash squeeze. The same Cash Flow Worksheet in Figure 1.9 can be filled out on both a monthly and a quarterly basis.

We have designed this worksheet to be as comprehensive as possible, providing you with lines for the most common sources of income and the most frequent expenses, broken down into familiar categories. If you currently do not have one of the sources of income listed, leave the lines blank. Even so, it will be instructive for you to see the many different potential sources of income.

The same holds true on the expense side. If you are not spending money for day care or a health club membership, leave it blank. Still, this list of expenses will give you some idea of the range of ways people spend their money.

The best way to complete this worksheet is to take your bank, brokerage, insurance and other statements, last year's tax return, along with your last year-end paycheck and other records you have accumulated for the past six months, and fill in the real numbers. This is not an exercise in wishful thinking; this is a document that will show you, for better or worse, how you actually are earning and spending your money now. It's no use inflating the income and lowballing the expenses because you're the only one who will be hurt by not knowing the truth. You don't have to show the results to anyone—not even your mother.

SOURCES OF INCOME

The income side of the Cash Flow Worksheet is broken into six categories: earned, self-employment, family, government, retirement and investment income. The following is a brief guide to what kinds of income fall into each category. (For each of the six categories, we have provided a line on the worksheet to subtotal the income, which will make it easier to add up your total income at the end of the worksheet.)

Earned income. The most common and largest source of income for most people, of course, is their salary from a job. You should note on the worksheet your net take-home pay, after deductions.

Other sources of earned income include commissions paid to salespeople, bonuses for extraordinary performance, overtime and tips. You may also be entitled to stock options, which give you the right to buy your company's stock at a preset price, usually below the current market value, and the right to sell the shares for a profit. There are also many forms of deferred compensation that can be paid out to you, based on your performance or in accordance with the provisions of a contract. If you expect to exercise stock options or receive deferred compensation in the next year, you should note this on the worksheet.

Self-employment income. If you work for yourself or a closely held partnership, most of your income will come from this income category. Because taxes or other deductions are not normally withheld from freelance income, you will have to pay income and self-employment taxes on this money on a quarterly basis through estimated tax filings. Finally, if you are a writer, a musician, a painter or an inventor, you may be getting regular royalty income from sales of your books, music, paintings or inventions.

Family income. If you are lucky enough to come from a family that has put money in a trust for you, this can be a significant source of regular income. You should list on the worksheet the income produced from the assets you inherited or the assets in a trust for you. If you receive regular (or even irregular) gifts from family members, the total amount should also be listed here. Finally, if you are divorced and receive alimony or child support, that income should be entered on the worksheet.

Government income. You might qualify to receive regular checks from the federal or state government. If your other income is low enough, you can get welfare or Aid to Families with Dependent Children (AFDC) funds. If you have had a disabling accident, you may qualify for disability insurance or workers' compensation insurance. If you had a job, but were laid off, you are entitled to unemployment insurance for several months. Note these amounts on the worksheet.

Retirement income. There are several sources of income once you have retired, assuming you have been building up retirement assets for most of your working life. You can receive a monthly payment from an annuity, issued by an insurance company, based on your lifelong contributions to the annuity. Alternatively, you can take the lump sum you receive from your employer once you retire (from any pension plan you may have had) and buy an annuity from an insurance company to ensure a fixed monthly income for the rest of your life. Similarly, starting at age 59½, you can take money out of your IRA or Keogh account without penalty. (You must pay a 10 percent penalty if you withdraw from these accounts sooner.) If you worked at a company that offered a profit-sharing plan, a salary reduction plan or a pension plan, you can have the earnings paid to you in monthly installments. Finally, as long as Social Security was keeping track of how many years you worked and what you were earning, you will get monthly Social Security checks as well.

Investment income. This category offers the most possibilities because there are so many kinds of bank instruments, bonds, stocks, mutual funds and limited partnerships designed to throw off income. Among bank products, you can earn regular interest income from certificates of deposit (CDs), money-market deposit accounts, NOW accounts, on which you can write checks, and other savings accounts such as passbook accounts. Two additional kinds of short-term interest-bearing accounts are money-market mutual funds, which come in both taxable and tax-exempt varieties, and Treasury bills, which come in three-month, six-month and one-year maturities.

Among income-producing bonds, your options include corporate bonds (issued by corporations); convertible bonds (also issued by companies, but with the added option of converting the bonds into company stock in the future); Treasury notes maturing in up to 10 years and Treasury bonds coming due in up to 30 years; municipal bonds (issued by states and localities and paying interest free from federal and usually state taxes); and foreign bonds (issued by non-U.S. corporations or foreign governments). In addition, you may be counting on income produced from selling any of these kinds of bonds for a profit, listed on the worksheet as capital gains from bond sales. Similarly, you can produce regular income by investing in bond mutual funds that buy any of these taxable or tax-exempt bonds.

Stocks also give you several options for producing regular income. Many individual stocks pay quarterly dividends, with some, like public utilities, yielding 5 percent or more. Many mutual funds investing in stocks also are designed to pay a significant monthly dividend to income-oriented investors. Plus, most mutual funds make a yearly payout of all the capital gains they have accumulated during the year, known as a capital gains distribution. If you plan to sell some of your stocks or stock funds to realize a profit, that should be entered on the worksheet as income from capital gains.

Limited partnerships, though their name has been tarnished by the many partnership debacles of the 1980s, still provide a viable vehicle for producing regular income. Partnerships can invest in rental real estate, oil and gas wells, or leasing of equipment such as airplanes or computers, all of which provide a monthly stream of income. If you have any interests in such partnerships, enter the annual income you expect from them on the worksheet.

Next, total the income you expect to receive in all six categories, and add any other income sources as well, to create your grand total: annual income.

EXPENSES

Now you're going to figure out where all of that income disappears every year. Your expenses can be divided roughly into two categories: what is *fixed*, meaning it must be paid on an annual or a monthly basis, and what is *flexible*, meaning you have more control over whether and when you spend it. By filling out the expense portion of the worksheet in these two categories, you will be able to see what percentage of your income is taken up by fixed expenses. This will give you a clearer idea of how much money you have left over for discretionary spending.

There are seven categories that should be considered *fixed expenses*: automobile-related expenses, family expenses, home-related expenses, insurance, savings and investments, taxes and utilities.

Automobile-related expenses. Most people either lease their car from the dealer or buy it with an auto loan. In either case, you will have to make a monthly payment until the lease is up or the loan is paid off. To keep the car running, of course, you will need gasoline in the tank and oil under the hood.

Family expenses. It's hard to raise children without feeding them (they will start to complain), so add food and beverages to your regular fixed expenses. If your children go to a school that charges tuition, this also goes into the fixed expenses column. If you are divorced and still supporting your spouse and your children, count alimony and child support as fixed expenses.

Home-related expenses. You've got to live somewhere, and if you own or rent, certain expenses are impossible to avoid. Owners must make their monthly mortgage payments, just as renters must keep the landlord happy on the first of the month. And if you want cable television, make an allowance in your budget for its charge.

Insurance. Somehow, paying the insurance company never feels like a good use of money—until you have a claim. Then you are glad that you kept up with your premiums. The most common forms of insurance you will have to pay are auto, disability, dental, excess liability, health, homeowner's and life insurance. (These are all discussed in more detail in Chapter 11, "All about Insurance.")

Savings and investments. At last, here is an expense category that lets you feel you are not spending money you will never see again. It may seem hard to think of saving and investing as fixed expenses, but it's the only way to accumulate funds. The easiest way to invest is through some kind of automatic savings plan, such as your salary reduction plan (called a 401(k) in companies, a 403(b) in nonprofit institutions and a 457 in government agencies). You can also save at your bank by building up your emergency fund, which should be kept at three months' salary, if possible. Such a fund is crucial if you suddenly become unemployed, must pay for a major auto or house repair, or have a major medical emergency. And even though you may not think of repaying debt as savings, it's one of the best savings moves you can make. Not many investments out there can guarantee you, for example, the instant 18 percent return you earn for paying off credit card debt. (For much more on savings and investments, read Chapters 2–8.)

Taxes. The federal, state and local governments seem to have this nasty habit of expecting you to pay taxes quite frequently. If you do not have enough withheld from your paycheck or you have a great deal of freelance income, you must make quarterly estimated payments to both the IRS and your state. Also, the freelancer should make regular Social Security self-employment tax payments as well. If you own your home, your city government expects you to pay property taxes, though often those taxes are actually paid by the bank that holds your mortgage and has set up your tax escrow account.

Utilities. If you want to keep the lights on, your electric utility gets its share of your budget. The same holds true for the gas company or oil dealer—if you want to stay warm. If you want to talk on the telephone, you must ante up each month to the utility. In some cities, you are also charged for water or sewage service.

These seven categories include most of what you absolutely have to pay every year. The typical American spends about 70 percent of his or her income on fixed expenses. With some good planning, you will have about 30 percent of your income left for more discretionary purchases, known by financial professionals as *flexible spending*. There are many more ways to spend money when you have some choice in the matter, so we've broken flexible expenses into 13 categories: children, clothing, contributions and dues, education, equipment and vehicles, financial and professional services, food, home maintenance, medical care, miscellaneous, recreation and entertainment, savings and investments, and travel and vacations.

Children. If you have children or are planning to have them, you know that the joys of parenthood don't come cheap. As children grow up, what they require and desire changes, and it usually gets more expensive. While your infant may be perfectly content with a pacifier for $.69, your teenager will not be satisfied with anything but the latest stereo equipment, starting at roughly $500. Many older children, even those who have graduated from college, often continue to need financial help (and often housing back in what was supposed to be the empty nest!) until they get a job and become established. So depending on their age, you might as well plan on spending something on allowances, babysitting, day care, books and toys. During the summer, the children will probably want to go to camp. And it will surely cost you something to rent a hall or restaurant for their birthday parties. Remember, they'll grow up faster than you can ever imagine, and soon they'll be out on their own—at least that's what everyone likes to tell you.

Clothing. You probably will need to augment your clothing budget if you are in a professional setting, where appearance is important. Set aside money not only for new clothes and shoes but also for the upkeep of your clothes, such as for dry cleaning, tailoring and pressing. All those trips to the dry cleaner may seem insignificant, but those bills can really add up over a year.

Contributions and dues. The amount you give to charities, religious institutions and political candidates is up to you. You may be able to deduct some or all of your contributions, which will give you a bit of a tax break. For the most part, though, give because you believe in the cause, not to get the write-off. If you are a member of a union, dues are normally not so voluntary. And gift giving can always take a big bite out of your budget because you can get carried away with your feelings of generosity toward the recipients.

Education. If you or your children plan on going to a school that charges tuition, it's never too early to start budgeting. Remember, you will have to pay not only for tuition but also room and board, books, software and supplies. And don't forget to budget for lessons on everything from ballet to violin.

Equipment and vehicles. Every time you buy a new vehicle or piece of equipment to make your life easier, you are adding potential expenses. Cars, boats, motorcycles and motor homes all need maintenance, registrations, licenses and a place to park. Televisions, videotape recorders, stereos, CD players and other consumer electronics need videotapes, audiotapes and CDs, along with occasional repairs. The same holds true for all of life's other conveniences, from Cuisinarts to washing machines.

Financial and professional services. Some areas of finance are too complicated for the average person, and it is worthwhile to pay an expert for advice. That can be particularly true with tax, legal and investment matters. Also, most of the time, you are charged fees to make financial transactions, from the pesky fees that banks charge to use automatic teller machines to brokerage fees you pay to buy or sell stocks or mutual funds. Some of these fees can be avoided; for example, you can buy a no-load mutual fund directly from a fund company that does not charge an up-front commission. Still, even no-load funds charge an annual management fee, which is taken out of your fund's return. If the advice you get from financial professionals is solid, the charges can be well worth it. But if the advice is biased in favor of the adviser, or you don't act on it because you don't understand the advice or you think the counsel is inappropriate for you, the fees can be a major money-waster.

Food. In addition to food you buy to serve at home, you should allow for food outside the home, including both restaurant meals and on-the-fly snacks. Count any purchases of alcohol and tobacco in this food category.

Home maintenance. The bigger your house or apartment, the more expensive it is to maintain. You should expect a certain amount of repairs every year, along with ongoing cleaning and household expenses, from soap to dishes to light bulbs. Remember the fees for outside maintenance as well, which include removing the garbage and snow and tending the lawn and garden. If you have a home office, you will have to keep it stocked with file folders, pens and probably computer supplies and fax paper. If you have suffered a break-in or damage to your house that is not covered by your insurance policy, you should count that, too.

Medical care. Even those workers with health insurance through their employers bear more and more medical costs these days. Often, employees have to pay part of the insurance premium, deductibles and copayments, as well as for drugs, eyeglasses and medical devices like wheelchairs and canes. In some cases, insurance companies limit the amount of a physician's, dentist's or hospital's bill that they will reimburse, leaving the insured holding the bag. In addition, you must budget to cover over-the-counter medicines, personal care items and toiletries, as well as haircuts, manicures and pedicures if they are part of your routine. You may also have to pick up medical expenses for your older parents if they do not have enough money, whether they live on their own or in a nursing home, because most insurance will not cover all of their expenses.

Miscellaneous. There are always going to be some expenses that just don't fit into any of the other categories. Unreimbursed business expenses and postage are two that come to mind. Quite frequently, the *recurring nonrecurring expense* hits. Generally each of these expenses happens only once, but a new one seems to occur every month or so. One month, the boiler breaks down. The next month, your parked car is hit, but the damage is just under your insurance deductible. By assuming such recurring nonrecurring expenses will pop up, you can budget for them.

And then there is always that big hole in your budget we like to call "mystery cash." You had cash in your wallet, and you have absolutely no idea what you spent it on by the end of the week. Try writing down what you spend every penny on during one week, and you might be able to unlock the secrets of mystery cash.

Recreation and entertainment. Most people can't exist without some kind of hobby, sport or recreation. You may like pets, books, movies, music, photography, plays, sporting events or videos, all of which can become expensive hobbies. You may be committed to your health, having joined a fitness club or playing a sport like golf, where greens fees are required. Nothing is wrong with any of these—except that they don't come free.

Savings and investments. While you should put aside a certain amount of money as part of your fixed expenses to keep your emergency fund solvent, you should also try to invest in bank instruments, stocks, bonds and mutual funds that will provide you with the wherewithal to reach the financial goals you set in a previous section of this book. If you don't start investing for these goals, the money will never be there when you need it, whether it be for your child's college education or your retirement. While some of the investments should be in a regular taxable bank, brokerage or mutual fund account, some of the money should be compounding tax deferred in an IRA or a Keogh account.

Travel and vacations. There are two kinds of travel—for business and for pleasure. You should set aside money for both. For business, you will spend money to commute to work, whether that means driving (paying tolls and parking your car) or taking a bus, subway or train. In addition, there are often expenses you incur while on the road for your business that your company might not reimburse, like watching a pay-per-view movie in your hotel room. Vacations are all on you, and you should be realistic about the cost of airfares, hotels, car rentals, food, tips and souvenirs. Vacations can be wonderfully relaxing, but somehow they always end up costing more than you expect.

So there you have it—the 13 major categories for which you spend your money. As you fill out the Cash Flow Worksheet in Figure 1.9, only certain sections may apply to you right now. Some day, you probably will use those sections you cannot use now. For the moment, feel free to skip those categories that do not apply.

After you've filled out both the income and expense sides of this worksheet, it will be time to get down to the bottom line. Subtract your expenses from your income, and you have your annual cash flow. If you are taking in more than you are spending, congratulations. You are in *positive cash flow.* Your next job is to figure out the best places for your extra cash—probably savings vehicles and investments.

If, on the other hand, your expenses total more than your income—not an unlikely situation—you are in *negative cash flow,* and it's time to start scrutinizing your expenses. Just because you have negative cash flow does not mean you are in trouble. For example, you may still be putting away money in your company savings plan, so you are investing more than you remember. But if the reason you are spending more than you are taking in is excessive debt, it's time to take notice. This exercise is your loud wake-up call, and the time to mend your ways is now. That's where we go in the next chapter—creating a financial plan and budget that will help you meet your goals.

Creating a Budget That Works

By now, you have assembled a pretty accurate picture of where you stand financially. You know what your assets and liabilities are, you have clearly prioritized your financial goals and you have analyzed how your income matches up with your expenses. Using this information as a base, you now must project into the future to create a budget that works for you.

Often, the word *budget* sounds constricting, foreboding and even a bit frightening. The word has a certain ring to it, vaguely resembling the word *homework* when you were in school.

Instead, you should see a budget as your friend. It is the document that gives you *control* over your finances—in a way that lets you decide what is most and least important to you. A budget is an intensely personal plan; there is probably no one you know who has exactly the same priorities you have. If you find it important to include in your budget a lavish ski vacation to the Alps every winter, so be it—as long as the numbers tell you that you can afford it.

Once you become accustomed to budgeting, you will wonder how you got through all those years without one. A budget is a living, breathing document that expands or contracts as your circumstances change. Think of it as a road map, allowing you to know the direction you want to go, but giving you several options on how to get there. For example, you might be planning to buy a house in three years, and you are carefully putting aside money for a down payment. Then you are involved in a car accident that puts you out of work for six months. Your budget must change, causing your down payment plans to be put off for a while. But this does not mean you will never buy the house, just that your budget priorities have had to adapt to altered circumstances.

When you've executed a budget, you will be able to answer those questions that you have asked yourself in the past but were never able to resolve conclusively. Here are a few examples:

- Do I have enough income to cover the payments on more debt?
- Do I have enough money available to cover quarterly tax payments?

Figure 1.9 Cash Flow Worksheet

Annual Income	$ Amount	$ Total
1. Earned Income		
Salary after Deductions	$ _____	
Bonuses	_____	
Commissions	_____	
Deferred Compensation	_____	
Overtime	_____	
Stock Options	_____	
Tips	_____	
Other	_____	
TOTAL EARNED INCOME		$ _____
2. Self-Employment Income		
Freelance Income	$ _____	
Income from Partnerships	_____	
Income from Running a Small Business	_____	
Rental Income from Real Estate	_____	
Royalties	_____	
Other	_____	
TOTAL SELF-EMPLOYMENT INCOME		$ _____
3. Family Income		
Alimony Income	$ _____	
Child Support Income	_____	
Family Trust Income	_____	
Gifts from Family Members	_____	
Inheritance Income	_____	
Other	_____	
TOTAL FAMILY INCOME		$ _____
4. Government Income		
Aid to Families with Dependent Children Income	$ _____	
Disability Insurance Income	_____	
Unemployment Insurance Income	_____	
Veterans Benefits	_____	
Welfare Income	_____	
Workers' Compensation Income	_____	
Other	_____	
TOTAL GOVERNMENT INCOME		$ _____

Figure 1.9   (continued)

	$ Amount	$ Total
5. Retirement Income		
Annuity Payments	$ _____	
Social Security Income	_____	
Pension Income	_____	
Income from IRAs	_____	
Income from Keogh Accounts	_____	
Income from Profit-Sharing Accounts	_____	
Income from Salary Reduction Plans (401(k), 403(b), 457 plans)	_____	
Other	_____	
TOTAL RETIREMENT INCOME		$ _____
6. Investment Income		
Bank Account Interest		
CDs	$ _____	
Money-Market Accounts	_____	
NOW Accounts	_____	
Saving Accounts	_____	
Bonds and Bond Funds		
Capital Gains	_____	
Dividends	_____	
Interest	_____	
Other	_____	
Limited Partnerships (real estate, oil, gas)	_____	
Money Funds and T-Bills		
Taxable Funds	_____	
Tax-Exempt Funds	_____	
T-Bills	_____	
Stock and Stock Funds		
Capital Gains	_____	
Dividends	_____	
Interest	_____	
Other	_____	
Other	_____	
TOTAL INVESTMENT INCOME		$ _____
7. Other Income (specify)		
_____	$ _____	
TOTAL OTHER INCOME		$ _____
TOTAL ANNUAL INCOME		$ _____

Figure 1.9   Cash Flow Worksheet (continued)

Annual Expenses	$ Amount	$ Total
1. Fixed Expenses		
Automobile-Related		
Car Payment (loan or lease)	$_____	
Gasoline or Oil	_____	
Other	_____	
Total		$_____
Family		
Alimony	_____	
Child Support Payments	_____	
Food and Beverage	_____	
School Tuition	_____	
Other	_____	
Total		_____
Home-Related		
Cable Television Fees	_____	
Mortgage Payments Home #1	_____	
Mortgage Payments Home #2	_____	
Rent	_____	
Total		_____
Insurance		
Auto	_____	
Disability	_____	
Dental	_____	
Health	_____	
Homeowners	_____	
Life	_____	
Other		
Total		_____
Savings and Investments		
Bank Loan Repayment	_____	
Emergency Fund Contributions	_____	
Salary Reduction Plans	_____	
Contributions (401(k), 403(b),		
457 plans)	_____	
Other	_____	
Total		_____
Taxes		
Federal	_____	
Local	_____	
Property	_____	
Social Security (self-employed)	_____	

Figure 1.9   (continued)

	$ Amount	$ Total
State	$ _____	
Other	_____	
Total		$ _____
Utilities		
Electricity	_____	
Gas	_____	
Telephone	_____	
Water and Sewage	_____	
Other	_____	
Total		
Other (specify)		
_____	_____	
Total		_____

TOTAL FIXED EXPENSES $ _____

2. Flexible Expenses
Children

	$ Amount	$ Total
Allowances	$ _____	
Babysitting	_____	
Books	_____	
Camp Fees	_____	
Day Care	_____	
Events (parties, class trips, etc.)	_____	
Toys	_____	
Other	_____	
Total		$ _____
Clothing		
New Purchases	_____	
Shoes	_____	
Upkeep (cleaning, tailoring, dry cleaning, etc.)	_____	
Total		_____
Contributions and Dues		
Charitable Donations	_____	
Gifts (Christmas, birthdays, etc.)	_____	
Political Contributions	_____	
Religious Contributions	_____	
Union Dues	_____	
Other	_____	
Total		_____
Education		
Room and Board	_____	

Figure 1.9   Cash Flow Worksheet (continued)

	$ Amount	$ Total
Books and Supplies (parents and/or children)	$ _____	
Tuition (parents and/or children)	_____	
Other	_____	
Total		$ _____
Equipment and Vehicles		
Appliance Purchases and Maintenance	_____	
Car, Boat and Other Vehicle Purchases and Maintenance	_____	
Computer Purchases, etc.	_____	
Consumer Electronics Purchases	_____	
Licenses and Registration of Cars, Boats, etc.	_____	
Parking	_____	
Other	_____	
Total		_____
Financial and Professional Services		
Banking Fees	_____	
Brokerage Commissions and Fees	_____	
Financial Advice	_____	
Legal Advice	_____	
Tax Preparation Fees	_____	
Other	_____	
Total		_____
Food		
Alcohol	_____	
Foods and Snacks away from Home	_____	
Restaurant Meals	_____	
Tobacco	_____	
Other	_____	
Total		_____
Home Maintenance		
Garbage Removal	_____	
Garden Supplies and Maintenance	_____	
Home Office Supplies	_____	
Home Furnishings	_____	
Home or Apartment Repairs and Renovations	_____	
Home Cleaning Services	_____	
Home Supplies	_____	
Lawn Care and Snow Removal	_____	
Linens	_____	

Figure 1.9   (continued)

	$ Amount	$ Total
Uninsured Casualty or Theft Loss	$ _____	
Other	_____	
Total		$ _____
Medical Care		
Dentist Bills	_____	
Drugs (over the counter)	_____	
Drugs (prescriptions)	_____	
Eyecare and Eyeglasses	_____	
Hospital (uninsured portion)	_____	
Medical Devices (wheelchairs, canes, etc.)	_____	
Medical Expenses (parents)	_____	
Nursing Home Fees (parents, etc.)	_____	
Personal Beauty Care (hair stylist, manicurist, etc.)	_____	
Personal Care (cosmetics, toiletries, etc.)	_____	
Physician Bills	_____	
Unreimbursed Medical Expenses	_____	
Other	_____	
Total		_____
Miscellaneous		
Mystery Cash	_____	
Postage and Stamps	_____	
Recurring Nonrecurring Expenses	_____	
Unreimbursed Business Expenses	_____	
Other	_____	
Total		_____
Recreation and Entertainment		
Animal Care	_____	
Books	_____	
Club Dues	_____	
Cultural Events	_____	
Health Club Memberships	_____	
Hobbies	_____	
Lottery Tickets	_____	
Magazine and Newspaper Subscriptions	_____	
Movie Admissions	_____	
Music Admissions	_____	
Photography (cameras, developing, film, etc.)	_____	
Play Admissions	_____	

Figure 1.9   Cash Flow Worksheet (continued)

	$ Amount	$ Total
Recreational Equipment (games, sports, etc.)	$ _____	
Sporting Events Admission	_____	
Videotape Rentals	_____	
Other	_____	
Total		$ _____
Savings and Investments		
Bank Savings Contributions	_____	
Stock, Bond and Mutual Fund Contributions	_____	
IRA Contributions	_____	
Keogh Account Contributions	_____	
Other	_____	
Total		_____
Travel and Vacations		
Bus Fares	_____	
Subway Costs	_____	
Tolls	_____	
Train Fares	_____	
Travel Expense (other than vacations)	_____	
Unreimbursed Business Travel Expenses	_____	
Vacations (airfare)	_____	
Vacations (car rental)	_____	
Vacations (food)	_____	
Vacations (hotel)	_____	
Vacations (other)	_____	
Other	_____	
Total		_____
Other (specify)		
_____	_____	
Total		_____

TOTAL FLEXIBLE EXPENSES		$ _____
TOTAL ANNUAL EXPENSES		$ _____
TOTAL ANNUAL INCOME		$ _____
(MINUS)		
TOTAL ANNUAL EXPENSES		(_____)
EQUALS		
TOTAL NET ANNUAL POSITIVE (OR NEGATIVE) CASH FLOW		$ _____

- Have I put aside enough to cover the Christmas presents I want to give?

- Will my Social Security and pension income be enough to live on and maintain my current lifestyle if I retire this year?

- What size mortgage payments can I afford?

Many such questions will continue to arise as you move through different stages of life, and you will finally be in a position to make rational, informed decisions based on the information in your budget worksheet.

Creating a written budget therefore accomplishes several tasks for you. It communicates your priorities in black and white when they may have been communicated only verbally in the past. The process of creating a budget will, in itself, motivate you to take charge of your financial life. As the year goes on, you will feel in control of your money because you will know whether you are spending more or less than you expected. And at the end of the year, you will be able to evaluate how you did based on accurate information, making next year's budget even better.

ANNUAL BUDGET

As you make out your budget (see Figure 1.10), keep in mind a few common-sense tips:

- A budget takes thought, so you probably can't do a good job of forecasting all your income and expenses in an afternoon. Plan to do it in several sessions over about a week's time.

- Do your first few rounds of budgeting in pencil so you can erase until all the numbers add up.

- Work out a budget with everyone who will be affected by it. A budget should not be handed down to the family like the Ten Commandments from Moses. Instead, it should be discussed with your spouse and children so they feel involved in the plan. This way, you have a much better chance of meeting your targets than if they had no input.

- Be realistic and specific to your situation. You should not count on levels of spending or income that you only wish you had, or that your neighbor has. That will only frustrate the exercise. Also, remember that a budget, in itself, will not increase your income or cut your spending; it only allows you to see what is going on so you can improve it.

- When setting priorities, refer back to the "Defining Your Financial Goals" section, in which you went through the exercise of determining what is most and least important to you.

- Use round numbers in your budget. You're not trying to drive yourself crazy by getting your spending down to the last penny.

- When making projections for the next year, don't automatically assume you will earn or spend the same amount in each category as you did the

Figure 1.10   Annual Budgeting Worksheet

YEAR _____

Annual Income	Actual Last Year	Budget This Year	Actual This Year	+/(−) Budget vs. Actual This Year
Earned Income	$	$	$	$
Self-Employment Income				
Family Income				
Government Income				
Retirement Income				
Investment Income				
Other Income				
TOTAL ANNUAL INCOME	$	$	$	$
Expenses				
Fixed Expenses				
Automobile-Related	$	$	$	$
Family				
Home-Related				
Insurance				
Savings and Investments				
Taxes				
Utilities				
Other				
Total Fixed Expenses	$	$	$	$
Flexible Expenses				
Children	$	$	$	$
Clothing				
Contributions and Dues				
Education				
Equipment and Vehicles				
Financial and Professional Services				
Food				
Home Maintenance				
Medical Care				
Miscellaneous				
Recreation and Entertainment				
Savings and Investments				
Travel and Vacations				
Other				
Total Flexible Expenses	$	$	$	$
TOTAL EXPENSES	$	$	$	$
TOTAL INCOME LESS TOTAL EXPENSES	$	$	$	$

Figure 1.11   Monthly Budgeting Worksheet

MONTH _____   YEAR _____

Income	Budget	Actual	YTD Budget	YTD Actual
Earned Income	$_____	$_____	$_____	$_____
Self-Employment Income	_____	_____	_____	_____
Family Income	_____	_____	_____	_____
Government Income	_____	_____	_____	_____
Retirement Income	_____	_____	_____	_____
Investment Income	_____	_____	_____	_____
Other Income	_____	_____	_____	_____
TOTAL INCOME	$_____	$_____	$_____	$_____

Expenses

Fixed Expenses

	Budget	Actual	YTD Budget	YTD Actual
Automobile-Related	$_____	$_____	$_____	$_____
Family	_____	_____	_____	_____
Home-Related	_____	_____	_____	_____
Insurance	_____	_____	_____	_____
Savings and Investments	_____	_____	_____	_____
Taxes	_____	_____	_____	_____
Utilities	_____	_____	_____	_____
Other	_____	_____	_____	_____
Total Fixed Expenses	$_____	$_____	$_____	$_____

Flexible Expenses

	Budget	Actual	YTD Budget	YTD Actual
Children	$_____	$_____	$_____	$_____
Clothing	_____	_____	_____	_____
Contributions and Dues	_____	_____	_____	_____
Education	_____	_____	_____	_____
Equipment and Vehicles	_____	_____	_____	_____
Financial and Professional Services	_____	_____	_____	_____
Food	_____	_____	_____	_____
Home Maintenance	_____	_____	_____	_____
Medical Care	_____	_____	_____	_____
Miscellaneous	_____	_____	_____	_____
Recreation and Entertainment	_____	_____	_____	_____
Savings and Investments	_____	_____	_____	_____
Travel and Vacations	_____	_____	_____	_____
Other	_____	_____	_____	_____
Total Flexible Expenses	$_____	$_____	$_____	$_____
TOTAL EXPENSES	$_____	$_____	$_____	$_____
TOTAL INCOME LESS TOTAL EXPENSES	$_____	$_____	$_____	$_____

previous year. Last year's figures should be a guide, not a straitjacket. Part of your budget is taking control of your finances, so move numbers on the expense side up or down, depending—to some extent—on what you would like to see happen in the next year.

In setting up your budget (see Figure 1.10), use the totals from the Cash Flow Worksheet from the previous section (see Figure 1.9) and add four columns to it. Label the first column, "Actual Last Year." In it, record what you actually earned and spent in each of the categories in the last year. This should be easy because all you have to do is transfer the figures from the Cash Flow Worksheet.

Next, you want to project what you think you will earn and what you want to spend in each of the categories over the next year. Label this second column, "Budget This Year."

As you proceed through the year, you will be keeping track of what you are actually earning and spending in each category. This should be entered in the third column, "Actual This Year." In the fourth column, you will calculate whether you are above or below what you projected in each category. Label this last column, "+/− Budget vs. Actual This Year" or "Difference."

With this design, you can instantly see whether your income and expenses are coming in over or under projections. When you total them, you can observe whether you are shooting above or below your total budget. If you are over budget, the culprit category usually sticks out like a sore thumb. If you are under budget, you might make a mid-course correction to see where else you can put some money, such as in savings or investments.

MONTHLY BUDGET

In addition to doing an annual budget, you should keep a running tab of how you are doing on a monthly basis in at least the major categories. The Monthly Budgeting Worksheet in Figure 1.11 will let you compare your budgeted amount with your actual income and spending. At the end of the worksheet, calculate whether you are over or under budget overall. Using this worksheet, you will be able to see month by month what kind of progress you are making toward meeting your budget and what items are at the greatest variance with your projections.

Assembling a Long-Term Financial Plan

While budgeting is crucial to balancing your income and spending over the coming months and years, you also have to take steps to project how your needs will evolve during the rest of your life. That is where long-term financial planning fits in. This process not only helps you avoid or at least be prepared for financial surprises and disasters; it helps those in good financial shape become even better prepared for the future. As you get older, certain financial events inevitably are bound to occur, and the more prepared you are for them, the easier they will be to handle. The relatively small amount of time you spend on long-term planning will pay off enormously for the rest of your life, both in terms of dollars and cents and in the security it gives you to know you will be able to deal with almost any twist or turn of your financial fate.

As you found out in the "Defining Your Financial Goals" section, there are short-, medium- and long-term dimensions to your financial life. While budgeting is aimed at satisfying your short-term goals, you might never get to the medium- and long-term objectives without a comprehensive financial plan.

Many of the aspects of long-term planning will be discussed in more detail later in this book. What follows is a brief introduction to all of the elements you will need to consider in setting up your strategy for long-term success.

Investment strategy. Your financial plan will outline how much capital you will need to accumulate to meet certain long-term goals, such as paying for your children's college education, buying or upgrading a home or providing for a secure retirement. Part of the investment strategy is assembling a portfolio of stocks, bonds, mutual funds and bank instruments that will get you where you want to go. One of the main risks you must overcome in a long-term plan is the slow but steady erosion of the worth of a dollar because of inflation. A good investment strategy will keep your dollars growing faster than inflation so that by the time you need to spend them, you will have enough. Another element of investing is finding a level of risk with which you feel comfortable. For more on investing, see Chapters 2–8.

Housing planning. Whether it is figuring out how to build a down payment on a first home, making an addition to your existing home or planning a move to a retirement community, your long-term housing needs must be planned far in advance because such decisions are expensive. Part of the planning entails deciding what kind of housing you would like at each stage of your life. You should then consider the different financial strategies you might use to pay for it. In some circumstances, it might make more sense to rent than to buy. In other cases, a 15-year mortgage might be better than a 30-year loan. A more detailed discussion of these matters appears in Chapter 8, "Inside Real Estate."

Debt planning. There are times in your life when it makes sense to borrow and other times when it is better to pay off debt. A young couple buying and furnishing their first home should expect to borrow to cover these enormous costs, while someone nearing retirement should already have his or her mortgage paid off (in an ideal world) and have as little debt as possible. If you do not plan carefully, debt can overwhelm your other financial plans because interest costs have a way of swallowing up much of your discretionary income. (For an extreme case, look at the federal government, which has to pay more and more for interest each year because of the soaring budget deficit, leaving less and less for programs.) When you do borrow, you must decide among various repayment alternatives in order to pay the lowest interest and still provide yourself with repayment flexibility. You will find more on debt planning in Chapter 9, "You and Your Credit—Managing It Wisely."

Automobile planning. Aside from your house and your children's education, your car will probably be the most expensive purchase you will make in your lifetime. Depending on what you will use your car for, how much you will drive it and how long you expect to keep it, there are different financial strategies to consider in obtaining a car. You might compare leasing versus taking out an auto loan to buy the car. You also should weigh the merits of buying a new versus a used car. You will find more on these questions in Chapter 10, "Getting the Most for Your Money When Buying a Car."

Insurance strategy. A key part of your long-term financial plan is to make sure you, your family and your major possessions are protected in case something unfortunate happens. That means finding the right kind of auto insurance, disability coverage, liability protection, health plans, homeowner's policies and life insurance. For a fuller explanation of these options, see Chapter 11, "All about Insurance."

Financing college. To accumulate the $50,000 to $100,000 or more that it will take to put your children through four years of a good college over the next few years, you would have had to start planning—and saving—as soon as they were born. This takes a discipline that will pay off as they approach their freshman year. The later you start saving, the more you will need to invest each year to end up with the same college kitty. In addition, it takes advance planning to understand and qualify for various kinds of student loan programs, both those offered by the government and those offered by individual schools. More details on college financing strategies can be found in Chapter 12, "How To Finance a College Education."

Tax planning. Without a systematic plan to minimize your federal, state and local tax liability, you will end up paying far more to the government than you need to. A key part of financial planning is determining in advance the tax implications of all your other moves. This might involve bunching deductions in one year rather than the next. Or tax considerations might dictate that you sell your business in installments over several years instead of taking all the cash in one lump sum, which would create a huge tax bill. To create more deductions, you might want to borrow against the equity in your home rather than on your unsecured line of credit, for which interest costs are nondeductible. For more on how you can plan to beat the tax man legally, read Chapter 13, "The Basics of Tax Planning."

Retirement planning. Even though it may be decades away, it is not too soon to plan for your retirement. Millions of people reach their supposedly "golden years" impoverished because they failed to plan. Millions of dollars passed through their hands during their lifetime, but very little of it was saved for their later years. The more capital you build up during your working years, the more options you will have when you retire. Considerations about retirement include whether you will stay in your home or move to another state; whether you will continue your career in modified form or even try a new career; or whether you will travel extensively. More on this topic appears in Chapter 14, "Retirement—How To Get There from Here."

Estate planning. You should think far in advance about how you want to dispose of your assets to your heirs. The scenes from old movies where the ancient patriarch signs over all of his assets to his children on his deathbed just don't apply to the real world anymore. In that situation today, the IRS would lump all of those assets back into his estate, which may have to pay estate tax at a rate of 37 percent or more. Estate planning, of course, involves writing a will, but it also might entail setting up different kinds of trusts and giving gifts to several people over several years. For more detail on this topic, read Chapter 15, "Estate Planning—Keeping Your Assets in the Family."

Employee benefit planning. Your biggest source of long-term capital, if you manage it well, could be the benefits your employer offers you. Quite often, the benefits are not explained very well by your benefits office, and you fail to take full advantage of what you are offered. By enrolling in salary reduction, savings bond payroll deduction, profit-sharing and flexible spending plans, among others, you can greatly enhance your long-term financial health with relatively little effort. For further details on these plans, see Chapter 16, "Making the Most of Your Employee Benefits."

Selecting financial advisers to prepare the plan. Each of the areas just mentioned is itself a specialty that requires expertise. This book will give you most of the basic knowledge you will need so that you can understand and make judgments about what advisers recommend. Still, it would probably be productive for you to sit down with them and go over your specific situation. If you bring in your completed net worth, goals, cash flow and budget worksheets from this book, you will already be miles ahead of most people who arrive at the door of financial planners—and you will save yourself a great deal of money because the planner will not have to take time to assemble that information for you. For you to create a workable plan that meets all legal requirements, you should assemble a team that includes a financial planner, a tax adviser, an estate lawyer, an insurance specialist and an investment professional. For more on how to choose members of this team, see Chapter 17, "Finding Financial Advisers Who Are Right for You."

Finally, the answers in all these areas of financial planning depend on your age and your situation (whether you are single, married, remarried, divorced, widowed, with or without children, etc.). The final chapter gives you brief outlines of some special planning rules that apply to different ages—whether you are in your 20s, 30s, 40s, 50s or retirement years.

Assessing Your Tolerance for Risk

Unfortunately, for many people, the word *risk,* just like the word *budgeting,* has a negative connotation. "Why would I want to risk my hard-earned money?" you say. "I'm very conservative."

The answer: If you take no risks with your assets, you will be unlikely to earn a return high enough to achieve your financial goals. To alter the universal saying seen in gymnasiums everywhere—"No pain, no gain"—when you get into the money world, the saying is "No risk, no return."

Now, we're not advocating that you take enormous risks with all of your money. Not every risky investment will earn a high return; if it did, it wouldn't be risky. By diversifying your assets carefully among high-risk, medium-risk and low-risk investments, you are assured of ending up with a larger pool of assets over time than if you keep all of your money in low-risk, low-return choices.

In general, the further in the future a return is expected, the greater the risk. Because it is tricky enough to predict what is going to happen over the next few months, it is even more difficult to know what the long-term future holds. Therefore, under normal circumstances, the longer you commit yourself to an investment, the more risk you are taking. But because you are taking more risk, you should be compensated in the long run by a higher return.

As you determine your tolerance for risk, you should understand several types of risk. There are ways to control and minimize each of these risks. But before we get to that later in the book, here are the most important risks you will face:

Currency risk. While most of your assets will probably be in dollar-denominated investments, you should be aware of the risk of currency movements if you own stocks or bonds denominated in other currencies. When you buy an individual stock or bond in another country, or a mutual fund that invests in foreign securities, the value of your investment fluctuates based on how many dollars it takes to buy a unit of the foreign currency. In effect, when you own a British stock, for example, your money has been converted into pounds. If the value of the pound falls against the U.S. dollar, your British shares will be worth less if you were to sell the stock and translate the pounds back into dollars. Conversely, if the pound gains value against the greenback, your British stock will be worth more if you were to sell it. Currency movements, which swing day to day based on each country's economic and political conditions, can therefore hand you substantial gains or losses.

Deflation risk. If prices are falling sharply because of a severe economic contraction, you face the risk that the value of your assets will drop just as sharply. This is what happened during the Great Depression of the 1930s, when stock prices, real estate prices and prices of just about everything else plummeted. To some extent, deflation was a problem in the early 1990s as well, particularly in commercial real estate, which had been vastly overbuilt during the boom times of the 1980s. The key to sidestepping deflation risk is to make sure you do not have too much of your wealth in assets that could get hit by a deflationary wave. Treasury bonds provide a good haven from deflation, for example, because it is safe to assume the government will always honor its obligations to bondholders.

Lack of diversification risk. This is commonly known as the risk of keeping all your eggs in one basket. If all your assets are in one kind of investment, like stocks or CDs, you are not protected if that asset falls sharply in value. Even more dangerous is to keep most of your money in just one stock, bond or CD because if something happens to it, you have no alternate assets to fall back on. Many people's biggest financial mistake is to have too much of their net worth tied up in their own company's stock. Even if it is a wonderful company that has a bright future, these people lack diversification. The way to lower risk in this realm is to spread your holdings among different kinds of assets as well as among several individual investments within each kind of asset. One easy way to diversify is to buy a mutual fund, which itself holds dozens of stocks or bonds. For more on this, see Chapter 4, "Selecting Mutual Funds."

Inflation risk. Even if prices are rising at about 5 percent a year, the value of your dollars is steadily eroding over time. If inflation is galloping at more than 10 percent, your purchasing power disappears much faster. Sometimes you don't notice inflation risk until you must buy something you have not bought for several years and you are hit with sticker shock when you see how much prices have risen. That can be true when you buy a new car or when you make your child's first tuition payment. You might mutter to yourself: "Why, when I went to college, it cost me $5,000 for all four years, and now that covers only the first semester of freshman year!" Welcome to inflation risk.

Interest rate risk. Over the past two decades, interest rates on bonds, money-market accounts, mortgages and all other types of interest-sensitive financial instruments have been extremely volatile. In the early 1980s, the prime rate reached as high as 21½ percent, and rates on bonds, CDs and mortgages also soared into double digits. By the 1990s, rates had plunged to the low single digits, and savers who had become accustomed to 14 percent CDs were crying, "Bring back the good old days of double-digit yields!" Interest-rate risk can therefore cut both ways. If you lock into a fixed-rate instrument like a bond or CD when rates are low, and then rates rise sharply, the value of your investment will plunge if you have to resell it. On the other hand, if you set your lifestyle according to the high yields you can earn in an environment of soaring interest rates, you will endure a painful shock when rates fall and your lifestyle suffers.

Lack of liquidity risk. There are times when you need to sell something, but the market for it has dried up temporarily. That leaves you with two options: You can hang on to what you had wanted to sell, or you can sell it anyway even if you must accept an artificially low price. In general, the more aggressive an investment is, the more subject it is to the risk of holding an illiquid asset. Stocks of small companies and junk bonds, for example, are relatively easy to buy and sell under normal circumstances. But when bad news hits these markets or investors become nervous, the ability to sell at a fair price temporarily disappears.

Playing it too safe risk. As mentioned at the beginning of this section, if you keep all your money in super-safe CDs, money-market funds and Treasuries, you run the risk of outliving your assets because your return has not kept you current with inflation. This risk is not frequently recognized, but it is probably the biggest risk people take. By the time you have figured out that you have been too conservative with your investments, it is often too late to recover.

Political risk. If you invest in countries where the political structure is not as stable as in the United States, you run the risk of a change in government, which will dramatically devalue the worth of your holdings. In the most extreme case, a new government that has run on the platform of "throwing out all the foreigners" might go so far as to nationalize all assets, which means you will get whatever the government decides to give you for your stocks and bonds. Fortunately, most countries have been going the opposite direction lately, as they realize it is better to encourage foreign investment than to scare it away.

A milder form of political risk that you should keep in mind for American investments is the change in government policy that favors one industry over another. This can be done by legislation, tax policy, tariffs, subsidies or many other means at the government's disposal. For example, in the 1970s, President Carter wanted to encourage the use of coal because it was available domestically and could reduce our dependence on foreign oil. By the 1990s, coal was considered an environmentally dangerous fuel, and natural gas was in vogue. Another striking example is the multi-billion-dollar buildup of the defense industry in the 1980s, unraveled in the 1990s, with devastating impact on the holders of defense-related stocks.

Repayment risk. There are two kinds of repayment risk. The most common, also known as *credit risk,* is the chance that you will not get repaid what you are owed when it is due. The second risk is the opposite: you are repaid before you want or expect to get your money back. You are taking credit risk whenever you buy a bond because your ability to collect on that obligation is only as good as the issuer's ability to repay it. Some issuers, like the U.S. government, which sells Treasury bonds, are above reproach, and, therefore, credit risk on such paper is considered to be virtually nonexistent. Bonds issued by corporations, municipalities and foreign governments also rarely default, but these issuers offer several gradations of credit risk. Credit risk ratings by agencies like Standard & Poor's and Moody's Investors Service, which range from AAA to D, will indicate how much repayment risk you are taking with a particular issue.

The other kind of repayment risk entails getting your money back faster than you expect. While you might not think this is a big problem, it is in two circumstances. First, suppose you lock in a 10 percent yield on a bond, and gradually the rate falls to 6 percent. Because interest rates have dropped, you will not be able to replace that bond with a new one at the same yield. Most bond issuers have the right to redeem (or *call,* as it is known) a bond a certain number of years after it has been issued. (One of the advantages of Treasury bonds is that they are usually noncallable.)

The other kind of investment that hits you with repayment risk is the mortgage-backed security. Known in the trade by the names Ginnie Mae, Fannie Mae or CMO (which stands for *collateralized mortgage obligation*), mortgage-backed securities are actually pools of thousands of individual mortgages that have been packaged for sale. The repayment problem occurs when mortgage rates fall sharply and homeowners rush to refinance their loans. While it is great for the homeowners, the holders of mortgage-backed securities lose because the securities repay most of their principal quickly. Because interest rates have fallen, holders of mortgage-backed securities have the same problem as owners of called bonds: They can't replicate the high rates they thought they had locked in for years. (For more on bonds, refer to Chapter 5, "All about Bonds."

Volatility risk. This risk occurs when an investment swings wildly in value, from a very low price to a high one in a short period of time. Of course, volatility gives you a greater chance to profit if you buy when the price is low and sell when it is high. But that's easier said than done. Often, your emotions will drive you to buy into a volatile investment when its price has been rising because you assume the price will continue to soar. The opposite usually holds true: You are most tempted to sell when the price has plummeted because you fear it will plunge even further. Just because an investment is volatile in the short run doesn't mean you should avoid it altogether. But you should realize what you've bought and feel psychologically able to ride out sudden air pockets when they strike, keeping in mind that you entered into the investment in the hope of long-term gain.

THE INVESTMENT PYRAMID

In assembling a portfolio that both achieves your financial goals and still allows you to sleep comfortably at night, think of your entire mix of assets in the form of an investment pyramid (see Figure 1.12).

At the top of your pyramid are the riskiest assets, which offer the greatest potential for high returns as well as big losses. The *high-risk* apex includes collectibles, foreign investments, futures contracts, junk corporate and municipal bonds, new stock issues, oil and gas limited partnerships, options, raw land, small growth stocks, tax shelters, unfinished real estate construction, venture capital and warrants.

The next tier of the pyramid, the *moderate-risk* sector, includes stock and bond mutual funds, income-oriented limited partnerships, mortgage-backed securities, individual growth stocks, corporate bonds and rental real estate.

Figure 1.12
Investment Risk Levels

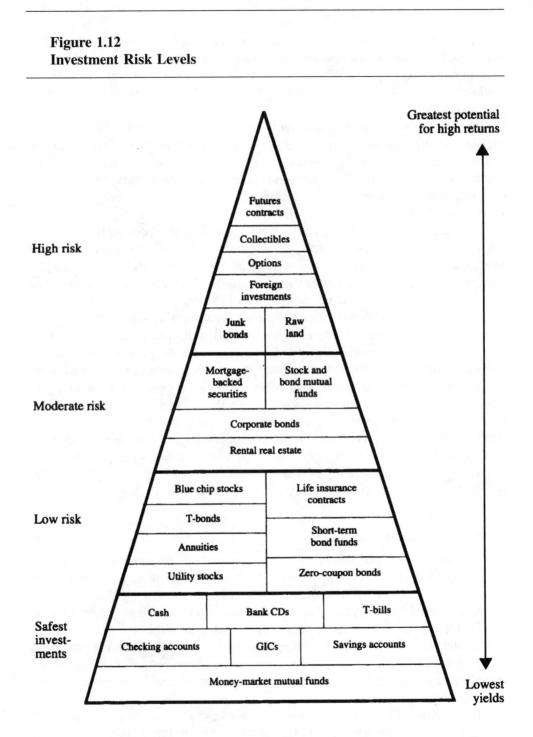

The third tier of the pyramid, called the *low-risk* sector, consists of annuities, blue chip stocks, Treasury bonds, life insurance contracts, municipal bonds with high credit ratings, short-term bond funds, utility stocks and zero-coupon bonds.

The *base* of the pyramid is composed of investments where there is almost no chance of losing your principal. This includes bank CDs, cash, checking accounts, money-market mutual funds and guaranteed investment contracts (GICs) found in salary reduction plans, savings accounts and Treasury bills.

There is, however, the risk of investments that are too safe. While your principal is not at risk, the investments earn low yields and therefore do not allow you to keep up with inflation.

No matter what your age or situation, you should probably have some of your assets in each of the four sectors of the pyramid at all times. What should change over time is how much you invest in each sector. You might be young and able to take more risk, so more of your money should be in the high-risk apex. Or you may be retired and need to live off your investments. More of your money should then be in low-risk and base investments. But the young person should still have a cash reserve in base investments, and the retiree should have a small amount of money in apex investments, so they both can stay ahead of inflation. The allocation of assets among the four pyramid sectors is discussed in more detail in Chapter 18, "Smart Money Strategies for Every Age and Situation."

A Quiz To Determine Your Risk Tolerance

Even though by now you should realize that you will have to take some calculated risks in order to attain your financial goals, this doesn't mean you are comfortable doing it. The quiz in Figure 1.13 will give you some insight into how much risk you feel able to take. Answer each of the questions, giving yourself one point for answer one, two points for answer two, up to four points for answer four. Then add up the points to see what kind of risk-taker you are.

Keep your risk score in mind as you read through the rest of the book. If you are a diehard conservative, you should resist the temptation to put much money in riskier investments even though they may sound promising. Keep the investment pyramid in mind, though; you still don't want to have all your assets in only the safest bets.

If you are a moderate-risk investor, put more of your money in the middle and top sectors of the investment pyramid as long as you carefully gauge the level of risk you are taking.

For high-risk investors, allocate more of your money to the apex of the investment pyramid, but don't neglect the pyramid base. You should be careful not to become so enthusiastic about an investing idea that you put too much of your capital at risk in something that goes bust.

Wherever you stand on the risk spectrum, keep in mind that dealing with your personal finances, in general, and investing, in particular, is not only about

Figure 1.13 Risk Tolerance Quiz

A. If someone made me an offer to invest 15 percent of my net worth in a deal he said had an 80 percent chance of being profitable, the level of profit would have to be

1. No level of profit would be worth that kind of risk.
2. seven times the amount I invested.
3. three times the amount I invested.
4. at least as much as I have invested in the first place.

Points: _____

B. How comfortable would I be assuming a $10,000 debt in the hope of achieving a $20,000 gain over the next few months?

1. Totally uncomfortable—I would never do it.
2. Somewhat uncomfortable—I would probably never do it.
3. Somewhat comfortable—I might do it.
4. Very comfortable—I would jump at the chance to do it.

Points: _____

C. I am holding a lottery ticket that has gotten me to the finals, where I have a one in four chance of winning a $100,000 prize. The least I would be willing to sell my ticket for before the drawing is

1. $15,000.
2. $20,000.
3. $35,000.
4. $60,000.

Points: _____

D. I have spent more than $150 on one or more of these activities: professional sports gambling, recreational betting on poker or basketball games I participate in, casino gambling.

1. I have never participated in any of these activities.
2. I have participated in these activities only a few times in my life.
3. I have participated in one of these activities in the past year.
4. I have participated in two or more of these activities in the past year.

Points: _____

E. Whenever I have to decide where to invest a large amount of money, I

1. delay the decision.
2. get somebody else (like my broker) to decide for me.
3. share the decision with advisers.
4. decide on my own.

Points: _____

Figure 1.13   (continued)

F.   If a stock I bought doubled in the year after I bought it, I would

   1.   sell all my shares.
   2.   sell half of my shares.
   3.   not sell any shares.
   4.   buy more shares.

   Points: _____

G.   Which of the following describes how I make my investment decisions?

   1.   Never on my own
   2.   Sometimes on my own
   3.   Often on my own
   4.   Always on my own

   Points: _____

H.   My luck in investing is

   1.   terrible.
   2.   average.
   3.   better than average.
   4.   fantastic.

   Points: _____

I.   My investments are successful mainly because

   1.   God is always on my side.
   2.   I was in the right place at the right time.
   3.   when opportunities arose, I took advantage of them.
   4.   I carefully planned them to work out that way.

   Points: _____

J.   I have a high-yielding certificate of deposit that is about to mature, and
interest rates have dropped so much that I feel compelled to invest in
something with a higher yield. The most likely place I will invest the
money is

   1.   U.S. savings bonds.
   2.   a short-term bond fund.
   3.   a long-term bond fund.
   4.   a stock fund.

   Points: _____

TOTAL SCORE: _____

How to score yourself:

0–19 points: You are a conservative investor who feels uncomfortable taking any risk.

20–29 points: You are a moderate investor who feels comfortable taking moderate risks.

30–39 points: You are an aggressive investor who is willing to take high risks in search of high returns.

maximizing the amount of dollars in your pocket. Finding your financial comfort zone is also important so that you feel psychologically secure about the decisions you are making. It's no use becoming rich if you die from the stress of attaining your wealth (even though your heirs might disagree!).

Using Your Computer To Keep Your Finances in Shape

Now that you have done the exercises in this chapter, it would be best if you could keep this data up-to-date on a regular basis so that you always know where you stand when you need to make financial decisions. The easiest way to accomplish this job is by using your personal computer. There are two ways to put your computer to work for you in this arena: (1) entering data in a personal finance software program and (2) using the Internet and its many Web sites to educate yourself about finance and track your progress towards your financial goals.

Personal Finance Software Programs

In the early days of the personal computer, there was a profusion of programs to help you manage your personal finances. Now many of the competitors have fallen by the wayside, leaving four major programs for you to choose from. They are all available at most bookstores and computer software stores, as well as through the Web sites listed here:

Kiplinger's Simply Money (617-642-1706). Perhaps the simplest package of the four, Simply Money allows you to track a budget, write checks, do basic financial planning, manage your investment portfolio and keep records for tax preparation. The program comes with the Financial Advisor, which imparts the wisdom of editors of Kiplinger's financial magazine and newsletters on almost any topic of personal finance. www.cdtitles.com

Managing Your Money (203-268-2797). This program has been continually improved since it first debuted in the early 1980s. Its distinguishing feel comes from the omnipresent character of financial adviser Andrew Tobias, who guides you through the many realms of personal finance with his humorous and sensible commentary. Managing Your Money features the SmartDesk interface, which sets up the main menu like your home office, with file drawers and tools representing the program's many functions. A fountain pen takes you to the check-writing section, for instance. The program offers a great amount of depth in both performing calculations and teaching you about personal finance. A sampling of the subjects it covers: tax preparation, budgeting, asset allocation, portfolio tracking, buying insurance, analyzing various borrowing alternatives, planning for financing college and credit management. www.mymnet.com

Microsoft Money (206-635-7131). This financial offering from the dominant software company in the world covers all the bases in a logical, easy-to-navigate style. The program allows you to track your portfolio, research potential investments, calculate your net worth, prepare and follow a budget, and prepare your taxes. The program is used by many banks for online banking systems, making electronic bill payment and recordkeeping easy. You can also prepare charts and graphs of different aspects of your personal finances that may help you understand your situation better than just looking at columns of numbers. Microsoft Money was designed to work with Windows software, and it does so very elegantly. Another helpful feature is that the program takes maximum advantage of the many offerings in the Microsoft Moneyzone, from information on stocks and mutual funds to tax-planning strategy and personal finance discussion groups. Microsoft comes out with a new version of this program every year, constantly adding new features that you might find useful in managing your money better. www.microsoft.com/moneyzone

Quicken Deluxe (520-295-3220). The bestselling Quicken is the most comprehensive, in-depth program in personal finance. If you are willing to spend a great deal of time and effort inputting data and doing analysis of your financial situation, you will get a lot out of Quicken. But if you are a novice, you may find the program a bit overwhelming. Quicken lets you set up detailed budgeting categories, a check register, a financial calendar, a credit card and mortgage loan tracking system, an asset-liability worksheet and an investment portfolio system. You can create numerous charts and graphs, showing, for instance, how much your income or expenses are varying from your projections. Quicken also provides a detailed tax-planning section, designed to work with Intuit's TurboTax program. The program is loaded with financial planning calculators to help you figure out the cost of refinancing a loan or how much you need to be saving towards retirement or your children's college education. Quicken is designed to work with CheckFree to let you pay bills online, and the special Intellicharge credit card downloads your credit card statement and automatically categorizes your transactions for you into Quicken. There is also the Mutual Fund Finder, which allows you to screen for mutual funds meeting your investment parameters using Morningstar data. All in all, Quicken probably provides the richest array of personal finance tracking, transaction and analysis software. You just have to be willing to devote enough effort to make the most of it. www.qfn.com

TAPPING THE ONLINE WORLD

There is a vast amount of information on the Internet and commercial online services to help you manage your finances. You can get news, search for price quotes on stocks, bonds, mutual funds and insurance policies, find the cheapest credit cards and learn about any area of personal finance that tickles your fancy. You can join in any of thousands of discussion groups and bulletin boards covering the broadest or the narrowest of financial interests. You must be careful when doing so, however, because you never really know who is giving advice or what their hidden motives might be, particularly when people are recommending investments.

Perhaps the easiest place to get started in the online world is by subscribing to America Online (800-827-3338). AOL has prepackaged an enormous amount of personal finance resources under its Personal Finance Channel button, so that you don't have to find Web site addresses on your own. AOL's Channel is divided into many subchannels, such as the Insurance Center, the Banking Center, the Mutual Funds Center and the Brokerage Center. Each center has an educational component that explains the basics and more sophisticated strategies to screen for stocks and mutual funds, or purchase home or car insurance, for example. Each also displays the icons of several major institutions, such as banks, brokers and insurance companies, beckoning you to visit their Web sites:

- In the Mutual Fund Center, you can screen among thousands of funds in the Morningstar database, consult the Sage for advice on funds, look at Fund Family Profiles and track a portfolio of funds.

- In the Insurance Center, you can learn about the ins and outs of auto, life and home insurance, and buy coverage online.

- In the Banking Center, you can perform online banking, look at rates on credit cards, mortgages and other loans in the Bank Rate Monitor section, find the highest-yielding certificates of deposit ranked by maturity, and find links to major bank Web sites. The banking sector also features the Money Whiz, who answers any questions relating to banking and credit.

- In the Investment Center, there is a plethora of information on stocks and bonds. You can look at current market news and quotes, maintain a stock portfolio, find links to several major online discount brokers and screen for stocks that meet specific criteria.

- Other features of the Personal Finance section include The Motley Fool area on investing tips and strategies; Shark Attack on hot stock tips; Family Finance from Parent Soup with advice for parents; Chart-O-Matic charts on individual stocks; Hoover's Business Resources with data on thousands of companies; Checks and Balances, a weekly finance newsletter; Advice from Your Financial Planner Ric Edelman, who is an author and radio show host; the New York Stock Exchange center; and links to various magazines and organizations including the American Association of Individual Investors, *Consumer Reports, The Economist, Investor's Business Daily* and *Worth Magazine.* Of course, the AOL site is constantly changing and adding new features and links, so this is by no means a definitive list of what the service offers. But it should give you a sense of the breadth of the service—for many people who are not spending all their time on their personal finances, it is plenty.

For those who want more, there is a seemingly endless number of Web sites devoted to personal financial topics. One way to find sites is to type in words like *Personal Finance* or *Money* into a web browser to come up with Web site addresses. Even better, narrow your search by typing in a word specifically related to what you are investigating at the moment. Here are just a few suggestions of some Web sites that will help you find out what you need to know:

- *Financenter.* A wealth of information on how to finance major assets like homes and cars. The site allows you to compare various borrowing alternatives so you can pick what is best for your situation. It also has an extensive section on how to get the best credit cards. Several companies allow you to apply for loans online, and some even offer special rates to Financenter users. www.financenter.com

- *Financial Electric Library.* The ultimate source of information to answer whatever question you have about personal finance. The Library draws on hundreds of magazines, books, wire services, newspapers and broadcast transcripts to get you what you need based on how you define the search criteria. www.elibrary.com/intuit/

- *Interactive Nest Egg.* An online finance magazine aimed at small investors. It includes an Equity Center, Initial Public Offering (IPO) Center, Mutual Fund Center, Planning Your Future section and a Special Topics sector. The site has numerous financial calculators to help you figure out, for instance, how much you need to save for a comfortable retirement, or whether you would be better off with a 15-year or 30-year mortgage. www.nestegg.iddis/com/nestegg.html

- *Personal Finance Network.* Loaded with articles and audio broadcasts on a wide variety of topics, including retirement planning, pensions, Social Security, 401(k) plans and women's finances. Also sponsors chat sessions with prominent government policymakers on various aspects of personal finance. www.wwbroadcast.com/pfn

- *Personal Finance Web Sites.* A source of links to many other useful personal finance Web sites. You choose a category, like College Financing, Investing or Credit, and it will tell you which Web sites you can visit to find out more. www.tiac.net/users/ikrakow/pagerefs.html

- *Personal Finance Magazine Web Sites.* All of the major financial magazines sponsor their own Web sites, which offer much more than articles
  from the publications. They host chat sessions with magazine staffers and
  experts featured in articles and provide investment news and portfolio
  tracking services, financial calculators, polls, links to other Web sites and
  much more. The magazine Web site addresses for *Bloomberg Personal,
  Family Money, Kiplinger's Personal Finance, Money, Smart Money* and
  Worth are listed under "Magazines" in the "Resources" section.

Resources

For further information on the topics presented in the first chapter of this book,
I recommend that you consult the following resources.

BOOKS

The Budget Kit: The Common Cent$ Money Management Workbook, by Judy
Lawrence (Dearborn Financial Publishing, 155 N. Wacker Dr., Chicago, IL 60606;
312-836-4400; 800-245-2665). An easy-to-use, hands-on workbook that helps you
keep track of your budget each month. www.realestate-ed.com

Consumer Reports Money Book, by Janet Bamford, Jeff Blyskal, Emily Card and
Aileen Jacobson (Consumer Reports Books, P.O. Box 10637, Des Moines, IA 50336;
800-500-9760). A comprehensive guide on how to acquire, save and spend money
wisely. www.consumer.org

Home Filing Made Easy!, by Mary E. Martin, CFP, and J. Michael Martin, JD,
CFP (Dearborn Financial Publishing, 155 N. Wacker Dr., Chicago, IL 60606; 312-
836-4400; 800-245-2665). Helps you set up an easy-to-find home filing system to keep
up with an incoming flood of papers—tax documents, credit-card statements, insurance policies, medical records, etc.

Lew Altfest Answers Almost All Your Questions about Money, by Lewis J. and
Karen C. Altfest (McGraw-Hill, Order Dept., 860 Taylor Station Rd., Blacklick, OH
43004; 800-233-1128). A book by husband and wife financial planners who cover 11
basic and sophisticated financial planning subjects in question-and-answer format.
www.McGraw-Hill.com

Money Dynamics for the 1990s, by Venita Van Caspel (Simon & Schuster, 1230
Avenue of the Americas, New York, NY 10020; 212-698-7000; 800-223-2348). A
detailed look at most major financial planning issues, with an emphasis on taking
advantage of trends in the 1990s. www.simonsays.com

Ninety Days to Financial Fitness, by Joan German Grapes (Macmillan Publishing,
866 Third Ave., New York, NY 10022; 212-702-2000; 800-428-5331). Offers a plan

for financial stability and provides model plans for people in different situations, including married couples, couples living together and singles. www.mcp.com

Smart Money: How To Be Your Own Financial Manager, by Ken and Daria Dolan (Berkley Books, 200 Madison Ave., New York, NY 10016; 212-951-8400; 800-631-8571). A breezy guide to personal finance, presented mostly in question-and-answer format. www.berkley.com

The Wealthy Barber: Everyone's Common-Sense Guide To Becoming Financially Independent, by David B. Chilton (Prima Publishing, P.O. Box 1260DC, Rocklin, CA 95677; 916-632-4400). A clever and folksy book on financial planning, written in novel form, that covers retirement planning, buying a home, investing and taxes, among other topics. www.primapublishing.com

Your Money or Your Life: Transforming Your Relationship with Money and Achieving Financial Independence, by Joe Dominguez and Vicki Robin (Viking Penguin, 375 Hudson St., New York, NY 10014; 212-366-2000). Offers a new financial road map to improve your financial well-being. www.penguin.com

Your Wealthbuilding Years: Financial Planning for 18- to 38-Year-Olds, by Adriane G. Berg (Newmarket Press, 18 E. 48th St., New York, NY 10017; 212-832-3575; 800-733-3000). A practical guide aimed at younger people wanting to get their finances organized.

Magazines

Bloomberg Personal (P.O. Box 888, Princeton, NJ 08542-0888; 609-279-3000; 888-432-5820). Sophisticated magazine, largely devoted to investing strategies, published by the Bloomberg Business News organization, which supplies news and data to the financial services industry. www.bloomberg.com

Family Money (1716 Locust Street, Des Moines, IA 50309-3023; 515-284-3450; 800-642-9607). Basic personal finance magazine published by Meredith Corporation, which also publishes *Better Homes and Gardens.* www.familymoney.com

Financial Planning (SDC Publishing, 40 W. 57th St., Suite 114, New York, NY 10019, 212-765-5311). A magazine that covers the financial planning industry and the latest trends in financial planning. www.fponline.com

Kiplinger's Personal Finance Magazine (The Kiplinger Washington Editors, Inc., 1729 H St., N.W., Washington, DC 20006-3938; 202-887-6400; 800-544-0155). Personal finance magazine aimed at readers less financially sophisticated than those who read *Money.* www.kiplinger.com

Money (Time Inc., a division of Time Warner, Time and Life, Rockefeller Center, New York, NY 10020; 212-522-1212; 800-633-9970). The largest circulation and most prestigious magazine bringing financial planning ideas to average Americans. Features advice and news on investing, taxes, real estate, insurance, retirement and all other topics in personal finance, written in an easy-to-understand style. Also features a monthly case study, called "One Family's Finances," of a particular financial situation. www.money.com

Smart Money Magazine (1790 Broadway, New York, NY 10019; 212-492-1300; 800-444-4204). Sophisticated magazine concentrating on investing strategies, stocks and mutual funds but also dealing with lifestyle and spending decisions. www.smartmoney.com

Worth Magazine (Capital Publishing, 575 Lexington Ave., New York, NY 10017; 212-751-4550; 800-727-9098). Magazine covering both investing and lifestyle choices to help you improve your personal financial decision making. www.worth.com

NEWSLETTERS

Digest of Financial Planning (College for Financial Planning, 4695 S. Monaco St., Denver, CO 80237-3403; 303-220-1200). Letter aimed at updating financial planners on industry trends.

The Kiplinger Washington Letter (The Kiplinger Washington Editors, Inc. 1729 H St., N.W., Washington DC 20006-3938; 202-887-6400; 800-544-0155). News on business and personal finance trends from Washington. The letter covers changes in government policies, interest rates, investment markets and tax rulings that affect your finances. www.kiplinger.com

The MoneyLetter (Hume Publishing, 2200 Yonge St., Suite 604, Toronto, Ontario, Canada M4S 2C6; 416-440-8260; 800-733-4863). A newsletter with solid tips on all aspects of financial planning. www.humegroup.com

NEFE Digest (College for Financial Planning, 4695 S. Monaco St., Denver, CO 80237-3403; 303-220-1200). Letter aimed at updating financial planners on industry trends. www.nefe.org

Personal Finance Letter (KCI Communications, 1705 Old Meadow Rd., McLean, VA 22102; 703-905-8000). Touches on all areas of personal finance but specializes in investment advice.

Straight Talk on Your Money, by Ken and Daria Dolan (Phillips Publishing, 7811 Montrose Rd., Potomac, MD 20854; 301-340-2100; 800-777-5015). Discusses general financial planning as well as tax planning, investing, real estate, college funding and more. www.phillips.com

SOFTWARE

Everyone's Money Software (1932 First Ave., Suite 605, Seattle, WA 98101-1051; 800-553-9997). Contains all the worksheets in *Everyone's Money Book* in an easy-to-use, interactive format. Available in DOS and Windows versions.

Kiplinger's CA-Simply Money (Computer Associates International, 1 Computer Associates Plaza, Islandia, NY 11788-7000; 516-342-5224; 800-225-5224). Designed to work with Microsoft's Windows program, *CA-Simply Money* is more graphically oriented than many other personal finance programs. The program lets you track income, expenses, track the amortization of mortgage payments, print personalized checks and forms, and pay bills electronically. It is also designed to connect to the CompuServe and Prodigy databases. The software also incorporates Kiplinger's *Financial Advisor,* which tracks every financial move you make and offers suggestions on how you might improve the implementation of your plan.

Managing Your Money (MECA Software LLC, 115 Corporate Dr., Trumbull, CT 06611; 203-268-2797; 888-808-6322). A wonderfully designed yet complex software package, filled with witty commentary from personal finance writer Andrew Tobias that will help you calculate your net worth, create and keep to a budget, set goals, track your investments, pay bills, do tax planning, determine how much insurance you need and much more. www.mymnet.com

Microsoft Money (Microsoft Corp., One Microsoft Way, Redmond, WA 98052-6399; 206-635-7131; 800-426-9400). A simple program designed to track your income, expenses and net worth, keep your checkbook and pay your bills electronically. www.microsoft.com

Money Counts (Parsons Technology, One Parsons Dr., Hiawatha, IA 52233; 319-395-9626). An easy-to-use program that uses checkbook entry screens to help you budget and manage cash, checking, credit, investments and savings. www.parsonstech.com

Quicken (Intuit, P.O. Box 7850, Mountain View, CA 94039-7850; 415-944-6000). When you must make a financial decision on investments, taxes or other matters, allows you to track every aspect of your personal finances and analyze alternatives, using color graphs. Offers a credit card, which can be connected to Intellicharge, that will automatically enter all credit card charges into your software. Also designed to pay bills automatically and import stock prices from Prodigy. Quicken Financial Network is a broad-based Web site that will help you in many areas of personal finance. Some examples: NetWorth for mutual fund information; Quicken InsureMarket for auto, home and life insurance information and price quotes; the Banking Center for links to online banking; the Retirement Planning section, which helps you project your financial needs in retirement. The site is run by Intuit, so there are many places throughout the site encouraging you to use Quicken. www.qfn.com

Smart Investor, Wealthbuilder and *Reality Online* (Reality Technologies, 2200 Renaissance Blvd., King of Prussia, PA 19406; 610-650-8600; 800-346-2024). Two software programs and an online service designed to work together to help you set your goals, determine your net worth and map out an investment plan to help you reach your goals. Allow you to set your risk level, then pick among thousands of stocks and mutual funds that meet your criteria. As part of *Smart Investor,* allows you to dial into a local phone number to retrieve the latest financial news and data on stocks, CDs, mortgage rates and mutual funds. www.moneynet.com

TRADE ASSOCIATIONS

American Financial Services Association (919 18th St., N.W., Suite 300, Washington, DC 20006; 202-296-5544). The trade group for consumer finance companies; will send you the *Consumer's Almanac* for a very low price. www.americanfinsvcs.com

College for Financial Planning National Endowment for Financial Education (4695 S. Monaco St., Denver, CO 80237-3403; 303-220-1200; 800-553-5343). Administers the mail-order test for financial planners seeking to become Certified Financial Planners. www.nefe.org

Consumer Information Center (Pueblo, CO 81009; 719-948-3334). The U.S. government's main distribution center for consumer information. Catalog lists consumer-oriented publications.

Council of Better Business Bureaus (4200 Wilson Blvd., Arlington, VA 22203; 703-276-0100). The national organization for local Better Business Bureaus; offers a book titled *Investor Alert! How To Protect Your Money from Schemes, Scams and Frauds.* www.bbb.org

Institute of Certified Financial Planners (3801 East Florida Ave., Suite 708, Denver, CO 80210; 303-759-4900; 800-282-7526). Represents planners who have passed their Certified Financial Planning examinations; will provide you with a list of CFPs in the town where you live. www.icfp.org

International Association for Financial Planning (5775 Glenridge Dr. Northeast, Suite B300, Atlanta, GA 30328-5364; 404-845-0011; 800-945-4237). Represents those in the financial services industry involved with financial planning; will refer you to a qualified financial planner near your home. Will send you the *Consumer Guide to Financial Independence* for a very low price. www.iafp.com

International Association of Registered Financial Planners (307 E. Texas Ave., El Paso, TX 79901; 915-544-7947; 800-749-7947). Represents an advanced category of financial planners who have had at least four years' experience in planning, a college degree in business, economics or law and a CFP, ChFC or CPA designation as well as a securities or insurance license.

National Association of Life Underwriters (1922 F St., N.W., Washington, DC 20006; 202-331-6000). Group of life insurance agents. www.nalu.org

National Association of Personal Financial Advisors (355 West Dundee Rd., Suite 107, Buffalo Grove, IL 60089; 847-537-7722; 800-366-2732). Represents financial planners who work on a fee-only basis and therefore earn no commissions by selling products they recommend. www.napfa.org

National Center for Financial Education (P.O. Box 34070, San Diego, CA 92163 or located on the Internet at www.ncfe.org; 619-232-8811). Nonprofit organization dedicated to helping people do a better job of spending, saving, investing, insuring and planning for their financial future to avoid depending entirely upon Social Security or Medicare. Publishes a bimonthly newsletter called *The Motivator* that touches on most areas of personal finance. Operates a Money Bookstore that offers discounts on books for members, publishes books, including *Prime Time: How To Enjoy the Best Years of Your Life,* about retirement and *Marta's Closet Book: Bargain Dressing for Fun, Flair and Extra Money.*

Maximizing Returns on Cash Instruments

If you are a beginner at investing, chances are that you have most of your money in cash instruments. By *cash*, we mean investments that are totally safe from loss of principal, including checking, savings and certificate of deposit (CD) accounts at banks and savings and loans, money-market mutual funds and Treasury bills (T-bills). When you got your first allowance as a child, you probably were taught to save at least part of it in the bank, where you were proud to earn 5½ percent. Many people have never broken this praiseworthy habit but put some of their money into investments, such as stocks and bonds, that can offer higher rates of return.

The Importance of Cash Instruments

Cash instruments play an important stabilizing role in your investment portfolio. No matter how much or how little your cash earns for you in interest, it cannot fall in principal value, which certainly cannot be said for stocks and bonds. Cash can therefore act as a haven when stock and bond prices are falling.

Clearly, it is important to have cash available to meet everyday living expenses. Many cash instruments, including money-market accounts, NOW accounts and passbook savings accounts, are instantly accessible either through a check privilege or by withdrawing cash at an automatic teller machine (ATM). Other cash vehicles, including CDs and T-bills, which have short maturities, allow you to get at your money when the instruments mature in a few months. The liquidity of cash is one of its main benefits.

The Benefits of Bank Insurance

Safety is another important benefit of cash. Despite the hundreds of bank and savings and loan failures of the last several years, no depositor with insured cash instruments of $100,000 or less has lost a penny of principal or interest due. Ever since the *Federal Deposit Insurance Corporation* (FDIC) was set up in 1933, bank depositors have been able to sleep safely knowing that whatever happens to their banks, their money is safe as long as they keep the amount on deposit under the legal maximum. This could not be said before the FDIC was established. In fact, many bank depositors were wiped out when their banks failed after the stock market crash of October 1929. As expensive as it has been over the years for the federal government to keep its promise to protect bank depositors—and it has cost hundreds of billions of dollars—that assurance has provided stability for the banking system, which has allowed the economy to prosper. In countries where there is no deposit insurance, people keep their money under the mattress, or they open a foreign bank account—usually in America or Switzerland.

It is important to understand exactly what federal deposit insurance covers and what it doesn't. Under current law, each account you have registered at a bank or savings and loan is insured up to $100,000. For example, a married man may have an account in his name, a separate account in his wife's name and a joint account in both their names. Each of the accounts would be separately insured to $100,000, for a total, in this case, of $300,000. You can extend your coverage by opening accounts at other banks. While the FDIC is the overall insurer of deposits, banks are covered by the *Bank Insurance Fund* (BIF), and savings and loans are covered by the *Savings Association Insurance Fund* (SAIF). Credit union accounts are insured up to the same limit by the *National Credit Union Share Insurance Fund,* administered by the *National Credit Union Administration* (NCUA). This structure was created as part of the savings and loan bail-out legislation in 1989.

While federal deposit insurance guarantees that you will get back your principal and all interest due, it does not guarantee that you will be able to withdraw your money at will if a bank is seized. In that case, you may have to give the bank up to 30 days' advance notice if you want to take money out of your account. This provision, designed to help banks withstand a flood of depositors demanding their money at once, is rarely enforced. Usually, when a bank is taken over (the Feds typically do it after closing on Friday), you have access to your money within a few days (often on Monday). The idea is to assure depositors that they have no need to worry, thus averting panic.

Even though you might think you will never have to worry about it, make sure not to keep more than $100,000 in one account at a time. The federal insurance agencies say explicitly that they do not insure more than $100,000 per account, and they may or may not cover any amount over that if a bank is seized or liquidated.

There have been horror stories of people receiving lump-sum distributions of well over $100,000 in pension benefits at retirement or in severance pay after they were laid off, which they deposited temporarily in a bank account, only to be struck by a surprise closing of the bank by federal regulators. In some cases, they lost all the money in their account over $100,000. Don't even tempt the fates: If you have more than $100,000 in cash at any time, spread it among various accounts at several banks.

Despite the protection of federal deposit insurance, you might still want to watch the condition of the bank where your life savings are invested. You do not want the upset and inconvenience of seeing your local bank closed, having swarms of federal agents comb through bank records, then seeing the bank reopen with a new name. There is now an easy way to check on the financial condition of any bank in the country. A firm called Veribanc (P.O. Box 461, Wakefield, MA 01880; 617-245-8370; 800-837-4226 (800-VERIBANc) has established a three-star rating system to grade the financial strength of banks. The highest rating is three stars, followed by two stars and then one star. Some banks get no stars. You can call Veribanc to find out the financial health of any bank and, for a fee, get a detailed written report on the bank. The Veribanc ratings are also published widely, including monthly in the "Monitor" section of *Money* magazine.

Earning Interest on Cash

Banks and Savings and Loans

For decades, the interest that banks and savings and loans could pay on checking and savings accounts was regulated by the federal government. Savings and loans could pay 5½ percent on passbook accounts, while banks could pay a maximum of 5¼ percent. The soaring inflation and interest rates of the late 1970s rendered those fixed rates obsolete, ushering in the era of bank deregulation. Ever since the banking industry was fully deregulated in the early 1980s, banks and savings and loans have been free to pay as much as they choose on checking and savings accounts. A bank that wants to generate a large amount of deposits to make loans will offer higher interest rates than a bank that does not anticipate much loan demand.

Though there are variations from bank to bank, the yields you earn on your cash are affected more by the general movement in interest rates than by individual banks themselves. If inflation is high and rising and the Federal Reserve pushes up interest rates to try to cool off the economy, cash instruments will pay rates from 8 percent to as much as 20 percent, as they did in the early 1980s. On the other hand, if the economy is weak and inflation has subsided, the Federal Reserve will push rates down to stimulate the economy. Under these circumstances, which persisted in the 1990s, yields on cash can fall dramatically to as low as 2 percent.

When you sign up for a bank account, take note of what kind of compounding the bank uses in calculating interest. The more frequent the compounding, the more you will earn. The fastest compounding is called *continuous compounding*. Other banks compound on a daily or monthly basis. While signing up with a bank that compounds interest more frequently is desirable, you will not earn so much more interest that it makes it worth sacrificing convenience or other useful bank services.

Remember that all interest you earn from a bank or savings and loan account is totally taxable at the federal, state and local levels. Deduct what you will be paying in taxes when you calculate what your return will be from a bank account of any type.

In choosing a bank, look closely at the minimum deposit levels required to avoid monthly service charges and other fees. Banks today say they are not in the banking business, but the "financial relationship" business. The more of your money you bring to a bank, the more you will be rewarded with higher yields and lower fees on your accounts, as well as lower interest rates on loans. If you keep small balances of less than $1,000, you may want to opt for a no-frills checking account, on which you pay a flat fee no matter how low your balance falls.

CREDIT UNIONS AND ASSET MANAGEMENT ACCOUNTS

There are two viable alternatives to banks and savings and loans for earning interest on your cash: *credit unions* and the *asset management accounts* offered by brokerage firms. Credit unions, which are run for the benefit of their members and not for the profit of stockholders, typically require lower minimum balances, charge lower service fees and pay higher interest rates than banks. To join a credit union, you must be able to show some common affiliation with other credit union members. That might mean you are an employee of a company, nonprofit institution, government agency, church or synagogue, or a member of a labor union or trade association. To find out whether there is a credit union near you that you would be eligible to join, contact the Credit Union National Association (CUNA, P.O. Box 431, Madison, WI 53701; 608-231-4000; 800-356-9655; www.cuna. org). Make sure that any account you open is insured by the NCUA because there are still a few privately insured credit unions that are subject to bank runs if something goes wrong. The most notable case of this problem came in the early 1990s when a failure at one bank in Rhode Island caused a failure of the fund that insured several banks and credit unions, which forced the governor to freeze credit union accounts insured by the private fund for more than a year, wreaking havoc with the lives of thousands of credit union members.

If you have stocks, bonds and mutual funds, a brokerage firm's asset management account may offer the highest return on your cash and the greatest convenience. Such an account automatically sweeps all interest and dividend income distributed by your securities into a money-market fund until you decide what to do with the money. You can also write checks on the account although there usually is a minimum check size of $100 to $500. The account also comes with credit and debit cards as well as margin loan capacity allowing you to borrow against the value of your securities. Most brokerage firms will open an account for about $5,000 to $10,000 in cash and securities, and they typically charge an annual management fee from $25 to $100. Assets in such accounts are insured against the bankruptcy of your brokerage firm for up to $500,000 in securities, including $100,000 in cash, by the federal Securities Investor Protection Corporation (SIPC, 805 15th St., N.W., Suite 800, Washington, DC 20005; 202-371-8300). However, it makes sense to maintain an asset management account only if you have enough money to make it worthwhile.

Types of Cash Instruments

In deciding how much money to allocate to the different kinds of cash accounts, you should consider both convenience and yield. Because all of these alternatives are absolutely safe, they belong on the bottom, or low-risk level, of your investment pyramid (described in the last chapter). What follows is a rundown of the advantages and disadvantages of the different kinds of cash instruments, starting with the lowest yielding and running through the highest yielding.

NOW AND SUPER-NOW CHECKING ACCOUNTS

Before the mid-1970s, checking accounts paid no interest. The introduction of the money-market mutual fund forced banks to respond by offering what was called a *negotiable order of withdrawal* (NOW) account. At first, these accounts could pay a maximum of 5.25 percent interest, but by the mid-1980s, banks were free to pay whatever they chose. Rates rose a bit higher but then fell to the 2 percent to 3 percent range in the 1990s.

NOW and super-NOW accounts allow unlimited writing of checks of any size. In return, banks often require minimum balances of at least $1,000, and they charge service fees if you do not keep enough money in the account. Some banks will also charge for every check you write if you do not maintain the minimum balance. Before you sign up for a NOW account, see whether you typically keep enough in your checking account to earn more in interest than you will pay in fees.

PASSBOOK SAVINGS ACCOUNTS

Long the staple of bank depositors, the passbook savings account is not as popular as it used to be. In the 1970s, it was about the only account a bank offered that paid interest—usually 5.25 percent—and that provided instant access to your money. The bank provided a passbook in which it would post your interest and balances.

These days, passbook accounts often don't even come with passbooks. Because you can put money into them or take money out whenever you want, they are called *day-to-day savings accounts*. Instead of receiving a passbook, you get a monthly statement from the bank updating your balance and the amount of interest earned.

Even when interest rates soared in the early 1980s, few banks paid more than about 5 percent on their passbook accounts because they noticed that depositors seemed to be struck with a case of inertia. The banks figured that if they could pay low rates and still not lose deposits, there was no reason to raise rates to competitive levels. When interest rates plunged in the early 1990s, however, the banks moved swiftly to lower rates on passbook accounts to the 2 percent to 3 percent range.

Unless you do not have enough money to meet minimum balance requirements on other higher yielding accounts, passbook savings plans are not very attractive investments. The fees a bank charges to maintain a passbook account may eat up a significant portion of your interest earnings unless you maintain a large enough balance.

MONEY-MARKET DEPOSIT ACCOUNTS

Money-market deposit accounts (MMDAs) are the banking industry's answer to the money-market mutual fund. They were first offered as banking was deregulated in the early 1980s to allow banks to compete against the money funds that were attracting billions of dollars in deposits.

Banks can pay whatever they wish on MMDAs. Their rates will always be higher than those on NOW or passbook savings accounts, though not always much higher. In the early days of deregulation, banks paid hefty double-digit rates, but by the 1990s, MMDA yields had plunged to about 3 percent to 4 percent. Bankers will usually adjust their MMDA rates on a weekly basis, based on what competing banks and money-market mutual funds are offering and what is happening to the general direction of interest rates, particularly short-term rates such as Treasury bills. Because MMDAs track the general direction of interest rates, you will benefit if yields rise sharply. However, this is a short-term rate, and you cannot lock in a high yield unless you convert to some form of fixed-income security, such as a bond or a long-term CD.

Unlike your access to a NOW account, your access to an MMDA is somewhat restricted. According to federal banking law, you can write three checks of any amount and make three electronic transfers a month on your MMDA. Those electronic transfers might be made by telephone, at an automatic teller machine or as an automatic payment to a third party, like a utility. Your best strategy is to make three large transfers a month into your checking account, for which you can write checks. This way, most of your money will be earning high interest for a longer period of time.

Like they do for other accounts, banks usually require a minimum balance of at least $1,000 to open an MMDA. Most banks also charge fees for keeping a low balance, though often they will pay higher interest if you keep more money in your account.

If you want to consolidate most of your cash at a bank in one liquid account, the MMDA is the best place to do it. It will pay the highest yields of any readily accessible product the bank offers.

MONEY-MARKET MUTUAL FUNDS

Though many people think money-market mutual funds are the same as MMDAs, there are several important differences between them:

Money-market mutual funds are run by fund management companies, and they buy short-term securities that offer the best yields available in the marketplace at that time. The money funds buy high-quality, short-term obligations called commercial paper, banker's acceptances, CDs, repurchase agreements and Treasury bills, and they pass on all of their income, minus management fees, to shareholders in the funds. In contrast, bank MMDA funds are not invested in the money markets directly. They are lent by the bank to corporations and consumers, and the bank keeps whatever difference there is between the loan proceeds and the money-market yield.

Money-market mutual funds are not insured by the FDIC or any other government agency, unlike bank MMDAs. Though there has never been a default or even a near-default in a money-market mutual fund, there is usually no insurance company guaranteeing that it will cover losses in the unlikely case of such a default. (A few money funds do carry such insurance.) Ultimately, the fund management company stands behind the guarantee that you will be able to withdraw your money from a money fund. In a few cases where there were temporary problems with a money fund, the fund company immediately bailed out shareholders. One advantage of having assets in a money fund that is part of a larger mutual fund family is that you can transfer money into or out of the money fund with a simple toll-free phone call.

Money-market mutual funds have a net asset value that is kept stable at $1 a share, while there is no price per share set for bank MMDAs. Money funds set up the $1-a-share system when they were introduced in the mid-1970s, and allowing people to know that the number of shares they own is exactly equal to the dollar value of their accounts has worked well. In the money fund business, it would be considered a violation of the worst kind to "break the buck," or $1 share price, for any reason.

Money-market mutual funds assess annual management fees of less than 1 percent annually, which is deducted automatically from a fund's yield. The industry average is .75 percent, and any fee over 1 percent is excessive. So if the fund earned an 8 percent yield last year and it levies a 1 percent management fee, you will earn 7 percent. Sometimes, if money funds get into a war for business, they will waive some or all of their management fees for a few months, which will instantly raise the funds' yields. In contrast, banks do not charge management fees. Instead, they impose minimum balance requirements and service fees.

Money-market mutual funds usually impose a minimum amount on checks that ranges from $100 to $500, while bank MMDAs usually allow checks of any amount. All brokerage asset management accounts come with money-market funds on which you can write checks.

Money-market mutual funds come in both taxable and tax-free varieties, while interest from bank MMDAs is always taxable. Money-market funds offer three *taxable* varieties: Treasury-only, government-only and general-purpose. Treasury-only funds buy exclusively Treasury bills and other direct obligations of the U.S. government. These are the safest but lowest yielding money funds. The government-only funds invest solely in paper that is backed either directly or indirectly by the government. These funds are extremely safe, yet they pay slightly higher yields than Treasury funds. General-purpose money funds buy obligations of both domestic and foreign governments and corporations. While these are also very safe, there is a bit more risk that a corporate issuer will default. As a result, these money-market funds pay the highest yields, which may be as much as a percentage point higher than government funds. Whether you opt for a government or a general-purpose fund depends on your tolerance for risk, though a general-purpose money-market fund should hardly be considered a trip to the roulette wheel.

Money-market mutual funds also are available in *tax-free* form. These funds buy the short-term debt of states and municipalities and pass all their income, minus management fees, to shareholders. There are hundreds of national tax-exempt funds to choose from, either directly from fund companies or indirectly through brokerage firm asset management accounts. The percentage yield on these funds will always be lower than that of taxable money-market funds, but if your tax bracket is high enough, you will have more money in your pocket after taxes with a tax-exempt money fund. In some high-tax cities like New York, there are even triple-tax-exempt money funds, which buy only debt of the city. Shareholders in these funds thereby avoid federal, state and city income taxes. For you to determine whether it makes more sense to keep cash in a taxable or a tax-free money fund, perform the following calculation, called *finding the taxable equivalent yield of your money fund*. It is the same method you would use when considering buying a municipal bond.

Deduct your federal tax bracket percentage from 100. In this example, we will use a 31 percent tax bracket. The result is known as the reciprocal of your tax bracket.

100 − 31 Tax bracket = 69 Reciprocal of tax bracket

Divide the tax-free yield on the money fund you are considering by the reciprocal of your tax bracket. In this case, we will assume that your tax-free money fund pays a 5 percent tax-free yield.

$$\frac{5\% \ \text{Tax-free money-fund yield}}{69 \ \text{Reciprocal of tax bracket}} = 7.25\% \ \text{Taxable equivalent yield}$$

This means that you would have to find a taxable money fund paying 7.25 percent to end up with the same dollars in your pocket after taxes that the 5 percent tax-free will pay you.

To determine whether a double-tax-free or triple-tax-free money fund makes sense, go through the same exercise, adding in your state and local tax brackets. If your combined federal, state and local tax brackets add up to 40 percent, for example, the taxable equivalent yield of a 5 percent triple-tax-free money fund would be an astounding 8.33 percent!

$$\frac{5\% \ \text{Tax-free money-fund yield}}{60 \ \text{Reciprocal of tax bracket}} = 8.33\% \ \text{Taxable equivalent yield}$$

Now you can see why tax-free money funds are so popular. Like taxable money funds, tax-free money funds permit you to write checks, usually with a minimum size of at least $100. (For names and addresses of the mutual fund companies offering money-market mutual funds, see the resources at the end of Chapter 4, "Selecting Mutual Funds.")

Money-market mutual fund yields are usually higher than those paid by bank MMDAs. Fund managers have a certain amount of flexibility in managing their funds that allows them to maximize yields. Money-market mutual funds, by law, cannot buy securities with maturities of longer than one year, and the average maturity of their entire portfolio cannot exceed 90 days. The longer the maturity of the paper they hold, the higher the funds' yields, and the longer those yields will last.

Fund managers who anticipate falling interest rates will lengthen the maturity of their holdings to be able to hang on to high yields for as long as possible. On the other hand, if managers think rates will rise, they will shorten the maturity of their holdings so they mature quickly, allowing them to buy more debt securities as soon as the yields are higher. The average maturity of all mutual funds is published every week in *The Wall Street Journal* and other financial newspapers, so you can tell whether maturities in the industry in general, and in any particular fund, are lengthening or shortening. Because of the different maturities of money funds, their yields tend to lag behind the movement in overall short-term rates. That is an advantage when rates are falling because you will be earning a high yield for a longer time. But when rates shoot up sharply, money fund yields take a while to catch up.

Money-market mutual funds are widely diversified. Securities and Exchange Commission (SEC) regulations prohibit money funds from investing more than 5 percent of their assets in the paper of a single company, or any more than 25 percent in one industry. In addition, SEC rules force money funds to buy commercial paper that is in either of the top two quality ratings—A1 or A2 by Standard & Poor's, or P1 or P2 by Moody's Investors Service. In contrast, all of your money is with one bank if it is in a bank MMDA, though if the funds are insured, there is nothing to worry about.

Money-market funds are credited with interest daily, and the interest is reinvested automatically in more fund shares. Banks can pay interest on MMDAs daily, weekly or monthly. When it is credited to your account, interest also compounds automatically.

Money-market fund yields are widely quoted in four ways: the annualized average 7-day simple yield, the annualized average 7-day compounded yield, the annualized average 30-day simple yield and the annualized average 30-day compounded yield. The simple yield measures what the fund is paying without compounding. The 7-day maturity yield will give you a sense of what the fund has been buying lately, while the 30-day yield will tell you what has happened over the last month. If the 7-day yield is lower than the 30-day yield, the fund's yield is falling. If the 7-day yield is higher, the fund's yield should be rising soon. The *IBC's Money Fund Report* (IBC USA, Inc., 290 Eliot St., Ashland, MA 01721-9104; 508-881-2800; 800-343-5413; www.ibcdata.com) compiles these numbers and also sells subscriptions to its weekly newsletter.

Here is what you will normally see in weekly newspaper listings of fund yields:

Money-Market Mutual Funds

Fund Name[1]	Assets in Millions[2]	Average Maturity[3]	7-Day Yield[4]
Taxable			
Fidelity Cash Reserves Fund	$9,749	55	3.20%
Select Government Fund	10	25	2.30
Tax exempt			
Dreyfus Investors Municipal Fund	370	76	2.35
Putnam California Fund	56	55	1.41

Explanation of Newspaper Listings

1. *The name of the money-market mutual fund.* The name will normally reveal whether it is a general-purpose fund or a government-only fund. Fidelity Cash Reserves is a general-purpose fund, while Select Government is a government-only fund. The tax-exempt funds are listed separately. The national tax-free funds, which buy securities from all over the country, are

mixed in with single-state funds, which buy securities only from one state. In this case, the Dreyfus Investors Municipal Fund is national, while the Putnam California Fund buys securities only from California-based issuers.

2. *Asset size in millions of dollars.* The larger the fund, the less its expenses tend to be. Any fund with more than $100 million in assets would be considered a large fund. In this case, the Fidelity Cash Reserves Fund has a massive $9.749 billion, while the Select Government Fund has only $10 million. The Dreyfus Investors Municipal Fund has $370 million, while the Putnam California Fund has $56 million.

3. *Average maturity of the fund's portfolio.* This figure tells you the average number of days it will take for the fund's securities to mature. The longer the maturity, the more the fund manager believes interest rates will fall. In this case, the Fidelity Cash Reserves Fund has an average maturity of 55 days, which is quite long, while the Select Government Fund's maturity is 25 days, which is quite short. The fund managers of these two funds clearly disagree on which way interest rates are headed. The manager of the Dreyfus Investors Municipal Fund, with a 76-day maturity, is even more convinced that interest rates will fall.

4. *The 7-day yield.* This is the average compounded yield for each fund. In this case, the Fidelity Cash Reserves Fund's yield of 3.2% is higher than the Selected Government Fund's 2.3% because Fidelity's maturity is longer and because government securities like Treasury bills yield less than the corporate securities in Fidelity's portfolio. Among the tax-exempt funds, the Dreyfus 2.35% is higher than the Putnam California's 1.41% because the Dreyfus Fund's maturity is longer and because the California-only securities in the Putnam Fund offer a lower yield than a national fund. Yet for high-tax-bracket residents of high-tax California, the Putnam Fund might offer a better after-tax return than the Dreyfus Fund.

Therefore, depending on the amount of money you have and your need for convenience and liquidity, a money-market mutual fund might be just right for you.

TREASURY BILLS

T-bills, as they are called, provide the ultimate in safety and liquidity and are therefore among investors' favorite havens for cash. Treasury bills are backed by the full faith and credit of the U.S. government, so for all practical purposes, they carry no risk of default.

Any Treasury security that is issued with a maturity of one year or less is called a Treasury bill. They are normally auctioned to the public every Monday in three-month and six-month maturities. (The Treasury calls them 13-week and 26-week bills). Once a month, the Treasury sells one-year (or 52-week) bills.

Normally, the longer you commit your money, the higher your yield will be. Yields on Treasury bills tend to be lower than yields on money-market mutual funds because of the extra security that T-bills offer.

You can buy a Treasury bill directly from any Federal Reserve Bank or branch (a list of them appears in the "Resources" section in Chapter 5, "All about Bonds"), either in person or by mail, with no fee. You can also write or visit the Bureau of Public Debt at the Treasury Department (Washington, DC 20239; www.publicdebt. treas.gov). You must fill out a form called a *tender* (see Figure 2.1), which means that you are making what is known as a *noncompetitive bid*, and submit a check for at least $10,000, the minimum accepted for a Treasury bill purchase. By submitting this bid, you are agreeing to accept whatever yield emerges from the Treasury auction at which you are bidding. Professional government securities traders submit competitive bids for millions of dollars of bills. The supply of and demand for bills ultimately determine the average yield on each T-bill auction.

Alternatively, you can buy a Treasury bill through any broker or bank for a minimal charge of about $25. That fee, of course, reduces your effective yield. Once you have bought a T-bill, your name will be kept in the Treasury's electronic records. Don't expect a fancy certificate to be sent to you.

The investment yield method. Once the yield on the T-bill has been set by the auction, which will be determined before 2 PM of that day and reported in newspapers the next day, the Treasury will immediately send you a refund check for what is known as the *discount*. The discount is the difference between $10,000 and the market price of the T-bill at that point. For example, if the auction produces a yield of 5.26 percent, you will receive a check for a discount of $500, which represents your return on investment. Your $9,500 remains with the Treasury until the bill matures. To calculate your yield for a one-year T-bill, divide the discount by the effective purchase price, which is $10,000 minus $500 in this case:

$500 Discount ÷ $9,500 Effective purchase price = 5.26% Investment yield

For a three- or six-month T-bill, you have to annualize the yield. For a three-month T-bill, you multiply the yield (5.26%) by 365, then divide by 91. For a six-month T-bill, you multiply the yield by 365, then divide by 182 as follows:

$$\frac{\$500 \text{ Discount}}{\$9,500 \text{ Effective purchase price}} \times \frac{365}{182} = 10.5\% \text{ Investment yield}$$

This yield is also known as the coupon-equivalent yield because it is measuring your return on the principal you have tied up in the T-bill until maturity. When the T-bill matures in three or six months, you receive a check for $10,000.

Like the interest on all Treasury securities, your T-bill's interest is taxable for federal income tax purposes, but it is not taxable at the state or local level. This gives a boost to the after-tax return you earn from the T-bill, particularly if you live

Figure 2.1
Tender for 13-Week Treasury Bill

FORM PD F 5176-1
(February 1990)

OMB No. 1535-0069
Expires: 09-30-92

TREASURY DIRECT®

TENDER FOR 13-WEEK TREASURY BILL

TENDER INFORMATION

AMOUNT OF TENDER: $ _____

FOR DEPARTMENT USE

BID TYPE (Check One) ☐ NONCOMPETITIVE ☐ COMPETITIVE AT _____ . _____ %

ACCOUNT NUMBER ▓▓▓ – ▓▓ – ▓▓

TENDER NUMBER
912794

INVESTOR INFORMATION

CUSIP

ACCOUNT NAME

ISSUE DATE

RECEIVED BY

DATE RECEIVED

ADDRESS

EXT REG ☐

FOREIGN ☐

BACKUP ☐

REVIEW ☐

CITY   STATE   ZIP CODE

TAXPAYER IDENTIFICATION NUMBER

CLASS ☐

1ST NAMED OWNER ▓▓▓ – ▓▓ – ▓▓▓ OR ▓▓ – ▓▓▓▓

SOCIAL SECURITY NUMBER   EMPLOYER IDENTIFICATION NUMBER

TELEPHONE NUMBERS

WORK (▓▓▓) ▓▓▓ – ▓▓▓ HOME (▓▓▓) ▓▓▓ –

PAYMENT ATTACHED

TOTAL PAYMENT: $ _____

NUMBERS

CASH (01): $ _____   CHECKS (02/03): $ _____

SECURITIES (05): $ _____ $ _____

OTHER (06): $ _____ $ _____

DIRECT DEPOSIT INFORMATION

ROUTING NUMBER ▓▓▓▓▓▓

FINANCIAL INSTITUTION NAME ▓▓▓▓▓▓▓▓

ACCOUNT NUMBER ▓▓▓▓▓▓▓

ACCOUNT TYPE (Check One) ☐ CHECKING

ACCOUNT NAME ▓▓▓▓▓▓▓

☐ SAVINGS

AUTOMATIC REINVESTMENT

1 2 3 4 5 6 7 8 Circle the number of sequential 13-week reinvestments you want to schedule at this time

AUTHORIZATION

For the notice required under the Privacy and Paperwork Reduction Acts, see the accompanying instructions.

I submit this tender pursuant to the provisions of Department of the Treasury Circulars, Public Debt Series Nos. 1-86 and 2-86 and the public announcement issued by the Department of the Treasury.

Under penalties of perjury, I certify that the number shown on this form is my correct taxpayer identification number and that I am not subject to backup withholding because (1) I have not been notified that I am subject to backup withholding as a result of a failure to report all interest or dividends, or (2) the Internal Revenue Service has notified me that I am no longer subject to backup withholding. I further certify that all other information provided on this form is true, correct and complete.

SIGNATURE   DATE

SEE INSTRUCTIONS FOR PRIVACY ACT AND PAPERWORK REDUCTION ACT NOTICE

★U.S.GPO 1990-268-403/20484

in a high-tax state like New York or California. Taxes are due in the year the T-bill matures or is sold; therefore, if you want to delay taxes into the next year, you can buy a T-bill that matures after the next January 1.

If you need to cash in your T-bill before maturity, you can sell it but may not receive the best price. However, if interest rates have risen between the time you bought it and when you want to sell it, the T-bill's price will have dropped.

To look up the price of your Treasury bill, consult the listings in *The Wall Street Journal, Barron's* or another financial newspaper. They will look like this:

Treasury Bills

Date[1]	Bid[2]	Ask[3]	Change[4]	Yield[5]
Mar 25	2.96	2.94	+0.03	2.99
Jul 29	3.16	3.13	+0.03	3.22

Explanation of Treasury Bill Listings

1. *This is the date the Treasury bill will mature.* Most listings will carry 33 dates, which is the number of T-bill maturity dates outstanding. In these two cases, the bills mature on March 25 and July 29.

2. *The bid price is the highest price dealers are willing to pay for a particular Treasury bill.* The number is actually the discount from face value, expressed as an annual percentage. In the first case here, dealers will buy the bill at 2.96 percent. The higher the discount, the lower the price of the T-bill.

3. *The ask price is the lowest price that dealers are willing to sell a particular Treasury bill.* It is also the discount, expressed as an annual percentage. In the first case here, it is 2.94 percent. Therefore, dealers are willing to sell at a smaller discount, which means the ask price of the T-bill is higher than the bid price.

4. *The change signals how much the discount rose or fell in yesterday's trading.* Paradoxically, a plus (+) refers to a rise in interest rates and means that T-bill prices dropped. In these cases, the interest rate rose yesterday by .03, meaning the prices fell by that amount. Think of it in terms of a store putting goods on discount. The bigger the discount, the lower the price of the goods to customers. A minus (−) means that T-bill prices have risen and interest rates fell because the discount has been reduced.

5. *The yield is the coupon-equivalent yield.* That is, it is based on your return on the capital you have tied up in the T-bill until maturity. In the first case here, the yield is 2.99 percent. It would be calculated as follows:

$$\$291 \text{ Discount} \div \$9,709 \text{ Remaining principal} = 2.99\%$$

This means that you would have $9,709 tied up until the T-bill matures, when you would receive a check from the Treasury for $10,000. Your interest would be $291.

Treasury bills might be right for you if you want total security and liquidity and you have a minimum of $10,000 to invest.

CERTIFICATES OF DEPOSIT (CDs)

CDs are bank, savings and loan or credit union instruments that allow you to lock in an interest rate for a specific period of time. If you withdraw your money from the CD before the CD matures, you face an early-withdrawal penalty set by each bank—often three months' interest. The most popular CDs mature in three months, six months and one year although banks offer CDs with maturities as long as five years. Some banks even offer so-called "designer" CDs, for which you decide the maturity and the bank quotes you a yield. Generally, the longer you commit your money, the higher your CD's yield will be. Banks usually set some minimum amount for CDs, which can be as low as $100 or as much as $1,000, but they never charge a fee to buy a certificate.

There are several methods that banks use to pay interest on CDs. In many cases, the interest is not paid until the CD matures. For longer term CDs, banks mail out checks every three or six months, or they deposit the money directly into your bank account. Most banks will also allow you to reinvest your interest in the CD if you wish. All interest from CDs is taxable at the federal, state and local levels in the year it is received, even if the interest is reinvested. Remember to calculate the effect of those taxes when you compare your potential CD returns against other alternatives, like tax-free money funds or municipal bonds.

Since the banking industry was deregulated in the 1980s, banks have been able to offer whatever rates they want on CDs. The yield that any particular bank is willing to pay depends on its executives' expectations of loan demand. If they expect a pickup in loan demand, they might raise the rates they pay on CDs to attract more funds to lend. If they do not see much demand for loans, they will not offer higher than market rates.

You do not have to restrict your search for high yields to your neighborhood or even your state. Many banks accept out-of-state deposits by wire or mail, and the highest yields around the country are publicized constantly in major financial newspapers such as *The Wall Street Journal* and *USA Today*, as well as the "Monitor" section of *Money* magazine. You can also subscribe to the newsletter *100 Highest Yields* (P.O. Box 088888, North Palm Beach, FL 33408; 800-327-7717), which surveys banks every week to uncover those with the top yields for 6-month, 1-year, 2½-year and 5-year certificates. In the 1980s, yields on CDs stayed in double digits for several years, then fell sharply, along with all interest rates. By the 1990s, CD yields had settled in the 3 percent to 6 percent range.

As with other bank products, different banks use different methods of compounding interest on their CDs. Some compound using simple interest, while others compound daily, weekly, monthly, quarterly, semiannually or annually. This affects what banks advertise as the "effective yield" on a CD, which, in fact, is mythical because it is unlikely that you will be able to capture exactly the same rate when the CD comes due in three or six months.

Make sure that you check with your bank to see what happens when your CD matures. Banks are not required to notify you when a CD is about to mature. Some will automatically reinvest the money in a new CD at the prevailing rate, which may or may not be what you want. Some banks will automatically mail you a check for the full amount of your CD, while others will put the money in a low-yielding passbook account until you give them further instructions.

To protect yourself against the ups and downs of interest rates, you might try a strategy called *laddering*. Instead of putting all your money in one CD with one maturity, spread it among several CDs maturing every few months. With this technique, CDs will constantly be maturing, which gives you the chance to reinvest at higher rates if rates have risen. If rates have fallen, you still have several CDs locked in at higher rates.

In addition to buying CDs directly from banks, you can buy CDs indirectly, from brokerage firms. Most brokerage firms sell CDs from banks across the country. For example, a bank contacts a brokerage firm because it wants to raise several million dollars quickly. Instead of relying on its branches to bring in cash, the bank pays a fee to the broker to solicit clients. Therefore, clients do not have to pay a fee to buy a CD through a broker because the bank has already paid the fee. From your point of view, you are able to buy a CD that is probably yielding more than your local bank's, and you are still protected by federal deposit insurance, as long as you invest less than $100,000 (which you should!). In addition, if you need to sell the CD before it matures, the brokerage firm maintains a ready market for it. If interest rates rose after you bought it, you will suffer a loss, while if rates fell, you will earn a profit.

Some banks have added wrinkles to the simple CD in recent years. One popular version is the *rising-rate* CD, which guarantees that if interest rates rise, your CD's yield will be increased as well every six months. Other versions allow you to switch to a higher rate for your CD once during its lifetime if interest rates have risen. Some banks offer *expandable* CDs. These permit you to add more money to an existing CD at the same rate, which would be advantageous if rates have fallen since you first bought the CD. Even dicier CDs are tied to stock market indexes. Citicorp in New York, Fleet Financial Group in Providence and others now sell a *market index* CD. There, you are guaranteed a certain level of return on your CD, as usual, but, in addition, you will receive a certain percentage of the market appreciation or depreciation in the Standard & Poor's 500 over the life of the CD.

Whether you invest in a traditional CD or a fancier version, it might have just the combination of high yields, convenience and safety that is right for you.

Using Your Computer for Home Banking

Today it's easy to use your home computer to improve the efficiency of all your banking transactions. Most major banks offer software allowing you to tap into their mainframes to do everything from checking your balances to buying securities and paying bills. Some banks offer proprietary software that only works with their system, while others allow you to use commonly available programs like Quicken, Managing Your Money or Microsoft Money to initiate transactions. The advantage to banking using these programs is that all of your records are already captured in the software, making it easier to keep your budget up-to-date or to do your taxes. More and more banks are offering their services over the Internet, either directly at their Web sites or through commercial services such as America Online. Some banks only have an online existence, allowing them to offer banking services at lower cost because they have minimal physical overhead from branches and tellers.

Whichever system you use, home banking allows you to stay on top of what is going on in your bank account in a far more convenient manner than was ever possible before. Some banks charge monthly or annual fees for access to home banking, while many others give the service away free because it saves the banks the cost of providing live tellers for routine transactions. Even if you have to pay a small fee, electronic banking is usually worth the cost if you use it wisely. You do not need to worry about the security of your bank account records because all of the information is protected by passwords. Just make sure that your password does not get into the hands of those who shouldn't have access to your account. Here are the main functions you can perform with home banking

MONITORING ACCOUNT BALANCES

There's no longer any reason to wonder how much money you have in your checking, savings and borrowing balances. All of your accounts are updated daily, so you can find out when checks have cleared, when your paycheck has been deposited, when certificates of deposit have paid their interest, when loan payments are due and much more. By tracking all of these balances carefully, you should be able to maximize the interest you earn on deposits and minimize the interest you pay on loans. For example, you can keep most of your money in a money market account earning interest until it is needed to cover checks in a checking account, which usually does not earn any interest. By keeping track of your balances, you can also be sure not to bounce checks because of insufficient funds, thereby avoiding the substantial fees that banks levy for bad checks. Home banking systems also will summarize your entire bank account, showing you how much money you have on deposit and in investments and how much you owe in various kinds of loans.

TRANSFERRING MONEY BETWEEN ACCOUNTS

Home banking also makes it easy to move money from one account to another electronically. With a few keystrokes, you can transfer funds from savings to checking or vice versa, pay off overdraft lines of credit or credit card balances, or buy a certificate of deposit. You not only can transfer funds on the day you are logged on, but you also can set up transfers several days ahead. For example, you can have funds transferred to cover a check even when you are out of town.

CUSTOMER SERVICE

You can take care of tedious housekeeping on your bank account by communicating with the bank's customer service people online. For example, you can open and close accounts, ask for a credit line increase, stop payment on a check, wire money or resolve errors by sending electronic messages. Never a need to stand in line to speak to a bank officer about these matters again!

PAYING BILLS ELECTRONICALLY

Perhaps the most useful feature of home banking is the ability to pay bills online. Once you get into the habit of doing it, you'll wonder how you ever paid bills the old-fashioned way. The first step is to set up a list of your payee's names and addresses with your account numbers. Many banks today provide a ready-made list of payees, such as the electric and gas utilities, other banks, credit card companies, schools, health care facilities and other local institutions that are equipped to receive payments electronically. It is far better to pay a bill electronically than to have a paper check cut and mailed to the payee, because the electronic payment is certain and immediate, while the paper check may get lost or delayed in the mail and may take several days to be posted to your account.

Check your bank's list of predetermined electronic payees before you enter your own. All you have to do is enter your account number and you're ready to use that payee. For payees that don't appear on the bank's list, such as individuals, contractors or others that you pay regularly, you must fill in the person's name, address and your account number, if any, on the bank's bill payment system. The bank will always have to cut a paper check and mail it to these personal payees.

Once you have your list of payees entered into the computer, your bill-paying chores become much easier. Assemble your bills before you go online, noting the amount to be paid to each payee and the date the payment should be made. For electronic payments, you can initiate the payment only a day or two before it is due, while payments made by check through the mail should be sent at least a week ahead of time. Once you are connected to the bank's computer, you just have to enter the amount due each payee and the date of the payment and you're done! No checks to write, no envelopes to stuff, no stamps to lick, no trips to the post office! Even when you are out of town or thinking about other more important things, your bills are being paid reliably.

Another advantage of home banking is that it gives you excellent records of the bills you have and are planning to pay. You can look into the history of payments to a particular payee to show when your payment was sent and when it cleared. You can also look at what payments you have coming up, so you can be sure to have enough funds in your account to cover those bills. You can also print out all your payments that may generate tax deductions, such as medical expenses or donations to charitable organizations.

If done correctly, electronic bill paying should also allow you to hold onto your money for a longer time, where it can earn interest, instead of having to send checks off in advance to make sure they arrive in a timely fashion. That's why it's best to make electronic payments whenever possible, because you can zip the necessary funds to the payee right before the bill is due.

If your bank does not offer electronic bill paying, you may still be able to pay bills online by establishing an account with Checkfree, which can be found on the Internet at www.checkfree.com. Checkfree allows you to pay any amount to anyone from any bank from anywhere at any time, because it accesses the Federal Reserve payments system directly. Checkfree includes a sophisticated security system so financial information about you or your payments to others is not stolen. The service is also compatible with major software packages like Microsoft Money, Quicken and Managing Your Money (discussed in greater detail at the end of Chapter 1).

INVESTING

Most home banking systems make it easy to buy stocks, bonds, mutual funds, CDs, options and other investments. One advantage in investing through your bank is that all of your holdings are consolidated in one place. That not only makes recordkeeping easier, but many banks will charge lower fees or even waive them altogether, if you keep all of your assets at the bank. The more money you keep at the bank, the higher the interest the bank pays on deposits and the lower interest it charges on loans. Another advantage is that you are able to comparison-shop online for yields on CDs and other bank products. Banks will list all of the different maturities of their certificates with the current yields, so you can pick the CD with the highest yield and maturity appropriate for your needs.

Banks will also automatically update the value of your securities portfolio, usually every night after the stock market has closed. In addition, the bank will keep track of reinvesting stock dividends and mutual fund capital gains distributions and will adjust for stock splits and bond redemptions. The bank also should keep track of your cost basis so that you can calculate your capital gains liability when you sell an investment. All of these recordkeeping chores would be a tremendous burden for you to track on your own.

The only disadvantage of investing electronically through a bank is that the bank may charge you fees and commissions that you might be able to avoid or reduce if you bought the investments directly from the source. For example, many banks will charge a commission to buy a no-load mutual fund that you could buy directly from the fund company on your own without a sales charge. Also, you should compare the commissions charged by your bank for buying stocks and bonds with the fees from discount brokers, which can in many cases be substantially less. You may find that the convenience of having all your assets in one institution outweighs the higher fees you may have to pay. But you should at least know how much extra you are paying for the privilege of convenience.

RESEARCHING THE BEST BANKING DEALS ONLINE

You can also use your computer to find the best opportunities for high yields from savings instruments and lower interest rates on loans. Today, there is a national market for banking services, so you should not feel limited by what your local bank is offering. Here are two online resources to help you shop for the best nationwide rates:

Bank Rate Monitor. BRM collects data from thousands of banks and displays the best deals on its Web site. It lists the highest-yielding certificates of deposit, separated by the CD's maturity, from one month to five years. All of the banks are federally insured. A toll-free phone number is provided so you can contact the bank directly and open an account. BRM also provides a huge amount of data allowing you to find the lowest-interest loans anywhere in the country. Their Web site has separate sections for credit cards, home equity loans, mortgages, auto loans and personal loans. You can sort their database for the kind of loan that fits your needs. For example, in the credit card arena you may want to isolate the card charging the lowest interest rate or one without an annual fee or a card that provides the biggest cash-back bonus. When looking for a mortgage, you have to screen for lenders who originate mortgages where you live. www.bankrate.com

BanxQuote. Their Web site provides yields on savings deposits, money market accounts and CDs throughout the country. It also shows loan rates on a variety of consumer loans. BanxQuote features state-by-state and regional benchmarks for savings and loan rates, so you can judge whether the investment or loan you are considering is above or below the local or regional average. www.banx.com

FINDING AN ONLINE BANK

Since you are not limited by geography when searching for an online bank, you should feel free to compare the fees and services of many banks before you decide to open an account. One resource you may find helpful is NETBanker (www.netbanker.com), which includes directories of online banks with Web addresses. NETBanker is a service of the newsletter *Online Banking Report.*

Another way to find good online banks is through the Online Banking Association (www.obanet.org), which lists many online banks and the services they offer, as well as extensive links to their Web sites.

Though there are many online banks to choose from, and new ones creating Web sites all the time, you may want to stick with an institution that has been doing electronic banking for a while. The first Internet-only bank was Security First Network Bank (www.sfnb.com), which offers no-fee checking, several free electronic payments per month, no minimum balance requirements and online banking statements. Security First also offers credit cards, CDs, money market accounts, stocks and mutual funds, and several kinds of loans. Instead of receiving cancelled paper checks, you can call up an electronic image of the cancelled check if you need to prove you paid a bill.

Another Internet-only bank that is worth checking out is the Atlanta Internet Bank (www.atlantabank.com), which tends to offer above-average yields on money market accounts, as well as bill paying and other banking services.

Most traditional banks also have Web sites allowing you to complete banking transactions and learn about ways to manage your money better. Usually the bank's name is listed in its Web site address. Here is a sampling of some of the more advanced bank Web sites you may want to look at:

Bank of America (www.bofa.com)
Chase Manhattan (www.chase.com)
Citibank (www.citibank.com)
First Chicago (www.fcnbd.com)
First Union (www.firstunion.com)
Fleet Bank (www.fleet.com)
Mellon Bank (www.mellon.com)
Nationsbank (www.nationsbank.com)
U.S. Bank (www.usbank.com)
Wells Fargo (www.wellsfargo.com)

ELECTRONIC CASH

One service that an online bank cannot provide is cash from an Automated Teller Machine right in your home. But they can offer something almost as good—electronic cash. By transferring funds electronically to an account, you can use this money to buy goods and services online. Some cities are also experimenting with electronic cash debit cards that you can reload and that can be used in stores in the same way as credit cards. Here are some of the Web sites that can give you more information on electronic cash alternatives:

CyberCash. Using CyberCash Wallet software, you can purchase goods and services online for as little as 25 cents. The Wallet software can be downloaded for free from this site. CyberCash makes sure that all transactions are secure by using its encryption systems. www.cybercash.com

Digicash. Payments can be made electronically using Ecash developed by Digicash. Their Web site provides links to providers of Ecash as well as the many online merchants who accept Ecash. www.digicash.com

First Virtual. You get a VirtualPIN (personal identification number) from First Virtual, which acts like a credit card online. You provide your VirtualPIN when you want to make a purchase from an online vendor. To confirm the transaction, First Virtual sends you an e-mail, to which you respond to complete the sale. First Virtual charges just $2 a year to enroll for its service, and you can even sign up online. www.fv.com

Banking from your home computer is only going to become easier, cheaper and more convenient as banks continue to innovate and compete online. The sooner you start banking online, the better!

Resources

BOOKS

The Bank Rating Service by Veribanc (Veribanc, P.O. Box 461, Wakefield, MA 01880; 617-245-8370; 800-VERIBANc; 800-837-4226). A series of publications published by Veribanc, a rating service that rates the financial strength of most banks in the country. They will send you reports on any bank, savings and loan, credit union or bank holding company for a fee. You can get instant ratings, a short form report, an in-depth research report or what is known as a VERIFAX, a faxed, in-depth report. You also can get lists of financial institutions that are particularly safe, broken down by state, region or financial condition. Veribanc also offers DEPOSITSURE, a private insurance program offering insurance against bank default up to $5 million, instead of the $100,000 offered by federal agencies. For more information on this program, call 800-723-3893.

The Cash Book: High Yields with Safety, by James Blanchard III (New York Institute of Finance, 2 Broadway, 5th Floor, New York, NY 10004; 212-859-5000). A broad overview of the different kinds of cash investments available, with their levels of safety and yield potential. www.nyif.com

How To Keep Your Savings Safe: Protecting the Money You Can't Afford To Lose, by Walter Updegrave (Crown Publishers, 201 E. 50th St., New York, NY 10022; 212-572-6071; 800-733-3000). Explains how to find the strongest banks, insurance companies and money-market mutual funds in the United States. Lists safe banks, insurers, savings and loans, and money funds. www.rh.com

IBC's Money Fund Directory (IBC Financial Data, 290 Eliot St., Ashland, MA 01721-9104; 508-881-2800; 800-445-5900). An annual book that provides in-depth information on more than 800 money-market mutual funds. Each fund listing includes the sponsoring company's name, toll-free number, and address. For every fund, listing includes the fund type, inception, portfolio manager, minimum initial and subsequent investment amounts, total assets, expense ratios and 12b-1 fees. Also lists services offered by each fund, such as check writing, exchange privileges and IRA and Keogh accounts, and shows the top ten funds in five categories based on the latest 12-month yields. www.ibcdata.com

The Money Market, by Marcia Stigum (McGraw-Hill Publishing, 1333 Burr Ridge Pkwy., Burr Ridge, IL 60521; 708-789-4000; 800-634-3961). The most comprehensive and authoritative guide to the money markets. www.McGraw-Hill.com

NEWSLETTERS

The Moneyletter (Agora Publishing, 1217 Saint Paul St., Baltimore, MD 21202; 410-223-2400; 800-433-1528). A twice-monthly newsletter that lists the top-yielding money-market mutual funds. The funds are separated into taxable, which includes government-only and general-purpose funds, and tax-exempt, which includes national funds and state-specific funds. The top six funds are listed in each category, with their 7-day, 30-day and 12-month compound yields. Also recommends no-load stock and bond mutual funds and an asset allocation for conservative, moderate and venturesome portfolios. Also covers economic trends and personal finance issues such as insurance, retirement planning and banking. www.agora.com

Income Fund Outlook (Institute for Econometric Research, 2200 Southwest 10th St., Deerfield Beach, FL 33442; 954-421-1000; 800-327-6720). Lists the top-yielding bank MMDAs and 30-day, 60-day, 3-month, 6-month, 1-year, 2½-year and 5-year CDs in the United States. Provides information on taxable and tax-free money-market mutual funds, including safety ratings, yields, telephone numbers, assets, portfolio maturity, expenses, minimum initial investments and check amounts, and loads. Also lists top-yielding bond mutual funds. www.mfmag.com

The International Bank Credit Analyst (BCA Publications, 1002 Sherbrooke St. West, Suite 1600, Montreal, Quebec H3A 3L6; 514-499-9550). A monthly journal that provides an outlook for the direction of interest rates and trends in banking safety. www.bcapub.com

Martin Weiss' Safe Money Report (Weiss Research, P.O. Box 109665, Palm Beach Gardens, FL 33410; 407-627-3300; 561-627-3300; 800-289-9222). Covers the risks of all types of investing and discusses troubled banks, savings and loans, insurance companies and brokerage firms. Predicts potential danger spots in the stock and bond markets. The Weiss organization also compiles safety ratings—from A (excellent) to F (failed or in the process of failing)—on thousands of banks and savings and loans, insurance companies and brokerages, and rates HMOs. www.weissratings.com

IBC's Money Fund Report (IBC USA, Inc., 290 Eliot St., Ashland, MA 01721-9104; 508-881-2800; 800-343-5413). A weekly newsletter that tracks more than 850 money-market mutual funds. Lists their assets, 7-day yields, both simple and compounded, 30-day simple yields, the average maturity of the holdings in their portfolios, and the kinds of securities they hold, broken down into nine categories, including government, municipal and corporate. Quoted widely in newspapers, also computes industry average yields for 16 money-market-fund categories. www.ibcdata.com

Jumbo Rate News and *CD Rate Watch* (Bauer Communications, P.O. Drawer 145510, Coral Gables, FL 33114-5510; 305-441-2062; 800-388-6686). *Jumbo Rate News* is a weekly eight-page newsletter that analyzes and surveys over one thousand select creditworthy institutions. The Bank Rater, a toll-free rating service, provides financial strength ratings on all U.S. banks, savings and loans, and credit unions on a five-star system. Institutions with 3½ to 5 stars are considered well capitalized, while those with zero to 2 stars are undercapitalized and may be in danger of being seized by federal regulators. *CD Rate Watch* lists the top-yielding bank MMDAs and CDs with maturities of 90 days, 180 days, 1 year, 1½ years, 2 years, 2½ years, 3 years, 4 years, and 5 years and long-term CDs with maturities up to 10 years. Only banks with 3.5 to 5 stars are listed. In addition to rates and yields, the publication details early withdrawal penalties, a contact person at each bank (with the person's telephone number) and whether the bank accepts IRAs and Keogh accounts. It also updates readers on news from the banking world. www.bauergroup.com

100 Highest Yields and *Bank Rate Monitor* (Financial Rates, Inc., P.O. Box 088888, North Palm Beach, FL 33408; 407-627-7330; 800-327-7717). List the 20 highest yielding bank MMDAs and 6-month, 1-year, 2½-year and 5-year CDs. Also show each bank's safety rating from Veribanc. Included are the highest yields for mini-jumbo CDs (those with $25,000 or $50,000 minimums) in the 3- and 6-month maturities and the highest yields for jumbo ($100,000 minimum) CDs in 1-, 3-, and 6-month maturities. Discuss other banking topics of interest to consumers, such as credit card, home-equity loan and car loan rates. www.bankrate.com

FEDERAL GOVERNMENT REGULATORS

Comptroller of the Currency (250 E St., S.W., Washington, DC 20219; 202-622-2000). The chief regulator of all national banks. Compliance Management handles consumer complaints against national banks. (The current telephone number for Compliance Management and the Consumer Affairs Office is 202-874-5280.)

Federal Deposit Insurance Corporation (FDIC, 550 17th St., N.W., Washington, DC 20429; 202-393-8400; 800-424-5488). The FDIC insures all banking deposits up to $100,000 per account. Examines banks regularly and handles consumer complaints about banks. www.fdic.gov

Federal Reserve System (20th St. and C St., N.W., Washington, DC 20551; 202-452-3946). Regulates the U.S. banking system, money supply and printing of currency. You can also buy Treasury securities through any Federal Reserve Bank or branch. (They are all listed in the "Resources" section in Chapter 5.) Will send you a copy of the following booklets: *The ABC's of Figuring Interest; The Arithmetic of Interest Rates; The Basics of Interest Rates; Buying Treasury Securities; Check Rights; Counterfeit? How To Spot Counterfeit Bills; Endorsing Your Check: What the New Endorsement Standard Means; The Federal Reserve Today; Investing in Government Securities; Fundamental Facts about United States Money; Making Deposits: When Will Your Money Be Available? The Expedited Funds Availability Act; Options for Depositors; Putting It Simply: A Basic Introduction to the Federal Reserve; Your Money: The Characteristics, Creation, Function* and *Value of Different Kinds of U.S. Currency.* www.fedweb.frb.gov

National Credit Union Administration (1775 Duke St., Alexandria, VA 22314-3428; 703-518-6300). Regulates federally chartered U.S. credit unions and handles consumer complaints against credit unions. Insures deposits through the National Credit Union Share Insurance Fund (the current telephone number for the National Credit Union Share Insurance Fund is 703-518-6570). www.ncua.org

Office of Thrift Supervision (1700 G St., N.W., Washington, DC 20552; 202-906-6000). Supervises and charters federal savings and loan associations and handles complaints from the public about savings and loans. The Consumer Affairs Office, designed to handle consumer complaints, can be reached at 202-906-6237 or 800-842-6929. www.ots.treas.gov

State Banking Regulators

The following state banking departments will pursue consumer complaints against banks in their states.

Alabama: 101 S. Union St., Montgomery 36130; 334-242-3452

Alaska: P.O. Box 110807, Juneau 99811-0807; 907-465-2521

Arizona: 2910 N. 44th St., Suite 310, Phoenix 85018; 602-255-4421

Arkansas: Tower Building, 323 Center St., Suite 500, Little Rock 72201-2613; 501-324-9019

California: 111 Pine St., Suite 1100, San Francisco 94111-5613; 415-263-8555

Colorado: 1560 Broadway, Suite 1175, Denver 80202; 303-894-7575

Connecticut: 260 Constitution Plaza, Hartford 06103; 203-240-8299

Delaware: 555 E. Loockerman St., Suite 210, Dover 19901; 302-739-4235

District of Columbia: Comptroller of the Currency, 250 E St., S.W., Washington 20219; 202-622-2000

Florida: State Capitol Building, Tallahassee 32399-0350; 904-488-0370

Georgia: 2990 Brandywine Rd., Suite 200, Atlanta 30341-5565; 770-986-1633

Hawaii: Division of Financial Institutions, P.O. Box 2054, Honolulu 96805; 808-586-2820

Idaho: P.O. Box 83720, 700 W. State St., Boise 83720-0031; 208-334-3678

Illinois: Office of Banks and Real Estate, 500 East Monroe St., Springfield 62701; 217-782-3000

Indiana: 402 W. Washington St., Room W066, Indianapolis 46204-2759; 317-232-3955

Iowa: Iowa Division of Banking, 200 E. Grand Ave., Suite 300, Des Moines 50319; 515-281-4014

Kansas: 700 Jackson St., S.W., Suite 300, Topeka 66603; 913-296-2266

Kentucky: Department of Financial Institutions, 477 Versailles Rd., Frankfort 40601; 502-573-3390

Louisiana: Office of Financial Institutions, P.O. Box 94095, Baton Rouge 70804-9095; 504-925-4661

Maine: State of Maine Bureau of Banking, 36 State House Station, Augusta 04333-0036; 207-624-8570

Maryland: Commissioner of Financial Regulations, 501 St. Paul Pl., Baltimore 21202-2272; 410-333-6808

Massachusetts: 100 Cambridge St., Room 2004, 20th Floor, Boston 02202; 617-727-3145 ext. 349

Michigan: Financial Institutions Bureau, P.O. Box 30224, Lansing 48909; 517-373-3460

Minnesota: Financial Examinations Divisions, 133 E. 7th St., 4th Floor, St. Paul 55101; 612-296-2715

Mississippi: P.O. Box 23729, Jackson 39225-3729; 601-359-1031

Missouri: Division of Finance, P.O. Box 716, Jefferson City 65102; 573-751-3242

Montana: 846 Front St., Helena 59620-0546; 406-444-2091

Nebraska: The Atrium, 1200 N St., Suite 311, Lincoln 68508; 402-471-2171

Nevada: Financial Institutions Division of the Department of Business and Industry, 406 E. Second St., Carson City 89710; 702-687-4259

New Hampshire: 169 Manchester St., Concord 03301; 603-271-3561

New Jersey: 20 W. State St., CN040, Trenton 08625; 609-292-3420

New Mexico: Financial Institutions Division, P.O. Box 25101, Santa Fe 87504; 505-827-7100

New York: 2 Rector St., New York 10006; 212-618-6557

North Carolina: 702 Oberlin Rd., Suite 400, Raleigh 27605; 919-733-3016

North Dakota: 700 East Main Ave., Bismarck 58502; 701-328-5600

Ohio: Division of Financial Institutions, 77 S. High St., 21st Floor, Columbus 43266-0121; 614-466-2932

Oklahoma: 4545 North Lincoln Blvd., Suite 164, Oklahoma City 73105; 405-521-2782

Oregon: 350 Winter St. Northeast, Room 21, Salem 97310; 503-378-4140

Pennsylvania: 333 Market St., 16th Floor, Harrisburg 17101-2290; 717-787-6991

Rhode Island: 233 Richmond St., Suite 231, Providence 02903-4231; 401-277-2405

South Carolina: 1015 Sumter St., Room 309, Columbia 29201; 803-734-2001

South Dakota: State Capitol, 500 E. Capitol Ave., Pierre 57501-5070; 605-773-3421

Tennessee: John Sevier Building, 4th Floor, Nashville 37243-0705; 615-741-2236

Texas: 2601 N. Lamar Blvd., Austin 78705; 512-475-1300

Utah: 324 S. State St., Suite 201, Salt Lake City 84111; 801-538-8830

Vermont: 89 Main St., Drawer #20, Montpelier 05620-3101; 802-828-3301

Virginia: 1300 E. Main St., Suite 800, P.O. Box 640, Richmond 23218-0640; 804-371-9657

Washington: P.O. Box 41200, Olympia 98504-1200; 360-902-8704

West Virginia: State Capitol Complex, Building 3, Room 311, Charleston 25305-0240; 304-558-2294

Wisconsin: Department of Financial Institutions, P.O. Box 7876, Madison 53707-7876; 608-266-1621

Wyoming: Herschler Building, 122 W. 25th St., 3rd Floor, East Wing, Cheyenne 82002; 307-777-7797

TRADE ASSOCIATIONS

American Bankers Association (1120 Connecticut Ave., N.W., Washington, DC 20036; 202-663-5000). The main trade group representing commercial banks offers several free brochures about dealing with banks. www.aba.com

Consumer Bankers Association (1000 Wilson Blvd., Suite 3012, Arlington, VA 22209; 703-276-1750). Represents banks, savings and loans, and credit unions and educates the public about banking. www.cbanet.org

Consumer Federation of America (1424 16th St., N.W., Suite 604, Washington, DC 20036; 202-387-6121). A consumer group that watches out for consumer interests.

Credit Union National Association (CUNA, P.O. Box 431, Madison, WI 53701; 608-231-4000; 800-356-9655). The trade group for credit unions. Lobbies on issues of importance to credit unions and helps people set up credit unions. www.cuna.org

Investment Company Institute (4201 H St., N.W., Suite 1200, Washington, DC 20005; 202-326-5800). The trade group for mutual funds, including money-market mutual funds; will send a free brochure entitled "Money Market Mutual Funds: A Part of Every Financial Plan." www.ici.org

The Savings and Community Bankers of America (900 19th St., N.W., Suite 400, Washington, DC 20006; 202-857-3100). Lobbies on behalf of savings and loans and savings banks and educates the public about banking and issues that face savings and loans and savings banks. Encourages policies that increase savings and keeps housing affordable through mortgage loans from its members. Was formed by the merger of the United States League of Savings and the National Council of Community Bankers. www.acbankers.org

Picking
Winning Stocks

If you've never invested in stocks or have only limited experience with them, you might be harboring a common misperception of the stock market: It's a dangerous, volatile place where thousands of sophisticated professional traders and brokers lurk to steal your hard-earned money.

The reality of the stock market—if you learn a little about it—could not be further from that myth. There are millions of small investors like you who have been able to finance their dreams by successfully buying and holding for years shares of profitable companies and of mutual funds that buy such shares. Millions of other investors depend on the regular income they earn from their stock and mutual fund holdings.

Sure, stock prices go down at times, as well as up. Sometimes, like in the 508-point crash of October 19, 1987 or the 554-point drop on October 27, 1997, they can plummet so fast that your heart palpitates. But this is the exception that proves the rule. If you look over the past few decades, prices of good-quality companies' stocks have invariably moved higher, as shareholders are rewarded by the performance of the firms they own. As a device to increase your net worth so you can achieve your financial goals, stocks or stock mutual funds are your best investment over the long run (see Figure 3.1).

Investing in Stocks

When you buy common shares in a company, you become a part owner in that firm, along with all the other people and institutions that own all the shares that have ever been issued. Because you are a part owner, you have a piece of equity in that company. That is why stocks are often called *equities*. The shares you own constantly rise and fall in value as investors buy and sell them based on their outlook for the company. The more people want to buy because they think profits will rise, the more

Figure 3.1
1925–1997 Chart of Stocks, Bonds, Bills and Inflation

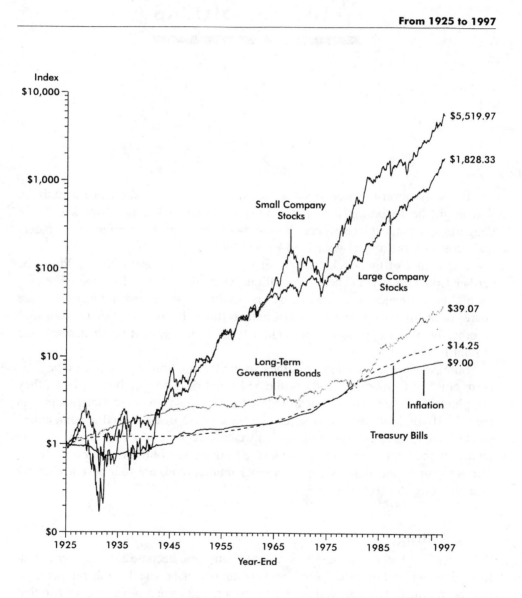

From 1925 to 1997

the share price increases. Theoretically, your opportunities for profit are boundless. However, if the firm's prospects start to sour and it looks like profits will turn down, more people will want to sell than buy, and the share price will fall.

Another way to own a piece of a company is through ownership of *preferred shares.* Owners of preferred shares, though they usually do not have voting rights on company matters, are entitled to receive their dividends before common shareholders, and if the company is liquidated, preferred claims are satisfied before common shareholders' claims. Preferred dividends are set at the time the shares are issued and therefore cannot rise over time as common dividends can if the company performs well. In general, preferred stock is not as volatile as common stock; thus, it does not offer as much appreciation or depreciation potential. Some preferred issues, known as *convertible preferreds,* can be converted into common shares at a preset price.

The Basics of Being a Shareholder

As a shareholder, you are also entitled to receive quarterly updates on how your company is doing. You will be mailed a report that tells you whether profits were up or down and what other major corporate developments occurred in the last three months. You will also get a more detailed annual report outlining how the numbers for the latest year compare with prior years, as well as the company's plan for the future. You will also be invited to vote at the firm's annual meeting, either in person at the meeting or by a mail proxy ballot. You will vote on important matters, such as whether a major acquisition should be completed. At most companies, you get one vote for every share you own. So unless you own an enormous number of shares, you shouldn't expect to have much influence over the company's strategic direction. For the most part, you are along for the ride while the professionals running the company do their best to maximize profits.

In addition to the profit potential from a rising share price, you can earn money from stocks by collecting dividends. If the corporation is profitable and the board of directors decides it is prudent, the firm will send you a quarterly check for your piece of the profits, known as a *dividend.* Dividends are normally paid by large, well-established companies that are sure they will achieve a certain level of profit each year. Smaller and newer firms usually do not pay dividends because they want to reinvest all of their profits back in the business to make it grow faster.

Unlike other investment vehicles such as bonds, certificates of deposit (CDs) or futures contracts, shares in a company never mature or expire. As long as the company stays in business, the shares have some value. If the company goes out of business, however, your stock will probably become worthless because when a corporation is liquidated, shareholders get what's left after the Internal Revenue Service (IRS), bankruptcy lawyers and all other creditors, including bondholders and preferred shareholders, are paid. In most cases, that means the shareholders' stake is wiped out. On the bright side, you might still appreciate your stock certificate as a wall hanging in your living room, as it might remind you of the hopes you had for the company issuing it.

Why would a profitable company want to give you a chance to participate in its growth? Because it needs the money that the sale of stocks generate in order to run and expand the business. When a company offers shares to the public for the first time, known as an *initial public offering,* the proceeds of the sale help the company open new factories, research and develop new products, acquire other businesses or pay down debt. Later, if the company needs more capital to grow, it can issue additional shares in what is known as a *secondary offering.*

Most of the time when you buy shares, however, your money is going to the person or institution selling the shares, not to the company. The company benefits by having a constant market price for its shares so it knows how much money it can raise if it wants to do a secondary offering.

The person selling you his or her shares might be doing so for several reasons. The person might have a big profit in the shares and want to cash in. The person might have found what he or she thinks is a better investment opportunity in another stock. He or she might need the money to meet expenses. Or the seller might think that the company's stock is about to fall because this year's profits will not be as high as people expect.

Whatever a person's reason may be, you will never know because you won't meet the person selling you your stock. Because it would be difficult for you to find someone on your own who has shares and wants to sell, just as it would be impossible for him or her to find someone who wants to buy the shares, a centralized marketplace called a *stock exchange* has been set up to facilitate buying and selling. You can't just go down to the stock exchange with your certificates and sell your shares on your own, however. You must execute trades through a brokerage firm that is a member of the exchange.

The following are the five most common kinds of orders you can give a broker to buy or sell shares.

Day order. This is an order to buy or sell a stock at a particular price on the day the order is placed. If the trade is not executed on that day, the order expires.

Good-this-month (GTM) order. A GTM order tells a broker to buy or sell a stock at a particular price any time during the current month. If the trade is not executed by the end of the month, the order expires. A variation of this order is a *good-this-week order,* which expires within a week.

Good-till-canceled (GTC) order. A GTC order tells your broker to buy or sell a particular stock when it hits a specific price, whenever that might be. Such an order remains in effect until it is canceled. As long as the GTC order is in effect, it is known as an *open order.*

Limit order. With a limit order, you are telling your broker to buy or sell a particular stock at a certain price or better. For example, if you want to buy a stock for $27 a share that is now trading at $30, you can place a limit order at $27. If the stock falls quickly below $27, your broker would execute the order at the lower price, saving you money. On the other hand, if you want to sell a stock at $40 that is now trading at $35 and the stock suddenly shoots up beyond $40, the broker would execute the limit order and obtain an even higher price for your shares.

Stop order. With a stop order, you are trying to protect a profit or limit further losses. The most frequently used stop order, known as a *stop-loss order,* tells your broker to sell your stock at whatever the market price is when the stock hits a specific price less than the price for which it is currently trading. For example, say you bought a stock at $40 a share and it has since risen to $60. If you want to protect your profit, you can place a stop-loss order at $50. However, if the company suddenly announces that its earnings were far less than expected in the latest quarter and the stock plummets to $45, your order will be executed at $45, which is the next market price after the stock hits $50. If you want to make sure you get $50 a share, you should place a limit order. If you are selling *short*—that is, betting that a stock will fall in price—you can use a stop order to buy back shares at a particular price to prevent your losses from mounting. The risk in placing stop orders is that they may be executed because of a momentary setback in a stock's price. This is why you should not set stop orders too close to the current market price. Most pros leave a 20 percent margin to avoid losing a stock that will bounce back.

The following are three principal exchanges where you can buy and sell stocks.

New York Stock Exchange (NYSE). Founded in 1792, the NYSE is the oldest, largest and most prestigious of the stock exchanges. Located on the corner of Wall and Broad streets in downtown Manhattan, the Big Board, as it is called, is home to about 3,000 of the largest and most well-established companies in the United States. In addition, many foreign companies offer their shares for trading on the NYSE in the form of American depositary receipts (ADRs), which for all practical purposes are the same as U.S. shares. The listing requirements to trade on the NYSE are much more stringent than those to trade on other exchanges.

The NYSE uses a specialist system for trading stocks, which means that a specialist is assigned to maintain a fair and orderly market in every stock. Under normal conditions, brokers representing buyers and sellers meet in front of the specialist's post to agree on a price. However, when there is a sudden surge of buyers or sellers because of some dramatic event, the specialist must step in to take the other side of the trade. For example, if a company announces that it is being acquired at a much higher than market price, a stampede of buyers will descend on the trading post. The specialist must sell shares to those buyers though it would be at a higher price than the price of the shares right before the good news was announced. Similarly, if a company announces that its earnings were much lower in the latest quarter than people expected, there would be a flood of sell orders. The specialist would have to buy shares from the crowd, though it would be at a lower price than the price of the shares right before the bad news was announced, until the market for the stock stabilized.

American Stock Exchange (AMEX). Known as the Curb Exchange until 1921 because it conducted trading on the street curb, the AMEX, as it is now known, is home to about 800 medium- and small-sized growth companies. The AMEX is located near the NYSE in lower Manhattan at 86 Trinity Place. Like the NYSE, the AMEX hosts many companies, particularly Canadian ones, trading in the form of ADRs. The AMEX also operates the Emerging Companies Marketplace for very small companies offering their shares to the public. The AMEX uses a specialist system just like that employed on the floor of the NYSE.

Nasdaq National Market System. Nasdaq (National Association of Securities Dealers Automated Quotation system) stocks are, for the most part, smaller and less established than NYSE or AMEX companies'. Though Nasdaq stocks may be riskier and more volatile than traditional blue chips, in many cases, they also have more growth potential. Unlike the NYSE and AMEX, the National Market System (NMS) has no centralized floor where all trading on Nasdaq occurs. Instead, Nasdaq is a network of broker-dealers connected by an elaborate telephone and computer system. Instead of a specialist system, Nasdaq uses what are known as *market makers* to compete against each other and offer the best prices to buy and sell a stock at all times. Before this system was set up in 1972, trading in such stocks was called *over-the-counter (OTC) trading,* so the Nasdaq market is still called the OTC market by some. From your perspective as a stock buyer or seller, though, it makes little difference whether your stock is traded on the NYSE, the AMEX or Nasdaq. You must know where it is traded only so that you can look up the stock's price in the newspaper because all three exchanges are listed separately.

Buying Stocks on Margin

Most of the time, you will probably pay for your shares of stock in full. However, if you're feeling so optimistic about a stock that you want to increase your risk in the hope of magnifying your return, you can look into buying on *margin,* or with borrowed funds. According to rules set by the Federal Reserve, brokers currently will lend you up to half the money you need to buy stocks, as long as they have some collateral of yours to seize in case your stocks lose value. That collateral must be in the form of other securities or cash, which would include money-market fund shares. A broker charges you interest on the loan at the *broker's loan rate,* which is typically about a percentage point over the prime rate.

By doubling your bets (borrowing to match your own funds), you can make twice as much money if your stock goes up than you would if you were paying for your stock in full. For a margin loan to pay off well, the stock should rise quickly so that you can sell the shares and pay off the margin loan.

But margin loans clearly have tremendous risks. The first risk is that the value of the stock you buy will either remain fixed or decrease, thereby not earning the money to repay your margin loan. For you to break even, your stock must rise by the amount of your interest costs. More disastrously, if your stock price falls by half, you will be hit by the second most dreaded event in investing—a *margin call*. (A stock market crash is the most dreaded on our list.) When you receive a margin call from your broker, you must put up additional collateral to cover your loan or your position in the stock will be sold immediately, meaning you will have lost your entire investment. Meanwhile, if your collateral has declined in value as well, you will owe your broker even more money.

Most beginning investors should stay clear of buying on margin because of such risks. Think of it as a game you can play with your excess profits when you've become a wildly successful investor.

Selling Short

If you think buying on margin is risky, wait until you hear about *selling short*. This technique is for people who think they can profit if a stock drops in price. Because, as we've said, stocks tend to rise in value over time, these people are trying to swim upstream.

Of course, stock prices do fall, and if you've sold short in the right stock at the right time, you can make a great deal of money. The flip side is that your losses are unlimited because the stock you have shorted can rise forever (theoretically). The following example illustrates how selling short works. Assume that you want to short the stock of Smith Company because you think its new product is a flop and its earnings will be less than anyone expects, causing the stock price to plummet. You essentially borrow the shares from someone who owns them, typically your broker, with the promise that you will return them later. You then immediately go out and sell the borrowed shares at the current market price, which you think is inflated. (If the stock pays a dividend while you have possession of them, by the way, you must pay that amount to the lender.)

When the share price plunges (if your hunch is right), you buy the same number of shares in the marketplace and return them to the lender. This is known as *covering your short*. Your profit is the difference between the price you sold the stock for in the first place and the price at which you bought it back.

The specifics of this ideal short sale might be as follows:

1. You "short" or borrow 100 shares of Smith Company stock at $70 a share, which you immediately sell for a total of $7,000.

2. Smith's poor earnings report comes out, and the stock plummets to $50 a share.

3. You buy 100 shares of Smith at $50 each for a total of $5,000 and return the shares to your broker. Your profit is $2,000.

However, suppose that Smith Company's earnings report is actually better, not worse, than expected, and the stock soars. You won't be happy, to put it mildly. The specifics of this short sale might be as follows:

1. You borrow 100 shares of Smith Company stock at $70 a share, which you immediately sell for a total of $7,000.

2. Smith's good earnings report comes out, and the stock soars to $100 a share.

3. You buy 100 shares of Smith at $100 each for a total of $10,000 and return the shares to your broker. Your loss is $3,000.

From time to time, you will hear that stock prices are up one day because of *short covering*. That happens when stock prices start to rise and short sellers capitulate before their losses become too great; therefore, they buy shares to settle their loans.

Short selling, like buying on margin, should be done only by experienced investors with nerves of steel. To make money at this game, you not only must accurately guess the direction of future stock prices but also the timing. It's a dangerous game that only a few people win.

How To Pick Winning Stocks

Before you buy any stocks, remember that they are vehicles that can enable you to reach your financial goals. When you hear an exciting story about a hot growth stock, you may be tempted to put your life savings in it so you can become a quick millionaire. Resist the temptation. Recall all the work you did at the beginning of this book. Now is the time to use the conclusions you drew from the budgeting exercise and, most important, the examination of your tolerance for risk. Also remember to put stocks in their place in the investment pyramid (see Figure 1.12) so that you are diversified against loss yet stand to gain.

With that said, it's time to discuss the different techniques you can use to pick winning stocks. First, a few general tips that should help you make profitable decisions follow.

Plan to invest for the long term. Despite endless predictions by market gurus that stocks are about to soar or plunge, no one really knows what will happen to stock prices over the short term. So, for the most part, you should ignore most of the prognostications. The same advice holds for the economy, which is just as unpredictable as the stock market.

Your emotions will probably get the best of you if you do a great deal of short-term trading. When prices are rising, you will tend to get caught up in the enthusiasm and buy more. When prices are falling, you will probably get depressed and sell out. Besides, excessive trading activity will generate hefty commissions for your broker and taxes on capital gains for Uncle Sam. Instead of trading for the short term, buy stocks that have good market positions, are financially strong and offer products or services that seem sensible. If you can't explain what a company does in about two sentences, you probably shouldn't invest in it.

Buy stocks systematically. Instead of putting all your money into a stock in one lump sum, buy a fixed dollar amount of shares on a regular basis, whether that be monthly, quarterly or annually. If you buy the same dollar amount of a stock, say $100 a month, you will automatically buy fewer shares when the price is high and more shares when the price is low, thereby assuring yourself of a low average price over time. This technique is known as *dollar cost averaging.* It's a lot safer and easier than trying to determine when a stock has hit its low or high point.

The following simple example demonstrates the value of dollar cost averaging (excluding the effect of commission costs).

If you have $10,000 to invest in a stock, either you could invest it all at once or, using dollar cost averaging, you could buy $1,000 worth every month for ten months. The stock's price most surely will rise and fall over those ten months, so let's say the stock starts the year at $50 a share, steadily descends to $25 a share by June 1, then returns to $50 a share by November 1. If you were to put your entire $10,000 to work in January, your results would look like Figure 3.2.

Figure 3.2
Investing $10,000 All at the Same Time

Month	Amount Invested	Share Price	Shares Purchased	Cumulative Shares	Cumulative Market Value
January	$10,000	$50	200	200	$10,000
February	0	45	0	200	9,000
March	0	40	0	200	8,000
April	0	35	0	200	7,000
May	0	30	0	200	6,000
June	0	25	0	200	5,000
July	0	30	0	200	6,000
August	0	35	0	200	7,000
September	0	40	0	200	8,000
October	0	45	0	200	9,000
November	0	50	0	200	10,000
Total	$10,000	$50*	200	200	$10,000

*average price

If, instead of investing all your money at once, you invested $1,000 on the first of every month, your results would look like Figure 3.3.

Figure 3.3
Investing $10,000 by Dollar-Cost-Averaging Strategy

Month	Amount Invested	Share Price	Shares Purchased	Cumulative Shares	Cumulative Market Value
January	$ 1,000	$50	20	20	$ 1,000
February	1,000	45	22.2	42.2	1,899
March	1,000	40	25	67.2	2,688
April	1,000	35	28.5	95.7	3,350
May	1,000	30	33.3	129	3,870
June	1,000	25	40	169	4,225
July	1,000	30	33.3	202.3	6,069
August	1,000	35	28.5	230.8	8,078
September	1,000	40	25	255.8	10,232
October	1,000	45	22.2	278	12,510
November	0	50	0	278	13,900
Total	$10,000	$37.5*	278	278	$13,900

*average price

Notice that you would have ended up with $3,900 (or 39 percent) more if you had used the dollar-cost-averaging strategy than if you had bought all of your shares in January. The reason is that as the share price fell to a low of $25 on June 1, you kept buying more shares for your $1,000 each month. By the time the stock recovered back to the $50 level on November 1, you would have accumulated 78 more shares than if you had bought 200 shares in January. By buying ten times instead of once, you would incur ten commission charges, which would greatly reduce your gains. To avoid this problem, you can execute dollar cost averaging using a no-load mutual fund (see Chapter 4 on mutual funds), or enroll in a company's dividend reinvestment plan (see later in this chapter), which allows you to buy shares commission free and in fractional share amounts.

Figures 3.2 and 3.3 present a best-case scenario for dollar cost averaging because the price of the shares fell and then rebounded. Even in a less optimal case, where share prices rose and then dropped, you would still come out ahead with dollar cost averaging compared to investing all your money at once. That's the power of systematic investing!

Invest in stocks that you know well. Use your professional knowledge to spot companies that seem to be up and coming. For example, if you are a doctor, what new drugs seem to be particularly effective, and who manufactured the new medical equipment that your hospital just installed? If you are a car mechanic, what company is making the best components for new cars? If you are a homemaker, what new stores seem to be crowded, and what new products seem to be hot sellers at the supermarket? You have many stock tips at your disposal. Use them for profit.

Research your choices carefully. For some reason, people will spend weeks investigating every feature of a car costing $15,000, but when it comes to stocks, they will spend $15,000 based on a hot tip, a broker's recommendation or a mention in a newspaper story. Before you invest any money, know exactly what business the company is in, how profitable it is, whether it has much debt, which companies are competing with it and what new products or services the company intends to introduce. Most of all, look at who is running the company. Firms can have great plans, but they need top-quality management to transform those plans into profitable reality. The best way to judge management is by looking at its track record. If the management team has succeeded in the past, chances are that the team can do it again.

Monitor the company after you've bought shares. Read the quarterly and annual reports to see whether your projections are, in fact, coming to pass. Was the new product line successful? Did the company pay down its debt as you thought it would? Also keep an eye on the company's stock price. You don't need to check it every day—maybe once a week or at least once a month. If the stock price rises or falls dramatically, someone knows something about the stock that you will probably find out later. Also, you shouldn't own so many stocks that you don't have time to track them all. It's possible to be overdiversified as well as underdiversified.

Don't be pressured to buy or sell just because everyone else is doing so. In fact, if everyone else is doing it, it's probably the wrong time to be joining in. It takes courage, but you will most likely make the majority of your money by buying stocks when they are down and everyone dislikes them and by selling them when they are rising and every taxi cab driver lets you in on this latest "hot" tip.

Don't worry about missing out on a good stock. The best ones rise in value for years at a time, so you have plenty of opportunity to get in on them. If you had bought Wal-Mart stock any time in the early 1970s, you would have made more than 30 times your money if you had held until the 1990s. Just because a good stock moves up a few dollars, it's not too late to invest.

Have a selling target price in mind when you buy a stock. If the stock reaches that price, either you can sell some or all of it, or you can reconsider your position based on the company's situation at that time. You should also know the price at which you would sell the stock at a loss. This might be between 25 percent and 50 percent less than you paid for it. One of the worst things you can do is to watch your stock's price melt away as you hope it will recover. Remember, your stock does not know or care what price you paid for it, so it has no obligation to return to that price.

Consider transaction costs before you buy. If you have only enough money to buy a few shares, the commission you will pay might not be worth the investment. Determine in advance whether you will buy the stock through a full-service broker, who offers advice but charges higher fees, or a discount broker, who only executes your order but at much lower commission rates.

Understanding Key Financial Ratios

With these general rules in mind, let's look at the key financial ratios you must understand in order to pick a winning stock.

Price-earnings (PE) ratio. The most common way to compare how investors value one stock against another is to measure how much they will pay for a dollar of earnings. To determine the PE ratio, divide the stock's latest price by its earnings for the latest four quarters. For example, if a stock is selling for $10 a share and it earned $1 a share last year, it has a PE ratio of 10.

$$\frac{\$10 \text{ Current stock price}}{\$1 \text{ Past earnings per share}} = 10 \text{ PE}$$

This PE ratio, called the *trailing* PE ratio because it is based on the past, is the figure shown in the newspaper listing under the heading "PE."

An even more useful PE ratio is based on estimates of future earnings. Investors value stocks not only on what the stocks have done in the past but even more for what they think a firm's profits will be in the future. Stock analysts specialize in projecting earnings per share for the next two years, and even if they are not right on the button, you can get a sense of how the stock is valued based on the analysts' expectations. In addition to looking at analysts' reports, which you can get from a broker, you can study estimates of future earnings from the *Value Line Investment Survey,* Standard & Poor's stock reports (available both in libraries and by subscription) and most newsletters' commentary about individual stocks. To calculate a future, or *forward,* PE ratio, as it is known, divide the current stock price by analysts' estimates of next year's profits.

$$\frac{\$10 \text{ Current stock price}}{\$2 \text{ Projected earnings per share}} = 5 \text{ PE}$$

Once you've calculated the PE ratio, you must put it in proper context. The higher the PE ratio, the more earnings growth investors expect from the company. Any PE ratio over 20, for instance, means that investors have high expectations that the company's profits will grow rapidly in the next year. A PE ratio between 10 and 20 signals that investors expect solid growth. However, a PE ratio below 10 is a sign that investors do not anticipate much growth from the firm.

Compare the stock you are investigating to both the overall market and its industry peers to determine whether the stock is in or out of favor. The best benchmark for the overall market is the PE ratio of the Standard & Poor's 500 Index, which is published in *Barron's* and in most analysts' reports. Over the years, that PE ratio has ranged from a low of about 8 in the valleys of bear markets to around 20 at the peaks of bull markets. Because each industry has its own dynamics, you should also compare your stock to similar stocks' PE ratios. For example, if you are looking into a major city bank's stock, compare it to other big-city bank stocks. Do the same for airlines, oil firms, retailers, semiconductor chip makers or any other industry. If your stock's PE ratio is higher than its peers, investors expect even better results from it than from its competitors. If your stock's PE ratio is lower than its peers, investors expect less than industry-average results.

You might be thinking that investing in stocks is easy because all you have to do is choose the stock with the highest PE ratio and, therefore, the brightest future. This is the essence of growth stock investing, described in more detail with the worksheet in Figure 3.5. Unfortunately, this strategy hardly ensures success; in fact, it almost guarantees disappointment. While stocks with high PE ratios do indeed have promising futures, they are also the most subject to disappointment. Let us assure you, one of the last places you want to have your money is in a stock with high expectations that, for whatever reason, lets down investors. The moment the bad news hits the streets, the stock's price will plummet.

Some investors use the opposite strategy: They purchase stocks with low PE ratios that have reason to improve. The thinking behind this approach is that a stock with a low PE ratio already has low investor expectations built into its price; therefore, if the company reports poor profits, the stock has little room to fall. If, however, the company reports better than expected profits, the stock has much room to rise. All of this sounds good in theory, but not every low-PE-ratio stock will spring to life some day. Some have low valuations for good reasons, and they will stay that way indefinitely. The kind of low-PE-ratio stock you want to buy is the one with a turnaround already underway that has not been perceived by most investors. For more on how to find such stocks, refer to the discussions with the worksheets in Figure 3.7 (out-of-favor stocks) and Figure 3.8 (value stocks).

Price-book value ratio. Instead of comparing a stock's current price to the company's earnings, you can compare the price to the worth of the company's assets, or what is known as the company's *book value.* This includes the company's real estate, patents, brand names and all other assets, minus debts and other liabilities. To compute the ratio, divide the stock's price by the book value per share, which you can get from the annual report, Standard & Poor's company reports or the *Value Line Investment Survey.*

$$\frac{\$10 \text{ Current stock price}}{\$5 \text{ Book value per share}} = 200\% \text{ Price-book ratio}$$

A company selling over its book value indicates that investors think highly of the company and therefore have put a high value on its assets. A company selling at or below its book value indicates that investors have low expectations for the company and do not prize its assets. Investors who specialize in buying under-valued stocks peruse stocks selling at or below book value because they think they are getting a bargain if they can buy the stock for less than the company's assets are worth. Such stocks might also be takeover bait because another company or a raider may smell the same bargain, acquire the company and sell off its pieces for more than their current price. For more on finding undervalued stocks, see the discussion with the worksheet on value stocks in Figure 3.8.

Measures of profitability. Another method used to size up a company is to analyze its level of profitability. In general, the more profitable a company is, the better its stock performs over the long term. Firms with high profitability usually have some proprietary niche product, or a large and growing market share, and strong finances that enable them to invest in research and development to improve their products or services. The more profitable a company is, the more it tends to attract competitors that want to replicate its success. So a company that is able to ward off imitators and retain a high level of profitability is probably a good company to invest in over the long run.

The most commonly used measure of profitability is called *return on equity* (ROE). It is calculated by dividing a company's earnings by total shareholders' equity.

$$\frac{\$20 \text{ million earnings}}{\$100 \text{ million shareholders' equity}} = 20\% \text{ ROE}$$

In general, a return on equity of more than 15 percent is considered excellent, so the company in this example is extremely profitable.

As is the case with PE ratios and price-book value ratios, return on equity varies greatly by industry, so it is important to compare a company against its peers.

Another way to determine profitability is by looking at a company's *net profit margin.* This measure shows a company's overall success not only in managing operations but in terms of borrowing money at a favorable rate, investing cash wisely and taking advantage of tax benefits. To calculate it, divide net income by net sales.

$$\frac{\$20 \text{ million net income}}{\$200 \text{ million net sales}} = 10\% \text{ Net profit margin}$$

Profit margins also vary widely by industry. Supermarkets are happy with 2 percent margins, while newspaper publishers expect 20 percent margins. Therefore, compare the company you're investigating to similar firms.

Measures of debt. Just as it is in your personal life, debt can be either beneficial or detrimental to a company's financial health, depending on what the company does with the borrowed money and how easily it is able to make the interest and principal payments. In general, the more debt a company owes, the riskier it is as an investment because if its profits sag, it may be overly burdened by interest payments.

When you investigate a stock, look for its *debt-equity ratio*—the most common measure of indebtedness. The ratio is calculated by dividing a company's total liabilities (debts) by total shareholders' equity.

$$\frac{\$20 \text{ million total liabilities}}{\$100 \text{ million total shareholders' equity}} = 20\% \text{ Debt-equity ratio}$$

In this case, the company has a debt-equity ratio of 20 percent, which is usually very manageable. As with all other ratios discussed so far, the amount of debt companies owe differs greatly by industry. Electric utilities frequently have a debt-equity ratio of more than 50 percent because they constantly borrow to upgrade their generating plants. Small high-tech companies might have high debt levels because they fund new product research, which will pay off in the future but creates little revenue in the present. On the other hand, a well-established food manufacturer might have little or no debt because it has a steady flow of cash coming in from sales of its products. In general, a debt-equity ratio of more than 50 percent means the company has a high level of debt.

Dividend payout ratio. This measure tells you how much of a company's profits is being paid out in dividends. To calculate it, divide the dividends per share by the earnings per share.

$$\frac{\$1 \text{ Dividends per share}}{\$2 \text{ Earnings per share}} = 50\% \text{ Dividend payout ratio}$$

In this case, 50 percent of the company's profits are going directly to the shareholders in the form of a cash dividend. In general, the more established a company, the higher its payout ratio. Electric utilities, which investors buy for their dividends, probably have the highest payout ratio of any industry, typically around 50 percent. Other manufacturers might pay 30 percent to 40 percent of their profits as dividends and reinvest the rest in their businesses.

A high dividend payout ratio—more than 70 percent—can signal that the dividend is about to be cut. If a company is paying out nearly all of its profits in dividends, it has little money left to reinvest in its business, which ultimately will make it less competitive. Therefore, don't search for companies with very high payout ratios because you're likely to find stocks about to slice their dividends.

Categories of Stock

Armed with an understanding of basic financial ratios, you are now equipped to choose individual stocks. There are many kinds of stocks, and some are more appropriate for you than others, depending on your risk profile and financial objectives. I will concentrate here on five categories of stocks (cyclical, growth, income, out-of-favor and value) and provide worksheets, adapted with permission from worksheets I developed for *Money* magazine, that will tell you whether a stock you are interested in passes the test.

CYCLICAL STOCKS

Certain companies' fortunes are very closely tied to the ups and downs of the economy, and if you time purchases and sales of such company stocks well, you can profit handsomely. Cyclical stocks, so called because they ride the economic cycle, are typically found in such heavy industries as auto manufacturing, paper, chemicals, steel and aluminum. These companies all have relatively large fixed costs to run their

Figure 3.4   Cyclical Stock Worksheet

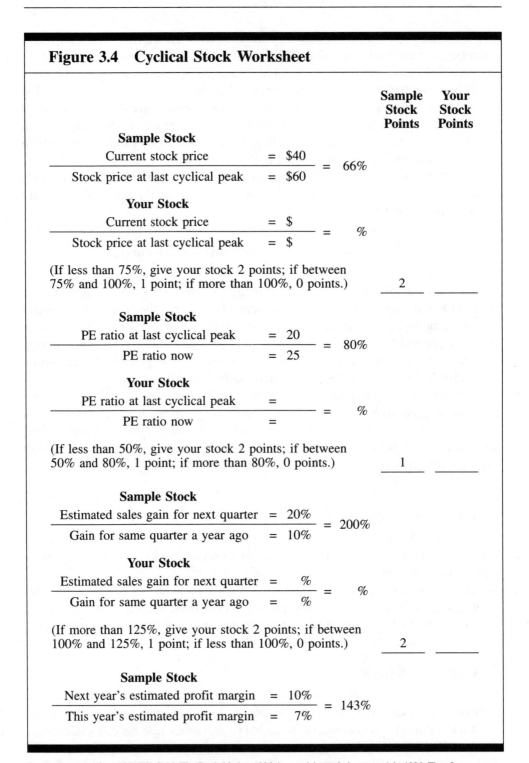

	Sample Stock Points	Your Stock Points

Sample Stock

$$\frac{\text{Current stock price} \quad = \$40}{\text{Stock price at last cyclical peak} \quad = \$60} = 66\%$$

Your Stock

$$\frac{\text{Current stock price} \quad = \$}{\text{Stock price at last cyclical peak} \quad = \$} = \ \%$$

(If less than 75%, give your stock 2 points; if between 75% and 100%, 1 point; if more than 100%, 0 points.)   2   _____

Sample Stock

$$\frac{\text{PE ratio at last cyclical peak} \quad = 20}{\text{PE ratio now} \quad = 25} = 80\%$$

Your Stock

$$\frac{\text{PE ratio at last cyclical peak} \quad =}{\text{PE ratio now} \quad =} = \ \%$$

(If less than 50%, give your stock 2 points; if between 50% and 80%, 1 point; if more than 80%, 0 points.)   1   _____

Sample Stock

$$\frac{\text{Estimated sales gain for next quarter} \quad = 20\%}{\text{Gain for same quarter a year ago} \quad = 10\%} = 200\%$$

Your Stock

$$\frac{\text{Estimated sales gain for next quarter} \quad = \ \%}{\text{Gain for same quarter a year ago} \quad = \ \%} = \ \%$$

(If more than 125%, give your stock 2 points; if between 100% and 125%, 1 point; if less than 100%, 0 points.)   2   _____

Sample Stock

$$\frac{\text{Next year's estimated profit margin} \quad = 10\%}{\text{This year's estimated profit margin} \quad = 7\%} = 143\%$$

Source: Reprinted from MONEY Guide/The Stock Market–1986, by special permission; copyright 1986, Time Inc.

Figure 3.4   (continued)

	Sample Stock Points	Your Stock Points

Your Stock

$$\frac{\text{Next year's estimated profit margin} = \quad \%}{\text{This year's estimated profit margin} = \quad \%} = \quad \%$$

(If more than 125%, give your stock 2 points; if between 100% and 125%, 1 point; if less than 100%, 0 points.)   2   _____

Sample Stock

$$\frac{\text{Next year's estimated return on equity} = 15\%}{\text{This year's return on equity} \quad = 10\%} = 150\%$$

Your Stock

$$\frac{\text{Next year's estimated return on equity} = \quad \%}{\text{This year's return on equity} \quad = \quad \%} = \quad \%$$

(If more than 125%, give your stock 2 points; if between 100% and 125%, 1 point; if less than 100%, 0 points.)   2   _____

Total Points   **9**   _____

If your stock scores 6 points or more, you have probably found a cyclical stock about to take off. The example here is clearly a good investment.

---

factories. As a result, if the volume of the product they sell is high and the prices they receive are rising because of strong demand, they stand to cover those costs easily and earn enormous profits. However, when demand is weak and prices are falling, they are still burdened by the same costs, so their earnings plummet.

Cyclical stock prices are even more volatile than the company's earnings. Investors are constantly trying to determine whether the cycle is turning up or down because it has a tremendous impact on the company's bottom line. While all stock prices reflect investors' expectations of future profits, cyclical stocks are even more sensitive to perceptions about the future.

The best time to buy cyclical stocks, as hard as it may be to do, is when they are still losing money in the bottom of a recession but their situation is no longer deteriorating. The moment that investors sense a turnaround, the stock will shoot up. Conversely, the time to sell a cyclical stock is when the company is earning record profits and everything seems to be going well. When investors sense that the rate of improvement is slowing or growth is stalling, the stock will decline rapidly.

The worksheet in Figure 3.4 will help you evaluate where a cyclical stock is in its cycle and therefore whether now is a good time to buy it. All the numbers needed to complete this worksheet are available from Standard & Poor's company profiles or the *Value Line Investment Survey.* We have provided sample numbers for a cyclical stock.

GROWTH STOCKS

The easiest way for most people to make money in stocks over the long term is to buy and hold shares in high-quality growth companies. If it is a true growth stock, its earnings will compound at 15 percent or more no matter what the overall economy is doing. Impossible, you say? Take a look at the track records of such stellar growth companies as tax preparation giant H&R Block, retailer Wal-Mart, tobacco and food company Philip Morris and software king Microsoft, for starters.

Growth stocks can perform so admirably because their companies offer proprietary niche products or services and have well-known brand names, strong finances and top-flight management. As long as these factors remain constant, growth can continue indefinitely. At a certain point, though, as a company becomes huge, it is more difficult to generate the same percentage profit increases; however, some firms seem to keep the increases coming, despite the odds.

So far, investing in growth stocks sounds like a breeze. But it isn't quite that easy. The better the record a growth company establishes, the higher investors' expectations soar and the higher the stock's PE ratio climbs. As long as the growth continues unabated, no problem occurs. But the moment such a company reports a slight slip in its upward trajectory, the stock can take a seemingly senseless pounding. As we stated earlier, one of the last investments you want to own is growth stock about to disappoint investors' earnings expectations. Also, successful companies attract imitators, which usually try to copy the original company's products or services and sell them cheaper. Sometimes that can slow the company's profit growth.

Growth stock investing is also plagued by fads. In the 1960s and early 1970s, stocks like Avon, Polaroid and Xerox were Wall Street darlings, until they plummeted by 50 percent or more in 1973. In the late 1970s, gambling stocks were the rage as Atlantic City casinos began to open. In the 1980s and 1990s, biotechnology, health maintenance organization, personal computer, software and specialty retailing stocks all had their day, only to fade after expectations got too high. Whenever you invest in a growth stock that seems like a fad, sell your shares the moment you think the fad is fading.

Growth stocks come in three sizes. The largest, with sales of at least $1 billion, are known as blue chip growth companies. Medium-sized growth companies, with sales of $500 million to $1 billion, are called *mid-cap* ("cap" for capitalization, which is the market value of the outstanding shares) growth stocks. Small companies, with sales of less than $500 million, are known as emerging growth companies. In general, the smaller the company, the bigger the growth potential because it is easier to grow quickly from a small base than from a big one. But investing in stocks of smaller companies also entails more risk because they do not have market positions as established as larger companies' positions.

One of the biggest mistakes people make when buying growth stocks is to get too excited by their prospects and pay too much for the stocks. An easy way to judge whether you are overpaying is to look at the stock's PE ratio. The higher the PE ratio, the more enthusiastic investors are about the company. Compare the PE ratio of your stock with that of similar companies in the same industry. If your stock's PE ratio is considerably higher, you could be paying too much.

The other key indicator growth stock investors look for is the *earnings growth rate,* or the rate at which profits grow from year to year. In general, the higher the growth rate, the higher the stock's PE ratio. The ideal growth stock is one selling at a PE ratio below its growth rate. For example, if Go-Go Computer's profits are growing at 30 percent a year, its stock would be considered a bargain if it were selling for a PE ratio of 20. While producing a solid growth rate is important, consistent growth is also highly prized. A company with profits up 40 percent one year and down 20 percent the next will not earn as high a PE ratio as one that grows 20 percent year after year.

The worksheet in Figure 3.5 will help you evaluate your own growth stock. All the numbers needed to complete this worksheet are available from Standard & Poor's company profiles or the *Value Line Investment Survey.* We have provided sample numbers for a growth stock.

INCOME STOCKS

While most people think of stocks as vehicles to achieve capital appreciation, they can also provide steady income. Good-quality income stocks have an advantage over bonds (see Chapter 5) for income investors. While the interest that a bond pays is fixed until the bond matures, a stock's dividend can rise year after year. So although a bond usually provides a higher current yield, a stock with a solid record of dividend increases can actually pay more over time. Because those higher dividends are paid out of ever-increasing profits, the stock price should climb over time as well.

Companies that pay high dividends usually are well-established, profitable firms. Some businesses that offer high-paying stocks include banking firms, real estate investment trusts, and electric, gas, telephone and water utilities. Unlike faster growing younger companies, which reinvest profits in their own businesses, such firms traditionally pay out at least half their profits to shareholders in the form of dividends.

Even more than prices of other stocks, high-yield stock prices are greatly influenced by the direction of interest rates. When rates on Treasury bonds fall, high-yield stock prices tend to rise because that stock's dividends are more

---

Figure 3.5   Growth Stock Worksheet

	Sample Stock Points	Your Stock Points

Sample Stock

Projected five-year annual growth rate   =   22%

Your Stock

Projected five-year annual growth rate   =   %

(If more than 20%, give your stock 2 points; if between
10% and 20%, 1 point; if less than 10%, 0 points.)   2   _____

Sample Stock

Earnings growth rate for last five years   =   25%

Your Stock

Earnings growth rate for last five years   =   %

(If more than 20%, give your stock 2 points; if between
10% and 20%, 1 point; if less than 10%, 0 points.)   2   _____

Sample Stock

Average return on equity for past three years   =   18%

Your Stock

Average return on equity for past three years   =   %

(If more than 20%, give your stock 2 points; if between
10% and 20%, 1 point; if less than 10%, 0 points.)   1   _____

Sample Stock

$$\frac{\text{Projected five-year earnings growth rate} = 22\%}{\text{Stock's current PE ratio} \qquad = 16\%} = 137\%$$

Your Stock

$$\frac{\text{Projected five-year earnings growth rate} = \%}{\text{Stock's current PE ratio} \qquad = \%} = \%$$

(If more than 160%, give your stock 2 points; if between
125% and 160%, 1 point; if less than 125%, 0 points.)   1   _____

Source: Reprinted from MONEY Guide/The Stock Market–1986, by special permission; copyright 1986, Time Inc.

Figure 3.5   (continued)

		Sample Stock Points	Your Stock Points
Sample Stock			
Earnings consistency	= Up 7% in each of last five years		
Your Stock			
Earnings consistency	= Up 7% in each of last five years		

(If up 10% or more for each of the last five years, give your stock 2 points; if up for each of the last five years, 1 point; if down in any of the last five years, 0 points.)   1   _____

Total Points   7   ══════

If your stock scores 6 points or more, it has long-term growth potential. The example here looks like an attractive growth stock.

---

competitive with bonds. Conversely, when interest rates rise, high-yield stocks look less attractive, and their prices tend to drop.

To make sure an income stock you are considering can continue to raise its dividend, you should determine that the company is financially strong. You can do this by analyzing the company's debt. Debt that is more than 50 percent of the company's equity may be a sign of trouble. Another quick way to gauge financial strength is to check the stock's rating with a reputable credit rating agency's ratings such as *Standard & Poor's Stock Guide.* Any rating over B+ means that the company is financially solid.

The final ratio to inspect before you buy a stock for income is the *payout ratio,* the percentage of earnings that is paid out in dividends. A payout ratio below 60 percent means that there is a sizable cushion for the company to fall back on before it has to cut its dividend. A low ratio also leaves room for the dividend to grow. On the other hand, a payout ratio above 60 percent might be a sign that the dividend may be cut.

Don't be entranced by a stock that sports an above-average yield, usually of more than 10 percent. There must be a reason why the yield is that high, and probably it is not positive. For example, the payout may be high because the stock price has fallen in anticipation of a dividend cut. Or it may be high because the company is in the process of liquidation, and the high payouts are actually a return of shareholders' capital. Whatever the reason, be suspicious of stocks with ultra-high yields.

Figure 3.6   Income Stock Worksheet

		Sample Stock Points	Your Stock Points

Sample Stock
Dividend yield   =   7%

Your Stock
Dividend yield   =   %

(If more than 6%, give your stock 2 points; if between
4% and 6%, 1 point; if less than 4%, 0 points.)   2

Sample Stock
Dividend growth rate for the past five years   =   9%

Your Stock
Dividend growth rate for the past five years   =   %

(If more than 8%, give your stock 2 points; if between
5% and 8%, 1 point; if less than 5%, 0 points.)   2

Sample Stock
Projected five-year earnings growth rate   =   10%

Your Stock
Projected five-year earnings growth rate   =   %

(If more than 8%, give your stock 2 points; if between
5% and 8%, 1 point; if less than 5%, 0 points.)   2

Sample Stock

$$\frac{\text{Dividends per common share} = \$\ 1}{\text{Earnings per common share} = \$\ 2} = \text{Dividend payout ratio—50\%}$$

Your Stock

$$\frac{\text{Dividends per common share} = \$}{\text{Earnings per common share} = \$} = \text{Dividend payout ratio— \%}$$

(If less than 60%, give your stock 2 points; if between
60% and 70%, 1 point; if more than 70%, 0 points.)   2

Source: Reprinted from MONEY Guide/The Stock Market–1986, by special permission; copyright 1986, Time Inc.

Figure 3.6 (continued)

	Sample Stock Points	Your Stock Points
Sample Stock		
Financial strength rating = A–		
Your Stock		
Financial strength rating =		
(If the credit rating agency's ratings is A or above, give your stock 2 points; if between B+ and A–, 1 point; if lower than B+, 0 points.)	1	
Total Points	9	

If your stock scores 6 points or more, it should provide steady, attractive income. The example here is a stock that any retiree could count on to pay uninterrupted dividends for years.

All the numbers needed to complete the worksheet in Figure 3.6 are available from Standard & Poor's company profiles or the *Value Line Investment Survey*. We have provided sample numbers for an income stock.

OUT-OF-FAVOR STOCKS

If the age-old way to make money in stocks is to buy low and sell high, then buying stocks when they are out of favor is a good way to buy low. Though this style of choosing stocks can be emotionally trying, it can be rewarding as well. Investors are not always rational. Just as they can bid up the price of a growth stock too high because they are so enthusiastic about its prospects, they can also pummel a stock that has momentarily slipped to unrealistically low prices. That's where bargain hunters swoop in. They sell out when the stock recovers.

The easiest way to spot neglected stocks is by looking for low PE ratios. A PE ratio of less than 10 signals that investors do not have much hope for the future of the company, which may, in fact, be an incorrect perception of the situation. The moment the company reports better-than-expected results, perceptions can change quickly, and the stock price can shoot up. Do your research first. Don't be tempted to buy any stock with a low PE ratio, however. Some companies deserve their lowly valuation and, in fact, will not recover.

In addition to a low PE ratio, bargain hunters usually look for industries that are currently out of favor. They also seek stocks with low price-book value ratios

Figure 3.7   Out-of-Favor Stock Worksheet

	Sample Stock Points	Your Stock Points

Sample Stock

$$\frac{\text{Current stock price} = \$40}{\text{Book value per share} = \$90} = 44\%$$

Your Stock

$$\frac{\text{Current stock price} = \$}{\text{Book value per share} = \$} = \quad \%$$

(If less than 25%, give your stock 2 points; if between 25% and 50%, 1 point; if more than 50%, 0 points.)   1   _____

Sample Stock

$$\frac{\text{Stock PE ratio} = 10}{\text{S\&P 500 PE ratio} = 15} = 66\%$$

Your Stock

$$\frac{\text{Stock PE ratio} =}{\text{S\&P 500 PE ratio} =} = \quad \%$$

(If less than 80%, give your stock 2 points; if between 80% and 100%, 1 point; if more than 100%, 0 points.)   2   _____

Sample Stock

Estimated five-year earnings growth rate   =   6%

Your Stock

Estimated five-year earnings growth rate   =   %

(If more than 7%, give your stock 2 points; if between 2% and 7%, 1 point; if less than 2%, 0 points.)   1   _____

Sample Stock

$$\frac{\text{Estimated capital expenditures for this year} = \$50 \text{ million}}{\text{Capital expenditures for last year} = \$20 \text{ million}} = 250\%$$

Source: Reprinted from MONEY Guide/The Stock Market–1986, by special permission; copyright 1986, Time Inc.

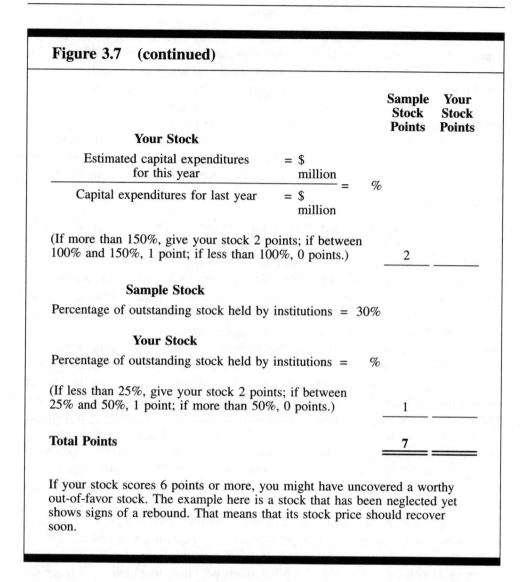

Figure 3.7   (continued)

	Sample Stock Points	Your Stock Points

Your Stock

Estimated capital expenditures = $ _____ million
for this year

Capital expenditures for last year = $ _____ million

$$\frac{\text{Estimated capital expenditures for this year} = \$ \_\_\_ \text{million}}{\text{Capital expenditures for last year} = \$ \_\_\_ \text{million}} = \_\_\_ \%$$

(If more than 150%, give your stock 2 points; if between
100% and 150%, 1 point; if less than 100%, 0 points.)   2

Sample Stock

Percentage of outstanding stock held by institutions = 30%

Your Stock

Percentage of outstanding stock held by institutions = _____ %

(If less than 25%, give your stock 2 points; if between
25% and 50%, 1 point; if more than 50%, 0 points.)   1

Total Points   7

If your stock scores 6 points or more, you might have uncovered a worthy
out-of-favor stock. The example here is a stock that has been neglected yet
shows signs of a rebound. That means that its stock price should recover
soon.

because such stocks are typically out of favor. Another sign of benign neglect is
when few of the shares are held by institutional investors, such as mutual funds or
banks, because it is not fashionable to own such depressed stocks. Finally, if
brokerage analysts do not pay attention to a stock, it is probably out of favor.

What you *should* look for is a stock with a fair chance at turnaround. You may
infer that a recovery is on the way if sales and earnings are no longer deteriorating
or if the company has a new product or service that has the potential to restart its
growth. Another way to check for signs of life is to determine whether company
executives are buying the stock themselves and whether they are increasing capital
expenditures. If the people who know the company best are investing in it heavily,
that could be a tip-off that recovery is at hand.

Not every ugly duckling turns into a swan, however. If your stock remains depressed after a year or more, you probably should turn it in for another one. It takes only one or two dramatic recoveries for this strategy to pay off.

All the numbers needed to complete the worksheet in Figure 3.7 are available from Standard & Poor's company profiles or the *Value Line Investment Survey*. We have provided sample numbers for an out-of-favor stock.

If your stock scores 6 points or more, you might have uncovered a worthy out-of-favor stock. The example here is a stock that has been neglected yet shows signs of a rebound. That means that its stock price should recover soon.

Value Stocks

If you could buy a stock worth $10 for $8, would you do it? Most people would because they know they are buying something for less than it is worth. In the stock market, this style of choosing stocks is known as *value investing*.

The key to value investing is being able to perceive when a stock's current price does not fully reflect the value of its assets. Those assets might include real estate, brand names, oil reserves, patented technology or even cash or stocks in other companies. Value investors make money by buying when the stock's assets are worth more than the stock's price and selling when the value of the assets has been realized.

Shareholders can be paid for the true value of their company's assets in one of several ways. A company can be taken over by another company or by a raider at a premium price because the acquirer thinks it can sell the assets for even more. The company can be broken into pieces, leaving shareholders with several stocks worth more separately than they were worth as a whole. The company's management can derive a way to make the formerly underused asset more productive, which would produce profits to boost the stock price. Or investors can finally realize the value of the the company's assets, and the stock price will rise to reflect that changed perception.

Trying to determine the true value of assets is tricky and subjective. A valuable asset to one analyst may have far less worth to another. Still, you can get a sense of whether a stock is selling for less than its breakup value by looking at the company's book value per share, tangible assets per share like land or oil reserves, and financial assets including cash and securities. A particularly stringent test is to compare the stock's price to so-called *net net working capital*. That is the amount of cash a company could raise in a hurry if it were liquidated today. To calculate it, subtract short- and long-term debts from such current assets as cash, securities, receivables and inventory. If the net net working capital of the stock you are looking at is 25 percent or more than the current price, you have found an undervalued stock.

The other way to identify a value stock is to see how much it would be worth if it continued in business. Take a look at the firm's cash flow (profits plus depreciation) per share, and divide it by the current stock price. The lower the price-cash flow ratio, the cheaper the stock is. At a certain point, the cash the company is throwing off could finance an acquisition of the company, making it a likely takeover target.

All the numbers needed to fill out the worksheet in Figure 3.8 are available from Standard & Poor's company profiles or the *Value Line Investment Survey.*

New Issues

Probably one of the most exciting yet dangerous opportunities in the stock market is *new issues,* the *initial public offerings* (IPOs) of former privately held companies. Such companies usually "go public" with great fanfare and hype, which can make their stock prices soar immediately after they begin trading. In the most famous case, when Genentech, the first biotechnology company to go public, made its offering at $35 a share in the early 1980s, its stock soared to more than $80 a share by the end of the first day of trading.

The new issues market is extremely sensitive to the general direction of the stock market. When stock prices are high and rising and investors are enthusiastic, many new issues go public. When prices are low and depressed and no one wants to hear about stocks, it is almost impossible to sell a new issue.

IPOs usually occur when their industries are popular with investors. What's hot goes in and out of fashion quite frequently. One year, semiconductor company stocks are popular; next, it can be environmental stocks. Biotech stocks have had their day, and specialty retailer stocks were the rage among new issues at one point. In the 1990s, stocks of companies that had been taken private in the leveraged buyout craze of the 1980s started going public again, making the hottest new issue a "reverse leveraged buyout." Who knows what Wall Street will think of next?

By their nature, new issues are speculative because they usually have no history of performance as public corporations. Some might have very promising-sounding products or services, but they may not be able to produce results when they finally get the money to bring the products or services to market. Several studies have shown that in the long term, about a third of all new issues do well, a third don't move much from the price at which they go public and a third go bankrupt. Another study found that IPOs jump an average of 15 percent on their first day of trading, then underperform the market by 44 percent over the ensuing three years.

In deciding whether to buy a particular new issue, use the standard analysis tools we've discussed earlier in this chapter. Also, you can get an offering statement, usually known as the *red herring,* from a broker, with all the company's financial history and plans. Other criteria to analyze include:

- How are the company's earnings affected by the issuance of millions of new shares in the IPO?

Figure 3.8   Value Stock Worksheet

			Sample Stock Points	Your Stock Points

Sample Stock

$$\frac{\text{Current stock price} \quad = \$40}{\text{Book value per share} \quad = \$45} = 89\%$$

Your Stock

$$\frac{\text{Current stock price} \quad = \$}{\text{Book value per share} \quad = \$} = \quad \%$$

(If less than 100%, give your stock 2 points; if between 100% and 140%, 1 point; if more than 140%, 0 points.)   2   _____

Sample Stock

$$\frac{\text{Cash per share} \quad = \$5}{\text{Current stock price} \quad = \$40} = 12.5\%$$

Your Stock

$$\frac{\text{Cash per share} \quad = \$}{\text{Current stock price} \quad = \$} = \quad \%$$

(If more than 25%, give your stock 2 points; if between 10% and 25%, 1 point; if less than 10%, 0 points.)   1   _____

Sample Stock

$$\frac{\text{Net net working capital per share} \quad = \$6}{\text{Current stock price} \quad = \$40} = 15\%$$

Your Stock

$$\frac{\text{Net net working capital per share} \quad = \$}{\text{Current stock price} \quad = \$} = \quad \%$$

(If more than 25%, give your stock 2 points; if between 0% and 25%, 1 point; if less than 0%, 0 points.)   1   _____

Sample Stock

$$\frac{\text{Current stock price} \quad = \$40}{\text{Cash flow per share} \quad = \$10} = 4$$

Source: Reprinted from MONEY Guide/The Stock Market–1986, by special permission; copyright 1986, Time Inc.

Figure 3.8   (continued)

			Sample Stock Points	Your Stock Points

Your Stock

$$\frac{\text{Current stock price} \quad = \$}{\text{Cash flow per share} \quad = \$} =$$

(If less than 5, give your stock 2 points; if between 5 and 7, give it 1 point; if more than 7, 0 points.)   2   _____

Sample Stock

$$\frac{\text{Outstanding debt} \quad = \begin{array}{c}\$19 \\ \text{million}\end{array}}{\text{Total capital} \quad = \begin{array}{c}\$100 \\ \text{million}\end{array}} = 19\%$$

Your Stock

$$\frac{\text{Outstanding debt} \quad = \begin{array}{c}\$ \\ \text{million}\end{array}}{\text{Total capital} \quad = \begin{array}{c}\$ \\ \text{million}\end{array}} = \%$$

(If less than 20%, give your stock 2 points; if between 20% and 30%, 1 point; if more than 30%, 0 points.)   2   _____

Total Points   8   _____

If your stock scores 4 points or more, you might be looking at an undervalued stock. The example here is a real bargain.

- What unique product or service does this company have that will allow it to compete with more established firms?

- How will the IPO's PE ratio compare with that of other companies in the same industry at the proposed initial offering price?

- Are company executives and other insiders on the board of directors using the IPO as a chance to unload their shares?

- What is the record of the brokerage firm underwriting the offering? How have other issues the firm has sold performed in the last year?

If a new issue with exciting prospects is coming to market, chances are that you will not be able to obtain many shares, if you get any at all. That's because hot IPOs are parceled out to brokers' best customers, almost as a favor. If the issue is so hot that its price soars immediately after it begins trading, many investors will "flip" the stock back into the market and pocket an instant profit. Don't expect to be a flipper, though, unless you are a steady customer of a broker with a great deal of pull at his or her firm.

In many cases, the best strategy for dealing with the new issues market is to wait for all the hype to calm down and buy the stock three months or so after the offering. By then, Wall Street will have moved on to other new issues, and these stocks tend to sink back to more reasonable levels.

For more information on new issues, consult the following newsletters:

- *Standard & Poor's Emerging and Special Situations* (25 Broadway, New York, NY 10004; 800-852-1641). www.infostandard&poor.com

- *New Issues* (The Institute for Econometric Research, 2200 Southwest 10th St., Deerfield Beach, FL 33442; 954-421-1000; 800-327-6720). www.mfmag.com

- *New Issues Outlook* (50 Main St., White Plains, NY 10606; 800-477-3331). This company also publishes an annual *New Issues Performance Directory.*

- *IPO Financial Network* (212 Short Hills Ave., Springfield, NJ 07081; 973-379-5100). www.ipofinancial.com

You can also use the Internet to find out the latest information about initial public offerings. By retrieving information about coming offerings online, you will be able to find out and act on the best deals earlier than if you had to wait for a mailed newsletter. Here is a sampling of the most prominent IPO Web sites:

- Alert IPO (www.ostman.com/alert-ipo)
- Capital Markets Financial Center (www.capmarkets.com)
- Interactive Nest Egg's IPO Center (www.nestegg.iddis.com/ipo/
- IPO Central (www.ipocentral.com)
- IPO Data Systems (www.ipodata.com)
- IPO Network (www.iponetwork.com)
- IPO Online Home Page (www.ipo-source.com)
- IPO Retriever (prospex.com//IPOs.html)
- IPOs Online (www.ipos-online.com)
- WebIPO (www.webipo.com)

Socially Conscious Investing

If you are one of the growing number of people who not only want their investments to do well, but to *do good* as well, you might be interested in socially conscious investing. This is the practice of seeking out companies that meet standards of social performance in addition to normal financial criteria. Most social criteria are positive; that is, they are attributes that people look for in a company. However, some criteria are negative; that is, they are aspects of a company that would keep people from investing in it.

The most common positive social criteria are clean environmental records; widespread advancement of women and minority employees; action on child care and AIDS for workers; safe, nonpolluting products; active investment in community and social projects; promoting alternative energy sources such as solar and geothermal power; commitment to worker safety; and fair bargaining with unions.

The most common negative social criteria are dealing with the military or arms business; supporting the South African apartheid regime; operating nuclear power facilities; testing products on animals in a way that is considered cruel; selling tobacco or liquor; fostering gambling; and creating water or air pollution.

The financial idea behind socially conscious investing is that if a company does not pollute and treats its workers well, in addition to promoting other progressive policies, it will probably be able to stay out of trouble with government agencies and the public. That will be good for business and, in the long run, the firm's stock price. Conversely, a company that is constantly fined by the government for polluting, suffers strikes by oppressed workers and experiences nuclear meltdowns is probably not going to offer profitable stock.

One group that monitors corporate performance on a broad range of social issues is the Council on Economic Priorities (30 Irving Pl., New York, NY 10003; 212-420-1133; 800-729-4237; www.accesspt.com/cep). Another company that issues social and financial reports on individual stocks is Franklin Research & Development (711 Atlantic Ave., Boston, MA 02111; 617-423-6655; www.frdc.com). It has published a book on the subject entitled *Investing for a Better World,* by Amy Domini. Domini has also produced, with Peter D. Kinder and Steven D. Lydenberg, a book titled *The Social Investment Almanac* (Henry Holt & Co., 115 W. 18th St., New York, NY 10011; 212-886-9200). Two more good books on the topic are *Socially Responsible Investing,* by Alan Miller (New York Institute of Finance, 2 Broadway, 5th Floor, New York, NY 10004; 212-859-5000; www.nyif.com), and *Investing with Your Conscience,* by John C. Harrington (John Wiley & Sons, 605 Third Ave., New York, NY 10158; 212-850-6000; www.wiley.com).

If you want a fund manager to make these sometimes tricky social screening decisions for you, there are about ten mutual funds that use ethical screens. Some of the better known funds include Calvert-Ariel Appreciation (800-368-2748; www.calvertgroup.com), Dreyfus Third Century (800-645-6561; www.dreyfus.com), Parnassus (800-999-3505; www.networth.quicken.com/parnassus), Pax World (800-767-1729; www.paxfund.com).

Stock Indexes and Averages

News reports about the stock market that you see or hear every day on television, on the radio and in newspapers normally track the action of stock indexes and averages, not individual stocks. These reports can give you a sense of the general direction of stocks though they will not tell you whether the stocks in your portfolio are up or down. Still, it is good to understand these indexes because they are commonly used as benchmarks for judging the performance of individual stocks. Each index is calculated slightly differently and measures a different sector of the market. The most commonly quoted indexes follow.

AMEX Composite Index. This index tracks the average of stocks traded on the AMEX, which tend to be medium- and small-sized growth stocks. The index is weighted by the market capitalization of its component stocks, meaning that stocks with a larger number of shares outstanding and with higher stock prices affect the index more than smaller companies with lower prices.

Dow Jones Industrial Average. The most commonly quoted average tracks the movement of 30 of the largest blue chip stocks traded on the NYSE. When people say, "How did the market do today?", they are usually referring to the performance of this average. The Dow Jones is a price-weighted average, so it is more affected by the movement of higher priced shares than by lower priced ones, no matter how many shares are outstanding.

The 30 component stocks in the Dow Jones industrials are Allied-Signal, Aluminum Company of America (Alcoa), American Express, AT&T, Boeing, Caterpillar, Chevron, Coca-Cola, Du Pont, Eastman Kodak, Exxon, General Electric, General Motors, Goodyear, Hewlett-Packard, IBM, International Paper, J.P. Morgan, Johnson & Johnson, McDonald's, Merck, Minnesota Mining and Manufacturing (3M), Philip Morris, Procter & Gamble, Sears Roebuck, Travelers, Union Carbide, United Technologies, Walt Disney and Walmart.

Dow Jones and Co., which maintains the average, also tracks utilities (electric and gas) in the Dow Jones Utilities Average and transportation stocks (airlines, railroads and truckers) in the Dow Jones Transportation Average. The combined industrial, utilities and transportation averages are called the Dow Jones Composite Average.

Nasdaq Composite Index. This index tracks the movement of all companies traded on the Nasdaq NMS. These tend to be smaller, more volatile companies than the blue chips in the Dow Industrial Average or the S&P 500. The Nasdaq Composite is market-value weighted, which gives more influence to larger and higher priced stocks.

NYSE Composite Index. This is the index for the trading of all NYSE stocks. It is market-value weighted and expressed in dollars and cents. When commentators say, "The average share lost 15 cents on the New York Exchange today," for example, this is the index to which they are referring.

Standard & Poor's 500 Index. The S&P 500 is the benchmark against which most portfolio managers compare themselves. It is composed of 500 blue chip stocks, separated by industry, so that almost all key industries are represented. The index always tracks 400 industrial company stocks, 60 transportation stocks and 40 financial stocks, like banks or insurance companies. The S&P 500 is the fairest yardstick against which you can measure the performance of your stocks.

Wilshire 5,000 Equity Index. The broadest measure of all indexes, the market-value-weighted Wilshire includes all major NYSE, AMEX and Nasdaq stocks and gives a good indication of the overall direction of all stocks, large and small.

Foreign indexes. The key indexes used to track stock prices in other countries include the CAC-40 in France; the DAX in Germany; the Financial Times 100 (known as the Footsie) in the United Kingdom; the Hang Seng Index in Hong Kong; the Nikkei 225 Index in Japan; the Toronto 300 Index in Canada; and the Zurich Index in Switzerland.

Dividend Reinvestment Plans (DRIPs)

If you own a stock that is paying a dividend, chances are that the company offers a terrific benefit called a *dividend reinvestment plan,* commonly known as a DRIP. If you don't need the cash from your dividend to live on, you can reinvest the payment with the company and buy more shares of stock. About 1,000 companies offer a DRIP.

Enrolling in a DRIP offers several advantages:

You put the magic of compounding to work for you. The shares that you buy with reinvested dividends earn more dividends, which buy more shares, and so on. Over time, the number of shares you own in the company grows steadily, without your having to contribute more cash.

Without even thinking about it, you are practicing dollar cost averaging. For example, say you receive $100 in dividends each quarter. When the share price is high, like $50, your dividends will buy fewer shares—in this case, two shares. But when the share price is low, like $20, the same dividends will buy more shares—in this case, five. This counteracts your normal emotional inclination to buy more shares when the price is high and rising and fewer when the price is low and falling. Over time, your average cost of buying shares will most likely be lower than it would if you tried to time your purchases.

Most DRIPs are free of brokerage commissions and other charges. Because the company offering the plan wants to encourage shareholders to use it, the firm normally absorbs all brokerage commissions for buying the stock and the administrative costs of the program.

More than 100 companies offer a sweetened version of the DRIP, called a discount DRIP. To encourage shareholder participation, the company gives up to an additional 5 percent discount on reinvested dividends. So, for example, if you reinvest $100 worth of dividends, you receive $105 worth of stock. This makes your holdings in the company grow even faster.

The following is a sample of the companies that offer a 1 percent to 5 percent discount on reinvested dividends, provided courtesy of Charles Carlson, author of *Buying Stocks Without a Broker* and *Free Lunch on Wall Street: Perks, Freebies, and Giveaways for Investors* (both by McGraw-Hill, Order Dept., 860 Taylor Station Rd., Blacklick, OH 43004; 800-722-4726; www.mcgraw-hill.com). The books explain how DRIPs work and provide a directory of all plans, including a profile of each company, with its address and telephone number, whether it offers optional cash purchase plans and other details of its plans. Carlson also is editor of the monthly newsletter *The DRIP Investor* (Dow Theory Forecasts, 7412 Calumet Ave., Hammond, IN 46324; 219-931-6480; www.dowtheory.com). Here is a list of such plans and the phone numbers of the companies and/or transfer agents (usually toll-free numbers) that can help you set up an account at any of these companies.

ADAC Laboratories; 800-356-2017
Aquarion Company; 800-288-9541
Argentina Fund; 800-426-5523
ATMOS Energy Corporation;
    800-543-3038; 800-774-4117
Austria Fund; 800-219-4218
Avalon Properties; 800-666-6431
Ball Corporation; 800-446-2617;
    765-747-6100
BanPonce Corporation; 787-764-1893
BCB Financial Services;
    800-368-5948
Beacon Properties Corporation;
    617-575-3120
Berkshire Gas Company;
    800-426-5523; 413-442-1511
Blount International;
    800-730-4001; 334-244-4000
Bradley Real Estate; 800-730-4001
Brazil Fund; 800-426-5523
Canadian Imperial Bank of
    Commerce; 800-387-0825
Capstead Mortgage Corporation;
    800-969-6715
Capstone Capital Corporation;
    205-581-7557

Carolina First Corporation;
    800-241-5568; 864-255-7913
Cathay Bancorp, Inc.; 800-937-5449
CBL & Associates Properties;
    800-733-5001; 423-855-0001
Chester Valley Bancorp; 800-937-
    5449
CNB Bancshares; 812-464-3416
Colonial Gas Company;
    617-575-3100
Columbia Bancorp; 800-368-5948
Columbus Realty Trust;
    800-730-6001
Commerce Bancorp, Inc.;
    800-526-0801; 609-751-9000
Commercial Net Lease;
    407-422-1574
Countrywide Credit; 818-225-3550
Cousins Properties; 770-955-2200
Crestar Financial; 800-756-3353;
    804-782-5619
CRIIMI MAE; 800-368-5948
CWM Mortgage Holdings;
    800-524-4458
Duff & Phelps Utilities Income
    Fund; 800-432-8224

Duke Realty Investments;
    800-278-4353; 800-774-4117
E'Town Corporation; 800-524-4458
Empire District Electric Company;
    888-261-6784
Equity Residential Properties;
    800-733-5001
Essex County Gas Company;
    800-278-4353; 508-388-4000
F&M Bancorp; 800-637-7549
FCNB; 301-662-2191
First American Corporation;
    615-748-1500
First Australia Prime Income
    Fund; 800-451-6788
First Colonial Group;
    610-746-7317
First Commerce Corporation;
    800-446-2617
First Commercial Corporation;
    800-482-8410
First Commonwealth Financial;
    800-524-4458; 412-349-7220
First Michigan Bank Corporation;
    800-441-3622
First Patriot Bankshares
    Corporation; 800-829-8432
First Union Corporation;
    800-347-1246
Fleming Companies;
    800-395-2662; 405-840-7200
Fuller H.B.; 800-468-9716;
    612-645-3401
Golden Triangle Industries;
    800-368-5948
GoodMark Foods; 800-829-8432
Green Mountain Power;
    800-647-4273; 802-864-5731
Health Care REIT; 800-851-9677;
    419-247-2800
Healthcare Realty Trust;
    617-575-3400

Hibernia Corporation;
    800-814-0305; 504-533-3333
Highwoods Properties Inc.;
    800-829-8432
Home Properties of New York;
    800-278-4353; 800-774-4117
Household International, Inc.;
    800-926-2335
Imperial Credit Mortgage
    Holdings; 714-556-0122
Independent Bank Corporation;
    800-257-1770; 616-527-9450
INMC Mortgage; 818-225-3550
IPL Energy; 800-387-0825
Irvine Apartment Communities,
    Inc.; 800-733-5001
Italy Fund; 800-331-1710
Kennametal, Inc.; 800-526-0801
Korea Fund; 800-426-5523
Lafarge; 703-264-3600
MDS Inc.; 416-813-4578
Media General, Inc.;
    800-633-4236; 804-649-6000
Mercantile Bankshares
    Corporation; 800-524-4458
Merry Land & Investment
    Company, Inc.; 800-829-8432;
    706-722-6756
MGI Properties; 800-730-6001
Mills Corporation; 201-324-0498
Monmouth Capital Corporation;
    800-526-0801
Monmouth REIT; 800-526-0801;
    908-542-4927
National City Corporation;
    800-622-6757
National Health Investors;
    615-890-9100
New Plan Realty Trust;
    800-730-6001; 212-869-3000
North Carolina Natural Gas;
    800-633-4236; 910-483-0315

Old National Bancorp; 800-264-6621
Omega Healthcare Investors, Inc.;
    800-519-3111
ONEOK, Inc.; 800-395-2662
Pennichuck Corporation;
    617-575-2000
Petroleum Heat & Power;
    800-278-4363
Philadelphia Suburban
    Corporation; 800-205-8314
Piccadilly Cafeterias;
    800-633-4236
Piedmont Natural Gas;
    800-633-4236
PMC Capital, Inc.; 800-278-4353;
    972-349-3200
PMC Commercial Trust;
    800-937-5449
Post Properties; 800-633-4236
Presidential Realty; 800-937-5449
Prestige Financial Corporation;
    800-368-5948
Price REIT; 800-284-9541
Public Service Company of North
    Carolina; 800-829-8432
Redwood Trust; 800-774-4117
ReliaStar Financial Corporation;
    800-468-9716
Resource Bancshares Mortgage
    Group, Inc.; 800-829-8432
Resource Mortgage Capital;
    800-829-8432
Saul Centers; 204-324-0498
Scudder New Asia Fund;
    800-426-5523
Scudder New Europe Fund;
    800-426-5523
Sea Containers Ltd.; 800-730-4001
Second Bancorp, Inc.; 800-756-3353
Security Capital Industrial Trust;
    800-730-6001
Southwest Water Company;
    800-356-2017

Sovereign Bancorp, Inc.;
    800-685-4524
Spain Fund; 800-219-4218
Suffolk Bancorp; 800-937-5449
Summit Properties; 800-829-8432
Sun Communities, Inc.; 800-257-1770
Sunstone Hotel Investors;
    888-261-6776
Taiwan Fund; 800-426-5523
Telephone & Data Systems;
    312-461-3310
Telus Corporation; 800-558-0046
Thornburg Mortgage Asset;
    800-426-5523; 800-509-5586
Time Warner; 800-279-1238
Trans Financial Bancorp;
    800-829-8432
TransCanada Pipelines Ltd.;
    403-267-6800
Union Planters National Bank;
    901-523-6656
UnionBanCal; 213-239-0671
United Cities Gas; 800-829-8432
United Dominion Realty Trust;
    800-526-0801
United Mobile Homes, Inc.;
    800-526-0801; 908-389-3890
UNITIL Corporation; 800-736-3001
Unocal Corporation; 800-279-1249
USBANCORP, Inc.;
    800-730-4001; 814-533-5319
USX-Marathon Group; 412-433-4801
USX-U.S. Steel Group;
    412-433-4801; 412-433-1121
Utilicorp United; 800-884-5426
Valley Resources, Inc.; 800-524-4458
Walden Residential Properties;
    617-575-3120
Weeks Corporation; 800-633-4236
Westcoast Energy, Inc.;
    604-661-0222
York Financial Corporation;
    800-278-4353; 717-846-8777

Several hundred companies not only allow you to reinvest your dividends; they offer optional cash purchase plans. These plans enable you to invest your own money, along with your dividends, in more shares at no cost. While that alone is a great deal, some firms even offer optional cash purchase at a discount. The companies that offer a 5 percent DRIP discount also extend the discount to any additional money you invest. Most of these programs, however, put limits on optional cash purchases, usually of about $25,000 a year. (The companies don't want to give away too much free money, after all.)

Several companies not only allow you to reinvest dividends and optional cash at no charge; they also make it easy to buy your original shares directly from the companies themselves, without commissions. Theoretically, you could buy shares in these firms, enroll in their DRIPs and optional cash programs, and build up a stake of hundreds of shares without ever paying a commission! (Don't tell your broker that you know about this one, or he or she won't return your calls!)

Another resource to keep you up-to-date on which companies are offering dividend reinvestment plans is the *DRP Authority* newsletter (The Moneypaper, Inc., 1010 Mamaroneck Avenue, Mamaroneck, NY 10543; 800-388-9993; www. moneypaper.com). In addition to the monthly newsletter listing new developments in the DRIP world, Moneypaper publishes a complete fact-filled *Guide to Dividend Reinvestment Plans* that has all the information you will ever need to get started with this sensible form of investing.

Direct Investing in Stocks

Another way to avoid brokerage commissions as you invest in individual stocks is by enrolling in the direct investment option at a growing number of companies. Following is a partial list of companies allowing direct initial stock purchases. This list is provided by Charles Carlson, editor of the *No-Load Stock Insider* newsletter (7412 Calumet Avenue, Suite 200, Hammond, IN 46324; 219-852-3230), which maintains a current list of such plans. Carlson refers to such stocks obtained through these plans as no-load stocks[TM]. The companies using the phone number 800-774-4117 are participating in the Direct Stock Purchase Plan Clearinghouse, which offers direct enrollment for many stocks around the world.

ABN AMRO; 800-749-1687
ABT Building Products;
   800-774-4117
Adecco; 800-749-1687
Advanta; 800-774-4117
Aegon; 800-774-4117
AFLAC; 800-774-4117
AGL Resources; 800-774-4117
Air Products & Chemicals;
   888-694-9458

AirTouch Communications;
   800-233-5601
Aktlebolaget Electrolux;
   800-749-1687
Akzo Nobel; 800-749-1687
Amcor Limited; 800-749-1687
American Electric Power;
   800-955-4740
American Express;
   800-463-5911

American Recreation Centers;
916-852-8005
Ameritech; 800-774-4117
Amoco; 800-774-4117
Amway Asia Pacific;
800-727-7033
Amway Japan; 800-749-1687
Aracruz Celulose; 800-749-1687
Arrow Financial; 518-745-1000
Asia Pulp and Paper Ltd.;
800-345-1612
Asia Satellite Telecommunications
Holdings; 800-749-1687
Ascent Entertainment; 800-524-4458
Astra; 800-345-1612
Atlantic Energy; 609-645-4506
Atlas Pacific; 800-345-1612
Atmos Energy; 800-774-4117
Augat; 617-575-3400
Banco de Galicia; 800-345-1612
Banco de Santiago; 800-749-1687
Banco de Santander; 800-749-1687
Banco Industrial Colombiano;
800-345-1612
Banco O'Higgins; 800-774-4117
Banco Wiese; 800-749-1687
Bank of Ireland; 800-345-1612
Bank of Tokyo-Mitsubishi;
800-345-1612
Barclays Bank PLC; 800-749-1687
Bard (C.R.); 800-828-1639
Bell Atlantic; 800-631-2355
BellSouth; 888-266-6778
Beneficial; 800-482-1595
Benetton Group; 800-749-1687
Biora AB; 800-345-1612
Blue Square-Israel; 800-345-1612
Bob Evans Farms; 800-272-7675
BOC Group; 800-749-1687
Boral Ltd.; 800-345-1612
Borg-Warner Automotive;
800-774-4117

Boston Beer; 888-266-6780
BRE Properties; 800-774-4117
British Airways; 800-749-1687
British Petroleum; 800-749-1687
British Telecommunications;
800-749-1687
Buckeye Partners LP;
800-519-3111
Bufete Industrial; 800-345-1612
Cadbury Schweppes;
800-749-1687
Cantab Pharmaceuticals;
800-345-1612
Capstead Mortgage; 800-969-6715
Carpenter Technology;
800-822-9828
CBT Group; 800-345-1612
Central & South West;
800-774-4117
Central Hudson Gas & Electric;
888-280-3848
Central Vermont Public Service;
800-354-2877 (permitted in
less than half the states)
Chevron; 800-774-4117
Chock Full O' Nuts; 888-200-3161
CILCORP; 800-774-4117
Coastal; 800-774-4117
Compania Cervecerias Unida;
800-749-1687
COMSTAT; 301-214-3200
Consorcio G Grupo Dina;
800-749-1687
Corporacion Bancaria de Espana,
S.A. Argentaria; 800-749-1687
Cresud; 800-345-1612
Cross Timers Oil; 800-774-4117
Crown American Realty Trust;
800-774-4117
CMS Energy; 800-774-4117
CSR Ltd; 800-749-1687
Curtiss-Wright; 888-266-6793

Dayton Hudson; 888-268-0203
Dassault Systemes SA;
    800-749-1687
Deere & Company; 800-268-7369
De Rigo; 800-345-1612
Digitale Telekabel; 800-345-1612
Disney (Walt); 800-948-2222
Dominion Resources;
    800-552-4034
Doncasters; 800-345-1612
DQE; 800-247-0400
Dr. Solomon's Group;
    800-345-1612
DTE Energy; 800-774-4117
Duke Realty; 800-774-4117
Durango; 800-774-4117
Durban; 800-345-1612
Eastern Company; 800-633-3455
Eastman Kodak; 800-253-6057
ECsoft Group; 800-345-1612
Elan; 800-345-1612
EMCEE Broadcast; 888-200-3167
Empresa Nacional De Electricidad;
    800-749-1687
Empresas ICA; 800-345-1612
Empresas La Moderna;
    800-345-1612
Energen; 800-774-4117
Enova; 800-307-7343
Enron; 800-662-7662
Entergy; 800-225-1721
Equifax; 800-887-2871
Equitables Cos.; 800-774-4117
Espirit Telecom Group;
    800-345-1612
Exxon; 800-252-1800
FAI Insurances Ltd; 800-345-1612
Fed One Bancorp; 800-742-7540
Fiat S.P.A.; 800-749-1687
Fila; 800-345-1612
Finova Group; 800-774-4117
First Commercial; 800-482-8410

First Financial Holdings;
    800-998-9151
Flamel Technologies;
    800-345-1612
Food Lion; 888-232-9530
Ford Motor Company;
    800-955-4791
Freepages Group; 800-345-1612
Fresnius Medical; 800-749-1687
Frontier Insurance; 888-200-3162
Gallaher Group; 800-345-1612
General Cable; 800-345-1612
General Growth Properties;
    800-774-4117
Gillette; 800-730-4001
Glenborough Realty;
    800-266-6785
Goodyear; 800-453-2440
Grand Metropolitan PLC;
    800-749-1687
Great Central Mines;
    800-345-1612
Groupe AB; 800-345-1612
Grupo Casa Autrey, S.A. de C.V.;
    800-749-1687
Grupo Elektra; 800-345-1612
Grupo IMSA; 800-345-1612
Grupo Industrial Durango;
    800-345-1612
Grupo Tribasa; 800-345-1612
Guangshen Railway Co.;
    800-749-1687
Guidant; 800-537-1677
Harland (John); 800-649-2202
Harmony; 800-345-1612
Harvey's Casino; 888-200-3164
Hawaiian Electric Industries;
    808-543-5662
Heidemij; 800-345-1612
Hillenbrand Industries;
    800-774-4117
Home Depot; 800-774-4117

Home Properties; 800-774-4117
Houston Industries; 800-774-4117
Huntingdon Life Sciences;
    800-345-1612
IBM; 888-421-8860
Illinova; 800-750-7011
Imperial Chemical Industries;
    800-749-1687
INA; 800-345-1612
Industrias Bachoco; 800-345-1612
Industrie Natuzzi; 800-345-1612
ING Group; 800-749-1687
Integon; 800-826-3978
Interchange Financial Services;
    201-703-2265
Invesco PLC; 800-749-1687
Investors Financial; 888-333-5336
IPALCO Enterprises;
    800-774-4117
IRSA Inversiones; 800-345-1612
ISPAT International; 800-345-1612
Israel Land Development;
    800-345-1612
Istituto Mobiliare Italiano SPA;
    800-749-1687
Johnson Controls; 800-524-6220
Kellwood; 314-576-3100
Kerr-McGee; 800-395-2662
Koninklijke Ahold NV;
    800-749-1687
Koor Industries; 800-345-1612
Lear; 800-524-4458
Libbey; 800-524-4458
Liberty Property Trust;
    800-944-2214
Lihir Gold Ltd.; 800-345-1612
Lilly (Eli); 800-451-2134
London International;
    800-345-1612
Longs Drug Stores; 888-213-0886
Lucent Technologies;
    800-774-4117

Luxottica Group; 800-345-1612
McDonald's; 800-774-4117
Macronix International;
    800-345-1612
Maderas y Sintecticos Sociedad
    Anonima; 800-345-1612
Madison Gas & Electric;
    800-356-6423
Makita; 800-345-1612
Matav; 800-345-1612
Mattel; 888-909-9922
Mavesa; 800-345-1612
Meadowbrook Insurance;
    800-649-2579
Merck; 800-774-4117
Micro Focus Group; 800-345-1612
MidAmerican Energy;
    800-247-5211
Mid-States; 800-345-1612
Minnesota Power & Light;
    800-774-4117
Mobil; 800-648-9291
Montana Power; 800-245-6767
Morgan Stanley, Dean Witter,
    Discover & Co.; 800-228-0829
Morton International;
    800-843-3445
National Westminster Bank PLC;
    800-749-1687
NEC Corporation; 800-345-1612
Nera A.S.; 800-345-1612
Netcom Systems; 800-345-1612
New Holland; 800-774-4117
Newport; 888-200-3169
New York Broker Deutschland;
    800-345-1612
Newport News Shipbuilding;
    800-649-1861
Nice Systems Ltd; 800-345-1612
Nippon Telephone & Telegraph;
    800-749-1687
NorAm Energy; 800-843-3445

Norsk Hydro A.S.; 800-749-1687
Norwest Bank; 800-774-4117
Novo-Nordisk AS; 800-749-1687
OGE Energy; 800-774-4117
Old National Bancorp;
   800-774-4117
OLS Asia; 800-345-1612
Oneok; 800-395-2662
Owens-Corning; 800-472-2210
OZEMail Ltd.; 800-345-1612
Pacific Dunlop; 800-749-1687
J.C. Penney; 800-565-2576
Peoples Energy; 800-774-4117
Petroleum Securities of Australia;
   800-345-1612
Pharmacia & Upjohn;
   800-774-4117
Philadelphia Suburban;
   800-774-4117
Piedmont Natural Gas;
   800-774-4117
Pinnacle West (AZ); 800-774-4117
Procter and Gamble; 800-764-7483
Providian Financial; 800-482-8690
P.T. Pasiflk Satelit Nusantara;
   800-345-1612
Portugal Telecom; 800-345-1612
Public Service Enterprise;
   800-242-0813
Public Service of New Mexico;
   800-545-4425
Public Service of North Carolina;
   800-774-4117
Questar; 800-729-6788
Randgold; 800-345-1612
Rank Group PLC; 800-749-1687
Reader's Digest; 800-242-4653
Redwood Trust; 800-774-4117
Regions Financial; 800-922-3468
Repsol S.A; 800-345-1612
Reuters Holdings PLC;
   800-749-1687

Ricoh Company Ltd.; 800-345-1612
Royal Bank of Scotland;
   800-345-1612
Royal Dutch Petroleum;
   800-749-1687
Santos Ltd.; 800-749-1687
Saville Systems; 800-345-1612
SCANA; 800-763-5891
SCOR; 800-345-1612
Sears Roebuck; 888-732-7788
Select Appointments;
   800-345-1612
Select Software Tools;
   800-345-1612
SEMCO Energy; 800-649-1856
Senetek PLC; 800-345-1612
SGS-Thomson Microeletronics;
   800-345-1612
Sierra Pacific Resources;
   800-662-7575
Small World; 800-345-1612
Smithkline Beecham;
   800-345-1612
Sonoma Valley Bank;
   888-200-3163
Sony; 800-749-1687
Southeastern Michigan Gas;
   800-649-1856
Southern Co.; 800-774-4117
Southern Union; 800-793-8938
STET-Societa Finanziara
   Telefonica PA; 800-749-1612
Stone Container; 800-346-9979
Sunstone Hotel Investors;
   800-774-4117
Supermercados Unimarc;
   800-345-1612
TAG Heuer; 800-749-1687
Taubman Centers; 800-774-4117
TDK Corporation; 800-749-1687
Telecom Argentina STET-France
   Telecom SA; 800-749-1687

Telecom Brasileiras; 800-345-1612

Telefonica del Peru SA;
    800-749-1687

Telefonos de Mexico SA;
    800-749-1687

Telex Chile (Empresas);
    800-345-1612

Tenneco; 800-446-2617

Texaco; 800-283-9785

Thorn PLC; 800-749-1687

Timken; 888-347-2453

TNP Enterprises; 800-774-4117

Tribune; 800-924-1490

Tubos de Acero de Mexico;
    800-749-1687

TV Azieca; 800-345-1612

Tyson Foods; 800-822-7096

Unilever NV; 800-749-1687

Unilever PLC; 800-749-1687

Unionamerica Holdings PLC;
    800-749-1687

Urban Shopping Centers;
    800-774-4117

US West Comm. Grp.; 800-537-0222

US West Media Group;
    800-537-0222

Utilicorp United; 800-647-2789

Valmet; 800-345-1612

Vimpel Communications;
    800-345-1612

Viad; 800-453-2235

Vodafone Group PLC;
    800-345-1612

Walgreen; 800-774-4117

Wal-Mart Stores; 800-438-6278

Warner Lambert; 888-767-7166

Waterford Wedgewood PLC;
    800-774-4117

Weingarten Realty; 888-887-2966

Western Resources; 800-774-4117

Westpac Banking; 800-749-1687

Wharf Holdings; 800-345-1612

Whitman; 800-660-4187

WICOR; 800-236-3453

Wisconsin Energy; 800-558-9663

WLR Foods; 540-896-7001

WMC Holdings; 800-345-1612

WPS Resources; 800-236-1551

Xeikon; 800-345-1612

Xenova Group; 800-345-1612

XXSYS Technologies;
    888-200-3166

York International; 800-774-4117

YPF Sociedad Anonima;
    800-345-1612

Zeneca Group PLC; 800-749-1687

This list of companies is always expanding, since more and more companies want to attract shareholders buying their stock directly. In addition to Carlson's newsletter mentioned above, you may be interested in the *Direct Investing* newsletter (The Moneypaper, Inc., 1010 Mamaroneck Ave., Mamaroneck, NY 10543; 800-388-9993; www.moneypaper.com), which also tracks developments in the field. You also can get a current list of no-load stocks at several Web sites, including: Direct Purchase Stock Plans (www.natcorp.com/ir/direct.html), NetStock Direct (www.netstockdirect.com) and No-Load Stocks (www.noloadbase.org).

To enroll in a company's dividend reinvestment plan, you must have the stock registered in your own name. Normally, if you buy stock through a brokerage firm, the broker holds it in its *street name*—that is, under a consolidated name for all of its accounts. A company offering a DRIP, however, must know the name of the participating shareholder so it can set up a reinvestment account. Therefore, if you have your stock with a broker, you must reregister it with the company, which the company will gladly take care of for you. After you're enrolled in the plan, you will receive quarterly statements from the company informing you how many shares your dividends purchased and how many total shares you now own.

Shareholder Freebies

In addition to dividends and DRIPs, many companies offer shareholders a variety of free and discounted products and services, which can make buying a company's stock even more rewarding. Companies do this to engender good will among their shareholders and to encourage them to hold onto their stock for the long term.

In some cases, you must attend the annual meeting, where the freebies are handed out to—or, in some cases, devoured by—shareholders. In other cases, you can receive discount coupons or tickets by writing to the company. To learn what a specific company offers, call its investor relations department. To learn about benefits, in general, consult the latest edition of Gene Walden's book, *The 100 Best Stocks To Own in America* (Dearborn Financial Publishing, 155 North Wacker Dr., Chicago, IL 60606; 312-836-4400; 800-322-8621). With his permission, the following are a few benefits companies now offer.

Abbott Laboratories. At the annual meeting, shareholders receive a sampling of Abbott's consumer products such as Selsun Blue, Murine, an ice pack and a bottle of vitamins.

Albertson's, Inc. At the annual meeting, shareholders receive some of Albertson's private label groceries, including canned vegetables, napkins, paper towels and other household products.

American Home Products Corp. Occasionally, the company sends out coupons for some of its foods and health care products along with the dividend check.

Anheuser-Busch Companies, Inc. New shareholders of record are sent a letter of welcome, a fact book on the company and a pamphlet on its dividend reinvestment plan. The company makes a point of moving its annual meetings around the country. Those who attend get a chance to sample all the company's brews. Shareholders are also entitled to a discount on admission to the company's amusement parks.

Berkshire Hathaway. Shareholders who attend the annual meeting receive discounts on company products like Dexter shoes and services like GEICO insurance.

Bristol-Myers Squibb. The company sends all new shareholders a welcome packet of its consumer products, including, for example, small bottles of Excedrin, Bufferin, Nuprin, Clairol hair care products and Ban deodorant.

Campbell Soup Company. The company hands out a bag of freebies at the annual meeting, including coupons, soup, cookies, chicken nuggets, Vlasic pickles and some new product samples.

Chalone Wine Group. Investors owning at least 100 shares in this winery get private tours of the partner winery in France, Chateau Lafite-Rothschild, as well as discounts on the company's wine. The company also subsidizes the cost of lavish dinners at the annual meeting. Some of Chalone's rare wines are only for sale to shareholders.

Circus Circus Enterprises, Inc. At the annual meeting, the company traditionally passes out small gifts to shareholders, such as a special coin set or free tokens for the slot machines.

ConAgra, Inc. At the annual meeting, the company passes out a gift pack of some of its foods to shareholders, and it sometimes sends out discount offers along with its quarterly earnings reports.

Deluxe Corp. Deluxe offers no dividend reinvestment plan, but it does offer one perk. At the annual meeting, shareholders are invited to a dinner—on the company—after the meeting. Meetings rotate around six locations, St. Paul, Chicago, Kansas City, Houston, Los Angeles and New Jersey, where the company has a large concentration of shareholders.

The Walt Disney Company. Shareholders qualify for a discount on the Magic Kingdom Club Gold Card. Gold Card membership provides a wide range of benefits, including savings on admission at the theme parks and select resort hotel accommodations, and discounts on travel arrangements with Delta Air, National Car Rental and Premier Cruise Lines. Gold Card members also receive a personalized embossed membership card, an informative newsletter, a two-year subscription to *Disney News* magazine, a Disney vacation planning video, and a toll-free number for the Magic Kingdom Club Travel Centers.

General Mills, Inc. General Mills occasionally sends out coupons for some of its products along with its quarterly reports. It also offers holiday gift boxes in December at very attractive prices. In one year, the boxes included nearly $50 worth of goods and coupons.

H. J. Heinz Company. At the annual meeting, shareholders receive a gift package of some of the company's newer products. The company puts out one of corporate America's best quarterly reports. Generally about 30 pages, the reports are packed with new product information and company developments. They also occasionally carry special offers or product discounts for Heinz shareholders.

Hershey Foods Corp. The company makes Christmas shopping a lot easier for shareholders with chocolate-loving friends. Hershey's Chocolate World Visitors Center mails its Christmas gift catalog to any shareholder requesting it and maintains a mailing list for annual receipt of the catalog. Shareholders may purchase special gift packages from the catalog and have them wrapped and mailed directly to their friends. At the annual meeting, shareholders are treated to a free packet of Hershey's candies and pasta.

International Business Machines. The computer maker occasionally sends out offers to shareholders along with dividend checks for substantial discounts on its computers and software products.

Kellogg Company. All new shareholders of record receive a welcome kit with brochures and reports on the company along with a pair of coupons for free grocery products. At the annual meeting in Battle Creek, shareholders also receive product samples and discount coupons. The company sometimes hands out special gifts such as decorative Kellogg's plates.

The Limited, Inc. The company sent out a coupon with its most recent annual report for 15 percent off merchandise at any of its stores.

Loctite Corp. At the annual meeting, the company hands out tubes of Super Glue.

McCormick & Company. Shareholders leave the spice and food company's annual meetings with a goody bag full of McCormick products such as jellies, cheeses and garlic sauce.

McDonald's Corp. A wealth of literature on McDonald's and its locations and product ingredients is available to shareholders (or anyone else requesting it). The company also provides an investor hot-line (not toll-free) that gives company news.

Newell Corp. At the annual meeting, the company often hands out a special gift. At a recent meeting, shareholders received a glass vase from the Anchor Hocking glassware division.

Nike, Inc. Each year at the annual meeting, the company passes out some promotional items. Don't expect to walk away in a pair of Air Jordans, but at a recent meeting, shareholders took home a cap like the one worn by tennis star Andre Agassi, a sports towel and a Nike pen.

Quaker Oats Company. Coupons for a percentage off some of Quaker's new products are often sent to shareholders along with their quarterly reports. The company puts out one of corporate America's best quarterly and annual reports. At the annual meeting, shareholders are sometimes given sample packets of some of Quaker's newer products.

Rubbermaid Inc. At the annual meeting, shareholders usually receive a free Rubbermaid product such as a file case, food tray or food storage container. Shareholders may also shop in the company store on annual meeting day and may take advantage of discounts on dozens of Rubbermaid products.

Sara Lee Corp. Each year at the annual meeting, Sara Lee shareholders receive a gift box of Sara Lee products, including such items as coupons, bath soaps and other company products.

Schering-Plough Corp. Schering-Plough gives a sample packet of products to shareholders at its annual meetings. The packets include such products as Coppertone sun tan lotion, Afrin nasal spray, Gyne-Lotrimin and other over-the-counter remedies.

Stanhome, Inc. At the annual meeting, the company hands out a gift pack of product samples, such as a collectible item, Stanley cologne and other personal care products.

Starbucks Coffee. In its annual report, Starbucks provides a coupon for a coffee or latte at one of its outlets.

UST, Inc. At the annual meeting, the company hands out samples of its products, such as pipe cleaners, a pipe, smokeless tobacco, a small bottle of wine and a video from its new Cabin Fever Entertainment subsidiary.

Walgreen Company. At the annual meeting, shareholders usually receive one or two Walgreen products.

Wal-Mart Stores, Inc. At the annual meeting, shareholders are often given Wal-Mart memorabilia such as hats, buttons and T-shirts.

William Wrigley Jr. Company. Wrigley sends out to shareholders a gift package each Christmas that includes several packs of Wrigley's gum.

Source: Adapted with permission from *The 100 Best Stocks To Own in America,* 5th edition, by Gene Walden (Chicago: Dearborn Financial Publishing, Inc., 1998).

Using Technical Analysis To Choose Stocks

Instead of concentrating on a company's earnings, book value or products, some analysts look only at its stock's trading action to see whether the stock is worth buying or selling. This way of choosing stocks is called *technical analysis,* in contrast to *fundamental analysis,* which we have focused on so far.

For the novice, technical analysis can be mysterious and intimidating. Instead of understanding a company's products, you must interpret charts and graphs. However, even if you want to concentrate mostly on fundamentals, it is still a good idea to glance at the charts and graphs to see what the market action can tell you about the stock. The two key indicators that technical analysts use to determine whether a stock is headed up or down are *price action* and *volume of trading.*

Price action. Technicians look at a stock's price history and draw many conclusions from it. For example, a stock's low point is often called its *support level,* meaning that it is likely to find support from stock buyers when it hits that price. Conversely, a stock's high is called its *resistance level,* meaning that in order to lock in their profits, shareholders will tend to sell when the stock reaches that price. In general, technicians recommend buying when a stock is near its support level and selling as it approaches resistance.

Volume of trading. The number of shares that a stock trades over a particular period of time gives technicians many clues about its future direction. High volume in a stock that is rising in price is considered bullish, and low volume in a stock that is falling in price is considered bearish.

People can dedicate their lives to analyzing each latest wrinkle in a stock's trading action. If you want to learn more about technical analysis, consult the following classics in the field: Martin Pring's *Technical Analysis Explained: The Successful Investor's Guide to Spotting Investment Trends and Turning Points* (McGraw-Hill, Order Dept., 860 Taylor Station Rd., Blacklick, OH 43004; 800-722-4726; www.mcgraw-hill.com) and *Technical Analysis of Stock Trends,* by

Robert E. Edwards and John Magee (Prentice Hall Professional Publishing, 200 Old Tappan Rd., Old Tappan, NJ 07675; 800-223-1360; www.prenhall.com).

Choosing Stocks with an Investment Club

If you don't want to choose stocks on your own, you have another alternative—starting an investment club or joining one that is already up and running. An investment club is a group of people, usually between 5 and 30, who pool their money and decide on stocks to buy or sell. Club members usually start the club by contributing $100 each, then make a monthly deposit of $25 or $50.

Investing through such a club has several advantages.

- You will hear about stocks you probably never would have heard about on your own. Because members of the club will come from all walks of life, they often will have insights into companies that are doing well in industries in which they work.

- You can gain valuable experience from other members that you can apply to your own portfolio.

- Through the club, you can be part of a more diversified portfolio than you could probably afford on your own.

- The club will probably pay lower commissions than you would because it is buying more shares in each transaction.

- You may make social or business contacts that are important beyond the investment club's scope.

You might think that putting a group of amateur investors together would be a recipe for disaster. In fact, just the opposite is true. The National Association of Investors Corporation (NAIC), the trade group for investment clubs, says that more than half of all clubs beat the Standard & Poor's 500 Index every year—a feat many investment pros fail to achieve. There seems to be some magic in the consensus-style stock selection process that makes many investment clubs successful. Most clubs would not agree to invest in the ideas of an eccentric member who recommends risky stocks.

Most successful investment clubs have a strategy that guides their stock selection. Some clubs might concentrate on local stocks, while others look for growth stocks or undervalued companies. Whatever the style, it provides a framework for club members to research companies that might be of interest to the club.

If you want to set up a club, hook up with a good broker who likes working with clubs. Although the broker can provide investment ideas and analysts' reports, do not let him or her dominate the club. Remember, the idea of the club is not only to make money; it is also to learn about choosing stocks by doing the research yourself. A good broker should offer the club attractive discounts on commissions not only because he or she wants to keep the club's business but also because the broker wants to capture club members as individual clients.

Another way to keep commission costs under control is to enroll in the NAIC's Low-Cost Investment Plan. This allows clubs to buy as little as one share of many blue chip companies at a minimal fee. It also allows dividends to be reinvested automatically at no charge.

The easiest way to get your club started is to send away for the step-by-step manual published by NAIC (711 W. 13 Mile Rd., Madison Heights, MI 48071; 810-583-6242; www.better-investing.org). The guide will tell you how to get a federal tax identification number, open a brokerage account and set up a record-keeping system so the club's treasurer can track deposits and withdrawals.

Club members are required to report realized gains or losses, as well as dividend income, from the club's portfolio on their personal tax returns every year. On the other hand, your portion of the club's expenses, such as subscriptions to newsletters or accounting fees, will earn you deductions if you qualify.

Most people enjoy their investment club experiences not only as a way to learn about and profit from investing but also as a way to have fun.

Foreign Stocks

When buying stocks, you do not have to limit yourself to U.S. shares. In fact, the U.S. market currently accounts for only about a third of the world's total stock market value. Europe and Asia account for the other thirds. So if you restrict yourself to domestic stocks, you exclude two-thirds of the world's growth potential.

You don't have to take an overseas trip to buy foreign stocks. In fact, hundreds of foreign-based-corporation stocks are available on the NYSE and AMEX, as well as on the Nasdaq NMS. When they trade here, foreign stocks are sold in the form of American depositary receipts (ADRs). Technically, an ADR is a receipt for shares of the foreign-based corporation and is held in the vault of a U.S. bank. The ADR entitles the bearer to all dividends and capital gains that shareholders in the home country receive. As a convenience, all dividends are converted from the home country currency into dollars before they are paid. Also, ADR holders receive quarterly and annual reports in English that adhere to U.S. accounting rules. For all practical purposes, ADRs trade just like U.S. stocks.

Like any investment in foreign securities, ADRs can be affected by swings in the value of the U.S. dollar against other currencies. In general, a declining dollar boosts the price of an ADR because the company does most of its business in foreign currencies that are appreciating. Conversely, a rising dollar tends to depress the price of an ADR.

Because today's world is so interdependent, you will surely recognize many ADR names because they have significant presence in U.S. consumer markets. There are hundreds of ADRs traded in the United States today, representing every

major industrialized country. Following are just a few names of some prominent
ADRs, along with their product lines and home countries.

Akzo: *pharmaceuticals, Netherlands*
Allied Irish Banks: *banking, Ireland*
Anglo American Gold Investment: *gold mining, South Africa*
Laura Ashley: *furnishings, United Kingdom*
Banco Central: *banking, Spain*
Bank Leumi: *banking, Israel*
Barclays Bank: *banking, United Kingdom*
Bayer: *chemicals and drugs, Germany*
Benetton Group: *clothing, Italy*
British Airways: *airline, United Kingdom*
British Gas: *gas, United Kingdom*
British Petroleum: *oil, United Kingdom*
British Telecommunications: *phone company, United Kingdom*
Cable and Wireless: *telecommunications, United Kingdom*
Cadbury Schweppes: *food, United Kingdom*
Canon: *copiers and cameras, Japan*
China Light & Power: *electricity, Hong Kong*
Cifra: *retailing, Mexico*
Club Mediteraneé: *vacation resorts, France*
DeBeers Consolidated Mines: *diamonds, South Africa*
Deutsche Bank: *banking, Germany*
Elf Aquitaine: *oil, France*
Fiat: *auto manufacturing, Italy*
Fuji Photo Film: *film manufacturing, Japan*
Glaxo Holdings: *drugs, United Kingdom*
Hanson: *conglomerate, United Kingdom*
Heineken: *beer, Netherlands*
Hitachi: *consumer electronics, Japan*
Honda Motor: *car and motorcycle maker, Japan*
Hong Kong Telecommunications: *phone company, Hong Kong*
Imperial Chemical Industries: *chemicals, United Kingdom*
L'Oréal: *cosmetics, France*
L.M. Ericsson: *telecommunications equipment, Sweden*
LVMH Moët Hennessy Louis Vuitton: *champagne and handbags, France*
Montedison: *chemicals, Italy*
NEC: *consumer electronics, Japan*
News Corporation: *media conglomerate, Australia*
Nikon: *photographic equipment, Japan*
N.V. Phillips*: *consumer electronics, Netherlands*

Pharmacia: *drugs, Sweden*
Reuters Holdings: *media conglomerate, United Kingdom*
Rolls Royce: *aircraft engines, United Kingdom*
Royal Dutch Petroleum*: *oil, Netherlands*
Sony Corporation: *consumer electronics, Japan*
Teléfonos de Mexico: *phone company, Mexico*
Unilever*: *consumer products, Netherlands*
Waterford Glass Group: *crystal and glassware, Ireland*
Wellcome: *drugs, United Kingdom*

*These are New York shares, which are foreign common shares traded on the NYSE.

For further information on ADRs, consult *The McGraw-Hill Handbook of American Depositary Receipts,* by Richard J. Coyle (McGraw-Hill, Order Dept., 860 Taylor Station Rd., Blacklick, OH 43004; 800-722-4726; www.mcgraw-hill.com). The book describes what ADRs are and how they work and offers a complete list of issues, with analyses of each company.

These three best newsletters follow ADRs: *The Mercer ADR Review* and *The Global Portfolio* (Mercer Inc., 379 W. Broadway, Suite 400, New York, NY 10012; 212-334-6212) and *Global Investing* (Vivian Lewis, 1040 1st Ave., Suite 305, New York, NY 10022; 212-758-9480; 800-388-4237; www.adrs@compuserve.com).

Making Sense of Stock Tables

To track the value of stocks in your portfolio or look up the prices of and activity in stocks you are thinking of buying, you must be able to decipher stock tables—the way most people get this information. They may look intimidating at first, but with a little explanation, they can reveal significant data that will help you choose stocks.

NEWSPAPER STOCK TABLES

Though there are slight variations between the tables displayed in your local newspaper and the ones in national publications like *Barron's, Investor's Business Daily* or *The Wall Street Journal,* the basic elements of the stock tables remain the same. These tables describe the consolidated trading activity in individual stocks, combining data from the NYSE, regional exchanges and the Nasdaq NMS. Most newspapers provide more detail for NYSE and AMEX listings than for Nasdaq listings. Following is a typical line in the tables.

52-Week High[1]	Low[2]	Stock[3]	Sym[4]	Div[5]	Yld[6]	PE Ratio[7]	Vol 100s[8]	High[9]	Low[10]	Close[11]	Net Chng[12]
35	12	Exxon	XON	1.00	2.8	17	3000	34¾	33	34¾	+½

The following explanations correspond to the number above each column.

1. *High* means the highest price that the stock has reached over the last 52 weeks, up to but not including, yesterday's trading. The difference between the high price and the low price (column 2) of the last year indicates whether the stock is stable or volatile. The wider the difference, the more volatile the stock's price.

2. *Low* means the lowest price that the stock has reached over the last 52 weeks, up to but not including yesterday's trading. By comparing the numbers in columns 1 and 2 to yesterday's closing price (column 11), you can determine whether the stock is currently trading near its high or low price for the last 12 months.

3. This column displays the common stock's name. Unless the company has a short name, it is abbreviated. The stocks are listed alphabetically by their full names, so the letters you see might look out of order.

    Several letters occasionally follow a stock's name. Some are upper case and some, lower case. Following are the letters you will see in the tables and an explanation of what they mean.

    A or **B**—There are different classes of stock, such as class A or class B, with different voting rights.

    dd—The company lost money in the most recent four quarters.

    f—The stock has changed exchanges within the last month.

    h—The company has a temporary exception to Nasdaq qualifications.

    n—The stock was a new issue during the last year.

    pf—It is a preferred stock issue.

    pp—The holder of the stock owes installments of the purchase price.

    pr—It is preference stock, which has a higher claim on dividends than preferred stock, in case of the liquidation of the company.

    rt—It is a right to buy a security at a specified price.

    s—The stock has split within the last year by at least 20 percent. (For example, a 2-for-1 stock split means that for every share you used to have, you now have two shares, and the price of the shares splits in half.)

    un—The stock is a unit, including more than one security.

    v—Trading has been suspended in the primary market.

    vj—The company is in bankruptcy or receivership or is being reorganized under bankruptcy law.

    wd—Trades will be settled when the stock is distributed.

wi—Trades will be settled when the stock is issued.

wt—The issue is a warrant, giving you the right to buy more stock.

ww—The stock trades with a warrant attached.

x—The stock is trading ex-dividend, which indicates that yesterday was the first day it traded without the right to receive the latest quarterly dividend. The price change is adjusted to reflect this fact.

xw—The stock trades without a warrant attached.

4. The *stock symbol* is the trading symbol used to identify the stock by computerized quotations systems.

5. The *dividend* is the dollar amount of the dividend per share paid in cash over the last four quarters. In the example, the dividend is $1. The dividend rate may have risen or fallen since the last quarterly payment, so you should not assume you will receive this amount over the next four quarters. Several letters might follow the dividend rate.

a—extra dividend

b—the annual rate plus another dividend paid in stock, not cash

c—a liquidating dividend, which implies that a company is selling off its pieces and distributing the proceeds to shareholders as dividends

e—an irregular dividend, which means that the annual dividend rate is based on the latest dividend figure

f—the dividend at an annual rate but increased for the latest quarter

g—a dividend paid in Canadian dollars

i—a dividend declared after a stock dividend or split

j—a dividend that was paid this year, but recently dividend payments were suspended

k—a dividend that was paid this year, which includes dividends that were owed from the past but still not paid (known as dividends in arrears)

m—the dividend on an annual rate but reduced starting with the latest quarter

p—initial dividend, or the first time this company has paid a dividend

r—declared or paid in the preceding 12 months, plus a dividend paid in stock

t—paid in stock in the preceding 12 months. This figure is the estimated cash value of the stock dividend on the ex-dividend date.

y—ex-dividend and volume that are noted in full, not in hundreds

6. The *yield* is how much dividend you receive as a percentage of the stock price, rounded off to the nearest tenth of a point. In the example, it is 2.8 percent, which is the $1 dividend (column 5) divided by the $34¾ stock price. The higher the dividend yield, the less volatile the stock usually is, and the more appropriate it is for income-oriented investors.

7. *PE ratio* means price-earnings ratio, which is the stock's price divided by the company's earnings for the last four quarters, rounded to the nearest whole number. In the example, the PE ratio of 17 shows investors expect Exxon Corporation to produce solid earnings gains over the next year. The higher the PE ratio, the more profit growth investors expect from the company. A PE ratio of 20 or more indicates a growth company. A PE ratio of less than 10 indicates the company's stock is not in great demand by investors. In two cases, a letter (or letters) follows the PE ratio. A **cc** means the PE ratio is 100 or more and therefore not meaningful. A **q** means that the stock is actually a closed-end fund, which has no PE ratio.

8. *Vol 100s* shows the stock's trading volume in yesterday's market in hundreds of shares. In the example, 3,000 means that 300,000 shares were traded. By watching the volume pattern over several days, you can tell whether the volume of trading is low or high. A **z** following the volume means that it is the total number of shares traded. An underlined **z** means that the volume on this day was particularly heavy, which might indicate that there were important corporate developments.

9. A stock's *high* is the highest price the shares traded during yesterday's session. In the example, that was $34¾ per share. A **u** following the high means that this price is a 52-week high as well.

10. A stock's *low* is the lowest price the shares traded during yesterday's session. In the example, that was $33 per share. A **d** following the low means that this price is a 52-week low as well.

11. The *close* (sometimes labeled *last*) is the price of the shares when trading stopped. In the example, Exxon Corporation stock closed yesterday at $34¾ per share, which was also its highest price of the day. The high, low and closing prices are all expressed in minimums of eighths of a point, or 12.5 cents. Lower-priced stocks also have their prices listed in sixteenths (6.25 cents) and even thirty-seconds (3.125 cents) of a point. The other fractions you will see stand for the following amounts of money: ¼ is 25 cents, ⅜ is 37.5 cents, ½ is 50 cents, ⅝ is 62.5 cents, ¾ is 75 cents and ⅞ is 87.5 cents.

12. The *net change* is the amount the price of the shares moved up or down compared to the previous day's close. In the example, the shares rose

onehalf of a point, or 50 cents per share. A "**+**" following the change means that the shares rose, and a "**–**" means the shares fell in price. Net changes are expressed in minimums of eighths of a point.

DIVIDEND AND EARNINGS REPORT TABLES

The other two important tables you will see in many newspapers report both action on dividends and quarterly earnings.

Dividend report tables. These tell you whether a corporation's board of directors declared a higher, a lower or the same dividend as the previous quarter or omitted the payout altogether.

Stock[1]	Period[2]	Amount[3]	Stock of Record[4]	Date Payable[5]
Exxon Corp.	Q	.25	3–10	3–30

The following explanations correspond to the number above each column.

1. The first column states the name of the company declaring the dividend.

2. *Period* refers to the time in which the dividend will be paid, normally **Q**, for quarterly. **A** means annually. **M** means monthly. **S** means semiannually.

3. *Amount* is the per-share amount of the dividend. In the example, a $.25 quarterly dividend means an annual rate of $1. An **h** following the figure means that the amount is paid from earned income. A **k** signifies that it is paid from realized capital gains, usually taken by a closed-end mutual fund. An **n** means that it is an initial distribution or the first one ever paid by this stock. A **t** signals that it is the approximate dollar amount of the dividend from a foreign company traded in the United States as an ADR.

4. The fourth column indicates that the dividend will be paid to shareholders of record on the date noted—in the example, March 10. The day after the record date, the stock goes ex-dividend, meaning that buyers will no longer receive the dividend. So if you buy the stock on March 11, in the example, you will not receive the $.25 dividend. However, the stock normally drops in price by the amount of the dividend when it enters the ex-dividend period.

5. The *date payable* is the date the dividend is actually paid.

Earnings report tables. Companies report their earnings on a quarterly basis, and newspapers usually run columns of reports that look like the following.

[1] **Exxon Corporation (N)**		
[2] *Quar Dec. 31:*	*This Year*	*Last Year*
[3] Revenues	$20,000,000	$18,000,000
[4] Net income	1,000,000	800,000
[5] Share earns	.10	.08
[6] Avg. shares outstanding	10,000,000	9,000,000

The following explanations correspond to the number beside each line.

1. The first line notes the company that is reporting earnings. A letter will follow in parentheses.

   A—American Stock Exchange

   B—Boston Stock Exchange

   F—foreign stock exchange

   M—Midwest Stock Exchange

   Mo—Montreal Stock Exchange

   N—New York Stock Exchange

   O—over-the-counter market

   P—Philadelphia Stock Exchange

   Pa—Pacific Stock Exchange

   T—Toronto Stock Exchange

   In the example, Exxon Corporation trades on the NYSE.

2. The *quarter* that is being reported ends on the date noted in line 2. In the example, the quarter ends on December 31.

3. *Revenues* is the gross sales figure for the company, comparing the latest quarter with the same quarter a year ago. In the example, sales rose from $18 million to $20 million.

4. The fourth line reports *net income,* the amount of profit earned in dollars during the quarter. This also is compared to the same quarter a year ago.

5. *Share earns* indicates how much of the profit noted in the previous line is attributable to each common share outstanding. This earnings-per-share number is used to compute the PE ratio. It also is compared to the same quarter a year ago.

6. Line 6 shows the number of common shares that were outstanding, on average, during the quarter. An increase in the number of shares means

that the same amount of earnings would create a lower earnings-per-share figure. Fewer shares outstanding means that the same earnings would create a high earnings-per-share result.

Often, earnings report tables will use additional lines to account for special circumstances. Some of the most common abbreviations you will see include the following.

Acctg adj—a significant accounting adjustment during the quarter

Extrd chg—an extraordinary charge during the quarter, such as a losing business was sold or a division's assets were written down to a lower value

Extrd cred—an extraordinary credit during the quarter, such as a business's value was upgraded or a large profit was made by selling securities

Inco cnt op—income from continuing operations, or businesses that continue as part of the company

Inco dis op—income from discontinued operations, which means the company received income during the quarter from a business that has since been sold or liquidated

Usually, earnings reports are released the trading day before you see them in the newspaper, so the stock market has already had time to react positively or negatively. Earnings report tables are only summaries of the most important aspects of the reports. As a shareholder, you will receive a more detailed quarterly earnings report in the mail a few weeks after it is released.

Using Your Computer To Invest in Stocks

Perhaps in no other area of personal finance is the computer better suited to help you make money than in picking and following a stock portfolio. The computer's ability to store and analyze data, get you online to find the latest news and execute trades with lightning speed are perfectly suited to investing in individual stocks.

The first step in buying stocks, of course, is analyzing what individual securities are worth buying at current prices. By using a combination of analysis software and Web sites, you can get the data you need and the tools to crunch numbers to produce the result you want. Some software does fundamental analysis, screening stocks for price-earnings ratios, earnings growth rates, yields, book values and the like. Other programs specialize in technical analysis, trying to predict future price movements based on trading patterns. There are online versions of both fundmental and technical analysis programs in the Web sites listed in the Resources section of this chapter.

Web sites also allow you to keep up with news developments as they affect individual stocks. You can either search out stocks that have announced major developments on a particular day, or look up a company's history and see all the news stories about that company for the past few months. In either case, it is a good idea for you to be familiar with a company's financial, management and operational history before you invest in it. The online world is loaded with financial advisers recommending individual stock trades. Before you take any of their counsel, you should know what you are getting into.

Once you have bought several stocks, software and Web sites will allow you to track your portfolio's value. You also can place price alerts so that the computer will signal you when a stock hits a certain price at which you want to buy or sell shares. You also can enter alerts to tell you when there is unusually heavy trading activity in a stock, which is often a signal that major news is about to break.

Of course, there are thousands of Web sites on the Internet offering help in picking individual stocks. In the following Resources section, I have chosen the best, easiest-to-use and most comprehensive sites to help you put the power of your computer to work for you picking winning stocks.

Resources

BOOKS

America's New Blue Chips: An Investment Guide to the Hottest Growth Stocks, by Gene Walden (Walden Books, Dept. 401, P.O. Box 7002, Lavergne, Tennessee 37086; 800-322-2000). Walden profiles 120 of the fastest-growing emerging growth stocks. This book includes five-year growth graphs on earnings revenue and stock price.

Beating the Street, by Peter Lynch (Simon & Schuster, 200 Old Tappan Rd., Old Tappan, NJ 07675; 800-223-2336; www.simon&schuster.com). Written by the legendary manager of the Fidelity Magellan Fund, who explains how he picks stocks. Details how he first heard about companies and where he found the information so critical to deciding whether to invest in them. Also offers advice on buying mutual funds and putting together an investment program.

Buying Stocks Without a Broker, by Charles Carlson (McGraw-Hill, Order Dept., 860 Taylor Station Rd., Blacklick, OH 43004; 800-722-4726; www.mcgraw-hill.com). Details how you can buy stock directly from companies and how you can sign up for DRIPs. Contains the most complete list of companies offering DRIPs.

The Dictionary of Finance and Investment Terms, by John Downes and Jordan E. Goodman (Barron's Educational Series, 250 Wireless Blvd., Hauppauge, NY 11788; 516-434-3311; 800-645-3476). The standard reference work of finance and investment, defining more than 5,000 terms in simple language.

Dividends Don't Lie, by Geraldine Weiss and Janet Lowe (Dearborn Financial Publishing, 155 N. Wacker Drive, Chicago, IL 60606; 312-836-4400; 800-322-8621; www.dearborn.com). Explains the value of buying stocks with high yields, both for income and because such stocks often rise in price over time.

Divining the Dow: 100 of the World's Most Widely Followed Stock Market Prediction Systems, by Richard J. Maturi (McGraw-Hill, Order Dept., 860 Taylor Station Rd., Blacklick, OH 43004; 800-722-4726; www.mcgraw-hill.com). Explains all of the major stock market prediction systems and how to use them to forecast stock price movements.

The Finance and Investment Handbook, by John Downes and Jordan E. Goodman (Barron's Educational Series, 250 Wireless Blvd., Hauppauge, NY 11788; 516-434-3311; 800-645-3476). The complete book about everything you need to know about finance and investing. Contains explanations of investment alternatives and how to read the financial pages of newspapers and annual reports, a dictionary of 5,000 terms and lists of stocks, mutual funds, futures and options, currencies and more.

Getting Started in Stocks, by Alvin Hall (John Wiley & Sons, 1 Wiley Dr., Somerset, NJ 08875-1272; 212-850-6000; 800-225-5945; www.wiley.com). A primer on the basics of stock investing.

How To Buy Stocks, by Louis Engel and Brendan Boyd (Bantam Books, 2451 S. Wolf Rd., Des Plaines, IL 60018; 212-354-6500, ext. 9479; 800-223-6834, ext. 9479; www.bantam.com). A readable book about the stock market that has become the classic in the field.

The Hulbert Guide to Financial Newsletters, by Mark Hulbert (Dearborn Financial Publishing, 155 N. Wacker Drive, Chicago, IL 60606; 312-836-4400; 800-322-8621; www.dearborn.com). Written by the person who tracks the performance of all major investment newsletter publishers. Describes the style and performance of the top 120 newsletters.

The Income Investor: Choosing Investments That Pay Cash Today and Tomorrow, by Donald R. Nichols (Dearborn Financial Publishing, 155 N. Wacker Drive, Chicago, IL 60606; 312-836-4400; 800-322-8621; www.dearborn.com). Explains the many types of stocks and bonds about which income-oriented investors need to know.

International Value Investing, by Charles H. Brandes and Glenn R. Carlson (McGraw-Hill, Order Dept., 860 Taylor Station Rd., Blacklick, OH 43004; 800-722-4726). A step-by-step guide to investing in stock markets outside the United States.

Investments: An Introduction to Analysis and Management, by Frederick Amling (Prentice Hall, 200 Old Tappan Rd., Old Tappan, NJ 07675; 800-223-2336; www.prenhall.com). Explains the fundamentals of investment analysis through case studies.

The New Contrarian Investment Strategy, by David Dreman (Random House, 201 E. 50th St., New York, NY 10022; 212-751-2600; 800-733-3000; www.randomhouse.

com). Written by a successful money manager, who explains the principles of buying stocks that no one likes and selling them when they become popular.

The New Money Masters, by John Train (HarperCollins, P.O. Box 588, Dunmore, PA 18512; 800-331-3761; www.harpercollins.com). Profiles some of the most successful money managers of all time—people you can emulate.

The 100 Best Stocks To Own in America, by Gene Walden (Dearborn Financial Publishing, 155 N. Wacker Drive, Chicago, IL 60606; 312-836-4400; 800-322-8621; www.dearborn.com). Profiles 100 top-quality growth companies and reveals shareholder perks each company offers.

One up on Wall Street, by Peter Lynch (Simon & Schuster, 200 Old Tappan Rd., Old Tappan, NJ 07675; 800-223-2336; www.simon&schuster.com). A compendium of sensible advice from the former manager of Fidelity's legendary Magellan Fund.

Plugging into Utilities: A Safe and Sound Way to Superior Returns in the Stock Market, by Donald I. Cassidy (McGraw-Hill, Order Dept., 860 Taylor Station Rd., Blacklick, OH 43004; 800-722-4726; www.mcgraw-hill.com). Explains how to evaluate stocks of electric, gas and water utilities to achieve high returns at a relatively low risk.

A Random Walk Down Wall Street, by Burton G. Malkiel (National Book Company, 800 Keystone Industrial Park, Scranton, PA 18512; 212-354-5500; 800-233-4830; www.wwnorton.com). This comprehensive guide to investing in the stock market is an investment classic; it covers stock analysis and investment strategies.

Security Analysis: Principles and Techniques, by Benjamin Graham and David Dodd (McGraw-Hill, Order Dept., 860 Taylor Station Rd., Blacklick, OH 43004; 800-722-4726). Written by the fathers of fundamental stock analysis, this book is their seminal work on the subject. Might be too dense for first-time investors.

Small Stocks Big Profits: Gerald Perritt on Investing in Small Companies, by Gerald Perritt (Dearborn Financial Publishing, 155 N. Wacker Drive, Chicago, IL 60606; 312-836-4400; 800-322-8621; www.dearborn.com). Explains the risks and rewards of investing in small-company stocks.

Stock Picking: The 11 Best Tactics for Beating the Market, by Richard Maturi (McGraw-Hill, Order Dept., 860 Taylor Station Rd., Blacklick, OH 43004; 800-722-4726; www.mcgraw-hill.com). Simple, time-tested techniques for choosing winning stocks in any market environment.

Understanding Wall Street, by Jeffrey Little and Lucian Rhodes (Tab Books/ McGraw-Hill, Order Dept., 860 Taylor Station Rd., Blacklick, OH 43004; 800-722-4726). An in-depth look at how to evaluate stocks and bonds and how the brokerage industry works.

Winning on Wall Street, by Martin Zweig (Warner Books, 1271 Avenue of the Americas, New York, NY 10020; 212-522-7200; 800-343-9204; www.warnerbooks. com). Written by a famous money manager and regular panelist on the *Wall Street Week* TV show, who explains how to choose winning stocks according to his theories on the economy and investor psychology.

MAGAZINES

Weekly and monthly investment magazines usually give far more detail on individual stocks than do newspapers. Articles are also researched in more depth, giving you a better basis to judge whether you are interested in a particular company. The best magazines are as follows.

Business Week (McGraw-Hill, 1221 Avenue of the Americas, 39th Floor, New York, NY 10020; 212-512-2511; www.businessweek.com). Although it concentrates more on the economy and business strategy, *Business Week* also has columns about Wall Street and personal investing.

Equities (160 Madison Ave., 3rd Floor, New York, NY 10016; 212-213-1300; 800-237-8400, ext. 21, for credit card orders and subscriptions only; members.aol. com/equitymag/index). Formerly known as *OTC Review,* focuses on the outlook for individual emerging growth stocks.

Forbes (60 Fifth Ave., New York, NY 10011; 212-620-2200; 800-888-9896; www.forbes.com). Known for its acerbic and witty style. Uncovers good stocks and exposes stocks it considers overpriced.

Fortune (1271 Avenue of the Americas, New York, NY 10020; 212-522-1212; 800-541-1000; www.fortune.com). A business magazine with extensive coverage of Wall Street and stock selection. Fortune also publishes an annual *Investor's Guide* with many stock ideas.

Financial World (1328 Broadway, 3rd Floor, New York, NY 10001; 212-594-5030; 800-829-5916; www.financialworld.com). Specializes in corporate strategies, which gives readers insight into which stocks look attractive.

Money (Time and Life Building, Rockefeller Center, New York, NY 10020; 212-522-1212; 800-541-1000; www.pathfinder.com/money). A popular magazine that publishes several articles each month on individual stocks, as well as the *Wall Street Newsletter,* which highlights a stock of the month. Also features the "*Money* Magazine Small Investor Index" (described in more detail in the appendix of this book), which will help you track your investment performance.

NEWSLETTERS

Hundreds of newsletters give stock advice. These letters usually reflect the personality and interests of the letter writer. Some use technical analysis and are therefore loaded with graphs and charts. Others rely on fundamental analysis and explain the prospects for a company's business. Still others focus on takeovers, foreign stocks, IPOs or emerging growth stocks. Some newsletters provide solid advice, but many do not. To some extent, the success of a letter's recommendations depends on how the kinds of stocks it favors are doing at the moment.

The referee for this chaotic field is Mark Hulbert, who publishes the *Hulbert Financial Digest,* which ranks the monthly performance of recommendations in the most influential newsletters. To find out which letter has had a good record recently, you can subscribe to the *Digest* at 316 Commerce St., Alexandria, VA 22314; 703-683-5905; www.hulbertdigest.com. Newsletter performance is also tracked by *Timer Digest* (P.O. Box 1688, Greenwich, CT 06836; 203-629-3503; 800-356-2527).

For more on what kind of stock information each letter contains, you can call or write it at the phone number or address given below. In many cases, the newsletter will send you a free sample so you can see what the letter is like. You can also get a trial subscription to most of these newsletters through Select Information Exchange (244 W. 54th St., New York, NY 10019; 212-247-7123; www.selectex.com). The following list of newsletters covers the ones tracked by Hulbert, which are the most widely followed publications.

The Addison Report (P.O. Box 402, Franklin, MA 02038; 508-528-8678)

The Aden Forecast (P.O. Box 66710, St. Louis, MO 63166; 888-ADE-NMKT)

Adrian Day's Investment Analyst (Agora, Inc., 824 East Baltimore St., Baltimore, MD 21202; 800-433-1528)

Analyst Watch (155 N. Wacker Dr., Chicago, IL 60606; 800-399-6659)

Richard E. Band's Profitable Investing (Phillips Publishing, 7811 Montrose Rd., Potomac, MD 20854; 301-424-3700; 800-777-5005; www.phillips.com)

Beating the Dow (P.O. Box 2069, Riverdale, NJ 07675; 800-477-3400)

Bert Dohmen's Wellington Letter (Suite 3801, 66 Queen St., Honolulu, HI 96813; 808-545-2243)

Better Investing (NAIC, 711 W. 13 Mile Rd., Madison Heights, MI 48071; 810-583-6242; www.better-investing.org)

BI Research (P.O. Box 133, Redding, CT 06875; 203-270-9244)

The Big Picture (Suite 301, 1750 Old Meadow Rd., McLean, VA 22102; 800-832-2330; www.investchoice.com)

Blue Chip Investor (575 Antone Blvd., Suite 510, Costa Mesa, CA 92626; 714-641-3579)

Bob Brinker's Marketimer (P.O. Box 229, Irvington, NY 10533; 914-591-2655)

The Bowser Report (P.O. Box 6278, Newport News, VA 23606; 757-877-5979)

The Buyback Letter (P.O. Box 84900, Phoenix, AZ 85071; 800-528-0559)

The Cabot Market Letter (176 North St. or P.O. Box 3067, Salem, MA 01970; 508-745-5532; 800-777-2658; www.cabotm.com)

California Technology Stock Letter (P.O. Box 308, Half Moon Bay, CA 94019; 415-726-8495; www.ctsl.com)

The Chartist (P.O. Box 758, Seal Beach, CA 90740; 310-596-2385)

The Clean Yield (P.O. Box 117, Garvin Hill Rd., Greensboro, VT 05841; 802-533-7178)

The Contrarian's View (132 Moreland St., Worcester, MA 01609; 508-757-2881)

Crawford Perspectives (1382 3rd Ave., Suite 403, New York, NY 10021-0403; 212-744-6973; www.astromoney.com)

Dennis Slothower's On The Money (Suite 9-D, 2230 N. University Parkway, Provo, UT 84604; 801-373-3381)

John Dessauer's Investor's World: Your Passport to Profits (Phillips Publishing, 7811 Montrose Rd., Potomac, MD 20854; 800-804-0942; www.phillips.com)

The Dines Letter (P.O. Box 22, Belvedere, CA 94920; 800-84-LUCKY)

Donoghue's Wealthletter (Money Market Square East, P.O. Box 309, Milford, MA 01757; 800-982-2455)

Dow Theory Forecasts (7412 Calumet Ave., Hammond, IN 46324; 219-931-6480; www.dowtheory.com)

Dow Theory Letters (P.O. Box 1759, La Jolla, CA 92038; 619-454-0481)

Elliott Wave Theorist (P.O. Box 1618, Gainesville, GA 30503; 770-536-0309; www.elliottwave.com)

Emerging and Special Situations (Standard & Poor's Corporation, 25 Broadway, New York, NY 10004; 212-208-8000; 800-852-1641; www.rating.com)

Equities Special Situations (160 Madison Ave., 3rd Floor, New York, NY 10016; 212-213-1300; 800-237-8400; members.aol.com/equitymag/index.html)

Financial World (P.O. Box 10750, Des Moines, IA 50340; 800-666-6639)

Ford Investment Review (11722 Sorrento Valley Rd., Suite 1, San Diego, CA 92121; 800-842-0207; www.fordinv.com)

Foreign Markets Advisory (P.O. Box 75, Fairfax Station, VA 22039; 703-425-5961)

F.X.C. Investors Corporation (62-19 Cooper Ave., Queens, NY 11385; 800-FXC-0992; www.fxcinv.com)

Garzarelli Outlook (7811 Montrose Rd., Potomac, MD 20854; 800-804-0939)

Ken Gerbino's Smart Investing (Phillips Publishing, 7811 Montrose Rd., Potomac, MD 20854; 301-340-2100; 800-777-5015; www.phillips.com)

Global Investing (P.O. Box 1945, Ft. Collins, CO 80522; 800-388-4237)

Good Fortune (P.O. Box 1500, Woodland, CA 95776; 916-661-7394)

The Granville Market Letter (P.O. Drawer 413006, Kansas City, MO 64141; 816-474-5353)

Ground Floor (P.O. Box 2069, Riverdale, NJ 07675; 800-477-3400)

Growth Stock Outlook (4405 E. West Highway, Suite 305, Bethesda, MD 20814; 301-654-5205)

Growth Stock Winners (1750 Old Meadow Rd., Suite 301, McLean, VA 22102; 800-832-2330)

Growth Stocks Report (107 Edinburgh South, Suite 207, Cary, NC 27511; 919-461-3960)

Harmonic Research (650 Fifth Ave., 5th Floor, New York, NY 10019; 212-484-2065)

The Sy Harding Hotline by Fax (169 Daniel Webster Highway, Suite 7, Meredith, NH 03253; 603-279-4783)

Hussman Econometrics (34405 W. Twelve Mile Rd., Suite 377, Farmington Hills, MI 48334; 800-487-7626; www.hussman.com)

Income Fund Outlook (The Institute for Econometric Research, 2200 Southwest 10th St., Deerfield Beach, FL 33442; 954-421-1000; 800-327-6720; www.mfmag.com)

Individual Investor Special Situations Report (1633 Broadway, 38th Floor, New York, NY 10019; 212-843-2777)

The Insiders (The Institute for Econometric Research, 2200 Southwest 10th St., Deerfield Beach, FL 33442; 954-421-1000; 800-442-9000; www.mfmag.com)

The International Harry Schultz Letter (FERC, P.O. Box 622, CH-1001, Lausanne, Switzerland)

Invest with the Masters (P.O. Box 60042, 7811 Montrose Rd., Potomac, MD 20859; 800-211-8559)

InvesTech Market Analyst (2472 Birch Glen, Whitefish, MT 59937; 406-862-7777; 800-955-8500; www.investech.com)

Investing with Barry Ziskin (1217 St. Paul Street, Baltimore, MD 21202; 800-433-1528)

Investment Quality Trends (7440 Girard Ave., Suite 4, La Jolla, CA 92037; 619-459-3818; www.iqtrends.com)

The Investment Reporter (133 Richmond St. West, Suite 700, Toronto, Ontario, Canada M5H 3M8; 416-869-1177)

Investors Intelligence (P.O. Box 2046, 30 Church St., New Rochelle, NY 10801; 914-632-0422)

Kinsman's Stock Pattern Recognition Service (1601 Sobre Vista Road, Sonoma, CA 95476; 707-935-6504)

LaLoggia's Special Situation Report (P.O. Box 167, Rochester, NY 14601; 716-232-1240)

Louis Rukeyser's Wall Street (1750 Old Meadow Rd., 3rd Floor, McLean, VA 22102; 800-892-9702)

The Low Priced Stock Survey (7412 Calumet Ave., Suite 200, Hammond, IN 46324; 219-852-3210)

Margo's Small Stocks (P.O. Box 642, Lexington, MA 02173; 617-861-0302)

The Marketarian Letter (P.O. Box 9803, Grand Island, NE 68802; 800-658-4325; www.marketarian.com)

Market Logic (The Institute for Econometric Research, 2200 Southwest 10th St., Deerfield Beach, FL 33442; 954-421-1000; 800-442-9000; www.mfmag.com)

Medical Technology Stock Letter (P.O. Box 40460, Berkeley, CA 94704; 510-843-1857)

The Moneyletter (Agora Publishing, 1217 Saint Paul St., Baltimore, MD 21202; 410-223-2400; 800-433-1528; www.moneyletter.com)

Motley Fool (918 Prince St., Alexandria, VA 22314; 703-838-3665)

MPT Review (1 East Liberty, 3rd Floor, Reno, NV 89501; 702-785-2300; 800-454-1395; www.navellier.com)

National Trendlines (National Investment Advisors, 14001 Berryville Rd., North Potomac, MD 20874; 800-521-1585)

Natural Contrarian (7720B El Camino Real #172, Rancho LaCosta, CA 92009; 619-793-3706)

New Issues (The Institute for Econometric Research, 2200 Southwest 10th St., Deerfield Beach, FL 33442; 954-421-1000; 800-442-9000; www.mfmag.com)

The Ney Report (P.O. Box 92223, Pasadena, CA 91109; 818-441-2222)

Bob Nurock's Advisory (P.O. Box 460, Santa Fe, New Mexico 87504-0460; 800-227-8883)

The Oberweis Report (951 Ice Cream Dr., Suite 200, North Aurora, IL 60542; 800-323-6166)

On Markets (31 Melkhout Crescent, Hout Bay 7800 South Africa; 2721-7904259)

The Option Advisor (P.O. Box 46709, Cincinnati, OH 45246; 513-589-3838; 800-327-8833; www.options-iri.com)

OTC Insight (P.O. Box 5759, Walnut Creek, CA 94596; 800-955-9566; www.icrm.com)

The Outlook (Standard & Poor's Corp., 25 Broadway, New York, NY 10004; 800-852-1641; www.standard&poor.com)

Overpriced Stock Service (P.O. Box 308, Half Moon Bay, CA 94019; 415-726-8495)

The PAD System Report (P.O. Box 43285, Cincinnati, OH 45243; 513-529-2863)

PEcom Stock Valuation (P.O. Box 22431, Minneapolis, MN 55422; 612-533-0474)

Personal Finance (1750 Old Meadow Rd., McLean, VA 22102; 800-832-2330)

Peter Dag Portfolio Strategy and Management (65 Lakefront Dr., Akron, OH 44319; 330-644-2782; 800-833-2782)

The Portfolio Advisor (320 Arizona St., Hollywood, FL 33019; 954-923-3553)

P.Q. Wall Forecast (P.O. Box 15558, New Orleans, LA 70175-5558; 504-895-4891)

Professional Investor (P.O. Box 2144, Pompano Beach, FL 33061)

Professional Tape Reader (P.O. Box 2407, Hollywood, FL 33022; 800-868-7857)

Professional Timing Service (P.O. Box 7483, Missoula, MT 59807; 406-543-4131)

Prudence and Performance (22112 NE 23rd St., Redmond,WA 98053; 206-836-4744)

Prudent Speculator (P.O. Box 1438, Laguna Beach, CA 92652; 714-497-7657; www.investools.com)

The Pure Fundamentalist (P.O. Box 7084, Deerfield, IL 60015; 847-945-4700)

Red Chip Review (P.O. Box 1059, Portland, OR 97207; 503-241-1265)

RHM Survey of Warrants, Options and Low-Price Stocks (172 Forest Ave., Glen Cove, NY 11542; 516-759-2904)

Richard Geist's Strategic Investing (1905 Beacon St., Waban, MA 02168; 617-332-3323)

The Ruff Times (757 S. Main St., Springville, UT 84663; 801-489-8681; www.rufftimes.com)

Safe Money Report (P.O. Box 109665, Palm Beach Gardens, FL 33402; 800-289-9222; www.weissinc.com)

Scientific Investing (1521 Alton St., Suite 368, Miami Beach, FL 33139; 800-232-8197)

Sector Selector (P.O. Box 642, Lexington, MA 02173; 617-861-0302)

Short on Value (2300 Route 208, Fair Lawn, NJ 07410; 210-794-8886)

Mark Skousen's Forecasts & Strategies (Phillips Publishing, 7811 Montrose Rd., Potomac, MD 20854; 301-340-2100; 800-777-5015; www.phillips.com)

Sound Advice (319 Diablo Rd., Suite 102, Danville, CA 94526; 510-838-6710)

Sound Mind Investing (2337 Glen Eagle Dr., Louisville, KY 40222; 502-426-7420)

Stockmarket Cycles (P.O. Box 6873, Santa Rosa, CA 95406; 707-579-8444)

Strategic Investment (824 E. Baltimore St., Baltimore, MD 21202; 410-234-0691; 800-433-1528; www.mcgraw-hill.com)

Street Smart Investing (13D Research, P.O. Box 2087, Ketchum, ID 83340; 208-726-1565)

Systems and Forecasts (150 Great Neck Rd., Great Neck, NY 11021; 516-829-6444)

Timer Digest (P.O. Box 1688, Greenwich, CT 06836; 203-629-3503)

Todd Market Timer (26861 Trabuco Rd., Suite E182, Mission Viejo, CA 92691; 714-581-2457)

The Turnaround Letter (225 Friend St., Suite 801, Boston, MA 02114; 800-468-3810; www.turnarounds.com)

United & Babson Investment Report (Babson-United Building, 101 Prescott St., Wellesley Hills, MA 02181; 617-235-0900)

U.S. Investment Report (Suite 4-C, 25 Fifth Ave., New York, NY 10003; 212-460-9200)

Utility Forecaster (1750 Old Meadow Rd., 3rd Floor, McLean, VA 22102; 800-832-2330)

Value Line Convertibles (220 E. 42nd St., New York, NY 10017; 800-634-3583; www.valueline.com)

Value Line Investment Survey (220 E. 42nd St., New York, NY 10017; 800-634-3583; www.valueline.com)

Value Line OTC Special Situations Service (220 E. 42nd St., New York, NY 10017; 800-634-3583; www.valueline.com)

VectorVest Stock Advisory (286 North Cleveland Massillon Rd., Akron, OH 44333; 800-533-3923; www.vectorvest.com)

Vickers Weekly Insider Report (601 Indiana Ave., Suite 616, Washington, DC 20004; 800-645-5043)

The Volume Reversal Survey (P.O. Box 1451, Sedona, AZ 86339; 520-282-1275; www.vrsurvey.com)

The Wall Street Digest (One Sarasota Tower, Two N. Tamiami Trail, Suite 602, Sarasota, FL 34236; 941-954-5500)

The Wall Street Generalist (Market Metrics, Inc., 630 S. Orange Ave., Suite 104, Sarasota, FL 34236; 941-366-5645)

World Investor (1217 St. Paul St., Baltimore, MD 21202; 410-234-0691)

Richard C. Young's Intelligence Report (Phillips Publishing, 7811 Montrose Rd., Potomac, MD 20854; 301-340-2100; 800-777-5015; www.phillips.com)

Zweig Forecast (P.O. Box 360, Bellmore, NY 11710; 516-223-3800; 800-633-2252)

Zweig Performance Ratings Report (P.O. Box 360, Bellmore, NY 11710; 516-223-3800; 800-633-2252)

NEWSPAPERS

While your local newspaper may have a few stories about companies in your region and a few general stock stories, it does not normally present enough information to expose you to a wide range of investment ideas. The best national newspapers aimed at investors are the following.

Barron's National Business and Financial Weekly (200 Liberty St., New York, NY 10281; 212-416-2700; 800-822-7229). Tabloid that features incisive articles on stocks and the stock market, and the best array of statistics around.

Investor's Business Daily (12655 Beatrice St., Los Angeles, CA 90066; 310-448-6000; 800-831-2525; www.investors.com). Daily paper with many short articles about individual companies, as well as many pages of statistics, graphs and charts.

The New York Times, "Business Day" section (229 W. 43rd St., New York, NY 10036; 212-556-1234; 800-631-2580; www.nytimes.com). An influential section that covers corporate news and features columns about individual stocks.

USA Today, "Money" section (1000 Wilson Blvd., Arlington, VA 22229; 703-276-3400; 800-872-8632; www.usatoday.com). A Gannett paper with many short articles on individual stocks and the stock market. Also carries a wide range of statistics on stock market activity.

The Wall Street Journal (200 Liberty St., New York, NY 10281; 212-416-2000; 800-228-3880; www.wsj.com). The most influential daily newspaper. Covers the stock market, particularly in the paper's third section, "Money and Markets."

TELEVISION AND RADIO

Several local TV and radio stations provide excellent coverage of the stock market. On radio, there are several all-business news stations, such as WBBR in New York City, which is run by Bloomberg Financial Markets. On a national level, several programs and cable channels can help you choose stocks. Among the best are the following:

Business News Network (5025 Centennial Blvd., Colorado Springs, CO 80919; 719-528-7040; www.ibnn.com). Airs programs on business topics, with interviews of investment experts. Appears in many markets around the country.

CNBC (Consumer News and Business Channel, 2200 Fletcher Ave., Ft. Lee, NJ 07024; 201-585-2622; www.cnbc.com). The only round-the-clock cable channel devoted to business and financial news. During trading day, stock market ticker crawls at the bottom of the TV screen. Features interviews with prominent market analysts, fund managers, economists and other stock gurus. Produces *This Morning's Business,* aired on local stations nationwide in the morning, which highlights the day's financial news and offers interviews with investment experts.

CNN Business News (Cable News Network, 5 Penn Plaza, New York, NY 10001; 212-714-7848; www.cnn.com). Airs two business news shows in the morning and one, called *Moneyline,* in the evening. Every hour while the market is open, updates what is happening to the stock market.

CNNfn (Cable News Network Financial Network, 5 Penn Plaza, New York, NY 10001; 212-714-7848). A 24-hour financial news network using staff members from Cable News Network devoted to business and financial news. CNNfn provides in-depth coverage of the financial markets, interviews with newsmakers, opportunities for viewers to call in with questions and comments, and much more. The service also has a Web site (www.cnnfn.com) that tracks the markets and offers information about programs on the channel.

Marketplace (USC Radio, University of Southern California, Los Angeles, CA 90089; 213-743-6555). A daily radio show aired on Public Radio International sta-tions. Covers the day's financial news in more depth than is commonly found on radio.

Nightly Business Report (14901 Northeast 20th Ave., Miami, FL 33181; 305-949-8321; www.nightlybusiness.org). A daily TV show that airs on PBS stations. Covers the action in the stock market and features interviews with investment experts.

Adam Smith's Money World. Airs on the Public Broadcasting System. Takes an in-depth look at a current business and economic issue and often focuses on the investment implications of the trend. You can call your local PBS station to see when the program airs.

Sound Money (45 E. 7th St., St. Paul, MN 55101; 612-290-1471; www.mpr.org). A weekly call-in radio show produced by Minnesota Public Radio that features hosts Bob Potter, Chris Farrell and other investment experts, who answer listeners' questions.

Wall Street Week with Louis Rukeyser (Maryland Public Television, 1167 Owings Mills Blvd., Owings Mills, MD 21117; 410-356-5600; www.mpt.org). The grand-daddy of TV shows about selecting stocks. A PBS offering, airs on Friday nights and stars host Louis Rukeyser, who, along with an esteemed panel of investment pros, interviews prominent stock analysts and money managers. You can call your local PBS station to find out when the show airs in your area.

SOFTWARE

You can identify stocks of interest to you by using a software package de-signed to select stocks. These programs allow you to enter certain criteria, such as earnings growth rates, PE ratios, dividend yields or debt levels, and screen for the stocks that fit your specifications. For a more detailed listing of software that chooses stocks, consult the *Individual Investor's Guide to Computerized Investing* (American Association of Individual Investors, 625 N. Michigan Ave., Suite 1900, Chicago, IL 60611; 312-280-0170; www.aaii.com). The best ones follow.

PC Stock Market Databank (American Investors Alliance, 219 Commercial Blvd., Ft. Lauderdale, FL 33308; 954-491-5100). An extensive database, sent in disk form on a monthly basis, allowing you to screen among hundreds of criteria.

Smart Investor (Reality Technologies, 2200 Renaissance Blvd., King of Prussia, PA 19406; 610-650-8600; 800-521-2471; www.moneynet.com). An online database with stock and bond price quotes and company data, mutual fund performance information, CD and money-market fund rates and samples of investment newsletters and magazine articles. Links to the Prodigy Service and allows you to execute trades electronically through a discount broker. Includes the Tour de Wealth Challenge—an online investment game in which you compete against other *Smart Investor* subscribers. Designed to work with *Wealthbuilder* software, also by Reality Technologies, which helps you assess your risk level and execute a financial plan to reach such goals as retirement or funding your children's educations.

Schwab Investor's Web Kit (Charles Schwab & Co., 101 Montgomery St., San Francisco, CA 94101; 800-4-SCHWAB; www.schwab.com). A complete package to help you get news and company reports and analyze stocks based on fundamental or technical techniques. Of course, you also can trade online and track your portfolio.

Value/Screen (220 E. 42nd St., New York, NY 10017; 800-634-3583). Monthly, weekly or quarterly, subscription to computer diskettes with data on all the companies followed by *Value Line*. Allows you to screen stocks by many different criteria.

Trade Associations and Stock Exchanges

American Association of Individual Investors (625 N. Michigan Ave., Chicago, IL 60611; 312-280-0170). A nonprofit group that educates individual investors about the stock market through publications, conferences and seminars. You also can contact them at their Web site (www.aaii.org), which includes the Information Guide, a directory of regulatory agencies, exchanges, NASD offices, financial journals, data sources and places to take complaints. The AAII Web site also provides extensive articles on the basics of investing, as well as a reference section allowing you to find information on a wide variety of topics, such as annuities, mutual funds, dividend reinvestment plans and discount brokers.

American Stock Exchange (86 Trinity Pl., New York, NY 10006; 212-306-1000). An exchange that lists mostly medium- and small-sized growth companies. Offers various pamphlets about investing in stocks.

Bond and Share Society (26 Broadway, New York, NY 10004; 212-943-1880; www.pawws.com/hrzg). Promotes the collection of stock and bond certificates and can help those who want to buy or sell a certificate.

Investment Counsel Association of America (20 Exchange Pl., New York, NY 10005; 202-293-4222; www.icaa.org). Represents money managers who select stocks for individual and institutional clients.

Investors Alliance (219 Commercial Blvd., Ft. Lauderdale, FL 33308-4440; 954-491-5100). A nonprofit group formed to help individual investors become more capable and knowledgeable through diverse programs of investment education and research. Offers easy-to-use software for screening stocks by various criteria, as well as software to help users choose mutual funds. Publishes the monthly *IA Investor Journal* letter for members, which provides information on stock and mutual fund investing techniques.

National Association of Investors Corporation (711 W. 13 Mile Rd., Madison Heights, MI 48071; 810-583-6242). Promotes the growth of investment clubs. The group's Web site (www.better.investing.org) provides a great amount of data for investors of all levels of sophistication. There are reprints from NAIC's *Better Investing* magazine, and you can download NAIC software programs to screen stocks based on fundamental factors. The site also makes it easy to find out about investment clubs near you, as well as investor fairs and other educational opportunities. You also can learn about NAIC's Low Cost Investment Plan, which allows you to purchase a single share of stock in many companies for a small fee over the purchase price. After that, you can buy additional shares of the stock directly from the company's dividend reinvestment plan at little or no commission.

National Association of Securities Dealers (1735 K St., N.W., Washington, DC 20006-1506; 202-728-8000; 800-289-9999; www.nasd.com). Oversees the Nasdaq NMS, and polices securities markets and brokers' actions. Offers the following publications: *NASD Disciplinary Procedures; Nasdaq/CQS Symbol Directory; Nasdaq Fact Book & Company Directory; Nasdaq: The Stock Market for the Next 100 Years; The Nasdaq Investor Relations Guide; The Nasdaq Handbook: The Stock Market for the Next 100 Years—A Complete Reference for Investors, Registered Reps, Researchers and Analysts; The Nasdaq Stock Market: One Billion Plus & Fastest Growing; OTC Bulletin Board Symbol Directory.*

New York Stock Exchange (11 Wall St., New York, NY 10005; 212-656-3000; www.nyse.com). The Big Board, where the largest and most well-known stocks trade. Offers many pamphlets and other literature about investing in stocks.

Securities Industry Association (120 Broadway, New York, NY 10271; 212-608-1500; www.sia.com). Represents the securities industry in lobbying activities and educates the public about the stock market. Offers *The SIA Yearbook,* a listing all of the brokerage houses that are SIA members. Sponsors *The Stock Market Game,* which teaches students about the stock market.

United Shareholders Association (1828 L St., N.W., Suite 402, Washington, DC 20036; 202-429-0300). Works to increase shareholders' rights and battle abuses by corporate management.

WEB SITES

Annual Report Gallery. A site to look at many corporate annual reports. The site also lists all the companies that publish their annual reports online. www.reportgallery.com

Data Broadcasting Corporation. (1900 South Norfolk Street, Suite 150, San Mateo, CA 94403; 415-571-1800; 800-762-7538). This quote service provides a wide variety of prices for stocks, bonds, futures, options, foreign exchange and mutual funds. DBC's Marketwatch feature allows you to create your own portfolio and is constantly being updated. DBC also offers quote services through its handheld QuoTrek and wireless receiver Signal system, which use radio receivers to get information so you do not have to pay telephone charges. www.dbc.com

EduStock. A Web site designed to help students learn about the stock market and how to pick individual stocks. The site includes a real-time stock market simulation and allows you to set up and track a stock portfolio. tqd.advanced.org/3088/

Hoover's Online. Extensive data on over 10,000 public and private companies, including financial performance, news, Web addresses and corporate profiles. www. hoovers.com

INVESTools. One of the most comprehensive Web sites available for analyzing stocks. The site has an online financial library, incorporating reports and newsletters from Standard & Poor's, Morningstar, Reuters, Zack's and many others. You also can keep track of a portfolio, get news about companies, see technical charts and join in discussion forums. For example, if you enter a company's stock symbol, you will not only get a panoply of fundamental and technical data, but the site also will link you to all issues of newsletters mentioning the stock. www.investools.com

InvestorGuide. A massive site with links to thousands of other investment-related sites. The site also has a great deal of basic information on the principles of finance and investing, and what to watch for when you take others' advice. The site links you to articles of interest in the major personal finance magazines, as well. www.investorguide. com

Investors Edge. One of the best sites around to track your portfolio and research stocks. Investors Edge will constantly update the value of your portfolio, so that you can see your net worth rising and falling with every market fluctuation. The site is also linked to IPO Online, allowing you to see monthly calendars of new stock issues. It also offers access to Nelson's Company Research Summaries, which provide the latest research on stocks from major brokerage firms. www.investorsedge.com

MarketGuide. This site provides a wealth of information on thousands of publicly traded companies. The Company Snapshot gives you the basics, which you can update daily with the latest prices and news events. MarketGuide's StockQuest feature lets you screen for stocks based on your criteria, such as PE ratio or earnings growth rates. www.marketguide.com

Microsoft Investor. A highly useful site that will help you track and research your investments. The service is linked to several online brokers, so it is easy to execute trades after your research is complete. www.msn.com

Money Online. Money magazine's personal finance Web site allows you to track your portfolio, get news and access articles in *Money*. The site also publishes *Money Daily,* a wrapup of events affecting individual investors and consumers. www.money. com

The Motley Fools. A popular investment site, also accessible through America Online, provides a great deal of educational material based on the Foolish theory popularized by founders Tom and David Gardner. The idea is that the average individual investor, usually considered "foolish" by the Wall Street establishment, can do better on their own than with advice from most financial newsletters and brokers and outperform many mutual funds, based on the commonsense approach used in the site. The site includes Fool's School for novice investors and several forums in which investors can communicate with each other about stocks and mutual funds. www. fool.com

Quote.com. One of the largest and best-known sites specializing in stock quotes. In addition to providing stock prices, Quote.com offers earnings, price-earnings ratios, yield and 52-week high and low prices. The service also presents technical charts and lists of major market movers each day. www.quote.com

Reuters Money Network on the Web. A Web version of the Reuters Money Network offering portfolio tracking, stock and bond price quotes, corporate and economic news and price charts. The network also offers extensive research and annual reports. www.moneynet.com

The Silicon Investor. A Web site devoted to coverage of high-tech stocks. You can find financial performance, charts, links to company Web sites, corporate profiles and discussion forums where you might turn up profitable tidbits on high-tech stocks. www.techstocks.com

The Small-Cap Investor. A site specializing in small-capitalization companies. They bill themselves as "The Unofficial Directory of Nasdaq SmallCap Stocks on the Web." They provide company summaries, stock price histories, SEC filings and links to small-cap Web sites. There is also a general introduction for novices investing in small companies. www.financialweb.com

Wall Street City. A wealth of stock market information awaits you at this site. There is market commentary, stock search capability and reports on companies. You can even create your own stock ticker with the issues you want to follow most. www.wallstreetcity.com

Zack's Analyst Watch. This site offers one of the best ways to track analysts' opinions and earnings estimates for publicly traded stocks. Since stock prices react quickly to changes in analyst opinion, this information can help improve your investment results significantly. The Web site can alert you to changes in opinion through daily e-mail. It also tracks positive and negative earnings surprises and allows you to screen stocks based on earnings estimates. www.zacks.com

FEDERAL GOVERNMENT REGULATORS

Securities and Exchange Commission (SEC, 450 5th St., N.W., Washington, DC 20549; 202-942-8088; www.sec.gov). The principal federal government agency that regulates the stock and bond markets. Offers the following free brochures: "Arbitration Procedures"; "Consumer's Financial Guide"; "Information on Bounties"; "Penny Stock Telephone Fraud"; "What Every Investor Should Know"; "The Work of the SEC." Has nine regional offices, the addresses and telephone numbers of which follow.

California: 5670 Wilshire Blvd., 11th Floor, Los Angeles 90036-3648; 213-965-3998

Colorado: 1801 California St., Suite 4800, Denver 80202-2648; 303-391-6800

Georgia: 3475 Lenox Rd., N.E., Suite 1000, Atlanta 30326-1232; 404-842-7600

Illinois: Citicorp Center, 500 W. Madison St., Suite 1400, Chicago 60661-2511; 312-353-7390

Massachusetts: 73 Tremont St., Suite 600, Boston 02109; 617-424-5900

New York: 7 World Trade Center, Suite 1300, New York 10048; 212-748-8000

Pennsylvania: Curtis Center, 601 Walnut St., Suite 1005 East, Philadelphia 19106-3322; 215-597-3100

Texas: 801 Cherry St., 19th Floor, Fort Worth 76102; 817-334-3821

Washington: 915 Second Ave., 3040 Jackson Federal Building, Seattle 98174; 206-220-7500

The SEC's huge database of all filings is now accessible directly to the public over the EDGAR system (www.sec.gov/edgarhp.htm). EDGAR stands for Electronic Data Gathering and Retrieval. The system offers all quarterly and annual reports, tender offers and takeovers, insider purchases and sales, and much more. The data is usually posted within 24 hours of being filed.

Securities Investor Protection Corporation (SIPC, 805 15th St., N.W., Suite 800, Washington, DC 20005-2207; 202-371-8300; www.sipc.com). The agency that insures your brokerage account against loss due to the failure of the brokerage firm. Offers the following free publications: "How SIPC Protects You."

STATE SECURITIES REGULATORS

North American Securities Administrators Association (1 Massachusetts Ave., N.W., Suite 310, Washington, DC 20001; 202-737-0900; www.nasaa.org). A group representing state securities enforcement agencies. Offers several free pamphlets on avoiding scams, including those on blind pool offerings, dirt pile gold swindles, penny stock fraud and unsuitable investments. Also offers a book titled

Investor Alert! How To Protect Your Money from Schemes, Scams and Frauds. The following are regional offices.

The following are the state offices of securities regulators:

Alabama: 770 Washington Ave., Suite 570, Montgomery 36130-4700; 334-242-2984

Alaska: P.O. Box 110807, Juneau 99811-0807; 907-465-2521

Arizona: 1300 W. Washington, 3rd Floor, Phoenix 85007; 602-542-4242

Arkansas: Heritage West Building, 201 E. Markham, 3rd Floor, Little Rock 72201-1692; 501-324-9260

California: 3700 Wilshire Blvd., Suite 600, Los Angeles 90010; 213-736-2741

Colorado: Colorado Division of Securities, 1580 Lincoln St., Suite 420, Denver 80203-1506; 303-894-2320

Connecticut: 260 Constitution Plaza, Hartford 06103; 203-240-8299

Delaware: State Office Building, 820 N. French St., 8th Floor, Wilmington 19801; 302-577-2515

District of Columbia: 450 5th St., Suite 821, Washington 20001; 202-626-5105

Florida: State Capitol Building, Suite LL-22, Tallahassee 32399-0350; 904-488-9805

Georgia: 2 Martin Luther King Dr., Suite 802, West Tower, Atlanta 30334; 404-656-2894

Hawaii: P.O. Box 40, Honolulu 96810; 808-586-2730

Idaho: P.O. Box 83720, Boise 83720-0031; 208-334-3684

Illinois: 520 South 2nd St., Springfield 62701; 217-782-2256

Indiana: 302 W. Washington, Suite E-111, Indianapolis 46204; 317-232-6690

Iowa: Iowa Securities Bureau, Lucas State Office Building, 2nd Floor, Des Moines 50319; 515-281-4441

Kansas: 618 S. Kansas Ave., 2nd Floor, Topeka 66603; 913-296-3307

Kentucky: Department of Financial Institutions, 477 Versailles Rd., Frankfort 40601-3868; 502-573-3390

Louisiana: 1100 Poydras St., Suite 2250, New Orleans 70163; 504-568-5515

Maine: 121 State House Station, Augusta 04333; 207-624-8551

Maryland: 200 St. Paul Pl., 20th Floor, Baltimore 21202-2020; 410-576-6360

Massachusetts: One Ashburton Place, Room 1701, Boston 02108; 617-727-3548

Michigan: The Michigan Department of Commerce, 6546 Mercantile Way, Lansing 48910; 517-334-6200

Minnesota: 133 E. 7th St., St. Paul 55101; 612-296-6848

Mississippi: 202 N. Congress St., Suite 601, Jackson 39201; 601-359-6364

Missouri: 600 W. Main St., Jefferson City 65101; 573-751-4136

Montana: Mitchell Building, 126 N. Sanders, Suite 270, Helena 59620; 406-444-2040

Nebraska: The Atrium, 1200 N St., Suite 311, Lincoln 68508; 402-471-3445

Nevada: 555 E. Washington Ave., Suite 5200, Las Vegas 89101; 702-486-2440

New Hampshire: State House, Room 204, Concord 03301-4989; 603-271-1463

New Jersey: 153 Halsey St., Newark 07102; 201-504-3600

New Mexico: P.O. Box 25101, 725 Saint Michaels Dr., Santa Fe 87501; 505-827-7140

New York: 120 Broadway, 23rd Floor, New York City 10271

North Carolina: Secretary of State Securities Division, 300 N. Salisbury St., Suite 100, Raleigh 27603; 919-733-3924

North Dakota: North Dakota Securities Commissioner, State Capitol, 600 E. Boulevard Ave., 5th Floor, Bismarck 58505; 701-328-2910

Ohio: 77 S. High St., 22nd Floor, Columbus 43215; 614-644-7381

Oklahoma: First National Center, 120 N. Robinson St., Suite 860, Oklahoma City 73102; 405-235-0230

Oregon: Department of Consumer and Business Services, Finance and Corporate Securities, 350 Winter St. Northeast, Room 21, Salem 97310; 503-378-4387

Pennsylvania: 1010 N. Seventh St., 2nd Floor, Harrisburg 17102-1410; 717-787-8061

Rhode Island: 233 Richmond St., Suite 232, Providence 02903-4232; 401-277-3048

South Carolina: Office of the Attorney General, Securities Section, P.O. Box 11549, Columbia 29211-1549; 803-734-1087

South Dakota: 118 W. Capitol Ave., Pierre 57501-2017; 605-773-4823

Tennessee: Davy Crockett Building, 500 James Robertson Pky., Suite 680, Nashville 37243-0575; 615-741-2947

Texas: P.O. Box 13167, Austin 78711; 512-305-8300

Utah: Box 146760, 160 E. 300 South, 2nd Floor, Salt Lake City 84114-6760; 801-530-6600

Vermont: 89 Main St., Drawer 20, Montpelier 05620-3101; 802-828-3420

Virginia: 1300 E. Main St., 9th Floor, Richmond 23219; 804-371-9051

Washington: 405 Black Lake Blvd., S.W., 2nd Floor, Olympia 98502; 206-753-6928

West Virginia: State Capitol Building, Room W-118, Charleston 25305; 304-558-2257

Wisconsin: Division of Securities, 101 E. Wilson St., 4th Floor, Madison 53703; 608-266-3431

Wyoming: State Capitol Building, Cheyenne 82002-0020; 307-777-7370

Securities Purchase Program

Another way to enroll in dividend reinvestment plans without paying brokerage commissions is to enroll in the First Share Program (P.O. Box 222, Westcliffe, CO 81252-0222; 719-783-2929). For an $18 enrollment fee, First Share allows you to buy one share of about 250 blue chip companies and sign up for direct purchase and dividend reinvestment programs.

4

Selecting
Mutual Funds

If the process of selecting individual stocks seems a bit overwhelming, one alternative offers the benefits of stock ownership without the complications of choosing stocks: mutual funds that invest in stocks.

Mutual funds, which have been around since the 1920s, have, in recent years, blossomed into the most commonly used vehicle for average Americans to own stocks. That's because they are easy to use and understand, and they provide several great services at a low cost.

Put simply, a stock mutual fund is a pool of money that a fund manager invests in stocks to achieve a specific objective. The fund is sponsored by a mutual fund company, which may be an independent firm, such as Fidelity, T. Rowe Price or Vanguard, or a division of a brokerage or insurance company, like Merrill Lynch, PaineWebber or Kemper.

Load Versus No-Load Funds

There are two basic kinds of mutual funds, differentiated by the method by which they are sold. When you pay a commission to a salesperson, financial planner or broker, that fee is called a *load*. One kind of fund therefore is called a *load mutual fund* because you have to pay a commission to buy it. The other kind of fund, called a *no-load fund*, is sold directly by the mutual fund company, with no salesperson involved. To buy no-load shares, you call the mutual fund company directly, usually at a toll-free 800 number, and it sends you the necessary prospectus and application forms. Sending them back with a check opens your account.

Both load and no-load funds have their roles in the marketplace, and you must decide which is best for your needs. The advantage of a load fund is that you receive professional advice on which fund to choose. Such advice may be well worthwhile because it might be difficult for you to isolate the few funds that are best for your situation among the more than 4,000 funds in existence. Ideally, the salesperson helping you will not only tell you when to buy the fund but also when to sell your shares and move your money into a better fund.

The disadvantage of a load fund is that the commission you must pay immediately reduces the amount of money you have at work in the fund. The load can amount to as much as 8.5 percent of your initial investment though many funds today charge 3 percent or 4 percent. Thus, for every dollar you sink into the fund, only 91.5 cents will earn money if you pay the full 8.5 percent load. If you pay a 3 percent load, 97 cents of every dollar will be invested in stocks. In the short term, therefore, you are starting at a disadvantage over a no-load fund, where all of your dollar is at work from the beginning. Over a longer time period, however, if the load fund performs better than the no-load fund, the up-front charge will pale in significance.

Clearly, the advantage of the no-load fund is that you have all of your money working for you from the moment you open your account. The disadvantage of a no-load fund is that you will not receive much, if any, guidance on which fund to buy. When you call a no-load company's toll-free number, the phone representative can explain the differences among all of the firm's offerings. He or she can describe each fund's investment objective, track record, dividend yield, size in assets, management style and fees, and the stocks currently in its portfolio. But because the person does not know you or your situation, and chances are will never speak to you again, he or she cannot advise you on which fund to buy. If you already have made up your mind based on information you have received about the fund from the fund company itself or reports in the press, that may be no problem. Just realize that you are taking full responsibility for your investment decisions when you buy a no-load fund. No salesperson will call to sell you more of the fund, and no one will tell you when to sell your shares and move to a better performing fund.

People often wonder how no-load companies can offer mutual funds if they do not charge for the service. In fact, they charge plenty, but it is not in the form of an explicit fee for which you must write a check. Both no-load and load funds levy what is known as a *management fee* every year to compensate them for the services they render. The management fee, which ranges from as little as .2 percent of your assets to as much as 2 percent, is deducted from the value of the fund automatically. So, if a fund charges a 1 percent management fee, for example, and the fund's stock portfolio rose 10 percent over the last year, you will earn a 9 percent return. As long as you keep your money in a fund, you will pay the management fee though you might never realize it. A management fee, listed in a fund's selling literature as part of the expense ratio, should not be much more than 1.25 percent of its (and therefore your) assets for it to be considered fair and reasonable.

The Advantages of Mutual Funds

Mutual funds offer several key advantages over individual stocks, which can make the management fee very worthwhile.

A professional skilled in choosing stocks does all of your work for you. Managers of stock mutual funds spend their entire day determining which stocks to buy and sell. They have instant access to information about every stock around the world at the push of a few computer keys. They work in companies where teams of research analysts pore over corporate quarterly and annual reports and managers and analysts visit company executives and factories to evaluate the firms' prospects firsthand. You have almost no opportunity to become as knowledgeable as these fund managers without quitting your job and taking up investing full time.

A mutual fund gives you instant diversification. If you have only $1,000 or $5,000 to invest, the money will not buy many shares of a single stock, and it will certainly not buy many different stocks. By putting your money in only two or three stocks, you are exposed to the possibility that one of them will plummet in price, wiping out much of your investment capital. Instead, when you put your $1,000 or $5,000 in a mutual fund, your money buys into a portfolio that may comprise 50 stocks, or maybe 500 different issues. If one or two stocks in the portfolio get hit hard, your losses will be much more limited because many of the other stocks will probably be going up at the same time.

A fund exists for every financial goal and risk tolerance level. Armed with your goals and risk level from the first chapter, you can find a fund that fits your situation. The different types of funds are described in more detail later in this chapter, but in broad terms, there are funds designed for various degrees of growth and for varying levels of income, as well as funds that combine both growth and income objectives.

Transaction costs are much lower. When you invest in a mutual fund, you benefit from the brokerage commission rates paid by the fund company, which are far lower than you would pay to make the same trades. Mutual funds are among the largest institutional investors on Wall Street, and because they buy and sell billions of dollars' worth of stock every day, they pay between $.02 and $.05 a share per trade. You would be lucky to pay $.10 a share at most brokerage firms, and if you trade in quantities of less than $1,000, you might have to pay as much as $.40 or $.50 a share. Over time, the lower transaction costs that the mutual fund pays will boost your return because you will have more money invested and less paid out in fees.

You can get into and out of a mutual fund easily. All it takes is a phone call to your broker or the fund. By law, a fund must allow you to buy shares at the fund's closing price on the day the fund gets your money. The closing price, called *net asset value* (NAV), is the value of the stock portfolio at the end of the day divided by the number of shares in the fund. Conversely, if you want to sell, the fund must redeem your shares at the NAV on the day you give your instructions. This instant liquidity can be a big advantage when you want to buy or sell stocks quickly. For example, say stock prices are shooting up and you still haven't determined which stocks to buy, or you can't get your broker on the phone. Instead of watching helplessly on the sidelines, you can participate in the rally by buying a stock fund. On the other hand, if stock prices are plunging, it may be difficult to get decent prices if you have only a handful of shares to sell. When you sell the mutual fund, you know you will receive the fund's closing price that day, no matter what problems the fund manager has selling stocks.

In addition to buying and selling fund shares on your request, mutual funds can set up automatic systems to add or subtract money from your account. Most mutual funds will automatically transfer a set amount—usually as little as $25—from your bank account or money-market mutual fund into the stock or bond fund of your choice on a regular basis, whether that be weekly, monthly or annually. Many mutual funds actually waive their normal initial minimum investment amount of $1,000 if you sign up for such a plan. This is a simple way to invest on autopilot. You probably won't even miss the money from your checking account, but over time, you will build up your capital in the mutual fund. On the other hand, if you are retired and want a regular income, most mutual funds will automatically withdraw a certain amount of money and send you a monthly check. This is called an *automatic withdrawal program,* which allows you to withdraw a regular amount of money from your funds every month. It is targeted mostly to retired people living off their funds.

You can easily switch from one fund to another within a fund family. Most mutual fund companies offer a broad array of mutual funds so that as your views of the stock market or your needs change, you can simply switch from one fund to another. This is known as an *exchange.* For instance, you may have invested money in a growth stock fund for years to build capital for retirement. When you retire, you can exchange some of the shares in the growth fund for shares in a stock fund paying high dividends on a monthly basis, on which you will live. All fund families allow exchanges not only between stock funds but also from stock funds to bond funds and money-market funds, which may act as havens when stock prices are falling.

The fund will reinvest dividends and capital gains automatically. If you want the power of compounding to work for you, you can instruct your mutual fund to reinvest in more fund shares all dividends it has earned from the stocks in its portfolio. In addition, as the fund captures capital gains by selling stocks at a profit, it disburses the proceeds as capital gains distributions. You can have the fund reinvest those distributions in more shares as well. Remember to pay taxes on both reinvested dividends and capital gains in the tax year you receive them even though you have reinvested the money unless you hold shares in a tax-deferred retirement account.

Over time, the shares you own from reinvestment produce more shares, and the compounding effect can dramatically increase your capital. For example, if you had invested $10,000 in the Denver-based Berger 100 Fund on September 30, 1974, you would have accumulated $258,771 by December 31, 1997, assuming you had reinvested all dividends and capital gains distributions. In contrast, your $10,000 would have grown to only $65,000 if you had taken the distributions. The graph in Figure 4.1 clearly illustrates the power of compounding.

More on Fund Fees

Some mutual funds levy additional charges, which you should be aware of before you invest. The funds cannot sneak these charges by you. They are all disclosed in a standardized fee table on the front of all mutual fund prospectuses. *Prospectuses* are the official legal documents describing funds. The section, titled "Fund Expenses," appears in the example in Figure 4.2.

Note that funds are required to detail their expenses by category for the last year. In addition, they must project what that level of expenses would cost investors if they invested $1,000 over the next year, three years, five years and ten years. You can use this section of the prospectus to compare one mutual fund with a similar fund in another fund family.

An explanation of the most common fund fees follows.

Back-end loads. To compete with no-load funds, many broker-sold funds now waive a charge when you buy them but hit you with a fee if you sell the funds before a particular period of time elapses. This is also called a *contingent deferred sales charge.* Usually, the back-end load operates on a sliding scale, so you will pay 4 percent of the money you invested if you sell the fund in the first year you hold it, 3 percent in the second year, 2 percent in the third year and 1 percent in the fourth year. If you hold the fund for at least four years, you will not pay the back-end load. A brokerage firm needs this system because it pays the broker his or her commission up front when you buy the fund even though the firm doesn't receive the money from you to pay the commission. If you sell the fund before the brokerage firm has had a chance to recoup that fee through management fees, it wants to be able to charge you.

Dividend reinvestment loads. Although most mutual funds do not levy a sales commission on reinvested dividends, some fund groups do. This fee usually amounts to 4 percent of the reinvested funds. Because dividend reinvestment is automatic and no sales advice is given, it is best to avoid funds that charge for counsel you are not receiving.

Exchange fees. Some fund groups charge a fee if you exchange one fund for another within a fund family. The fee covers administrative costs and usually amounts to about $5 per transaction.

Figure 4.1
The Effect of Compounding on a Berger 100 Fund Investment

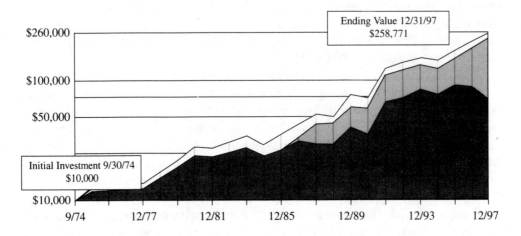

BERGER 100 FUND
Growth

Dividends and Capital Gains Reinvested

Ending Value 12/31/97
$258,771

Initial Investment 9/30/74
$10,000

Past performance shows the fund's history and does not guarantee future results. The figures include changes in share price and reinvestment of dividends and capital gains, which will fluctuate so that shares, when redeemed, may be worth more or less than their original cost. The figures include the deduction of 12b-1 fees beginning in June 1990.

Source: Reprinted by permission of Berger Associates and Tower Data Systems.

Figure 4.2
Sample Charges That Funds Levy

Fund Expenses

The following table sets forth the fees that an invest-
or in the Fund might pay and expenses paid by the
Fund during its fiscal year ended December 31, 1991.

Shareholder Transaction Expenses

Maximum Sales Charge on Purchases	
(as a percentage of offering price)	5.75%
Sales Charge on Reinvested Dividends	None
Redemption Fee	None
Deferred Sales Load	·None*
Exchange Fee	$5.00

Annual Fund Operating Expenses (as a percentage of average net assets)

Management Fees	.65%
12b-1 (Distribution Plan) Fees	.08%
Other Expenses	.22%
Total Fund Operating Expenses	.95%

*Certain purchases of $1 million or more are not
subject to front-end sales charges but a contingent
deferred sales charge of 1% is imposed on the proceeds of such shares redeemed within 18 months of
the end of the calendar month of their purchase, subject to certain conditions. See "How to Buy Shares—
Contingent Deferred Sales Charge," below.

The purpose of this table is to assist an investor in
understanding the various costs and expenses that
an investor in the Fund will bear directly (shareholder transaction expenses) or indirectly (annual fund
operating expenses). The sales charge illustrated is
the current maximum rate applicable to purchases of
Fund shares. Investors may be entitled to reduced
sales charges based on the amount purchased or the
value of shares already owned and may be subject to
a contingent deferred sales charge in limited circumstances (see "How to Buy Shares"). "Other
Expenses" includes such expenses as custodial and
transfer agent fees, audit, legal and other business
operating expenses, but excludes extraordinary
expenses.

The following example applies the above-stated
expenses to a hypothetical $1,000 investment in
shares of the Fund over the time periods shown
below, assuming a 5% annual rate of return on the
investment and also assuming that the shares were
redeemed at the end of each stated period. The
amounts below are the cumulative costs of such hypothetical $1,000 investment for the periods shown.

1 year	3 years	5 years	10 years
$67	$86	$107	$167

**This example should not be considered a
representation of past or future expenses or
performance. Expenses are subject to change
and actual performance and expenses may be
less or greater than those illustrated above.
For further details, see the Fund's Financial
Statements included in the Additional
Statement.**

12b-1 fees. These charges, like management fees, are deducted automatically from the fund's assets each year. They cover distribution costs, which include advertising, promotion, literature and sales incentives to brokers, and range from .25 percent to as much as 1.25 percent of the fund's assets each year. The idea behind these fees is that if a mutual fund increases its assets through more promotion, fund shareholders will benefit because the fund's expenses will be spread over a wider customer base, thereby lowering each shareholder's cost. In many cases, however, expenses do not decrease as fund assets grow. In general, unless you invest in a fund that has a superb record or some other compelling reason to buy it, avoid funds that impose 12b-1 fees.

Buying and Monitoring Shares in a Stock Mutual Fund

THE PROSPECTUS

Mutual fund companies have made it as easy as possible to open an account, but there is still a certain amount of legal paperwork you must go through in the process. In protecting consumers and making sure they receive enough information about a fund, the Securities and Exchange Commission (SEC) requires that potential fund shareholders receive a prospectus and an application form from the fund. While you shouldn't expect the prospectus to compete with your favorite novel for light reading, it does contain several important facts you should understand before you give the fund any money. The following are the most important areas the prospectus covers.

- *The fund's investment objective.* It may be aiming for aggressive growth, steady income or something in between.

- *The investment methods the fund uses to achieve its goals.* It may restrict itself to certain kinds of stocks, or it may use complex hedging strategies involving futures and options to prevent losses. The fund will also tell you what kinds of stocks it will not buy.

- *The fund's investment adviser.* The prospectus will outline the background of the fund company and usually tell you which portfolio manager makes the decisions about what stocks to buy and sell. Ultimately, the fund's performance is determined by the quality of the investment adviser. Some firms use a team approach, while others are run by an individual who decides what to buy or sell.

- *The amount of risk the fund will assume.* Depending on the type of fund, the prospectus will reveal how volatile the fund's price is. The more risks the fund takes, the more its price will jump around.

- *The tax consequences of holding the fund.* For example, the prospectus will mention that you must pay taxes on all dividend and capital gains distributions.

- *A list of services provided by the fund.* The prospectus will tell you whether the fund is suitable for individual retirement accounts (IRAs) and Keogh accounts, whether you can reinvest dividends and capital gains automatically and whether you can set up an automatic investment or withdrawal program. The prospectus will also tell you the minimum initial investment to get into the fund, as well as the minimum amount to make subsequent investments.

- *A financial summary of the fund's performance for the last ten years if it has been around that long.* A table will track the fund's price, dividends and capital gains distributions that have been paid and expenses.

- *A listing of all fund fees.* This table will summarize the management fee, 12b-1 fees, sales charges and any other fees charged to shareholders.

THE APPLICATION FORM

When you've decided that you want to invest in a particular fund, you must fill out the application and return it to the fund with a check. Once you've completed this form, you will not have to do so again for this fund group. To guide you through the application process, we have reproduced a sample form here (see Figure 4.3), printed with permission from the Oppenheimer group of funds. Following are the key areas of information about which you will be questioned, coded by number according to the sections on the sample application.

1. *Account owner(s).* You should record the exact name(s) in which you want the fund registered. If you hold assets in joint name with your spouse, include both names. If the fund is for your child, fill in your name as the custodian for the account. Also note your Social Security number, which is needed for tax-reporting purposes.

2. *Mailing address.* Enter the address to which you want your statements sent—normally your home address.

3. *Fund selection.* Check off the fund in which you want to invest. This section will also tell you the minimum initial investment amount. On some applications, you must check off all the funds you potentially would ever want to invest in so you can easily exchange into them once your account is opened.

4. *Dividends and capital gains distributions.* On the application, you must tell the fund what to do with payouts. You can reinvest them in the same fund, reinvest them in a different fund within the same fund family, receive the payments in the form of a check or have them deposited automatically in your bank account.

5. *Signature(s).* Make sure that you and anyone else on the account sign the form. Such signature is very important because it will be used for

Figure 4.3
Oppenheimer's New Account Application Form

OppenheimerFunds Selection

Specialty Stock Funds
Global Bio-Tech Fund
Global Environment Fund
Gold & Special Minerals Fund

Stock Funds
Discovery Fund
Time Fund
Target Fund
Special Fund
Global Fund
Oppenheimer Fund
Value Stock Fund

Stock & Bond Funds
Total Return Fund
Global Growth & Income Fund
Equity Income Fund
Asset Allocation Fund

Bond Funds
High Yield Fund
Champion High Yield Fund
Strategic Income & Growth Fund*
Strategic Income Fund*
Strategic Investment Grade Bond Fund*
Strategic Short-Term Income Fund*
Investment Grade Bond Fund
GNMA Fund
U.S. Government Trust
Government Securities Fund

Tax-Exempt Funds
New York Tax-Exempt Fund'
California Tax-Exempt Fund'
Pennsylvania Tax-Exempt Fund
Tax-Free Bond Fund
Insured Tax-Exempt Bond Fund
Intermediate Tax-Exempt Bond Fund

Money Market Funds
Money Market Fund
Cash Reserves
Tax-Exempt Cash Reserves

* Also available in B shares
' Available only to residents of that state

Oppenheimer Funds are distributed by
Oppenheimer Fund Management, Inc.
Two World Trade Center
New York, NY 10048-0203

AO 001 (1/93)

New Account Application

Oppenheimer Fund Management, Inc.
1960 South Quebec Street
Denver, CO 80231-3234

For Retirement Plans
Do not use this form for Oppenheimer-
sponsored retirement plans, such as
Individual Retirement Accounts. For
a special retirement plan application
form, call:

Oppenheimer Shareholder Services
1-800-525-7048.

 OppenheimerFunds℠

Figure 4.3
(continued)

OppenheimerFundssm   **New Account Application**

Type of Account
(choose one only)

1 **Account Owner(s) and Other Information** Please print clearly.

☐ **Individual**

First Name	Middle Initial	Last Name	Social Security Number

(first individual only)

☐ **Joint Tenant**

Joint Tenant's First Name   Middle Initial   Last Name
Joint tenants with rights of survivorship and not tenants in common will be presumed unless otherwise specified.
No joint tenants with rights of survivorship registrations are permitted for residents of Louisiana.

☐ **Gift/Transfer to Minors**

Custodian's Name (one only)   Minor's Name (one only)

Under Uniform Gift/Transfer to Minors Act of (State)   Minor's Social Security Number

☐ **Corporation, Partnership,
Trust or Other Organization**   Exact Name of Corporation, Partnership, or other Organization   Tax Identification Number

Trustee Accounts Only: Name(s) of all Trustee(s) required by trust agreement to sell/purchase shares

Date of Trust Agreement   Name of Trust or Beneficiaries   Tax Identification Number

2 **Mailing Address**

Street Address   Apartment No.   City   State   Zip

(   )   (   )   Citizenship: ☐ U.S. ☐ Other
Business Phone   Home Phone   Indicate Country

3 **OppenheimerFunds Selection** ($1,000 minimum investment; $25 if opening through an Asset Builder Plan.)

Fund Name(s)   Type of Shares   Amount

                            ☐ Class A   ☐ Class B* $

                            ☐ Class A   ☐ Class B* $

                            ☐ Class A   ☐ Class B* $

                            ☐ Class A   ☐ Class B* $

                            ☐ Class A   ☐ Class B* $

                            Total Amount Enclosed $

*Please check OppenheimerFunds Selection for the availability of Class B shares. Class A shares will be purchased if no class of share is indicated. Please make checks payable to Oppenheimer Fund Management, Inc. All optional features selected below will apply to all accounts established.

4 **Dividends and Capital Gains Distributions**

Dividends (check one)   **Capital Gains (check one)**
☐ **Reinvest dividends in Fund that pays them**   ☐ **Reinvest capital gains in Fund that pays them**
☐ Reinvest dividends in another Fund*   ☐ Reinvest capital gains in another Fund*

Fund Name   Account Number (if known)   Fund Name   Account Number (if known)
☐ Send dividends by check to above address   ☐ Send capital gains by check to above address
☐ Deposit dividends in my bank account   ☐ Deposit capital gains in my bank account
   through AccountLink (complete Section 6)   through AccountLink (complete Section 6)
If not specified, dividends and capital gains will be reinvested in the Fund that pays them.
*Dividends and capital gains on Class B shares can only be reinvested into that fund's or another fund's Class B shares.

5 **Signature(s)**

I/we are of legal age and capacity, have legal authority to purchase shares, have received and read a current prospectus for each Fund selected and agree to the terms and conditions on this Application and those contained in the current prospectus(es) (including the statement(s) of additional information) of the Fund(s) selected for purchase. I/we acknowledge that the account will be subject to the telephone exchange and redemption privileges described in the Fund's current prospectus and agree that the Fund, its Distributor and Transfer Agent will not be liable for any loss in acting on written or telephone instructions reasonably believed by them to be authentic.

Under penalties of perjury, the undersigned whose Social Security (Employer I. D.) number is shown on this application certifies that (i) the number is my correct taxpayer identification number and (ii) currently I am not under IRS notification that I am subject to backup withholding (line out (ii) if under notification). If no such number is shown, the undersigned further certifies, under penalties of perjury, that either (a) no such number has been issued, and a number has been or will soon be

Figure 4.3
Oppenheimer's New Account Application Form (continued)

applied for; if a number is not provided to you within sixty days, the undersigned understands that all payments (including redemptions) are subject to maximum withholding under Federal tax law, until a number is provided; or (b) that the undersigned is not a citizen of the U.S., and either does not expect to be in the U.S. for 183 days during each calendar year and does not conduct business in the U.S. which would receive any gains from the fund, or is exempt under an income tax treaty. My signature below constitutes my agreement and acceptance of all the terms, conditions and account features selected in any and all parts of this Application.

Individual, Joint or
Custodian Accounts

X

Signature of Individual Owner or Custodian   Date

X

Signature of Joint Registrant, if any   Date

Corporate, Partnership,
Trust or Other Accounts

X

Signature of Authorized Officer, General Partner, Trustee, etc.   Date

Title of Corporate Officer, General Partner, Trustee, etc.

Special Services for More Convenient Investing (optional)

6 **AccountLink**

I would like to be able to transfer assets by phone or in writing between my Oppenheimer fund account(s) listed in section 3 and my bank or financial institution account. Please establish AccountLink for the following account(s):

Fund Name(s)   **Account Number(s)**

Bank Account Information (check one only)

☐ Checking Account (please attach a voided check)   ☐ Savings Account (please attach a pre-printed deposit slip)

Bank Name   Account Number

Street Address   City   State   Zip

X   X

Signature of Depositor   Signature of Joint Depositor   Date

Dealer (Financial Advisor) AccountLink Instruction Option

☐ I do *not* want my Dealer Representative of record to have authority to give AccountLink instructions.

By selecting AccountLink or Asset Builder options below, I am requesting that Oppenheimer Shareholder Services ("OSS") arrange to debit or draw checks on my bank account to pay for share purchases. A separate debit or check will be drawn for each account. OSS is preparing these debit entries or checks at my request and shall not be liable for any loss arising from delays in processing or failure to prepare debit entries or checks. If a debit cannot be made to purchase shares or a check to purchase shares is returned for any reason, this plan may be cancelled by OSS and I shall return any amount paid to me from the redemption of those shares.

7 **Asset Builder Plan**

I would like to automatically purchase additional shares of the Oppenheimer fund(s) indicated below. (Check *one box only* to indicate where payments for the purchase of additional shares will come from.)

☐ From my Cash Reserves Account Number
☐ From my Tax-Exempt Cash Reserves Account Number
☐ From my Checking or Savings Account (complete Bank Account Information in Section 6).

Purchase shares in the fund(s) listed below (up to 5 funds, minimum of $25 per fund).

Fund Name(s)   **Amount of Purchase**

$ ☐ New Account   ☐ Existing Account
                                                    Number

$ ☐ New Account   ☐ Existing Account
                                                    Number

$ ☐ New Account   ☐ Existing Account
                                                    Number

$ ☐ New Account   ☐ Existing Account
                                                    Number

$ ☐ New Account   ☐ Existing Account
                                                    Number

Make investments on the (check one or more)   ☐ 5th   ☐ 10th   ☐ 20th   ☐ 25th   days of each month.

If you are making payments from a bank account, your bank account will be debited 1-2 business days prior to the investment dates selected above. Monthly investments will be debited automatically from your bank account and used to buy shares for your Oppenheimer fund account(s) listed above. Neither OSS nor the fund shall be liable for any loss arising from delays in processing or failure to prepare debit entries or checks. If a check to purchase shares is returned for any reason, this plan may be cancelled by OSS and I/we agree to return any amount paid to me/us from the redemption of shares.

**Figure 4.3
(continued)**

8 Automatic Withdrawal and Exchange Plan

I would like to make ☐ monthly ☐ quarterly ☐ annual withdrawals and/or exchanges from the following Oppenheimer fund account:

Fund Name   Account Number

Amount of Withdrawal/Exchange $ To begin on the   of
(minimum amount $50)   Day   Month   Year

Automatic Withdrawal Plan ☐ Make check payable to the account owner(s) and send to the address of record; or

☐ Make check payable to and send to the person whose name and address appear below; or

First Name   Middle Initial   Last Name

Street Address   Apartment No.   City   State   Zip

☐ Deposit payments in my bank account (complete Bank Account Information in Section 6).

Automatic Exchange Plan ☐ Automatically exchange, as indicated, shares of the Oppenheimer fund listed above for shares of:

☐ New Account ☐ Existing Account

Fund Name   Number

See "Exchange Privilege" in the prospectus for terms and conditions. Class B shares can only be exchanged for another fund's Class B shares. Shares are normally redeemed pursuant to the Automatic Withdrawal Plan 3 business days before the date you select. If a contingent deferred sales charge applies to the redemption, the amount of the check or payment will be reduced accordingly. OSS and the Fund cannot guarantee that you will receive your Automatic Withdrawal Plan payment on the exact date selected. OSS and the Fund reserve the right to amend or terminate the Automatic Withdrawal or Exchange Plan at any time.

Dealer (Financial Advisor) Information Your Dealer/Advisor should complete this section.

Dealer's Name   Oppenheimer Dealer Number

Dealer's Head Office Street Address   City   State   Zip

Representative's First Name   M.I.   Last Name   (   )
Office Telephone Number   AE Number

Representative's Branch Office Street Address   City   State   Zip

9 Telephone Exchange and Redemption Privileges

All shareholders and their Dealer Representatives will automatically receive telephone exchange and redemption privileges, **unless** refused by checking the appropriate box below.

Telephone Exchange Privilege ☐ No Telephone Exchange Privilege for me or my Dealer Representative
☐ No Telephone Exchange Privilege for my Dealer Representative only

Telephone Redemption Privilege ☐ No Telephone Redemption Privilege for me or my Dealer Representative
☐ No Telephone Redemption Privilege for my Dealer Representative only

This authorization will remain in effect unless and until OSS receives written notice of termination or change signed by a shareholder of record.

10 Right of Accumulation (Class A shares only)

If you already have an Oppenheimer fund account(s), you may be eligible for reduced sales charges. Check the box below and indicate your fund account number(s).

☐ I would like to use the combined assets in the following Oppenheimer fund account(s) to qualify for reduced sales charges. (See "Reduced Sales Charges" in the prospectus for eligibility guidelines.)

Fund Name(s)   Account Number(s)

Figure 4.3
Oppenheimer's New Account Application Form (continued)

Letter of Intent (Class A shares only)

If you intend to invest a certain amount over a 13-month period in one or more Oppenheimer funds, you may be entitled to reduced sales charges.

☐ I plan to invest over a 13-month period a total of at least:

☐ $25,000   ☐ $50,000   ☐ $100,000   ☐ $250,000   ☐ $500,000   ☐ $1,000,000 or more*

If the amount indicated is not invested within 13 months, reduced sales charges do not apply.

☐ I am already investing under an existing Letter of Intent.

*A contingent deferred sales charge may apply to proceeds of shares redeemed within 18 months of purchase. Please refer to the prospectus for complete terms and conditions.

Checkwriting Application (Class A shares only) Minimum check amount $100.

For Oppenheimer Use Only   Check Control Number   Account Number

Note: Accounts with shares subject to a contingent deferred sales charge cannot have checkwriting privileges.

I would like to have checkwriting privileges in the following fund

(see reverse side for eligible funds)

☐ **Joint Accounts.** Check here if only one signature is required on checks.

All joint owners' signatures will be required unless this box is checked.

☐ **Corporate, Partnership, Trust Accounts.** Check if more than one signature will be required on checks.

Indicate number of signatures required

Listed below are the names of all persons authorized to sign checks for this account. Only the registered owners (or, in the case of corporations, partnerships, general partners, or trusts, duly authorized persons listed below) are authorized to sign checks. The undersigned investor(s) guarantees that all signatures appearing on this checkwriting application are genuine and agree that use of the Fund's checkwriting privileges shall be governed by the terms and conditions set forth on the reverse side of this form and contained in the prospectus of the Fund in effect at the time each check is presented.

All joint owners and all authorized signatories, in the case of a corporation, partnership or trust account, must sign

Name (please print)	**X** Signature	Title (if required on checks)
Name (please print)	**X** Signature	Title (if required on checks)
Street Address	City	State	Zip	Date

Checkwriting Authorization and Specimen Signature Card

The person(s) signing the reverse side of this card (1) represent(s) that they are either the registered owner(s) of the shares of each fund for which checkwriting privileges are requested, or are an officer, partner, trustee, or other fiduciary or agent, as applicable, duly authorized to act on behalf of such registered owner(s); (2) authorize(s) the fund, its Transfer Agent and any bank through which the fund's drafts ("checks") are payable (the "Bank") to honor all checks drawn on the fund account of such person(s) and to effect a redemption of sufficient shares in that account to cover payment of such checks; (3) specifically acknowledge(s) that if this card is marked on the reverse side to permit a single signature on checks drawn against joint accounts, or accounts for corporations, partnerships, trusts or other entities, the signature of any one signatory on a check will be sufficient to authorize payment of that check and a redemption from an account, even if that account is registered in the names of more than one person or even if more than one authorized signature appears on the reverse side of this card; and (4) understand(s) that this checkwriting privilege may be terminated or amended at any time by the fund and/or the Bank and neither shall incur any liability for such amendment or termination or for honoring and effecting redemptions to pay checks reasonably believed to be genuine, or for returning or not paying checks which have not been accepted for any reason.

The following Oppenheimer Funds offer checkwriting privileges:

California Tax-Exempt	High Yield	New York Tax-Exempt	Tax-Exempt Cash Reserves
Cash Reserves	Insured Tax-Exempt Bond	Pennsylvania Tax-Exempt	Tax-Free Bond
Champion High Yield	Intermediate Tax-Exempt Bond	Strategic Income A	U.S. Government Trust
GNMA	Investment Grade Bond	Strategic Investment Grade Bond A	
Government Securities	Money Market	Strategic Short-Term Income A	

comparison if you ever want to withdraw your funds or close your account. At that point, the fund will request a signature guarantee to prove that you are the rightful owner of the funds.

6.   *Special services.* You may want to sign up for additional services the fund offers. For instance, you can link your fund account to your bank account so that you can transfer money easily between them without having to write a check. This allows you to invest a specific dollar amount in the fund automatically on a regular basis. You can also have money wired to or from the fund easily once you set up this system.

7.   *Asset builder plan.* You may want to transfer money from your money-market fund or bank account into any of the fund family's offerings automatically on a set schedule.

8.   *Automatic withdrawal and exchange plans.* If you indicate your desire to receive one, the fund will send you a regular check. The money will be taken first from any fund dividends. If your dividends don't cover it, the fund will automatically sell enough of your shares to meet the monthly payment.

     You can also set up an automatic exchange, where you move money from one fund—usually a money fund—to another fund on a monthly, a quarterly or an annual basis.

     Along with this information, you must enter the name of the broker, financial planner or other adviser who recommended that you invest in the fund. The fund needs this information so it knows who gets the commission check.

9.   *Telephone privileges.* Checking the appropriate box allows you to transfer money from one fund to another by a phone call, either from you directly or from your broker or financial adviser. Otherwise, you will be able to buy or sell fund shares only by mail.

10. *Right of accumulation.* At some funds, you can pay lower sales charges if you have accumulated enough money in the entire family of funds. By listing all your fund holdings, you may qualify for this discount.

11. *Letter of intent.* If you promise to invest a certain amount of money in the fund family over a particular period of time, you might qualify for a sales charge discount. In Oppenheimer's case, you must invest at least $25,000 over 13 months to qualify.

12. *Checkwriting application.* Completing this information allows you to write checks on your account. Usually, these checks debit your money-market fund in the same fund family. Most funds stipulate a minimum check size—which, in Oppenheimer's case, is $100.

Once you have completed and mailed the application, your account should be established within a few days. You will receive a confirmation statement from the fund showing how much you invested, how many shares you received and the current price per share. Unlike stocks, certificates are not usually issued as evidence of ownership of mutual fund shares. Some mutual fund companies will issue certificates but only if requested.

MONITORING YOUR FUND

Tracking the value of your fund holdings is simple. Just multiply the current price (NAV) by the number of shares you own. For example:

500 Shares of Oppenheimer Total Return Fund × $10 Per share =
$5,000 Total value

If you reinvest your distributions in more shares (which is probably a good idea), remember that the number of shares you own will continue to increase. Make sure to use the latest number of shares on your statement in calculating the value of your holdings.

The easiest way to determine the current price is to call your fund company or broker. Most fund companies have automated voice systems so you can even call after hours.

You can also look up your fund's NAV in a local newspaper or in national papers like the *New York Times*, *USA Today* or *Investor's Business Daily*. Following is a typical listing, along with an explanation of each column.

	NAV[2]	Offer Price[3]	NAV Change[4]
OppenheimerFunds[1]			
Asset Allocation	11.63	12.34	+.02
Blue Chip	16.76	17.78	−.03
Discovery	33.91	35.98	+.10
Total Return	7.80	8.28	+.15
Vanguard Group			
Explorer	43.69	N.L.	+1.43

1. The *fund family's name* comes first, followed by the names of all the funds in the family. The *fund names* are usually abbreviated. Each family lists several types of funds, including different kinds of stock and bond funds.

2. The NAV (*net asset value*) is the per-share price of the fund's assets, including expenses. This is the price per share, in dollars and cents, you would receive if you sold the shares on this day. In the example, the price

of the Oppenheimer Blue Chip Fund is $16.76 per share. Some newspapers list this column under the heading "Sell."

3.   *Offer price* means the amount you must pay, in dollars and cents, to buy shares on this day. For load funds that carry a sales charge, the difference between this column and the NAV column is the commission that goes to the broker. In the case of the Blue Chip Fund, that difference is $1.02 per share, or 5.7 percent. To calculate the load, divide the difference by the offer price. No-load funds, because they do not charge commissions, usually record an "N.L." (which stands for *no-load*) in this column. The example's Vanguard Explorer Fund, for instance, is a no-load. Some newspapers list this column under the heading "Buy."

4.   The *NAV change* shows, in dollars and cents, how much the price of the shares changed in the last day's trading. In the example, the Oppenheimer Blue Chip Fund lost $.03, while the Total Return Fund gained $.15 and the Vanguard Explorer Fund gained $1.43.

Various abbreviations appear in the mutual fund tables found in local and national newspapers. Among the most common are the following:

e—ex-distribution, which signifies that the fund just distributed capital gains and the share price has been adjusted downward to reflect the payout

f—previous day's closing price, if no price was available for the latest day

N.L.—no load, signifying the fund charges no sales commission

p—Distribution costs, such as a 12b-1 fee, apply to the fund.

r—Redemption charges or back-end loads may apply if you sell the fund before such charges have been phased out. Usually, such charges are levied on a sliding scale. For example, one fund provides that if you sell the fund in the first year, you are assessed a 4 percent charge; in the second year, 3 percent; in the third year, 2 percent; in the fourth year, 1 percent. There would be no charge if you sold the fund after having held the shares four years.

s—stock split or dividend, if the fund split its price (A fund at $50 a share might split 2 for 1, which would lower its price to $25 a share and double the number of shares outstanding.)

t—Both 12b-1 fees and redemption charges may apply to the fund.

x—ex-dividend, which signifies that the fund just distributed a dividend and the share price has been adjusted downward to reflect the payout

The Wall Street Journal enhances the traditional listing of mutual funds. Following is a *Journal* listing, along with an explanation of each additional column.

	Investment Objective[1]	NAV	Offer Price	NAV Change	**Total Return**			
					YTD[2]	26 Weeks[3]	4 Years[4]	R[5]
Oppenheimer Funds								
Asset Allocation	S&B	11.63	12.34	+.02	+10.30	+15.65	+9.5	A
Blue Chip	STK	16.76	17.78	−.03	+12.45	+13.56	+10.6	C
Discovery	SML	33.91	35.98	+.10	+15.43	+12.57	+20.6	D
Total Return	STK	7.80	8.28	+.15	+10.43	+20.56	+14.7	B
Vanguard Group								
Explorer	SML	43.69	N.L.	+1.43	+11.23	+23.45	+15.6	A

Source: Reprinted by permission of *The Wall Street Journal*, © 1993 Dow Jones & Company, Inc. All Rights Reserved Worldwide.

1. The fund's investment objective may be growth, income or a combination of the two. The fund may achieve its objective by investing in stocks, bonds or a combination of stocks and bonds. The *Journal* provides the following abbreviations for ten categories of mutual funds:

Stock Funds

SEC—sector funds, which invest in only one industry. These include environmental, financial services, gold-oriented, health/biotechnology, natural resources, real estate, science and technology, specialty and miscellaneous, and utility industries.

SML—small-company funds, which buy shares in small growth companies

STK—general U.S. stock funds, which buy shares in U.S. companies. These include capital appreciation, equity income, growth, growth and income, and option income companies.

WOR—world stock funds, which invest in companies around the world. These include Canadian, European region, global, international, Japanese, Latin American, Pacific region, and small-company global companies.

Bond Funds

BHI—bond high-yield funds, which buy high-current-yield bonds, commonly known as junk bonds

BND—intermediate and long-term bond funds, which buy bonds maturing in about 3 years to as long as 30 years. These include intermediate U.S. Treasury, intermediate U.S. government, general U.S. Treasury, general U.S. government, GNMA (Ginnie Mae), U.S. mortgage, corporate debt—A-rated, corporate debt—BBB-rated, intermediate investment grade, general, flexible income, and target maturity bonds, which use zero-coupon bonds to mature at a particular date in the future.

BST—bond short term, which buy short-term bonds maturing in three years or less. These include adjustable rate preferred, adjustable rate mortgage, short U.S. Treasury, short U.S. government, and short investment grade bonds.

MUN—municipal bonds of all maturities, which buy tax-free bonds issued by states and local municipalities. These include short municipal debt, general municipal debt, intermediate municipal debt, insured municipal debt, high-yield municipal debt, single-state municipal, single-state insured municipal, and single-state intermediate municipal bonds.

WBD—world bond funds, which buy bonds issued by governments and corporations around the world. These include short world multi-market, short world single-market, and general world income bonds.

Stock and Bond Funds

S&B—stock and bond blended funds, which buy varying combinations of equities and fixed-income securities. These include balanced, balanced target maturity, convertible security, flexible portfolio, global flexible portfolio, and income fund bonds.

2. The *total return, year to date* (YTD), is the gain or loss in value of the fund's shares, plus any dividends and interest paid out so far this year. These mutual fund tables assume that all capital gains and dividend payouts are reinvested in more shares of the fund. For example, the Oppenheimer Asset Allocation Fund's total return has been 10.30 percent so far this year. That return might have been composed of 5 percent in dividends and 5.3 percent in capital gains.

3. *Total return, 26 weeks* shows the capital gain or loss, plus interest and dividends received, over the last 26 weeks, or half a year.

4. *Total return, 4 years* shows the capital gain or loss, plus interest and dividends received, over the last four years, expressed as an annual average rate. In the case of the Oppenheimer Asset Allocation Fund, for instance, shareholders have received an average annual return of 9.5 percent for each of the past four years.

The Wall Street Journal publishes long-term total returns for several time periods. On Tuesdays, it lists 4-week and 1-year performances. On Wednesdays, it reports 13-week and 3-year results. On Thursdays, it lists 26-week and 4-year performances. On Fridays, it prints 39-week and

5-year results. By looking at how a fund has performed over various time periods, you will get a better sense of the consistency of its performance.

5.   **R** stands for ranking, which indicates how each fund's total return performance ranks for the longest time period published that day. Funds are separated into five groups: **A** funds finish in the top 20 percent for their investment objective for a particular time period; **B** funds, in the second 20 percent; **C** funds, in the third 20 percent; **D** funds, in the fourth 20 percent; and **E** funds, in the bottom 20 percent. In the example, the Oppenheimer Asset Allocation Fund has an A ranking, meaning its 9.5 percent average annual return over the last four years puts it among the top 20 percent of all stock and bond funds.

In addition to these listings, the *Journal* publishes sales charge and annual expense data every Monday. Under the heading "Maximum Initial Charge," a percentage of up to 8.5 percent will be listed. This means that a sales fee of up to 8.5 percent of the amount you invest will be deducted as a commission to the salesperson.

The *Journal* also lists a total expense ratio. This number represents the total annual operating expenses of the fund, expressed as a percentage of the fund's assets in the prior year. Operating expenses include management fees, 12b-1 distribution fees and other charges levied on shareholders. A figure of 1 percent in this column, for example, means you will automatically be charged an annual fee amounting to 1 percent of your fund's value.

Types of Stock Funds: Choosing the Best for You

Now that you understand the mechanics of buying and monitoring stock funds, it's time to determine which is best for you. As with all investments, before you sink your money into any fund, you should review your financial goals, your risk tolerance level and everything else you assessed in the first chapter of this book. Also, you should place each fund you consider at its appropriate level in the investment pyramid.

The following is a rundown of the different categories of stock funds, separated into the sectors of the investment pyramid.

High-Risk Apex Funds

Aggressive growth funds. These funds buy stocks of fast-growing companies or of other companies that have great capital gains potential. Or they might buy stocks in bankrupt or depressed companies, anticipating a rebound. Such funds often trade stocks frequently in hope of catching small price gains. They are also known as maximum capital gains funds.

Foreign stock funds. These funds buy stocks of corporations based outside of the United States. In addition to the usual forces affecting stock prices, fluctuations in the value of the U.S. dollar against foreign currencies can dramatically affect the price of these funds' shares, particularly over the short term.

Sector funds. Sector funds buy stocks in just one industry or sector of the economy. Some examples would be environmental stocks, oil company shares and stocks in automakers and gold-mining companies. Because these funds are undiversified, they soar or plummet on the fate of the industry in which they invest.

Small-company growth funds. Such growth funds invest in stocks of small companies, typically those having outstanding shares with a total market value of $500 million or less. These companies have enormous growth potential, yet the stocks they invest in are much less established—and therefore riskier—than blue chip stocks.

Special situation funds. These funds often place large bets on a small number of stocks, anticipating a big payoff. The "special situation" the fund manager looks for might be a takeover or a liquidation of the company at a price higher than the shares currently sell for. Some funds offer venture capital financing for privately held firms, hoping to cash in when the companies offer shares to the public in the future.

Moderate-Risk Sector Funds

Growth funds. Growth funds invest in shares of well-known growth companies that usually have a long history of increasing earnings. Because the stock market fluctuates, growth funds rise and fall over time as well though not as much as funds holding smaller, less proven stocks.

Equity-income funds. Such funds own shares in stocks that pay higher dividends than do growth funds. Whereas a growth fund's payout may be 1 percent or 2 percent, an equity-income fund might yield 4 percent or 5 percent. That higher yield tends to cushion the fund's price when stock prices fall. When stock prices rise, equity-income funds tend to increase less sharply than do pure growth funds. A slightly more aggressive version of an equity-income fund is called a *growth and income fund* or a *total return fund* because it strives for gains from both income and capital appreciation.

Index funds. These funds buy the stocks that make up a particular index to allow investors' returns to match the index. The most popular index used is the Standard & Poor's 500. Proponents of index funds argue that because many money managers fail to match or beat the S&P 500 each year, investors can come out ahead by just matching the index. The management fees of an index fund are much lower than those of a regular stock fund because the fund manager just replicates an index; he or she does not research or make decisions on which stocks to buy and sell.

Option-income funds. These funds buy stocks and write options on the shares, which generate more income for shareholders. This usually results in a higher dividend than growth funds offer. On the other hand, if stock prices rise, the funds lose their position in the stocks because the options are exercised. Therefore, these funds have limited appreciation potential.

Socially conscious funds. Such funds look for companies that meet certain criteria, such as advancing minority and women employees or helping clean up the environment. These funds screen out stocks of companies that are major polluters, defense contractors or promoters of gambling or tobacco. (See the section on socially conscious investing in Chapter 3 for more on these funds.)

Low-Risk Sector Funds

Balanced funds. Balanced funds keep a fairly steady mix of high-yielding stocks and conservative bonds. This allows the funds to pay a fairly high rate of current income and still participate in the long-term growth of stocks.

Flexible portfolio funds. These funds have the latitude to invest in stocks, bonds or cash instruments, depending on the fund manager's market outlook. If he or she thinks stock prices are about to fall, the manager can shift all the fund's assets into cash instruments, thereby avoiding losses. If he or she thinks stock prices are about to rise, the manager can move all the fund's assets into stocks. Usually, the fund will have some money in stocks, bonds and cash, which tends to stabilize its performance. These funds are also known as *asset allocation funds.*

Utilities funds. Such funds buy shares in electric, gas, telephone and water utilities. Because all these companies are regulated monopolies, they have steady earnings and pay high dividends. Utilities funds are subject to swings in interest rates, however. Nonetheless, for a high-yielding and relatively stable stock fund, it's hard to beat a utilities fund.

Another way to look at this trade-off between risk and return is illustrated in the dial in Figure 4.4.

Selecting a Fund Within a Category

Once you have chosen the fund category that fits your needs, you must narrow your options further by looking at the best funds within the category.

Performance. The first criterion in selecting a particular fund is *performance.* You want to choose a fund that has established a solid long-term record of achieving its objectives. It is also preferable if the fund has had the same manager for a long time so that you can be assured that the fund's style will remain consistent.

Several independent fund-monitoring organizations rank fund performance. The two biggest and best known are Lipper Analytical Services (74 Trinity Pl., New York, NY 10006; 212-393-1300) and Morningstar (225 West Wacker Dr., Chicago, IL 60606; 800-876-5005). Results from both are published regularly in *The Wall*

Figure 4.4
Trading Risk for Return: A Mutual Fund Dial

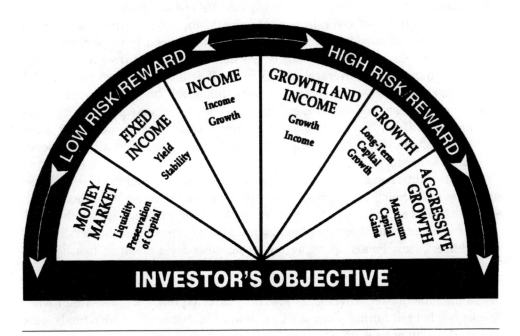

Source: *The Investor's Guide to Low-Cost Mutual Funds.* Reprinted by permission of The Mutual Fund Education Alliance.

Street Journal, USA Today and *Investor's Business Daily,* as well as *Money* magazine and other reputable personal finance journals. You can also track fund performance in the many newsletters that follow this action. The names, addresses and telephone numbers of these newsletters are listed at the end of this chapter.

The best measure of fund performance is called *total return.* This combines all dividends and capital gains distributions with changes in a fund's price. It is a far better yardstick to use when comparing funds than just the change in a fund's price over a period of time. The listings for total return you will see from the ratings services and in the media normally show a fund's results thus far in the current year, over the last 52 weeks and over the last three, five and ten years. They will also refer to the *average annual return,* which is the averaging of returns over longer periods of time. Any average annual return of more than 15 percent for at least five years is considered exemplary.

In choosing a fund, you should feel comfortable with its *style.* What exactly *is* a fund's style? It is a methodology of selecting stocks that differentiates one fund from another. Some styles work well at certain points in a stock market cycle, while others take over as the stock market changes. The two broadest kinds of stock-choosing styles are growth and value. *Growth* refers to selecting stocks with ever-rising earnings, while *value* means buying stocks temporarily out of favor that the manager expects will become popular again. Therefore, you can often determine a fund's style by its name. For instance, the Kemper Growth Fund is a classic growth stock fund, while the T. Rowe Price Small-Cap Value Fund looks for small stocks that are currently out of favor. In general, growth stocks shine when the economy is well into an economic recovery, while value stocks tend to outperform others when the economy is in recession or is just starting to emerge from a recession.

It is difficult for the average investor, as well as the Wall Street professional, to evaluate whether growth or value stock funds are on the upswing at any particular moment. For that reason, the best long-term strategy is to diversify among styles. If half your holdings are in growth stocks and the other half are in value stocks, you will perform better over time than if you invest all your money in one style of stock.

Another difference in investment styles is based on whether the fund manager makes *market timing* decisions. A fund run by a market timer, even though it is a stock fund, can sell most or all of its stocks if the manager senses the stock market is about to tumble. This fund is designed to protect shareholders' capital from huge losses. Funds operating under the other style maintain that it is impossible to time the stock market's ups and downs, so it is best to be nearly fully invested in stocks at all times. These funds will be more volatile than funds that try to time the market. This means that fully invested funds will rise faster when stocks rise but fall further when stocks tumble. The managers of such funds leave the market timing to you.

Convenience. The second criterion you should use to choose a fund is convenience. Though you might receive a higher return by having holdings in the top ten funds in ten different fund families, the recordkeeping and headaches in following so many funds are most likely not worth the higher return. It's probably best to find a top-quality fund family or two and keep most of your capital with them. Most families offer consolidated statements, meaning you can see all of your fund holdings on one statement. Also, you will be able to transfer money from one fund to another easily if you keep most of your assets in one place.

You have one way around this problem of proliferating fund families. Several discount brokers, including Charles Schwab, Fidelity and Jack White, allow you to buy almost any mutual fund in any family and keep it in one account. Schwab calls its service the Mutual Fund Marketplace or OneSource; Fidelity calls its equivalent FundsNetwork. For many funds, you pay no loads, transaction fees or commissions. By consolidating all of your fund holdings under one custodian, you can save yourself much frustration and still participate in the best funds.

Quality of service. The quality of the service you receive is also important in choosing a fund family. While most fund complexes offer good service, there are variations. Following are a few services that top fund groups offer. You should have access to each of them.

- *Automated phone answering systems* that can give you prices, yields and other information about your funds, as well as allow you to make transactions. In many cases, these systems operate 24 hours a day, seven days a week.

- *Knowledgeable and helpful telephone service representatives.* Remember that phone reps at no-load funds will describe funds but will not advise you on which fund to buy. Some large fund companies have walk-in investor centers in large cities where you can discuss your investing needs with a fund representative in person.

- *Easy-to-read statements.* You should not have to be a lawyer or mutual fund expert to be able to make sense of your statement. It should clearly spell out how many shares you have, how many shares you bought or sold in your latest transactions, the yields on your funds and other relevant data. Most funds will calculate your *cost basis,* which is the amount of money you spent to buy your shares. That can be quite complex to ascertain on your own if you have been buying shares with reinvested dividends and capital gains for years. You will need your cost basis to determine the amount of taxes you owe when you sell fund shares.

Once you have opened an account with a fund that meets your criteria, hold onto it unless its performance starts to deteriorate, its fees shoot up, its star manager leaves, its style changes dramatically or you have some other major reason to sell the fund. That includes, of course, a change in your financial situation or your stage in the life cycle. Otherwise, continue to add to the fund and watch it grow!

Closed-End Mutual Funds

So far, all of our discussion of mutual funds has pertained to open-end funds. Another variety of fund is called a *closed-end fund,* which has its own advantages and disadvantages.

Like open-end funds, closed-end funds offer the advantages of professional management, diversification, convenience and automatic reinvestment of dividends and capital gains.

The difference between the two types of funds comes in the way they sell shares. Open-end funds create new shares continually, as more money is invested in them. When cash is taken out of the fund, the number of outstanding shares shrinks. The portfolio manager therefore is faced with an ever-changing pool of assets that can be small one month and huge the next. This can make it difficult to manage the fund because millions of dollars usually pour into the fund after it has had a hot record and stock prices are high, and millions leave the fund when it has underperformed the market and stock prices are falling. This pattern of volatile cash flow can severely harm the fund's performance because the manager is forced to buy stocks when prices are high and sell them when prices are low.

Closed-end funds are designed to avoid this problem. Instead of constantly creating and redeeming shares, these funds issue a limited number of shares, which trade on the New York or American Stock Exchange or on the Nasdaq National Market System. Instead of dealing with the fund company directly when you buy or sell shares, as you do with open-end funds, you trade closed-end shares with other investors, just as you do any publicly traded stock. You pay standard brokerage commissions to buy and sell them, and you can look up the fund's price in the stock tables of the newspaper every day.

From the closed-end fund manager's point of view, there is no need to worry about huge flows of cash into and out of the fund. The manager knows how much money he or she must invest and selects stocks based on the fund's investment objective. This allows the manager to concentrate on meeting long-term objectives because he or she does not have to keep a stash of cash around to meet redemptions.

Like an open-end fund, a closed-end fund always has a certain NAV (the worth of all the stocks in its portfolio divided by the number of shares). But unlike an open-end fund, a closed-ender can sell for more or less than the value of its portfolio, depending on demand for the shares.

When the fund sells for more than its portfolio is currently worth, that is called *selling at a premium.* This usually happens when the fund is extremely popular and it offers some unique style or investing niche, which make investors willing to pay a high price for it. For example, the Korea Fund, which was the only fund granted permission to invest in fast-growing Korea by the Korean government, soared to a 100 percent premium at one point because investors had no other way of investing in Korea. That means that investors were willing to pay $20 a share—or double the $10 that the underlying portfolio of Korean stocks was worth. Another reason a fund might sell at a premium is that it is named after a famous money manager with a good track record, so brokers actively sell it. Funds that meet this description include the Gabelli Fund, the Templeton Emerging Markets Fund and the Zweig Fund.

In general, closed-end funds tend to jump to premiums immediately after they first issue shares to the public because the brokerage firms that underwrite the issues actively promote them for a few months. Often, once the brokers have moved on to the next closed-end issue, the older funds drop to a discount. The moral of the story: It almost never pays to buy a new issue of a closed-end fund.

On the other hand, a fund investing in an unpopular category of stocks can fall to a steep discount. For example, the Brazil Fund dropped to a 35 percent discount when the country was suffering through a bout of political scandals and hyperinflation. That means a buyer paid only $6.50 per share, or 65 percent of the $10 value of the Brazilian stock portfolio. Closed-end funds can also drop to discounts because few people pay attention to them and, therefore, there is little demand for them. That can provide an opportunity to buy assets cheaply. In fact, if a fund's discount remains too deep for too long a time, raiders will often swoop in. Their game is to buy millions of shares at a discount, then force a vote to convert the fund from closed-end to open-end status. Because open-end funds always trade at the worth of their underlying portfolios, the raiders can walk off with huge profits.

Therefore, you should assess two factors when you buy a closed-end fund. The first is the fund manager's record in choosing winning stocks that allow the fund to achieve its investment objective. The second factor is whether you are buying the fund at a premium or a discount. Some investors' entire strategy with closed-end funds is to buy them at a discount and wait for them to rise to a premium, at which point they sell.

To determine whether a fund is selling at a premium or a discount, you can look in Monday's *Wall Street Journal* in the "Money and Investing" section or in *Barron's*. A sample table, along with an explanation of each column, follows.

Fund[1]	Stock Exchange[2]	Net Asset Value[3]	Stock Price[4]	% Difference[5]
Baker Fentress Fund	AMEX	$9.00	$10.00	+11%
China Fund	NYSE	$13.00	$10.00	−23%

Source: Reprinted by permission of *The Wall Street Journal,* © 1993 Dow Jones & Company, Inc. All Rights Reserved Worldwide.

1. Column 1 lists the name of the fund. Funds are broken down alphabetically by categories, such as diversified funds, specialized equity funds and bond funds.

2. The second column notes the exchange where the fund's shares are traded. In the example, Baker Fentress shares trade on the American Stock Exchange, and the China Fund trades on the New York Stock Exchange.

3. The *NAV* is the total per-share worth of the underlying portfolio of securities on this day. In the example, all of the stocks in the Baker Fentress Fund, divided by the number of fund shares, are worth $9 per mutual fund share.

4. The *stock price* is the dollar amount that the fund currently sells for on the New York or American Stock Exchange.

5. The *difference* is the percentage difference between the stock price and the NAV. In the example, the Baker Fentress Fund is trading at an 11 percent premium, while the China Fund is selling at a 23 percent discount.

There are several kinds of closed-end funds, each with its own objective and risk characteristics. Some of the most common types follow.

Balanced funds. Balanced funds buy a mix of stocks and bonds to provide shareholders with both capital appreciation and hefty dividends. They are for conservative investors.

Diversified equity funds. These funds buy a portfolio of stocks in many industries. If the fund manager is bearish (the manager thinks that the stock prices are about to fall), though, the fund can hold cash or some bonds. The objective of diversified equity funds is usually growth.

Dual-purpose funds. Such funds require two classes of shares. One class, called *capital shares,* is designed for capital appreciation; and the other, called *income shares,* is designed to provide high current income. Capital shareholders receive all the changes in the value of the fund's portfolio, and income shareholders receive all investment income from dividends and interest.

International funds. International funds buy stocks in countries around the world. Their prices are therefore affected not only by changes in stock prices but also by fluctuations of foreign currencies against the U.S. dollar. Some international funds specialize in a particular area of the world, like Europe or Asia. Some specialize in stocks of developing countries. Some funds buy stocks in a particular industry, like health care or telecommunications, on a worldwide basis.

Single-country funds. Such funds invest in the stocks of a single country. This makes them more volatile than broadly diversified international funds. For example, on the euphoria about the possibilities of German reunification, the Germany Fund shot up sharply to a huge premium after the Berlin Wall fell. A few years later, when it was clear that reunification would take longer and be more costly than expected, shares in the Germany Fund fell to a deep discount.

Using Your Computer to Pick Mutual Funds

The World Wide Web provides a great resource to help you pick and monitor a mutual fund portfolio. By tapping into several of the Web sites listed in the Resources section of this chapter, you can screen databases of funds, such as the one maintained by Morningstar, to identify funds that meet your investment objectives. For example, you could search for funds with the highest long-term total return that take the lowest risk. Or if you are an income investor, you can search for funds with the highest, safest yields. You also can identify funds with low expense ratios, which automatically gives you an advantage over buying high-expense funds. Once you have identified funds that sound promising, you can go to their Web sites to find out more detail and even ask for applications and prospectuses online. Many mutual funds, and discount brokers offering mutual funds, make it easy to buy shares right from your computer.

By participating in online discussions and chat groups, you may be able to pick up useful information on good mutual funds. Be careful, however, to know who is in these groups and what their hidden agendas and levels of expertise may be. Two good places to look for chat groups are the Mutual Funds section of America Online and the various discussion groups hosted by major personal finance magazines such as *Money, Mutual Funds Magazine, Smart Money* and *Worth.*

Once you have opened an account with a mutual fund company, you can use its Web page to monitor the value of your holdings and receive information on how the fund is doing and what its current investment strategy is. Many mutual fund company Web sites also have extremely helpful tools to help you in all areas of personal finance, such as calculators to help you figure out your financial needs in retirement, or the pros and cons of rolling over money from a regular IRA to a Roth IRA. You also can ask your mutual fund questions online, such as how to calculate your cost basis if you have been reinvesting dividends and capital gains for years.

The profusion of thousands of mutual funds may at first make it seem more difficult than ever to pick the funds that are right for you. But adept use of your computer for research and portfiolio monitoring may make your job of fund-picking significantly easier.

For both beginning and sophisticated investors, there is probably no better way to set up a diversified portfolio than through mutual funds. Both open and closed-end funds offer many services at reasonable cost. The wide array of choices of different types of funds means that there is a fund for every investing need you may ever have, from the most aggressive to the most conservative. Millions of share-holders who have studied about and invested in funds are satisfied with their holdings. With the explanation of mutual funds provided by this chapter, you should now feel confident about choosing the best fund for your situation.

Resources

For further information on stock mutual funds, we recommend that you con-sult the following list of resources. It includes the names, addresses and telephone numbers, where applicable, of books, newsletters, software, major fund compa-nies, ratings services and trade associations. The fund companies will provide a list of their funds, along with such data as current performance and fees.

There are several ways to follow the action in closed-end funds. Some bro-kerage house analysts issue research reports on the funds, and you will spot occasional stories about closed-end funds in financial newspapers and magazines. For more in-depth coverage, consult those books and newsletters in the following list written specifically about closed-end funds.

BOOKS ABOUT STOCK MUTUAL FUNDS

Bogle On Mutual Funds: New Perspectives for the Intelligent Investor, by John C. Bogle (McGraw-Hill, Order Dept., 860 Taylor Station Rd., Blacklick, OH 43004; 800-722-4726; www.mcgraw-hill.com). Bogle, the founder and chairman of the Van-guard mutual funds group, gives sage advice on setting up a portfolio of funds to meet investment objectives, spotting excessive fees and false advertising claims, and inter-preting mutual fund data.

Building Wealth with Mutual Funds, by John H. Taylor (McGraw-Hill, Order Dept., 860 Taylor Station Rd., Blacklick, OH 43004; 800-722-4726; www.mcgraw-hill.com). Offers a step-by-step approach to investing in mutual funds. Covers, among other topics, international investing, index funds, variable annuity funds and socially responsible investing.

Business Week's Guide to Mutual Funds, by Jeffrey M. Laderman (McGraw-Hill, Order Dept., 860 Taylor Station Rd., Blacklick, OH 43004; 800-722-4726; www. mcgraw-hill.com). A comprehensive guide to mutual funds, using *Business Week*'s Scoreboard system, which shows how every type of fund performed over the last year, five years and ten years. Also describes each fund's risk levels, objectives, management, fees and largest stock holdings.

CDA Wiesenberger Mutual Funds Update (CDA Wiesenberger, 1355 Piccard Dr., Suite 220, Rockville, MD 20850; 800-232-2285). A detailed monthly compilation of mutual fund performance statistics.

The Fidelity Guide to Mutual Funds, by Mary Rowland (Simon & Schuster, 1230 Avenue of the Americas, New York, NY 10020; 212-698-7000; www.simon&schuster. com). A well-written guide to selecting top-performing mutual funds.

The Handbook for No-Load Fund Investors, by Sheldon Jacobs (McGraw-Hill, Order Dept., 860 Taylor Station Rd., Blacklick, OH 43004; 800-722-4726; www.mcgraw-hill.com). The definitive guide to mutual funds that do not levy sales commissions.

How To Buy Mutual Funds the Smart Way, by Stephen Littauer (Dearborn Financial Publishing, 155 N. Wacker Dr., Chicago, IL 60606; 312-836-4400; 800-322-8621; www.dearborn.com). A thorough introduction to mutual funds for the financial do-it-yourselfer who likes to be in control, reduce costs and rely on his or her own judgment.

How To Select Top-Performing Mutual Fund Investments, by Aaron H. Coleman and David H. Coleman (McGraw-Hill, Order Dept., 860 Taylor Station Rd., Blacklick, OH 43004; 800-722-4726; www.mcgraw-hill.com). Outlines mutual fund strategies and gives tips for choosing winners and avoiding losers. Also presents extensive data on mutual fund performance.

The Individual Investor's Guide to No-Load Mutual Funds (American Association of Individual Investors, 625 N. Michigan Ave., Suite 1900, Chicago, IL 60611; 312-280-0170; www.aaii.com). A comprehensive listing of all mutual funds not charging sales commissions. Also provides useful guidance on buying mutual funds.

Investing for a Lifetime: Paul Merriman's Guide to Mutual Fund Strategies, by Paul Merriman (McGraw-Hill, Order Dept., 860 Taylor Station Rd., Blacklick, OH 43004; 800-722-4726; www.mcgraw-hill.com). A lucid book that will guide you through the many strategies for investing in mutual funds.

Kurt Brouwer's Guide to Mutual Funds: How To Invest with the Pros, by Kurt Brouwer (John Wiley & Sons, 605 Third Ave., New York, NY 10158; 212-850-6000; www.wiley.com). A good book explaining how mutual funds work and the best strategies for buying and selling them.

Mutual Fund Directory (McGraw-Hill, Order Dept., 860 Taylor Station Rd., Blacklick, OH 43004; 800-722-4726; www.mcgraw-hill.com). A listing of most major mutual funds, with their features and services. Provides no performance data.

The Mutual Fund Encyclopedia, by Gerald W. Perritt (Dearborn Financial Publishing, 155 N. Wacker Dr., Chicago, IL 60606; 312-836-4400; 800-322-8621; www. dearborn.com). A complete annual listing of mutual fund performance and services.

Mutual Fund Performance Guide (Charles Schwab & Co., P.O. Box 7780, San Francisco, CA 94120-7780; 800-526-8600; www.schwab.com). A quarterly report with long-term performance data on many mutual funds.

Mutual Funds Sourcebook (Morningstar, 225 W. Wacker Dr., Chicago, IL 60606; 800-876-5005; 312-424-4288; www.morningstar.net). An enormous volume with full descriptions of most mutual funds.

Straight Talk about Mutual Funds, by Dian Vujovich (McGraw-Hill, Order Dept., 860 Taylor Station Rd., Blacklick OH 43004; 800-722-4726; www.mcgraw-hill.com). A primer on the basics of mutual funds.

The Ultimate Mutual Fund Guide: 17 Experts Pick the 46 Top Funds You Should Own, by Warren Boroson (McGraw-Hill, Order Dept., 860 Taylor Station Rd., Blacklick, OH 43004; 800-722-4726; www.mcgraw-hill.com). Identifies the best mutual funds according to leading fund experts in all major categories, including money-market, stock, bond and sector funds. Presents performance data and an interview with the fund manager for each of the highlighted funds.

BOOKS ABOUT CLOSED-END MUTUAL FUNDS

Herzfeld's Guide to Closed-End Funds, by Thomas J. Herzfeld (McGraw-Hill, Order Dept., 860 Taylor Station Rd., Blacklick, OH 43004; 800-722-4726; www. mcgraw-hill.com). A thorough review of everything you need to know to profit in closed-end funds. Profiles more than 300 fund portfolios and provides statistical analysis and rankings for most closed-end funds.

Investing in Closed-End Funds: Finding Value and Building Wealth, by Albert Freedman and George Cole Scott (New York Institute of Finance, 2 Broadway, 5th Floor, New York, NY 10004-2283; 212-859-5000; 800-227-6943; www.nyif.com). A more sophisticated overview of strategies for buying and selling closed-end funds.

The Thomas J. Herzfeld Encyclopedia of Closed-End Funds, by Thomas J. Herzfeld (Thomas J. Herzfeld & Co., P.O. Box 161465, Miami, FL 33116; 305-271-1900). An annual book filled with detail on the performance of all closed-end funds, along with strategies for buying and selling funds.

NEWSLETTERS ABOUT STOCK MUTUAL FUNDS

All Star Funds (P.O. Box 203427, Austin, TX 78720; 800-299-4223)

Asset Allocator (2408 Chestnut St., Joliet, IL 60435; 800-850-1522)

Cabot's Mutual Fund Navigator (P.O. Box 3067, Salem, MA 01970; 508-745-5532; www.cabotm.com)

CDA Mutual Fund Report (CDA Investment Technologies, 1355 Piccard Dr., Rockville, MD 20850; 301-975-9600; www.cda.com)

The Chartist Mutual Fund Timer (P.O. Box 758, Seal Beach, CA 90740; 310-596-2385)

Czeschin's Mutual Fund Outlook and Recommendations (P.O. Box 1423, Baltimore, MD 21203-1423; 410-235-0983)

Equity Fund Outlook (P.O. Box 76, Boston, MA 02117; 617-397-6844)

Fabian Premium Investment Resource (P.O. Box 2538, Huntington Beach, CA 92647; 800-950-8765)

Fidelity Forecaster (Institute for Econometric Research, 2200 SW 10th St., Deerfield Beach, FL 33442; 800-442-9000)

Fidelity Independent Advisor (P.O. Box 387, Williamstown, MA 01267; 800-548-3797)

Fidelity Insight (Mutual Fund Investors Association, 20 William St., P.O. Box 9135, Wellesley Hills, MA 02180; 800-444-6342)

Fidelity Monitor (P.O. Box 1270, Rocklin, CA 95677; 800-397-3094; www.fidelitymonitor.com)

Fund Exchange (1200 Westlake Ave. N., Suite 700, Seattle, WA 98109; 800-423-4893; www.paulmerriman.com)

Fund Kinetics (2841 23rd Ave. W., Seattle, WA 98199; 800-634-6790)

Fundline (P.O. Box 663, Woodland Hills, CA 91365; 818-346-5637)

FundNet Insight (Mutual Fund Investors Association, 20 William St., Wellesley Hills, MA 02181; 617-369-2500)

Fund Profit Alert (P.O. Box 46709, Cincinnati, OH 45246; 800-327-8833; www. optionresearch.com)

Gerald Perritt's Mutual Fund Letter (12514 Stancey Rd., Largo, FL 33773; 800-326-6941)

Graphic Fund Forecaster (6 Pioneer Circle, P.O. Box 673, Andover, MA 01810; 800-532-2322)

Growth Fund Guide (P.O. Box 6600, Rapid City, SD 57709; 605-341-1971)

Hot Funds Analyst (107 Edinburgh S., Suite 207, Cary, NC 27511; 919-461-3960)

Independent Adviser for Vanguard Investors (Fund Family Shareholder Association, 7811 Montrose Rd., Potomac, MD 20854; 800-777-5005)

Investech Mutual Fund Advisor (2472 Birch Glen, Whitefish, MT 59937; 406-862-7777; 800-955-8500; www.investech.com)

Louis Rukeyser's Mutual Funds Newsletter (1750 Old Meadow Rd., Suite 300, McLean, VA 22102; 800-892-9702)

Morningstar Mutual Funds (225 W. Wacker Dr., Chicago, IL 60606; 312-424-4288; www.morningstar.com)

The Mutual Fund Advisor (One Sarasota Tower, Two North Tamiami Trail, Suite 602, Sarasota, FL 34236; 941-954-5500; www.wallstreetdigest.com)

Mutual Fund Forecaster (Institute for Econometric Research, 2200 SW 10th St., Deerfield Beach, FL 33442; 954-421-1000; 800-442-9000; www.mfmag.com)

Mutual Fund Guide (Commerce Clearing House, 4025 W. Peterson Ave., Chicago, IL 60646; 312-583-8500; www.cch.com)

Mutual Fund Letter (12514 Starkey Rd., Largo, FL 34643; 813-585-3801; 800-326-6941; www.mutletter.com)

Mutual Fund Specialist (Royal R. LeMier & Co., P.O. Box 1025, Eau Claire, WI 54702; 715-834-7425)

Mutual Funds Magazine (Institute for Econometric Research, 2200 SW 10th St., Deerfield Beach, FL 33442-8799; 954-421-1000; 800-442-9000)

Mutual Fund Strategist (P.O. Box 446, Burlington, VT 05402; 802-658-3513; 800-355-3863)

Mutual Fund Technical Trader (P.O. Box 4560, 1971 Spear St., Burlington, VT 05406; 802-864-3128)

Mutual Fund Timer (P.O. Box 6275, Jacksonville, FL 32236; 904-693-0355)

Mutual Fund Values (Morningstar, 225 W. Wacker Dr., Chicago, IL 60606; 312-424-4288; www.morningstar.net)

No-Load Fund Analyst (4 Orinda Way, Suite 230D, Orinda, CA 94563; 510-254-9017)

No-Load Fund Investor (P.O. Box 318, Irvington-on-Hudson, NY 10533; 914-693-7420; 800-252-2042; www.adpad.com)

NoLoad Fund*X (235 Montgomery St., Suite 662, San Francisco, CA 94104; 415-986-7979; 800-763-8639; www.investools.com)

No-Load Mutual Fund Selections and Timing Newsletter (100 N. Central Expressway, Suite 1112, Richardson, TX 75080-5328; 800-800-6563)

No-Load Portfolios (8635 W. Sahara, Suite 420, The Lakes, NV 89117; 702-871-4710)

Jay Schabacker's Mutual Fund Investing (Phillips Publishing, 7811 Montrose Rd., Potomac, MD 20854; 301-340-2100; 800-777-5005; www.phillips.com)

Sector Funds Newsletter (P.O. Box 270048, San Diego, CA 92198; 619-748-0805)

Switch Fund Timing (P.O. Box 25430, Rochester, NY 14625; 716-385-3122)

Telephone Switch Newsletter (2100 Main St., Suite 300, Huntington Beach, CA 92648-2489; 800-950-8765)

United Mutual Fund Selector (101 Prescott St., Wellesley Hills, MA 02181-7528; 617-235-0900)

Value Line Mutual Funds Survey (220 E. 42nd St., New York, NY 10017; 800-634-3583)

Vantage Point: An Independent Report for Vanguard Investors (2927 West Liberty Ave., Suite 195, Pittsburgh, PA 15216; 412-594-4749)

NEWSLETTERS ABOUT CLOSED-END MUTUAL FUNDS

Closed-End Country Fund Report (725 15th St., N.W., Suite 501, Washington, DC 20005; 202-783-7051)

Closed-End Fund Digest (1224 Coast Village Circle, Suite 11, Santa Barbara, CA 93108; 805-565-5651; 800-282-2335)

Investor's Guide to Closed-End Funds (Thomas J. Herzfeld Advisors, P.O. Box 161465, Miami, FL 33116; 305-271-1900)

SOFTWARE AND WEB SITES

Closed-End Fund Investor A comprehensive site focusing on closed-end funds. It provides profiles, charts, holdings and reports on hundreds of funds. There is also a tutorial on how to invest in closed-end funds. www.icefi.com

Fundlink A site loaded with information about mutual fund investing, such as a glossary of terms and a list of frequently asked questions about funds. You also are provided with many links to hundreds of other mutual fund resources on the World Wide Web. www.webcom.com/~fundlink

Fundscape A service allowing you to update data about your mutual fund holdings. You can calculate the value of your portfolio and your rates of return in a series of customized reports. www.fundscape.com

INVESTools A large part of this comprehensive investing Web site is devoted to mutual funds. It offers access to the Morningstar OnDemand service, in which you can screen thousands of mutual funds by their track records, Morningstar star rating, investment objective and other measures. www.investools.com

Investors Alliance Personal Computer Mutual Fund Databank (P.O. Box 11209, 219 E. Commercial Blvd., Fort Lauderdale, FL 33339-1209; 954-491-5100). A program loaded with data on thousands of mutual funds. Allows you to search for the best-performing mutual funds that meet your criteria.

Manhattan Analytics A sophisticated Web site to help pick mutual funds. The company offers Monocle software to help you track fund performance, screen for funds meeting your criteria and keep track of tax liabilities in fund portfolios. www. manhattanlink.com

Mutual Funds Magazine Online The Institute for Econometric Research offers many tools to pick mutual funds. There is access to current and back issues of *Mutual Funds Magazine.* The site also features extensive performance rankings, fund profiles and screening capability. www.mfmag.com

Mutual Fund Investor's Center Sponsored by the Mutual Fund Education Alliance, a group of no-load fund families, this site is designed to educate you about how to invest in mutual funds. It also provides links to the Web sites of all the Alliance's member fund groups. www.mfea.com

NetWorth One of the most comprehensive mutual fund sites on the Internet. It provides complete information on many fund families, including performance, fees, prospectuses and Morningstar profiles. Users can access the Morningstar screening tool to identify funds that meet their investment objectives. Fund prices also can be graphed over different time periods. The site is part of the Quicken Financial Network, and it also includes numerous tools to track and analyze individual stocks. networth.galt.com

100% No-Load Mutual Fund Council This is the Web site for mutual funds that do not charge any front-end, back-end or marketing fees. The site provides a directory of member fund companies and facts and figures about each fund. There is also a great deal of educational material about mutual fund investing. www.galt.com/www.home/mutual/100/

MUTUAL FUND COMPANIES

Most mutual fund firms offer Web sites that provide information about the company's funds and often far more. If you have an account with a fund family, you can look up how many shares you own, how much you have invested in them and the value of your holdings. Some sites allow you to buy and sell shares online. Funds provide a large amount of educational material about asset allocation, how funds are taxed, profiles of fund managers, commentary on the state of the economy and the stock and bond markets, and much more. Here is a list of all the major mutual fund companies, along with their addresses, phone numbers and Web sites (if they have one):

AAL Mutual Funds (222 W. College Ave., Appleton, WI 54913-8004; 414-734-5721; 800-553-6319; www.aal.org)

AARP Funds (42 Longwater Dr., Norwell, MA 02061; 800-253-2277; www.scudder.com)

ABT Funds (340 Royal Palm Way, Palm Beach, FL 33480; 561-655-7255; 800-553-7838)

Achievement Funds Trust (One Freedom Valley Dr., Oaks, PA 19456; 800-472-0577)

Acorn Funds (227 W. Monroe St., Suite 3000, Chicago, IL 60606; 800-922-6769)

Advantus Funds (400 Robert St. N., St. Paul, MN 55101; 800-443-3677)

AEGON USA Managed Portfolios (4333 Edgewood Rd., N.E., Cedar Rapids, IA 52499; 319-398-8511)

Aetna Mutual Funds (151 Farmington Ave., Hartford, CT 06156; 203-273-2843; 800-367-7732; www.aetna.com)

AIM Funds Group (AIM Funds Services, P.O. Box 4739, Houston, TX 77210-4739; 713-626-1919; 800-959-4246; 800-457-0630; 800-347-1919; www.aimfunds.com)

Alger Funds (75 Maiden Lane, New York, NY 10038; 212-806-8800; 800-992-3863; www.algerfund.com)

Alliance Funds (1345 6th Ave., New York, NY 10105; 212-969-1000; 800-221-5672; www.alliancecapital.com)

ALLMERICA (ALLMERICA Financial Corp., 4400 Computer Dr., Westboro, MA 01581; 800-628-0414; www.allmerica.com)

American Century Funds (4500 Main St., Kansas City, MO 64111; 800-345-2021; 816-531-5575; www.americancentury.com)

American Express Financial Advisors (IDS Tower 10, Minneapolis, MN 55440; 800-328-8300)

American Funds Distributors (333 S. Hope St., Los Angeles, CA 90071; 800-421-0180)

American General Funds (2929 Allen Pkwy., Houston, TX 77019; 713-526-5251)

American Investors Funds (44 Wall St., 2nd Floor, New York, NY 10005; 212-495-4105; 800-677-4400—closed-end funds only; www.dhblair.com)

American National Funds (One Moody Plaza, Galveston, TX 77550; 800-231-4639)

American Odyssey Funds (Two Tower Center, East Brunswick, NJ 08816; 908-214-2000)

American Performance Funds (BISYS Fund Services, 3435 Stelzer Rd., Columbus, OH 43219-3035; 800-762-7085)

American Skandia Trust (One Corporate Dr., Shelton, CT 06484; 800-628-6039)

AmeriPrime Funds (1793 Kingswood Dr., Suite 200, Southlake, TX 76092; 800-298-1995)

AmSouth Mutual Funds (3435 Stelzer Rd., Columbus, OH 43219; 800-451-8382)

Anchor Pathway Funds (733 Third Ave., New York, NY 10017; 800-858-8850)

Aquila Group (380 Madison Ave., Suite 2300, New York, NY 10017; 212-697-6666; 800-762-5955; www.aquilafunds.com)

Aquinas Funds (5310 Harvest Hill Rd., Suite 248, Dallas, TX 75230; 800-423-6369)

Arbor Funds (One Freedom Valley Dr., Oaks, PA 19456; 800-342-5734)

Arch Funds (3435 Stelzer Rd., Columbus, OH 43219; 800-551-3731)

Ariel Funds (307 N. Michigan Ave., Chicago, IL 60601; 800-29ARIEL)

Ark Funds (One Freedom Valley Dr., Oaks, PA 19456; 800-624-4116)

Artisan Funds (1000 N. Water St., Suite 1770, Milwaukee, WI 53202; 800-399-1770)

ASM Fund (15438 N. Florida St., Suite 107, Tampa, FL 33613; 800-445-2763)

Astra Funds (11400 W. Olympic Blvd., Suite 200, Los Angeles, CA 90064; 800-441-7267)

Atlas Funds (794 Davis St., San Leandro, CA 94577; 800-933-2852; www. atlasfunds.com)

Avesta Funds (P.O. Box 2558, Houston, TX 77252; 713-216-6433)

Bankers Trust Family of Funds (4 Albany St., New York, NY 10006; 800-422-6577)

Bartlett Capital Trust, 36 E. Fourth St., Suite 400, Cincinnati, OH 45202; 513-621-4612; 800-543-0863)

Baron Funds (767 Fifth Ave., New York, NY 10153; 800-99-BARON)

BB&K Funds (950 Tower Lane, Suite 1900, Foster City, CA 94404; 800-882-8383)

BB&T Mutual Funds Group (3435 Stelzer Rd., Columbus, OH 43219; 800-228-1872)

BEA Advisor Funds (153 E. 53rd St., New York, NY 10022; 800-293-1232)

Bear Stearns Funds (245 Park Ave., New York, NY 10167; 800-766-4111)

Benchmark Funds (50 S. LaSalle St., Chicago, IL 60675; 800-621-2550)

Berger Funds (210 University Blvd., Suite 900, Denver, CO 80206; 303-329-0200; 800-333-1001)

Bernstein Funds (767 Fifth Ave., New York, NY 10153; 212-756-4097; www. bernstein.com)

Biltmore Funds (Federated Investors Tower, 1001 Liberty Ave., Pittsburgh, PA 15222; 800-341-7400)

BNY Hamilton Funds (125 W. 55th St., New York, NY 10019; 800-426-9363)

Bramwell Funds (745 Fifth Ave., New York, NY 10151; 800-272-6227)

Bridgeway Funds (5650 Kirby Dr., Suite 141, Houston, TX 77005; 800-661-3550)

Brinson Funds (209 S. LaSalle St., Chicago, IL 60604; 800-448-2430)

Bull & Bear Funds (11 Hanover Square, New York, NY 10005; 212-785-0900; 800-847-4200; www.mutualfunds.net

Calamos Funds (1111 E. Warrenville Rd., Naperville, IL 60563; 800-823-7386)

Calvert Funds (4550 Montgomery Ave., Bethesda, MD 20814; 800-368-2745; www.calvertgroup.com)

Capital Research and Management Funds (333 S. Hope St., Los Angeles, CA 90071; 800-421-0180; www.americanfunds.com)

Capital Value Funds (2203 Grand Ave., Des Moines, IA 50312; 800-798-1819)

Capstone Funds (5847 San Felipe, Suite 4100, Houston, TX 77057; 713-750-8000; 800-262-6631)

Cardinal Family of Funds (155 E. Broad St., Columbus, OH 43215; 800-848-7734)

Carillon Funds (1876 Waycross Rd., Cincinnati, OH 45240; 513-595-2600; 800-999-1840)

CGM Funds (222 Berkeley St., 10th Floor, Boston, MA 02116; 617-737-3225; 800-345-4048; www.cgmfunds.com)

Charles Schwab & Co. (101 Montgomery St., San Francisco, CA 94104; 800-526-8600; www.schwab.com)

Chicago Trust Funds (171 N. Clark St., Chicago, IL 60601; 800-992-8151)

Chubb America Funds (One Granite Place, Concord, NH 03301; 603-224-7741; 800-258-3648)

CitiSelect Funds (153 E. 53rd St., 6th Floor, New York, NY 10022; 800-625-4554)

Citizens Trust (One Harbour Place, Portsmouth, NH 03801; 603-436-5152; 800-223-7010; www.efund.com)

Cohen & Steers Funds (767 Fifth Ave., 27th Floor, New York, NY 10017; 800-437-9912)

College Retirement Equities Fund (CREF) (730 Third Ave., New York, NY 10017; 800-842-2733)

Colonial Funds Group (One Financial Center, Boston, MA 02111-2621; 617-426-3750; 800-225-2365; www.lib.com/colonial/colonial.html)

Columbia Funds (1301 S.W. 5th Ave., Portland, OR 97201-5691; 503-222-3600; 800-547-1707; www.columbiafunds.com)

Commerce Funds (922 Walnut St., Kansas City, MO 64199; 800-993-6365)

Common Sense Trust (2800 Post Oak Blvd., Houston, TX 77056; 800-421-5666)

Compass Capital Group (Compass Capital Funds in care of PFTC, 400 Bellview Pkwy., Wilmington, DE 19809-3710; 800-422-6538; www.compassfunds.com)

Composite Group of Funds (1201 Third Ave., Suite 1400, Seattle, WA 98101; 800-543-8072)

Conseco Mutual Funds (11815 N. Pennsylvania St., Carmel, IN 46032; 800-888-4918)

Countrywide Funds (312 Walnut St., Cincinnati, OH 45202; 800-543-8721)

Coventry Group (3435 Stelzer Rd., Columbus, OH 43219; 800-438-6375)

Cowen Funds (One Financial Sq., New York, NY 10005; 800-262-7116)

Crabbe Huson Funds (121 S.W. Morrison, Portland, OR 97204; 800-541-9732; www.contrarian.com)

Davis Funds (124 E. Marcy St., Santa Fe, NM 87504; 800-279-0279)

Dean Witter Funds (Dean Witter Trust Co., 72nd Floor, 2 World Trade Center, New York, NY 10048; 800-869-6397; www.deanwitter.com)

Delaware-Voyageur Group Funds (1818 Market St., Philadelphia, PA 19103; 800-523-4640)

Diversified Investor's Fund Group (4 Manhattanville Rd., Purchase, NY 10577; 800-666-9800)

DLB Fund Group (David L. Babson & Co., One Memorial Dr., Boston, MA 02142; 888-722-2766)

Dodge & Cox Funds (1 Sansome St., 35th Floor, San Francisco, CA 94104; 800-621-3979)

Dreyfus Mutual Funds (200 Park Ave., New York, NY 10166; 800-645-6561; www.dreyfus.com)

Eaton Vance Funds (24 Federal St., Boston, MA 02110; 617-482-8260; 800-225-6265)

Eclipse Funds (144 E. 30th St., New York, NY 10016; 800-872-2710)

Elfun Funds (3003 Summer St., Stamford, CT 06905; 800-242-0134)

Endeavor Series Trust (2101 East Coast Highway, Suite 300, Corona Del Mar, CA 92625; 714-760-0505; 800-854-8393; www.endeavorgroup.com)

Enterprise Group of Funds (3343 Peach Tree Rd. N.E., Suite 450, Atlanta, GA 30326; 404-261-1116; 800-432-4320; www.enterprisegroup.com)

Evergreen Funds (2500 Westchester Ave., Purchase, NY 10577; 914-694-2020; 800-807-2940; www.evergreenfunds.com)

Excelsior Funds (U.S. Trust Co., 114 W. 47th St., New York, NY 10036; 800-446-1012)

FAM Value Fund (P.O. Box 339, Cobleskill, NY 12043; 800-932-3271)

FBL Series Funds (5400 University Ave., West Des Moines, IA 50266; 515-225-5400; 800-247-4170)

Federated Group of Funds (Federated Investors Tower, Pittsburgh, PA 15222-3779; 412-288-1900; 800-341-7400; www.fedservco.com)

FFTW Funds (200 Park Ave., New York, NY 10166; 800-762-4848)

Fidelity Group of Funds (82 Devonshire St., Boston, MA 02109; 800-544-8888; www.fidelity.com)

59 Wall Street Funds (40 Water St., Boston, MA 02109; 800-625-5759)

First American Funds (One Freedom Valley Dr., Oaks, PA 19456; 800-637-2548)

First Investors Funds (95 Wall St., New York, NY 10005; 212-858-8000; 800-423-4026; www.firstinv.com)

First Pacific Mutual Fund (2756 Woodlawn Dr., Honolulu, HI 96822; 808-988-8088)

Flag Investors Funds (One South St., Baltimore, MD 21202; 800-767-3524)

Flex-Funds (6000 Memorial Dr., Dublin, OH 43017; 614-766-7000; 800-325-FLEX; www.flexfunds.com)

Fortis Funds (P.O. Box 64284, St. Paul, MN 55164; 800-800-2638; www.ffg.us.fortis.com)

Forum Funds (2 Portland Sq., Portland, ME 04101; 800-943-6786)

Founders Funds (2930 E. Third Ave., Denver, CO 80206; 303-394-4404; 800-525-2440; www.founders.com)

Fountain Square Funds (3435 Stelzer Rd., Columbus, OH 43219; 800-554-3862)

FPA Funds (11400 W. Olympic Blvd., Suite 1200, Los Angeles, CA 90064; 800-982-4372)

Franklin/Templeton Group of Funds (777 Mariners Island Blvd., San Mateo, CA 94403-7777; 415-312-2000; 800-632-2180; www.franklin-templeton.com)

Frank Russell Mutual Funds (909 A St., Tacoma, WA 98402; 800-972-0700)

Fremont Mutual Funds (50 Beale St., San Francisco, CA 94105; 800-548-4539)

Fundamental Family of Funds (90 Washington St., New York, NY 10006; 800-225-6864)

FundManager Portfolios (One Beacon St., Boston, MA 02108; 800-638-1896)

Furman Selz (237 Park Ave., New York, NY 10169; 212-808-3900; 800-845-8406; www.furmanselz.com)

Gabelli Funds (One Corporate Center, Rye, NY 10580; 914-921-5100; 800-422-3554; www.gabelli.com)

Galaxy Funds (4400 Computer Dr., Westboro, MA 01581; 800-628-0414)

GAM Funds (135 E. 57th St., New York, NY 10022; 800-426-4685)

Gateway Trust (400 TechneCenter Dr., Suite 220, Milford, OH 45150; 513-248-2700; 800-354-6339)

GCG Funds (280 Park Ave., New York, NY 10017; 800-243-3706)

General Electric Funds (3003 Summer St., Stamford, CT 06905; 800-242-0134)

Gintel Funds (Number 6 Greenwich Office Park, Greenwich, CT 06831; 203-622-6400; 800-243-5808)

Goldman Sachs Funds (4900 Sears Tower, Chicago, IL 60606; 800-621-2550; www.gs.com)

Govett Funds (250 Montgomery St., San Francisco, CA 94104; 800-634-6838)

Gradison Funds (580 Walnut St., Cincinnati, OH 45202; 513-579-5700; 800-869-5999; www.mcdonald.com)

Griffin Funds (5000 Rivergate Rd., Irwindale, CA 91706; 800-676-4450)

G.T. Global Growth Funds (50 California St., 27th Floor, San Francisco, CA 94111; 415-392-6181; 800-824-1580; www.gtglobal.com)

Guiness Flight Investment Funds (225 S. Lake Ave., Pasadena, CA 91101; 800-434-5623)

John Hancock Group of Funds (101 Huntington Ave., Boston, MA 02199-7603; 617-375-1500; 800-225-5291; www.jhancock.com)

Harbor Funds (Harbor Funds c/o Harbor Transfer, One SeaGate, Toledo, Ohio 43666; 419-247-1940; 800-422-1050)

Harris Insight Funds (One Exchange Place, Boston, MA 02109; 800-982-8782)

Hartford Funds (200 Hopmeadow St., Hartford, CT 06104; 800-862-6668)

Heartland Funds (790 N. Milwaukee St., Milwaukee, WI 53202; 800-432-7856)

Heitman Funds (180 N. LaSalle St., Suite 3600, Chicago, IL 60601; 800-435-1405)

Heritage Funds (880 Carillon Pkwy., St. Petersburg, FL 33716; 813-573-8143; 800-421-4184)

Highmark Group of Funds (One Freedom Valley Dr., Oaks, PA 19456; 800-433-6884; www.networth.galt.com/www/hone/mutual/highmark)

Horace Mann Funds (P.O. Box 4657, Springfield, IL 62708-4657; 217-789-2500; 800-999-1030)

HSBC Funds (3435 Stelzer Rd., Columbus, OH 43219; 800-634-2536)

Hudson River Trust (1345 Avenue of the Americas, New York, NY 10105; 800-221-5672)

IAA Trust Funds (808 IAA Dr., Bloomington, IN 61702; 309-557-3222; 800-245-2100; www.iaatrust.com)

IAI Funds (601 Second Ave. S., Minneapolis, MN 55402; 612-376-2700; 800-945-3863; www.iaifunds.com)

ICON Funds (12835 E. Arapahoe Rd., Englewood, CO 80112; 800-828-4881)

IDEX Funds (201 Highland Ave., Building #2, Largo, FL 33770; 813-585-6565; 800-851-9777)

IDS Group of Funds (IDS Tower 10, Minneapolis, MN 55440; 612-671-3131; 800-328-8300)

Independence Capital Group of Funds (600 Dresher Rd., Horsham, PA 19044; 800-818-8184)

Integrity Mutual Funds (1 N. Main St., Minot, ND 58703; 800-562-6637)

INVESCO Advisor Funds (1355 Peachtree St., N.E., Atlanta, GA 30309; 800-241-5477; www.invesco.com)

INVESCO Funds Group (7800 E. Union Ave., Denver, CO 80237; 303-930-6300; 800-525-8085; www.invesco.com)

Ivy MacKenzie Group of Funds (700 S. Federal Hwy., Suite 300, Boca Raton, FL 33432; 800-456-5111)

Janus Group of Funds (100 Fillmore St., Suite 300, Denver, CO 80206; 303-333-3863; 800-525-8983; www.janusfunds.com)

John Hancock Funds (101 Huntington Ave., Boston, MA 02199; 800-225-5291)

Jones and Babson Funds (2440 Pershing Rd., Suite G15KCMO, Kansas City, MO 64108; 816-471-5200; 800-422-2766; www.jbfunds.com)

JNL Series Trust (Jackson National Life, 5901 Executive Dr., Lansing, MI 48909; 800-322-8257)

JPM Pierpont Funds (522 Fifth Ave., New York, NY 10036; 800-766-7722)

Jurika & Voyles Fund Group (1999 Harrison St., Oakland, CA 94612; 800-852-1991)

Kaufmann Fund (140 E. 45th St., New York, NY 10017; 212-922-0123)

Kent Funds (P.O. Box 182201, Columbus, OH 43218; 800-633-5368)

Keystone Family of Funds (200 Berkeley St., Boston, MA 02116; 617-338-3200; 800-343-2898)

Kobren Insight Funds (20 William St., Wellesley Hills, MA 02181; 800-456-2736)

Lancaster Funds (1225 L St., Lincoln, NE 68501; 800-279-7437)

Landmark Funds (153 E. 53rd St., New York, NY 10022; 800-625-4554)

Lazard Funds (30 Rockefeller Plaza, 58th Floor, New York, NY 10020; 800-823-6300)

Lebenthal Funds (120 Broadway, New York, NY 10271; 800-221-5822)

Legends Funds (515 W. Market St., Louisville, KY 40202; 800-634-0142)

Legg Mason Funds (111 S. Calvert St., Baltimore, MD 21203; 800-822-5544; www.leggmason.com)

Lexington Group of Funds (Park 80 West, Plaza Two, Saddle Brook, NJ 07663; 201-845-7300; 800-368-2558)

Longleaf Partners Funds (6075 Poplar Ave., Memphis, TN 38119; 800-445-9469)

Loomis Sayles Funds (600 Fifth Ave., New York, NY 10020; 800-676-6779; www.loomisayles.com)

Lord Abbett Funds (767 5th Ave., General Motors Building, New York, NY 10153; 212-848-1800; 800-223-4224; www.lordabbett.com)

Lutheran Brotherhood Funds (625 4th Ave. S., Minneapolis, MN 55415; 612-339-8091; 800-328-4552; www.luthbro.com)

MainStay Mutual Funds (260 Cherry Hill Rd., Parsippany, NJ 07054; 800-624-6782; 201-331-2000; www.mainstayfunds.com)

Managers Funds (40 Richards Ave., Norwalk, CT 06854; 800-835-3879)

Manning & Napier Funds (P.O. Box 41118, Rochester, NY 14604; 800-466-3863; www.oppenheimerfunds.com)

ManuLife Series Funds (P.O. Box 633, Buffalo, NY 14201-0633; 800-827-4546)

Mariner Funds Trust (700 W. Hillsboro Blvd., Deerfield Beach, FL 33441; 800-826-5439)

Markman MultiFund Trust (6600 France Ave. S., Edina, MN 55435; 800-395-4848)

Marquis Funds (One Freedom Valley Dr., Oaks, PA 19456; 800-342-5734)

MAS Funds (One Tower Bridge, West Conshohocken, PA 19428; 800-354-8185)

Massachusetts Financial Services Funds (500 Boylston St., Boston, MA 02116; 617-954-5000; 800-343-2829; www.mfs.com)

Mass Mutual (1295 State St., Springfield, MA 01111; 800-788-8411; www.massmutual.com)

MassMutual Life Funds (1295 State St., Springfield, MA 01111; 413-788-8411; www.massmutual.com)

Masterworks Funds (111 Center St., Little Rock, AR 72201; 800-458-6589)

Mentor Funds (901 E. Byrd St., Richmond, VA 23219; 800-382-0016)

Meridian Funds (60 E. Sir Francis Drake Blvd., Larkspur, CA 94939; 800-446-6662)

Merrill Lynch Mutual Funds (P.O. Box 9011, Princeton, NJ 08543-9011; 609-282-2800; 800-637-3863; www.ml.com)

Merriman Funds (1200 Westlake Ave. N., Seattle, WA 98109; 800-423-4893)

MIMLIC Funds (400 N. Robert St., 10-4252, St. Paul, MN 55101; 612-223-4252; 800-443-3677; www.minnesotamutual.com)

Monitor Funds (One Freedom Valley Dr., Oaks, PA 19456; 800-342-5734)

Monitrend Mutual Funds (2000 Richard Jones Rd., Suite 123, Nashville, TN 37215; 800-251-1970)

Montgomery Funds (101 California St., San Francisco, CA 94111; 800-572-3863)

MONY Series Funds (1740 Broadway, New York, NY 10019; 800-786-6244)

Morgan Stanley Funds (1251 Avenue of the Americas, New York, NY 10020; 800-548-7786; www.ms.com)

Mosaic Funds (1655 Fort Myer Dr., Arlington, VA 22209; 800-336-3063)

Munder Funds (P.O. Box 9755, Providence, RI 02940; 800-239-3334)

Mutual of America Funds (320 Park Ave., New York, NY 10022; 212-244-1600; 800-468-3785)

Mutual of Omaha Funds (10235 Regency Circle, Omaha, NE 68114; 402-397-8555; 800-228-9596; www.mutualofomaha.com)

NASL Funds (116 Huntington Ave., Boston, MA 02116; 800-344-1029)

Nations Funds (111 Center St., Little Rock, AR 72201; 800-321-7854; www.nationsbank.com/nationsfunds)

Nationwide Funds (P.O. Box 1492, Columbus, OH 43216; 614-249-7855; 800-848-0920; www.nationwide.com)

Navellier Funds (1 E. Liberty, Reno, NV 89501; 800-887-8671)

Neuberger and Berman Funds (605 3rd Ave., 2nd Floor, New York, NY 10158; 212-476-8800; 800-877-9700; www.nbfunds.com)

New England Funds (399 Boylston St., Boston, MA 02116; 617-267-6600; 800-225-7670; www.tne.com)

Nicholas Family of Funds (700 N. Water St., Suite 1010, Milwaukee, WI 53202; 414-272-6133)

Nicholas-Applegate Funds (600 W. Broadway, San Diego, CA 92101; 800-551-8643; www.nacm.com)

Ni Family of Mutual Funds (Numeric Investors, 1 Memorial Dr., Boston, MA 02142; 800-686-3742)

Northern Trust Mutual Funds (50 S. LaSalle St., Chicago, IL 60675; 800-595-9111)

Northstar Funds (Northstar Investment Management Corp., 2 Pickwick Plaza, Greenwich, CT 06830; 800-595-7827)

Nottingham Investment Trust (105 N. Washington St., Rocky Mount, NC 27802; 800-525-3863)

Nuveen Mutual Funds (333 W. Wacker Dr., Chicago, IL 60606; 800-621-7227; www.nuveen.com)

Oberweis Funds (951 Ice Cream Dr., North Aurora, IL 60542; 800-323-6166)

Ohio National Mutual Funds (One Financial Way, Cincinnati, OH 45242; 513-861-3600; 800-578-8078; www.ohionatl.com)

One Group Funds (1111 Polaris Pkwy., Columbus, OH 43271; 614-213-1684; 800-480-4111; www.onegroup.com)

Oppenheimer Funds Family (6803 S. Tucson Way, Englewood, CO 80112; 303-671-3200; 800-525-7048; www.oppenheimerfunds.com)

O'Shaughnessy Funds (60 Arch St., Greenwich, CT 06830; 800-797-0773)

Overland Express Funds (Stephens Bldg., 111 Center St., Little Rock, AR 72201; 501-374-4361; 800-458-6589; www.wellsfargo.com)

Pacific Advisors Funds (206 N. Jackson St., Suite 201, Glendale, CA 91206; 800-989-6693)

Pacific Capital Funds (3435 Stelzer Rd., Columbus, OH 43219; 800-451-8377)

Pacific Financial Research Funds (9601 Wilshire Blvd., Suite 800, Beverly Hills, CA 90210; 800-776-5033)

Pacific Horizons Funds (3435 Stelzer Rd., Columbus, OH 43219; 800-332-3863)

PaineWebber Funds (1285 Avenue of the Americas, New York, NY 10019; 212-713-2000; 800-647-1568; www.painewebber.com)

Papp & Associates Funds (4400 N. 32nd St., Suite 280, Phoenix, AZ 85018; 800-421-4004)

Park Avenue Portfolio Funds (201 Park Ave. S., New York, NY 10003; 800-221-3253)

Parkstone Group of Funds (3435 Stelzer Rd., Columbus, OH 43219; 800-451-8377; www.parkstone.com)

Parnassus Funds (One Market St., San Francisco, CA 94105; 800-999-3505)

Pasadena Group of Mutual Funds (600 N. Rosemead Blvd., Pasadena, CA 91107; 818-351-4276; 800-648-8050; www.secapl.com/rea)

Pax World Fund (222 State St., Portsmouth, NH 03801; 800-767-1729)

Payden & Rygel Funds (333 S. Grand Ave., Los Angeles, CA 90071; 800-5PAYDEN)

PBHG Funds (One Freedom Valley Dr., Oaks, PA 19456; 800-809-8008)

Pegasus Funds (3435 Stelzer Rd., Columbus, OH 43219; 800-688-3350)

Phoenix Duff & Phelps Family of Funds (101 Munson St., Greenfield, MA 01301; 800-243-1574)

Pilgrim America Funds (40 N. Central Ave., Two Renaissance Square, Suite 1200, Phoenix, AZ 85004; 800-331-1080; www.pilgramamerica.com)

Pillar Funds (One Freedom Valley Dr., Oaks, PA 19456; 800-342-5734)

PIMCO Funds (840 Newport Center Dr., Suite 360, Newport Beach, CA 92660; 800-927-4648)

Pioneer Funds (60 State St., Boston, MA 02109, 617-742-7825; 800-225-6292; www.pioneerfunds.com)

Piper Capital Funds (222 S. Ninth St., Piper Jaffray Tower, Minneapolis, MN 55402; 800-866-7778)

Planco Financial Services Funds (16 Industrial Blvd., Suite 201, Paoli, PA 19301; 800-523-7798)

Portico Funds (615 E. Michigan St., Milwaukee, WI 53201; 800-982-8909)

PNC Family of Funds (345 Park Ave., 29th Floor, New York, NY 10154; 212-409-3700; www.pnc.com)

Preferred Group of Funds (100 NE Adams St., Peoria, IL 61629; 800-662-4769)

Primary Trends Funds (700 N. Water St., Milwaukee, WI 53202; 800-443-6544)

Principal Preservation Funds (215 N. Main St., West Bend, WI 53095; 800-826-4600)

Princor Mutual Funds (711 High St., Des Moines, IA 50392; 515-247-5711; 800-247-4123; www.principal.com)

Protective Investment Funds (2801 Hwy. 280 S., Birmingham, AL 35223; 800-627-0220)

Provident Investment Funds (300 N. Lake Ave., Pasadena, CA 91101; 800-618-7643)

Prudential Mutual Funds (One Seaport Plaza, New York, NY 10292; 800-225-1852; www.prusec.com/Prudential/prumutfd.htm)

Putnam Group of Mutual Funds (One Post Office Square, Boston, MA 02109; 617-292-1000; 800-225-2465; www.putnam.inv.com)

Qualivest Funds (3435 Stelzer Rd., Columbus, OH 43219; 800-743-8637)

Quantitative Group of Funds (55 Old Bedford Rd., Lincoln, MA 01773; 800-331-1244)

Rainier Mutual Funds (601 Union St., Suite 2801, Seattle, WA 98101; 800-280-6111)

Reich & Tang Mutual Funds (600 Fifth Ave., New York, NY 10020; 800-676-6779)

Rembrandt Funds (One Freedom Valley Dr., Oaks, PA 19456; 800-443-4725)

Republic Funds (6 St. James Ave., Boston, MA 02116; 800-782-8183)

Rightime Funds (Forst Pavilion, 218 Glenside Ave., Wyncote, PA 19095; 215-887-8111; 800-866-9393; www.rightime.com)

Rimco Funds (1001 Liberty Ave., Pittsburgh, PA 15222; 800-341-7400)

Robertson Stephens Funds (555 California St., San Francisco, CA 94104; 800-766-FUND; www.rsim.com)

Rochester Funds (350 Linden Oaks, Rochester, NY 14625; 716-383-1300; 800-552-1149)

Rodney Square Funds (Rodney Square North, 1100 N. Market St., Wilmington, DE 19890; 302-651-1923; 800-336-9970)

T. Rowe Price Mutual Funds Group (100 E. Pratt St., Baltimore, MD 21202; 410-547-2000; 800-638-7890; www.troweprice.com)

Royce Family of Funds (1414 Avenue of the Americas, New York, NY 10019; 800-221-4268)

Frank Russell Investment Company (909 A St., Tacoma, WA 98402; 206-627-7001; 800-972-0700; www.russell.com)

Rydex Series Trust (6116 Executive Blvd., Suite 400, Rockville, MD 20852; 800-820-0888)

SAFECO Family of Funds (SAFECO Plaza, Seattle, WA 98185; 206-545-7319; 800-426-6730)

Salomon Brothers Funds (Seven World Trade Center, New York, NY 10048; 212-783-7000; 800-725-6666; www.salomon.com)

Saturna Capital Funds (1300 N. State St., Bellingham, WA 98227; 800-728-8762)

Schield Portfolios Series (390 Union Blvd., Suite 410, Denver, CO 80228; 303-985-9999; 800-275-2382; www.smcl.com)

Schroder Fund Advisers (787 Seventh Ave., New York, NY 10019; 800-344-8332)

Charles Schwab Funds (101 Montgomery St., San Francisco, CA 94104; 415-627-7000; 800-526-8600; www.schwab.com)

Scudder Group of Mutual Funds (Two International Pl., Boston, MA 02110; 800-225-2470; www.scudder.com)

Security Benefit Funds Group (700 S.W. Harrison St., 10th Floor, Topeka, KS 66636; 913-295-3127; 800-888-2461; www.securitybenefit.com)

SEI Funds Group (One Freedom Valley Dr., Oaks, PA 19456; 800-342-5734)

Select Advisors Funds (311 Pike St., Cincinnati, OH 45202; 800-669-2796)

Selected Funds (124 E. Marcy St., Santa Fe, NM 87504; 800-279-0279)

Seligman Funds Group (Seligman Mutual Funds, 100 Park Ave., New York, NY 10017; 212-850-1864; 800-221-7844; www.seligman.com)

Seneca Funds (909 Montgomery St., Suite 600, San Francisco, CA 94133; 800-828-1212)

Sentinel Group Funds (One National Life Dr., Montpelier, VT 05604; 802-229-3900; 800-282-3863)

Sessions Group of Funds (3435 Stelzer Rd., Columbus, OH 43219; 800-874-8376)

1784 Funds (One Freedom Valley Rd., Oaks, PA 19456; 800-252-1784)

Sierra Trust Funds (9301 Corbin Ave., Northridge, CA 91324; 800-221-9876)

Sit Mutual Funds (90 S. 7th St., 4600 Norwest Center, Minneapolis, MN 55402; 612-334-5888; 800-332-5580; www.sitfunds.com)

Skyline Funds (311 S. Wacker Dr., Suite 4500, Chicago, IL 60606; 800-458-5222)

Smith Barney Mutual Funds (388 Greenwich St., New York, NY 10013; 212-464-6000; 800-544-7835; www.smithbarney.com)

Smith Breeden Mutual Funds (100 Europa Dr., Suite 200, Chapel Hill, NC 27514; 800-221-3138)

SoGen Funds (1221 Avenue of the Americas, New York, NY 10020; 212-278-5800)

SSgA Funds (2 International Pl., Boston, MA 02110; 800-647-7327)

Stagecoach Funds (111 Center St., Little Rock, AR 72201; 800-222-8222)

Standish, Ayer & Wood Investment Trust (One Financial Center, Boston, MA 02111; 800-221-4795)

State Farm Funds (One State Farm Plaza, D-Z, Bloomington, IL 61710; 309-766-2029)

State Street Research Funds (One Financial Center, 3rd Floor, Boston, MA 02111; 617-357-7800; 800-562-0032; www.ssrm.com)

SteinRoe Mutual Funds (1 S. Wacker Dr., Chicago, IL 60606; 312-368-7700; 800-338-2550; www.steinroe.com)

STI Classic Funds (One Freedom Valley Dr., Oaks, PA 19456; 800-342-5734)

Strategist Mutual Fund Group (IDS Tower 10, Minneapolis, MN 55440; 800-297-7378)

Stratton Mutual Funds (610 W. Germantown Pike, Suite 300, Plymouth Meeting, PA 19462; 800-634-5726)

Strong Capital Management (100 Heritage Reserve, Menomonee Falls, WI 53051; 414-359-3400; 800-368-3863; www.strong-funds.com)

SunAmerica Fund Group (733 3rd Ave., 3rd Floor, New York, NY 10017; 212-551-5100; 800-858-8850; www.sunamerica.com)

Templeton Group of Funds (700 Central Ave., St. Petersburg, FL 33701; 813-823-8712; 800-342-5236; www.franklin-templeton.com)

Third Avenue Value Funds (767 Third Ave., New York, NY 10017; 800-443-1021)

TMK/United Funds (6300 Lamar, Shawnee Mission, KS 66202; 800-366-5465)

Tocqueville Funds (1675 Broadway, New York, NY 10019; 212-698-0800)

Transamerica Premier Funds (1150 S. Olive St., Los Angeles, CA 90015; 213-742-5995; 800-892-7587)

T. Rowe Price Family of Funds Group (100 E. Pratt St., Baltimore, MD 21202; 410-547-2000; 800-638-5660; www.troweprice.com)

Tweedy Browne Funds (52 Vanderbilt Ave., New York, NY 10017; 800-432-4789)

UAM Funds (211 Congress St., Boston, MA 02110; 800-638-7983)

Ultra Series Fund (2000 Heritage Way, Waverly, IA 50677; 800-798-5500)

Unified Funds (429 N. Pennsylvania St., 4th Floor, Indianapolis, IN 46204; 317-634-3300; 800-862-7283)

United Group of Mutual Funds (6300 Lamar, Shawnee Mission, KS 66202; 913-236-2000; 800-366-5465; www.waddell.com)

U.S. Global Investors Funds (7900 Callaghan Rd., San Antonio, TX 78229; 800-873-8637; www.usfunds.com)

USAA Funds (9800 Fredericksburg Rd., San Antonio, TX 78288; 210-498-8000; 800-531-8181; 800-531-8448; 800-382-8722)

VALIC Funds (2929 Allen Pkwy., Houston, TX 77019; 713-526-5251)

Value Line Funds (220 E. 42nd St., New York, NY 10017; 212-907-1500; 800-223-0818; www.valueline.com)

Van Eck Funds (99 Park Ave., 8th Floor, New York, NY 10016; 212-687-5200; 800-221-2220; www.vaneck.com)

Vanguard Group of Mutual Funds (Vanguard Financial Center, P.O. Box 2600, Valley Forge, PA 19482; 800-662-7447; www.vanguard.com)

Van Kampen American Capital (One Parkview Plaza, Oakbrook Terrace, IL 60181; 708-684-6000; 800-225-2222; www.vankampen.com)

Variable Investors Series Trust (10 Post Office Sq., Boston, MA 02109; 617-457-6700)

Victory Portfolios (3435 Stelzer Rd., Columbus, OH 43219; 800-539-3863)

Virtus/Blanchard Funds (Federated Investors Tower, 1001 Liberty Ave., Pittsburgh, PA 15222; 800-356-2805)

Vista Family of Funds (125 W. 55th St., New York, NY 10019; 800-367-6075; www.vista-funds.com)

Vontobel Funds (1500 Forest Ave., Suite 223, Richmond, VA 23229; 800-527-9500)

Voyageur Funds (90 S. 7th St., Suite 4400, Minneapolis, MN 55402; 612-376-7000; 800-553-2143)

Waddell & Reed Funds (6300 Lamar, Shawnee Mission, KS 66202; 800-366-5465; www.waddell.com)

Wanger Funds (227 W. Monroe St., Suite 3000, Chicago, IL 60606; 800-592-6437)

Warburg Pincus Funds (466 Lexington Ave., New York, NY 10017; 800-927-2874)

Wasatch Funds (68 S. Main St., Suite 400, Salt Lake City, UT 84101; 800-551-1700)

Wayne Hummer Funds (300 S. Wacker Dr., Chicago, IL 60606; 800-621-4477)

Weiss Peck and Greer Funds Trust (One New York Plaza, New York, NY 10004; 800-223-3332)

Weitz Funds (One Pacific Pl., 1125 S. 103rd St., Suite 600, Omaha, NE 68124; 800-232-4161)

Westcore Funds (370 17th St., Suite 2700, Denver, CO 80202; 800-392-2673)

William Blair Mutual Funds (222 W. Adams St., Chicago, IL 60606; 312-236-1600)

Williamsburg Investment Trust (312 Walnut St., Cincinnati, OH 45201; 800-443-4249)

WNL Series Trust (5555 San Felipe, Suite 900, Houston, TX 77056; 800-262-4764)

Woodstock Common Trust Fund (P.O. Box 8000, Wisconsin Rapids, WI 54494-8000; 715-423-7600)

Wood Struthers & Winthrop Funds (277 Park Ave., New York, NY 10172; 800-922-9004)

World Funds (1500 Forest Ave., Suite 223, Richmond, VA 26229; 804-285-8211; 800-527-9500; www.vusa.com)

Wright Funds (Wright Investors' Service Distributors Inc., Attention Mutual Fund Distribution Dept., 24 Federal St., Boston, MA 02110; 800-225-6265; www.wisi.com)

Zurich Kemper Funds (200 S. Riverside Plaza, Chicago, IL 60606; 312-781-1121; 800-621-1048)

Zweig Fund Group (900 Third Ave., New York, NY 10022; 800-272-2700)

CLOSED-END STOCK FUNDS

Following is a list of some of the biggest and most actively traded closed-end stock funds. Each entry includes the fund's name, its stock symbol, the exchange where the fund is traded (NYSE—New York Stock Exchange; AMEX—American Stock Exchange; Nasdaq—Nasdaq National Market System), its address and its telephone number. Upon request, the fund will send its latest quarterly or annual report, which lists the fund's performance history and holdings.

Adams Express Company, ADX, NYSE (7 St. Paul St., Suite 1140, Baltimore, MD 21202; 410-752-5900)

Allied Capital Corp., ALLC, Nasdaq (1666 K St., N.W., Suite 901, Washington, DC 20006; 202-331-1112; www.alliedcapital.com)

Allied Capital Corp. II, ALII, Nasdaq (1666 K St., N.W., Suite 901, Washington, DC 20006; 202-331-1112; www.alliedcapital.com)

Charles Allmon Trust, GSO, NYSE (4405 East-West Hwy., Suite 305, Bethesda, MD 20814; 301-986-5866)

Argentina Fund, AF, NYSE (345 Park Ave., New York, NY 10154; 617-330-5602)

ASA Limited, ASA, NYSE (P.O. Box 269, Florham Park, NJ 07932; 201-377-3535)

Asia Pacific Fund, APB, NYSE (One Seaport Plaza, New York, NY 10292; 212-214-3334; www.prudential.com)

Austria Fund, OST, NYSE (1345 Avenue of the Americas, New York, NY 10105; 800-247-4154)

Baker Fentress & Co., BKF, AMEX (200 W. Madison St., Suite 3510, Chicago, IL 60606; 312-236-9190)

Bando McGlocklin Capital Corp., BMCC, Nasdaq (13555 Bishops Ct., Suite 205, Brookfield, WI 53005; 414-523-4300)

Bergstrom Capital, BEM, AMEX (505 Madison St., Suite 220, Seattle, WA 98104; 206-623-7302)

Blue Chip Value Fund, BLU, NYSE (633 17th St., Suite 1800, Denver, CO 80202; 303-293-5999)

Brazil Fund, BZF, NYSE (345 Park Ave., New York, NY 10154; 617-330-5602)

Brazilian Equity Fund, BZL, NYSE (One Citicorp Center, 153 E. 53rd St., 58th Floor, New York, NY 10022; 212-832-2626; www.bea.com)

Capital Southwest Corp., CSWC, Nasdaq (12900 Preston Rd., Suite 700, Dallas, TX 75230; 972-233-8242)

Central Fund of Canada, CEF, AMEX (P.O. Box 7319, Ancaster, Ontario, Canada L9G 3N6; 416-648-7878)

Central Securities Corp., CET, AMEX (375 Park Ave., Suite 3404, New York, NY 10152-0055; 212-688-3011)

Chile Fund, CH, NYSE (One Citicorp Center, 153 E. 53rd St., New York, NY 10022; 212-832-2626; www.bea.com)

China Fund, CHN, NYSE (Oppenheimer & Co., One World Financial Center, 200 Liberty St., New York, NY 10281; 212-667-7866; 800-421-4777; www.oppenheimer funds.com)

Clemente Global Growth Fund, CLM, NYSE (152 W. 57th St., 25th Floor, New York, NY 10019; 212-765-0700; www.clementecapital.com)

Convertible Holdings, CNV, NYSE (P.O. Box 9011, Princeton, NJ 08543; 609-282-2800; www.ml.com)

Counsellors Tandem Securities Fund, CTF, NYSE (466 Lexington Ave., New York, NY 10017; 212-878-9204)

Dover Regional Financial Shares, DVRFS, Nasdaq (1521 Locust St., Suite 500, Philadelphia, PA 19102; 215-735-5001)

Duff and Phelps Utilities Income Fund, DNP, NYSE (55 E. Monroe St., Suite 3800, Chicago, IL 60603; 312-368-5510; www.duff.com)

Emerging Germany Fund, FRG, NYSE (One Battery Park Plaza, New York, NY 10004; 212-429-2800; www.dresdner.com)

Emerging Markets Telecommunications Fund, ETF, NYSE (One Citicorp Center, 153 E. 53rd St., New York, NY 10022; 212-832-2626; www.bea.com)

Emerging Mexico Fund, MEF, NYSE (PaineWebber 1285 Avenue of the Americas, New York, NY 10019; 212-713-3857; 800-553-8080; www.painewebberedge.com)

Engex, EGX, AMEX (44 Wall St., New York, NY 10005; 212-495-4200)

European Warrant Fund, EWF, NYSE (Julius Baer Securities, 330 Madison Ave., New York, NY 10017; 800-331-1710)

Europe Fund, EF, NYSE (780 3rd Ave., New York, NY 10017; 212-751-8340; www.prusec.com)

First Australia Fund, IAF, AMEX (One Seaport Plaza, New York, NY 10292; 212-214-3334; 800-451-6788; www.prudential.com)

First Financial Fund, FF, NYSE (One Seaport Plaza, New York, NY 10292; 212-214-3334; 800-451-6788; www.prudential.com)

First Iberian Fund, IBF, AMEX (345 Park Ave., New York, NY 10154; 617-330-5602)

First Israel Fund, ISL, NYSE (One Citicorp Center, 153 E. 53rd St., New York, NY 10022; 212-832-2626; www.bea.com)

First Philippine Fund, FPF, NYSE (152 W. 57th St., New York, NY 10019; 212-765-0700; www.clementecapital.com)

France Fund, FRN, NYSE (535 Madison Ave., New York, NY 10022; 212-701-2845; www.dillon.com)

France Growth Fund, FRF, NYSE (1230 Avenue of the Americas, New York, NY 10020; 800-852-4750)

Franklin Multi-Income Trust, FMI, NYSE (777 Mariners Island Blvd., San Mateo, CA 94404; 800-331-1710; www.franklin-templeton.com)

Future Germany Fund, FGF, NYSE (31 W. 52nd St., New York, NY 10019; 800-GERMANY; www.deutsche-bank.de)

Gabelli Equity Trust, GAB, NYSE (One Corporate Center, Rye, NY 10580; 914-921-5070; www.gabelli.com)

Gemini II, GMI, NYSE (Vanguard Financial Center, Valley Forge, PA 19482; 800-662-2739; www.vanguard.com)

General American Investors Co., GAM, NYSE (450 Lexington Ave., Suite 3300, New York, NY 10017; 212-916-8400)

Germany Fund, GER, NYSE (31 W. 52nd St., New York, NY 10019; 800-GERMANY; www.deutsche-bank.de)

Global Health Sciences Fund, GHS, NYSE (7800 E. Union Ave., Suite 800, Denver, CO 80237; 800-528-8765; www.invesco.com)

Greater China Fund, GCH, NYSE (1285 Avenue of the Americas, New York, NY 10019; 212-713-2000; www.painewebber.com)

Growth Fund of Spain, GSP, NYSE (120 S. LaSalle St., Chicago, IL 60603; 800-621-1148; www.kemper.com)

GT Greater Europe Fund, GTF, NYSE (50 California St., 27th Floor, San Francisco, CA 94111; 415-392-6181; www.kemper.com)

Hampton Utilities Trust, HU (capital shares), HU pr (income shares), AMEX (777 Mariners Island Blvd., San Mateo, CA 94403; 415-312-2000; 800-DIAL-BEN; www. franklin-templeton.com)

H&Q Healthcare Investors, HQH, NYSE (50 Rowes Wharf, Suite 420, Boston, MA 02110; 617-574-0500; www.namquist.com)

H&Q Life Sciences Investors, HQL, NYSE (50 Rowes Wharf, Suite 420, Boston, MA 02110; 617-574-0500; www.namquist.com)

India Growth Fund, IGF, NYSE (1285 Avenue of the Americas, New York, NY 10019; 212-713-2000; 800-553-8080)

Indonesia Fund, IF, NYSE (One Citicorp Center, 153 E. 53rd St., New York, NY 10022; 212-713-3857; www.painewebber.com)

Irish Investment Fund, IRL, NYSE (Boston Company Advisors, Inc., Exchange Place, Boston, MA 02109; 800-468-6475)

Israel Investors Corp., IICR, Nasdaq (475 Park Ave. S., New York, NY 10016; 212-213-2200)

Italy Fund, ITA, NYSE (Two World Trade Center, New York, NY 10048; 212-298-6263)

Jakarta Growth Fund, JGF, NYSE (180 Maiden Ln., New York, NY 10038; 800-833-0018)

Japan Equity Fund, JEQ, NYSE (Daiwa Securities Trust Co., One Evertrust Plaza, Jersey City, NJ 07302; 800-933-3440)

Japan OTC Equity Fund, JOF, NYSE (180 Maiden Ln., New York, NY 10038; 800-833-0018)

Jardine Fleming China Region Fund, JFC, NYSE (100 E. Pratt St., Baltimore, MD 21202; 800-638-8540; www.troweprice.com)

Jundt Growth Fund, JF, NYSE (P.O. Box 9011, Princeton, NJ 08543-9011; 800-543-6217; www.ml.com)

Jupiter National, Inc., JPI, AMEX (5454 Wisconsin Ave., Chevy Chase, MD 20815; 301-656-0626)

Korea Fund, KF, NYSE (345 Park Ave., New York, NY 10154; 212-326-6200; 617-330-5602; www.scudder.com)

Korean Investment Fund, KIF, NYSE (1345 Avenue of the Americas, New York, NY 10105; 800-247-4154; www.alliancecapital.com)

Latin American Discovery Fund, LDF, NYSE (1221 Avenue of the Americas, New York, NY 10020; 212-296-7100)

Latin American Equity Fund, LAQ, NYSE (One Citicorp Center, 153 E. 53rd St., New York, NY 10022; 212-832-2626; www.bea.com)

Latin American Investment Fund, LAM, NYSE (One Citicorp Center, 153 E. 53rd St., New York, NY 10022; 212-832-2626; www.bea.com)

Liberty All-Star Equity Fund, USA, NYSE (600 Atlantic Ave., Boston, MA 02210; 800-542-3863; www.lamco.com)

Malaysia Fund, MF, NYSE (1221 Avenue of the Americas, New York, NY 10020; 215-669-8503)

Merrill Lynch & Co. S&P 500 Fund, MIT, NYSE (P.O. Box 9011, Princeton, NJ 08543-9011; 609-282-8837; www.ml.com)

Mexico Equity and Income Fund, MXE, NYSE (200 Liberty St., New York, NY 10291; 212-667-5018; www.oppenheimerfunds.com)

Mexico Fund, MXF, NYSE (Impulsora del Fondo Mexico, 77 Aristoleles St., 11560 Mexico DF Mexico; 212-750-4200; 525-280-1636)

Morgan Grenfell SMALLcap Fund, MGC, NYSE (855 3rd Ave., Suite 1740, New York, NY 10022; 212-230-2600)

Morgan Stanley Emerging Markets, MSF, NYSE (1221 Avenue of the Americas, New York, NY 10020; 212-296-7100)

New Germany Fund, GF, NYSE (31 W. 52nd St., New York, NY 10019; 212-474-7000; www.deutsche-bank.de)

Patriot Premium Dividend Fund I, PDF, NYSE (101 Huntington Ave., Boston, MA 02199; 617-375-1500; 800-843-0090; www.jhancock.com)

Patriot Premium Dividend Fund II, PDT, NYSE (101 Huntington Ave., Boston, MA 02199; 617-375-1500; 800-843-0090; www.jhancock.com)

Patriot Select Dividend Trust, DIV, NYSE (101 Huntington Ave., Boston, MA 02199; 617-375-1500; 800-843-0090; www.jhancock.com)

Petroleum and Resources Corp., PEO, NYSE (7 St. Paul St., Suite 1140, Baltimore, MD 21202; 410-752-5900; 800-638-2479)

Pilgrim Prime Rate Trust, PPR, NYSE (10100 Santa Monica Blvd., Los Angeles, CA 90067; 800-331-1080)

Pilgrim Regional Bank Shares, PBS, NYSE (10100 Santa Monica Blvd., Los Angeles, CA 90067; 800-331-1080)

Portugal Fund, PGF, NYSE (153 E. 53rd St., New York, NY 10022; 212-832-2626; www.bea.com)

Preferred Income Fund, PFD, NYSE (301 E. Colorado Blvd., Pasadena, CA 91101; 818-795-7300)

Preferred Income Opportunity Fund, PFO, NYSE (301 E. Colorado Blvd., Pasadena, CA 91101; 818-795-7300)

Pro-Med Capital, PMC, AMEX (1380 N.E. Miami Gardens Dr., Suite 225, North Miami Beach, FL 33179; 305-949-5900)

Putnam Dividend Income Fund, PDI, NYSE (One Post Office Square, Boston, MA 02109; 617-292-1000; www.putnaminv.com)

Quest for Value Dual Purpose Fund, KFV (capital shares), KFVpr (income shares), NYSE (Oppenheimer Tower, World Financial Center, New York, NY 10281; 800-232-FUND; 800-525-1103; www.oppenheimerfunds.com)

Real Estate Securities Income Fund, RIF, AMEX (757 3rd Ave., New York, NY 10017; 212-832-3232)

Regional Financial Shares Investment Fund, BNC, NYSE (1285 Avenue of the Americas, New York, NY 10019; 212-713-2000; www.painewebber.com)

R.O.C. Taiwan Fund, ROC, NYSE (100 E. Pratt St., Baltimore, MD 21202; 410-752-2880; 800-343-9567)

Royce Value Trust, RVT, NYSE (1414 Avenue of the Americas, New York, NY 10019; 212-355-7311; www.roycefunds.com)

Salomon Brothers Fund, SBF, NYSE (Seven World Trade Center, New York, NY 10048; 212-783-1301; 800-725-6666; www.salomon.com)

Scudder New Asia Fund, SAF, NYSE (345 Park Ave., New York, NY 10154; 212-326-6200; 617-330-5602; www.scudder.com)

Scudder New Europe Fund, NEF, NYSE (345 Park Ave., New York, NY 10154; 212-326-6200; 617-330-5602; www.scudder.com)

Singapore Fund, SGF, NYSE (Daiwa Securities Trust Co., One Evertrust Plaza, Jersey City, NJ 07302; 201-915-3020; 800-933-3440; www.daiwa.com)

Source Capital, SOR, NYSE (11400 W. Olympic Blvd., Los Angeles, CA 90064; 310-996-5406)

Southeastern Thrift and Bank Fund, STBF, Nasdaq (1 Beacon St., Boston, MA 02108; 800-225-5291; www.jhancock.com)

Spain Fund, SNF, NYSE (1345 Avenue of the Americas, New York, NY 10105; 800-247-4154; www.alliancecapital.com)

Sterling Capital Corp., SPR, AMEX (635 Madison Ave., New York, NY 10022; 212-980-3360)

Swiss Helvetia Fund, SWZ, NYSE (630 Fifth Ave., Suite 915, New York, NY 10111; 212-332-7930; www.swz.com)

Taiwan Fund, TWN, AMEX (82 Devonshire St., Boston, MA 02109; 800-334-9393; 800-544-4774; www.fidelity.com)

Templeton Emerging Markets Fund, EMF, NYSE (700 Central Ave., St. Petersburg, FL 33701; 813-823-8712; www.franklin-templeton.com)

Templeton Global Utilities Fund, TGU, NYSE (700 Central Ave., St. Petersburg, FL 33701; 813-823-8712; www.franklin-templeton.com)

Thai Capital Fund, TC, NYSE (Daiwa Securities Trust Co., One Evertrust Plaza, Jersey City, NJ 07302; 201-915-3020; 800-933-3440; www.daiwa.com)

Thai Fund, TTF, NYSE (126 High St., Boston, MA 02110; 800-221-6726; www.ms.com)

Tri-Continental Corp., TY, NYSE (130 Liberty St., New York, NY 10006; 800-221-2450)

Turkish Investment Fund, TKF, NYSE (Vanguard Financial Center, Valley Forge, PA 19482; 215-669-8503)

United Kingdom Fund, UKM, NYSE (245 Park Ave., New York, NY 10167; 212-272-6404; 800-524-4458; www.stkxser.bankofny.com)

Worldwide Value Fund, VLU, NYSE (111 S. Calvert St., Baltimore, MD 21202; 410-539-0000; www.leggmason.com)

Z-Seven Fund, ZSEV, Nasdaq-Pacific Exchange (2651 W. Guadalupe Rd., Suite B-233, Mesa, AZ 85202; 602-897-6214)

Zweig Fund, ZF, NYSE (900 3rd Ave., New York, NY 10022; 212-755-9860)

Zweig Total Return Fund, ZTR, NYSE (900 3rd Ave., New York, NY 10022; 212-755-9860)

RATINGS SERVICES

The following companies rate the performance of mutual funds:

AMG Data Services (5440 Ericson Way, Arcata, CA 95521; 707-822-4888; www.amgdata.com)

CDA (1355 Piccard Dr., Suite 220, Rockville, MD 20850; 301-975-9600; 800-232-2285; www.cda.com)

CDA Weisenberger (1355 Piccard Dr., Suite 220, Rockville, MD 20850; 301-975-9600; 800-232-2285; www.cda.com)

Computer Directions Advisors (1355 Piccard Dr., Rockville, MD 20850; 301-975-9600; www.cda.com)

Lipper Analytical Services (74 Trinity Pl., New York, NY 10006; 212-393-1300; www.lipperweb.com)

Morningstar (225 W. Wacker Dr., Chicago, IL 60606; 800-876-5005; www. morningstar.net)

Trade Associations

Investment Company Institute (1401 H St., N.W., Suite 1200, Washington, DC 20005; 202-326-5800; www.ici.org www.msdc.com). The trade group for lobbying and public education on mutual fund issues. Will send you a copy of the following free pamphlets: "A Close Look at Closed-End Funds"; "Money Market Mutual Funds: A Part of Every Financial Plan"; "Planning for College? The Mutual Fund Advantage Becomes a Parent"; "Reading the Mutual Fund Prospectus"; "What Is a Mutual Fund?" To receive a copy of any of these brochures, write to the ICI at P.O. Box 66140, Washington, DC 20035-6140.

Mutual Fund Education Alliance (100 N.W. Englewood Rd., Suite 130, Kansas City, MO 64118; 816-454-9422; www.mfea.com). An educational group composed mostly of no-load mutual funds. Some of its members charge low loads, back-end loads or 12b-1 fees. For a small fee, the Alliance will send you the *Investor's Guide to Low-Cost Mutual Funds,* which lists hundreds of funds, with their investment objectives, minimum investment requirements, sales fees, assets, expense ratios and long-term returns. For anothercharge, it will send you *Directing Your Own Mutual Fund Investments,* a booklet that covers the basics of mutual fund investing, and an audiocassette on the same topic.

National Investment Company Services Association (850 Boylston St., Suite 437, Chestnut Hill, MA 02167; 617-277-1855). The trade group specializing in mutual fund service issues.

100% No-Load Mutual Fund Council (1501 Broadway, Suite 1809, New York, NY 10036; 212-768-2477). Represents mutual funds that charge no sales commissions of any type. Upon request, it will send you a free copy of the "100% No-Load Mutual Fund Council Investment Guide and Member Directory."

Society of Asset Allocators and Fund Timers (165 S. Union Blvd., Suite 415, Lakewood, CO 80228; 313-642-6640). A group of investment professionals who manage mutual fund assets for their clients through the use of dynamic asset allocation and market-timing strategies.

All about Bonds

When you invest in a *bond,* you are loaning the issuer of that bond your money in return for a fixed rate of interest for a specific amount of time. Normally, you receive interest payments every six months, and when the bond matures, you receive your original principal, no matter how much the price of the bond fluctuated since it was issued.

Investing in Bonds

Bonds are one of the key investment vehicles available for your use in achieving your financial goals. They allow you to lock in a set rate of income for a long period of time, which can give your financial plan a rock-solid foundation. In addition, if you want to trade bonds more actively, you can earn capital gains by buying them when their prices fall and selling them when their prices rise, just as you can do with stocks.

For many decades, bonds were quite simple. For years, interest rates remained remarkably stable at about 1 percent or 2 percent because inflation was low. Few, if any, bonds defaulted, which happens when bond issuers fail to honor their pledge to pay interest or principal on time. Bond prices hardly budged.

But starting in the mid-1970s, when the Arab oil embargo and soaring government budget deficits ignited inflation, all of that changed. Interest rates jumped from 4 percent or 5 percent in the early 1970s to more than 20 percent in the early 1980s, giving rise to tremendous volatility in the bond market. Even as rates fell back from those heights during the 1980s and 1990s, bond yields remained higher than they had been in the 1950s, and bond prices continued to jump around. On top of gyrating rates, the number of bond defaults increased dramatically, as many companies, and a few municipalities, were unable to handle the increased interest payments required from higher yielding bonds.

The bond market was changed not only by increased volatility of interest rates, prices and defaults but also by an explosion in the variety of new bond types. For decades, the major issuers of bonds had been the federal government and its agencies, state and local governments and related agencies, foreign governments and blue chip corporations. Starting in the 1980s, billions of dollars' worth of *junk* bonds were issued by small and risky growth companies or by raiders, who used the money to take over major corporations. Another new class of bond called *asset-backed securities,* which back the promise to repay the bond with interest from assets like mortgages, credit cards and auto loans, was created and took in hundreds of billions of dollars.

Also, the bond market, which had formerly been the preserve of the rich, was democratized by the introduction of the *bond mutual fund.* Like stock funds, bond funds allowed average people access to the huge and complicated world of investing for a small amount of money and reasonable fees. Bond funds became the haven for millions of income-oriented investors who had always kept their money in bank products like CDs and money-market funds.

With all these recent developments in the world of bonds, there is much to learn about the opportunities and pitfalls of today's bond market. Chances are that fixed-income securities will play an important role in your financial plan at some stage in your life.

The Basics of Holding Bonds

When you buy bonds issued by a government agency or a company, you become a lender to that entity. This is very different from being a stockholder, which you become when you buy a company's stock. As a bondholder, you are entitled to receive the bond's stated interest rate when interest is due and your principal when the bond matures—nothing more. You will not receive quarterly or annual reports. You will not be invited to a firm's annual meeting. You will not earn dividends. If a company's earnings soar, you will not participate in that success.

On the other hand, the yield you will receive from the bond will typically be higher than the stock dividend yield because bondholders must be compensated for reduced purchasing power in the future because of inflation. (Of course, there is no way to buy stock in most government agencies—although you can buy stock in some, as noted later—so bonds are the only way to participate in the government.)

As with stocks, the money that you pay to buy bonds goes to the issuers only when the bonds are first sold to the public. After that, you buy bonds from the existing owners, or you sell bonds to other investors. Most bond trading is done automatically in a computer-driven system without specialists or dealers. In addition, bonds are bought and sold through competing dealers, who communicate with each other by computer and telephone.

Bonds are normally quoted on a price scale of 0 to 200, with 100 being the price at which the bond was issued, or what is known as *par.* Because bonds are sold in minimum denominations of $1,000, a price of 100 means that the bond is trading at $1,000 per bond. If the bond's price rises to 110, your holdings are now worth $1,100.

Unlike stock transactions, bond buy-and-sell transactions normally occur without a separate commission charge. Instead, a broker makes money from a transaction by taking a piece of the spread between the buying and selling prices. For example, if a broker buys you a bond at a price of 100, he or she might charge you 102 for it and keep the two points as his or her commission. If you try to sell the bond for a price of 100, you might get only 98 for it. Because the bond market is generally dominated by large institutions that trade millions of dollars' worth of bonds, you will pay a wider spread if you buy only a small number of bonds. Many bond dealers won't even execute a trade for fewer than 25 bonds, or $25,000, though some might go as low as five bonds, or $5,000. Because it is a competitive market, you should shop around among brokers to get the best deal.

The only way you can avoid paying a large spread for small purchases, other than to buy bonds through a mutual fund, is to buy government bonds directly from the Treasury. You can buy bills, notes and bonds whenever the Treasury auctions new issues. You can also buy U.S. savings bonds for only $25 through any bank or by payroll deduction. (Government bonds will be discussed in more detail later in this chapter.)

For decades, bondholders received fancy bond certificates with attached coupons entitling the coupon owners to the cash interest payment on the date due. These were known as bearer bonds because whoever bore a bond coupon would be paid the interest. Bearer bonds have not been issued since 1982; therefore, for the most part, the days of bearer bond certificates are long gone. Instead, bonds are now issued in either *registered* or *book entry form.* Registered bonds still have certificates, and the owner of the bond is named on the back of the certificate. To sell a registered bond, the owner must endorse it and have his or her name changed to the new owner's name in the issuer's records. The more common form of bond issued today, however, is the book entry bond, for which interest payments are tracked by computers. If you hold a bond in a brokerage account, interest and principal payments will be made automatically. Book entry bonds provide no certificate you can hold in your hands; the record exists only in the computer data banks of your brokerage firm. Because the bond is electronic, however, it is much easier to trade because no endorsement is needed for the bond to change hands.

How Bond Prices Move

When you consider investing in bonds, you should understand that one cardinal rule about the movement of bond prices: *Bond prices move in the opposite direction of interest rates.* Normally, you might think that rising interest rates would be good for your bond, but nothing could be further from the truth. Even though it may sound illogical at first, it is true that when interest rates rise, bond prices fall. When interest rates fall, bond prices rise. The following example explains why.

Say you buy a bond yielding 10 percent at a price of 100 (the par price). If interest rates plummet to 5 percent over the next several years, your 10 percent bond would become very valuable, indeed. Its price would soar—maybe to a dollar value of 150—because people would be willing to pay a big premium to get their hands on a 10 percent bond in an environment where bonds pay only 5 percent. Notice that as interest rates fell, your bond's value rose.

Now let's take the opposite situation. You buy your 10 percent bond at 100, and instead of dropping, interest rates soar to 15 percent. Your bond won't be popular now because people would rather buy a new bond paying 15 percent than your old bond paying 10 percent. Therefore, if you want to sell your bond to buy a newer one at the higher current rate, you would suffer a loss. The price of your bond might drop to half, from 100 to 50. Notice that as interest rates rose, your bond's value fell.

Bond prices move so perversely because bonds are a fixed-rate instrument. Because the bond's rate is locked in at whatever level it was when the bond was first issued, the bond becomes more or less valuable as interest rates fall or rise. Figure 5.1 might help you better understand the inverse relationship between interest rates and bond prices.

The longer the maturity of your bond, the more its price will react to the ups and downs of interest rates. A bond that locks in a high interest rate for 20 or 30 years is much more valuable to an investor if interest rates have fallen than a bond that matures in a year or two. Conversely, if interest rates have risen, the investor would rather get his or her money back quickly so he or she can reinvest at higher rates.

When calculating the effect of interest rates on an investor's holdings, analysts usually look at the total return—that is, the price change of the bond added to the income it is paying. Figure 5.2 shows how an interest rate increase of from one to four percentage points over one year would affect the total returns of several bond maturities, from 6 years to 30 years. This table assumes that 6-year bonds yield 6 percent, 10- and 20-year bonds yield 7 percent and 30-year bonds yield 8 percent. Notice that the longer the bond maturity, the more the bond loses value as rates rise.

Figure 5.3 shows how much total returns on different bond maturities rise as interest rates fall over one year.

This bond volatility should always factor into your decision to buy bonds.

WHY INTEREST RATES FLUCTUATE

Many factors influence interest rate movements. In the long term, the outlook for inflation is the most important determinant of interest rates. If inflation is high

Figure 5.1
Relationship Between Bond Funds and Interest Rates

When interest rates move up or down, the price of a bond usually moves in the opposite direction.

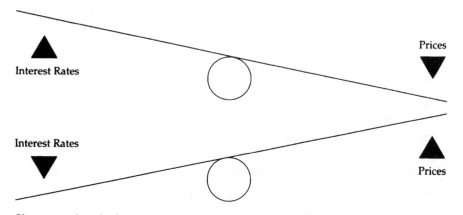

Short-term bonds (bonds that are close to maturity) are usually less affected by changes in interest rates than long-term bonds.

and rising, investors demand a higher yield to protect the value of their money from erosion. If inflation is low and declining, investors settle for a lower yield because they are not as threatened by the loss of purchasing power. One way to measure investors' fear of inflation is to subtract the current inflation rate from a bond's yield. This produces what is known as the *real interest rate.* For example:

Current interest rate	10%
Consumer price index inflation rate	− 6
Real interest rate	4%

Figure 5.2
Percentage Points Rate Increase in a Year

Maturity	Unchanged	+1%	+2%	+3%	+4%
6 years	+6%	+2%	−2%	−5%	−9%
10 years	+7	+1	−5	−10	−15
20 years	+7	+1	−7	−13	−19
30 years	+8	−3	−11	−19	−25

Source: Reprinted by permission of The Leuthold Group, an investment advisory firm in Minneapolis, Minnesota.

Figure 5.3
Percentage Points Rate Decrease in a Year

Maturity	Unchanged	−1%	−2%	−3%	−4%
6 years	+6%	+10%	+15%	+20%	+25%
10 years	+7	+13	+20	+28	+37
20 years	+7	+18	+28	+42	+57
30 years	+8	+20	+35	+51	+69

Source: Reprinted by permission of The Leuthold Group, an investment advisory firm in Minneapolis, Minnesota.

If the resulting number is positive, it is known as a *positive real interest rate.* In the example, bondholders receive four percentage points more than the current inflation rate. Historically, positive real rates usually average around 3 percent, but they have stretched to 5 percent or 6 percent at times.

If bond rates are lower than inflation, it is known as a *negative interest rate.* For example:

Current interest rate	10%
Consumer price index inflation rate	− 13
Real interest rate	− 3%

In the example, a likely scenario during the late 1970s, bond investors actually lose money because their 10 percent rate is adjusted for rampant inflation.

Because the 1970s lesson was so painful to bond investors, real interest rates have stayed positive since then and are likely to continue to do so because investors want a protective cushion over the current inflation rate. Still, there is no guarantee that yields won't shoot up sharply again in the future and investors will be stuck earning negative real interest rates again.

In addition to the outlook for inflation, supply and demand influence interest rates. If you think of an interest rate as the price of money, you will understand that as demand for money increases and supply decreases, the price, or interest rate, goes up. This situation might occur when the economy is picking up and businesses and consumers want to borrow money to expand and spend, while lenders—including banks and bond buyers—are reluctant to lend because they fear higher interest rates.

Interest rates tend to fall when the economy is declining or in recession because there is little demand for borrowing; businesses are retrenching, and consumers are more interested in paying off existing debts than in taking on new loans. At the same time, a larger supply of money is available to lend because bond buyers want to lock in high interest rates.

Over the last two decades, a new factor has grown in influence on the interest rate level: the federal budget deficit. When the difference between what the government received in taxes and what it spent for programs each year was modest—less than $50 billion—the deficit was easy to cover with national savings. But as the size of the annual deficit grew—first to $100 billion, then to $200 billion, then to a staggering $300 billion—the government consumed more and more of the supply of capital available in the United States. This enormous demand for money by the government as it sells billions of dollars' worth of new bonds, compounded by the fear of an ever rising national debt, has kept interest rates much higher than they normally would have been if the deficit had been controlled. By the late 1990s, those huge federal deficits had all but disappeared. The dramatically reduced amount of government borrowing helped interest rates on long-term bonds fall sharply from early 1990s levels.

While these broad factors influence the general level of interest rates, more specific supply and demand issues affect the interest rates and prices of individual bonds. Whether a bond is issued by a corporation or a municipal agency, investors evaluate it by the strength of its financial condition. The better its financial shape, the more confident investors are that their interest and principal will be repaid on time and, therefore, the lower the bond's interest rate will be. One major factor influencing investors' perceptions of the bond is the rating it receives from one of the three big bond-rating agencies: Standard & Poor's, Moody's and Fitch. Analysts at these agencies, using detailed financial information and judgment based on years of experience, assign a rating to each bond issuer. The ratings scales of the three services appear in Figure 5.4.

Figure 5.4
Bond Rating Services' Rating System

	Rating Service		
Explanation of Bond Rating	*Standard & Poor's*	*Moody's*	*Fitch*
Highest quality	AAA	Aaa	AAA
Very High quality	AA	Aa	AA
High quality	A	A	A
Medium quality	BBB	Baa	BBB
Predominantly speculative	BB	Ba	BB
Speculative, low grade	B	B	B
Poor to default	CCC	Caa	CCC
Highest speculation	CC	Ca	CC
Lowest quality, not paying interest	C	C	C
In default, in arrears, of questionable value	D		DDD
			DD
			D

Source: Reprinted by permission of Standard & Poor's Corporation, Moody's Investors Service and Fitch Investors Service, Inc.

In addition to regular letter grades, Fitch and Standard & Poor's modify ratings with + or − signs. A corporate bond may be rated AA− or BBB+, for instance. Moody's uses numbers from 1 to 3 to signify gradations. The same corporate bonds might have a Moody's rating of Aa2 or Baa1, for example.

Although ratings agencies do not always agree on the risk of default by a particular issuer, their assessments are usually fairly similar. Therefore, such ratings, as well as the prospect for upgradings or downgradings in those ratings, can significantly affect a bond's interest rate and price.

THE MEANING OF YIELD

While a bond has only one interest rate, there are four ways to calculate its *yield*—that is, your return at the bond's current price. They are as follows:

1. **Coupon rate.** The coupon rate is the interest the bond pays. It may equal the bond's yield when it is trading at its issue price of 100, or its $1,000 face value. A bond with a 10 percent coupon therefore would pay $100 a year in interest.

2. **Current yield.** This yield adjusts the bond's coupon rate for the bond's current price to determine what percentage you would receive if you bought the bond at its current price. In the example above, if the bond dropped in price from 100 to 90, for instance, the bond's value would fall from $1,000 to $900. At that price, the current yield would rise to 11.1 percent. Current yield is calculated as follows:

$$\frac{\$100 \text{ Annual interest payment of the bond}}{\$900 \text{ Current market price of the bond}} = 11.1\% \text{ Current yield}$$

    Remember that rising interest rates cause bond prices to fall. Therefore, in the example, if the bond's price rose from 100 to 110, the bond's value would rise from $1,000 to $1,100. Current yield is calculated as follows:

$$\frac{\$100 \text{ Annual interest payment of the bond}}{\$1,100 \text{ Current market price of the bond}} = 9.09\% \text{ Current yield}$$

    Don't worry about having to calculate the yield of every bond you consider buying. Current yields are displayed on your broker's computer screen and also in any newspaper's bond listings. (For more on this, see "Reading the Bond Tables in Newspapers" later in this chapter.)

3. **Yield to maturity.** This yield takes into account the bond's coupon rate, its current price and the years remaining until the bond matures. It is a more complicated calculation, but your broker should be able to tell you the yield to maturity on any bond you are considering. You can also consult a book with yield-to-maturity tables or figure it using a programmable calculator. If you want only to approximate the yield to maturity,

you can use the following calculations. This example will use a bond with a 10 percent coupon (paying $100 a year) trading at a price of 85 (now worth $850) with ten years before it matures.

First, subtract the current bond value (in this case, $850) from par ($1,000) to arrive at the *discount*.

Par	$1,000
Current bond value	− 850
Discount	$150

Divide the discount ($150) by the number of years remaining until the bond matures (10) to calculate the annual gain in the bond's price as it moves from $850 currently to $1,000 at maturity.

$$\frac{\$150\ \text{Discount}}{10\ \text{Years to maturity}} = \$15\ \text{Annual gain}$$

Combine the annual gain ($15) with the bond's annual interest ($100) to get the bond's yearly total gain.

$15	Annual gain
+ 100	Annual interest
$115	Yearly total gain

Divide the yearly total gain ($115) by the bond's current price ($850) to calculate the yield to maturity.

$$\frac{\$115\ \text{Yearly total gain}}{\$850\ \text{Current price of the bond}} = 13.5\%\ \text{Yield to maturity}$$

4. **Yield to call.** This is the yield up to the first potential date at which the issuer can *call,* or redeem, the bond—usually several years before the bond is scheduled to mature. You calculate the yield to call exactly the same way you calculate the yield to maturity, except that you replace the number of years to maturity with the number of years to the first call date.

    You should always assume that a corporation or municipality will put its shareholders' or constituents' interests ahead of bondholders'. Therefore, if interest rates have fallen sharply from the time the bond was issued to the first date that the bond can be called, you should assume the bond will be redeemed. The yield to call is the most realistic yield you can calculate for a bond because you can never assume the bond will remain outstanding between its first call date and its stated maturity.

EARLY REDEMPTION

A bond can be redeemed before it is scheduled to mature? That sounds illegal. But it isn't—as long as the issuer's ability to redeem the bond is written into the thick legal document that accompanies the original bond issue. In that document, called the *indenture,* bondholders are guaranteed a certain number of years before which the bond cannot be redeemed. This can be as little as 5 years or as many as 15 to 20 years although 10-year call protection is more typical.

When the first date of a potential call arrives, the issuer decides whether it makes more sense to continue to pay interest on the bond or to pay off the bond and issue another one at a lower interest rate. For example, if the bond was issued at 10 percent and rates have dropped to 7 percent over the last few years, the issuer would probably refinance. If rates have dropped only to 9 percent, though, refinancing might not be worthwhile. In many cases, bondholders whose bonds are called before maturity will receive a slight premium over par for the bonds. Therefore, they might receive 102 per bond, or $1,020, at redemption. Otherwise, they would receive only par, or $1,000, per bond.

Whenever you consider buying a bond, find out how many years of call protection you have. The more years you know your bond will pay interest, the better.

THE YIELD CURVE

Because bonds mature at some point in the future, the amount of time between now and that maturity point is key in determining the bond's yield and price. In general, the further off an event will occur, the less sure you are about exactly what will happen in the meantime. You might have a pretty good idea of what the next five minutes hold, but you're sure to be a lot fuzzier about what will happen 20 years from now. This uncertainty about the future, and the related risk, are normally built into bond prices.

As we discussed earlier, the longer the maturity of a bond, the more its price fluctuates with any movement in interest rates. For example, if yields on 30-year Treasuries are 7.5 percent, a 1 percentage point rise in interest rates to 8.5 percent might make a 1-year bond's price fall by 5 percent, while a 30-year bond's price might plunge 30 percent. Conversely, a 1 percent drop in interest rates would translate into a 5 percent rise in a 1-year bond's price but a 40 percent rise in the price of a 30-year issue. Keep this extra volatility in mind if you plan to buy a longer term bond. While you usually receive a higher yield, it comes at the price of much more price fluctuation over the life of the bond.

The *yield curve* is a convenient chart allowing you to compare the current yields of short-term, medium-term and long-term bonds. Though there are yield curves for many different kinds of bonds, the curve you will see most often is for Treasury securities. The Treasury curve is printed daily in *The Wall Street Journal* and other newspapers and also appears in financial magazines. A typical yield curve looks like Figure 5.5.

Across the bottom of the chart are the various bond maturities, from the shortest maturity of three months to the longest maturity of 30 years. Down the

Figure 5.5
Sample Treasury Yield Curve

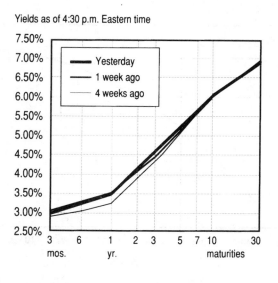

Yields as of 4:30 p.m. Eastern time

Legend:
— Yesterday
— 1 week ago
— 4 weeks ago

side of the chart are the various yields on Treasury securities. This particular chart shows potential yields ranging from a high of 7.5 percent to a low 2.5 percent yield. The curve illustrates how much more interest a bond with a longer maturity earns. In this case, for instance, a 30-year bond pays nearly 7 percent, while a 3-month bill pays only about 3.25 percent. The difference between the long and the short maturity—in this case, 4.25 percentage points—is the premium investors currently demand for committing their money for a long time. When long-term interest rates are much higher than short-term rates, as in this case, bond experts call the resulting curve a *steeply sloped positive yield curve* (see Figure 5.6).

At other times, the difference between short- and long-maturity bonds can be very slight, producing a yield curve that looks like Figure 5.7. Here, there is virtually no difference between 3-month Treasury bills and 20-year bonds; both yield about 7 percent. This is known as a *flat yield curve.*

An *abnormal yield curve* occurs when short-term rates are actually higher than long-term rates, usually when the economy is about to head into a recession. In this case, yields on 3-month bills are 9.2 percent, while yields on 20-year bonds are 5 percent. This is known as a *negative,* or an *inverted,* yield curve (see Figure 5.8). An inverted yield curve occurred briefly in the early 1980s, for instance, when the Federal Reserve pushed up interest rates sharply to combat inflation, while long-term rates rose more gradually.

Figure 5.6
Sample Positive Yield Curve

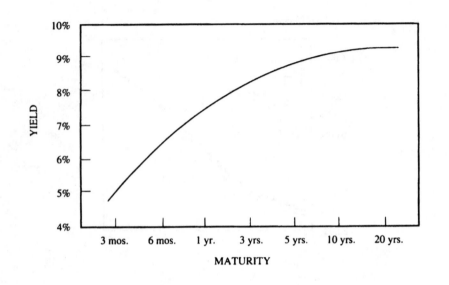

Figure 5.7
Sample Flat Yield Curve

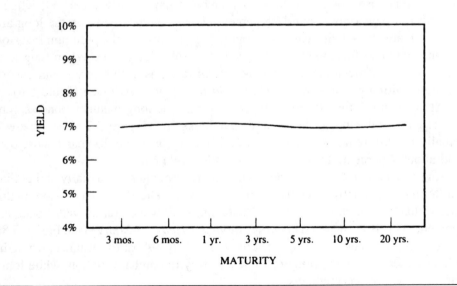

When choosing the maturity of a bond, you might look for the "sweet spot" on the yield curve. This is the maturity at which you receive the highest possible yield for the lowest possible risk. No definitive sweet spot exists; it varies according to the shape of the yield curve and your view of the direction of interest rates.

READING THE BOND TABLES IN NEWSPAPERS

Corporate bonds. The most complete corporate bond listings, which cover the most actively traded bonds, appear in *The Wall Street Journal, Investor's Business Daily* and other financial newspapers though your local newspaper may feature limited bond listings as well. Even the most complete listings, however, highlight just a fraction of the outstanding bonds traded every day. The following is an example of the form most corporate bond tables take, along with an explanation of each column.

Sample Corporate Bond Table

Bonds[1]	Current Yield[2]	Volume[3]	Close[4]	Net Change[5]
ATT 7½ 06	7.0	272	106	+2
Texaco 8½ 03	7.7	100	111	−½

1. Column 1 lists the issuer of the corporate bond. The corporate name is abbreviated, sometimes differently than you see in stock tables. After the company name are the coupon rate of the bond and the final two numbers of the year the bond is scheduled to mature. In the example, the first bond is issued by AT&T, has a 7 percent coupon rate and is scheduled to mature in 2006. The second bond is issued by Texaco, carries an 8½ percent coupon rate and is scheduled to mature in 2003.

2. The *current yield* column shows the annual interest payment as a percentage of the current bond price. You would receive this effective yield if you bought the bond at the current price. This column allows you to compare one bond's yield with those of competing issues. In the example, the AT&T bond yields 7 percent, while the Texaco bond pays 7.7 percent.

3. *Volume* means the number of trades in the bond in yesterday's trading. It is expressed in sales of $1,000 bonds. The trading volume will tell you how actively traded the bond is. In the example, 272 AT&T bonds traded yesterday, and 100 Texaco bonds changed hands.

4. *Close* means the closing price for the bond in yesterday's trading. The number is quoted in $100 units, so to calculate the value of the bond, multiply by ten. In the example, the AT&T bond, now selling at $106,

Figure 5.8
Sample Inverted Yield Curve

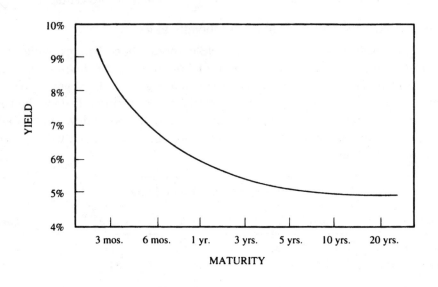

would bring $1,060. The Texaco bond, trading at $111, would cost $1,110.

5. The *net change* column indicates whether the bond's price rose or fell from the previous day's closing price. In the example, the AT&T bond rose 2 in yesterday's trading, or $20 per bond. The Texaco bond fell ½, or $5 per bond. As the price on the AT&T bond rose, its current yield fell. As the price on the Texaco bond fell, its yield rose.

Corporate bond tables also contain various footnotes.

cf—certificates, meaning the bond comes with certificates

cld—called, meaning the bond is in the process of being redeemed

cv—convertible, allowing the bond's owner to convert it into common shares at some point in the future

dc—deep discount, signifying the bond is selling far below its par value of 100. A deep discount bond may be selling at 20, for instance.

ec—denominated in European currency units, not dollars

f—flat, signifying the bond is not paying interest. A bond that has defaulted is flat, for instance.

m—matured, meaning it has limited trading potential because it is in the process of being paid off

na—no accrual, signifying the bond is not accruing interest

r—registered, meaning the bond has a registration certificate

t—floating rate, signifying the bond's rate is tied to some index that changes over time, unlike most bonds, which are fixed at a certain rate when they are issued

vj—an issuer currently in bankruptcy or receivership. In many cases, this means the bond is not currently paying interest.

wd—when distributed, indicating the bond has not actually been distributed to investors yet

ww—with warrants, meaning that when you buy this bond, you also get warrants (or rights) to buy more bonds

x—ex-interest, meaning the bond just made its interest payment. If you buy it now, you will receive the next interest payment, probably in six months.

xw—without warrants attached

zr—zero-coupon, meaning the bond has a coupon of 0 but is sold at a deep discount. The bond gains value each year until it matures at a par price of 100.

Treasury bonds. Depending on how many years remain to maturity, federal government fixed-income securities are called bills (up to 1 year to maturity), notes (1 to 10 years) or bonds (10 years or more). Because Treasury bills are considered an alternative to cash investments like CDs and money-market funds, they are covered in Chapter 2 on cash instruments.

Treasury note and bond prices are listed in the same tables in *The Wall Street Journal, Investor's Business Daily* and other financial newspapers. The tables present a long list of bonds in order of maturity, from the closest to maturity to the furthest from maturity. If there is a normal yield curve, you will notice that the yields rise as you look down the column because longer maturity bonds tend to pay higher yields.

Because the government bond market is run by dealers trading with each other and not by an exchange like the New York Stock Exchange, the prices you see in Treasury bond tables are the prices at which dealers are willing to buy and sell those maturity bonds on that particular day. The government bond market also uses denominations of 32nds rather than 100ths, so the decimal points do not mean what you might think. A price of 101:01 means 101⅓₂, for example.

Following is a typical Treasury bond table, plus an explanation of each column.

Sample Treasury Bond Table

Rate[1]	Month/Year[2]	Bid[3]	Asked[4]	Change[5]	Asked Yield[6]
5½	Feb 99	99:24	99:26	−1	5.66
6¼	Feb 03	102:01	102:03	−6	5.77
8⅛	May 21	125:10	125:16	−25	6.07

1. The first column notes the bond's *coupon rate.* In the example, the first bond has a coupon of 5½ percent; the second, 6¼ percent; and the third, 8⅛ percent.

2. Column 2 lists the month and year the bond is scheduled to mature. The month is abbreviated, and only the final two numbers of the year are shown. In the example, the bonds listed will mature in February 1999, February 2003 and May 2021.

3. The *bid price* is the dollar amount dealers will pay for the bond. The decimal point refers to 32nds, not 10ths or 100ths. Each 32nd is worth 31¼ cents. In the example, the 99:24 price of the first bond equals 99 and 24/32nds. If 24/32nds amounts to $7.68, the bond is worth $997.68. The price of the second bond, at 102:01, amounts to $1,020.31¼. The price of the third bond, at 125:10, equals $1,253.12½.

4. The *asked price* is the dollar amount for which dealers will sell the bond. The method of showing prices is exactly the same as in column 3. Note that the asked price is slightly higher than the bid price. The difference is the dealers' profit, or *spread.*

5. Column 5 notes the *change* in the bond's price from the previous day's closing price, based on the bid price.

6. *Asked yield* means the bond's yield to maturity. This yield combines the bond's current yield and the difference between the current price and the bond's value when it is redeemed.

Major newspapers like *The Wall Street Journal* will also list prices of government agency bonds, such as those issued by the Federal National Mortgage Association (Fannie Mae), the Federal Home Loan Bank (FHLB) and the Student Loan Marketing Association (Sallie Mae). The newspapers use exactly the same listing format as they do for Treasury bonds.

Municipal bond prices are generally not quoted in newspapers because thousands of such bonds exist, and many trade infrequently. The best way to obtain municipal bond prices is to contact a dealer, who can bring up current quotes on a computer.

Types of Bonds: Choosing the Best for You

Now that you understand the basics of bonds, it is time to discuss the advantages and disadvantages of the many kinds of bonds that exist. Selecting the best bond for you depends on the size of your assets, your financial goals, your risk tolerance, your tax situation and your knowledge level. The following sections touch on each kind of bond, starting with the most conservative (Treasuries) and ending with the most speculative (junk bonds).

TREASURY BONDS

Bonds issued by the U.S. government are considered the safest around because Uncle Sam has a weapon to back these bonds that no other entity has: the printing press. If the government does not have enough funds to honor its debts, it can always print more money. When Congress raises the national debt ceiling every year or two, the government is, in effect, giving itself permission to borrow more money. This is known as the full faith and credit of the U.S. government, and it backs every Treasury security.

From a bond investor's point of view, *Treasury bonds* trade as though they are free from the risk of default. No one can even envision a default on Treasury bonds; the government must borrow money constantly in order to operate. It would be totally against the government's interest to default because the government would never again be able to sell bonds in the market, thus ensuring the government's instant collapse.

Because Treasuries are considered immune from default, they are the benchmark against which all other bonds are compared. Treasuries are to the bond world what diamonds are to the precious gem world: Nothing is more secure than a Treasury, and no stone is harder than a diamond. Whenever you investigate another bond's default risk, yield, after-tax return and ease of trading, compare it to what a Treasury offers. Treasury notes work just like bonds except that notes are shorter maturities.

Treasury bonds are issued in minimum denominations of $1,000 and also in $5,000, $10,000, $100,000 and $1 million sizes. To invest in Treasury bonds, you put up your $1,000 (or more) and receive interest checks every six months. Under a program called Treasury Direct, you can have your interest checks deposited electronically in any bank or financial institution you choose.

Treasury bills, discussed in more detail in Chapter 2 on page 73, mature in a year or less and come in minimum denominations of $10,000. To invest in Treasury bills, you pay less than the $10,000 face amount but receive $10,000 when the bill matures. So, for example, you might pay $9,500 for a three-month Treasury bill, and in three months, you get $10,000. The $500 in interest you received means the bill yielded 5.26 percent. To calculate your yield on a Treasury bill, divide the interest by the amount you invested (see page 78 for more explanation).

$$\frac{\$500 \text{ Interest earned}}{\$9,500 \text{ Capital invested}} = 5.26\% \text{ Yield on Treasury bill}$$

If you buy Treasury securities directly from a Federal Reserve bank or branch (a list of them appears in the "Resources" section) or the Bureau of Public Debt (1300 C St., S.W., Washington, DC 20239), you do not have to pay any fees. The easiest way to buy directly is to put in a so-called noncompetitive bid at one of the Treasury's quarterly auctions, which usually occur in February, May, August and November. Entering such a bid means you will accept whatever average rate emerges for the securities you want to buy. If you buy a Treasury security through a regular bank or brokerage firm, it will charge a modest fee of between $50 and $60.

Because literally trillions of dollars' worth of outstanding Treasury securities exist, the market for them is huge, and it is extremely easy to buy or sell them. But remember, just because Treasuries are free from default risk does not mean you can't lose money on them. If you buy when rates are low and sell after rates have risen, the value of your Treasury bond will fall. On the other hand, if you buy when rates are high and sell after rates have fallen, you can capture a capital gain, on which you must pay a capital gains tax.

Treasuries have another feature quite unique in the bond world. Almost all Treasury bonds are *noncallable.* That means the Treasury cannot redeem them before maturity, as many corporations and municipalities can do with their bonds. In some rare cases, Treasuries may be redeemed early, but for the most part, you are able to lock in the current rate on a Treasury for much longer than you are with any other bond. Just ask any of those happy investors who, in the early 1980s, bought 30-year Treasury bonds with 13 percent yields. Despite the decade-long plunge in rates that followed, they are still collecting their 13 percent interest every six months.

U.S. government bonds have another advantage that many people do not realize: All the interest you earn is exempt from state and local taxes. As part of the U.S. Constitution, a separation of federal and state powers was set up so that states cannot tax federal securities. In addition, the federal government cannot tax state and local securities (for more information, see page 227). This is why, for residents of the issuing state, municipal bonds are exempt from federal taxes. By avoiding state and local taxes on Treasury securities, your effective after-tax yield is actually a bit higher than you might think, particularly if you live in a high-tax city or state. For example, say you own a Treasury bond worth $10,000 that is yielding 10 percent, or $1,000, a year. If your combined city and state tax rate is 10 percent, you have avoided paying the $100 in local taxes that would have been due if Treasury interest were not exempt. You still must pay federal income tax on your Treasury bond interest, of course.

Treasuries have all these wonderful features, but what is their disadvantage? In return for the safety, liquidity and tax advantages, you receive a lower yield than is available from other bonds. How much lower depends on the current market conditions and the bonds to which you compare Treasuries. But for conservative income-oriented investors, there's no match for Treasuries.

U.S. SAVINGS BONDS

Even though savings bonds are another form of Treasury security, they have several features that are worth discussing separately. Like other Treasuries, savings bonds have the backing of the full faith and credit of the U.S. government (see Figure 5.9), and the interest they pay is free from state and local taxes. Unlike other Treasuries, though, savings bonds have the following features.

- *They are available in much smaller denominations.* You can buy a savings bond at any bank, or through your company by payroll deduction, for as little as $25 apiece. They also come in denominations of $50, $75, $100, $200, $500, $1,000, $5,000 and $10,000. The government limits you to investing a maximum of $15,000 a year in savings bonds.

- *Series EE savings bonds are issued at half their face value.* When you buy a $50 bond, for example, you pay $25 for it. They have no set maturity date and pay no current interest, but you can redeem them any time—from within six months of buying them to as long as 30 years later, according to a redemption schedule published by the Treasury Department. Depending on when the bond was issued, it has a different original maturity date, which is the maximum amount of time it takes for the bond to reach face value. This table shows the original term for Series EE bonds issued since 1980:

Issue Date	*Original Term*
1/80–10/80	11 years
11/80–4/81	9 years
5/81–10/82	8 years
11/82–10/86	10 years
11/86–2/93	12 years
3/93–4/95	18 years
5/95–Present	17 years

After a savings bond reaches its original maturity, it automatically enters one or more extension periods, usually of ten years duration. For bonds issued before May 1995, the interest is either based on a guaranteed yield or a market-based rate. If a guaranteed rate applies, it is the one in effect at the time the bond entered the extension period. If the bond was issued after April 1995, there is no guaranteed minimum yield, but instead a market rate of interest based on the rules applying to savings bonds at the time they enter the extension period.

Savings bonds stop earning interest when they reach final maturity. For Series EE bonds, that is 30 years, and for Series HH bonds, it is 20 years.

Figure 5.9
Savings Bond

Source: Courtesy of the United States Savings Bonds Division, Department of the Treasury.

- *Savings bond interest is exempt from state and local income and personal property tax.* You owe federal income tax on the interest earned when you redeem the bonds. When you cash in a savings bond at a bank, you will receive a Form 1099 INT from the bank telling you how much interest to report on your federal income tax return. Savings bond principal and interest are also subject to gift, estate, inheritance and other federal and state excise taxes.

- *You can swap noninterest-bearing Series EE bonds for a minimum of $500 worth of Series HH bonds, which pay cash interest at a 4 percent rate.* You must pay taxes on the cash interest for the tax year in which you receive the checks. But when you swap, you do not have to pay taxes on all the interest your EEs accumulated until you redeem the HHs. Series HH bonds mature in ten years.

- *Yields on U.S. savings bonds are not fixed.* Instead, for bonds issued May 1997 or later, they earn interest based on 90 percent of the average yields of five-year Treasury securities for the preceding six months. These bonds increase in value every month, and interest is compounded semiannually. The new rate is announced each May 1 and November 1. Series EE bonds issued from May 1995 through April 1997 earn short-term market-based rates during their first five years and long-term based rates from 5 through 17 years. The rate this bond earns is adjusted to market-based rates every six months. Series EE bonds issued before May 1995 earn market-based yields based on 85 percent of the average five-year Treasury yields, if you've held them for at least five years, as long as this rate is higher than the guaranteed minimum yields available at that time.

- *The government no longer guarantees a minimum yield.* For many years, the Treasury guaranteed that you would earn a minimum of 6 percent if you held a savings bond for at least five years. In 1993, the minimum was lowered to 4 percent, and in 1995, the minimum was dropped altogether for all newly issued savings bonds.

- *If your modified adjusted gross income is between $50,850 and $65,850 for individuals or $76,250 and $106,250 for couples married filing jointly at the time you redeem your savings bonds (this amount is adjusted slightly upward for inflation every year), the interest you earn from the bonds is either fully or partially tax exempt if you use it for college tuition for either yourself, your spouse or your children.* This version of savings bonds is called an Education Bond, and it can apply to any bond purchased after Dec. 31, 1989. Make sure to keep the savings bonds in your own name if you plan on using the proceeds for educational expenses.

As you can see, savings bonds have a lot going for them. If you sign up to receive them as part of a payroll savings plan, you receive an added benefit: You build capital automatically, which will come in handy if you need quick cash for an emergency or when you need capital to live on in retirement.

To find out more about how savings bonds work, you can contact any Federal Reserve Bank (see the list at the end of this chapter), or write the Savings Bond Office at the U.S. Treasury, 999 E St. NW, Washington DC 20004. You can call that office at 202-447-1775 or find the latest savings bond rates at 800-872-6637. Another good source of information is the Treasury's Web site (www.publicdebt.treas. gov/sav/sav.htm), which answers frequently asked questions and includes a Savings Bond Earnings Report telling you what your bonds are earning. The site also includes a Savings Bond Wizard, which displays the current value and interest earned for each of your bonds and the total of all your bonds, and allows you to change the redemption date so you can see what the bond's value will be on the new redemption date.

Another source of information about savings bonds is the Savings Bond Informer (P.O. Box 09249, Detroit, MI 48209; 313-843-1910; 800-927-1901). This private-sector service will help you figure how much your savings bonds are worth, when the best time to redeem them arrives and whether you have bonds that have stopped earning interest.

GOVERNMENT AGENCY SECURITIES

One notch more risky than Treasuries and savings bonds are the securities issued by a plethora of federal-government-backed agencies. Though they do not have the full faith and credit of the U.S. government behind them, you can be certain Congress would find a way to make sure these agencies don't default on their debt. Take the savings and loan crisis, for example. Congress appropriated a few hundred billion dollars to make sure depositors covered by the Federal Savings and Loan Insurance Corporation (FSLIC) would not lose their money. Though the specific laws backing each agency are different, the effect is the same: A default is almost unthinkable.

Because agency securities are not considered as completely risk free as Treasury securities, they pay slightly higher yields. If a Treasury bond yields 8 percent, a federal agency security of the same maturity might pay from 8.25 percent to 9 percent, for instance. Like interest from Treasuries, interest from agency securities is usually taxable at the federal level but exempt from state and local taxes. As with any bond, you must pay a capital gains tax if you sell a federal agency bond for a profit. The two major exceptions to this rule are mortgage-backed securities of the Federal National Mortgage Association (Fannie Mae) and the Government National Mortgage Association (Ginnie Mae). (The next section discusses mortgage-backed securities in more detail.)

Unlike Treasuries, federal agency securities are not auctioned directly to the public; they are sold by a network of bond dealers and banks. Nonetheless, they are easy to buy through any brokerage firm. The dealer usually does not charge an explicit commission on agency securities (or on most other bonds), but he or she marks up the bonds and earns a profit on the spread between the price the dealer paid for them and the price at which he or she sells them. Depending on the agency, the bonds come in minimum denominations of $1,000 to $25,000.

The agencies that issue securities to the public are numerous and varied in their public purpose. The following is a list of the biggest issuers of government-backed paper, with their acronyms or nicknames, where applicable.

Asian Development Bank
College Construction Loan Insurance Corporation (Connie Lee)
Export-Import Bank of the United States
Farmers Home Administration (FmHA)
Federal Agricultural Mortgage Corporation (Farmer Mac)
Federal Farm Credit System
Federal Home Loan Bank System (FHLB)
Federal Home Loan Mortgage Corporation (Freddie Mac)
Federal Housing Administration (FHA)
Federal National Mortgage Association (Fannie Mae)
Government National Mortgage Association (Ginnie Mae)
International Bank for Reconstruction and Development (World Bank)
Resolution Funding Corporation (Refcorp)
Small Business Administration (SBA)
Student Loan Marketing Association (Sallie Mae)
Tennessee Valley Authority (TVA)
United States Postal Service

Some of these agencies are fully owned by the government; therefore, their securities are considered nearly as safe as Treasuries. Such agencies include the Export-Import Bank, the Farmers Home Administration, the FHA, Ginnie Mae, the TVA and the Postal Service. Many of the agencies that are fully owned by the government issue securities through the Federal Financing Bank, established in 1974 as a central clearinghouse for federal agencies to issue debt.

Most of the other agencies listed were originally fully owned by the government but have since been transferred either to public ownership or to ownership by the organizations that benefit from the agency's services. For example, Fannie Mae, Freddie Mac and Sallie Mae are all publicly traded corporations, with their stocks trading on the NYSE. The FHLB is owned by its member banks.

Whether a federal agency bond is right for you depends on its current yield and whether you feel comfortable with the slightly greater risk involved in owning one. For most conservative income-oriented investors, it can be a fine choice.

MORTGAGE-BACKED SECURITIES

You may not realize it, but when you take out a mortgage from your local bank or savings and loan, your monthly mortgage payments are probably funneled by the bank or S&L through a federally designed system to investors who buy mortgage-backed securities. These securities, which go by the names of the agencies that guarantee timely payment of the securities' interest and principal, such as Ginnie Mae, Fannie Mae and Freddie Mac, offer higher yields than Treasury bonds at slightly higher levels of risk.

A *mortgage-backed security* works as follows: Soon after a bank or savings and loan issues a mortgage to a homeowner, the loan is sold along with thousands of other loans to a federal agency, which repackages them in the form of a mortgage-backed security. The federal agency then guarantees it will pay investors interest and principal as they come due, even if a homeowner is late with his or her mortgage payments or defaults on the mortgage. The homeowner continues to make payments to the local bank, which collects a fee from the agency for providing this go-between service. Once the bank receives this money, it can make another mortgage loan and start the process again.

From the investor's point of view, a mortgage-backed security provides regular monthly interest as it is paid by homeowners. In addition, each month, a certain amount of the mortgage principal is repaid, and that money is also passed through to the investor. The investor's brokerage statement will distinguish the two types of income he or she receives from the security each month.

The mortgage-backed securities market, which began in 1970 when Ginnie Mae introduced the concept, has mushroomed. Hundreds of billions of dollars' worth of outstanding mortgage-backed securities now exist, and billions of dollars' worth more are created every year. These securities are actively traded, and plenty of such bonds are always available from any major brokerage firm.

However, several problems exist for small investors buying individual mortgage-backed securities. First, the minimum denomination is $25,000 though some older issues trading at lower prices may require less than that. Second, the timing of interest and principal payments is not totally predictable. This is the biggest difference between a mortgage-backed security and a Treasury bond, which pays interest every six months and is not callable for years.

The interest and principal repayment schedule is uncertain because the homeowners making the payments can be unpredictable. If mortgage rates fall enough to make it worthwhile, they will refinance their higher interest mortgages. On the other hand, if mortgage rates rise, homeowners will hold onto their mortgages for dear life. And if a homeowner sells the residence, he or she may have to pay off the mortgage and take out another loan for his or her new home. Because the mortgage-backed security is a conduit through which homeowner payments pass, all of this activity greatly affects the cash flow received by investors.

In certain situations, the investors in a mortgage-backed security lose whichever way interest rates go. For instance, say an investor buys a Ginnie Mae filled with 10 percent mortgages, and mortgage rates drop over the next few years to 7 percent. Many of the homeowners in that Ginnie Mae pool will refinance their mortgages to lock in 7 percent, causing the investor to receive a flood of principal at a time when interest rates have fallen and it is impossible to replicate that 10 percent yield. In another scenario, if interest rates soar from 10 percent to 13 percent, exactly the reverse would happen. Few, if any, homeowners would refinance their mortgages at higher rates, so the investor would receive only a small amount of principal. With rates at 13 percent, though, the investor would love to receive principal so he or she could reinvest it at the higher rates.

As the mortgage-backed securities market has matured over the last two decades, these problems have become well recognized. The mortgage-backed securities industry has reacted in two ways: by raising yields and by creating new forms of mortgage-backed paper. To compensate investors for the uncertainty about the pace of repayment, mortgage-backed securities now pay between 1 and 2 percentage points more than Treasury securities of similar maturities. So, if a 10-year Treasury is paying 8 percent, you might be able to earn as much as 10 percent from a Ginnie Mae or Fannie Mae.

As though regular mortgage-backed securities were not complicated enough, a newer and even more complex version called a *collateralized mortgage obligation* (CMO) or a *real estate mortgage investment conduit* (REMIC), has been invented to ease the prepayment worry. In theory, a CMO or REMIC works by slicing a mortgage-backed securities pool into *tranches* (the French word for slice). All prepayments from underlying mortgages are applied to the first tranche until it is paid off. Then prepayments are applied to the next tranche until it is redeemed, and so on, until all the tranches are eventually retired. The idea behind this slice-and-dice routine is that investors will be able to choose a tranche that most closely meets their maturity needs and will have a better chance that the security will last that long. Yet because tranches still do not guarantee prepayment schedules, investors receive a yield that is 1 to 3 percentage points higher than they would earn on similar maturity Treasuries.

Even though all this sounds extremely complicated, billions of dollars flow into mortgage-backed securities, CMOs and REMICs these days, as people search out higher yields than are available from bank CDs and money-market funds. Realizing this, brokers market CMOs aggressively. (See Figure 5.10.) Mortgage-backed securities may be right for you, as long as you understand what you are getting into.

In addition to mortgage-backed securities, there exist several new classes of securities backed by other types of loans. These work exactly like mortgage-

Figure 5.10
Sample CMO (Collateralized Mortgage Obligation) Brochures

backed paper. The latest forms of asset-backed securities include pools of credit card loans, car loans, mobile home loans and college loans. If you consider buying into one of these innovative loan pools, apply the same criteria you used with mortgage-backed securities.

MUNICIPAL BONDS

Though riskier than Treasury or agency securities, *municipal bonds* (munis) are extremely popular. These bonds, issued by states, cities, counties, towns, villages and taxing authorities of many types, have one feature that separates them from all other securities: The interest they pay is totally free from federal taxes. In most cases, bondholders who are also residents of the states issuing the bonds do not have to pay state or local taxes on the interest either. (For a list of which states tax bonds and which do not, see the end of this section). Bonds not taxable by the resident state are known as *double-tax-free bonds,* and those also not taxable by a locality are called *triple-tax-free issues.* The exemption from federal taxation is based on the 1895 Supreme Court case of *Pollock vs. Farmers' Loan and Trust Company,* which applied the constitutional doctrine of "intergovernmental tax immunity." The High Court ruled that this doctrine means that states are immune from federal interference with their ability to borrow money.

The fact that the interest from municipal bonds is federally tax free allows issuers to float bonds with yields lower than taxable government and corporate bond issuers must pay. Investors are satisfied to earn 6 percent tax free, compared to 8 percent on a Treasury, on which federal taxes are due. The higher an investor's federal, state and local tax bracket, the more attractive munis become because they permit the investor to escape more taxes. At the same time, the lower yields that municipalities pay make it affordable for them to build roads, schools, sewer systems, hospitals and other public facilities.

The market for municipal bonds is huge: Several hundred billion dollars' worth of bonds are outstanding, and billions of dollars' worth of new bonds are issued every year. While there exist millions of bonds and thousands of issuers, no centralized marketplace trades munis as it does stocks. Instead, municipal bonds are bought and sold by the many brokerage firms and banks that specialize in them. These dealers communicate with each other through a telephone and computer network. To buy municipal bonds, you must go through a broker or bank that can plug into this complex system of competing dealers. As with other bonds, brokers usually do not charge a separate commission to buy or sell your municipal issue. Instead, they make their money by marking up the bond from their cost by about 2 percent.

Municipal bonds are usually issued in minimum denominations of $5,000 though some are issued in lots as small as $1,000. Brokers usually require a minimum order of $5,000, but they prefer dealing in blocks of five bonds, or $25,000.

Small orders invariably are hit with markups as high as 5 percent. Depending on the dollar volume of the bonds when they are issued, trading can be very active or almost nonexistent. Many municipalities have issued only a few bonds during their history, so the bonds are hard to buy or sell. If you plan to buy a bond and hold it until maturity, the fact that little trading activity occurs should be of little concern to you. When shopping for a municipal bond, ask how many years of protection against early redemption you will receive. Many municipal bond investors have been shocked in recent years when they received their principal back much sooner than they expected it.

Two main types of municipal bonds exist: *general obligation* and *revenue* bonds. General obligation bonds (GOs) are issued by a state or local entity and are backed by the taxing power of that state, city or town. In general, the proceeds from these issues are used to finance general capital expenditures, as well as ongoing municipal operations. Revenue bonds, on the other hand, finance specific revenue-producing projects, such as toll roads, bridges, tunnels, sewer systems or airports. The interest and principal paid by the bonds comes from the economic activity generated by the bonds. For instance, a revenue bond might be floated to finance a new highway. The proceeds of the issue will be spent to build the road, and tolls collected on the road for the next several years will pay the interest and principal on the bonds. You can buy many other forms of revenue bonds, some riskier than others. For example, so-called private purpose bonds can be issued on behalf of hospitals, universities or other nonprofit organizations. Industrial revenue bonds are sponsored by municipalities to finance construction of factories or industrial parks that will bring jobs into a district.

Aside from different kinds of general obligation and revenue bonds, some municipal issues can be taxable under certain circumstances. For example, some bonds are issued to be subject to federal income tax but exempt from state and local taxes to in-state residents who buy them. Other bonds, known as *alternative minimum tax* (AMT) bonds, can be taxed if the holder falls into the alternative minimum tax trap, which is designed to keep wealthy people from avoiding federal taxes altogether. If the holder will not be hit by the AMT, these bonds, which pay a slightly higher yield than regular munis, would provide totally tax-free income.

Debates rage among bond analysts over whether general obligation or revenue bonds are safer for investors. To some extent, the safety of the bond depends on the financial situation of the issuing entity and the revenue potential of the project the issue funds. Though defaults by states and cities are exceedingly rare, they can happen if political gridlock occurs in a state or city where expenses are soaring, revenues are falling and residents are moving out. Revenue projects normally are a safe bet as well, but they can be disrupted if an economic contraction (the area's economy takes a downturn) in the area of the project causes revenues to come in under projections. The best way to judge the safety of any particular issue is to look at the bond's safety rating by Standard & Poor's, Moody's or Fitch. (For more on ratings, see page 210.)

If you would rather not worry at all about safety, a conservative alternative called *municipal bond insurance* is becoming more widely available on a broad range of municipal bonds. You cannot buy insurance on your bonds individually, but you can purchase bonds that already have insurance attached to them. The municipal bond insurers, such as the Municipal Bond Investors Assurance Corporation (MBIA), the American Municipal Bond Assurance Corporation (AMBAC) and several others, guarantee that you will receive timely payments of interest and principal for the life of the bond if the issuer defaults. (A list of the top nine bond insurance companies appears at the end of this chapter.) Insured bonds usually trade as though they have an AAA rating because no risk of default exists. However, the cost of the insurance is passed on to the investor; insured bonds usually yield a little less than similar noninsured bonds.

Determining your taxable equivalent yield. To calculate whether a municipal bond makes sense for you, compare its yield with taxable alternatives to see which bond leaves you the most money after taxes. The following exercise helps you determine the taxable equivalent yield of your muni.

First, deduct your federal tax bracket from 100. (This example uses a 31 percent tax bracket.) The result is known as the reciprocal of your tax bracket.

$$
\begin{array}{lr}
& 100 \\
\text{Tax bracket} & -31 \\
\hline
\text{Reciprocal of tax bracket} & 69 \\
\end{array}
$$

Divide the tax-free yield on the municipal bond you are considering by the reciprocal of your tax bracket. (In this case, assume the bond pays a 7 percent tax-free yield.)

$$
\frac{7\% \text{ Municipal bond yield}}{69 \text{ Reciprocal of tax bracket}} = 10.14\% \text{ Taxable equivalent yield}
$$

The above calculation means you would have to buy a taxable bond paying 10.14 percent to end up with the same dollar amount after taxes that the 7 percent muni will pay. To earn that high a yield, you would normally have to take on far more risk than a municipal bond entails.

To make munis look even more attractive, go through the same exercise adding in your state and local tax brackets. For example, if your combined federal, state and local tax brackets total 40 percent, the taxable equivalent yield of a 7 percent muni would be an astounding 11.6 percent! You can see why munis are so popular.

The following table will give you a few taxable equivalent yields for various tax-free muni yields. As you can see, the higher the tax bracket, the more you would have to earn in a taxable bond to end up with the same after-tax return.

Federal Tax Bracket	Tax-Exempt Yield				
	4%	5%	6%	7%	8%
15%	4.71%	5.88%	7.05%	8.23%	9.41%
28	5.56	6.94	8.33	9.72	11.11
31	5.80	7.25	8.70	10.14	11.59
36	6.25	7.81	9.37	10.93	12.50
39.6	6.62	8.27	9.93	11.58	13.24

Which states tax which bonds. In almost every state, interest from bonds issued by that state is tax free to state residents. The only exceptions are Illinois, Iowa, Kansas, Oklahoma and Wisconsin. For residents of those states, interest from some, but not all, in-state bonds is tax exempt.

The following states never impose state taxes on interest earned by residents who buy bonds issued by other states: Alaska, the District of Columbia, Indiana, Nevada, South Dakota, Texas, Utah, Washington and Wyoming.

The following states do impose state taxes on interest earned by residents who buy bonds issued by other states:

Alabama	Mississippi
Arizona	Missouri
Arkansas	Montana
California	Nebraska
Colorado	New Hampshire
Connecticut	New Jersey
Delaware	New Mexico
Florida	New York
Georgia	North Carolina
Hawaii	North Dakota
Idaho	Ohio
Illinois	Oklahoma
Iowa	Oregon
Kansas	Pennsylvania
Kentucky	Rhode Island
Louisiana	South Carolina
Maine	Tennessee
Maryland	Vermont
Massachusetts	Virginia
Michigan	West Virginia
Minnesota	Wisconsin

Keep these taxation rules in mind when you are deciding whether it makes more sense to buy an in-state bond or an out-of-state bond. Your return will depend on whether the out-of-state bond is taxable and on your state tax rates.

Clearly, if you are in a high enough tax bracket, it could be quite worthwhile to investigate municipal bonds. They are not only safe; their after-tax yields can often beat any other taxable alternative.

CORPORATE BONDS

The next rung down the ladder of bond risk are bonds issued by corporations. While the U.S. government and its agencies, states, and municipalities are not going to disappear, corporations may not be around forever. Thousands of companies go bankrupt each year. Firms thrive or crash based on their success in the marketplace, and that is never ensured. Because corporations, no matter how solid financially, are thus perceived as vulnerable to changes in the business environment, the bonds they issue are considered riskier than government issues and therefore always pay a higher yield than government issues of the same maturity.

Still, only a tiny percentage of corporate bonds—typically less than 1 percent —ever default. Thousands of perfectly solid issues are outstanding, and many more come to market every year. Even in the worst-case scenario of a company going bankrupt, bondholders' claims are settled before stockholders receive any compensation.

As an individual investor, you have many opportunities to increase your income by holding corporate bonds. Most bonds pay interest semiannually and use the electronic book-entry system, so interest payments can be sent automatically to your brokerage account. Depending on the financial creditworthiness of the issuing company, a corporate bond can yield from 2 to 6 percentage points more than Treasuries of the same maturity.

As with all bonds, you can profit by buying them when interest rates are high and selling them after rates have fallen and bond prices have climbed. Corporate bond prices react to general fluctuations in interest rates, as well as the financial fortunes (or misfortunes) of the issuing companies. For example, a bond's price will rise if the company's finances improve because investors anticipate that the bond's safety rating from agencies like Standard & Poor's might be upgraded. On the other hand, a series of financial setbacks will cause the bond's price to sink, as investors fear a rating downgrade. If the situation deteriorates enough, the bond's price might plummet to very low levels because investors think the firm might declare bankruptcy and default on its bond payments.

Corporate bonds typically are issued in denominations of $1,000 and quoted in units of $100, like Treasury bonds. (Refer back to the discussion on page 243 about reading corporate bond tables.) Most bond dealers don't like trading in lots of fewer than five bonds, or less than $5,000. For smaller lots, brokers' markups can be quite high. In some cases, brokers will charge a minimum per-bond commission of as much as $20.

Many of the thousands of outstanding corporate bonds trade quite actively and are therefore easy to buy and sell. Some smaller issues may not trade as frequently, which means there will be a wider spread between the buying price and the selling price.

As with municipal bonds, you must research your protection against premature calls carefully. Many corporate bonds offer ten years guaranteed against early redemption though call protection varies widely. Among the most frustrating experiences for investors is to have a high-yield corporate bond plucked from their grasp after interest rates have fallen sharply. Corporate treasurers will always do whatever is in the best interest of their stockholders—which is to refinance high-yield debt at the first possible moment.

Most corporate bonds are unsecured, meaning they are backed only by the companies' general ability to repay them out of cash flow and profits. Such unsecured bonds are generally called *debentures*. Other corporate bonds are secured by a particular asset, which becomes the property of bondholders if a company defaults. Examples of secured corporate bonds include mortgage bonds, backed by real estate, and equipment trust certificates, backed by equipment such as airplanes or railroad cars.

While most corporate bonds are fairly conservative, junk bonds allow riskier investment. (An upcoming section describes junk bonds in more detail.)

FOREIGN BONDS

You need not restrict your search for solid, income-producing bonds to U.S. securities. There's a big world beyond our shores, and it is filled with opportunities in highly rated, high-yielding bonds issued by foreign governments and foreign-based corporations.

Foreign government bonds, like U.S. Treasuries, are backed by the full faith and credit of the issuing countries. While that sounds comforting, the guarantee has more weight coming from an industrialized country like Germany or France than from a developing country like Kenya or Costa Rica. In some places where political turbulence seems to be a local tradition, like Argentina or Haiti, protecting the interests of bondholders is not usually high on the latest ruler's priority list. Because most investors do not want to have to worry about receiving their interest and principal, the foreign government bonds that trade most actively in the United States are issued by industrialized countries.

Most U.S. brokers can sell foreign government bonds, though the easiest ones to trade are so-called *Yankee bonds,* which are issued in the United States by foreign governments and are denominated in dollars. It is probably not worth the hassle of buying a bond denominated in a foreign currency and having to convert interest payments in francs, pounds or deutsche marks into dollars. Most foreign bonds, even Yankee bonds, come in minimum denominations much higher than the denominations of domestic issues. Depending on the country, you might have to invest at least $25,000 to buy one German or French bond, for instance.

Foreign corporate bonds have drawbacks similar to foreign government bonds. The bonds that are most actively traded are those issued by large, well-known, foreign-based corporations like Sony in Japan, Barclays Bank in the United Kingdom, Michelin in France or Siemens in Germany. In many cases, you can find a Yankee bond that pays interest in U.S. dollars. Minimum investments still tend to be higher than they are for domestic bonds, often running in the $25,000 range.

Foreign bonds might make sense for you for two reasons. First, the yields on foreign bonds can be significantly higher than those on similar domestic issues. Other governments may have large budget deficits, or their central banks want to slow their economies to stop inflation, causing high yields.

The other reason foreign bonds can be profitable is that their value to U.S. investors can rise if the U.S. dollar falls against the foreign currencies. So, in the best of all worlds, your foreign bond can give you not only a high yield but capital gains as well.

When you buy a foreign bond, you are, in effect, converting your dollars into the bond's foreign currency. If that currency appreciates against the dollar, you will have earned a profit when you convert the bond back into dollars. To take a highly exaggerated example, say you buy a $1,000 bond denominated in British pounds when you get two pounds for one U.S. dollar. If, over the next few years, the British pound appreciates so you get one pound for each dollar, you will double your money from $1,000 to $2,000. The following breaks down this exaggerated example to determine your potential gain (this example is for illustration only; the dollar-pound relationship does not fluctuate this widely).

When buying the bond:

$1,000 = 2,000 pounds, with an exchange rate of 1 dollar for 2 pounds

When selling the bond:

2,000 pounds = $2,000, with an exchange rate of 1 dollar for 1 pound

Profit: $1,000, or 100%

Of course, if the value of the dollar appreciates against the foreign currency, you will lose money when you translate the bond back into dollars. Therefore, when you consider buying a foreign bond, evaluate whether the dollar seems to be getting stronger or weaker. It's best to wait until you think the dollar is getting weaker.

Despite the potential high yields and profits from foreign bonds, most individuals play this market by buying mutual funds that specialize in foreign bonds. Funds allow investors to avoid the complexities and high cost of buying individual foreign bonds, yet they offer high yields and the play on the U.S. dollar. (For more on foreign bond funds, see page 276 later in this chapter.)

Zero-Coupon Bonds

Zero-coupon bonds—called zeros for short—can, paradoxically, be the safest of all investments or the riskiest. It all depends on how you use them.

A zero-coupon bond gets its name from the fact that the bond is issued with a 0 percent coupon rate. Because people buy bonds to collect interest at the coupon rate, who would ever be interested in a bond that pays no interest? Plenty of people, and here's why:

Instead of making regular interest payments, a zero is issued at a deep discount from its face value of 100, or $5,000. The return on a zero comes from the gradual increase in the bond's price from the discount to face value, which it reaches at maturity.

This slow but steady rise in value yields three benefits.

1. You know exactly how much money you will receive when the bond matures.

2. You know exactly when you will receive that money.

3. You do not have to worry about reinvesting the small amounts of interest regular full-coupon bonds pay.

Very few investments can guarantee you will receive a specific dollar amount years from now. Because zeros have a specific schedule of appreciation, you can use a zero as an integral part of a financial plan to fund specific expenses years in advance. For example, if you are the parent of a newborn, you know to the month when his or her first college tuition payment will be due. Therefore, you can buy a zero maturing in 18 years. Or, if you are a 40-year-old who plans to retire at age 65, you can buy a 25-year zero that will mature on the day your company gives you the gold watch.

When you contact a broker about buying a zero, he or she will usually quote the current price of a bond that will mature at a face value of $1,000 a number of years in the future, (one advantage is that you can buy almost any amount, not a minimum of $5,000) and he or she will tell you what yield you are locking in at that price. The broker's quote will include the markup, so you do not have to figure in an additional commission. Markups can vary widely from broker to broker, so it is important that you shop around. Get at least three quotes, asking for:

• the amount of money you must invest now, including all fees and commissions;

• the amount of money you will receive when the zero matures on the date you choose; and

• the yield to maturity you will be locking in for the years you hold the zero.

Once you have the data for various zeros, choose the bond selling for the lowest price and boasting the highest yield to maturity for the date you want.

For example, if you want to have a lump sum of $10,000 available to you at various times in the future, the following is a table typical of one a broker might give you. It outlines your bond options and lays out the prices and yields you might achieve.

Notice that the longer in the future you want your money back, the fewer dollars you must pay now because you are allowing more time for the zero to compound.

The other attraction of a zero is that your interest is reinvested automatically at the zero's yield. This can be a particularly significant advantage if you lock in a high interest rate. With a regular interest-paying bond, you receive interest checks every six months, which can be helpful if you need the money for living expenses. But if you would rather reinvest the interest to make your capital grow, prevailing interest rates constantly rise and fall, making it impossible to lock in a constant rate of reinvestment. Also, the dollar amount of your interest payment may be so small that you would not be able to afford the minimum needed to buy another bond.

Many issuers of zero-coupon bonds exist, but most investors buy zeros based on Treasury bonds. These zeros are commonly known as *STRIPS,* which stands for *separate trading of registered interest and principal of securities.* Like any other Treasury, they are backed by the full faith and credit of the U.S. government and are noncallable. Some brokerage firms have launched their own versions of STRIPS, with names like Salomon Brothers' *CATS* (certificates of accrual on Treasury securities) and Merrill Lynch's *TIGRs* (Treasury investment growth receipts). In a sense, U.S. savings bonds are also zeros; they work exactly the same way but are issued in much smaller denominations. Also, several large corporations issue zero-coupon bonds that allow you to lock in higher yields than do government issues. For the most part, though, it is best to invest in STRIPS because you do not want to wait 20 years with no payoff, only to discover that the issuing corporation went bankrupt recently.

If you want a diversified portfolio of zeros, you can buy shares in a zero-coupon bond mutual fund for a minimum of $1,000. The largest fund company offering zero-coupon funds is the American Century Benham Group (4500 Main St., Kansas City, MO 64111; 800-345-2021; www.twentieth-century.com). The company offers no-load funds called Benham Target Maturities Trusts that are set to mature every five years (such as 2000, 2005, 2010, 2015, 2020 and 2025). You pay annual expenses of .62 percent of your assets. You can avoid these expenses by buying STRIPS directly. But the fund does offer you a more diversified portfolio, and it is easy to buy and sell without having to pay the large spread some brokers charge.

Taxable zero-coupon bonds have one major pitfall. The Internal Revenue Service (IRS) has ruled that the scheduled yearly growth in the value of a zero-coupon bond (the IRS calls it the bond's accretion) must be considered interest income in the year it is earned even though you do not receive any cash interest

	Current Price	Cost in Dollars	Yield
5-year zero	71.80	$7,180	6.05%
10-year zero	48.12	$4,812	7.05
15-year zero	31.61	$3,161	7.54
20-year zero	20.86	$2,086	7.77
25-year zero	14.28	$1,428	7.76

payments. The IRS publishes an accretion table, telling you how much "imputed" interest you must report each year. This rule can take much of the zip out of zeros because every year, you must pay taxes on interest without having received the interest to pay the taxes.

You have two ways to get around this dilemma: buying zeros only in tax-sheltered accounts or buying tax-free municipal zero-coupon bonds. If you buy a zero through an individual retirement account (IRA), a Keogh account, an annuity, a salary reduction plan or some other vehicle that allows you to defer tax liability until you withdraw money from the account, the IRS accretion rules do not affect you. The zero compounds year after year, untouched by taxes. You pay taxes on the increased value only when you withdraw the money, usually at retirement.

Because you never owe taxes on the interest paid by municipal bonds, the same holds true for muni zeros. You can therefore buy muni zeros in your regular account and watch them compound tax free until they mature. The fact that muni zeros offer such superb benefits makes them extremely popular, which often means they sell out soon after they are issued. Therefore, if you think a muni zero is right for you, contact your broker before a new bond is issued so he or she can prepare to grab a few bonds while they last. When shopping for muni zeros, look carefully at the call provisions of the issues because many allow issuers to redeem them before their scheduled maturity, which could defeat your whole purpose in buying them. Figure 5.11 is an illustration of how a municipal zero would grow from $5,000 when you bought it to $20,000 in 20 years.

The risky side of zeros. So far, we have described zeros as the safest and surest way to fund a distant financial goal, despite one major pitfall. However, another far more volatile side to zeros exists if you use zeros to earn capital gains.

Because zeros lock in a fixed reinvestment rate of interest for a long time, their prices react to fluctuations in interest rates far more than does any other type of bond. For every one-point drop in interest rates over a year, for example, a normal 30-year coupon bond paying 8 percent would produce a total return (price change plus income) of 20 percent, while a 30-year zero with an 8 percent reinvestment rate would soar by 42 percent. Conversely, if interest rates rose by 1 percentage point over a year, the full-coupon bond would suffer a negative total return of 3 percent, while the zero would plunge by 19 percent. The fact that the zero

Figure 5.11
The Growth of a 20-Year Municipal Zero-Coupon Bond Yielding 7%

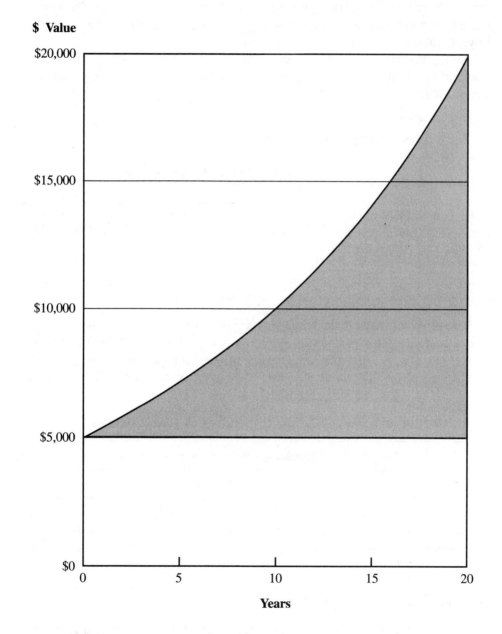

Source: Adapted with permission by Public Securities Association.

compounds its yield automatically for many years magnifies the impact of interest rate changes.

Figure 5.12 shows how the total return of a 30-year zero-coupon Treasury bond with an 8 percent reinvestment rate is affected by interest rate changes of 1 percentage point upward and downward over a year, compared to the effect on a 30-year full-coupon bond paying 8 percent.

Notice that the effect of a 1-percentage-point change is not symmetrical. A 1-point drop yields a 43 percent gain on a zero, while a 1-point rise yields an 18 percent loss.

Figure 5.12
Zeros Versus Full-Coupon Bonds

	Percentage Point Change in a Year								
	+4	*+3*	*+2*	*+1*	*Unchanged*	*−1*	*−2*	*−3*	*−4*
30-year zero	−64%	−53%	−38%	−18%	+8%	+43%	+89%	+139%	+220%
30-year full-coupon	−24	−18	−11	−2	+8	+20	+35	+54	+76

Source: Courtesy of Ryan Labs, Inc., a bond research firm in New York, New York.

The effect of interest rate changes on zeros is lessened if the zeros are of a shorter maturity. This is obvious in Figure 5.13, which illustrates the effect of interest rate changes of 1 percentage point upward and downward on 5-, 10-, 20- and 30-year zeros. (The table assumes 30-year Treasury rates are at 8 percent.)

Figure 5.13
5-, 10-, 20- and 30-year Zeros Responding to Rate Changes

	Percentage Point Change in a Year								
	+4	*+3*	*+2*	*+1*	*Unchanged*	*−1*	*−2*	*−3*	*−4*
30-year zero	−64%	−53%	−38%	−18%	+8%	+43%	+89%	+139%	+220%
20-year zero	−47	−37	−25	−10	+8	+30	+56	+88	+117
10-year zero	−23	−16	−9	0	+8	+18	+29	+40	+53
5-year zero	−7	−4	0	+4	+8	+12	+17	+21	+26

Source: Courtesy of Ryan Labs, Inc., New York, New York.

Notice that if interest rates drop by 4 percentage points, the 30-year zero would soar 220 percent, while the 5-year zero would rise only 26 percent. On the other extreme, if rates shoot up by 4 percentage points, the 30-year bond would plummet

64 percent, while the 5-year zero would fall only 7 percent. This dramatically illustrates that the longer the maturity of the zero, the more volatile its price will be.

As a result of zeros' volatility, they are the favorite weapon for speculators who want to bet that interest rates will fall. This is a game for serious investors, however, because if interest rates rise instead of fall, they can lose big. For most investors, though, zeros are far from a speculative investment.

CONVERTIBLE BONDS

Convertible bonds are hybrids—one part bond and the other part stock. In their role as bonds, they offer regular fixed income though usually at a yield lower than straight bonds of the same issuer. In their role as stocks, convertibles offer significant appreciation potential and a way to benefit from the issuing companies' financial success. However, owners of convertibles will not benefit as much as common stockholders if the companies' fortunes soar. To some investors, convertibles offer the best of both worlds—high income and appreciation potential. To others, convertibles offer the worst of both worlds—lower income than bonds yield and less appreciation potential than common stock offers. Whichever way you view them, convertibles can make a solid contribution to your investment portfolio.

Convertibles come in two forms: *preferred stock* and *debentures,* which are unsecured bonds. Both pay a fixed rate of interest and are convertible into common stock of the issuer when the common stock reaches a certain price, known as the *conversion price.* That conversion price is always set at a level higher than the common stock's price at the time the convertible is first issued. It can be as low as 15 percent above the common price or as high as 50 percent above. When the underlying stock hits the conversion price, the convertible bond can be changed into a specified number of shares at what is called the *conversion ratio.* For example, ABC Corporation may issue a convertible that allows its holders to convert each bond into 50 shares of ABC common when ABC hits $100 a share.

Convertible bond prices are influenced by several factors. Because they are bonds, they are affected by the general ups and downs of interest rates. Also, the market evaluates convertibles as straight fixed-income securities. This gives them their investment value. The market also evaluates convertibles based on their underlying common stock. This gives them their conversion value. When the market takes a dim view of an underlying company, the convertible's investment value is more important than it would be otherwise. If the underlying company is a hot growth stock, however, the convertible will trade more on its conversion value because investors expect the common stock price to rise, and the convertible will eventually be changed into common shares.

You can judge what kind of growth potential the market expects of a convertible by looking at what is known as the *premium over conversion value.* As the underlying common stock rises in value, the convertible is viewed increasingly as a common stock. At a certain point, usually when the dividend on the underlying common stock is more valuable than the interest return from the convertible, it makes sense to convert into common shares. The price of the common shares will rise beyond the convertible price when this happens, signaling that it is time to convert.

The higher the conversion premium, the riskier the bond, however, because the premium can shrink quickly if the hot growth company stumbles. Any premium of more than 20 percent to 25 percent should be seen as a warning sign of increased risk. One way to protect yourself from paying too high a premium is to determine how long it will take to earn back that premium. The following example—in which the conversion premium is 20 percent, the underlying common stock yields 2 percent, and the convertible yields 7 percent—shows you how to do this.

First, subtract the common stock yield from the convertible yield.

Convertible yield	7%
Common stock yield	− 2%
Yield difference	5%

Then divide the premium by the yield difference.

$$20\% \div 5\% = 4 \text{ Years}$$

The answer indicates how long it would take to recover your conversion premium if all else stayed the same. In this case, it would take four years.

Convertible prices tend to fall less than stock prices when the stock market declines because convertibles offer a higher level of income than most stocks, which tends to cushion the convertibles' descent. On the other hand, when the stock market surges, convertibles tend to rise less than stocks.

Convertible bonds are usually denominated in minimums of $1,000 though most brokers like to trade at least ten bonds, or $10,000 worth, at a time. Smaller trades will subject you to larger dealer markups. Depending on the size of the convertible issue, the stature of the issuer and the credit rating of the bond from the ratings agencies, trading may be very active or inactive. As with other bonds, you must determine how much call protection the convertible offers. You don't want the bond redeemed quickly if interest rates fall and the issuer decides to refinance at a lower rate.

Convertibles offer no special tax breaks. All interest paid is fully taxable at the federal, state and local levels. Although no taxes are due when you convert from a bond to common stock, you must pay all the normal taxes on the stock dividends. As with any other security, you must pay capital gains taxes if you sell a convertible for a profit.

Before you buy any convertible, decide whether you want to own the issuer's common stock. If you think the underlying company has a bright future, the convertible can be an excellent choice to improve your current income and profit from the firm's success. However, if you are considering the convertible only for the income, and you would not want to be caught holding the underlying stock, move on to another option. Despite all the bells and whistles of convertibles, they are ultimately just another way to invest in a company's prospects.

If you want the benefits of convertibles without the complications discussed here, you can invest in a convertible bond mutual fund. It offers a high yield and appreciation potential, and the fund manager is an expert in picking through the somewhat bewildering world of convertibles.

For those seeking more information about convertibles, many brokerage firms publish research reports on widely traded issues. The two best newsletters that track the field are the *Value Line Convertibles* (220 E. 42nd St., New York, NY 10017; 800-634-3583) and the *RHM Convertible Survey* (172 Forest Ave., Glen Cove, NY 11542; 516-759-2904).

JUNK BONDS

The riskiest type of bond is known in the brokerage industry as *high-yield bonds,* but colloquially they are known as *junk bonds.* These bonds barely existed before the 1980s takeover, leveraged buyout and junk bond boom made them famous—or infamous, depending on your experience with them.

Junk bonds are issued by corporations that have less than an investment-grade rating. That means Standard & Poor's and Fitch rate them below BBB, and Moody's rates them below Baa. Companies earn such low ratings for two reasons: They are either on their way up or on their way down, financially speaking. The up-and-comers are companies that do not have the long track record of sales and earnings that the ratings agencies require to merit an investment-grade rating. Just because they do not have a top rating, however, does not make them bad companies; it just means they need more seasoning before their rating rises from the B into the A category.

The companies on their way down, often called fallen angels, are a different story. These corporations attained an investment-grade rating in years past by diligently increasing sales and profits. But some event or series of events changed all that, causing the ratings agencies to downgrade the firms' bonds. Possible events include a takeover financed with millions of dollars in new debt, a failed market strategy that saddles a firm with operating losses instead of profits, or a general downturn in the economy that undermines a firm's profitability so severely that the ratings agencies doubt its ability to pay interest on its outstanding bonds.

While a low safety rating might be bad news for a company, it is good news for investors because it means that the firm's bonds will pay a substantially higher yield than will securities issued by blue chip corporations. How much more depends on which issuers you compare, but decent-quality junk bonds often yield between 2 and 5 percentage points more than investment-grade issues. That can translate into yields of 9 percent to 15 percent. Lower-quality junk issues can pay up to 20 percent.

Think you've found your dream investment? Well, hold onto your money because those higher yields obviously come with higher risks. The chief risks follow.

- *The company can default.* The higher the yield, in fact, the more likely it is that the bond's interest rate will drop suddenly one day, from high double digits to 0, as the high cost of servicing the debt becomes too much for the company to handle. When a company seeks protection from creditors in bankruptcy, interest payments to bondholders often cease. Default rates on junk bonds vary and, to a large degree, depend on the overall health of the economy. A vibrant economy will allow companies to earn the profits they need to meet their interest costs, meaning only 1 percent or 2 percent of all junk bonds might default in a year. But in a recession, junk bond default rates can soar to 8 percent or 10 percent if reduced sales and profits make it impossible to pay bond interest.

- *The company's bonds can be downgraded further.* Though not as serious as outright default, a junk bond with a BB rating can be downgraded to a B or even into the Cs, which would pummel the bond's price.

- *Interest rates can rise.* While that hurts the value of all bonds, it can be particularly harmful to companies already in a weakened financial condition.

- *The stock market can fall.* Because a junk bond's price is tied closely to the fate of the underlying company, a general drop in stock prices can spill over to the company's stock price, which will affect its bond price negatively.

- *There can be an imbalance of supply and demand.* In the 1980s, when billions of dollars' worth of new junk bonds were brought to market every year, the supply eventually outran the demand, causing bond prices to decline sharply. In addition, because of junk-bond-related scandals and losses suffered by junk bond holders, Congress forced savings and loans to sell their junk bonds. Insurance companies were later ordered to liquidate their portfolios for the same reasons. And many other large institutions, such as pension funds, were also banned from buying junk bonds. All of this reduced demand for junk bonds even further. The main buyers of junk bonds now are individuals and mutual funds that raise money from individuals.

- *The liquidity of junk bond trading can dry up.* If bad news hits the market, such as an unexpected default, it can become very difficult to buy or sell bonds at a reasonable price. Dealers will execute trades only at enormous spreads that make it unattractive for investors to complete transactions.

- *Junk bonds can be called.* Companies do not voluntarily pay double-digit yields on their bonds; they are forced to do so. If their financial fortunes improve, or if interest rates fall, they will refinance those high-yielding bonds with lower yielding bonds at the first possible opportunity.

Despite the risks, junk bonds can provide very high returns if they are chosen well. In selecting a high-yield bond, look for a company with improving finances rather than worsening finances that you hope will turn around some day.

Most junk bonds come in minimum denominations of $1,000, but if they are depressed, they may sell for far less than that. Brokers normally like to sell bonds in lots of at least five, or $5,000. They will charge a wide spread or a steep commission on smaller orders.

The interest you receive from a junk bond is fully taxable at the federal, state and local levels. If you sell the bond for a gain, you must pay capital gains tax. If the company defaults on its bonds and ultimately liquidates, you can use the bond certificates to wallpaper your living room (unless you would rather not be reminded of your investment). You can also write off your losses against other capital gains and $3,000 of ordinary income.

If you feel skittish about buying individual junk bonds (and you should), a safer alternative is to buy a mutual fund that purchases a widely diversified portfolio of the toxic issues. That way, you have a professional manager picking through the junk for you.

Whether you invest in junk bonds depends on your ability to tolerate high risk in return for high yields and some potentially large capital gains. However, don't put too much of your money into junk bonds. The risk is just not worth the angst.

Bond Mutual Funds

If the process of choosing individual bonds seems too complicated, bond mutual funds might be right for you. For a fuller discussion of the benefits of mutual funds in general, refer back to Chapter 4, "Selecting Mutual Funds."

Mutual funds offer several advantages to bond investors. For the most part, the bond market is designed for large institutional players that buy blocks of bonds, millions of dollars at a time, rather than small investors who buy a few thousand dollars' worth of securities. Bonds can be difficult to trade in small lots, so funds offer much better liquidity than do individual bonds. Plus, you can buy or sell a mutual fund at that day's net asset value (NAV) and not have to worry about taking a bad price on a solo bond. By having a professional mutual fund manager on your side, you also pay much less in commission costs than you would as an individual investor. And it is difficult to obtain good research on some bond types, particularly municipal, convertible and junk bonds. Professionals will always have access to more detailed and timely information than you could get on your own.

Bond mutual funds offer other advantages. If you are an income-oriented investor, a bond fund portfolio can send you a monthly dividend check that will smooth out your cash flow. Individual bonds usually pay every six months, so you may receive a large amount of interest, then have to wait several months before the next payment. If you do not need the cash, bond funds offer automatic dividend reinvestment, which makes it far easier to buy more bonds than waiting for interest to accumulate until you meet the minimum for individual bonds. Finally, a bond fund is made up of tens, if not hundreds, of bonds, diversified by maturity, issuer and quality. By spreading the risk around, you soften considerably the impact of a negative development on any particular bond. You could not afford such a diversified portfolio on your own, and you are exposed to serious loss if a problem develops with an individual bond.

One disadvantage of bond funds compared to individual bonds is that bond funds (except for zero-coupon bond funds) never mature. Bonds within a portfolio might mature, but the fund is constantly reinvesting the proceeds of matured or sold bonds back into more bonds. This means you have no guarantee that a bond fund will ever return to the price you purchased it at originally. For example, if you buy a fund when interest rates are low and then they rise a great deal, you might have to wait a long time for your principal value to return to where you started. With individual bonds, you can count on a fixed maturity date at which you will receive your original principal. The bond's price will bounce around while it is outstanding, but you can be assured that, in the end, you will get your money back—as long as the issuer does not default.

As with all individual bond prices, bond fund prices move inversely to interest rates. If rates rise, bond fund shares decline in price. As rates fall, bond fund prices rise. If you sell bond fund shares for more than you paid for them, you must pay capital gains tax on the difference. The income you receive from a bond fund is taxable if the fund buys taxable bonds, and it is tax free if the fund invests in municipal securities. To allow bond fund shareholders to keep the taxation of dividends straight, the same bond fund does not buy both taxable and tax-exempt bonds.

As with other kinds of mutual funds, you can choose between no-load bond funds you buy directly from a fund company or load funds you buy indirectly through a broker or financial planner. Loads can have an even bigger effect on your bond fund's return than on a stock fund's return because if the commission is taken off the top, you will have less money earning interest. *12b-1 fees,* which take .5 percent to 1.5 percent of your assets annually, are used for promotional expenses by the fund in order to increase fund assets. Expenses, such as management fees and 12b-1 charges, also have a direct impact on your bond fund's yield. The higher the expenses, the lower the yield. So, as you shop around among bond funds, compare not only the yields but also the effect fees and expense levels will have on your return over time.

Types of Bond Funds: Choosing the Best for You

Over the last several years, the number and variety of bond funds have mushroomed, as has the amount of money invested in them. Hundreds of funds now compete for your attention—plus the hundreds of billions of dollars in current total bond fund assets and the billions of dollars more that pour into bond funds each year. And bond fund companies continue to introduce new features already tested on other types of funds.

Two factors distinguish funds: the kinds of securities they buy and the average maturity of the bonds in their portfolios. In general, the longer the fund's portfolio maturity, the higher its yield, and the higher its risk. The following list describes different kinds of bond funds in terms of these two factors.

They have been separated according to the levels of the investment pyramid, from the most conservative to the most aggressive. For the names, addresses and telephone numbers of the mutual fund companies offering these funds, refer to the list on page 206 in Chapter 4. For a fuller discussion of the risks and rewards of different types of bonds, see the sections on those bonds earlier in this chapter.

As with any investment, you should review your financial goals, your risk tolerance level and the other lessons covered in the first chapter of this book before you buy any bond fund.

Low-Risk Sector

Government bond funds. Government bond funds invest exclusively in securities issued by the U.S. government or its agencies. No risk of default exists in any of the underlying securities; therefore, these are the safest bonds around. Long-term bond funds do carry substantial risk due to interest rate volatility, however.

Municipal bond funds. These funds invest solely in tax-exempt bonds, so all the dividends they pay are not subject to federal income tax. Depending on your tax bracket, these funds might allow you to keep more interest than you could earn on a higher yielding but taxable bond fund. Three kinds of muni bond funds are available: national, state and local.

- *National funds* buy bonds from municipalities across the country. In a few cases, interest from a state's bonds is taxable to out-of-state residents, so national bond funds will tell shareholders at the end of the year what percentage of the income they received came from such a state.

- *State-specific funds* are designed by states for residents of those states who want to avoid both federal and state taxation. Large, high-tax states, such as New York, California, Pennsylvania and Michigan, offer many single-state funds because so much demand for them exists.

- *Local muni funds* buy bonds only from a locality that levies an income tax, such as New York City. These bonds are therefore triple-tax-free because they allow residents to sidestep federal, state and local income taxes.

Municipal bond funds also are sold with portfolios composed totally of insured bonds. This insurance protects investors against the possibility of default by any issue a fund holds.

While state and local bond funds offer beneficial tax shelter, they are riskier than national funds because they are not diversified geographically. If a particular state or locality suffers a sharp downturn in its economy, the entity's bonds will probably be downgraded, which could cause shareholders in funds holding those bonds to suffer losses. Still, municipal bond funds, as a whole, are extremely safe; very few defaults have occurred.

Short- and intermediate-term bond funds. Such funds, which come in both taxable and tax-free varieties, buy bonds with maturities no longer than ten years, and usually as short as five years. Because short-term bonds fluctuate in price far less than long-term bonds during the same interest rate volatility, these funds' prices remain quite stable. Many short-term funds offer check-writing privileges; therefore, many people use them as higher yielding alternatives to money-market funds. In cases where there exists a significant difference between money-market and medium-term rates, intermediate-term bond funds can offer yields 4 or 5 percentage points higher than money funds. Unlike money funds, however, these funds' net asset values (NAVs) fluctuate and will fall if interest rates rise sharply.

MODERATE-RISK SECTOR

Convertible bond funds. Convertible bond funds buy convertible debentures and convertible preferred stocks. Though convertible yields are lower than those on straight corporate bonds, convertible bond funds offer more appreciation potential. These funds will provide their highest returns when the stock market is rising. The convertible market can be particularly confusing, and a good fund manager's expertise can be well worth the management fee.

High-grade corporate bond funds. Such funds buy bonds issued by investment-grade corporations, or those with ratings of BBB or higher. The funds will pay yields of one or two percentage points higher than will government funds of similar maturities. Yet they remain quite safe because they buy top-quality bonds and diversify widely among hundreds of issues.

Mortgage-backed securities funds. These funds invest in mortgage-backed securities issued by quasi-governmental agencies, such as Ginnie Mae, Fannie Mae and Freddie Mac. The securities they buy are guaranteed against default by those agencies but not against price fluctuations caused by interest rate movements. The other uncertainty that plagues mortgage-backed securities—the early prepayment of mortgage principal by homeowners—is taken care of by the fund manager, who automatically reinvests principal payments back into more securities. This is a big advantage over holding individual Ginnie Maes or Freddie Macs because it is often difficult to reinvest the small amount of principal paid each month. Mortgage-backed securities funds tend to pay yields of 1 to 3 percentage points higher than similar maturity Treasury funds. Some mortgage-backed funds even permit check writing.

HIGH-RISK APEX

Global bond funds. Global bond funds purchase bonds issued by governments and corporations from around the world. When interest rates are higher in countries other than the United States, as they were in the early 1990s, these funds can pay yields two or three percentage points higher than similar domestic funds. What makes them a higher risk is that currency fluctuations can create large swings in the value of fund shares. Because you are, in effect, putting your money in foreign currencies when you buy one of these funds, you will profit if the U.S. dollar falls in value against other currencies. But if the greenback rises in value, you can suffer losses. Some funds try to use complicated futures and options strategies to hedge against currency swings, but the hedges do not always work, and they can be expensive, cutting the funds' yields. The bonds these funds purchase are typically from top-rated governments and corporations, so there is little, if any, default risk. Global bond funds also come in short-term and long-term varieties. Short-term funds usually are less sensitive to currency swings, while long-term funds react more sharply both to interest rate movements and to changes in currency values.

High-yield junk bond funds. Junk bond funds buy bonds of corporations that are below investment grade, meaning they have ratings of less than BBB. The companies backing these bonds are financially weaker than top-rated blue chip corporations; therefore, the bonds pay higher yields to compensate investors for the increased risk of default. Junk bond funds can pay yields four to six percentage points higher than government or high-grade corporate bond funds of similar maturities. High-yield fund prices are much more volatile than more conservative bond funds because of rapidly changing values of the bonds they hold. In general, junk bond funds perform well when the stock market rises because junk bonds mirror the performance of their issuers' stocks.

Zero-coupon bond funds. Such funds buy portfolios of zero-coupon bonds, which are issued at a deep discount to face value and mature at a specific time in the future. These funds should be considered very conservative if they are held until they liquidate, which occurs when the bonds mature. However, because zero-coupon bonds are the most volatile of all bonds, these funds fluctuate more dramatically than any other kind of bond fund while the bonds are outstanding. Zero-coupon bond funds, which pay no dividends, soar in price when interest rates fall and plunge in price when interest rates rise. If you time your purchases and sales correctly, you can make a lot of money. But if you buy when rates are low and then rates surge, you must hold the funds to maturity to get back your principal.

Closed-End Bond Funds

All of the funds described above are open-end funds, meaning that they continually offer new shares to the public as new money flows into the funds. You should also consider shares in closed-end bond funds, which issue a limited number of shares and trade on the NYSE, AMEX Nasdaq NMS. (For a more detailed discussion of how closed-end funds work, as well as their advantages and disadvantages, see "Closed-End Mutual Funds" in Chapter 4).

Closed-end bond funds, like all closed-end funds, sell at either a premium or a discount to the current value of their bond portfolios. They typically sell at a premium to, or for more than, the portfolios' value when interest rates decline and investors scramble into closed-end bond funds in search of higher yields. But when interest rates rise, fund prices tend to shrink to a discount.

A good strategy is to buy closed-end bond funds when they are at a discount because this will boost your yield. To calculate your effective yield, divide the annual dividend by the current price of the fund. For example, assume that a bond fund pays a $.70 annual dividend, and the NAV of the fund's portfolio—or the exact worth of its portfolio—is $10 per share. If the fund is selling at its NAV, its effective yield is 7 percent.

$$\frac{\$.70 \text{ Annual dividend}}{\$10 \text{ Current price of the fund}} = 7\% \text{ Effective yield}$$

If investors temporarily lose confidence in the fund and its price falls to $9, it is selling at a 10 percent discount. Because the annual dividend remains at $.70, the effective yield will rise to 7.77 percent.

$$\frac{\$.70 \text{ Annual dividend}}{\$9 \text{ Current price of the fund}} = 7.77\% \text{ Effective yield}$$

If investors become enthusiastic about the fund again and its price rises to $11, it is selling at a 10 percent premium. Therefore, the effective yield will fall to 6.36 percent.

$$\frac{\$.70 \text{ Annual dividend}}{\$11 \text{ Current price of the fund}} = 6.36\% \text{ Effective yield}$$

While it is easy enough to calculate the effective yields of closed-end funds, you can also look up these payouts in financial newspapers like *The Wall Street Journal* (on Mondays) and *Barron's*. They will list each bond fund's current price, NAV and effective yield. You can also find the price and yield in NYSE, AMEX and Nasdaq NMS tables because closed-end funds trade through these systems.

Closed-end bond funds, like their open-end cousins, come in both general and specialized categories. General funds can invest in any kind of bond that the fund's manager thinks will produce capital gains and income. These funds might have a combination of government, municipal, corporate, foreign, convertible, junk and zero-coupon bonds as well as mortgage-backed securities in their portfolios. Their wide diversification makes them less risky than specialized funds, which buy only one type of those bonds listed above. Still, a specialized fund might yield higher income if it invests only in tax-free municipal bonds or in high-yielding junk bonds, for example.

You have several ways to follow the action in closed-end bond funds. Some brokerage house analysts issue research reports on the funds. Also, you will occasionally spot stories about the funds in financial newspapers and magazines. And for more in-depth coverage, consult the books and newsletters listed in the "Resources" section at the end of this chapter.

Unit Investment Trusts

Instead of buying an open-end or a closed-end bond fund, you have another alternative if you are income-oriented. *Unit investment trusts* (UITs), sometimes called defined asset trusts, buy a fixed portfolio of bonds and hold them to maturity. These contrast with bond funds, which constantly buy and sell bonds and never mature.

You can buy a UIT from any broker for a minimum of $1,000. You usually pay a sales charge of about 4 percent or 5 percent when you buy it, then minimal management expenses thereafter of .15 percent per year. The underwriter of the portfolio also profits by marking up the bonds it buys for the portfolio. Over the long term, though, these fees are less than the typical annual management fees of 1 percent or more on more actively managed bond funds. A few large brokerage firms, including Merrill Lynch, Nuveen and Van Kampen Merritt, dominate the UIT business. The trusts are usually sold through syndicates of brokerage firms that unite to sell one trust after another.

UITs offer several advantages.

- You buy into a widely diversified, professionally selected portfolio that would be impossible to replicate on your own.

- You know exactly what assets the trust contains before you buy it. That is why they are called defined asset trusts.

- You receive fixed monthly income checks, as opposed to payments every six months from individual bonds.

- If you need access to your capital, you can sell your units back to the sponsoring company, though you might have to sell at a discount.

- You receive your principal back when the portfolio of bonds matures (usually in about 20 years) unlike a bond fund, which never matures.

- You can choose a UIT that fits your income needs. Many trusts specialize in municipal bonds and therefore pay tax-free interest. Within that category, some trusts buy only bonds from a particular state, yielding double-tax-free income. For investors who want extra security, other municipal trusts buy only insured bonds. In addition to municipal bonds, UITs buy mortgage-backed securities, high-quality corporate bonds, foreign bonds and even junk bonds.

Because they own fixed portfolios of bonds, UITs can get hurt if there is a problem with some of the bonds in their portfolios. For example, in the early 1980s, a consortium of municipalities that had banded together to build nuclear power plants in Washington state (called the Washington Public Power Supply System and commonly known as WHOOPS) defaulted on billions of dollars in bonds, many of which were held in UIT portfolios. While some of the bonds were insured, leaving trustholders unaffected, others were not. Thus, many UITs suffered losses and had to reduce monthly payouts. In extreme cases, UIT managers can sell bonds if they sense trouble coming, but such active management is the exception. When bonds are sold, however, the principal is returned to UIT holders because UITs are not allowed to add new bonds to a portfolio once it has been sold.

When shopping for a UIT, look carefully at the prospectus describing the portfolio. Notice the average maturity of the bonds, which may range from 10 years to as many as 30 years. Inspect the bonds' safety ratings, making sure that they fall in the A category if you want to depend on the trust for income for many years. Determine what kind of call protection comes with the bonds in the portfolio. Ideally, you would like at least ten years before the bonds can be redeemed.

With a little homework, you may find a UIT that meets your needs for dependable monthly income.

Resources

To learn more about bonds, read financial newspapers like *The Wall Street Journal* and *Barron's,* as well as personal finance magazines like *Money,* which feature articles about bonds regularly. For more in-depth information on bonds, consult the following books, newsletters and trade associations.

BOOKS

All about Bonds from the Inside Out, by Esme Faerber (McGraw-Hill, Order Dept., 860 Taylor Station Rd., Blacklick, OH 43004; 800-722-4726; www.mcgraw-hill.com). Explains the basics of bonds, including the different types of bonds, varying levels of risk, how to spot undervalued and overvalued bonds, how to read yield curves and calculations for interest rates and returns.

The Basics of Bonds, by Gerald Krefetz (Dearborn Financial Publishing, 155 N. Wacker Dr., Chicago, IL 60606; 312-836-4400; 800-322-8621; www.dearborn.com). Covers everything a beginner needs to know about the bond market.

Bond Markets: Analysis and Strategies, by Frank Fabozzi (Prentice Hall, 200 Old Tappan Rd., Old Tappan, NJ 07675; 201-592-2000; 800-947-7700; www.prenhall.com). Offers more sophisticated bond market strategies.

Buying Municipal Bonds: The Common Sense Guide to Tax-Free Personal Investing, by John Andrew (Free Press, division of MacMillan, 866 3rd Ave., New York,

NY 10022; 212-702-2000; 800-223-2348; www.simon&schuster.com). A guide to the municipal bond market for beginners.

The Fixed-Income Almanac: The Bond Investor's Compendium of Key Market, Product and Performance Data, by Livingston G. Douglas (McGraw-Hill, Order Dept., 860 Taylor Station Rd., Blacklick, OH 43004; 800-722-4726; www.mcgraw-hill.com). Provides years of performance data for the bond markets, including yield levels, measures of bond volatility, information on ratings upgrades and downgrades, and levels of new bond issuance.

Fixed-Income Investments: A Personal Seminar (New York Institute of Finance, 2 Broadway, 5th Floor, New York, NY 10004-2283; 212-859-5000; 800-227-6943; www.nyif.com). Overviews the fixed-income markets.

Fundamentals of Municipal Bonds (Public Securities Association, 40 Broad St., 12th Floor, New York, NY 10004-2373; 212-809-7000; www.psa.com). An excellent overview of everything you need to know about municipal bonds.

The Handbook of Asset-Backed Securities, by Jess Lederman (New York Institute of Finance, 2 Broadway, 5th Floor, New York, NY 10004-2283; 212-859-5000; 800-227-6943; www.nyif.com). A comprehensive book about the mechanics and economics of asset-backed securities, including those backed by mortgages, credit cards and auto loans.

The Handbook of Fixed-Income Securities, by Frank Fabozzi (McGraw-Hill, Order Dept., 860 Taylor Station Rd., Blacklick, OH 43004; 800-722-4726; www.mcgraw-hill.com). A complete guide to the bond market, with great detail on every aspect of the subject.

The Thomas J. Herzfeld Encyclopedia of Closed-End Funds (Thomas J. Herzfeld Advisors, P.O. Box 161465, Miami, FL 33116; 305-271-1900). Self-published encyclopedia of closed-end funds. Includes data on all funds and methods for choosing the best funds.

How the Bond Market Works (New York Institute of Finance, 2 Broadway, 5th Floor, New York, NY 10004-2283; 212-859-5000; 800-227-6943; www.nyif.com). An explanation of the ins and outs of the bond market.

The Income Investor, by Donald R. Nichols (Dearborn Financial Publishing, 155 N. Wacker Dr., Chicago, IL 60606; 312-836-4400; 800-322-8621; www.dearborn.com). A thorough review of different bonds and stocks that are appropriate for income-oriented investors.

Investing in Closed-End Funds: Finding Value and Building Wealth, by Albert Freedman and George Cole Scott (New York Institute of Finance, 2 Broadway, New York, NY 10004-2283; 212-859-5000; 800-227-6943; www.nyif.com). Provides strategies for picking the best closed-end funds.

Investing in Convertible Securities: Your Complete Guide to the Risk and Rewards, by John P. Calamos (Dearborn Financial Publishing, 155 N. Wacker Dr., Chicago, IL 60606; 312-836-4400; 800-322-8621; www.dearborn.com). Takes you through the sometimes bewildering world of convertible securities. Provides clear explanations.

Mortgage-Backed Securities: Investment Analysis and Advanced Valuation Techniques, by Andrew S. Davidson and Michael D. Herskovitz (McGraw-Hill, Order Dept., 860 Taylor Station Rd., Blacklick, OH 43004; 800-722-4726; www.mcgraw-hill.com). Explains the complex world of mortgage-backed securities, including how to calculate prepayment risk and find the highest yields with the least risk.

Mortgage-Backed Securities: Products, Analysis, Trading, by William Bartlett (New York Institute of Finance, 2 Broadway, 5th Floor, New York, NY 10004-2283; 212-859-5000; 800-227-6943; www.nyif.com). Aimed at sophisticated investors in the mortgage-backed securities market.

Mortgage Securities: The High-Yield Alternative to CDs, the Low-Risk Alternative to Stocks, by Daniel R. Amerman (McGraw-Hill, Order Dept., 860 Taylor Station Rd., Blacklick, OH 43004; 800-722-4726; www.mcgraw-hill.com). Explains how to invest in mortgage securities, which are the highest yielding of all government-insured securities. Explains mortgage-backed securities mutual funds, how to buy and sell individual mortgage-backed bonds, how prepayment risk is factored into bond prices, and the difference between Ginnie Mae, Fannie Mae and other issuers of mortgage-backed securities.

The New Business One Irwin Guide to Zero-Coupon Investments, by Donald R. Nichols (McGraw-Hill, Order Dept., 860 Taylor Station Rd., Blacklick, OH 43004; 800-722-4726; www.mcgraw-hill.com). A complete guide to the many varieties of zero-coupon bonds. Includes the Treasury, corporate and mortgage-backed markets. Explains how zeros can be used for capital growth or stability, aggressive gains or lump-sum distributions.

The New High-Yield Bond Market, by Jess Lederman and Michael P. Sullivan (McGraw-Hill, Order Dept., 860 Taylor Station Rd., Blacklick, OH 43004; 800-722-4726; www.mcgraw-hill.com). Explains how the high-yield junk bond market works, how to reduce risk without sacrificing return and how to play the risky game of buying bonds from bankrupt companies.

The Personal Investor's Complete Book of Bonds, by Donald R. Nichols (Dearborn Financial Publishing, 155 N. Wacker Dr., Chicago, IL 60606; 312-836-4400; 800-322-8621; www.dearborn.com). Offers a complete rundown of all types of bonds.

Treasury Securities: Making Money with Uncle Sam, by Donald R. Nichols (Dearborn Financial Publishing, 155 N. Wacker Dr., Chicago, IL 60606; 312-836-

4400; 800-322-8621; www.dearborn.com). An easy-to-understand explanation of different kinds of Treasury securities.

Understanding Corporate Bonds, by Harold Kerzner (McGraw-Hill, Order Dept., 860 Taylor Station Rd., Blacklick, OH 43004; 800-233-1128; www.mcgraw-hill.com). A primer on the complex world of corporate bonds.

Yield Curve Analysis: The Fundamentals of Risk and Return, by Livingston Douglas (New York Institute of Finance, 2 Broadway, 5th Floor, New York, NY 10004-2283; 212-859-5000; 800-227-6943; www.nyif.com). An explanation of how investing in different bond maturities can bring high returns and high risks.

NEWSLETTERS

Bondweek (Institutional Investor, 488 Madison Ave., 12th Floor, New York, NY 10022; 212-303-3300). Covers the bond market and is aimed at professional bond investors and bond dealers.

Closed-End Country Fund Report (Suite 501, 725 15th St., N.W., Washington, DC 20005; 202-783-7051). Recommends favorite closed-end funds and provides up-to-date performance data on the funds.

Closed-End Fund Digest (1224 Coast Village Circle, Suite 11, Santa Barbara, CA 93108; 800-282-2335). Recommends favorite closed-end funds and provides up-to-date performance data on the funds.

Defaulted Bonds Newsletter (Bond Investors Association, P.O. Box 4427, Miami Lakes, FL 33014; 305-557-1832). Advises individual investors about opportunities in the riskiest of all bonds—those that have already defaulted.

Grant's Interest Rate Observer (30 Wall St., 6th Floor, New York, NY 10005-2201; 212-809-7994; www.grantspub.com). A witty and provocative look at the bond markets and interest rates from well-known bond analyst James Grant.

Income Fund Outlook (Institute for Econometric Research, 2200 SW 10th St., Deerfield Beach, FL 33442; 800-442-9000).

Investor's Guide to Closed-End Funds (Thomas J. Herzfeld Advisors, P.O. Box 161465, Miami, FL 33116; 305-271-1900). Chooses best closed-end funds and provides up-to-date performance data on the funds.

Lynch Municipal Bond Advisory (P.O. Box 20476, New York, NY 10025; 212-663-5552). Aimed at individual investors wanting to select high-quality municipal bonds or bond funds.

Moody's Bond Survey (99 Church St., New York, NY 10007; 212-553-0300; www.moodys.com/fis). Provides data and commentary on the economy and fixed-income markets. Includes calendars of recent offerings and Moody's commodity and scrap metal price indices, yield averages and market commentaries.

Mortgage-Backed Security Letter (IDD Enterprises, Two World Trade Center, Suite 1810, New York, NY 10048; 212-227-1200; www.gfoa.org). Follows the mortgage-backed and asset-backed securities markets.

Public Investor (Government Finance Officers Association, 180 N. Michigan Ave., Suite 800, Chicago, IL 60601-7476; 312-977-9700). Tracks developments in the municipal bond market and is aimed at public investors.

RHM Convertible Survey (172 Forest Ave., Glen Cove, NY 11542; 516-759-2904). Recommends convertible bonds and convertible preferred stocks.

Standard & Poor's Corporation (25 Broadway, New York, NY 10004; 212-208-8000) publishes several newsletters about the bond market. They include *Blue List* (212-770-4300), which lists upcoming municipal bond offerings; *Bond Guide,* which lists corporate bonds; *Called Bond Record,* which tracks bonds that have been redeemed; *Creditweek,* which analyzes the overall bond market, as well as specific bond issues; *Municipal Bond Book,* which lists municipal bonds; and *Unit Investment Trusts,* which tracks UITs.

Value Line Convertibles (220 E. 42nd St., New York, NY 10017; 800-634-3583). Recommends the convertible bonds that Value Line (a bond-rating service) likes best.

NEWSPAPER

The Bond Buyer (One State Street Plaza, 31st Floor, New York, NY 10004; 212-943-8200). A trade newspaper that covers the municipal bond business.

PAMPHLET

"Investing in Municipal Bonds" (North American Securities Administrators Association, One Massachusetts Ave., N.W., Suite 310, Washington, DC 20001; 202-737-0900). Explains the basics of the municipal bond market.

TRADE ASSOCIATIONS

Association of Financial Guaranty Insurors (52 Vanderbilt Ave., 21st Floor, New York, NY 10017; 212-953-2550). The trade group representing the insurance companies that insure municipal bonds against default. Will send you a free copy of the following three brochures and guide: "Anatomy of an Insured Bond Default"; "Insured Municipal Bonds in the Secondary Market"; "Monoline vs. Multiline: Comparison of Financial Guaranty Insurors to Property/Casualty and Life/Health Insurors" and "An Investors Guide to Triple A-Rated Insured Municipal Bonds."

Bond Investors Association (P.O. Box 4427, 6175 N.W. 153rd St., Suite 221, Miami Lakes, FL 33014; 305-557-1832). A nonprofit group that educates the public about bonds and keeps statistics on defaulted bonds. Offers a pamphlet about the association entitled "Staying Informed on Your Bond Investments in the 90's." Also offers subscriptions to three newsletters: *Bond Investors Association Newsletter; Defaulted Bonds Newsletter* and *High-Yield Securities Journal.*

Public Securities Association (40 Broad St., 12th Floor, New York, NY 10004-2373; 212-809-7000). The industry group representing brokerage firms, dealers and banks that trade government, municipal and mortgage-backed securities. Will send you one free copy of several pamphlets containing helpful information about bonds, including: "An Investor's Guide to Mortgage Securities"; "An Investor's Guide to Real Estate Mortgage Investment Conduits (REMICs)"; "An Investor's Guide to Tax-Exempt Unit Investment Trusts"; "An Investor's Guide to Triple-A Rated Insured Municipal Bonds"; "An Investor's Guide to Zero-Coupon Municipal Bonds." Also publishes a book called *A Guide to Certificates of Participation (COPs).*

WEB SITES

The Blue List. Standard & Poor's offers daily updates on all municipal and corporate bonds coming to market. The site also provides commentary on the bond market and individual bonds. www.bluelist.com

Bonds Online. A comprehensive database about corporate, government, municipal bonds and bond mutual funds. The site features commentary on the bond market from well-known analysts, yield curves for different kinds of bonds and a bond map allowing you to look for municipal bond offerings in your state. www.bondsonline.com

Bureau of Public Debt—Treasury Bills, Bonds and Notes. The complete source for information about Treasury securities. You will be able to find out about upcoming Treasury auctions, and how the Treasury Direct program works. The site also answers frequently asked questions about Treasury bills, notes and bonds and inflation-indexed securities. www.publicdebt.treas.gov/sec/sec.htm

Bureau of Public Debt—Savings Bonds Division. The complete source for information about savings bonds. The site explains all the rules affecting savings bonds, including how to buy and redeem them and how to calculate their value. It also features the Savings Bond Wizard, which calculates the current redemption value of your savings bond holdings. www.publicdebt.treas.gov/sav/sav.htm

Duff & Phelps Credit Rating Company. A Web site to look up the credit ratings of most corporate debt. Duff & Phelps is a major rating agency of corporate debt, and this site will let you find the ratings for American and international companies for bonds and preferred stock. It lists Duff & Phelps, as well as Moody's and Standard & Poor's ratings. You also can find ratings changes announced in the last 90 days and a list of companies on ratings watch, meaning that their ratings may be upgraded or downgraded soon. www.dcrco.com

Nuveen Research. One of the largest sites devoted to tax-exempt securities. Nuveen provides extensive research on individual municipal bonds, both existing and new issues. The site also offers municipal bond market commentary and investment strategy advice. As you might expect, there is also plenty of information on Nuveen's municipal bond fund offerings. www.nuveenresearch.com

Standard & Poor's Rating Services. The largest rating service for corporate, municipal and government bonds provides extensive listings in its Web site. S&P not only provides the ratings, but also why an issuer's rating has risen or fallen. You also can look at the Credit Wire for recent ratings changes. www.ratings.standardpoor.com

FEDERAL RESERVE BANKS AND BRANCHES

For more information about government bonds, write the Consumer Information Center (Pueblo, CO 81009) for the following pamphlets: "Information about Marketable Treasury Securities (Bills, Notes and Bonds)"; "The Savings Bond Question and Answer Book"; and "U.S. Savings Bonds: Now Tax Free for Education." To purchase Treasury securities, visit the bank nearest you. You can use the telephone numbers and addresses below either to call or visit the Federal Reserve department to get information on buying Treasury bills, notes and bonds directly.

Alabama: P.O. Box 830447, Birmingham 35283-0447; 205-731-8500
Arkansas: 325 W. Capitol Ave., Little Rock 72203; 501-324-8275
California: 950 S. Grand Ave., Los Angeles 90015, 213-683-2300; 101 Market St., San Francisco 94120, 415-974-2330
Colorado: P.O. Box 5228, Denver 80217-5228; 303-572-2473
District of Columbia: 20th Street and C Street, N.W. 20551; 202-452-3000
Florida: P.O. Box 929, Jacksonville 32231-0044, 904-632-1000; P.O. Box 520847, Miami 33152-0847, 305-591-2065
Georgia: 104 Marietta St., N.W., Atlanta 30303; 404-521-8653
Illinois: 230 S. LaSalle St., Chicago 60604; 312-322-5369
Kentucky: P.O. Box 32710, Louisville 40232; 502-568-9236
Louisiana: 525 St. Charles Ave., New Orleans 70130; 504-593-3200
Maryland: 502 S. Sharp St., Baltimore 21201; 410-576-3300
Massachusetts: 600 Atlantic Ave., Boston 02106; 617-973-3805
Michigan: 160 W. Fort St., Detroit 48231; 313-961-6880
Minnesota: P.O. Box 291, Minneapolis 55480-0291; 612-340-2345
Missouri: 925 Grand Blvd., Kansas City 64198, 816-881-2000; P.O. Box 14935, St. Louis 63178-4935, 314-444-8703
Montana: 100 Neill Ave., Helena 59601; 406-447-3800
Nebraska: 2201 Farnam, Omaha 68102; 402-221-5500
New York: 160 Delaware Ave., Buffalo 14202, 716-849-5000; 33 Liberty St., New York 10045, 212-720-5000
North Carolina: 530 E. Trade St., Charlotte 28202; 704-358-2100

Ohio: 150 E. 4th St., Cincinnati 45202, 513-721-4787; 1455 E. 6th St., Cleveland 44101, 216-579-2490

Oklahoma: 226 Dean McGee Ave., Oklahoma City 73125; 405-270-8652

Oregon: 915 S.W. Stark St., Portland 97208; 503-221-5932

Pennsylvania: Ten Independence Mall, Philadelphia 19106, 215-574-6680; 717 Grant St., Pittsburgh 15230, 412-261-7802

Tennessee: 200 N. Main St., Memphis 38103, 901-523-7171; 301 8th Ave. North, Nashville 37203-4407, 615-251-7100

Texas: 2200 N. Pearl St., Dallas 75201, 214-922-6000; 301 E. Main St., El Paso 79901, 915-544-4730; 1701 San Jacinto St., Houston 77001, 713-659-4433; 126 E. Nueva St., San Antonio 78295, 512-224-2141

Utah: 120 S. State St., Salt Lake City 84130; 801-322-7844

Virginia: 701 E. Byrd St., Richmond 23219; 804-697-8000

Washington: 1015 2nd Ave., Seattle 98104; 206-343-3600

MUNICIPAL BOND INSURANCE COMPANIES

The following insurance companies insure municipal bonds against default.

AMBAC Indemnity Corporation (One State Street Plaza, 17th Floor, New York, NY 10004; 212-668-0340; www.ambac.com)

Capital Markets Assurance Corporation (885 3rd Ave., 14th Floor, New York, NY 10022; 212-755-1155)

Capital Reinsurance Company (1325 Avenue of the Americas, 18th Floor, New York, NY 10019; 212-974-0100)

Enhance Reinsurance Company (335 Madison Ave., 25th Floor, New York, NY 10017; 212-983-3100; www.efsgroup.com)

Financial Guaranty Insurance Company (115 Broadway, New York, NY 10006; 212-312-3000; 800-352-0001)

Financial Security Assurance (350 Park Ave., 13th Floor, New York, NY 10022; 212-826-0100)

FSA (One Market Plaza, Steuart Tower, 22nd Floor, San Francisco, CA 94105; 415-995-8020)

Connie Lee Insurance Company (1299 Pennsylvania Ave., Suite 800 West, Washington, DC 20004; 202-835-0090; www.connielee.com)

Municipal Bond Investors Assurance Corporation (113 King St., Armonk, NY 10504; 914-273-4545; www.mbia.com)

6

Speculating with Futures and Options

If taking my advice in this book has left you in such good financial shape that you have a few thousand dollars left over with which to take risk, you might want to learn more about futures and options. Otherwise, you should probably not even be tempted by these high-stakes games in which you can make or lose thousands of dollars in days, hours or even minutes. If you are like the typical small investor who gets lured into speculative futures and options trading, you will end up losing some or all of your invested capital by the time you throw in the towel. So, if you have built up only a modest pool of capital, it's not normally worth assuming the enormous risks inherent in these markets. In the investment pyramid described in Chapter 1, futures and options trading would be at the top of the high-risk apex.

The Basics of Futures Trading

Despite the enormous risks of futures trading, the tremendous potential for quick profits attracts thousands of new investors to the markets every year.

A *futures contract* is an obligation to buy or sell a specific quantity of a commodity, financial instrument or stock index at a fixed price at a particular date in the future. Buying a contract obligating you to take delivery of the underlying commodity is known as *taking a long position*. For example, you might buy a futures contract obligating you to accept delivery of 100 troy ounces of gold for $350 on June 20. This particular contract is available on the Chicago Board of Trade (CBOT). If you were to follow through on the contract and buy all the gold, it would cost you $35,000 ($350 × 100 ounces).

The profit potential—and danger—of futures trading stem from the fact that you must put up only a small percentage, usually between 5 percent and 10 percent, of the contract's value to play the game. This money, a form of good faith deposit, is known as *margin*. In the example, if you had to put up 5 percent, it would cost you $1,750 to control the $35,000 contract.

As the price of the underlying commodity rises or falls, the worth of your contract surges or plunges. For example, if the price of gold rises from $350 to $400, the value of the underlying contract would soar to $40,000. Your profit would be $5,000 because the contract you bought that was worth $35,000 is now worth $40,000. Of course, if you had bought ten contracts, you would have earned a $50,000 profit.

On the other hand, if gold fell from $350 to $332.50, you would have lost all your $1,750 deposit money. If gold prices dropped from $332.50 to a lower price, your broker would send you a *margin call* (i.e., more money to cover your additional losses above and beyond your original $1,750 deposit). If gold dropped to $300, you would need an additional $3,250 to maintain your market position. If you don't meet the margin call, the contract would be liquidated immediately. If you do meet the margin call, you would maintain your position in the futures contract. When the delivery date arrives, you would have to buy $35,000 worth of gold, which would then be worth only $30,000, thus saddling you with a $5,000 loss per contract. If you were the seller of this contract, you would not have to worry about losing money if the buyer cuts his or her losses and runs—or even skips town. The commodity brokerage firm and, ultimately, the commodity exchange on which the trade was made guarantee that the buyer's obligations will be met.

If you believe that the price of the underlying commodity will fall, you can sell a futures contract short, or take a *short position*. The previous example would then work in reverse: You would profit if the price of the commodity fell and lose money if the commodity's price rose.

Another more conservative way to play futures is to buy or sell what is known as a *spread*. Instead of taking a pure bet that a commodity's price will rise if you are a buyer or fall if you are a seller, you can play both sides of a trade and profit by the spread widening or narrowing. For example, you might buy a long gold contract for one month and sell short another gold contract for another month. The spread between the price from one month to another would widen or narrow over time, giving you the chance to profit. Or you can spread one commodity against a similar one and hope to profit from the differential. For instance, you might buy a gold contract for one month and sell a silver contract for the same month, trying to profit from a change in the relationship between gold and silver.

While, in theory, you could actually accept delivery of the underlying commodity by taking possession of the 100 troy ounces of gold (to use the previous example), almost no one does. Only about 1 percent of futures contracts traded are settled by delivery, and that is done at a designated warehouse designed to transfer ownership of commodities. Most contracts are liquidated long before they expire. To cancel a contract, you would close out your position by taking the opposite side, netting you either a profit or a loss. In the earlier example, if you had gone long by buying a contract for gold, you could close out your position by selling the contract. Investing in futures is known as a *zero-sum game* because for every contract that profits, someone holds an offsetting contract that loses.

READING THE FUTURES TABLES IN NEWSPAPERS

Because so much rides on your futures positions, you must keep up with what happens in the futures markets. While you would need a computer to track moment-to-moment price changes, you can get a sense of the action from the daily listings in *The Wall Street Journal, Investor's Business Daily* and other financial newspapers.

Futures are grouped in the newspaper by broad categories, such as agricultural products (grains, oils, sugar, etc.), metals (copper, gold, silver, platinum, etc.), industrial goods (lumber, cotton, heating oil, etc.) and financial products (foreign currencies, stock market indexes, Treasury securities, etc.). Following is a typical listing for a futures contract—in this case, gold futures traded on the COMEX—along with an explanation of each column.

Gold (100 troy ounces; dollars per troy ounce)

Season's			Daily or Weekly			Net Change[7]	Open Interest[8]
High[1]	Low[2]		High[4]	Low[5]	Close[6]		
404.20	326.30	Feb.[3]	330.40	326.90	328.60	+1.60	42,183
330.10	328.40	Mar.	330.10	329.00	329.10	+1.60	30,012
410.00	327.00	Apr.	331.30	328.00	329.40	+1.40	21,350
418.50	328.00	June	332.60	329.10	330.50	+1.40	16,533
383.00	333.40	Dec.	336.50	334.00	334.70	+1.20	7,550

[9] Est. sales 20,151, Tuesday's sales 19,164
[10] Total open interest 117,628 +4,471

Above the table is a brief description of the contract and how prices are quoted. The example is a contract for gold, and prices are quoted in dollars per troy ounce.

1. The first column notes the highest price the contract has reached so far during its life.

2. The second column notes the lowest price the contract has reached so far during its life. The February contract, for example, has swung between a high of $404.20 and a low of $326.30, for example.

3. Column 3 indicates the different maturity months for the gold contracts—in this case, from February through December.

4. Column 4 records the highest price the contract sold for during the day's or week's trading.

5. The next column records the lowest price the contract sold for during the day's or week's trading. For example, during the last week, the February contract traded between a high of 330.40 and a low of 326.90.

6. Column 6 indicates the closing price of the contract at the end of the trading day or week. In the example, the February contract closed the week at 328.60.

7. The *net change* is how much the contract rose or fell in price during the trading day or week. The February contract, for instance, rose $1.60 last week.

8. *Open interest* is the number of contracts that are still being traded and have not been closed by delivery of the commodity or offsetting contracts. In the example, 42,183 contracts remain open on the February future. Note that the nearer the month of maturity, the more open interest there tends to be. This is because you incur less risk in committing your money for a shorter time than a longer time, and most people want to limit their risk by trading in the most actively traded "near month."

9. Line 9 estimates the total number of contracts traded today (in the example, 20,151) and the actual numbers for the previous day (19,164).

10. The final line estimates the total number of contracts still trading in the previous sessions (in the example, 117,628) and whether that number has risen or fallen (risen by 4,471).

Largest futures exchanges. While all futures contracts work the same way, you have many options as to which commodity, financial instrument or stock index to speculate on and which futures exchange will execute your trade. Each exchange sets different margin requirements, minimum and maximum amounts that a contract can move, expiration dates and trading hours for each contract. Following are the largest futures exchanges and the most popular contracts traded on each.

Chicago Board of Trade: corn, Dow Jones Industrial Average, Federal funds gold, municipal bonds, oats, silver, soybean meal, soybean oil, soybeans, Treasury bonds, Treasury notes, wheat.

Chicago Mercantile Exchange: Australian dollar, British pound, Canadian dollar, German mark, Eurodollars, feeder cattle, Goldman Sachs Commodity Index, Japanese yen, LIBOR 1-Month Rate, live cattle, lumber, Major Market Stock Index, Mexican peso, pork bellies, Nasdaq 100 Index, Nikkei 225 Average, Russell 2000 index, S&P 500 Index, S&P Midcap 400 Index, S&P Mini Index, Swiss franc, Treasury bills.

Coffee, Sugar and Cocoa Exchange: cocoa, coffee, International Market Index, sugar.

Commodity Exchange: copper, Eurotop 100 Index, gold, silver.

Kansas City Board of Trade: Mini Value Line Index, Value Line Index, Western Natural Gas, wheat.

MidAmerica Commodity Exchange: British pound, Canadian dollar, corn, deutsche mark, Eurodollars, gold, Japanese yen, live cattle, live hogs, oats, platinum, rice, silver, soybean meal, soybeans, Swiss franc, Treasury bills, Treasury bonds, wheat.

Minneapolis Grain Exchange: high fructose corn syrup, oats, wheat.

New York Cotton Exchange: Cotlook World cotton, cotton, European currency units, orange juice, Treasury notes, U.S. Dollar Index.

New York Futures Exchange: Commodity Research Bureau Price Index, New York Stock Exchange Composite Index.

New York Mercantile Exchange: crude oil, gasoline, heating oil, light sweet crude oil, natural gas, palladium, platinum, propane, sour crude oil, unleaded gasoline.

If you are thinking of playing the futures game, keep these guidelines in mind:

- *Play only with money you can afford to lose.* Don't speculate with money you need to rely on to cover your mortgage payment or your child's tuition.

- *Figure out in advance at what level you would promise yourself to take a profit or at what price you would promise to cut your losses.* This is important because the futures game can get you so entangled psychologically that you lose all perspective. Many people have seen profits slip from their grasp as they became greedy to earn even more. Others have stubbornly refused to cut their mushrooming losses on the foolish conviction that "the market will come around to my way of thinking." One way to impose this discipline on yourself is to set an automatic level at which you sell to capture a profit and an automatic stop-loss level at which your losses will be limited to a predetermined amount.

- *Don't assume you will win with every trade.* If you continue to cut your losses so they do not get out of hand, you will be in a position to let your profits run when you hit a big winner.

- *Figure in the costs of brokerage commissions in assessing your chances for profits or losses.* Brokers love futures trading because it involves so many transactions, each of which generates a commission. The costs of overtrading have sunk many investors.

- *Leave a cash cushion in your futures account* so that if the market goes against you, you do not have to scramble to come up with cash to meet a margin call.

- *Understand what you are getting into before you invest any money.* Work with an experienced broker, and study the factors that influence a particular market and what has happened in that market recently. You might do this by subscribing to one of the newsletters listed at the end of this chapter. Also, before you actually invest money, you could try some hypothetical trading. However you learn about futures, don't hurry to get into futures trading; the markets will be there whenever you decide you're ready.

Futures Pools and Discretionary Accounts

If you're not able to devote the time and emotional energy involved in trading futures (that includes most investors!), you have two ways to let professional futures traders do the work for you. First, you can invest in a futures pool, which is similar to a mutual fund. Investors pool millions of dollars with an established futures money management firm, which then buys and sells contracts in many different markets simultaneously, including agricultural, financial, industrial, metal and foreign currency futures.

Two advantages of participating in these pools are that you have a professional money manager watching your positions at all times, and you will never be subject to a margin call. If the manager runs into a serious losing streak, the pool may be dissolved earlier than anticipated, and you may get back only part of your principal. If everything goes well, on the other hand, the pool will be liquidated in five or ten years, and all profits will be distributed to pool participants, minus the fees that have been deducted every year. These fees, which amount to as much as 6 percent of managed assets each year, are charged on top of brokerage commissions of as much as 10 percent of your capital. In addition, the management company may take up to a 30 percent incentive fee from the fund's new profits. Unlike stock and bond mutual funds, it is not easy to get out of a futures pool once you have invested in one. Most brokerage firms require you to keep your capital in the pool at least three, and usually six, months.

The performance of these pools varies widely from pool to pool and year to year. They do best when the markets move sharply upward or downward and the pools are invested on the correct side of the move. They tend to do little when the markets are placid. And if they are on the wrong side of a market move, they can lose a lot of money in a hurry. Most brokerage firms sell participations in futures pools. You can size up an offering by looking at the futures manager's track record; however, that is no guarantee of future performance. Brokers want to sell to managers with hot records, and what worked before may not work again as the fast-moving markets change.

The best way to follow the performance of different money managers and the pools they manage is to subscribe to Managed Account Reports (220 5th Ave., 19th Floor, New York, NY 10001; 212-213-6202). This rating service provides monthly updates and industry averages for futures pools. In addition, several firms track the performance of futures money managers and will place your money with the top managers. One such firm is A.T.A. Research (5910 N. Central Expressway, Suite 1520, Dallas, TX 75206; 214-373-7606).

The second way to let professional futures traders invest your money for you is to sign up for a discretionary account with a futures trading adviser. Such an account gives a professional trader full discretion to buy and sell futures contracts without your prior authorization. The adviser receives an annual management fee of about 2 percent of your capital. In many cases, the trading adviser will also take an annual percentage—up to about 20 percent—of any profits he or she generates. You must be extremely careful in signing up for such an account, no matter how brilliant the track record of the trading adviser. Once he or she has your money and your signature on the dotted line, you have no power to stop the adviser's trading activity unless you revoke the agreement altogether.

Many brokerage firms will recommend futures trading advisers with good records. You can also contact the Managed Futures Association (471 Emerson St., Suite 200, Palo Alto, CA 94301; 415-325-4533).

The Basics of Options Trading

Though they are also speculative, options have one advantage over futures: The amount of money you can lose is limited to the amount of money you invested in the option. In futures, remember, you can actually lose more than you invest if you are hit with a margin call. While this limited-loss feature of options may provide some comfort, it doesn't change the fact that you can lose every penny of your investment.

Options come in two varieties: a *call* and a *put*. You buy a call when you think the underlying stock, stock index or futures contract will rise in value, and you buy a put when you think the underlying investment will fall in value. Following is an explanation of how each works.

Calls. When you buy a *call option,* you receive the right but not the obligation to buy a stock, an index or a futures contract at a set price for a particular period of time, usually a few months. For example, you might purchase the right to buy General Motors stock at $35 a share from now until February 20, which, let us say, is about a month from now. The person who sells you the option, known as the *option writer,* receives in return a nonrefundable payment called a *premium.* In this case, the premium might be $4 a share, or $300 total, because options are traded in minimums of 100 shares.

Assume that when you buy it, GM stock is trading at $38 a share. You are about even because your option gives you the right to buy at $35, and you paid $4 for the option. If GM stock shoots up from $38 to $45, or 18 percent, in the next month, your option's price will rocket from $4 to $10—a 150 percent gain. You could now do one of two things. First, you could exercise your right to buy 100 shares of GM stock at $35 a share for $3,500, then sell it in the open market for $45 a share, or $4,500 total, pocketing a $10-per-share, or $1,000, gain. Alternatively, you could sell the option for $10 per share, or $1,000 total, taking home a $600 gain ($1,000 minus the original $400 you paid for the premium). Most of the time, investors sell the option for a profit and do not actually exercise their right to buy the underlying shares.

If, instead of shooting up to $45 per share, however, GM stock either remains the same or falls, your option would expire worthless on February 20. You would lose your entire $400 premium.

Puts. When you buy a put, you want the underlying investment to fall in price—exactly the opposite of what you want to happen when you buy a call. A put gives you the right but not the obligation to sell a stock, an index or a futures contract at a set price for a particular period of time, usually a few months. If you think General Motors stock is about to fall in price, for instance, you could buy a General Motors put giving you the right to sell General Motors stock at $35 a share any time over the next month to February 20. With GM stock at $38, that right might cost you a premium of only ¼ of a point, or $25 (100 shares times .25).

If GM stock plummets from $38 to $30 over the next month, a 21 percent decline, your put would soar in value from ¼ to $5, or 19 times your premium investment. You could now do one of two things. You could exercise your option by selling General Motors stock at $35 per share for $3,500, then buy it back on the open market for $30 a share, or $3,000 total, and pocket the $500 difference. Or you could sell your option for $5 per share, or $500 total, and walk off with a $475 profit ($500 minus your $25 premium).

On the other hand, if GM stock either remains the same or rises in price before February 20, your put would expire worthless. You would lose your $25 premium.

As you can see, profits or losses in options can be significant and achieved in a short amount of time. If you buy a call or a put, the underlying investment must move up or down far enough and fast enough for you to make a profit. If you buy a call and the stock moves up, but not before your option expires, you still lose.

A key factor in whether you profit in options is the price of the premium. This price is determined by several factors, including the general direction of the underlying investment, the volatility level of the underlying investment and the time remaining before the option expires. Options are known as *wasting assets,* meaning that they waste away as time goes on. If you buy an option, time is your enemy because the option is worth less and less each day. If you sell an option, time is your friend because you want the option to expire without being exercised.

As with futures, you can hedge your bets with options by buying combinations of options called *spreads* or *straddles.* You can buy a call option with one date, like February, and a put option with another date, like April, and hope to profit from the change in the relationship between the two. Or you can buy a call on gold, for instance, and a put on silver and, again, hope to profit as the difference between the two options widens or narrows.

Another way to play options is to sell them on your existing holdings instead of buying them on investments you don't own. This is known as *writing covered options.* For example, say you own 100 shares of General Motors stock. If you write, or sell, a call option when the stock is at $38 a share, you will receive $4 a share, or $400 total, in premium, which is yours to keep no matter what happens to GM's stock price. (The $4 a share is a function of the bullishness or bearishness of the marketplace, time remaining in the option's life as well as several other factors.) If the price goes up enough, you might have to sell your stock to the option buyer because that is a right you grant when you sell the option. If, on the other hand, GM stock doesn't move or even goes down, you keep your stock and the $400 premium. Therefore, writing options can be a conservative strategy to boost the income you receive from a stock in addition to its dividends.

As long as you own the underlying shares and are able to deliver them if the option is exercised, selling options is a rather conservative strategy because you know in advance the worst that can happen: You would have to sell your shares to the option buyer at the predetermined price. In the previous example, that means you would receive a $400 premium and $35 a share, or $3,500, for your stock. You would not feel too happy, however, if the shares rose to $45 or more because you would no longer own the stock.

Daredevils in the options market sell options without owning the underlying shares, a strategy known as "naked" option writing. If the stock's price remains fixed or falls, someone who has sold a call for a $400 premium can keep the cash without having invested any money. However, if the stock price shoots up, the investor must buy shares in the market at the higher price to be able to deliver shares when the option is exercised. Most investors shouldn't try naked options writing until they are quite knowledgeable about the options market—and probably not even then.

READING THE OPTIONS TABLES IN NEWSPAPERS

If you buy or sell options, you should track your positions closely. The following listing is typical of those published in most major financial newspapers, such as *The Wall Street Journal* and *Investor's Business Daily*, along with an explanation of each column.

Listed Options Quotations

Option[1]	Strike Price[2]	Volume[3]	Last[4]	Net Change[5]	Close[6]	Open Interest[7]
General Motors	Feb35	8221	4	+1	38	6212
General Motors	Feb35p	2315	1/4	-1/2	38	1656

1. Column 1 names the underlying investment on which the option is written. In the example, that is General Motors stock.

2. The second column notes the date on which the option expires and the price at which the option can be exercised (the *strike price*). In the example, both options expire in February at a price of $35 per share. A *p* following the strike price means the option is a put option; no notation means the option is a call.

3. *Volume* refers to the volume of trading in the last day or week. In the example, the GM call traded 8,221 contracts, and the GM put option traded 2,315 contracts.

4. *Last* is the closing price for the option, or the premium per share (minimum 100 shares), you must pay to buy the contract. The price of the GM call is $4 a share, or $400 total, and the price of the put is ¼ a share, or $25 total.

5. *Net change* refers to the change in the option's price, or the previous day's closing price. In the example, the General Motors call option shows a +1.

6. *Close* is the closing price for the underlying investment. In the example, General Motors stock closed at $38 a share.

7. *Open interest* is the total number of options of that maturity still outstanding. In the example, 6,212 call options remain outstanding, and 1,656 put options have not yet expired.

Most important option exchanges. In addition to trading options on individual stocks like General Motors, you can trade options on stock indexes like the Standard & Poor's (S&P) 500 Index and on many futures contracts. Following is a list of the most important exchanges that trade options and the investments on which you can trade options contracts.

American Stock Exchange: individual stock options, stock index options including Airline Index, Biotechnology Index, BRG Leaps Index, BTK Leaps Index, Computer Technology Index, Eurotop Index, Hong Kong Index, Institutional Index, Internet Index, Japan Index, Major Market Index, Mexico Index, Morgan Stanley Cyclical Stock Index, Morgan Stanley Consumer Stock Index, Morgan Stanley High Technology 35 Stock Index, North American Telecommunications Index, Oil Index, Pharmaceutical Index, Standard & Poor's Depositary Receipts (SPDR) Index, Standard & Poor's Mid-Cap Index, XMI Leaps Index.

Chicago Board of Trade: options on futures contracts for corn, municipal bonds, silver, soybean meal, soybean oil, soybeans, Treasury bonds and 5-year and 10-year Treasury notes, wheat.

Chicago Board Options Exchange: Dow Jones Industrial Average, Dow Jones Transportation Average, Dow Jones Utility Average; FT-FE Index, individual stock options, Israel index, Mexico index, Nasdaq 100 Index, New York Stock

Exchange composite index, Nikkei 300 Index, Russell 2000 Index, Small Cap 600 Index, stock options and LEAPS on the S&P 100 Index, options and LEAPS on the S&P 500 Index, Standard & Poor's Banks Index, Technology Index.

Chicago Mercantile Exchange: options on futures contracts for Australian dollars, British pounds, Canadian dollars, deutsche marks, Eurodollars, feeder cattle, Japanese yen, live cattle, live hogs, lumber, pork bellies, S&P 500 Index, Swiss francs, Treasury bills.

Coffee, Sugar and Cocoa Exchange: options on futures contracts for cocoa, coffee, sugar.

Commodity Exchange: Eurotop 100 Index, options on futures contracts for copper, gold, silver.

Kansas City Board of Trade: Mini Value Line Index, Value Line Index, wheat.

MidAmerica Commodity Exchange: options on futures contracts for corn, gold, rice, soybeans, Treasury bonds, wheat.

Minneapolis Grain Exchange: oats, options on futures contracts for wheat, shrimp.

New York Cotton Exchange: Cotlook World Cotton, options on futures contracts for cotton, orange juice, Treasury notes, U.S. Dollar Index.

New York Futures Exchange: options on futures contracts for the Commodity Research Bureau Price Index, New York Stock Exchange Composite Index.

New York Mercantile Exchange: gasoline, heating oil, light sweet crude oil, natural gas, options on futures contracts for crude oil, platinum, unleaded gasoline.

New York Stock Exchange: index options on the NYSE Options Index.

Pacific Stock Exchange: index options on Morgan Stanley Emerging Growth Index, PSE Technology Index, Taiwan Stocks Index, Wilshire Small Cap Index.

Philadelphia Stock Exchange: options on the foreign currencies of Australian dollars, British pounds, Canadian dollars, Deutsche marks, European currency units, French francs, Japanese yen, Swiss francs; index options on Bank Stock Index, Gold/Silver Index, National OTC Index, Oil Sector Index, Phone Sector Index, Semiconductor Index, Top 100 Index, Utilities Index, Value Line Composite Index.

Using Your Computer To Trade Futures and Options

The fast-moving world of futures and options almost necessitates the use of a computer and online services if you have a chance of profiting. Prices change so fast based on the latest news or market sentiment shifts, that you will likely be left behind if you trade based on yesterday's newspaper reports. There are many computerized technical trading systems designed to spot trends in both the futures and options markets that will crunch data for you. However, it is ultimately up to you to decide which system is most understandable to you and has a good track record. To get your feet wet, you might want to subscribe to some of the newsletters or magazines listed in the Resources section of this chapter and also log on to their Web sites. Most brokers specializing in futures and options also offer helpful advice on their sites. If you have become more sophisticated, you might try some of the private trading-oriented Web sites listed in the Resources section of this chapter. There is also a wealth of information on trading strategies and current market trends on the Web sites of the Futures and Options Exchanges themselves, also listed at the end of this chapter.

You can pursue many strategies in the options market, from the very conservative to the extremely aggressive. As in futures, the excitement of potential profits can lure you into taking more risk than you probably should. Therefore, study the options market carefully before you invest. For more information, consult the books and newsletters listed in the following Resources section. Exchanges that trade options also will send helpful explanatory brochures.

Resources

BOOKS

All about Options from the Inside Out, by Thomas A. McCafferty and Russell R. Wasendorf (McGraw-Hill, Order Dept., 860 Taylor Station Rd., Blacklick, OH 43004; 800-722-4726; www.mcgraw-hill.com). Aimed at beginning investors who want to learn more about stock options and options on futures. Describes various high-return, low-risk strategies and how to hedge a stock portfolio against loss.

A Complete Guide to the Futures Markets: Fundamental Analysis, Technical Analysis, Trading, Spreads and Options, by Jack Schwager (John Wiley & Sons Inc., 605 3rd Ave., New York, NY 10158-0012; 212-850-6000; www.wiley.com). A guide for sophisticated investors in the futures markets.

The Day Trader's Manual: Theory Art and Science of Profitable Short-Term Investing, by William F. Eng (John Wiley & Sons Inc., 605 3rd Ave., New York, NY 10158-0012; 212-850-6000; www.wiley.com). The most comprehensive book on techniques used to time entry and exit points on various markets. Contains a good section on options spreading.

Futures Trading, by Robert E. Fink and Robert B. Feduniak (New York Institute of Finance, 2 Broadway, 5th Floor, New York, NY 10004-2283; 212-859-5000; 800-227-6943; www.nyif.com). A comprehensive examination of every aspect of futures trading.

Getting Started in Commodity Futures Trading, by Mark J. Powers (McGraw-Hill, Order Dept., 860 Taylor Station Rd., Blacklick, OH 43004; 800-722-4726; www. mcgraw-hill.com). The basics of futures trading.

Getting Started in Futures, by Todd Lofton (John Wiley & Sons Inc., 605 3rd Ave., New York, NY 10158-0012; 212-850-6000; www.wiley.com). Introduces futures trading.

Getting Started in Options, 2nd Edition, by Michael Thomsett (John Wiley & Sons Inc., 605 3rd Ave., New York, NY 10158-0012; 212-850-6000; www.wiley.com). Introduces the complex world of options.

The Handbook of Financial Futures: A Guide for Investors and Professional Financial Managers, by Nancy H. Rothstein and James M. Little (McGraw-Hill, Order Dept., 860 Taylor Station Rd., Blacklick, OH 43004; 800-722-4726; www.mcgraw-hill.com). Explains the various kinds of financial futures, including Treasury bonds, stock indexes and foreign currencies.

Handbook of Futures Markets: Commodity, Financial, Stock Index and Options, by Perry J. Kaufman (John Wiley & Sons Inc., 605 3rd Ave., New York, NY 10158-0012; 212-850-6000; www.wiley.com). A complete reference work about the futures, index and options markets and how to invest in them.

The Handbook of Stock Index Futures and Options, by Frank J. Fabozzi and Gregory M. Kipnis (McGraw-Hill, Order Dept., 860 Taylor Station Rd., Blacklick, OH 43004; 800-722-4726; www.mcgraw-hill.com). A complete guide to the complex world of stock index futures and options, designed for more sophisticated investors.

How the Options Markets Work, by Joseph A. Walker (New York Institute of Finance, 2 Broadway, 5th Floor, New York, NY 10004-2283; 212-859-5000; 800-227-6943; www.nyif.com). A primer that explains how options work and how to trade them.

Inside the Financial Futures Market, by Mark J. Powers (John Wiley & Sons Inc., 605 3rd Ave., New York, NY 10158-0012; 212-850-6000; www.wiley.com). Explains how the financial futures markets work and how you can profit by investing in them. Designed for sophisticated investors.

LEAPS (Long-Term Equity Anticipation Securities): What They Are and How To Use Them for Profit and Protection, by Harrison Roth (McGraw-Hill, Order Dept., 860 Taylor Station Rd., Blacklick, OH 43004; 800-722-4726; www.mcgraw-hill.com). Explains LEAPS, or long-term options, which mature in a few years and differ from short-term options, which mature in a few months. Discusses different strategies for each.

Managed Futures Portfolio Strategies: Investment Analysis and the Evaluation and Selection of Commodity Trading Advisors, by John P. Lass and Sol Waksman (McGraw-Hill, Order Dept., 860 Taylor Station Rd., Blacklick, OH 43004; 800-722-4726; www.mcgraw-hill.com). Explains how to evaluate, select and track a commodity trading adviser if you want to participate in the futures market but don't feel able to do the trading yourself.

The New Options Market, by Max G. Ansbacher (Walker & Co., 720 5th Ave., 14th Floor, New York, NY 10019; 212-265-3632). The classic work explaining how to invest in the options market for profit.

19 Options Strategies; Tools of the Trade, Volumes I & II; Understanding Options; by *Futures Magazine* (Oster Communications, P.O. Box 6, 219 Parkade, Cedar Falls, IA 50613; 319-277-6341; 800-635-3936; www.osterinc.com). Four booklets that explain the basics of the options markets for beginners.

The Options Manual, by Gary G. Gastineau (McGraw-Hill, Order Dept., 860 Taylor Station Rd., Blacklick, OH 43004; 800-722-4726; www.mcgraw-hill.com). A comprehensive guide explaining the ins and outs of the complex options market.

Options on Futures: A Hands-on Workbook of Market-Proven Trading Strategies, by Ronald J. Frost (Oster Communications, P.O. Box 6, 219 Parkade, Cedar Falls, IA 50613; 319-277-6341; 800-635-3936; www.osterinc.com). A clearly written book explaining the complex world of options on futures.

Options: Trading Strategies That Work, by William F. Eng (Dearborn Financial Publishing, 155 N. Wacker Dr., Chicago, IL 60606; 312-836-4400; 800-322-8621; www.dearborn.com). For sophisticated investors, outlines the myriad ways to use options to generate profits. Contains 12 contributed chapters from industry experts on how they make money with options.

Starting Out in Futures Trading, by Mark J. Powers (McGraw-Hill, Order Dept., 860 Taylor Station Rd., Blacklick, OH 43004; 800-722-4726; www.mcgraw-hill.com). Primer to the futures market for beginning investors. Explains how orders are sent to the trading floor and how to develop a trading plan by limiting your risks. Provides trading exercises you can try before you start trading.

The Technical Analysis of Stocks, Options and Futures, by William F. Eng (McGraw-Hill, Order Dept., 860 Taylor Station Rd., Blacklick, OH 43004; 800-722-4726; www.mcgraw-hill.com). Explains the technical analysis techniques thoroughly. Includes sections on how and why the indicator should be used.

Trading in Options on Futures, by James T. Colburn (New York Institute of Finance, 2 Broadway, 5th Floor, New York, NY 10004-2283; 212-859-5000; 800-227-6943; www.nyif.com). Sophisticated strategies for using the options on futures markets.

Trading Rules: Strategies for Success, by William F. Eng (Dearborn Financial Publishing, 155 N. Wacker Dr., Chicago, IL 60606; 312-836-4400; 800-322-8621; www.dearborn.com). Presents 50 proven principles for traders.

Warrants: Trading, Hedging and Speculating, by Donald T. Mesler and John J. Kilgannon (McGraw-Hill, Order Dept., 860 Taylor Station Rd., Blacklick, OH 43004;

800-722-4726; www.mcgraw-hill.com). Explains how to analyze warrants and find undervalued issues. Runs through the process of determining the risk/reward characteristics of different warrants.

Winning in the Futures Markets, by George Angell (Oster Communications, P.O. Box 6, 219 Parkade, Cedar Falls, IA 50613; 319-277-6341; 800-635-3936; www.osterinc. com). Provides in-depth coverage of the market mechanics of futures. Also explains how to set up a trading plan and what strategies you can use to profit from futures.

MAGAZINES AND NEWSLETTERS

Bullish Review of Commodity Futures Markets (14600 Blaine Ave. East, Rosemount, MN 55068; 612-423-4949)

Commodity Closeup (Oster Communications, P.O. Box 6, 219 Parkade, Cedar Falls, IA 50613; 319-277-1271; 800-635-3936; www.osterinc.com)

Commodity Futures Forecast (Commodex, Mall at the Galaxy, 7000 Boulevard East, Guttenberg, NJ 07093; 201-868-2600; www.commodex.com)

Commodity Traders Consumer Report (P.O. Box 7605, New York, NY 10150-7603; 212-736-2330; 800-832-6065; www.ctcr.investors.net)

CRB Futures Perspective (135 S. LaSalle St., Dept. 2212, Chicago, IL 60674-2212; 800-621-5271; www.crbindex.com)

Dunn & Hargitt Commodity Service (P.O. Box 1100, 22 N. 2nd St., Lafayette, IN 47902; 317-423-2624; 800-927-7289)

Futures Charts (Commodity Trend Service, P.O. Box 32309, Palm Beach Gardens, FL 33420; 407-694-0960; 800-331-1069; www.cts.dearborn.com)

The Futures Industry (Futures Industry Association, 2001 Pennsylvania Ave., N.W., Suite 600, Washington, DC 20006; 202-466-5460; www.fiafii.org)

Futures Magazine (Oster Communications, P.O. Box 6, 219 Parkade, Cedar Falls, IA 50613; 319-277-6341; 800-635-3936; www.futuresmag.com). A comprehensive look at the futures industry, including market news and articles from past issues. The Learning Center provides educational resources like books, software and videotapes about futures, while Futures Talk provides a place for online discussion groups.

Gann Angles (495 Trinity Ave., Suite A, Seaside, CA 93955; 408-393-2000; www.gannangles.com)

Managed Account Reports (220 5th Ave., 19th Floor, New York, NY 10001; 212-213-6202; 800-638-2525; www.marhedge.com)

Spread Scope Commodity Spread Charts (Spread Scope, Inc., P.O. Box 950841, Mission Hills, CA 91345; 818-782-0774; 800-232-7285; www.trading-advice.com)

Technical Analysis of Stocks and Commodities Magazine (3517 S.W. Alaska St., Seattle, WA 98126; 206-938-0570; 800-832-4642; www.traders.com)

Tomorrow's Commodities, Tomorrow's Options, Tomorrow's Stocks (Techno-Fundamental Investments, P.O. Box 14111, Scottsdale, AZ 85267-1411; 602-996-2908)

WEB SITES

Bruck Babcock's Reality Based Trading Company. The founder of *Commodity Traders Consumer Reports* and author of several books on futures and options, Babcock provides a great deal of educational material and trading ideas on his Web site. He even has a special section designed for beginners. www.lloyd.com/~babcock

Club 3000—Commodity Traders Network. A network of computerized commodity traders discussing trading opportunities. Many members contribute commentary to the network's frequent newsletters. ison.com/club3000

Commodity Traders Advice. A complete Web site offering price updates, analysis and trading recommendations on all futures and options markets. infomatch.com/~adas/adv.html

EzTrade. A sophisticated EZAnalyser program looks at all the activity in the futures, index options and stock markets to propose trades with the best chances for success and the lowest risk. The site also keeps prices of futures and options positions up-to-date and produces illustrative graphs showing price trends. Beginners will find several tutorials to help them learn the ropes of options and futures trading. www.eztrade.com

INO Global Markets. One of the most complete Web sites around, INO gives you price updates, charts and graphs, news summaries affecting all markets, and links to most industry associations and exchanges. There are several online newsletters, loaded with advice on specific trades and trading techniques. www.ino.com

Monthly Profits. A site covering options call-writing strategies. It gives you a manual describing how the system works and recommends specific trades. www.napanet.net/vi/monthlyprofits

XYZ for Commodities. An artificial intelligence Web site aiming to catch potentially profitable trends in many futures and options markets. www.fastfwd.com/xyz

TRADE ASSOCIATIONS

Futures Industry Association (2001 Pennsylvania Ave., N.W., Suite 600, Washington, DC 20006; 202-466-5460; www.fiafii.org). Represents brokers in the futures and options business and lobbies on issues affecting the futures and options industry. Also educates the public about investing in futures and options.

Managed Futures Association (471 Emerson St., Suite 200, Palo Alto, CA 94301; 415-325-4533; www.mfahome.com). Represents and educates money managers who offer managed futures programs. Can help consumers find a futures-oriented money manager.

Managed Futures Association of Trading Advisors (1150 Connecticut Ave., Suite 700, Washington, DC 20036; 202-872-9186; www.mfahome.com). Represents commodity futures trading advisers in lobbying before government agencies.

National Futures Association (200 W. Madison St., Suite 1600, Chicago, IL 60606; 312-781-1300; www.nfa.futures.org). Represents firms dealing in futures trading. Will resolve any dispute with a member firm. Offers the following free publications: "Arbitration: A Way To Resolve Futures-Related Disputes"; "Buying Options on Futures Contracts: A Guide to Their Uses and Risks"; "Glossary of Futures Terms"; "Investment Swindles: How They Work and How To Avoid Them"; "Investor's Bill of Rights"; "Swindlers Are Calling"; "Understanding Opportunities and Risks in Futures Trading."

The Options Industry Council (440 S. LaSalle St., Suite 2400, Chicago, IL 60605; 800-566-9642; www.optionscentral.com). The Options Industry Council provides educational material about trading in the options market. They offer several free publications, including "Characteristics and Risks of Standardized Options," "Understanding Stock Options," "Directory of Exchange Listed Options," "LEAPS/ Long Term Equity Anticipation Securities," "Taxes and Investing" and "Blueprint." Their Web site offers price quotes, answers to frequently asked questions about options and a list of educational resources such as books and software. There is also a Strategy of the Month, which describes how a particular options strategy works.

FEDERAL GOVERNMENT REGULATORS

Commodity Futures Trading Commission (1155 21st St., N.W., Washington, DC 20581; 202-418-5000; www.cftc.gov). The federal regulator of all futures and options markets in the United States. Investigates charges of fraud against dealers and approves all new contracts before they begin trading. Answers questions about the futures and options markets and takes complaints against futures brokers. Offers the following free brochures: "Before Trading, Get the Facts"; "The CFTC"; "Economic Purposes of Futures Trading"; "CFTC Glossary." The CFTC also offers a Web site at (www.cftc.gov) with online editions of CFTC literature, statistical data, details of enforcement actions against futures brokers and information on how to file claims against brokers.

FUTURES AND OPTIONS EXCHANGES

American Stock Exchange (AMEX, 86 Trinity Pl., New York, NY 10006; 212-306-1000; www.amex.com)

Chicago Board of Trade (CBOT, 141 W. Jackson Blvd., Chicago, IL 60604; 312-435-3500; www.cbot.com)

Chicago Board Options Exchange (CBOE, 400 S. LaSalle St. at Van Buren, Chicago, IL 60605; 312-786-5600; www.cboe.com)

Chicago Mercantile Exchange (CME), Index and Options Market (IOM) and International Monetary Market (IMM) (30 S. Wacker Dr., Chicago, IL 60606; 312-930-1000; www.cme.com)

Chicago Rice and Cotton Exchange (CRCE, 141 W. Jackson Blvd., Chicago, IL 60604; 312-341-3078; www.cbot.com)

Chicago Stock Exchange (CHX, 440 S. LaSalle St., Chicago, IL 60605-1070; 312-663-2222; www.chicagostockex.com)

Coffee, Sugar and Cocoa Exchange (CSCE, Four World Trade Center, New York, NY 10048; 212-742-6000; www.ino.com/gen/csce.html)

Commodity Exchange (COMEX, Four World Trade Center, New York, NY 10048; 212-390-1420)

Kansas City Board of Trade (KCBT, 4800 Main St., Suite 303, Kansas City, MO 64112; 816-753-7500; www.kcbt.com)

MidAmerica Commodity Exchange (MIDAM, 141 W. Jackson Blvd., Chicago, IL 60604; 312-341-3000; www.cbot.com)

Minneapolis Grain Exchange (MGE, 400 S. 4th St., Suite 130, Minneapolis, MN 55415; 612-338-6212; www.mgex.com)

New York Cotton Exchange (NYCE, Four World Trade Center, New York, NY 10048; 212-938-2650; www.nyce.com)

New York Futures Exchange (NYFE, Suite 5572, Four World Trade Center, New York, NY 10048; (800) THE-NYFE; www.nyce.com)

New York Mercantile Exchange (NYMEX, Four World Trade Center, New York, NY 10048; 212-938-2222)

New York Stock Exchange (NYSE, 11 Wall St., New York, NY 10005; 212-656-3000; www.nyse.com)

Pacific Stock Exchange (PSE, 301 Pine St., San Francisco, CA 94104; 415-393-4000; www.pacificex.com)

Philadelphia Stock Exchange (PSE) and Philadelphia Board of Trade (PBOT) (1900 Market St., Philadelphia, PA 19103; 215-496-5000; www.phlx.com)

7

Investing in Gold and Collectibles

Since 3000 B.C., gold has been recognized as the ultimate medium of exchange. Because gold is rare, in continuous demand and portable, it is considered the supreme store of value. In contrast, paper money, printed by governments, can be eroded by inflation or the collapse of those governments. Gold is an asset in its own right; it does not require a government, a corporation or any other entity to validate it. For example, when Vietnam was falling to the Communists in 1975, Vietnamese refugees weren't interested in escaping with South Vietnamese currency; it would be worthless. They fled with gold coins and bars, which they knew would have value wherever they ended up.

Is there a place for gold in your investment portfolio? The answer depends on your outlook for inflation and the total mix of your portfolio.

Gold and Other Precious Metals

Gold is an investment that prospers when the economy suffers. The last great increase in gold prices occurred during the late 1970s, when interest rates and inflation soared into double digits, tension between the United States and the Soviet Union mounted over the Soviet invasion of Afghanistan, Iran held Americans hostage, and Arab oil embargoes caused oil prices to skyrocket. Gold had been fixed at $35 an ounce in 1934, and it was declared illegal for individuals to own gold bullion. These restrictions were removed in late 1974, after which gold eventually shot up in price to a peak of $875 per ounce in January 1980. However, as inflation and interest rates plunged to low single digits, the Soviet Union disintegrated, oil prices fell to stable levels and the economy rebounded in the 1980s and 1990s, an ounce of gold dropped back to the $250 to $400 range.

Traditionally, gold has been seen as a hedge not only against high inflation but also against high international tension. This was certainly true during the 1970s, when gold shot up dramatically in a day based on the latest rumors of war in the Middle East or in some other part of the world. But over the past few years, gold seems to have lost its appeal even during times of turmoil. Despite such dramatic events in the 1990s as the collapse of Communism and the related outbreaks of ethnic tension throughout the former Soviet empire, the Persian Gulf War, the strife in the former Yugoslavia, and the meltdown on many Asian economies and currencies, gold fell from about $400 an ounce to below $300. This was because inflation remained well under control, and investors did not feel the need to hedge themselves against rising prices as they had in the late 1970s.

Though it seems unlikely that a repeat of the 1970s inflation and gold price surge will occur, gold may still have a role to play in your investment portfolio. Studies show that over the long term, portfolios containing gold are more stable and have higher returns than gold-free portfolios because gold tends to move in the opposite direction of paper assets, such as stocks and bonds. This counterweight effect—again, over the long term—provides protection against unforeseen events, even though in the short term gold holdings may severely underperform stocks and bonds.

All this holds true for other precious metals as well, though to a lesser degree. Silver and platinum are also used by investors as inflation hedges, but they are not seen as the ultimate store of value, as is gold. Gold is used in the jewelry, dentistry and electronics industries; however, its price is determined mainly by the supply from gold mines and by investment demand, not as much by industrial factors. The other precious metals have wider industrial uses—silver in photography, electrical and electronics, jewelry and silverware; diamonds in jewelry and as cutting tools; and platinum and palladium in jewelry and catalytic converters for automobiles. These metals tend to fluctuate in price based more on industrial supply and demand than on investment demand (see Figure 7.1).

Investing in precious metals is, by its nature, risky. Most forms of metals investing do not provide income, so you depend totally on an increase in the metal's price in order to profit. While profits can be enormous at certain times in the economic cycle, metals prices may remain depressed for several years in a row and yield little or no return. Because metals investing is so risky, it should be placed in the high-risk apex of the investment pyramid described in Chapter 1. Most investment advisers recommend that you invest between 5 percent and 10 percent of your portfolio in one form of gold, silver or platinum to serve as a long-term hedge.

Investors looking to hedge their portfolios with gold and other precious metals have five principal ways of participating in the markets: coins and bars; certificates; shares in precious-metals-mining companies; mutual funds that buy precious-metals-mining stocks; and futures and options on gold, silver and platinum.

Figure 7.1
Platinum Typically Trades at a Premium to Gold

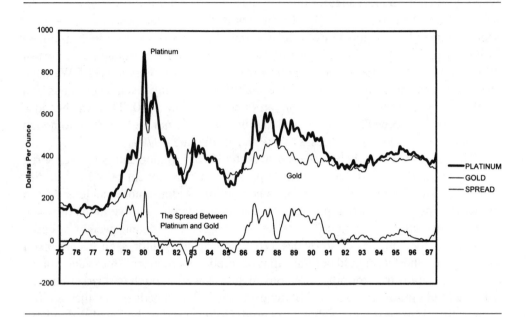

Source: Reprinted by permission of Platinum Guild International (USA) Inc. (Nearby Nymex Contract; Avg. Monthly Close - 2nd Quarter, 1997)

Coins and Bars

The most convenient and direct way to invest in the precious-metals markets is to buy coins and bars that have been minted specifically for investors. Coins fall into two categories: *bullion* and *numismatic*. Bars are always bullion. Bullion coins and bars are pure or near-pure gold, silver or platinum and therefore trade almost solely on their metal content. Numismatic coins are minted in limited quantities, sometimes for a specific event, like the Olympics or the coronation of a king. They trade on supply and demand for the specific coin and on the artistic traits and condition of the coin.

THE CASE FOR BULLION

For investment purposes, you should stick with bullion coins and bars. They trade for a small markup of from 1 percent to 15 percent more than the price of the underlying metal. Gold coins and bars come in many sizes, from a one-gram bar or a ¹⁄₂₅-ounce coin to a one-ounce coin (a one-kilo coin by the Australian mint is the exception) to a 400-ounce bar. Don't expect to find one of these large bars, which would be worth $120,000 if gold were $300 an ounce, in your local coin dealer's front window, however. They are normally used by central banks and governments to settle debts. If you're interested, you can see several hundred of them in the vault at the Federal Reserve in New York City or at Fort Knox, Kentucky.

The best size coin to purchase is the one-ounce variety because it is easiest to buy and sell. Many countries produce one-ounce gold coins, but the most popular (in alphabetical order by country) are the Australian Nugget, the Austrian Philharmonica, the British Britannia, the Canadian Maple Leaf, the Mexican Peso, the South African Kruggerand and the U.S. Gold Eagle. As part of the now lifted apartheid-related ban on South African products, no new Kruggerands were imported into the United States for years, though an active secondary market in Kruggerands still exists worldwide.

Among one-ounce silver coins, the most popular are the Australian Kookaburra, the Canadian Silver Maple Leaf and the U.S. Silver Eagle. Silver can also be purchased in bags of coins worth about $1,000 per bag and bars of many sizes ranging from 1 ounce to 1,000 ounces. Silver usually sells for far less per ounce than gold and might therefore be more affordable for starting bullion investors.

Platinum coins usually sell for more than either gold or silver because platinum is rarer. The most popular one-ounce platinum coins are the Australian Koala Bear, the Canadian Platinum Maple Leaf and the Isle of Man Noble. So few palladium coins circulate that they are not worth buying for investment purposes.

When buying bullion coins, you should shop around among coin dealers, banks and brokerage houses because they all charge slightly different markups or sales charges. Because many fly-by-night coin dealers charge excessive markups, it is best to associate with a dealer who is a member of the Professional Numismatists Guild (3950 Concordia Lane, Fallbrook, CA 92028; 760-728-1300; www. pngdealers.com), which holds its members to high ethical standards. Be particularly wary of dealers who solicit you over the phone but have no office nearby. Many stories circulate about firms that set up shop, deliver high-pressure sales pitches promising huge instant profits, collect investors' money, then disappear as quickly as they appeared. Another safe way to buy coins is through coin conventions or shows, where you haggle with other investors over prices. You can find out about such shows from the American Numismatic Association (818 N. Cascade Ave., Colorado Springs, CO 80903; 719-632-2646).

If you build up a sizable collection of bullion coins, keep them in a secure place, preferably a safe-deposit box, even though this adds to your cost of owning the coins. You might also consider a rider on your home insurance policy to cover theft of your coins if you insist on keeping them at home.

If you want to buy bars instead of coins, you can choose among more than 19 sizes and weights, from the tiny one-gram to the one-ounce, five-ounce, ten-ounce and kilo bar, which equals 32.15 troy ounces. Bars are usually engraved with the name of the company that created them. When you buy, look for the most recognized names: Englehard Metals, Johnson Matthey and Credit Suisse. Bars are generally sealed in a plastic container to protect them from scratching and chipping. If your bars have been removed from their plastic, or they are marked with an unfamiliar company name, the dealer you want to sell them to may require that the bars be assayed, or weighed and inspected, to make sure they are acceptable. This process will cost you up to 1 percent of the bars' price, which will cut into your return.

THE INS AND OUTS OF NUMISMATICS

While bullion coins and bars are priced solely on the value of the metal, numismatic coins are much trickier to price because they are subject to the condition of the coins, their scarcity and their popularity. The price of a sought-after numismatic coin will be much higher than its gold content—in some cases, double or more.

To make money in numismatics, you must spend time studying the market. By consulting numismatic magazines and newsletters (listed at the end of this chapter), attending coin conventions and swap meets and getting to know your local coin dealer, you will be able to determine which coin has appreciation potential and which is merely a flash in the pan. Don't expect to get rich quickly with numismatics; those who do almost always lose money.

Among gold coins, two of the most popular—and therefore easy-to-trade—coins are the U.S. $20 Liberty piece, issued from 1850 through 1907, and the followup coin, the $20 U.S. St. Gaudens, produced from 1907 through 1932. Also frequently traded are the $1, $2½, $3, $5 and $10, U.S. gold pieces. The United States resumed minting one-ounce and smaller gold coins in 1986.

Among silver numismatics, the U.S. Morgan dollar, issued from 1878 through 1921, and the U.S. Peace dollar, dating from 1921 through 1935, are the most popular.

The wide variation in prices for the same pieces results from competition in the marketplace and the grade of the coin. Knowing your coin's grade will largely determine whether you receive a fair price for it. The market is flooded with counterfeit coins and coins being passed off as a higher grade than they really are. Even one grade can make a significant difference in the price of a coin. For example, an MS-63 $20 gold piece might sell for between $500 and $550, while an MS-64 might sell for more than $700. (Ratings are explained below.) As the coin size gets smaller, the spread between grades grows dramatically. For example, a small $5 Indian coin with an MS-63 grade might sell for $2,800, while an MS-64 might fetch $5,500.

The only sure way to protect yourself when buying a coin is to buy one that is already certified to be a particular grade or to get the coin certified before you buy it. Three professional services grade coins: Professional Coin Grading Service (PCGS), Numismatic Guaranty Corporation of America (NGC) and American Numismatic Association Certification Service (ANACS). (The addresses and phone numbers of all three are listed in the "Resources" section of this chapter.)

These services will certify any coin you send them for $11 plus postage. They will ascertain its correct grade and mail it back to you in a hard plastic holder known as a slab. The services will guarantee the authenticity of the coin's grade as long as the slab remains unopened. (Opening the slab trips its security device, automatically voiding the guarantee.) Having your coin professionally graded is inexpensive insurance for an expensive item, and the slab will protect the coin from mishandling and atmospheric conditions, which could slash your coin's value.

The following* is a brief rundown, supplied by the American Numismatic Association, of the different quality grades assigned to coins, from the top grade to the bottom.

Proof. A specially made coin distinguished by sharpness of detail and usually with a brilliant mirrorlike surface. "Proof" refers to the method of manufacture and not to a condition, but normally the term implies perfect mint state unless otherwise noted and graded. 0

Mint state (MS). A term used interchangeably with "uncirculated (Unc.)" to describe coins showing no trace of wear. Such coins may vary to some degree because of blemishes, toning or slight imperfections, as described in the following subdivisions.

Perfect uncirculated (MS-70). Perfect new condition, showing no trace of wear; the finest quality possible, with no evidence of scratches, handling or contact with other coins. Very few regular issue coins achieve this grade.

Gem uncirculated (MS-65). An above-average uncirculated coin that may be brilliant or lightly toned and that has very few contact marks on the surface or rim. MS-69 thru MS-61 indicates a slightly higher or lower grade of preservation, respectively.

Uncirculated (MS-60). No trace of wear but may show a number of contact marks. Surface may be spotted or lack some luster.

Choice about uncirculated (AU-55). Barest evidence of light wear on only the highest points of the design. Most of the mint luster remains.

About uncirculated (AU-50). Traces of light wear on many of the high points of the design. At least half of the mint luster is still present.

Choice extremely fine (EF-45). Light overall wear on the highest points of the design. All design details are very sharp. Some of the mint luster is evident.

Extremely fine (EF-40). Design lightly worn throughout but all features sharp and well defined. Traces of luster may show.

Choice very fine (VF-30). Light, even wear on the surface and highest parts of the design. All lettering and major features are sharp.

Very fine (VF-20). Moderate wear on the high points of the design. All major details are clear.

*Source: Used with permission of the American Numismatic Association.

Fine (F-12). Moderate, considerable, even wear. The entire design is bold, with an overall pleasing appearance.

Very good (VG-8). Well worn with the main features clear and bold although rather flat.

Good (G-4). Heavily worn, with the design visible but faint in areas. Many details are flat.

About good (AG-3). Very heavily worn, with portions of the lettering, date and legends worn smooth. The date may be barely readable.

Clearly, the condition of a numismatic coin will have an enormous impact on the price at which you buy or sell it. Take good care of it, and enjoy it—but don't count on profiting from it.

Certificates

If you want to invest in precious metals for profit and don't care about holding the metal itself, a certificate may be the best thing to buy. A gold, silver, platinum or palladium certificate represents ownership of a particular amount of metal, which is stored in a bank vault. Certificates are sold in minimum lots of $1,000 by banks, brokerage firms and coin dealers at commissions ranging from 1 percent to 3 percent of the purchase price, depending on the size of the order. When you cash in your certificate, the bank or broker will usually charge a 1 percent sales commission. In addition, the bank holding the metal will charge an annual storage and insurance fee of up to another percentage point of the certificate's value. But make sure that you deal only with reputable companies.

Precious-Metals Stocks

An even more volatile way to ride the ups and downs of the gold, silver and platinum markets is to invest in publicly traded mining companies. Their stocks, like all stocks, rise and fall based on investors' expectations of future profits. This means that investors' projections of higher or lower gold and silver prices, or hopes that a new "mother lode" gold mine will be found, can cause sharp increases or decreases in a mining company's stock price. Gold mining shares usually shoot up faster and fall more sharply than gold bullion prices.

Two kinds of gold-mining shares exist: North American-Australian mine issues and South African mine issues. North American-Australian mines tend to pay lower dividends than South African mines and are influenced more by developments at the company. South African issues are frequently affected by political turmoil and labor strikes in South Africa, as well as by fluctuations in the value of the South African rand against the U.S. dollar. It might be possible, for instance, that strife in South Africa that threatens to shut down gold mines would cause the price of gold to soar because the markets fear a gold shortage, while South African gold-mining shares would plunge because of the mines' lost production.

North American-Australian mining shares, on the other hand, can rise in price even if the price of gold is stagnant or falling slightly. Improved technology often allows some companies to extract more gold from their mines, so the firms' profits will rise because of increased output. You have plenty of solid, well-known North American mining companies to choose from, such as American Barrick Resources, Newmont Mining and Homestake Mining, all traded on the New York Stock Exchange (NYSE). Don't be tempted by small, penny-stock firms that hope to strike it rich someday. They are far too risky an investment for your hard-earned capital.

If you want to invest in even riskier platinum and palladium, you can buy shares in two South African companies—Rustenberg Platinum and Impala Mines, both available in the form of American depositary receipts (ADRs). Remember, though, that these shares are subject to the volatility of the South African political situation.

Precious-Metals Mutual Funds

A safer way to invest in gold- and silver-mining stocks is to buy shares in one of the many *open-ended mutual funds* that specialize in precious metals. Because they invest in mining stocks, the funds tend to be more volatile than the price of bullion, but because they are diversified, the funds are safer than investing all your money in one stock. Like all mutual funds, precious-metals funds are run by a professional manager who dedicates all his or her time to analyzing mining stocks. Some funds specifically avoid South African gold-mining companies, while others mix South African, North American and Australian shares. These mutual funds pay dividends, which can easily be reinvested in more shares.

The following are the largest precious-metals mutual funds, with their toll-free numbers, supplied courtesy of the Morningstar Mutual Fund Data Service of Chicago:

American Century Global Gold Fund; 800-345-2021
Blanchard Precious Metals Fund; 800-829-3863
Bull & Bear Gold Investors; 800-847-4200
Cappiello-Rushmore Gold Fund; 800-343-3355
Dean Witter Precious Metals and Minerals; 800-869-3863
Fidelity Select American Gold Fund; 800-544-8888
Fidelity Select Precious Metals and Minerals Fund; 800-544-8888
Franklin Gold Fund; 800-342-5236
Gabelli Gold Fund; 800-422-3554
IDS Precious Metals Fund; 800-328-8300

Invesco Strategic Gold Fund; 800-525-8085
Keystone Precious Metals Fund; 800-343-2898
Lexington Goldfund; 800-526-0056
Lexington Strategic Investments; 800-526-0056
Lexington Strategic Silver Fund; 800-526-0056
MFS Gold & Natural Resources Fund; 800-637-2929
Midas Fund; 800-400-6432
Monterey OCM Gold Fund; 800-251-1970
Morgan Stanley Institutional Gold Fund; 800-548-7786
Oppenheimer Gold & Special Minerals Fund; 800-525-7048
PIMCO Precious Metals Fund; 800-426-0107
Pioneer Gold Fund; 800-225-6292
Rydex Precious Metals Fund; 800-820-0888
Scudder Gold Fund; 800-225-2470
SoGen Gold Fund; 800-334-2143
U.S. Gold Shares Fund; 800-873-8637
U.S. World Gold Fund; 800-873-8637
U.S. Global Resources Fund; 800-873-8637
USAA Gold Fund; 800-382-8722
Van Eck Gold Opportunity Fund; 800-826-1115
Van Eck Gold Resources Fund; 800-826-1115
Van Eck International Investors Gold Fund; 800-826-1115
Vanguard Gold & Precious Metals Fund; 800-662-7447

You have two options among *closed-end funds* for investing in gold and silver. One is called the Central Fund of Canada (P.O. Box 7319, Ancaster, Ontario, Canada L9G 3N6; 416-648-7878), and it trades on the American Stock Exchange (AMEX). The fund owns a large cache of gold and silver bullion, which it keeps in a bank vault. This fund therefore offers no risk of exploration or production of gold. It is as pure an investment in bullion as you can get without holding the metal in your hands.

The other closed-end fund is ASA Limited (ASA LTD, P.O. Box 269, Florham Park, NJ 07932; 201-377-3535). This fund invests almost exclusively in shares of South African mining companies and is therefore subject to all the ups and downs of the South African market and the fluctuations of the South African rand against the U.S. dollar.

Precious-Metals Futures and Options

If all of the vehicles for investing in precious metals discussed so far are too tame for your taste, you might try a foray into the extremely speculative world of gold, silver, platinum and palladium futures and options. (For a more detailed discussion of how futures and options work, see Chapter 6, "Speculating with Futures and Options.")

Profits and losses are magnified when you use futures or options to speculate—and that is what you are doing—on short-term price swings in precious metals. With futures, you invest only a small amount, perhaps 5 percent to 10 percent, of what the futures contract is worth. This investment is known as the *margin* (a kind of good-faith deposit). You can bet that the price will rise, called a *long position,* or you can speculate that the price will fall, called a *short position.* If you guess correctly, you stand to make a great deal of money. If you guess incorrectly, your margin will be wiped out, and you will be subject to a *margin call,* meaning that you must put up more cash or lose the money you have invested so far.

If that sounds like fun, you may like options on futures even more. With options, you not only bet on the direction of gold, silver, platinum or palladium prices; you also speculate on what will happen to the price of the futures contract on each metal. It's like doubling your bet at the blackjack table in Las Vegas. To win at options on futures, you must guess correctly what will happen to the crowd psychology in the metals markets. Because the futures markets are incredibly volatile in the first place, trying to predict how people will speculate on futures is an even more daunting challenge. You might see or hear pitches on television, on the radio or in the mail for options claiming, "All you can lose is your original investment." That's true, and you should plan on doing just that. If you are lucky enough to guess correctly the direction of the underlying futures, you can make a quick fortune. But if you get the direction wrong, or even if you get the direction right and your timing is off, you can easily lose every cent you put into the option.

One other way to speculate with options is to buy contracts on indexes of gold- and silver-mining stocks. The Philadelphia Stock Exchange offers trading in a gold and silver index option based on the movement of seven gold- and silver-mining stocks. With an index option, you invest a certain amount of money, called a *premium,* which grows or shrinks in value as the index you are betting on rises or falls. If you don't sell before your index option expires, you end up with either a profit or nothing at all.

Trading in futures, options and index options on precious metals ranks at the top of the high-risk apex of the investment pyramid discussed in Chapter 1. In fact, it might be outside the pyramid altogether! However, if you are determined to try futures and options on precious metals, the following list notes the exchanges on which various contracts are traded. Consult the list of futures and options exchange addresses and telephone numbers following Chapter 6 if you need to contact an exchange for further information about any of these contracts.

GOLD

Futures: Chicago Board of Trade (CBOT);
Commodity Exchange (COMEX) in New York;
MidAmerica Commodity Exchange (MIDAM) in Chicago

Options on futures: Commodity Exchange (COMEX) in New York; MidAmerica Commodity Exchange (MIDAM) in Chicago

Index options: gold/silver index of seven stocks on the Philadelphia Stock Exchange (PSE)

SILVER

Futures: Chicago Board of Trade (CBOT);
Commodity Exchange (COMEX) in New York;
MidAmerica Commodity Exchange (MIDAM) in Chicago

Options on futures: Chicago Board of Trade (CBOT);
Commodity Exchange (COMEX) in New York

Index options: gold/silver index of seven stocks on the Philadelphia Stock Exchange (PSE)

PLATINUM

Futures: MidAmerica Commodity Exchange (MIDAM) in Chicago;
New York Mercantile Exchange (NYMEX)

Options on futures: New York Mercantile Exchange (NYMEX)

PALLADIUM

Futures: New York Mercantile Exchange (NYMEX)

Antiques and Collectibles

Stocks, bonds, cash instruments, mutual funds, futures and options play an important role in your investment portfolio. However, while you might take personal satisfaction in how well your portfolio performs, you cannot bring home any of these traditional investments to impress friends and family and to look at whenever you choose. That's the fun of antiques collectibles: You get to buy a physical object that you think is aesthetically pleasing and keep it around the house as long as you like. In addition to the pleasure you get from seeing and touching your collectibles, you may earn a profit—if you learn enough about the collectible to buy when prices are low and sell after they've risen. Because they do not produce current income, the only way you can earn a return from antiques and collectibles is to buy and sell them.

Buying collectibles primarily for investment purposes is treacherous. Many factors affect the prices of collectibles, and it is difficult, if not impossible, to predict which particular collectible will get hot. A trend that you think is making your collectible increasingly popular may, in fact, be petering out just as you learn enough about the collectible to start trading. To a great extent, overall interest in collectibles is related to inflation expectations. When inflation roars, as it did in the United States in the late 1970s, people flee "paper" investments like stocks and bonds in favor of "hard" assets like real estate, gold and collectibles. Investors feel that hard assets will retain their value better than paper money when inflation erodes the worth of currency. In the extreme case of hyperinflation, whether it be in Argentina, in Russia or anywhere else, the paper currency becomes nearly worthless, and everyone flocks to the security of physical assets, including antiques and collectibles, which can rise in value as fast as the currency depreciates.

Since inflation in the United States peaked in the late 1970s and early 1980s, prices of many collectibles have slumped because inflation hedges are no longer as necessary. In the Carter and early Reagan years, fevered investment-oriented collectors pushed up the prices of everything from Chinese porcelains to comic books to astronomical heights. As inflation subsided throughout the 1980s and into the 1990s, the prices of almost all collectibles settled down to more reasonable levels, as most fast-buck artists left the game to people who enjoy collecting for its own sake. Unless inflation returns with a vengeance, the antiques and collectibles market will probably remain rational.

Just because the collectibles market will not likely be hit with another speculative binge any time soon does not mean you cannot make money at this game, however. Following are key factors you should keep in mind to profit from buying and selling collectibles.

Available supply. Determine the available supply of the collectible that holds your interest. Clearly, the fewer the existing stamps, paintings, baseball cards or other collectibles, the more rarity value they have. Also, the more historical significance an item has, the higher its value.

Most experienced collectors and dealers have a good idea of how many of each item were originally produced. In some cases, that is easy to determine. For instance, the U.S. mint knows how many of a particular issue of stamps it printed, and art dealers know how many pictures Van Gogh painted.

In most cases, however, the supply of an item is unclear, and this tends to hurt the value of all existing collectibles in that field. For example, you might think you have a valuable set of Roman coins until an archeological dig in Tunisia uncovers several thousand coins just like yours. Or your set of George Washington autographs from his days at Valley Forge can suddenly plummet in value if hundreds of such papers turn up in someone's attic near Philadelphia.

Current demand. Get a sense of the current demand for the collectible. This is always tricky to ascertain because something in hot demand this year can fall from favor the next year. Still, you can get a sense of demand by watching prices at auctions, flea markets and galleries and in catalogs and collector publications.

It is important to determine not only how much demand exists for a collectible but, if possible, who the investors are. For example, when Japanese investors became infatuated with Impressionist paintings in the mid-1980s, prices soared beyond all reason for a few years. Once the Japanese economy started to contract, the prices of Impressionist paintings slid sharply because the Japanese demand for them evaporated. If you see demand for some collectible from investors who have not normally been interested in it, be careful. It's fine to ride the wave of increased demand, but be sure to get out before the hot investors move on to the next trend.

Condition. The condition of antiques and collectibles is crucial. In general, try to buy a collectible in the best condition possible because it will invariably hold its value better than the same object in poorer shape. From an investment point of view, you will be better served by fewer objects of higher quality than by many objects of fair-to-low quality.

Also, do what you can to protect your object from wear and from damage caused by carelessness, fire or theft. For example, keep coins in protective plastic cases; put stamps in books that will keep them flat; polish brass objects; and don't subject antique furniture to heavy use.

Authenticity. Make sure the object you buy is authentic. The rise of collectible prices has, unfortunately, spawned an industry of unmarked reproductions and counterfeit artists who try to sell their fakes at the original's price. Some collectibles, such as coins, use an official grading system to ensure that you know what you are buying. But most collectibles have no such system of authentication. If you deal with a reputable dealer or auction house, your chances of obtaining a reproduction or counterfeit are greatly reduced though not eliminated. You can also have an object appraised by a professional, who should be able to spot a phony before you buy it.

Educating yourself. Spend time learning about the type of collectibles in which you are interested. Before you buy anything, get a sense of the marketplace by visiting a few auctions, antique shows and flea markets. Subscribe to collector's periodicals and buy a few books on the subject. You can probably locate collector's clubs or trade shows in your home town. There may even be courses on collecting antiques or other collectibles at a local school. The more you know about the history of the object, the less chance that you have of paying too much—the beginner's most common mistake.

Appraisal. Use an appraiser if you need an expert opinion. Unless you have specialized in one aspect of collectibles for a long time, you should not expect to know the value or authenticity of an object you plan to buy or sell. Contact the Appraisers Association of America (AAA) or the International Society of Appraisers (ISA) for a referral of member appraisers near your home. Members of the AAA have completed a voluntary certification program and members of both associations pledge to abide by a strict code of ethics. All full members of the ISA have completed the CAPP program, which makes them Certified Appraisers of Personal Property in their chosen specialty area.

Ask any potential appraiser for his or her qualifications, how long he or she has worked in the field, whether he or she will supply references and whether he or she uses a network of specialists to appraise objects out of his or her area of expertise. You should obtain a written, signed appraisal report describing the property and specifying the reasons for the value the appraiser has assigned. This appraisal can be used not only for investment purposes but also to prove your cost basis to the IRS when you report a profit from the purchase or sale of a collectible. However, different purposes require different appraisals. Don't assume that an appraisal done for *investment* purposes can also be used for IRS donation purposes. Appraisers normally charge an hourly rate or a preset price, plus expenses. If an appraiser gives you an accurate idea of what your object is worth, his or her opinion can be well worth the expense.

Prices. When buying or selling, be prepared to dicker over prices. Because no central exchange sets prices, each transaction results in a different price. You may buy or sell an object for one price while—at exactly the same time in a different place—someone else buys or sells the same object at another price. Your ability to discern value, acquired through your self-education process, should enable you to buy objects for prices less than you have seen elsewhere. To get a higher price when you sell, you must find buyers who are passionate about your object. When buying through a dealer, expect to pay a little more than if you were to buy at a flea market because the dealer must cover his or her overhead. For the same reason, expect to receive a bit less if you sell to a dealer.

Illiquid markets. Some collectibles markets are very illiquid, which means that it can take a long time to find a buyer or seller. For example, if you want to buy one of the 50 copies of a particular Chagall print, you might have to wait a while before an owner decides to sell. On the other hand, if you own a rare teddy bear or Batman comic book, it might be difficult to find a buyer interested in what you've got at a price you think is fair. It's much easier to get an appraiser to give you an estimate of an object's worth than it is to find a buyer who agrees with that appraisal. You can try to locate buyers through collector's clubs, specialized journals and advertisements in mass-market antiques and collectibles newspapers.

The easiest way to buy or sell collectibles is through a widely advertised auction. General merchandise auctions are held frequently. However, specialty auctions usually are held by category, so you must wait for your category of collectibles to come up, which may be once or twice a year. An auction's wide exposure comes at a price. Sellers must pay an auctioneer's commission of as much as 25 percent of the object's selling price. The seller's commission is almost always negotiable, especially for big-ticket items. *Always* ask for the lowest sales commission. Some auction houses will also tack on a 10 percent commission that buyers must pay.

When you purchase through a dealer, you must pay retail prices. When you sell to a dealer, you must accept wholesale prices, which are usually 50 to 60 cents on the dollar. Therefore, the object must appreciate significantly just to cover the spread between wholesale and retail prices, which can be as much as 100 percent of the collectible's worth. The illiquidity of most collectibles as investments can be a drawback if you ever need to get at your money quickly.

Reporting gain. If you sell collectibles at a profit, you must report the gain to the IRS on your tax return and pay capital gains taxes on the profit. You should always hold onto documents showing the price you paid for an item so you can verify your gain when you sell it.

If you can prove that you invest in collectibles as a profession, many of your expenses for buying and selling objects would be tax deductible. Such expenses might include appraisal fees, insurance premiums, travel expenses to auctions or trade shows and subscriptions to journals. You can deduct these expenses only to offset your gross profit and not against other sources of income. Be cautious, however, because collectibles deductions are vulnerable to IRS audit. If the IRS determines that you engage in a hobby instead of a bona fide business, it will deny your deductions and impose severe tax penalties.

With these general principles in mind, you may want to investigate specific types of collectibles. The best book on the subject of collectibles—providing lists of periodicals, auction houses and other resources—is *Maloney's Antiques & Collectibles Resource Directory*. Following this chapter is an extensive list of resources for many kinds of collectibles, as well as the addresses and phone numbers of all publications mentioned in the proceeding paragraphs. You will also find a list of auction houses.

Antiques include aged furniture, pottery, porcelain, glass, dinnerware and many other objects. Within the furniture category, several different periods of specialization exist, including French, Continental, English, Early American, Art Nouveau, Art Deco and Modern. If you collect furniture as an investment, using it extensively will harm its value. With glass and figurine antiques, invest in well-known brand names such as Royal Doulton, Lalique, Steuben or Tiffany. A few of the publications that follow antiques include *Antique & Collectables, Antiques and the Arts Weekly, Antique Week* and *Maine Antique Digest.*

Art encompasses paintings, prints, posters and sculpture. You have many schools of art to choose from, including old masters, impressionist, cubist, surrealist and modern. Some collectors specialize in the work of one country, such as England, France, Italy or Japan. Others specialize in individual artists with well-known names like Picasso, Lichtenstein or Warhol. The work of new and unknown artists also can rise in value quickly if their work becomes popular, though buying art of an unknown artist is quite risky. The value of any particular piece of art depends on its aesthetic qualities, the level of collector interest in that genre of art, who owned the work previously (at least, if he or she was famous) and how many renditions of the work exist.

Prints typically are produced in limited editions. The fewer copies made, the more valuable each print. Numbered prints tell you the placement of your copy in the full print run. For example, 115/250 means that the print is the 115th copy out of a total print run of 250. Signed prints are always worth more than unsigned works.

Sculpture is usually one of a kind and therefore more valuable and expensive. Make sure you've thought about where to put that huge statue or where you will hang that mobile before you bid for it at auction.

A few of the more important publications covering art include *Art/Antiques Investment Report, Art in America, ARTnews* and *Leonard's Annual Price Index of Art Auctions.*

Autographs are worth collecting for investment purposes only if the people who signed them were or are (if currently living) famous and didn't sign too many autographs. Serious autograph collectors are more interested in complete signed documents, letters or manuscripts written by a particular famous person than they are in merely a clipped signature. The more significant the document's historical value, the more money it will bring in the marketplace. Signatures from political figures like George Washington, Abraham Lincoln and Franklin Roosevelt usually bring much higher prices than those of entertainment or sports stars whose celebrity status may be fleeting. (Be careful not to buy the signature of a recent president written by autopen!) Because it is relatively easy to forge a signature, you should authenticate an autograph before you buy it. A few publications that focus on autographs are *Autograph Collector, Autograph Quarterly & Buyers Guide* and *The Autograph Review Newsletter.*

Cars, particularly classic roadsters, were among the hottest collectibles in the 1980s. Car buyers, perhaps trying to relive their teenage years, paid outlandish prices for chrome-laden classics of the 1950s. Some top-of-the-line Rolls Royces, Bentleys and Dusenbergs from the 1930s fetched more than $100,000. That is just the tip of the iceberg, however, as much more modest cars also trade actively at car shows and auctions. If you want to buy such a car, check out its mechanical condition closely in advance of the sale. If you're not mechanically inclined, bring your mechanic. A few of the publications that follow this market include *Deals on Wheels, Hemmings Motor News* and *Old Cars.*

Comic books have become enormously popular collectibles. Books chronicling the adventures of Batman, Spiderman, Superman, Captain America, Thor, Popeye and Zorro have appreciated significantly, depending on the print run for each title. You can buy and sell comic books through hundreds of dealers and fairs around the country. The best comic book reference guide is the *Overstreet Comic Book Price Guide,* and the best periodicals are the *Comic Buyer's Guide* and *Overstreet's Comic Book Monthly.*

Dolls of every type, including Kewpie dolls, Shirley Temple dolls, Barbies and even teddy bears, have become popular collectibles. The best periodicals covering dolls include *Dolls—The Collector's Magazine* and *National Doll & Teddy Bear Collector.*

Gems are treacherous investments because a small difference in grading can have a major effect on a gem's worth. Gem prices fluctuate widely and can fall sharply if a new source of gems is found. The most commonly collected gems are rubies, emeralds, sapphires and semiprecious stones, including tourmalines, aquamarines, topazes and garnets.

Related to gem investing is the field of antique and costume jewelry collecting. As is true of other collectibles, the condition and design of old brooches, pins or watches are key to their value. For costume jewelry, the designer's name is also an important factor. One notable publication in this field is *Jewelry Price Report*, which reports on auction sales of antique and period jewelry.

Hollywood memorabilia provides an outlet for movie buffs who collect movie posters, magazines, autographs, silent and talking pictures, theater advertising and cartoon cells. As with all collectibles, prices are driven by the scarcity and condition of the material and the level of investor interest. The best periodical following this field is *Movie Collector's World.*

Fine Oriental rugs can be traded as investments if they are in good condition. A huge supply of modern rugs from India, Iran, Turkey, Afghanistan, Pakistan and China in recent years has limited appreciation. Authenticate any rug before you purchase it because it is easy to overpay if you don't know exactly what you are buying. In general, the older the rug, the more valuable it is for investment purposes, as long as it is in top condition. You can follow the rug market by subscribing to *Oriental Rug Review* or *Rug News.*

Photographs by renowned photographers like Ansel Adams, Edward Steichen, Alfred Stieglitz and Edward Weston have become extremely popular as collectibles. Prices rise when a print is of top quality, is aesthetically pleasing and is rare. Experts in the field tend to know how many prints a photographer made of a particular picture; the fewer produced, the more each is worth. Be careful with color photos because colors can fade if you hang a photo in sunlight, and this will, of course, cut the picture's value. The periodical *Photograph Collector* will help you keep up with this field.

Quilts have come a long way since they were turned out by the local quilting bee in the Wild West. They have taken off as hot collectibles for lovers of Americana. Because each quilt is handmade, they are all unique and therefore provide good scarcity value. Still, choose a design you like because you might have to keep it several years before you can sell it at a profit. For more on quilts, consult the *Quilters Newsletter* or the *Quilt Price Guide,* published as part of the Confident Collector Series by Avon.

Rare books have been collected since the Gutenberg Bible came off the first press in the 15th century. The rarest books, such as those written by medieval monks, William Shakespeare or Martin Luther, can sell for hundreds of thousands of dollars. Still, plenty of more inexpensive books exist that are rare enough to have some investment value. Collectors tend to specialize in certain types of books, like children's books, military history volumes or James Bond adventure stories. In general, the earlier the book's printing, the higher its value. If you find a rare book autographed by the author, grab it because it is worth more than one without such a signature. One periodical will help you collect rare books: *Book Source Monthly.*

Sports collectibles have become an enormous business because of the popularity of college and professional sports. This field includes trading cards, uniforms, baseball bats and gloves, footballs and baseballs, programs from historic games, golf clubs and autographs of sports stars, as well as other memorabilia. As with other collectibles, rarity and condition are key to determining an object's value. The most valuable sports cards are the rookie cards of athletes who go on to become stars—for example, a Mickey Mantle or Reggie Jackson first-year card. If you want to get your children interested in collectibles, sports memorabilia is often a good place to start. The three best periodicals in this field are *Baseball Hobby News, Sports Cards* and *Sports Collectors Digest.*

Stamps are one of the most established ways of participating in collectibles. Usually, dealers know precisely how many stamps are printed, which gives each issue some scarcity value. Prices are determined by the forces of supply and demand, but many catalogs and price guides can help ensure that you don't pay too much for your stamps or sell them for too little. For example, stamps printed with errors, such as an upside down airplane, are particularly rare and valuable. You can trade at stamp shows or with local stamp dealers. It is important to keep stamps as close to their original condition as possible, which means that you should not put hinges on stamps to attach them to an album page because hinges remove some of their glue. The American Stamp Dealers Association attaches a certificate of authenticity to every stamp of great value to prevent forgeries. The best publications in this field include *Linn's Stamp News, Mekeel's Weekly Stamp News, Scott's Stamp Monthly, Stamp Auction News* and *Stamps.*

Collecting stock and bond certificates is known as *scripophily.* Before most trading of stocks and bonds was handled electronically, companies issued beautiful certificates to stock- and bondholders. The certificates currently most valuable are those issued by famous companies, like John D. Rockefeller's Standard Oil or American Express shares signed by Henry Wells and William Fargo of Wells-Fargo fame. If you locate some old certificates of companies no longer around, you might inquire of a firm like R. M. Smythe, (26 Broadway, New York, NY 10004; 800-622-1880; www.rm-smythe.com) or Stock Search International, (4761 W. Waterbuck Dr., Tucson, AZ 85742; 800-537-4523; www.stocksearchintl.com) to determine their worth. Smythe and other companies run scripophily auctions regularly. Collectors in this field also trade bank notes, checks and paper money from the United States and foreign countries. Followers of scripophily may be interested in the *Friends of Financial History* and *Bank Note Reporter* newsletters.

Toys have also become popular as collectibles. We're not talking about recently mass-produced GI Joes here but, instead, the handcrafted tinplate toys, trains, model soldiers, robots, piggybanks and wind-up toys that were made in limited quantity. Condition and scarcity dictate prices, as does the interest among toy collectors. To follow the toy market, you might want to subscribe to *Model & Toy Collector* or *Collectible Toys & Values.*

Vintage wines have even become hot collectibles. Because the quantity of wine produced by a vineyard in a particular year is well known, scarcity value is preserved. Ancient bottles—for example, wines from French chateux in the 18th century—may sell for more than $100,000, but many more modestly priced vintages exist that are suitable for investment. The most actively traded wines are French Bordeaux, including such famous labels as Lafite-Rothschild, Cheval Blanc and Latour. Wine connoisseurs may end up drinking some of their investment and selling some of it. It is hoped that the profits from the sales would cover the cost of imbibing so valuable a commodity. Those who want to follow the vintage wine market can consult the periodical *Wine Price File.*

In the end, collect any of the objects discussed here or the many other collectibles available because you enjoy having them around. This way, even if you are not able to sell a collectible for a profit, you will have made a good investment.

Resources

BOOKS, BOOK SERIES AND BOOK PUBLISHERS

Best Buys in Rare Coins: What Expert Dealers and Collectors Advise, by Donn Pearlman (Bonus Books, 160 E. Illinois St., Chicago, IL 60611; 312-467-0580; 800-225-3775; www.bonus-books.com). A basic guide to the different types of rare coins and investing in them. Devotes chapters to the main kinds of rare coins, including U.S. silver commemorative coins, Morgan dollars, buffalo nickels, mercury dimes, Saint-Gaudens double eagles, ancient Greek and Roman coins, Indian head cents, European coinage and other coins.

Confident Collector Series, by Susan Theran (Avon Books, Hearst Corporation, 1350 Avenue of the Americas, New York, NY 10019; 800-238-0658; www.avonbooks. com). A series of books that help you identify and price collectibles. Books in the series include *Fine Art: Identification and Price Guide, Original Comic Art Guide* by Jerry Weist; *Overstreet's Comic Book Price and Grading Guides* by Robert M. Overstreet and *Quilts: Identification and Price Guide* by Liz Greenbacker and Kathleen Barach.

The Gold Companion, by Timothy Green (The Gold and Silver Institutes, 1112 16th St., N.W., Suite 240, Washington, DC 20036; 202-835-0185; www.goldinstitute. com). Published by the trade group for gold- and silver-mining companies. Describes the different ways to invest in gold and silver.

Gold: Myth and Reality (Swiss Bank Corporation, 10 E. 50th St., New York, NY 10022; 212-574-3000; www.swissbank.ch www.sbcwarburg.com). Looks at gold throughout history and explains the current ways to invest in it.

High Profits from Rare Coins Investment, by Q. David Bowers (Bowers and Merena Galleries, P.O. Box 1224, Wolfeboro, NH 03894; 603-569-5095; www.bowersandmerena. com). The classic book describing the intricacies of investing in rare coins.

Hobby House Press (One Corporate Dr., Grantsville, MD 21536; 800-554-1447). A publishing company that produces many books and price guides to dolls, teddy bears and crafts. For example, Hobby House publishes the annual *Blue Book of Dolls & Values.*

How To Profit from the Coming Boom in Gold, by Jeffrey A. Nichols (McGraw-Hill, Order Dept., 860 Taylor Station Rd., Blacklick, OH 43004; 800-722-4726; www.mcgraw-hill.com). A complete guide to the many ways of investing in gold, including coins, bars, gold-mining shares, mutual funds, futures and options on gold futures. Provides technical analysis that can be applied to all these ways of buying gold. Also covers how to set up a gold portfolio. Makes a bullish case for gold prices in the 1990s, based on supply and demand.

The International Directory for Collectors by Art & Auction Magazine (440 Park Ave. South, 14th Floor, New York, NY 10016; 800-777-8718). A complete list of reputable art dealers throughout the United States and the world.

Kovel's Antiques & Collectibles Price List (Crown Publishing Group, 201 E. 50th St., New York, NY 10022; 800-733-3000; www.random.com). The definitive guide, published annually, to prices of more than 50,000 collectibles, from plates to figurines, glass to furniture, paintings to toys, and much more. The Kovels have also published many other books with Crown Publishing, including *American Silver Marks; Antiques & Collectibles Fix-It Source Book; Bottles Price List; Depression Glass & American Dinnerware;* and *Dictionary of Marks—Pottery and Porcelain.*

Leonard's Annual Price Index of Art Auctions (Auction Index, Inc., 30 Valentine Park, Newton, MA 02165; 617-964-2876). Provides a complete picture of auction results for paintings, drawings and sculpture. Lists prices for every artist who has sold work in the United States, whether or not the artist is American. For each work sold, provides its selling price, whether it is signed and dated, its dimensions and the birth date, death date and nationality of the artist. Auction Index also publishes a separate *Leonard's Annual Price Index of Prints, Posters and Photography.*

Linn's Stamp News (P.O. Box 29, Sidney, OH 45365; 513-498-0801; 800-831-3158). Linn's publishes many books about stamp collecting, including *Classic United States Imperforate Stamps; Fun and Profit in Stamp Collecting; An Introduction to Stamp Collecting; Philatelic Forgers; Stamp Club Handbook; Stamp Collecting Made Easy; U.S. Postal History Sampler;* and *Who's Who on U.S. Stamps.*

Maloney's Antiques & Collectibles Resource Directory (Collector's Information Clearinghouse, P.O. Box 2049, Frederick, MD 21702-1049; 301-695-8544; 800-836-2403). The most complete guide in existence for resources on every kind of antique and collectible. Provides nearly 10,000 resources on 2,600 categories of collectibles, from A&P items to zeppelins. Lists appraisers, auction houses, buyers, clubs, collectors, dealers, experts, matching services, museums, periodicals and restorers and much more.

The One Minute Coin Expert, by Scott A. Travers (Dell Publishing, 1540 Broadway, New York, NY 10036; 212-354-6500; www.bdd.com). A simple guide to coin collecting aimed at beginners.

Scott Standard Postage Stamp Catalogue (Scott Publishing, 911 Vandemark Rd., P.O. Box 828, Sidney, OH 45365; 513-498-0802; 800-5-SCOTT-5; www.amospress. com). The most widely used annual catalog of stamp prices. Scott's Amos Press Division also distributes *Fun and Profit in Stamp Collecting,* by Herman Herst, Jr.

Stamp Collector Books (700 E. State St., Iola, Wisconsin 54990; 715-445-2214; www.krause.com). The publisher of the *Stamp Collector Newspaper.* Also sells books on stamp collecting, including *Basic Philately; How To Detect Damaged, Altered and Repaired Stamps; On the Road; Stamp Collecting Is Fun; This Is Philately; Top Dollar Paid!; U.S. Errors; Where in the World: Unique Stamp Atlas;* and *The Wild Side.*

Warman's Antiques and Their Prices (Wallace-Homestead Book Company, 201 King of Prussia, Radnor, PA 19089; 800-695-1214). For nearly half a century, Warman's has maintained a distinctive margin of superiority over its competition and imitators—more than 50,000 fresh items in each edition, hundreds of photographs and factory marks to aid in identification, annual state of the market report, reproduction alerts, collector's clubs, sources, historical background, museums. Wallace-Homestead Book Co. publishes a complete line of antiques reference books covering collectibles, country, furniture, glass, jewelry and precious metals, paper ephemera, pottery and porcelain.

Warman's Encyclopedia of Antiques & Collectibles Series (Wallace-Homestead Book Company, 700 E. State St., Iola, Wisconsin 54990; 715-445-2214; www. krause.com). These books help you identify and price several categories of antiques and collectibles. Included in this series are *Country Antiques & Collectibles, Furniture, English & Continental Pottery & Porcelain, Oriental Antiques, Americana & Collectibles,* and *Glass.*

Wine Price File (P.O. Box 1007, Darien, CT 06820; 203-655-0566). Annually published book covers the vintage-wine-collecting industry.

MAGAZINES

American Ceramics (9 E. 45th St., New York, NY 10017; 212-309-6886). Provides information about trading in ceramic art.

Antiques and the Arts Weekly Magazine (Bee Publishing, 5 Churchill Rd., Newtown, CT 06470; 203-426-3141; www.thebee.com). The most comprehensive weekly guide to the arts and antiques trade. A tabloid-sized journal, discusses auctions, antique shows and flea markets for every kind of collectible.

Art & Auction (P.O. Box 11344, Des Moines, IA 50340; 800-777-8718; editorial office: 250 W. 57th St., New York, NY 10107). Updates the international art and auction scene.

Art in America (P.O. Box 11292, Des Moines, IA 50340; 800-925-8059). Focuses mostly on contemporary art.

ARTnews (48 W. 38th St., 9th Floor, New York, NY 10018; 212-398-1690; 800-284-4625). The bible of the art-collecting world. Covers exhibitions, openings, new and old painters and art collectors.

Autograph Collector (510-A South Corona Mall, Corona, CA 91719; 909-734-9636; www.odyssey.com). Covers autograph and historical document collecting in such fields as entertainment, politics and sports.

Bank Note Reporter (Krause Publications, 700 E. State St., Iola, WI 54990; 715-445-2214; 800-258-0929; www.krause.com). Covers the marketplace for collectors of U.S. and foreign paper money, notes, checks and other financially oriented paper.

Baseball Hobby News (4540 Kearny Villa Rd., San Diego, CA 92123; 619-565-2848). A monthly magazine with news of auctions and fairs trading baseball memorabilia. Issues an annual price guide for baseball-related items.

Book Source Monthly (P.O. Box 567, Cazenovia, NY 13035; 315-655-8499). Serves both members of the antiquarian book trade as well as private investors.

CameraShopper (P.O. Box 1086, New Canaan, CT 06840; 203-972-5700; www.camera-shopper.com). Covers the vintage photograph and antique camera markets.

COINage Magazine (James Miller Publications, 4880 Market St., Ventura, CA 93003; 805-644-3824)

Coins (700 E. State St., Iola, WI 54990; 715-445-2214; www.krause.com)

Collectible Toys & Values (15 Danbury Rd., Ridgefield, CT 06877; 203-438-9652; members.aol.com/AlexMalloy/agmalloy.htm). A monthly price guide with articles, tips, and book reviews.

Deals on Wheels Magazine (Deals on Wheels, P.O. Box 205, Sioux Falls, SD 57101; 605-338-7666; 800-334-1886; www.dealsonwheels.com). Provides listings of antique cars for sale nationwide.

Doll Reader (P.O. Box 420235, Palm Coast, FL 32142-0235; 717-540-6640). Gives both the beginner and advanced collector information on antique, collectible and modern dolls.

Dolls—Collector Communications (170 5th Ave., New York, NY 10010; 212-989-8700; 800-588-1691). Full-color magazine covering antique and contemporary dolls.

Doll World (306 East Parr Rd., Burn, IN 46711; 219-589-8741; 800-829-5865). Provides information about doll collecting, including doll history, and interviews with doll artists. Also produces an annual *Doll Collector's Price Guide.*

Friends of Financial History (American Financial History, 26 Broadway, Suite 200, New York, NY 10004; 212-908-4110; www.mash.org). Gives background on collecting stock and bond certificates. Smythe is in the business of valuing old certificates, and it runs auctions for buying and selling them.

Hemmings Motor News (P.O. Box 100, Bennington, VT 05201; 802-442-3101; www.hmm.com). For antique and special-car enthusiasts. Lists upcoming auctions and sources of services—such as restoration and insurance—for old cars.

Linn's Stamp News (P.O. Box 29, Sidney, OH 45365; 513-498-0801). The sister publication of *Scott's Stamp Monthly;* the standard reference for stamp collectors following stamp prices and new stamp releases.

The Magazine Antiques (Brant Publications, 575 Broadway, New York, NY 10012; 212-941-2800; 800-925-9271). A top-of-the line, slick magazine covering all aspects of antiques collecting, including arts and crafts, auctions, dolls, folk art, furniture, games, paintings, porcelain and toys. Advertisers include the finest antique dealers in the country.

Movie Collector's World (P.O. Box 309, Fraser, MI 48026; 810-774-4311; www. mcwonline.com). Covers the Hollywood memorabilia market of posters, videos, stills and other star-struck objects.

Old Cars Weekly (Krause Publications, 700 E. State St., Iola, WI 54990; 800-258-0929; www.krause.com). Features news about antique cars, car shows, auctions and swap meets.

Oriental Rug Review (P.O. Box 709, Meredith, NH 03253; 603-744-9191; www. rugreview.com). An online journal focusing on aged rugs. Carries news of auctions and reviews about Oriental rugs.

Overstreet's Comic Book Monthly (801 20th St. NW, Suite 3, Cleveland, TN 37311; 615-472-4135). Monthly comic book price guide.

Photograph Collector (301 Hill Ave., Langhorne, PA 19047; 215-757-8921). Covers the photography market. Also publishes an annual compilation of photo auction prices.

Rug News (Museum Books, 90 John St., New York, NY 10038; 212-587-1340; www.rugnews.com). Covers the oriental rug market and the machine-made rug market, including news of auctions and rug shows.

Scott's Stamp Monthly Magazine (P.O. Box 828, 911 Vandemark Rd., Sidney, OH 45365; 800-5-SCOTT-5; 800-488-5351). The principal magazine covering developments in the stamp collector's market. Gives notice of upcoming stamp issues from the U.S. Postal Service.

Silver Magazine (P.O. Box 1243, Whittier, CA 90609; 310-696-6738)

Sports Cards (Krause Publications, 700 E. State St., Iola, WI 54990; 715-445-2214; 800-258-0929; www.krause.com). Full-color magazine featuring baseball, basketball, hockey and football cards from all eras.

Sports Collectors Digest (Krause Publications, 700 E. State St., Iola, WI 54990; 715-445-2214; 800-258-0929; www.krause.com). A weekly news magazine with information about all aspects of sports memorabilia.

NEWSLETTERS

Art/Antiques Investment Report (100 Wall St., New York, NY 10005; 212-747-9500; www.twist.com). A biweekly newsletter about the art market for the art connoisseur, collector, curator and dealer. Features interviews with prominent dealers and publishes the latest prices for fine objects.

Art Newsletter (48 W. 38th St., 9th Floor, New York, NY 10018; 212-398-1690; 800-284-4625). A biweekly newsletter containing the latest news on auctions and trends in the art markets.

Autograph Review (305 Carlton Rd., Syracuse, NY 13207; 315-474-3516). For the serious autograph collector.

Coin Dealer Newsletter and *Certified Coin Dealer Newsletter* (P.O. Box 7939, Torrance, CA 90504; 310-515-7369; www.graysheet.com)

Coin World (911 Vandemark Rd., Sidney, OH 45365; 937-498-0800; www.collect.com/coinworld)

Dines Letter (P.O. Box 22, Belvedere, CA 94920)

Free Market Gold & Money Report (P.O. Box 4634, Greenwich, CT 06830)

Gold & Money: A Commentary on Precious Metals and Monetary Matters (P.O. Box 4634, Greenwich, CT 06830; 203-661-5474; www.goldmoney.com)

Gold Monitor (M. Murenbeeld & Associates, P.O. Box 6187, Victoria, British Columbia, Canada V8P 5L5; 604-477-7579)

Gold Newsletter (1112 16th St., N.W., Suite 240, Washington, DC 20036; 202-835-0185; www.goldinstitute.com)

Gold Newsletter (Jefferson Financial, 2400 Jefferson Hwy., Suite 600, Jefferson, LA 70121; 800-877-8847)

J. Taylor Gold and Gold Stocks (P.O. Box 770871, Woodside, NY 11377; 718-457-1426)

Moneypower (4257 46th Ave. North, Suite 207, Minneapolis, MN 55422; 612-537-8096)

Numismatic News (Krause Publications, 700 E. State St., Iola, WI 54990; 715-445-2214; www.krause.com)

Powell Gold Industry Guide and *International Mining Analyst* (Reserve Research, 181 State St., Portland, ME 04101; 207-774-4971)

Quilters Newsletter (P.O. Box 4101, Golden, CO 80402; 800-477-6089). Covers the quilt market.

Rare Coin Review (Bowers and Merena, P.O. Box 1224, Wolfeboro, NH 03894-1224; 603-569-5095; 800-458-4646; www.bowersandmerena.com)

Red Book (Western Publishing, 1220 Mound Ave., Racine, WI 53404; 414-633-2431; www.goldenbks.com). Provides prices from coin auctions.

Ruff Times (757 S. Main, Springville, UT 84663; 801-489-8681; www.rufftimes.com)

Silver and Gold Report (4176 Burns Rd., Palm Beach Gardens, FL 33410; 800-289-9222; www.weissinc.com)

Silver News (1112 16th St., N.W., Suite 240, Washington, DC 20036; 202-835-0185; www.goldinstitute.com)

Winning Edge (Ellesmere Numismatics, P.O. Box 402, Brookfield, CT 06804; 800-426-3343)

World Coin News (Krause Publications, 700 E. State St., Iola, WI 54990; 715-445-2214; www.krause.com)

NEWSPAPERS

Antique & Collectables (P.O. Box 1565, El Cajon, CA 92022; 619-593-2933; 619-593-2925). Follows several collectibles markets, including dolls, toys and teddy bears. Reports auction results and publishes trade show dates and events. Available by subscription or through many antique stores.

Antique Week (Mayhill Publications, P.O. Box 90, Knightstown, IN 46148; 800-876-5133; www.antiqueweek.com). A leading weekly newspaper containing feature articles, auction results, genealogy section, reproduction column and buy/sell ads.

Buyer's Guide for Comic Fandom (15800 Route 84 North, East Moline, IL 61244; 309-496-2353). A weekly newspaper covering the comic book industry.

Comic Buyer's Guide (Krause Publications, 700 E. State St., Iola, WI 54990; 715-445-2214; 800-258-0929; www.krause.com). A weekly newspaper serving comics fans and collectors, with news of upcoming comic book events. Publisher also produces a quarterly price guide.

Maine Antique Digest (P.O. Box 1429, Waldoboro, ME 04572-1429; 207-832-5745; 800-752-8521; www.maineantiquedigest.com). A monthly tabloid filled with information about the antiques market. Articles and advertising feature furniture, pewter, paintings, porcelain, quilts, weathervanes, clocks, maps and much more. Also publishes a calendar of upcoming antique shows and auctions.

Mekeel's Weekly & STAMPS (P.O. Box 5050, White Plains, NY 10602; 914-997-7261; 800-635-3351). Features news and articles for the active adult stamp collector. Covers auctions, new stamp issues and trading in classic stamps.

National Doll & Teddy Bear Collector (P.O. Box 4032, Portland, OR 97208; 503-771-1490). A monthly newspaper for doll, kewpie doll and teddy bear collectors.

Stamp Collector (700 E. State St., Iola, WI 54990; 715-445-2214; 800-258-0929). A weekly newspaper for both beginning and expert collectors. Provides how-to articles, release dates for new stamps around the world, schedules of stamp shows, buying and selling prices and a question-and-answer column. Van Dahl also publishes *The Stamp Wholesaler,* a biweekly newspaper for stamp dealers.

Stamps (HL Lindquist Publications, 85 Canisteo St., Hornell, NY 14843; 607-324-2212). Provides the latest news about stamp collecting, including auction results, upcoming stamp shows and new editions of stamps. Lindquist also publishes the monthly journal *Stamps Auction News,* which tracks auction prices.

TRADE ASSOCIATIONS

American Numismatic Association (818 N. Cascade Ave., Colorado Springs, CO 80903-3279; 719-632-2646; 800-367-9723; www.money.org). Chartered by Congress to educate collectors of coins, paper money, tokens and metals. Offers free pamphlet entitled "Coin Collecting: A Fascinating Hobby for Young and Old."

American Stamp Dealers Association (3 School St., Glen Cove, NY 11542; 516-759-7000; www.exposonline.com/asda). Represents stamp dealers. Issues free lists of dealers in various local areas and by areas of interest. Sponsors national and regional stamp shows, as well as educational programs, throughout the United States. Offers the following free brochures: "Expertizing Philatelic Materials"; "Getting Started in Stamp Collecting"; "Selling a Stamp Collection . . . What You Need To Know!"; and "The Stamp Dealer's Obligations and Responsibilities When Selling Stamps as an Investment."

Appraisers Association of America (60 E. 42nd St., Suite 2505, New York, NY 10165; 212-867-9775). The professional association of appraisers that sets standards for appraisers of personal property. Offers a membership directory, a free referral to three members near your home and a free copy of "Elements of a Correctly Prepared Appraisal" and "Frequently Asked Questions of Appraisers."

Gold and Silver Institutes (1112 16th St., N.W., Suite 240, Washington, DC 20036; 202-835-0185; www.goldinstitute.com). Composed of gold- and silver-mining companies, refiners, traders and wholesalers. Lobbies on issues affecting the gold and silver industries and publishes research on gold and silver mining and the metals markets. Offers several publications, including brochures entitled "Your Guide to Investing in Gold" and "Your Guide to Investing in Silver."

Industry Council for Tangible Assets (P.O. Box 1365, Severna Park, MD 21146-8365; 410-626-7005). Tracks regulations and legislation that affect the rare-coin and precious-metals industry. Publishes a quarterly newsletter called the *Washington Wire.*

International Precious Metals Institute (4905 Tilghman St., Suite 160, Allentown, PA 18104; 215-395-9700). An international association of producers, refiners, fabricators, scientists, users, merchants, private and public sector groups and the general precious-metals community. Encourages the exchange of information and technology; seeks and promotes efficient and environmentally acceptable uses of precious metals; conducts educational meetings and courses; and serves as a primary resource for factual information for industry and government agencies worldwide.

International Society of Appraisers (500 N. Michigan Ave., Suite. 1400, Chicago, IL 60611-3796; 312-661-1700). The largest association of personal property appraisers in the world for many kinds of personal property, including antiques, fine art, gems and jewelry, machinery and equipment, residential contents and other collectibles. All full members are educated and tested. Will send a free copy of the following publications: "The Absolutes of Professional Appraisings"; "Be Certain of Its Real Value"; "What Is a CAPP (Certified Appraiser of Personal Property)?"; and "When You Need an Informed, Skilled Appraiser."

National Antique and Art Dealers Association of America (12 E. 56th St., New York, NY 10022; 212-826-9707). Represents art and antique dealers. Sponsors antique and art exhibitions, including the International Antique Dealers Show every October in New York City. Also promotes ethical trade practices among its members. Offers a free copy of its membership directory, which lists about 50 reputable dealers, as well as fine museums, areas of dealer specialization (including furniture, ceramics, folk art, glass, paintings and tapestries) and U.S. stylistic periods from pilgrim to mission.

Platinum Guild International (150 E. 58th St., 25th Floor, New York, NY 10155; 212-758-6767; www.researchmag.com/platinum). Represents producers and marketers of platinum and palladium. Publishes *Platinum Investor Update,* a regular newsletter on trends in the platinum industry. Offers free brochures titled "Platinum: The Strategic Precious Metals Investment" and "Platinum: Today and Tomorrow."

Professional Numismatists Guild (3950 Concordia Lane, Fallbrook, CA 92028; 760-728-1300; www.pngdealers.com). The organization of professional coin dealers. Offers binding arbitration on consumer disputes with any PNG member and maintains strict standards for coin dealer members. Offers a free book entitled *The Pleasure of Coin Collecting* and a free brochure entitled "What You Should Know before You Buy Rare Coins for Investment!" Provides a fax hot-line number (760-728-8507) for complaints against dealers or questions about investing in rare coins.

World Gold Council (900 3rd Ave., 26th Floor, New York, NY 10022; 212-688-0005; www.gold.org). Represents gold-mining companies and offers information about investing in gold. Publishes a quarterly report titled *Gold Demand Trends,* which tracks demand for physical gold around the world.

Federal Government Regulators

Federal Trade Commission (6th St. and Pennsylvania Avenue, N.W., Washington, DC 20580; 202-326-2000; www.ftc.gov). Protects consumers from scams, including precious-metals scams. Has jurisdiction over art dealers. Offers free brochures titled "Investing in Rare Coins" and "Art Fraud."

North American Securities Administrators Association (One Massachusetts Ave., N.W., Suite 310, Washington, DC 20001; 202-737-0900; www.nasaa.org). Represents state securities administration associations. Protects the public against scams, many of them precious-metals fraud. Offers the free publications "Investing in Coins" and "Precious Metals Bank Financing."

Coin-Grading Organizations

The following organizations will issue a grade for a coin and guarantee its authenticity.

ANACS (P.O. Box 182141, Columbus, OH 43218-2141; 800-888-1861; www.anacs.com)

Numismatic Guaranty Corporation of America (NGC, P.O. Box 1776, Parsippany, NJ 07054; 201-984-6222; www.numismatists.com/ngc.html)

Professional Coin Grading Service (PCGS, P.O. Box 9458, Newport Beach, CA 92658; 800-447-8848; www.pcgs.com)

Auction Houses

The following are the leading auction houses in the United States. Upon request, each will send a schedule of upcoming auctions.

Alderfer Auction Company (501 Fairground Rd., Hatfield, PA 19440; 215-368-5477; www.alderfercompany.com)

Arman Absentee Auctions (P.O. Box 4037, Middletown, RI 02840; 401-847-7453; www.antiquechina.com)

F.O. Bailey Antiquanans (137-141 Middle St., Portland, ME 04101; 207-774-1479)

Berman's Auction Gallery (33 W. Blackwell St., Dover, NJ 07081; 201-361-3110)

Butterfield & Butterfield (7601 Sunset Blvd., Los Angeles, CA 90046; 213-850-7500; www.butterfield&butterfield.com)

Christie's Inc. (502 Park Ave., New York, NY 10022; 212-546-1000; www.christies.com)

Collectors Auction Services (R.D. 1, P.O. Box 431, Oakwood Rd., Oil City, PA 16301; 814-677-6070)

Jim Depew Galleries (1860 Piedmont Rd., N.E., Atlanta, GA 30324; 404-874-2286)

Douglas Auctioneers (Route 5, South Deerfield, MA 01373; 413-665-3530)

Doyle Auctioneers (109 Osborne Hill Rd., Fishkill, NY 12524; 914-896-9492; www.auctionweb.com/aar-ny)

William Doyle Galleries (175 E. 87th St., New York, NY 10128; 212-427-2730; www.doylegalleries.com)

Dumouchelle Art Galleries (409 E. Jefferson Ave., Detroit, MI 48226; 313-963-6255; www.dumouchelles.com)

Dunning's Auction Service (755 Church Rd., Elgin, IL 60123; 847-741-3483; www.dunnings.com)

Freeman/Fine Arts of Philadelphia (1808 Chestnut St., Philadelphia, PA 19103; 215-563-9275)

Garth's Auctions (2690 Stratford Rd., Delaware, OH 43015; 614-362-4771)

Chase Gilmore Art Galleries (724 W. Washington St., Chicago, IL 60606; 312-648-1690)

Guernsey's Auction (108½ E. 73rd St., New York, NY 10021; 212-794-2280)

Hanzel Galleries (1120 S. Michigan Ave., Chicago, IL 60605; 312-922-6234)

Harris Auction Galleries (875 N. Howard St., Baltimore, MD 21201; 410-728-7040)

Leslie Hindman Auctioneers (215 W. Ohio St., Chicago, IL 60610; 312-670-0010)

F.B. Hubley & Co., Inc. (364 Broadway, Cambridge, MA 02139; 617-876-2030)

Iroquois Auction Gallery (P.O. Box 736, Brewerton, NY 13029; 315-668-2346)

Bob Koty Professional Auctioneers (P.O. Box 625, Freehold, NJ 07728; 908-780-1265)

Lubin Galleries (110 W. 25th St., New York, NY 10001; 212-929-0909)

Manion's Auction House (P.O. Box 12214, Kansas City, KS 66112; 913-299-6692; www.manions.com)

Mapes Auction Gallery (1729 Vestal Pkwy. West, Vestal, NY 13850; 607-754-9193; www.mapesauction.baka.com)

Marc J. Matz Gallery (366½ Broadway, Cambridge, MA 02139; 617-661-6200)

Mid-Hudson Auction Galleries (1 Idlewild Ave., Cornwall-on-Hudson, NY 12520; 914-534-7828)

Charles Moore Americana (32 E. 57th St., New York, NY 10022; 212-751-1900)

Northeast Auctions (694 Lafayette Rd., Hampton, NH 03842; 603-926-9800)

Richard Opfer Auctioneering (1919 Greenspring Dr., Timonium, MD 21093; 410-252-5035)

Pettigrew Auction Company (1645 S. Tejon St., Colorado Springs, CO 80906; 719-633-7963)

Pioneer Auction of Amherst (P.O. Box 9593, North Amherst, MA 01059; 413-253-9914; www.pioneerauction.com)

Savoia Auction, Inc. (Route 23, South Cairo, NY 12482; 518-622-8000)

Skinner, Inc. (357 Main St., Bolton, MA 01740; 508-779-6241)

C.G. Sloan & Co., Inc. (4920 Wyaconda Rd., Rockville, MD 20852; 301-468-4911; www.sloanesauction.com)

Sotheby's (1334 York Ave., New York, NY 10021; 212-606-7000; www.sothebys.com)

South Bay Auctions, Inc. (P.O. Box 303, East Moriches, NY 11940; 516-878-2909)

Swann Galleries, Inc. (104 E. 25th St., New York, NY 10010; 212-254-4710)

Weschler's (909 E Street, N.W., Washington, DC 20004; 202-628-1281)

Gustave White Auctioneers (P.O. Box 59, Newport, RI 02840; 401-847-4250)

Willis Henry Auctions, Inc. (22 Main St., Marshfield, MA 02050; 617-834-7774; www.willishenry.com)

Winter Associates, Inc. (P.O. Box 823, Plainville, CT 06062; 203-793-0288)

Wolf's Fine Arts Auctioneers (1239 W. 6th St., Cleveland, OH 44113; 216-575-9653; www.wolfs-auctions.com)

Woody Auction Company (P.O. Box 618, Douglass, KS 67039; 316-747-2694)

WEB SITES

Several Web sites allowing you to buy and sell collectibles through online auctions have started to spring up. A few examples you may want to try out include:

Antique-Shop.Com (www.antique-shop.com)

Early American History Auctions (www.earlyamerican.com)

Golden Age Antiques and Collectibles (www.goldnage.com)

Internet Antique Shop (www.tias.com)

Up4Sale (www.up4sale.com)

8

Inside Real Estate

Purchasing a home is probably the single biggest investment you will ever make. The entire process of finding, financing and maintaining a home is fraught with complexities, both financial and emotional. Despite the difficulties and high cost of home ownership, it remains the ultimate American dream for most people. Home ownership provides several major benefits, including tax breaks, appreciation potential and the pride of controlling the place where you live. In addition, if you pay off your mortgage by the time you retire, you will be able to live free and clear of mortgage payments. In contrast, renters often feel that they throw their money away each month because they do not build any equity in the place they live. Once they retire, their rent continues unabated.

Throughout the 1970s and early 1980s, real estate was the sure-fire way to accumulate wealth. The combination of a housing shortage, a surging number of baby boomers entering the real estate market, generous tax advantages and high inflation expectations resulted in startling gains in home prices. That bubble burst in the mid 1980s and into the 1990s, however, as most housing markets became overbuilt, fewer baby boomers could afford homes, tax breaks were curtailed and inflation plunged. The real estate landscape is therefore much more treacherous now, particularly if you purchase a home as an investment rather than just a nice place to live.

Many people who bought homes at inflated prices, especially in the late 1980s, now feel burdened by huge mortgage payments on property that has fallen sharply in value. Such a homeowner often rationalizes his or her purchase by saying, "I couldn't stand not earning any mortgage interest deductions to lower my taxes" or "I had to buy before prices got out of reach." In retrospect, however, these buyers' total financial situation might have been improved had they rented for less than their current monthly mortgage payment, owed a bit more in taxes and invested the difference between their rent and their mortgage in the surging stock and bond markets.

Buying Versus Renting

The first question you must ask yourself in deciding where to live is whether to buy or rent. The following factors will help you make your decision.

ADVANTAGES OF BUYING

- You build up equity, or ownership, in your home over time as you pay off your mortgage, as long as your home is appreciating in value. Having to make those payments becomes a form of forced savings.

- If you buy right and your home is well maintained and in a good location, you have a good chance of substantial capital appreciation over time. Homes provide one of the best hedges against inflation.

- You can remodel your home to suit your needs and tastes. You are unlikely to do so for rental property.

- Owning your home gives you a deeper sense of commitment to your community. Homeowners, wanting to maintain property values, tend to take care of their homes better than renters. They also tend to be more involved in civic issues, such as education and neighborhood improvement.

- As a homeowner, you qualify for several significant tax advantages. First, all mortgage interest you pay up to $1 million qualifies as a deduction, reducing both your federal and state income tax burdens. In addition, you can deduct any interest charged on home equity loans of up to $100,000 taken out against the value of your home. Local property taxes are also deductible from your federal income tax. If you sell your home, you do not have to pay any capital gains tax as long as you have lived in the home as your principal residence for two of the previous five years, and your profit does not exceed $500,000 if you are a married couple filing taxes jointly, or $250,000 if you are filing taxes as a single.

- Your home can be a source of cash in the future. Whether you borrow against it through a second mortgage or a home equity loan, or pull out the cash slowly through a reverse annuity mortgage (explained in more detail later in this chapter), you can put your equity to work for you when you need it most.

ADVANTAGES OF RENTING

- The costs of home ownership, from the down payment to the monthly mortgage and maintenance costs, may take a large bite out of your household budget. Many people sacrifice their entire lifestyle by sinking 50 percent or more of their income into home ownership costs. If you can rent for 30 percent or less of your income, you may live a less stressful life.

- Prices of homes may fall in your neighborhood. By renting, you will not be hurt by eroding real estate prices. Once you think a market has bottomed out, you can get a good deal on a house. The fact that you will not have to sell your rental property to do so is an added bonus.

- You can invest the money you save by renting in stocks, bonds and mutual funds, which may rise in value faster than home prices. This is particularly true if you are lucky enough to pay below-market rent or live in a rent-controlled apartment. If you have the discipline to follow through with this strategy, you may be able to build up much more equity over time by renting, then funneling the money you would be paying in mortgage payments and maintenance costs into a diversified portfolio of securities. Stocks, bonds and mutual funds are much more liquid than real estate, allowing you to buy and sell easily to take advantage of the latest trends. Also, securities, unlike a home, generate regular income, which you can reinvest.

- Homeowners with adjustable rate mortgages risk higher mortgage payments if interest rates rise. Depending on the strength of your local rental market, you may be able to avoid rent increases or even pay below-market rent.

- If you already know that you may relocate several times during your career, it may make more sense to rent than to buy and sell a home each time you move. Unless your local real estate market is extremely active, you probably cannot expect enough appreciation in a year or two to compensate for the significant costs of buying and selling a home.

- You may be at a life stage that sees many changes in a relatively short time, meaning your housing needs may be different several years from now. For example, if you are young and single, it might make more sense to rent a small apartment if you anticipate getting married and having children in a few years. And those going through a divorce may be too unsettled to purchase a home.

The buy-versus-rent decision should therefore not be based only on finances but also on expectations for future lifestyle. To calculate the purely financial trade-offs, however, you might try one of the real estate software packages on the market, such as *Buying Your Home* or *Buy or Rent* (information for which can be found in the "Resources" section). They will help you sort through the true value of housing tax benefits, the realistic costs of buying and maintaining a home, the alternative returns on your money if you rent, the number of years you must stay in a house for it to pay off and other complex factors you should consider.

If You Decide To Rent

When you've completed the buy-versus-rent analysis, you may conclude that it makes more sense to rent your housing and invest your money in securities that may grow faster than property values over time. If you plan to rent, the following tips can help you get the most for your money.

- *Before beginning your search for an apartment or a home to rent, refer back to the budget exercise in Chapter 1 to determine how much rent you can afford.* You should be able to meet comfortably your rent plus all your other expenses—which include saving and investing. Remember, one of the main advantages of renting is that it should leave you with enough cash to invest about 10 percent of your gross income. Clearly, that won't happen if you saddle yourself with too high a rent. Ideally, your rent (including utilities) should absorb no more than 30 percent of your gross income or 25 percent of your net income.

- *Next, hone in on a good location.* The best is usually close to your job or provides convenient transportation options to get there. The neighborhood you choose should also offer quality stores, schools, parks and other recreational facilities; and it should feel safe. Before you settle on a neighborhood, tour it extensively during the day and at night, on weekdays and weekends, to get a feel for it.

- *Once you've decided on a location, look for rental homes or apartments advertised in newspapers, at REALTORS®' offices and on billboards in local supermarkets, schools and bank lobbies.* Depending on the strength of the market, you or the landlord will have to pay a fee if you find your apartment or rental home through a real estate agent. If there are few rentals in the local market, the renter usually pays the fee; if there are many apartments for rent, the landlord tends to pay the fee. However, you can avoid that cost if you deal directly with a landlord or with a renter who offers a sublease.

- *Don't rent the first home or apartment you see.* The more time you take, the better the deal you will find.

- *When looking at apartments or rental homes, check everything carefully.* Run all the appliances and facilities, including the dishwasher, washing machine, toilet, shower, sink, stove and waste disposal system. Also, make sure the refrigerator is in good condition and that heating and air conditioning systems work well. Inquire about parking facilities, security procedures, pest control and grounds maintenance, if applicable. Determine which utility costs are included in and excluded from your rent. Finally, visit the property both in the day and at night to see—and even chat with—your potential neighbors and to determine the property's or neighborhood's noise level.

- *Once you've found a place that meets your needs, lock in as low a rent as possible.* You will have much more leverage if a surplus of rentals exists in the area, of course. Your landlord will probably ask for references from your employer or past landlords. Have them ready, in writing, in advance. Landlords will also require at least a month's security deposit and maybe two months' rent. In many states, landlords are required to put that money in an escrow bank account and credit you with any interest it earns.

- *If you plan on staying in the apartment or rental home at least a year, insist on getting a year-long lease.* Otherwise, you will rent under a *tenant-at-will agreement,* which means that you can leave whenever you want, but the landlord can evict you at will. If you plan to stay awhile, you should sign a *renewable lease.* In addition to allowing you to extend your rental, the lease gives you the right to have the landlord maintain the basic facilities in your apartment at an acceptable level. Ask the landlord whether your lease grants you the right to sublease to another renter and under what conditions you can get out of your lease before it officially terminates.

- *If you like your apartment or rental home so much that you may want to own it someday, ask the landlord whether he or she would apply your rent toward a down payment on the purchase of the property. Rent-to-own agreements* are gaining popularity and may work to your advantage if you can lock in a price now that may be profitable if real estate prices rise later. Most rent-to-own agreements do not obligate you to buy, however, so you can walk away from the purchase if your situation changes or real estate values fall.

If You Decide To Buy

If you conclude from the buy-versus-rent analysis that you should buy a home, you have a much more complex task ahead of you than if you decide to rent. You now must determine how much house you can afford, what kind of house to buy, where you want to live, how to find the best deal, how to make an offer that is accepted and how to finance your home with a mortgage. After you've done all of this, you must maintain the home and possibly remodel it to fit your needs.

The first step to take before you house hunt is to determine how much of a mortgage you can afford. To qualify for a home loan, you must pass certain tests that all banks will impose. Therefore, you might as well apply those tests yourself before you ever meet with a banker. In summary, if you make a 10 percent down payment on a home, banks will approve a loan only if your monthly real estate obligation—which includes mortgage principal and interest payments, real estate taxes, homeowner's insurance and maintenance costs (for a cooperative or condominium)—is 28 percent or less of your gross monthly income. In addition, all of your debt—including payments on credit cards, car loans, student loans and revolving lines of credit, as well as mortgage debt—should not total more than 36 percent of your gross monthly income.

The Monthly Mortgage Worksheet in Figure 8.1 will help you determine how much of a mortgage you can afford using these rules. The worksheet includes sample figures. To determine how much money you can borrow for the purchase of a home, you must assume an interest rate and a mortgage term. Figure 8.2 lists *factors* for the two most popular term loans, 15 years and 30 years, at various interest rates, from 7 percent to 13 percent. When you have located the proper factor, multiply the loan amount by this factor to arrive at a monthly payment. For example, a $200,000, 30-year loan at 8 percent interest would require a $1,468 monthly payment ($200,000 × .00734 = $1,468). If item 10 on your Monthly Mortgage Worksheet is greater than this monthly payment, you can afford the mortgage.

Using these factors, you can try different combinations of terms and interest rates to see how much money you can borrow. To do this, divide item 10 from the Monthly Mortgage Worksheet by various factors to produce different loan amounts. Some examples follow.

Rate/Term	Item 10	Factor	Loan Amount
7%/30 years	$1,500	.00666	$225,225
10%/30 years	1,500	.00878	170,843
13%/30 years	1,500	.01107	135,501
7%/15 years	1,500	.00899	166,852
10%/15 years	1,500	.01075	139,535
13%/15 years	1,500	.01266	118,483

Notice that the longer the loan term and the lower the mortgage interest rate, the higher the loan amount you can afford.

The following table will also help you determine how large a mortgage you can afford. It cites monthly payments at different interest rates and mortgage amounts. All these payments are calculated for a 30-year, fixed-rate mortgage and include both principal and interest repayment.

Mortgage Amount	Interest Rates									
	7.5%	8%	8.5%	9%	9.5%	10%	10.5%	11%	11.5%	12%
$ 50,000	$350	$367	$384	$402	$420	$439	$457	$476	$495	$514
$ 60,000	420	441	461	483	505	527	549	571	594	617
$ 70,000	490	514	538	563	589	614	640	667	693	720
$ 80,000	560	587	615	644	673	702	732	762	792	823
$ 90,000	630	661	692	724	757	790	823	857	891	926
$100,000	700	734	769	805	841	878	915	952	990	1,029

Figure 8.1 The Monthly Mortgage Worksheet

	Example	Your Loan
1. Percentage of monthly income available for total mortgage payment, including principal, interest, real estate taxes and homeowner's insurance	28%	
2. Percentage of monthly income available for real estate taxes and homeowner's insurance	4%	
3. Percentage of monthly income available for mortgage principal and interest payments	24%	
4. Gross monthly income	$6,250	
5. Multiply item 3 by item 4	$1,500	
6. Percentage of monthly income available for principal, interest, real estate taxes and homeowner's insurance, plus other debts (subtract item 2 from 36%)	32%	
7. Amount of monthly income available for principal and interest, plus other debts (multiply item 6 by item 4)	$2,000	
8. Amount of monthly income available for other debts	$ 450	
9. Subtract item 8 from item 7	$1,550	
10. Enter either item 5 or item 9, whichever is less	$1,500	

Armed with the knowledge of how large a mortgage you can afford and how much you must pay each month toward that mortgage, you can now determine what price you can pay for a home. It is safe to assume that closing costs, which include *points* (prepaid interest charged by the lender—one point is 1 percent of the loan amount), legal fees, title searches, transfer taxes and other charges, will amount to about 2 to 4 percent of your mortgage amount. You should deduct all of these closing costs from the cash you have available for a down payment.

Most sellers and lenders require at least a 10 percent down payment, though some will accept 5 percent. If you can make a down payment of 20 percent or more of the home's purchase price, you will save thousands of dollars of interest over the

Figure 8.2
Monthly Payment Factors

Interest Rate Percentage	30-Year Loan	15-Year Loan
7%	.00666	.00899
7.5	.00700	.00928
8	.00734	.00956
8.5	.00769	.00985
9	.00805	.01015
9.5	.00841	.01045
10	.00878	.01075
10.5	.00915	.01106
11	.00953	.01137
11.5	.00991	.01169
12	.01029	.01201
12.5	.01068	.01233
13	.01107	.01266

mortgage's life, you can avoid the cost of private mortgage insurance (known as PMI), and your loan will be approved much more readily.

If you plan to make a traditional 10 percent down payment, the Purchase Cost Worksheet in Figure 8.3 will help you determine how much home you can afford. Sample numbers are provided.

ASSEMBLING A DOWN PAYMENT

Buying a home depends on your ability to put together a down payment. The inability to do so is the single most common reason that many people are shut out of the housing market. Many people have enough income to make mortgage payments but are never able to assemble that up-front lump sum. If this is your dilemma, the following suggestions may help.

- *Borrow the money from your parents or other relatives.* If they are in better financial shape than you, Mom and Dad or another family member might lend you the down payment, which you should repay as you pay off your mortgage.

- *Put securities or bank deposits in escrow to act as your down payment.* For example, in the Merrill Lynch Mortgage 100 program (800-854-7154), if you can place a bit over 30 percent of the home's purchase price in escrow in the form of stocks, bonds, mutual funds and certificates of deposit,

Figure 8.3   Purchase Cost Worksheet

	Example	Your Purchase
Start with the mortgage amount qualified for (assuming $700/mo., 7.5%, 30 yr.)	$100,000	$
Add down payment cash	11,000	
Total price of home	111,000	
Add closing costs (at 4% of loan amount)	4,440	
Total Purchase Cost	$115,440	$

Merrill will lend you 100 percent of your home's purchase price. One advantage of this system is that you do not have to sell securities and pay capital gains taxes on any realized gains to assemble your down payment. Over time, as you pay down the principal of your mortgage or the value of your home increases, you will be able to take securities out of escrow, because you will have built up enough home equity. If you do not have enough securities to participate in the Mortgage 100 program, Merrill also offers the Parent Power Program, which permits parents to fund the escrow account with their securities or bank deposits, allowing their children to get 100 percent financing for their home. As the children pay down the mortgage or as the value of the home increases, the parents' securities can be released from the escrow account.

- *Take out a loan against your equity in your employer's profit-sharing, thrift or 401(k) plan.* Most firms allow you to borrow at the prime rate or at a little more than prime and pay the loan back through payroll deduction.

- *Make saving a priority.* The sooner you start putting money aside and investing it for growth, the sooner you will accumulate the down payment you need now or in the future. (One path to increased savings is decreased spending, particularly frivolous spending on disposable items. Think of all those Chinese dinners you pick up on the way home from work instead of cooking and those spur-of-the-moment vacations as assaults on your down payment fund.)

- *Get a Federal Housing Administration (FHA) or Department of Veterans Affairs (VA) loan, both of which require lower or, in some cases, no down payments.* Although maximum FHA loan amounts vary depending on the area, they range between $100,000 and $115,000 for a single-family house.

VA loans are given to members of the armed forces, veterans and widows of veterans.

- *Obtain private mortgage insurance with your lender.* If your creditworthiness qualifies you to receive it, you will be able to reduce the size of your down payment because your lender is now protected against your default.

- *Buy a foreclosed home.* Local lenders, as well as the FHA and VA, will usually accept low down payments to induce buyers to buy homes on which the lenders have foreclosed. You might have to fix up the property and it might not be located in a prime area, but the investment can get you into the housing market.

Finding the Right Home

Once you have determined how large a mortgage you can afford, what price you will pay for a home and how you will assemble a down payment, it's time to establish what kind of housing will best serve your needs, both today and in the future.

THE BEST LOCATION

Before you explore the different homes available, determine where you want to live. For example, are you most comfortable in the city, country or suburbs? Examine the trade-offs between different locations. Would you exchange a quick trip to the office, for instance, for acres of trees and grass many miles away? Do a short trip to work and nearby cultural opportunities outweigh a shortage of parking? Also, evaluate available shopping, public and private schools, recreational and cultural facilities and transportation options, as well as the composition of the local population and the cost of living in the area. Lifestyle considerations often outweigh financial ones when choosing a place to live.

In addition to choosing where to live, you must decide how to live. What size home suits your present and future needs? First, determine how long you plan to stay in the home you are about to buy. A young, childless couple might need only a small condominium now but a larger house in five years when they begin a family. On the other hand, an empty-nester couple nearing retirement might find a large home a burden to maintain. Next, establish realistically how much space you need, both now and in the future. If you plan to move in a few years, it might not make sense to buy more house than you need now because it may strain your budget. Conversely, a house in which you plan to live for the rest of your life shouldn't be too small if it will seem cramped as your children grow or when you add a new member to the family.

A Home for Your Lifestyle

Next, assess what type of home bests suits your lifestyle. For instance, would you rather own a new structure, which may offer many modern conveniences, or an older home, which you may find more charming, though less energy efficient and more in need of repair? You might prefer the traditional American dream home—a single-family detached house, which gives you much privacy. Or you may favor buying a multifamily house or small apartment building, which earns rental income that offsets your mortgage and maintenance costs.

Finally, you may like the idea of purchasing an apartment in a cooperative or condominium building. In a cooperative, you actually buy shares in the entire property, which grants you a proprietary lease to occupy an apartment. Condominiums allow you to buy the property outright. In many cases, the cooperative or condominium board of directors must approve anyone to whom you want to sell the apartment, which can make the property difficult to sell. Both coops and condos assess a monthly maintenance charge to pay for such shared costs as the property's underlying mortgage, heat, elevators, electricity, grounds maintenance, security and recreational facilities, such as swimming pools or tennis courts. If the coop or condo must undertake a particularly large repair job, like replacing a roof or boiler, you may have to pay an extra assessment to cover your share of the bill. Living in a well-run coop or condo can liberate you from much of the maintenance of a single-family home. On the other hand, you must make sure that the board of directors runs the organization well. If the board continually defers essential maintenance, for example, the value of your unit could erode.

Conducting the Search

Once you have zeroed in on the location, size and style of the home that best suits your needs, you may begin your search. You have many ways to find your dream home.

- *Tell friends and neighbors you're in the market for a home.* They might know of a good deal.

- *Contact a real estate agent.* Unless you hire a broker who represents the buyer, you will deal with an agent whose job it is to represent the seller. Agents and brokers can be extremely helpful in showing you homes that fit your housing and budgetary needs, but always remember that the seller pays their commission, which is based on their getting as high a price for the property as possible. (See "Real Estate Brokers" in Chapter 17 for more information about selecting a real estate broker.)

- *Read classified ads in newspapers.* With practice, you will learn to scan the thousands of listings with an eye for a bargain. Your best chance to buy a great home at a good price occurs when the seller is under pressure to sell. She might be going through a divorce. He may be on the verge of foreclosure. She may have taken a job in another city. Whatever the reason, look for what real estate professionals call motivated sellers. You might not only get a good price but also induce the seller to offer attractive financing. Also notice whether a newspaper ad has been placed directly by the homeowner, which would allow you to sidestep an agent's commission, or by an agency. Even though the seller pays the broker's fee of up to 7 percent, that fee is built into the price you pay.

- *Place a classified ad.* If you can't find a home you like through the newspapers, you can place an ad explaining what you are looking for. You may hear from a seller or real estate agent who can tell you about a property that you don't know about.

- *Look for vacant homes.* By driving or walking through the neighborhood you are interested in, you may spot a vacant home with an overgrown lawn, peeling paint and a lot of junk mail in the mailbox. A for-sale sign may or may not be posted on the property. To determine who owns the home, look up records at City Hall, question the neighbors or ask the post office whether it has a forwarding address. The home may be owned by a motivated seller who would be overjoyed to receive your bid.

- *Purchase real estate about to be or already foreclosed upon.* The ultimate motivated seller is the person about to lose property to the bank because he or she has not kept up with the payments. You can buy from the owner before foreclosure, from the trustee at foreclosure or from the bank that holds the property after foreclosure. If the FHA or VA insured the loan, it may also be involved in the foreclosure. Foreclosed-upon properties are frequently offered at auctions; however, you will probably do better if you can buy the property directly from the owner before it gets to auction.

- *Use a buyer's broker.* If you've never searched for a house before, it may be useful to have a buyer's broker on your side. These brokers are unlike traditional brokers whose job it is to get the highest price for the home-seller. They work exclusively to get you, the homebuyer, the best possible deal. Buyer's brokers are fully licensed real estate professionals, with total access to all multiple listed, unlisted, and "for sale by owner" properties. They assist you with the entire homebuying process, from helping you define your wants and needs to making price comparisons and offering strategies. They will help you objectively look at a property's strengths and weaknesses. During negotiations with the seller or the seller's agent, the buyer's broker will do his or her best to help you get the best price and terms. One strategy that can save you thousands of dollars is not to disclose your highest price intentions, or how motivated you are to buy the house.

Buyer's brokers can help you by acting as an intermediary with the seller, only divulging the information that is needed to seal the deal. A buyer's broker usually gets paid on a normal commission structure—make sure you know how much your broker gets before you agree to use their services. To find a buyer's broker near you, look in the Yellow Pages, or you can contact the national Buyer's Homefinding Network at 800-893-0864 for a local referral.

As you evaluate various properties, write in a notebook the location, layout, features and financial details—such as price, taxes and maintenance costs—of each home you consider. When you look at many homes, you may have difficulty keeping all these details straight.

ARRANGING AN INSPECTION

Once you have found the home, including condominiums, that meets your housing and financial needs, you should have it professionally inspected to detect any problems with the property. You can find a professional inspector through one of the following: the American Society of Home Inspectors (85 W. Algonquin Rd., Arlington Heights, IL 60005; 847-290-1959) or the National Association of Property Inspectors (303 W. Cypress, San Antonio, TX 78212-0528; 800-486-3676). A qualified home inspector will be impartial, will have years of experience and a good reputation in the community and will stand behind his or her inspection. Some companies will even offer a one-year warranty on their inspections that covers any defect not detected during the inspection.

The following is a brief rundown of things your inspector should check.

- Structural components, including foundations, floors, walls, columns, ceilings and roofs
- Exterior conditions, including wall flashings and trim, doors, windows, chimneys, decks, balconies, stoops, steps, porches, eaves, vegetation, grading, drainage, driveways, patios and walkways
- Plumbing systems, including pipes, drains and traps, and the operation of showers, toilets and faucets
- Electrical systems, including wiring, grounding equipment, amperage and voltage ratings, circuit breakers, lighting fixtures and receptacles
- Heating systems, including boilers, thermostats, heat pumps, insulation, radiators and automatic safety controls
- Air conditioning systems, including central controls and distribution systems such as fans, pumps, ducts and air filters
- Interiors, including walls, ceilings, floors, cabinets, doors, windows and stairs

In general, the inspector assesses the structural and mechanical components of the home. Features the inspector will usually not examine include paint, wallpaper, carpeting, household appliances and draperies. He or she also will not look for termites, fleas, rodents or other pests. It is your task to scrutinize the aspects of the home the inspector does not. You should also learn about the state of the local environment. You don't want to pay for damages caused by leakage of toxic or hazardous wastes that have been buried on the land.

OBTAINING AN APPRAISAL

If the home passes both your inspection and examination by a professional inspector, you should obtain an independent appraisal to make sure you don't pay too much for the property. Your lender may select an appraiser for you, whose fees you will probably pay. But if you want your own appraisal as well, you can find a professional appraiser through the National Association of Master Appraisers (P.O. Box 12617, 303 W. Cypress St., San Antonio, TX 78212-0617; 210-271-0781; 800-229-NAMA; www.nfbhousing.com/lgc) or the Appraisal Institute (875 N. Michigan Ave., Suite 2400, Chicago, IL 60611-1980; 312-335-4100; www.appraisalinstitute.org). If the appraisal indicates a lesser amount than the seller is asking, you may be able to use it as a bargaining chip to get a better price. The appraisal will also be useful in the mortgage application process because banks lend only a certain percentage of a home's appraised value.

NEGOTIATING THE PRICE

With your inspection and appraisal in hand, you can now set the lowest possible price to which the seller will agree. Whether you deal directly with the seller or bargain through a real estate agent, you should know how much you can afford to bid, based on your budget and the mortgage for which you can qualify. You should also determine whether you or the seller has a stronger bargaining position. If the local market is active and many other buyers have expressed interest in the home, the seller will likely be inflexible. On the other hand, if the market is glutted and the seller desperate to move, you can expect to receive much better terms.

Using your inspection report, you can point out defects in the home, estimate how much it will cost to fix them and ask that this amount be deducted from the property's price. You can also negotiate what fixtures, appliances and draperies will remain in the home and, if the seller offers you financing, what interest rate he or she will charge. The entire negotiation process can be unnerving and intimidating; however, you should stand firm because thousands of dollars are at stake.

THE SALES CONTRACT

When you come to an agreement with the seller, note all terms in the sales contract. These terms should include the:

- sales price;

- address and legal description of the property;

- amount of your earnest money deposit, which reserves the house for you while the contract is prepared and executed;

- amount of the down payment—perhaps 5 percent or 10 percent of the sales price—which holds the house for you while you apply for a mortgage;

- terms of your mortgage, allowing you to withdraw from the sales contract if you cannot qualify for a mortgage or if interest rates rise so much that you can no longer afford to buy the home;

- terms of assuming the seller's mortgage, if applicable, which may allow you to obtain a lower rate than is currently available in the market;

- details of owner financing, if applicable, which should include repayment terms, interest rates and down payments (The contract should not impose a prepayment penalty.);

- closing details, such as when and where the closing will take place;

- date of occupancy so that it is clear when you can move into your new home;

- type of deed required to be transferred from the seller to the buyer at closing;

- personal property and fixtures included with the house, such as appliances, carpeting, draperies and lighting fixtures (The contract can define something as a fixture or as personal property, which thus establishes what goes with the property and what does not.);

- repairs the seller agrees to make, including necessary inspections for such problems as termites (This list should also include any required inspections by the city or county to ensure that the building has no code violations and has a valid certificate of occupancy.);

- explanation of easement rights, which give someone else—such as a utility—the legal right to use your land;

- amount of the real estate broker's fee, if any, and who will pay it (usually the seller, but this should be spelled out in the contract);

- account where your earnest money and down payment will be kept, usually in escrow in a special bank account (Another clause should explain the conditions under which you can receive a refund.);

- proration of homeownership costs, specifying how property taxes, utility bills and rent from tenants will be split during the period between the signing of the contract and the time you take possession of the home;

- provisions about title insurance, specifying which title insurance company will issue a policy (Title insurance protects the buyer in case someone later challenges the seller's right to sell the property in the first place. If the title is unclear, the home cannot be sold easily. The contract should also specify who must pay for the title search—usually the seller although in some areas of the country it is the buyer.);

- warranty against liens, stating that all renovation or repair bills and taxes have been paid (You don't want to take possession, then have to deal with a contractor trying to collect an unpaid bill dated several months or years ago.);

- financing arrangements, specifying that you will apply for a mortgage loan (The entire sale will usually be contingent on your obtaining financing. There should be a clause in the contract stating that if you can't get a mortgage, the contract is void. If the seller provides financing, the terms should be included in the sales contract. The seller has the right to run a credit check on you to ensure that you are creditworthy.).

To make sure all of these provisions are handled correctly, it is best to have an experienced real estate lawyer represent you in the sales contract process.

CLOSING THE SALE

The last step in buying your dream home is the closing, where the many players involved in the transaction come together and checks for thousands of dollars are distributed. You should enter the final leg of this house-buying marathon knowing who will be present, what legal documents you must bring and how much money you must hand over to finish the deal.

Generally, the cast of characters attending a closing include the buyer, the seller, a real estate attorney for both parties, a representative of the bank making the mortgage, an escrow agent from the bank holding your down payment and earnest money, a representative of the title insurance company and the real estate broker for both parties.

The entire settlement procedure is covered by a federal law called the Real Estate Settlement Procedures Act (RESPA) that helps you anticipate the costs of closing. Settlement services often arrange the details of a closing, and if you use such a service, you should shop around to get the best price on a closing cost package. Your real estate agent may have a suggestion.

The following list names the most common closing costs.

- First mortgage payment
- Mortgage application fees
- Loan origination fees (fees the bank charges to process your loan)
- Points, or prepaid interest, charged by the lender (One point equals 1 percent of the loan amount. You may have to pay between 1 and 3 points.)

- Loan assumption fee (if you are assuming the seller's mortgage)
- Mortgage insurance premiums (This insurance covers the lender's risk if the buyer fails to make loan payments.)
- Credit report fees
- Survey, inspection and appraisal fees
- Recording deed fee
- Homeowner's insurance premiums for the first year
- Escrow account reserves that the lender might require to cover insurance or property taxes over the coming year
- Property tax payments for the first year (prorated to the closing date)
- Legal fees for your lawyer and the bank's attorney
- Settlement company's fees
- Title search fees and title insurance premiums (usually paid by the seller)
- Down payment (which should include the earnest money you have already set aside)

Depending on the price of your home and the price you get for all these items, your closing costs may amount to between 2 percent and 4 percent of the cost of your home.

Choosing the Best Mortgage

The entire process of uncovering and qualifying for a mortgage is crucial to making the most of your real estate dollar. You must pay off this debt for years; therefore, to find the best possible deal, you should understand the various sources and types of loans available.

Loan Sources

The first step in shopping for a mortgage is to identify loan sources. The following are the most likely lenders.

- *Savings and loans* (S&Ls) are the largest traditional lender to the home mortgage market. Despite the thrift crisis and subsequent bail-out in the late 1980s and early 1990s, the S&Ls that survived are strongly committed to originating mortgages. They have great expertise in this area and frequently offer the lowest rates.
- *Savings banks,* largely the same as S&Ls, are found mostly on the East Coast and specialize in mortgage lending.
- In recent years, *commercial banks* have been aggressively pursuing the S&L's bread-and-butter business of making mortgage loans. They may

offer the best deal around, particularly if you combine your mortgage with your checking, savings and investment accounts at the bank.

- Members of *credit unions* may be able to get the best mortgage terms from this nonprofit organization designed to serve its participants.

- *Mortgage bankers* borrow money from banks or investors, make mortgage loans and resell the loans to investors at a profit. They may be able to tap into mortgage pools created by insurance companies, pension funds and other institutional lenders you would not normally have access to on your own. Frequently, mortgage bankers will collect both your monthly payments and a fee from the lender for providing this service. You can find a mortgage banker through a local real estate agent, the *Yellow Pages* or the Mortgage Bankers Association of America (1125 15th St., N.W., Washington, DC 20005; 202-861-6500; www.mbaa.org).

- *Mortgage brokers* find the best loans for home buyers for a fee paid by the lender. They get these good deals because they bring in many loans to a particular lender and therefore can obtain better terms than you, individually, could from the same lender. In addition to the loan fee, you normally must pay the mortgage broker an application fee. Generally, mortgage brokers do not lend any of their own money. You can locate a broker through a local real estate agent or the *Yellow Pages*.

- *Sellers* may offer the best financing option if you are not able to qualify with another lender and the seller is desperate to move. The amount of seller financing rises sharply when interest rates at traditional lenders shoot up.

In addition to traditional home loans, most of these lenders will make loans guaranteed by the FHA or VA. These agencies set certain standards for the kinds and sizes of loans and borrower qualifications to qualify for their guarantees. For example, many VA loans require little or no down payment for qualified veterans. Many states also sponsor housing finance agencies that offer below-market mortgages for low- or moderate-income home buyers. These agencies usually raise the money for such loans by issuing municipal bonds backed by the home loans.

When you shop for a mortgage, compare not only the interest rate but also the closing costs (points and other fees), which can add to your total cost significantly. A few services—such as the *Home Buyer's Mortgage Kit* run by HSH Associates (1200 Route 23N, Butler, NJ 07405; 800-873-2837)—can give you, for a small fee, a current comparison of rates and terms for lenders in your area.

In today's mortgage market, many lenders do not retain the loans they make. They sell the loans in the multi-billion-dollar secondary market to such quasi-governmental agencies as Ginnie Mae (Government National Mortgage Association), Fannie Mae (Federal National Mortgage Association) and Freddie Mac

(Federal Home Loan Mortgage Corporation). Ginnie, Fannie and Freddie then package these loans, guarantee them against homeowner default and sell them as mortgage-backed securities. This secondary market continually brings in new dollars to the mortgage market for lending at the local level. So even though you continue to send your mortgage payments to the lender that financed your loan, your payments may very well be passed on to holders of mortgage-backed securities across the country.

KINDS OF MORTGAGES

Most lenders offer several types of mortgages. The most common options follow.

Fixed-rate. The traditional 30-year *fixed-rate mortgage* is still the industry standard because it offers long-term predictability. Your total payments are spread over so many years that your monthly payments are lower than they would be on a shorter term loan. In the long run, however, you will pay thousands of dollars more in interest on a 30-year loan than on a less extended obligation. This interest is usually tax deductible, though, which lowers your actual after-tax cost of paying it.

Lately, 15-year loans have become particularly popular. They usually offer slightly lower interest rates than 30-year loans, but you must make substantially larger monthly payments. If you want to prepay your mortgage on such a faster schedule, contact your lender to arrange a prepayment schedule, and make sure that you will not be assessed any prepayment penalties. Because you pay off the loan balance faster, a smaller portion of your monthly payment goes for interest. This means that you will deduct less on your tax return but own your home sooner than you would with a 30-year loan. Making biweekly payments on a 30-year loan rivals making monthly payments on a 15-year mortgage.

In the early years of either a 30-year or a 15-year fixed-rate loan, you pay mostly interest. By the end of the loan, you pay almost all principal. Therefore, over time, ownership in your home gradually shifts from the lender to you.

Adjustable-rate. Instead of offering an interest rate fixed for the life of the loan, an *adjustable-rate mortgage* (ARM) features an interest rate that moves up and down with prevailing rates. Early in the ARM's term, its rate will almost always be less than that on a fixed-rate loan. Because the borrower agrees to risk fluctuating rates over the life of the loan, he or she is rewarded with a low initial rate.

ARMs come in many varieties. Some adjust their rates every year, while others alter them every three or five years. Loan rates are tied to a number of interest rate indexes. A bank will charge a *margin,* or spread, over the underlying index of up to 2 or 4 percentage points. The most popular loan rates include the national average mortgage rate as calculated by the Federal Home Loan Bank (FHLB) Board; U.S. Treasury bill rates; one-year constant maturity Treasury rates; the prime lending rate; and the 11th District cost of funds index rate (known as a COFI loan), which is the average cost that S&Ls must pay depositors for their money.

You can learn these rates from most lenders, from publications like *The Wall Street Journal* or from the "Monitor" department in *Money* magazine.

In general, the more short term the index that your ARM is tied to, the more volatile your payments will be. That's good if interest rates fall but can cause trouble if interest rates rise. Rates on T-bills and one-year Treasuries and the prime rate will fluctuate much faster than the cost of funds rate or the national average mortgage rate. If you hesitate to take the risk of short-term rates, consider an ARM tied to the more slowly moving indexes.

Most ARMs offer two built-in caps to protect you from enormous increases in monthly payments. A *periodic rate cap* limits how much your payment can rise at any one time. For example, your loan agreement might stipulate that your rate cannot go up more than 2 percentage points a year. An *aggregate,* or a *lifetime, cap* limits how much the rate can rise over the life of the loan. The same loan that limits increases to 2 percent a year may also impose a 6 percent cap for the duration of the loan. Such caps can also apply to rate decreases. Therefore, the example loan may not fall more than 2 percentage points in one year or 6 points during its lifetime.

In addition to rate caps, many ARMs feature *payment caps,* which limit the amount your payment can rise over the life of the loan. Therefore, if the underlying index shoots up, your payment would increase only to the limit of the payment cap. Even though you do not pay the difference now, however, you owe it to the lender over the long term. When your mortgage payment does not cover the full interest and principal due, this is called *negative amortization.* The lender will apply more, and possibly all, of your payment to interest, which means that your home equity will grow more slowly or, in the extreme case, will actually shrink.

Convertible. A *convertible mortgage* is an ARM that can be changed to a fixed-rate mortgage at a specified rate. You may have one chance or several to make the switch. The conversion feature gives you the opportunity to start with a low adjustable rate, then lock into a low fixed rate for a long time.

Balloon. A *balloon mortgage* requires a series of equal payments, then a large payment (balloon) at the loan's termination. The mortgage term may be from three to ten years. Usually, balloon mortgages are offered at fixed rates, though some adjustable-rate balloons are also available. The payments on a balloon mortgage generally cover interest only, so you do not build equity in the home over time. If you take on such a loan, you should know what you will do when the balloon arrives. Most homeowners refinance the payment. Some lenders will promise to refinance the loan when the balloon comes due, though they will not lock in an interest rate in advance. In many cases, home sellers offer buyers balloon mortgage options to help the deals go through.

Graduated payment. A *graduated payment mortgage* (GPM) begins with a low monthly payment that rises steadily over time until it reaches a plateau for the duration of the loan. This might be ideal if you are a young person with little money but with the potential to earn much more in the future. As your income grows over time, you can make the rising payments. Usually, GPMs offer a fixed rate. In the loan's early years, you actually pay less than the interest rate would normally dictate. In the loan's later years, you make up the difference by paying more. Nonetheless, GPMs are dangerous because they assume your income will rise steadily over time. If you are laid off or if your salary does not rise as much as you expect, you could be in trouble.

Growing equity. A *growing equity mortgage* (GEM), often known as a rapid payoff loan, offers a fixed rate and a changing monthly payment. Formally, the loan is for 30 years but, in fact, may be paid off in 15 years or less because your payments reduce the outstanding principal quickly. Your payment amount is usually tied to some index, such as the Commerce Department's per capita income index. In this case, as income rises, your payments increase. You can also create your own GEM by sending in extra principal payments or by paying your mortgage biweekly instead of monthly. All of these methods of payment will help you build equity faster and pay off your mortgage sooner.

Shared appreciation. If you are willing to surrender to your lender some of your home's appreciation potential, you may want to opt for a *shared appreciation mortgage* (SAM). With this loan, you pay a below-market interest rate on your mortgage and, in return, offer the lender between 30 percent and 50 percent of the increased value of your home when you sell it in a specified number of years. If that day comes and you do not want to sell, you must pay the lender its share of the property's appreciation. If you don't have the cash to do so, you might have to sell the property anyway. On the other hand, if the property has not appreciated or has, in fact, decreased in value, you will owe nothing. SAMs were much more popular in the 1970s and 1980s, when housing appreciation was more assured. They are far trickier in the 1990s for both lenders and borrowers because of the unsettled real estate market.

Buy-down. If you buy a home from a developer, it may offer a *buy-down,* or mortgage subsidy, to help you afford the property. For example, to help you qualify, the developer may cut the interest rate on your mortgage by 2 or 3 percentage points for the first three years of your loan. While this may help you obtain the mortgage, you may not be able to afford the payments when the subsidy lapses. If you count on a higher income in the future to help you meet those higher payments, you could be in trouble if your income does not rise sufficiently.

Choosing the best mortgage for you is a matter of weighing the pros and cons of each. For example, you might treasure the security of a fixed-rate mortgage, particularly if you lock in a favorable rate for a long time. However, the higher interest rate attached to a fixed loan can be a significant price to pay for that sense of security.

On the other hand, you might be better off taking the risk of an ARM and investing the difference between an ARM payment and a fixed loan payment. If you put the money in a few top-performing stocks, bonds or mutual funds, your financial picture might improve far more with the adjustable mortgage, even if interest rates rise over time.

The other types of loans discussed here—convertibles, balloons, graduated payment loans, growing equity mortgages, shared appreciation loans and buy-downs—all have their place, depending on your situation. As with adjustable-rate and fixed-rate loans, weigh the disadvantages against the advantages of each.

REFINANCING YOUR MORTGAGE

If you locked yourself into what you thought was a good fixed-rate mortgage and rates have since dropped, you may want to consider refinancing your loan to save what could total thousands of dollars over the long term.

The rule of thumb in the industry used to be that your new mortgage had to be at least 2 percentage points less than your existing mortgage for the transaction to be worthwhile. Recently, however, the competition among lenders has shaved closing costs significantly, and in many cases, it might pay off to refinance if the difference is 1 percentage point or possibly even less. It all depends on how much the new bank charges in closing costs, and how long you plan to stay in your home.

In order for you to refinance, your home must have enough value to justify a new loan. Many people who bought homes at peak prices in the late 1980s were disappointed to learn that they could not refinance their homes in the 1990s when mortgage rates dropped so sharply because the worth of their homes had plunged as well.

Most lenders will make you go through the same application process when you refinance as you did when you applied for your original mortgage. Even though it doesn't seem fair or necessary, you must again pay loan origination fees, credit report charges, appraisal charges, inspection fees, points, mortgage recording taxes, title insurance and legal fees. Also, determine whether your current loan imposes prepayment penalties. If so, refinancing can be significantly more expensive.

To determine whether you should refinance your current mortgage, calculate your refinancing costs, then complete the Refinancing Worksheet in Figure 8.4. Sample figures are provided.

In the example in Figure 8.4, it would take the borrower ten months of lower payments to recover the $3,000 in up-front refinancing costs. Therefore, the borrower should plan to stay in his or her home at least ten months after the refinancing. In other cases, the savings would be less and the payback period would be longer. Again, it is worthwhile to refinance only if you live in your house for a significant amount of time after you refinance.

When you refinance, you will pay less interest on the new loan. That saves you money but means that you will receive fewer mortgage interest deductions to lower

Figure 8.4   Refinancing Worksheet

	Example	Your Mortgage
1. Present Monthly Mortgage Payment	$1,000	
2. Mortgage Payment after Refinancing	$ 700	
3. Monthly Savings (subtract item 2 from item 1)	$ 300	
4. Total Fees, Closing Costs and Prepayment Penalties	$3,000	
5. Time Needed To Break Even (divide item 4 by item 3)	10 months	

your tax bill. Also, any points you pay on the new mortgage can be deducted only over the life of the loan, not up-front in a lump sum.

While most people refinance a fixed-rate loan with another such loan, you can also exchange a fixed-rate loan for an ARM or an ARM for a fixed-rate loan. When you convert a fixed-rate mortgage to an ARM, you should invest your savings in stocks, bonds or mutual funds that will give you long-term capital appreciation. Then, if interest rates on the ARM rise, you will have accumulated capital on which to draw to make the higher payments. One of the worst moves you can make is to convert from a fixed- to an adjustable-rate mortgage and spend the difference on a more extravagant lifestyle.

If rates drop low enough, it may make sense to exchange an ARM for a fixed-rate loan. Just realize that you are increasing your monthly mortgage payment in order to gain peace of mind. If you can live with a little more uncertainty, invest the money you save on an ARM in top-quality securities.

Another way to refinance is to convert a long-term loan, such as a 30-year mortgage, to a shorter term loan, such as a 15-year mortgage. You might find that your monthly payment stays about the same, but you will pay off your mortgage much faster.

A good way to determine whether refinancing makes sense and what refinancing options are best for you is to analyze your situation using some of the personal finance software packages now on the market. You might try *Interest Vision* (Parsons Technology, 1700 Progress Dr., Hiawatha, IA 52233-0100; 319-395-9626; 800-779-6000; www.parsonstech.com); *Managing Your Money* (MECA Software LLC, 115 Corporate Dr., Trumbull, CT 06611; 203-268-2797; 888-808-6322; www.mymnet.com); *Mastering Your Mortgage* (Home Equity Software,

202 Montebello Ave., Suite 9, Mountain View, CA 94043; 415-967-4965; www. isnetwork.com); *Mortgage Analyzer* (Insight Software Solutions, P.O. Box 354, Bountiful, UT 84011-0354; 801-295-1890; www.wintools.com); or *Wealthbuilder* (Reuters Money Network, 2200 Renaissance Blvd., King of Prussia, PA 19406; 800-346-2024; www.moneynet.com). You can also calculate whether refinancing makes sense using some of the Web sites described at the end of this chapter.

If the math indicates refinancing, try your existing lender first. In order to keep your business, it will probably give you the best deal and might even waive certain procedures or fees, such as the appraisal or prepayment charges. Your lender should be particularly accommodating if you have made all your mortgage payments on time, your new payments are not more than 15 percent higher than your old payments and you make at least the income you earned when you took out the original loan. Still, before you recommit to your lender, shop around to several other lenders to see whether you can obtain an even better deal.

HOME EQUITY LOANS

Once you have built up equity in your home, you have the privilege of arranging a home equity line of credit, which allows you to borrow against that equity inexpensively and conveniently. Most financial institutions—banks, savings and loans, brokerage firms, finance companies, credit unions and others—have entered the home equity market, so you have plenty of options when you shop for the best loan.

In effect, a home equity loan is a second mortgage on your home. You usually get a line of credit up to 70 percent or 80 percent of the appraised value of your home, minus whatever you still owe on your first mortgage. For example, if your home is worth $100,000 and you owe $20,000 on your mortgage, you might receive a home equity line of credit for $60,000 as your lender subtracts your $20,000 owed on the first mortgage from your $80,000 worth of equity. You will qualify for a loan not only on the value of your home but also on your credit-worthiness. For instance, you must prove that you have a regular source of income to repay a home equity loan. Because only the first $100,000 of home equity debt creates deductible interest, many people limit themselves to that amount although banks will loan much more if you qualify.

Like other mortgages, the home equity loan requires you to go through an elaborate process to qualify for and open a line of credit. You will usually need a home appraisal and must pay legal and application fees and closing costs. Many banks also charge loan origination fees or points. In addition, they may collect an annual fee of up to $50 to maintain the account.

Because a home equity loan is backed by your home as collateral, it is considered more secure by lenders than unsecured debt, such as on credit cards. And because the loans are less risky for banks, you benefit by paying a much lower interest rate than you would on credit cards or most other kinds of loans. Typically, home equity credit lines charge a variable rate 1 to 3 percentage points more than the prime lending rate. In many cases, home equity lenders will start you off with an introductory rate of one-half to one percentage point below the prime rate for six months to as long as a year. Home equity loans can therefore offer extremely attractive rates when the prime is low but subject you to much higher interest costs if the prime shoots up. You can tap the credit line simply by writing a check, and you can pay back the loan as quickly or as slowly as you like, as long as you meet the minimum payment each month. In theory, you must repay outstanding balances in five or ten years in one balloon payment. In practice, the bank will probably not require the balloon as long as you pay your minimum.

Home equity loans have become popular because they are flexible and offer attractive rates and tax deductions. However, you should be careful about how you spend the proceeds from your home equity loan. It is best if you use the money for major capital expenditures on which you might earn a return instead of on impulse items. For example, you might use home equity money to renovate your home, finance your children's tuition, buy a car or furniture or pay off high-cost, nondeductible credit card debt. Don't, however, tap the credit line for a Caribbean vacation or a spin of the roulette wheel in Las Vegas. Remember, your home is on the line. If you spend the money frivolously and don't repay the loan, you'll lose your home quickly. If you know that you will be tempted to spend the money unwisely, it's best not to open a home equity credit line.

REVERSE MORTGAGES

Another way to tap the equity in your home, particularly if you are retired and own your home free and clear, is to assume a *reverse mortgage*. Instead of borrowing against your equity and paying interest, you contract with a bank to convert some of your home equity to cash while you retain ownership. These are called reverse mortgages because they are the opposite of traditional mortgages— the *bank* makes payments to *you*. You can use the money for anything you want though it is prudent to use it for living expenses such as taxes, insurance, heat or food.

With a reverse mortgage you can take your proceeds in a lump sum, in monthly checks or through a line of credit you can tap whenever you want. The amount you can borrow depends on your age, the value of the equity in your home and the interest rate charged by the lender. Some loans charge a fixed rate of interest, while others charge a variable rate. When obtaining a reverse mortgage, you normally must pay closing costs and insurance premiums and sometimes a monthly service fee. The reverse mortgage comes due when you die, sell the home or move permanently. At that point, you or your heirs must pay off the loan, or the bank will take title to your home.

Reverse mortgages increase the amount of interest you owe every month. Over time, the interest owed can become considerable, and your equity stake can shrink dramatically. However, a reverse mortgage can be a good way to use the equity in your home if you do not mind leaving your heirs a far smaller estate when you die.

All payments you receive from a reverse mortgage (technically, they are loan advances) are considered nontaxable income. Therefore, they do not lower your Social Security or Medicare benefits. On the other hand, the interest you pay on reverse mortgages is not tax deductible until you pay off all or part of your total reverse mortgage debt.

You have three basic types of reverse mortgages from which to choose.

FHA-insured. You need not pay off an FHA-insured reverse mortgage as long as you live in your home. You can change your payment options from monthly advances to a line of credit at any time at little or no cost. The FHA guarantees your payments even if the lender defaults.

Lender-insured. A lender-insured plan generally offers a heftier line of credit or larger monthly payments than an FHA-insured plan. Also, you do not have to borrow against the full equity in your home, as you do with an FHA-insured loan. Often, however, a lender-insured loan imposes a number of higher costs, which means that your loan balance will grow quickly, leaving you with less equity.

Uninsured. An uninsured plan pays a fixed monthly payment for a certain number of years—which you choose when you open the line—then terminates. At that point, the loan balance comes due, and the lender may take title to your home. An uninsured plan usually charges a fixed interest rate and requires no mortgage insurance. The plan can work well if you know how long you will need payments. But if you run through the equity in your home and still need more money, you will likely lose your home to an uninsured lender.

A related technique to tap your home's equity when you retire is to assume a *reverse annuity mortgage* (RAM). With this plan, you use the proceeds generated by a mortgage on your home to buy an annuity from an insurance company. The insurer pays the interest on your mortgage and sends the rest of the money to you in monthly installments. Upon your death, the insurer usually sells your home and repays the mortgage balance. Remaining funds are passed on to your heirs through your estate.

The amount of monthly income you receive from a RAM depends on the interest rate the insurer pays, your life expectancy and the equity you have accumulated in your home. Because the insurance company risks that you will live longer than its actuarial tables predict, the insurer makes smaller monthly payments than you might receive through a traditional reverse mortgage.

For more detailed information on how reverse mortgages work and which institutions currently grant them, contact the National Center for Home Equity Conversion (7373 147th St. West, Suite 115, Apple Valley, MN 55124; 612-953-4474). It publishes a book titled *Retirement Income on the House: Cashing in on Your Home with a "Reverse" Mortgage,* which describes how reverse mortgages work. The book includes a "Reverse Mortgage Locator," which lists all reverse mortgage lenders in the country.

Protecting the Value of Your Home

You can help ensure the value of your home through regular maintenance, renovation and home warranty.

MAINTAINING AND IMPROVING YOUR HOME

Because your home is probably your largest single asset, it pays to maintain and improve it over the years to enhance its value. It's great if you can do much of the work yourself, but most people don't have the time or expertise to handle plumbing, electrical and carpentry repairs, as well as mow the lawn and paint occasionally. That is why you should assemble a team of reliable plumbers, electricians, carpenters, lawn maintenance workers, painters and others to keep your home in tip-top shape. They not only solve problems and perform regular maintenance to keep problems from occurring, but, if you employ them consistently, they know your home perhaps better than you do.

Remodeling your home can cost thousands of dollars but can greatly add to the pleasure you derive from it—once the workers finally leave. In general, you should not expect to recoup all your money from most remodeling jobs when you sell, though some improvements hold their value better than others. The more customized your renovations, the more chance that future buyers will not like what you have done. If you take on major remodeling, you should plan to stay in your home for at least five more years.

Remodeling that pays off most includes those renovations that add living space and those that improve kitchens and bathrooms. Buyers like large master bedrooms, many bathrooms (even half-baths), modern appliances and open kitchen layouts.

Upgrading that costs the most and probably returns the least includes the addition of major recreational facilities like swimming pools, spas or tennis courts. Similarly, decks and patios may be nice but often don't recoup the money it costs to build them.

When you take on a renovation project, obtain several written bids from qualified contractors before you choose one. The following list names some of the key items that should be included in the contract.

- Full name, address and phone number of the company
- Contractor's name and license number
- Detailed specification of the job, including brand names, styles, colors and model numbers of any materials or appliances being installed. The contractor should also agree in writing to give you a credit or refund for any materials not used.

- Start and completion dates, with a clause allowing you to withhold money if certain deadlines are not met
- Statement from the contractor stating that he or she will obtain all necessary building permits or variances before work begins
- Proof that the contractor carries liability and workers' compensation coverage
- Written warranty on all work performed
- Promise that the contractor will clean up the site when he or she is finished
- Statement that all changes to the contract must be approved and signed by you and the contractor
- Payment schedule specifying the deposit and progress payments

You should aim to pay contractors as slowly as possible, with perhaps a third of the money up front, a third after half the job is finished and the final third when the job is completed to your total satisfaction. If you want a major overhaul of your home, you may need a general contractor to coordinate all the subcontractors. Otherwise, you must act as the general contractor and stay on top of the subcontractors to ensure that they keep to the schedule. The process usually takes much longer than you expect and costs far more (many times double) than you planned. But if the renovation turns out well, your home will give you many years of enjoyment.

HOME WARRANTIES

Another way to protect your investment is through a home warranty. Many builders of new homes participate in the *HOW* (Home Owners Warranty) program, which insures a home against major system and structural defects for up to ten years. You can learn more about the program by contacting HOW (P.O. Box 152087, Irving, TX 75015-2087; 800-433-7657; www.howcorp.com).

Warranties also exist for occupied homes. If you have your home examined by a warranty inspector, you can get a policy to cover your major systems for several years. Policies issued without inspections restrict coverage greatly and usually are not worthwhile.

Selling Your Home

When the time comes to sell your home, you must do just as much homework as you did when you bought the property.

The first step in getting the highest price possible for your home is to obtain a realistic appraisal of its current value. If you have paid little attention to the market for the past several years, you may have an outdated sense of what your home is worth. You should get a feel for the market by scanning newspaper ads for similar properties and by visiting nearby open houses. Real estate agents will be glad to give you a free assessment of your home's strengths, weaknesses and fair price range. For a fee, you can also obtain a professional appraiser's opinion.

If you want to avoid the real estate broker's fee, you can try to sell your home yourself with newspaper ads and a for-sale sign on your front lawn. Although you will have to deal with browsers and people unqualified to buy your property, you may be lucky enough to find someone who falls in love with your home and places a bid on it.

Before you let anyone past the front door, make sure your home is in tip-top shape. Add a fresh coat of paint. Locate plants and flowers strategically. Mow the lawn. Spruce up the exterior. Clean every room thoroughly. Remove excess clutter and furniture to maximize the appearance of living space. Distribute a one-page fact sheet listing your home's selling points and illustrating the layout. If you're located in an active real estate market, you might be able to sell within a few weeks. It is always best, however, to sell your home before you buy another property. You don't want to owe two mortgage payments if your home sells more slowly than you had anticipated.

More and more states require that you disclose all of your home's problems in writing to prospective buyers. The document covers a property's structure, utilities (such as plumbing, air conditioning and water system) and municipal status (such as building permits, zoning restrictions, certificate of occupancy and property tax rates). If the buyer signs this sales disclosure form acknowledging that he or she has been informed of the home's problems, the buyer has little right to sue you later if any problems crop up for any of the items listed.

If you cannot sell your home on your own, bring in several real estate agents to compete for your listing. Unless you deal with a flat-fee or discount broker, you must pay the agent you choose a commission of 6 percent to 8 percent of your home's selling price, but if he or she can find a buyer when you can't, the fee is worthwhile. For much more on how to work with a real estate broker, see Chapter 17, "Finding Financial Advisers Who Are Right for You."

When you sell your home, either on your own or through a REALTOR®, you must deduct all selling and closing costs from the gross sales price to arrive at your net proceeds. The worksheet in Figure 8.5 lists some of the costs you might incur and helps you determine your profit.

Investment Real Estate

Buying a home is the primary, but by no means the only, way to profit from real estate. Investing in real estate for profit is tricky and can take a great deal of time and expertise. Real estate has the advantages of appreciation potential, rental income and tax benefits. On the other hand, it can be extremely illiquid (hard to sell) and management intensive. The real estate market is also subject to the

Figure 8.5   Net Proceeds Worksheet

Gross Equity	$ Amount	Total
Sale Price of Property	$_____	
Minus Remaining Mortgage Balance	(_____)	
Minus Other Home-Related Debts	(_____)	
TOTAL GROSS EQUITY		$_____
Selling and Closing Costs		
Escrow or Other Fees	$_____	
Legal and Document Preparation Fees	_____	
Title Search and Insurance Fees	_____	
Transfer Taxes	_____	
FHA, VA or Lender Discounts	_____	
Mortgage Prepayment Penalties	_____	
Real Estate Taxes Owed	_____	
Appraisal Fees	_____	
Survey Fees	_____	
Termite and Other Pest Inspection Fees	_____	
Fees for Repair Work Required by Sales Contract	_____	
Home Protection or Warranty Plan Fees	_____	
Unpaid Assessments	_____	
Real Estate Commissions	_____	
Other Selling or Closing Costs	_____	
TOTAL SELLING AND CLOSING COSTS		$_____
TOTAL GROSS EQUITY MINUS		_____
TOTAL SELLING AND CLOSING COSTS EQUALS		(_____)
NET PROCEEDS		$_____

influence of national trends, such as changes in tax laws and interest rates, as well as local trends in economic growth and supply and demand for similar properties.

When seeking advice about investing in real estate, make sure that you know whom you listen to. The field is rife with self-promoters promising instant riches for no money down. Their so-called seminars are, in fact, high-pressure sales pitches. These scam artists usually show off their wealth to impress you; however, they have probably earned their millions by *giving* bad real estate advice, not *taking* it. Some tout enormous riches to be made in foreclosed property. Others guarantee wealth through government loan programs. A few want you to believe your road to easy street is paved with *multilevel marketing,* another term for a pyramid or Ponzi scheme. Be extremely careful when dealing with these promoters. Their presentations are slick and convincing, but the chances that you will end up as rich as they are slim or nonexistent.

If you wish to invest legitimately in real estate, you have seven principal ways to do so. They are ranked and discussed below from the safest to the most speculative: real estate mutual funds; real estate investment trusts; real estate limited partnerships; rental real estate; vacation homes; timeshares; and raw land.

REAL ESTATE MUTUAL FUNDS

Several mutual funds invest in publicly traded real-estate-oriented stocks. As do all mutual funds, they provide a widely diversified portfolio of securities, professional management and reasonable management fees of about 1 percent of your assets each year. Because many of these funds buy real estate investment trusts (REITs) that pay high dividends, the funds can pay yields of 2 percent to about 5 percent. In addition to REITs, these funds buy stocks of home builders and suppliers to the home-building industry.

Real estate funds tend to perform well when interest rates fall and when occupancy and rental rates rise. Conversely, they tend to underperform during periods of rising interest rates and when gluts of real estate exist on the market. Some funds buy only U.S. real estate companies, while other global funds invest in real estate companies around the world.

The popularity of real estate investing through mutual funds has spawned a profusion of funds. The funds that have been around the longest are: AIM Advisor Real Estate Portfolio (11 Greenway Plaza, Houston, TX 77046; 800-554-1156); Alliance Real Estate Investment Fund (P.O. Box 1520, Secaucus, NJ 07096; 800-227-4618); Alpine U.S. Real Estate Equity Fund and Alpine International Real Estate Equity Fund (Alpine Management and Research, 2500 Westchester Ave., Purchase, NY 10577; 914-694-2020); Brazos/JMIC Real Estate Securities Portfolio (1105 N. Market St., Wilmington, DE 19801; 800-426-9157); CGM Realty Fund (222 Berkeley St., Suite 1013, Boston, MA 02116; 800-598-0765); Cohen and Steers Realty Shares (757 Third Ave., New York, NY 10017; 800-437-9912); Columbia Real Estate Equity Fund (1301 SW Fifth Ave., Portland, OR

97207; 800-547-1707); Davis Real Estate Fund (124 E. Marcy St., Santa Fe, NM 87501; 800-279-0279); Fidelity Real Estate Investment Portfolio (82 Devonshire St., Boston, MA 02109; 800-544-8888); Flag Investors Real Estate Securities Fund (135 E. Baltimore St., Baltimore, MD 21202; 800-767-3524); Franklin Real Estate Securities Trust (777 Mariners Island Blvd., San Mateo, CA 94403-7777; 800-342-5236); Heitman Real Estate Fund (180 N. LaSalle St., Chicago, IL 60601; 800-435-1405); Munder Real Estate Equity Investment Fund (480 Pierce St., Birmingham, MI 48009; 800-438-5789); Phoenix Real Estate Securities Fund (100 Bright Meadow Blvd., Enfield, CT 06083; 800-243-4361); Pioneer Real Estate Shares (60 State St., Boston, MA 02109-1820; 800-225-6292); U.S. Global Investors Real Estate Fund (7900 Callaghan Rd., San Antonio, TX 78278; 800-873-8637); Van Kampen American Capital Real Estate Securities Fund (One Parkview Plaza, Oakbrook Terrace, IL 60181; 800-421-5666); Victory Real Estate Investors (P.O. Box 8527, Boston, MA 02266; 800-539-3863).

REAL ESTATE INVESTMENT TRUSTS (REITS)

REITs are publicly traded stocks that invest in office buildings, apartment complexes, industrial facilities, shopping centers and other commercial spaces. Under current law, they do not pay taxes at the corporate level as long as they distribute at least 95 percent of their earnings to shareholders in the form of dividends each year. Shareholders then pay taxes on the dividends as regular income. In some cases, a portion of the dividends may be considered a return of capital for tax purposes and therefore is not taxed.

Three primary types of REITs exist:

Equity. These trusts buy properties, fix them up, collect rents and sometimes sell the properties at a profit. Equity REIT share prices greatly reflect the general direction of real estate values. Some equity REITs buy different kinds of properties across the country. Others specialize in a particular type of real estate. For example, several REITs, including Meditrust (128 Technology Center, Waltham, MA 02154; 617-736-1500) and Health Care REIT, Inc. (One Seagate, Suite 1500, P.O. Box 1475, Toledo, OH 43603; 419-247-2800), concentrate on health care facilities. Others buy properties in one region of the country. For example, Washington REIT (10400 Connecticut Ave., Concourse Level, Kensington, MD 20895; 301-929-5900; www.shareholdernews.com/wre) buys properties in the Washington, D.C., market, while Weingarten Realty Investors (2600 Citadel Plaza Dr., Suite 300, Houston, TX 77708; 713-866-6000; www.weingarten.com) specializes in shopping centers in Texas and Louisiana. Equity REITs can provide some protection against inflation because they usually include rent escalator clauses in their contracts with tenants so that price increases can be passed along in the form of higher rents.

Mortgage. This form of REIT originates or buys mortgages on commercial properties. Mortgage REITs offer yields of about 6 percent to 10 percent—much more than the 4 percent to 7 percent paid by equity REITs. But mortgage REITs offer little capital appreciation potential. If mortgages get into trouble or default, share prices can plunge.

Hybrid. These REITs combine equity and mortgage holdings. Hybrid trusts pay yields of 6 percent to 9 percent and offer some appreciation potential.

The REIT industry has become notorious for a boom and bust cycle. Its first boom occurred in the early 1970s, which led to an enormous bust in the 1973–1974 recession, when many REITs went bankrupt in the wake of massive overbuilding. The industry recovered and prospered for much of the 1980s until the real estate market again became glutted in the late 1980s and early 1990s. By the mid and late 1990s, REIT shares were popular again as lower interest rates and tightening rental markets in many places boosted share prices.

REAL ESTATE LIMITED PARTNERSHIPS

Limited partnerships (LPs), which saw their heyday in the 1980s, raise money from limited partners and invest it in new or existing commercial real estate. Decisions on what to buy and how to manage the properties are made by a general partner.

Unlike real estate funds or REITs, LPs are not easy to buy and sell. When you buy, you must pay onerous sales charges and other fees that may amount to as much as 10 percent of your invested capital. On top of that, you remit annual management fees of 2 percent or 3 percent of your principal. If you want to withdraw from the partnership before it is liquidated, which occurs up to ten years after its launch, you must sell in a tricky secondary market where investors offer to buy your units at deep discounts.

In theory, a good real estate partnership produces high current income from rents and mortgage interest it collects. Upon liquidation, partners receive magnificent capital gains when the partnership's properties are sold for huge profits. The reality of the past decade has been far from the hype, as many partnerships have suffered defaults, plunging property values and declining rental income.

Another form of real estate partnership that offers more liquidity is a *master limited partnership* (MLP). These operate just like traditional partnerships except that they trade on exchanges like any other stock. In some cases, an MLP has been formed by combining the assets of several troubled illiquid partnerships into one giant, publicly traded vehicle. MLPs typically pay high dividends of 5 percent to 10 percent.

RENTAL REAL ESTATE

Becoming a landlord has its advantages and disadvantages. If you own a good property, it can appreciate handsomely over time and provide solid rental income. In addition, you can reap substantial tax benefits, such as writing off losses up to $25,000 against other income, if you meet certain IRS restrictions.

On the other hand, few people think being a landlord is fun. Tenants often complain. You are responsible if the plumbing breaks down in the middle of the night or the heat shuts off in the dead of winter. Not every renter pays his or her rent on time. You must constantly guard against vandalism. You must sometimes evict a tenant. And in some localities, rent controls prevent you from raising rents enough to cover increased expenses.

The key to successful rental real estate is to buy properties in good locations that attract the type of tenant who takes care of his or her unit and is so happy living on the property that he or she never objects to rent hikes every year. Easier said than done!

When looking for profitable rental properties, you might begin in working-class neighborhoods, where prices are more reasonable and tenants more reliable than they are in the elite neighborhoods of town. To find a bargain, you could focus on properties with problems that are relatively easy to resolve. The problem—be it asbestos, a leaky roof or some other repair—might scare the current owner so much that he or she will sell at a large discount from the property's real value. Before buying, determine how much it will cost to resolve the problem, and estimate the rent you could collect once the place is in tip-top shape.

Another way to get the best possible value when buying rental real estate is to look for a building that sits on a lot providing extra land that could be developed. You might be able to add onto the building, erect a new home or even sell part of the land to offset your purchase cost. Before you contemplate such a strategy, however, determine whether you will need a zoning variance to subdivide the land.

Vacation Homes

One of the more pleasurable forms of real estate investment is a vacation home because you can live there up to 14 days a year or 10 percent of the amount of time you rent it, whichever is less (according to the tax code). If you own a home in a desirable location near a beach, lake, ski resort or tourist attraction, you should be able to rent out the property for at least part of the year. In the best of all worlds, your annual rental income would cover your expenses or even exceed them. That would mean that you could live in the house rent free during your vacations. Unless your property is extremely popular, however, you should not expect to enjoy a positive cash flow.

A vacation home can provide tax benefits if it produces negative cash flow—in other words, costs more than it earns in rent. That's because the tax law allows you to deduct up to $25,000 of business losses from your *adjusted gross income* (AGI), as long as you actively rent and maintain the property. You qualify for the full $25,000 write-off if your AGI is less than $100,000. From $100,000 to $150,000 in income, the tax benefit is phased out. If you earn more than $150,000, you can deduct business losses only against rental income, not against regular income from your job or other investments. (See Chapter 13 on taxes for more information.) In calculating business losses, you can count all your expenses for maintaining the property, including depreciation, painting, yard maintenance, property taxes, insurance and utility bills. You are also allowed to count any trips you take to inspect or repair the property. If you abuse this right of visitation, the IRS may consider your vacation home a personal, not a rental, property.

If you take out a mortgage to purchase a vacation home, you can deduct your mortgage interest on your tax return. While that deduction may be sizable, it also increases your expenses considerably and makes it more difficult to generate positive cash flow.

When looking for a vacation home to buy as a rental, you should hunt for a property that has already been rented for several seasons. This will earn you a return clientele and give you a realistic indication of the level of rent to expect. If you improve the property, you might even be able to increase the rent somewhat. If you're going to charge a hefty rent, though, the property must be in excellent condition, offer comfortable furnishings and provide modern appliances that work. You might be able to rent the property yourself with ads in the local newspaper, but if that doesn't work, you will have to hire a rental agent, who might charge as much as 25 percent of the rent you collect.

In the end, you should not purchase a vacation home primarily as an investment that you expect will earn substantial capital appreciation. Instead, aim to generate a positive cash flow and maximize your tax benefits. If you get to live at the home two weeks every year for free, you've got yourself a good deal.

TIMESHARES

While they are often sold as real estate investments, timeshares are, in fact, not investments at all. When you purchase a timeshare, you own a specific block of time—usually a week—at a particular place—usually a condominium in a resort area. Before you buy, you must be convinced that you like the unit, development and surrounding area so much that you will want to come back year after year on your vacation.

Owners of timeshare units built by developers that are members of the Resort Property Owners Association (P.O. Box 2395, Northbrook, IL 60062; 708-291-0710) can swap their units with other members at properties around the world. Another company that facilitates exchanges of timeshare units is Interval International (62 Sunset Dr., Miami, FL 33243; 305-666-1884; 800-843-8843; www. interval-intl.com). However, unless you own a share in a very popular resort at a highly desirable time of year, you may not be able to trade for a place you want to go. If you become ill or an emergency arises in your week for the timeshare, you probably will have to forfeit that week unless you can make a last-minute swap.

The high-pressure salespeople who sell timeshare units usually pitch the excellent resale potential of their developments. Don't believe it. Hundreds of thousands of people can't find buyers because the salespeople direct most potential purchasers to new units. If you still want to buy a timeshare, you will probably get the best deal by purchasing an existing unit at a deep discount.

Be particularly wary of telemarketing firms that sell timeshares. Some of them claim to have extensive lists of sales agents and buyers lining up for their resale units. The more audacious promoters will even charge up to $500 for an "advance listing," promising that you can resell your unit for a quick profit. Some actually offer money-back guarantees.

Timeshare units are not only illiquid; they impose maintenance charges you must pay whether you use the your unit or not. Even those who try to abandon their timeshares meet with little luck. The developer and timeshare owners association pursue them to collect the money due according to the contract.

Nevertheless, if you want to own a timeshare, begin by renting an apartment a few times in the development in which you are interested. If you really like the development and want to return frequently, it might be worth buying into it. However, try to buy into a development backed by a major, well-known corporation—such as Marriott, Disney or Hilton—rather than some fly-by-night operation. Consider your purchase a way to lock in a long-term price for a vacation. It's unlikely to be an investment that grows in value over time.

To learn more about timeshares from the industry's point of view, contact the American Resort Development Association (1220 L St., N.W., Suite 500, Washington, DC 20005; 202-371-6700; www.arda.org).

Raw Land

Picture the following: You buy a piece of raw land cheaply from owners who have been sitting on it for years, unaware of its true value. Knowing that the area is about to be developed, you sell the acreage to developers and reap huge profits. That's the dream. The reality of investing in raw land is usually quite different.

Most raw land is purchased by developers assembling a site for a housing project, a shopping center, a factory or another commercial use. The land's value rises once utilities, roads, sewers and other amenities are installed. The prospect of quick gains usually encourages investment houses to sponsor *raw land,* or *predevelopment, limited partnerships,* but most fail. The combination of high interest rates and a glut of commercial properties in many markets hurt the value of raw land throughout the United States in the 1990s.

Raw land is usually illiquid, meaning that it can be difficult to sell. In addition, unless you rent the land to someone, the property produces no income. Meanwhile, you incur expenses such as maintenance and property taxes. If you borrow to buy the land, you must meet regular interest payments as well. This negative cash flow can drain your budget and makes sense only if you feel sure the land will rise in value soon.

Many factors affect the selling price of land, including the state of the local economy, the direction of interest rates, local zoning and environmental regulations and changing tax laws. Any one of these factors can turn against the owner of raw land. For example, the property may be rezoned to a use with less commercial potential, hurting the land's value. Or the land may be classified as a wetland, making it unsaleable. Or an inspector may find traces of toxic waste from a previous owner that you must clean up before you sell the property. Even if the land is clean, you should determine how difficult it will be to get water, electricity, sewage systems and roads to the site. Before you buy, know everything about a piece of land, including its present condition and development potential.

In most cases, it has been difficult for raw land values to rise much in the face of increasing property tax burdens, strict zoning enforcement and slow economic growth. Buying raw land is therefore the most speculative real estate investment. You might hit it big with a combination of luck and inside knowledge, but don't count on it.

Using Your Computer To Buy and Sell Real Estate

The real estate market has always been considered local. But the advent of the computer and the Internet is quickly transforming bringing real estate into a national marketplace, making it easier for you to buy and sell your home and get financing from lenders anywhere in the country.

All of the major institutions involved in the homebuying and selling business now have a significant presence on the World Wide Web. Mortgage lenders, REALTORS®, builders, relocation firms, home-oriented magazines, housing-related government agencies and many others now have Web sites (listed in the "Resources" section of this chapter) that can educate you about real estate and help you go through much of the homebuying process online:

- *You can use various buy versus rent calculators to evaluate whether it makes sense for you to be buying in the first place.* Other calculators help you determine how much of a mortgage you can afford based on your income and assets.

- *You can shop for homes online through the many REALTOR®-sponsored Web sites.* These sites offer information about various communities you may be interested in, as well as pictures and details about houses for sale. Just type in the name of your REALTOR®'s company to browse these sites. A few examples: Century 21: (www.c21realty.com); Coldwell Banker: (www.coldwellbanker.com); RE/MAX: (www.remax.com).

- *You can shop for the most competitive mortgage rate online.* There now is a national market for mortgages, and you do not have to be limited to what your local lender is offering. These sites are constantly updated with the latest rates on fixed and adjustable loans, points, fees, closing costs and even online applications. A few sample sites to help you tap into this market include: American Mortgage Online (www.amo-mortgage.com); HSH Mortgage Information (www.hsh.com); Mortgage Mart (www. mortgage-mart.com); Mortgage-Net (www.mortgage-net.com) and the Mortgage Rate Shopper Service of the United Homeowners Association, reachable through keyword UHA on America Online.

One of the most complete online services to help you in your real estate decisions is the Real Estate section of America Online. Here is a sample of what it includes:

- *Apartments Plus.* An online listing of apartments for rent in most areas of the country. You can take a Virtual Tour of your choices, with pictures of the interior and exterior of the building and apartment and common areas like lobbies and pools. There are also listings of movers and relocation services to help you find the apartment you can afford.

- *Home Magazine Online.* A wealth of resources from *Home* magazine including information on gardening, decorating, how to build your own home and buyers' guides for home appliances and electronics. The site also hosts chat sessions with housing experts.

- *The Homeowner's Forum,* sponsored by the United Homeowners Association. This site includes sections on home improvement, how to sell your home without a broker, how to get the lowest-interest mortgage, how to find a good home inspector and how to find a qualified remodeling contractor.

- *Homes.com,* sponsored by *Homes and Land* magazine. This site allows you to view homes for sale in almost every state in the country, as seen through free magazines distributed in those states. You can also advertise your home for sale on this site.

- *NAREIT Online.* The National Association of Real Estate Investment Trusts has a site giving you all the information you need on investing in REITs.

- *NARI Online.* The National Association of the Remodeling Industry promotes sound business practices for remodelers. Their Web site has sections on developing a budget, selecting contractors, what should be in a contract and how to satisfy local zoning and housing code laws.

Other features of the AOL Real Estate section are Community Profiles by Century 21, Appliances Online with links to major manufacturers and retailers like General Electric, Home Depot and Whirlpool, and School Match, giving you details on the quality of schools in the district you are thinking of moving into.

As in many other areas of personal finance, the computer is making the real estate market much more efficient. If you take advantage of the power of the computer, you can save thousands of dollars on financing, and end up with the home of your dreams that you might never have found the old-fashioned way.

Investing in real estate—both in your home and in other investment property—will always hold great appeal for Americans. More people in this country have amassed fortunes in real estate than in any other asset. By buying a home, you not only acquire pride of ownership; you get real value out of your property by using it every day, even if its market value falls. Investment real estate offers potential capital appreciation, income and tax breaks—as well as headaches.

The era of the 1970s and early 1980s, when almost every piece of real estate appreciated dramatically, has passed, probably forever. To succeed in real estate investment now, you must study the markets carefully and understand the complex financing options and tax laws that cause values to rise and fall. You need to depend less on luck and more on expertise.

Resources

BOOKS

Art of Real Estate Appraisal, by William L. Ventolo, Jr. and Martha R. Williams, (Real Estate Education Company, 155 N. Wacker Dr., Chicago, IL 60606; 800-322-8621; 800-829-7934; www.dearborn.com). The complete reference on how to appraise the value of your home or evaluate appraisal reports. Up-to-date information on financing techniques, energy efficient construction and home depreciation.

Barron's Real Estate Handbook (Barron's Educational Series, 250 Wireless Blvd., Hauppauge, NY 11788; 516-434-3311; 800-645-3476). Defines real estate terms and gives tips on buying and selling real estate.

Buying More House for Less Money, by Ceil R. Lohmar (McGraw-Hill, Order Dept., 860 Taylor Station Rd., Blacklick, OH 43004; 800-722-4726; www.mcgraw-hill.com). Techniques for house hunting and bargaining to get the best value for your housing dollar.

The Common-Sense Mortgage: How To Cut the Cost of Home Ownership by $100,000 or More, by Peter G. Miller (HarperCollins, 10 E. 53rd St., New York, NY 10022-5299; 212-207-7000; 800-242-7737; www.harpercollins.com). Practical advice about using computerized mortgage loan shopping services, refinancing and the different kinds of mortgages.

Dictionary of Real Estate Terms, by Jack Friedman (Barron's Educational Series, 250 Wireless Blvd., Hauppauge, NY 11788; 516-434-3311; 800-645-3476). A complete guide to the many terms used in the real estate market.

Essentials of Real Estate Finance, by David Sirota (Real Estate Education Company, 155 N. Wacker Dr., Chicago, IL 60606; 800-322-8621; 800-829-7934; www. dearborn.com). Comprehensive reference for consumers and real estate practitioners on qualifying for and selecting the right loan for a home or investment property. Workbook format and questions increase its usefulness as a resource and self-study guide.

Handbook of Real Estate Terms, by Dennis Tosh (Prentice Hall Professional Publishing, 200 Old Tappan Rd., Old Tappan, NJ 07675; 800-223-2336; www.prenhall. com). Defines more than 2,900 real-estate-related terms. Also includes standardized forms for trusts, deeds, appraisals and other real estate transactions.

Home Buyer's Checklist, by Joseph Scutella and D. Heberle (McGraw-Hill, Order Dept., 860 Taylor Station Rd., Blacklick, OH 43004; 800-722-4726; www.mcgraw-hill.com). Provides helpful hints on buying a house.

The Home Buyer's Inspection Guide, by Warren Boroson (John Wiley & Sons Inc., 605 3rd Ave., New York, NY 10158-0012; 212-850-6000; www.wiley.com). Explains how to find and work with a home inspector and what to look for in a home.

The Homebuyer's Kit, by Edith Lank (Dearborn Financial Publishing, 155 N. Wacker Dr., Chicago, IL 60606; 312-836-4400; 800-322-8621; www.dearborn.com). A complete kit designed to take you from the planning stage to the purchase of a home.

The Homeowner's Property Tax Relief Kit, by Vincent and Laurence Czaplyski (McGraw-Hill, Order Dept., 860 Taylor Station Rd., Blacklick, OH 43004; 800-722-4726; www.mcgraw-hill.com). Describes how to lower your property tax bill through protesting assessments and other proven techniques.

The Homeseller's Kit, by Edith Lank (Dearborn Financial Publishing, 155 N. Wacker Dr., Chicago, IL 60606; 312-836-4400; 800-322-8621; www.dearborn.com). Helps you attain the highest possible price for your home with the fewest headaches.

How To Buy Your Own Home in 90 Days, by Marc Stephen Garrison (Doubleday, 1540 Broadway, New York, NY 10036; 800-223-6834; www.bdd.com). A step-by-step workbook that illustrates what it takes to buy the home of your dreams.

How To Evaluate Real Estate Limited Partnerships, by Robert Stanger (Robert A. Stanger & Company, 1129 Broad St., Shrewsbury, NJ 07702; 732-389-3600). Describes how to size up limited partnerships before you invest.

How To Find Hidden Real Estate Bargains, by Robert Irwin (McGraw-Hill, Order Dept., 860 Taylor Station Rd., Blacklick, OH 43004; 800-722-4726; www.mcgraw-hill.com). Explains the process of purchasing attractively priced real estate from distressed sellers and foreclosures, among other techniques.

How To Get the Best Home Loan, by W. Frazier Bell (John Wiley & Sons Inc., 605 3rd Ave., New York, NY 10158-0012; 212-850-6000; www.wiley.com). Describes different types of home loans and how to choose the best one for you.

How To Make or Save Thousands When You Buy or Sell Your House, by Jens and Jackie Nielsen (Doubleday, 1540 Broadway, New York, NY 10036; 800-223-6834; www.bdd.com). A guide, loaded with practical tips, to buying or selling a house.

How To Sell Your Home Without a Broker, by Bill Carey (John Wiley & Sons Inc., 605 3rd Ave., New York, NY 10158-0012; 212-850-6000; www.wiley.com). Explains how to prepare your property for sale and how to find buyers so you can avoid paying the real estate broker's commission.

How To Sell Your House in 90 Days, by Marc Stephen Garrison (Doubleday, 1540 Broadway, New York, NY 10036; 800-223-6834; www.bdd.com). A ten-step plan to sell your house with or without a broker.

Investing in Real Estate, by Andrew James McLean (John Wiley & Sons Inc., 605 3rd Ave., New York, NY 10158-0012; 212-850-6000; www.wiley.com). Explains how to find properties worth buying, how to negotiate the best deal, how to obtain financing and when to sell the properties.

Landlording: A Handy Manual for Scrupulous Landlords and Landladies Who Do It Themselves, by Leigh Robinson (Express Publishing, P.O. Box 1639, El Cerrito, CA 94530; 510-236-5496; www.landlording.com). Describes the rights and responsibilities of landlords, including security deposits, leases, rent control and other matters.

The Landlord's Handbook, by Daniel Goodwin and Richard Rusdorf (Dearborn Financial Publishing, 155 N. Wacker Dr., Chicago, IL 60606; 312-836-4400; 800-322-8621; www.dearborn.com). A complete guide to managing small residential properties. Features more than 50 forms and checklists covering everything from finding good tenants to maximizing tax deductions.

Language of Real Estate, by John W. Reilly (Real Estate Education Company, 155 N. Wacker Dr., Chicago, IL 60606; 800-322-8621; 800-829-7934; www.dearborn.com). Virtually an encyclopedia of real estate with more than 2,800 detailed definitions on appraising, mortgaging, listing, selling or exchanging your property. The ultimate technical reference for real estate owners, practitioners, attorneys or students.

The McGraw-Hill Real Estate Handbook, by Robert Irwin (McGraw-Hill, Order Dept., 860 Taylor Station Rd., Blacklick, OH 43004; 800-722-4726; www.mcgraw-hill.com). A comprehensive treatment of almost every aspect of real estate, including financing techniques, taxes, property management, real estate brokers and investment opportunities in residential, commercial, office and industrial properties.

Modern Real Estate Practice, by Fillmore W. Galaty, Wellington J. Allaway and Robert C. Kyle (Real Estate Education Company, 155 N. Wacker Dr., Chicago, IL 60606; 800-322-8621; 800-829-7934; www.dearborn.com). *The* reference book on every aspect of home buying and selling: the sales transaction, real estate laws, leasing, financing and appraising your home or real estate investment. Includes standardized forms for listing and sales contracts, deeds, appraisals, environmental assessments and a sample mortgage. Also prepares you to become a real estate agent or broker. Available in 20 individual state editions or supplements.

The Mortgage Book, by John R. Dorfman (Consumer Reports Books, P.O. Box 10637, Des Moines, IA 50336; 515-237-4903). Covers the basics of mortgages, including different kinds of loans and how to qualify for a mortgage.

No-Nonsense Landlord: Building Wealth with Rental Properties, by James Jorgenson (McGraw-Hill, Order Dept., 860 Taylor Station Rd., Blacklick, OH 43004; 800-722-4726; www.mcgraw-hill.com). A helpful book if you are thinking of buying a building to generate income.

Real Estate Exchange, edited by Howard A. Zuckerman and Rochelle Stone (McGraw-Hill, Order Dept., 860 Taylor Station Rd., Blacklick, OH 43004; 800-722-4726; www.mcgraw-hill.com). Explains both the investment and the tax aspects of exchanging one property for another.

Real Estate Investing from A to Z, by William Pivar (McGraw-Hill, Order Dept., 860 Taylor Station Rd., Blacklick, OH 43004; 800-722-4726; www.mcgraw-hill.com). A step-by-step guide to successful real estate investing strategies. Describes creative financing techniques, foreclosure and tax sales, subdividing property and managing real estate profitably.

The Real Estate Investor's Survival Guide, by Stuart M. Saft (John Wiley & Sons Inc., 605 3rd Ave., New York, NY 10158-0012; 212-850-6000; www.wiley.com). Covers the basics of real estate investment for the novice.

Real Estate on the Brink: Making Money in Distressed Properties, by Skip Lombardo (McGraw-Hill, Order Dept., 860 Taylor Station Rd., Blacklick, OH 43004; 800-722-4726; www.mcgraw-hill.com). Describes how to make money buying and selling distressed real estate.

Refinance Kit (HSH Associates, 1200 Route 23, Butler, NJ 07405; 201-838-3330; 800-873-2837; www.hsh.com). Explains how to calculate what different mortgages will cost you.

The Saavy Renter's Kit, by Ed Sacks (Dearborn Financial Publishing, 155 N. Wacker Dr., Chicago, IL 60606; 312-836-4400; 800-322-8621; www.dearborn.com). Discusses where to find good rentals, how to inspect the property, how to negotiate a fair lease, how to manage the details of the move and how to resolve disputes with your landlord.

Semenow's Questions and Answers on Real Estate, by Frank J. Blankenship (Prentice Hall, 200 Old Tappan Rd., Old Tappan, NJ 07675; 800-223-2336; www.prenhall.com). A reference book covering the gamut of real estate issues. Includes a fill-in-the-blank, true/false and multiple-choice test on real estate math. Discusses land use, financing techniques, tax laws and real estate buyers' and sellers' rights. Features a glossary of more than 400 commonly used real estate terms.

The Smart Money Guide to Bargain Homes: How To Find and Buy Foreclosures, by James I. Wiedemer (Dearborn Financial Publishing, 155 N. Wacker Dr., Chicago, IL 60606; 312-836-4400; 800-322-8621; www.dearborn.com). A complete guide to finding quality homes in foreclosure with banks and government agencies. Describes how to evaluate foreclosed properties, obtain financing and prepare the paperwork required by government agencies.

Tips and Traps for Making Money in Real Estate, by Robert Irwin (McGraw-Hill, Order Dept., 860 Taylor Station Rd., Blacklick, OH 43004; 800-722-4726; www.mcgraw-hill.com). Reveals the best techniques for buying when prices are low and selling as prices peak. Filled with practical advice for novice real estate investors.

Tips and Traps for Saving on All Your Real Estate Taxes, by Robert Irwin and Norman Lane (McGraw-Hill, Order Dept., 860 Taylor Station Rd., Blacklick, OH 43004; 800-722-4726; www.mcgraw-hill.com). Explains all tax aspects of real estate. Discusses how to reduce property taxes, avoid taxes when selling a home, exchange properties to avoid taxes and plan for tax consequences when you buy a home.

Tips and Traps When Buying a Home, by Robert Irwin (McGraw-Hill, Order Dept., 860 Taylor Station Rd., Blacklick, OH 43004; 800-722-4726; www.mcgraw-hill.com). Reveals how to get a good deal on a home. Discusses how to inspect the home and negotiate for the best price.

Tips and Traps When Mortgage Hunting, by Robert Irwin (McGraw-Hill, Order Dept., 860 Taylor Station Rd., Blacklick, OH 43004; 800-722-4726; www.mcgraw-hill.com). Explains the pros and cons of different kinds of mortgages and helps you determine which is best for you.

Tips and Traps When Selling a Home, by Robert Irwin (McGraw-Hill, Order Dept., 860 Taylor Station Rd., Blacklick, OH 43004; 800-722-4726; www.mcgraw-hill.com). Offers strategies for getting the highest price possible for your home. Gives advice on sprucing up your property, using a real estate broker and negotiating with buyers.

Bob Vila's Guide to Buying Your Dream House, by Bob Vila (Little Brown, 34 Beacon St., Boston, MA 02108; 617-227-0730). A practical guide to inspecting and buying a high-quality house from the man made famous by his TV renovation projects.

Your Home Mortgage, by Michael Thomsett (John Wiley & Sons Inc., 605 3rd Ave., New York, NY 10158-0012; 212-850-6000; www.wiley.com). Explains the basic types of mortgages and how to choose the right one for you.

Your Money and Your Home, by Sidney Lenz (Countrywide Credit, 155 N. Lake Ave., Pasadena, CA 91109-7137; 818-304-8400; 800-669-6064; www.countrywide.

com). A free book from a leading mortgage lender explaining the entire process of acquiring a mortgage, from applying for a loan to closing on the property. Describes how to qualify for a loan, how to balance mortgage debt against your income, how to distinguish different kinds of mortgages and how to refinance a mortgage.

PUBLISHER

Foreclosure Research of America (P.O. Box 10236, Rockville, MD 20849; 301-590-1177; 800-888-7313). Publishes material on purchasing foreclosed properties at bargain prices, then fixing them up and reselling them at a profit. Will send a free brochure titled "The Pre-Foreclosure Hot List." To learn about foreclosed properties, you can subscribe to *Real Estate Owned: Bank Repossessed Properties* and *Houses at Bargain Prices.* Also teaches the public about different types of mortgages available for investment.

MAGAZINES

Creative Real Estate Magazine (Drawer L, Rancho Santa Fe, CA 92067; 619-756-1441). Covers the gamut of real estate investing issues. Features columns on mortgages, tax aspects of real estate, exchanging real estate, single-family homes and distressed property. Includes a directory of real estate exchange groups and a listing of real estate seminars and home-study courses. Incorporates the *Real Estate Observer* and *Investors Association* newsletters. Published since 1972, this magazine is for anyone who wants to make money in real estate. Also sells memberships for the Tape-of-the-Month Club, which presents excerpts from seminars by renowned real estate experts on audiocassette. Offers the home-study course, "The Key to Creative Real Estate Success."

Financial Freedom Report Quarterly (2450 Fort Union Blvd., Salt Lake City, UT 84121; 801-272-5300). A quarterly magazine covering many areas of real estate investment, geared to the individual investor. Discusses property management, finance, negotiation strategies, distressed-property purchases, foreclosure and discounted mortgage investment. Subscription includes an audiocassette featuring interviews with leading real estate experts, as well as membership in the META Institute, which is an academic institution granting a master in real estate investing or professional certification through home-study courses.

Stanger Report (Robert A. Stanger & Company, 1129 Broad St., Shrewsbury, NJ 07702; 732-389-3600). Tracks the limited partnership industry and provides terms of upcoming partnership offerings.

NEWSLETTERS

Real Estate Investing Letter (861 Lafayette Rd., Number 5, Hampton, NH 03842-1232; 603-929-1600). Monthly publication aimed at real estate investors. Discusses tax implications of real estate transactions, how to analyze a real estate deal, how to prepare real estate documents such as loan proposals, partnership agreements and financing packages. Also covers real estate maintenance and employee relations. Provides case studies of failed real estate transactions.

Realty Stock Review (Dow Jones Financial Publishing, 170 Avenue at the Commons, Shrewsbury, NJ 07702; 732-389-8700; www.djfoc.com). Covers real estate investment trusts and recommends REITs to buy and sell.

John T. Reed's Real Estate Investor's Monthly (John T. Reed Publishing, 342 Bryan Dr., Danville, CA 94526; 510-820-6292; 800-635-5425). Aimed at serious investors in real estate. Features such subjects as apartment conversion projects, bargain hunting, equity sharing, investment strategies, limited partnerships, property exchanges, refinancing techniques and tax laws. In addition to newsletter, publisher offers the following publications: *Aggressive Tax Avoidance for Real Estate Investors; Distressed Real Estate Times: Offensive and Defensive Strategy and Tactics; How To Buy Real Estate for at Least 20% below Market Value; How To Do a Delayed Exchange; How To Increase the Value of Real Estate; How To Manage Residential Property for Maximum Cash Flow and Resale Value; How To Use Leverage to Maximize Your Real Estate Investment Return; Office Building Acquisition Handbook; Real Estate Investment Strategy; Residential Property Acquisition Handbook;* and *Single-Family Lease Options.*

REIT Line (National Association of Real Estate Investment Trusts, 1129 20th St., N.W., Suite 705, Washington, DC 20036; 202-785-8717; www.nareit.com). Covers the real estate investment trust industry.

NEWSPAPERS

National Mortgage News (1110 Plaza, New York, NY 10001; 212-967-7000; www.faulknergray.com). Covers the mortgage market and mortgage lenders, such as savings and loans and mortgage bankers.

Real Estate Weekly (1 Madison Ave., Suite 25A, New York, NY 10010; 212-679-1234). The only weekly real estate newspaper in the United States. Concentrates on the New York real estate market.

SOFTWARE AND SERVICES

America Online (8619 Westwood Center Dr., Vienna, VA 22182; 800-827-6364, ext. 5764; www.aol.com). A nationwide electronic bulletin board accessible to DOS, Windows and Macintosh users. Members may ask real estate questions, check daily mortgage rates, download software, read articles and post messages on the AOL MLS to buy, sell, exchange or rent property anywhere in the country. Open to brokers and nonbrokers.

Buying Your Home and *Mastering Your Mortgage* (Home Equity Software, 202 Montebello Ave., Suite 9, Mountain View, CA 94043; 415-967-4965; www.isnetwork.

com). Help you determine whether to buy a home or to rent, given your financial situation, and what mortgage best suits your needs.

Buy or Rent (Real Estate Consultants, 46 A Myerhoss Pl., Oradell, NJ 07649-2654; 800-289-6773). Helps you analyze whether to buy a home or to rent based on a number of factors, including your tax rate, housing costs and potential housing appreciation.

Home Buyer's Mortgage Kit (HSH Associates, 1200 Route 23N, Butler, NJ 07405; 800-873-2837; www.hsh.com). For a nominal fee, provides a list of banks and savings and loans that might offer a mortgage on a property based on its location and your income. You are given a computer print-out listing the lending institutions' latest interest rates, points and fees, as well as other details. You then choose several mortgages that interest you, and the service has the banks or savings and loans contact you. Can save you an enormous amount of time and money and introduce you to lenders you might not find on your own.

MacFreedom (Financial Freedom Report, 240 E. Morris Ave., Salt Lake City, UT 84115; 801-463-6502). Analyzes investment real estate; property management; real estate forms such as leases, purchase agreements and contracts; mortgage reduction plans; utility bill reduction systems; and property tax reduction software.

Mortgage Analyzer (Insight Software Solutions, P.O. Box 354, Bountiful, UT 84011-0354; 801-295-1890; www.wintools.com). Helps you assess your mortgage options. Determines whether you can qualify for a loan, whether it is worth refinancing your mortgage and how various mortgages affect your taxes. Includes amortization tables and information on closing costs, points, property taxes, mortgage insurance and other aspects of mortgage finance.

TRADE ASSOCIATIONS

American Homeowners Foundation (1724 S. Quincy St., Arlington, VA 22204; 703-979-4663). Dedicated to helping homeowners maintain and upgrade their homes. Offers model home-improvement contracts. Offers free brochure about the foundation.

American Resort Development Association (1220 L St., N.W., Suite 500, Washington, DC 20005; 202-371-6700; www.arda.com). Represents the vacation ownership industry, including timeshares, lot sales, golf resorts, recreational vehicles and campground resorts. Lobbies on issues related to timeshare resorts and provides information about buying and selling timeshares. The most popular publications offered by ARDA include *The Benefits of Timeshare Ownership: Results from a Nationwide Survey of Timeshare Owners; Consumer's Guide to Resort and Urban Timesharing; Financial Performance in the Timeshare Industry; Guide for Fractional Vacation Ownership and Development; Guide to Timeshare Housekeeping; Timeshare Property Assessment and Taxation;* and *Vacation Ownership: Time of Your Life! Consumer Guide.*

American Society of Home Inspectors (85 W. Algonquin Rd., Arlington Heights, IL 60005; 847-290-1959). Publishes guidelines detailing what home inspectors are and are not expected to do. For example, they are expected to inspect a home's structural components, roofing, doorways, windows, plumbing, heating and electrical systems and insulation; they are not expected to estimate the life expectancy of a component, offer warranties, perform engineering services or inspect home appliances. Will send a free *Standards of Practice* publication giving details on dealing with a home inspector.

Appraisal Institute (875 N. Michigan Ave., Suite 2400, Chicago, IL 60611-1980; 312-335-4100; www.appraisal institute.org). Represents real estate appraisers. Formed out of the unification of the American Institute of Real Estate Appraisers and the Society of Real Estate Appraisers. Sets minimum standards for real estate appraising and confers several professional designations. Publishes the *Appraiser News* and *Appraisal Journal* newsletters. Will refer you to a qualified appraiser near your home.

Commercial Investment Real Estate Institute (430 N. Michigan Ave., Suite 600, Chicago, IL 60611; 312-321-4460; www.ccim.com). Represents those involved in commercial and investment-oriented real estate. Confers the Certified Commercial Investment Member (CCIM) designation on developers, brokers, property managers, corporate real estate executives, asset managers, institutional lenders or others involved in any aspect of commercial real estate. Can help those interested in learning more about investing in commercial property.

Investment Program Association (607 14th St., N.W., Suite 1000, Washington, DC 20005; 202-775-9750). The trade association for limited partnerships, many of which are real estate partnerships sold by brokerage firms.

Mortgage Bankers Association of America (1125 15th St., N.W., Washington, DC 20005; 202-861-6500; www.mbaa.org). The trade group of mortgage bankers. Offers the following publications: *A Consumer's Glossary of Mortgage Terms; A Consumer's Guide to Mortgage Lock-ins; A Consumer's Guide to Mortgage Settlement Costs; A Consumer's Guide to Refinancing Your Mortgage; Deducting Your Mortgage Interest under the Tax Code; How Much House Can I Afford: A Self-Test; How To Save Half on Interest Costs: A Consumer's Guide to 15-Year Fixed-Rate Mortgages; How To Shop for a Mortgage; What Happens after You Apply for a Mortgage; When Your Loan Is Transferred to Another Lender—A Consumer's Guide;* and *Why Mortgage Escrows?*

National Association of Home Builders (1201 15th St., N.W., Washington, DC 20005; 202-822-0200; 800-368-5242; www.nahb.com). Represents single-family and multifamily home builders, remodelers and others associated with the home-building industry, such as those involved in mortgage finance and building products and services. Some local associations run consumer dispute resolution programs. The association's Home Builders Institute develops educational and job-training programs related to home building. Offers information on various home-buying issues, such as settling problems with builders and buying a new home. Sells two books titled *Dreams to Beams: A Guide to Building the Home You've Always Wanted* and *Understanding House Construction* through the following toll-free phone number: 800-223-2665. Operates the Home Builder Bookstore, which publishes a book catalog you can obtain at no charge. Books in the catalog include *Land Development; Managing a Home Building Business; Marketing and Selling New Homes; Multihousing; New Home Design and Construction;* and *Remodeling.* Publishes the following brochures aimed at the home-buying public: "Choosing Your Builder"; "How To Choose a Remodeler Who's on the Level"; "Make Your Move to a New Home . . . Now"; "Your Home Buying Power"; and "Your New Home and How To Take Care of It."

National Association of Master Appraisers (P.O. Box 12617, 303 W. Cypress St., San Antonio, TX 78212-0617; 210-271-0781; 800-229-NAMA; www.mfahousing. com/lqc). Represents those involved in real estate appraisal, including appraisers, assessors, brokers, salespeople, developers and bankers. Publishes guidelines detailing appraisers' responsibilities and offers continuing education for appraisers. Will send free brochures titled "Issues in Appraising" and "Your Real Estate Appraisal." The association is also home to the Real Estate Law Institute, which compiles an annual *Registry of Real Estate Specialists,* which is available free of charge when you call 800-486-3676 or write to P.O. Box 12528, San Antonio, TX 78212-0528.

National Association of Real Estate Investment Trusts (1129 20th St., N.W., Suite 305, Washington, DC 20036; 202-785-8717; www.nareit.com). Offers a free brochure titled "Most Frequently Asked Questions about REITs." Also produces the *REIT-Watch* newsletter, the *REIT Report,* the *REIT Fact Book* and the *REIT Handbook: The Complete Guide to the Real Estate Investment Trust Industry,* which names all publicly traded REITs and provides statistics on the industry.

National Association of REALTORS® (430 N. Michigan Ave., Chicago, IL 60611; 312-329-8200; 800-874-6500; www.realtor.com). The trade group for real estate agents. Offers the following consumer-oriented publications: *Buying a Home? Working with a Realtor; If You Are Thinking Investment, Think Real Estate; Selling or Buying a Home . . . It Pays To Work with a REALTOR®; Selling Your Home? Work with a REALTOR®; Sixteen Essentials for Greater Profits; Speed the Sale of Your Home—Sell It for Every Dollar It's Worth!;* and *Your American Dream Home—The Complete Guide to Buying or Selling Your Home.* Affiliated with the following groups at the same address: American Society of Real Estate Counselors, which confers the Counselor of Real Estate (CRE) designation on those who give real estate investment advice; Institute of Real Estate Management, which confers the Certified Property Manager (CPM) and Accredited Residential Manager (ARM) designations on those who manage real estate properties; REALTORS® Land Institute, which confers the Accredited Land Consultant (ALC) designation on those experts in all facets of buying and selling agricultural, urban, transitional and recreational land; REALTORS® National

Marketing Institute, which confers the Certified Real Estate Brokerage Manager (CRB) and Certified Residential Specialist (CRS) designations on brokers experienced in running brokerage offices and active in residential real estate; Society of Industrial and Office REALTORS®, which confers the Professional Real Estate Executive (PRE) designation on experts in industrial and office real estate transactions; and Women's Council of REALTORS®, which confers the Leadership Training Graduate (LTG) designation on women who have exhibited leadership.

National Center for Home Equity Conversion (7373 147th St. West, Suite 115, Apple Valley, MN 55124; 612-953-4474). Helps those with equity in their homes find a lender that will grant a reverse mortgage. Publishes a book titled *Retirement Income on the House: Cashing in on Your Home with a "Reverse" Mortgage,* which describes how reverse mortgages work. The book includes a *Reverse Mortgage Locator,* which lists all reverse mortgage lenders in the country.

National Real Estate Investors Association (4250 Perimeter Park South, Suite 124, Atlanta, GA 30341; 770-451-4900). A parent organization for independent chapters of real estate associations in large metropolitan areas across the United States. Provides such services to investors as seminars, home-study courses, property management materials and group purchasing power to buy supplies such as carpeting and paint. Acts as a clearinghouse for lobbying on real-estate-related issues. Its newsletter is incorporated in *Creative Real Estate* magazine.

United Homeowners Association (1511 K St., NW, Washington DC, 20005; 202-408-8808). Group representing American homeowners. They are a resource for helping homeowners save money when buying or selling a home, remodeling, financing or refinancing, and getting homeowner's insurance. The UHA also lobbies for homeowner rights with the federal government. Members receive a great deal of educational material on buying, financing and maintaining their homes and are eligible for discounts on appliances, insurance, and housing-related publications. Members also have access to UHA's Mortgage Rate Shopper, which is designed to help you get the most advantageous mortgage rate. Their Web site, accessible through keyword UHA on America Online, explains their services in more detail and answers many questions you may have about home ownership.

WEB SITES

American Mortgage Online A great place to look for a home lender. The site lets you search out the best deals by state and even apply for prequalification online. It also has many articles about the mortgage qualification and approval process. www. amortgage.com

America's HomeNet A detailed database of home listings in most areas of the country. Also includes data about local schools, businesses and lenders. www.netprop. com/homenet.htm

Consumer Mortgage Information Network A great source to find the best mortgage. The site has links to many realtors and lenders around the country, and hundreds of useful educational articles on the entire homebuying and mortgage-finding process. www.pacificrim.net/~proactiv/cmin/first.html

Cyberhomes Listings of homes for sale over the Internet, including pictures, the listing REALTOR®'s name and phone number, and e-mail addresses. www.cyberhomes.com/

Homebuyer's Fair A complete site about homebuying, including an affordability analyzer, a buy-versus-rent calculator, articles on home costs around the country, listings of mortgage rates and much more. www.homefair.com

Interactive Homebuying on the Web A basic rundown of the steps in buying a house, financing the purchase and closing the deal. www.maxsol.com/homes/steps.html

Mortgage Mart A comprehensive hubsite for mortgage information, including current rates, a long list of lenders, online loan applications, mortgage calculators and details about government lending programs. www.mortgage-mart.com/

Mortgage Terms A compendium of the language you will need to buy or sell a house. www.yournewhouse.com/mtgterms.html

National Average Mortgage Rates A complete listing of national mortgage rates so you can compare what you are considering against national averages. www.interest.com/ave.htm

FEDERAL GOVERNMENT REGULATORS

Department of Housing and Urban Development (451 7th St., S.W., Washington, DC 20410; 202-708-1422; www.hud.gov). The main regulatory agency overseeing housing and real estate issues. HUD's Office of Fair Housing and Equal Opportunity (800-669-9777) can be contacted if you think you have been a victim of housing discrimination.

Federal National Mortgage Association (3900 Wisconsin Ave., N.W., Washington, DC 20016; 202-752-7000; www.fanniemae.com). Creates a secondary market in mortgage-backed securities. Offers several brochures about real estate, including "Fannie Mae National Housing Survey"; "Home Equity Conversion Mortgages: You've Worked Years To Own Your Home. Now It's Time Your Home Worked for You"; "Housing America: Fannie Mae and the Dream of Homeownership"; "How To Buy a Foreclosed Home"; and "Unraveling the Mortgage Loan Mystery."

Federal Reserve Board (20th Street and C Street, N.W., Washington, DC 20551; 202-452-3946; www.fedweb.frb.gov). Oversees bank and savings and loan mortgage lending. Branches offer several free brochures, including "Comparing Average Mortgage Costs"; "Comparing Mortgage Rates"; "Consumer's Guide to Mortgage Closing Costs"; "Consumer's Guide to Mortgage Lock-Ins"; "Consumer's Guide to Mortgage Refinancing"; "Consumer Handbook on Adjustable Rate Mortgages";

"Financing Your Home"; "Home Improvement Credit: Avoiding Second Mortgage Fraud"; "Home Mortgages: Understanding the Process and Your Right to Fair Lending"; "Homeownership"; and "When Your Home Is on the Line: What You Should Know about Home Equity Lines of Credit."

Federal Trade Commission (6th Street and Pennsylvania Avenue, N.W., Washington, DC 20580; 202-326-2222; www.ftc.gov). Has jurisdiction over many real-estate-related practices. Will send a free copy of the following brochures: "Getting a Loan: Your Home as Security"; "Home Equity Credit Lines"; "Home Financing Primer"; "Land Sales Scams"; "Lawn Service Contracts"; "The Mortgage Money Guide"; "Mortgage Servicing"; "Real Estate Brokers"; "Refinancing Your Home"; "Reverse Mortgages"; "Second Mortgage Financing"; "Timeshare Resales"; "Timeshare Tips"; "Using Ads To Shop for Home Financing"; and "Your Home, Your Choice (Living Choices for Older Americans)."

Office of Thrift Supervision (1700 G St., N.W., Washington, DC 20552; 202-906-6000; www.ots.treas.gov). Oversees the nation's savings and loan industry.

Frequent Flier Miles Mortgage Programs

Some airlines have started to link up with mortgage lenders, allowing you to accumulate thousands of frequent flier miles while you buy and pay for your house. The largest such program is run by American Airlines. Under their AAdvantage Program for Mortgages, you can earn 15,000 AAdvantage miles per $100,000 of purchase or sale price of your home, if you use a real estate broker enrolled in the program. If you sign up for a mortgage through a lender enrolled in the program, you qualify for one AAdvantage mile for each dollar in interest you pay on your mortgage. This applies whether you are refinancing your existing home or financing a new one. For more information on this program, call 800-852-9744 or visit their Web site at www.americanair.com. United Airlines offers a similar program called Residential Rewards at 800-717-5330 or www.unitedair.com. TWA has hooked up with the Better Homes and Gardens real estate network at 800-654-5409 or www.twa.com. Continental Airlines has affiliated with the Prudential Referral Services at 800-732-7391 or www.flycontinental.com. Check with your favorite airline to see if they have added such a program recently.

No-Down-Payment Mortgages

Several mortgage lenders will now finance 100 percent of your home's purchase price if you can put a certain amount of securities in escrow to act as your down payment. For example, Merrill Lynch's Mortgage 100 program (800-854-7154; www.ml.com) requires that you place 30 percent of your home's purchase price in escrow in securities. If you were buying a $100,000 house, you would have to place a bit more than $30,000 worth of CDs, stocks, bonds or mutual funds in escrow to get full financing. Merrill also offers the Parent Power program at the same phone number, which allows parents to place their securities in escrow for a bit over 30 percent of the purchase price for their children's home purchase. Since the securities put in escrow do not have to be sold, you can avoid the capital gains tax that would normally be required if you sold securities to assemble a down payment.

WARRANTY SERVICE

Home Warranty (P.O. Box 152087, Irving, TX 75015-2087; 800-433-7657; www. howcorp.com). Helps those who have purchased homes covered by the Home Owners Warranty (HOW) program resolve complaints against builders. HOW, funded voluntarily by home builders and originally established by the National Association of Home Builders, provides liability insurance to home builders. That insurance, in turn, allows the builders to give buyers of newly built homes a two-year limited warranty on workmanship and on materials, systems and major structural defects.

PART
II

Financing Your Present and Future Needs

9

You and Your Credit—
Managing It Wisely

Credit has become indispensable to everyday life in the United States. To some people, it is a convenience; to others, a necessity. Whatever your attitude toward credit and loans, the subject is hard to ignore. If you take control of your credit obligations, you can increase your wealth, cut your taxes and buy what you need when you need it without paying a king's ransom in interest. On the other hand, if you relinquish control of your credit obligations and let your debts mount, credit payments can consume a disproportionate amount of your disposable income. The choice is yours.

Credit provides the ability to buy something now, when you lack cash, and pay for it later. Whether you purchase a small toy or a large house, the principle remains the same. For the convenience of obtaining the item on credit, you must pay a fee called *interest*. Think of interest as rent on money you borrow from a lender, whether that be a bank, credit union, savings and loan or retail store. When you have the cash to pay off the loan, either in a lump sum or over an extended period of time, you can stop paying "rent" (until you borrow again).

The ability to buy something with an instant loan is a double-edged sword. On one hand, it is a privilege to take home something of value without having the cash to pay for it. On the other hand, it creates an obligation to repay the debt. The longer you take to pay off the loan, the more it will cost you in interest. Since it is so tempting to say "charge it" and to worry about the bills later, proper use of credit requires more self-discipline than do many other areas of personal finance. In general, you should borrow when you must finance the purchase of something that will grow in value over time, like a house or a college education. The worst things to finance include items that are consumed quickly—such as food or vacations—and, worst of all, other debts.

Credit has become so ingrained in the U.S. consumer's psyche that it is hard to imagine our lives without it. For example, you would find it difficult to check into a hotel, rent a car or buy an airline ticket without a credit card. You probably could not afford a home without assuming a mortgage. And you might never make it through the Christmas season without charging your purchases on your retail store accounts and paying for the gifts over the next several months. Yet many people who have abused their borrowing privileges find themselves cut off from this normal world of commerce because they no longer qualify for credit. To ensure that you do not join these ranks, learn all you can about credit and how to make the most of it.

Open-End Versus Closed-End Credit

Two general categories of credit exist: *open-end* and *closed-end.*

OPEN-END CREDIT

Open-end credit, also known as *revolving credit*, provides a line of borrowing that you can tap into at will and pay back as quickly or slowly as you want (as long as you pay the minimum required each month.) Open-end credit is extended by stores, credit card issuers, banks and other lenders and can be drawn upon by check or credit card. Each month, you receive a bill from the lender specifying the total amount you owe, the interest you must pay and your minimum payment. To stay current, you can pay the minimum, the full amount or anything in between. If you pay your bills responsibly over time, the lender will probably increase your credit line, giving you more borrowing power.

When shopping for open-end credit, compare the following elements of one loan with the same elements of another loan to get the best deal.

Annual percentage rate (APR). A loan's interest cost must be stated as an annual percentage. The finance charge rate may be as high as 21 percent or as low as 8 percent, but when the rate is stated as an APR, you can easily compare one loan to another. In general, the more creditworthy you are, the lower your APR will be. Each month, personal finance magazines, such as, *Money, Kiplinger's Personal Finance* and others publish a list of the banks charging the lowest APRs in the country. You can also get such a list from various Web sites listed in the "Resources" section at the end of this chapter. Some lenders charge a fixed APR, while others levy a finance charge that rises and falls based on the movement of an underlying index, such as the prime rate or yields on government securities.

Finance charge calculations. Lenders use varying methods to determine your average daily balance, on which finance charges are calculated. The most common method is the *average daily balance level,* in which each month's daily balances are added together, then divided by the number of days in the month. Some banks include new purchases when calculating the average daily balance, and some exclude them. Other banks calculate the average daily balance for two billing cycles—the current and the previous—while some calculate the balance based on the current cycle only. When shopping for open-end credit, look for a loan that calculates charges based on the most recent cycle and that excludes new purchases.

While these methods of calculating finance charges can be confusing, they can result in vastly different amounts of interest due. In one example, banks can calculate the finance charges on one account four different ways. The account begins its first month with a zero balance. The account holder then charges $1,000 and makes the minimum payment. The next month, the account holder charges another $1,000 and pays off the balance due. The account's interest rate is 19.8 percent. The calculations result in the following figures:

Average daily balance method, including new purchases: $33
Average daily balance method, excluding new purchases: $16.50
Two-cycle average daily balance method, including new purchases: $49.05
Two-cycle average daily balance method, excluding new purchases: $32.80

To make the situation even more confusing, some lenders use the *previous balance method*, in which they base the finance charge on the amount owed at the end of the previous billing period. Still other lenders use the *adjusted balance method*, in which they subtract all payments made during the month, then add finance charges. The only way to avoid this morass is to pay off your balance every month.

Grace period. The amount of time a lender allows before charging interest on the loan is called the *grace period*. Typically, many credit card companies give 25 days from the date of the bill before they assess finance charges. If a company offers no grace period, you pay interest from the moment the bank learns of a charge to your account even though you haven't received a bill yet. Clearly, having a grace period is a plus because it allows you to stretch out your payments over several weeks. To take maximum advantage of the grace period, note when your bank usually sends out its bills. Then, you should charge items on an account immediately after the bill goes out. For example, if a bank mails bills on the 15th of the month, your charges from the 16th on will appear on next month's bill, giving you almost a two-month grace period. To maximize this strategy, it is best to have three credit cards, each billing in a different part of the month. So, for example, if one card bills on the 5th, the second on the 15th and the third on the 25th, you will always have a time during the month when the bill was put in the mail recently. Use that card when you make a purchase.

Annual fees. Many credit grantors charge an annual fee that ranges from as little as $15 for a simple credit card to as much as $300 for a platinum American Express card. Banks justify these fees by the services they offer, including discount travel and buying plans, 24-hour service and other extras. In general, the higher the annual fee, the larger your credit line. To some extent, a trade-off may exist between the annual fee and the interest rate: The lower the rate, the higher the fee. Some banks even have had the audacity to charge annual fees if you do *not* use your card, or if you do not pay any finance charges because you pay off your balance every month. Still, many banks, such as those listed each month in the "Monitor" department of *Money* magazine, offer credit cards with no annual fee.

Minimum payment. Depending on your credit record and the lender's policy, the minimum amount you must pay on your loan each month will vary. Some banks set a high minimum if they are unsure of your reliability. Others set a low minimum in hopes you will pay only that amount, thereby accruing more interest charges on your outstanding balance.

Late fees. Most lenders charge a set fee of about $10 to $20 if they do not receive payment by the due date. Many banks also assess such a penalty if you exceed your credit limit. This is called an *over-limit fee.*

Transaction fees. Some banks charge pesky little fees every time you make a purchase or take a cash advance against your credit line. Each fee may total only a few dollars, but they can add up if you initiate many transactions.

CLOSED-END CREDIT

The other type of credit, known as *closed-end credit*, provides a fixed amount of money to finance a specific purchase for a preset period of time. Lenders such as banks, savings and loans, credit unions, retailers, mortgage companies and others offer loans to help fund major purchases, such as cars, houses, appliances, boats or furniture. Borrowers must make set monthly payments for a number of months or years until the loans are retired.

Like lenders of open-end loans, lenders of closed-end loans—under the Truth-in-Lending Act—must disclose every loan's APR and finance charge. They also must inform you of other such fees as appraisal fees, service charges, credit insurance premiums and processing fees.

Closed-end loans offer both *fixed-interest rates* and *variable-interest rates.* Fixed-rate loans guarantee that you will pay the same interest rate for the life of the loan, which protects you if the general level of interest rates rises. Adjustable-rate loans charge interest rates that shift up or down based on the movement of an underlying index, such as the prime rate or yields on Treasury securities. To induce you to assume the increased risk of an adjustable-rate loan, lenders typically start off such loans with interest rates lower than fixed-rate loans offer. If interest rates remain constant or fall, you win. But if interest rates rise sharply over the term of the loan, you can end up owing substantially more than you expected. Adjustable-rate loans offer annual caps as well as lifetime caps, so you know how high your APR can rise each year, and over the life of the loan.

Whether you should choose a fixed- or an adjustable-rate loan depends on several factors. First, look at the index to which the adjustable-rate loan is tied. If it is a short-term rate that is particularly volatile, such as the prime rate or yields on Treasury bills, you expose yourself to far more risk than you do if the loan is tied to the average mortgage rate or to long-term Treasury bonds. Also, determine how frequently the loan rate can change. Some reset every month, while some change once every year or even every five years. Clearly, the less frequent the changes, the less risk you assume. Some adjustable-rate loans, called *convertible loans,* offer the option of converting to a fixed-rate loan at several specific dates in the future.

You should also consider whether you could afford the adjustable-rate loan if the rate soared to its lifetime cap. If that level of interest would drain your income or savings, you probably should not assume the loan. On the other hand, if you think you could invest wisely the extra cash resulting from the adjustable-rate loan's lower interest charge, the added risk may be worthwhile.

For instance, if you borrow $10,000 for five years at a fixed rate of 10 percent, you must pay $1,000 each year in interest, or a total of $5,000 over the life of the loan. If, instead, you borrow the same $10,000 at an adjustable rate of 7 percent, you must pay only $700 the first year. If you invest the $300 difference in a stock mutual fund that provides a 15 percent, you will collect about $600 in five years, which could be more than you must pay in interest—even if rates rise a bit. If you continue to invest the $300 in interest every year, your capital will compound far more than it will under the fixed loan, and you will find yourself ahead of where you would have been with the fixed loan and $5,000 in interest charges.

Secured Versus Unsecured Credit

Lenders use two other terms to distinguish loans: *secured* and *unsecured.* One type of secured loan is backed by a particular asset, known as *collateral,* which the lender can seize if you stop payments on your loan. The lender will try to ensure that the collateral is worth more than the outstanding balance on the loan, so if you default, the lender can sell the asset at market prices to recoup its losses. Collateral can be a diamond ring, a car, a boat, a home or anything else of quantifiable value.

Another form of secured loan is a *secured credit card.* In this case, you deposit a certain amount of cash with the credit card issuer in return for a credit line of the same size. For instance, you might deposit $1,000 with a bank to qualify for a $1,000 credit line. The bank will pay some interest, usually 2 percent or 3 percent, on that deposit. If you default on your credit card payments, the bank can seize enough money from your deposit to cover your debt. Opening a secured credit line is one way to establish a good credit record if you don't yet have a credit history or to re-establish good credit if you have a history of poor credit. You can obtain a list of secured credit card issuers from CardTrak (800-344-7714 or various Web sites listed in the "Resources" section of this chapter). Some banks that consistently rank at the top of the best secured credit card lists include:

Amalgamated Bank of Chicago; 800-365-6464
American Pacific Bank; 800-610-1201
Bank One Arizona; 800-544-4110
Chase USA; 800-482-4273

Community Bank of Parker; 800-779-8472
Orchard Bank; 800-488-2720
Union Planters Bank; 800-628-8946
United National Bank; 800-937-4600

With unsecured credit, lenders do not demand that a specific asset be pledged as collateral. Instead, lenders extend credit to you because of your general record of reliability and stable source of income.

In general, the interest rates charged on unsecured credit are higher than those levied on secured loans because lenders take a greater risk, relying on your promise to pay rather than on their ability to seize collateral.

Truth-in-Lending Rules

No matter what kind of credit you desire, the federal Truth-in-Lending Act requires that lenders provide certain information so that you can compare one loan to another. Some of the most important facts lenders must provide include the following:

- Company providing the loan or credit line
- Size of the loan or credit line in dollars
- List of those charges that your payments cover, including taxes, fees, interest, etc.
- Finance charge, in dollars and as an APR
- Expected repayment schedule, including when payments must be made and the minimum payments required
- Total payments due for an installment loan or a mortgage, as well as the sales price of the item financed
- Annual fees, if any
- Length of grace period, if any, before payment must be made
- Prepayment penalties, if any, and how they are calculated
- Late payment fees, if any, and how they are calculated
- Rules under which a lender can seize your security deposit if you do not make scheduled payments
- Fees for credit insurance, if any, which pays off your loan if you die before the debt is fully repaid

Types of Loans

Within the broad categories of open-end, closed-end, secured and unsecured credit, many types of loans exist, depending on your borrowing needs. Following is a rundown of the most common forms of credit, with tips to help you snare the best deal in each.

CREDIT CARD LOANS

Credit cards, issued by banks, savings and loans, credit unions, airlines, retail stores, oil companies, brokerage firms and other financial institutions, assign you a preset credit limit. You can charge any amount up to that limit, either to purchase merchandise or to obtain a cash advance. Most credit cards offer a grace period that allows you to avoid paying interest on your purchases. Others charge interest from the moment your sales slips arrive at the banks.

The majority of credit card companies charge a fixed-interest rate, which the companies adjust upward or downward over time. A few credit card issuers provide variable-rate cards, on which the interest rate floats on a month-to-month basis in line with market interest rates.

Most credit cards collect an annual fee; however, many no longer levy such a charge. If your cards carry hefty balances on which you pay interest every month, opt for the cards charging the lowest interest you can find. If you tend to pay off your balance in full every month, obtain a card with no annual fee and a slightly higher interest rate, which will not affect you.

In addition to company credit cards' interest rates and annual fees, compare their benefits and services. Cards often offer discounts on merchandise, hotels, car rentals and auto clubs and free mileage on airline frequent-flier plans. Some cards offer free replacement of lost or stolen merchandise, extensions of product warranties, automatic air travel insurance and lost or damaged baggage insurance and a free collision damage waiver when you rent a car. Other credit card companies provide emergency medical and legal service, emergency cash and card replacement and credit card registry services. Many cards offer 24-hour customer-service phone lines. Increasingly, card companies provide a year-end statement separating your purchases into various categories to help you budget and detect tax deductions. Most card issuers also provide a gold version of their card, which has a higher credit line and more benefits at an increased annual fee.

Visa and MasterCard, which authorize the two most frequently issued cards, actually do not distribute credit cards themselves. Instead, they act as franchise organizations that license member banks to offer cards featuring the Visa or MasterCard name. Each issuer then sets its own policies within broad guidelines prescribed by Visa and MasterCard covering the interest rate the issuer charges, the applicants it accepts and the benefits and services it provides.

Traditionally, only banks issued Visas and MasterCards. In recent years, however, manufacturing companies like General Motors and General Electric, as well as long-distance phone companies like AT&T, have begun distributing the cards. They all compete to offer credit cards that earn "credits" they hope you will spend on GM cars, GE appliances or AT&T long-distance calls. Before you obtain one of these issuer's cards, however, determine whether you want the products or services that these credits earn.

Another outpouring of credit cards originates from affinity groups, which might include your professional association, college alumni group or favorite charity. Every purchase you charge on the card earns the group a certain amount of money, without costing you anything extra.

Another card emblazoned with the Visa or MasterCard symbol, called a *debit card*, is not a credit card. Debit cards are accepted by merchants like credit cards; however, when you use such a card, the charge is immediately withdrawn from your bank checking account. You do not receive a bill, nor do you pay interest. However, you lose the benefit of floating your money during the grace period of a credit card.

Travel and entertainment (T&E) cards like American Express, Carte Blanche and Diners Club are both like and unlike regular and gold bank credit cards. Like credit cards, they let you charge purchases and pay for them later. T&E cards also charge an annual fee based on whether you have a regular, a gold or even a platinum card. The higher the card level, the more benefits and services offered, though you might not find them useful.

Unlike bank cards, T&E cards do not impose a spending limit. They allow you to charge whatever you want; however, they track your spending patterns. If a company's representatives are asked to authorize a purchase much larger than you normally make, they will question it to make sure you can pay the bill. The other major difference between bank and T&E credit cards is that the entire T&E balance is due in full each month. If you want to extend payment, most T&E cards will offer a credit line. You just fill in the check provided with your bill, and the bank issuing the credit line will charge you interest. The credit line issuer is always different from the T&E card issuer. You can also tap this credit line by withdrawing cash from an automatic teller machine, such as the Express Cash machines operated by American Express in airports and hotels across the country.

When you have sized up your credit, debit and T&E card needs, settle on two or three cards that offer the best benefits at the most favorable interest rates and fees. (You might want to consult *CardTrak* 800-344-7714 or the Web sites listed at the end of this chapter, to find the best deals.) Consolidate all of your purchases on these cards, and cut up or send back any other cards that you will no longer use. It's best to eliminate the temptation of owning too many cards.

HOME EQUITY LOANS

If you have accumulated equity in your home, you might take out a *home equity loan* to pay off other installment loans. First, home equity interest is generally fully deductible up to $100,000 on your federal and state income tax. And because they are secured, home equity loans charge a much lower interest rate than do unsecured credit cards. You usually must pay only 1 percent to 2 percent more than the current prime rate on a home equity loan. However, if the prime rate rises sharply, your interest costs also increase. Most home equity lines offer a *periodic cap,* usually the maximum your rate can jump in one year, as well as a *lifetime cap,* the highest your rate can ever climb. These provide some, but not too much, protection against soaring rates because lifetime caps are usually very high—often 15 percent to 20 percent.

Generally, home equity loans are not inexpensive or easy to qualify for. Most lenders put you through several procedures similar to applying for a mortgage and impose a litany of up-front charges, including title search, appraisal, application and attorney's fees. In some cases, you can negotiate with the lender to absorb some of these costs. The largest up-front cost, however, called *points*, is really an add-on fee in the form of prepaid interest to the lender. One point equals 1 percent of the credit line you open. For instance, if you establish a $100,000 home equity line of credit, one point would total $1,000, due at the time your loan closes. Some lenders charge two or three points, which would amount to $2,000 or $3,000 on a $100,000 loan. Nonetheless, competition in the marketplace has induced some lenders to offer *no-points home equity loans*, though such loans may charge higher interest rates than loans requiring points. You can consult an updated list of the home equity loans charging the lowest rates and points in the "Monitor" section of *Money* magazine each month.

In addition to up-front fees, some lenders levy an annual fee or a transaction charge every time you write a check on your credit line. Make sure you know about these fees before you commit to a particular lender.

Lenders will typically provide a credit line of up to about 80 percent or 85 percent of the appraised value of your home minus the balance you owe on your first mortgage. Some plans set a fixed time, known as the *draw period*, during which you can tap the account. Unless the draw period is renewed, you may not be able to access the credit line after the time expires. In some cases, *balloon loans* require you to pay off the entire balance when the draw period ends. Avoid such a plan if possible because you might have to scramble to come up with so much cash all at once. If you sell your home, lenders will normally require you to pay off your outstanding home equity balance.

In addition to the low interest rate, one of the main advantages of home equity loans—once you've gone through the agonizing process of obtaining one—is convenience. You can tap the credit line with a check and pay back the loan as quickly or as slowly as you like. Most plans impose a minimum check size of $100 to $250. Some banks also allow you to use automatic teller machines to obtain cash or to make payments.

While a home equity loan can save you thousands of dollars in interest costs, you place your home on the line. If you are consistently late with your payments or miss payments and end up defaulting, the lender will repossess your house. Therefore, don't take a home equity loan lightly.

INSTALLMENT LOANS

Installment loans are usually designed to help pay for a particular item with a set number of payments over a specified period of time. They may be used to purchase furniture, home appliances, cars, boats, computers or any other major item. When considering an installment loan, compare the terms and rates available from the product's manufacturer or the retailer selling the product against a loan from a local bank, credit union or savings and loan. Often, such a lender offers better rates than the manufacturer or retailer, particularly if you already have an account with that lender.

Your monthly payments will be calculated as follows: The lender takes the sales price of the item, adds the interest you would pay over the life of the loan, then divides the total by the number of months over which you will pay. For instance, say you buy living room furniture for $10,000, which you will pay over five years at 10 percent interest. Therefore, on top of the $10,000, you will owe $1,000 in interest a year over the term of the loan, for a total of $15,000. Because you will pay off that amount over 60 months (five years), your monthly payment will total $250 ($15,000 divided by 60). In the early months or years of your loan, almost all of the monthly payment will pay off interest. In the final months or years, almost all of the payment will pay off principal. This process of adjusting the portion of your monthly payment applied to interest and principal is known as *amortization.*

Installment loan contracts sometimes allow you to pay off the loan early if you wish. Some impose a penalty fee for early prepayment; some do not. If such a fee exists, it must be explicitly stated in your loan contract.

LIFE INSURANCE LOANS

If you have built up cash value in your life insurance policy, you might find that you can borrow against that asset inexpensively and easily. All insurance companies will lend cash up to the full face value of your policy at an interest rate from as little as 5 percent to as much as 15 percent. Some older policies permitted loans at a guaranteed rate of 5 percent as long as the policy remained in force. Policies issued more recently usually offer a variable-rate loan tied to some index of interest rates, such as the prime rate or yields on Treasury securities. Like other consumer interest, the finance charges you pay on a life insurance loan are not deductible.

All you must do to borrow from your policy is to inform your insurance agent how much money you want, and he or she will process your loan application. You need not explain your plans for the loan proceeds, and no one will check your credit record. You should receive a check within a few days or weeks.

Your loan affects the value of your insurance policy in various ways. First, your death benefit is automatically reduced by the amount you borrow, so if you die while the loan is outstanding, your heirs receive less of a payout from the insurer. Some companies also lower the return they credit you on your cash value by the amount of your loan. Therefore, the cash value remaining in your policy might grow more slowly than if you hadn't borrowed.

Still, a loan from your insurance policy can be a good idea, particularly if it is used for a worthwhile investment that will allow you to pay off the loan later. However, don't borrow so much that you seriously impair your insurance coverage.

MARGIN LOANS

Borrowing against the value of your stocks, bonds, mutual funds and other securities held by your broker can save you thousands of dollars in interest costs over installment or credit card loans. Margin loans charge a floating interest rate slightly higher than the broker's loan rate, which itself is tied to yields on short-term securities such as Treasury bills. The larger your credit line and the more active a trader you are, the lower your interest rate. In the 1990s, margin loans charged about 6 percent to 8 percent interest versus the 10 percent to 20 percent charged on installment and credit card debt.

Not only are margin loans inexpensive; they are convenient. Most brokerage firms allow you to access your margin loan line by writing a check or using a debit card tied to your asset management account. You can spend the borrowed money to buy more securities or to purchase anything else you desire. No fixed schedule exists for repayment of the loan, which can be extended indefinitely.

Like other consumer interest, finance charges on margin debt are not tax deductible unless you use the loan proceeds to buy taxable securities like Treasury or corporate bonds or dividend-paying stocks. You can then deduct up to the amount of net investment income generated by those securities. If you use the loan proceeds to purchase tax-exempt municipal bonds, you earn no deductions.

However, understand the risks of borrowing on margin before you assume such a loan. When you use margin debt, you pledge the value of your securities as collateral. You can borrow up to 50 percent of the value of your stocks or mutual funds and up to 90 percent of the worth of your bonds, depending on the type of bonds and their maturity. If the value of those securities falls sharply, you must put up more cash, or your broker will automatically sell your securities to meet the *margin call.*

Borrowing on margin can therefore be cost effective and convenient—as long as you consider the risk of falling securities prices before you open a margin account.

MORTGAGE LOANS

Probably the largest loan you will ever undertake is the mortgage to buy or renovate a home. Mortgages are secured loans, allowing the mortgage lender to repossess your home if you fail to meet your payments. Mortgages come in many varieties, including fixed- and variable-rate, as well as several maturities, though 10-, 15- and 30-year mortgages are most common.

Most mortgages require that you invest a certain amount of money as a down payment, which can be as little as 5 percent or as much as 25 percent of the purchase price of your home. Different lenders require varying levels of down payments, depending on their rules and how creditworthy they find you. Clearly, the more money you invest in the home, the less chance exists that you will walk away from your obligation and give up your equity.

The lender then calculates how much of your gross income the monthly mortgage payments will absorb. Depending on the lender, it normally doesn't want the payments to consume more than 28 percent of your gross income. The lender then determines your other debt obligations to make sure that you can also afford the mortgage payments. Once you have passed all of these tests, the lender verifies your employment and income and checks your credit record to satisfy itself that you are a worthy borrower. For a more detailed discussion of the mortgage process, as well as choosing a mortgage, see Chapter 8, "Inside Real Estate."

RETIREMENT PLAN LOANS

If you have built up equity in a retirement plan, such as a 401(k) salary reduction plan, a Keogh account or an individual retirement account (IRA), you may be able to borrow at attractive rates, as long as you follow certain rules.

Most companies allow you to borrow up to a certain amount of the assets accumulated in your 401(k) plan. Often, you must shift the amount of funds you want to borrow into an extremely conservative investment option, such as a guaranteed investment contract (GIC), for the duration of the loan. The interest rate on the loan varies by company, but it is usually 1 or 2 percentage points more than the prime rate. Because your company wants to make sure that you repay the loan, it will insist that you do so through regular payroll deductions. (Of course, this will reduce your take-home pay.) You choose how many years you need to repay the loan, usually from one to five. The longer you take to pay off the loan, the lower your monthly payments but the higher your interest costs over the life of the loan. Most companies allow you to prepay the loan in full at any time.

Borrowing from Keoghs and IRAs is possible, though tricky, and should be a short-term last resort. IRS rules permit you to withdraw from your Keogh or IRA without penalty for up to 60 days once a year. If you fail to replace the money within those two months, you must pay income taxes on the borrowed amount, plus a 10 percent penalty.

SERVICE LOANS

Though you may not even think of it as credit, you receive many interest-free loans to pay for services you use each month. For example, utilities bill you for telephone, gas, water and electric services every month, long after you've used them. Hospitals, doctors, lawyers, dentists and other service providers also, in effect, grant you a loan if you do not pay them immediately after they serve you. If you don't reimburse them within a certain number of days after receiving your bill, service providers often assess a late charge or interest.

To smooth out your monthly payments, many utilities offer a *level-payment plan* in which you remit the same amount each month over a year's time. Otherwise, you pay small heating bills in the summer and enormous ones in the winter, wreaking havoc on your budget. Such level-billing plans are a form of service credit.

In some cases, particularly with utilities, you must submit a security deposit to prove your creditworthiness. After a few months of paying your bills on time, you can get back your security deposit. If you don't pay on time, your utility service is cut off after several warnings. If you qualify as a low-income or an elderly customer, local laws may protect you from such a cutoff.

Qualifying for Credit

When a lender sizes you up to determine how much credit, if any, to grant you, it usually looks for the *three Cs*: character, capacity and capital.

"Character" summarizes a lender's sense of how responsibly you handle your credit obligations. Good character is established over a long period of time when you promptly pay principal and interest on your mortgage, student loans, credit cards and other loans. In the lender's eyes, you also exhibit character if you do not buy too much on credit for your level of income. By demonstrating a strong sense of character, you persuade the lender to trust that you will make a good-faith effort to pay your bills even if you run into financial difficulties. Good character means contacting the lender if you have problems repaying a debt. This way, you can work together to establish a new repayment schedule.

Lenders assess your character in many ways. For example, they determine how many years you have lived in or owned your home or apartment and how many years you have held your job. The longer you have lived at one address or held one job, the more lenders feel comfortable with your character. If you have never before borrowed and therefore have not established a repayment history, lenders have difficulty assessing your character.

"Capacity" measures your financial ability to assume a certain amount of debt. Lenders ask the annual income from your job, the value of your investment portfolio and the income you earn in dividends and interest from those investments. Many banks set minimum income requirements you must meet to qualify for specific dollar amounts of credit. In general, the longer you have earned a certain income, the larger your credit capacity because that income is considered fairly secure.

Lenders are required to consider all sources of income, such as alimony, Social Security, pensions and consulting fees, in addition to wages. Though creditors are supposed to assess all sources of income equally, they rely on income more than assets, which can fluctuate sharply in value and can be sold quickly. If you do not earn enough income to obtain credit on your own, you may qualify for a loan by having a friend or relative with a good credit rating cosign your loan. If you default, the cosigner must pay back the loan. But if you repay your obligations faithfully, you might qualify for the credit line on your own over time.

In addition to evaluating your assets, creditors measure your capacity by analyzing the amount of debt you already owe. They prefer it if no more than a maximum of 36 percent of your income pays your total fixed expenses and no more than 28 percent of your income pays for housing, whether that be mortgage payments or rent. The more debt you incur, the less credit that lenders extend.

"Capital" consists of the financial assets at your disposal to pay off debts if your character and capacity do not prove sufficient. Lenders include as capital stocks, bonds, mutual funds, real estate, collectibles, cars and other assets that you could sell to raise money to meet your obligations. Even if you refused to sell them, lenders could seize these assets, sell them and use the proceeds to retire your debt.

BUILDING A GOOD CREDIT RATING

Your ability to obtain credit ultimately depends on how lenders score your credit rating, based on how you fare on the three Cs. Though you may not be aware of it, all of your financial habits are tracked by your credit grantors, such as banks and retail stores, which report their experiences to credit bureaus. Credit bureaus then compile the information they receive regarding such things as how quickly or slowly you pay your bills, how long you have lived in your home and how many years you have been employed at your company. When you apply for a loan, the lender checks with the credit bureau to learn other lenders' experiences with you.

The lender then uses a credit scoring system to judge whether you meet its criteria. You receive more points if you own your home and have lived there several years, have held a job for a long time, are highly educated, work in a professional or managerial position, have large balances in your checking and savings accounts and have handled credit responsibly with previous creditors. On the other hand, if you earn a low income, float from job to job, have moved several times in the last few years, have low balances in your bank accounts and frequently remit debt payments late, you receive far fewer points. You never see your credit score, which is compiled each time you apply for credit based on the information the grantor obtains from your credit report.

Most lenders will lower your score if you have too much credit available from other sources. Even though you may have a spotless payment history, lenders are concerned that you could go on a spending binge if you have more credit at your disposal. To make sure that your credit application is not denied for this reason, close any credit lines and cancel any credit cards you do not use—and tell the lender to inform the credit bureau of your action. To be sure the lender has done so, contact the credit bureau in writing in a month or two to make sure the bureau knows that these credit lines have been terminated.

If you know you have a low score because you have not established a credit history, take small steps to build that record. Apply for a department store or gasoline company credit card, which are relatively easy to qualify for, and pay your bills on time. Take out a secured credit card by depositing money with the issuing bank, and make several charges, which you repay in a timely manner. Or persuade someone to co-sign your application; then take care of the bills responsibly. Over time, your credit score will rise, and you will qualify for loans on your own.

Also realize that every person has his or her own credit report and is scored separately. This knowledge is particularly critical for women who work in their homes. When their husband dies or they get divorced, these women frequently are shocked to discover that they have little credit history because they never established an individual credit identity. This can make it difficult for them to qualify for credit on their own. The Equal Credit Opportunity Act (ECOA) provides that women cannot be discriminated against on credit decisions because of their sex, but this law won't help if they cannot show that they earn an income and can manage credit responsibly. Therefore, married women should have credit cards and other loans issued in their name (Mary Smith rather than Mrs. John Smith).

The Equal Credit Opportunity Act does not apply only to women. The federal law states that lenders cannot deny credit because of age, sex, marital status, race, color, religion or national origin or because the applicant receives public income, such as a veteran's pension, Social Security or welfare. That means that creditors cannot ask questions about whether you are single, married, widowed or divorced, whether you plan to have children or whether you receive alimony or child support, for example. Nevertheless, while lenders may not legally consider these factors, they may consider others to ensure that you possess the character, capacity and capital to repay your loans on time.

Credit bureaus typically acquire information from major lenders that issue credit cards, such as retail stores and banks, and from T&E card issuers, such as American Express, Diners Club and Carte Blanche. Credit bureaus also record car loans, airline credit cards and any liens or legal actions pending against you. Other debts you may accumulate, including mortgages, utility or telephone bills and medical bills, normally are not reported to a credit bureau unless you miss payments over an extended period of time. Of course, credit bureaus also track whether you have declared bankruptcy or whether the IRS chases you with a tax lien.

If you have been denied credit because of something in your financial background, you are entitled to a free report so you can see the evidence that credit grantor relied on to make its decision. Even if you have not been denied credit, you can receive a copy of the report—often for a fee—to determine its accuracy.

Though many local credit bureaus exist, the industry consists of three major players: Equifax, Experian and Trans Union. (Their addresses and phone numbers are listed in the "Resources" section at the end of this chapter, along with a listing for CreditComm Services, 800-777-9700, which compiles a credit report combining all three credit bureaus' information.) Each bureau uses its own form to report your credit status. All three forms have been simplified in recent years so consumers can better understand them.

Figure 9.1 illustrates the Equifax credit report; Figure 9.2, the Experian report; and Figure 9.3, the Trans Union report.

All three of these reports share the following elements:

- Basic identifying information, such as your name, address, date of birth, Social Security number and spouse's name.

- Your credit history, including companies that have loaned you money in the past, along with the account numbers, size of your credit lines, dates the lines were opened, dates you last used the credit lines, lines' repayment terms, amounts you presently owe, status of your payments (current or in arrears) and number of months your payments are past due, if applicable.

- Collection agencies that have been assigned to collect overdue debts, including the original creditor's name, which collection agency oversaw which account, the amount it tried to collect and whether you paid.

- Courthouse records obtained from federal, state or local courts, showing liens, bankruptcy filings or other judgments.

- Additional information about your history, such as former employers or addresses.

- Listing of inquiries made by potential credit grantors. (Whenever an institution checks your credit record in deciding whether to approve your loan, its inquiry will be noted here.)

At the end of a credit report, the credit bureau normally offers a dispute form to complete if you find anything in the report inaccurate. (You have the right to correct mistakes under the Fair Credit Reporting Act, and the bureau must finish their investigation of your claim within 30 days of receiving it.) On the form, you must explain why you think the information is incorrect. For example, you may contend that some data do not belong to your account. Or you may have paid a debt that the lender contends you have not. The more evidence you can show to back up your claims, the better the chance your credit report will be altered. If the credit bureau agrees to correct your record, it must notify the credit grantor requesting the report, which—based on the new information—may change its decision to reject your application.

If the credit bureau finds your credit report accurate after you've disputed parts of it, do not give up. Instead, write a letter (maximum of 100 words) presenting your

Figure 9.1
Sample Equifax Credit Report

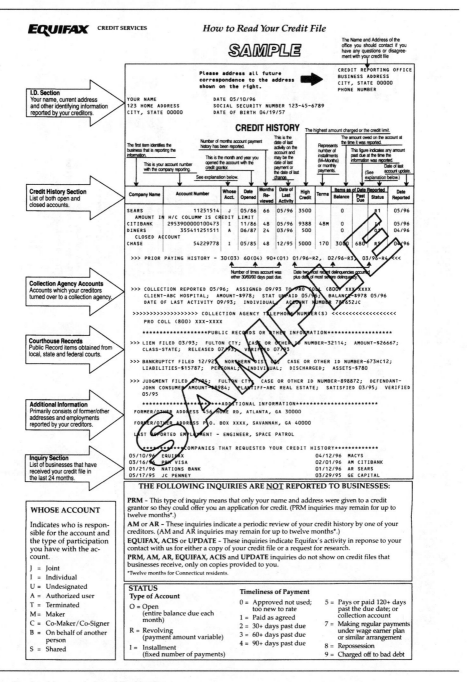

Source: Reprinted by permission of Equifax Inc.

Figure 9.2
Sample Experian Credit Report

experian

Prepared for
John Q. Consumer

Report date
May 1, 1998

Report number
123456-173634738

Page 1 of 4

Experian
PO Box 949
Allen, TX 75013-0949

Personal Credit Report

About this report

Experian collects and organizes information about you and your credit history from public records, your creditors and other reliable sources. We make your credit history available to your current and prospective creditors and employers as allowed by law. We do not grant credit or evaluate your credit history. Personal data about you may be made available to companies whose products and services may interest you.

Important decisions about your creditworthiness are based on the information in this report. You should review it carefully for accuracy.

Information affecting your creditworthiness

Below is a summary of the information contained in this report.

Potentially negative items listed

Public records (see page 2)	1
Accounts with creditors and others (see page 2)	2

Accounts in good standing   1

Other information

Total items listed in this report	8
Last potentially negative item reported	4-1998
Total inquiries you initiated	2
Last inquiry you initiated	12-1997

Analysis of most recent information reported

Total revolving credit available	$0
Total outstanding balances	$36,421
Total monthly payments	$366
Total amount past due	$548

Where to find details   page

Public record information about you	2
Your statement	2
Credit information about you	2
Others who have requested your credit history	4
Personal information about you	4

If you have questions
For all questions about this report, please call us toll-free at:
888 397 3742
M-F 7:30am - 7pm
Central Time

To learn more about Experian or for other helpful information, including tips on how to improve your credit-worthiness, visit our web site:
http://www.experian.com

JOHN Q CONSUMER
123 MAIN STREET
ANYTOWN CA 90001-9999

Figure 9.2
(continued)

experian

Prepared for John Q. Consumer	Report date May 1, 1998
	Report number 123456-173634738
	Questions? Call 888 397 3742
	Page 2 of 4

Information affecting your creditworthiness

Items listed with dashes before and after the number, for example –1–, may have a potentially negative effect on your future credit extension and are listed first on the report.

Credit grantors may carefully review the items listed below when they check your credit history. Please note that account information connected with some public records, such as bankruptcy, also may appear with your credit accounts listed later in this report.

Your statement

At your request, we include the following statement every time your credit report is requested. If you wish to change or delete this statement, please call us at 888 397 3742.

"My identification has been used without my consent on applications for credit. Please call me at 999 9999 before approving credit in my name."

Public record information about you

Source/ Identification number	Location number	Date filed/ Date resolved	Responsibility	Claim amount Liability amount	Comments
–1– U.S. Bankruptcy Court Bridgeport Bridgeport, CT 06604		8-1993/ 11-1993	Joint	Unknown/ $13,579	Status: voluntary chapter 7 bankruptcy discharged. 26% adjusted, 26% of original amount repaid. This item is scheduled to continue on record until 8-2003. Your statement "My ex-spouse filed bankruptcy without my participation."

Credit information about you

Source/ Account number (except last few digits)	Date opened/ Reported since	Date of status/ Last reported	Type/ Terms/ Scheduled payment	Responsibility	Credit limit or original amount/ High balance	Most recent balance	Comments
–2– B.B. Credit 835 Washington St. Dedham, MA 02026/ 547631236... **Original creditor: Tony's Health Club**	10-1990/ 4-1995	4-1998/ 4-1998	Installment/ 60 months/ $34	Individual	$8,500/ $8,500	$1,321 as of 4-1998	Status: collection/past due 90 days. $548 past due as of 6-1996. Account past due: Collection as of 9-1995 thru 6-1996; 90 days as of 7-1995; 60 days as of 11-1994, 6-1-1995, 6-29-1995; 30 days as of 9-1994, 1-1995 and 2 other times. This account is scheduled to continue on record until 2-2001. This item was verified and updated on 6-1996.

Figure 9.2
Sample Experian Credit Report (continued)

experian

Prepared for	John Q. Consumer
Report date	May 1, 1998
Report number	123456-173634738
Questions?	Call 888 397 3742
	Page 3 of 4

Credit information about you *continued*

Source/ Account number (except last few digits)	Date opened/ Reported since	Date of status/ Last reported	Type/ Terms/ Scheduled payment	Responsibility	Credit limit or original amount/ High balance	Most recent balance	Comments
-3- America's Best Bank PO Box 7871 SROC, Ft. Lauderdale, FL 33329/ 547632536...	1-1985/ 3-1992	4-1998/ 4-1998	Installment/ 180 months/ $332	Joint with Jane Consumer	unknown/ $55,000	$35,100 as of 4-1998	Status: open/current; was past due 60 days. Balloon payment of $1,348 due 12-1999. Account past due: 60 days as of 3-1994, 6-1995; As of 4-1998, this account is scheduled to go to a positive status 3-2001.
-4- America's Best Bank 547638896....	5-1990/ 7-1992	6-1996/ 6-1996	Revolving/ NA/ $0	Authorized User	$5,000/ $145	$0/paid as of 6-1996	Status: closed/never late. This account is scheduled to continue on record until 6-2003. Creditor's statement "Credit line closed - reported by subscriber."

Your use of credit

The information listed below provides additional detail about your accounts, showing up to 24 months of balance history and your credit limit or original loan amount. Not all balance history information is reported to Experian, so some of your accounts may not appear. Balance history information missing from your accounts is indicated by a dash (—).

Source/Account number	Date	Balance	Date	Balance	Date	Balance	Date	Balance	Date	Balance	Date	Balance
-3- America's Best Bank 547632536...	4-1998	35,100	12-1997	35,300	8-1997	35,700	4-1997	36,100	12-1996	36,500	—	—
	3-1998	35,200	11-1997	35,400	7-1997	35,800	3-1997	36,200	11-1996	36,600	—	—
	—	—	10-1997	35,500	6-1997	35,900	2-1997	36,300	—	—	—	—
			9-1997	35,600	5-1997	36,000	1-1997	36,400	—	—	—	—
-4- America's Best Bank 547638896....	4-1998	0	12-1997	0	8-1997	0	4-1997	0	12-1996	0		
	3-1998	0	11-1997	0	7-1997	0	3-1997	0	11-1996	0		
	—		10-1997	0	6-1997	0	2-1997	0	10-1996	0		
			9-1997	0	5-1997	0	1-1997	0	9-1996	0		

Between 2-1997 and 1-1998, your credit limit was $5,000.

Between 8-1996 and 1-1997, your credit limit was $3,000.

Figure 9.2
(continued)

experian

Prepared for	Report date		
John Q. Consumer	May 1, 1998		
	Report number	Questions?	Page 4 of 4
	123456-173634738	Call 888 397 3742	

Others who have requested your credit history

Listed below are all those who have received information from us in the recent past about your credit history.

Requests initiated by you

You took actions, such as completing a credit application, that allowed the following sources to review your information. Please note that the following information is part of your credit history and is included in our reports to others.

Source	Date	Comments
Bank of Binginton	12-9-1997	Extension of credit. This
1666 Spring St.		inquiry is scheduled to
Springfield, MA 01103		continue on record until 12-1999.
Superior Lenders	7-13-1997	Real estate loan of
42501 Albrae St.		$200,000 on behalf of
Fremont, CA 94538		Chase Manhattan Bank with 30 year repayment terms. This inquiry is scheduled to continue on record until 7-1999.

Other requests

You may not have initiated the following requests for your credit history, so you may not recognize each source. We offer credit information about you to those with a permissible purpose, for example, to:

- your current creditors to monitor your accounts;
- other creditors who want to offer you preapproved credit;
- an employer who wishes to extend an offer of employment;
- a potential investor in assessing the risk of a current credit obligation;
- Experian Consumer Assistance to process a report for you.

We report these requests only to you as a record of activities, and we do not include any of these requests on credit reports to others. These items will continue on record for two years from the date below.

Source	Date	Source	Date
Experian	7-1996	**ABC/Promotional**	4-1996
PO Box 949		802 Delaware Avenue	
Allen, TX 75013		Wilmington, DE 19801	

Personal information about you

The following information associated with your records has been reported to us by you, your creditors and other sources. As part of our fraud-prevention program, a notice with additional information may appear in your report.

Names

John Q. Consumer
John Consumer
Jack Q. Consumer

Residences

Our records show you currently are a homeowner. The geographical code shown with each address identifies the state, county, census tract, block group and Metropolitan Statistical Area associated with each address.

Address	Type of address	Geographical code
123 Main Street	NA	23-914-629331-
Anytown, CA 90001		1-1234
7 Buckingham Drive	Single family	14-167-353800-
Southwick, MA 01077		6-6464
125 Main Street, Apt. 305	Apartment complex	75-344-896002-
Westfield, MA 01085		9-7436

Social Security numbers

123-45-6789
123-54-6789

Date of birth

9/27/1959

Driver's license number

CA X123456

Telephone numbers

999 999 9999 home
999 999 9009
999 999 8888

Spouse's name

Jane

Employers

ABC Corporation
456 Main Street
Anytown, CA 90001

City of Newton

Notices

This is a non-residential address: 123 Main/Anytown CA 90001.

A Social Security number reported to us does not match any of your personal information.

Figure 9.3
Sample Trans Union Credit Report

```
1561 E. ORANGETHORPE AVENUE          YOUR TRANS UNION FILE NUMBER: 98AA0001-006
FULLERTON, CA 92831-5207             PAGE  1 OF  4 (INTL USE: CC      12VN 05)
                                     DATE THIS REPORT PRINTED: 01/02/98
RETURN SERVICE REQUESTED
                                     SOCIAL SECURITY NUMBER: 666-77-8886
                                     BIRTH DATE:             07/33
                                     YOU HAVE BEEN IN OUR FILES SINCE: 02/78
                                     AKA: CARL MONROE


CONSUMER REPORT FOR:


   *****
   MONROE, RANDY, R
   5550 PILLERO RD
   SPRINGFIELD, CA 99999


FORMER ADDRESSES REPORTED:

   9990 POTRERO RD, SPRINGFIELD, CA 99999
   4440 EL CAMINO REAL, SPRINGFIELD, CA 99999

EMPLOYMENT DATA REPORTED:

   WELLS FARGO                          SOUTHLAND CORP
   POSITION: DRIVER                     POSITION: CLERK
   DATE REPORTED: 05/90                 SALARY:     $12000
                                        DATE REPORTED: 05/89

                    INVESTIGATION RESULTS
───────────────────────────────────────────────────────────────
WE HAVE COMPLETED OUR INVESTIGATION OF THE ITEM(S) YOU DISPUTED. OUR FINDINGS
ARE SUMMARIZED AS FOLLOWS:

ITEM                           DESCRIPTION         RESULTS
────                           ───────────         ───────
LOMAS MT USA                   # 51515151          NEW INFORMATION BELOW
CITIBK VISA                    # 67676767898989    DELETED

ANY CORRECTIONS TO YOUR IDENTIFICATION REQUESTED BY YOU HAVE BEEN MADE AS NOTED
ABOVE. IF OUR INVESTIGATION HAS NOT RESOLVED YOUR DISPUTE, YOU MAY ADD A 100
WORD CONSUMER STATEMENT TO YOUR REPORT. YOUR UPDATED CREDIT INFORMATION
FOLLOWS:
───────────────────────────────────────────────────────────────

                    YOUR CREDIT INFORMATION
───────────────────────────────────────────────────────────────
THE FOLLOWING ITEMS OBTAINED FROM PUBLIC RECORDS APPEAR ON YOUR REPORT. YOU MAY
BE REQUIRED TO EXPLAIN PUBLIC RECORD ITEMS TO POTENTIAL CREDITORS.  ANY BANK-
RUPTCY INFORMATION WILL REMAIN ON YOUR REPORT FOR 10 YEARS FROM THE DATE OF
FILING.  UNPAID TAX LIENS ARE REPORTED INDEFINITELY.  ALL OTHER PUBLIC RECORD
INFORMATION, INCLUDING DISCHARGED CHAPTER 13 BANKRUPTCY AND ANY ACCOUNTS
CONTAINING ADVERSE INFORMATION, REMAIN FOR 7 YEARS.

DOCKET #9898989      FEDERAL DISTRICT     CHAPTER 13 BANKRUPTCY DISMISSED
PLAINTIFF:           COUNTY OF HARRIS                    ENTERED:   09/96
PLAINTIFF ATTORNEY: EDWIN J RAMBY                        PAID:      01/97
                                 ASSETS:     $0    LIAB:          $0

                                                 80108C    1   1/7
───────────────────────────────────────────────────────────────
```

Source: Reprinted by permission of Trans Union.

Figure 9.3
(continued)

```
REPORT ON MONROE, RANDY, R                                    PAGE  2 OF  4
SOCIAL SECURITY NUMBER: 666-77-8886     TRANS UNION FILE NUMBER: 98AA0001-006


DOCKET #BB77887        SUPERIOR COURT        CIVIL JUDGMENT
PLAINTIFF:             SINSHEIMER SCHIEBELHUT               ENTERED:    02/95
PLAINTIFF ATTORNEY: ANDREW STEIN                           AMOUNT:     $25629


THE FOLLOWING ACCOUNTS CONTAIN INFORMATION WHICH SOME CREDITORS MAY CONSIDER TO
BE ADVERSE.  THE ADVERSE INFORMATION IN THESE ACCOUNTS HAS BEEN PRINTED IN
>BRACKETS< FOR YOUR CONVENIENCE, TO HELP YOU UNDERSTAND YOUR REPORT.  THEY ARE
NOT BRACKETED THIS WAY FOR CREDITORS. (NOTE: THE ACCOUNT # MAY BE SCRAMBLED BY
THE CREDITOR FOR YOUR PROTECTION).

  HHLD BANK                # 5455555666661290   REVOLVING ACCOUNT
>PROFIT AND LOSS WRITEOFF<
    UPDATED   12/96  BALANCE:       $12056   AUTHORIZED ACCOUNT
    OPENED    11/90  MOST OWED:     $12056   CREDIT LIMIT:     $12000
    CLOSED    09/96 >PAST DUE:      $12056<
    >STATUS AS OF 09/96: CHARGED OFF AS BAD DEBT<
    >MAXIMUM DELINQUENCY OF  60 DAYS OCCURRED IN   4/97<

  GRT WSTRN SL             # 30888888888        MORTGAGE ACCOUNT
                                               REAL ESTATE
    VERIF'D   06/93  BALANCE:          $0      JOINT ACCOUNT
    OPENED    01/92  MOST OWED:    $157500     PAY TERMS: 30 MONTHLY $1239
    CLOSED    06/93                            CREDIT LIMIT:         $0
    >STATUS AS OF 06/93: 90 DAYS PAST DUE<
    >IN PRIOR 18 MONTHS FROM DATE CLOSED  2 TIMES   90 DAYS,
      2 TIMES 60 DAYS,   3 TIMES 30 DAYS LATE<

  GLNDLE FD BK             # 5444445555         MORTGAGE ACCOUNT
                                               CONVENTIONAL REAL ESTATE MTG
    VERIF'D   11/97  BALANCE:     $157621      JOINT ACCOUNT
    OPENED    05/93  MOST OWED:   $165500      PAY TERMS: 360 MONTHLY $1457
    STATUS AS OF 11/97: PAID AS AGREED
    >IN PRIOR 26 MONTHS FROM DATE VERIF'D  2 TIMES  60 DAYS,
      5 TIMES 30 DAYS LATE<

  CITIBANK FSB             # 1111111111153013   LINE OF CREDIT ACCOUNT
>CANCELLED BY CREDIT GRANTOR<                   LINE OF CREDIT
    UPDATED   10/97  BALANCE:       $4427    JOINT ACCOUNT
    OPENED    10/87                          PAY TERMS:  MINIMUM $134
    CLOSED    09/96                          CREDIT LIMIT:      $7000
    STATUS AS OF 09/96: PAID AS AGREED
    IN PRIOR  1 MONTH   FROM DATE CLOSED NEVER LATE

  LOMAS MT USA             # 51515151           MORTGAGE ACCOUNT
  TRANSFERRED TO ANOTHER LENDER                 CONVENTIONAL REAL ESTATE MTG
    VERIF'D   03/96  BALANCE:       $3400    JOINT ACCOUNT
    OPENED    03/94  MOST OWED:   $100000    PAY TERMS: 360 MONTHLY $1118
                    >PAST DUE:      $1118<
    STATUS AS OF 03/96: UNRATED
    IN PRIOR 24 MONTHS FROM DATE VERIF'D NEVER LATE


THE FOLLOWING ACCOUNTS ARE REPORTED WITH NO ADVERSE INFORMATION
```

Figure 9.3
Sample Trans Union Credit Report (continued)

```
REPORT ON MONROE, RANDY, R                              PAGE  3 OF  4
SOCIAL SECURITY NUMBER: 666-77-8886      TRANS UNION FILE NUMBER: 98AA0001-006


    MERRILL LYNC              # 63333333332222294   MORTGAGE ACCOUNT
                                                    CONVENTIONAL REAL ESTATE MTG
        UPDATED   11/94   BALANCE:     $162325      JOINT ACCOUNT
        OPENED    05/93   MOST OWED:   $165500
        STATUS AS OF 11/94: PAID AS AGREED
        IN PRIOR  7 MONTHS FROM LAST UPDATE NEVER LATE


    MEDALLION MO              # 144444               INSTALLMENT ACCOUNT
                                                    CONVENTIONAL REAL ESTATE MTG
        VERIF'D   05/94   BALANCE:     $166275      PARTICIPANT ON ACCOUNT
        OPENED    07/93   MOST OWED:   $168000      PAY TERMS: 360 MONTHLY $10
        STATUS AS OF 05/94: PAID AS AGREED
        IN PRIOR 11 MONTHS FROM DATE VERIF'D NEVER LATE


    HHLD BANK                 # 5437000100589508     REVOLVING ACCOUNT
    CREDIT CARD LOST/STOLEN                          CREDIT CARD
        UPDATED   03/96    BALANCE:        $0        JOINT ACCOUNT
        OPENED    09/92    MOST OWED:       $0
        STATUS AS OF 03/96: UNRATED
        IN PRIOR 30 MONTHS FROM LAST UPDATE NEVER LATE
```

```
THE FOLLOWING COMPANIES HAVE RECEIVED YOUR CREDIT REPORT.  THEIR INQUIRIES
REMAIN ON YOUR CREDIT REPORT FOR TWO YEARS. (NOTE: "TU CONSUMER DISCLOSURE"
INQUIRIES ARE NOT VIEWED BY CREDITORS).

INQUIRY TYPE   DATE        SUBSCRIBER NAME
PARTICIPANT    12/29/97    CBR
PARTICIPANT    12/01/97    TU CONSUMER DISCLOSURE
JOINT          08/12/97    CBSLO/CB STA MARIA RE
JOINT          10/17/96    CBSLO/CB STA MARIA RE
PARTICIPANT    02/20/96    IMPERIAL THRIFT & LOAN
INDIVIDUAL     01/19/96    WELLS FARGO BK LINEOFCR
```

Figure 9.3
(continued)

```
REPORT ON MONROE, RANDY, R                              PAGE  4 OF  4
SOCIAL SECURITY NUMBER: 666-77-8886    TRANS UNION FILE NUMBER: 98AA0001-006


THE COMPANIES LISTED BELOW RECEIVED YOUR NAME, ADDRESS AND OTHER LIMITED
INFORMATION ABOUT YOU SO THEY COULD MAKE A FIRM OFFER OF CREDIT OR INSURANCE.
THEY DID NOT RECEIVE YOUR FULL CREDIT REPORT, AND THESE INQUIRIES ARE NOT SEEN
BY ANYONE BUT YOU.

   SUBSCRIBER NAME        DATE        SUBSCRIBER NAME        DATE
   CITIBANK NA            07/97       BANK OF AMERICA R.M.C.  02/97
   CAPITAL ONE BANK       02/97


THE COMPANIES LISTED BELOW RECEIVED INFORMATION ABOUT YOU IN CONNECTION WITH
THEIR REVIEW OF AN EXISTING ACCOUNT YOU HAVE WITH THEM. THESE INQUIRIES ARE NOT
SEEN BY ANYONE BUT YOU.

   SUBSCRIBER NAME        DATE        SUBSCRIBER NAME        DATE
   CITIBANK NA            09/97       CITIBANK NA            11/97


CONSUMER STATEMENT:
       #HK# FRAUD VICTIM; DO NOT EXTEND CREDIT WITHOUT FIRST CONTACTING
       ME PERSONALLY AND VERFYING ALL APP LICANT INFORMATION. CONTACT
       ME FOR VERIFICATION AT: 555-1212


SPECIAL MESSAGES:

       CONSUMER STATEMENT ON FILE RELATES TO TRUE NAME FRAUD OR CREDIT FRAUD


IF THERE HAS BEEN A CHANGE IN YOUR CREDIT HISTORY RESULTING FROM OUR
INVESTIGATION, OR IF YOU ADD A CONSUMER STATEMENT, YOU MAY REQUEST TRANS UNION
TO SEND AN UPDATED REPORT TO THOSE WHO RECEIVED YOUR REPORT WITHIN THE LAST TWO
YEARS FOR EMPLOYMENT PURPOSES, OR WITHIN THE LAST ONE YEAR FOR ANY OTHER
PURPOSE. IF INTERESTED, YOU MAY ALSO REQUEST A DESCRIPTION OF HOW THE
INVESTIGATION WAS CONDUCTED ALONG WITH THE NAME, ADDRESS, AND TELEPHONE NUMBER
OF ANYONE CONTACTED FOR INFORMATION.

IF YOU BELIEVE ANY OF THE INFORMATION IN YOUR CREDIT REPORT IS INCORRECT,
PLEASE LET US KNOW.  PLEASE ADDRESS ALL CORRESPONDENCE REGARDING YOUR CREDIT
REPORT TO:

TRANS UNION CONSUMER RELATIONS
1561 E. ORANGETHORPE AVENUE
FULLERTON, CA 92831-5207
1-800-555-5555
```

Figure 9.3
Sample Trans Union Credit Report (continued)

Your Credit Rights As A Consumer

Reviewing Your Credit Report

Knowing and understanding what is in your credit report is one of your most important consumer rights. If you request within 60 days of being denied credit, insurance, an employment opportunity or any other benefit, due in part to information found in your credit report, we will provide you with a copy of your report free of charge. There is a fee if you request copies for any other reason. If you have any questions concerning a credit denial, please contact that creditor.

You can receive and review your credit file any business day by applying either in person with reasonable notice and proper identification; by phone preceded by a written request and proper identification; or by any other reasonable means available and authorized by you. When appearing in person, you can be accompanied by one other individual, although you may be asked for written permission to have your credit file discussed in that person's presence.

Disputing Incorrect Information

If you disagree with any of the information in your credit report, you have the right to request Trans Union to recheck it without cost. It is our responsibility to have the source of the information reverify their records. Likewise, you may submit court papers/schedules of creditors, or any other relevant information you may have to assist in resolving the dispute. We cannot accept canceled checks as proof of account status without further reverification from the creditor. Investigations will be concluded within 30 days of the day we receive your request, and a revised report, reflecting the results of the investigation, will be sent to you within five business days.

Should we be unable to resolve your dispute in the 30 days, or if the disputed information is found to be incorrect, we will send you a revised report indicating that the disputed information has been corrected.

If adverse information has been deleted from your file because it could not be verified and it is later found to be accurate, we will send you a written notice within 5 business days informing you that it has been reinserted into your file.

If our investigation has not resolved the dispute, you may add a 100 word explanatory statement to your report. At your request, we will assist you in preparing the statement. If interested, you may also request a description of how the investigation was conducted along with the name, address and telephone number of anyone contacted for information.

Who Has Received Your Report

Your credit report can be obtained only by companies that have a legally permitted use for the information. The names of those companies that have received your credit report in the past two years are shown in your credit report. If there has been a change in your credit history resulting from our investigation, or if you add a consumer statement, you may request Trans Union to send an updated report

to those who received your report, within the last two years for employment purposes, or within the last one year for any other purpose.

Mailing Preference

Credit reporting companies, such as Trans Union, occasionally give your name to direct marketing companies offering goods and services which would seem of interest to you. If you do not want to receive these mailings, you have the right to deny permission of the use of your name for these purposes. Simply write Trans Union, Consumer Relations Department, Post Office Box 7245, Fullerton, California 92834. Include your name, address, signature, social security number and your name will be removed from these mailings.

Understanding Credit "Repair" Clinics

Many states have laws regulating the practices of companies that claim they can "repair" your negative credit information. No one can have accurate information removed. You may wish to check with your Attorney General, or local consumer protection agency before contracting or paying for credit repair services. If something on your report is incorrect, you can have it corrected at no cost by filling out the enclosed "Investigation Request Form".

Fair Credit Reporting Act

How far back does your credit history go? The Fair Credit Reporting Act allows credit reporting agencies to list negative credit and public record information for 7 years from the date of delinquency, charge-off or placement for collection; or for 10 years from the date of filing chapter 7, 11, 12, or 13 bankruptcy. Our policy is to delete discharged Chapter 13 bankruptcies after 7 years.

California Residents

If we investigate the information in your report at your request, you will receive an updated credit report, and another copy of this notice, to indicate that we have completed our investigation. The results of our investigation will be shown in that report. Items that we cannot verify will not appear in your updated credit report or in future reports, unless the information is later verified. Items that we verify will appear on the updated report with an indication that they were verified, and any items that we change will show those changes on your updated report.

You can obtain your credit report at a reasonable fee not exceeding $8. You also have the right to bring civil action against anyone who improperly gains access to your file or knowingly or willfully misuses file data.

**Figure 9.3
(continued)**

A Summary of Your Rights Under the Fair Credit Reporting Act

The federal Fair Credit Reporting Act (FCRA) is designed to promote accuracy, fairness, and privacy of information in the files of every "consumer reporting agency" (CRA). Most CRAs are credit bureaus that gather and sell information about you -- such as if you pay your bills on time or have filed bankruptcy -- to creditors, employers, landlords, and other businesses. You can find the complete text of the FCRA, 15 U.S.C. §§ 1681-1681u, at the Federal Trade Commission's web site *(http://www.ftc.gov)*. The FCRA gives you specific rights, as outlined below. You may have additional rights under state law. You may contact a state or local consumer protection agency or a state attorney general to learn those rights.

♦ **You must be told if information in your file has been used against you.** Anyone who uses information from a CRA to take action against you -- such as denying an application for credit, insurance, or employment -- must tell you, and give you the name, address, and phone number of the CRA that provided the consumer report.

♦ **You can find out what is in your file.** At your request, a CRA must give you the information in your file, and a list of everyone who has requested it recently. There is no charge for the report if a person has taken action against you because of information supplied by the CRA, if you request the report within 60 days of receiving notice of the action. You also are entitled to one free report every twelve months upon request if you certify that (1) you are unemployed and plan to seek employment within 60 days, (2) you are on welfare, or (3) your report is inaccurate due to fraud. Otherwise, a CRA may charge you up to eight dollars.

♦ **You can dispute inaccurate information with the CRA.** If you tell a CRA that your file contains inaccurate information, the CRA must investigate the items (usually within 30 days) by presenting to its information source all relevant evidence you submit, unless your dispute is frivolous. The source must reveiw your evidence and report its findings to the CRA. (The source also must advise national CRAs -- to which it has provided the data -- of any error.) The CRA must give you a written report of the investigation, and a copy of your report if the investigation results in any change. If the CRA's investigation does not resolve the dispute, you may add a brief statement to your file. The CRA must normally include a summary of your statement in future reports. If an item is deleted or a dispute statement is filed, you may ask that anyone who has recently received your report be notified of the change.

♦ **Inaccurate information must be corrected or deleted.** A CRA must remove or correct inaccurate or unverified information from its files, usually within 30 days after you dispute it. **However, the CRA is not required to remove accurate data from your file unless it is outdated (as described below) or cannot be verified.** If your dispute results in any change to your report, the CRA cannot reinsert into your file a disputed item unless the information source verifies its accuracy and completeness. In addition, the CRA must give you a written notice telling you it has reinserted the item. The notice must include the name, address and phone number of the information source.

♦ **You can dispute inaccurate items with the source of the information.** If you tell anyone -- such as a creditor who reports to a CRA -- that you dispute an item, they may not then report the information to a CRA without including a notice of your dispute. In addition, once you've notified the source of the error in writing, it may not continue to report the information if it is, in fact, an error.

Figure 9.3
Sample Trans Union Credit Report (continued)

- **Outdated information may not be reported.** In most cases, a CRA may not report negative information that is more than seven years old; ten years for bankruptcies.

- **Access to your file is limited.** A CRA may provide information about you only to people with a need recognized by the FCRA -- usually to consider an application with a creditor, insurer, employer, landlord, or other business.

- **Your consent is required for reports that are provided to employers, or reports that contain medical information.** A CRA may not give out information about you to your employer, or prospective employer, without your written consent. A CRA may not report medical information about you to creditors, insurers, or employers without your permission.

- **You may choose to exclude your name from CRA lists for unsolicited credit and insurance offers.** Creditors and insurers may use file information as the basis for sending you unsolicited offers of credit or insurance. Such offers must include a toll-free phone number for you to call if you want your name and address removed from future lists. If you call, you must be kept off the lists for two years. If you request, complete, and return the CRA form provided for this purpose, you must be taken off the lists indefinitely.

- **You may seek damages from violators.** If a CRA, a user or (in some cases) a provider of CRA data, violates the FCRA, you may sue them in state or federal court.

The FCRA gives several different federal agencies authority to enforce the FCRA:

FOR QUESTIONS OR CONCERNS REGARDING:	PLEASE CONTACT:
CRAs, creditors and others not listed below	Federal Trade Commission Consumer Response Center - FCRA Washington, DC 20580 *202-326-3761
National banks, federal branches/agencies of foreign banks (word "National" or initials "N.A." appear in or after bank's name)	Office of the Comptroller of the Currency Compliance Management, Mail Stop 6-6 Washington, DC 20219 *800-613-6743
Federal Reserve System member banks (except national banks, and federal brances/agencies of foreign banks)	Federal Reserve Board Division of Consumer & Community Affairs Washington, DC 20551 *202-452-3693
Savings associations and federally chartered savings banks (word "Federal" or initials "F.S.B." appear in federal institution's name)	Office of Thrift Supervision Consumer Programs Washington, DC 20552 *800-842-6929
Federal credit unions (words "Federal Credit Union" appear in institution's name)	National Credit Union Administration 1775 Duke Street Alexandria, VA 22314 *703-518-6360
State-chartered banks that are not members of the Federal Reserve System	Federal Deposit Insurance Corporation Division of Compliance & Consumer Affairs Washington, DC 20429 *800-934-FDIC
Air, surface, or rail common carriers regulated by former Civil Aeronautics Board or Interstate Commerce Commission	Department of Transportation Office of Financial Management Washington, DC 20590 *202-366-1306
Activities subject to the Packers and Stockyards Act, 1921	Department of Agriculture Office of Deputy Administrator - GIPSA Washington, DC 20250 *202-720-7051

case, which will become part of your record. Subsequent lenders that ask to see your credit record will therefore get your side of the story and will know that you are concerned enough about keeping your credit record clean that you defend it.

Nevertheless, if your credit report contains negative but true information, nothing you can do will erase it, although improving your repayment habits will help convince lenders that you are creditworthy. Credit bureaus can keep negative information in their files for seven years, and they are permitted to report bankruptcies—even if they are dismissed later—for up to ten years.

A thriving industry of so-called credit repair clinics has sprung up across the country, claiming the ability to clean up your credit record. They often offer debt consolidation loans, debt counseling or other plans "guaranteed" to rid you of persistent creditors and delete any negative items in your credit report.

Credit repair clinics also offer a new credit identity through a procedure called file segregation. They claim that you can hide the unfavorable information contained in your credit record and that your new identity will be clean as a whistle. The problem is that this scheme is illegal, and you could be fined or even go to prison if you participate.

In fact, such clinics have no ability to deliver on any of these promises. They can do nothing to improve your record, despite the outrageous fees they charge. Use any money you might spend on such clinics to repay debts.

Problems with Billing

You have certain legal rights to correct any errors in bills on open-end loans, particularly credit card loans. Some of the most common billing mistakes include the following:

- Your bill includes charges that you or anyone authorized to use your account never made.
- Your bill lists an incorrect dollar amount for a purchase.
- You never agreed to accept delivery of the goods listed because they were defective or you returned them.
- Your bill does not reflect payments you have already made.

In these and similar cases, the federal Fair Credit Billing Act stipulates that you must write a letter within 60 days of the statement's postmark date explaining the error. You can call the card issuer, and the representative can note your complaint, but no investigation will begin until the company receives your letter. Many people call but forget to follow up with a letter, so they lose their right to protest the error after two months elapse.

Some guidelines for writing a complaint letter follow:

- Include your name, address and credit card account number.

- Explain the error you think has been made, the dollar amount you dispute, the merchant involved and the date of the error.

- Send the letter to the special address for billing disputes listed on your statement. It will be a different address from the one to which you normally send your payments. To be able to prove that you mailed the letter when you did, send it certified mail, return receipt requested.

While the creditor investigates your complaint, you do not have to pay the charges in dispute or the finance charges that accrue on that amount. However, the dollar amount under dispute will still be applied against your credit limit.

The credit grantor must answer your complaint within 30 days. Either it can resolve the matter in your favor, or it can claim it needs to investigate the case further. Within 90 days, the creditor must either correct the error or explain to you in writing why it thinks no error occurred.

If the creditor finds no error after investigating the matter, you must pay the disputed amount, including finance charges that accumulated during the time of the investigation. If you still think the error exists, write another letter to your lender refusing to pay. At that point, the creditor will start its usual collection procedures and may report you as deliquent to the credit bureau. Therefore, unless a huge amount of money is involved, you should probably pay the bill rather than mar your credit history.

Managing Your Credit Wisely

The best way to establish a solid credit rating is to handle your debt obligations prudently. First, assess how much debt, as a percentage of your income, you can afford, and limit your borrowing to that amount. Consult the budget you prepared in Chapter 1 to see how much money you have left over, if any, to make debt payments. Use the worksheet in Figure 9.4 to determine your debt limit.

If you are young and earn a stable or growing income, your debt percentage may be as high as 30 percent, though it is preferable to keep it under 20 percent. If you are older or earn a less reliable income, try to limit your debt to about 10 percent of your income.

Before you assume any new debt, in the form of either an open-end credit card or a closed-end installment loan, make sure that the payments will not push your debt percentage over your limit.

Try to consolidate your borrowing to a few lines of credit. You may be one of those people who own a wallet or purse bulging with credit cards, only a few of which you use regularly. Similarly, you may have several small installment loans for cars, boats, education, furniture and other purposes. You will save not only money but also bill-paying time by transferring your credit card balances to one or two credit cards with the lowest interest rates and annual fees. However, if you

Figure 9.4   Debt Limit Worksheet

Loan	Monthly $ Payment
	$ _____
	_____
	_____
	_____
	_____
Total Monthly Loan Payments	$ _____
Annual Income	$ _____
Percentage of Income Absorbed by Payments (divide payments by income)	_____ %

consolidate your loans, don't assume more debt on your now-clear credit lines. If you don't think you can resist such temptation, cut up your cards and close down the lines.

Ever since consumer interest became nondeductible in 1991, it has become far more expensive to borrow with after-tax dollars. Previously, when consumer interest was fully deductible and tax rates were 50 percent or higher, it made much more sense to take out loans. For example, if you paid 18 percent on a loan and $1,000 in interest and taxes at a 50 percent rate, your real, after-tax cost was only 9 percent, or $500. When the deduction was abolished, however, that cost doubled from 9 percent back to a real 18 percent, or $1,000.

At the same time, inflation has dropped from the double digits of the late 1970s and early 1980s to single digits. What economists call the *real interest rate,* which is the interest rate minus inflation, has soared from 5 percent in 1980 (when inflation was 13 percent and credit cards charged 18 percent) to an astronomical 16 percent in the 1990s (with inflation at 2 percent and card companies still charging 18 percent). Therefore, to pay 18 percent or so in today's economic environment is extraordinarily expensive. As Americans have seen their after-tax, inflation-adjusted cost of borrowing skyrocket, they have either cut back on their borrowing or shifted their balances to home equity loans, which provide tax write-offs and much more reasonable rates.

CREDIT CARD SURFING

If you are willing to spend a little time and effort at it, you can "surf" your credit card balance from one issuer to another to maintain a consistently lower interest rate than if you stayed with one credit card all the time. Credit card surfing has become the new national sport, as many people constantly transfer their balances from one card to another to keep their interest charges under control. There are two types of credit card surfing:

1. *Active surfing.* This technique involves taking advantage of issuers' introductory "teaser" rates of 5.9 percent or 6.9 percent, which usually last six months to a year. When the rate is about to expire, you prepare to move your balance to a competitor's introductory rate for the next few months. Before you switch, however, it is worth a call to your bank asking them to extend the teaser rate for another six months or so. If you have been a good customer and paid on time consistently, they may do so in order to hold onto your business. If they refuse to go along, transfer the balances to another card. In order to stay out of trouble and avoid the temptation of using up the old card's credit line when the balance has been transferred to the new one, it is best to close the old account. Many people actively surf from one card to the next and end up with far too much of their debt capacity used up. When they apply for a large loan, like a mortgage or car loan, they are turned down because of the huge amount of *potential* debt they have taken on.

2. *Passive surfing.* If the effort of jumping from one introductory rate to another is too much for you, you may want to be a passive surfer instead. This involves transferring your balances once from a high-interest (15 percent to 20 percent) account down to a low-interest (8 percent to 10 percent) account. If you have a good payment history and a decent income and have not taken on too much debt already, this should not be a problem. Open an account at one of the banks offering the lowest interest and pay off your existing balances at high-interest banks, and then close the old accounts. Of course, banks charging the lowest interest have the strictest credit criteria, because they have a much slimmer margin to cover write-offs from bad debts. If you are paying a high double-digit interest rate, in effect what you are doing is subsidizing other people's bad credit habits. If you have good credit, it's far better to get a card from a bank serving responsible people who pay off their debts in a timely manner.

There are several ways to find banks charging credit card rates of 10 percent or below. You can consult CardTrak (800-344-7714), the Bank Rate Monitor Web site or other Web sites listed in the "Resources" section of this chapter. Many banks consistently show up on the list because they maintain tight credit standards. Several of the banks are based in Arkansas, which has usury ceilings preventing banks from charging more than 5 percent over the federal funds rate. Here is a list of some of the banks that frequently offer credit cards with interest rates below 10 percent. You should check with the bank to find out their latest offer:

AFBA Industrial Bank of Colorado; 800-776-2265
Arkansas Federal; 800-477-3348
Federal Savings Bank of Arkansas; 800-374-5600
Huntington National Bank of Ohio; 800-480-2265
Metropolitan National Bank of Arkansas; 800-883-2511
Pulaski Bank & Trust of Arkansas; 800-980-2265
Simmons First National of Arkansas; 800-636-5151
Wachovia Bank of Georgia; 800-842-3262

If it's not a low rate, but frequent flier miles that you are looking for as you surf from one credit card to the next, you may be interested in one of the many cards offered by banks affiliated with a major airline. Typically, for every dollar you spend on the card, you get one frequent flier mile on that airline. It's best to pick the airline you use the most and concentrate all your spending on one card, if you want to accumulate enough points to get a free trip. Most of these cards charge high interest rates of about 18 percent, which they will not reduce because they know you want the frequent flier miles. They also usually charge annual fees of about $50. But if you pay your balance off in full every month, these cards can be a great ticket to free travel:

Alaska Airlines; 800-552-7302
American Airlines; 800-359-4444
America West Airlines; 800-678-2632
British Airways; 800-700-4240
Continental Airways; 800-850-3144
Delta Airlines; 800-759-6453
Northwest Airlines; 800-360-2900
Southwest Airlines; 800-792-8472
TWA Airlines; 800-322-8921
U.S. Airways; 800-282-2273
United Airlines; 800-247-3927

You also can save money on gasoline by using a gasoline rebate card associated with one of the large oil companies. Rebates range from about 2 percent to 4 percent of the purchase price of the gas and are applied at the end of each month retroactively to that month's purchases. Here are the phone numbers for some of the major oil company programs:

Amoco; 800-254-9695
British Petroleum (BP); 800-347-2683
Exxon; apply at local station
Gulf; 800-367-4853
Phillips; 800-884-1930
Shell; 800-373-3427

Sunoco; 800-786-3003
Unocal; 800-638-3673

If you pay your balance off in full every month, the interest rate the bank charges does not really affect you. In this case, you may want a credit card that charges no annual fees. Some of the banks that typically do not charge annual fees and still offer a relatively low interest rate when you do revolve balances include:

AFBA Industrial Bank of Colorado; 800-776-2265
Amalgamated Bank of Chicago; 800-723-0303
AmTrust of Boca Raton; 888-268-7878
Broadway National Bank of Texas; 800-531-7650
First USA Bank of Delaware; 800-451-2491
Metropolitan Savings Bank of Cleveland; 800-837-6058
Perpetual Savings Bank of Iowa; 800-914-4953
Pullman Bank & Trust of Chicago; 800-785-5626
USAA Savings Bank; 800-922-9092
Wachovia of Georgia; 800-842-3262

WHEN YOU'VE ASSUMED TOO MUCH DEBT

With lenders making it convenient and easy to borrow, you might find yourself over your head in debt. The following warning signs will alert you that you are assuming too much debt.

- You juggle your bills, paying one company one month and another company the next.

- You frequently receive overdue notices from lenders.

- You make only the minimum payments on your debt, and you never pay off the principal owed.

- You have reached your limits on most or all your credit cards and credit lines.

- You pay for everyday necessities like food, rent or gasoline with credit because you have run out of cash.

- You constantly dip into the overdraft credit line accompanying your checking account to make bill payments. (Such overdraft lines usually charge a very high interest rate of 15 percent to 20 percent, sinking you even deeper in the hole.)

- You do not know how much you owe or what you spend on interest.

- You are afraid to open your monthly credit card statement.

- You pay so much in interest that no money remains for saving or investing. Typically, this will occur if more than 40 percent of your take-home income pays off interest.

- You have not accumulated much of an emergency fund, or you constantly dip into this fund because you run out of cash.

- Whenever you pay off a large balance, you run up an even bigger balance soon after.

- You borrow heavily against your stock and bond portfolio on margin. (If the value of the securities falls enough, you may be subject to a margin call, in which case your broker might sell your assets to satisfy your debt.)

- You apply for credit but are denied because of negative notations on your credit report.

If you find that your debts are out of hand, the worst step you can take is to ignore them. Hiding your bills in a drawer or refusing to open your mail will not make the payments go away, as much as you might like it to. The sooner you deal with your credit problems by discussing them with your lenders, the more lenient and the less painful your exit from debt will be. Most lenders would rather help you work out a debt repayment schedule than seize your property or send a collection agency after you. They take these steps only when you have been unresponsive to their inquiries and they think that they have no alternative.

If creditors assign collection agencies to your case, you still have certain rights under the federal Fair Debt Collection Practices Act.

- Collection agencies must send a written notice telling you how much you owe, to whom and what to do if you dispute the debt.

- If you send an agency a letter within 30 days saying that you do not owe the debt in question, the agency cannot contact you again unless it mails you proof of the debt, such as a copy of the bill that remains unpaid.

- Debt collectors cannot use techniques to collect the money that are abusive, deceptive or unfair.

- Collection agencies cannot threaten you with violence, curse at you, force you to accept collect telephone calls or advertise your debt to try to embarrass you into paying. They are prohibited from telling anyone (except your lawyer, if you have one) that you are behind in your debt payments.

- Agencies cannot lie to you about how much you owe or threaten you with arrest or imprisonment unless they possess the legal power to do so (which is difficult to obtain).

- Collectors planning to repossess your property or *garnish* (deduct from) your wages must inform you in advance so you have time to avoid these drastic actions.

- Bill collectors cannot call you at all hours of the day or night, such as before 8:00 AM or after 9:00 PM, unless you allow it. Also, they cannot call you at work if they know your employer disapproves.

- If collectors violate any of the above rules, you can sue in court for damages. However, if the court finds that you have acted in bad faith with the collectors, you might have to pay the collectors' legal bills incurred for your case.

While the Fair Debt Collection Practices Act protects you from abusive collection agencies, it does not absolve you of your debts. Creditors can still seize your assets, attach your wages or foreclose on your home if you don't pay. It's far better to avoid all this trouble in the first place by not borrowing too much and by staying on top of your bills.

If contacting your creditors about your problem does not work, you might want to consult the local chapter of the nonprofit Consumer Credit Counseling Service (CCCS). To find the counseling center nearest to you, call 800-388-2227. The national CCCS will send you an information packet explaining their services. It also will include a form in which you explain your financial situation to them, which you should fill out and return. They will then refer you to the counseling center nearest you. Often, the chapter is a member of the National Foundation for Consumer Credit (8611 2nd Ave., Suite 100, Silver Spring, MD 20910; 301-589-5600). The CCCS is financially supported by creditors and offers its services to the public free of charge or for a small fee. Under the guidance of the CCCS, one of your first acts—as painful as it might sound—will be to cut up most or all of your credit cards in front of your credit counselor. After that, your counselor will help you work out a realistic budget and debt repayment plan. Your credit counselor's job is to ensure that you pay back your debts over time. When the CCCS informs your lenders that you are working out a repayment plan, they will probably leave you alone. Your credit counselor will keep your creditors up to date on your progress.

Once you have dug yourself out of debt, with or without the help of a credit counselor, make sure that you change your spending and credit habits forever. Refer back to the budgeting exercise in Chapter 1 to help you gain control of your spending habits, and continue working with a counselor, if necessary.

THE LAST RESORT: BANKRUPTCY

If you have accumulated so much debt and have so many creditors hounding you for payment that you see no escape, you might have to consider the last resort: bankruptcy. Declaring bankruptcy is not a decision to be taken lightly because it will haunt your credit record for ten years and will impair your ability to obtain credit in the future. Potential employers and landlords may also learn that you declared bankruptcy. Therefore, bankruptcy is not exactly the fresh start that many bankruptcy lawyers advertise.

The main advantage of declaring bankruptcy is that you obtain relief from many of your debts. Depending on which form of bankruptcy you choose and the laws in your state, you may get to keep some or most of your assets. For example, some states allow you to keep your clothes and a car, while other states permit you to retain your home, car and other assets. However, you cannot discharge all your debts. For instance, you must continue to pay alimony, taxes, child support and student loans.

Two basic forms of bankruptcy exist: Chapter 13 and Chapter 7. Most people choose a Chapter 13 filing when their debts overwhelm them. If you have accumulated less than $100,000 in unsecured debt, such as debt on credit cards, and less than $350,000 in secured debt, such as car or furniture loans or home mortgages, you can formulate a plan to pay off all or part of your debt under the guidance of the bankruptcy court. Chapter 13 bankruptcy does allow you to discharge a large part of your debt, and it allows you to pay whatever debt is left over at a reasonable pace if you earn a regular income. You get to keep more of your assets under a Chapter 13 filing than you do under a Chapter 7.

Working with a lawyer who specializes in bankruptcy, you begin by filing a Chapter 13 petition with the court. The judge appoints a bankruptcy trustee to oversee your affairs. The trustee goes over your budget with you to make sure that it is realistic. To save on legal fees, you can try to do most of the work yourself, using one of the bankruptcy kits described in the "Resources" section following this chapter. However, you should be confident that you know what you are doing if you plan to execute the petition yourself. You may also be able to get help from a legal clinic or from a local law school, where students often work for free.

Your petition includes a repayment plan, as well as a listing of all your income, assets and debts, including the names and addresses of your creditors. Never try to hide assets or give them away temporarily to friends. If the court learns of your actions, it will seize these assets and distribute them to creditors. If the judge really gets upset, he or she can deny your bankruptcy petition and charge you with fraud.

Your petition also includes a budget of your living expenses, like the one you completed in the first chapter of this book. Your plan proposes extending the time you take to repay creditors and offers to pay less than the full amount. Some states require that you pay 90 cents on the dollar, while others allow you to pay far less.

Your plan is then sent to your creditors. Once your creditors have accepted your plan, the trustee will dispense a specific amount of money each month to your creditors, according to the plan. With this done, you send him or her a specific amount of money each month from your income, which the trustee dispenses to your creditors, according to the plan. As long as you make these payments in a timely way, your creditors legally cannot bother you. You also owe no interest or finance charges on your debt when it is supervised by the court. Chapter 13 is therefore not a total escape from your creditors. Rather, it functions as a way of paying them off in a controlled manner.

Chapter 7 is far more drastic. In this case, you must turn over all your assets to the bankruptcy court except for certain items the law allows you to keep. That usually includes $7,500 in home equity, $1,200 in equity in a car or truck, $200 per household item up to a total of $4,000, life insurance with a cash value of up to $4,000, $750 worth of trade tools or professional books and $500 worth of jewelry and other personal possessions. The court then distributes any excess assets—or possibly sells the assets in an auction and disburses the cash raised—to creditors. Once this process has been completed, you are legally discharged from your debt and have no obligation to repay your past loans.

Declaring bankruptcy is not a pleasant experience, as the millions of people who have done so can testify. By establishing a good credit record and managing your credit wisely, you should never need a bankruptcy lawyer, and the inner workings of bankruptcy court will forever remain a mystery to you.

Using Your Computer To Improve Your Credit Management

Your personal computer and the many Web sites related to credit issues can help you save a great deal of money and manage your debts better. (See the list of Web sites in the "Resources" section of this chapter.) The first way to lower your credit expenses is to apply for credit cards charging lower interest rates than your present cards. Searching Web sites such as CardTrak, Bank Rate Monitor and the Credit Card Network will help you identify cards with the lowest rates, no annual fees, rebates, frequent flier miles and other perks. In some cases, these sites will link you to sites sponsored by the issuing banks, which will allow you to apply for the card online.

There are also many Web sites designed to help you avoid getting into trouble with debt in the first place and resolve existing credit problems. These sites are sponsored by Credit Reporting Bureaus and Consumer Credit Counseling organizations. You can request a copy of your credit report online from Equifax, Experian and Trans Union, which often will get you the report quicker than a mail request. Credit bureaus still do not let you see your report online for security reasons; they still have to mail it to your address of record. If you are contemplating bankruptcy, it would be worth looking at some of these sites so you understand what your alternatives really are. No matter what your questions about credit, there is an online resource to help you answer them.

Resources

BOOKS

Bankruptcy: Is It the Right Solution to Your Debt Problems?, by Robin Leonard (Nolo Press, 950 Parker St., Berkeley, CA 94710; 510-549-1976; 800-992-NOLO; www.nolo.com). This compassionate guide can help you, if you feel overwhelmed by debts, to evaluate your options for getting back on your feet. It answers questions such as if you will lose your house or car, or if you will have trouble keeping or getting a job.

The Bankruptcy Kit, by John Ventura (Dearborn Financial Publishing, 155 N. Wacker Dr., Chicago, IL 60606; 312-836-4400; 800-322-8621; www.dearborn.com). Explains the entire bankruptcy process, from dealing with creditors to the discharge hearing.

Chapter 13 Bankruptcy: Repay Your Debts, by Robin Leonard (Nolo Press, 950 Parker St., Berkeley, CA 94710; 510-549-1976; 800-992-NOLO; www.nolo.com). Chapter 13 allows you to reorganize your debts into a manageable repayment plan without losing your property. This book shows you how the process works from beginning to end, including many sample letters and forms you will need to file.

Consumer Handbook to Credit Protection Laws (Consumer Information Center, Dept. 345C, Pueblo, CO 81009; 719-948-3334; www.pueblo.gsa.gov). A booklet published by the Federal Reserve Bank. Explains the cost of credit, how to apply for credit, how to build a good credit history and how to complain about being denied credit. Also includes other useful information about credit.

Credit Repair—Quick and Legal Series, by Robin Leonard (Nolo Press, 950 Parker St., Berkeley, CA 94710; 510-549-1976; 800-992-NOLO; www.nolo.com). A guide to improving your credit record by fixing errors, getting positive information added and negotiating with credit bureaus.

The Credit Repair Kit, by John Ventura (Dearborn Financial Publishing, 155 N. Wacker Dr., Chicago, IL 60606; 312-836-4400; 800-322-8621; www.dearborn.com). Explains how to read your credit report and correct errors you find. Also examines the credit reporting industry.

Guide to Personal Bankruptcy, by Gail J. Koff (Henry Holt, 115 W. 18th St., New York, NY 10011; 212-886-9200; www.hholt.com). A complete guide to the pros and cons of declaring bankruptcy. Also describes the steps to filing for Chapter 11 protection from creditors. Part of a series produced by the Jacoby and Meyers law firm.

How to File for Bankruptcy, by Stephen Elias, Albin Renauer and Robin Leonard (Nolo Press, 950 Parker St., Berkeley, CA 94710; 510-549-1976; 800-992-NOLO; www.nolo.com). This book will give you a clear overview of the bankruptcy process, showing you whether it makes sense to file for Chapter 7 or Chapter 13 in your situation. It explains which debts can and cannot be eliminated in bankruptcy, which property you risk losing and how to rebuild your credit.

How To Get Out of Debt, by Michael C. Thomsett (McGraw-Hill, Order Dept., 860 Taylor Station Rd., Blacklick, OH 43004; 800-722-4726; www.mcgraw-hill.com). Lists steps to correct your debt problem.

The Insider's Guide to Managing Your Credit, by Deborah McNaughton (Dearborn Financial Publishing, 155 N. Wacker Dr., Chicago, IL 60606; 312-836-4400; 800-245-2665; www.dearborn.com). A complete guide to establishing and maintaining a good credit history; also covers how to restore your credit reports when there are problems. The book explains your rights relating to collection agencies and guides you in reestablishing credit after bankruptcy.

Money Troubles: Legal Strategies To Cope with Your Debts, by Robin Leonard (Nolo Press, 950 Parker St., Berkeley, CA 94710; 510-549-1976; 800-992-NOLO; www.nolo.com). Helps those behind in their debts negotiate with lenders, challenge wage attachments, force bill collectors to stop their badgering and contend with property repossessions. Explains credit, student loans, taxes, alimony, child support and bankruptcy and what to expect if you are sued.

No-Nonsense Credit: An Insider's Guide to Borrowing Money and Managing Debt, by James Jorgenson (McGraw-Hill, Order Dept., 860 Taylor Station Rd., Blacklick, OH 43004; 800-722-4726; www.mcgraw-hill.com). Explains the best ways to borrow money at the cheapest rates.

Personal Bankruptcy, by Steven Elias, Albin Renauer, Robin Leonard and Lisa Goldoftas (Nolo Press, 950 Parker St., Berkeley, CA 94710; 510-549-1976; 800-992-NOLO; www.nolo.com). For those in serious debt trouble, a kit providing explanations of and forms for every step of a bankruptcy filing. Explains how to hold onto as many assets as possible as you go through the process. The same authors and publisher have issued a more detailed book on the subject titled *How To File for Bankruptcy.*

The Ultimate Credit Handbook: How To Double Your Credit, Cut Your Debt and Have a Lifetime of Great Credit, by Gerri Detweiler (Plume Press, Penguin-Putnam, 375 Hudson St., New York, NY 10014; 212-366-2000; 800-526-0275; www.penguin.com). Written by the former executive director of the Bankcard Holders of America. Explains in simple terms how to obtain your credit rating and improve a poor credit rating. Explains the ins and outs of credit cards, including interest rates, annual charges and hidden fees. Also discusses the alternative of bankruptcy, your rights to privacy and solving billing problems with banks or credit card issuers.

PAMPHLET

Tips on Consumer Credit (Council of Better Business Bureaus, 4200 Wilson Blvd., Arlington, VA 22203; 703-276-0100; www.bbb.org). An inexpensive brochure explaining different kinds of credit and loans, credit cards and your credit record.

TRADE ASSOCIATIONS

American Financial Services Association (919 18th St., N.W., Suite 300, Washington, DC 20006; 202-296-5544; www.americanfnsvcs.com). Offers free publications titled *The Consumer's Almanac* and *What You Should Know before Declaring Bankruptcy.*

Associated Credit Bureaus (1090 Vermont Ave., N.W., Suite 200, Washington, DC 20005-4905; 202-371-0910; www.acb-credit.com). The trade association for credit bureaus; it is involved in government relations, public affairs and education. Offers brochure titled "Consumers, Credit Bureaus and the Fair Credit Reporting Act."

Consumer Bankers Association (1000 Wilson Blvd., Suite 3012, Arlington, VA 22209-3908; 703-276-1750; www.cbanet.org). Represents banks and savings and loans and educates the public about credit issues.

Debtors Anonymous (General Service Board, P.O. Box 400, Grand Central Station, New York, NY 10163-0400). National organization with local support groups established to help people who consistently take on too much debt. Operates under many of the same guidelines and principles of Alcoholics Anonymous.

Family Service America (11700 W. Lake Park Dr., Park Place, Milwaukee, WI 53224; 414-359-1040; 800-221-2681; www.fsanet.org). An international nonprofit association dedicated to strengthening family life through services, education and advocacy. Member agencies throughout the United States provide family counseling services, including credit counseling. Also helps with marital problems, parent-child tensions, drug and alcohol problems, child abuse, family violence and other family problems.

International Credit Association (243 N. Lindbergh Blvd., St. Louis, MO 63141; 314-991-3030; www.ica-credit.org). A broad-based trade association representing all segments of the credit industry. Provides information services, professional development opportunities and credit education to the public and credit industry. Offers publications, including *Resource Guide to Credit* and *How to Use Consumer Credit Wisely.*

MasterCard International (2000 Purchase St., Purchase, NY 10577; 914-249-4600; www.mastercard.com). The organization of financial service firms issuing MasterCards. Offers these free publications, available by calling 800-999-5136: "Building a Credit History that Works for You"; "Credit Card Basics"; "Defending Yourself against Credit Card Fraud"; "In the Driver's Seat: A Guide to Managing Your Personal Information"; "Knowing Your Credit Card Bill of Rights"; "Learning About Smart Cards"; "Protecting your Financial Future"; "Schemes, Scams and Flim-Flams"; and "You Are Here: Managing Your Debt." Also offers "Debit Cards: The Smart New Way To Pay" brochure; available at 800-647-1756.

National Foundation for Consumer Credit (8611 2nd Ave., Suite 100, Silver Spring, MD 20910; 301-589-5600; 800-388-CCCS; www.nfcc.org). Aids consumers who have taken on too much debt. Has local consumer credit counseling centers across the country that help consumers restructure their debt and negotiate with creditors.

Visa U.S.A. (800 Metro Center Blvd., Foster City, CA 94404; 650-432-3200; www.visa.com). Organization of financial institutions issuing Visa cards. Signs up merchants for Visa acceptance. Offers free brochures titled "Credit Cards: An Owner's Manual" and "Managing Your Debt" to consumers who call 800-Visa-511.

FEDERAL GOVERNMENT REGULATORS

Federal Reserve System (20th Street and C Street, N.W., Washington, DC 20551; 202-452-3946; www.fedweb.gov). Regulates the U.S. banking system and the granting of credit by banks. Offers the following brochures about credit: "Consumer Credit Protection: Do You Know Your Rights?"; "Consumer Handbook to Credit Protection Laws"; "Consumers and the Fed"; "Credit Guide"; "Fair Credit Billing"; "Fair Debt Collection Practices Act"; "Give Yourself Credit"; "A Guide to Business Credit for Women, Minorities and Small Businesses"; "How the Equal Credit Opportunity Act Affects You"; "How To Establish and Use Credit"; "How To File a Consumer Credit Complaint"; "Paying a Loan Off Early: Things You Should Know"; "Plastic Fraud: Getting a Handle on Debit and Credit Cards"; "The Story of Consumer Credit"; and "Your Credit Rating."

Federal Trade Commission (6th Street and Pennsylvania Avenue, N.W., Washington, DC 20580; 202-326-3650; www.ftc.gov). Credit Practices Division has jurisdiction over many credit-related issues and enforces the following laws: Consumer Leasing Act; Credit Practices Rule; Electronic Funds Transfer Act; Equal Credit Opportunity Act; Fair Credit Billing Act; Fair Credit Reporting Act; Fair Debt Collection Practices Act; Holder-in-Due-Course Rule; and Truth-in-Lending Act. Oversees trends in credit card fraud, 900 phone numbers, mortgage escrow and the credit repair industry. Will send a free copy of the following brochures: "Advance Fee Loan Scams"; "Building a Better Credit Record"; "Buying and Borrowing: Cash in on the Facts"; "Choosing and Using Credit Cards"; "Cosigning a Loan"; "Credit and Charge Card Fraud"; "Credit and Older Americans"; "Credit Billing Errors"; "Credit Practices Rule"; "Credit Repair Scams"; "A New Credit Identity: A New Credit Repair Scam"; "Electronic Banking"; "Equal Credit Opportunity"; "Fair Credit Billing"; "Fair Credit Reporting"; "Fair Debt Collection"; "Fix Your Own Credit Problems and Save Money"; "Getting a Loan: Your Home as Security"; "Home Equity Credit Lines"; "Lost or Stolen: Credit and ATM Cards"; "Making Smart Choices"; "Protecting Your Money"; "Scoring for Credit"; "Solving Credit Problems"; "Truth in Leasing"; "Using Plastic: A Young Adult's Guide to Credit Cards"; "Utility Credit"; "Vehicle Repossession"; "What's Going on at the FTC?"; and "Women and Credit Histories."

CREDIT BUREAUS

Three major credit bureaus retain your credit profile for use by credit grantors deciding whether to give you credit. You can call or write these bureaus to obtain a copy of your credit report, usually for a fee.

CreditComm Services (2700 Prosperity Avenue, Suite 100, Fairfax, VA 22031; 703-207-1600; 800-777-9700; www.creditfaqs.com). For a fee of about $30, this company compiles a CreditCompare profile, which combines your credit reports as currently listed by Equifax, Experian and Trans Union. The report is reformatted from the styles of all three credit bureaus, making it easier to understand.

Equifax Credit Information Services (corporate headquarters: 1600 Peachtree St., NW, Atlanta, GA 30309; 404-885-8000; consumer inquiries: P.O. Box 740241, Atlanta, GA 30374-0241 for a copy of your credit report; P.O. Box 740256 to dispute items on your credit report; 800-685-1111; www.equifax.com). Offers free brochures titled "Consumer Information and Privacy" and "You Have a Right To Know . . . Facts about the Fair Credit Reporting Act."

Experian, formerly TRW Information Services (corporate headquarters: 505 City Pkwy. West, Orange, CA 92868; 714-385-7500; consumer inquiries for a copy of your credit report: Experian National Consumer Assistance Center, P.O. Box 949, 701 Experian Pkwy., Allen, TX 75013; to dispute information on your credit report, P.O. Box 2106 at the same address 888-EXPERIA (397-3742); 800-422-4879; 800-682-7654; www.experian.com). Experian produces a series of Reports on Credit that are available free for consumers from the company's Consumer Education Department, directly at P.O. Box 1239, Allen, TX 75013, or on Experian's Web site. Some of the titles for reports on credit include: "Basic Questions About Credit Reports and Credit Reporting"; "Creating a Positive Credit History"; "Divorce and Your Credit"; "Facts About Mailing Lists and Preapproved Credit Offers"; "The Fair Credit Reporting Act, Privacy and Your Credit Report"; "How Lenders Make—and Monitor—Credit Decisions"; "Obligations When Signing or Cosigning a Loan"; "Protecting Yourself Against Credit Card Fraud"; "Reviewing Your Credit Report"; and "The Use of Credit Reports for Employment Purposes." Experian also offers a brochure titled "12 Common Questions About Consumer Credit and Direct Marketing."

Trans Union Corporation (corporate headquarters: 555 W. Adams, Chicago, IL 60661; 312-258-1717; consumer inquiries: 760 W. Sproul Rd., P.O. Box 390, Springfield, PA 19064; 800-888-4213; www.tuc.com).

CREDIT CARD RATING SERVICE

CardTrak (RAM Research, P.O. Box 1700, Frederick, MD 21702; 800-344-7714; www.ramresearch.com). Publishes a list of banks offering credit cards with low finance charges, low or no annual fees, full grace periods, frequent flier mileage credits, gold cards, rebates and secured credit cards for consumers rebuilding their credit history. This list is available for a nominal fee.

WEB SITES

Associated Credit Bureaus Consumer Credit Information. The site sponsored by the Credit Reporting Agencies's trade group, Associated Credit Bureaus. It explains what a credit report is, how mistakes can be corrected and whether bad credit can really be repaired. It also has an explanation of various federal laws relating to credit, such as the Fair Credit Reporting Act. www.acb-credit.com/

Bank Rate Monitor. A service that will help you find the best credit card for your needs. You can sort credit cards by the lowest interest rates on a conventional or gold card, cards with no annual fees, cards with rebates, frequent flier miles and other perks, or secured cards for those with past credit problems. www.brm.com

Center for Debt Management. A comprehensive Web site on debt sponsored by the Family Debt Arbitration and Counseling Services organization. This group specializes in debt counseling and negotiations with creditors. The site has an extensive library of articles and resources on almost all aspects of debt management. www.members.aol.com/DebtRelief/

Consumer Credit Counseling Service. A site devoted to helping people resolve their debt problems. It includes a detailed question and answer section with debt counselors, and links to CCCS offices around the country. Many topics are covered, including dealing with creditors and credit bureaus, choosing credit cards, and how to handle rejected applications for credit. www.powersource.com/cccs/

Credit Card Network. A site linking you to many other credit-card-related sites. You can search for the lowest-interest card and even apply for a card online. www.creditnet.com/

Fair, Isaac Consumer Credit Information. Fair Isaac is the company that provides the scoring system to creditors that in many cases determines if you will be granted a loan or not. This Web site explains the credit scoring system, which might help you understand why you will or will not be accepted when you apply for credit. www.fairisaac.com /consumer/

National Credit Counseling Services. The site sponsored by the National Consumer Credit Counseling Service gives you advice if you are having trouble with credit and debts. It gives you a confidential credit evaluation quiz, and you can read articles on many credit-related topics like bankruptcy, credit reports and applying for credit cards. www.nccs.org/welcome.html

Getting the Most
for Your Money
When Buying a Car

Along with purchasing a home and funding college tuition, buying a car numbers among the largest investments you will ever make. Long gone are the days when you could spend $5,000 for an economy car that would last for years. Today, cars come in a staggering variety of styles and price ranges and offer an incredible array of options.

The process of buying a car comprises two separate but related steps. First, you must determine your transportation needs and what type of car will best meet them. Second, you must decide how to pay for the car. A car purchase entails weighing the pros and cons of dealer or bank financing, leasing or paying cash. This chapter will guide you in both choosing your car and paying for it.

Determining What Kind of Car You Need

Before you visit a dealer's showroom or pick up your first car review magazine, carefully evaluate your transportation needs. By writing down the features you want in a car and how much you will spend, you can avoid making a hasty or costly decision you will regret later. Many buyers' emotions have overtaken their common sense, leaving them with beautiful, option-filled cars that boost their self-esteem but take unnecessarily large bites out of the buyers' wallets.

Following are a few questions you should consider when deciding what kind of car to buy.

- How long do you plan to keep the car?

- Will you use it mostly for short, local trips or for long drives?

- How important is good gas mileage? (In general, the more luxurious the car, the worse its gas mileage.)

- If you have children: What will be your family's transportation needs in the short and long term?

- If you do not have children: Do you anticipate having children during the years that you will own the car? What will be your family's transportation needs then?

- How many passengers will normally use the car? What is the maximum number of people the car will need to carry?

- What kinds of storage will you need from the car? Will you mostly carry groceries from the supermarket, or will you frequently lug heavy suitcases as well? Do you need a storage rack on top of the car, as well as ample trunk space?

- Will you tow trailers behind the car; if so, how big will they be? (If you rent large trailers, you will need a car with more horsepower.)

- What facilities are available—at home, at work, at a train or bus station— for parking the car?

- How safe are the neighborhoods where you will park the car? (This will help determine how expensive a car to acquire, the antitheft devices the car will require and how essential a garage will be.)

- How important is car safety? Will you pay a premium for a very safe car?

- How important is comfort? (Today's automakers offer many luxurious features that are nice to have but can cost thousands of dollars.)

- How much attention will you pay to maintaining the car? (You may be a car buff who relishes the thought of tuning and waxing your beauty every Saturday. Or your definition of maintenance might be telling a gas station attendant to check the oil.)

- What are the weather and road conditions where you will drive the car? For example, do you live in an area so hot during the summer that air conditioning is a must? Will you drive the vehicle off main roads? If so, four-wheel drive will be necessary.

- What options are vital, and which are expendable?

A list of the most rudimentary auto options follows. Determine those options that you must have and those you can live without.

Adjustable steering column. This feature allows you to move the steering wheel up or down to adjust to your height. Tilting the wheel upward also makes it easier to get into the car.

Air bag for driver. This air bag pops out of the steering wheel automatically when the air bag's sensor system detects high-speed contact with another car or some other obstruction. The air bag deflates immediately after inflating and must be replaced thereafter, often along with the steering column.

Air bag for passenger. This air bag works the same way as the driver's, except that it is usually bigger and is mounted in the dashboard.

Air conditioning. Air conditioning not only cools you in the summer; it helps defog the car's windows. Some cars offer *automatic temperature control,* allowing you to choose the interior temperature. The system determines when to turn on or shut off to achieve that temperature. Using the air conditioning worsens fuel economy.

AM-FM sound system. You may desire a traditional radio system in the car. The best systems provide graphic equalizers and reverberation controls designed to create sound for the car's interior. If you live in a high-crime area, you might want to obtain a removable radio.

AM-FM cassette sound system. In addition to the radio, this system provides the ability to play cassette tapes. Because such a sound system is even more attractive to thieves than a radio alone, you might want to buy a removable system.

AM-FM compact disc sound system. This top-of-the-line system allows you to play compact discs, as well as the radio. The CD system is designed to withstand bumps in the road. Your best bet is a removable system because most thieves find CD players easy to sell.

Antilock brakes. These brakes, unlike traditional brakes, let you steer effectively while the car stops on a wet surface, thereby avoiding skids.

Antitheft devices. You have many ways to protect your car from theft or vandalism, including alarms, steering column locks, flashing headlights and engine disablers. While they all deter thieves, none probably will stop a professional. Many antitheft devices qualify you for discounts on your auto insurance.

Automatic transmission. This transmission shifts the car from one gear to another automatically, in contrast to manual transmission, for which you must use a shift stick and clutch to move among several gears. Automatic transmission is less fuel efficient than manual transmission, but it makes driving significantly easier and less tiring.

Bumper protection and body trim. Bumpers are designed to withstand gentle contact from another vehicle or some other obstruction. Body side moldings protect the car from nicks obtained in parking lots and other tight parking places.

Cellular telephone. A car phone can make you more productive if you find yourself sitting in traffic frequently. Many phones today offer hands-free operation, which helps you keep your eyes on the road. You often save money by installing a cellular phone after you've bought a car instead of taking the factory-installed version. Remember to budget for monthly cellular phone charges, which can be significant if you use your phone frequently.

Child-safety seats. Many cars today provide built-in child seats, which usually fold out of the middle back seat. When you don't need them, they fold away neatly.

Cruise control. This feature allows you to hit a button to maintain the car's current speed while you take your foot off the accelerator. The moment you put your foot on the brake (or the clutch in a manual transmission auto), you deactivate the cruise control.

Dual remote-controlled mirrors. This feature allows you to adjust both the driver's and passenger's side mirror with an electronic control. The feature is helpful when it works but can be difficult and expensive to repair. Some more luxurious cars provide heated mirrors to combat snow and ice in the winter.

Electronic instrument-panel display. Many panels today provide digital miles-per-hour read-outs, as well as digital temperature displays. (The moving needle is quickly becoming obsolete.) Some panels incorporate a computer that helps you estimate how long it will take to arrive at your destination. Other panels warn you if doors are not properly closed, if your car is out of oil, if your taillights are burned out or if anything else in the car is not functioning properly. Aside from an instrument panel's features, however, look for a display that is easy to read. The most sophisticated display information will do you little good if you cannot interpret it.

Four-wheel drive. If you drive off main roads, on beaches, in deserts or in snow, four-wheel drive is a must. It greatly improves traction although it reduces fuel economy.

Full-size spare tire. This spare tire is the same size as your regular tires; therefore, you can use it when you rotate your tires. However, a full-size spare tire takes up far more room in the trunk than a compact spare tire, which is designed for short-term, emergency use.

Intermittent wipers. You can set intermittent wipers at various speeds, depending on the weather's severity. They cut down on wiper wear and may distract you less than continuous wipers, which are standard on all cars.

Power brakes. These brakes make it much easier to apply the brake pedal than do traditional brakes.

Power lock system. This electrical system allows you to lock all the car's doors from either the driver's or the passenger's door. It is certainly more convenient than locking each door manually. Some locking systems even provide remote infrared devices and keyless entry. Just be careful not to lock yourself out of the car with these fancy systems.

Power seat adjustments. These controls let you move your seat forward, backward, up and down to fit your size and allow the driver and passenger to adjust their seats individually. Some cars offer *seat adjustment memory* so the seat moves to a preset position for a particular person.

Power steering. This system makes steering easy and is especially helpful when you park the car.

Radial tires. The longest lasting tires made, radials often can be used in all seasons and elements, including snow, rain and other foul weather.

Rear window defogger. This system helps keep the rear window clear when snow, rain or humidity causes it to fog.

Rear window wiper/washer. This feature allows you to wipe rain or snow off the back window by flicking a switch on the dashboard. It sure beats getting out of the car and wiping the window by hand.

Roof rack. A handy place to carry things that won't fit in the car, a roof rack provides special attachments for skis, boats and other large objects.

Rustproofing. Many dealers sell a rustproofing package that is supposed to increase corrosion protection. However, most auto consumer groups recommend against additional rustproofing. In some cases, additional rustproofing will even void an automaker's rustproofing warranty.

Special lighting systems. To help you lock up, some cars offer a lighting system that will stay on for a few seconds after you leave the car.

Sun roof. You can open this panel in a car's roof to let in sunshine or improve air circulation.

Upholstery options. You have several options in seat coverings. Cloth is the most practical and comfortable because it "breathes" during the hot summer. Vinyl protects against spills but can get sticky in the summer. Leather is the most luxurious but requires the most upkeep.

Windshield heating system. This system warms the windshield faster than does the defroster alone, making it easier to clean off snow and ice.

Finally, carefully consider how much you want to spend annually for gasoline. The table in Figure 10.1, reprinted courtesy of *The Car Book* (see "Resources" section at the end of this chapter), shows how much you should expect to pay for gas, assuming you drive your car 15,000 miles a year. The first column lists the number of miles per gallon your car might get, from a low of 22 to as many as 50. At the head of each remaining column are different prices for a gallon of gas, from $1 to $1.50. Notice that you would pay as little as $450 a year (with gas at $1.50) for an economical 50-miles-per-gallon car, while you would pay more than twice as much—$1,023—for a gas guzzler averaging only 22 miles per gallon.

The Shopping Process

After you have considered the questions listed earlier in the chapter, determined which options are most important to you and decided how much you want to spend each year on gasoline, it's time to set a target price for the car you want to buy. Because you won't know exactly what car is right for you until you've shopped around, set a wide range at first, perhaps in increments of $5,000. You should have an idea of whether you can afford a car for less than $10,000, $10,000 to $15,000, $15,000 to $20,000 or more than $20,000.

Once you've chosen a price range, your options will narrow quickly. Consult magazines like *Motor Trend* and *Car and Driver* to learn what they say about the models that interest you. For a complete write-up of all cars, consult *Consumer Reports'* April auto issue or its *New Car Buying Guide* (Consumer Reports Books, P.O. Box 10637, Des Moines, IA 50336; 515-237-4903; 800-500-9760). This definitive and unbiased guide, updated every year, is based on *Consumer Reports'* extensive testing of all new cars. For data on injury records and collision loss

Figure 10.1
Annual Cost of Fuel (Based on 15,000 Miles Per Year)

	Price per Gallon					
MPG	$1.50	$1.40	$1.30	$1.20	$1.10	$1.00
50	$450	$420	$390	$360	$330	$300
48	469	438	406	375	344	313
46	489	457	424	391	359	326
44	511	477	443	409	375	341
42	536	500	464	429	393	357
40	563	525	488	450	413	375
38	592	553	513	474	434	395
36	625	583	542	500	458	417
34	662	618	574	529	485	441
32	703	656	609	563	516	469
30	750	700	650	600	550	500
28	804	750	696	643	589	536
26	865	808	750	692	635	577
24	938	875	813	750	688	625
22	1023	955	886	818	750	682

Source: Table on page 62 of *The Car Book 1992* by Jack Gillis. Copyright © 1991, 1989, 1988, 1987, 1986, 1985, 1984, 1983, 1982, 1981 by Jack Gillis. Reprinted by permission of HarperCollins Publishers, Inc.

experience from a particular manufacturer's products, contact the Highway Loss Data Institute (listed in the "Resources" section at the end of this chapter).

Once you've selected a few cars that meet your criteria, visit a dealership for a test drive or drop by a local auto show to better compare the vehicles. If you visit a dealer, tell the salesperson that you are considering several models and just want to test drive now. You will return if you are interested. (Many salespeople try not to let you escape the showroom if you display much interest in a car.) Test drive the car on different types of roads for a long enough time that you develop a good feel for the car's acceleration, braking, steering and handling. Turn on the radio to see how the system sounds while you are under way. Then turn off the radio to determine how well the car blocks out street noises. If you fall in love with the car, don't let the salesperson know it. Swoon in private, and you will save a lot of money.

YES! Please send me the latest issue of the

MONEY ANSWERS CATALOG.

A $3 cover price – **FREE** with this coupon!

(For more information about the catalog, see page xxiii.)

Name: _____
(please print)

Address: _____

_____

City: _____ State: _____ ZIP: _____

Phone: ( ) _____ FAX: ( ) _____

Please let us know if you are interested in any of the following:

☐ CDs, Mutual Funds, & Investing

☐ Home Buying & Mortgages

☐ Real Estate Investment

☐ Debt Management

☐ Insurance

☐ Credit Card Rates

☐ College Financing

☐ Travel

☐ Car Buying

☐ Retirement Planning

☐ Estate Planning

YES! Please send me the latest issue of the

MONEY ANSWERS CATALOG.

A $3 cover price – **FREE** with this coupon!

(For more information about the catalog, see page xxiii.)

Name: _____
(please print)

Address: _____

_____

City: _____ State: _____ ZIP: _____

Phone: ( ) _____ FAX: ( ) _____

Please let us know if you are interested in any of the following:

☐ CDs, Mutual Funds, & Investing

☐ Home Buying & Mortgages

☐ Real Estate Investment

☐ Debt Management

☐ Insurance

☐ Credit Card Rates

☐ College Financing

☐ Travel

☐ Car Buying

☐ Retirement Planning

☐ Estate Planning

BUSINESS REPLY MAIL

FIRST-CLASS MAIL PERMIT NO. 1403 SEATTLE WA

POSTAGE WILL BE PAID BY ADDRESSEE

NO POSTAGE
NECESSARY
IF MAILED
IN THE
UNITED STATES

MONEY ANSWERS
1932 1ST AVE STE 605
SEATTLE WA 98101-9903

Also, ask about the car's warranty coverage. Automakers now compete aggressively to offer the longest and most complete warranties, and you should benefit from this competition. Often, auto warranties run for either three years or 36,000 miles or five years or 50,000 miles, whichever comes first. Many are even more generous. Warranties tell you exactly what parts they cover, for how many years and what you must do to rectify the problem if a part malfunctions. Most warranties are limited, meaning that they cover some but not all of a car's systems. Usually, warranties cover the *power train,* which includes the transmission, engine and driveline. Some warranties stipulate a deductible—a dollar amount of repairs you must pay before the warranty takes effect. A long warranty does not mean that the car will remain trouble free for a long time; however, it protects you from significant out-of-pocket costs if you end up with a lemon.

In addition to offering basic warranties, most automakers offer *extended warranties,* or service contracts. The extended warranty goes into effect when the basic warranty lapses. However, most extended service contracts are not good deals. They can be quite expensive, and they contain so many exclusions that you often find they do not cover what has broken. Many extended warranties also require a deductible each time you bring in your car for repair. In addition, the extended service contract often duplicates the basic warranty coverage, and many of the extended warranty's other provisions, such as towing service and car rental during repairs, are covered by your basic auto insurance policy or membership in an auto club.

If you still desire a service contract, make sure that you know who backs it, the auto manufacturer, the dealer or an independent company called an *administrator,* which uses claims adjusters to authorize the payment of claims to the dealer. If the dealer or an administrator backs the warranty, know who will fulfill your extended service if either goes out of business. In some cases, the contract is also backed by an insurance company that would pick up any expenses if your primary service agent is unable to do so. Also, learn whether the service contract is transferable if you sell the car. Sometimes the service company charges a fee to transfer the contract. If you consider buying a service contract, wait several months after you purchase the car to determine whether the vehicle is likely to need many repairs.

Closing the Deal

After you've narrowed your search to one or two models, it's time to concentrate on getting the best price. The easiest way to accomplish this is to arm yourself with knowledge of the dealer's cost. You should bargain from the dealer's cost upward, not the sticker price downward. Typically, the dealer will settle for a profit margin from 3 percent to 7 percent more than the dealer's cost if the car is not in great demand. That might amount to $200 to $500 more than the dealer paid. The suggested retail price might build in a profit margin as high as 12 percent.

If several dealers operate in your neighborhood, bargain with all of them, and play one off against another. Dealers often brag that they offer the lowest prices in town—so make them prove it. On the other hand, if the car you want is a hot seller, you have less bargaining power and may have to pay close to the suggested retail price. (Other ways to get a good deal on a car include checking prices in classified ads in newspapers or visiting used-car dealers or car rental agencies, which might offer the same car—slightly used or a year old—for thousands of dollars less than the price of a brand-new car.)

Although you might not endear yourself to the salesperson by knowing the dealership's costs, most have come to expect this from cost-conscious consumers. Four services—CarBargains, Car/Puter International, Consumer Reports' Auto Price Service and *Money* Magazine's Auto Cost Comparison—can tell you a dealer's cost for every model and all options. (These services' addresses and phone numbers are listed in the "Resources" section at the end of this chapter.) The services also provide data on projected repair histories, annual expenses and manufacturer's incentive or rebate programs currently in effect. Salespeople at local dealerships may contest the numbers on the print-outs from these services, but the figures are updated continuously and accurate.

Determining what price you should bargain from can often be confusing. Dealers refer to the following four prices:

- The *invoice price* is the price the automaker charges the dealer. It always includes *freight,* or what are commonly called destination and delivery charges. The dealer's actual cost may be less than the invoice price because it may qualify for various rebates, incentives and other discounts.

- The *base price* is the cost of the car with standard equipment and a basic warranty but no options.

- The *Monroney sticker price* is the price listed on the sticker on the car window. It includes the base price, the cost of installed options, destination charges and fuel economy.

- The *dealer sticker price* equals the Monroney sticker price plus the suggested retail price of any options installed by the dealer.

If you hate to haggle, you might use an auto broker or a buyer's service to obtain a good price. *Brokers* usually buy a high volume of cars through a dealer's fleet sales department and can therefore obtain a better deal than you could get on your own. Brokers usually take possession of the car first and then resell it to you. However, dealing with brokers has a few drawbacks. For example, brokers usually do not accept trade-ins, tend to work with a limited number of dealers and cannot find all models of all car makes. You can locate local brokers through your local *Yellow Pages,* or you may try the two largest national auto brokers, Nationwide Auto Brokers (17517 W. 10 Mile Rd., Southfield, MI 48075; 800-521-7257; www.car-connect.com) or Car/Puter International (1500 Cordova Rd., Suite 309, Fort Lauderdale, FL 33316; 305-462-8905; 800-645-2960).

Buyer's services can usually work with all makes and models in all 50 states. These services do not take possession of the vehicle. After the buyer's service has found a factory-authorized dealer that will give you the lowest price, you buy directly from the dealer. Buyer's services can also handle trade-ins. Two of the biggest such services are offered by the American Automobile Association and AutoAdvisor, Inc. (see "Resources" section for more information).

When negotiating to buy a new car, limit the conversation to the car's price until you agree on a deal. Do not discuss trade-in allowances for your existing car, rebates or financing options until the price is firm. Many dealers will extract a higher price from you by giving you less than your old car is worth or by adjusting financing terms. To get an idea of your trade-in's value, consult the *N.A.D.A. Official Used Car Guide,* Retail Edition (discussed in more detail later in this chapter) and *Edmund's Used Car Prices,* available on most newsstands.

While most dealers expect to haggle over price, a recent trend started by GM's Saturn division has emerged—the *fixed-price dealer.* These dealers are not allowed to sell the car for less than the suggested retail price, which is supposedly marked down to prevent the need for bargaining. However, you still have to negotiate the value of your trade-in.

When you have agreed on a price, a trade-in allowance and financing terms, don't drop your guard. Read the fine print in your sales agreement (you might bring along a magnifying glass), and make sure you understand everything in it. If you have a question, ask. Don't rely on verbal promises, and don't sign a contract containing blank spaces. Be sure that you can get your deposit back if the car delivered to you does not meet your standards. And it's best to have the manager of the dealership, as well as the salesperson, sign the sales agreement to ensure that the contract is legally binding.

Once you've signed the contract, you have plenty of paperwork to complete before you can drive your new car out of the dealer's lot. You or the dealer must obtain the following.

- *Title forms.* These are your proof of ownership of the car and must be obtained from the state motor vehicle department. If you lease, the title goes to the leasing company.

- *Registration certificate.* This is proof from the state that the car has been properly registered.

- *License plates.* You can either transfer the plates from your old car (after notifying the state) or obtain new plates. If the state doesn't send you license plates by the time you take possession of the car, the dealer will provide temporary plates, which are usually good for 30 days.

- *Proof of insurance.* You usually need to show the dealer your insurance forms to receive your registration. If you lease, you must show your insurance policy to the leasing company.

- *Proof of sales tax payment.* Before you receive your registration, the state needs proof that you paid sales tax. Many cities and counties also require that you display a tax license on your windshield.

- *Inspection sticker.* Many dealers perform an official inspection and attach a sticker to your windshield to prove it.

Buying a Used Car

Most of the advice about buying a new car also pertains to buying a used car. Here are a few extra tips.

First, choose which of the following five sources of used cars suits your needs:

- *New-car dealers usually sell the cars they have purchased as trade-ins.* The cars have often been repaired in the firm's service department before being offered for sale, and they may provide a limited warranty.

- *Used-car dealers usually sell cars with more mileage and wear and tear than the trade-ins on new-car dealers' lots.* Used-car dealers may offer limited warranties.

- *Car rental agencies offer vehicles that have been rented several months— perhaps as much as six months and up to 8,000–15,000 miles.* Because the cars have been used by many drivers, they probably are not as well cared for as cars driven by one person. However, often this is reflected in the price, which means that you can get a good deal.

- *Banks sell repossessed cars to pay off defaulted loans.* The vehicles can often be purchased at auctions or directly through the banks. The quality of your deal depends totally on who drove the car and how well he or she took care of it.

- *Individuals sell their cars through newspaper ads.* However, have the car checked out thoroughly by a mechanic before you buy it because you may not receive any warranties or other protections once you purchase the vehicle.

When you've located a car that interests you, examine the following features particularly carefully:

- Battery (date purchased, power test)
- Body (damage, repair, rust, welding)
- Doors and window glass (operation, rattle)
- Fluids such as oil and radiator and transmission fluid (clear, full, leakage)
- Heater and air conditioner (leakage, noises, operation)
- Interior upholstery (clean, holes)
- Lights (headlight alignment, operation)

- Radio (operation)
- Shock absorbers or struts (damage, leakage)
- Tailpipe (connectors, holes, rust)
- Tires (sidewall, tread, wear)

Test drive the car extensively to check the steering, the brakes and other major systems. While you drive, pay attention to unusual vibrations, noises or odors, which could be tip-offs to larger problems.

Once you've found a car that passes all these tests, bargain with the seller as you would with the salesperson at a new-car dealership. Use as a guide the prices listed in the National Automobile Dealers Association's *N.A.D.A. Official Used Car Guide,* Retail Edition, published quarterly (NADA, 8400 Westpark Dr., McLean, VA 22102; 800-248-6232). The book provides a low, a high and an average retail price for most used cars.

Financing Versus Leasing

The most inexpensive way to buy your new car is to pay cash for it because you then have no financing costs. However, most people can't come up with $10,000 to $30,000 or more in cash at one time. That leaves two main options: financing and leasing.

THE INS AND OUTS OF CAR LOANS

Obtaining a car loan was much more attractive in the days when consumer interest was fully deductible. If you paid 10 percent interest when you were in a 50 percent tax bracket, your real, after-tax cost of borrowing was only 5 percent. But starting in 1991, when taxpayers could no longer deduct consumer interest, that same loan's real cost doubled from 5 percent to 10 percent. However, today many low-interest options are available to qualified buyers.

The monthly loan payment includes loan fees, the fee the lender paid to obtain your credit report and charges for credit life insurance. *Credit life insurance* will pay off the auto loan for you if you die with a balance. Most financial advisers recommend against credit life coverage because it is very expensive and your regular life insurance should pay your bills if you die prematurely.

When shopping for the best loan, look at the *annual percentage rate* (APR)— that is, the interest rate you pay each year on the unpaid loan balance. To some extent, the interest rate, or APR, you get on your car loan will depend on your credit history. The more creditworthy you are, the lower your rate will be.

In addition to looking at the interest rate, also determine how much down payment each lender requires. If your trade-in does not cover the down payment, most lenders ask for between 10 percent and 20 percent of the value of the car you're buying, depending on your creditworthiness. The less you invest up front, the higher your financing costs and monthly payments over time. All lenders require that the total loan be covered by collateral—your car. If you miss a few payments, you lose your car to repossession.

Several sources for car loans exist. *Dealers* offer financing, often through the captive finance arm of the automaker. Expect a GM dealer to direct you to the General Motors Acceptance Corporation (GMAC), a Ford dealer to suggest Ford credit and so on. Usually, the interest rates charged by captive finance companies are higher than those available at local banks or credit unions. However, for many buyers, this may be the only available credit source depending on your level of credit risk. Dealers push financing with captive finance companies because they receive money for every car loan they arrange. If car sales are slow and the manufacturer wants to stimulate buying, it will sweeten financing deals considerably. In the most extreme cases, captive finance companies tout 0 percent financing. It's hard to beat 0 percent interest—except that such deals often come with many strings attached, and you must pay a higher price for the car than if you financed it through another source or paid cash. Many low-interest-rate loans apply only to cars on the dealer's lot, not to cars ordered with special options from the factory. In many cases, these low-rate loans cover short terms of two or three years, which raises the monthly loan payments significantly. And often they require down payments of 25 percent to 30 percent instead of the normal 10 percent. Some dealers require you to surrender the manufacturer's rebate if you obtain a low-interest loan.

Local banks frequently offer lower interest rates on car loans than do dealers. For a detailed listing of low loan rates, consult *Bank Rate Monitor* (P.O. Box 088888, North Palm Beach, FL 33408; 407-627-7330; 800-327-7717). This publication tracks car loan rates at most banks in the country on a weekly basis.

If you belong to a *credit union,* you might obtain an even better loan. Because credit unions, unlike banks, are designed to serve their members rather than shareholders, they often charge lower interest rates and offer more lenient terms. In many cases, however, credit unions require larger down payments than do banks or finance companies.

Finally, *insurance companies* often loan money to policyholders. Many auto insurance companies offer attractive rates, and most life insurance companies provide a single-payment loan on the cash value in your policy, which can be used to pay for your car. You can repay the loan as part of your regular premium payments.

When deciding on a financing package, determine how much you can afford to pay each month. (Use the budget you established in Chapter 1 to set a comfortable amount.) One way to lower your monthly payment is to increase your down payment—although this maximizes up-front, out-of-pocket expenses. You can also reduce your monthly outlay by opting for a loan term of five years instead of three or four. Realize, however, that you will pay much more interest over five years than you would if you paid off your debt in three years. (Remember also that none of that interest is deductible.) In addition, you will build up equity in your car more slowly with a longer term loan.

Before you commit to any car loan, know the answers to the following questions:

- From which company are you borrowing money?

- Where do you send your monthly payments?

- Do you hold title to your car, or does the lender hold title until the loan is paid?

- Must you obtain credit life insurance? (Most lenders encourage you to do so because it is profitable for them; some banks even require it. However, as discussed earlier, credit life insurance is very expensive, and your regular life insurance should already cover your debt.)

- What rights do you have if you default on your loan and the car is repossessed?

- What is the grace period on making your car payment each month?

- Does the lender charge prepayment penalties or other fees if you pay off the loan early? Can you get a refund of your down payment if you prepay the loan?

THE LEASING ALTERNATIVE

Before you obtain an auto loan, investigate leasing the car of your dreams. Leasing contracts can be tricky, but you often come out ahead leasing instead of financing a car. That's why every year more people lease their cars instead of buying them.

Two kinds of leases exist: closed-end and open-end. A *closed-end lease,* often called a *walk-away lease,* allows you to return the car when the agreement expires and walk away from any further responsibility. The leasing company assumes all the risks and headaches of reselling the car. You must, however, bring back the car in good condition, which includes normal wear and tear. If your lease specified a limit to the number of miles you could drive the car during the agreement, you must make sure that you have not exceeded that limit. If you do exceed it, you must pay a penalty of up to $.15 per mile. (When you sign the lease, do not agree to fewer miles than you would normally drive if you owned the car.) Because you are not responsible for the car's worth when the lease terminates, your monthly payments will usually be higher with a closed-end lease than with the open-end variety.

Closed-end leases usually give the leasing company the right to sell the car when the lease expires if you don't want to buy the vehicle. You should obtain a provision in your contract stating that you must approve of the sales price. According to most leases, if the company receives less than the residual value, you must make up the difference. Usually, though, dealers will not force you to make this payment because it alienates you as a customer. When your lease expires, you are a prime candidate to lease another car; therefore, the dealer wants to keep you happy.

An *open-end lease* exposes you to the risk of your car's resale value when the lease expires. When you enter into an open-end lease, you bet that the car will be worth a certain amount, known as the *residual value,* when the lease ends. When you return the car to the leasing company, it is appraised to determine its current market value. If you disagree with the appraisal, you usually have the right to acquire your own independent appraisal from a local car dealer or car appraisal service. Once you and the leasing company agree on the car's worth, you compare that number to the residual value assumed in the lease contract. If the car's value is equal to or greater than the residual value, you owe nothing. Depending on your contract, you may even receive a refund if the appraisal value is considerably more than the residual value.

However, if the appraisal value is less than the residual value, you must make up most or all of the difference in cash, depending on the terms of your lease contract. For example, if your contract assumes the car will have a residual value of $10,000 and the appraisal assumes it is worth $9,000 when the lease ends, you owe the leasing company $1,000. This settlement is usually referred to as a *balloon payment.* Most open-end leases also give you a purchase option—that is, the right to buy the car at residual value. These are known as *lease-purchase contracts.*

Many companies offer leases. Captive finance companies of auto dealers, banks, credit unions and companies that specialize in leasing all compete for auto lease business. Therefore, shop around for the lease that offers the most favorable terms. Bargain just as hard for good lease terms as you would for the best price on a new or used car. You don't have to accept a leasing company's first offer, just as you don't have to pay a car's sticker price.

The federal Consumer Leasing Act, administered by the Federal Trade Commission, provides certain protections for consumers entering both closed- and open-ended leases. For example, the balloon payment you make under an open-end lease can never be more than three times your monthly lease payment unless the car has suffered far more damage than could be described as normal wear and tear. Under the act, you must also be told the following information:

- The size of any security deposit due at the beginning of the lease
- The date each payment is due and the amount your payments will total over the term of the lease
- How much you must pay for licenses, car registrations, taxes and maintenance costs
- The type of auto insurance required
- What warranties cover the car
- Who is responsible for maintaining the car and exactly what is meant by normal wear and tear

- What happens if your car is stolen or demolished in an accident (Some contracts consider a stolen car to be an early termination of the lease and force you to pay fees in excess of the insurance settlement.)

- The penalties for making late lease payments or defaulting on the contract

- Whether you can terminate the lease before it is scheduled to expire (If you bail out early, you will probably have to pay some kind of penalty, which should be specified in your contract.)

- Under what conditions you or the leasing company can cancel the contract

- The price you will pay for the car—if you so desire—when the lease expires

- Whether you can renew the lease once it has expired (Some dealers will offer lower lease payments if you ask for a contract extension clause.)

In deciding whether to lease or finance your car, add up the following costs, as well as the others listed in the Leasing Costs Worksheet in Figure 10.2.

Then compare these costs to the annual outlays for financing the car with a bank or finance company loan (as listed in the Car Loan Worksheet in Figure 10.3).

- *The security deposit,* required up front. This money can be retained by the leasing company if you fail to make a payment or you owe a balloon payment at the termination of the lease. It can also be applied to damage to the car or to mileage charges if you exceed your limit. If you do owe none of this money when the lease expires, the leasing company should return your deposit.

- *The first and last monthly lease payment,* typically required up front.

- *The down payment,* technically called the *capitalized cost reduction.* The larger the down payment, the less your monthly lease costs. Because one main advantage of leasing is the low up-front, out-of-pocket cost, keep the down payment as low as possible. Some dealers will permit you to use the trade-in value of your old car to make the down payment. However, make sure that they give you a value close to the amount for which you could sell the car in the open market.

- *Fees and maintenance charges,* which include sales taxes, registration, title and license fees, and insurance premiums. In some cases, leasing dealers will include repair and maintenance costs in your lease if you promise to bring the car into the dealership on a regular basis for a checkup.

- *The costs of concluding the lease,* which include default charges, excess mileage and wear-and-tear fees, and balloon payments. Some dealers will also levy *final disposition charges* for cleaning, tuning and making final repairs on the car.

Figure 10.2   Leasing Costs Worksheet

	Leasing Costs
Security Deposit	$
First Lease Payment	
Last Lease Payment	
Monthly Lease Payment	
Down Payment	
Sales Taxes	
Registration Fees	
Title Fees	
License Fees	
Insurance Premiums	
Dealer-Provided Maintenance Costs	
Default Charges	
Excess Mileage Charges	
Excess Wear-and-Tear Charges	
Final Disposition Charges	
Balloon Payments	
TOTAL LEASING COSTS	$

Choosing between leasing and financing a car is not a purely financial decision. First, determine how long you plan to own the car. If you like to turn over your car every three or four years, leasing might make more sense than buying. As you pay off your loan, you will accumulate equity in your car, but that may not be desirable if you plan to trade it in soon. On the other hand, if you plan to hold onto your car for ten years or so, buying might make more sense than leasing.

If you expect your transportation needs to change over the next few years, leasing might be the better option. For example, if you plan to have children—or more children—you might need a larger car in three or four years than you do now. Also consider how much you will drive the car. If you drive more than 15,000 miles a year, leasing can be very expensive, and buying probably makes more sense. On the other hand, if you use your car only for short runs to the supermarket or the train station, leasing might be preferable. And if you plan to use your car partly for business, you can deduct a portion of your lease payments as a business expense, which you cannot do if you purchase the car.

Those who decide to lease must choose between an open-end and a closed-end lease. Most consumer groups recommend the closed-end lease because you assume much less risk when the lease expires.

Figure 10.3   Car Loan Worksheet

	Car Loan Costs
Down Payment	$ _____
Monthly Interest Costs	_____
Sales Taxes	_____
License Fees	_____
Registration Fees	_____
Insurance Premiums	_____
Estimated Maintenance Charges	_____
Trade-in Allowances	_____
TOTAL CAR LOAN COSTS	$ _____

Whichever car you end up buying, the method you use to finance it or the lease you choose will have a major impact—positively or negatively—on your personal finances. Even though it might require a great deal of concentrated effort to purchase and finance your car, a careful consideration of your options will pay off for years to come.

Using Your Computer To Buy Your Car

The online world is revolutionizing the car-buying process, and if you learn to navigate the Internet as part of your car search, you can very likely save yourself hundreds, possibly thousands of dollars over walking into a dealer's showroom and negotiating over the sticker price.

Before you start haggling online, make sure you have all the information you need to pick the car that's best for you. There are many Web sites that will give you all the data you could ever desire, including:

- *All Things Automotive Directory.* Offers a staggering amount of detail on car models, auto clubs, service records, online car enthusiast magazines and much more. www.webcom.com/-autodir

- *Auto Site.* Provides thousands of Web pages of information on auto specifications, crash test results, maintenance records and buying tips. www.auto site.com

- *Car and Driver.* One of the most reliable review magazines. Its Web site offers current reviews and a helpful buyer's guide. www.caranddriver.com

- *Consumer Reports.* Offers test results on all cars and articles from past issues of the magazine. The site also offers a New Car Price Service (also available by calling 800-933-5555) to help you know dealers' costs, and a Used Car Price Service (also available by calling 900-446-0500) so you have a good idea of the value of used cars. www.ConsumerReports.org

- *Motor Trend.* The other highly respected provider of car reviews, easily accessible through this Web site. www.motortrend.com/

- *Vehicle Marketplace.* The place for data on new cars and leasing and financing options in your state, including links to competing vendors offering the most attractive terms. www.nfsn.com/Vehicle.htm

Once you have decided on the car and options that fit your needs, it's time to start shopping online. There are several online car-buying services that you can access over the Internet that give you comparative prices on the car and options you want from several dealers around the country. In effect, you can conduct a mini-auction online by saying what car and options you are looking for and asking dealers to make their best bid online. Because dealers have far lower costs in the online world (such as advertising in newspapers), they usually will offer you a lower price than if you walked into the same dealer's showroom. You also can go into this auction process well armed with knowledge of the dealer's costs, so that you know how much of a margin the dealer has to work with when they negotiate. Here are some of the major car-shopping Web sites you might check out:

- *Autobytel.* One of the first of the online car-buying services, Autobytel links you to dealers near where you live and makes sure you get a competitive bid. www.autobytel.com

- *Autovantage.* Performs a car-buying search for you through America Online. You also can reach them by calling 800-AUTOVAN. www.autovantage.com

- *Autoweb.* Similar to Autobytel, Autoweb is accessed through the Yahoo search engine and can help you find the lowest price on a car in your geographical area. www.autoweb.com

- *Car-link.* The source for shopping for a used car. This site features hundreds of pictures of used models offered by dealers and individuals. Be careful to check out the car with a mechanic before you buy, as you should whenever buying a used car. www.car-link.com

- *Carpoint.* The Microsoft Network's car-buying service will find you the lowest price and refer you to local dealers. The site also provides reviews from car magazines and statistics on the latest models. www.carpoint.msn.com

- *DealerNet.* By linking you to auto dealers throughout the country, you can make sure you get the best price by browsing their Web sites and even requesting bids by e-mail. This Web site also includes the Confidential Credit service (www.dealernet.com//credit/ccredit.htm), which allows you to ensure that your credit is in good standing before you apply for a car loan or lease. www.dealernet.com/

- *Edmunds.* Provides comparative prices on most car models using its extensive database built up over many years in the business. www.edmunds.com

- *Intellichoice's CarCenter.* Allows you to pick a car by price range using its AutoExplorer service and also gives you its recommended best cars based on customer feedback in whatever price category you pick. www.intelli choice.com

- *Kelley's Blue Book.* Similar to Edmund's, finding out dealer's costs on most models from the Kelley Blue Book will help you bargain for a better deal. www.kbb.com

- *Price Auto Outlet.* This car outlet lists cars from the Oxford Financial portfolio that are coming off lease and can be purchased online at substantial discounts from their original retail price. www.priceautooutlet.com

All the major auto manufacturers now have Web sites that may be helpful in getting a good deal on a car. For example, General Motors offers the GMBuyPower service that lets you compare prices on GM cars and other brands, look for your car in dealer inventories and get dealers to offer you their best price online. Some sites even offer "virtual test drives" of some of their models. Others permit you to assemble the options package that you want online, and use that customized package in asking for bids from dealers. The Web site addresses for carmakers are self-evident—they all begin with *http://www.* and you just insert the manufacturers name and *.com.* So it is easy to find ford.com, gm.com, chrysler.com, toyota.com, etc. Another way to get all your links to carmakers in one place is by calling up the Automobile Manufacturers' Web pages (www.autoinfocenter.com/makers.html).

You no longer have to settle for the financing package offered by your dealer. Check out www.carloan.com/ or 800-CARLOAN to make sure you get the best possible terms from lenders anywhere in the country.

As you can see, the computer can empower you to get the information you need to find the car of your dreams and make sure you get the best price and financing package.

If You Have Problems with Your Car

After you've owned your car for a while, you might run into various mechanical difficulties. It is important to report major problems to the federal government's Auto Safety Hotline (800-424-9393) because it allows regulators to determine whether a pattern of problems exists with a particular car model. Lodging a complaint is quite easy. Simply call the hot-line, and the operator will mail you the form illustrated in Figure 10.4.

If regulators determine that a pattern of problems does persist with your model, the National Highway Traffic Safety Administration (NHTSA) will order

Figure 10.4
Vehicle Owner's Complaint Form

Form Approved: O.M.B. No. 2127-0008

AUTO SAFETY HOTLINE **VEHICLE OWNER'S QUESTIONNAIRE** NATIONWIDE 1-800-424-9393 DC METRO AREA 202-366-0123 US Department of Transportation National Highway Traffic Safety Administration	**FOR AGENCY USE ONLY** DATE RECEIVED — od.or rt.dt od-rt up-ltr REFERENCE NO.

OWNER INFORMATION (TYPE OR PRINT)

NAME and ADDRESS

DAY TIME TELEPHONE NO. (AREA CODE)

Do you authorize NHTSA to provide a copy of this report to the manufacturer of your vehicle? YES ☐ NO ☐
In the absence of an authorization, NHTSA *WILL NOT* provide your name or address to the vehicle manufacturer.

SIGNATURE OF OWNER   DATE

VEHICLE INFORMATION

VEHICLE IDENTIFICATION NO.*	VEHICLE MAKE	VEHICLE MODEL	MODEL YEAR

*LOCATED AT BOTTOM OF WINDSHIELD ON DRIVER'S SIDE

CURRENT ODOMETER READING | DATE PURCHASED _____ ☐ NEW ☐ USED | DEALER'S NAME, CITY & STATE | ENGINE SIZE (CID/CC/L) — ☐ TURBO ☐ DIESEL ☐ GAS ☐ FUEL INJECTN NO. CYLINDERS __

TRANSMISSION TYPE	ANTILOCK BRAKES	RESTRAINT SYSTEM	CRUISE CONTROL	DRIVETRAIN	BODY STYLE
☐ MANUAL ☐ AUTOMATIC	☐ YES ☐ NO	☐ DRIVERSIDE AIRBAG ☐ MOTORBELT ☐ PASSENGERSIDE AIRBAG ☐ 3-POINT BELT ☐ 2-POINT BELT	☐ YES ☐ NO	☐ FRONT ☐ REAR ☐ 4-WHEEL	STAWAG ___ HATCH BK ___ 4 DR ___ VAN ___ 2 DR ___ PK UP TRK ___ OTHER ___

FAILED COMPONENT(S)/PART(S) INFORMATION (REPORT TIRE INFORMATION ON BACK)

COMPONENT	PART NAME(S)	LOCATION ☐ LEFT ☐ RIGHT ☐ FRONT ☐ REAR	FAILED PART(S) ☐ ORIGINAL ☐ REPLACEMENT
NO. OF FAILURES	DATE(S) OF FAILURE(S) _____ MILEAGE AT FAILURE(S) _____ VEHICLE SPEED AT FAILURE(S)	MANUFACTURER CONTACTED ☐ YES ☐ NO	NHTSA PREVIOUSLY CONTACTED ☐ YES ☐ NO

APPLICABLE ACCIDENT INFORMATION

ACCIDENT ☐ YES ☐ NO	FIRE ☐ YES ☐ NO	NUMBER PERSONS INJURED	NUMBER OF FATALITIES.	PROPERTY DAMAGE EST$ ___	POLICE REPORTED ☐ YES ☐ NO

NARRATIVE DESCRIPTION OF FAILURE(S), ACCIDENT(S), INJURY(IES)

CONTINUE ON BACK IF NEEDED

The Privacy Act of 1974
Public Law 93-579
This information is requested pursuant to authority vested in the National Highway Traffic Safety Act and subsequent amendments. You are under no obligation to respond to this questionnaire. Your response may be used to assist the NHTSA in determining whether a manufacturer should take appropriate action to correct a safety defect. If the NHTSA proceeds with administrative enforcement or litigation against a manufacturer, your response, or a statistical summary thereof, may be used in support of the agency's action.

HS-Form 350 (Rev. 5-92)

Source: Courtesy of National Highway Traffic Safety Administration, U.S. Department of Transportation.

**Figure 10.4
(continued)**

Fold to show Return Address (no stamp needed) Fasten with tape or staple and mail

INFORMATION ON TIRE FAILURE(S) (IF APPLICABLE)

TIRE IDENTIFICATION NO.*											MANUFACTURER/TIRE NAME	SIZE
D	O	T										

* The identification number consists of 7 to 10 letters and numerals following the letters DOT. It is usually located near the rim flange on the side opposite the whitewall or on either side of a blackwall tire.

NARRATIVE DESCRIPTION (CONTINUED)

☆ U.S. G.P.O.: 1992 – 623-897 / 60086

U.S. Department
of Transportation

**National Highway
Traffic Safety
Administration**

400 Seventh St., S.W.
Washington, D.C. 20590

Official Business
Penalty for Private Use $300

BUSINESS REPLY MAIL
FIRST CLASS PERMIT NO. 73173   WASHINGTON, D.C.

POSTAGE WILL BE PAID BY NATL HWY TRAFFIC SAFETY ADMIN.

U.S. Department of Transportation
National Highway Traffic Safety Administration
Auto Safety Hotline, NEF–11 HL
400 7th Street, SW
Washington, DC 20590

NO POSTAGE
NECESSARY
IF MAILED
IN THE
UNITED STATES

the manufacturer to recall the car and fix the problem. Because you will be on the NHTSA's list of complainants, you will be notified by mail of any recall.

If you, unfortunately, have purchased a lemon, you are protected under so-called *lemon laws* in most states. These laws define a lemon as a car that has been repaired for the same defect at least four times or is out of service for at least 30 days. Lemon laws establish a period of coverage—usually one year from the date you took possession of the car—and require arbitration out of court. For further details on how these laws work and how to resolve your complaint under them, consult *The Lemon Times,* a quarterly newsletter, and the *Lemon Book* by Ralph Nader and Clarence Ditlow, executive director of the Center for Auto Safety (see "Resources" section at the end of this chapter for more information). The newsletter will, of course, be more up to date than the book.

Resources

BOOKS

The Car Book, by Jack Gillis (HarperCollins Publishers, 1000 Keystone Industrial Park, Scranton, PA 18512; 800-242-7737; www.harpercollins.com) complete annual guide to buying a new car. Presents the latest safety ratings, dealer prices, fuel economy numbers, insurance premiums, warranty coverages, tire grades and maintenance costs. Also gives advice on getting the best deal and having your complaints resolved satisfactorily. Same author and publisher also produce a yearly *Used Car Book* and *Minivan, Pickup and 4×4 Book.*

How To Buy a New Car (Consumer Reports Books, P.O. Box 10637, Des Moines, IA 50336; 515-237-4903; 800-500-9760). A comprehensive book explaining how to negotiate when you buy a new car; the advantages and disadvantages of leasing; and how to get the best trade-in value for your old car. Consumer Reports also publishes its annual *New Car Buying Guide.*

The Lemon Book, by Ralph Nader and Clarence Ditlow at the Center for Auto Safety (Moyer Bell Publishers, Kymbold Way, Wakefield, RI 02879; 401-789-0074). Offers advice on how to avoid scams by car dealers and what to do if you end up with a lemon.

TRADE ASSOCIATIONS

American Automobile Association (1000 AAA Dr., Heathrow, FL 32746-5063; 407-444-7000; www.aaa.com). A federation of motor clubs throughout the United States and Canada. Offers information about cars and travel and provides emergency road service and towing; emergency check acceptance; travel agency services; tour books and Triptiks to help you find the most efficient way to get where you're going; hotel discounts; accident insurance; TripAssist, a 24-hour emergency hot-line for legal, medical or travel-related problems; traveler's checks; discounts on car rentals; AAA credit cards; AutoTest, which provides performance and specification details for most new cars; and auto repair referral service. Sponsors the AUTOSOLVE hot-line, which helps arbitrate disputes between consumers and car dealers. Also performs research and provides driver education to improve automotive safety.

Center for Auto Safety (2001 S St., N.W., Suite 410, Washington, DC 20009; 202-328-7700). A nonprofit consumer organization working to reduce deaths and injuries from car accidents through safer design of automobiles and highways. Publishes two periodicals, *IMPACT* and *Lemon Times,* which keep you up to date on car safety issues. Also offers booklets on car safety and quality, auto defects, fuel economy and emissions.

Council of Better Business Bureaus (4200 Wilson Blvd., Arlington, VA 22203; 703-276-0100; www.bbb.org). Takes complaints about local car dealers and offers the following brochures: "Tips on Buying a New Car"; "Tips on Buying a Used Car"; and "Tips on Renting a Car."

Highway Loss Data Institute (1005 N. Glebe Rd., Suite 800, Arlington, VA 22203; 703-247-1600; www.hwysafety.org). Provides research information on the ways that insurance losses vary among different types of vehicles. Publishes the following free publication: *Injury and Collection Loss Experience by Make and Model.*

Insurance Institute for Highway Safety (1005 N. Glebe Rd., Suite 800, Arlington, VA 22201; 703-247-1500; www.hwysafety.org). Promotes car safety and offers the following free publications: *Shopping for a Safer Car* and *Teenage Drivers* as well as films on a variety of highway safety issues that are available on a free loan basis.

National Automobile Dealers Association (8400 Westpark Dr., McLean, VA 22102; 703-821-7000; 800-252-6232; www.nadanet.com). Publishes the *N.A.D.A. Official Used Car Guide,* Retail Edition, which provides low, high and average retail prices for most used cars. The *Guide* is also available as a computer diskette (call 800-544-NADA for more information). Will send a free copy of the brochures "At Your Service," "Buckle Up Baby," "Your Money, Your Car." Operates a consumer hot-line called the Automotive Consumer Action Program (AUTOCAP—703-821-7144) to handle complaints against automobile dealers who sell new cars and trucks.

National Vehicle Leasing Association (P.O. Box 34579, Los Angeles, CA 90034-0579; 310-838-3170). The trade group for automotive leasing companies. Can provide guidance on understanding leasing contracts and terms. Offers the *Leasing News Automotive Views,* a newsletter, and *Vehicle Leasing Today,* a magazine.

National Tire Dealers and Retreaders Association (1250 I St., N.W., Suite 400, Washington, DC 20005; 202-789-2300). Operates a hot-line (800-876-8372) to help resolve disputes between consumers and tire dealers.

FEDERAL GOVERNMENT REGULATORS

Federal Highway Administration (U.S. Department of Transportation, 820 1st St., N.E., Suite 750, Washington, DC 20002; 202-523-0163). Oversees all transportation policies relating to highways, cars and trucks. Offers a very helpful brochure titled "The Cost of Owning and Operating Automobiles, Vans and Light Trucks." The brochure explains the various annual costs of operating a car, including insurance, repairs, taxes, registration and gasoline. It provides detailed benchmarks of car ownership for the first through the twelfth year of ownership, against which you can judge the projected operating costs of any car you contemplate purchasing. This brochure is also available through the Consumer Information Center (Pueblo, CO 81009).

Federal Trade Commission (6th Street and Pennsylvania Avenue, N.W., Washington, DC 20580; 202-326-2222; www.ftc.gov). Has jurisdiction over car dealers and many auto-related issues. Will send a free copy of the following brochures: "Auto Service Contracts"; "Buying a Used Car"; "Car Ads: Low Interest Loans and Other Offers"; "Car Financing Scams"; "Car Rental Guide"; "A Consumer Guide to Vehicle Leasing"; " 'Gas-Saving Products"; "New Car Buying Guide"; "Octane Ratings"; "Truth in Leasing"; and "Vehicle Repossession."

National Highway Traffic Safety Administration (400 7th St., S.W., Washington, DC 20590; 202-366-9550; www.nhtsa.dot.gov) and its Auto Safety Hotline (202-366-0123; 800-424-9393). The federal agency that oversees car safety issues, and its hot-line, which provides information on motor vehicle safety recalls and safety defect investigations and explains how to complain about defects in your car so they can be brought to the manufacturer's attention. NHTSA conducts yearly crash tests on new cars, called the New Car Assessment Program (NCAP). Will also send free copies of the following brochures: "Auto Defects and Recall Campaigns"; "Child Safety Seat Package"; "Consumer Guide to Uniform Tire Quality Grading"; "Drunk Driving Package"; "Gas Mileage Guide"; "Lap/Shoulder Belt Kits for Rear Seats"; "Motorcycle Safety"; "Seatbelts and Air Bags Package"; and "Uniform Tire Quality Grading." In addition, sends free copies of consumer information pamphlets on the following topics: "Antilock Braking Systems"; "Bumpers"; "Insurance Discounts"; "Lighting"; "Motorcycle Safety Helmets"; "Odometer Fraud"; "Pregnancy—Protecting Your Unborn Child in a Car"; "Safety Belts—Proper Use"; "Tires"; "Traffic Safety Tips for Older Drivers"; and "Transporting Your Children Safely."

CAR MANUFACTURER CUSTOMER ASSISTANCE CENTERS

The following addresses and phone numbers are for problem resolution and customer assistance centers at all the major automakers that operate such services.

Acura Division of American Honda (1919 Torrance Blvd., Torrance, CA 90501; 310-783-2000)

Alfa Romeo (6220 S. Orange Blossom Trail, Suite 200, Orlando, FL 32859; 407-856-5000)

American Honda Motor Company (1919 Torrance Blvd., Torrance, CA 90501; 310-783-3260)

American Isuzu Motors (2300 Pellissier Rd., P.O. Box 995, Whittier, CA 90608; 800-255-6727)

Audi of America (3800 Hamlin Rd., Auburn Hills, MI 48326; 248-340-5000)

BMW of North America, Inc. (1 BMW Plaza, Montvale, NJ 07645; 800-831-1117)

Buick Motor Division (902 E. Hamilton Ave., Flint, MI 48550; 800-521-7300)

Cadillac Motor Car Division (P.O. Box 9025, Warren, MI 48090-9025; 800-458-8006)

Chevrolet (P.O. Box 7047, Troy, MI 48007-7047; 800-222-1020)

Chrysler Corporation (12000 Chrysler Dr., Highland Park, MI 48288; 313-956-5741)

Ferrari North America (250 Sylvan Ave., Englewood Cliffs, NJ 07632; 201-816-2600)

Ford Motor Company (P.O. Box 43360, 300 Renaissance Center, Detroit, MI 48243; 800-392-3673)

General Motors Truck Central Office (31 Judson St., Pontiac, MI 48342-2230; 800-462-8782)

Hyundai Motor America (10550 Talbert Ave., Fountain Valley, CA 92728; 714-965-3508)

Infiniti Division of Nissan Motor Corporation (18701 S. Figueroa St., Carson, CA 90248; 800-662-6200)

Jaguar Cars, Inc. (555 MacArthur Blvd., Mahwah, NJ 07430; 201-818-8500)

Lamborghini U.S.A. (7601 Centurion Pkwy., Jacksonville, FL 32256; 904-565-9100)

Land Rover North America (4390 Parliment Pl., Lanham, MD 20706; 301-731-9040)

Lexus Division of Toyota Motor Sales (19001 S. Western Ave., Torrance, CA 90509; 800-255-3987)

Lincoln-Mercury Division of Ford Motor Company (300 Renaissance Center, Detroit, MI 48243; 800-392-3673)

Lotus Cars U.S.A. (1655 Lakes Pkwy., Lawrenceville, GA 30243; 770-822-4566)

Mazda Motor of America (P.O. Box 5900, Sumerset, NJ 08875; 800-222-5500)

Mercedes-Benz (1 Glenview Road, Montvale, NJ 07645; 201-476-6200)

Mitsubishi Motor Sales of America (6400 W. Katella Ave., Cypress, CA 90630; 714-372-6000)

Nissan Motors (Nissan Motors Corporation, P.O. Box 191, Gardena, CA 90248; 800-647-7261)

Oldsmobile Central Office (920 Townsend St., Lansing, MI 48921; 800-442-6537)

Pontiac Division (One Pontiac Plaza, Pontiac, MI 48340; 800-762-2737)

Porsche Cars North America (P.O. Box 30911, Reno, NV 89520-3911; 702-348-3000)

Rolls-Royce Motor Cars (120 Chubb Ave., Lyndhurst, NJ 07071; 201-967-9100)

Saab Cars USA (P.O. Box 9000, Norcross, GA 30091; 800-955-9007)

Saturn Division of General Motors Corporation (1420 Stephenson Hwy., Troy, MI 48007; 800-553-6000)

Subaru of America (Subaru Plaza, Cherry Hill, NJ 08034; 609-488-8500)

Suzuki Motor Corporation (3251 E. Imperial Hwy., Brea, CA 92621; 714-996-7040)

Toyota Motor Sales (USA, Inc., 19001 S. Western Ave., Dept. A102, Torrance, CA 90509; 800-331-4331)

Volkswagen United States (3800 Hamlin Rd., Auburn Hills, MI 48326; 800-822-8987)

Volvo Cars of North America (15 Volvo Dr., Rockleigh, NJ 07647; 201-767-4737)

CAR-BUYER AND CAR-PRICING SERVICES

AutoAdvisor, Inc. (3123 Fairview Ave. E., Seattle, WA 98102; 206-323-1976; 800-894-2155; www.autoadvisor.com). A national car buyer's service that can help you find any make and model at the guaranteed lowest price. They can handle trade-ins, and they do all the negotiation with the dealer for you.

Auto Cost Comparison and Automotive Just the Facts (Intelli Choice Inc., 471 Division St., Campbell, CA 95008; 800-777-1880; www.intellichoice.com). By calling this number, you can compare dealers' costs on several cars and all available options on those cars. Also provides data on repair records and resale values. The Just the Facts service offers all the data you need on one car model.

CarBargains (733 15th St., N.W., Suite 820, Washington, DC 20005; 202-347-7283; 800-475-7283; www.checkbook.org). Helps you identify the dealer nearest you with the lowest price on the car that interests you.

Car/Puter International (2190 Southeast 17th St., Suite 212, Fort Lauderdale, FL 33316; 800-645-2960). This voice-interactive system provides dealers' costs for any car you name for $2 a minute. They also sell a printout with all the options and features you want on a particular car. You can then call back and talk to a personal counselor who will take an order for a vehicle.

CarSource (700 Larkspur Landing, Suite 199, Larkspur, CA 94939; 415-927-2886; 800-517-2277; www.carsource.com). A national car buyer's service that will help you find the model you want at the best possible price and terms. CarSource will also refer you to a car buying service in your state, if that service is a certified member of the National Association of Buyer's Agents (NABA). The Association requires that their members work for fees from consumers only and receive no compensation from car dealers.

Consumer Reports Auto Price Service (P.O. Box 8005, Novi, MI 48376; 800-203-5454). Provides a computer printout comparing the sticker price to the dealer's invoice for the makes and models you choose. Tells you exactly what the dealer paid for the car and every option. Also informs you of factory-to-customer and factory-to-dealer incentive programs. Consumer Reports also offers a Used-Car Price Service (900-988-0828) that provides the current market-value price in your region of any car you describe. Trade-in, buying and selling prices of used cars are based on the car's age, mileage, options and condition.

Nationwide Auto Brokers (17517 W. 10 Mile Rd., Southfield, MI 48075; 800-521-7257; www.car-connect.com). A national car broker that will send you an invoice and sheet listing a car's options. If you use the service to buy a car, they will refund the cost of the option sheet and tell you the suggested markup and vehicle cost.

11

All about Insurance

When you spend money on insurance, you might feel like you are wasting hard-earned cash on something that produces no tangible benefit. You may, in fact, go for years without collecting a dime from your insurance company. However, the opposite could also be true; you could have an accident or get sick soon after your insurance coverage starts. At that point, the benefits of insurance become very real.

Insurance assumes the risk of bad things happening to policyholders. Fortunately for insurance companies, not everyone becomes ill, has a car accident or sustains a burglary at his or her home simultaneously. By collecting and investing premiums from millions of policyholders, insurance companies have the capital to pay claims as they arise.

The field of insurance is difficult to understand, and as a result, many people pay for more insurance coverage than they actually need. The insurance industry is notorious for using jargon and complex presentations that baffle most people. What you don't know about insurance can hurt you in two ways.

- You may pay too much for a policy that you could have bought much cheaper if you had understood how to compare insurers and policies.

- The coverage you purchase may be too much or too little for your needs, or it may duplicate existing coverage in some areas and leave you unprotected in others. If you have a large claim that is not covered, you could be ruined financially.

This chapter will help you cut through the complexities of insurance so you can buy the most coverage for the fewest dollars possible. Learning about insurance is not as stimulating as uncovering the intricacies of the stock market or mutual funds, but it is equally important to your total financial plan.

The Basics of Insurance

Insurance is designed to distribute the risk of adverse events among a company's policyholders. When such an event occurs, whether it be a car accident, a heart attack or a death, the insurance company calls it a *loss*. When that loss affects a policyholder directly, it is known as a *first-person loss*. When the loss is sustained by another person but the policyholder is liable, it is termed a *third-party loss*. For example, a third-party loss occurs when the policyholder injures someone in a car accident or when someone slips and falls in the policyholder's home. If you are uninsured, you might have to pay the full cost of the loss. If you are covered by an insurance policy, the insurance company pays most of it.

In return for this protection, you must pay the insurance company what is known as a *premium*. People who purchase insurance figure that it is better to surrender a specific amount of money in a premium up front than to expose themselves to unlimited and unpredictable expenses later. The insurance company, on the other hand, thinks the opposite. Statistically, the chances that you or any other individual will suffer a major catastrophe are rather small. The insurance company is willing to cover the occasional large loss in return for millions of policyholders' premiums. The company then invests the cash in stocks, bonds, real estate and other vehicles that provide income and capital gains. If the company limits its losses by careful underwriting and invests well, it can earn enormous profits. Conversely, if it must pay more claims than it expects and also loses money on its investment portfolio, the insurer may have to dig deeply into its reserves. If the losses become big enough, the insurance company may, in fact, be forced out of business. In this case, policyholders will have to cover the expenses themselves or, more commonly, their policies will be taken over by a new insurance company. When insurance companies fail, their obligations may also be assumed by a state guaranty fund, which could step in to cover policyholder claims.

INFLUENCES ON PREMIUM PRICES

The key element that links the policyholder and the insurance company is the cost of the policy's premium. The insurance company sets the premium based on several factors.

- *The risk that you will file a claim.* The larger the chance that you will collect, the higher your premium. For example, if your home is located in a high-crime area, a greater chance exists that it will be burglarized—and therefore that you will file a claim—than if you live where crime is rare and security is good. Similarly, if you smoke and have already suffered two heart attacks, you stand a much greater chance of dying than you would if you exercised regularly and had no health problems. Clearly, your premium would be higher if you smoke or live in a high-crime locale.

- *The liability to which the insurance company is exposed.* The more losses the insurance policy covers, the more potential claims exist. And the more potential claims exist, the higher the premium climbs. For example, a homeowner's policy that insures a small house with few possessions would carry a much smaller premium than would a policy covering a mansion filled with valuable artwork and antiques.

- *The percentage of the loss the insurance company covers.* In some cases, such as life insurance, the company must pay 100 percent of the loss. In other cases, policyholders pay for part of the loss by signing up for a *deductible.* For example, a policy might stipulate that the policyholder will pay the first $1,000 in health or auto insurance claims, and the insurance company will cover any amount exceeding $1,000. A policy with such a deductible would charge a much lower premium than would a contract on which the insurance company covers claims starting at the first dollar of loss.

- *The insurance company's level of expenses and investment expertise.* The greater an insurance company's expenses for administration and marketing, the higher its premiums tend to be. On the other hand, the better its investment performance, the lower its premiums usually are. A company confident in its ability to invest premium dollars successfully can be profitable with lower premium rates.

- *The general level of competition in a particular line of insurance.* The law of supply and demand rules the insurance industry as much as it does the stock market, for example. If only a few insurance companies will take on a specific risk, they can charge higher premiums. For instance, a policy insuring a pianist's fingers or a contract to pay for injuries from skydiving would cost a great deal because only a few companies will assume these risks. On the other hand, if many companies offer standard insurance coverage, premiums tend to be lower due to increased competition.

TYPES OF INSURERS

Though the principles of insurance remain the same no matter what insurer issues a policy, it is important to understand the four types of insurers. Each has its own set of incentives, which affect the quality of the policies they offer.

Stock companies. Insurance companies owned by shareholders are in business to earn a profit for their shareholders and to make their stock price rise over time. As such, they tend to raise premiums or cut dividends on policies to bolster profits. Of course, stock companies can't go too far; otherwise, their policies would become uncompetitive. If a stock company profits significantly, the benefits flow to its shareholders, not its policyholders. On the other hand, if the company is marginally profitable or sustains losses, policyholders will pay higher premiums and earn lower dividends on their policies. Despite all of this, do not necessarily avoid buying a policy from a stock company. Firms such as Allstate, Equitable, Travelers, Chubb and American International Group are all extremely strong financially because they raise capital by selling shares and therefore offer very competitive policies.

Mutual companies. Insurers organized in mutual form are owned by their policyholders. No shares of a mutual firm's stock are publicly traded. When you buy a policy from a mutual company, you benefit if the company does well, and you lose if the firm performs badly. For example, if you own a life insurance policy from a mutual company that keeps its expenses down, pays few death claims and enjoys superior investment performance, your policy dividends will rise. Part of your premiums go to building up the company's financial cushion, called a *surplus.* If you cancel your policy, however, you keep none of the surplus to which you have contributed. Several mutual insurance companies have accumulated enormous surpluses over the years and are therefore extremely strong financially. The biggest mutual insurers include Prudential, State Farm, John Hancock, Northwestern Mutual and Penn Mutual.

Cooperatives. Groups of people or companies that band together to provide insurance for themselves are called *cooperatives.* These groups hire professional managers to perform administrative duties such as collecting premiums and paying claims. But each cooperative is designed only to provide insurance protection to its members, not to earn a profit for shareholders or to build a surplus for policyholders. One form of cooperative, known as a *producer's cooperative,* is formed by service providers to make it easier for people to afford their services. The best example of such a cooperative is the Blue Cross/Blue Shield system, which was established by doctors, hospitals and the health care industry to give patients access to medical care and to ensure payment to doctors and other health care providers.

Government entities. A panoply of federal and state government programs provides insurance for millions of people. In many cases, the government supplies insurance that private companies cannot or will not offer. Just a few examples at the federal level include Social Security, Medicare, Department of Veterans Affairs (VA) benefits and bank deposit insurance from the Federal Deposit Insurance Corporation (FDIC). States offer workers' compensation, disability and unemployment insurance.

INSURANCE RATINGS SYSTEMS

Before you buy a policy from an insurance company or contact one of its sales representatives, have some idea of the firm's financial condition. Several large insurance companies, notably Executive Life, based in California, and Mutual Benefit Life, based in New Jersey, failed in the early 1990s when their investment portfolios soured and thousands of policyholders rushed to redeem their contracts. These dramatic cases underlined the importance of knowing the strength of the company that issues your policy.

Five principal independent firms rate insurance companies' financial strength. (Addresses, phone numbers and descriptions of their publications and services appear in the "Resources" section at the end of this chapter.) The four traditional agencies are A.M. Best, Duff & Phelps, Moody's Investors Service and Standard & Poor's (S&P) Corporation. The newest entrant in the field, Weiss Research, is considered a maverick by the insurance industry because it uses a different, and far more conservative, method of assessing insurers' financial condition.

Ratings agencies base their grades of insurance companies on a combination of factors. Some of the key determinants of a rating include how widely the company spreads risk; how sufficient its reserves and surplus are; the quality of its management; its profitability, investment returns, mortality experience, expense ratios and debt levels; the amount of cash it has available to pay claims; and the quality of the firm's assets, including whether or not it holds risky junk bonds or speculative real estate.

Once these factors are analyzed, rating companies assign one of the following grades. Each rating service uses a different combination of letters and symbols to signify the same ranking.

Superior. Companies have achieved superior overall performance when compared to industry averages. They have a very strong ability to meet policyholder obligations over a long period of time and under a variety of economic and underwriting conditions. Best: A++ and A+; Duff & Phelps: AAA; Moody's: Aaa; S&P: AAA; Weiss: A.

Excellent. Companies have achieved excellent overall performance when compared to industry averages. They have a strong ability to meet policyholder obligations over a long period of time. Best: A and A−; Duff & Phelps: AA+ to AA−; Moody's: Aa; S&P: AA+ to AA−; Weiss: A.

Very good and good. Companies have achieved good overall performance when compared to industry averages. They have adequate ability to meet policyholder obligations, but their financial strength is susceptible to unfavorable changes in underwriting or economic conditions. Best: B++ to B−; Duff & Phelps: BBB+ to BBB−; Moody's: Ba; S&P: A+ to BBB−; Weiss: B.

Fair. Companies have achieved fair overall performance when compared to industry averages. They have reasonable ability to meet policyholder obligations, but their financial strength is susceptible to unfavorable changes in underwriting or economic conditions. Best: C++ to C+; Duff & Phelps: BB+ to BB−; Moody's: B; S&P: BB+ to BB−; Weiss: C.

Marginal. Companies have achieved marginal overall performance when compared to industry averages. They have a current ability to meet policyholder obligations, but their financial strength is very vulnerable to unfavorable changes in underwriting or economic conditions. Best: C to C−; Duff & Phelps: B+ to B−; Moody's: Caa; S&P: B+ to B−; Weiss: D.

Below minimum standards. Companies meet minimum size and experience requirements but do not meet minimum standards for financial strength. Best: D; Duff & Phelps: CCC; Moody's: Ca; S&P: CCC; Weiss: E.

Under state supervision, in liquidation or failed. Companies that are placed under some form of supervision, control or restraint by a state insurance regulatory authority. Best: E or F; Duff & Phelps: CCC or DD; Moody's: C; S&P: R; Weiss: F.

Plenty of insurance companies offer ratings in the A range; therefore, you have little reason to take a risk of a lower rated company. Because the five ratings agencies sometimes differ in their opinions of a particular company's financial condition, you should purchase policies from a company with high ratings in at least three or four ratings systems.

In addition to checking commercial ratings, ask your state insurance department whether it knows of any problems with an insurance company you are considering. A list of the insurance departments in all 50 states appears in the "Resources" section at the end of this chapter.

DIFFERENT WAYS INSURANCE IS OFFERED

Depending on the kind of policy you need and the company you deal with, different ways to obtain insurance exist. The principal methods are as follows:

Your employer. When you become an employee of a company or a member of a labor union, you automatically qualify for whatever insurance that the organization offers its employees or members. This usually includes accident insurance (if you are traveling on company business), disability insurance, health insurance, life insurance, and workers' compensation insurance. The company or union shops for the best coverage and offers it to all employees or members. You also benefit because the organization receives group rates, which are far less expensive than the rates you would pay for the same coverage as an individual. In the past, employees did not pay for any of this coverage. In recent years, however, many employees are being required to contribute at least part of the premium cost, particularly for health insurance.

Insurance agents. These sellers of insurance must be licensed in the state where they do business. The ideal agent assesses your needs and finds the policy that provides the coverage you need for the lowest premium. In return, he or she gets a commission for making the sale and often receives a fee, called a *renewal commission,* every year that you retain the policy.

Two types of agents exist: independent and exclusive. *Independent agents* sell policies for many companies and therefore can shop among competing firms to get you the best coverage and price. *Exclusive agents,* also called *captive agents,* represent only one company.

No hard and fast rule says that you will do better with either an independent or an exclusive agent. Independents, in theory, can get you a better price by comparison shopping. However, independents are not always familiar with the provisions of each company's policies. Also, they may steer you to a contract that pays them the highest commission, rather than to one that offers you the lowest premium. On the other hand, a top-producing independent agent might be able to get you a discount on the price of a policy because he or she sells a large volume of insurance for the company.

Exclusive agents usually know their company's product better than independent agents do because that is all they sell. If they work for a top-notch company, they often incur lower selling costs because they are more careful to offer policies to people unlikely to make a claim. For example, a captive life insurance agent tries to sell policies to people in good health, which lowers his or her company's death benefit expenses. Nevertheless, exclusive agents often must meet certain sales goals set by their company, which means that they might use high-pressure tactics to sell you a policy that generates a certain level of commissions even though it may not meet your needs exactly.

For more on choosing a good agent, consult Chapter 17, "Finding Financial Advisers Who Are Right for You."

Insurance brokers. Brokers are employed by the insurance buyer to find the best policy at the most competitive price. They may buy the policy directly from the insurance company, or they may go through an agent. Either way, they earn a commission based on the premium you pay. Because their goal is to please you, the customer, brokers may bargain harder with an insurance company to get you the best deal than agents will. Like agents, brokers must be licensed to sell insurance in the state where they practice.

A relatively new kind of insurance broker is the *independent quote service.* Firms like Insurance Quote, Selectquote and Termquote (see "Resources" section for addresses and phone numbers) maintain databases of term life insurance policy rates from many companies. When you call the toll-free number of one of these companies, tell the customer service representative your age, your health condition and how much coverage you need. The company will then send you a printout of the terms of four or five policies with the lowest premiums. If you like one of the offerings, you can buy the policy through the quote service. It receives a commission from the insurance company like any other broker.

Insurance advisers. The latest way to find the best insurance policy is by consulting an independent insurance adviser. Unlike agents and brokers, advisers earn no commissions from policies they sell. They charge a flat fee—which varies depending on the size of the policy you seek—for finding the cheapest policy providing the coverage you need. Because they are not tied to insurance companies, advisers usually recommend insurers paying no or very low commissions to salespeople and giving the highest returns. (A list of the top low-load insurance companies appears in the "Resources" section at the end of this chapter.) To find an adviser near you, call the Life Insurance Advisers Association at 800-521-4578. Another source for such advice is INSurance INFOrmation (Cobblestone Court #2, 23 Route 134, South Dennis, MA 02660; 800-472-5800).

Direct marketing. To reduce the cost of maintaining an expensive sales force, many insurance companies offer you coverage directly, through the mail or over the telephone. Such coverage can be less expensive than policies sold in person, but you will have little, if any, contact with a company's representative. Scrutinize such offers, and compare them to policies you could get through an agent or a broker. Direct mail policies are not always as attractive as insurance companies make them sound, but they can be better than the alternatives if you research the contracts carefully.

Assessing Your Insurance Needs

The first step in selecting any insurance policy is determining how much coverage you need and what you can afford. To assess your need, start by identifying your potential losses. Then determine how you could cope with those losses if you did not have insurance. For example, ask yourself whether your spouse could support your children if you died unexpectedly. If the answer is no, you need life insurance to cover that risk. Or if you live where earthquakes, tornados or hurricanes are commonplace, you need coverage against such calamities, though premiums will be high. If the risk of such events is low, however, you probably would waste your money buying earthquake, tornado or hurricane insurance. If you would not be financially burdened by a loss, don't insure against it. For example, you would probably be able to cover the cost of minor scratches to your car, so purchase a policy that covers only significant damage.

Once you determine your need for coverage, calculate how much you can afford to pay for insurance premiums. Consult the budgeting exercise in Chapter 1 to see how much money you allocated to insurance coverage. You might not be able to afford all the policies that you ideally would like to own. Therefore, you must make a few choices about which coverage is more important than another. Prioritize your insurance needs by the size of the potential loss. The greater the risk, the higher priority the insurance. Make sure that you are covered against catastrophic losses, such as the total destruction of your home or car.

Having determined what you need covered and how much you can afford, look into any methods and incentives an insurance company offers to slash your premiums. For example, if you agree to cover a certain amount of loss out of your own pocket (your deductible), your premiums would be lower. Therefore, you might cut your car insurance premiums significantly by increasing your deductible from $500 to $1,000. You might also qualify for special rates if you meet certain criteria. Nonsmokers pay lower health and life insurance premiums than smokers, for example. Also, auto insurers will often discount your premiums if you buy coverage for two cars instead of one or if you take a special safety-oriented driver education course.

Another way to earn lower rates is to live your life so that you present less risk to insurance companies. For example, your auto insurance rates will stay low if you never have an accident. Your life insurance premiums will be far less expensive if you don't smoke and if you exercise and eat healthy foods. And your home insurance rates will fall if you maintain good security around your home or install an alarm system.

With these guidelines in mind, consider the five major types of coverage you will probably need: auto, disability, health, homeowner's and life insurance.

Auto Insurance

Most states require drivers to carry some kind of auto insurance before they will issue a car registration, so it is a policy you cannot avoid if you own a car. The lingo of car insurance can be particularly difficult to understand, but it is worth learning if you don't want to pay excessive premiums.

The first principle of car insurance is that your policy covers a specific automobile. That means you are not covered when driving other cars, such as your cousin's jalopy, unless your policy specifically includes them. In addition to potential damage to your car itself or injuries caused by your car, your policy also insures the people who drive or ride in the vehicle. Mainly, your auto policy covers you and your family. However, if you give someone else permission to drive your car, such as a friend or relative, he or she also is covered by your policy.

Your auto insurance is really several kinds of coverage combined in one policy. The primary components of coverage are bodily injury, property damage, collision, comprehensive, medical payments, personal injury and uninsured or underinsured motorist. A brief explanation of each follows:

Bodily injury. If you hit someone with your car and cause injury or death because you were driving negligently, you must pay for the damages caused by the accident. These damages include the medical bills and lost wages of the person you injured. The person can also sue for pain and suffering if you live in a state that assesses fault for accidents. If you kill someone, you may also be responsible for the loss of income to the deceased person's family. Most states require that you carry a minimum amount of bodily injury liability coverage—usually between $15,000 and $25,000. If you own a substantial amount of property and earn a regular income, obtain far more coverage than the minimum. Because potential liabilities are enormous, coverage for at least $100,000 per individual you harm and $300,000 for each accident you cause would not be excessive.

Property damage. This liability insurance covers any damage that you cause to another person's property by driving negligently. This may include damage to another car or other property, such as a fence or a tree. Because it is usually less expensive to damage property than to injure people, property liability is cheaper and generally purchased in smaller amounts. Most states require a minimum of $5,000 to $25,000 in coverage; however, you should probably obtain at least $25,000 worth because today's cost of repairing cars is extremely high.

Following are the minimum amounts of bodily injury and property damage liability insurance required by all 50 states. The first two numbers are the minimum amounts of bodily injury liability coverage required. The listing 20/40, for example, means coverage up to $40,000 for all persons injured in an accident, subject to a limit of $20,000 for one individual. The third number is the minimum property damage coverage required, so for example, 10 means $10,000.

State	Bodily Injury	Property Damage
Alabama	20/40	10
Alaska	50/100	25
Arizona	15/30	10
Arkansas	25/50	15
California	15/30	5
Colorado	25/50	15
Connecticut	20/40	10
Delaware	15/30	10
District of Columbia	25/50	10
Florida	10/20	10
Georgia	15/30	10
Hawaii	20/40	10
Idaho	25/50	15
Illinois	20/40	15
Indiana	25/50	10
Iowa	20/40	15
Kansas	25/50	10
Kentucky	25/50	10
Louisiana	10/20	10
Maine	20/40	10
Maryland	20/40	10
Massachusetts	20/40	5
Michigan	20/40	10
Minnesota	30/60	10
Mississippi	10/20	5
Missouri	25/50	10
Montana	25/50	10
Nebraska	25/50	25
Nevada	15/30	10
New Hampshire	25/50	25
New Jersey	15/30	5
New Mexico	25/50	10
New York	25/50	10
North Carolina	25/50	15

State	Bodily Injury	Property Damage
North Dakota	25/50	25
Ohio	12.5/25	7.5
Oklahoma	10/20	10
Oregon	25/50	10
Pennsylvania	15/30	5
Rhode Island	25/50	25
South Carolina	15/30	5
South Dakota	25/50	25
Tennessee	20/50	10
Texas	20/40	15
Utah	25/50	15
Vermont	20/40	10
Virginia	25/50	20
Washington	25/50	10
West Virginia	20/40	10
Wisconsin	25/50	10
Wyoming	25/50	20

Collision. One of the main reasons you buy auto insurance is to reimburse you if your car is seriously damaged in a collision. Your policy will pay you to fix the car and bring it back to its condition before the accident. Most policies will pay your repair bills in full, less the deductible. If the repairs total $3,000, for example, you receive a check for $3,000. Policies, however, reimburse you only for the book value of the damaged property. In this case, the insurance company would rather pay you what the car was worth before the accident (assuming plenty of depreciation), knowing that this amount could not bring it back to a usable condition. No insurance settlement pays enough for a new car. Therefore, try to obtain a policy that reimburses you for the replacement cost, not the book value.

The older and less valuable your car becomes, the less collision coverage you need. You can also cut your collision premiums by raising your deductible as the car ages. You might start with $250 and increase it to $1,000 or more after two or three years of ownership. Once your car's value drops below $1,000, it probably makes sense to drop collision and/or comprehensive coverage because what you might collect from a claim will not replace the car.

Usually, collision coverage also protects you when you drive a car you don't own but are authorized to use, such as a car owned by your relatives or friends.

Comprehensive. This coverage pays for losses sustained by your car other than in collisions with cars or property. Comprehensive coverage includes fire, theft, storm damage, falling objects, explosions, earthquakes, floods, riots and collisions with birds or other animals. For example, if a thief breaks your window and takes your car stereo, you would file a claim under the comprehensive portion of your policy. As with collision insurance, the less valuable your car becomes over time, the less comprehensive coverage you need. You can also save money by raising your deductible from about $250 to $1,000 or more.

If your car is stolen, your comprehensive coverage normally pays you a certain amount, perhaps $10 to $15 a day, to cover your transportation costs while you replace the car. All policies limit the money they will pay for such temporary transportation, however.

Medical payments. Medical coverage, known as *med pay,* pays doctor and hospital bills—as well as funeral expenses, if needed—brought about by injuries that you and your passengers sustain in a car accident. Med pay also kicks in if you or a family member is hit by a car when walking as a pedestrian or if you or a family member is hurt when riding in someone else's car. Medical bills are covered up to the limit specified in the policy, regardless of who causes the accident. Most policies limit coverage for each injured individual in a car, up to as much as $5,000 apiece. For example, if three people are in your car when you have an accident, the insurer may have to pay as much as $15,000 in medical bills.

Some people skimp on med pay coverage because they figure that their bills will be covered by their health insurance. Economizing on such coverage, however, is usually not a good idea for two reasons. First, while your health insurance may be topnotch, your passengers may not have good coverage. (If you don't have good health insurance coverage, med pay is even more important.) Second, med pay covers funeral expenses, which are not reimbursed by health insurance. For the relatively small med pay premium, the extra coverage is worthwhile. In some states, med pay is not optional, so you don't have a choice over whether to carry it or not.

Personal injury. In states with no-fault insurance laws, *personal injury protection* (PIP) covers a broader assortment of medical charges than med pay does. In addition to covering doctor's bills, PIP also replaces lost wages or pays to replace the services of someone injured in a car accident. For example, if a stay-at-home mother is laid up because of an auto accident, PIP payments would cover babysitter fees until the mother can care for her children again. PIP is often required in states with no-fault plans though it is also usually available in states assessing fault. It is relatively inexpensive and usually worth adding to your policy.

Uninsured or underinsured motorist. This coverage protects you if you are involved in an accident with a driver who is either totally uninsured or severely underinsured. It also protects you if you are injured by a hit-and-run driver.

With auto insurance premiums skyrocketing these days, some people drive around with little or no coverage. If such an uninsured or underinsured driver causes an accident, your uninsured motorist coverage pays you what you would be entitled to if the other driver had full insurance. You can collect not only for medical bills caused by the accident but also for lost wages and pain and suffering.

Uninsured or underinsured motorist coverage is very inexpensive because the odds of hitting an uncovered driver are relatively small. Obtain at least $100,000 of

Figure 11.1   Auto Insurance Pricing Worksheet

	Amount of Coverage	Company 1 Premiums	Company 2 Premiums
Bodily Injury	$	$	$
Property Damage			
Collision (no deductible)			
With $100 Deductible			
With $500 Deductible			
With $1,000 Deductible			
Comprehensive (no deductible)			
With $100 Deductible			
With $500 Deductible			
With $1,000 Deductible			
Medical Payments			
Personal Injury			
Uninsured or Underinsured Motorist			
TOTAL BEFORE DISCOUNTS		$	$

Figure 11.2   Auto Insurance Discount Worksheet

Discount	Company 1 Discount		Company 2 Discount	
Defensive Driving Course	$		$	
		%		%
Good Driving Record	$		$	
		%		%
Car Pool	$		$	
		%		%
Limited Annual Mileage	$		$	
		%		%
Antitheft Devices	$		$	
		%		%
Antilock Brakes	$		$	
		%		%
Passive Restraint Systems	$		$	
		%		%
Nonsmoker	$		$	
		%		%
Older than Age 50	$		$	
		%		%
Good School Grades	$		$	
		%		%
Total Discount Savings	$		$	
TOTAL PREMIUM BEFORE DISCOUNTS (see Figure 11.1)	$		$	
(MINUS) TOTAL DISCOUNT SAVINGS	$ (	)	$ (	)
EQUALS				
NET PREMIUM	$		$	

coverage per individual riding in your car and a total of $300,000 per accident. Many states require proof of this coverage before they issue a driver's license or a car registration. Even if the insurance is optional in your state, obtain it to protect yourself.

When buying your auto insurance policy, assess each of these components to determine what you need and how much you can afford. By accepting higher deductibles and lower coverage limits, you can reduce your premium. But don't limit your coverage or raise your deductibles so much that the policy won't protect you when you really need it.

You can also qualify for a lower premium if you insure several cars with the same company or if you buy several types of policies, such as home, life and auto, from the same insurer. Most companies will also shave your premium by 5 percent to 10 percent if you meet any of the following conditions:

- You successfully complete a defensive driving course.
- You have a good driving record.
- You use recognized antitheft devices.
- Your car has antilock brakes.
- You do not smoke.
- Your car has passive restraint systems like automatic seat belts and air bags.
- You drive a limited number of miles each year.
- You participate in a car pool.
- You are older than age 50.

Some companies establish even more specific conditions, such as getting good grades if you are a high school or college student. In this case, the insurance company figures that you spend much of your time studying and therefore have less opportunity to get into an accident.

The auto insurance business is extremely competitive, so it pays to shop around. Get a quote from a captive agent who works for a large insurer like Allstate, State Farm or Geico, and compare it to the best price that you obtain from an independent agent who represents several companies.

The worksheet in Figure 11.1 summarizes the elements of auto insurance. Use it to compare premium prices between companies. When choosing among policies with different deductibles, list all the alternatives on the worksheet, but choose only one when you total the premiums.

After you complete the Auto Insurance Pricing Worksheet, total the discounts for which you qualify in Figure 11.2's worksheet. On the first line, enter your dollar savings; on the second line, the percentage discount you receive on comprehensive premiums.

The price you are quoted for auto coverage depends not only on the insurer's rates but also on your driving record, where you live and the kind of car you wish to insure. Your gender and marital status also affect your premium because women and married people are statistically less likely to have accidents than men and singles. Your price will be quite low if you have never had an accident, live in a quiet suburb and drive a modest sedan. On the other hand, expect to pay a high premium if you have a history of collisions, you live in a high-crime area and you own a sports car or luxury sedan. Many companies will not even insure certain cars at any price.

Before you commit to a company, check the claim procedure. Make sure that the firm has claims adjusters near your home who can examine your car, assess the damage and process your claim quickly and efficiently. Also inquire whether your rates will soar or the company will drop you altogether if you file a claim. Some companies take such a drastic step after only one claim—even if the accident was not your fault. It is better to work with a company a bit more understanding.

If, for whatever reason, you are not able to find a commercial insurance company that will issue you a policy at a reasonable cost or that will issue you a policy at all, you may have to obtain a state-sponsored insurance plan. Unfortunately, because these plans must accept everyone—no matter what the risk—their premiums are far higher than those under commercial policies. Your state's plan might be called a *joint underwriting association* (JUA) or an *assigned-risk plan*. But whatever its name, it is far less preferable than qualifying for coverage with a private insurance company.

Fault Versus No-Fault

To fully understand your auto insurance coverage, know whether you live in a fault or a no-fault state. In a no-fault state, your insurance coverage pays for any injuries sustained in an auto accident, no matter who was to blame. In a fault state, the insurance company of the person who caused the accident pays for injuries. That means you must establish whose fault the accident was, usually through a lengthy court proceeding.

The problem with the fault system is that it can take years for a court to rule on who was to blame for a collision. Meanwhile, the victims of the accident receive no compensation to cover medical bills or lost wages. In addition, even if you win your case, legal fees can devour a substantial piece of your settlement.

In a no-fault state, medical and repair bills are paid promptly, and far fewer lawsuits exist. In return for speedier settlement of claims, however, you give up the right to sue for damages in all but the most serious cases. Each no-fault state defines its coverage slightly differently. Some offer generous no-fault benefits in exchange for strict prohibitions against lawsuits. Others provide generous benefits and make it relatively easy to sue. Some states offer a choice between the no-fault option and the traditional fault system, which allows you to sue.

The following list of states, provided by the American Insurance Association, stipulates various no-fault laws and coverage. The states marked with an asterisk allow you to choose between the no-fault option and the traditional liability system.

Compulsory personal insurance protection coverage; some restrictions on lawsuits:

Colorado	Minnesota
Hawaii	New Jersey*
Kansas	New York
Kentucky*	North Dakota
Massachusetts	Pennsylvania*
Michigan	Utah

Compulsory personal insurance protection coverage; optional liability insurance; some restrictions on lawsuits:

Florida	Puerto Rico

Compulsory personal insurance protection and liability insurance; no restrictions on lawsuits:

Delaware	Oregon
Maryland	

Compulsory liability; optional personal insurance; no restrictions on lawsuits:

Arkansas	South Dakota
District of Columbia	Texas
South Carolina	Washington

Insurance not compulsory; personal insurance protection benefits optional; no restrictions on lawsuits:

New Hampshire	Wisconsin
Virginia	

   *These states allow you to choose between the no-fault option and the traditional liability system.

By spending a little time learning the ins and outs of auto insurance, you can save a tremendous amount of money over the long term. Once you have chosen a policy, it is a good idea to comparison shop every two or three years or, if you like, each time it is renewed—usually every six months. Insurance rates constantly change, and you may get an even better deal the next time if you maintain a clean driving record.

Disability Insurance

Though you might think it highly unlikely that you will ever become disabled, either on the job or outside of work, you are mistaken. According to the Health Insurance Association of America, at age 40, for example, you have a 19 percent probability of suffering at least one disability lasting more than 90 days.

If you miss work for a short time, your employer will probably provide short-term sick leave. You might also collect benefits from workers' compensation if you were injured on the job. Other government programs, such as veterans benefits, civil service disability, black lung insurance for miners and Medicaid for low-income people, might also kick in. If you were injured in a car accident, your auto insurance will pay you a certain amount of cash for a limited period of time. And if you are a union member, you might be eligible for group union disability coverage.

You will qualify for Social Security disability benefits if you become severely disabled. How much you receive depends on your salary and the number of years you have been covered by Social Security. Following are the ground rules for receiving Social Security disability payments:

- *You must be disabled for at least five months and expect to be out of commission for at least a year, total.* Expect the Social Security Administration to take at least three months to process your claim, so file as soon as you think you will be eligible.

- *The amount you receive from Social Security will be reduced by other payments you get from other government disability programs.* For example, any money you receive from military, civil service or government pensions or from workers' compensation is subtracted from your Social Security benefit. All of these income sources combined cannot exceed 80 percent of your average earnings before you became disabled.

- *You must not be able to perform any job whatsoever,* not just the work you did before you were injured.

- *You qualify for Medicare after receiving Social Security payments for two years.* You must enroll and pay the monthly premium to receive both medical and hospital coverage under Medicare.

- *You must pay federal income tax on your disability benefits if your income exceeds a certain limit.* The most recent limit for adjustable gross income (AGI) plus nontaxable interest income and half of all Social Security benefits is $34,000 for a single person and $44,000 for a couple filing jointly.

Even if you collect from several government programs, you probably will not receive enough money to live comfortably. This is where individual long-term disability insurance becomes crucial. If you qualify, you can receive between 60 percent and 80 percent of your regular salary, depending on the policy, plus cost-of-living adjustments in some policies. Companies do not pay 100 percent of your salary because they want you to have an incentive to go back to work.

Many clauses in disability contracts can be crucial in determining the benefits you receive if you are injured.

Definition of disability. Some policies pay if you are unable to perform your customary job. Others stipulate that you must be unable to do *any* job before they consider you disabled. Many use a combination of the inability to perform your own job for an initial period (usually the first year of your disability) and then the inability to perform at any job for which you are suited based on your education and experience. Some policies require that you be totally disabled; others pay if you are only partly disabled.

Cause of disability. Some policies provide benefits only if you are injured in an accident. Others pay if you become injured and ill. The best policies cover both accidents and illness, and they pay no matter how you become disabled.

Exclusions. Insurers usually will not pay disability benefits if an injury is caused by a suicide attempt, drug abuse, a crash of a noncommercial aircraft, military service or a normal pregnancy.

Residual benefits. Residual benefits are partial benefits. For example, if you are healthy enough to work one day a week or earn 20 percent of your former income by performing less demanding tasks, a policy offering residual benefits will pay you 80 percent of the full benefit. The more you work, the less residual funds you receive.

Payment amount. Your monthly benefit is based on your level of income before you become disabled. You can expect anywhere from 60 percent to 80 percent of your predisability income from all sources combined. Higher paid workers tend to receive a smaller percentage of their former pay than do lower paid workers. If you pay your own premiums on a disability insurance policy, they will cost less if you accept a smaller percentage of your predisability pay. You can also add a cost-of-living-adjustment clause to your policy for an extra premium. This clause would raise your disability payments based on an index tied to the yearly change in the Consumer Price Index (CPI).

Benefit payment method. Some policies call for weekly checks, but most pay monthly. A policy also might include a provision allowing the insurance company to pay the entire benefit in one lump sum, cutting short any further liability.

Beginning payment date. Some policies begin paying benefits within a month of your disability; others wait six months or even a year. The longer you can go without receiving insurance benefits, the lower your premiums will be. Before you choose a longer waiting period, however, make sure you have enough savings and other resources to cover your expenses over that time.

Payment caps. All policies limit the monthly amount of disability benefits paid to recipients. It could be as much as $2,000 or $3,000 or far less, depending on the policy. Try to estimate realistically how much income you would need if you were disabled.

Ending payment date. Disability insurance is designed to replace earned income, so benefits may last from one year to the rest of your life, depending on when you get injured and what other sources of income are available to you. If you agree to receive benefits for a shorter time, your premiums will be lower. Most people buy policies that pay benefits until age 65 when they qualify for various government programs.

Renewability. The last thing you want to happen if you are disabled is for your insurance company to cancel your policy. Make sure that the coverage you buy is guaranteed noncancelable and renewable at the original premium price.

If you become disabled and you have paid the premiums for disability insurance, any benefits you receive are free of federal, state and local income taxes. However, if your employer has paid some or all of the premiums, your benefits are partially or totally taxable. Though prices vary widely among disability policies, expect to pay about $1,000 a year for $12,000 worth of annual disability income coverage. While several kinds of insurance companies offer disability coverage, life insurers specialize in the product and will offer the best options at the lowest prices. You will obtain a much better price and more generous benefits if you buy through a group plan. However, if you cannot purchase coverage through your employer, union or trade association, it often makes sense to purchase a supplemental individual policy.

A specialized type of disability insurance is tied to your ability to repay loans. Banks, finance companies, car dealerships and other lenders sell *credit disability insurance,* which covers your loan payments if you become disabled. Mortgage lenders push mortgage *disability insurance,* which makes your home payments if you have an accident. In general, both credit and mortgage disability insurance policies are not good investments because they are overpriced. You are better served by more comprehensive forms of disability coverage.

The worksheet in Figure 11.3 will help you total your potential sources of disability income. Fill in the monthly amount you would receive from each policy, the waiting period before benefits begin and the number of years you would receive benefits.

By completing the Disability Income Worksheet when you are not disabled, you will have a better idea of how you might cope if such a tragedy ever occurred. By adding your potential sources of disability income, you can also calculate how much private insurance you need to buy, either through your employer or on your own.

Health Insurance

The soaring cost of medical care and the resulting pressure on health insurance premiums have become top-priority issues for employers, employees, the self-employed, the federal government and recipients of various government health insurance plans. The current health insurance system is not only costly but also extremely complex and constantly changing.

Figure 11.3 Disability Income Worksheet

Disability Insurance Program	Monthly $ Amount	Waiting Period (Months)	Benefits For How Long (Years)
Government Programs			
Black Lung	$ _____	_____	_____
Civil Service	_____	_____	_____
Department of Veterans Affairs	_____	_____	_____
Medicaid	_____	_____	_____
Social Security	_____	_____	_____
Workers' Compensation	_____	_____	_____
Group Programs			
Employer	_____	_____	_____
Sick Leave	_____	_____	_____
Union	_____	_____	_____
Individual Programs			
Auto	_____	_____	_____
Credit Disability	_____	_____	_____
Individual Disability	_____	_____	_____
Mortgage Disability	_____	_____	_____
Other (while disabled)			
Savings and Investments	_____		
Spouse's Income	_____		
Other	_____		
TOTAL MONTHLY INCOME (while disabled)	$ _____		

Years ago, health insurance was relatively simple. You went to the doctor of your choice. He or she billed your insurance carrier directly, or you paid the bill and submitted it for reimbursement. If you worked for a large company, you paid no premiums, and your co-payments, if any, were minor.

Now, you have many more choices to make. Do you want the traditional fee-for-service indemnity plan? How about opting for the health maintenance organization (HMO) or preferred provider organization (PPO) alternative? Should you participate in a flexible spending account (FSA) plan? Today, you have a much bigger stake in these decisions because you are often required to pay part of the health insurance premiums, and your deductibles and co-payments are far more costly than they used to be. On top of what is occurring between private employers and their workers, massive changes in health insurance coverage provided by the government promise to cost you even more money and angst.

Despite these complexities, it is crucial to understand your health insurance options and maximize your benefits at the least possible cost. A good health insurance plan can be the best employee benefit you receive because its coverage would be extremely expensive to replicate on your own. For this reason, many employees fear losing their job or are reluctant to switch companies if health benefits at the new company are not equal. Adequate health insurance is critical because you can easily be devastated financially if you or a family member needs major surgery or long-term medical care.

The optimal traditional fee-for-service indemnity policy is divided into two plans. The *basic plan* reimburses you for doctor's bills, drugs, outpatient surgical procedures and other medical expenses up to a certain annual dollar limit. The second plan, called *major medical,* covers extended hospital visits and other major medical procedures. Both the basic and major medical plans, if offered by an employer, usually cover the employee, his or her spouse and any children age 23 or younger if the children attend school.

The basic plan, which may be offered directly by your employer or by an outside insurance company, usually applies deductibles of $100 to $1,000 or more before your bills are reimbursed. Some companies impose a fixed annual deductible of $100 or $200 for all employees; others tie the deductible to your salary level. After you pay the deductible out of your pocket, all further bills are usually reimbursed for 80 percent of your cost, up to a specified annual limit. Once you have spent more than that limit, you are reimbursed 100 percent.

Some basic plans are far less generous than others. Depending on the company you work for and the insurance carrier, reimbursement for some procedures might be limited or omitted altogether. This includes such expenses as home health care, dentist bills, psychiatric care and drug or alcohol abuse treatment.

Your major medical plan normally pays 100 percent of the cost of a semi-private hospital room up to a certain length of time, such as 120 days. After that time limit, the plan typically covers 80 percent of your bills. Hospitalization charges usually include room and board, nursing care, drugs, medical devices, food and fees for specialists, such as surgeons, who work in the hospital. If your surgery can be performed on an outpatient basis, these expenses are also usually covered. Most major medical policies have either an annual or a lifetime cap, typically between $250,000 and $1 million. Some major medical plans, such as those offered by Blue Cross and Blue Shield, require you to cover the first $2,000 to $5,000 worth of hospital costs as a deductible before they pay hospital bills directly. This stipulation is often called the *stop-loss clause* because it limits your loss to the deductible. You are responsible for the initial deductible (say $250) after which the insurer will pay 80 percent of the covered medical costs, and you will pay 20 percent. When your total out-of-pocket expenditures reach a certain amount, such as $2,000, the insurer pays 100 percent.

For even more protection, you can buy excess major medical coverage to supplement a regular major medical policy with a low lifetime limit. *Excess major medical policies,* often called *catastrophic policies,* usually have a very high deductible of about $15,000 but can be vital if you need an expensive medical procedure.

Taking Your Policy with You

If you switch companies, you have a right to carry your group health insurance coverage with you to your new job for up to 18 months under the *Congressional Omnibus Budget Reconciliation Act* (COBRA). (You do not receive this benefit if you are fired for cause or due to misconduct.) You must pay the full premium for the coverage, but at group rates, it is far less expensive than buying a similar policy at individual rates. Health insurance coverage under COBRA, with the same payment requirement, also applies to the following people:

- Employees who leave a company to become unemployed or self-employed (for up to 18 months)

- Widows or widowers and children of employees who die while still working for the company (for up to three years)

- Spouses and children of employees who reach age 65 and qualify for Medicare, at which time a company usually stops paying for health benefits (for up to three years)

- Spouses who divorce employees, as well as the employees' children, even if they live with the ex-spouses (for up to three years)

- Employees' children who reach maturity (for up to three years). Normally, a child graduating from school at age 23 would no longer be covered under his or her parent's group policy.

If you will need COBRA benefits, fill out the appropriate forms from your employer's benefits department. If you take no action within 60 days of leaving a company, you may be denied continued coverage.

If you remain unemployed or self-employed when your COBRA benefits expire, you must purchase health insurance on your own. First, inquire of your former company whether you can convert your group policy to individual coverage with the same carrier. Your rates will be higher and the benefits more limited, but the terms are probably better than you could obtain on your own. Alternatively, you might be able to sign up for your spouse's plan at group rates if he or she is employed at a company with good health coverage.

The next best strategy is to join an organization that gives you access to group rates. For example, the American Association of Retired Persons (AARP) sells a decent group health care policy. Or you might already be a member of a trade association, an alumni group, a union or another group that offers policies. Also, check with your credit card companies to see whether they offer health insurance.

If all else fails, buy an individual policy. The rates can be frighteningly high— up to several thousand dollars a year—and coverage can be limited. If you should be self-employed, however, you can deduct 25 percent of your health insurance premiums as a business expense.

You need health insurance because you shouldn't be exposed to the potentially devastating financial impact of a major medical problem—unless such a policy is totally unaffordable. If you can purchase health insurance, obtain a policy that guarantees you can renew it, no matter how many times you make claims. And, of course, get as low a limit as possible on your out-of-pocket expenses, such as co-payments.

You might contact a health insurance agent or broker to help you find the policy that best suits your needs. Many agents today have access to computerized services that help them locate the policies offering the most coverage for the least price. The three largest insurance services are Quotesmith (800-556-9393); Dinan (800-346-2610); and Group Benefit Shoppers (800-231-8495). If the agent you choose does not have access to these services, call one of them and ask for an agent near you who does subscribe.

If you are a particularly bad risk because of some health problem, you might not be able to obtain an individual policy at any price. In this case, consider applying for Blue Cross and Blue Shield coverage during one of their open enrollment periods. Or try your state's health insurance risk pool, which is designed to offer coverage to those considered uninsurable. As you might suspect, however, the premiums for risk pool coverage are usually extremely expensive.

MEDICARE

For those age 65 or older, Medicare provides substantial health insurance benefits—whether you are retired or still working. Medicare is designed to cover part of your expenses for short-term acute medical problems rather than long-term conditions requiring custodial care. It pays for hospitalization, surgery, doctor bills, home health care and skilled nursing care considered to be medically necessary and within reasonable cost limits.

Medicare coverage is divided into two parts. *Part A* is hospital insurance. If you are eligible, you can enroll without charge; however, if you are not covered by Social Security, you must pay part of the premium. When you apply for Social Security benefits, you automatically apply for Medicare. If you plan to work past age 65, you should still apply for Medicare. Following are those expenses that Medicare Part A covers.

- *Hospitalization.* After you meet your deductible, Medicare pays all costs from your 1st through 60th day in the hospital. From your 61st through 90th day, Medicare covers your full costs after you meet your co-insurance payments, which are the daily cost of hospitalization that you pay.

- *Nursing-home care.* Medicare pays 100 percent of approved amounts for your first 20 days of care in a skilled-nursing facility after you have been in the hospital for at least three days. From your 21st through 100th day in the nursing facility, Medicare pays all costs after you meet your co-insurance payments.

- *Home health care.* Medicare pays 100 percent of any approved home health care services, as well as 80 percent of approved medical equipment.

- *Hospice care.* Medicare covers all costs, though it sets limits for outpatient drugs and inpatient respite care.

- *Blood.* Medicare pays for all blood after the first three pints, which you must cover.

Medicare Part B is a medical insurance program covering charges from doctors, surgeons and other outpatient providers, as well as fees for medical supplies. Part B is optional if you are eligible for Part A. To take advantage of Part B, you must enroll and pay a monthly premium. Medicare Part B covers the following expenses:

- *Medical services.* After you meet your deductible, Part B pays 80 percent of approved amounts for doctors, surgeons, supplies and medical equipment.

- *Tests.* Part B pays 100 percent of approved amounts for medical tests, laboratory work, biopsies and bloodwork.

- *Home health care.* Part B pays for all costs of approved home health care services, with no deductible. In addition, it covers 80 percent of the cost of medical equipment used in the home, after a deductible.

- *Outpatient hospital care.* Part B covers 80 percent of any approved procedures performed in a hospital on an outpatient basis.

- *Blood.* The plan pays for 80 percent of the cost of approved amounts of blood after the first 3 pints.

For more details on the expenses Medicare covers, as well as the cost of deductibles, co-payments and premiums, call the Social Security Administration's

Medicare hot-line at 800-772-1213, or obtain a copy of the *Medicare Handbook* from any Social Security office.

While the list of services that Medicare covers seems extensive, many medical expenses are excluded. For example, you will not be reimbursed for the following:

- Nursing care beyond 100 days in a skilled-nursing facility; private nursing care; and any care in a center not approved by Medicare

- Custodial and intermediate nursing care

- Prescription drugs not given in a hospital

- Routine physicals, dentistry, acupuncture, immunizations, cosmetic surgery and foot, eye and hearing care

- Doctor charges that exceed approved Medicare levels or that Medicare does not consider medically necessary. Each year, the government publishes a fee schedule listing maximum Medicare payments, which are usually far less than doctors charge regular commercial patients.

- Care in foreign countries, except in certain limited circumstances in Canada and Mexico

Because Medicare coverage is limited in so many ways, several plans have been designed to fill in the gaps. These plans are called *Medigap* policies and are discussed in more detail on the next page.

SPECIALIZED HEALTH INSURANCE POLICIES

In addition to the usual health insurance plans, several more specialized policies are marketed aggressively.

Hospital indemnity plans. The most widely advertised policies are hospital indemnity plans, which pay a specified amount of cash each day that you are hospitalized. The plans are usually advertised on television or through the mail. Such pitches announce that you can get $75 a day, for example, for only pennies in premiums. The problem is that hospitals charge an average of $750 a day, and most of the hospital's services are already covered by your comprehensive health insurance plan. In addition, hospital indemnity plans often limit pre-existing conditions, which may prevent you from receiving benefits. Most plans also have elimination periods, meaning that you must be hospitalized a certain number of days before you collect benefits. Nowadays, most hospitals try to shorten patients' stays, so it can be very difficult to collect on these policies.

Long-term care policies. Such policies cover the health costs of long-term custodial care either in a nursing home or at home. While the coverage from long-term care policies can offset some of the costs of such care, they rarely pay all the bills. Nursing homes charge between $30,000 and $70,000 a year, and home health aides can cost between $7,000 and $10,000 a year for three visits a week. Long-term care policies pay between $40 and $100 a day for nursing homes and half that amount for at-home care. While some policies offer inflation-adjustment clauses, these policies should be seen as a supplement to, not a replacement of, more comprehensive policies. When evaluating long-term care policies, avoid coverage naming exclusions like Alzheimer's disease, which is frequently a reason for long-term care. For a more detailed look at the best long-term care solutions, obtain a copy of the booklet *Long-Term Care: A Dollars and Sense Guide,* published by the United Seniors Health Cooperative (1331 H St., N.W., Suite 500, Washington, DC 20005; 202-393-6222; www.ushc-online.org). The publication discusses the many aspects of long-term care, including continuing care communities, nursing homes and veterans' options.

Medicare supplement policies. Known as either *Medigap* or *MedSup plans,* these policies are designed to pick up where Medicare leaves off, covering Medicare co-payments and deductibles. Some supplemental policies also pay for products and services not covered by Medicare, such as outpatient prescription drugs. As long as you enroll in Medicare Part B within six months after enrolling in Medicare Part A, you cannot be rejected when you apply for a Medicare supplement policy if you are at least 65 years old. Currently, ten standard Medicare supplement policies exist. They are labeled letter A through letter J for easier comparison. Policy A is the most basic and is available to all Medicare recipients. Policies B through J offer more and more benefits, and more and more people are excluded from qualification.

All ten Medigap policies cover at least the daily co-insurance amount for hospitalization under Medicare Part A. The more inclusive policies pay additional benefits for such services as preventive medical care, coverage in a foreign country, hospice care, prescription drugs or home visits—all of which Medicare does not cover. The table in Figure 11.4, provided courtesy of the National Association of Insurance Commissioners (NAIC), lists the benefits included in each supplemental policy.

A new form of Medicare supplement insurance called *Medicare Select* is being tested in several states. It is a form of private Medigap insurance designed to be less costly to policyholders because policyholders must use a designated group of health care professionals and facilities. The insurance company selects the providers, which may include HMOs and PPOs (described in more detail later in this chapter). The medical service providers offer discount prices because they are assured a steady flow of patients.

The Medicare Select test began with 15 states in 1992 and is likely to expand to more states if the program proves successful. The original test states are Alabama, Arizona, California, Florida, Indiana, Kentucky, Michigan, Minnesota, Missouri, North Dakota, Ohio, Oregon, Texas, Washington and Wisconsin.

When shopping for a Medigap policy, watch for pre-existing conditions clauses that preclude you from receiving benefits if you already have developed an ailment. Also, make sure that your policy is guaranteed renewable, and deter-

Figure 11.4
Benefits Offered by Medicare Supplemental Policies

A	B	C	D	E	F	G	H	I	J
Basic benefits	Basic benefits	Basic benefits	Basic benefits	Basic benefits	Basic benefits	Basic benefits	Basic benefits	Basic benefits	Basic benefits
		Skilled nursing co-insurance	Skilled nursing co-insurance	Skilled nursing co-insurance	Skilled nursing co-insurance	Skilled nursing co-insurance	Skilled nursing co-insurance	Skilled nursing co-insurance	Skilled nursing co-insurance
	Part A deductible	Part A deductible	Part A deductible	Part A deductible	Part A deductible	Part A deductible	Part A deductible	Part A deductible	Part A deductible
		Part B deductible			Part B deductible				Part B deductible
				Part B excess (100%)		Part B excess (80%)		Part B excess (100%)	Part B excess (100%)
		Foreign travel emergency	Foreign travel emergency	Foreign travel emergency	Foreign travel emergency	Foreign travel emergency	Foreign travel emergency	Foreign travel emergency	Foreign travel emergency
			At-home recovery			At-home recovery		At-home recovery	At-home recovery
							Basic drugs ($1,250 limit)	Basic drugs ($1,250 limit)	Extended drug benefit ($3,000 limit)
				Preventive care					Preventive care

Source: Used by permission of the National Association of Insurance Commissioners.

mine whether your premiums rise as you age. Finally, examine the elimination periods imposed for hospital stays. You may have to be hospitalized several days before benefits kick in, which may mean that you never collect a dime.

The process of choosing a Medigap policy can be quite complex and confusing. Many people are pressured into making quick decisions by commission-hungry salespeople. Instead, take your time, and make sure you that understand exactly what you are buying. Don't make a common mistake and purchase too much insurance; one comprehensive Medigap plan should be all you need. According to federal law, even after you buy a policy, you have 30 days to review it and obtain a full refund of all premiums paid.

Specific disease policies. Also known as *dread disease policies,* these policies play on people's fears by covering a specific disease, most commonly cancer. These pay limited benefits if you contract the illness named in the policy; each policy establishes a strict definition of a specific disease. For example, health problems caused by cancer usually don't entitle you to benefits. As with hospital indemnity coverage, a good comprehensive policy costs far less money and pays benefits more readily than a disease-specific plan. In some states, insurance regulators have prohibited the sale of cancer insurance, due to the questionable sales practices they could invite that take advantage of people's fears of this disease.

THE HMO (HEALTH MAINTENANCE ORGANIZATION) ALTERNATIVE

Instead of choosing your own doctors and getting reimbursed for expenses under the traditional fee-for-service health insurance plan, your employer might offer you the HMO alternative. Hundreds of HMOs across the country offer full medical services for a flat annual fee, which you may pay part of on a monthly basis. That fee might be several hundred or several thousand dollars, depending on the HMO, your employer and the plan coverage.

When you become an HMO member, you have unlimited access to the organization's medical services. You can visit a doctor for preventive checkups, minor problems or emergencies, sometimes for a small fee of $5 or $10 per visit. If the HMO runs a central medical facility, you must go there for all procedures. However, if you are out of town, the HMO will reimburse you for visits to approved doctors or hospitals. In a true life-or-death emergency, you can go to any hospital and still get reimbursed.

An HMO offers several advantages, primarily that your total out-of-pocket costs are limited to the annual HMO fee, plus small charges for special services. Because the HMO charges group rates, the premium will be less than the fee you normally would pay for traditional insurance coverage. In addition, you no longer must deal with deductibles, co-payments or coverage limits. And neither must you search for a generalist or specialist practitioner because the HMO employs every type of physician you probably will ever need. If you have an extremely rare condition that no one on the HMO's staff can handle, the HMO will locate a specialist for you. You will also receive prescription drugs either free of charge or at very low cost because the HMO buys them at bulk prices directly from manufacturers. Finally, all of your medical records are kept in one place, so your medical history is immediately available to whatever doctor treats you.

If HMOs offer so many advantages, why doesn't everyone join one? What you gain in financial control you lose in medical choice. You cannot bring your existing doctor to the HMO, so you must choose a new primary care physician from a list provided by the HMO. If your chosen doctor is not available on the day you visit the clinic, you must see whoever is working. If you need a specialist, you must select one from the HMO's approved list, regardless of whether he or she is the best person in town. In addition, many HMO generalists hate to refer patients to specialists because it costs the HMO more, and one of the main goals of HMOs is to control costs. Some HMOs also have a reputation for discouraging medical tests. Also, services such as vision, hearing and dental care and psychiatric treatment are considered basic in some HMO plans but not all.

The same lack of choice applies to hospitals: You go where the HMO sends you, not where you might prefer. If you seek help at a hospital not specifically authorized by your HMO, you will probably have to pay the entire bill on your own.

Before you join an HMO, ask plenty of questions. Following are a few areas to explore.

- What kinds of experiences have fellow employees had with the plan?

- How competent are the doctors? What percentage are board-certified? (The more doctors who are *board-certified,* meaning that they successfully passed a specialty test, the better. The average certification rate is about 70 percent.)

- How long do patients wait for an appointment to see a specialist?

- Is preventive medicine encouraged or discouraged? If encouraged, specifically what does the HMO do to minimize medical problems?

- How are HMO members treated at HMO-affiliated hospitals?

- Is the HMO accredited? (This is not required, but it is certainly better to join an accredited HMO than an unaccredited one. Agencies such as the National Committee for Quality Assurance set the most stringent standards.)

- Is there is a high staff turnover rate at the HMO you are interested in? (A high rate can mean that the patient load is too large and that doctors are unhappy.)

- What is the member retention rate? (A higher rate indicates a better level of member satisfaction. Good HMOs conduct annual patient surveys. Review them to gain insight into member satisfaction.)

For an evaluation of a managed care plan you are thinking of using, contact the National Committee for Quality Assurance (2000 L St., NW, Suite 500, Washington, DC 20036; 202-955-3500; 800-839-6787; www.ncqa.org). NCQA is a private, not-for-profit organization dedicated to assessing and reporting on the quality of managed care plans. To find out whether a managed care program you are thinking of signing up for is accredited by NCQA or not, call their Accreditation Status Line at 800-275-7585, or download their Accreditation Status List from their Web site. NCQA also provides two-page Accreditation Summary Reports giving you more detail on the performance of a particular plan. NCQA also measures the performance of managed care, looking at the results achieved by the plans. The performance is kept in a national database called Quality Compass, making it easy for you to compare your local plan against national averages in 71 performance measures.

THE PPO (PREFERRED PROVIDER ORGANIZATION) ALTERNATIVE

Somewhere between the traditional fee-for-service plan and the HMO is a relatively new form of health coverage called a PPO. Under this type of insurance, your employer, union or health insurance company enlists the services of generalist and specialist doctors, hospitals and many other health care providers. These caregivers receive a set monthly fee to provide a set level of services. If they give more care than was agreed upon, they earn more money.

From your point of view, your costs will probably be lower under a PPO than a traditional plan because the medical professionals and hospitals in the network offer discounts in exchange for a steady flow of patients. In some cases, doctors will accept your insurance reimbursement—usually 80 percent of PPO costs—as the entire payment. Like doctors in HMOs, caregivers in PPOs are encouraged to contain costs by discouraging tests and referrals to specialists unless they are absolutely necessary. However, PPOs give you more choice over which doctor you see because you can go to anyone who is part of the network. If you visit a doctor who does not work for the PPO, you will be reimbursed by the health insurance company at a reduced rate. For example, you might get back 70 percent of the bill instead of 80 percent. When investigating a PPO, ask questions similar to those posed for HMOs.

Homeowner's Insurance

The process of buying insurance to protect your home and its contents is similar in many ways to buying auto, disability and health insurance. The clauses in the policies are filled with unfamiliar jargon, and it can be quite difficult to determine how much coverage you really need. Nevertheless, you should wade through this morass because you need to protect yourself against all forms of disaster that might afflict your home and your possessions.

PROPERTY DAMAGE

The primary reason that you buy homeowner's insurance is to compensate you for property damage or loss. Two sources of damage exist: natural occurrences and man- or equipment-made disasters. Some of the more common natural causes include earthquakes, fire, floods, hurricanes, mudslides, storms, tornados, volcanos, wind, hail and weight of snow. Losses caused by people or the malfunctioning of equipment include arson, burglary, electrical fires, explosions, riots, theft, vandalism and water pipe breaks.

Insurers offer two policies to cover these risks: *named peril insurance* and the *all-risk insurance.* Named peril coverage protects you against only the specific dangers spelled out in the insurance contract. The perils usually named are fire, wind, hail, riots, smoke, vandalism and theft, among others. Under this policy, if you have a claim, you must show that the loss or damage was caused by one of the named perils. All-risk insurance, on the other hand, covers almost every possible source of loss or damage *except* those specifically named, such as floods, earthquake, nuclear war, dry rot, termites and insect damage wear and tear. You will need special insurance—for example, from the National Flood Insurance program—to cover those risks. Because the all-risk policy is more comprehensive, its premiums are usually higher than those on a named peril policy covering the same property.

Six basic types of homeowner's policies exist, each offering protection against certain losses on both your home's structure and its contents. They are all labeled HO (which stands for *homeowner's*), followed by a number. The most basic plan is HO-2. The most comprehensive plan, HO-3, is an all-risk policy that also provides special coverages. Policies for renters are labeled HO-4 and for condominium owners, HO-6. If you own an older home, you will need an HO-8 policy.

Both the basic HO-2 policy and the HO-8 policy for older homes protect you against the following specific perils:

1. Fire or lightning

2. Windstorm or hail

3. Explosion

4. Riot or civil disturbance

5. Damage from an aircraft

6. Damage from a vehicle

7. Smoke damage

8. Vandalism or malicious mischief

9. Theft

10. Breakage of glass that is part of a building

11. Volcanic eruption

The HO-2, or broad coverage, policy covers all of the perils of an HO-1, as well as the following:

12. Falling object

13. Weight of ice, snow or sleet

14. Freezing of a plumbing, a heating or an air conditioning system, of an automatic fire protective sprinkler system or of a household appliance

15. Accidental discharge or overflow of water or steam from a plumbing, a heating or an air conditioning system

16. Sudden and accidental discharge from an artificially generated electric current

17.   Sudden and accidental tearing apart, cracking, burning or bulging of a heating, an air conditioning or a protective sprinkler system or of an appliance for heating water

The HO-4 for renters and the HO-6 for condo owners cover the same perils as the HO-2. In addition, these policies cover contents and some structural aspects of an apartment or condominium, such as a wall that is not shared with another unit or separate balcony.

The special homeowner's HO-3 policy covers a house for all perils except those explicitly excluded from the contract, such as flood, earthquake, war, nuclear accidents, wear and tear, dry rot, or termite or insect damage. Clearly, because the HO-3 offers the most protection, it costs more than the HO-2 and HO-8, the renter's HO-4 and the condo owner's HO-6.

The purpose of homeowner's insurance is to replace what has been lost or damaged; therefore, in determining how much coverage to buy, follow the most important rule of homeowner's insurance: *Buy enough to replace most or all property at risk.* Frequently, homeowners insure their homes and the contents of their homes for what they paid for them, perhaps years ago. When these home-owners suffer a loss, they find—to their dismay—that they are reimbursed only for the present market value of the objects, which is usually far less than it costs to replace them. Unless your homeowner's policy specifically stipulates that it pays replacement cost, the insurer covers only the actual, depreciated value of the goods. Though you will pay premiums that are 10 to 20 percent higher for replacement cost insurance, the coverage is worth the extra money.

If you cannot afford the premiums on full replacement cost insurance, the least you should settle for is 80 percent replacement cost. Cutting back from 100 percent to 80 percent will slash your premiums by as much as a quarter. However, if you settle for less than 80 percent, you expose yourself to too much financial risk. Whether you opt for 100 percent or the 80 percent, though, always insist on a clause that indexes your coverage to changes in inflation.

In addition to your regular homeowner's coverage, you might want to purchase special insurance, known as a *rider* or a *floater,* for particularly valuable artwork, collectibles, silver, furs, jewelry or other items. Without these riders, you would collect nowhere near their true value if such precious objects were damaged or stolen.

HOME-BASED BUSINESSES

If you run a home-based business, you probably need extra insurance protection for all your equipment. Most homeowner's policies provide only $2,500 in coverage for property used for business purposes. Therefore, acquire an endorsement, or an additional clause that specifies particular items, to cover your computers, fax machines, office furniture, copiers, file cabinets and other equipment. Many insurance companies offer special-rate policies tailored to cover small businesses. Usually, homeowner's policies do not cover liabilities arising out of business activities. For example, you would not be covered against a suit filed by a delivery person who falls on your property while delivering a package for your business. A *small-business specialty policy* insures against such an event. You might also investigate *business interruption insurance,* which pays for your temporary relocation to other quarters while your office is being repaired due to fire or another disaster.

RENTERS AND CONDO OWNERS

While your landlord's insurance covers the building in which you live, you should buy a separate policy to cover your possessions if you rent. The provisions of a renter's policy are nearly identical to those of homeowner's coverage. You are protected against loss or damage from the most common perils, such as fire, explosion, water damage, vandalism or theft. If you own valuables, such as jewelry or computers, you probably need a floater to provide coverage beyond the typical limits. Most renter's policies impose a $1,000 limit on jewelry, $3,000 to $10,000 on computers and $2,500 to $10,000 on silverware. As with homeowner's insurance, *it is best to buy replacement cost coverage rather than a policy based on cash value.*

If you rent an apartment with several roommates, many companies write policies allowing you to cover all the contents of your apartment, no matter who they belong to. If you get a new roommate, you will probably have to tell the insurance company and list his or her name on the policy. Unmarried couples living together can also obtain coverage if it is specifically allowed in the contract. Some policies automatically extend coverage to any future resident of a policyholder's household who is considered a domestic partner.

In addition to property coverage, most renter's policies provide liability insurance if someone claims injury due to your negligence. For example, bodily injury liability pays medical costs, as well as your legal defense fees, if you injure or kill someone.

Insurance for condominium owners is similar to coverage available for renters. The condominium association buys insurance that protects the buildings, grounds and common areas, while each owner must obtain special condominium coverage for the contents of their apartments, walls that are not shared with other apartments and other things that are not commonly owned, as well as liability claims.

TAKING INVENTORY

Keeping those general guidelines in mind, determine how much homeowner's insurance you need. First, take a household inventory to see what actually needs insuring. Walk around your home, and list on an inventory sheet each item you own, what you paid for it and how much it might cost to replace. Also note model and serial numbers. If you have no idea what things cost today, you might consider bringing in an appraiser to help you. The worksheet in Figure 11.5, divided by rooms in your house, will help you inventory the contents of your home.

Figure 11.5   Household Inventory Worksheet

Article and Description	Purchase Price	Replacement Cost	Total Purchase Cost	Total Replacement Cost
Bathrooms				
Carpets/Rugs	$ _____	$ _____		
Clothes Hampers	_____	_____		
Curtains	_____	_____		
Dressing Tables	_____	_____		
Electrical Appliances	_____	_____		
Lighting Fixtures	_____	_____		
Linens	_____	_____		
Scales	_____	_____		
Shower Curtains	_____	_____		
Other	_____	_____		
Total for Bathrooms			$ _____	$ _____
Bedrooms				
Beds/Mattresses	_____	_____		
Books/Bookcases	_____	_____		
Carpets/Rugs	_____	_____		
Chairs	_____	_____		
Clocks	_____	_____		
Clothing	_____	_____		
Curtains/Drapes	_____	_____		
Desks	_____	_____		
Dressers	_____	_____		
Lamps	_____	_____		
Mirrors	_____	_____		
Plants	_____	_____		
Records/Tapes/CDs	_____	_____		
Stereos/Radios	_____	_____		
Tables	_____	_____		
Televisions	_____	_____		
Wall Hangings/Pictures	_____	_____		
Wall Units	_____	_____		
Other	_____	_____		
Total for Bedrooms			$ _____	$ _____
Dining Room				
Buffets	_____	_____		
Carpets/Rugs	_____	_____		
Chairs	_____	_____		
China	_____	_____		
Clocks	_____	_____		
Curtains/Drapes	_____	_____		
Glassware	_____	_____		

Figure 11.5 (continued)

Article and Description	Purchase Price	Replacement Cost	Total Purchase Cost	Total Replacement Cost
Lamps/Fixtures	$	$		
Silverware				
Tables				
Wall Hangings/Pictures				
Other				
Total for Dining Room			$	$
Garage/Basement/Attic				
Furniture				
Ladders				
Lawn Mowers				
Luggage				
Shovels				
Snowblowers				
Sports Equipment				
Sprinklers/Hoses				
Tools/Supplies				
Toys				
Washer/Dryer				
Wheelbarrows				
Work Benches				
Other				
Total for Garage/ Basement/Attic			$	$
Kitchen				
Buffets				
Cabinets				
Chairs				
Clocks				
Curtains				
Dishes				
Dishwasher				
Disposal/Trash Compactor				
Food/Supplies				
Freezer				
Glassware				
Lighting Fixtures				
Refrigerator				
Pots/Pans				
Radio/Television				

Figure 11.5   Household Inventory Worksheet (continued)

Article and Description	Purchase Price	Replacement Cost	Total Purchase Cost	Total Replacement Cost
Small Appliances	$_____	$_____		
Stove	_____	_____		
Tables	_____	_____		
Washer/Dryer	_____	_____		
Other	_____	_____		
Total for Kitchen			$_____	$_____
Living Room				
Books/Bookcases	_____	_____		
Carpets/Rugs	_____	_____		
Chairs	_____	_____		
Clocks	_____	_____		
Curtains/Drapes	_____	_____		
Desks	_____	_____		
Lamps	_____	_____		
Mirrors	_____	_____		
Musical Instruments	_____	_____		
Plants	_____	_____		
Records/Tapes/CDs	_____	_____		
Sofas	_____	_____		
Stereo/Radio	_____	_____		
Tables	_____	_____		
Television	_____	_____		
Wall Hangings/Pictures	_____	_____		
Wall Units	_____	_____		
Other	_____	_____		
Total for Living Room			$_____	$_____
Porch/Patio				
Carpets/Rugs	_____	_____		
Chairs	_____	_____		
Lamps	_____	_____		
Outdoor Cooking Equipment	_____	_____		
Outdoor Furniture	_____	_____		
Plants/Planters	_____	_____		
Tables	_____	_____		
Other	_____	_____		
Total for Porch/Patio			$_____	$_____
TOTAL HOUSEHOLD			$_____	$_____

In addition to listing your household possessions, photograph or videotape each room. If you videotape, talk about the objects you are taping, and estimate how much they cost. Keep the pictures or tape somewhere other than your home, such as at work so you will have access to it if your house is destroyed or damaged. These physical records can be invaluable if you ever must file a claim and convince an adjuster that you owned a particular item or what an item is worth.

LIABILITY COVERAGE

In addition to reimbursing you for lost or damaged property, homeowner's insurance protects you and members of your household against claims and lawsuits for injuries or property damage that you or your family members may have caused accidentally. For example, if your son throws a baseball through your neighbor's window, your neighbor can sue you to pay for the damage. If your dog bites the mail carrier, your liability insurance would cover his or her medical expenses. Someone who slips on ice on your sidewalk may also sue you for negligence. This general liability coverage does not apply to any damage you do in your car, which is covered by your auto liability insurance.

If you think the chances of being sued are remote, think again. The courts are clogged with thousands of seemingly frivolous liability suits. Such a lawsuit can cost thousands of dollars and waste days of your time—even if you end up winning. If you are unfortunate enough to get sued, your insurance carrier will pay for your legal defense, as well as any settlement or jury verdict against you, up to the liability limits of your policy.

To protect against a huge jury award, purchase extra liability coverage as part of your regular policy. This is generally known as *umbrella coverage*, and it usually extends your liability insurance to $1 million or more.

LIVING EXPENSES

If your home sustains so much damage that you are not able to live there while it is being repaired, your homeowner's insurance will pay for your living expenses until you can move back home. This might include the cost of hotels and restaurant meals. Don't expect to take on a luxury lifestyle, however; policies impose strict limits on how much they will pay for living expenses, both on a daily basis and in total.

MINIMIZING YOUR PREMIUM

The best way to qualify for the lowest insurance rates is to guard against accidents, thefts and losses. Some of the more obvious precautions you can take, which often qualify for direct discounts, include the following:

- Install deadbolt locks on doors and key locks on windows. If your home or apartment is at street level, add grates or grilles to protect windows.

- Install a burglar alarm system that attaches to doors and windows, that rings loudly if activated and that automatically notifies the local police department or alarm company of an intruder.

- Keep wiring in top condition.

- Maintain stairs, railings, carpets and flooring to minimize the possibility of slips or falls.

- Keep fresh batteries in smoke detectors, and install a sprinkler system and fire alarm that automatically alerts the fire department when it senses smoke.

- Install exterior lights to make it difficult for a burglar to work in secrecy.

- Stop smoking cigarettes because nonsmokers are less likely to start fires than smokers.

Most companies also shave your premiums if you are a long-time customer who has never filed a claim or if you have policies for auto or life insurance with the same company.

Rates on homeowner's policies are also based on the neighborhood in which your home is located. Obviously, owners of homes in crime-infested areas will pay higher premiums than those whose neighborhoods boast tight security and few crimes. Also, the closer your home is to fire and police protection, the lower your premiums. In general, newer homes qualify for lower rates than older homes because more can go wrong in older buildings as wiring, plumbing and heating systems deteriorate over time.

Another way to cut your premiums is to accept higher deductibles. If you increase the amount of loss you cover out of your own pocket from $100 to $500 or more, your premium cost plummets. Even when you agree to a substantial deductible, however, you gain protection against the enormous losses that home-owner's insurance is designed to cover.

KEEPING YOUR POLICY UP TO DATE

Once you purchase a homeowner's policy, keep it up to date as your home and lifestyle change. For example, tell your insurance agent if you build an addition on the house or remodel the kitchen. It might be worth increasing your coverage to protect the enhanced value of your property. The same holds true if you add several valuable possessions, such as artwork, computers or electronic gear. Re-assess your policy to determine whether you have enough insurance to cover the new valuables or whether you need to add any riders.

FILING A CLAIM

If your property sustains damage or if you suffer a property loss, report it to your insurance agent immediately. Take pictures of any damage as soon as possible in case the insurance adjuster cannot examine the scene right away. Also report thefts or burglaries to the police at once because your insurance agent will request the police report.

When you call your agent to report damage or loss, ask the following questions:

- Does my policy cover this damage or loss?
- Does my claim exceed my deductible?
- How long should I expect the processing of my claim to take?
- What is the procedure for getting estimates to repair or replace the items that were damaged or lost?

For safety's sake, follow up your phone conversation with a letter detailing the damage or loss. With the letter, include any evidence of the claim, such as photographs. Your agent should immediately send you a claims form, in which you provide as much detail as possible about the property damaged or lost.

If your home has been damaged, you can make temporary repairs to prevent further damage. Your insurer should reimburse you for those repairs if you send the company receipts substantiating your costs. Also, save receipts for additional living expenses—for example, hotel bills—that you may incur while repairs are made to your home.

After receiving all necessary information, your insurance agent and adjuster will either accept or reject your claim. If they accept your claim, your agent will offer you a settlement that he or she thinks fair. If you disagree, ask your agent for an explanation. You do not have to accept an agent's first offer. Often, he or she will negotiate the settlement with you until you are satisfied. If your agent still does not offer what you think you deserve after such negotiations or if your claim was rejected, you can take the following steps of appeal:

- *Send a copy of your original letter as well as a new letter explaining your dispute to the chief claims officer at the executive offices of your insurance company.* All reputable companies have internal investigation departments to help resolve disputes.

- *Call the National Insurance Consumer Helpline (800-942-4242; www.iii. com).* This industry-sponsored service might be able to intercede with your insurance carrier if its experts agree that you have not been offered a fair settlement.

- *Complain to your state insurance department.* All insurance companies are regulated, and the insurance department should be able to help you obtain justice if it agrees with your complaint. A list of the insurance departments in all 50 states appears in the "Resources" section at the end of this chapter.

- *Have an independent arbitrator decide whether the settlement offer is fair.* Your insurance company may be able to recommend such an arbitrator through Arbitration Forums, Inc. (220 White Plains Rd., 1st Floor, Tarry-town, NY 10591; 914-332-4113; www.arbfile.org), which supplies insur-ance arbitration specialists. Or you may obtain an arbitrator on your own through the American Arbitration Association (140 W. 51st St., New York, NY 10020-1203; 212-484-4000; www.adr.org).

- *As a last resort, hire a lawyer, and sue the insurance company to collect a fair settlement.* This process could cost hundreds or thousands of dollars and take many months or even years of litigation. Therefore, your claim must be substantial enough to make all of this trouble worthwhile. Your lawyer should also give you an honest opinion about your odds of winning the case. For more on choosing a lawyer, see Chapter 18, "Finding Fi-nancial Advisers Who Are Right for You."

Life Insurance

For many people, life insurance is probably the most unpleasant type of insurance to discuss. As is true of other insurance policies, when you buy life insurance, you confront arcane language, complex charts and tables and pushy salespeople. However, pure life insurance offers one difference: The insured is not the primary beneficiary from the policy. Life insurance is really designed to protect the survivors of the insured. This is not to say that a life insurance policy yields no advantages while the insured lives. Nevertheless, the main reason to purchase a policy is for the death benefit, which you hope that your dependents collect a long time in the future.

If your family or other people depend on your income, you need life insurance to help them live without your support if you pass away. The insurance contract requires that the insurance company pay your beneficiaries a set amount, called the *death benefit,* if you should die for almost any reason. (For example, suicide is usually excluded for the first two to three years of a policy.) Your beneficiaries can receive the money in one lump sum, free of federal income taxes. The funds should be enough to replace the insured's paycheck, cover daily living expenses and pay the insured's final medical bills and burial costs. In addition, the insurance proceeds should provide income for long-term needs such as retirement, estate taxes or college costs.

How Much Is Enough?

The key question in buying life insurance is how much coverage your ben-eficiaries really need. You should determine this before you listen to insurance agents' sometimes confusing pitches or the details of different policies. Unfortu-nately, assessing how much is enough is not a simple process because each family is different. No general formula exists. You will require more coverage if you have several young children and a nonworking spouse, for instance, than you will if your spouse earns a good salary and you have only one child.

The first step in determining your ideal amount of insurance is to examine your current family situation and your potential family situation. The following describe a few typical family scenarios, broken down into high-need, medium-need and low-need categories:

High need. You will need a significant amount of insurance if you die as a:

- *Working spouse married to a nonworking spouse, with children.* Life insurance proceeds should pay for your family's living expenses and your children's education and should replace your income as sole wage earner.

- *Working spouse married to a nonworking spouse, with no children.* Your spouse should receive a death benefit that will generate enough investment income to replace your paycheck and cover his or her living expenses for the rest of your spouse's life.

- *Single parent.* Because your children depend on you totally for both short- and long-term expenses, life insurance proceeds should replace your income.

- *Business owner.* If you are the sole owner of a small business or are in partnership with someone else, your life insurance proceeds should replace your income for your family and enable your partner to carry on with the business. A special arrangement called a *buy/sell agreement* can be funded with life insurance proceeds to smooth the transition for both your family and your partner.

Medium need. You will need some insurance if you die as a member of a:

- *Dual-income household, with no children.* Though your spouse may be able to survive on his or her own if you die, he or she might have to adopt a significantly lower standard of living. The insurance benefit, if invested wisely, should permit your spouse to maintain a quality life.

- *Retired couple, with self-supporting children.* Assuming that you have not set aside enough money in savings and investments, life insurance proceeds should provide enough income to maintain your spouse's lifestyle.

Low need. You will need little or no insurance if you die as a:

- *Single person with no children.* If no one depends on your income, you have little need for life insurance.

- *Nonworking spouse, with no children.* Because a homemaker produces no income that needs to be replaced, your spouse should be able to maintain his or her standard of living if you die.

- *Young child.* While the insurance on children is inexpensive, it is usually unnecessary because they do not support anyone—unless they happen to be supermodels or famous child actors.

As you can see, the common thread in determining need in all of these situations is whether survivors will have enough money to maintain their quality of life if the insured dies. Calculating how much insurance you need is where this whole process can get very complicated. For an exhaustive analysis, consult a good insurance agent, or run through some of the exercises available on software like Managing Your Money, Microsoft Money or Quicken (listed in Chapter 1's "Resources" section). Or you can contact an independent insurance adviser through the Life Insurance Advisers Association (800-521-4578). Such advisers will counsel you about your insurance needs; they sell no policies.

No matter what route you take, you will start by using the Death Expense Worksheet in Figure 11.6. Total the immediate expenses your family would incur if you were to die today.

Next, determine your family's ongoing future income and expenses if you were to die. The worksheet in Figure 11.7 provides you with space to record one year's net cash flow, but you must project this amount many years into the future if your family is young. When calculating income, include any benefits your family might be entitled to, due to your death, from government programs, such as Social Security and veterans survivor's programs, as well as from life insurance provided by your employer. To learn how much these programs pay, call the Social Security Administration, the Department of Veterans Affairs (VA) or your employee benefits office. Use the Cash Flow Worksheet in Chapter 1 as a guide in completing the Survivor's Worksheet.

After you complete the worksheet, combine your total immediate expenses with your total net cash flow to see how much of a gap exists between your expenses and your income. This gap is what your life insurance should fill. Depending on your life situation, you will probably discover that this gap is larger than you thought it would be.

Some simple rules of thumb can give you an idea of how much life insurance you need. At the least, you probably need three times your annual income; at the most, ten times. Many people require at least $100,000 of coverage, and most need several hundred thousand dollars more if they truly want to cover all of the immediate and future expenses listed above and in the Survivor's Worksheet.

Types of Life Insurance

Now that you have determined how much insurance you need, consider the pros and cons of the four basic types of coverage: *term, whole life, universal life* and *variable life.* The debates about which type is best will rage forever among insurance professionals. You must decide what is best for you based on how much coverage you need, how much premium you can afford and whether you want insurance only for its death benefit or also for its savings potential. Term insurance merely pays off if you die; whole life, universal life and variable life insurance are versions of *cash-value insurance,* which combines a death benefit and an investment fund.

Figure 11.6   Death Expense Worksheet

Expense	$ Amount
Federal Estate Taxes	$ _____
State Death Taxes	_____
Probate Costs and Attorney Fees	_____
Funeral Expenses	_____
Unreimbursed Medical Costs (for deceased's last illness)	_____
Other (specify) _____	_____
TOTAL IMMEDIATE EXPENSES	$ _____

Both term and cash value policies come in two varieties: participating and nonparticipating. With *participating (or "par") insurance*, you are entitled to receive dividends from the policy, which are considered a refund of the portion of your premium that the insurance company did not pay in death benefits or administrative expenses over the previous year. The premiums on participating policies are more than *nonpar premiums*, so the insurance company has more money to invest to pay dividends.

If you buy a participating policy, you can use your dividends in several ways. You can take them in cash, though you would have to pay income tax on your dividends in the year you receive them. Or you can reinvest the dividends in the policy to reduce future premiums and perhaps earn higher investment returns, or buy additional paid-up insurance. Most policyholders reinvest the dividends to enhance the value of their policies.

Nonparticipating policies pay no dividends for you to reinvest. Instead, your premiums are fixed when you buy a policy at a set amount. Though nonpar premiums may, at first, be less than par premiums, the ability to receive and compound dividends usually makes participating policies a better deal over the long term.

TERM INSURANCE

Term insurance offers financial protection on your life for a specified and finite period of time, usually 1, 5, 10 or 20 years. The only way your term policy will pay out is if you die during this period. In this case, your beneficiaries will

Figure 11.7   Survivor's Worksheet

Income	Annual $ Amount
Benefits Income	
Life Insurance	$ _____
Pensions	_____
Social Security	_____
Trusts	_____
Veterans	_____
Other	_____
Investment Income	
Annuities	_____
Dividends (from stocks, mutual funds)	_____
Interest (from bank accounts, bonds, mutual funds)	_____
Rent (from owned real estate)	_____
Other	_____
Survivor's Salary	_____
Other Income	_____
TOTAL ANNUAL INCOME	$ _____

Expenses	
Child Care	$ _____
Children's Education	_____
Clothing	_____
Entertainment and Recreation	_____
Food	
At Home	_____
Outside the Home	_____

Figure 11.7   (continued)

Expenses	Annual $ Amount
Housing	
Mortgage	$ _____
Rent	_____
Utilities	_____
Other	_____
Insurance Premiums	
Auto	_____
Disability	_____
Health	_____
Life	_____
Other	_____
Loan Repayments	_____
Medical and Dental	_____
Taxes	
Federal Income	_____
State Income	_____
Local Income	_____
Property	_____
Other	_____
Transportation	_____
Other Expenses	_____
TOTAL ANNUAL EXPENSES	$ _____
Total Annual Income	$ _____
Minus Total Annual Expenses	$(_____)
Equals **TOTAL NET CASH FLOW**	$ _____

probably be offered a lump-sum payout or a series of annuity payments. When the period expires, you can usually renew the policy, though at a higher premium because you are older and statistically more likely to die. If your policy offers a *guaranteed renewability feature,* you do not have to take a medical test or otherwise prove insurability to continue coverage for another term. You can also buy term insurance that provides a *convertibility feature*, which allows you to convert some or all of the coverage into whole life insurance without a medical exam. If you stop paying premiums on a term policy, your coverage ceases.

You can purchase far more protection for your dollar with term insurance than you can with a cash-value policy. Term insurance is therefore ideal if you have a large insurance need for a specific period of time. For example, you might need coverage for the years before your children become self-supporting, which should be in their mid-20s.

The chief advantage of term insurance is that it is very inexpensive. Hundreds of companies offer term; therefore, the market is extremely competitive. You can obtain price quotes on term coverage through any insurance agent, many direct mail insurers, banks or quote services such as AccuQuote, BestQuote, Choice Quote, INSurance INFOrmation, Insurance Quote, QuickQuote, QuoteSmith, Selectquote, TermQuote, and others described in the "Resources" section at the end of this chapter. Make sure that the policy you buy is not only low-priced but also backed by a financially strong insurance company. Preferably, the carrier should have at least an A rating from two or three of the major ratings agencies.

If you decide to purchase term insurance, check whether your employer offers such coverage and, if so, how much. As part of their employee benefits package, many companies provide the equivalent of one year's salary, while others pay double your annual income. You may also be able to get a good deal by buying more group term through your employer's plan, though you should compare those premium prices carefully with premiums on policies that you can obtain on your own. You may also be able to obtain a good group term policy through a trade association, an alumni group or another organization to which you belong.

The disadvantage of term insurance is that the premium rises over time. As mentioned earlier, your premium stays the same during the term of a policy but increases each time you renew. This is because your chance of dying becomes greater as you age, and the insurance company needs to collect a higher premium to offset the greater risk of having to pay a claim. Term premiums rise slowly while you are in your 20s and 30s but start to get much more expensive as you progress through your 40s and 50s. By the time you reach your 60s, term insurance is astronomically expensive and probably should be dropped.

CASH-VALUE INSURANCE

Instead of buying term insurance, which offers pure protection, you can choose to purchase one of several varieties of cash-value insurance. All of these policies, which are called *whole life, universal life* or *variable life*, add a tax-deferred savings feature to the insurance protection component of the policy.

Whole life insurance. Whole life insurance, often called *straight life* or *permanent insurance* by agents, is the opposite of term. While term starts with low premiums that rise over time upon renewal and provides you with no investment reserves, whole life locks in for life one premium rate, part of which is invested for your benefit. However, whole life premiums are much more expensive than term premiums, particularly when you are in your 20s and 30s.

Whole life remains in force as long as you live and pay your premiums. You need not renew it frequently, as you do term. The younger you are when you buy a whole life policy, the lower your lifelong premium rate. The insurance company uses your premium dollars to cover three expenses: death claims, administrative costs and investments. Most of your money ends up invested in stocks, bonds, real estate and other capital assets that can appreciate and produce income over time. The cash value that your whole life policy accumulates results from those investments that are paid in the form of policy dividends, minus death claims and administrative expenses.

In the 1960s and 1970s, whole life policies paid very low returns of about 5 percent because insurance companies were locked into long-term, low-rate bonds. But as those bonds matured and insurers replaced them with the high-coupon issues of the 1980s, returns on investments gradually rose into the 8 percent to 12 percent range. As bond rates fell again in the 1990s, yields on insurance portfolios also started to recede but at a much slower pace than returns on portfolios holding shorter term money-market instruments. All whole life policies, however, make a minimum earnings guarantee, usually of about 4 percent.

One big advantage of all forms of cash-value insurance is that your investment dollars compound tax-deferred. The insurance industry has fought off numerous attempts to repeal this tax shelter and is likely to do so for a long time. If you ever cancel or surrender your whole life policy, you can withdraw in a lump sum whatever cash value has accumulated, and you will pay taxes only if your cash value and policy dividends exceed the total amount of premiums you paid during the life of the policy.

You have several other ways to use any accumulated cash value in a whole life policy.

- You can borrow up to the full amount of your cash value. You must pay nondeductible interest that usually floats 2 or 3 percentage points above the prime rate, which is far better than the rate you would pay on a credit card. If you have an older policy, it may even offer a low fixed rate. If you die before the loan is repaid (and there is no requirement that the loan must be repaid), your loan balance plus any interest due will be deducted from the death benefit paid to your beneficiaries.

- You can tap your cash value to pay some or all of your premiums if you have built up enough value in the policy.

- Once you reach retirement age, you can convert your accumulated cash value into an annuity, which can pay you a guaranteed monthly income for life.

Insurance companies have invented numerous twists on traditional whole life plans. Mostly, they offer different ways of paying premiums. Some of the most frequently sold varieties include the following:

- *Modified life versions* start with lower premiums when you are younger, then compensate by charging higher premiums when you are older. Your cash value buildup occurs more slowly in such a policy than it does in a traditional whole life policy.

- *Limited-payment life* allows you to pay premiums for a certain number of years, usually between 7 and 20, then stop. Premiums will be higher in such a plan, but cash values will build faster as a result.

- *Single-premium life* is paid in one lump sum up front. Such a premium usually costs thousands of dollars, but you need not make another payment for the rest of your life. You must be careful to avoid adverse tax consequences with single-premium life if you want to withdraw money from the policy under some circumstances.

Universal life insurance. Born in the high-interest-rate years of the early 1980s, universal life offered policyholders very high rates of return from investments in money-market instruments. When rates dropped by the 1990s, universal life became much less popular. This form of cash-value insurance offers much more flexibility than traditional whole life policies, however. Universal life policyholders can pay premiums at any time and in any amount, as long as certain minimum levels are met. Also, the amount of insurance protection can be increased or decreased easily to meet your current needs. In addition, you always can tell exactly how much of your premium dollar is allocated to insurance protection, administrative expenses and savings. These figures are never clearly disclosed when you own a whole life policy.

Unlike whole life premiums, which are invested in long-term bonds and mortgages, universal life premiums reflect the current short-term rates available in the money markets. Insurance companies set a rate of return for one year, then readjust the yield up or down, depending on the level of interest rates. However, universal life policies guarantee a minimum yield of about 4 percent or 5 percent.

A final advantage of universal life therefore is that the returns you earn on your cash value will reflect a sharp upturn in interest rates far more quickly than the returns on a traditional whole life policy. However, if rates fall or remain depressed, you may have to settle for lower returns for many years.

Variable life insurance. If you are willing to take higher risks in search of juicier returns, variable life offers the option of investing your cash value in stock, bond or money-market funds managed by the insurance company. As with other cash-value policies, these returns compound tax deferred until you withdraw your principal. A good fund manager operating in a bull market can easily provide double-digit gains and outperform a traditional whole-life portfolio. But markets do not always rise, and this year's hero can become next year's goat. You have the option of shifting your money among stocks, bonds and cash vehicles, but the chances of selling at just the right moment are remote.

Your investment timing affects not only the appreciation or depreciation of your cash value in a variable life policy. The death benefit also rises and falls based on investment performance. However, the death benefit will never drop below the original amount of insurance coverage for which you contracted.

Because the stock, bond and money-market funds within variable insurance policies are legally considered securities, the life insurance agent who sells you a policy must be a licensed registered representative of a broker-dealer. He or she must give you a prospectus, as with any mutual fund, and explain the risks as well as the potential rewards of the plan.

When choosing a variable life policy, study the long-term track record of the funds offered. It is very difficult and expensive to switch out of one variable contract and into another under the management of a new insurance company if performance starts to lag.

Two newer versions of variable life exist: *scheduled premium variable life* and *flexible premium variable life.* The scheduled variety fixes the amount and timing of premium payments. The flexible style allows you to adapt the amount and timing of premiums to your changing needs.

Second-to-die insurance. One of the trendiest new forms of cash-value insurance, called *second-to-die* or *survivorship life* is usually acquired in the names of a husband and wife. The policy pays a death benefit, intended to cover estate taxes, upon the demise of the insured who survives longer. Survivorship life premiums can be invested in either traditional whole life vehicles or in universal or variable options. Because the policy is based on the joint life expectancy of both husband and wife, the premiums cost less than they would if you bought traditional cash value policies on both lives.

Before you obtain this kind of insurance, however, make sure that your estate taxes will be significant enough to warrant the coverage. Ask a financial planner or an estate lawyer if he or she can set up trusts to reduce your estate taxes so you won't have to pay survivorship life premiums.

Accelerated death benefit insurance. Another recent development in life insurance is the introduction of policies that allow you, in particular cases, to access your death benefit while you are still living. These are known as *accelerated death benefit* or *living benefits policies.* These policies usually will make payments while you are alive under three circumstances.

- If you need long-term care, either in a nursing home or at home

- If you are struck by a catastrophic illness or disease that runs up enormous medical bills. The policy lists specific diseases and surgeries covered, most commonly heart attacks, strokes, life-threatening cancers, coronary-artery bypass surgeries, renal failures, paralyses and major organ transplants.

- If you are diagnosed as terminally ill. If your doctor confirms in writing that you have only weeks or months to live, you can tap your death benefit.

Remember, however, that if you withdraw part or all of your death benefit while you are still living, your beneficiaries receive less when you die.

SIZING UP TERM VERSUS CASH-VALUE INSURANCE

When you understand the differences between term and the myriad forms of cash-value life insurance, you must decide which is best for you. Some people believe that you come out ahead if you buy the cheapest term policy you can find and invest the difference between the term premium and the premium that you would pay on cash value insurance in stocks, bonds and mutual funds of your choice. Indeed, if you actually follow through on this strategy and build a sizable portfolio on your own through a disciplined savings regimen, you probably would come out ahead. By the time you retire, you not only would have had the insurance coverage you needed at a low price, but you also would have avoided paying the high commission charges wrapped into a cash-value policy.

Proponents of cash-value insurance say that, as well intentioned as most people might be, they do not, in fact, exercise the discipline to invest the difference between premiums every year for the long term. The higher premiums paid into a cash-value policy are therefore a form of forced savings. In addition, the cash value accumulates tax deferred, while your personal investments are subject to yearly taxation unless they occur within an individual retirement account (IRA), a Keogh account, a salary reduction plan or another tax-deferred plan. Furthermore, the investments made on your behalf by the insurance company are chosen by a full-time staff of investment professionals. You may or may not be skilled at selecting investments that perform consistently well over time.

You do not have to opt for only term or only cash-value life insurance. Your best choice might be to put together a combined policy that gives you adequate protection from term but also builds investment reserves from cash-value insurance. If your salary rises over time and you feel you can afford it, convert some of the term into cash-value insurance.

ANNUITIES

In addition to term and cash-value life insurance, insurance companies sell *annuities.* Although annuities are issued by life insurance companies, they work quite differently than cash-value or term insurance policies. Annuities pay a regular stream of income while you live, usually after you retire, in contrast to life insurance, which pays your beneficiaries a lump sum when you die. Annuities also provide the advantage of tax-deferred compounding on the investment portion of the account.

Two basic kinds of annuities exist: immediate and deferred. *Immediate annuities* are purchased with a lump sum (and begin to generate an income stream immediately). Typically they are purchased by people in retirement to provide a guaranteed stream of income. The lump sum might come from a distribution by a pension plan, a salary reduction plan, an IRA, a Keogh plan or investments that you have built up over the years. Different insurance companies offer varying levels of monthly income, depending on how long you will receive payments.

Deferred annuities are bought by younger people who want to save tax deferred for many years, then convert to a payout schedule once they retire. You can purchase a flexible premium retirement annuity through regular monthly or annual deposits of as little as $25. You are not required to pay a premium every year, but the more you invest, the greater your annuity's value grows. You can also buy an annuity with one lump sum. This is called a *single-premium deferred annuity* (SPDA). Most companies require at least $2,500, though they prefer $10,000 or more. Annuities also have a life insurance component because your beneficiaries receive the entire accumulated value of your annuity (what you paid in plus the interest earned) if you die before receiving annuity payments.

If your life insurance policy accumulates enough cash value, you can convert that value into an annuity to boost your income stream in retirement. Take this step, however, only if your children are self-supporting and you no longer need as much life insurance.

Fixed versus variable annuities. You have two annuity options. The more conservative route is a *fixed-dollar annuity,* which the insurance company invests in bonds or mortgages. Each year, the company announces the *fixed return* for the next year, depending on the current investment portfolio. The fixed return is the rate the company will credit to your annuity. In the mid-1980s, double-digit annual returns were routinely promised, but by the 1990s, rates had dropped to the 7 percent to 9 percent range. The insurance company provides some level of guaranteed minimum return, however—usually about 4 percent. Do not be lured by a high first-year rate, which often drops dramatically in subsequent years. To protect yourself, make sure that your policy offers a *bail-out provision.* This gives you the right to liquidate all or part of your annuity without cost if your renewal rate is ever less than 1 percent of the previously offered rate. Usually, you must notify the insurance company within 30 days of receiving notice of the renewal rate that you plan to bail out. Nevertheless, do not rely on the bail-out clause if you opt for a fixed annuity. Choose a company that has paid a consistently above-average return; chances are that its record will continue.

Your other option is a *variable annuity,* which offers the potential for higher returns, though at greater risk. The variable annuity contract gives you a choice among several stock, bond and money-market portfolios. Within the stock category, you will normally be offered a selection of sector, aggressive growth, growth, growth and income, international and balanced funds. With bonds, you may shift among corporate, government, high-yield and international fixed-income portfolios. You can allocate your money among stock and bond options any way you like and transfer the funds as market conditions charge. As the stock and bond markets swing in value over the years, your annuity's value also rises and falls.

If you select a company with a proven investment performance, you can probably do far better in the long term with a variable annuity than with a fixed-dollar annuity. The key is to purchase a contract with top-notch investment managers. The easiest way to find such an annuity is to consult a recent issue of *Variable Annuity Research & Data Service Large Report* (P.O. Box 1927, Roswell, GA 30077-1927; 770-998-5186), *Comparative Annuity Reports* (P.O. Box 1268, Fair Oaks, CA 95628; 916-487-7863), or *Annuity & Life Insurance Shopper* (8 Talmadge Rd., Monroe TWP., NJ 08831; 800-872-6684; 908-521-5110). Because it is difficult and expensive to switch from one company's variable annuity to another's, it is worthwhile to research your decision carefully.

Payout options. Once you reach retirement age, annuities offer many different payout options. In general, the longer you obligate the company to pay benefits, the lower your monthly check. Whether you think that you will live a short or a long time determines your regular stipend. Each company determines its payout scale by estimating survival rates and the company's expected earnings on investments. The duration of annuity payments can be based on a life contingency, a certain period of time or on a combination of the two. The following are the usual choices that you will be offered.

Ten-year term certain annuity. If you think that you will live ten years or less after retirement, you can choose an annuity that will pay you or your heirs for only ten years. This option provides the highest monthly benefit. However, if you live more than ten years, you're out of luck (at least as far as the company's obligation goes). This is a very risky strategy—unless you are in very poor health when you retire—because the average life expectancy today is well into a person's 80s, or more than 20 years from the usual retirement age of 65.

Life annuity with 10-year term certain. This annuity will pay a fixed monthly amount for the rest of your life. However, if you die before the annuity has paid you benefits for ten years, your beneficiary (usually your spouse), will receive your payments only for the remainder of the original ten years. This form of annuity pays less than the ten-year term certain. It also is significantly risky for your spouse, who would not receive payments after ten years from the date of your retirement, assuming that you have died. If you select this option, make sure that your spouse has enough other sources of income to fall back on to cover the shortfall.

Life annuity. This plan would cut your monthly payout from the ten-year term certain significantly but would assure you of an income for life. After you die, your beneficiary receives no payments.

Joint and survivor annuity. If you are married or if someone depends on your income, you may want to select this option, which pays a fixed amount until both you and your spouse or dependent die. When you die, your spouse or dependent receives *qualified joint and survivor annuity* (QJSA) payments until he or she dies. These payments are usually less than the amount you received, but by law they cannot be less than 50 percent of your payment. Because both you and your spouse or dependent may live a long time, the joint and survivor plan offers the lowest monthly payment of those options discussed here. However, it is also the safest plan because it ensures that your spouse or dependent will receive a monthly income after you are gone.

If you are married and want to receive your benefits on the life annuity option or assign your survivor benefit to someone other than your spouse, you must obtain written spousal consent confirming that your spouse knows what he or she is relinquishing and that he or she does so willingly. (If you are asked to sign such a consent form, don't unless you fully understand the financial impact of the alternate election and are so wealthy that you can't envision ever needing the money.)

Once you start receiving payouts from annuities, you must pay income tax on a portion of those payouts. Each payment is considered part investment earnings and part return of your original principal. You must pay tax on the investment earnings but not on the return of capital. The insurance company informs you how much of each payment constitutes earnings and principal.

Unless you absolutely need access to your annuity money before retirement, don't touch it. If you take distributions from your annuity before age 59½, you not only must pay income tax on the earnings but you also owe the IRS a stiff 10 percent early withdrawal penalty. The only ways around this penalty before age 59½ are if you suffer a disability or if you die and the annuity proceeds are distributed to your beneficiaries.

Annuity fees and expenses. Pay careful attention to the many fees attached to every annuity contract. Most companies do not explicitly charge an *up-front commission,* or *load.* Instead, they levy a hefty surrender charge of as much as 10 percent of your principal if you want to transfer your annuity to another company within the first five or ten years of the contract. After that time, the surrender charges may disappear. However, many annuities offer a free withdrawal provision after the first year and for every year thereafter that surrender charges apply. This allows the contract holder to withdraw a certain percent (usually ten percent) of the accumulated account value. (Prior to age 59½, these partial withdrawals would be subject to penalty tax).

In addition, most annuity marketers charge annual maintenance fees of $25 to $50 to cover the administrative costs of maintaining an account. For variable annuity contracts, annual asset management fees of ¼ percent to 2 percent are also assessed, just as they are in regular stock and bond mutual funds. All of these fees are deducted automatically from your investment account.

Most annuity charges do not apply to immediate annuities because once you have purchased such a contract, you cannot surrender the contract. Therefore, they impose no surrender, sales, maintenance or asset management fees.

MINIMIZING SALES CHARGES AND OTHER EXPENSES

Whichever type of life insurance policy or annuity contract you choose, be particularly wary of high fees and expenses. Some insurers pay their salespeople much higher commissions than others, and you can be sure that those sales charges will come out of your pocket one way or another. Sales commissions usually are not stated explicitly in an insurance contract, but they are most often paid out of your first few years of premiums. High commissions might hit you in the form of slower cash value buildup, reduced dividends or greater expenses. One way to get around such high fees is to buy from one of the growing number of *low-load insurance carriers* that sell mostly over the phone and through the mail. A list of some of the larger low-load companies is provided in the "Resources" section at the end of this chapter.

Whenever you purchase a policy, determine the cancelation fees or surrender charges for pulling out of the contract. These fees can be quite high, such as 7 percent of your accumulated cash value, particularly if you want to withdraw in the first few years of your policy. Think long and hard about switching from your current policy to a new one, despite any strong encouragement you receive from an agent. It takes years for your cash value to accumulate significantly, and you can lose a good deal of your investment reserves to fees if you transfer to another policy.

COMPARING COSTS

When you have narrowed your search for the best policy to a few companies, you can use the *interest-adjusted net cost index* to help you make your final decision. This index, available for both term and cash value policies, factors in all financial elements of an insurance policy, such as the company's dividend record, expenses, premium costs and timing of payments. The result allows you to compare the price of policies, all things being equal.

The index is expressed as a cost per $1,000 of insurance. For example, a policy with a $5 cost index costs $5 per $1,000 of coverage per year, or $500 for a $100,000 policy. These index costs range from a low of about $1 to as much as $10. Ask your agent for this cost index on two or more comparable policies, though he or she may not volunteer the data eagerly. The lower the cost index, the more insurance your money buys. Another objective source from which to obtain this data is the latest issue of *Consumer Reports* that examined life insurance.

While you size up the insurer, the insurer also evaluates you as a potential risk. On the insurance application form, it asks your family medical history, occupation, age, sex and health habits (such as smoking or drinking), as well as other factors that affect your chances of living a long time. The insurer may even ask you to undergo a medical exam from a doctor of the company's choosing. Once it compiles your profile, the insurance company rates you a preferred, standard or substandard risk. Preferred risks have the least likelihood of dying prematurely and therefore pay the lowest rates. Standard risks are a bit more likely to die early because of health problems and therefore pay higher rates than preferred risks. Substandard risks smoke, drink, are overweight and have a history of medical problems in their families. As a result, they pay high rates for coverage.

Choosing a Life Insurance Company

Because life insurance is a long-term commitment, you want to make sure that the company you choose will be around years from now to fulfill its part of the bargain. Therefore, examine a company's financial strength ratings as published by A.M. Best, Standard & Poor's, Moody's, Duff & Phelps and Weiss Research. Also, evaluate the service you receive from the company's representatives. After you buy your policy, you probably will not have much contact with your agent, but he or she should be able to answer questions knowledgeably and readily. For example, when your family situation changes, such as when you have a child, you might wonder how your need for insurance changes. (For more tips on choosing an insurance agent, see Chapter 17, "Finding Financial Advisers Who Are Right for You.") The agent should go over the insurance contract with you carefully before you sign so you understand its key clauses.

Using Your Computer To Buy Insurance

The computer can save you a substantial amount of money in the insurance-buying process in three ways: analyzing your needs, educating yourself about insurance and finding the cheapest policy.

By using software that is part of broader-based personal finance packages like *Quicken, Microsoft Money* or *Managing Your Money,* or online calculators that are the feature of many insurance-oriented Web sites, you can make an accurate assessment of how much insurance you really need. That is the first step to saving money, because such an analysis makes sure you don't buy too much coverage and waste money in excess premiums, or too little, exposing yourself to significant financial risk. For example, in the Insurance Center on America Online, there are calculators in the Life Insurance section to help you figure how much coverage you need and whether it is better to get term, whole life, variable life or universal life in your situation. Other sites offering calculators include Quicken's Insuremarket (www.insuremarket.com), InsWeb Consumer Center (www.insweb.com), LifeNet (www.lifenet.com) and the Insurance Marketplace sponsored by National Financial Services Network (www.nfsn.com). Many of the insurance-company–

sponsored sites also include calculators, including Metropolitan Life (www.metlife. com), Prudential (www.prudential.com), Allstate's Need Analysis Worksheet (www.allstate.com) and Lincoln Benefit Life's (www.moneyforum.com).

There is also a wealth of information online to teach you everything you wanted to know about all forms of insurance. In addition to the Web sites just listed, take a look at the Insurance News Network (www.insure.com), Insurance and Risk Management Central's Advice for Consumers Page (www.irmcentral. com) and Life-Line, sponsored by the Life and Health Insurance Foundation for Education (www.life-line.org). For even more ideas, look at the Web sites listed for the trade associations in the "Resources" section of this chapter.

America Online provides a great deal of educational guidance on all kinds of insurance. Some of the basic sections in the Insurance Center include: "Insuring Your Home"; "Types of Home Policies"; "Insuring Your Car"; "Money-Saving Insurance Tips"; "Do's and Don'ts of Life Insurance"; "Insure Your Paycheck"; "Before You Buy Disability Insurance"; and "Insurance Mumbo-Jumbo." They are constantly adding new features, and you also can have your questions answered by insurance experts in ongoing chat sessions. AOL also features The Money Whiz from Bank Rate Monitor, who gives sage advice on insurance matters. The AOL Insurance Center also provides several links to major insurance company sites, such as those sponsored by Prudential, Nationwide, Colonial Penn and AARP.

Finally, the Internet can be a powerful tool for searching for the least expensive insurance policy. The art of locating the best policy is most highly refined in the term life insurance market, because term is a simple product that is relatively simple to compare based on price. There are many Insurance Quote Services with Web sites that allow you to get quotes instantly, based on your health condition and how much insurance you need. Some of the largest quote services include Accu-Quote, InsuranceQuote Services, QuickQuote, QuoteSmith, Selectquote and Term-Quote. These are all described in more detail, including Web site addresses and phone numbers, in the "Resources" section of this chapter under the Insurance Quote Services heading. Other Web sites specialize in specific product lines, such as annuities. Two examples in this genre are Annuities Online (www.annuity.com) and WebSaver Annuity (www.Websaver.com). One of the best overall places to shop for insurance is Quicken's Insuremarket (www.insuremarket), which provides price quotes and referrals to local insurance agents.

The emergence of computers and Web sites is revolutionizing the process of buying insurance. No longer do you need to be the captive of whatever your local insurance agent tells you. By exploring some of the Web sites listed here, you can probably find a much better deal, saving yourself hundreds or thousands of dollars while increasing your coverage.

No one ever said buying insurance was going to be much fun. Picking your way through the complexities of auto, disability, health, homeowner's and life insurance is a chore you probably want to postpone indefinitely. But don't. Once you go through the process of obtaining the proper kind and amount of coverage, you will have earned a benefit that is hard to put a price on: peace of mind.

Resources

BOOKS AND BROCHURES

Aetna Life & Casualty Insurance Company (151 Farmington Ave., Hartford, CT 06156; 203-273-2843). A large insurance company that offers the following helpful free brochures: "Auto Insurance: Issues & Answers"; "Fifteen Money Blunders . . . How To Avoid Them"; "An Insurance Blueprint for Homeowners"; "Making Auto Insurance More Affordable"; and "Who's Ripping Off Who? (About Insurance Fraud)."

Building Your Future with Annuities: A Consumer's Guide (Consumer Information Center, Pueblo, CO 81009; 719-948-3334; www.pueblo.gsa.gov). A free brochure by Fidelity Investments that explains various types of annuities and how they should be used. Can also be obtained directly from Fidelity (800-544-2442).

Family Insurance Handbook: The Complete Guide for the 1990's, by Les Abro-mowitz (McGraw-Hill, Order Dept., 860 Taylor Station Rd., Blacklick, OH 43004; 800-722-4726; www.mcgraw-hill.com). A complete guide to life, health, auto and other insurance coverage.

Individual Investor's Guide to Low-Load Life Insurance, by Glenn Daily (McGraw-Hill, Order Dept., 860 Taylor Station Rd., Blacklick, OH 43004; 800-722-4726; www.mcgraw-hill.com). Discusses how to buy life insurance at the lowest possible cost.

Life Insurance: A Consumer's Handbook, by Joseph M. Belth (Indiana University Press, 601 N. Morton St., Bloomington, IN 47404; 812-855-4203; 800-842-6796). Written by a long-time consumer advocate on insurance matters. Helps you find the best policy for your needs and answers the following key questions: How much life insurance do you need? What type of life insurance is appropriate for you? From what company should you buy your policy? Also explains how to select a life insurance agent and when to consider replacing an existing policy.

Managed Care Made Easy: Survival in the HMO Era, by Vikram Khanna (People's Medical Society, 462 Walnut St., Allentown, PA 18102; 610-770-1670). Comprehensive guide to getting the most out of managed health care. The book explains what managed care is, how to select a managed care provider, how managed care treats special needs like mental health, vision and dental care and prescription drugs, and how to complain effectively if you have been mistreated by a managed care institution.

Medicare/Medigap: The Essential Guide for Older Americans and Their Families, by Carl Oshiro and Harry Snyder (Consumer Reports Books, 111 10th St., Des

Moines, IA 50309; 515-237-4903; 800-500-9760). Clears away all confusion about the Medicare system and explains how to receive maximum benefits from Medicare and Medigap policies.

Winning the Insurance Game: The Complete Consumer's Guide to Saving Money, by Ralph Nader and Wesley J. Smith (Doubleday/Main Street Books, 1540 Broadway, New York, NY 10036; 800-223-6834; www.bdd.com). Discusses how to get the best coverage and fair prices for auto, health, homeowner's and life insurance. Also explains government insurance programs, including Social Security and Medicare, as well as specialized insurance coverage, such as senior citizens insurance, workers' compensation and prepaid legal insurance.

Your Life Insurance Options, by Alan Lavine (John Wiley & Sons, 605 3rd Ave., New York, NY 10158-0012; 212-850-6000; 800-225-5945). Explains how to choose the best life insurance policies to meet your needs.

NEWSLETTERS

Annuity & Life Insurance Shopper (8 Talmadge Rd., Monroe TWP., NJ 08831; 800-872-6684; 908-521-5110). Provides updated performance on immediate, deferred, fixed and variable annuities. Covers other product offerings of insurance companies as well as their financial strength ratings.

Comparative Annuity Reports (P.O. Box 1268, Fair Oaks, CA 95628; 916-487-7863). Tracks the rates paid by insurance companies on their fixed annuities in its monthly *CAR* newsletter, as well as different payout options offered by insurance companies. Conducts studies on both single-premium deferred annuities (SPDAs) and flexible-premium deferred annuities (FPDAs).

Insurance Forum (P.O. Box 245, Ellettsville, IN 47429; 812-876-6502). Devoted to insurance issues and directed mostly at insurance professionals. Discusses what is being done and what should be done to protect policyholders. Also alerts readers to changes in insurance company ratings. Once a year, publishes a special issue that lists the ratings of all life and health insurance companies ranked by at least one of the four major ratings agencies. Also includes explanatory material on what ratings mean and how to use them.

Variable Annuity Research & Data Service Report (P.O. Box 1927, Roswell, GA 30077-1927; 770-998-5186). Tracks the investment performance of hundreds of variable annuities sold by insurance companies. Will send, for a fee, a monthly performance report on variable annuities. Also provides a short Standard Contract Data Profile on every outstanding annuity policy, which outlines all expenses, minimum investment amounts and past performance data. Also compiles *National Contract Expense Reports* that list the total expenses charged on every annuity. Subscribers to VARDS reports also receive the Executive Series of articles pertaining to the variable annuity business.

TRADE ASSOCIATIONS

American Association of Health Plans (1129 Twentieth St. NW, Suite 600, Washington, DC 20036; 202-778-3200; www.aahp.org). A trade group for managed health care plans including HMOs, PPOs, and point-of-service plans that upholds strict standards of financial soundness and medical excellence among its members. Can supply a list of members in your state to help you locate a managed care plan. Offers a free publication called "A Common-Sense Guide to Choosing a Health Plan."

American Council of Life Insurance (1001 Pennsylvania Ave., N.W., 5th Floor South, Washington, DC 20004-2599; 202-624-2000; www.acli.com). A trade group of life insurance companies that lobbies on life insurance matters and provides information about insurance to the public. Upon written request, will send the following free publications: *Accelerated Death Benefit Update; A Consumer's Guide to Annuities; A Consumer's Guide to Life Insurance;* and *Life Insurance Fact Book.*

American Insurance Association (1130 Connecticut Ave. NW, Suite 1000, Washington, DC 20036; 202-828-7100; www.aiadc.com). Property and casualty trade group that provides a forum for the discussion of problems. Promotes safety programs and lobbies on behalf of the insurance industry.

American Society of CLU & ChFC (270 S. Bryn Mawr Ave., Bryn Mawr, PA 19010-2194; 610-526-2500). Chartered life underwriters specialize in life and health insurance, education funding and estate planning; chartered financial consultants provide overall financial planning. Will send the following free publications: *Consumer's Guide to Insurance and Financial Services; The Initial Advantage: Chartered Life Underwriter and Chartered Financial Consultant;* and *30 Years of Retirement.* Also publishes three newsletters titled *Assets: A Business, Tax and Financial Newsletter; The Financial Monitor;* and *Query: Questions and Answers about Your Financial Security.*

Association of Health Insurance Agents (1922 F St., N.W., Washington, DC 20006; 202-331-2160; www.agents-online.com). Lobbies for health insurance matters and educates the public about health insurance issues.

Consumer Federation of America Insurance Group (1424 16th St., NW, Suite 604, Washington, DC 20036; 202-387-6121). A consumer-oriented group frequently critical of the insurance industry. For a $40 fee, they will help you evaluate life insurance policy proposals and analyze the projected rates of return on your insurance policies. They also offer several helpful publications about shopping for insurance, including "An Analysis of Cash Value Life Insurance Policies"; "Most Credit Life Insurance Still a Rip-Off"; "Medical Malpractice Insurance"; and "Consumers Waste More Than $6 Billion Annually on Life Insurance Premiums."

Health Insurance Association of America (555 13th St., N.W., Suite 600 East, Washington, DC 20004; 202-824-1600; www.hiaa.org). The lobbying group for health insurance companies. Also educates the public about health insurance.

Independent Insurance Agents of America (127 S. Peyton St., Alexandria, VA 23314; 703-683-4422; 800-221-7917; www.iiaa.org). Association of independent insurance agents who are not tied to selling any particular insurance company's products. The IIAA offers several free Consumer Education Guides on various insurance topics that are available by calling 800-261-4422. They include "The Consumer's Independent Guide to Auto Insurance"; "The Consumer's Independent Guide to Homeowners Insurance"; "The Consumer's Independent Guide to Small-Business Insurance"; "The Graduate's Independent Guide to Insurance"; "The Women's Independent Guide to Insurance"; "Non-Profits' Essential Handbook on Insurance"; and "Don't Get Soaked by a Flood." The Association also offers these free brochures, which are available by calling 800-447-6788: "After an Accident"; "Filing Your Auto Insurance Claim"; "Filing Your Home Insurance Claim"; "Insuring Your Sports and Recreational Vehicles"; "Protecting Your In-Home Business"; "Protecting Your Small Business"; "Renter's Insurance"; and "Taking Inventory of Your Home."

Insurance Education Foundation (3601 Vincennes Rd., Indianapolis, IN 46268; 317-876-6046; www.ins-ed-fdn.org). Organization dedicated to educating high school teachers and students about how the insurance industry works. Among their offerings is a multimedia program called "Choice, Chance and Control" that helps explain insurance to teenagers. The foundation also sponsors Insurance Education Institutes for teachers.

Insurance Information Institute (110 William St., 24th Floor, New York, NY 10038; 212-669-9200; 800-942-4242—National Insurance Consumer Hotline; www.iii.org). The association of property and casualty insurance companies. Offers the following helpful free publications: "Am I Covered?"; "Here Today . . . Gone Tomorrow"; "Home Security Basics"; "How To File An Insurance Claim"; "Hurricane Awareness"; "Insurance for Your Home and Personal Possessions"; "Insuring Your Home Business"; "Insuring Your Business Against a Catastrophe"; "Nine Ways To Lower Your Auto Insurance Costs"; "OOPS!!"; "Settling Insurance Claims After a Disaster"; "Taking Inventory"; "Tornado Safety: Before, During and After"; "Twelve Ways To Lower Your Homeowners Insurance Costs."

Insurance Institute for Highway Safety (1005 N. Glebe Rd., Suite 800, Arlington, VA 22201; 703-247-1500; www.highwaysafety.org). Research and education organization dedicated to reducing loss, death, injury and property damage on the highways. Ranks safety of different car models. Offers several free publications, including "Shopping for a Safer Car," which includes a listing of the ratings of all the vehicles IIHS has crash-tested. Other publications include "About Your Airbags"; "Beginning Drivers, Helping Them Make It Home"; "Crashworthiness Evaluations"; "Driver Death Rates by Make and Series"; "Fatality Facts"; "Get an Airbag On/Off Switch? Probably Not"; and "Kids and Airbags." For a copy of these publications, write to IIHS at P.O. Box 1420, 1005 N. Glebe Rd., Arlington, VA 22210.

Life Insurance Advisers Association (800-521-4578). A group of independent life insurance consultants who provide advice for a fee and do not sell insurance policies. This set up not only can save you a great deal of money; it also guarantees that your adviser has no financial interest in the insurance that he or she proposes. Such independent advisers can help you find the best deal in life insurance by recommending no-load or low-commission policies at wholesale prices.

Medical Information Bureau (MIB) (160 University Ave., Westwood, MA 02090; 617-426-3660). Organization of life insurance companies operating a confidential exchange of underwriting information about consumers' medical records. This allows insurers to verify the health claims of consumers applying for life, health and disability insurance. At the above phone number, you can inquire whether an MIB record on you exists and what your MIB reference number is.

National Association of Health Underwriters (1000 Connecticut Ave., NW, Suite 810, Washington, DC 20036; 202-223-5533; www.nahu.org). Represents professionals who sell disability income, hospitalization and major medical health insurance policies. NAHU offers a free brochure called "Are You Using a Health Insurance Benefit Advisor? Are You Getting the Service You Are Paying For? Would You Even Know It?"

National Association of Life Underwriters (1922 F St., N.W., Washington, DC 20006-4387; 202-331-6000; www.nalu.org). The association of health and life insurance agents involved in lobbying for insurance matters and educating the public about life and health insurance. Will send a free copy of brochures titled "Annuities: Building Your Retirement Nest Egg"; "Disability Income Protection: Don't Leave Home Without It!"; "Life Insurance: Choosing Your Best Buy"; "Long-Term Care Insurance: Is It in Your Future?"; "Points To Ponder if You're Considering Replacing Your Life Insurance"; "Shaping Your Financial Fitness"; "Supplementing Your Medicare Coverage"; and "Term & Permanent Life: What's the Difference?"

National Committee for Quality Assurance (2000 L St., NW, Suite 500, Washington, DC 20036; 202-955-3500; 800-839-6787; www.ncqa.org). NCQA is a private, not-for-profit organization dedicated to assessing and reporting on the quality of managed care plans. NCQA's mission is to provide information enabling purchasers and consumers of managed care to distinguish among plans based on quality. NCQA accredits managed care organizations by surveying them and making sure they meet certain standards in both clinical and administrative functions. To find out whether a managed care program you are thinking of using is accredited by NCQA or not, call their Accreditation Status Line at 800-275-7585, or download their Accreditation Status List from their Web site. NCQA also provides two-page Accreditation Summary Reports, giving you more detail on the performance of a particular plan. NCQA also measures the performance of managed care, looking at the results achieved by the plans. The performance is kept in a national database called Quality Compass, making it easy for you to compare your local plan against national averages in 71 performance measures. NCQA also publishes a free brochure titled "Choosing Quality: Finding the Health Plan That Is Right for You."

National Insurance Consumer Helpline (800-942-4242; www.iii.org). A consumer information service sponsored by insurance industry associations. Answers your questions about auto, health, homeowner's and life insurance, refers any complaints to the appropriate sources and sends informational brochures.

United Seniors Health Cooperative (1331 H St., N.W., Suite 500, Washington, DC 20005; 202-393-6222; www.ushc-online.org). Dedicated to helping seniors obtain good health care coverage and insurance. Advises seniors on selecting both private Medigap insurance and federal Medicare coverage that best meet their needs. Offers two books for a nominal charge titled *Long-Term Care: A Dollars and Sense Guide* and *Managing Your Health Care Finances.* Also issues occasional pamphlets, such as "Insurance To Pay for Long-Term Care" and "Medicare and Medigap Update."

Workers Compensation Research Institute (101 Main St., Cambridge, MA 02142; 617-494-1240). Organization founded to research workers compensation issues on behalf of insurers and employers.

GOVERNMENT REGULATORS

Federal Insurance Administration (500 C St., SW, Washington, DC 20472; 202-646-4600; www.fema.gov). Administers the federal flood insurance and crime insurance programs.

Health Care Financing Administration (7500 Security Blvd., Baltimore, MD 21244-1850; 410-786-3000; www.hcfa.gov). The federal agency that oversees the Medicare and Medicaid health insurance system. Offers free publications titled *Consumer's Guide to Long-Term Care Insurance; Guide to Health Insurance for People with Medicare;* and *Medicare and Prepayment Plans.*

National Association of Insurance Commissioners (120 W. 12th St., Suite 1100, Kansas City, MO 64105; 816-842-3600; www.naic.org; Washington office: 444 N. Capitol St. NW, Suite 701, Washington, DC 20001-1512; 202-624-7790). A nonprofit association of the chief state insurance regulatory officials in the United States. Coordinates the regulation of insurance—particularly interstate issues, such as solvency regulation. Proposes model laws, regulations and guidelines designed to protect consumers against insurance company insolvency. Offers a free copy of these publications from the Kansas City office: "Guide to Health Insurance for People with Medicare"; "Guide to Auto Insurance"; "Long Term Care Shoppers Guide"; "Guide to Home Insurance"; "Guide to Cancer Insurance"; "Life Insurance Buyers Guide."

INSURANCE QUOTE SERVICES

The following services quote insurance rates and help evaluate insurance policies based on your age and health condition.

AccuQuote (237 Melvin Dr., Northbrook, IL 60062; 800-442-9899). An Internet-based insurance quote service for term policies. Their Web site has a helpful explanation of how to figure how much insurance you need, how to qualify for coverage, what criteria are used to rate the financial strength of insurance companies and much more. The site includes a Life Insurance Needs Calculator. You can apply for coverage online by sending an e-mail to the company.

Best Quote (23600 Mercantile Rd., Beachwood, OH 44122; 800-896-8006; 216-292-7900). Offers free quotes on various term insurance policies and is able to sell you the policies that fit your needs.

Choice Quote (887 Oak Grove Ave., Menlo Park, CA 94025; 800-778-2001; 650-327-4571). Quote service that spends time assessing your needs over the phone and recommends the lowest-cost term life policy you can qualify for that will suit your needs. Choice Quote also sells Survivorship Life, also known as second-to-die insurance.

Consumer Reports Auto Insurance Price Service (800-807-8050). To get the best deal on auto insurance, try this unique service from Consumer Reports. You supply the make and model of your car, how many drivers are in your household, each person's driving record, the annual mileage you drive and how much insurance you want. Consumer Reports will then compare as many as 70 policies based on the information you have provided to come up with a list of the lowest-priced policies for the drivers in your household. Also included for the $12 fee is a guide on how to buy auto insurance and the Consumer Reports Insurance Company Ratings Scores for most companies.

INSurance INFOrmation (Cobblestone Court #2, 23 Route 134, South Dennis, MA 02660; 800-472-5800). Offers to find the lowest cost term insurance policy. Will either suggest a new policy if you do not have one or evaluate a policy you already own to determine whether the service can recommend one less expensive. Provides only advice; does not sell insurance.

Insurance Quote Services (Building C, 3200 N. Dobson Rd., Chandler, AZ 85224; 602-345-7241; 800-972-1104; www.iquote.com). A database with term insurance prices. Asks your age, how much insurance you want and your health condition. Then sends an IQ Analysis listing the five lowest cost term insurance policies in the country, based on your situation. Will sell any of these policies. Will also send a free brochure titled "Simple Guide to Insurance Savings."

QuickQuote (987 Tahoe Blvd., Incline Village, NV 89451; 800-867-2404; 702-831-2404; www.quickquote.com). Founded as an Internet-based real-time insurance and annuity quoting service. When connected to the QuickQuote Web site, you fill out a brief questionaire to help determine what insurance you qualify for based on your health condition and personal profile. You then get an immediate quote on the least expensive and best term or annuity policy for your needs. Then, if you want to buy a policy, you fill out a short form application, which is submitted electronically to

QuickQuote. Their Web site also has basic information on how annuities work, how to exchange one annuity for another without tax penalty and how IRA rollovers work, among other topics. QuickQuote also markets a full line of life insurance products, including universal life, second-to-die and whole life policies over the Internet, although you receive your price quote by e-mail within 24 hours instead of instantly on these products.

Quotesmith (8205 S. Cass St., Suite 102, Darien, IL 60561; 800-556-9393; www. quotesmith.com). Quotes prices for term insurance policies from over 140 companies. Also provides safety ratings from A.M. Best, Duff & Phelps, Moody's, Standard & Poor's and Weiss Research on all its quotes. Also quotes prices on annuities, medicare supplement policies, second-to-die policies and health insurance policies.

SelectQuote (595 Market St., 6th Floor, San Francisco, CA 94105; 800-343-1985; www.selectquote.com). Tracks term insurance prices across the country. Quotes the lowest rate for your situation and can sell you the policy.

TermQuote (6706 Loop Rd., Centerville, OH 45459; 937-434-8989; 800-444-8376). Searches its database of about 70 companies to find the lowest cost term insurance policy for your age and health condition. Employs a Certified Financial Planner and Chartered Life Underwriter to help you determine how much insurance you need. Will also sell a policy for which it has quoted rates.

INSURANCE RATINGS SERVICES

The following services rate insurance companies based on financial strength and investment performance.

A.M. Best & Co. (A.M. Best Rd., Oldwick, NJ 08858; 908-439-2200; 900-555-BEST; www.ambest.com). Provides ratings on life and property/casualty insurance companies. A top rating of A++ means that the company has a very strong ability to meet its policyholder obligations over a long period of time. A bottom rating of F means that the company is being liquidated. To learn Best's ratings on individual companies, call 900-420-0400; you will be charged a small fee. For more in-depth information on insurance companies, Best's offers the following publications: *Best's Aggregates & Averages; Best's Experience by State; Best's Flitcraft Compend; Best's Insurance Reports; Best's Intelligencer; Best's Key Rating Guide; Best's Quantitative Analysis Report; Best's Retirement Income Guide; Best's Review;* and *Best's Underwriting Newsletter.*

Duff & Phelps, Inc. (55 E. Monroe St., 35th Floor, Chicago, IL 60603; 312-368-3157; www.dcrco.com). Offers the Insurance Claims Paying Ability Service for life, health, annuity and property/casualty insurers. Rates companies on a scale from AAA for the highest claims-paying ability to DD, which indicates that the company is being liquidated.

Moody's Investors Services (99 Church St., New York, NY 10007; 212-553-0300; www.moodys.com). The Moody's Insurance Financial Strength Ratings, from Aaa to

Ca, are available for all North American corporate bond, life, private mortgage bond and property/casualty insurance companies, as well as all major reinsurance companies. Not only provides current ratings but also informs you whether a company is on its Watchlist for possible upgrading or downgrading.

Standard & Poor's Insurance Ratings Services (25 Broadway, New York, NY 10004; 212-208-1527; www.standardandpoor.com). Provides extensive ratings of life, health and property/casualty insurance companies. Ratings range from AAA to CCC, which means that the company is extremely vulnerable financially. R rating indicates the company is under the supervision of insurance regulators and may be in receivership or liquidation. Also offers the CLASSIC Database Service, which provides on a computer diskette a massive amount of data on most insurance companies. For S&P's ratings on a particular insurance company, call 212-208-1527 at no charge for the rating. Publications include *S&P's Insurance Book; S&P's Insurance Digest; S&P's Insurer Ratings List; S&P's Insurer Solvency Review; S&P's Selective Ratings Package,* and *S&P's Select Reports.*

Weiss Research (4176 Burns Rd., Palm Beach Gardens, FL 33410; 800-289-9222; www.weissratings.com). Issues conservative ratings of insurance company financial stability. For a small charge, you can get a Weiss Verbal Rating over the telephone (a grading system from A [excellent] to F [failed or in the process of failing]). For a higher charge, the firm will send a more detailed *Personal Safety Report* on any life insurance, health insurance or annuity company. These reports are explained in great detail in the *Weiss Approach to Insurance Company Safety Ratings* booklet. Weiss also rates Blue Cross and Blue Shield insurance programs and offers a booklet titled *Rating the Blues: The Weiss Approach to Hospital, Medical and Dental Indemnity Plans.*

Low and No-Load Insurance Companies

These companies offer various kinds of life insurance, annuities and auto insurance direct to the consumer. Since there is no salesperson involved in the sale, you pay little or no sales commission to buy the policy. This allows the savings to be passed on to you in the form of lower premiums and higher cash value buildup than you would receive from a standard load policy. Most of the policies sold by these companies also impose no surrender charge, which is the fee traditional insurance companies assess if you try to get out of your policy within the first few years after having purchased it. Low and no-load companies provide service on your policy 24 hours a day over a toll-free phone line.

American Life of New York (320 Park Ave., New York, NY 10022; 212-224-1600; 800-392-4082). For term, variable universal insurance policies; fixed and variable annuities.

Ameritas Life Insurance Corp. (5900 O St., Lincoln, NE 68510; 800-255-9678; www.ameritas.com). For survivorship (second-to-die) life, term insurance, universal life, variable annuities and variable universal life policies.

Charles Schwab (101 Montgomery St., San Francisco, CA 94104; 800-542-5433; www.schwab.com). For term from Zurich America Insurance and survivorship life, universal and variable annuities from Great West Life and Annuity Company.

Fidelity Investments Life Insurance Co. (P.O. Box 1306, Boston, MA 02104-9907; 800-544-2442; www.fidelity.com). For term insurance and variable annuities.

GEICO (1 Geico Plaza, Washington, DC 20046; 800-841-1587; 800-841-3000; www.geico.com). For auto insurance only.

Jack White (9191 Towne Centre Dr., 2nd Floor, San Diego, CA 92122; 800-622-3699). For variable annuities.

Lincoln Benefit (134 S. 13th St., Lincoln, NE 68508; 800-525-9287; www.money forum.com)

USAA Life (9800 Fredericksburg Rd., San Antonio, TX 78288; 800-531-8000; www.usaa.com). For auto insurance, fixed annuities, term insurance, universal insurance, variable universal life, variable annuities and whole life policies.

Veritas (a division of Ameritas Life) (1800 W. Loop South, Suite 1000, Houston, TX 77027; 713-621-1104; 800-552-3553; www.ameritas.com/veritas). For survivorship life (second-to-die) insurance, term insurance, universal insurance, variable annuities and variable universal insurance.

STATE INSURANCE DEPARTMENTS

Alabama: P.O. Box 303351, 135 S. Union St., Room 200, Montgomery 36130-3551; 334-269-3550

Alaska: 3601 C. St., Suite 1324, Anchorage 99503-5948; 907-465-2515

Arizona: 2910 N. 44th St., Suite 210, Phoenix 85018-7256; 602-912-8400

Arkansas: University Tower Building, 1123 S. University Ave., Suite 400, Little Rock 72204-1699; 501-686-2900

California: 300 Capitol Mall, Suite 1500, Sacramento 95814; 916-445-5544

Colorado: 1560 Broadway, Suite 850, Denver 80202; 303-894-7499

Connecticut: P.O. Box 816, Hartford 06142-0816; 203-297-3800

Delaware: The Rodney Building, 841 Silver Lake Blvd., Dover 19904; 302-739-4251

District of Columbia: 441 Fourth St. NW, 8th Floor N., Washington, DC 20001; 202-727-8000

Florida: Plaza Level 11, State Capitol, Tallahassee 32399-0300; 904-922-3101

Georgia: 2 Martin Luther King Dr., 7th Floor West Tower, Atlanta 30334; 404-656-2056

Hawaii: 230 S. King St., 5th Floor, Honolulu 96813; 808-586-2790

Idaho: 700 W. State St., Boise 83720; 208-334-4250

Illinois: 320 W. Washington St., Springfield 62767; 217-782-4515

Indiana: 311 W. Washington St., Suite 300, Indianapolis 46204; 317-232-2385; 800-622-4461

Iowa: Lucas State Office Building, Des Moines 50319; 515-281-5705

Kansas: 420 S.W. 9th St., Topeka 66612-1678; 913-296-7801; 800-432-2484

Kentucky: 215 W. Main St., Frankfort 40602; 502-564-6027

Louisiana: P.O. Box 94214, Baton Rouge 70801-9214; 504-342-5423

Maine: State House Station 34, Augusta 04333; 207-624-8475

Maryland: Maryland Insurance Administration, 501 St. Paul Pl., Baltimore 21202; 410-333-2521; 800-492-6116

Massachusetts: 280 Friend St., Boston 02114; 617-727-7189

Michigan: 611 W. Ottawa St., 2nd Floor N., Lansing 48933; 517-373-9273

Minnesota: 133 E. 7th St., St. Paul 55101; 612-296-6848; 800-657-3602

Mississippi: 1804 Walter Sillers Building, Jackson 39201; 601-359-3569; 800-562-2957

Missouri: 301 W. High St., Truman Building, 6th Floor, Room 630, Jefferson City 65101; 573-751-4126

Montana: P.O. Box 4009, 126 N. Sanders St., Helena 59604-4009; 406-444-2040

Nebraska: 941 O St., Suite 400, Lincoln 68508; 402-471-2201

Nevada: 1665 Hot Springs Rd., Suite 152, Carson City 89710; 702-687-4270; 800-992-0900 ext. 4270

New Hampshire: 169 Manchester St., Concord 03301-5151; 603-271-2261; 800-852-3416

New Jersey: 20 W. State St., CN 325, Trenton 08625; 609-292-5360

New Mexico: State Corporation Commission, Department of Insurance, P.O. Drawer 1269, Santa Fe 87504-1269; 505-827-4500

New York: Agency Building 1, Empire State Plaza, 8th Floor, Albany 12257; 800-342-3736; 25 Beaver St., New York, NY 10004; 212-480-6400

North Carolina: Dobbs Building, Suite 4140, 430 N. Salisbury St., Raleigh 27603; 919-733-7349; 800-662-7777

North Dakota: State Capitol Building, 600 E. Boulevard Ave., Bismarck 58505; 701-328-2440

Ohio: 2100 Stella Court, Columbus 43215-1067; 614-644-2658; 800-686-1526

Oklahoma: 1901 N. Walnut St., Oklahoma City 73105; 405-521-2686

Oregon: 350 Winter St. Northeast, Salem 97310; 503-378-4271

Pennsylvania: 1326 Strawberry Square, Harrisburg 17120; 717-787-5173

Puerto Rico: Fernandex Juncos Station, 1607 Ponce de Leon Ave., Santurce 00910; 809-722-8686

Rhode Island: 233 Richmond St., Suite 233, Providence 02903-4233; 401-277-2223

South Carolina: 1612 Marion St., Columbia 29202; 803-737-6160; 800-768-3467

South Dakota: 500 E. Capitol Ave., Pierre 57501-5070; 605-773-3563

Tennessee: 500 James Robertson Pkwy., Nashville 37243; 615-741-2241; 800-342-4029

Texas: 333 Guadalupe St., Austin 78701; 512-463-6169

Utah: State Office Building, Room 3110, Salt Lake City 84114; 801-538-3800

Vermont: 89 Main St., Drawer 20, Montpelier 05620-3101; 802-828-3301

Virginia: 1300 E. Main St., Richmond 23219; 804-371-9741

Virgin Islands: Kongens Gade #18, St. Thomas 00802; 809-774-2991

Washington: Insurance Building, 14th Ave. & Water St., Olympia 98504; 360-753-7301; 800-562-6900

West Virginia: 1124 Smith St., Charleston 25301; 304-558-3386; 800-642-9004

Wisconsin: Office of the Insurance Commissioner, 121 E. Wilson St., Madison 53702; 608-266-0102; 800-236-8517

Wyoming: Wyoming Insurance Department, Herschler Building, 122 W. 25th St., 3rd Floor East, Cheyenne 82002-0440; 307-777-7401

How To Finance a College Education

For your children to have a bright economic future, they will need a college education. As the world continues to grow more competitive and technologically sophisticated, most of the high-paying jobs will require skills learned in college and graduate school. Numerous studies have shown that the gap between earnings of college and high school graduates widens every year. Years ago, most employers expected workers to have at least a high school diploma; today, a college degree is considered a minimum requirement for most well-paying jobs.

While it has never been more worthwhile to attend college, neither has the cost of college been greater. Four years of tuition, room and board at a public university in your home state can easily run between $20,000 and $50,000, and the cost of four years at an Ivy League school ranges from $100,000 to $150,000. With college costs expected to increase between 4 and 7 percent a year, today's prices could look like bargains 20 years from now. For example, unless the pace of college cost inflation dramatically (and unexpectedly) slows, parents of a baby born in 1998 should expect to pay a whopping $100,000 to $150,000 for their child's public education and a mind-boggling $300,000 to $400,000 for four years at a top-ranked private university.

Before you become discouraged and convinced that you could never amass such a sum, realize that you can take many steps today to make college education a reality for your children tomorrow. Despite the obstacles, millions of people finance their children's college education, and you can be one of them. It will take long-term saving and investing in the years before college, combined with borrowing from several sources once your children enroll. If you develop a realistic plan and commit seriously to it, you can meet most or all of the massive expenses. If you ignore or put off the problem, the challenge of college funding becomes only more daunting, and you may end up unable to send your children to school.

Estimating College Costs

Rather than dwelling on the hundreds of thousands of dollars that college *could* cost, you might put your mind at ease a bit by calculating how much you might actually pay for your child's education. Although it is hard to know what school your toddler might aspire to more than a decade from now, ask yourself the following questions.

- Is he or she more likely to attend a public university in the state where you live or an out-of-state public institution?

- Is there a chance he or she might want to enroll at a top-ranked private college, such as an Ivy League university or its equivalent?

- How much chance is there that your child will want to go to graduate school?

- Might a junior or community college be the most realistic choice?

The more prestigious the school on which your child sets his or her sights, the more it will cost, and the more you will have to save or borrow to meet tuition. Many schools charge far less tuition than Ivy League universities. These schools also provide high-quality education, though they may not have as prestigious a reputation. Sending your child to one of these institutions may ease some of the financial pressure.

Though you cannot answer with much certainty the hypothetical questions posed above, you force yourself to confront the reality of how much to save. Most parents save far less than they ultimately need for college costs, so if you can motivate yourself to invest more, you will be that much further ahead of most Americans in your situation. After all, what's the worst that could happen if you save too much? In the unlikely event that you accumulate more than enough money for college tuition, room, board and other expenses such as books and transportation, you will have plenty of other uses for the assets—like your retirement, for instance. However, if you save too little, you and your child will be forced to assume debt that will take years to repay and cost thousands of dollars in non-deductible interest.

For a rough idea of how much college might cost and how much you must save, either ask a financial planner to calculate the amounts, or use the software on the market or the many calculators on college financing Web sites listed in the "Resources" section of this chapter to do so yourself. In most of these calculators, you enter the number of years until your child starts college, your assumed inflation rate, your estimated return on investments and other factors to arrive at likely college costs. As you change your assumptions, note how the cost of college and the amount you must save change. A similar exercise is also available in *Managing Your Money, Quicken* and *Microsoft Money* and other software packages described in the "Resources" section of Chapter 1.

The worksheet in Figure 12.1 will help you estimate college costs and your savings needs. It assumes that your child will enter college at age 18, that you will continue to save throughout your child's college years, that education costs will escalate 7 percent a year. We are also assuming that you earn 7 percent per year after taxes on your investments. To complete the worksheet, you must know the current annual cost of a school your child might attend. You can locate this figure in the book *Meeting College Costs: What You Need to Know Before Your Child and Your Money Leave Home* (for more information, consult the "Resources" section at the end of this chapter under College Board, "Trade Associations").

Sample figures in the worksheet are based on a current college cost of $10,000 per year and a 6-year-old child.

As you will see by trying various combinations of factors on the worksheet, the earlier you start to save, the less you must put aside each month or each year. And, of course, the longer you wait, the more you must save every month. As a rule of thumb, set aside between $2,000 and $4,000 a year if you begin when your child is a newborn. If you start saving when he or she is in second or third grade, reserve between $4,000 and $8,000 a year.

To give you an idea of how much money you will accumulate if you save $100 a month, use Figure 12.2. Find the number of years until your child enrolls in college in the left column. Across the top, you can see how your money will compound at different after-tax rates of return. If you save more than $100 a month, multiply these numbers by the appropriate multiple of $100. For example, if you save $400 a month, multiply these numbers by four.

Investing To Pay College Bills

The higher the return you earn on your savings and investments, the less money you must set aside for your children's college tuition. Unfortunately, because no guarantees of high returns exist in the investment world without commensurate high risks, you should put together a balanced portfolio of high-, medium- and low-risk investments to fund your children's college. In general, the longer you have until you need the money, the more risk you can take in search of high returns. As the tuition bills draw closer and closer, you should take less and less risk so that, ideally, all the money you need is sitting in your money-market account on the day you write your first huge check to the institution of your child's choice.

Before examining the appropriateness of specific investments for funding college, let's look at whose name the investments should bear. Before the Tax Reform Act of 1986, it made sense for parents to fund college trusts because all assets in a child's name were taxed at the child's low income tax rate. Tax reform limited the amount of income taxed at the child's rate to $1,400. For a child younger than age 14, the first $700 of income from interest and dividends is totally tax-free, and the second $700 is taxed at the child's tax rate, usually 15 percent.

Figure 12.1   College Costs and Savings Needs Worksheet

	Example (Assumes 7% Return)	**Your Child**
1. Current Annual College Costs	$10,000	$ _____
2. Age of Your Child	6	_____
3. Future Cost of First Year of College (Multiply item 1, above, by number in column A next to your child's age, below.)	$22,520	$ _____
4. Total Cost of Four Years of College (Amount needed at the beginning of college. Multiply item 3 by 3.624.)	$81,626	$ _____
5. Amount You Must Save/Invest Each Year (Multiply item 4 by number in column B next to your child's age.)	$ 4,563	$ _____
6. Amount You Must Save/Invest Each Month (Divide item 5 by 12.)	$ 380	$ _____

Age of Child	A	B
Newborn	3.380	0.0294
1	3.159	0.0324
2	2.952	0.0359
3	2.759	0.0398
4	2.579	0.0443
5	2.410	0.0496
6	2.252	0.0559
7	2.105	0.0634
8	1.967	0.0724
9	1.838	0.0835
10	1.718	0.0975
11	1.606	0.1155
12	1.501	0.1398
13	1.403	0.1739
14	1.311	0.2252
15	1.225	0.3110
16	1.145	0.4831
17	1.070	1.0000

Figure 12.2
Money Accumulated by Investing $100 Per Month

# of Years until College	Rates of Return					
	5.5%	*7%*	*8%*	*9%*	*10%*	*12%*
1	$ 1,236	$ 1,246	$ 1,253	$ 1,260	$ 1,267	$ 1,281
2	2,542	2,583	2,611	2,638	2,667	2,724
3	3,922	4,016	4,081	4,146	4,213	4,351
4	5,380	5,553	5,673	5,795	5,921	6,183
5	6,920	7,201	7,397	7,599	7,808	8,249
6	8,546	8,968	9,264	9,572	9,893	10,576
7	10,265	10,863	11,286	11,730	12,196	13,198
8	12,080	12,895	13,476	14,091	14,740	16,153
9	13,998	15,073	15,848	16,672	17,550	19,482
10	16,024	17,409	18,417	19,497	20,655	23,234
11	18,164	19,914	21,198	22,586	24,085	27,461
12	20,425	22,602	24,211	25,964	27,874	32,225
13	22,814	25,481	27,474	29,660	32,060	37,593
14	25,537	28,569	31,008	33,703	36,684	43,642
15	28,002	31,881	34,835	38,124	41,792	50,458
16	30,818	35,432	38,979	42,961	47,436	58,138
17	33,793	39,240	43,468	48,251	53,670	66,792
18	36,936	48,323	48,329	54,037	60,557	76,544

Any earnings exceeding $1,400 are taxed at the parent's rate, which may be 28 percent or more. The $1,400 limit is indexed upward for inflation annually. Once the child turns 14, all earnings are again taxed at his or her rate.

As a result of this rule, you should fund a Uniform Gifts to Minors Act (UGMA) custodial account with investments that produce little, if any, taxable income but, instead, provide long-term capital growth. Stocks of high-growth companies or aggressive-growth stock mutual funds are two examples of appropriate investments for your child's account. Another is municipal bonds or municipal bond funds, which pay tax-exempt interest. You can also give up to $10,000 a year to each of your children without incurring gift tax.

Putting assets in your child's name has a few disadvantages. Once your child reaches the age of 18, he or she has full discretion over how to use the money in the UGMA account. Therefore, if your child spends it on a sports car instead of college tuition, you can't do anything about it. You hope your child would never squander all this carefully invested capital, but you never know when looking at your two-year-old. Another downside of building up a child's portfolio is that if your child applies for financial aid, the college will require that a high percentage of the assets—usually about 35 percent—be used to pay for tuition. In contrast, colleges insist that parents spend only about 6 percent of their assets for their child's college costs. Therefore, if you want to be totally safe and able to have your child qualify for the maximum amount of financial aid, keep all college funds in your name, and pay tuition bills out of your account.

Following, then, is a brief look at some of the investment alternatives for your child's college fund.

Growth stocks or growth-stock mutual funds. Over the long term, you earn the highest return from stocks with sharply rising earnings or from mutual funds that invest in growth companies. Individual growth stocks pay few or no dividends because they reinvest most of their profits in their companies to accelerate the businesses' growth. Individual stocks can perform spectacularly but can also plunge if competitors reduce the firm's profitability. A safer and easier way to achieve rapid growth is to invest in growth-oriented mutual funds. These funds often accept small amounts of money, such as $100 a month, which would be difficult to invest in individual stocks. Most importantly, fund managers constantly buy the most promising growth stocks and sell the fading stars, so you have the best chance of achieving maximum returns. Though such funds are volatile from month to month or year to year, chances are that a well-managed fund could provide an average annual return of 10 to 15 percent or more. Therefore, invest most of your college savings in growth-stock funds for the first 10 to 12 years of your child's life.

Bonds or bond mutual funds. Fixed-income securities or the mutual funds that invest in them provide much more current income than stocks but much less growth potential. If interest rates are very high—more than 10 percent—invest a significant percentage of your money in bonds to build a college fund. But if bonds yield only 5 to 8 percent, invest a smaller amount of your assets, perhaps 30 percent, in them while your child is young. By the time your child becomes a teenager, you can put more money in bonds, which have less risk of falling sharply in value than do stocks. Bond funds offer the advantage of a diversified portfolio and the ease of continuously buying small amounts. But bond funds never mature, so you never know exactly what a fund will be worth until you sell it. If you buy individual bonds, purchase those that mature in the year your child starts college, which will ensure a hefty amount of principal when you need it. To carry this strategy even further, buy a series of bonds that mature in each of the four years that your child attends college. Make sure that the bonds you buy are not callable before the date you need the money.

Zero-coupon bonds. Another way to make sure that a certain amount of principal will be available when you must pay tuition bills is to purchase zeros, which are deeply discounted from their face value. The best strategy is to buy them so they mature when your child will start school. The higher the interest rate on the bond, the faster it will appreciate over time. Zeros come in two principal varieties: *Treasuries* and *municipals*. Treasury zeros, usually called *STRIPS* (which stands for *separate trading of registered interest and principal of securities*), have no risk of default, cannot be redeemed before maturity and usually pay higher yields than municipal bonds. The problem with STRIPS is that the IRS expects you to pay taxes every year on the growth of the bonds attributable to interest even though you do not receive that interest in cash. This is more of a nuisance than a reason to avoid STRIPS, however. If you buy a zero-coupon bond issued by a municipality, you can sidestep the tax problem altogether. Because the bond's interest is tax exempt, you never owe taxes on the growth of the bond. However, be careful to select a zero-coupon municipal that cannot be redeemed before maturity. You do not want your well-laid plans upset by an early return of your principal.

Education IRA. A new type of account, similar to an individual retirement account, called the Education IRA, was created as part of the Taxayer Relief Act of 1997. It allows parents to save up to $500 per year per child under age 18 to help pay educational expenses. Contributions were allowed starting on January 1, 1998. The money invested does not generate a deduction when placed in the Education IRA, but the principal and all income and capital gains can be withdrawn completely tax-free to pay for college expenses such as tuition, fees, books, and room and board. Only couples with joint adjusted gross incomes of $150,000 or less and singles with incomes of $95,000 or less qualify for the full Education IRA. The $500 limit is phased out for couples with incomes between $150,000 and $160,000, after which no Education IRA is allowed. The limit is phased out for singles with incomes between $95,000 and $110,000.

Another related rule allows parents to withdraw money from regular IRAs before age 59½ without penalty if the proceeds are used for college or vocational school expenses. However, the money withdrawn must be reported as income in the year it is taken from the IRA. So the Education IRA is probably a better deal for those eligible to open one. If you do not use the assets in an Education IRA by the time your child is age 30, the account must be liquidated and taxes paid on the proceeds at regular income tax rates. If one child does not go to school, the Education IRA proceeds can be used for another child in the family who does attend college. The best way to invest money in an Education IRA is with aggressive growth vehicles such as growth stocks or growth-oriented mutual funds, because you will not pay taxes on capital gains, no matter how much the account grows, as long as you use the money to pay for college expenses.

Baccalaureate bonds. A special-purpose municipal zero-coupon bond, nicknamed a baccalaureate bond, is issued by more than 20 states to help residents pay for tuition at an in-state school. These bonds typically cost between $1,000 and $5,000 apiece, and mature between 5 and 20 years. It is best to buy one that matures in the year your child is expected to go to college. Unlike other municipal zeros, however, baccalaureate bonds cannot be redeemed early if interest rates fall. They are extremely popular and usually sell out quickly when offered to the public. If you buy them when interest rates are high—more than 6 percent, for example— they can be a good deal. However, compare the yields on baccalaureate bonds to those on EE savings bonds. The interest on baccalaureate bonds is exempt from federal and state taxes no matter what your income; with savings bonds, you receive a tax break only if your income falls under a certain limit. Therefore, if your income exceeds the limit, you will probably do better with baccalaureates. If your child decides not to attend an in-state school or go to college at all, you can cash in the bonds and use the proceeds however you choose.

Savings bonds. Series EE savings bonds, though they do not have the growth potential of growth mutual funds, can provide a solid base for funding at least part of your child's college education. Savings bonds formerly had a guaranteed mini- mum rate, but that policy was discontinued in May 1995. The yields on savings bonds issued on May 1, 1997, or later are based on 90 percent of the average yields on five-year Treasury securities for the preceding six months. These bonds in- crease in value every month and interest is compounded semiannually. Therefore, if interest rates rise, savings bond returns will also rise, but if rates fall, yields will drop. Savings bonds are easy to accumulate through a payroll savings plan in denominations as little as $25. These bonds also offer a special advantage to parents saving for their children's education: If your modified adjusted gross income is between $50,850 and $65,850 for individuals or $76,250 and $106,250 for married couples filing jointly at the time you redeem your savings bonds (this amount is adjusted slightly for inflation every year), the interest you earn from the bonds is either fully or partially tax exempt if you use it for college tuition for either yourself, your spouse or your children. The bonds must be redeemed in the same calendar year that tuition and fees are paid. Make sure to secure the bonds in the parent's name, not the child's name, if you want to take advantage of this tax break. This version of savings bonds is called an education bond, and it can apply to any bond purchased after December 31, 1989. For more information on how savings bonds can be used to finance college education, take a look at the Treasury's savings bond Web site at www.publicdebt.treas.gov/sav/sav.htm.

COLLEGESURE CERTIFICATES OF DEPOSIT

College Savings Bank (5 Vaughn Dr., Princeton, NJ 08540-6313; 800-888- 2723; www.collegesavings.com), sells what it calls the *CollegeSure* certificate of deposit (CD). The bank, as a member of the Federal Deposit Insurance Corpo- ration (FDIC), provides $100,000 of bank insurance per depositor. The CD is sold in maturities from 1 to 25 years and pays a variable rate of return indexed to the change in a measure of college costs compiled annually by the College Board. The Savings Bank guarantees that the CD's value will grow by at least the college inflation rate. The bank guarantees a 4 percent minimum interest rate floor;

therefore, at the very least, your investment will double over 18 years if college inflation remains below 4 percent for that many years—a highly unlikely event.

Like you do with a zero-coupon bond, you buy the CD at a deep discount from its face value. The longer the maturity of the CD, the deeper the discount. You can purchase the CD either with one up-front lump sum (minimum of $500) or with periodic deposits (minimum of $250 per payment). You can even arrange to have the funds transferred automatically from your bank.

If you must withdraw money before the CD matures, you will pay stiff penalties. Any principal that you take out within the first three years of opening the CD will be hit with a 10 percent penalty. Between three years and the year before the CD matures, you will pay a 5 percent early-withdrawal charge. In the final year before maturity, the penalty declines to 1 percent.

The CollegeSure CD is sold in units, with one unit guaranteed to cover one year's tuition, fees, room and board at the average four-year college. Half a unit will pay for a year of public school, and a unit and a half will pay for a year at the priciest Ivy League university. The CD levies no sales charges, fees or commissions, and if your child decides not to attend school, you can cash in your CD and do whatever you like with the money. However, you must pay taxes on the interest earned each year, although you can avoid $700 of the interest being taxed by putting the CD in your child's name if he or she is younger than age 14.

The CollegeSure CD also may be purchased through a number of qualified state tuition programs such as in Arizona and Montana. Both programs offer the depositor federal income tax deferral (the child's tax rate is applied when the child matriculates in college), no means test and generous contribution limits. There are also no residency requirements, so you can participate no matter where you live. For more information on these programs, call College Savings Bank at 800-888-2723 or Arizona's Web site at www.acpe.asu.edu or Montana's Web site at www.montana.edu/wwwoche.

The CollegeSure CD is designed to protect you against quickly spiraling college costs. However, if college inflation rates decline, you will earn a low return on your money over time. Therefore, compare the return you might earn on a CollegeSure CD with that of growth-stock funds or EE savings bonds before you make a long-term commitment to such a program. This program might be best for you only if you find the CD's guarantees psychologically satisfying.

PREPAID TUITION PLANS

Several states, including Alabama, Alaska, Colorado, Florida, Illinois, Maine, Maryland, Massachusetts, Michigan, Mississippi, Missouri, Nevada, Ohio, Oregon, Pennsylvania, South Carolina, Tennessee, Texas, Virginia, Washington, West Virginia, and Wisconsin, offer plans that allow you to prepay college tuition bills years in advance. (The phone numbers to get more information on these plans are listed in the "Resources" section of this chapter.). If you pay with either a lump sum or a series of payments, your child is guaranteed up to four years at a state school when he or she reaches college age, no matter what the tuition at that time. The price of college is deeply discounted. The younger your child, the steeper the discount. These plans can be a good deal if you are fairly sure that your children will want to attend college in your state.

However, prepaid tuition plans have drawbacks. If your child attends school out of state, each program has different refund policies. Some states will pay you the equivalent of a current state tuition. Others will give back only your initial investment, plus a low rate of interest (like 5 percent in Florida). Some will refund only your initial investment without interest and also hit you with a cancelation fee. In addition, the IRS has ruled that you must pay federal income tax on the difference between your initial investment and the cost of tuition when your child enrolls. For a detailed listing of all state prepaid tuition plans and the features of each plan, look at the Web site for the College Savings Plans Network of the National Association of State Treasurers at www.collegesavings.org.

Many states also offer savings programs in which your money is invested and grows tax-deferred inside a trust according to the tax rules of IRS Section 529. Most states invest the money very conservatively in Treasuries and CDs and offer a guaranteed floor rate of return of 3 or 4 percent, while others, such as Indiana, put at least some of the assets in stocks, offering higher return potential but also more risk. For a complete list of state programs with phone numbers to call for more information, look in the "Resources" section of this chapter under State College Savings Programs. In these plans, assets are kept in the parent's name but are taxed at the child's more advantageous 15 percent tax rate when the child matriculates in college. If the child decides not to go to school, the assets can be used for subsequent children who do. If the money is not used for college education, the parents can take it back, though they would pay taxes on the money and have to fork over a 10 percent penalty as well. So, it is best to sign up for such a program only if you are fairly sure that your child will use the money for college expenses.

More than 500 colleges offer a more limited form of prepaid tuition plan, often known as a tuition discount program. These programs allow you to pay for four years of tuition in a lump sum when your child enrolls as a freshman. Most schools will lend you the money to participate in this program. Interest rates vary widely. You might take advantage of this program if you think the school's tuition will rise faster than the interest rate on the loan and if the interest rate is competitive to one you could obtain elsewhere, such as on a home-equity loan.

INVESTMENTS TO AVOID

Several forms of savings and investments are frequently touted as being ideal for college savings but truly are inappropriate. A few examples include cash value life insurance, annuities, limited partnerships, unit investment trusts and highly speculative devices such as options or futures. All of these are designed to achieve other financial goals, such as insuring a life or providing retirement income, and therefore are inefficient and costly ways to pay for your children's college education.

Winning the Financial Aid Game

Even if you have saved diligently and amassed a large college fund—and particularly if you haven't been so conscientious—you will need to apply for financial aid to cover at least part of your children's college costs. Many grants, loans, scholarships and other programs exist, some offering better opportunities than others.

GRANTS

Begin your search for cash with grants, which cost you nothing and do not have to be repaid. The most common sources of grants follow.

Pell grants. Pell grants are given mostly to students in low-income families. The grants range from about $400 to as much as $3,000 a year, with the higher amount reserved for the families earning the least. To determine whether your child is eligible for a Pell grant, calculate your *expected family contribution* (EFC) using the standard formula reproduced on the application for the grant. If your EFC is low enough, your child might receive a grant. To calculate the amount of your Pell grant, subtract your EFC from the maximum authorized Pell grant, which is currently $3,000. The grant will depend somewhat on the cost of tuition at your child's school, whether he or she will be a full- or part-time student and whether he or she will attend school for a full academic year. Your child should apply for a Pell grant even if your child knows that he or she will not receive one because colleges normally won't consider a student for another grant unless he or she has been rejected for a Pell. For more information on the Pell grant application process, call 800-4-FED-AID.

Supplemental Educational Opportunity Grants (SEOGs). These grants are funded by the federal government and administered through college financial aid offices. The grants to undergraduates range from $100 to $4,000 a year, with larger amounts of money going to lower income students. The priority goes to those receiving Pell grants. SEOG funds are limited, so it is important to submit an application as early as possible.

State programs for residents. Most states provide student grants based on a combination of merit and financial need. To be eligible for some grants, your child must meet a certain academic threshold, such as a B average; then your family's financial status is considered. Other grants are made solely on academic accomplishment, no matter what your family's level of need. Your child's high school guidance counselor should know the details of grants available in your state. A complete list of the addresses and phone numbers of all state financial aid offices can be found in the "Resources" section of this chapter.

College grants. Most institutions offer several kinds of grants, which may or may not be based on financial need. Many merit scholarships are awarded purely on superlative high school academic achievement and high SAT test scores. Some colleges give cash grants, while others offer tuition discounts. Colleges also award grants to athletes, musicians and others with special skills that the schools prize.

Private grants. Thousands of grants and scholarship programs are available to students with superior academic records, special interests and other qualifying characteristics. The National Merit Scholarship program awards grants purely on academic performance. Some grants are given by companies to their employees' children; others, by the local chamber of commerce. Some trade groups offer scholarships to students wanting to pursue careers in the groups' industries. To locate private grants or scholarships for which your child may be eligible, consult some of the books listed in the "Resources" section at the end of this chapter. Two particularly helpful books are *Winning Money for College,* by Alan Deutschman, and *The A's and B's of Academic Scholarships.* You may want to consult a scholarship search service such as the National Scholarship Research Service (2280 Airport Blvd., Santa Rosa, CA 95403; 707-546-6777; 800-432-3782; www. 800headstart.com), Scholarship Resource Network (Daigle and Vierra, 555 Quince Orchard Rd., Gaithersburg, MD 20878; 301-670-1281; www.rams.com/srn) or other similar services with Web sites that will send you, for a fee, a printout of grants and scholarships that your child may be eligible to receive.

You must be careful about claims made by many commercial scholarship search services. The Federal Trade Commission has launched Project $cholar$cam to alert consumers about potential fraud in this arena and how to avoid it. The FTC's Web site on the subject can be found at www.ftc.gov/bcp/conline/pubs/scholarship/index.htm.

Here are the FTC's six promises some services make that are warning signs to tell you the service is not legitimate:

1. "Scholarships are guaranteed or your money back." No one can legitimately guarantee you will receive a scholarship or grant, and refunds may be difficult to get.

2. "You can't get this information anywhere else." There are a multitude of books and Web sites listed in the "Resources" section of this chapter with just about every scholarship in existence.

3. "Please give me your credit card number so I can hold this scholarship for you." Since no one can guarantee you will get a scholarship, it is dangerous to give your credit card number over the phone.

4. "We'll do all the work for you." Services may be able to identify potential scholarships, but you or your child have to write the essay and fill out the application to win the money.

5. "This scholarship will cost you some money." No one can hold a scholarship or grant for a fee. You win the grant because of your qualifications, not because you pay for it.

6. "You've been selected by a national foundation to receive this scholarship." It is highly unlikely that a foundation has selected you if you did not apply in the first place. In the same vein, be suspicious if someone has told you that you have won a contest that you don't remember entering.

If your child is awarded a grant or scholarship, the college will deduct that amount from the financial aid it would otherwise give your child, as required by federal rules, because the award is considered a source of income, and parents must declare all sources of income when applying for loans. Nevertheless, the scholarship could save you money if you wouldn't have qualified for much financial aid. Or if the college awards your child a grant instead of a loan, the scholarship can reduce the amount you must borrow.

WORKING FOR CASH: COOPERATIVE EDUCATION

By combining a full- or part-time job and a college career, your child can finance some or all of his or her education. The federal government sponsors thousands of students who take jobs in the armed forces, the Treasury Department, the Department of Health and Human Services, the Department of Agriculture, the General Services Administration, the Department of Justice, the Department of Labor and many other agencies. Hundreds of private employers also offer co-op education opportunities.

The scheduling of work and school is flexible. Some students opt for parallel study and work, in which they attend school in the morning and work in the afternoon, or vice versa. The other option is to alternate semesters—one at work, then one at school. For federal programs, pay is based on the civil service pay schedule.

Federal work-study programs not only help students pay for schooling; they also expose students to real-world careers they would not experience in a classroom. To learn more about federal co-op education, contact the employment divisions of federal agencies directly or the Federal Job Information Center in Atlanta, Chicago, Dallas, Philadelphia, San Francisco or Washington, D.C. You can also get a free copy of the *Cooperative Education Undergraduate Program Directory* from the National Commission for Cooperative Education (360 Huntington Ave., Boston, MA 02115; 617-373-3778). The best book on the subject is *Earn & Learn: An Introduction to Cooperative Education* (see "Resources" section at the end of this chapter).

Federal work-study. This program, available for both middle- and low-income students, allows your child to work a certain number of hours each week to earn a college grant and at least the minimum wage. Usually, your child works on campus in the cafeteria, library or gym. In some cases, your child works for a local business in a field related to his or her course of study. Other jobs are offered at local, state or federal public agencies. The program is administered by the college financial aid office, which sets the work schedule. Your child cannot work more hours than the office approves and cannot earn more money than the work-study award.

Americorps. The National Community Service Trust Act of 1993 established the Americorps program, in which students can finance some or all of their college education in return for agreeing to perform specified community service. Americorps volunteers receive a living stipend of about $7,500 a year and get the opportunity to accrue educational awards of $4,725 a year that can be used to pay tuition costs or repay student loans. Applicants must be U.S. citizens who are at least 17 years old and who have graduated from high school. Americorps volunteers typically work in underprivileged areas of American cities and rural districts in four fields: education, public safety, human services and the environment. You can get all the details by contacting the Americorps Web site at www.cns.gov/americorps.html. One book describing this option in more detail is *Americorps: Serve your Country and Pay for College* from Conway Greene Publishing Company.

The military. Your child's entire college tuition, plus a monthly allowance, will be paid if he or she attends one of the military academies, such as West Point for the U.S. Army, Annapolis for the U.S. Navy, or the Air Force Academy. Your child must then serve in the military for a specified number of years after graduation. To get into these academies, however, your child must be nominated by your congressional representative or senator. Your child should apply to the academies during his or her junior year in high school.

If your child would rather combine military training with education at a public or private university, he or she can apply to a Reserve Officer Training Corps (ROTC) program. The U.S. Army and Air Force run their own ROTC programs, while the U.S. Navy and Marines operate a combined program. All ROTC programs offer both two-year and four-year terms. To enroll in ROTC, your child must be a high school graduate and be physically and academically qualified. After graduation and at least two years in the reserves, your child must serve at least four years of active duty in the service for which he or she was trained.

ROTC programs also offer various specialty training courses, such as for doctors, nurses and engineers. These programs can give your child a solid, marketable skill, making it easier to get a job once your child completes his or her military career. ROTC programs require that reservists attend both regular classes and ROTC courses while on campus. For more details about the ROTC, talk to a military recruiter, or contact the addresses and phone numbers provided in the "Resources" section at the end of this chapter.

LOANS

If the combination of savings, grants, scholarships and work-study programs falls short of tuition costs, your child can apply for one of the many loans intended to finance college costs. Three main sources of loans exist: the federal or state government; colleges; and commercial enterprises such as banks or firms that specialize in college loans. Taking out a loan to finance college is a serious commitment that will probably take many years to repay, so help your child shop diligently for the best deal.

Government loans. Several types of local and federal government loans exist.

Perkins loans. The college or university granting Perkins loans acts as the lender, using money provided by the federal government. These loans, named after former Kentucky representative Carl Perkins, used to be called National Direct Student Loans. They are designed for undergraduate and graduate students with *exceptional need*—meaning that their families earn $30,000 or less annually. Exceptional need is determined by the school's financial aid officer. Students can usually borrow up to $3,000 for each year of undergraduate study, up to a maximum of $15,000. Graduate students can usually borrow up to $5,000 a year, with total debt—including loans for undergraduate study—of no more than $30,000. If you go to a school with a default rate of under 7.5 percent, you can qualify for even more—$4,000 per undergraduate year up to $20,000 and $6,000 per graduate year up to $40,000.

Perkins loans are extremely attractive for several reasons. First, they charge a flat 5 percent interest rate, which is lower than most other loans. Second, they allow a nine-month grace period following graduation before repayment must begin. Finally, the loans can be repaid over ten years, which reduces the monthly payment considerably from shorter term student loan programs.

Stafford loans. Once known as Guaranteed Student Loans, Stafford loans were renamed for former Vermont Senator Robert Stafford. They are available to all students, without regard to financial status. Children of families that demonstrate need receive interest subsidies, while those considered less needy pay a higher interest rate. Your child can apply for a Stafford loan at financial institutions such as banks, savings and loans, credit unions and state loan-guarantee agencies. Your child should apply as soon as he or she is accepted by a school because the application procedure and processing can take several months.

The Stafford program imposes certain limits on how much your child can borrow each year. Currently, first-year students enrolled in a program of study that is at least a full academic year can borrow up to $2,625. For those who have completed their first year of study and the remainder of their program is at least one full academic year, a total of $3,500 can be borrowed. You can borrow up to $5,500 if you have completed two years of study and the remainder of your program is at least one full academic year. If you are an independent undergraduate student or a dependent student whose parents can't get a PLUS loan, you can borrow up to $6,625 if you're a first-year student and $7,500 if you've completed your first year of study and you have at least one full academic year to go. For those who have completed two years of study with at least one year to go, the limit is raised to $10,500. All undergraduate loans (for dependent students) combined cannot exceed $23,000, and the maximum total for independent undergraduates is $46,000. Graduate students who are still dependents can assume loans for $8,500 a year, up to a maximum of $65,000, which includes any money borrowed as an undergraduate. For independent graduate students, the maximum rises to $18,500 per year with a lifetime cap of $138,500, including undergraduate loans. For students attending school part-time, lower lending limits are imposed.

Lenders of subsidized Stafford funds often charge a 5 percent loan origination fee, as well as an insurance fee of up to 3 percent, which are deducted from the loan proceeds. For unsubsidized Stafford loans, the combined origination and insurance fee might total 6.5 percent. Not all lenders charge the same fees, however; it pays to shop around.

Once a year, on June 30, the interest rate on Stafford loans is fixed at 3.1 percent more than the yield on a 91-day Treasury bill. By law, however, the rate cannot rise above 8.5 percent. If your child demonstrates financial need, the government will pay the interest on the loan while your child attends school, as well as for a 6-month grace period after graduation. If borrowing is not based on need, an unsubsidized Stafford loan accrues interest while your child attends school, though he or she does not have to begin repaying the loan until after graduation. The minimum annual repayment amount on a Stafford loan is $600, and your child can repay the loan in five to ten years.

Parent Loans to Undergraduate Students (PLUS). PLUS loans are made to parents and are available through banks, savings and loans, credit unions and some state lending agencies.

PLUS loans allow parents to borrow an unlimited amount to finance college costs. However, PLUS loans and other financial aid cannot exceed the student's cost of attending school. The interest rate on PLUS loans is set at 3.1 percent more than the one-year Treasury bill rate and is adjusted annually in June. The rate on PLUS loans cannot exceed 9 percent. Repayment of these loans must begin within 60 days of receiving the loan proceeds, and the loans can be repaid in five to ten years.

Legislation passed under the Clinton Administration will affect the student loan program in many ways. Many loans that formerly were processed through banks or other lending institutions are now granted directly through the Department of Education in the Federal Direct PLUS Program. For more information on this and other forms of student aid, ask for "The Student Guide" from the U.S. Department of Education Office of Student Financial Assistance (P.O. Box 84, Washington, DC 20044; 800-433-3243). In addition, thousands of students will be able to pay off their government loans through work in a National Service Corporation. Such work may include positions in state or local government, as well as in educational, environmental, law-enforcement or social activities. Those entering the program could pay off as much as $5,000 worth of student loans for every year of service up to $10,000. For the latest information on all of the federal loan programs described here, call 800-4-FED-AID.

State loan programs. In addition to the federal aid, most states offer their own loan programs. Usually, these programs are designed for state residents; however, in some cases, even out-of-state students can qualify. The terms, interest rates, repayment schedules and amounts of loans vary widely from state to state. Several states offer special incentive programs to train teachers, doctors, nurses and other professionals in short supply. Other states offer programs aimed at veterans or those enlisted in the state's National Guard. For a list of each state's offerings, including descriptions of some of the most innovative state programs, consult *Don't Miss Out: The Ambitious Student's Guide to Financial Aid,* by Robert and Anna Leider (see "Resources" section at the end of this chapter).

College loans. Most colleges, seeking to fill the gaps created by federal and state programs, offer their own loan programs. Rules vary widely, as some loans are designed for parents, others for students and still others for both parents and students. Interest rates—usually tied to some index of Treasury securities—also range from very low to quite high, and repayment terms can be strict or lenient. Ask a school's financial aid officer about specific programs, preferably when your child applies to the school but certainly once he or she is accepted.

Commercial loans. In addition to the loans made by banks through government programs and as personal loans based on creditworthiness, several commercial lenders specialize in college lending. These programs allow your child to repay the principal on a loan after he or she has graduated, though he or she must pay interest while still in school. Following are some of the major players in this market. Consult the "Resources" section at the end of this chapter for addresses and further explanation.

College Board. Its CollegeCredit program offers ExtraCredit loans to cover the full cost of your child's education. The minimum loan is $2,000. The loan's rate floats at 4½ percentage points over the 91-day Treasury bill rate, adjusted quarterly. There is a 3 percent loan fee, and your child has 15 years to repay. Another loan that is part of the CollegeCredit program is called the ExtraTime loan, which is designed to pay for a single year of education expenses. It has similar features to the ExtraCredit loan, except that you have the option of monthly payments of interest only while a student is enrolled, or monthly payments of principal and interest after the education is complete. For more information on these loans, call the College Board's College Answer Service line at 800-831-5626.

ConSern. ConSern Loans for Education lend up to $25,000 each year per child at the 30- or 90-day commercial paper rate plus 4.6 percentage points, adjusted monthly. ConSern charges a 4½ percent origination fee and allows your child to repay a loan over as long as 15 years. These loans are designed for employees of companies that have adopted the ConSern program. For more information on how to qualify, call ConSern at 800-767-5626; for a company to join this program call: 800-207-9416 ext. 1415.

The Education Resources Institute (TERI). TERI lends a minimum of $2,000 up to the cost of education minus financial aid per year per child at the prime rate plus 1½ to 2 percentage points, adjusted monthly with no cap. There are no fees and your child can repay in as long as 25 years. TERI also offers the Professional Education Plan (PEP) for graduate students. For more information, call TERI at 800-255-8374.

Key Education Resources. Key offers private supplemental loans, such as the Key Alternative Loan, which allows undergraduates enrolled full-time to share the cost of their education. Key also offers the AchieverLoan to parents with three different ways to finance college or prep school tuitions. This loan charges 4½ percentage points over the 91-day Treasury bill rate, adjusted quarterly. Fees range from 3 percent to 5 percent of the loan amount, depending on the repayment method. The Key CareerLoan is designed for adult students attending college part-time. Key also offers the Monthly Payment Plan, an interest-free budget plan administered through the school that allows families to make equal monthly payments to meet annual expenses. Key also offers several programs tailored to graduate students in specific fields such as law, business, medical and dental schools. For more information, call Key at 800-KEY-LEND.

Nellie Mae. Formerly known as the New England Education Loan Marketing Association, Nellie Mae offers the EXCEL and SHARE programs. They will lend from $2,000 up to the cost of education minus the amount of other financial aid received by the student. One-year renewable loans charge the prime rate plus ½ percent for the first year and plus 1 percent in subsequent years and are adjusted monthly. You can repay both principal and interest on the loan or interest only for up to four years while the student is still enrolled in school. These loans charge a guarantee fee of 7 percent. Your child can repay the loan over as many as 20 years. For more information, call 800-634-9308 or visit the Nellie Mae Web site at www. nelliemae.org or see the "Resources" section at the end of this chapter.

Sallie Mae (formerly the Student Loan Marketing Association). Sallie Mae, which buys and services federally insured educational loans made by lenders, has introduced several programs to reward borrowers who make on-time payments on their Stafford loans by reducing their interest rates. Great Rewards enables Stafford loan borrowers who make their first 48 scheduled monthly payments on time to receive an interest rate reduction of two full percentage points for the remaining term of the loan. SMART REWARDS is a similar program for SMART LOAN (consolidation) borrowers who make their first 48 scheduled payments on time. They are rewarded with an interest rate reduction of one full percentage point for the remaining repayment term. The Great Returns Program helps heavily indebted Stafford borrowers who make their first 24 scheduled payments on time to receive an account credit equivalent to federal origination fees up to 3 percent (less $250). The SMART LOAN program helps students consolidate their loans into one loan on advantageous terms. Another Sallie Mae program is called Direct Repay, which allows you to repay your student loans through an automatic debit on your checking or savings account and earns you a quarter-point interest rate reduction on your loan as long as you make payments through the plan. For more details on these programs, call the Sallie Mae Service Center at 800-524-9100 or the College Answer Service at 888-888-3460. You also can get more detail on these programs at Sallie Mae's Web site at www.salliemae.com.

Applying for Financial Aid

The process of applying for financial aid can be daunting. You must fill out several confusing forms and provide a detailed profile of your financial situation to colleges, federal agencies, banks and other lenders. The entire ordeal is so strenuous that an industry of financial aid counselors has emerged to help you work through the procedure—for a fee that can run several hundred dollars. Before you contact such a consultant, however, give the financial aid application process a try.

Basically, to receive financial aid, a student must prove that his or her family needs the money. To determine how much, a standard *needs analysis* examines what the parents can afford to pay and what the student can contribute. Financial aid is designed to supplement, not replace, a family's contribution to college costs. Therefore, all lenders expect a family to pay as much as possible. The factors that determine how much financial aid a family qualifies for include the parents' and student's income and assets, the size of the family and the number of children attending college. The more income and assets a family has, the more college costs it is expected to pay.

The financial aid forms you obtain from the school your child wants to attend will help you go through the application process step by step. To complete the forms, it will be helpful if you complete the worksheets in Chapter 1 and if you have your latest tax return and bank and brokerage statements available for reference.

Begin by totaling your family's income and assets. Then, deduct the amount of money your family needs to live, which includes a certain allocation to savings. The remainder, known as the *parental contribution,* you are expected to spend for college tuition and expenses. Once you determine the cost of tuition, room and board and other fees and expenses, apply your parental contribution—plus any money your child can pay out of his or her income or assets—to the total school costs. Whatever remains is considered your family's financial need.

The sample table from the College Board shown in Figure 12.3 will give you some sense of how much parents are expected to contribute to college costs, based on their pretax income, assets and number of children. The Board made the following assumptions when assembling this table.

Figure 12.3
Estimating Parental Contributions

Net assets: $25,000

Family size:	3	4	5	6
Parents' Pretax Income		Parental Contribution		
$ 20,000	$ 0	$ 0	$ 0	$ 0
30,000	1,304	631	1	0
40,000	2,926	2,179	1,548	836
50,000	5,251	4,121	3,238	2,394
60,000	8,134	6,853	5,672	4,437
70,000	10,615	9,334	8,142	6,776
80,000	13,602	12,321	11,129	9,763
90,000	16,589	15,308	14,116	12,750
100,000	19,576	18,294	17,102	15,737

Net assets: $50,000

Family size:	3	4	5	6
Parents' Pretax Income		Parental Contribution		
$ 20,000	$ 12	$ 0	$ 0	$ 0
30,000	1,560	887	257	0
40,000	3,254	2,452	1,804	1,092
50,000	5,717	4,517	3,576	2,685
60,000	8,681	7,400	6,208	4,866
70,000	11,162	9,881	8,689	7,323
80,000	14,149	12,868	11,676	10,310
90,000	17,136	15,855	14,663	13,297
100,000	20,123	18,841	17,650	16,284

Net assets: $100,000

Family size:	3	4	5	6
Parents' Pretax Income		Parental Contribution		
$ 20,000	$ 1,332	$ 660	$ 29	$ 0
30,000	2,958	2,207	1,577	864
40,000	5,303	4,165	3,275	2,426
50,000	8,534	7,097	5,749	4,481
60,000	11,501	10,220	9,028	7,534
70,000	13,982	12,701	11,509	10,143
80,000	16,969	15,688	14,496	13,130
90,000	19,956	18,675	17,483	16,117
100,000	22,943	21,661	20,470	19,104

Source: Reprinted with permission from *College Costs & Financial Aid Handbook* by the College Entrance Examination Board, New York

Figure 12.3
(continued)

Net assets: $150,000

Family size:	3	4	5	6
Parents' Pretax Income		Parental Contribution		
$ 20,000	$ 2,699	$ 1,980	$ 1,349	$ 571
30,000	4,889	3,813	2,977	2,184
40,000	8,047	6,610	5,333	4,129
50,000	11,354	9,917	8,569	7,048
60,000	14,321	13,040	11,848	10,354
70,000	16,802	15,521	14,329	12,963
80,000	19,789	18,508	17,316	15,950
90,000	22,776	21,495	20,303	18,937
100,000	25,763	24,481	23,290	21,924

- The older parent is 45 years old and both parents are employed at equal wages.
- Income is derived solely from both parents' jobs.
- The family's circumstances are not unusual, and it has no out-of-the-ordinary expenses.
- The family claims the standard deductions on its income tax return, Form 1040.
- One undergraduate family member attends college.
- Any equity in the family's home or farm is not included in its net assets for the purpose of determining federal aid eligibility.

Additional unusual circumstances are also considered when calculating the expected family contribution.

The numbers in the table are guidelines that financial aid officers must use to calculate your *expected family contribution* (EFC). Your child might qualify for more aid if unusual circumstances, such as a recent divorce, job loss or unusual medical expenses, can be documented. If you or your child explains why your family's situation is exceptional in a well-crafted letter, he or she might receive more aid than the guidelines normally allow. Financial aid officers have more flexibility in dispensing their own school's funds.

You can take a few other steps to improve your child's financial aid package. When completing the aid application, be honest, but don't overstate the value of family assets because it will reduce the amount of aid for which your child qualifies. For example, be conservative when estimating the value of your home. You can also invest money in retirement plans such as individual retirement accounts

(IRAs), Keogh plans and 401(k) salary reduction plans because you do not report these assets on financial aid forms. And refrain from selling assets such as stocks, bonds or mutual funds in the year before you apply for aid because any capital gains those sales generate are counted as income on financial aid forms. Capital gains weigh more heavily against you than do assets in the assessment of need.

Mail in the financial aid application—which might include the Free Application for Federal Student Aid (FAFSA), the CSS/Financial Aid PROFILE form from the College Board's College Scholarship Service, the Family Financial Statement (FFS) from ACT, Inc. (formerly the American College Testing Program), as well as any specific college aid application forms—soon after January 1, even before your child is accepted by a school. Once he or she has been accepted, your child will receive an award letter from the school's financial aid office. This letter details how your child's eligibility for government aid was determined, how his or her need for college aid was calculated and what kind and how much aid is being offered, if any. Your child doesn't necessarily have to jump at the first offer. If he or she has been accepted by several schools, weigh the pros and cons of all the offers. If a school wants your child's enrollment badly enough, it might sweeten the initial offer. In the end, however, the financial aid package—while important— should not be the main determinant of which college your child attends. He or she should believe that the academic and social offerings and the physical facilities will yield the best education you can afford.

The worksheet in Figure 12.4 summarizes the sources of assistance discussed in this chapter to give you an idea of the financial aid package you might expect for your child and let you calculate the gap between that financial aid and what you still need to finance.

Borrowing Against Your Assets

If the total financial aid package for which your child qualifies is not adequate, or if you want to cut down on outside borrowing, you might consider your last option: taking a loan against your assets. You may have accumulated substantial equity in certain assets that you can borrow against at a lower interest rate and with less hassle than applying for government, college or commercial loans. The most obvious places to look for equity include the following.

Your home. If you have paid down your mortgage and built up substantial equity in your home, you might be able to open a home-equity line of credit that charges only 1 to 2 percentage points more than the prime rate and allows you to repay it as quickly or as slowly as you wish, as long as you meet each month's minimum payment. An extra bonus is that all borrowing up to $100,000 is tax deductible. Remember, however, your home is on the line; if you default, the bank will foreclose. You can open a home-equity credit line with a bank, savings and loan, credit union or brokerage firm.

Figure 12.4   Financial Aid Package Worksheet

Item	$ Amount
1. **Costs of College** (tuition, room, board, fees)	$
2. **Expected Family Contribution** (parents and students)	$
3. **Financial Need** (subtract item 2 from item 1)	$
4. **Sources of Aid**	
Grants and Scholarships	
Pell	$
SEOG	
State	
College	
Private	
Work-Study	
Federal Work-Study	
ROTC or Other Military Aid	
Cooperative Education	
Loans	
Perkins	
Stafford (subsidized)	
Stafford (unsubsidized)	
PLUS/SLS	
State	
College	
Commercial	
Sources of Aid Total	$
GAP BETWEEN FINANCIAL NEED AND FINANCIAL AID (subtract item 4 from item 3)	$

Your company savings plan. If you have participated in a salary reduction or profit-sharing plan at work for several years, you probably have accumulated a substantial sum of money. Most employers will let you borrow against that money and have you repay the loan through payroll deduction. Interest rates charged on such loans are often quite favorable at 1 or 2 percentage points more than the prime rate. However, borrow against your retirement savings only as a last resort. These plans are designed to provide long-term growth for your golden years, not to pay huge college costs for your children. While you're investigating options at your company, ask the employee benefits department whether your firm makes college loans to employees. Some companies, particularly large corporations, offer such loans at attractive, below-market interest rates.

Your life insurance. If you have amassed a large amount of cash value in your insurance policy, you can usually borrow against it at a favorable interest rate. Again, consider this a last resort because such a loan will retard the growth of your cash value and lower your death benefit by the amount of the loan.

Using Your Computer To Finance College Education

The computer can make the search for financial aid much more efficient and productive than the old-fashioned way of wading through books and filling out application and financial aid forms by hand. There are enormous resources available through the Internet to help you calculate how much financial aid you need and help you find as much as possible. Many of the Web sites listed in the "Resources" section that follows contain calculators that help you figure out how much colleges will expect parents to pay, how much will be provided in financial aid, depending on the parent's financial circumstances, and what kind of loan repayment schedule you can expect. Other Web sites contain mountains of information on scholarships, grants and loans that your child may be able to qualify for. There are also several CD-ROMs allowing you to search for scholarships that your child might have a good chance of getting—these disks often are sold along with scholarship listing books, also detailed in the "Resources" section.

Most colleges and universities also have elaborate Web sites allowing you to take a "virtual tour" of their campus, find out about course offerings and the amount of financial aid available. It is certainly a lot cheaper and less time consuming to tour several campuses online than it is to go there in person.

You also can fill out applications for college, as well as financial aid forms, and submit them electronically. This can save your child a great deal of time and effort retyping the forms many times.

I have assembled a significant sample of the Web sites on the Internet in the following "Resources" section to help you understand the entire financial aid process. Using these resources can potentially save you thousands of dollars in college costs, so they are definitely worth investigating.

Whether you assemble the money to pay for your children's college education from savings and investments, grants, scholarships or loans, the costs are burdensome. The earlier you develop a plan to fund college, the easier you will handle this burden. While the sacrifice of paying for college is great, the reward—a bright future for your children—can be even greater.

Resources

BOOKS

The A's and B's of Academic Scholarships, (Octameron Press, P.O. Box 2748, Alexandria, VA 22301; 703-836-5480; www.octameron.com). A comprehensive listing of academic scholarships and grants at almost every college and university in the United States. Describes award criteria, whether aid is need based, what fields of study each school offers and each school's restrictions.

Barron's Guide to American Colleges (Barron's Educational Series, 250 Wireless Blvd., Hauppauge, NY 11788; 516-434-3311; 800-645-3476). A definitive guide to most major U.S. colleges and universities, with profiles of the campuses and academic specialties and tips on obtaining financial aid from each school.

The College Blue Book: Scholarships, Fellowships, Grants and Loans (MacMillan Books, 200 Old Tappan Rd., Old Tappan, NJ 07675; 800-428-5331; www.mgr.com). Lists thousands of scholarships, many of which go unclaimed because they are not well known.

College.Edu: On-Line Resources for the Cyber Saavy Student, by Lisa Guernsey (Octameron Press, P.O. Box 2748, Alexandria, VA 22301; 703-836-5480; www.octameron.com). This book will give you a road map to the many resources on college financing and the admission process available on the Internet. It describes the ins and outs of applying to college online, what to look for in virtual campus tours and how to make sure the information you're getting is objective.

College Financial Aid (MacMillan Books, 200 Old Tappan Rd., Old Tappan, NJ 07675; 800-428-5331; www.mgr.com). A complete guide to all grants, loans and scholarships available from federal and state government, corporate and private foundation sources.

College Financial Aid for Dummies, by Dr. Herm Davis and Joyce Lain Kennedy (IDG Books, 919 E. Hillsdale Blvd., Suite 400, Foster City, CA 94404; 800-762-2974; www.dummies.com). A step-by-step explanation of the entire financial aid process, from qualifying to filling out the forms to repaying loans. It has an extensive list of financial aid resources.

College Money Handbook (Peterson's Publishing, 202 Carnegie Center, Princeton, NJ 08543-2123; 800-338-3282; www.petersons.com). Helps identify sources of college financing. Includes a CD-ROM to help you estimate college costs. Profiles hundreds of colleges and what financial aid they have to offer.

College Scholarships and Financial Aid, by Jonathan Schwartz (Arco-MacMillan General Reference, 1633 Broadway, New York, NY 10019; 800-428-5331; www.mgr.com). Long listings of scholarships and a Scholarship Search CD-ROM that allows you to search by fields of study, merit status, religion, sports, residence and many other criteria.

Don't Miss Out: The Ambitious Student's Guide to Financial Aid, by Anna and Robert Leider (Octameron Press, P.O. Box 2748, Alexandria, VA 22301; 703-836-5480; www.octameron.com). Detailed descriptions of qualifications for financial aid. Also lists many sources of government and private aid. Contains complete tables and worksheets for family contribution under federal methodology.

Earn & Learn: An Introduction to Cooperative Education, by Joseph Re (Octameron Press, P.O. Box 2748, Alexandria, VA 22301; 703-836-5480; www.octameron. com). Describes how cooperative education programs work, allowing you to combine off-campus work with on-campus schooling. Also discusses distance learning in which you attend college via modem or correspondence so you can earn college credits where you live.

Financial Aid Financer: Expert Answers to College Financing Questions (Octameron Press, P.O. Box 2748, Alexandria, VA 22301; 703-836-5480; www.octameron. com). Explains how to apply for financial aid, how to put together a financial aid package, strategies for financing college and financing strategies for graduate students.

Financial Aid Officers: What They Do to You and for You, by Donald Moore (Octameron Press, P.O. Box 2748, Alexandria, VA 22301; 703-836-5480; www. octameron.com). Describes who financial aid officers are and their role in granting students financial aid. Helps you fill out a financial aid application and explains how applications are processed.

Financing College, How to Use Savings, Financial Aid, Scholarships, and Loans to Afford the School of Your Choice, by Kristin Davis (Times Books, Random House, 201 East 50th Street, New York, NY 10022; 212-751-2600; 800-733-3000; www. randomhouse.com). Davis, an editor at *Kiplinger's Personal Finance* magazine, demystifies the financial aid process and walks parents through the process of finding scholarships, low-cost loans and other ways to make higher education affordable.

Financing Graduate School: A Guide to Financial Aid for Graduate and Professional Education, by Patricia McWade (Peterson's Publishing, P.O. Box 2123, 202 Carnegie Center, Princeton, NJ 08543-2123; 609-243-9111; 800-338-3282; www. petersons.com). Discusses how to determine your qualification for graduate school financial aid and how to apply for it so that you have the best chance of receiving the aid you need. Also lists government programs, private sources of aid and grants for specific student groups. Peterson's also publishes *Grants for Graduate Study* and *Grants for Post-Doctoral Study.*

Financing Your Child's Education, by Nicholas Basta (John Wiley & Sons Inc., 605 3rd Ave., New York, NY 10158-0012; 212-850-6000; www.wiley.com). Explains the ins and outs of financial aid, how schools evaluate financial aid needs and how to present your family's financial status in the financial aid application. Also details school and government funding programs and scholarships.

The Fiske Guide to Colleges, by Edward B. Fiske (Times Books, Random House, 201 E. 50th St., New York, NY 10022; 212-751-2600; 800-733-3000; www.randomhouse. com). The most frequently asked questions about attending college, from academics to social life. Includes a section on getting a first-rate education at public university prices.

Free Money for Graduate School, by Laurie Blum (Henry Holt & Co., 115 W. 18th St., New York, NY 10011; 212-886-9200; www.henryholt.com). A comprehensive guide to graduate school grants. Lists scholarships by subject and also features a section on study and research abroad.

Free Money from Colleges and Universities, by Laurie Blum (Henry Holt & Co., 115 W. 18th St., New York, NY 10011; 212-886-9200; www.henryholt.com). A comprehensive guide to scholarships in a wide variety of disciplines. Lists scholarships by state and subject and provides sample applications.

Loans and Grants from Uncle Sam: Am I Eligible and for How Much? (Octameron Press, P.O. Box 2748, Alexandria, VA 22301; 703-836-5480; www.octameron.com). Describes the major federal loan and grant programs, such as Staffords, Perkins, PLUS loans and Direct loans. Details loan limits, interest rates, repayment plans, deferments and consolidation options. Helps you increase your eligibility and find the best lenders. Worksheets help you assess your eligibility and estimate the size of your award.

Lovejoy's College Guide, by Charles T. Straughn II and Barbara Lovejoy (MacMillan Reference, 1633 Broadway, New York, NY 10019-6785; 800-428-5331; www.mgr.com). Profiles most U.S. colleges to help students choose the one that best meets their needs. Also includes a CD-ROM for College Search, which allows you to enter the criteria you are interested in and produce a list of suitable colleges. Lovejoy also provides a counseling service at 302-698-0597 that will help you select an appropriate college.

Paying Less for College: The Complete Guide to $28 Billion in Financial Aid (Peterson's Publishing, P.O. Box 2123, 202 Carnegie Center, Princeton, NJ 08543-2123; 609-243-9111; 800-338-3282; www.petersons.com). A huge book detailing all government and private aid programs and explaining how to obtain financial aid at 1,600 undergraduate colleges. Ranks colleges by their net costs for freshman year based on the average financial aid package. Also covers the most frequently asked questions about financial aid.

The Scholarship Book, by Daniel Cassidy (Prentice-Hall Publishing, Englewood Cliffs, NJ 07632; 800-223-2336; www.phdirect.com). The ultimate listing of private-sector scholarships, loans and grants assembled by the founder of the National Scholarship Research Service.

Scholarships, Grants & Prizes (Peterson's Publishing, 202 Carnegie Center, Princeton, NJ 08543-2123; 800-338-3282; www.petersons.com). Extensive listings of scholarships, including a CD-ROM with search capabilities. The listings are broken down into ten categories, including academic field-career goals, civic affiliation, employment experience, impairment, military service, nationality-ethnicity, religious affiliation, state of residence, special talents and special interests.

Take Control of Your Student Loans, by Robin Leonard (Nolo Press, 950 Parker St., Berkeley, CA 94710; 510-549-1976; 800-992-NOLO; www.nolo.com). Lays out simple and effective ways for students to get out of student loan debt. It explains various repayment options, how to postpone repayment, how to avoid default, how to handle collection efforts by the government, how to get out of default and when bankrupcty makes sense. The book includes sample letters and forms to show you how to get back on your feet.

Tips on Financial Aid for College (Council of Better Business Bureaus, 4200 Wilson Blvd., Suite 800, Arlington, VA 22203; 703-276-0100; www.bbb.org). A helpful free brochure explaining different kinds of college financial aid and how to apply for them.

Winning Money for College, by Alan Deutschman (Peterson's Publishing, P.O. Box 2123, 202 Carnegie Center, Princeton, NJ 08543-2123; 609-243-9111; 800-338-3282; www.petersons.com). A complete guide to scholarship money. Describes contests and scholarships for specific professions, from arts to sciences.

SOFTWARE

Expected Family Contribution (EFC) (Octameron Associates, P.O. Box 2748, Alexandria, VA 22301; 703-836-5480; www.octameron.com). A simple software program designed to help you compute your expected family contribution to college costs. By changing the income or assets that your family reports, you easily can see how your expected contribution changes. May also help you find ways to lower your expected family contribution and, thus, qualify for more student aid.

TRADE ASSOCIATIONS AND COMPANIES SPECIALIZING IN COLLEGE FINANCING

ACT Inc. (formerly American College Testing) (2201 N. Dodge St., P.O. Box 168, Iowa City, IA 52243; 319-337-1000; www.act.org). Administers tests and advises financial aid administrators and students. Publishes the *ACTIVITY* newsletter for counselors, admissions officers and teachers. For students and their parents, offers a free brochure titled "Applying for Financial Aid: A Guide for Parents and Students." For a nominal charge, will also prepare a Financial Aid Need Estimator, which will give you an estimate of college costs, your expected family contribution and financial aid you could possibly receive. Does process the Free Application for Federal Student Aid (FAFSA).

The College Board (45 Columbus Ave., New York, NY 10023-6992; 212-713-8000; www.collegeboard.org). Publishes many books on financing college. The three most popular books are *College Costs & Financial Aid Handbook; Meeting College Costs: What You Need to Know Before Your Child and Your Money Leave Home;* and the *College Board Scholarship Handbook.* Another book, designed for adult students, is *Financing Your College Degree.* Also offers a scholarship search program called *College Cost Explorer—Fund Finder* on the College Board's Web site, allowing you to match your characteristics against a database of thousands of scholarship sources. Also sponsors a loan program called CollegeCredit (call 800-831-5626 for more information). The Board's College Scholarship Service also administers the CSS/Financial Aid PROFILE program, used by many colleges to help determine a student's need for financial aid.

College Savings Bank (5 Vaughn Dr., Princeton, NJ 08540-6313; 800-888-2723; www.collegesavings.com). Sells the CollegeSure CD, designed to let parents prepay college education costs, either in a lump sum or in smaller amounts over time. CD pays a variable rate indexed to the change in college costs.

Distance Education & Training Council (1601 18th St., N.W., Suite 2, Washington, DC 20009; 202-234-5100; www.detc.org). The accrediting agency for correspondence schools, which provide lessons for home study, sometimes for degrees. When you complete a lesson, you mail it to the school, where a professor corrects, grades and comments on your work. The assignment is then returned to you, and you move on to the next lesson in the course. Subjects taught by correspondence schools include advertising, bookkeeping, cartooning, desktop publishing, engine tune-up, floristry, gemology, hotel operations, interior decorating, jewelry sales, kindergarten instruction, landscaping, music appreciation, nutrition, oil painting, paralegal work, robotics, screenwriting, travel, VCR repair, window display and yacht design. Its *Directory of Accredited Institutions* can tell you where to find a home-study course teaching the subject in which you are interested. Other free publications offered by the Council include "What Does Accreditation Mean to You?" and "Using Your Distance Education To Earn an Academic Degree."

EduCap (205 Van Buren St., Suite 200, Herndon, VA 20170; 703-709-5626; 800-697-5626; 800-230-4080; www.consern.com and www.uss.org). Sponsors the ConSern Loans for Education program, in which about 5,000 employers offer education loans to their employees at advantageous rates. Loan proceeds can be used for either undergraduate or graduate study. Loan applications and processing are done directly through the main EduCap office in Virginia.

The Education Resources Institute (330 Stuart St., Suite 500, Boston, MA 02117-9123; 781-426-0681; 800-255-8374; www.teri.org). A nonprofit group known as TERI. Offers loans based on creditworthiness, not income limitations or needs. Loans are guaranteed and administered by TERI, and the funds come from participating lending banks. Will send the following free brochures describing these loan programs:

"PLEASE (Parent Loans for Elementary and Secondary Education)"; "Professional Education Plan for Graduate and Professional Study"; "TERI Supplemental Loan Program for Undergraduate and Graduate Study"; and "TERI Continuing Education Loan." TERI offers what they call FONEFUNDS, allowing you to apply for a loan over the phone. Their loans do not require collateral, but they do charge a guarantee fee of between 5 and 10 percent of the loan amount. TERI loan rates are usually close to the prime rate, which is lower than the rates offered by traditional bank lenders.

Key Education Resources (745 Atlantic Ave., Boston, MA 02111-2735; 617-348-0010; 800-KEY-LEND; www.keybank.com/educate.htm). Key is one of America's largest education lenders. They provide federal and private financing options, payment plans, and counseling from prep school through graduate school. Besides the traditional federal Stafford loans and PLUS loans for parents, Key offers private supplemental loans, such as the Key Alternative Loan, which allows undergraduates enrolled full-time to share the cost of their education. Key provides the AchieverLoan to parents with three different ways to finance college or prep school tuitions. The Key Career-Loan is designed for adult students attending college part-time. Key also offers the Monthly Payment Plan, an interest-free budget plan administered through the school that allows families to make equal monthly payments to meet annual expenses. Key provides several programs tailored to graduate students in specific fields such as law, business, medical and dental schools. Key's Web site features KeyScape, a software program allowing you to calculate your estimated family contribution and project a typical budget for repaying loans once you have graduated, among other features.

National Scholarship Research Service (2280 Airport Blvd., Santa Rosa, CA 95403; 707-546-6777; 707-546-6781; 800-432-3782; www.800headstart.com). A databank with more than 250,000 listings of private-sector scholarships, grants, fellowships and loans exceeding $25 billion. If you complete an application listing your educational background and intended area of study, the service—for a fee—will send you a customized list of grant and scholarship possibilities and other related materials.

Nellie Mae (Nellie Mae Inc., 50 Braintree Hill Office Park, Suite 300, Braintree, MA 02184; 800-634-9308; 781-849-1325; www.nelliemae.com). Formerly known as the New England Education Loan Marketing Association, Nellie Mae offers the EXCEL and SHARE student loan programs for undergraduate or graduate study. Nellie Mae also offers a loan consolidation program, allowing you to consolidate several student loans into one manageable payment. Nellie Mae offers two free brochures explaining the college financing process: "Get Ready for College" is designed for parents with children in elementary or junior high school; "Steps to Success" is aimed at those with high-school-age children.

USA Group (P.O. Box 7039, Indianapolis, IN 46207-7039, 30 S. Meridian St., Indianapolis, IN 46204-3503; 317-849-6510; 800-LOAN-USA; 800-562-6872; www. usagroup.com). Does not lend directly to students but guarantees education loans made by lending institutions. Will send a free copy of its "Education Loan Guide," which describes federal loan programs such as the Stafford and PLUS programs. USA also offers a loan consolidation service with no fee, allowing borrowers to consolidate several student loans into one and extending the repayment terms. They offer a free brochure called "In Your Interest: A Common-Sense Guide to Repayment Strategies for Federal Education Loans," which explains different repayment strategies such as ten-year level repayment, long-term level repayment, graduated repayment, income-sensitive repayment and income-contingent repayment, as well as how loan consolidation works. The USA Group's Web site offers calculators to help you figure how much different repayment plans will cost you.

FEDERAL GOVERNMENT REGULATORS

Sallie Mae (formerly Student Loan Marketing Association) (11600 Sallie Mae Dr., Reston, VA 20193; 703-810-3000; www.salliemae.com). Makes a secondary market in student loans and helps students consolidate their existing loans. Offers the SMART LOAN program at 800-524-9100 to enable borrowers to consolidate their student loans. Offers the Great Rewards and Smart Rewards programs, which allow borrowers who repay their loans on time to get a reduction in the interest rate on the remaining balance of their loan. Great Rewards enables Stafford loan borrowers who make their first 48 scheduled monthly payments on time to receive an interest rate reduction of two full percentage points for the remaining term of the loan. Smart Rewards is a similar program for SMART LOAN (consolidation) borrowers who make their first 48 scheduled payments on time. They are rewarded with an interest rate reduction of one full percentage point for the remaining repayment term. The Great Returns program helps heavily indebted Stafford borrowers who make their first 24 scheduled payments on time to receive an account credit equivalent to federal origination fees up to 3 percent (less $250). Another Sallie Mae program is called Direct Repay, which allows you to repay your student loans through an automatic debit on your checking or savings account and earns you a quarter-point interest rate reduction on your loan as long as you make payments through the plan. For questions on these programs or other college financing questions, call Sallie Mae's College Answer line at 888-888-3460.

United States Department of Education (Federal Student Aid Program; 400 Maryland Ave., S.W.; Washington, DC 20202; 800-433-3243; www.ed.gov). Oversees all federal aid programs. Will send brochures titled "Loan Default Blots Your Record" and "The Student Guide: Financial Aid from the U.S. Department of Education," which explains Pell grants, SEOGs, college work-study programs, Perkins loans, Stafford loans and PLUS and SLS loans. Also publishes a useful guide titled *Preparing Your Child for College: A Resource Book for Parents,* available free from the Consumer Information Center (Pueblo, CO 81009). Guide answers questions about college, such as why your child might want to attend college, how to choose a school and how to finance a college education; also lists sources of further information about educational financing programs. Department's Office of Student Assistance will also send a booklet titled *School Shopping Tips: Valuable Information about Choosing a Career, Finding the Right School and Getting Financial Aid for School.* For information on the Education Department's direct loan origination and consolidation program, call the Federal Direct Student Loan Origination Center at 800-557-7392 or 800-557-7394. If you already have an existing loan and have a question about it, you can call the Direct Loan Servicing Center at 800-848-0979.

MILITARY SOURCES OF FINANCIAL AID

Air Force ROTC (HQ/RROO, 551 E. Maxwell Blvd., Maxwell Air Force Base, AL 36112-6106; 205-953-2091; 800-522-0033, ext. 2091; www.thunder.rotc.af.mil), or see a local recruiter. Offers the following free brochures: "Air Force Curriculum Planning Guide"; "The Air Force Puts You Where the Action Is: ROTC Air Force"; "Air Force ROTC and Your Future"; "Air Force ROTC: An Opportunity To Succeed"; "ROTC Scholarships for Medical and Nursing Students"; and "Science and Engineering."

Army ROTC (GoldQUEST Center, P.O. Box 3279, Warminster, PA 18974-0128; national headquarters at Fort Monroe, VA 23651-5238; 800-USA-ROTC; www.tradoc.army.mil/rotc/index.html), or see a local recruiter. Offers the following explanatory brochures: "Army Nursing"; "The Army ROTC Two-Year Program"; "The Facts about Army ROTC"; "Nurse Summer Training Program"; and "Reserve Officers Training Corps: An Investment in Your Future."

Navy and Marines Corps ROTC (250 Dallas St., Naval Air Station, Pensacola, FL 32508-5220; 904-452-4960; 800-NAV-ROTC; www.cnet.navy.mil), or see a local recruiter. Will send a free brochure titled "The Navy-Marine Corps ROTC College Scholarships Bulletin."

PREPAID STATE COLLEGE TUITION PLANS

Many states offer residents the opportunity to prepay college tuition costs at schools anywhere in the country years in advance. These plans allow parents or grandparents to lock in the current price of tuition at the state's participating public or private universities. Most systems allow your child to go to any school in the country. If you choose a nonprogram school, you receive the tuition cost of a program school or a specified rate of return on your investment, typically about 5 percent. For more details on the plans available in your state, contact the programs at these phone numbers:

Alabama Prepaid Affordable College Tuition; 800-252-7228
Alaska Advance College Tuition Payment Plan; 800-478-0003
Colorado Prepaid Tuition Fund; 800-478-5651
Florida Prepaid College Program; 800-552-4723
Illinois Prepaid Tuition Plan; 847-831-8580

Maine Prepaid Tuition Plan; 207-287-2771
Maryland Prepaid College Trust; 888-463-4723
Massachusetts U-Plan; 800-449-6332
Michigan Education Trust; 800-638-4543
Mississippi Prepaid Affordable College Tuition Plan; 888-987-4450
Missouri Prepaid Tuition Plan; 573-751-2411
Nevada Prepaid College Tuition Plan Trust Fund; 702-687-5200
Ohio Tuition Trust Authority; 800-233-6734
Oregon Prepaid Tuition Plan; 503-378-4329
Pennsylvania Tuition Account Program; 800-440-4000
South Carolina Tuition Prepayment Program; 803-253-6217
Tennessee BEST Program; 888-486-2378
Texas Tomorrow Fund; 800-445-4723
Virginia Higher Education Tuition Trust Fund; 888-567-0540
West Virginia Prepaid College Plan; 304-558-5000
Wisconsin Education Investment (EDVEST) Plan; 888-338-3789

STATE COLLEGE SAVINGS PROGRAMS

Many states offer plans in which residents can save money for college expenses and also get a tax break. The money in the account accumulates tax deferred. Even though the assets are held in the name of the parents, they are taxed at the child's lower tax rate when they matriculate in school. Most state programs keep the money in conservative investments like Treasury securities and therefore pay a relatively low rate of return. Other states, such as Indiana, invest the money in a mix of stocks and bonds, offering participants higher potential rates of return, though with more risk. Check with your state to see how the money is invested.

Arizona Family College Savings Account; 602-229-2592
Arkansas Tax Deferred Tuition Savings Plan; 501-682-5888
California College Savings Plan; 916-526-7294
Connecticut Higher Education Trust; 888-799-2438
Delaware College Savings Program; 302-577-3240
Georgia HOPE Scholarship Program; 800-776-6878
Indiana Family College Savings Act; 888-814-6800
Iowa College Savings Plan; 515-281-8261
Kentucky Educational Savings Plan Trust; 800-338-0318
Louisiana START Program; 800-259-5626
Minnesota College Tuition Savings Program; 800-657-3866
Montana Family Education Savings Program; 406-444-0610
New Hampshire College Savings Plan; 603-271-2621
New Jersey Better Educational Savings Trust; 800-792-8670
New Mexico College Savings Plan; 505-827-6226

New York College Choice Tuition Savings Program; 518-473-9009
North Carolina College Vision Fund; 919-834-2893
Rhode Island College Savings Plan; 401-277-2397
Utah Educational Savings Plan Trust; 800-418-2551
Vermont Higher Education Savings Plan; 802-655-9602

STATE FINANCIAL AID AGENCIES

In many cases, you might be able to qualify for financial aid designed for state residents going to in-state schools. The following is a list of each state's financial aid office, which can direct you to what is available in your state and how to apply for it.

Alabama Commission on Higher Education, 100 N. Union St., Montgomery, AL 36130-2000; 334-242-1998

Alaska Commission on Post-Secondary Education, 3030 Vintage Blvd., Juneau, AK 99801; 907-465-2962; 800-441-2962

Arizona Commission on Post-Secondary Education, 2020 N. Central Ave., Phoenix, AZ 85004; 602-229-2591

Arkansas Department of Higher Education, 114 E. Capitol, Little Rock, AR 72201; 501-371-2000; 800-54-STUDY

California Student Aid Commission, P.O. Box 510845, Sacramento, CA 94245; 916-445-0880

Colorado Commission on Higher Education, 1300 Broadway, Denver, CO 80203; 303-866-2723

Connecticut Department of Higher Education, 61 Woodland St., Hartford, CT 06105; 860-566-5766

Delaware Higher Education Commission, 820 N. French St., Wilmington, DE 19801; 302-577-3240

District of Columbia Office of Postsecondary Education, 2100 Martin Luther King Jr. Ave., Washington, DC 20020; 202-727-3685

Florida Department of Education, Office of Student Financial Assistance, 325 W. Gaines St., Tallahassee, FL 32399; 850-487-0649

Georgia Student Finance Commission, 2082 E. Exchange Pl., Tucker, GA 30084; 800-546-4673

Hawaii State Postsecondary Education Commission, 2444 Dole St., Honolulu, HI 96822; 808-956-6624

Idaho State Board of Education, 650 W. State St., Boise, ID 83720; 208-334-2270

Illinois Student Assistance Commission, 1755 Lake Cook Rd., Deerfield, IL 60015; 847-948-8550; 800-899-4722

Indiana State Student Assistance Commission, 150 W. Market St., Indianapolis, IN 46204; 317-232-2350

Iowa College Student Aid Commission, 200 Tenth St., Des Moines, IA 50309; 515-281-3501; 800-383-4222

Kansas Board of Regents, 700 SW Harrison, Topeka, KS 66603; 913-296-3517

Kentucky Higher Education Assistance Authority, 1050 U.S. 127 S., Frankfort, KY 40601; 502-564-7990; 800-928-8926

Louisiana Student Financial Assistance Commission, P.O. Box 91202, Baton Rouge, LA 70821; 504-922-9202; 800-259-5626

Maine Finance Authority, 119 State House Station, Augusta, ME 04333; 207-626-8200; 800-228-3734

Maryland Higher Education Commission, 16 Frances St., Annapolis, MD 21401; 410-974-5370

Massachusetts Higher Education Coordination Council, 330 Stuart St., Boston, MA 02116; 617-727-9420

Michigan Higher Education Assistance Authority Office of Scholarships and Grants, P.O. Box 30462, Lansing, MI 48909; 517-373-3394

Minnesota Higher Education Services Office, 550 Cedar St., St. Paul, MN 55101; 612-296-3974; 800-657-3866

Mississippi State Insitutions of Higher Learning Financial Assistance Board, 3825 Ridgewood Rd., Jackson, MS 39211; 601-982-6623; 800-327-2980

Missouri Coordinating Board for Higher Education, 3515 Amazonas Dr., Jefferson City, MO 65109; 573-751-2361

Montana University System, 2500 Broadway, Helena, MT 59620; 406-444-6570

Nebraska Coordinating Commission for Postsecondary Education, 140 N. Eighth St., Lincoln, NE 68509; 402-471-2847

Nevada Office of Financial Aid, University of Nevada-Reno, Reno, NV 89557; 702-784-6181

New Hampshire Postsecondary Education Commission, 2 Industrial Park Dr., Concord, NH 03301; 603-271-2555

New Jersey Office of Student Financial Assistance, 4 Quakerbridge Plaza, Trenton, NJ 08625; 609-588-3268; 800-792-8670

New Mexico Commission on Higher Education, 1068 Cerrillos Rd., Santa Fe, NM 87501; 505-827-7383; 800-279-9777

New York State Higher Education Services Corporation, One Commerce Plaza, Albany, NY 12255; 518-473-7087

North Carolina State Education Assistance Authority, P.O. Box 2688, Chapel Hill, NC 27515; 919-549-8614; 800-700-1775

North Dakota Student Financial Assistance Program, 600 E. Boulevard Ave., Bismarck, ND 58505; 701-328-2960

Ohio Student Aid Commission, 309 S. Fourth St., Columbus, OH 43218; 614-644-5230

Oklahoma Tuition Aid Grant Program, 500 Education Building State Capitol Complex, Oklahoma City, OK 73105; 405-524-9120

Oregon State Scholarship Commission, 1500 Valley River Dr., Eugene, OR 97401; 541-687-7400

Pennsylvania Higher Education Assistance Agency, 1200 N. Seventh St., Harrisburg, PA 17102; 717-720-2800; 800-692-7435

Rhode Island Higher Education Assistance Authority, 560 Jefferson Blvd., Warwick, RI 02886; 401-736-1100; 800-922-9855

South Carolina Higher Education Tuition Grants Commission, 1310 Lady St., Columbia, SC 29201; 803-734-1200

South Dakota Department of Education and Cultural Affairs, 700 Governors Dr., Pierre, SD 57501; 605-773-3134

Tennessee Higher Education Commission, 404 James Robertson Pkwy., Nashville, TN 37243; 615-741-1346; 800-447-1523

Texas Higher Education Coordinating Board, P.O. Box 12788, Capitol Station, Austin, TX 78711; 512-427-6340

Utah Education Assistance Authority, 355 W. North Temple, Salt Lake City, UT 84180; 801-321-7200; 800-418-8757

Vermont Student Assistance Corporation, Champlain Mill, P.O. Box 2000, Winooski, VT 05404; 802-655-9602

Virginia State Council of Higher Education, James Monroe Building, 101 N. Fourteenth St., Richmond, VA 23219; 804-225-2137

Washington State Higher Education Coordinating Board, 917 Lakeridge Way, SW, Olympia, WA 98504; 360-753-7850

West Virginia College and University System, 1018 Kanawha Blvd. E., Charleston, WV 25301; 304-599-2691

Wisconsin Higher Educational Aids Board, P.O. Box 7885, Madison, WI 53707; 608-267-2208

Wyoming Community College Commission, 2020 Carey Ave., Cheyenne, WY 82002; 307-777-7763

WEB SITES

CollegeEdge. Scholarship search Web site giving you access to thousands of colleges and scholarship opportunities. You fill out a short questionnaire, allowing the Web site to match your qualifications to the available sources of financial aid. The site also has details on tuition and fees at many colleges, financial aid application forms and payment plans. www.CollegeEdge.com

College Express. This site presents information on hundreds of private colleges and universities. It also has an extensive section on the financial aid process, including the best ways to apply for federal and college-based aid and how to negotiate a lower tuition cost from the school. www.collegexpress.com

College Funding Company. This nonprofit issuer of private and student loans explains its offerings on this Web site. Their primary loan is the Flexible College Funding Loan, designed to cover college costs not paid by a regular financial aid package. The site also includes various calculators, such as how much you need to be saving to meet college costs depending on your child's age and the rate of return on your investments. For more information on this company, you also can call 800-745-6646. www.collegefundingco.org/

Department of Education's Office of Postsecondary Education. The federal government's site allows you to file your Free Application for Federal Student Aid (FAFSA) online. The site offers detailed instructions on filling out the form and is loaded with links to colleges and other financial-aid-related Web sites. Part of this site is called FAFSA Express, at www.ed.gov/offices/OPE/express.html, which allows you to complete and electronically submit the FAFSA form and get it processed quicker than the old-fashioned paper form. If you have questions about filling out these forms, you can call the FAFSA Service Center at 800-801-0576. The site also has information on the DOE's Direct Loan program at www.ed.gov/offices/OPE/DirectLoan/. www.ed.gov/offices/OPE/Students

Dollars for Scholars. The Dollars for Scholars pages from *U.S. News and World Report*'s annual college edition provide a list of what the magazine evaluates as the best college values. Another part of the site guides you through the financial aid process. The Answer Zone answers frequently asked questions about financing college. The site also lists other financial aid Web sites, a loan center and much more. www.usnews.com/usnews/edu/dollars/dshome.htm

Educational Resources Information Center. This federally funded center's site acts as a clearinghouse for an enormous amount of educational information. You can find publications, sources of financing and discussions of college admissions procedures. www.eryx.syr.edu

FastWEB! (Financial Aid Search Through the Web). This site allows you to conduct a personalized search of potential loans and scholarships you or you child may qualify for. You fill in a detailed form about you or your child, and the site searches its vast database for financing options, with the details about each program. For more information on fastWEB, call 800-327-8932. www.fastweb.com

FinAid: The Financial Aid Information Page. A comprehensive site sponsored by the National Association of Student Financial Aid Administrators (NASFAA), allowing you to ask questions of financial aid counselors and track down whatever information you need about financial aid. There are sections on loans, government programs, schools, special interests and vendors, each linking to a variety of relevant Web sites. There are other links allowing you to search for scholarships, loans, fellowships, grants and other tuition payment plans that you might qualify for. The site has 15 calculators, allowing parents, for example, to figure out how much colleges will cost, how much schools will expect you to pay and how much you can expect in financial aid. The Student Loan Advisor will calculate the maximum loan payment students will be able to handle given their expected career. www.finaid.com

KapLoan. This site sponsored by the Kaplan test-preparation company offers information on loans and an online form to request more information about a specific source of aid. The site also includes the KapLoan Financial Contribution Estimator, which displays your Expected Family Contribution after you have entered your income, expenses and assets. The site also offers Application Editing, in which staff members look over your financial aid application for incorrect or missing data, and Credit Pre-Approval, in which you are told if you are likely to receive the loan you are applying for. www.kaploan.com

Parent Soup's Guide to College Planning. This site for parents has extensive resources on finding the best college and financing college education. www.parent soup.com

Peterson's Education Center. The publisher of many financial aid books has a useful site explaining the entire process. There is a college admissions calendar reminding you of various filing deadlines, a glossary of terms and definitions of various types of financial aid. www.petersons.com

RSP Funding Focus. Reference Service Press provides a one-stop information resource for scholarships, fellowships, loans, grants, awards and internships. The site features a financial aid library, a listing of state financial aid agencies and a mailing list you can get on that provides a free electronic newsletter filled with the latest information about financial aid programs. You also can contact RSP at 5000 Windplay Dr., Suite 4, Eldorado Hills, CA 95762; 916-939-9620. RSP also publishes two books titled *Financial Aid for the Disabled and Their Families* and *High School Senior's Guide to Merit and Other No-Need Funding.* www.rspfunding.com; on America Online type keyword RSP

Student Services. A commercial database with tens of thousands of financial aid and scholarship sources, mostly in the private sector, that you can search through using your student's characteristics. For more information, you can call them at 847-785-8000. www.studentservices.com/search

13

The Basics of
Tax Planning

Taxes are probably the most unpleasant aspect of personal finance. However, just because you do not like thinking about how much you must pay in federal, state and local taxes every year does not mean that you should avoid the subject. If you pay little or no attention to the tax consequences of every financial move you make, you will certainly owe the government more money, not less. On the other hand, if you learn basic tax-saving strategies, you can maximize the amount of money you spend and invest while you minimize your tax bite.

If you concentrate on learning the thousands of pages of complex tax laws and regulations, you will surely be overwhelmed. The fact is, most obscure tax laws do not apply to the typical taxpayer. However, you should understand basic tax strategies, know how to file your taxes and implement the best methods to cut your tax bill, including legal deductions, credits and other tax-sheltered plans. Even if a tax preparation professional fills out your return, you are the one who must act in a tax-smart manner throughout the year. (For more on choosing a tax expert, see Chapter 17, "Finding Financial Advisers Who Are Right for You.")

The Basics of Filing a Tax Return

The first rule of taxes is that you must file a return if your gross income meets certain minimums. Over the years, millions of people have not filed for many reasons. Some protest that the government has no legal right to impose taxes. Others claim that filing taxes violates their religious beliefs. And other less high-minded Americans simply think that they will go unnoticed if they don't submit a return.

Whatever the excuse, it won't work with the IRS. There never has been, and probably never will be, a court ruling upholding the right of anyone to refuse to file a tax return. (If such a court ruling were ever handed down, everyone would try to find a way to qualify for the exception.) The requirement to file is absolute.

As mentioned, the government sets minimum income levels. You must file a federal return if your gross income exceeds the following amounts, which are adjusted annually.

- *Single:* Younger than age 65, $6,800; age 65 or older, $7,800

- *Married, filing jointly:* Both spouses younger than age 65, $12,200; one spouse age 65 or older, $13,000; both spouses age 65 or older, $13,800. (A married couple will almost always pay less tax if they file jointly.)

- *Married, filing separately:* All ages, $2,650. (A couple might file separately if they like to keep their financial affairs distinct).

- *Head of household:* Younger than age 65, $8,700; age 65 or older, $9,700. (You can claim to be the head of a household if you are single and pay for at least half the cost of keeping an unmarried child or grandchild in your home. You can also file as the head of a household if you support and claim as a dependent your married children or grandchildren, your parents or another close relative.)

- *Widow or widower supporting a dependent child:* Younger than age 65, $9,550; age 65 or older, $10,350

Even if you do not earn a gross income high enough to qualify under any of these income categories, you must file a return if you meet any of the following conditions.

- You have self-employment earnings of $400 or more.

- You are due a refund from withheld wages because (1) you qualify for the earned income credit for low-income working families or (2) you received an earned income credit payment from your employer.

- You are subject to the alternative minimum tax (AMT).

- You owe tax or paid a penalty for withdrawing money from an individual retirement account (IRA) or other qualified retirement plan before age 59½.

- You owe Social Security taxes on income earned from tips (if, for example, you are a waiter).

- You are a nonresident alien with an American business or you owe taxes that have not been covered by withholding.

If you legally must file but don't and the IRS catches you, not only will you pay hefty fines; you may end up in prison. The harshest penalties are imposed for fraudulently failing to file. In this case, you may pay up to 75 percent of what you owe in *addition* to the amount you owe. If you file late, you must pay 5 percent of the amount you owe for each month you are tardy—up to 25 percent of the taxes you owe—on top of interest and negligence penalties. If you file but don't remit the taxes due, you must pay a ½ percent per month up to 25 percent of what you owe. Therefore, you should file your return even if you don't have the money to pay your taxes because the penalties for not paying are lighter than the fines for not filing at all. The more you try to evade the IRS, the harder they will judge you.

If you can't file your return by the April 15 deadline, obtain an extension using Form 4868. This will automatically give you until August 15 to file. An extension does not mean that you don't have to remit your tax bill on April 15, however. You must pay based on your best estimate of what you will owe.

Electronic filing of tax returns has become increasingly popular, particularly with those taxpayers to whom the IRS owes a refund. Many accountants now offer the service for a fee of $25 to $50, or you can file electronically through a national tax service such as H&R Block. Many of these tax services will actually lend you your refund money up front, collecting your refund when it arrives. However, this instant gratification comes at a high price. The effective interest rate charged by such rapid refund services can be extremely high—such as 30 percent or more—even though the loan term is only a few weeks. Unless you need your refund money immediately, wait the few weeks and obtain your full refund.

TAX RATES

Depending on your filing status (single, married, etc.), different levels of income are taxed at different rates. The United States has a *marginal tax rate system*, which means that all income up to a certain limit is taxed at one rate. Income over that limit and under the next limit is taxed at a higher rate, and so on. Over the years, there have been many marginal rates and brackets as the government has expanded and contracted these numbers to generate more income. For example, the Tax Reform Act of 1986 greatly reduced the number of brackets, as well as the tax rates. Since then, both the number of brackets and the rates have been creeping upward. The Revenue Reconciliation Act of 1993 (RRA '93) added another marginal bracket of 36 percent, as well as a 10 percent surtax, which in effect created a fifth bracket of 39.6 percent. Each year, the income that qualifies in each bracket is adjusted upward slightly for inflation. Figure 13.1 shows the tax rates and brackets that applied in 1997.

DEFINING YOUR INCOME

When you determine how much you must pay on your income, examine what constitutes income under the tax rules. Three broad categories of income exist: *gross, adjusted gross* and *taxable.*

Gross income. This is the income you receive on which taxes are due before you take any deductions, credits or exemptions. The main components of gross income include wages and salary, interest from bonds and bank accounts, dividends from stocks and mutual funds, tips, alimony, pension payments, rent you collect, royalties you've earned and any other money you receive from working

Figure 13.1
1997 Tax Rates and Brackets

Filing Status	Marginal Tax Rate	Taxable Income
Single	15%	$ 1 to $24,650
	28	24,651 to 59,750
	31	59,751 to 124,650
	36*	124,651 to 271,050
	39.6*	271,050 and up
Married, filing jointly	15%	$ 1 to $41,200
	28	41,201 to 99,600
	31	99,601 to 151,750
	36*	151,751 to 271,050
	39.6*	271,050 and up
Married, filing separately	15%	$ 1 to $20,600
	28	20,601 to 49,800
	31	49,801 to 75,875
	36*	75,876 to 135,525
	39.6*	135,525 and up
Head of household	15%	$ 1 to $33,050
	28	33,051 to 85,350
	31	85,351 to 138,200
	36*	138,201 to 271,050
	39.6*	271,050 and up

*On taxable income greater than $271,050, there is a surtax that raises the effective rate to 39.6 percent. The 36 percent bracket and the surtax are indexed for inflation annually.

or investing. Some money is excluded from gross income, including interest from tax-exempt municipal bonds and bond mutual funds that hold such bonds; insurance settlements from personal injuries or death benefits; and reimbursement of health insurance claims.

Adjusted gross income (AGI). Your AGI is your total gross income minus any allowable losses generated from the operation of a business, the sale of a capital asset, any passive-activity losses and certain partnership and shareholder interest. Deductible contributions to qualified retirement plans such as IRAs and Keoghs also are used in computing your AGI.

Taxable income. You calculate the taxable income by subtracting all your exemptions and deductions from your adjusted gross income. These deductions might include unreimbursed employee business expenses or medical bills, mortgage interest or moving expenses. Taxable income is the income on which you pay taxes.

LEGAL DEDUCTIONS

To lower your taxable income, you will want to take steps to qualify for as many deductions as possible. Remember, however, when you take a deduction, it lowers your taxes by your marginal tax rate. Therefore, the lower the tax rate, the less money you save from each deduction.

To take an oversimplified example, if you have $1,000 worth of mortgage interest deductions and pay taxes at a 50 percent marginal rate, the value of the deductions is $500. If your tax rate drops to 30 percent, the value of that same $1,000 is $300. So when you pursue deductions, keep in mind how much they will actually save you in taxes.

Each year, everyone qualifies for the standard deduction, which is a part of your income on which you do not pay taxes. In 1997, a single person could claim a standard deduction of $4,150; a head of household, $6,050; a married couple filing jointly, $6,900 and a married couple filing separately, $3,450. A person age 65 or older or blind could add as much as $1,000 to the standard deduction. People who are claimed as dependents by others receive a $650 standard deduction, unless they have earned income of more than $650. Each year, these amounts are adjusted slightly for inflation.

If your individual deductions total more than your standard deduction, it makes sense to itemize those individual deductions. However, if your income is too high (according to IRS standards), you do not get the full benefit of your deductions. If your adjusted gross income is more than $121,200 for a married couple filing jointly, or $60,600 for a married couple filing separately, some of your itemized deductions are disallowed. To figure out how much, you should first total up your itemized deductions under the regular rules. Then subtract deductions generated by medical and dental expenses, investment interest, and casualty, theft and gambling losses. The remaining deductions are reduced by 3 percent of the amount of your AGI over the $121,200 threshold. The higher your income, the less the deductions are worth. In effect, this reduction in the value of your deductions increases the taxes you pay on each extra dollar of income you earn.

With these limitations in mind, the following are some of the most common deductions that you can take under current federal tax law.

Casualty and theft losses. If you have suffered a major property loss due to damage or theft and are not reimbursed by an insurance policy, you may qualify for a deduction. First, you must deduct the loss in the year it occurred even if you do not repair or replace the property that year. Damage loss must be the result of a sudden, destructive force like a hurricane or tornado rather than progressive deterioration taking place over several years. Theft loss qualifies for a deduction. Make sure to file a stolen property report with the police documenting a break-in, or obtain testimony from neighbors who saw someone suspicious near your home or car. You may not claim a theft loss deduction if you have no proof that your property was stolen. Generally, you can claim a theft deduction if you were a victim of fraud, embezzlement or riots or if you had to pay ransom to a kidnapper.

Even if you have suffered a casualty or theft loss, you may not be able to deduct it if the loss isn't costly enough. You can deduct such losses only if they exceed 10 percent of your AGI. In addition, each loss has a $100 floor, so you can deduct only the amount over $100.

Charitable contributions. You can deduct contributions made to qualified charities in cash, securities, real estate or physical property. If you contribute at least $250 to a charity, you must get a written receipt from the organization to substantiate your claim—a cancelled check is not enough proof for the IRS. If you do volunteer work for a qualified charity, you can deduct your unreimbursed expenses. If you donate property such as clothing or furniture to a charity and that property is worth more than $500, you must attach Form 8283 to your 1040 form. If you donate property and claim a deduction of more than $5,000, you should attach a written appraisal supporting your claim. The amount you can deduct as a charitable contribution is limited to 50 percent of your AGI in cash or 30 percent of your AGI in capital assets such as stocks or bonds. You not only get a deduction for their current market value; you also escape taxation on any capital gains you have earned on these investments.

Interest expenses. Five kinds of interest that you pay can generate deductions: home mortgage interest, points on a mortgage, interest on business loans, investment interest and interest on student loans. Consumer interest, such as the interest you pay on credit cards or on car or personal loans, is no longer deductible.

Home mortgage interest on your first and second homes is fully deductible. However, the total amount of loans on which interest is deductible is limited to $1.1 million if you assumed the loans after October 13, 1987. That limit comprises $1 million of straight mortgage debt for married couples filing jointly ($500,000 if married filing separately) and $100,000 of home equity loans if filing jointly, or $50,000 if filing separately.

Points—the up-front fees charged by lenders on a mortgage—are deductible because they are considered a form of prepaid mortgage interest. They are usually deductible over the term of the loan, but may also be deductible in a lump sum the year you paid them. If you use the loan to buy or improve your principal residence, the bank computes the points as a percentage of the loan and calls it either "points," "loan origination fees" or "loan discount," and you pay the points directly to the lender. Points are not deductible if the fees you are paying are for other lender services such as appraisals or mortgage document preparation fees.

Interest on business loans is deductible because it is considered an expense of doing business. Interest should be listed on Schedule C as one of the many expenses of running your business.

Investment interest, paid on margin accounts to brokerage firms, is deductible up to the amount of net investment income you earn that year. If you pay more investment interest than you earn in income from stocks, bonds and mutual funds, you can carry the interest forward to offset next year's investment income. Interest you pay to buy tax-free municipal bonds is not deductible. You are generally prohibited from offsetting investment interest expenses with capital gains generated by selling stocks or bonds.

Students paying interest on student loans can claim an "above-the-line" deduction (deducted from gross income) of up to $1,000. Loans to pay higher educational expenses for yourself, a spouse or a dependent qualify. The deduction is allowed only for the first 60 months (five years) the loan is outstanding. After five years, the deduction no longer applies. This deduction increases to $1,500 in 1999, $2,000 in 2000 and is capped at $2,500 in 2001. There are income limitations on who can claim this deduction: Singles with modified adjusted gross income under $40,000 can get the full deduction, and it is phased out up to $55,000. For married couples filing jointly, the phaseout begins at $60,000 and extends to $75,000. Therefore, singles with incomes over $55,000 and couples earning over $75,000 will not qualify for this deduction. Students claimed as dependents by their parents cannot claim this deduction.

Medical expenses. You can deduct unreimbursed medical expenses that exceed 7.5 percent of your AGI. The IRS has issued a long list of the medical expenses that are deductible. In general, they include the services of a licensed specialist such as a neurologist, pediatrician or surgeon; dental services such as x-rays, cleaning and tooth extraction; medical equipment such as braces, crutches, hearing aids and wheelchairs; medical treatments such as blood transfusions, insulin treatments and organ transplants; prescription drugs; lab tests; hospital bills; and premiums for health care insurance and long-term health care expenses for the chronically ill.

Medical treatments you cannot deduct are generally performed for cosmetic or quasi-medical reasons and are not prescribed by a doctor. Athletic club fees, ear piercing, maternity clothes, tattooing and weight loss programs are all nondeductible.

State, local and foreign taxes. You can deduct any income taxes you have paid to your state, your locality or a foreign government. In addition, all state, local and foreign real estate taxes are deductible on your federal return. If you hold shares in a cooperative apartment building, you can deduct your shares' worth of the property taxes paid by the co-op. Finally, all state and local personal property taxes generate federal tax deductions. If you live in a high-tax state or locality, these taxes can add up to a significant deduction.

Miscellaneous expense deductions. The IRS has approved as deductibles many other expenses, all falling in the miscellaneous category. To qualify for this deduction category, however, all miscellaneous expenses must total at least 2 percent of your AGI. You can deduct any amount over that threshold. For example, if your AGI is $10,000, all qualified expenses exceeding $200 are deductible. If your income is $50,000, expenses exceeding $1,000 would qualify as deductions. And if your AGI is $200,000, you can deduct expenses of more than $4,000.

In general, the expenses that qualify as deductions are those related to the performance of your job for which your employer will not reimburse you. Some examples follow.

- *Dues and subscriptions to professional organizations and publications,* including professional societies, trade associations, stock exchanges and unions.

- *Uniforms and work clothes necessary to perform your job.* For example, you can claim a deduction for special clothing if you work as a pilot, baseball player, firefighter, letter carrier or railroad conductor.

- *Expenses you incur while looking for a new job.* Only expenses related to finding a job in the same line of work are deductible. For example, travel costs associated with job interviews or printing of resumes generates a deduction.

- *Equipment required by your employer,* including computers, cellular phones, fax machines, copiers, calculators, typewriters, special tools and a car. Costs associated with personal use of the equipment, including commuting to work in your company car are not deductible.

- *Home office expenses.* If your office at home is your primary place of business and where you meet clients, you can deduct your expenses for the separate work space. The IRS is strict about home office expenses; therefore, follow its guidelines closely when claiming deductions. Starting in 1999, you can claim deductions for an office in your home where you perform only administrative or management activities for your business if you do not perform these activities elsewhere. You are allowed a home office deduction even if you provide services to customers or patients at another location outside your home. Employees are allowed the home office deduction only if the office is for the convenience of the employer.

- *Education required by your job,* including tuition for courses taken to maintain or improve your job skills or to retain professional certification.

- *Investment and tax advice expenses.* You can deduct the costs of investing, including bank and brokerage account fees, investment management fees, subscriptions to investment publications and travel costs incurred while inspecting rental property that you own. Also deductible are fees charged by tax preparers and accountants.

- *Legal fees.* Legal expenses are generally deductible if the dispute arises either in the course of your business or employment or involves income-producing property. Legal expenses for personal matters are generally not deductible.

- *Business travel and entertainment expenses not reimbursed by your employer.* You can deduct 100 percent of the cost of business travel, including airfare and hotels but only 50 percent of the cost of meals and entertainment.

- *Moving expenses.* If you move at least 50 miles from one residence to another when you take a new job, some moving expenses are deductible, assuming that your employer does not reimburse you for them. The main expenses that qualify are the costs, including travel, of moving your household from one residence to another. Moving expenses are an "above-the-line" deduction like alimony, so you do not have to itemize your return to qualify for the tax break.

PERSONAL AND FAMILY EXEMPTIONS

You can claim at least one exemption for everyone in your household. In 1997, each exemption equaled a deduction of $2,650 (an amount adjusted slightly for inflation each year). If you are married with dependent children, you can claim an exemption for yourself, your spouse and each of your children. You can also claim an exemption for a dependent parent living with you. (The parent is a dependent if you provided at least 50 percent of his or her income in the past year.)

In the case of divorce, the exemptions for any children automatically go to the parent who has custody. If this parent signs an agreement, he or she can give the exemptions to the noncustodial parent.

For certain high-income taxpayers, exemptions are phased out at various levels of AGI. For example, for a married couple filing jointly, you start to lose your exemption if your AGI totals $181,800 ($90,900 for a married couple filing separately). If you are single, the value of your exemption diminishes when you report an AGI of $121,200, and for heads of households at $151,500. You reduce the dollar value of your exemptions by 2 percent for each $2,500 that your AGI exceeds the threshold. For married couples filing jointly, the exemption disappears completely if the reported AGI is over $304,300. For married couples filing separately, the exemption is gone if AGI is over $152,150.

TAX CREDITS

The best tax-saving device is a *tax credit,* which lowers your tax bill by one dollar for every dollar of credit you receive. Therefore, if you receive a $1,000 credit, you can take $1,000 off your tax bill. A tax credit is far better than a deduction, which lowers your taxes only by your marginal tax rate.

The credit for which you are most likely to qualify pertains to dependent and child care expenses. This tax break is designed to help ease the financial burden of caring for dependents. If you pay for more than half the yearly expenses of a child or another dependent, such as a parent, you can qualify for a credit based on a percentage of your expenses.

The earned income tax credit either reduces your taxes or can result in a refund if you earn too little to owe taxes. In 1997, if you had one child, you could claim the credit if your earned income, such as wages, or your adjusted gross income was less than $25,760. If you had two or more children, you qualified for the credit if your income was less than $29,290. You don't have to have children to claim the credit. If you are childless and earned under $9,770, you still qualify. The more you earn, the less credit you receive. The maximum credit for a one-child family was $2,210, while the top credit for a two-child family was $3,656 and $332 is the most you can get if you are childless. To find out what credit you may qualify for, look at the IRS Earned Income Credit (EIC) tables, which are updated annually.

Adoption credit. You can earn a credit up to $5,000 if you adopt a child under age 18, or someone who is mentally or physically handicapped. Such a "special needs" child adoption can qualify for a $6,000 tax credit. That credit is phased out if your adjusted gross income is between $75,000 and $115,000. To claim these adoption credits, you must show what your adoption expenses included, such as attorney's costs and court fees.

Child tax credit. Starting in 1998, you can claim a tax credit of $400 for each child you support under age 17. The child must be a U.S. citizen and can be your own child, a grandchild, stepchild or foster child who you can claim as a dependent. The credit increases to $500 for tax year 1999 and every year thereafter. However, the credit is phased out if your modified adjusted gross income is more than $110,000 for a married couple filing jointly, $55,000 for a married couple filing separately and $75,000 for single parents. For each $1,000 of adjusted gross income over those limits, the credit is reduced by $50. So, for a married couple filing jointly, the credit disappears if their AGI exceeds $119,000.

Education tax credits. The Hope Scholarship Credit is available for expenses incurred in the first two years of postsecondary education. The credit became effective in 1998 and is a maximum of $1,500 per student per year. The credit can be used to offset tuition and related expenses such as registration fees, but not for room and board. The Lifetime Learning Credit applies to tuition costs for undergraduates, graduates and those improving their job skills through a training program, even through a part-time program, starting June 30, 1998. This credit is worth up to 20 percent of up to $5,000 of qualified expenses, or $1,000. Starting in the year 2002, the credit increases to a maximum of 20 percent of $10,000 in expenses, or $2,000. There are income limitations on who can benefit from both these credits. For married couples filing jointly, the credits start to phase out when modified adjusted gross income reaches $80,000 and are completely phased out once income hits $100,000. The phaseout range for singles is $40,000 to $50,000.

Elderly and disabled credit. You may qualify for a tax credit if you are age 65 or older and earn a low income or you have a permanent disability preventing you from working. The tax credit you can get is 15 percent of the base amount provided under the law. If you are single, the head of a household or a widow or widower, or you file a joint return and only one spouse is eligible for the credit, the base amount is $5,000. If you file a joint return and both spouses are eligible, the base amount is $7,500. If you are married and file separately, the base amount is $3,750.

For those with permanent disabilities who are under age 65, the base amount is the base amount listed above or last year's disability income, whichever is less. For example, if you are single and received $4,800 in disability income, you would figure the credit based on $4,800 instead of the $5,000 for singles.

Business tax credits. If you run a business, the government offers various tax credits as incentives to hire disadvantaged people and invest in certain areas. In the hiring arena, there are credits for hiring the disabled, those in empowerment zones, Native Americans and former welfare recipients who have just started to work under the "welfare-to-work" program. Other credits are available for businesses who invest in research and development, electric vehicles, low-income housing, enhanced oil recovery and renewable electricity production or who contribute to community development corporations.

Two kinds of real estate partnerships qualify for credits.

Low-income housing. If you invest in a limited partnership that either builds new low-income housing or substantially rehabilitates existing low-income housing that was put into service after 1986, you can obtain a credit. You claim the tax credit for ten years in annual installments, using Form 8586. The housing agency that certifies that you deserve the credit does so on Form 8609.

Certified historic housing. You can earn a credit of 20 percent of your investment when you participate in a partnership that rehabilitates certified historic structures built before 1936. You can earn a 10 percent credit for investing in a partnership that restores buildings built before 1936 that have not been certified as historic by the Department of the Interior. You must spend at least $5,000 in renovation costs to qualify for the credit.

CAPITAL GAINS AND LOSSES

If you sell an asset like a stock, bond or mutual fund for a profit, you must pay capital gains tax on that profit. Under current law, you are taxed at a maximum rate of 20 percent on the gain if you have held the asset for at least 18 months. That 20 percent maximum tax rate is far preferable to the maximum marginal tax rate of 39.6 percent on regular income. That 20 percent maximum rate applies to people whose regular top tax brackets are 28 percent, 31 percent, 36 percent and 39.6 percent. For those in the 15 percent tax bracket, the capital gains rate is even more advantageous—10 percent. So the tax code provides a large incentive for you to invest in assets that generate capital gains instead of regular income, such as dividends or interest.

If you held the asset you sold for more than 18 months, report the profit as a long-term capital gain. If you owned it for less than 18 months, report the profit as a short-term capital gain. Long-term gains pay the maximum 20 percent tax rate. Short-term gains pay regular income tax rates. Starting in the year 2000, you can qualify for an even lower capital gains rate if you hold onto an asset for at least 5 years. For assets bought after January 1, 2000 and held at least five years, the maximum capital gains rate is 18 percent (instead of 20 percent) and for those in the 15 percent tax bracket, the maximum capital gains tax rate is merely 8 percent (instead of 10 percent).

If, instead of choosing a winning stock, you select a loser, you can still squeeze some tax benefit out of the capital loss. Married couples filing jointly can deduct up to $3,000 in such losses from capital gains ($1,500 for married couples filing separately), thereby reducing capital gains taxes. If you have no gains to offset your losses, you can deduct up to $3,000 ($1,500 for married filing separately) from your ordinary income. If you still have losses left over, you can carry them to future years to offset capital gains and regular income. Using tax losses to reduce your tax bill should make you feel a little better about investments that do not work out as you hope.

Another way to reduce capital gains is to arrange an installment sale, in which you sell an asset over a period of years in order to stretch out your tax payments.

Special rules apply to capital gains and losses when you sell your primary residence. If you sold your home or cooperative apartment on May 7, 1997 or later for a profit of up to $500,000 for a married couple filing jointly, or up to $250,000 for a single, you owe no capital gains tax. You can sell your primary residence without capital gains taxes every two years. The IRS defines your primary residence as a home in which you have lived for at least two of the past five years. This rule, which went into effect as part of the Taxpayer Relief Act of 1997, repealed the two-year rollover and over-55 rules that formerly applied to home sales. If you sell your home at a loss, you cannot deduct the loss or use it to offset gains elsewhere.

However, for those selling a home with a profit of $500,000 or more ($250,000 for singles), there could be significant capital gains taxes to pay. Under old rules, such gains could be rolled into a new house of the same or greater value. But such rollovers are no longer allowed, so capital gains taxes of as much as 20 percent will be due on sale, even if the proceeds are reinvested in a more expensive house.

ALTERNATIVE MINIMUM TAX

The government wants everyone to pay his or her fair share of taxes, so it has instituted the *alternative minimum tax* (AMT) to snare wealthy people who have created so many deductions and credits that they might avoid paying taxes altogether. If you are one of these people, calculate your tax with both the regular tax tables and the AMT tables, which charge 26 percent on income up to and including $175,000 for a married couple filing jointly ($87,500 for a married couple filing separately) and 28 percent on income over $175,000 for a married couple filing jointly ($87,500 if filing separately).

To determine whether you will be hit by the AMT, add up your preference item deductions, including accelerated depreciation, percentage depletion and intangible drilling costs for oil and gas drilling, and other tax shelter losses. Even if you don't have such elaborate preference items, you might have to pay the AMT if you have huge itemized deductions from state and local income taxes, interest expenses, interest on AMT municipal bonds issued after August 7, 1986, or other miscellaneous deductions.

To calculate what you owe under the AMT (and probably only your accountant with a good computer program can actually figure it out), add all your tax preference items to your taxable income and take one big exemption—$45,000 if you are married, filing jointly; $33,750 if you are single or the head of a household; and $22,500 if you are married, filing separately or for estates and trusts.

Just to make the AMT more complicated, Congress mandated that these exemptions be phased out when your AMT taxable income exceeds $150,000 if you file jointly, $112,500 if you file singly or as the head of a household or $75,000 if you file separately while married. The exemptions are reduced by $.25 for each dollar over these limits. In practice, this means that you lose the exemption altogether when your AMT taxable income exceeds $330,000 on a joint return, $247,500 on a single or head-of-household return or $165,000 on a married-filing-separately return.

Although determining whether you must pay the AMT is extremely complex, do not avoid the exercise if you have enough preference items or deductions to make it possible to qualify. You must show the IRS that you have calculated your AMT and that your regular income tax is higher.

WITHHOLDING

The IRS not only wants your money; it wants your money frequently and quickly. That is why the agency has instituted tough withholding rules to make sure that your employer takes a percentage of your paycheck and passes it on to the federal government.

Withholding is imposed on several kinds of income: wages and salaries, sick pay, tips, pensions, payouts from retirement plans, supplemental unemployment insurance benefits and some gambling winnings. If you do not give your taxpayer ID (usually your Social Security number) to a bank or brokerage firm, you may be subject to backup withholding on any interest or dividends due you. The backup withholding rate is 20 percent.

To establish the amount of money withheld from your paycheck, you must submit a *W-4 form*—also called an *Employee's Withholding Allowance Certificate* —to your employer's payroll department. On this form, you claim a certain number of exemptions based on your anticipated deductions and credits for the coming year. By the end of January, your employer must give you a W-2 form that details how much of your pay was withheld in federal, state, local and Social Security taxes the previous year.

IRS rules mandate that you pay at least 90 percent of the current year's tax liability through a combination of withholding and quarterly estimated tax payments by January 15 of the following year. In addition, if you receive a surge of income during the year, you should increase your quarterly estimated tax payments accordingly.

You might think that you should have enough withheld from your paycheck that come April 15 you receive a large refund. While many people do this, they probably don't realize that they give the government an interest-free loan every year. It is better to cut your withholding so that you receive a larger paycheck throughout the year and receive only a small—or, perhaps, no—refund at tax time. You will come out ahead if that extra money earns you interest in the bank or in another investment. Having too little withheld, however, will trigger IRS penalties.

ESTIMATED TAXES

If you have sources of income other than wages or you are self-employed, you must send the IRS quarterly estimated tax payments. You also must pay estimated taxes if you receive significant income from dividends, interest or capital gains or significant business income, such as rent, royalties or freelance fees. In addition, you must pay estimated taxes if you owe the government at least $500.

Similar to withholding, the idea behind estimated taxes is to pay enough taxes throughout the year that by year's end you have given the IRS at least 90 percent of your current year's tax liability. If your income jumps during the year because you earned a large capital gain or you sold your business, for example, increase your estimated taxes to reflect your good fortune. The IRS is your silent partner; whatever profitable happens to you increases the taxes you pay. If you report more than $150,000 as a married couple filing jointly (or $75,000 for married, filing separately), in taxable income in the prior year, you must assume your income will rise by 10 percent over the coming year when calculating your quarterly estimated taxes. So your quarterly tax payments must amount to 110 percent of the tax you paid in the prior year.

To pay estimated taxes, submit Form 1040-ES to your local IRS service center by April 15, June 15, September 15 and January 15 of each year. If your state has an income tax, follow the same procedure and remit state estimated tax to the state center by the same dates.

If you fail to make estimated tax payments or you underpay what the IRS thinks you owe, you must file Form 2210. This form either calculates your penalty or explains to the IRS why you didn't pay enough. The IRS can waive its normal penalties if you suffered a major casualty or disaster, if you retired after turning age 62, if you became disabled or if you convince the agency otherwise that you didn't demonstrate willful neglect.

THE MOST COMMONLY USED TAX FORMS AND SCHEDULES

The plethora of forms required by the IRS can be quite confusing. In fact, you might pay more in taxes than you should because you do not use the correct form or schedule. You can obtain forms at any IRS office or from most accountants or national tax preparation services. Following is a brief rundown of the forms you will encounter, the major schedules corresponding to each tax form and an explanation of how to use each form.

Form 709: Gift Taxes. You must file a gift tax return if you give a gift worth more than $10,000 to an individual during one tax year. If it is a simple gift, you may use the short form 709-A.

Form 1040EZ. Use this basic form if you are single, have no dependents, plan to take the standard deduction, earn less than $50,000 in wages and earn less than $400 in interest income.

Form 1040A. Use Form 1040A, known as the *short form,* if you will report less than $50,000 in wages, interest, tips, dividends, interest or unemployment compensation. The short form does not allow itemization or any adjustments to income other than the IRA; therefore, you must use the standard deduction.

Form 1040. Remit a 1040, known as the *long form,* if you will report $50,000 or more in income. You will also need this form to list dividends, interest and other forms of income. You can itemize deductions, claim credits and make other adjustments to your income, such as Keogh account contributions. The schedules that you can file with your 1040 include the following:

- *Schedule A: Itemized deductions,* such as state and local income taxes, home mortgage interest, gifts to charity, casualty losses, moving expenses, medical and job-related expenses.

- *Schedule B: Interest and dividend income from bonds, bank accounts, stocks and mutual funds.* This schedule also includes capital gains distributions from mutual funds and nontaxable distributions.

- *Schedule C: Profits or losses from a business.* On this schedule, list your business's income and expenses, and declare a profit or loss. A professional activity code identifies the type of business in which you are engaged. You may also use a short version of this schedule called Schedule C-EZ.

- *Schedule D: Short- and long-term capital gains and losses* resulting from the buying and selling of stocks, bonds, real estate, mutual funds and other assets, including futures and options contracts.

- *Schedule E: Supplemental income and loss.* On this schedule, report income from rental real estate and royalties from books, records or other sources. List the income you received, deduct your expenses for producing that income, and pay tax on your net income. This schedule is also used to report income and losses from partnerships, small businesses organized as "S" corporations, estates and trusts, and *real estate mortgage investment conduits* (REMICs), which are a form of mortgage-backed security.

- *Schedule F: Profit or loss from farming.* On this form, you report all income earned from farming activities and all expenses incurred while farming. The bottom line shows your net farm profit or loss.

- *Schedule H: Household employment taxes.* On this form, you list all wages paid to your household employees of $1,000 or more. You also list the amount of taxes due for Social Security, Medicare and the amount of federal income tax withheld and federal unemployment tax (FUTA).

- *Schedule K-1: Partner's share of income, credits and deductions.* This schedule, part of Form 1065, is mailed to you if you participate in a partnership. It lists the income paid to you during the year, expenses incurred by the partnership and credits due you, such as for building low-income housing or rehabilitating historic structures.

- *Schedule R: Credit for the elderly or disabled.* On this schedule, note the age of the person qualifying for the credit, and attach a statement of permanent and total disability, certified by a doctor's signature.

- *Schedule SE: A self-employment tax schedule that comes in both a short and a long version.* The schedule indicates the type of business in which you are engaged, as well as your net earnings and the amount of self-employment tax you owe.

Form 1040ES. Submit this form with your estimated quarterly tax payments.

Form 1040NR. Tax form for a nonresident alien. Generally, nonresident aliens pay taxes only on income earned from U.S. sources.

Form 1040PC. A condensed tax form that many tax preparation software programs permit you to print out that only shows the lines on which you have entries. This form is easier for the IRS to process electronically, allowing them to speed your refund directly into your bank account through electronic funds transfer.

Form 1040X. Use this form when you amend a previous tax return. (You can amend an original return any time for three years after the original return was due.) Form 1040X explains why you want to amend the return and whether you are now owed a refund or must now pay more taxes.

Form 1041: Estate Income Tax. This form reports the income earned by the estate of a deceased person and must be filed if the gross income is $600 or more.

Form 1098: Mortgage Interest Statement. This form reports how much interest you paid on your mortgage in the past year so that you can deduct that amount on your tax return. You should receive this statement from your mortgage lender during January.

Form 1099: Reports income from various sources such as dividends and interest income. There are several versions of the 1099 form, including B for gross proceeds from sales of stocks, bonds, futures and options contracts; DIV for dividends; G for state income tax refunds; INT for interest; MISC for miscellaneous income such as prizes and awards and compensation for personal services, rents and royalties; OID for original issue discount bonds and time deposits; PATR for patronage dividends paid by cooperatives; R for retirement plan distributions like pension, profit-sharing or IRA payouts; and S for sales of real estate.

Form 1116: Foreign Tax Credit. Use Form 1116 if you paid taxes to a foreign country that you want to recoup on your U.S. taxes.

Form 1127: Application for Extension of Time for Payment of Tax. Use this form if you want to file your return on time but do not have the money to pay the tax due.

Form 2106: Statement of Employee Business Expenses. This form lists all the business expenses for which you have paid but have not been reimbursed by your employer.

Form 2119: Statement Concerning Sale or Exchange of Personal Residence. Use Form 2119 when you sell or exchange your primary home.

Form 2120: Multiple Support Agreements. Use this form to designate which parent is eligible to claim the exemption for child support when parents are filing separately.

Form 2210: Statement Relating to Underpayment of Estimated Tax. This form explains your failure to pay enough in your quarterly estimated-tax filing.

Form 2441: Credit for Dependent Care Expenses. On this form, claim the tax credit for child or other dependent care expenses.

Form 2555: Exclusion for Income Earned Abroad. Use Form 2555 if you live overseas and must exclude certain income from your U.S. taxes. The short version of this form is 2555-EZ.

Form 2688: Application for Additional Extension of Time To File Tax Return. Form 2688 is a request to automatically extend by up to four months the time you have to file your return. You must pay what you think you owe, however, when you file this form. You can use Form 4868 for an initial extension.

Form 2848: Power of Attorney. To be used when a spouse is unable to sign a joint tax return.

Form 3115: Changing Reporting Period on Savings Bond Interest Accrual. If you have been reporting annual increases in value in your savings bonds, you can change your method and defer reporting the interest earned until the bonds are redeemed or mature. Use Form 3115 and attach it to your tax return, specifying which bonds you are choosing to change reporting methods on.

Form 3903: Moving Expenses. This form lists deductible moving expenses when you relocate from one home to another.

Form 4070: Employee Tip Income Reported. You must list income from tips if you work as a waiter, waitress or hairstylist or you work in another profession that relies on tips. Form 4070A provides space to record daily tips received. Form 4137 helps you compute the Social Security tax due on unreported tip income.

Form 4506: Request for Copy of Tax Return. If you forget to keep a copy of your tax return, use Form 4506 to obtain one from the IRS.

Form 4562: Depreciation. This form helps you calculate depreciation on real estate or equipment.

Form 4684: Casualties and Thefts. Use this form to claim losses from casualties or thefts, which can be deductible.

Form 4797: Recapture of First-Year Expensing for Real Estate Depreciation. If you have sold depreciated real estate property after May 6, 1997, you may be subject to recapture rules, with your capital gains earned from previous depreciation deductions being taxed as much as 25 percent. Form 4797 helps you figure out how much tax you might owe in this situation.

Form 4810: Prompt Assessment of an Estate. Use Form 4810 to expedite the closing of a decedent's estate. Once this form has been filed, the IRS has 18 months to assess any additional taxes, instead of the usual three years from the due date of the final income tax return. Form 4810 should be sent directly to the District Director of the district in which the return is filed.

Form 4952: Investment Interest Deduction. Calculate on this form the interest you have paid to purchase investments, which is deductible up to the amount of investment income you earn, not counting capital gains.

Form 5305: Self-Directed Individual Retirement Account. Use this form to set up a model trust for a self-directed IRA, which gives you wide latitude in the kinds of investments you can make. (Form 5305-A is for a model custodial account agreement.)

Form 5329: Additional Taxes Attributable to Qualified Retirement Plans (Incuding IRAs), Annuities, Modified Endowment Contracts and Medical Savings Accounts. Use this form to calculate taxes owed on early or excess distributions from qualified retirement plans, or excess contributions to IRAs or medical savings accounts. Usually, such distributions result in a 10 percent penalty. This form also can be used to claim exceptions to the 10 percent penalty rules, applicable under certain circumstances.

Form 5500: Annual Return/Report of Employee Benefit Plan with 100 or More Participants. On this form, list expenses, contributions, investment income and claims of pension plans. Form 5500-C/R applies to pension plans with fewer than 100 participants. Form 5500EZ applies to one-person plans such as Keoghs. Use this form to claim a deduction for a Keogh contribution.

Form 5884: Work Opportunity Credit. Businesses use this form to claim the work opportunity credit for hiring certain kinds of workers.

Form 6198: Deductions for Losses When You Are Not at Risk. If you have invested an amount for which you are not at risk, such as a nonrecourse loan, use Form 6198 to figure out the amount of your deductible loss.

Form 6251: Alternative Minimum Tax. Form 6251 helps you calculate whether you must pay the AMT.

Form 6252: Computation of Installment Sale Income. Use this form to report capital gains when selling an asset over several years through an installment sale.

Form 6478: Alcohol Fuels Credit. Use this form to claim the credit for using alcohol fuels for a business.

Form 6765: Research Credit. Use this form to claim the credit for research expenses for a business.

Form 8283: Noncash Charitable Contributions. You must record noncash gifts to charity, which must be independently appraised.

Form 8300: Reporting Business Cash Receipts. Every time your business receives more than $10,000 in a cash transaction, it must be reported to the IRS on Form 8300 within 15 days of the transaction.

Form 8332: Release of Claim to Exemption for Child of Divorced or Separated Parents. This form is statement and proof that the spouse with custody over a child agrees to relinquish his or her deduction for the child to the other spouse.

Form 8582: Passive Activities. This form assembles income and expenses from passive activities in order to determine the effects of passive loss rules on your tax liabilities. Using this form, income from passive sources is reported as regular income and deductions are applied in the correct schedules.

Form 8586: Low-Income Housing Credit. You can claim this tax credit if you have invested in a low-income housing limited partnership.

Form 8606: Nondeductible IRA Contributions, IRA Basis and Nontaxable IRA Distributions. Complete this form when you make nondeductible contributions to your IRA or receive distributions from your IRA after your retirement.

Form 8615: Reporting Investment Income Exceeding $1,400 of Children under Age 14. Report of investment income beyond the limit allowed on which children pay taxes at their rate. Any amount exceeding $1,400 is taxed at the parent's rate.

Form 8721: Tax Shelter Registration. Form used to report the registration number of a tax shelter to the IRS.

Form 8801: Alternative Minimum Tax (AMT) Credit. Use Form 8801 to figure out if you qualify for a tax credit based on paying an alternative minimum tax in the prior tax year.

Form 8815: Exclusion of Interest from Series EE U.S. Savings Bonds Issued after 1989. File Form 8815 when you redeem savings bonds and use the interest for tuition. This makes the interest tax free if you meet certain income limitations.

Form 8822: Address Changes. File Form 8822 to notify the Internal Revenue Service when you change your address. The form lists your old and new address, along with your Social Security or employer identification number.

Form 8824: Like-Kind Property Exchanges. Use this form to report an exchange of like-kind property, which can generate a profit or loss. On this form you also report the tax basis of like-kind property received.

Form 8826: Disabled Access Credit. Use this form if your business can claim the credit for hiring disabled employees.

Form 8829: Expenses for Business Use of Your Home. Use this form when you claim a home office deduction.

Form 8834: Electric Vehicle Credit. Use this form to claim the 10 percent credit for the cost of a qualified electric vehicle, up to a maximum of $4,000 per vehicle.

Form 8839: Qualified Adoption Expenses. Use this form to figure out how much of an adoption credit you can claim if you have adopted an eligible child.

Form 8844: Empowerment Zone Wages Credit. Use Form 8844 if your business can claim a credit for wages paid to employees in an empowerment zone.

Form 8845: Indian Employment Credit. Use Form 8845 if your business can claim a credit for wages paid to qualified Native American employees.

Form TDF 90-22.1: Report of Foreign Bank and Financial Accounts. You need to file this form if you have a financial interest over a foreign bank or securities account that was valued at more than $10,000 at any time in the past tax year. This form is due by June 30 of the year following the year in which you had the financial interest.

Strategies To Cut Your Taxes

The two basic tax-saving techniques are to delay paying taxes using *tax-deferral strategies* and to sidestep taxes altogether. Most of the specific strategies that follow are discussed in more detail elsewhere in this book. They are the most popular and practical ways to cut your taxes.

CHARITABLE CONTRIBUTIONS

You can accumulate deductions by donating cash or property to qualified charities. If you donate an asset such as stocks, bonds or real estate that has appreciated sharply, you avoid the capital gains taxes you would have paid, had you sold the asset for a profit, and you qualify for a charitable contribution deduction. If you do volunteer work for a charity, you can also deduct your unreimbursed expenses, such as the travel costs involved in doing your job.

CHILDREN

There are various tax benefits associated with having children. You can qualify for a Child Tax Credit, and the Hope Scholarship and Lifetime Learning Credit for your children. You also may claim an Adoption Tax Credit if you adopt a child. (See "Tax Credits" in this chapter for more details.) Under certain circumstances, interest on student loans may be deductible as well. (See "Deductions" in this chapter for more details.) You also may be able to save up to $500 a year tax-free in an educational IRA for your kids.

EMPLOYEE BENEFITS

You can shelter investment capital from taxes until you retire—when you probably will be in a lower tax bracket—by contributing to Keogh plans, 401(k) or 403(b) salary reduction plans, simplified employee pension (SEP) plans, IRA and profit-sharing plans. Certain fringe benefits, such as the first $50,000 of group life insurance coverage and medical insurance premiums paid by your employer, are not taxed. Many companies also offer flexible spending accounts, which allow you to put aside pretax money to cover certain health care and dependent care costs. Your company also may offer a medical savings account (MSA) to which you contribute through payroll deduction. You get to deduct your MSA contributions from your personal taxes, and all the money in the account accumulates tax-free and can be withdrawn tax-free as long as it is used for qualified medical expenses. Using an MSA allows you, in effect, to pay for medical expenses and receive a tax break that would probably not be possible otherwise. Normally, medical expenses have to exceed 7.5 percent of your adjusted gross income to generate deductions, which most people find difficult to achieve in one year. MSAs are generally available for employees of small businesses with 50 or fewer employees and for the self-employed. All these employee benefit plans are described in more detail in Chapter 16, "Making the Most of Your Employee Benefits."

GROWTH STOCKS

Because you control when you sell a stock, the growth in the value of the stock is, in effect, a tax shelter. Particularly if the stock pays little or no dividend, all of the company's profits are reinvested in the business and, hopefully, making the stock's value rise over time. When you sell a stock you have held for at least 18 months, you pay a preferential capital gains tax rate of 20 percent at most, and 10 percent if you are in the lower 15 percent tax bracket. This is a significantly lower tax than you pay at regular income rates on dividend or interest income. See Chapter 3, "Picking Winning Stocks," for more information on this aspect of growth investing.

INCOME SHIFTING

By transferring a tax burden from someone in a high tax bracket to someone in a lower tax bracket, you can reduce the total amount of taxes your family pays. To sidestep gift taxes, such gifts must not exceed $10,000 each. Before the Tax Reform Act of 1986, many more income-shifting strategies existed than do today. Nevertheless, you can still shift some income-producing assets to your children younger than age 14. The first $700 of unearned income—that income generated by stock dividends or bond interest, as opposed to money a child might earn by working a paper route, for example—goes completely untaxed. The next $700 of unearned income is taxed at the child's rate, usually 15 percent versus as much as 39.6 percent rate of the parents. However, any unearned income the child receives that exceeds $1,400 is taxed at the parents' rate. This is usually known as the *kiddie tax.*

Once your child turns 14 years old, all of his or her unearned income is taxed at the child's rate, which may open up some income-shifting possibilities. For example, you might give your child a gift of $10,000 or less to invest for college. Your spouse could donate another $10,000. Realize, however, that you relinquish control of that money, and your child can do whatever he or she likes with it once the child reaches the age of majority, normally 18. Income-shifting techniques are discussed in more detail in Chapter 15, "Estate Planning—Keeping Your Assets in the Family."

INDIVIDUAL RETIREMENT ACCOUNTS

You can save a significant amount of taxes in the long run by maximizing all the different kinds of IRA accounts available to you. Depending on the kind of IRA and your income level, you may be able to deduct your initial contribution. But most important in the long run is your ability to have earnings grow tax-deferred in a regular IRA and tax-free in a Roth IRA, as long as you hold the assets in a Roth for at least five years. For regular tax-deductible IRAs, you can earn a full or partial deduction if your income is up to $60,000 for a married couple filing jointly, or $40,000 for a single. Those limits will gradually climb to top out at $100,000 for couples and $60,000 for singles in the year 2007. You will pay taxes on such IRA distributions when you withdraw the money in retirement after age 59½. With the Roth IRA, you do not get a deduction up front but can take the capital out totally tax-free in retirement. Unlike regular IRAs, you do not have to start withdrawing money from a Roth IRA at age 70½. You can, in fact, keep it in the account forever and pass the proceeds to your beneficiaries tax-free. See Chapter 14 for more details on IRAs.

You also can save on taxes by establishing an Education IRA for your children. You can contribute up to $500 per year for each child in your household up to the age of 18. That $500 limit is reduced if you report adjusted gross income of more than $95,000 for a single or $150,000 for a married couple filing jointly. Assets inside an Education IRA grow tax-free and can be withdrawn tax-free as long as the proceeds are used to pay for education expenses at a postsecondary school, including tuition, fees, books, supplies, and room and board. If your first child does not use the Education IRA money because they do not go to college, the assets can be transferred to your second child and used for their college bills as long as this is done before the child reaches age 30.

If you are self-employed, you can contribute even more to IRA-like vehicles such as Keogh, SIMPLE and SEP plans that give you upfront deductions and tax-deferred growth. (See Chapter 16 for more details on these plans.)

INSURANCE

The tax-deferred buildup of cash value in an insurance policy provides a major long-term tax benefit. This applies to whole life, variable life and universal life policies, as well as to variable and fixed annuities. Unlike IRAs, Keoghs and 401(k) plans, no rules limit how much you can invest in insurance policies to take advantage of this tax shelter. Insurance also offers certain tax breaks when benefits are paid out. See Chapter 11, "All about Insurance," for more details.

MUNICIPAL BONDS

The interest on tax-free municipal bonds is not taxed by the federal government and usually is not taxed by the state government for its residents if the bonds are issued in the state. Otherwise, a state tax may be due on municipal bonds issued by other states. This often provides a higher after-tax equivalent yield than you can get from a taxable bond of similar quality and maturity. Municipal bond interest goes untaxed if it is received through individual bonds, bond mutual funds or unit investment trusts. See Chapter 5, "All about Bonds," for more details.

PROTESTING YOUR PROPERTY TAX ASSESSMENT

While most of the strategies discussed in this book affect your federal and state tax burden, you may also save a significant amount of money by protesting the assessment on your home. This assessment forms the basis of your local property tax. To determine whether to protest, first find out your home's official assessed value. Then multiply this fair market value by the assessment ratio in your town. By asking local real estate agents for the recent sales prices of similar homes in your neighborhood, you can ascertain whether your home's fair market value is too high. You can also research at city hall the assessed value of nearby homes to determine whether your assessment is out of line. If it is, file a formal protest with your town assessor, who may reduce your home's official assessed value, thereby cutting your property taxes.

REAL ESTATE

You can qualify for mortgage interest deductions on a qualified residence mortgage up to $1 million. In addition, you can deduct the interest you pay on a home equity credit line up to $100,000, no matter how you spend the proceeds of the loan. You may also deduct property taxes you pay to your locality. When you sell your home, you do not have to pay any capital gains taxes if your profit is $500,000 or less for a married couple filing jointly, or $250,000 or less for a single.

This applies only to your primary residence if you have lived there for at least two of the past five years.

If you rent real estate for a living, you may also merit certain tax benefits. When you actively manage a property you own by finding tenants, collecting rents and supervising maintenance, you can deduct up to $25,000 in losses, if any, generated by the property. This can help reduce your taxable income. Certified real estate professionals can deduct losses on rental property against any form of income. You qualify as a professional if you spend at least 750 hours a year and half your time working in real estate or a related industry such as construction. You may also deduct costs of maintaining or upgrading your property. In addition to being actively involved in management, you must own at least 10 percent of the property and report an AGI of less than $100,000 a year. If your AGI falls between $100,000 and $150,000, your deductions phase out until they disappear at $150,000.

You may obtain some tax benefits by buying publicly offered real estate limited partnerships. For example, a portion of the distributions paid out to you may be sheltered by depreciation or may be considered nontaxable return of capital. You also may deduct your share of any mortgage interest or property taxes paid by the partnership. However, the days of high-write-off partnerships are long gone. If you purchase shares in a Real Estate Investment Trust (REIT), you also are gaining tax advantages because the REIT does not pay taxes at the corporate level. You are not taxed doubly on your dividends as you are with most other publicly traded stocks.

You also can generate tax credits by investing in a low-income housing development or the renovation of a certified historic building. (See "Tax Credits" in this chapter for more details.)

STARTING A BUSINESS

As long as you can show the IRS that you are trying to profit from a business venture that you start, many expenses legitimately incurred by your company qualify for business-related deductions. For example, you can deduct the business-related portion of your car lease payments. You can also deduct certain travel and entertainment expenses and the cost of a home office if it is your primary place for meeting customers and conducting the business. However, if you don't profit in three out of five consecutive years, the IRS may claim that you are pursuing a hobby and not running a legitimate business. You may be able to counter this claim by documenting all the steps you have taken to become profitable.

TREASURY BONDS

Interest on bonds, bills and notes issued by the U.S. government is not taxable at the state or local level. This gives these bonds a slightly higher effective yield than other taxable bonds, such as corporate bonds, particularly in states with higher state tax rates. This shelter is also valid for U.S. savings bonds. If your modified adjusted gross income is between $50,850 and $65,850 for individuals or $76,250 and $106,250 for married couples filing jointly at the time you redeem your savings bonds (this amount is adjusted slightly upward for inflation every year), the interest you earn from the bonds is either fully or partially tax exempt if you use it for college tuition for either yourself, your spouse or your children. This version of savings bonds is called an education bond and it can apply to any bond purchased after December 31, 1989. See Chapter 5, "All about Bonds," for more details.

TRUSTS

By establishing various kinds of trusts, you can sidestep estate-tax bills. See Chapter 15, "Estate Planning—Keeping Your Assets in the Family," for a more detailed explanation.

Dealing with the IRS

Though no one relishes the thought of dealing with the IRS, you may have to someday. If you are organized, come well prepared and keep good records, however, the experience does not have to be totally unpleasant.

The IRS publishes many helpful brochures explaining the tax law. All are available free from local IRS offices or when you call the toll-free number in your state. A list of the titles and numbers of these publications appears in the "Resources" section at the end of this chapter. In addition, the IRS offers Tele-Tax— a system of prerecorded phone explanations of various aspects of the tax code. Information about Tele-Tax is also included in the "Resources" section. You can also call the IRS help line for information about the tax law (if you can get through), but do not rely solely on what IRS representatives tell you. Many of their answers to questions are not correct, and the IRS does not stand behind its representatives.

In recent years, the IRS has substantially improved its computer capability, making it harder for people to cheat on their taxes. For example, all statements of interest and dividends you receive from your bank and brokerage firm also go to the IRS. The IRS also receives records of many other transactions, such as contributions to IRAs, state and local tax refunds, mortgage interest you pay and gross proceeds you receive when you sell a stock or bond.

When you don't report income that the IRS thinks you received, a computer will send a letter inquiring why you didn't report this revenue. If you don't answer satisfactorily, the IRS will ask you to pay the taxes quickly or face harsh penalties. However, don't capitulate immediately if you still believe you are right. Many times, the IRS has outdated or incorrect information. In that case, fight back by writing a more specific letter, backed by documentation, proving your case.

If you have a dispute with the IRS, you may be able to obtain help through the agency's *Problem Resolution Program* (800-829-1040). PRP personnel have authority to cut through red tape to try to resolve your problem. They can investigate delayed refund checks, unanswered inquiries or incorrect billing notices.

Congress has enacted an extensive Taxpayer Bill of Rights, which among other features, holds that:

- IRS employees will explain and protect your rights as a taxpayer.

- The IRS will not disclose the information you give to them to anyone except as authorized by law. You have the right to know why you are being asked for information, how the IRS will use it and what happens to you if you do not provide the requested data.

- IRS employees are to treat you in a professional and courteous manner. If they don't, you have the right to notify the employee's supervisor. If the supervisor's response is inadequate, you should report the incident to the IRS district director.

- You can either represent yourself or have someone else represent you at an IRS audit or interview. You can tape-record any examination or collection proceedings if you notify the IRS you are planning to do so at least ten days before the meeting.

- You are responsible for paying the correct tax, no more or no less.

- You have the right of appeal if you disagree with IRS rulings or collection practices.

- The IRS can waive penalties if you can show you acted reasonably and in good faith or relied on incorrect advice from an IRS employee.

IF YOU'RE AUDITED

Though the chances that you will be audited are slim, it might happen to you some day. If you have proper documents to back up what you claimed on your tax return, do not fear the audit process. Many taxpayers emerge from audits owing no more than they paid originally, and some even receive refunds. Even if the auditor finds that you unintentionally underreported income or overstated deductions, you may be able to work out a settlement that keeps penalties to a minimum. However, if the IRS agent determines that you purposefully evaded paying taxes, you will be charged both interest (calculated from the date your return was due) and severe penalties.

In theory, the IRS can audit you up to three years after the date your return was due or was filed, whichever is later; in practice, it usually audits people within the first 18 months. Even if you don't hear from the IRS for three years after you submit a return, however, save a copy of your return and the supporting documents for at least five years.

Because the IRS audits so few returns—usually fewer than 2 percent per year—it uses computers to pinpoint the most suspicious returns. The IRS employs a system called *Discriminate Function* (DIF) to spot returns that deviate sharply from the IRS computer models for particular types of taxpayers. For example, DIF is programmed to expect a certain number of credits, deductions and exemptions for a particular level of income. The more your return deviates from the model, the greater your risk of an audit.

If you are selected for an audit, you will have a month or two to prepare your defense. Many audits do not take place in person but are completed through the mail when you send your documentation to the auditor. If the auditor requests a meeting, you can go alone or with your tax preparer. Most auditors don't even require you to show up; they will complete the audit with your preparer. Usually, your CPA or accountant will charge extra—perhaps several hundred dollars—to represent you in an audit. If you decide to save your preparer's fees and handle the audit yourself, approach the situation calmly. Bring every piece of documentation the auditor might ask for, such as receipts, bills, W-2 forms and bank records, and answer his or her questions respectfully but unemotionally. Don't volunteer information beyond the answers to questions because it may open up a new avenue of inquiry that the auditor had not planned to pursue. And don't act suspicious or combative.

When the audit is complete, the auditor will determine whether you owe more taxes and penalties, owe nothing or are owed a refund. If you know that you've violated the law, capitulate quickly and pay up. However, you can dispute the auditor's decision if you feel a great injustice has been done to you. First, appeal to the auditor's supervisor, who will look at the evidence and judge whether the auditor made a proper decision. If you are still found to be wrong, complain formally, in writing, to an appeals officer. Make sure that you stand on extremely solid ground when you take your case to this level because the appeals officer can reevaluate your entire return, not just the portion you question.

If you are again voted down and you feel it is worthwhile, appeal the decision to the U.S. Tax Court or U.S. Claims Court in Washington. Such a step is expensive, time consuming and unlikely to succeed, however. Usually, you must pay the taxes that the IRS claims you owe before your case can be considered. Of course, most taxpayers never have to take such drastic steps to protect their rights, and it is unlikely that you will ever fight the IRS so vigorously.

Key Provisions of the Taxpayer Relief Act of 1997

The landmark legislation called the Taxpayer Relief Act of 1997, which was signed into law by President Clinton in August 1997, was part of a larger act designed to balance the federal budget. The 900-page tax legislation makes hundreds of changes in the law, and provides many new opportunities for you to save money on your taxes and establish new kinds of tax-free retirement and educational accounts. Here is a brief rundown of the major provisions of the law and how you can take advantage of them:

Tax credits for children. Parents or grandparents supporting children under the age of 17 can now claim a tax credit of $400 per child in 1998 and $500 per child in 1999 and every year thereafter. Credits are worth much more than deductions because they are dollar-for-dollar reductions in the amount of tax you owe. For instance, if you have one child and owe $1,000 in taxes, the credit, starting in 1999, cuts your taxes to $500. The credit is used in addition to the existing deduction for each dependent. At least part of the credit can be claimed by families with incomes as low as $18,000 owing little or no income tax. This tax credit is phased out for families with higher incomes. The phaseout begins for families reporting an adjusted gross income of $110,000 on a joint return, $55,000 if you are married filing separately and $75,000 for a single filer. The credit is reduced by $50 for each $1,000 of the threshold. The credit disappears altogether for couples with incomes of $119,000 or more and singles with incomes of $85,000 or higher. A tax credit of $5,000 also was added for taxpayers adopting children, and up to $6,000 for adopting "special needs" children.

Estate tax exclusion raised. The amount of assets that can be excluded from estate taxes was boosted from $600,000 to $1 million for everyone, and $1.3 million for small businessmen and farmers. The increase in the universal estate tax exclusion is phased in over a nine-year period, with the limit rising to $625,000 in 1998, $650,000 in 1999, $675,000 in 2000 and 2001, $700,000 in 2002 and 2003, $850,000 in 2004, $950,000 in 2005 and topping out at $1 million in 2006 and later years. However, the $1.3 million limit for farmers and small businesses went into effect fully on January 1, 1998. Figuring out whether you qualify as a small business is complex, however. There are many qualifying rules you must pass. For example, your estate's business assets must be at least 50 percent of its total assets. In addition, to preserve the tax break, heirs must be "materially participating" in running the business for at least five of the eight years within ten years of the owner's death. If heirs sell the business to nonfamily members within ten years after the owner's death, they will be required to pay some of the taxes from which they were originally exempt. To maximize the full estate tax exclusion, make sure to revise your wills to reflect the new limits. For any assets you have accumulated in excess of the limits, you may want to set up trusts or start giving the assets to your children over several years to avoid estate taxes that can be as high as 55 percent.

Three other estate tax limits were indexed to inflation, rounded to the next lowest multiple of $10,000, in the Tax Act:

1. The $1 million exemption from the generation-skipping transfer (GST) tax

2. The $750,000 maximum reduction in value on special use valuation of real property used in farming or a closely held business

3. The $1 million maximum value of a closely held business eligible for a special 4 percent interest rate on estate tax installment payments

Gift tax limit indexed to inflation. For many years, people have been able to give up to $10,000 a year to anyone they want without incurring a gift tax liability. A provision in the tax bill increases that $10,000 limit, tied to the rate of inflation, in $1,000 increments, starting on January 1, 1999.

Lower capital gains tax rates. The top tax rate on profits from the sale of assets like stocks, bonds, mutual funds and real estate was lowered from 28 percent to 20 percent. Before this law, those in the 15 percent and 28 percent income tax brackets paid the same tax rate on capital gains as on regular income. Only those in higher tax brackets benefitted from the 28 percent capital gains tax rate cap. Under the 1997 law, those in the 28 percent bracket will pay a maximum rate of 20 percent, while those in the 15 percent tax bracket will pay a maximum of just 10 percent when they realize capital gains. The new rules apply to anyone selling assets after May 6, 1997. The new rules do not apply to sales of hard assets like art, antiques, stamps, coins, gems and collectibles, for which the top capital gains tax rate remains 28 percent. By lowering capital gains rates and keeping regular income tax rates unchanged, Congress has given you a great incentive to invest in taxable accounts in assets like growth stocks that provide capital gains instead of bonds and high-yield stocks that pay interest and dividends that are taxable. It makes more sense to put income-oriented assets in tax-deferred accounts like IRAs and Keogh plans. The lower capital gains rates also increase the attractiveness of receiving compensation in the form of regular or incentive stock options, which can be exercised over time at preferential capital gains tax rates. The new capital gains tax rates apply for alternative minimum tax (AMT) purposes as well as for regular federal taxes.

New tax rate for property that has taken accelerated depreciation. If you sell a business or investment real estate on which you took accelerated depreciation, the portion of your capital gains representing the depreciation is eligible for a maximum tax rate of 25 percent, if the asset is sold after May 6, 1997.

New longer-term capital gains rates created. For assets like stocks, bonds and mutual funds purchased after January 1, 2000 and held for at least five years, the top capital gains rate was lowered to 18 percent for those in the 28 percent tax bracket or higher. The tax rate for holding assets for five years was lowered to just 8 percent for those in the 15 percent tax bracket. This provision provides a major incentive for buying and holding assets with appreciation potential for at least five years.

Changed holding period for capital gains. Previous law stated that assets had to be held for at least 12 months to qualify for long-term capital gains rates. Under the new law, to qualify for the advantageous capital gains tax rates, assets must be held for at last 18 months. (One exception: assets sold between May 6, 1997, and July 29, 1997, qualify for the lower rates if they were held for 12 months. Also, old capital gains rates still apply to assets sold after July 29, 1997, but held between 12 and 18 months.)

Expanded tax deductibility for individual retirement account contributions. Under previous law, a taxpayer could not fully deduct his or her contributions to individual retirement accounts if their adjusted gross income exceeded $40,000 on a joint tax return or $25,000 for a single tax return. Starting in 1998, the new law raised those income caps to $50,000 for a joint return and $30,000 for a single. The caps gradually climb over ten years (by 2007) to $80,000 for a couple and $50,000 for a single. Over those limits, the deduction phases out for the next $10,000 in income. For singles, the deduction is phased out completely once income tops $40,000 in 1998, climbing to $60,000 in 2005. For married couples filing jointly, the deduction is phased out once income exceeds $60,000 in 1998, rising to $100,000 in 2007. This rule change means you have a much greater chance to deduct your IRA contribution than under previous law. Also, if you are part of a married couple in which one spouse is eligible for a retirement plan like a 401(k) and the other spouse is not, the spouse without the plan will more likely be able to deduct their IRA contribution. However, this advantage applies only to couples reporting adjusted gross income of less than $150,000. The deduction is phased out for income between $150,000 and $160,000, after which no deduction is allowed.

Introduction of the Roth IRA. A new kind of individual retirement account was created called the Roth IRA, named after Delaware Senator William V. Roth Jr., who championed the idea of expanded IRAs. Starting January 1, 1998, you can put up to $2,000 a year into a Roth IRA, even after you reach age 70½. You can withdraw all the principal and earnings totally tax-free after age 59½, as long as the assets have remained in the IRA for at least five years. Unlike regular IRAs, you do not have to take distributions from a Roth IRA starting at age 70½. In fact, you don't have to take distributions at all in your lifetime if you prefer, allowing you to pass the assets in the Roth IRA to your beneficiaries income-tax-free. You do not receive a tax deduction for making the contribution in the first place. But the value of completely tax-free withdrawals should far exceed the tax break from an up-front deduction. The Roth IRA rules also permit you to withdraw assets without the usual 10 percent early withdrawal penalty if you use the money for the purchase of a first home (withdrawals are limited to up to $10,000), for college expenses or if you become disabled. Only married couples with adjusted gross incomes of $150,000 or less and singles with adjusted gross incomes of $95,000 or less can contribute the full amount to Roth IRAs. The amount you can contribute is phased out for income between $150,000 and $160,000 for married couples, and between $95,000 and $110,000 for singles. No contributions are allowed over those income limits. For those with adjusted gross incomes of $100,000 or less, the new law allows you to roll over existing deductible and nondeductible IRA balances into a Roth IRA. When you do so, however, you must pay income tax on all previously untaxed contributions and earnings. If you execute such a rollover before January 1, 1999, you can spread the resulting tax bill over four years. Starting in 1999, the rollover is fully taxable in the year it is completed. If you do not qualify for a Roth or deductible IRA, you can still fund a nondeductible IRA with up to $2,000 a year.

"Cash-out" threshold for 401(k) plans raised. Under previous law, an employer could "cash out" any departing employee whose 401(k) balance was $3,500 or less. The employee can either take the money and pay taxes on it or roll it over into an IRA rollover account. The new tax law raised that limit to $5,000, meaning more workers will be "cashed out" of their 401(k) plans than before.

New investments allowed in IRAs. Starting in 1998, you can invest in metals such as gold, silver, platinum and palladium inside an IRA. Previously, such investments were banned in IRAs.

Repeal of the "short-short" rule. Under previous law, mutual funds lost their tax pass-through status if more than 30 percent of their gross income was generated from short-term investment gains under what was known as the "short-short" rule. As a result, fund managers were afraid to use trading strategies, such as options contracts, hedging and short-selling, that would generate short-term profits on holdings, even though the fund manager wanted to do so for investment reasons. The short-short rule was repealed in the tax bill, freeing up managers to trade with less fear of losing their tax pass-through status.

Eliminates "Shorting against the box" tax delay technique. A popular way for some investors to delay paying taxes was to "sell short against the box." In this technique, an investor who owns a particular stock would sell borrowed shares of the stock rather than the shares already owned. This tactic is similar to selling because the investor no longer has any economic interest in the stock. But previous tax law did not treat it as a sale. Under the new law, shorting against the box after June 8, 1997, is considered a "constructive sale" and will result in a capital gains tax liability. In effect, this law change will mean it no longer makes sense to use this technique.

Simplifies reporting of taxes on foreign investments. Starting with 1998 tax-year returns, many investors with holdings in foreign stocks, bonds or mutual funds will have an easier time filling out their tax returns. Single investors who pay up to $300 a year in foreign taxes ($600 on a joint return) on their overseas income will no longer need to fill out a complicated Form 1116 to claim the foreign tax credit. The amount of foreign earned income that you can exclude from taxation increases to $72,000 in 1998, $74,000 in 1999, $76,000 in 2000, $78,000 in 2001, and $80,000 in 2002 and later years.

Repeal of excess accumulation and excess distributions tax. In earlier legislation, Congress had imposed a 15 percent "excess accumulation tax" on lump sums of more than $800,000 from pension plans and a 15 percent "excess distributions tax" on payouts from individual retirement accounts of more than $160,000. Under the Taxpayer Relief Act of 1997, all of these taxes were repealed for distributions made after December 31, 1996.

New capital gains rules for home sales. Congress created what may be the largest tax break of all time for many Americans. Under previous law, you could avoid capital gains taxes on the sale of your home only if you bought a home within two years and reinvested the proceeds into a home of the same or greater value. Those over age 55 could escape capital gains tax when selling their homes up to $125,000 once in their lifetime. The new tax law changed all of that by allowing people to avoid all capital gains taxes on profits up to $500,000 for married couples filing jointly and up to $250,000 for those filing singly. The rule applies to anyone selling their home after May 6, 1997. It only applies to a person's primary residence, defined as a home you occupied for at least two of the five years prior to the sale. Remember that you must count not only the gain on your present home but also any gains created by previous home sales that you sheltered when trading up when you calculate the $500,000 exemption.You can claim a new $500,000 capital gains tax exemption every two years. The old $125,000 exemption for those over 55 was repealed because it was superseded by the new law. This new law can be particularly advantageous if you have lived in a home for many years that is now too big for your needs. If you sell it for a profit of $500,000 or less, you are no longer forced to reinvest the proceeds in a house of the same or larger size. You may choose to rent or buy a smaller home and take the remainder of the proceeds to invest in stocks, bonds or mutual funds that may have greater appreciation and income potential. There is one change that might trip up those with housing profits of more than $500,000, however. In the past, someone with such gains could avoid taxes by rolling over the profits into a larger home. Under the new law, no such rollover is allowed. Capital gains taxes of up to 20 percent are due upon the sale of a home with profits of more than $500,000. One other twist affects real estate investors who have been depreciating their property over the years. When these investors sell the property, they will have to pay a maximum of 25 percent capital gains tax for the part of their gain that is due to depreciation. That, of course, is higher than the maximum 20 percent capital gains tax rate for securities.

Tax credits for college education. The new law created the Hope Scholarship, which is a tax credit to help pay for the first two years of tuition and fees for students attending college or vocational school. The tax credit starts at $1,500 in 1998 and rises to $2,000 in 2003. Starting on July 1, 1998, a yearly Lifetime Learning Credit of up to $1,000 for 20 percent of tuition and school fees up to $5,000 is available for third- and fourth-year college students, graduate students and people returning to school to sharpen their job skills. This credit rises to 20 percent of $10,000, or a maximum of $2,000, in 2002. These tax credits are only available to married couples filing jointly with adjusted gross incomes of $80,000 or less, or singles with $40,000 or less. The credit is phased out and disappears altogether for couples with incomes of $100,000 and singles earning over $50,000.

Education-related interest becomes deductible. Starting in 1998, up to $1,000 in interest on student loans is deductible for taxpayers repaying loans for their own or a dependent's college or vocational school expenses. The interest is deductible only for the first 60 months (five years) the loan is outstanding. The $1,000 cap increases by $500 a year until it reaches a maximum of $2,500 in 2001. Taxpayers can get this deduction even if they don't file an itemized return. This deductible interest is only fully available to married taxpayers with $60,000 or less in income if filing jointly or $40,000 or less for singles. The deduction phases out for couples with incomes between $60,000 and $75,000 and for singles with incomes between $40,000 and $55,000. The interest is not deductible for those with incomes over those thresholds. These income levels will be adjusted for inflation starting in 2003.

Tax-free employer-paid education. Employees are entitled to receive up to $5,250 per year from their employers for undergraduate classes without having to declare that money as taxable income. This rule applies to classes that are not directly related to the employee's job. The tax break remains in effect for courses beginning before June 1, 2000. Reimbursement for schooling that is directly job-related remains tax-free without limitation.

Creation of the Education IRA. A new type of account, similar to an individual retirement account, called the Education IRA, was created that allows parents to save up to $500 per year per child under age 18 to help pay educational expenses. Contributions begin on January 1, 1998, and must be made each year by December 31. The money invested does not generate a deduction when placed in the Education IRA, but the principal, income and capital gains are completely tax-free when withdrawn to pay for college expenses such as tuition, fees, books, and room and board. Only couples with joint incomes of $150,000 or less and singles with incomes of $95,000 or less qualify for the full Education IRA. The $500 limit is phased out for couples with incomes between $150,000 and $160,000, after which level no Education IRA is allowed. The limit is phased out for singles with incomes between $95,000 and $110,000, after which no Education IRA is allowed.

Another related rule allows parents to withdraw money from regular IRAs before age 59½ without penalty if the proceeds are used for college or vocational school. However, the money withdrawn must be reported as income in the year it is taken from the IRA. So the Education IRA is probably a better deal for those eligible to open one. If you do not use the assets in an Education IRA by the time your child is age 30, the account must be liquidated and taxes must be paid on the proceeds at regular income tax rates. If one child does not go to school, the Education IRA proceeds can be used for another child in the family who does attend college.

Tax relief for children. Children who have income from part-time jobs and investments got a bit of tax relief from the law. Under prior law, children earning more than $650 a year in wages could not use their standard deduction to shelter investment income from taxes. Beginning in 1998, children will be able to use the standard deduction to shelter their earnings from a job plus up to $250 in investment income.

Bigger deductions for health insurance premiums for the self-employed. Under previous law, only a portion of health insurance premiums paid by the self-employed were deductible, while all premiums paid by larger companies were deductible. This inequity was phased out by the new law. In 1997, 40 percent of the premium paid by the self-employed is deductible. In 1998 and 1999, it is 45 percent. In 2000 and 2001, it rises to 50 percent; in 2002 to 60 percent. From 2003 through 2005, the deduction rises to 80 percent; in 2006 to 90 percent and from 2007 on, the deduction is 100 percent.

Creation of the medical savings account (MSA). You may be eligible to participate in a medical savings account if you are covered only under a high-deductible health plan. You can deduct MSA contributions even if you do not itemize your deductions. MSAs are generally available for small employers with fewer than 50 workers and the self-employed.

Social Security and Medicare taxes. The maximum wages subject to Social Security tax (6.2 percent) was raised to $65,400. All wages are subject to the Medicare tax of 1.45 percent.

Liberalization of the home office deduction. For many years, the IRS rules and court decisions had greatly restricted what kind of home office qualified as a deductible business expense. The new tax law eased the rules a bit. Starting in 1999, home office deductions are allowed if the space used is essential to running the venture, even if it is just to administer the business. No longer does the space have to be the only place where you meet clients or do your work. However, the home office space still must be used exclusively and regularly for business purposes. Remember that if you take deductions for depreciation on the part of your house that is used as an office, you will have to adjust your home's cost basis when you sell it.

Higher exemption from filing quarterly estimated taxes. The new law exempts those expecting to pay less than $1,000 in taxes from having to make quarterly estimated tax payments, starting in 1998. That is double the previous limit of $500. However, in figuring your estimated tax, you must include any expected employment taxes for household workers that you will owe.

Higher deduction for charitable use of your car. The deduction for using your automobile to benefit a charity rose from 12 cents to 14 cents a mile, starting in 1998.

Repeal of motorboat gas tax. The 24.3-cents-a-gallon tax on diesel fuel for recreational motorboats was repealed.

Paying taxes by credit card. The bill authorized the Internal Revenue Service to accept payment of taxes by credit or debit card or electronic funds transfer, though the IRS is prohibited from paying fees to card issuers.

Higher cigarette taxes. The excise tax on cigarettes rises by 10 cents a pack to 34 cents in 2000, and by an additional 5 cents to 39 cents in 2002.

Higher airline ticket taxes. The excise tax on airline tickets rose from $6 to $12 on departures to international destinations, and a new $12-per-ticket-fee was added on international arrivals. A new $3 airport-to-airport segment tax also was added on all domestic flights. The airline ticket tax was gradually scaled back from 10 percent to 7.5 percent.

Using Your Computer To Prepare Your Taxes

The computer can be an extremely valuable tool in both planning tax strategy and filling out your tax return. The two main tax preparation software packages on the market today are Kiplinger's TaxCut and TurboTax, both described in more detail in the "Resources" section of this chapter. With these packages, you can enter your tax-related data during the year to see the tax effects of various personal financial actions you take. For example, you might calculate the after-tax effects of buying a home and taking on a mortgage compared to renting to see how much the mortgage interest deductions will actually reduce your tax liability. When it comes to tax filing season, these programs can actually prepare your return. If you have been keeping your financial data on a program like Quicken or Microsoft Money, you can download the data right into the tax program, saving hours of re-entering numbers. These programs also make it easy to file your return electronically to the IRS and some state tax departments. Filing by computer should speed your refund, if you are due one.

In addition to planning your tax strategy and filing your return, you can use your computer to get the latest information on taxes from the Web sites of private organizations and the government. Note the Web sites listed in the "Resources" section of such companies as Commerce Clearing House and Research Institute of America for tax information from the private sector. The IRS has an extensive Web site (www//irs.ustreas.gov) that has all the tax forms and publications and explanations of the tax code you would ever need. Most state tax departments also have Web sites offering information on state regulations and forms.

While the subject of taxes and tax planning may be unappealing, learning about the tax consequences of your financial decisions is well worth your time and effort. It is your right as a citizen to take full advantage of the tax laws as Congress has created them. To accomplish this, however, you must be familiar with the tax code and develop an awareness of all the legal strategies available to make that code work for you.

Resources

BOOKS

Ernst & Young Tax Guide (John Wiley & Sons Inc., 605 3rd Ave., New York, NY 10158-0012; 212-850-6000; 800-225-5945; www.wiley.com). Annual guide that explains the tax code and provides all the forms you need to file your taxes.

The Ernst & Young Tax Saver's Guide (John Wiley & Sons Inc., 605 3rd Ave., New York, NY 10158-0012; 212-850-6000; 800-225-5945; www.wiley.com). Strategies you can use to save on your taxes.

J.K. Lasser's™ Your Income Tax (MacMillan Books, 135 S. Mount Zion Rd., Lebanon, IN 46502; 800-428-5331; www.superlibrary.com). Everything you need to know to fill out your tax return. A new edition with the latest tax laws is published every year.

J.K. Lasser's™ Year-Round Tax Strategies, by David DeJong and Ann Gray Jakabcin (MacMillan Books, 135 S. Mount Zion Rd., Lebanon, IN 46502; 800-428-5331; www.superlibrary.com). Covers the main areas of tax planning, including deductions, write-offs, credits, marriage and divorce, estate planning, investments and more.

Stand Up to the IRS, by Frederick W. Daily (Nolo Press, 950 Parker St., Berkeley, CA 94710; 510-549-1976; 800-992-NOLO; www.nolo.com). Gives details on how to fight back when the IRS challenges your return. Explains how to handle an audit and how to respond to IRS notices that may be in error. Also covers dealing with the U.S. Tax Court and IRS collectors and discusses how an IRS ombudsman can help you.

U.S. Master Tax Guide (Commerce Clearing House, 4025 W. Peterson Ave., Chicago, IL 60646; 312-583-8500; 800-248-3248; www.cch.com). A complete guide to the tax code, aimed mostly at professional tax preparers. Includes examples, tables and checklists of deductions and other tax-related lists.

PUBLISHERS OF NEWSLETTERS AND TAX GUIDE SERVICES

Boardroom Reports (Boardroom Inc., 55 Railroad Ave., Greenwich, CT 06836-2614; 203-625-5900; 800-288-1051; www.boardroom.com). Publishes *Tax Hotline,* a simply written newsletter containing short explanations of legal tax strategies. Also publishes special reports titled *Tax Audits Confidential* and *New Tax Traps/New Opportunities,* as well as a comprehensive book titled *Tax Loopholes.*

Commerce Clearing House (4025 W. Peterson Ave., Chicago, IL 60646; 312-583-8500; 800-248-3248; www.cch.com). Commerce Clearing House publishes many reports detailing changes in tax laws, usually in loose-leaf binders. Some of the most important publications include *Family Law Tax Guide; Federal Tax Advisor; Federal*

Tax Guide; Income, Estate and Gift Taxes; IRS Letter Rulings Report; State Tax Reports; Tax Court Decisions; Taxes on Parade; Tax Planning Review; and *U.S. Master Tax Guide.*

Kiplinger Washington Editors, Inc. (1729 H St., N.W., Washington, DC 20006; 202-887-6400; 800-544-0155; www.kiplinger.com). Publishes *The Kiplinger Tax Letter,* which provides news on changes in the tax laws and strategies to minimize taxes.

Research Institute of America (117 E. Stevens Ave., Valhalla, NY 10595; 914-241-7500; 800-431-9025; www.riag.com). Publishes in-depth analysis of tax laws in all formats, including print, CD-ROM, and the World Wide Web. *Federal Tax Coordinator,* which analyzes the tax code so you know how to optimize tax planning, and the *United States Tax Reporter* are both loose-leaf binder services that are updated weekly. *Weekly Alert* is a weekly newsletter explaining the latest changes in tax rulings and law. The *Federal Tax Handbook* answers about 1,150 questions that people ask most frequently about the tax code. Also publishes many manuals and reports about state and local taxes. Publishes a wide array of guidance for estate tax planning. CD-ROMs include *OnPoint System* for tax law analysis, *Estate Planning System, Wealth Transfer Planning,* and more. The Web product, CHECKPOINT, offers a comprehensive tax and tax planning library.

Warren Gorham and Lamont (The Park Square Bldg., 31 St. James Ave., Boston, MA 02116; 800-950-1210; www.riag.com). Provides journals, books and loose-leaf services for all aspects of taxation, including corporate, partnership, international, real estate, state and estate-planning specialties. The broadest of its services is called Tax Ideas, which provides ideas and strategies for all aspects of business and personal tax planning.

SOFTWARE

Kiplinger TaxCut (Block Financial Corporation, 4435 Main St., Kansas City, MO 64111; 816-751-6000; 800-235-4060; www.taxcut.com). A comprehensive tax planning and preparation software package. It comes in software and CD-ROM versions, with TaxCut Deluxe Multimedia offering a CD-ROM with two hours of explanatory videos. It has over 100 IRS worksheets and forms you can print from your computer. It also is designed to import data from the most popular personal finance programs such as Microsoft Money, Quicken and Managing Your Money. TaxCut is not as thorough as TurboTax, but it may be appropriate for your needs if your tax situation is relatively simple. TaxCut also includes software for the most populous state tax returns, whereas TurboTax charges extra for state-specific software. TaxCut has a feature allowing you to file your tax return electronically for free.

TurboTax and *TurboTax Deluxe* (Intuit, 2698 Marine Way, Mountain View, CA 94043; 415-944-6000; 800-446-8848; www.turbotax.com). Takes you through a tax preparation exercise using a series of questions and answers. Provides valuable advice and planning tips in preparing your tax strategy and returns. Also will print out completed federal and state tax returns and allow you to file your federal return electronically. TurboTax is available in both software and CD-ROM versions, as well as on the TurboTax online Web site. The Web site is designed for preparing simple tax returns. TurboTax Deluxe is available only in CD-ROM format. It has far more extensive resources, including video clips explaining various parts of the tax code.

FEDERAL GOVERNMENT REGULATORS

Internal Revenue Service (1111 Constitution Ave., N.W., Washington, DC 20224; 202-622-5000; www.irs.ustreas.gov). The main tax collection organization for the government. If you have a problem with the IRS, you can contact its Problem Resolution Program at 800-829-1040 for help. The current toll-free telephone number for the IRS, for the hearing impaired is: 800-829-4059.

The IRS has offices in every state. Generally, they have the same toll-free telephone number: 800-829-1040. For the hearing impaired, the number is 800-828-4059. Some offices have a different telephone number for questions about the tax code. In the list that follows, this phone number appears after the initials TH (tax help). The IRS also provides the Tele-Tax system—recorded information on more than 140 tax topics. Usually, the Tele-Tax telephone number is 800-829-4477. In cases where the number differs, it is noted in the following list after the initials TT (Tele-Tax). If you are calling the tax help or the Tele-Tax number from the city or county indicated in parentheses after the local phone number, use this local number; *no "1-800" is necessary before dialing the number.* If you are calling from elsewhere in the state, *use the general 800 number.* In each state, you must send your tax return to a specified mailing address. The following list provides these addresses. Simply mail your return to the Internal Revenue Service Center, along with the city and zip code. No street address is needed. For states with more than one mailing address, use the address indicated for your city or county. If your city or county is not listed under your state category, use the general address listed for your state. If you are an American citizen working abroad or are a service member of the Armed Forces with an APO or FPO address, file with the IRS Service Center at Philadelphia, PA 19255-0002.

Alabama Memphis, TN 37501-0002

Alaska Ogden, UT 84201-0002; (TH) 561-7484 (Anchorage)

Arizona Ogden, UT 84201-0002; (TH) 640-3900 and (TT) 640-3933 (Phoenix)

Arkansas Memphis, TN 37501-0002

California All other counties: Fresno, CA 93888-0002; (TH) 839-1040 and (TT) 839-4245 (Oakland); counties of: Alpine, Amador, Butte,

Calaveras, Colusa, Contra Costa, Del Norte, El Dorado, Glenn, Humboldt, Lake Lassen, Marin, Mendocino, Modoc, Napa, Nevada, Placer, Plumas, Sacramento, San Joaquin, Shasta, Sierra, Siskiyou, Solano, Sonoma, Sutter, Tehama, Trinity, Yolo, Yuba: Ogden, UT 84201-0002

Colorado Ogden, UT 84201-0002; (TH) 825-7041 and (TT) 592-1118 (Denver)

Connecticut Andover, MA
05501-0002
Delaware Philadelphia, PA
19255-0002
District of Columbia Philadelphia,
PA 19255-0002; (TT) 628-2929
Florida Atlanta, GA 39901-0002;
(TH) 354-1760 (Jacksonville)
Foreign country residents Phila-
delphia, PA 19255-0002
Georgia Atlanta, GA 39901-0002;
(TH) 522-0050 and (TT) 331-6572
(Atlanta)
Hawaii Fresno, CA 93888-0002
Idaho Ogden, UT 84201-0002
Illinois Kansas City, MO 64999-0002;
(TT) 312-886-9614 (Chicago and
708 area code); (TT) 789-0489
(Springfield)
Indiana Cincinnati, OH 45999-0002;
(TH) 226-5477 and (TT) 631-1010
(Indianapolis)
Iowa Kansas City, MO 64999-0002;
(TT) 284-7454 (Des Moines)
Kansas Austin, TX 73301-0002
Kentucky Cincinnati, OH 45999-0002
Louisiana Memphis, TN 37501-0002
Maine Andover, MA 05501-0002
Maryland Philadelphia, PA
19255-0002; (TH) 962-2590 and
(TT) 244-7306 (Baltimore)
Massachusetts Andover, MA
05501-0002; (TH) 536-1040 and
(TT) 536-0709 (Boston)
Michigan Cincinnati, OH
45999-0002; (TH) 237-0800 and
(TT) 961-4282 (Detroit)
Minnesota Kansas City, MO
64999-0002; (TH) 644-7515 and
(TT) 644-7748 (Minneapolis and
St. Paul)
Mississippi Memphis, TN
37501-0002

Missouri Kansas City, MO
64999-0002; (TH) 342-1040 and
(TT) 241-4700 (St. Louis)
Montana Ogden, UT 84201-0002
Nebraska Ogden, UT 84201-0002;
(TT) 221-3324 (Omaha)
Nevada Ogden, UT 84201-0002
New Hampshire Andover, MA
05501-0002
New Jersey Holtsville, NY
00501-0002
New Mexico Austin, TX 73301-0002
New York New York City, Nassau,
Rockland, Suffolk and Westchester
counties: Holtsville, NY 00501-0002;
All other counties: Andover, MA
05501-0002; (TH) 685-5432 and
(TT) 685-5533 (Buffalo)
North Carolina Memphis, TN
37501-0002
North Dakota Ogden, UT 84201-0002
Ohio Cincinnati, OH 45999-0002;
(TH) 621-6281 and (TT) 421-0329
(Cincinnati); (TH) 522-3000 and
(TT) 522-3037 (Cleveland)
Oklahoma Austin, TX 73301-0002
Oregon Ogden, UT 84201-0002;
(TH) 221-3960 and (TT) 294-5363
(Portland)
Pennsylvania Philadelphia, PA
19255-0002; (TH) 574-9900 and
(TT) 627-1040 (Philadelphia); (TH)
281-0112 and (TT) 261-1040
(Pittsburgh)
Rhode Island Andover, MA
05501-0002
South Carolina Atlanta, GA
39901-0002
South Dakota Ogden, UT
84201-0002
Tennessee Memphis, TN 37501-0002;
(TH) 834-9005 and (TT) 781-5040
(Nashville)

Texas Austin, TX 73301-0002; (TH) 742-2440 and (TT) 767-1792 (Dallas); (TH) 541-0440 and (TT) 541-3400 (Houston)
Utah Ogden, UT 84201-0002
Vermont Andover, MA 05501-0002
Virginia Philadelphia, PA 19255-0002; (TH) 698-5000 and (TT) 783-1569 (Richmond)

Washington Ogden, UT 84201-0002; (TH) 442-1040 and (TT) 343-7221 (Seattle)
West Virginia Cincinnati, OH 45999-0002
Wisconsin Kansas City, MO 64999-0002; (TT) 273-8100 (Milwaukee)
Wyoming Ogden, UT 84201-0002

The following are the TeleTax topic numbers you can enter on your touch-tone telephone when you call the service.

#	Subject
101	IRS services—Volunteer tax assistance, toll-free telephone, walk-in assistance, and outreach programs
102	Tax assistance for individuals with disabilities and the hearing impaired
103	Small Business Tax Education Program (STEP)—Tax help for small businesses
104	Problem Resolution Program—Help for problem situations
105	Public libraries—Tax information tapes and reproducible tax forms
911	Hardship assistance applications
151	Your appeal rights
152	Refunds—How long they take
153	What to do if you haven't filed your tax return (nonfilers)
154	Form W-2—What to do if not received
155	Forms and publications—How to order
156	Copy of your tax return—How to get one
157	Change of address—How to notify the IRS
201	The collection process
202	What to do if you can't pay your tax

#	Subject
203	Failure to pay child support and other federal obligations
204	Offers in compromise
251	1040PC tax return
252	Electronic filing
253	Substitute tax forms
254	How to choose a tax preparer
255	TeleFile
301	When, where, and how to file
302	Highlights of tax changes
303	Checklist of common errors when preparing your tax return
304	Extensions of time to file your tax return
305	Recordkeeping
306	Penalty for underpayment of estimated tax
307	Backup withholding
308	Amended returns
309	Tax fraud—How to report
310	Tax-exempt status for organizations
311	How to apply for exempt status
312	Power of attorney information
999	Local information
351	Who must file?
352	Which form—1040, 1040A, or 1040EZ?
353	What is your filing status?
354	Dependents
355	Estimated tax
356	Decedents

#	Subject	#	Subject
401	Wages and salaries	512	Business entertainment expenses
402	Tips	513	Educational expenses
403	Interest received	514	Employee business expenses
404	Dividends	515	Disaster area losses
405	Refunds of state and local taxes	551	Standard deduction
406	Alimony received	552	Tax and credits figured by IRS
407	Business income	553	Tax on a child's investment income
408	Sole proprietorship		
409	Capital gains and losses	554	Self-employment tax
410	Pensions and annuities	555	Five- or ten-year tax options for lump-sum distributions
411	Pensions—The General Rule and the Simplified General Rule		
		556	Alternative minimum tax
412	Lump-sum distributions	557	Estate tax
413	Rollovers from retirement plans	558	Gift tax
414	Rental income and expenses	601	Earned income tax credit (EITC)
415	Renting vacation property and renting to relatives	602	Child and dependent care credit
		603	Credit for the elderly or the disabled
416	Royalties		
417	Farming and fishing income	604	Advance earned income tax credit
418	Earnings for clergy		
419	Unemployment compensation	651	Notices—What to do
420	Gambling income and expenses	652	Notice of underreported income—CP 2000
421	Bartering income		
422	Scholarship and fellowship grants	653	IRS notices and bills and penalty and interest charges
423	Nontaxable income		
424	Social security and equivalent railroad retirement benefits	701	Sale of your home—General
		702	Sale of your home—How to report gain
425	401(k) plans		
426	Passive activities—Losses and credits	703	Sale of your home—Exclusion of gain, age 55 and over
		704	Basis of assets
451	Individual Retirement Arrangements (IRAs)	705	Depreciation
		706	Installment sales
452	Alimony paid	751	Social Security and Medicare withholding rates
453	Bad debt deduction		
454	Tax shelters	752	Form W-2—Where, when, and how to file
455	Moving expenses		
501	Should I itemize?	753	Form W-4—*Employee's Withholding Allowance Certificate*
502	Medical and dental expenses		
503	Deductible taxes		
504	Home mortgage points	754	Form W-5—*Earned Income Credit Advance Payment Certificate*
505	Interest expense		
506	Contributions		
507	Casualty losses	755	Employer identification number (EIN)—How to apply
508	Miscellaneous expenses		
509	Business use of home	756	Employment taxes for household employees
510	Business use of car		
511	Business travel expenses		

#	Subject	#	Subject
757	Form 941—Deposit requirements	855	Foreign earned income exclusion—What qualifies?
758	Form 941—*Employer's Quarterly Federal Tax Return*	856	Foreign tax credit
759	Form 940/940-EZ—Deposit requirements	901	Who must file a U.S. income tax return in Puerto Rico
760	Form 940/940-EZ—*Employer's Annual Federal Unemployment Tax Return*	902	Deductions and credits for Puerto Rico filers
761	Form 945—*Annual Return of Withheld Federal Income Tax*	903	Federal employment taxes in Puerto Rico
762	Tips—Withholding and reporting	904	Tax assistance for Puerto Rico residents
801	Who must file magnetically	951	IRS services—Volunteer tax assistance, toll-free telephone, walk-in assistance, and outreach programs
802	Acceptable media and locating a third party to prepare your files		
803	Applications, forms, and information	952	Refunds—How long they should take
804	Waivers and extensions	953	Forms and publications—How to order
805	Test files and combined federal and state filing	954	Highlights of tax changes
806	Electronic filing of information returns	955	Who must file?
		956	Which form to use?
807	Information reporting program bulletin board system	957	What is your filing status?
		958	Social security and equivalent railroad retirement benefits
851	Resident and nonresident aliens		
852	Dual status alien	959	Earned income tax credit (EITC)
853	Foreign earned income exclusion—General	960	Advance earned income tax credit
854	Foreign earned income exclusion—Who qualifies?	961	Alien tax clearance

The IRS offers many free publications on all aspects of the tax code. These are available when you call 800-829-3676. You also can download these publications and copies of all tax forms from the IRS Web site (www//irs.ustreas.gov) or by dialing directly by modem to the IRS bulletin board at 703-321-8020.

The following lists the major publications by number and name.

#	Free Publication	#	Free Publication
1	*Your Rights as a Taxpayer*	15	*Employer's Tax Guide (Circular E)*
3	*Tax Information for Military Personnel (Including Reservists Called to Active Duty)*	17	*Your Federal Income Tax (For Individuals)*
4	*Student's Guide to Federal Income Tax*	51	*Agricultural Employer's Tax Guide (Circular A)*

#	Free Publication	#	Free Publication
54	*Tax Guide for U.S. Citizens and Resident Aliens Abroad*	520	*Scholarships and Fellowships*
80	*Federal Tax Guide for Employers in the Virgin Islands, Guam, American Samoa, and the Commonwealth of the Northern Mariana Islands (Circular SS)*	521	*Moving Expenses*
		523	*Selling Your Home*
		524	*Credit for the Elderly or the Disabled*
		525	*Taxable and Nontaxable Income*
		526	*Charitable Contributions*
		527	*Residential Rental Property*
179	*Federal Tax Guide for Employers in Puerto Rico*	529	*Miscellaneous Deductions*
225	*Farmer's Tax Guide*	530	*Tax Information for First-Time Homeowners*
334	*Tax Guide for Small Business*	531	*Reporting Tip Income*
349	*Federal Highway Use Tax on Heavy Vehicles*	533	*Self-Employment Tax*
		534	*Depreciating Property Placed in Service Before 1987*
378	*Fuel Tax Credits and Refunds*	535	*Business Expenses*
448	*Federal Estate and Gift Taxes*	536	*Net Operating Losses*
463	*Travel, Entertainment, Gift and Car Expenses*	537	*Installment Sales*
		538	*Accounting Periods and Methods*
501	*Exemptions, Standard Deduction, and Filing Information*	541	*Tax Information on Partnerships*
502	*Medical and Dental Expenses*	542	*Tax Information on Corporations*
503	*Child and Dependent Care Expenses*	544	*Sales and Other Dispositions of Assets*
504	*Divorced or Separated Individuals*	547	*Casualties, Disasters, and Thefts (Business and Non-Business)*
505	*Tax Withholding and Estimated Tax*		
508	*Educational Expenses*	550	*Investment Income and Expenses*
509	*Tax Calendars*	551	*Basis of Assets*
510	*Excise Taxes*	552	*Recordkeeping for Individuals*
513	*Tax Information for Visitors to the United States*	553	*Highlights of 1997 Tax Changes*
514	*Foreign Tax Credit for Individuals*	554	*Older Americans Tax Guide*
515	*Withholding of Tax on Nonresident Aliens and Foreign Corporations*	555	*Federal Tax Information on Community Property*
516	*Tax Information for U.S. Government Civilian Employees Stationed Abroad*	556	*Examination of Returns, Appeal Rights, and Claims for Refund*
517	*Social Security and Other Information for Members of the Clergy and Religious Workers*	557	*Tax-Exempt Status for Your Organization*
519	*U.S. Tax Guide for Aliens*	559	*Survivors, Executors, and Administrators*

#	Free Publication	#	Free Publication
560	Retirement Plans for Small Business	721	Tax Guide to U.S. Civil Service Retirement Benefits
561	Determining the Value of Donated Property	850	English-Spanish Glossary of Words and Phrases Used in Publications Issued by the Internal Revenue Service
564	Mutual Fund Distributions		
570	Tax Guide for Individuals with Income from U.S. Possessions	901	U.S. Tax Treaties
571	Tax-Sheltered Annuity Programs for Employees of Public Schools and Certain Tax-Exempt Organizations	904	Interrelated Computations for Estate and Gift Taxes
		907	Tax Highlights for Persons with Disabilities
575	Pension and Annuity Income (Including Simplified General Rule)	908	Tax Information on Bankruptcy
		911	Tax Information for Direct Sellers
578	Tax Information for Private Foundations and Foundation Managers	915	Social Security and Equivalent Railroad Retirement Benefits
583	Starting a Business and Keeping Records	917	Business Use of a Car
		919	Is My Withholding Correct?
584	Nonbusiness Disaster, Casualty, and Theft Loss Workbook	924	Reporting of Real Estate Transactions to IRS
587	Business Use of Your Home (Including Use by Day-Care Providers)	925	Passive Activity and At-Risk Rules
		926	Household Employer's Tax Guide
589	Tax Information on S Corporations	929	Tax Rules for Children and Dependents
590	Individual Retirement Arrangements (IRAs) (Including SEP IRAs and SIMPLE IRAs)	936	Home Mortgage Interest Deduction
		938	Real Estate Mortgage Investment Conduits (REMICs) Reporting Information
593	Tax Highlights for U.S. Citizens and Residents Going Abroad	939	General Rule for Pensions and Annuities
594	Understanding the Collection Process	945	Tax Information for Those Affected by Desert Storm
595	Tax Guide for Commercial Fishermen	946	How To Depreciate Property
596	Earned Income Credit	947	Practice Before the IRS and Power of Attorney
597	Information on the United States–Canada Income Tax Treaty	950	Introduction to Estate and Gift Taxes
598	Tax on Unrelated Business Income of Exempt Organizations	953	International Tax Information for Businesses
686	Certification for Reduced Tax Rates in Tax Treaty Countries	954	Tax Incentives for Empowerment Zones and Enterprise Communities

#	Free Publication	#	Free Publication
957	*Reporting Back Pay and Special Wage Payments to the Social Security Administration*	1212	*List of Original Issue Discount Instruments*
967	*The IRS Will Figure Your Tax*	1244	*Employee's Daily Record of Tips and Report to Employer*
968	*Tax Benefits for Adoption*	1542	*Per Diem Rates*
969	*Medical Savings Accounts (MSA)*	1544	*Reporting Cash Payments of over $10,000 (Received in a Trade or Business)*
1004	*Identification Numbers under ERISA*		
1045	*Information for Tax Practitioners*	1546	*How To Use the Problem Resolution Program of the IRS*

U.S. Tax Court (400 2nd St., N.W., Washington, DC 20217; 202-606-8754). Hears cases involving disputes between taxpayers and the IRS.

14

Retirement—How To Get There from Here

Achieving financial security in your retirement years has never been more important. Massive changes in society mean that more people than ever before in human history will live in retirement for longer periods of time. For example, advances in modern medicine commonly extend lives into the 80s, 90s and even 100s. At the same time, budget-cutting corporations nudge—and, in some cases, push—employees into accepting early retirement packages. And millions of baby-boomers who married and started families in their 30s advance toward retirement supporting young children, meaning that they will be paying college bills just about the time they begin their retirements.

The only solution to the coming retirement crunch is to understand your options, plan carefully to meet your goals and follow through on your plan. Your alternatives for how you will live the last 20 to 40 years of your life could not be more stark. If you plan and save methodically, you could enjoy your golden years traveling, doing volunteer work, taking courses or pursuing whatever interests you. Alternatively, if you defer retirement planning, you could spend your final years financially impoverished like millions of senior citizens today.

The key to achieving a financially secure retirement is to start early. The younger you begin, the more you capitalize on your biggest ally: time. If you make the magic of compound interest work for you while you are in your 20s or 30s rather than your 40s or 50s, you will have a much better chance of amassing the capital you need to live on in retirement. To give you a dramatic example, if you earn $30,000 a year and save 6 percent of your salary each month, or $150, starting at age 30, and if you earn a 10 percent average annual return, you will end up with $574,242 by the time you reach age 65. If you start saving at age 55, assuming all other variables remain constant, you will reap only $30,983 ten years later. While retirement is probably the furthest thought from most people's minds when they are in their 20s and 30s, you can see that investing a small amount of money wisely can yield an enormous payoff.

Both employers and the government increasingly try to reduce their obligation to support you in retirement. Companies have become stingier about offering the traditional defined benefit pension plan, to which employees do not have to contribute. Today, they often replace the pension plan with a defined contribution profit-sharing plan, which may or may not include a 401(k) salary reduction plan. 401(k) plans benefit only employees who contribute some of their salary. The federal government, weighed down by trillions of dollars in debt, is in no position to increase Social Security benefits sharply and probably will reduce them as the baby-boomers near retirement. At the very least, people who have higher levels of income and assets will most likely see their Social Security benefits trimmed at retirement if the government adopts some form of means testing. Therefore, with the institutions that prior generations relied on for much of their retirement income likely to continue cutbacks in the future, your actions in building your savings and investments are going to be largely responsible for the quality of your retirement.

Projecting Expenses and Income in Retirement

The first step in assembling a realistic retirement plan is to calculate how much money you will likely need in retirement and to pinpoint your potential sources of income. To some extent, how much money you need depends on the lifestyle you lead in retirement. Traditionally, financial planners have suggested that retirees plan on spending between 60 and 80 percent of the amount they spent during their working lives. Some expenses, such as business clothing, Social Security taxes, life insurance premiums and transportation costs, should certainly decrease. In addition, you should be able to cut costs somewhat by taking advantage of senior citizen discounts. However, you might spend more for other expenses, such as leisure travel, health care and gifts to children and grandchildren. In addition, inflation will continue to increase your costs over time. To estimate what percentage of your working-years expenses you might continue to pay in retirement, go back over the cash flow exercise (see Figure 1.9) in Chapter 1, adjusting your likely expenses for a retired lifestyle. Then calculate your retirement expenses as a percentage of your working-years expenses (as mentioned, somewhere between 60 and 80 percent).

For a rough idea of your expenses in retirement, use the simple worksheet in Figure 14.1. It is designed to adjust your working-years level of expenses for retirement and to factor in a long-term inflation rate of 4.5 percent. The savings called for in item 2 include all regular savings plus contributions to retirement plans such as 401(k)s and individual retirement accounts (IRAs). The worksheet's sample figures assume an annual income of $50,000, an annual savings of $5,000, a 70 percent level of retirement spending and 20 years remaining before retirement. In completing this worksheet, refer to the numbers you used for income and savings in the Cash Flow Worksheet (Figure 1.9) in Chapter 1.

Figure 14.1 Retirement Expenses Worksheet

		Example	Your Situation
1.	Present Gross Annual Income	$50,000	$ _____
2.	Present Annual Savings	$ 5,000	$ _____
3.	Current Spending (Subtract item 2 from item 1.)	$45,000	$ _____
4.	Retirement Spending Level (Between 60% and 80%, depending on your assumptions of lifestyle)	70%	_____ %
5.	Annual Cost of Living (in present dollars) if You Retired Now (Multiply item 4 by item 3.)	$31,500	$ _____
6.	4.5% Inflation Factor (From table below)	2.4	_____
7.	Estimated Annual Cost of Living (in future dollars) at Retirement (Multiply item 6 by item 5.)	$75,600	$ _____

Years until Retirement	Inflation Factor
40	5.8
35	4.7
30	3.7
25	3.0
20	2.4
15	1.9
10	1.6
5	1.2

With this general idea of how much money you will need each year in retirement, examine your potential sources of income. The three main income sources for retirees are Social Security, pensions, and private savings and investments. The Social Security Administration will estimate for you your benefit in current dollars, based on your earnings and years of service. Your company's employee benefits department can tell you in today's dollars what you should expect to receive from your pension based on your current age and salary level. Adjust both the pension and Social Security figures by the same 4.5 percent inflation factor used in the Retirement Expenses Worksheet. To calculate the amount of savings and investments you will need to make up the difference, subtract the adjusted pension and Social Security amounts from your projected annual living expenses.

Finally, to estimate the amount of capital you must amass to generate that level of annual investment income, assuming a 5 percent rate of return, multiply the number by 20. (For example, you need $20,000 in capital to produce $1,000 in interest if it earns 5 percent annually.) If you want to assume a higher rate of return than 5 percent, multiply by a smaller number. For example, multiply by 10 if you want to assume a 10 percent average annual return (because $10,000 will produce $1,000 in interest at 10 percent).

Using the assumptions in the Retirement Expenses Worksheet, you would therefore need to amass $312,000 over the next 20 years until retirement if you want to maintain a lifestyle similar to your current lifestyle (see the Capital Accumulation Worksheet in Figure 14.2). Of course, many factors can change the amount of capital you need to accumulate. If your pension or Social Security benefit does not rise as fast as inflation, for example, you will require more in private savings. However, if you earn a higher return on your investments, you will need to save less.

The next step is to figure out how much money you must save each year before retirement to accumulate the needed capital. The amount of money calculated in item 8 in the Capital Accumulation Worksheet is not all the money you will need to fund your retirement. It is the amount needed to fund your first year of retirement. To keep pace with inflation, you must increase your savings by at least 5 percent a year until you reach retirement age. The Annual Savings Worksheet in Figure 14.3 will help you determine how much money you must save each year to meet this goal. The sample figures assume an after-tax rate of return of 7.5 percent on all investments and 20 years before retirement.

After running your numbers through the three worksheets, you should have a sense of how much money you need to save and invest each year to meet your retirement savings goal. If you would like to apply different rates of return and inflation rates and change other factors, investigate the software on the market that is designed to help you calculate how much you need to save for retirement. One simple program, called the *Retirement Planning Analyzer,* is available for $20 from

Figure 14.2   Capital Accumulation Worksheet

		Example	Your Situation
1.	Estimated Annual Cost of Living (in future dollars) at Retirement (Item 7 from Retirement Expenses Worksheet)	$ 75,600	$ _____
2.	Annual Pension Income	10,000	_____
3.	Inflation-Adjusted Pension Income (Multiply item 2 by appropriate inflation factor on page 645.)	24,000	_____
4.	Annual Social Security Benefit	15,000	_____
5.	Inflation-Adjusted Social Security Benefit (Multiply item 4 by appropriate inflation factor.)	36,000	_____
6.	Inflation-Adjusted Pension and Social Security Income (Add items 3 and 5.)	60,000	_____
7.	Amount by which Expenses Exceed Pension and Social Security Income (Subtract item 6 from item 1.)	15,600	_____
8.	Needed Capital (Multiply item 7 by 20.)	$312,000	$ _____

T. Rowe Price Associates (100 E. Pratt St., Baltimore, MD 21202; 800-541-1472; www.troweprice.com). Other personal finance programs such as *Quicken, Microsoft Money* and *Managing Your Money,* described in more detail in Chapter 1, also have retirement planning sections.

Social Security

An important aspect of the retirement income calculation is the amount that you will receive from Social Security. Don't believe the prophecies that the Social Security system will go broke and people now paying into it will receive no benefits. Millions of voters, including those receiving Social Security and those paying Social Security taxes, will make sure that politicians don't scrap the system. Nevertheless, the ratio of workers to retirees continues to shrink as the baby-boomers head into

Figure 14.3 Annual Savings Worksheet

		Example	Your Situation
1.	Capital Needed To Fund Retirement (Item 8 from Capital Accumulation Worksheet)	$312,000	$ _____
2.	Current Investment Assets (Value of stocks, bonds, mutual funds, etc.)	$ 30,000	$ _____
3.	7.5% Appreciation Factor (From table below)	4.2	_____
4.	Appreciation of Your Investment Assets until Retirement (Multiply item 2 by item 3.)	$126,000	$ _____
5.	Other Assets Required by Retirement Age (Subtract item 4 from item 1.)	$186,000	$ _____
6.	Savings Factor for Years until Retirement (From table below)	.0231	_____
7.	Savings Needed over the Next Year (Multiply item 5 by item 6.)	$ 4,296	$ _____

Years until Retirement	7.5% Appreciation Factor
40	18.0
35	12.6
30	8.8
25	6.1
20	4.2
15	3.0
10	2.1
5	1.4

Years until Retirement	Savings Factor
40	.0044
35	.0065
30	.0097
25	.0147
20	.0231
15	.0383
10	.0707
5	.1722

retirement, and Social Security rules are sure to change in coming years. Following are just a few ways that Social Security will or may be altered:

- *A means test may allocate a smaller benefit to higher income people.*

- *You will be penalized for retiring earlier than age 65.* Even under today's law, you receive only 80 percent of your full Social Security benefit if you retire at age 62. Under current rules, starting in the year 2000, this percentage will drop annually until it reaches 70 percent by the year 2022. It is certainly possible that the percentage will drop even more than that as Congress seeks ways to trim Social Security spending.

- *The minimum age for receiving full Social Security benefits will rise gradually from age 65 to 67, starting in the year 2003.* This affects people born in 1938 and later. For example, if you were born in 1940, your minimum retirement age will be 65½. If you were born in 1950, your minimum retirement age will be 66. If you were born in 1960 or later, you will be eligible for full retirement benefits at age 67. In the future, the minimum age will probably be extended even further.

- *You will be encouraged to retire later.* Under current law, your Social Security benefit grows 5 percent a year for every year you delay retirement, up to age 70. This rate will increase in the future until it reaches 8 percent per year for people turning 65 in 2008 or later. This incentive might be sweetened even more over time.

- *You may pay higher taxes on Social Security benefits.* You must pay tax on as much as 85 percent of your benefits if your provisional income, which includes tax-exempt municipal bond interest, plus one half of your Social Security benefit exceeds $44,000 for married couples filing jointly or $34,000 for all other filers except married couples filing separately. Those married filing separately are also subject to the 85 percent threshold when provisional income is greater than $0.

- *The percentage of your preretirement pay that Social Security is designed to replace will likely be reduced from the current 24 percent to 20 percent or less.*

- *Social Security payroll taxes will increase from the current 7.65 percent for employees to as much as 15 or 20 percent.* How high these tax rates can be pushed without causing a taxpayer revolt remains uncertain.

All of these changes mean that Social Security will likely make up an increasingly smaller percentage of your retirement income in the years ahead.

To be eligible to receive Social Security, you must work and pay taxes into the system. As you work, you earn Social Security credits, up to four quarters of credit per year. In 1998, you receive one quarter of credit for each $700 you earn during

Figure 14.4
Personal Earnings and Benefits Estimate Request Form

First Class Postage Required

SOCIAL SECURITY ADMINISTRATION
WILKES-BARRE DATA OPERATIONS CENTER
P.O. BOX 20
WILKES-BARRE, PA 18711-2030

SOCIAL SECURITY . . . It never stops working!

Figure 14.4
(continued)

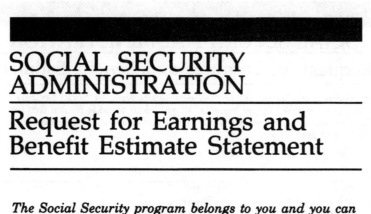

SOCIAL SECURITY ADMINISTRATION

Request for Earnings and Benefit Estimate Statement

The Social Security program belongs to you and you can count on it to be there for you. Social Security can protect you in many ways. It can help support your family in the event of your death and provide monthly payments and health insurance when you retire or if you become disabled.

To help you learn how Social Security is a part of your life, we are pleased to offer you a free Personal Earnings and Benefit Estimate Statement.

The Personal Earnings and Benefit Estimate Statement shows your Social Security earnings history and estimates how much you have paid in Social Security taxes. It also estimates your future benefits and tells you how you can qualify for benefits. When you receive your earnings statement, we hope you will use it to start planning for a strong financial future.

To receive your statement, please fill out the form on the reverse and mail it to us. You should receive your statement in 6 weeks or less. We look forward to sending it to you.

GWENDOLYN S. KING
Commissioner of Social Security

Figure 14.4
Personal Earnings and Benefits Estimate Request Form (continued)

SOCIAL SECURITY ADMINISTRATION
Request for Earnings and Benefit Estimate

To receive a free statement of your earnings covered by Social Security and your estimated future benefits, all you need to do is fill out this form. Please print or type your answers. When you have completed the form, fold it and mail it to us.

1. Name shown on your Social Security card:

    _____
    First   Middle Initial   Last

2. Your Social Security number as shown on your card:

    ☐ ☐ ☐ — ☐ ☐ — ☐ ☐ ☐ ☐

3. Your date of birth: _____ _____ _____
                        Month   Day   Year

4. Other Social Security numbers you have used:

    ☐ ☐ ☐ — ☐ ☐ — ☐ ☐ ☐ ☐
    ☐ ☐ ☐ — ☐ ☐ — ☐ ☐ ☐ ☐

5. Your Sex: ☐ Male   ☐ Female

6. Other names you have used (including a maiden name):

    _____

    _____

7. Show your actual earnings for last year and your estimated earnings for this year. Include only wages and/or net self-employment income covered by Social Security.

    A. Last year's actual earnings:

        $ ☐ ☐ ☐ , ☐ ☐ ☐ . [0] [0]
          Dollars only

    B. This year's estimated earnings:

        $ ☐ ☐ ☐ , ☐ ☐ ☐ . [0] [0]
          Dollars only

8. Show the age at which you plan to retire: ☐ ☐
                                                (Show only one age)

Form **SSA-7004-PC-OP1** (9-89) Destroy Prior Edition

Figure 14.4
(continued)

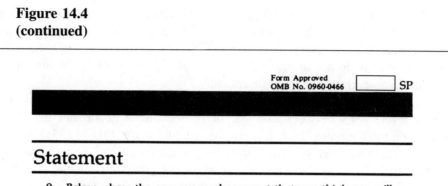

Form Approved
OMB No. 0960-0466   SP

Statement

9. Below, show the average yearly amount that you think you will earn between now and when you plan to retire. Your estimate of future earnings will be added to those earnings already on our records to give you the best possible estimate.

   Enter a yearly average, not your total future lifetime earnings. Only show earnings covered by Social Security. Do not add cost-of-living, performance or scheduled pay increases or bonuses. The reason for this is that we estimate retirement benefits in today's dollars, but adjust them to account for average wage growth in the national economy.

   However, if you expect to earn significantly more or less in the future due to promotions, job changes, part-time work, or an absence from the work force, enter the amount in today's dollars that most closely reflects your future average yearly earnings.

   Most people should enter the same amount that they are earning now (the amount shown in 7B).

   Your future average yearly earnings:

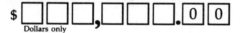

   $ ☐☐☐,☐☐☐.0 0
   Dollars only

10. Address where you want us to send the statement:

   _____
   Name

   _____
   Street Address (Include Apt. No., P.O. Box, or Rural Route)

   _____   _____   _____
   City   State   Zip Code

   I am asking for information about my own Social Security record or the record of a person I am authorized to represent. I understand that if I deliberately request information under false pretenses I may be guilty of a federal crime and could be fined and/or imprisoned. I authorize you to send the statement of earnings and benefit estimates to the person named in item 10 through a contractor.

▶
_____
Please sign your name (Do not print)

_____   _____
Date   (Area Code) Daytime Telephone No.

the year; the dollar amount is indexed to inflation annually. Most people need 40 credits, or 10 years of work, to qualify for benefits. If you work for many years, you will probably earn more credits than you need to qualify for Social Security. These extra credits do not increase the size of your benefit. Only the amount of income that you earn increases your check.

If you would like a current estimate of your Social Security benefit based on your pay level, years of work and age of retirement, write or call the Social Security Administration (8515 A Liberty Rd., Randalstown, MD 21133; 800-772-1213). Ask them to send you their *Request for Earnings and Benefit Estimate Statement,* also known as Form SSA-7004-PC. Once you complete and mail back the form, you will receive your payment history and a table of the benefits you might expect. A copy of the form appears in Figure 14.4.

Request this form every few years to make sure that the Social Security Administration correctly records your earnings. You may find that your employer has not reported all your earnings or that the Social Security Administration has not credited your wages to the correct Social Security number. If you find a discrepancy, point it out to the administration, and back up your claim with past W-2 forms from your employer. You want to receive every penny you deserve when you retire.

The table in Figure 14.5 shows what you and your spouse might expect to collect from Social Security if you both retire at full retirement age and had the same steady lifetime earnings. The calculations assume that you and your spouse are the same age. Your spouse may qualify for a greater or lesser retirement benefit based on his or her work record. The table is based on 1998 numbers, which are adjusted upward for inflation every year.

Your Social Security benefit will be reduced if you work part time in retirement. Between the ages of 62 and 65, you can earn up to $9,120 (1998 number) and still collect your full benefit. However, for every $2 you earn over that limit, your Social Security benefit decreases by $1. If you work between the ages of 65 and 69, you can earn up to $14,500 and still receive the full benefit. However, for every $3 you earn over that limit, $1 is withheld from your Social Security benefit. Once you reach age 70, you can earn as much money as you like; your Social Security income remains unaffected. Each year, these limits are adjusted upward for inflation. Only a salary or self-employment income is applied to the limits. Earnings from pensions, annuities, investments, Social Security or other government benefits do not count. Therefore, when deciding whether to work in retirement, consider the impact that income will have on your Social Security benefit.

SUPPLEMENTAL SECURITY INCOME (SSI)

For those with extremely low incomes and few assets, an additional source of retirement funds is *Supplemental Security Income* (SSI). The SSI program is run by the Social Security Administration, though benefits are paid from the U.S.

Figure 14.5

Approximate Monthly Benefits if You Retire at Full Retirement Age and Had Steady Lifetime Earnings

Your Age in 1998	Your Family	Your Earnings in 1997				
		$20,000	$30,000	$40,000	$50,000	$65,400 or More
45	You	$ 809	$1,076	$1,265	$1,390	$1,592
	You and your spouse	1,213	1,614	1,897	2,085	2,388
55	You	809	1,076	1,265	1,377	1,525
	You and your spouse	1,213	1,614	1,897	2,065	2,287
65	You	784	1,043	1,197	1,269	1,342
	You and your spouse	1,176	1,564	1,795	1,903	2,013

Source: *Social Security: Understanding The Benefits,* a booklet by the Social Security Administration.

Treasury, not the Social Security Trust Fund. To qualify for SSI, you must be a U.S. citizen living in the United States, and you must be 65 years or older, blind or disabled. The maximum income you can receive from private or government pensions or earn from a job differs by state. However, the government sets a national limit of $2,000 worth of assets for one person and $3,000 for a couple to qualify for SSI. When totaling assets, the Social Security Administration does not include the value of your home, your car or many of your personal belongings. Instead, it focuses on assets in bank and brokerage accounts and cash.

If you qualify for SSI, your benefit depends on how much you earn and where you live. However, the basic national benefit, which changes over time, is $494 a month for one person and $741 a month for a couple. Many states augment this basic benefit as well. SSI is also available for nonretired people, including children, with disabilities. To learn more about rules for qualification and benefit levels in your state, contact a local Social Security office, or call the Social Security Administration (800-772-1213; www.ssa.gov).

DISABILITY BENEFITS

In addition to regular Social Security retirement benefits, you can collect disability benefits if you become disabled. The government defines a disability as a physical or mental impairment that is expected to keep you from doing substantial work (earning $500 or more a month) for at least a year. Also, you may have a condition that a doctor certifies as terminal. If you qualify under these definitions, Figure 14.6 notes the monthly disability benefit you might receive from Social Security, based on your work and earnings history.

Figure 14.6
Approximate Monthly Benefits if You Become Disabled in 1998 and Had Steady Earnings

Your Age in 1998	Your Family	Your Earnings in 1997				
		$20,000	$30,000	$40,000	$50,000	$65,400 or More
25	You	$ 809	$1,076	$1,265	$1,390	$1,566
	You, your spouse and child	1,214	1,614	1,897	2,085	2,349
35	You	809	1,076	1,265	1,390	1,559
	You, your spouse and child	1,214	1,614	1,897	2,085	2,338
45	You	809	1,076	1,265	1,390	1,528
	You, your spouse and child	1,214	1,614	1,897	2,085	2,293
55	You	809	1,076	1,257	1,348	1,442
	You, your spouse and child	1,214	1,614	1,886	2,023	2,164
64	You	783	1,041	1,195	1,266	1,340
	You, your spouse and child	1,174	1,562	1,793	1,900	2,010

Source: *Social Security: Understanding The Benefits,* a booklet by the Social Security Administration.

SURVIVORS BENEFITS

Social Security will also provide regular income to your family if you die, no matter how old you are or whether you have accumulated enough work credit hours. Not everyone is entitled to *survivors benefits,* however. Family members can collect if they are a(an):

- widow or widower at least 60 years old;
- widow or widower at least 50 years old who is disabled;
- widow or widower of any age who cares for a child 16 years old or younger or a disabled child receiving Social Security benefits;
- unmarried child younger than age 18;
- unmarried child younger than age 19 who is enrolled in an elementary or a secondary school full time;
- unmarried child 18 years or older who has a severe disability that started before he or she reached age 22;

- parent who depended on the deceased for at least half his or her income;

- ex-spouse who is at least 60 years old (or 50 years old and disabled) and was married to the deceased for at least ten years before the divorce; or

- ex-spouse of any age if he or she still cares for a child eligible for benefits on the deceased's record.

A family's survivors benefits can total between 75 and 100 percent of the basic Social Security retirement benefit, depending on several factors. However, survivors can receive no more than between 150 and 180 percent of the basic monthly benefit. If the combined benefits from all family members exceed that amount, the total survivors benefit will be reduced proportionately.

The table in Figure 14.7 gives several examples of the benefits your surviving spouse and children might receive, depending on your age, your number of children and your level of earnings when you die.

Pensions

No matter how much Social Security you qualify for, as a sole source of income, it is clearly not enough to maintain a comfortable standard of living. You will need a regular source of pension income to enhance your retirement lifestyle. Two forms of pensions exist: one your employer provides without any contribution from you, and one to which you contribute part of your earnings during your working years, either through your employer or through a separate plan, such as an IRA or a Keogh account. In the best of all worlds, you would qualify for both types of pensions. However, if your employer does not fund a pension for you, you should build your own pension fund through a consistent savings strategy.

DEFINED BENEFIT PLANS

If you work for a company, government agency or nonprofit organization that provides a *traditional defined benefit pension plan,* you are fortunate. Many such plans are being cut back or eliminated because they are expensive to fund and administer. For those employees who qualify, defined benefit plans can provide a substantial portion—from 10 to 40 percent—of your total retirement income. The amount you receive often depends on how many years you worked for your employer and your salary in your final few years at the company. The longer you worked for the employer and the higher your salary, the fatter your monthly pension check.

Companies use several formulas to determine the size of your pension benefit. The best pension plan averages your salary for your final three or five years of work, when your income should be at its peak. A less generous plan averages your salary over your entire career. And you will receive the lowest benefit if your pension plan pays a flat dollars-per-month amount for every year you worked at

Figure 14.7

Approximate Monthly Survivors Benefits For Your Family if You Had Steady Earnings and Die in 1998

Your Age in 1998	Your Family	Your Earnings in 1997				
		$20,000	$30,000	$40,000	$50,000	$65,400 or More
35	Spouse and 1 child	$1,214	$1,614	$1,897	$2,085	$2,348
	Spouse and 2 children	1,459	1,914	2,215	2,434	2,741
	1 child only	607	807	948	1,042	1,174
	Spouse at age 60	578	769	904	994	1,119
45	Spouse and 1 child	1,214	1,614	1,897	2,085	2,302
	Spouse and 2 children	1,459	1,914	2,215	2,434	2,687
	1 child only	607	807	948	1,042	1,151
	Spouse at age 60	578	769	904	994	1,097
55	Spouse and 1 child	1,214	1,614	1,886	2,023	2,164
	Spouse and 2 children	1,459	1,914	2,201	2,361	2,526
	1 child only	607	807	943	1,011	1,082
	Spouse at age 60	578	769	899	964	1,031

Source: *Social Security: Understanding The Benefits,* a booklet by the Social Security Administration.

the company. This arrangement is usually used for union members. In anticipating the size of your pension benefit, know which of these methods of calculation your company uses.

To get a sense of what you might receive, contact your employee benefits department. You should get a yearly statement from the department detailing all your benefits, including your pension. If you don't receive one, request a personalized benefits statement, which will describe your monthly pension benefit starting at age 65 if you were to leave the company today. If you are young or haven't been at the company very long, the benefit may not amount to much; however, if you stay several years or even decades, the benefit can grow substantially.

Defined benefit pension plans are so named because they guarantee in advance the size of your monthly pension benefit. The company is responsible for funding the pension plan and choosing managers to invest the funds to earn a high return at a reasonable level of risk. The money managers invest in stocks, bonds, real estate, money-market securities, venture capital or other vehicles to produce a return high enough to make the promised payments to pensioners. If the company does not make the needed contributions, if investment returns fall short or, in the most extreme case, if the company goes out of business, pension payments are made from the remaining pension fund and, if necessary, from the federally backed *Pension Benefit Guaranty Corporation* (PBGC). (However, the PBGC does impose a maximum annual pension benefit of about $35,000, which increases with inflation every year.) With defined benefit plans, therefore, you do not have to worry very much about how the pension fund is invested because your benefit is guaranteed under almost all circumstances. However, examine the yearly statement of pension fund assets and liabilities you receive. You should feel comforted if the fund is fully or almost fully funded, and you should express some concern if the fund is severely underfunded.

To qualify for a pension, you must work for your employer a certain number of years to become vested. Under current law, most plans allow you to become fully vested after five years. This is known as *cliff vesting*. Alternatively, you can become vested on a graduated vesting schedule over seven years, during which you are 20 percent vested after the first three years and then vested 20 percent more in each subsequent year.

While you might be assured of receiving pension payments, you are by no means guaranteed that those payments, combined with Social Security, will adequately fund your retirement. Most pension benefits are fixed at the time you retire, so inflation slowly erodes the value of the benefits. (A few generous pension plans provide a cost-of-living adjustment for benefits, but don't count on it.) In addition, companies looking for ways to cut expenses can institute payment formulas that will reduce your benefit.

In the most extreme cases, companies will terminate their pension plans altogether and substitute an annuity purchased from an insurance company that will provide a fixed benefit, usually less than you would have earned from the pension plan directly. Such a substitution also replaces the ultimate backing of your pension payment from the federal PBGC with that of the insurance company. Although no one used to worry about this, it did affect thousands of pensioners whose annuities were backed by Mutual Benefit Life Insurance and Executive Life Insurance when those firms were taken over by regulators in the early 1990s. While no pensioner's payments were terminated, some payments were reduced, and many retirees were frightened about the possibility of losing their pension income.

As long as you are vested, your spouse will receive pension benefits if you die. Ask your benefits department how much your spouse might get in survivor's coverage if you were to die before retirement. Usually, the benefit is half the amount you would have received once retired, and it is paid starting in the year you would have stopped working, usually age 65. This is known as a *preretirement survivor's annuity*. If your spouse signs a document waiving the right to this annuity, the two of you will earn a larger pension benefit when you retire. However, if you die before retirement, your widow will not receive a pension from the company. Usually, it is not a good idea to take this risk, which could leave your spouse without pension income on which he or she had been counting. Most pension plans will also continue payments to spouses once the primary employees die if they opt for a *joint and survivor payout,* which is discussed in more detail in Chapter 16, "Making the Most of Your Employee Benefits."

Many insurance agents will advise you to choose a straight life annuity payout option instead of the joint and survivor option. This strategy is often called *pension maximization.* While the straight life choice pays a higher monthly amount, it ceases payments once you die. Insurance salespeople advocate taking a portion of the higher payments and buying an insurance policy to provide capital to cover your spouse's needs once you die. While this strategy may sound good in theory, it is usually not so in practice. The cost of the insurance policy, which includes large sales commissions, can consume most or all of the extra income provided by the straight life annuity. And the size of the death benefit may not adequately support your spouse for the rest of his or her life; therefore, your spouse will have to manage the money to produce extra income, which he or she may not have the expertise to do. It is therefore safer to choose the joint and survivor plan to make sure your spouse is covered until death.

The size of your pension benefit should weigh heavily in your decision to leave your employer for another. Every time you hook up with a new company, you start at square one in accumulating pension credits. The pension benefit you receive from your former employer is locked at the level earned when you left the company.

If you leave your present company for another, you may be offered the option to receive your pension benefit in a *lump sum,* which should be rolled over into the new firm's plan or an individual retirement account (IRA). When you accept a lump sum, you receive an amount that is discounted into today's dollars based on an assumed rate of return. Ask your employer what this rate of return is. If you think you can beat the return by investing on your own, consider taking the lump sum. However, if you fear that you won't do as well, you might leave the money with your employer's plan.

Also, complex rules mandate how that lump sum will be taxed. Under some conditions, you may be able to qualify for a favorable form of taxation called *five- or ten-year averaging,* which will greatly reduce your tax bite. However, you will not qualify for this kind of taxation once you've rolled the cash into an IRA. You must be extremely careful to make sure that any lump sum is deposited directly into an IRA through a *trustee-to-trustee transfer,* or the IRS will withhold 20 percent of the cash.

The decision to take all of your pension money at once is extremely complicated, so consult a qualified financial planner before you grab what may look like a huge chunk of cash. In many cases, you have no option in taking a lump sum. You must wait until retirement age to begin drawing payments from the plan. If, by chance, you return to a former employer, you will again earn pension credits, and depending on how long you were away, you may not be penalized much for your absence. In any case, for most people who will depend on that monthly pension check, it is far safer to opt for an annuity than to take on the responsibility of investing the lump sum.

DEFINED CONTRIBUTION PLANS

If your employer does not offer a traditional defined benefit pension plan, it probably offers a *defined contribution plan,* which gives you the opportunity to put aside money from your salary on a tax-deferred basis until you retire. Unlike a benefit plan, a contribution plan does not obligate your company to pay a certain pension benefit. Instead, you may set aside a certain contribution, which your employer may or may not match. Either way, however, you must choose among various investment options. This decision makes you responsible for the ultimate size of your pension benefit. Like income from all other pension plans, investment earnings from defined contribution plans grow tax deferred.

Your company may make its contributions to your plan in cash, which you can allocate among various investment options. Or it may give you company stock, which you can hold onto or, possibly, sell. Some companies offer a combination of cash and stock. The amount of your company's contribution is determined either by a percentage of its profits, in which case it is called a *profit-sharing plan,* or by a percentage of your salary, in which case it is called a *money-purchase plan.* In a profit-sharing plan, when the firm has a very profitable year, you might receive an additional 10 to 15 percent of your salary in your defined contribution account. But when profits fall or the company suffers a loss, you may get 5 percent or less, or possibly no contribution at all.

To qualify for participation in a company's plan, you usually must work there at least one year. Once you enroll in the plan, most companies give you the chance to match their contribution through payroll deduction. Some companies will contribute only if you do. Their match may be as generous as 100 percent or as little as 10 percent. A more typical match is 50 percent. So, if you set aside 6 percent of your salary in such a plan, the company would kick in another 3 percent every year. Few investments offer such an instant 50 percent return!

Any money that you contribute to a defined contribution plan is always vested, meaning that you can take it with you or roll it over into another firm's plan or an IRA if you change employers. However, to provide you with an incentive to stay, most firms make you wait three or four years before their contributions are fully vested.

SALARY REDUCTION PLANS

The most common type of defined contribution plan is a *salary reduction plan.* If you work for a private company, it is named a *401(k) plan* after the obscure section of the IRS code that permits it. If you are employed by a tax-exempt organization, such as a religious, an educational or a charitable group, it is called a *403(b) plan.* State and local government workers are offered *457 plans,* and federal employees can sign up for the *federal thrift savings fund*. Though these plans have their differences, they work basically the same way.

In each of these plans, your employer deducts a percentage of your salary— usually between 2 and 10 percent, according to your wishes—and deposits the funds in your plan account. The money is deducted from your salary before being taxed at the federal, state or local level and before Social Security taxes are deducted. As a result, the earnings you report to the IRS are lessened by the amount of your annual contribution. The money you set aside, whether or not it is matched by your employer, is invested in a range of stock, bond and money-market options, and all investment earnings accumulate tax deferred. You pay taxes only when you withdraw the money at retirement.

The IRS limits how much you can contribute annually to your salary reduction plan; that amount is increased each year for inflation. Currently, the limit for 401(k)s and federal thrift plans is about $10,000, while the cap for 403(b)s is $9,500 and you are limited to $7,500 for 457 plans. Although you should always try to contribute the maximum that your employer matches, you can add extra cash to boost you to the maximum if you can afford it. However, the IRS mandates that you cannot invest more than 25 percent of your salary or $30,000, whichever is less, into all company savings plans combined. The maximum contribution to all pensions is based on income up to $160,000, which may limit how much you can contribute to various retirement plans.

Once you see the money accumulate steadily in your account, you must allocate it among the various investment options presented. Some plans allow you to switch from one option to another every day (if you wish), while others limit you to quarterly or even annual shifts. You usually receive quarterly written reports describing your funds' progress, and often you can call the plan's representatives to learn the status of your account.

Usually, you will choose among various stock funds, bond funds or funds that combine stocks and bonds. Each category may offer many options. For example, among stock funds, you may be able to select aggressive, international, equity-income or index funds. Among bond funds, you may be offered government, corporate, international or junk bond funds. Some combined stock and bond options might include balanced and asset-allocation funds. In addition, most salary reduction plans offer money-market funds, company stock, and *guaranteed investment contracts* (GICs), which are similar to certificates of deposit (CDs). GICs pay a fixed rate for a set time, usually one to five years, and are backed by the insurance company or bank that issued them.

When deciding how to spread your money among investment options, apply the principles explained in this book. Assess your tolerance for risk, and balance that against the length of time before you need the money. Also, look at how you have allocated your money outside the salary reduction plan. If you hold mostly conservative bonds and CDs, you may want to invest more pension plan money in aggressive options. On the other hand, if you possess a large portfolio of aggressive stocks and mutual funds outside the salary reduction plan, you might want to put more of your pension money in conservative assets. In general, the younger you are, the more money you should invest in aggressive options; in the long run, growth-oriented vehicles like aggressive stock funds will outperform stodgy fixed-income bonds and GICs. The biggest mistake most people make is to sink most or all of their pension plan money in money-market accounts, GICs or bonds, thus depriving themselves of the opportunity for significant long-term gains from stocks.

As a rule of thumb, invest between 60 and 80 percent of your defined contribution money in stock funds while you are in your 20s, 30s and 40s. As you enter your late 40s and early 50s, cut that percentage to between 30 and 50 percent. From your late 50s into retirement, consider trimming stock investments to between 20 and 40 percent.

If you invest in stocks, however, don't sink too much money in your own company's stock. If your company matches your contributions in company stock, you will surely benefit if the firm does well. As wonderful as your company's prospects may be, you do not want to have too high a concentration of your plan's assets in your own company in case it runs into trouble. The worst thing that can happen to you, financially speaking, is that you invest most of your assets in your company's stock and its price plummets just as you are about to retire.

Withdrawing cash from a salary reduction plan before retirement. Consider withdrawing money from your salary reduction plan only if you desperately need to and have no other sources of funds. You have two ways of tapping your account. The better way is to borrow against your accumulated assets. Most plans allow you to borrow for whatever purpose you like; others let you borrow only for a major expense, like the down payment on a home or your children's tuition bills. Usually, you can borrow up to half the value of your account balance or $50,000, whichever is less, though some companies impose lower maximums. You normally have up to five years to repay the loan through payroll deduction. Most companies charge an interest rate either equal to or slightly above the prime lending rate. Because this is considered consumer interest, it is normally not tax deductible. (You may qualify for a deduction, however, if you use the proceeds to purchase investments that produce income.) If you leave your company while the loan remains outstanding, you must repay it, or the money due will be deducted from your account balance.

The other, less advantageous way to tap your salary reduction plan is to withdraw funds. In order to receive the money at all, however, you must prove that you suffer from a financial hardship. That means you have no other way of raising the money to pay huge unreimbursed medical bills, make post-secondary tuition payments, buy a home or prevent foreclosure or eviction. If you qualify for one of these hardships, you still must pay a 10 percent penalty on all withdrawals if you are younger than age 59½, as well as income taxes in the year you receive the funds. In addition, you forfeit all the tax-deferred compounding of investment interest and capital gains you would have earned if you had left the money in the account. Unless you find yourself in an extreme situation, it is therefore far better to borrow against your account balance than to withdraw from it.

Pension Plans for the Self-Employed

When you are self-employed, no one looks out for your interests—except you. Because you do not have the luxury of working for a company that offers a defined benefit or defined contribution plan, you must take a more active role in funding your retirement. If you never set up one of the pension plans that the IRS code allows, you will have to survive on only your personal investments and Social Security when you retire.

If you are self-employed, either full time or part time, you can contribute to either a *Keogh plan* or a *simplified employee pension plan* (SEP). Both allow you to make tax-deductible contributions, which you can invest in vehicles such as stocks, bonds, mutual funds and CDs. Here, the funds' earnings compound tax deferred.

All the money you stash in a self-employment retirement plan must be self-employment income. That means income from freelance writing, consulting, moonlighting, arts and crafts or any other way you earn money on your own. Farmers, doctors, lawyers and other professionals who are not covered by corporate plans may also fund a self-employment plan. Some such plans require you to contribute a certain amount of money every year. Other plans allow you to contribute whatever you please, up to an annual maximum, or nothing at all if you can't afford it or produce no self-employment income one year. As with other retirement plans, you must pay a 10 percent penalty and income taxes if you withdraw funds from a self-employment retirement plan before age 59½. Therefore, invest only funds that you will not need for living expenses or emergencies before you retire.

KEOGH PLANS

Named after U.S. Representative Eugene James Keogh, who first introduced the idea in the 1960s, Keogh plans come in both defined contribution and defined benefit form.

Defined contribution. The most common type of Keogh is the defined contribution variety, of which three forms exist: money-purchase, profit-sharing and combination.

A *money-purchase Keogh* requires you to choose a fixed percentage of your earnings and contribute it every year to the plan. That percentage can be as low as 1 percent or as high as 20 percent, up to a maximum of $30,000. You must contribute the money annually, no matter how profitable your business. If you don't contribute, you may be penalized by the IRS. Therefore, if you think you might have trouble meeting such a fixed obligation, consider investing in a profit-sharing Keogh.

A *profit-sharing Keogh* allows you to contribute up to 13.04 percent of your earnings, up to $30,000 a year. However, you can contribute the full amount one year and nothing the next, depending on how your business does.

A Keogh that *combines* both money-purchase and profit-sharing plans offers the option of contributing up to the maximum $30,000 but doesn't lock you into high payments. You can start with a profit-sharing plan, then add a money-purchase plan with a set annual contribution level, such as 8 or 10 percent. In good years, you can add money to your profit-sharing plan up to the maximum of $30,000; in lean years, you can pay only the minimum 8 or 10 percent.

Not only are Keogh plans available if you are the sole employee of your business; you can also enroll others who work for you. Rules for other employees regarding contribution limits, percentages of salary contributed and other matters differ slightly from those for single-worker plans. In general, you must contribute at least the same percentage of income for your employees as for yourself. Before you set up a Keogh for employees, check with a financial planner, an accountant or an employee benefits expert who can explain the rules.

Defined benefit. This less common variety of Keogh, which can be costly to establish and administer, allows you to contribute much more than the $30,000 limit imposed on defined contribution plans. In addition, each year the amount of money you add can be significantly greater or less than the amount you invested in previous years. With the help of an actuary, you should project your defined benefit at retirement, then contribute enough money while you are still working to fund that level of benefits. Defined benefit Keoghs usually are established by high-income people in their 50s with very successful businesses who have so far neglected to set up a pension plan. In effect, these plans allow them to catch up by investing a greater amount of capital at once to create a large pension benefit in retirement.

Other Keogh rules. Unlike you can an IRA, you cannot open a Keogh account right up until the April 15 tax-filing deadline. Instead, you must establish the Keogh by December 31 of the year in which you will file for the deduction. This is a key point to remember because one of the biggest advantages of a Keogh is that all your contributions are tax deductible. While you must open the account by the end of the year, you can make a contribution, or add to your existing account, any time up to April 15 (plus extensions) to claim the deduction for the previous year.

In general, it is difficult to withdraw cash from a Keogh before you reach age 59½ if you are an employer. Loans to employer-owners are barred and subject to severe IRS penalties. Employees enrolled in a Keogh can borrow up to half their vested balance, up to $50,000, which must be repaid through payroll deduction over five years.

Some paperwork goes along with establishing and maintaining a Keogh. If you deal with a reputable mutual fund company, stock brokerage, insurance company or bank, it should be able to help you complete and file the necessary forms though the firm will probably charge for the service. Accountants or financial planners can also prepare Keogh documents, such as the original application form and IRS Form 5500, which is the annual report required if the plan's assets exceed $100,000.

SIMPLIFIED EMPLOYEE PENSION (SEP) PLANS

SEPs are even easier to establish than Keoghs and involve much less paperwork. They combine some of the best features of IRAs and Keoghs. Like an IRA, a SEP establishes an account for each participant. As in a profit-sharing Keogh, you can contribute to a SEP one year and not the next if you desire. And as with other pension plans, you must pay a 10 percent penalty plus income tax if you withdraw money from a SEP before age 59½. In addition, you cannot borrow against SEP assets, the same way such loans are banned for holders of IRAs and employers with Keoghs. However, the government does not require annual filings of SEP plan assets, as it does for Keoghs. You can invest the assets of a SEP with a mutual fund, bank, credit union or stock brokerage.

To qualify for a SEP, your company must employ 25 or fewer workers who are considered eligible for the plan during the prior tax year. Eligibility is attained if an employee is at least 21 years old, has worked for the firm at least three of the past five years and has earned a certain minimum (currently about $400 although the number is indexed to inflation each year) from the employer. Half of your firm's employees must agree to participate before the plan can become effective. If you are the sole employee in your firm, you can set up a SEP just for yourself. Like a Keogh, a SEP allows a self-employed person to contribute up to 15 percent of his or her annual income, up to $30,000.

SEPs can be set up just like salary reduction plans, with each employee's contributions deducted before taxes and deposited in the investment account, where the funds grow tax deferred. A current maximum contribution of about $9,000 applies to SEPs, as well as to salary reduction plans. All of an employee's contributions are immediately fully vested, and an employer usually matches part or all of the employee's investment. And, finally, an employer earns a deduction for contributing up to 15 percent of each employee's wages.

As with an IRA, you can set up and fund a SEP until the April 15 tax deadline or an extension date to qualify for a tax deduction for the prior year. Therefore, if you miss the December 31 deadline for opening a Keogh, consider establishing a SEP instead. You also might look into setting up a SIMPLE (Savings Incentive Match Plan for Employees), which can be established as a SIMPLE IRA or SIMPLE 401(k) for firms with 100 or fewer employees.

Individual Retirement Accounts (IRAs)

Even if you have a defined-benefit or defined-contribution plan through your employer, or a Keogh or SEP if you are self-employed, you can also establish an IRA as a tax-sheltered vehicle to save for retirement. It can be quite complex to determine whether or not you qualify for a deduction for your IRA contribution. But in any case, the funds inside the IRA grow tax deferred, and in the case of a Roth IRA, tax free. Many people who formerly contributed to IRAs do not do so any longer because of the complexities of the law and the possibility that they will not be able to deduct their contributions. That may be a big mistake, particularly because of the attractiveness of Roth IRAs. Funding your IRA must be accomplished totally on your own initiative because no employer will offer you one. But the flexible account, allowing you to manage it however you want and offering an enormous range of investment options, is worth the extra effort.

WHEN CONTRIBUTIONS ARE DEDUCTIBLE

Depending on your employment status and level of income, the contribution you make to an IRA may or may not be deductible. If you are *not* eligible to participate in any qualified retirement plan, which includes the defined benefit and defined contribution plans discussed above, your IRA contribution of up to $2,000 a year and $2,000 for a nonworking spouse is tax deductible, no matter what your income. Also, if you earn less than $30,000 in adjusted gross income (AGI) as a single filer, or $50,000 as a couple filing jointly, you can deduct your IRA contribution, even if you are eligible for a qualified retirement plan.

The Taxpayer Relief Act of 1997 mandated that these limits be raised annually through the year 2007 until they reach $50,000 for a single and $80,000 for a married couple filing jointly. For singles, the limit rises $1,000 a year from 1998 through 2002, then jumps to $40,000 in 2003, $45,000 in 2004 and hits the $50,000 ceiling in 2005. For married couples filing jointly, the ceiling rises from $50,000 by $1,000 a year through 2002, then jumps to $60,000 in 2003, $65,000 in 2004, $70,000 in 2005, $75,000 in 2006 and tops out at $80,000 in 2007.

Once your income exceeds these levels and you are eligible to participate in a qualified plan, it gets trickier to determine whether your IRA is deductible. If you file a tax return as a single, your deduction gets phased out by $200 for every $1,000 you earn over $30,000. So, if you earn $40,000 or more, you can deduct none of your contribution. This cap is scheduled to rise gradually each year until it reaches $60,000 in 2005. For married couples filing jointly, the deduction disappears once adjusted gross income exceeds $60,000. That cap is scheduled to rise gradually until it reaches $100,000 in 2007.

If you earn somewhere in the middle of this scale, you can mix a deductible contribution with a nondeductible contribution to reach your $2,000 maximum. For example, a single filer earning $35,000 could make a deductible investment of $1,000, as well as a nondeductible contribution of $1,000.

If you earn more than the maximum level and are eligible for a qualified plan, you can still make a nondeductible contribution to an IRA. You and your spouse can each invest up to $2,000 a year from earnings. If your spouse does not work, you can contribute up to $2,000 for him or her in a spousal IRA. When you add a nondeductible contribution to your IRA, you must file IRS Form 8606 because the tax treatment of those funds will be different from the treatment of deductible contributions when you withdraw the money at retirement. When you contribute after-tax, nondeductible dollars, you will not be taxed on any distributions of your original capital, though you will be taxed on your accumulated earnings.

While a nondeductible IRA is certainly not as lucrative up front as a deductible IRA, it can still be a potent long-term tax shelter in which to accumulate a retirement nest egg. Because all dividends and capital gains are tax deferred until you are at least age 59½, you gain the advantage of tax-free compounding. In the long run, that shelter can be worth far more than the one-time tax reduction resulting from a deductible IRA contribution.

You can open an IRA account until the April 15 tax deadline and, if you are eligible, deduct your contribution on the previous year's tax return. However, do not wait until the last minute to invest your money because you lose valuable time for your earnings to compound tax deferred. It is far better to make your IRA deposit soon after January 1 of the year you will claim the deduction. This way, you have the full year of tax shelter. For example, it would be better to contribute $2,000 on January 3, 1999, for the 1999 tax year than to wait until April 15, 2000, because you will gain more than 15 months of additional tax-deferred compounding. You can continue to contribute to your IRA until you reach age 70½, at which point you must start withdrawing capital according to an IRS schedule.

ROTH IRAS

In addition to traditional IRAs, which permit your investments to compound tax deferred, the Taxpayer Relief Act of 1997 created a new breed of IRA called the Roth IRA. The Roth IRA allows your capital to accumulate tax free if you follow certain rules. It is named after Delaware Senator William V. Roth, Jr., who championed the idea of expanded IRAs. You and your spouse can each put up to $2,000 a year into a Roth IRA, even after you reach age 70½. You can withdraw all the principal and earnings totally tax free after age 59½, as long as the assets have remained in the IRA for at least five years after making the first contribution. The assets also can be withdrawn tax free if you are hit by a major disability. If you die before you start withdrawing from a Roth, the proceeds go to your beneficiaries tax free. Unlike regular IRAs, you do not have to take distributions from a Roth IRA starting at age 70½. In fact, you don't have to take distributions at all in your lifetime if you prefer, allowing you to pass the assets in the Roth to your beneficiaries income tax free.

You do not receive a deduction for contributing to a Roth IRA in the first place, unlike some other kinds of IRAs. But the value of completely tax-free withdrawals should far exceed the tax break from an up-front deduction.

Unlike regular IRAs, the Roth IRA rules permit you to withdraw assets without the usual 10 percent early withdrawal penalty, if you use the money for the purchase of a first home (withdrawals are limited to $10,000), for college expenses or if you become disabled.

There are income limitations on who can open Roth IRAs. You can contribute the full $2,000 if you are a married couple with an adjusted gross income of $150,000 or less or a single with adjusted gross income of $95,000 or less. The amount you can contribute is phased out for income between $150,000 and $160,000 for couples filing jointly and between $95,000 and $110,000 for singles. If your income is over those limits, you are not allowed to make a Roth contribution.

You can roll over assets from a traditional IRA to a Roth IRA under certain circumstances. If your adjusted gross income is $100,000 or less, you can roll over existing nondeductible and deductible IRA balances into a Roth without owing the 10 percent prepayment penalty. However, when you undertake such a rollover, you must pay income tax on all previously untaxed contributions and earnings. Figure out where you will get the money to pay this potentially large tax bill before you initiate this transaction. The two most likely sources for paying these taxes are your regular earnings or other savings. You should try to avoid selling a large part of your non-IRA portfolio and incurring capital gains taxes to raise the money to pay the taxes generated by a Roth rollover. This would not only decimate your portfolio, but it could also throw you into a higher tax bracket in the year you do it. It is preferable if you do not pay the taxes out of the proceeds from the IRA to preserve the maximum tax advantage of the Roth. For such rollovers completed before January 1, 1999, the tax bill is spread over four years, easing the pain at least somewhat. Starting in 1999, the rollover is fully taxable in the year it is completed.

Whether it makes sense to roll over money into a Roth from a traditional IRA depends on several factors. In general, the more you have accumulated in a traditional IRA, the more tax you will pay when you roll over to a Roth and the more time you need to recover those taxes from tax-free withdrawals. It probably does not make sense to roll over money into a Roth if you expect to be in a lower tax bracket when you retire, because you will pay lower taxes when you make withdrawals than you will when you roll over the funds during your working years. If you are young and have not accumulated very much in a traditional IRA, it might make more sense to roll over your balances to a Roth than if you have amassed a large sum that would generate a huge tax when rolled over. Many mutual fund and brokerage firms, including Fidelity, T. Rowe Price, Vanguard, Merrill Lynch and Salomon Smith Barney, offer customers free or low-cost software programs and sections on their Web sites allowing them to figure out whether or not a rollover to a Roth makes sense in their situation. The best way to take advantage of the Roth is to set one up when you are in your 20s, contribute the maximum allowed every year, invest the money for maximum capital gains and withdraw huge sums totally free of tax as needed in retirement.

TRANSFERRING IRA FUNDS

Once you build a substantial amount of capital in your IRA, you may want to transfer the funds from one institution to another. Your broker may have moved to a different brokerage house, for example, or you may want to relocate your money to a mutual fund company that has performed better than the one holding your money now.

Be extremely careful when transferring IRA assets. Your funds must go directly from one institution to another, without your ever touching the money. The IRS imposes a whopping 20 percent penalty on any transfer that does not flow directly between institutions. This law also applies to rollovers of funds from pension and profit-sharing accounts into your IRA. These transfers can often take a long time and get caught in administrative gridlock. Therefore, make sure that they are handled correctly, or you will end up with only 80 percent of the money you deserve when the funds finally arrive at the new custodian.

It is a good idea to deposit all your IRA assets with one custodian. You do not want to drown in the sea of paperwork that might result from filing IRS forms with many custodians. In addition, you will pay fewer fees if you keep all your assets in one place. The best custodian is one that offers a wide array of options so you can shift assets into whatever security or mutual fund suits your needs.

IRA WITHDRAWAL RULES

To maximize an IRA tax shelter, keep your money in it as long as possible. You are allowed to withdraw from the account without penalty starting at age 59½, and you must begin distributions by age 70½. If you take out money before age 59½, you will owe a 10 percent early withdrawal penalty, and you must pay income taxes on your distribution in the year you receive it. (Unlike salary reduction plans, IRAs do not allow you to borrow against your IRA assets under any circumstances.) However, a few exceptions to this penalty rule exist. IRA distributions can be made without penalty before age 59½ under the following conditions:

- you die and the IRA proceeds are distributed to your beneficiary or estate;
- you become permanently disabled; or
- the amount distributed is paid out as an annuity over your lifetime or your life expectancy in substantially equal amounts.

If you have made maximum use of your IRA tax shelter and not touched your proceeds by the time you turn 70½, you have to begin withdrawing at least a minimum amount of money each year thereafter. You must receive the first payment by April 1 of the year after you turn 70½. (*Note:* Your second distribution must be taken by December 31 of that same year.) The IRS requires you to withdraw an increasing proportion of your account each year so you will have withdrawn all your money by the time the actuarial tables predict you will die. If you designate your spouse as the beneficiary, you can calculate IRA withdrawals based on a combined life expectancy. The process of determining the minimum you must withdraw each year is quite complex, and you should ask your accountant or the company holding your IRA account, whether it be a mutual fund, bank or stock brokerage, to help you compute the amount. If you don't take out enough, the IRS will impose a whopping penalty of 50 percent of the difference between what you withdrew and what you should have withdrawn.

Another way to draw on your IRA is to take the entire balance in a *lump sum.* However, this subjects you to an enormous tax, which leaves less money to reinvest to generate the income on which you must live during retirement. You may also use the proceeds of your IRA to buy an *annuity.* As discussed previously, an annuity makes monthly payments to you for the rest of your life or, if you choose a joint and survivor payout option, for the rest of your life and that of your spouse. (For more detail on annuities, see Chapter 11, "All about Insurance.") To learn more about the different options you have in rolling over assets into an IRA from your company retirement plan, obtain the following free booklet published by T. Rowe Price: *Managing Your Retirement Distribution Rollover Kit* (available by calling 800-541-7894).

As with any other asset, when you open an IRA, designate a beneficiary who will receive the account's proceeds when you die. If you are married, most likely you will name your spouse as beneficiary. Once you die, your spouse will roll your IRA assets into his or her IRA. However, if you name someone who is not a spouse to receive your IRA proceeds, you must spell out in the plan to whom you want the money distributed.

INVESTING IRA FUNDS

When you understand the rules of contribution and withdrawal, learn to maximize your investment options. IRAs offer many investment vehicles, including individual stocks, bonds, mutual funds, unit investment trusts (UITs), limited partnerships, futures funds, CDs, options, gold and silver coins minted by the U.S. government such as the American Eagle and platinum and palladium. The two classes of investments in which you cannot legally deposit IRA funds are collectibles and physical real estate. *Collectibles* is defined as artwork, stamps, numismatic coins, gems, antiques, or gold or silver coins minted outside the United States. *Physical real estate* includes both your own home and rental real estate you own as an investment. Although it is legal to invest in municipal bonds within an IRA, it doesn't make sense because you do not need tax-exempt income in a tax-sheltered account.

Two philosophies exist regarding the best way to take advantage of the tax-deferred feature of IRAs. Some investment advisers favor growth and maintain that you want the fastest growing investments possible, such as aggressive growth stocks or futures funds, because an IRA is a long-term vehicle that allows you to accumulate a significant amount of assets by retirement. You can trade in and out of stocks, bonds and options without caring about the tax consequences of your actions because all gains are tax deferred for years.

Other investment advisers believe that you should stuff your IRA with the highest yielding investments available, such as high-yield stocks, bonds, mortgage-backed securities, income mutual funds, CDs and UITs. They reason that because all IRA income compounds tax deferred, you want to earn the highest income possible. Therefore, if interest rates are high, probably the best IRA investment is a zero-coupon bond, which automatically locks in that high rate of reinvestment until the bond matures. You also know exactly how much capital you will have accumulated as many as 30 years in the future. No other investment guarantees that.

Both ways of thinking are valid. You can decide to go with one strategy or the other, or you can mix the two. However you allocate your IRA funds, though, integrate your IRA into your total investment portfolio to achieve a proper balance. For instance, if your salary reduction plan is invested in conservative GICs or bonds, sink your IRA funds in more aggressive growth stocks. On the other hand, if you own many growth stocks in your personal portfolio, as well as growth mutual funds in your 401(k), be more conservative with your IRA money, and select high-quality bonds or bond funds.

However you allocate the money, it is more important to open an IRA early in your working life and contribute to it year after year. The capital that accumulates in your IRA could make the difference between a comfortable and a meager retirement.

Other Savings and Investments

In addition to Social Security, pensions and IRAs, the capital you accumulate through your regular savings and investment program will provide retirement income. Depending on how much you receive from Social Security, company-sponsored pension plans and your own tax-sheltered IRA, Keogh or SEP, your private savings may amount to anywhere from 30 to 50 percent of your retirement income. If you are not eligible for pensions and have not funded your own tax-sheltered plan, your private savings are all that separates you from living on Social Security—often a meager existence.

As a general rule, try to save as much as possible as early in your career as possible for maximum growth. Aim to save about 10 percent of your gross income each year, allocated among salary reduction plans, IRAs and Keoghs, as well as your independent savings accounts and investments.

Ideally, you should invest most of your capital aggressively while you are in your 20s, 30s and 40s to accumulate the largest pool of capital possible. This means buying all of the investment vehicles at the apex of the financial pyramid of risk described in Chapter 1. These include growth stocks, aggressive growth mutual funds, junk bonds and international investments. As you move into your 40s and mid 50s, scale back the risk level of your investments, emphasizing the middle tier of the pyramid. Purchase equity-income funds, convertibles, balanced funds and other vehicles that offer income as well as growth. By the time you retire, if you have accumulated a substantial amount of capital, you can become even more conservative and invest 60 percent or more of your money in low-growth vehicles, such as government and municipal bonds, CDs, money-market funds and Treasury bills, that will produce regular income on which you can live. However, do not sink all of your money in totally safe investments once you retire. You will probably live many years yet, and to keep up with inflation, you need the continuous growth of capital that stocks provide. For more detail on all of these investments and others, consult Part 1 of this book, "Maximizing Your Investment Options."

One investment designed for retirees is the *annuity,* which is sold by insurance companies. Annuities are discussed in great detail in Chapter 11, "All about Insurance." They can provide a steady stream of income for as long as you and your spouse live. You might find that the best way to convert a large portion of your accumulated savings into a reliable monthly check is to buy an annuity with a good payout plan. To find the best annuities, consult the newsletter *Annuity & Life Insurance Shopper* (United States Annuities, 8 Talmadge Rd., Monroe TWP., NJ 08831; 908-521-5110; 800-872-6684). The newsletter compares the current rates paid by most immediate annuities, as well as the returns on fixed and variable annuities.

Another way to boost your retirement income is to cash in on the value you have built up in your home. You may want to sell your home and buy a smaller one or rent an apartment that will cost less and be easier to maintain. If you are a married couple filing jointly, you can avoid all capital gains when selling your primary residence if your profit is $500,000 or less. If you are single, you avoid all capital gains taxes if your profit is $250,000 or less. Your primary residence is defined as a home in which you lived for at least two of the past five years. You can sell your primary residence every two years and take advantage of this rule. There is no requirement that you reinvest your home sale proceeds in another house, so if you like, you can rent another home and invest the proceeds in stocks, bonds, mutual funds, annuities and other investments that will pay you a regular income.

You don't have to move or sell your home to cash in on it, however. You can get a *reverse mortgage,* also known as a *home-equity conversion,* in which a lender—such as a bank or thrift—makes a loan against the value of your home and sends you a monthly check for as long as you live in the residence. How much you get depends on your life expectancy, the amount of equity in your home and the interest rate charged by the lender. When you die or move to another home, the lender usually takes title to the property and sells it to pay off the loan balance. Reverse mortgages are discussed further in Chapter 8, "Inside Real Estate." You can also contact the National Center for Home Equity Conversion (7373 147th St. West, Suite 115, Apple Valley, MN 55124; 612-953-4474; www.reverse.org), which publishes a book titled *Your New Retirement Nest Egg: A Consumer Guide to the New Reverse Mortgages.* This text describes in detail how reverse mortgages work and includes the *Reverse Mortgage Locator,* which lists all reverse mortgage lenders in the country. You may also want to consult *Home-Made Money: Consumer's Guide to Home Equity Conversion,* published by the American Association of Retired Persons (listed under "Trade Associations" in the "Resources" section at the end of this chapter).

Evaluating an Early Retirement Offer

From a purely financial point of view, the later you retire, the more generous your benefits. That applies to Social Security and pensions, as well as to IRAs, SEPs and Keoghs, which will have more time to compound tax deferred. However, you might not want to work into your late 60s for health or other reasons. Or your employer may offer you early retirement, which you should evaluate. Many people retire at much younger ages today, either voluntarily or because they have been forced out of their jobs.

Let's begin by assuming that your employer does propose early retirement. In some cases, all chosen employees are offered the same deal; however, individual negotiation often sweetens the package considerably. When weighing the proposal, first review the exercise at the beginning of this chapter to ascertain how much money you will need in retirement and how much you will receive from Social Security, pensions and other benefits, in addition to whatever early-retirement lump sum your employer offers. Calculate the value of your accumulated savings and investments to determine how much income they might provide. Remember to factor inflation into your expenses as you assess how much capital you will need to live comfortably in future years. If you find that you might have enough to retire on, look at the details of the severance package more closely.

Ask your employer the following questions:

- *What benefits can I keep?* It is particularly important to be able to purchase health insurance at group rates because it is expensive to buy as an individual. Also, ask whether dental and life insurance coverage continue.

- *Do I have a choice in how my severance package is paid out?* Some firms offer only a lump sum, while others distribute funds through an annuity. Depending on your ability to invest the money wisely, you may be better off taking the lump sum. You will probably want to roll that money into an IRA, which will allow the capital to grow tax deferred.

- *What are the components of my package?* Some plans add several years to your actual years of service to boost your pension payouts. Others give you a fixed-dollar amount for every year of service. Still others let you keep your retirement funds in company savings plans though they probably won't let you contribute any more.

- *What happens if I don't take the offer?* Depending on whether the offer is made to a few select employees or to a whole division, you can decide whether you are being targeted for elimination. You want to feel rather certain that if you turn down the package, you will not be laid off anyway. Also, investigate the situation on your own to assess whether the company has run into serious trouble and is cutting costs every way it can, or whether its prospects are bright and it is offering packages to cut costs and boost profitability.

- *Can I work out some kind of continuing relationship with the company if I take the package?* Many valued employees become freelancers or consultants when they leave.

Then, ask yourself a few questions:

- *If I take the offer, how do my chances look for getting other work?* You may have skills that are in high demand and therefore be able to land another job quickly. Or you may have always wanted to write a book, open a restaurant or buy a bed-and-breakfast in the country. But if you think you will have a hard time landing or creating another job, you might want to hang onto your present position, if possible.

- *If I don't take the offer, what will the working environment be like?* If the cutbacks are so severe that the remaining employees will be overburdened with work, morale might plummet, and you might wish that you no longer worked there.

- *If I take the offer, how will I feel about not going to my usual place of work every day?* If you have hated your job for years, the thought of leaving the office or factory might gladden your heart. But if your job is your main source of self-fulfillment, you might feel a tremendous emotional loss if you give it up.

- *Do I really have a choice?* Even if the incentive package is officially considered voluntary, you may feel that you really have little choice but to accept the offer. For example, you might be threatened with a layoff if you don't accept the package. Or your employer may offer a small window of eligibility, which pressures you to accept. However, you cannot be forced out of your job purely because of your age, according to the federal *Age Discrimination in Employment Act* (ADEA) of 1967. In addition, based on the *Older Workers Benefit Protection Act* (OWBPA) amendments to ADEA, which were passed in 1990, retirement incentives cannot discriminate against older workers.

Even if you never receive an early-retirement offer, you must decide when to stop working full time. Study after study has shown that the people who enjoy their retirement years most are those who participate enthusiastically in some endeavor, whether it be a job or a hobby. In fact, many companies hire older workers part time these days because retirees often have such a strong work ethic. Therefore, even though you may leave full-time employment, you don't have to wither away in a rocking chair.

Choosing a Retirement Lifestyle

If you have done everything right and you have set up a reliable stream of retirement income, you still must decide on the lifestyle you want to live in your golden years. In addition to deciding how much you will work in retirement, also consider your housing alternatives; possibilities for continuing education, hobbies and volunteering; and travel opportunities.

HOUSING OPTIONS

Probably the most important decision you must make is where you want to live as you grow older. Most people remain in the homes they lived in while working, but many retirees move to a warmer climate or a town that imposes less of a tax burden. While the lure of a warm and possibly faraway place and fresh start may be appealing in theory, think through such a decision carefully. It can be difficult to put down new roots at a stage in your life when you may want to relax. You might also find that moving farther from your children and close friends means that you see them less. You will also have to replace your entire network of professionals, from doctors and plumbers to financial planners, which took years to assemble. On the other hand, you might make this transition easily and thrive in your new setting.

If you want to move, consider the following factors as you evaluate potential locations:

- access to high-quality medical care
- cost of housing, as well as ongoing cost of living
- crime rate
- cultural and recreational attractions
- ease of making friends

- educational opportunities
- estate tax rules
- proximity to friends and family
- quality of shopping
- state and local income taxes
- weather

To help you choose, consult one of the guidebooks that rate retirement communities, such as Rand McNally's *Places Rated Retirement Guide.* Wherever you pick to move, it is a good idea to rent in the new place for a few months to make sure that you like it before you sell your home and move there. You do not want to go through the ordeal of selling your home of many years and moving all your possessions to a new place, only to discover that you do not like to live there after all.

For the most adventurous retirees, a move to a foreign country makes sense. The U.S. dollar often goes much further in other countries than it does at home, and you may be able to find an enclave of retired Americans, which will make you feel almost like you still live in the States. The countries with the largest concentrations of expatriate Americans are Mexico, Canada, Italy, the Philippines, Greece, Germany, Great Britain and Israel.

If you are thinking of retiring abroad, evaluate the political stability of the country, as well as the exchange rate for the dollar. Some developing countries like Mexico and the Philippines offer a lower cost of living, while industrialized nations like Great Britain and Germany are far more expensive. Inquire about your tax obligations if you move abroad. As long as you remain a U.S. citizen, you owe U.S. taxes. In some countries, you must pay local income tax as well. Usually, you can claim a foreign tax credit on your U.S. return to offset those local taxes. Also, look into health insurance coverage because it is unlikely that Medicare will cover you if you live abroad.

RETIREMENT HOUSING ALTERNATIVES

As you age, you might find that maintaining your home is becoming too much of a burden. If so, several options offer varying levels of independence combined with help with everyday living. The most common alternatives follow:

Independent living facility. Such facilities include government-subsidized housing developments designed for retirees in good health who need minimum assistance. They also include private retirement communities with separate housing for each resident.

Manufactured home park. If you own a mobile home, you can move it to a retirement-oriented park, where you pay rent and a service fee for electricity, water and recreational facilities. In some cases, retirees band together and run such parks as nonprofit cooperatives, in which each resident owns a share of the corporation that owns the park.

Congregate housing facility. In such facilities, you live independently in your own apartment and share with other residents common services such as a dining room, social and recreational programs and housekeeping.

Assisted-living facility. If you are less able to take care of yourself, such a place offers private or semiprivate rooms, meals, housekeeping and ongoing medical attention. Help with dressing, grooming and other personal care is available.

Continuing-care community. This housing development is designed for all stages of a retiree's life, including independent living, assisted living and nursing home care. As your needs change, you move from one facility to another within the community. You usually sign a long-term continuing-care contract with the community, which provides that the community's administrators will make sure you receive the level of aid you need as you age. You also must pay an entrance fee plus a regular monthly charge that cover you for as long as you live in the community. Contact the American Association of Homes for the Aging (AAHA, 901 E St., N.W., Suite 500, Washington, DC 20004; 202-783-2242; www.aahsa.org) for a list of continuing-care communities that are accredited by the association.

In evaluating any of these housing alternatives, ask yourself the following questions:

- *Does the facility offer the services I need now and am likely to need in the future?*

- *Do I like the facility's location?* Does it offer nearby recreational or cultural attractions?

- *What is the track record of the company running the facility?* Is it financially solid? How long has it been in the business of operating retirement facilities? What is the facility's occupancy level? (An 80 percent occupancy level within a year or two of opening means that clients are satisfied.)

- *What kind of contract must I sign?* You may be offered a rental agreement for a few months or years. You may have to buy the housing unit to live there. Or you may have to pay a life-use fee, which guarantees you the right to live in the facility until you die for a one-time investment of several thousand dollars as well as a monthly fee. In this case, if you move out, some of your investment may be refunded.

- *What services are available in the facility?* Ask about appliances, parking, utilities, exercise and recreation classes, security, housekeeping, meals and transportation.

- *What is the quality of medical care provided?* Look into the availability of general practitioners and specialists, dentists, home health care aides, drug dispensaries, physical therapists and psychiatric care. Ask whether the facility is certified to receive Medicare and Medicaid.

- *Does the facility accept Medicare assignment or Medicaid patients?* For example, ask whether the facility accepts Medicare and your Medicare supplement as payment in full. Do you have to pay the difference between the actual charge and Medicare's allowable charge? What other fees do you have to pay? What are optional services that could add to your fees?

Finally, tour the facility extensively, and talk to as many residents as possible to learn whether they are satisfied with the condition of the physical plant and the level of service provided. If a residents association or council exists, attend a meeting to get a sense of how well the facility is managed.

The decision about where to live is an important one and shouldn't be made hastily or without plenty of investigation.

Continuing Education, Hobbies, Volunteering and Traveling

To live a fulfilled life in retirement, you might cultivate activities that you never had time for during your working life. After you've cleaned the house and caught up on your reading, you will probably want to get involved in something that gives you a sense of satisfaction. The four most common pursuits for active retirees are continuing education, hobbies, volunteering and travel.

Continuing education. Most colleges offer courses aimed at retirees on almost every subject you can imagine. You can take them either for credit toward a degree or on a noncredit basis, just to expand your knowledge. Some courses take only a few weeks, while others last for a quarter or a semester. In addition, many communities offer free or low-tuition programs aimed at seniors and funded by the state or local government. And some universities sponsor *learning-in-retirement institutes* (LIRs), in which members of the institutes serve as instructors. A few of the better known LIRs include the Institute for Retired Professionals at the New School for Social Research in New York City; the Academy of Lifelong Learning at the University of Delaware; and the College for Seniors at the University of North Carolina at Asheville.

Aside from contacting local schools and community centers, another way to learn about continuing education programs is through *Elderhostel* (75 Federal St., Boston, MA 02110-1941; 617-426-7788; www.elderhostel.org). This organization conducts classes in many subjects in about 40 countries. Each course usually lasts a week and is held on a college campus, where you stay in a college dormitory and eat at the college cafeteria. You may also want to look into *Interhostel,* a two-week program combining courses and touring in many countries. It has links with universities and cultural institutions around the world that host the program. Contact Interhostel (University of New Hampshire, 6 Garrison St., Durham, NH 03824; 603-862-1147; 800-733-9753; www.learn.unh.edu) for more information.

If you don't want to travel for your courses, bring them into your home. For a copy of the National University Continuing Education Association's *Guide to Independent Study,* a list of correspondence classes, contact Peterson's Publishing (P.O. Box 2123, Princeton, NJ 08543-2123; 609-243-9111). If you are interested in more technical or vocational programs, contact the National Home Study Council (1601 18th St., N.W., Washington, DC 20009; 202-234-5100; www.detc.org).

Hobbies. Once retired, you will have more time to pursue a new hobby or develop one you could only dabble in during your working years. Most of the hobbies discussed below are inexpensive though some can become costly for avid hobbyists. These are just a few of the hobbies you might find interesting.

- *Collecting.* You can collect stamps, coins, antiques, artwork or anything else that interests you.

- *Crafts.* You can become an expert in many crafts, including quilting, needlework, photography, model building, ceramics, furniture repair and stained glass.

- *Games.* You might take up bingo, bridge, card games, checkers, chess, Monopoly, backgammon and many other sociable games.

- *Group activities.* You can join civic, political, religious or social clubs that might draw on your professional experience.

- *Outdoor activities.* You may enjoy birdwatching, camping, gardening or hiking.

- *Pets.* You might get satisfaction from raising cats, dogs, horses, ducks or fish.

- *Reading.* You can join or start a book club or frequent your local library to enrich your knowledge.

- *Sports.* To stay in shape and have fun, you might participate in boating, bicycling, tennis, bowling, fishing or swimming, to name a few.

- *Theater.* You can join a local theater group to learn acting or attend plays with a group and discuss the performance in a structured way.

Volunteering. One of the most rewarding ways to spend your time in retirement is to volunteer to help others who can learn from your experience or benefit from your time. For example, if you ran a business, help a struggling entrepreneur turn a profit. If you know art, volunteer to be a museum guide. If you are a member of a church or temple, volunteer your help wherever necessary. And to help those who are less fortunate, volunteer at the Salvation Army or almost any social service organization. The following organizations can help you locate the volunteer opportunity that is best for you:

- ACTION (1100 Vermont Ave., N.W., Washington, DC 20525; 800-424-8867; www.cns.gov). The federal agency that coordinates all volunteer activities. Some of its programs include the Foster Grandparent Program, the Retired Senior Volunteer Program (RSVP), the Senior Companion Program, the Service Corps of Retired Executives (SCORE) and Volunteers in Service to America (VISTA).

- Corporation of National Services (CNS, 1201 New York Ave., N.W., Washington, DC 20525; 800-942-2677; www.cns.gov). A nonprofit management consulting group that places top-caliber, retired executives who volunteer their time and expertise to nonprofit organizations in education, the arts and social services. CNS also operates the Senior Career Planning and Placement Service and the Math-Science Education Program, which places retirees with technical skills in schools.

- National Association of Partners in Education (901 N. Pitt St., Suite 320, Alexandria, VA 22314; 703-836-4880; www.NAPEhq.org). Will direct you to volunteer programs in schools.

- National Council on the Aging (409 3rd St., S.W., Suite 200, Washington, DC 20024; 202-479-1200; www.ncoa.org). An advocacy organization for retired people. Publishes the magazine, *Senior Citizen News,* which covers topics of interest to older Americans.

- National Council of Senior Citizens (8403 Colesville Rd., Suite 1200, Silver Spring, MD 20910; 301-578-8800; www.ncscinc.org). Offers volunteer opportunities in community agencies, such as child care, home health and adult education programs.

- Peace Corps (1990 K St., N.W., Washington, DC 20526; 202-606-3010; www.peacecorps.com). Appeals to hardy retirees who want to make a difference in impoverished parts of the world. You must first go through training and then live under spartan conditions, where you earn a small monthly stipend.

Whatever retirement activities you choose, you have myriad opportunities to learn and help others.

Traveling in Retirement

One of the biggest joys of retirement can be the opportunity to travel to places you have always wanted to visit—and to do it at your own pace. Not only do you have the advantage of time; you also can qualify for discounts of as much as 50 percent on tours designed for seniors.

If you travel with a group on a prepackaged tour, you will pay a better price than if you booked airfare and hotels on your own, and you will be shown the highlights of the places you visit. The tour operator will also take care of your luggage and other arrangements. However, you may not want to spend your entire trip sightseeing with the group. Therefore, make sure that any tour you choose leaves enough time for you to explore on your own, at your own pace. A convenient way of visiting many locations without constantly packing and unpacking is to board a cruise ship that stops in several ports.

If you want to plan your own itinerary, do plenty of research before you book airfares and hotels. Many good books will guide you to the best accommodations at the best prices. Before making reservations, set up a budget that details how much you will spend for transportation, hotels, food and souvenirs. It is easy to get carried away once you arrive at the destination of your dreams.

Use your senior power to get the biggest discounts possible. Following is just a sampling of the perks available:

- All U.S. national parks are free to any U.S. citizen 62 years or older who has a Golden Age Passport. This document, which you can apply for in person with proof of age at any National Park or Forest Service Station, allows you to pay half price for boating, parking, camping and other park services. Make sure to reserve your spot months in advance.

- Most U.S. airlines offer discounts of as much as 25 percent to seniors who buy airline coupon books. Some airlines provide special frequent flier clubs for seniors that offer extra discounts.

- Amtrak, Greyhound and Trailways offer price breaks of 10 to 15 percent for seniors on most of their fares.

- Membership in some senior organizations grants you substantial discounts. You can qualify for discounts at certain hotels if you show that you are a member of AARP, the National Council of Senior Citizens or the National Alliance of Senior Citizens (all listed in the "Resources" section of this chapter).

- Membership in some senior organizations grants you substantial discounts. The AARP Travel Experience (800-927-0111) provides hundreds of discount tour packages. You also qualify for hotel discounts if you prove that you are a member of the National Council of Senior Citizens or the National Alliance of Senior Citizens (both listed in the "Resources" section at the end of this chapter).

For more information on travel for seniors, subscribe to the *Mature Traveller* newsletter (see "Resources" at the end of this chapter for more information). Also, consult one of the many travel agencies that specialize in arranging travel for seniors, such as Grand Circle Travel in Boston (347 Congress St., Boston, MA 02210; 800-221-2610). Call for its free booklet titled *Going Abroad: 101 Tips for Mature Travelers.*

If you are willing to spend a little time and effort contacting specialized travel sources, you can save a great deal of money on hotels, cruises, dining and airfare. In the "Resources" section of this chapter, I have listed several hotel services that book rooms in particular cities like New York, Los Angeles, San Diego, San Francisco and Washington, D.C., that usually will get you a far better rate than if you called the hotels directly. There is also a national service called Hotel Reservations Network at 800-964-6835 offering the same service in many cities. For cruises, many deals are available, and one source you may try is the Cruise Travel Club at 800-685-6518. To get discounts or rebates on dining, you might try several of the services that sign up thousands of restaurants and either give you a 20 percent discount on the spot, such as Transmedia (11900 Biscayne Blvd., North Miami, FL 33181; 800-422-5090) or Dining a La Card (800-253-5379), which send you a 20 percent rebate check once a month based on your total spending, including tax and tips, in participating restaurants. Several airlines, including American and United, also have established Dining Discount programs that allow you to cut the cost of eating at participating establishments and earn frequent flier miles for every dollar you spend on meals.

By using the Web sites sponsored by various airlines, you also can save a considerable amount of money on airfares. Most airlines post their available inventory of seats on a regular basis on their sites. If you find that space is available for the destination and time that suits your needs, you can book the flight online, often at substantial savings over the regular fares. Airlines would rather sell their seats at 50 percent off regular fares than have the seats go empty. So the nearer a flight is to taking off, the larger the discounts become. There is a complete list of all the airline Web sites in the "Resources" section of this chapter.

If you plan on traveling overseas, update your passport, and obtain any needed visas. Also, check whether the country to which you are headed requires or recommends immunizations. Because health insurance policies, and particularly Medicare, often do not cover medical problems when you are out of the United States, it may be worth paying for the Medical Assistance Program, which provides short-term coverage for health problems while traveling in a foreign country. You can obtain it through either your regular health insurer or your travel agent. Make sure to bring plenty of whatever medication you are taking because the drug may be difficult, if not impossible, to find outside the United States. In addition, you might look into buying travel insurance, which covers canceled or delayed trips, lost baggage, accidents and other mishaps of the road. These maladies are not normally covered by your regular homeowner's policy although they may be included in insurance attached to your credit or American Express card.

Taking Care of the Next Generation

If you save for and enjoy your retirement years, you should have assets remaining to pass on to your children, your grandchildren and others dear to you when you die. If you have not already dealt with the complex and difficult subject of estate planning, do so now. Read the following chapter, "Estate Planning—

Keeping Your Assets in the Family," and follow its suggestions to transfer the remainder of your wealth to people you choose—not to the government.

Resources

BOOKS, BOOKLETS AND PAMPHLETS

Beat the Nursing Home Trap, by Joseph Matthews (Nolo Press, 950 Parker St., Berkeley, CA 94710; 510-549-1976; 800-992-NOLO; www.nolo.com). All the information you need to make the best choices for long-term care, such as how to protect your assets, arrange home health care, find nursing and non-nursing home residences, rate nursing home insurance policies and get the most from Medicare, Medicaid and other benefit programs.

A Common Sense Guide to Your 401(k), by Mary Rowland (Bloomberg Press, 100 Business Park, Princeton, NJ 08542). This book explains the retirement landscape in America and why 401(k)s have become so important. It goes through the basics of 401(k) plans, how to get money into and out of them, and how to invest the money when it is in the plan. The volume covers steps to take in planning for retirement and provides several sample portfolios. It also touches on 403(b) and 457 plans.

The Complete Idiot's Guide to 401(k) Plans, by Wayne Bogosian and Dee Lee (Alpha Books, MacMillan Reference USA, 1633 Broadway, New York, NY 10019; 800-428-5331; www.mgr.com). Describes how 401(k) plans work, how to allocate investments inside them, how to take money out of 401(k)s and much more. Loaded with worksheets.

The Complete Retirement Workshop: Your Guide to Planning a Secure and Rewarding Future, by Bureau of Business Practice (Prentice Hall Incorporated, 200 Old Tappan Rd., Old Tappan, NJ 07675; 800-223-1360). Describes what to expect from Medicare and Social Security, how to get good investment and insurance advice, what the best places to retire are and how to plan far in advance so you will have the money you need to retire in style.

Ernst & Young's Retirement Planning Guide (John Wiley & Sons, One Wiley Dr., Somerset, NJ 08875; 800-225-5945; www.wiley.com). This comprehensive guide has extensive sections on investment strategy, choosing financial advisers, and how to maximize 401(k)s, IRAs and Keogh plans. It addresses unique retirement issues facing executives, the self-employed, women and non-traditional families, and has a section on overcoming adverse financial events like corporate downsizing and personal disability. It provides worksheets, quizzes, Web sites and resources to help retirees.

Feathering Your Nest: The Retirement Planner, by Lisa Berger (Workman Publishing Co., 708 Broadway, New York, NY 10003; 212-254-5900; 800-722-7202;

www.workmanweb.com). Explains how to map out your retirement needs, invest prudently, take care of estates and wills, minimize taxes in retirement and live a rewarding lifestyle when retired.

Fidelity Investments Retirement publications (P.O. Box 500, Merrimack, NH 03051; 800-544-8888; www.fidelity.com). Fidelity offers a wide range of free publications on retirement planning and investment strategy, and also has an extensive retirement section on their Web site. Some of the publications include *401*(k) *Briefing Plan, Guide to Retirement Plans for Self-Employed People, Individual Retirement Account Kit, Keogh Kit, Retirement Planning Guide, Rollover Kit, SEP-IRA Kit, SIMPLE Plan Kit* and the *Spousal IRA Kit.*

How To Pay Less Tax on Your Retirement Savings, by Seymour Goldberg (JK Lasser Press, MacMillan Publishing, 1633 Broadway, New York, NY 10019; 800-428-5331; www.mgr.com). Explains the tax advantages of 401(k) and 403(b) plans, Roth IRAs and other tax-favored vehicles. Covers the best way to take distributions and minimize taxes, using careful estate planning and trusts.

How To Plan for a Secure Retirement, by Barry Dickman and Trudy Lieberman (Consumer Reports Books, P.O. Box 10637, Des Moines, IA 50336; 515-237-4903; 800-500-9760). Helps you estimate your income and expenses in retirement so you can plan ahead. Also covers health care plans, housing options and estate-planning topics.

How To Protect Your Life Savings from Catastrophic Illness, by Harley Gordon (Senior Planning Group Publications, 214 Lincoln St., Suite 110, Allston, MA 02134; 617-783-4365; 800-582-2889). Explains Medicaid system, including the latest Spousal Impoverishment Act regulations. Describes the pitfalls in Medicaid planning. Helps you get the best long term health care coverage to pay for nursing homes and other long-term health care. Updated to reflect the Kennedy-Kassebaum health care legislation.

How To Retire Young and Rich, by Joseph Coyle (Warner Books, 1271 Avenue of the Americas, New York, NY 10020; 212-522-1212). Gives you the basics on planning for and enjoying retirement. Coyle, a longtime *Money* magazine editor, explains how to figure out how much you will need in retirement, how to pick the right age to retire and how to pick mutual funds for building a retirement nest egg. The book draws on articles from past issues of *Money,* such as how to locate the best places to retire.

Legal Rights for Seniors: A Guide to Health Care, Income Benefits and Senior Legal Services (HALT, An Organization of Americans for Legal Reform, 1612 K St. NW, Suite 510, Washington, DC 20006; 202-887-8255; 888-367-4258; www.halt.org). A self-help book containing information for seniors on Medicare, Medicaid, Medigap policies, Social Security, estate planning, pensions, life insurance, guardianships, nursing home care, veterans benefits and other issues. Also provides a listing of state agencies that help the aging, as well as other senior-oriented organziations.

Maximize Your IRA: Make the New Rules Work for You, Choose the Right Plan, Discover New Ways To Use Your IRA, by Neil Downing (Dearborn Financial Publishing, 155 N. Wacker Dr., Chicago, IL 60606; 312-836-4400; 800-245-2665; www.dearborn.com). The complete guide to the many individual retirement choices you now have available. It covers the new Roth IRA, traditional tax-deferred IRAs and all the rules surrounding them.

The Only Retirement Guide You'll Ever Need, by Kathryn and Ross Petras (Fireside Books, 1230 Avenue of the Americas, New York, NY 10020). A comprehensive guide to retirement planning, including sections on investments, insurance, IRAs, Social Security, health care, working in retirement, estate planning and housing options.

Price Waterhouse Retirement Planning Advisor (Pocket Books, Simon & Schuster, 200 Old Tappan Rd., Old Tappan, NJ 07675; 800-223-2336). A complete guide to planning for a financially secure retirement.

Retirement Income Guide (A.M. Best Company, A.M. Best Rd., Oldwick, NJ 08858; 908-439-2200). Provides detailed information on the multibillion-dollar annuities market. Includes latest comparative data on more than 450 annuity plans.

Retirement Made Easy (Aetna Insurance Co., 151 Farmington Ave., Hartford, CT 06156; 203-273-0123; 800-US-AETNA). A simple booklet, available free from this major insurance company, that helps you save, invest and determine your insurance needs. Comes with a Save and Earn Wheel, which tells you how much you will have at retirement assuming different monthly and annual contributions to savings and an 8 percent annual return. Wheel tells you how much you will have accumulated after 5, 10 and 20 years of saving.

Retire Worry-Free: Financial Strategies for Tomorrow's Independence, by Michael E. Leonetti (Dearborn Financial Publishing, 155 N. Wacker Dr., Chicago, IL 60606; 312-836-4400; 800-322-8621; www.dearborn.com). Explains easy ways to plan for a financially secure retirement.

T. Rowe Price Retirees Financial Guide (T. Rowe Price Associates, P.O. Box 89000, Baltimore, MD 21289-0250; 800-638-5660; 800-225-5132). A helpful kit about retirement planning. Available free from T. Rowe Price, a large mutual fund marketing organization. Kit includes three publications: "Investing Your Retirement Assets: The Risk of Being Too Safe"; "Retirees Planning Workbook"; and "Retirement Living: Challenges to Financial Security." Firm also offers publications on financial planning once you are retired. For example, will send a free packet called *Managing Your Retirement Distribution,* which includes the brochure "Deciding What To Do with Your Company Retirement Money." Brochure explains different options, such as rolling over your funds into an IRA, taking a lump-sum distribution or leaving the money in your employer's plan.

Social Security, Medicare and Pensions: Get the Most Out of Your Retirement and Medical Benefits, by Joseph Matthews and Dorothy Matthews Berman (Nolo Press, 950 Parker St., Berkeley, CA 94710; 510-549-1976; 800-992-NOLO; www.nolo. com). This guide shows those over age 55 how to maximize benefits and make sure they get what they are entitled to. It explains the rules surrounding Social Security retirement and disability benefits, Supplemental Security income, Civil Service retirement benefits, Medicare, Medicaid and Medi-gap health insurance. Loaded with charts and graphs showing what to expect at what age.

Ten Minute Guide to Retirement for Women, by Kerry Hannon (Alpha Books, MacMillan Publishing, 1633 Broadway, New York, NY 10019; 800-428-5331; www.mgr. com). A brief outline of the basics of personal finance in retirement for women. The book covers insurance, creating a portfolio, choosing a financial planner, covering medical expenses, estate planning, working in retirement, annuities and company stock plans.

The Working Woman's Guide to Retirement Planning, by Martha Priddy Patterson (Prentice Hall Incorporated, 200 Old Tappan Rd., Old Tappan, NJ 07675; 800-223-1360). Describes how to accumulate retirement savings in 401(k) plans, pension plans and other company retirement plans. Discusses a woman's right to her husband's or ex-husband's retirement benefits. Covers the financial impact of marriage and divorce on retirement planning. Explains how to weigh the pros and cons of an early-retirement offer.

Your Next 50 Years: A Completely New Way To Look at How, When and If You Should Retire, by Victoria Collins and Ginita Wall (Henry Holt & Co., 115 W. 18th St., New York, NY 10011; 212-886-9200; 888-330-8477; www.henryholt.com). This book challenges baby boomers who have saved little and seen their pensions cut look at retirement as a renaissance. By that, the authors mean a time to renew, refocus and recharge based on long-range dreams and goals. They explore practical alternatives to retirement such as sabbaticals, flextime and part-time retirement. The book is loaded with worksheets to help you do insurance, investment and estate planning.

Your Retirement Benefits, by Peter E. Gaudio and Virginia Nicols (John Wiley & Sons, One Wiley Dr., Somerset, NJ 08875-1272; 800-225-5945; www.wiley.com). Focuses on all current major retirement plans and how to make them work for you. The book uses a question and answer format to guide you through an understanding of IRAs, 401(k)s, ESOPs and defined benefit plans. It also provides worksheets so that readers can apply the advice to their own situations. There are also extensive reference tables providing statistical data on life expectancy, the power of compounding and more.

"Your Rights over Age 50" (American Bar Association, 541 N. Fairbanks Ct., Chicago, IL 60611-3314; 312-988-5000; www.abanet.org). A pamphlet in question-and-answer format covering such topics as age discrimination in employment, credit, higher education, pensions, Social Security, Medicare and Medicaid.

MAGAZINES

Mature Outlook (Mature Outlook, Meredith Corp., 1716 Locust St., Des Moines, IA 50309-3023; 515-284-2007; 800-336-6330). Covers topics of interest to preretirees and retirees, including travel, fitness and health, people and relationships, food and nutrition, role models and lifestyle adventures. Associated with the Mature Outlook Club, which offers a newsletter, car rental and hotel discounts and discount coupons at Sears stores.

Modern Maturity (601 E St., N.W., Washington, DC 20049; 800-424-3410; www. aarp.org). The official magazine of AARP. Covers legislative issues facing retirees and provides inspirational stories and informative features to help people achieve more fulfilled retirement years.

New Choices for Retirement Living™ (Retirement Living Publishing Co., Inc., 28 W. 23rd St., New York, NY 10010; 212-366-8800; 800-388-6111; www.seniornews. com). Dedicated to helping readers enjoy retirement. Offers 50-Plus Pre-Retirement Services, a program that provides the following booklets: *Finding the Right Place for Retirement; How To Cope with the IRS; Personal Information and Records Inventory; Planning Your Tomorrow: What You Don't Know Can Hurt You!; Single Living; 65 Mistakes To Avoid in Retirement; What I Wish Someone Had Told Me about Retirement; What You Should Know about Ripoffs;* and *Your Social Security Benefits.* "Health and Your Successful Retirement: A Head-to-Toe Guide to Good Health"; "Housing and Your Successful Retirement: Home and Lifestle Options for Better Living"; "The Law and Your Successful Retirement: Important Facts about the Law You Should Know Now"; "Leisure and Your Successful Retirement: Planning Your Leisure Time for an Active and Fulfilling Life"; "Money and Your Successful Retirement: A Guide to Financial Success in Your Retirement"; "Planning for Your Successful Retirement: Prepare Now for a Happy and Rewarding Future"; and "Working in Retirement: Working for Financial Gain and Psychological Well-Being" are also offered.

NEWSLETTERS

Annuity & Life Insurance Shopper (United States Annuities, 8 Talmadge Rd., Monroe TWP., NJ 08831; 908-521-5110; 800-872-6684). Provides updated performance records of immediate, deferred, fixed and variable annuities. Also covers financial strength and product offerings of insurance companies.

Elderlaw News (Ampersand Solutions, 40 Beerborn St., Newton MA 02165; 617-350-5600). Covers developments in the law relating to retired people. Frequently discusses the latest estate-planning techniques.

Finance Over 50: Building Your Retirement Wealth (360 Grand Ave., Suite 133, Oakland, CA 94610; 510-704-9490; 800-769-6310). A monthly newsletter to guide retirees on safe investing strategies. Recommends individual stocks and mutual funds.

Mature Traveller (P.O. Box 50400, Reno, NV 89513-0400; 702-786-7419). Provides the latest information on discounts and tours for seniors.

Retirement Letter (Phillips Publishing, 7811 Montrose Rd., Potomac, MD 20854; 301-340-2100; 800-777-5005; www.phillips.com). A monthly newsletter covering many issues related to retirement. Offers investment suggestions, tax-planning ideas, travel advice, home repair tips and news from Washington that affects retired people.

Retire with Money (P.O. Box 60001, Tampa, FL 33660-0001; 800-633-9970). Newsletter published by *Money* magazine aimed at preretirees and retirees, with a heavy emphasis on investing and mutual funds. Also covers regulations and tax and health news affecting retirees.

United Retirement Bulletin (United & Babson Investment Report, 101 Prescott St., Wellesley Hills, MA 02181-3319; 617-235-0900). A monthly newsletter that tracks retirement trends. Covers estate-, tax- and financial-planning techniques and investment ideas. Also provides book reviews on topics of interest to retired people and offers suggestions on travel and hobbies.

SOFTWARE

Harvest-Time™ (Retirement Planning Software, 1824 Walker Lane, Henderson, NV 89014; 702-433-2695; 800-397-1456). Helps you calculate how much you must save to enjoy a comfortable retirement. Makes it easy to track the growth of tax-free municipal bonds, tax-deferred qualified retirement plans such as IRAs and Keoghs, and nonqualified tax-deferred plans such as annuities. Allows you to do "what-if" testing on saving and spending strategies allowing you to figure out how much you need to save to retire at different lifestyles. Also publishes the Harvest Time Professional program, which is aimed at financial planners and other professionals.

Retirement Planning Analyzer (T. Rowe Price Associates, 100 E. Pratt St., Baltimore, MD 21202; 800-541-1472; 800-638-5660; www.troweprice.com). A simple piece of software available for a nominal charge. Allows you to estimate your expenses in retirement and determine how much you must save to generate the capital you need to live comfortably. Also lets you enter your assumptions about inflation, rate of return on your investments, taxes, life expectancy and many other factors to see how they change the amount you should accumulate.

TRADE ASSOCIATIONS

Aging Network Services (4400 East West Highway, Suite 907, Bethesda, MD 20814; 301-657-4329; www.agingnets.com). Provides referrals to social workers specializing in caring for the aged.

American Association of Homes for the Aging (901 E St., N.W., Suite 500, Washington, DC 20004; 202-783-2242; www.aahsa.org). Helps the elderly find appropriate housing. Tracks the accreditation of health facilities and can recommend well-run communities.

American Association of Retired Persons (AARP, 601 E St., N.W., Washington, DC 20049; 202-434-2277; 800-424-3410; www.aarp.org). One of the largest trade associations in the country. Represents people nearing retirement and those who have retired. Offers to its members credit cards, discount drug purchase programs, educational seminars, insurance, mutual funds, travel opportunities and many other services. Publishes many publications, including *Borrowing Against Your Home; Consumer's Guide to Accessory Apartments; Consumer's Guide to Homesharing; Consumer's Guide to Probate; Guide to Local Housing Resources for Older Persons; Home-Made Money: Consumer's Guide to Home Equity Conversion; Housing Choices for Older Homeowners; Look before You Leap: A Guide to Early Retirement Incentive Programs; Medicare's Prospective Payment System: Knowing Your Rights; Medicare: What It Covers, What It Doesn't; Medigap: Medicare Supplement Insurance—A Consumer's Guide; Planning Your Retirement; Product Report: Life Insurance for Older Adults; Product Report: Living Trusts and Wills; Product Report: Personal Emergency Response Systems; Product Report: Prepaying Your Funeral?; Relocation Tax Guide; Rental Housing; Selecting Retirement Housing; A Single Person's Guide to Retirement Planning; Social Security: Crucial Questions and Straight Answers; Your Credit: A Complete Guide;* and *Your Home, Your Choice: A Workbook for Older People and Their Families.*

Children of Aging Parents (1609 Woodbourne Rd., Suite 302A, Levittown, PA 19057; 215-945-6900; www.experts.com). A national clearinghouse for information resources and support for caregivers of the elderly and allied health professionals. Sponsors a helpline and support groups and publishes a newsletter helpful to those having problems with an elderly relative.

Distance Education & Training Council (1601 18th St., N.W., Washington, DC 20009-2529; 202-234-5100; www.detc.org). The accrediting agency for correspondence schools, which provide lessons for home study, sometimes for degrees. You can contact them for information on technical and vocational programs. Its Directory of Accredited Institutions can tell you where to find a home-study course teaching the subject in which you are interested. Other free publications offered by the Council include *What Does Accreditation Mean to You?* and *Using Your Distance Education To Earn an Academic Degree.*

Eldercare Locator (1112 16th St., N.W., Suite 100, Washington, DC 20036; 800-677-1116). Refers you to appropriate agencies that offer services to senior citizens. For example, they can help you find adult day care, home-delivered meals, transportation, home health care and local centers for seniors.

Legal Counsel for the Elderly (Building A, 601 E St., N.W., 4th Floor, Washington, DC 20049; 202-434-2120; www.aarp.com). A nonprofit legal support center, sponsored by AARP, dealing with issues of concern to the elderly. Sells a series of self-help publications for consumers, including *Planning for Incapacity: A Self-Help Guide.* The guides, customized according to each state's law, offer answers to commonly asked questions about estate-planning, living-will and health care power of attorney forms, as well as instructions, a glossary of legal and medical terms and a wallet card. Other publications include *Organizing Your Future: A Guide to Decisionmaking in Your Later Years; The Rights of Older Persons—A Basic Guide to the Legal Rights of Older Persons under Current Law;* and *Your Legal Rights in Later Life.*

National Academy of Elder Law Attorneys, Inc. (1604 N. Country Club Rd., Tucson, AZ 85716; 520-881-4005; www.naela.org). Offers a directory of lawyers specializing in problems faced by retirees. Will send the free booklet *Questions and Answers When Looking for an Elder Law Attorney.*

National Association of Partners in Education (901 N. Pitt St., Suite 320, Alexandria, VA 22314; 703-836-4880; www.NAPEhq.org). Will connect you with volunteer programs in schools.

National Council of Senior Citizens (1331 F St., N.W., Washington, DC 20004-1171; 202-347-8800; www.ncscinc.org). An advocacy organization for retired people. Tries to increase Social Security benefits, protect Medicare and Medicaid, and secure funding for senior centers and nutrition sites, community employment projects and low-income senior housing projects. Sells Medicare supplement insurance, in-hospital insurance program and long-term care insurance. Offers a discount mail order drug prescription service, a senior travel service and discounts on hotels, motels and rental cars. Publishes the magazine, *Senior Citizens News,* which covers topics of interest to older Americans. Also publishes the *Coping with Aging* series. Offers the following free brochures: "An NCSC Guide to Social Security for Women" and "For a Good Retirement: Some Things You Should Know!"

National Council on the Aging (409 3rd St., S.W., Suite 200, Washington, DC 20024; 202-479-1200; www.ncoa.org). A nonprofit group specializing in issues affecting senior citizens. Lobbies on various issues. Offers 11 program areas of special concern allowing you to focus on your interests, including Health Promotion Institute; National Association of Older Worker Employment Services; National Center for Voluntary Leadership in Aging; National Center on Rural Aging; Institute of Senior Centers; National Institute of Senior Housing; National Institute on Adult Daycare; National Institute on Community-based Long-Term Care; National Institute on Financial Issues and Services for Elders; National Interfaith Coalition on Aging; and National Voluntary Organizations for Independent Living for the Aging. Offers various programs to help you plan for retirement. Publishes many books and pamphlets, including *Eating Well To Stay Well; Employees and Eldercare; A Guide for Selection of Retirement Housing; Home Security; Housing Options;* and *The Reality of Retirement.* Also publishes the magazine *Perspective on Aging.*

National Family Caregivers Association (9621 E. Boxhill Dr., Kensington, MD 20895; 301-949-3638; 800-896-3650). A membership organization based on the belief that the needs of the family caregiver are different from the needs of the person for whom they care. They want to improve the overall quality of life of America's caregivers and educate the public about the difficulties caregivers face. Primarily educational in their focus, their services include a newsletter and national speakers bureau.

National Organization of Social Security Claimants' Representatives (6 Prospect St., Midland Park, NJ 07432; 201-444-1415; 800-431-2804; www.nosscr.org). A group of lawyers who specialize in resolving disability and SSI benefits claims problems with the Social Security Administration. Lawyers affiliated with the organization can help you determine whether you are disabled enough to qualify for benefits and will represent you if you have been denied benefits. Such lawyers usually work on a contingency-fee basis, meaning that they receive 25 percent of past-due benefits if they win your case, and you owe them nothing if they lose. The organization will send a free pamphlet titled "Social Security Disability and SSI Claims: Your Need for Representation." Call the toll-free telephone number for a referral to a specialized lawyer near your home.

National Senior Citizens Law Center (1815 H St., N.W., Suite 700, Washington, DC 20006; 202-887-5280; www.nsclc.org). A group of lawyers practicing law that lobbies for legal services programs on behalf of the elderly. Specializes in litigation, research, lobbying, and training lawyers on issues of concern to retired people. Subjects covered include age discrimination; guardianship; home care; mandatory retirement; Medicaid; Medicare; nursing homes; pensions; Social Security and SSI. In addition to publications on all of these topics, publishes the following newsletters: *Disability Advocates Mailing; Memorandum on Law and Aging;* and *NSCLC Washington Weekly and Nursing Home Law Letter.*

Older Women's League (666 11th St., N.W., Suite 700, Washington, DC 20001; 202-783-6686). A group dedicated to the interests of mid-life and older women. Publishes the *Owl Observer,* which tracks issues such as health insurance and pension rights. Offers several pamphlets, including "COBRA Health Insurance Continuation"; "Taking Charge of the End of Your Life"; and "The Universal Health Care Action Kit." Also offers books of interest to older women, including *Making Ends Meet: Midlife and Older Women's Search for Economic Self-Sufficiency Through Job Training and Employment* and *Women and Money: The Independent Woman's Guide to Financial Security for Life.*

Pension Rights Center (918 16th St., N.W., Suite 704, Washington, DC 20006; 202-296-3778; www.pwsnrights@aol.com). A nonprofit organization that helps educate the public about pension issues. Offers a lawyer referral service for pension-related problems. The center offers the following brochures: "Can You Count on Getting a Pension?"; "The Pension Plan Almost Nobody Knows About: SEPs"; and "Your Pension Rights at Divorce."

FEDERAL GOVERNMENT REGULATOR

Social Security Administration (6401 Security Blvd., Baltimore, MD 21235; 410-965-7700; 800-772-1213; www.ssa.gov). Regulates distribution of Social Security benefits to eligible, retired or disabled Americans. Also administers programs for the aged, the blind and dependents. For a free copy of the following booklets, write to Public Information Distribution Center (Social Security Administration, P.O. Box 17743, Baltimore, MD 21235): *Disability; Food Stamps and Other Nutrition Programs; Guide for Representative Payees; How To Earn Social Security Credits; Medicare; The Medicare Handbook; Retirement; Social Security Numbers for Newborns; Supplemental Security Income; Survivors; Social Security: Understanding the Benefits; When You Get Social Security Disability Benefits . . . What You Need To Know; Working While Disabled . . . How Social Security Can Help; Your Right To Question the Decision Made on Your Social Security Claim; Your Right To Question the Decision Made on Your SSI Claim;* and *Your Social Security Taxes: What They're Paying For and Where the Money Goes.*

TRAVEL DISCOUNT SERVICES

There are several services that will help you save a considerable amount of money on travel: Hotel Reservations Network (800-964-6835; www.180096hotel. com) offers hotel rooms at up to 65 percent off retail rates; Express Hotel Reservations (800-356-1123; www.express-res.com) offers significant discounts on New York and Los Angeles hotels; and Quickbook (800-789-9887; www. quikbook.com) allows you to qualify for big discounts on last-minute hotel reservations in Atlanta, Boston, Chicago, Los Angeles, New York, San Francisco and Washington, D.C. Accommodations Express (800-444-7666; www.accommo dationsexpress.com) offers hotel rooms in many major U.S. cities. Central Reservations Service (800-548-3311) books in Atlanta, Boston, Los Angeles, Miami, New Orleans, New York, Orlando and San Francisco. Room Exchange (800-846-7000; www.hotelrooms.com) reserves rooms at hotels in over 200 cities in the U.S., the Caribbean, Europe and Asia, and RMC Travel Center (800-245-5738) books in 50 American cities. Other services specialize in booking discounted hotel rooms in just one city, such as California Reservations (800-576-0003) for most West Coast cities, Citywide Reservations Services (800-468-3593; www.cityres. com) in Boston, Hot Rooms (800-468-3500; www.hotrooms.com) in Chicago, Capitol Reservations (800-847-4832; www.hotelsdc.com) in Washington, D.C., San Francisco Reservations (800-333-8996; www.hotelres.com) and San Diego Reservations (800-728-3227; www.savecash.com); Cruise Travel Club (800-685-6518; www.cruiseline.com) helps you get the best deals on cruises.

Dining a La Card (P.O. Box 4405, Carol Stream, IL 60197; 800-253-5379) pays a 20 percent rebate check when you purchase a meal in one of their participating restaurants. You also can get a rebate on various hotels, rental car agencies and entertainment events. The rebate is figured on the total amount you charge on your credit card, including taxes and tips.

Best Fares Discount Travel Magazine (1301 S. Bowen Rd., Suite 490, Arlington, TX 76013; 817-860-5761; 800-880-1234; www.bestfares.com). A magazine loaded with the latest travel bargains on airfares, hotels, car rentals, cruises and package tours. Author Tom Parsons keeps track of the latest frequent flier promotions, coupons and tie-ins to travel companies, allowing you to accumulate frequent flier miles.

AIRLINE WEB SITES

Many airlines allow you to book trips directly on their Web sites, and many will give you substantial discounts for doing so. Most airlines will post their available inventory on a regular basis, and if they have seats for a destination you want, you can book it online for a discount. Some airlines have specific names for these fares—American calls them NetSAAvers, Northwest calls them Cybersavers and US Airways calls them E-savers. The airline would rather sell the seat to you at a discount than have it go empty. Here are the Web sites for the major North American airlines so you can take advantage of these discounts:

> Aeromexico Airlines; www.wotw.com/aeromexico
> Air Canada Airlines; www.aircanada.ca
> AirTran Airlines; www.airtran.com
> Alaska Air Airlines; www.alaska-air.com
> Aloha Air Airlines; www.alohaair.com
> America West Airlines; www.americawest.com
> American Airlines; www.americanair.com
> Canadian Airlines; www.cdnair.ca
> Continental Airlines; www.flycontinental.com
> Delta Airlines; www.delta-air.com
> Frontier Airlines; www.flyfrontier.com
> Mexicana; www.mexicana.com
> Midwest Express Airlines; www.midwestexpress.com
> Northwest Airlines; www.nwa.com
> Pan Am Airlines; www.flypanam.com
> Reno Airlines; www.renoair.com
> Southwest Airlines; www.iflyswa.com
> TWA Airlines; www.twa.com
> United Airlines; www.ual.com
> US Airways; www.usairways.com
> Western Pacific Airlines; www.westpac.com

15

Estate Planning—
Keeping Your
Assets in the Family

Though thinking about it may make you uncomfortable, you will die someday. When that unfortunate event occurs, whether it be tomorrow or decades from now, your assets will be distributed, and your estate may have to pay estate taxes. What you should decide now is whether you want to control how your estate is settled or you want to leave it up to the probate court, which might distribute your property in a manner that would not please you if you were alive.

If you ignore the rather daunting process of estate planning, you not only lose control of how your worldly possessions will be handed out, but your estate might pay thousands of dollars in onerous estate taxes that could have been easily avoided. On the other hand, if you make the effort to maximize basic estate-planning techniques, your spouse, children, grandchildren and others for whom you care deeply will receive a far greater inheritance to enrich their lives. Therefore, even though you won't benefit personally after your death, you will live with the satisfaction of knowing that you have done all you can to pass on the fruits of your life's labor to your loved ones.

Many people never plan their estates because they are intimidated by the subject, they think they have nothing of value to pass on, or they are concerned about how much lawyers charge to draw up wills and other estate-planning documents. More likely, however, these people never think about the subject at all and go through life assuming that their estates will somehow take care of themselves when they die. Only about one out of every three Americans has a will.

The two-thirds of Americans who do no estate planning might be shocked to learn that when people die without wills (or, as lawyers put it, *intestate*), the probate court takes over and can dominate survivors' lives for years. It is not a simple process. After all, estate planning settles not only the disposition of possessions and money but also other major life decisions, including custody of children. If you never express your preferences before you die, a judge who probably never met you must determine what's best for your family. The small amount of time and money you must invest now to dictate what happens when you die is well worth the effort. Most of all, planning your estate gives you peace of mind that your affairs will be handled properly and according to your wishes when you die.

What Estate Planning Entails

Because the term *estate planning* is mysterious to many people, the following list takes a quick look at some of the key areas covered by the term.

- Choosing who gets how much of your money and possessions that remain after the costs of settling the estate are subtracted.

- Preparing a strategy to give away many of your assets as tax-free gifts while you live to minimize the assets socked by estate taxes when you die.

- Selecting a guardian for your children if they are younger than age 18. This guardian, who may be an individual or a couple, would take your children into their home and raise them, so you must feel as certain as possible that they would bring up your children in a manner of which you would approve.

- Selecting a trustee to administer any trusts you may establish.

- Nominating an executor of your estate, who should be an independent person you trust, to carry out the provisions of your will faithfully. Often, this is a lawyer familiar with your family.

- Deciding what should be done with your body after you die. You may want it donated for medical research or cremated, for instance. Also, specifying how and where you want to be buried. Some people even limit what they want spent on their funerals.

- Appointing a successor custodian for the assets of a child or grandchild if you currently act as a custodian for a Uniform Gifts to Minors Act account. If you don't specify the successor custodian, a court will decide for you.

- Planning to make gifts of either money or property to your favorite charity, university, church or synagogue. Without your specific written instructions, no such gifts can be authorized by the executor of your estate.

- Preparing for the time you are unable to care for yourself. You can prepare what are called advance directives giving instructions on what kinds of health care you want provided or withheld in the event you cannot communicate your wishes. You can specify in a *living will,* for instance, whether you want extraordinary treatment to keep you alive if you go into a coma. You can also appoint someone you trust with a *health care power of attorney* to make difficult decisions about your medical treatment if you are unable to make these decisions yourself.

If you don't make all of these crucial decisions before you die, they will be settled for you, often by people you don't know, in ways you may not approve of. By taking care of these decisions in a calm, unhurried way far in advance of your death, you avoid any need for a hastily drawn document or, even worse, a *deathbed will,* which most likely will be contested later. Clearly, it is far better to determine how you want your estate handled long before the inevitable day comes when such decisions must be made.

Though the process of estate planning usually involves several professionals, such as lawyers, financial planners, insurance agents and accountants, it does not have to be so involved. Several do-it-yourself books on the market can help you draw up a simple will and prepare other documents that will be useful in various life situations. If you own a computer, several easy-to-use computer programs—such as *Living TrustMaker, Quicken Family Lawyer* and *WillMaker*—ask you a series of questions, then format your answers into legal documents that protect you and your estate against almost every eventuality. (See the "Resources" section at the end of this chapter for more information.) Or you may want to obtain from a legal clinic or local law firm a standard will that you could customize to meet your circumstances.

Legal books, software and clinics will take care of most common situations and are adequate if you have few assets and a limited number of people to whom you want those assets distributed. However, if you hold substantial assets, or your wishes for giving away assets are complicated, you should think about assembling a team of financial experts to make sure that your will covers every contingency. And because estate and probate laws vary from state to state, it is important to have your will drawn in accordance with local laws by an attorney familiar with them.

The Basics of Writing and Executing a Will

Whether you do it yourself or with the help of financial advisers, writing a will is key to estate planning. A *will* is, quite simply, a legal declaration that gives instructions on how to dispose of your assets when you die. You can divide your assets any way you want, as long as guidelines are presented clearly in writing. (Some states prohibit clauses in wills that are considered illegal, bizarre or against public policy.) The portion of your estate covered by the will includes both tangible assets, like homes, cars, boats, artwork, collectibles and furniture, as well as intangible assets, like bank accounts, stocks, bonds and mutual funds. To specify that certain people should inherit particular tangible assets, insert in your will a provision known as a *tangible personal property memorandum* (TPPM).

Other rights and benefits, like pension rights and life insurance proceeds, are normally handled outside of your will. For example, life insurance proceeds are usually payable directly to beneficiaries. And property owned jointly, such as a home held with your spouse, is not affected by the will because, by law, it passes to that joint owner automatically when you die. Also, any property that you have placed in a trust passes to the beneficiary without going through your will or probate. Because trusts take assets out of your probate estate, they can save you a lot of money.

Usually, you will create what is known as a *simple will,* which provides for the outright distribution of assets to beneficiaries. If your will establishes trusts to receive assets, it is a *testamentary trust will.* If you set up trusts before your death and the will passes assets into those trusts, it is a *pour-over will.*

Husbands and wives can write their wills either jointly or separately. Most estate lawyers suggest separate wills because it is difficult to establish who owns which property in a joint will. In addition, after one spouse dies, it is troublesome for the surviving spouse to change the provisions in a joint will. And if you're not careful, a joint will might deprive you of the full lifetime tax-exempt inheritance that both husband and wife are allowed to pass on to heirs free of federal estate tax.

Another important aspect of your will is choosing an *executor* of your estate. This can be either a long-time, trusted friend with knowledge of financial affairs or an institution, like a bank or law firm, with financial and legal expertise. The executor's task is to carry out your wishes as set forth in the will as efficiently as possible. This process may take several months, or it may drag on for years. If you trust the executor completely, give the executor enough authority to take action so that he or she does not have to buy a *surety bond* (sometimes called a *fidelity bond*), which insures your estate against malfeasance by the executor. The cost of that bond, which can be substantial, is paid by your estate.

When you visit a lawyer about your will, be well prepared. Bring with you the following information:

- A list of your real property, such as homes, and your tangible personal property, such as cars and furniture, along with how much you paid for it and where it is located. Bring deeds, bills of sale and any other relevant documentation to prove your ownership. Also, indicate whether you own the property solely or jointly.

- A list of intangible property, such as bank accounts, stocks, bonds and mutual funds. Bring your latest bank and brokerage statements.

- A list of all insurance policies and all pension and other employee benefits. Bring your latest statements.

- A list of all your debts, including debts to banks, insurance companies, your employer, the IRS and individuals. Bring any documents outlining your liabilities.

- The names, addresses and telephone numbers of any professional you want contacted, such as your insurance agent, broker or banker or another lawyer. Also bring the names, addresses and phone numbers of the executor and any guardians named for your children. Include, of course, the names, addresses and telephone numbers of your spouse and children.

Once the will has been completed, review it every five years or so to keep it up to date. If new circumstances have developed, change the will accordingly. For example, amend your will if you have a child, divorce or sell a major asset listed in the will. Also revise your will if you acquire a major new asset like a home or move to another state. If someone you name in the will as a beneficiary, an executor or a guardian dies, appoint another person in his or her place. You can either revoke the earlier will and replace it with a new one or add a *codicil,* or an amendment, to the earlier will. If you issue a new will, make sure that the earlier one is destroyed. If you add a codicil, make sure that it is signed and dated so it is clear that the amendment was adopted after the will was originally drawn up.

When you sign and date the will, have it witnessed by at least two, and preferably three, people with no connection to the will so you receive what is known as *proof of will.* Do *not* have someone who is a potential beneficiary of the will witness your signature. For example, employees in your lawyer's office normally act as witnesses. All the witnesses should sign the will in the presence of each other and should note their addresses so they can be contacted later, if necessary. With these signatures, your will is *self-proved,* allowing your executor to avoid the complex process of proving the authenticity of your will in probate court. Your will becomes effective only after you die and a probate court accepts the will as legally valid.

Once your will is complete, keep the signed original and several unsigned copies. (If all the copies are signed, no one will know which is the actual, fully executed will.) Preserve the original in a secure place other than a safe-deposit box, which may be sealed at your death, making it very difficult for the executor to administer your will. Keep copies in several locations, such as in a file cabinet at home, with your banker or lawyer and with the executor of your estate. You can even file a copy with the probate registrar at your county courthouse for a small fee.

If you leave nothing to someone who expects to be included in your will—especially a relative—expect your heirs to face a battle. People will fight like cats and dogs over property if they feel they have been slighted. They often contest the will on some technicality, claiming the document was not properly executed. For example, they might propose that someone with evil intent unduly influenced you while you drafted the will. Or they might say you had no mental capacity to make decisions when you excluded them from the will. Or they might even try to prove that the will was altered fraudulently and should therefore be overruled. In any case, when someone contests your will for whatever reason, it can create enmity among your heirs for years and prevent your beneficiaries from receiving expeditiously what you wanted them to have.

The Living Will and Health Care Power of Attorney

While a traditional will distributes your assets upon your death, a *living will* must be enforced while you live. It declares that you do not wish to be kept alive by extraordinary artificial life-support systems and authorizes doctors and named relatives to disconnect any equipment keeping you alive. A living will is activated when you become mentally or physically incapacitated and have no realistic hope of returning to your normal life.

Most states now recognize your *right to die.* Courts usually side with patients who have given explicit instructions in advance that they do not want their lives extended artificially. Valid living wills usually do not expire unless they are revoked. However, it's a good idea to review the document every five years or so. Initial and date it at each review to make sure readers know that it still reflects your wishes.

The easiest way to execute what is called an advance directive, which includes a living will and medical power of attorney, is to use one of the standardized forms available from most estate-planning lawyers or from Choice in Dying (1035 30th St. N.W., Washington, DC 20007; 202-338-9790; 800-989-9455; www.choices. org). Sign your living will in front of two impartial adults who are not related to you, who stand to inherit nothing from you and who are not doctors or hospital employees who might be in a position to disconnect your life-support equipment.

Once you have executed a living will, keep a copy of it with your medical records. Make sure that the people closest to you know of its location so they can retrieve it in the appropriate situation. Also, give a copy of the living will to the executor of your estate. In conjunction with the living will, sign a *health care power of attorney form,* which gives someone you trust the power to make medical decisions for you if you are unable to do so.

The Probate Process

Probate court will not be enjoyable for your loved ones, but it is unavoidable whether you die with or without a will. (Without a will, the process can be much more difficult and take considerably longer.) The first step in the probate process is establishing that the will, if one exists, is valid as the last statement of the deceased, declaring the person's wishes for distributing his or her assets.

Next, the probate court appoints an executor to administer the estate. Usually, the court designates the person named in the will. If no will exists, the court assigns an administrator, often a family member. The court then oversees the executor's or administrator's work, which consists of identifying, or marshalling, all the assets; paying off all debts, taxes and administrative costs; and, finally, disposing of the remaining assets to the beneficiaries. A federal and state estate-tax return must be filed within nine months of death if the estate's value exceeds the lifetime estate tax exemption, which starts at $625,000 in 1998 and gradually climbs to $1 million in 2006. If the surviving family needs money immediately to meet living expenses, the executor can distribute some income, or even principal, as needed while the probate process continues.

The executor receives a fee. The amount of the fee may be stated in the will, although the court may limit the fee to a set percentage of the estate as a commission—for example, 3 percent of all amounts paid and received in administering the estate. Usually, an independent executor, such as a lawyer or bank, collects between 2 percent and 5 percent of the estate's value, depending on the amount of assets involved and the complexity of the case. A family member executor usually charges far less than an independent one or may refuse to accept a fee out of love for the family—or perhaps because the fees are considered taxable income. However, dealing with the conflicting demands of family members can be a thankless job and one well worth the remuneration. All fees—which can amount to thousands of dollars—are paid by the estate.

If the will is clear, with no one contesting it, the executor can distribute the assets. Usually, executors like to pass on actual physical assets to beneficiaries, whether the assets are tangible or intangible. However, this is not always possible. For example, an executor might have to sell some assets to raise cash for estate taxes. Once all assets are distributed and all taxes are paid, the executor closes the estate. This may require filing a form with the court, which must approve everything the executor did. If the court and beneficiaries receive no challenges to the disposition of the estate, the matter is closed. The probate process lasts from several months to several years.

One disadvantage of probate, in addition to its slowness, is that all proceedings are public knowledge. The court may even require that certain notices be placed in newspapers to ensure that potential beneficiaries know that the will is being probated. Because your will becomes a matter of public record, certain financial details about you or your family might be revealed that you would rather be kept private.

In some states, the probate process has been streamlined and simplified. If you own less than $50,000 in assets, your estate may qualify for expedited treatment, which will save on legal and executor fees.

How To Avoid Probate

People are attracted by any alternative that is faster, cheaper and more private than probate court. Avoiding probate may be desirable, but it takes a great deal of planning and thorough comprehension of estate-planning rules.

Four main ways to avoid probating your estate follow.

- Giving away your assets as gifts while you are still alive

- Holding assets in joint tenancy
- Entering into certain contractual arrangements, such as life insurance or pensions
- Setting up trusts

The following sections cover each of these four separately.

GIFTS

Though giving away your assets to avoid probate may sound simple enough, it isn't. Years ago, people signed over their assets to their children on their deathbed to avoid estate taxes. Since then, government rules have tightened considerably. Current law allows you to give $10,000 a year, in either cash or property, to each of any number of people without incurring a gift tax. (The Taxpayer Relief Act of 1997 indexes the $10,000 limit to inflation, but each increase in the limit is in increments of $1,000.) When you make gifts during your lifetime, they are known as *inter vivos gifts*.

While this rather low limit on annual gifts might make it difficult to dispense your assets, giving away assets might also be troublesome if you need to live on them. Because you don't know how long you will live, you don't want to impoverish yourself by jettisoning your assets too soon. If you give gifts to relatives who are named in your will, add a provision that these gifts should not be considered advances on their inheritance. Otherwise, your gifts could be deducted from their share of your assets upon your death. If you give $100,000 to a sister who needs money for a down payment on a house, for instance, she might receive $100,000 less than you wanted her to have when you die unless that provision instructs your executor not to subtract the $100,000.

Most large gifts must be transferred to recipients at least three years before your death. If you die before the three years have lapsed, the gifts will probably be added to your estate, which might trigger the estate taxes you wanted to avoid.

Since 1982, federal estate tax law has allowed husbands and wives to make unlimited gifts of property to each other under the *gift tax marital deduction*. This deduction allows you and your spouse to balance your assets among both of your estates to take maximum advantage of the $625,000 (rising to $1 million by the year 2006) you each can pass on to heirs estate-tax free.

Another way to use gifts is to dispense assets that you believe will appreciate sharply in value. For example, say you give your child 100 shares of a growth stock, which he or she receives with your tax cost. Any future appreciation would be taxed only when your child sells the stock. You also may give assets that have appreciated sharply to a charity in return for an annuity. The charity can sell the asset without paying capital gains tax, and you may take a charitable deduction.

The annuity may be used to purchase insurance and establish a *wealth replacement trust* (see section titled "Insurance Trusts" in this chapter for more information).

Joint Tenancy

By holding assets in joint tenancy with right of survivorship with your spouse or another when you die, everything you own automatically transfers to the survivor without going through probate court. While the approach sounds simple, it has its problems.

For couples, if both you and your spouse die simultaneously, your entire estate will be settled at once—and chances are that the estate will have to pay enormous taxes. Current federal estate-tax law allows each person to pass up to $625,000 tax free to a beneficiary. Under the Taxpayer Relief Act of 1997, this lifetime estate tax exemption is scheduled to increase to $650,000 in 1999, $675,000 in 2000, $700,000 in 2002, $850,000 in 2004, $950,000 in 2005 and $1 million in 2006. By holding assets jointly, however, you may lose one of the two lifetime exemptions you would receive if you held your assets separately. For example, if you were in the year 2006 and you and your spouse had an estate worth $2 million, all $2 million passes free of tax from one spouse to the other when one dies. If the surviving spouse wants the estate to escape estate taxes, he or she must dispense $1 million before death.

If you hold your assets in joint tenancy with a person who is not your spouse, the same estate tax consequences apply, except no marital deduction is allowed. Also, the assets will be valued in the deceased's estate for 100 percent of their value at death unless the joint tenant can prove that he or she paid for some or all of the assets.

Contracts

You can avoid probate on some of your assets by using employee benefit plans and insurance contracts skillfully. Most retirement pension plans start paying benefits to your spouse as soon as you die, whether or not you are retired. Because these plans take effect so quickly after you die, they avoid probate altogether. If you die once you are retired and receiving pension checks, annuity payments to your spouse can continue until his or her death. Check with your employee benefits department to make sure that you have chosen the options that will protect your spouse when you die.

Life insurance contracts also provide proceeds directly to your beneficiaries without going through probate, if you choose to have them do so. This is one of the main advantages of insurance: It provides a source of ready cash if settling your estate drags on in probate court. However, under certain circumstances, it might be better to have the life insurance proceeds paid into a trust—either a trust you established during your lifetime or one that springs into existence when you die.

For example, if you have children younger than age 18, you might want the insurance money to go into a trust administered by a responsible trustee rather than directly to the children. Sometimes a trust pays lower taxes on the earnings of the insurance proceeds than your survivors would pay if they received the insurance money directly. Always consult a skilled insurance specialist or estate attorney when setting up such insurance arrangements.

TRUSTS

The most common technique used to avoid probate is to set up a lifetime, or *inter vivos,* trust. A trust holds assets so that when you die, those assets will not be considered part of your estate for probate and possible estate-tax purposes. A trust agreement permits you to set aside assets for the ultimate benefit of another person, called the *beneficiary*. In some cases, the beneficiary will receive income from the trust assets for life, while in other cases, he or she will receive principal from the trust.

Three parties take part in any trust set-up. The *grantor,* or donor, is the person whose assets are placed in trust. The *beneficiary* is the person who receives benefits—whether income or principal—from the trust. The *trustee* is an independent manager who administers the trust to make sure that the grantor's wishes are fulfilled. You may name as trustee yourself, a relative, a trusted friend or business associate, a financial professional like a lawyer or an accountant or an institution like a bank or a brokerage firm.

A trust must be established with a formal, written, legal document. Though you may be able to write a trust with the help of do-it-yourself books or software, show the results to a qualified lawyer to make sure that you have covered all your bases legally. If you establish a more complicated trust, consult an attorney who specializes in estate planning. Though it might cost several hundred or even a thousand dollars up front, seeking this expertise could save you and your family tens of thousands of dollars in the future.

Two basic kinds of trusts exist: *revocable* and *irrevocable*. Revocable trusts can be changed or even canceled any time after they are established. For this reason, they do not remove assets from a grantor's taxable estate; the government considers those assets as being under the grantor's control. With a revocable trust, you must pay income taxes on revenue generated by the trust and possibly estate taxes on those assets remaining at your death.

Irrevocable trusts, on the other hand, cannot be altered or canceled once they are established. The assets placed into an irrevocable trust are permanently removed from your estate and transferred to the trust. The trust becomes a separate taxable entity that pays taxes on the income and capital gains it generates. Therefore, when you die, the appreciation of those assets is not considered part of your estate and thus avoids estate taxes.

Both revocable and irrevocable trusts can help you transfer assets to beneficiaries after your death, and they can be used to hold the assets of someone who is mentally or physically incapacitated. Trusts are also useful if you want your assets held separately for your young children. Upon your death, the trustee must report expenditures annually to a judge. If the trustee and the guardian of your children differ, this requirement acts as a check against the guardian's running off with your children's inheritance.

Trusts not only can help you transfer assets and minimize estate taxes; they also provide far more privacy than probate court proceedings. Trust documents normally are not made public and therefore allow you to dispense assets without public disclosure.

While most of your assets can be transferred to trusts, they cannot hold everything. For example, it is unwise to deposit the stock of a closely held corporation or stock options in a trust. Nevertheless, a trust can greatly simplify the process of settling your estate.

You have many kinds of trusts from which to choose, depending on the size of your assets and your family situation. A rundown of the most common trusts follows.

Living trust. Also known as a *revocable inter vivos trust,* a *living trust* permits you to place assets into trust while you live. By naming yourself trustee, you control the assets during your lifetime; however, if you become mentally or physically incompetent, your successor or co-trustee can take over easily because your assets are already held in the trust. When you die, all the assets in the living trust automatically circumvent probate court, saving your heirs big headaches, costs and delays. Also, if you deposit many of your assets in a living trust, you may be able to write a simpler will because you have far less to pass on through it. You should still have a pour-over will, which provides for the distribution to the trust of assets left out of the trust. Another advantage of an inter vivos trust is that it is rarely contested, in contrast to wills, which often give rise to heated debates and expensive legal wrangles.

A great deal of hype often exaggerates the benefits of living trusts and understates the costs of establishing them. For example, living trusts offer no tax advantages not provided by a well-written will. You have a lifetime exemption of $625,000 (rising to $1 million in 2006) in assets that you can pass on to your heirs tax free, either through a will or through a living trust. Also, be careful not to pay too much to set up a living trust. Some marketers charge several thousand dollars, which is excessive, particularly if you do not own hundreds of thousands of dollars' worth of assets.

You can establish a living trust either by consulting self-help books or software or through a qualified estate lawyer. The living trust names the beneficiary of the trust and appoints both you and someone else as trustees. Or, if you prefer, the document can name you as the only trustee and designate some other trustworthy person as the successor trustee to take over when you die or no longer can serve. Like a will, the living trust stipulates who gets what property when you die.

Once you have set up a living trust, it is crucial that you transfer title of your assets to the trust. Otherwise, the trust remains an empty shell that does not serve its intended purpose. So, for instance, instead of keeping your assets in the name of Mary Pinkett, you should change ownership to the Mary Pinkett Trust. This applies to your home, your stocks, bonds, mutual funds and bank accounts, and all your other major assets. Quite often, people establish living trusts, then forget to fund them.

Support trusts. If you have a spouse and children who depend on your income, you might want to set up a *support trust.* Trustees of such vehicles are instructed to provide enough money to support beneficiaries in a comfortable lifestyle. If possible, the trust should generate enough income to accomplish this goal. If the income from bond interest and stock dividends is insufficient, the trustee might spend some principal to continue the support. Usually, he or she is reluctant to invade principal, however, because depleting it makes it more difficult to maintain a high level of income in the future.

Discretionary trusts. A *discretionary trust* is similar to a support trust, except that it gives the trustee even more latitude in deciding how much income and principal must be spent to support the beneficiaries' lifestyle. The trustee must use his or her discretion in deciding what is fiscally prudent, even if the beneficiaries desire higher payouts.

Spendthrift trusts. If you have a child or spouse who appears to be irresponsible about spending money, a *spendthrift trust* may be right for you. In such a trust, you instruct the trustee to set strict limits on how much money can be doled out at any time and not to accede to demands for more. Such a trust may also be appropriate if the beneficiary is mentally or physically incompetent. A spendthrift trust can protect your assets against the claims of creditors if your beneficiaries get in trouble with the law or pile up debts.

Standby or convertible trusts. A *standby trust* stands ready to receive your assets at a particular time in your life. The trust remains empty, awaiting the moment when it needs to be converted into an active trust. To establish such a trust, have your lawyer draw up a *durable power of attorney,* which gives permission to move assets into the trust at the established time, then manage them for your benefit. For example, assets may be moved into the trust if you become incapacitated.

Bypass trusts. When a couple's assets exceed the $625,000 (rising to $1 million in 2006) unified credit limit, a *bypass,* or *credit shelter, trust* may help provide for the surviving spouse and pass principal on to the children free of estate taxes. For example, assume that in 2006 that a couple owns $2 millon in assets—$1 million in the husband's name and $1 million in the wife's name. If the husband leaves all of his assets to his wife, her $2 million estate would be hit with huge estate taxes when she dies. Instead, the husband sets up a bypass trust, which stipulates that his $1 million goes into the trust when he dies. Upon his death, his widow receives income generated by that $1 million for the rest of her life, plus the option of receiving principal if she needs it. Because she has only limited access to the capital in the bypass trust, that money is not counted as part of the marital deduction. When the wife dies, the $1 million in the bypass trust, along with her $1 million estate, pass to their heirs free of estate taxes. Bypass trusts therefore accomplish two goals: They provide assets on which the surviving spouse can live, and they minimize estate taxes by reducing the surviving spouse's taxable estate.

Q-TIP trusts. The idea behind *qualified terminable interest property* (Q-TIP) *trusts* is to make the most of your unlimited marital deduction and still control who inherits your assets after your spouse dies. For example, as a husband, you can set up a Q-TIP trust so your assets will transfer into the trust when you die. Someone other than your wife must be appointed trustee. Upon your death, your wife receives income generated by those assets for as long as she lives. She is the only person allowed to receive income from the trust. Neither she nor anyone else can give away the money because the IRS fears that the funds will be shifted to someone in a lower tax bracket. This way, the IRS ensures that estate taxes will be paid on the assets in the trust when your wife dies if her assets total more than $625,000 (rising to $1 million in 2006).

While many uses for Q-TIP trusts exist, they are often used by wealthy people who have remarried and want to pass their assets on to the children of their first marriage while providing income for life to the current spouse.

Insurance trusts. *Life insurance trusts,* which are irrevocable, ensure that the death benefit from your life insurance policy does not transfer into your estate, which could push the estate's value beyond the lifetime estate tax exemption threshold and trigger estate taxes. The trust receives the insurance proceeds when you die, thereby circumventing both estate taxes and probate proceedings. You can stipulate how and when the insurance money will be dispensed to beneficiaries. For example, you might want only the income paid to them for a few years, after which they receive the principal. Or you may want them to receive the principal immediately in a lump sum. You might also allow the trustee to use the life insurance proceeds to pay your estate taxes. This is called a *wealth replacement trust.* When establishing a life insurance trust, buy a new policy in the trust's name; you may have gift-tax problems with an existing policy. Make sure that the new policy names you as the insured and the trust as the owner and beneficiary. Have your estate attorney carefully prepare and review this trust to make sure that it accomplishes what you want.

Charitable trusts. To pass on assets to your favorite charitable institution, you may want to consider a *charitable remainder trust.* You can make such an arrangement with your alma mater, a hospital that once cared for you, or your church or synagogue. If you deposit assets such as stocks or bonds in the trust, you receive an immediate income tax deduction for your contribution. During your lifetime, you also receive an annuity generated by the trust assets. When you die, the assets are retained by the charity.

You can usually give an unlimited amount of assets to a qualified charity with no gift or estate-tax limitations. Income tax charitable deduction limitations do apply, however. It makes sense to give assets that have appreciated sharply in value so you benefit from a tax deduction for the fully appreciated price but do not have to pay income or estate tax on any capital gains. A charitable trust coupled with an irrevocable insurance or a wealth replacement trust can be a fantastic vehicle for saving income, gift and estate taxes while you satisfy your charitable inclinations. Consult your tax adviser, your favorite charity and your estate lawyer for help with these complex trusts.

Estate tax trusts. Estate taxes can be burdensome. The federal estate tax (formally called the *estate transfer tax*) starts at a rate of 37 percent and graduates up to about 55 percent—much higher than the top income tax rate of 39.6 percent. In addition, some states levy a 5 percent tax on your estate even if it is worth less than $625,000 (rising to $1 million in 2006). All estate taxes reduce the amount that your beneficiaries receive.

Federal estate-tax law allows every individual to pass on to heirs $625,000 worth of assets free of estate taxes. This amount is scheduled to rise gradually until it reaches a cap of $1 million in 2006. This is known as the *unified credit exemption.* While you may think that your estate is worth nowhere near $625,000, you might be miscalculating. Refer back to the net worth calculation you performed in Chapter 1, and update it where necessary. For instance, you might add the current cash value of your life insurance policies, the updated worth of all your employee benefits and the appreciated value of your home. With the inflation we've experienced over the past few years, it is not as difficult to reach the credit exemption as you may think. Even if you haven't yet accumulated $625,000 worth of assets (rising to $1 mllion in 2006), you may in the future as the value of your existing assets grows and you add more assets over time.

The Taxpayer Relief Act of 1997 created two exceptions to the lifetime estate-tax exemption limit. Owners of family farms and small businesses can exclude up to $1.3 million of the value of their farm or business from estate taxes effective January 1, 1998. To qualify for this higher limit, the farm or business must represent at least 50 percent of the farmer's or small business owner's net worth. In addition, the heirs of the farm or small business must materially participate in the business or farm for at least five of eight years within ten years following the farmer's or small business owner's death. For small businesses, the executor of the estate can choose to pay the estate taxes in installments over a 14-year period. These provisions were put in place to help the families of farmers and small business owners to hold onto their properties. In the past, families often had to sell the family farm or small business in order to pay estate taxes.

Estate tax law allows a spouse to transfer all of his or her assets to the other spouse free of estate tax when the first spouse dies. This is called the *unlimited marital deduction.* While this rule allows the surviving spouse to avoid taxes, it may set up a huge estate tax when the surviving spouse dies. For example, say in 2006 you share a $2 million estate with your wife in joint name. When you die, the entire $2 million will be transferred into your wife's name untaxed under the marital deduction. However, unless your wife begins dispensing gifts or creating trusts, the $1 million in assets over $1 million will be subject to heavy estate taxes. The marital deduction may lull you into a false sense of security; however, it does not replace the need for careful estate planning.

Planning Your Funeral and Burial

As distasteful as planning your estate and writing your will may be, you probably dread even more the thought of making your funeral and burial arrangements. It is difficult enough to deal with the concept of your own demise in the abstract, but it is often even harder to select burial plots, mausoleums and caskets.

Yet you must take care of these matters. Funerals and related items like burial plots can cost thousands of dollars and may, in fact, be the largest purchases your family will ever make, after your home and your children's education. The further in advance of your death you consider your options, the less chance you have of wasting money. You also acquire peace of mind knowing what will happen when you die. This is a far better way to leave this earth than to have your family, already in deep emotional distress, trying to find a place to bury you and select a good funeral home.

The first decision you should make is what kind of final disposition you want for your remains. Knowing your wishes gives not only you but also your survivors peace of mind. The funeral process is, after all, an emotional event that your spouse, children, relatives and friends will remember long after you have died. If handled well, it will act as a confirmation that you are gone—a fact every survivor must deal with in order to get on with life.

The most common way to lay a person's remains to rest is, of course, *earth burial.* A burial plot gives you a physical final resting place, often near your parents or other relatives. Here your spouse and children can seek solace in the days ahead. You may want to be buried in a municipal cemetery or one run by your church or synagogue. If you are a veteran, you can be buried in a military cemetery at the government's expense.

If you choose an earth burial, you will also need a marker over your grave. If you have a preference, make your desires known. Some markers are grandiose, constructed of marble or bronze with ornate carving and inscriptions. Others are very simple. Some people install a bench near their family plot. Of course, the fancier the grave marker, the higher its expense. Many cemeteries also levy an annual charge for *perpetual care* of the gravesite. Be aware of how much that charge will run.

Those who want a grander burial choose a *mausoleum.* This above-ground structure can be simple or extremely ornate, holding one person or an entire family. Instead of listing merely their birth and death dates, some people use mausoleums to chronicle their accomplishments. Clearly, mausoleums are far more expensive than simple burial plots. Whichever you choose, however, you must also select a casket, which can be as simple as a pine box or as lavish as a wood and metal box with luxurious interiors and adjustable bedding.

The third alternative is *cremation,* a process in which your body is burned until it is reduced to a few pounds of bone and ash that fit in a small container or urn. Some people want to be cremated because it reduces the body to ashes far more quickly than does the gradual decomposition that occurs in a casket. For the religious, cremation completes the "dust-to-dust, ashes-to-ashes" philosophy. For the practical, cremation is far less expensive than burial in either a plot or a mausoleum.

Once your remains have been cremated, your survivors have several options. The container holding your ashes can be housed in a *columbarium*—a shrine holding many cremated remains. Some survivors bury the container in a traditional grave. Other families take the container home to be cared for appropriately. Before their death, some people ask that their cremated remains be scattered at sea or in a nearby river or stream.

However you choose to handle the funeral and burial, a good funeral director earns his or her fees by relieving the family of many details. The director transports the body to the funeral home, arranges for the wake and gets information to the proper authorities for the death certificate. (He or she should obtain at least ten death certificates; your survivors will need them for insurance companies, the probate court, Social Security offices and other purposes.) The funeral director places obituary notices in newspapers and even helps fill out claim forms for Social Security survivors benefits, veterans benefits and life insurance. He or she also sets a time for the funeral and contacts your clergyman to preside over the service. In addition, the funeral director explains options for various kinds of caskets and memorial tablets. On the day of the funeral, he or she takes care of transportation and other logistics.

If you are not careful, the cost of your funeral can add up quickly. For example, many funeral directors sell the entire funeral as a package, including items—such as pallbearers—that your family may not want. Obtain an itemized list of what the package includes, and eliminate the expendables. Also, investigate the full range of alternatives, from the least expensive casket to the most elaborate. Often, funeral directors keep the cheapest and least profitable caskets out of sight or discourage you from selecting among them. Funeral directors can also quote prices over the phone so you can comparison shop. (A 1984 Federal Trade Commission order prohibited funeral directors from refusing to quote prices over the phone and other practices that were found to be widespread and objectionable.)

PREARRANGED FUNERALS

One way that people deal with the whole unpleasant subject of death and funerals is to invest in a *prearranged funeral package* (as mentioned in the preceding section). You can shop for a prearranged funeral more calmly now than your family can at your death. This should allow you to bargain and obtain a better deal than your survivors could. In addition, by researching and choosing among the various burial options, caskets and so forth, you know exactly what will happen to you after your death, and your family knows that your funeral will be conducted according to your wishes.

A prearranged funeral requires a fixed, up-front fee. (Therefore, if you arrange your own funeral, your family will not have to raise the funds to cover your burial when they are least capable of doing so.) You can pay this fee in one lump sum, in several installments or by buying an insurance policy specifically designed to cover funeral expenses. In this case, your money is placed in a trust fund to cover your burial costs. One such fund is a *Totten Trust*—an individual savings plan earmarked for your funeral. While you live, you control the money, which is usually invested in a certificate of deposit or a money-market account. When you die, the funds are available immediately to pay for your funeral.

Another such fund is a *regulated trust,* in which your money is invested by the funeral home or cemetery to pay for your burial. You have no access to this money. This trust is enormously profitable for the funeral home or cemetery because it keeps the earnings that your capital generates after you die if your funeral costs less than the funds you deposited. The best prearranged packages will refund any unused money to your estate.

Before you sign up for a prefunded funeral, find out whether you can get a total or partial refund if you change your mind about the package. For example, you might want to be buried in another state if you move away. Or you might not have the money to make your installment payments and want a refund of what you have already paid. Also learn whether your current payment protects you against future price increases for funerals and related services. Most policies do, but make sure that yours is one of them. In addition, find out what happens if the funeral home you are dealing with goes out of business. Normally, its contracts will be transferred to another home, but you should know which home that might be.

MEMORIAL SOCIETIES

One way to defray the high cost of funeral services is to join a local *memorial society.* These societies, which act as consumer advocates for funeral planning, are nonprofit, voluntary associations of people from all walks of life who want simple, dignified alternatives to elaborate and expensive funeral services.

Local societies can guide you to more affordable burial alternatives in your hometown. For example, it might not be necessary to use a funeral home to conduct a burial in your state. In other cases, memorial societies make arrangements with local undertakers to provide inexpensive funerals at a preset cost for members. When you join, you will be sent a prearrangement form allowing you to choose burial, cremation or donation. You can also describe the kind of service you want.

In general, funerals provided by memorial societies dispense with expensive extras such as embalming, cosmetic make-up, open-casket viewing, fancy caskets and elaborate services. In fact, many memorial societies conduct their services without the body present.

ORGAN DONATION

Whatever method of disposition or type of funeral you choose, you can also donate your body to medical science. Experimentation performed on cadavers is extremely important to the advancement of medical research, and many people feel that they make a significant contribution by offering their body to science. For more information on donating your body to medical science, contact the National Anatomical Service (28 Eltingville Blvd., Staten Island, NY 10312; 718-948-2401; 800-727-0700), which is in the business of procuring cadavers and transporting them to medical schools. In some cases, the medical schools will pay to transport the body; in other cases, your estate must foot the bill.

Similarly, you may be able to donate organs like your heart and kidneys for transplant to help someone else live through your death. If you decide to donate any organs, you can indicate which organs to donate. The donor recipients pay for any costs incurred for removing the organs, but you are financially responsible for how you want your body to be taken care of after the organ donation, such as cremation, earth burial, donation to science, etc. For more information on donating your organs, contact The Living Bank (P.O. Box 6725, Houston, TX 77265-6725; 713-528-2971; 800-528-2971; www.livingbank.org), a nonprofit organization. Clearly, the decisions on whether to donate your organs to people in need and/or your body to medical research should be made calmly well in advance of your death.

To make sure that your body is donated to a medical school or your organs are donated for transplant purposes, carry a Uniform Donor Card in your wallet. You can obtain a card if you join the Funeral & Memorial Societies of America (802-482-3437) or from The Living Bank. Figure 15.1 illustrates the Uniform Donor Card.

While the entire subject of estate planning, wills, trusts and funerals may be unappealing, don't ignore it. The further in advance you plan and finance your inevitable death, the more at ease you will feel, and the better off your family will be for the rest of their lives.

Figure 15.1
Uniform Donor Card

Of
_____

(Your name)

in the hope I may help others, I hereby make this anatomical gift, if medically acceptable, to take effect upon my death. The words and marks below indicate my desires.

I give   (a) _____   any needed organs or parts.

         (b) _____   only the following organs or parts

_____

(Specify the organs or parts.)

                     for the purpose of transplantation, therapy, medical research or education.

         (c) _____   my body for anatomical study if needed.

_____

(Limitations or special wishes, if any)

Signed by the donor and the following two witnesses in the presence of each other:

_____   _____

Signature of Donor   Donor's Birthdate

_____   _____

Date Signed   City and State

_____   _____

Witness   Witness

This is a legal document under the Uniform Anatomical Gift Act or similar laws.

Resources

BOOKS

The American Way of Death Revisited, by Jessica Mitford (Alfred Knopf, 201 E. 50th St., New York, NY 10017; 212-751-2600). An expose of funeral industry practices, warning consumers about the many ways they can overpay for burials and funerals.

Caring for the Dead: Your Final Act of Love, by Lisa Carlson (Upper Access Press, P.O. Box 457, Hinesburg, VT 05461; 800-356-9315). A comprehensive guide to arranging a low-cost but dignified funeral, written by the executive director of the Funeral and Memorial Societies of America. Also lists all the laws pertaining to the funeral industry in every state in America.

The Common Sense Guide to Estate Planning, by Robert H. Runde and J. Barry Zischang (McGraw-Hill, 860 Taylor Station Rd., Blacklick, OH 43004; 800-722-4726; www.mcgraw-hill.com). The complete guide to estate planning for the layperson. Defines terms and identifies various options in estate planning.

The Complete Book of Trusts, by Martin M. Shenkman (John Wiley & Sons Inc., 605 3rd Ave., New York, NY 10158-0012; 212-850-6000; www.wiley.com). Describes the major forms of trusts, including living trusts, bypass trusts, children's trusts, charitable trusts and many more.

The Complete Will Kit, by Jens C. Appel III (John Wiley & Sons Inc., 605 3rd Ave., New York, NY 10158-0012; 212-850-6000; www.wiley.com). Contains all the forms you need to write a will, as well as state-by-state legal requirements for wills.

Estate Planning Made Easy, by David Phillips and Bill Wolfkiel (Dearborn Financial Publishing, 155 N. Wacker Dr., Chicago, IL 60606; 312-836-4400; 800-322-8621; www.dearborn.com). Provides a step-by-step guide to protecting your family, safeguarding your assets and minimizing estate taxes.

Everything Your Heirs Need To Know: Your Assets, Family History and Final Wishes, by David S. Magee (Dearborn Financial Publishing, 155 N. Wacker Dr., Chicago, IL 60606; 312-836-4400; 800-322-8621; www.dearborn.com). Guides you in assembling the information you need to help your heirs settle your estate, including insurance, benefit, bank account, real estate, asset, debt and burial arrangement information, as well as wills and trusts.

Financial Power of Attorney Workbook, by Shae Irving (Nolo Press, 950 Parker St., Berkeley, CA 94710; 510-549-1976; 800-992-NOLO; 800-992-6656; www.nolo.com). This book shows you how to give another person the legal authority to handle your financial matters, such as paying bills and taxes and managing real estate, if it becomes ncessary. Comes with all the necessary legal forms as tear-outs and on a floppy disk.

How To Avoid Probate! by Norman F. Dacey (HarperCollins Publishers, 100 Keystone Industrial Park Dr., Scranton, PA 18512; 800-242-7737; www.harpercollins. com). A classic book providing trust forms that help you avoid the cost and delay of probate proceedings.

How To Use Trusts To Avoid Probate and Taxes: A Guide to Living, Marital, Support, Charitable, and Insurance Trusts, by Theresa Meehan Rudy, Kay Ostberg and Jean Dimeo (Random House, 201 E. 50th St., New York, NY 10017; 212-751-2600; 310-582-8800; www.randomhouse.com). A complete guide written in everyday language explaining estate planning and the many types of trusts. Also discusses the varying estate laws in each of the 50 states in America. The book is also available through HALT (see entry under "Trade Associations") and the American Association of Retired Persons (AARP).

Keeping What's Yours: Proven Asset Strategies for Everything from Handling Creditors to Becoming Legally Judgement Proof, by Brett K. Kates (Dearborn Financial Publishing, 155 North Wacker Dr., Chicago, IL 60606; 312-836-4400; 800-322-8621; www.dearborn.com). Describes how to protect your assets from being seized by creditors. Also gives guidance about what names to hold assets in under different circumstances.

Introduction to Estate Planning, by Chris Prestopino (Kendall-Hunt Publishing, 4050 Westmark Dr., Dubuque, IA 52004; 319-589-1000; www.kendallhunt.com). An authoritative overview of estate planning, with an extensive glossary of terms, tax information and strategies for many situations. Especially readable because of many examples and charts.

The Living Trust Revolution: Why America Is Abandoning Wills and Probate, by Robert A. Esperti and Renno L. Peterson (Viking Penguin, 375 Hudson St., New York, NY 10014; 212-366-2000; www.penguin.com). Explains the living trust and other kinds of trusts that help you avoid probate.

Living Wills and More, by Terry J. Barnett (John Wiley & Sons Inc., 605 3rd Ave., New York, NY 10158-0012; 212-850-6000; www.wiley.com). Explains what a living will must include and provides forms to complete, as well as state-by-state guidelines for living wills.

Make Your Own Living Trust, by Denis Clifford (Nolo Press, 950 Parker St., Berkeley, CA 94710; 510-549-1976; 800-992-NOLO; 800-992-6656; www.nolo. com). Explains the living trust—how it works, how property is transferred to the trust, when you need one and how to create one. It also provides all the tear-out forms and instructions necessary to create a basic living trust, a marital life estate trust (an A-B trust), and a back-up will.

Plan Your Estate with a Living Trust: Wills, Probate Avoidance, and Taxes, by Denis Clifford and Cora Jordan (Nolo Press, 950 Parker St., Berkeley, CA 94710;

510-549-1976; 800-992-NOLO; 800-992-6656; www.nolo.com). Provides simplified explanations of estate planning. Covers gift giving, wills, trusts and tax planning. Includes a sample will and revocable living trust form.

Nolo's Will Book, by Denis Clifford (Nolo Press, 950 Parker St., Berkeley, CA 94710; 510-549-1976; 800-992-NOLO; 800-992-6656; www.nolo.com). Explains why you need a will and shows you what the will must cover to be legally valid. Discusses guardianship, creating trusts and avoiding probate. Also comes with a floppy disk with will forms on it.

Software

Living TrustMaker (Nolo Press, 950 Parker St., Berkeley, CA 94710; 510-549-1976; 800-992-NOLO; 800-992-6656; www.nolo.com). CD-ROM and floppy disk designed to help nonlawyers write a revocable living trust to avoid probate and transfer property to heirs safely and quickly while avoiding legal fees.

Quicken Family Lawyer (Parsons Technology, P.O. Box 100, 1700 Progress Dr., Hiawatha, IA 52233-0100; 319-395-9626; 800-779-6000; www.parsonstech.com). Provides 83 common legal documents, automatically customized for each state, including an estate-planning worksheet, a living will, a simple will and a living trust. Also offers powers of attorney forms, letters of credit, real estate leases, alimony and child support forms, prenuptial agreements, and responses to IRS notices, among others.

WillMaker (Nolo Press, 950 Parker St., Berkeley, CA 94710; 510-549-1976; 800-992-NOLO; 800-992-6656; www.nolo.com). CD-ROM and floppy disk leading you step by step through the process of writing a will. Also designed to help you establish testamentary and other types of trusts. Includes a living will or health-care directives module allowing you to specify what kinds of health care you want provided or withheld in the event you cannot communicate your wishes. Also includes funeral planning and burial arrangements documents.

Trade Associations

American College of Trust & Estate Counsel (3415 S. Sepulveda Blvd., Suite 330, Los Angeles, CA 90034; 310-398-1888; www.actec.org). The professional organization of trust and estate lawyers. Publishes a quarterly journal called *ACTEC Notes* with the latest news in the field. Upon written request, will refer you to qualified trust and estate lawyers in your state.

Cemetery Consumer Service Council (P.O. Box 3574, Washington, DC 20007; 703-379-6426). Represents cemetery operators and sponsors a hot-line to resolve disputes between consumers and cemetery operators.

Choice in Dying (1035 30th St., N.W., Washington, DC 20007; 202-338-9790; 800-989-9455; www.choices.org). Can help you set up advance directives such as a living will and medical powers of attorney and can explain the various medical and legal options available at the end of your life. Offers the following question-and-answer series of booklets for a nominal fee: *Artificial Nutrition and Hydration and End of Life Decisions; Dying at Home; Medical Treatments and Your Advanced Directives; Advance Directives and End-of-Life Decisions; Cardiopulmonary Resuscitation, Do Not Resuscitate Orders and End-of-Life Decisions; You and Your Choices; The Physician-Assisted Suicide Debate: Understanding the Issues; Health Care Agents: Appointing One and Being One.*

Funeral & Memorial Societies of America (P.O. Box 10, Hinesburg, VT 05461; 802-482-3437; 800-765-0107; www.funerals.org/famsa). A consumer group for non-profit funeral and memorial societies, which are associations of people wanting simple, dignified and meaningful and affordable alternatives to traditional funeral services. The group emphasizes consumer education and information about how the funeral industry works, leading to more informed choices. Will send copies of the following brochures: "Beat the High Cost of Funerals"; "Body Donation: A Gift to Science"; "Cremation Explained: Answers to Frequently Asked Questions"; "Earth Burial: Simplifying a Tradition"; "Guide to Funeral Planning: Affordable Options"; "How To Help Grieving People: What You Can Say and What You Can Do"; "No One Wants To Talk about Death: How To Help"; and "Prepaying Your Funeral: Benefits and Dangers"; "Ten Tips for Saving Funeral Dollars"; "Understanding the Tricks of the Funeral Trade"; "12 Reasons Why People Pay Too Much For A Funeral"; "Did You Forget: the Most Important Part of Funeral Planning"; "Eco-Friendly Death and Funeral Choices"; "Veterans Funeral and Burial Benefits: Including Spouses and Dependent Children."

HALT (Help Abolish Legal Tyranny): An Organization of Americans for Legal Reform (1612 K St. N.W., Suite 510, Washington, D.C. 20006; 202-887-8255; 888-367-4258; www.halt.org). A nonprofit public interest group dedicated to the principle that everyone should be able to dispose of their legal affairs in a simple, affordable and equitable manner. Achieves its reform goals through education and advocacy work. Offers a series of self-help books, including *Everyday Contracts: If You Want To Sue a Lawyer; How To Use Trusts To Avoid Probate and Taxes; Probate: Settling an Estate—A Step-by-Step Guide; Small Claims Court, Real Estate; Using a Lawyer . . . and What To Do if Things Go Wrong;* and *Wills: A Do-it-Yourself Guide.* Also offers *The Everyday Law Series,* which provides information on the court system, estate planning and probate, consumer law, bankruptcy and other legal issues. Two other helpful publications are: *The Legal Resource Directory: Your Guide to Help Hotlines and Hot Websites,* a book answering common legal questions filled with resources to help you resolve problems, file complaints against lawyers and seek free legal advice; and *Legal Rights for Seniors: A Guide to Health Care, Income Benefits, and Senior Legal Services.*

Legal Counsel for the Elderly (601 E St., N.W., 4th Floor, Building A, Washington, DC 20049; 202-434-2120; 800-423-3410; www.aarp.com). A nonprofit legal support center, sponsored by the American Association of Retired Persons, dealing with issues of concern to the elderly. Sells a series of self-help publications for consumers, including *Planning for Incapacity: A Self-Help Guide.* Each guide, customized according to state law, offers answers to commonly asked questions about estate-planning, living-will and health-care power of attorney forms, with instructions, a glossary of legal and medical terms and a wallet card to fill out and carry. Other publications include *Organizing Your Future: A Guide to Decisionmaking in Your Later Years; The Rights of Older Persons—A Basic Guide to the Legal Rights of Older Persons under Current Law;* and *Your Legal Rights in Later Life.*

Monument Builders of North America (3158 S. River Rd., Suite 224, Des Plaines, IL 60018; 847-803-8800; 800-233-4472; www.monumentbuilders.org). The association for manufacturers of burial monuments and plaques. Will recommend reputable local monument dealers.

National Funeral Directors Association (11121 W. Oklahoma Ave., Milwaukee, WI 53227; 414-541-2500; 800-228-6332; www.nfda.org). The association of funeral directors helps run the Funeral Service Consumer Assistance Program (FSCAP; 800-662-7666), which resolves disputes between consumers and funeral directors. Offers the following free brochures: "A Caring Response to an AIDS Related Death"; "Anatomical Gifts"; "Are You Interested In: Have You Considered Working in the Funeral Service Business"; "Children and Death"; "Choosing a Funeral Ceremony"; "Co-Worker Death"; "Cremation"; "Embalming"; "Grief: A Time To Heal"; "Living When Your Spouse Has Died"; "Living With Dying"; "Making Funeral Arrangements"; "Parent Death"; "Suicide"; "What Can We Do To Help?"; "When a Baby Has Died"; "Will I Ever Stop Hurting? A Parents Grief."

PART III

Controlling Your Financial Destiny

16

Making the
Most of Your
Employee Benefits

Whether you work for a large or a small company, a nonprofit organization, a for-profit firm or a government agency, the package of employee benefits available to you is crucial in putting together your personal financial plan. If you take the time and effort to understand and fully utilize your benefits package, you will end up in much better financial shape than if you toss your employee benefits handbook in a drawer and vow to yourself, "I'll get to it as soon as I can."

Most companies offer various employee benefits. This chapter discusses the most common: pension and retirement savings programs; health care and dependent care assistance programs; education and legal services; and life and disability insurance. Each of these has its own complex rules, both in terms of the tax treatment of benefits and in the choices you make in signing up for the benefits and maintaining your accounts.

While your employee benefits or human resources department can explain your benefits, don't expect it to take the initiative in doing so. Millions of employees go their entire career without talking to anyone from the employee benefits department until the day they retire or otherwise leave the company. By that time, of course, it is far too late to maximize the value of employee benefits. The best time to begin is when you first join a company. The earlier you enroll in certain programs, particularly retirement savings programs, the more time your assets have to grow and help meet your financial goals.

Many employers, both to cut costs and to give employees more ability to tailor their benefits to their individual circumstances, these days offer *cafeteria plans,* which give employees several choices to combine benefits. While the flexibility of such plans is desirable, they force you to order your priorities and allocate your benefits dollars in a way that best suits your situation. If you are in your 20s or

30s, are healthy and have young children, for example, consider shifting more of your dollars into life insurance and dependent care programs that can help pay for child care. If you are in poor health and nearing retirement, you might allocate more of your dollars into retirement savings plans and health insurance.

Whatever stage your career is in, understanding your employee benefits options is key to financially maximizing your working years. Learn to take advantage of all the opportunities offered by your benefits programs.

Pension and Retirement Savings Programs

The most financially significant benefit employers offer their workers are plans that allow the employees to build substantial savings for retirement. People who work many years at companies with generous pension and retirement savings plans have much more financially secure later years than those who never participate in such plans. Through years of federal legislation, the government has encouraged employers to offer retirement plans, partly because the government does not want millions of people to depend exclusively on Social Security when they retire.

Retirement savings programs can be divided into two classes: those in which the company promises to provide a specified retirement benefit known as *defined benefit plans,* and those in which the company promises to make certain contributions, known as *defined contribution plans.* In the latter case, employees are often allowed to make contributions to the plan, sometimes on a pretax basis. For most of the years employee benefits have been offered in U.S. companies, defined benefit plans have been more common. These plans place the employer in a paternalistic role: setting aside money for employees' retirement, determining the optimal way to invest it, then doling out benefits.

While defined benefit plans, usually offered in the form of pension plans, remain widespread, they have been giving way to defined contribution plans. These programs shift much of the responsibility for contributing, investing and distributing retirement assets from the employer to the employee. Contribution plans take many forms, but they are usually known as employee stock ownership plans, money purchase pension plans, profit-sharing plans, salary reduction (401[k]) plans, stock bonus plans or thrift plans. If you participate, you can build substantial savings by the time you retire and enjoy several major tax breaks along the way. If you do not enroll, you might end up with little or no retirement fund.

Companies have been shifting from traditional defined benefit plans to defined contribution plans not only because they may be less expensive for the firms but also because the companies want to encourage employees to take more responsibility for their own financial futures. Employees who switch companies fairly frequently also prefer defined contribution plans, which may allow the employees to transfer their accumulated savings to the new company. Defined benefit plans require at least five years of service at one firm for full vesting. This shift to defined contribution plans has been a wrenching change for many employees who had become accustomed to the idea of letting their companies take care of them. Because the shift seems irreversible, it becomes more important than ever that you learn about and participate in your company's retirement savings plan.

Traditional Defined Benefit Pension Plans

The idea of an employer providing a retirement pension plan for its employees started in the United States in 1759 when the Presbyterian Church created a fund to care for the widows and children of ministers. More than a century later, in 1875, American Express formed the first corporate pension plan. Now, hundreds of thousands of companies offer pension plans, and tens of millions of workers are covered. Pension plans have grown to become one of the biggest pools of assets in the United States, worth trillions of dollars. As such, pension plans are among the largest and most influential investor classes in the country because they own billions of dollars' worth of stocks, bonds, real estate and other assets.

The basic idea behind a defined benefit pension plan is that the company sets aside a certain amount of money in a trust fund for each employee every year. It then invests the money wisely so that it will grow. When you retire, the plan pays a monthly pension benefit normally based on how long you worked at the firm and the salary level you attained. The employer not only puts up all of the money that goes into the pension fund; it also hires money managers to invest it for both capital growth and regular income, which is distributed to pensioners. From the employer's point of view, all contributions to the pension plan are deductible as a business expense, providing a big tax break to the company. In addition, all the capital gains, dividends and interest earned by the company's pension fund accumulate tax free. Pension money is taxed only when it is paid to employees, who must report it as regular income in the year they receive it.

VESTING RULES

To qualify for pension benefits, you must work at a company long enough to become *vested.* Being vested means having enough years of service to give you the legal right to receive some or all of your benefits when you reach retirement age, even if you no longer work for that employer. Earning a year of service normally requires working at least 1,000 hours that year, or the equivalent of about 20 hours a week. Those hours are defined as time you were paid or were entitled to be paid, including vacation days, sick days and back pay days.

Most companies sponsoring their own pension plans use a system of *cliff* vesting, which requires that you work at a company for five years before you are eligible for benefits. In some plans that are co-sponsored by many employers, it may take as many as ten years for you to become vested. Other firms use the *graded* vesting method, in which you are 20 percent vested after three years of work, 40 percent vested after four years, and so on until you are fully vested after seven years of service. If you join a company near retirement age, you are automatically vested when you retire, even if you have not served the required number of years.

If you leave a company and then return, it is considered a *break in service,* which may reduce your pension benefit. For example, if you work for a company four years, then leave for another job and return more than a year later, you probably would lose credit for your first four years of service. Time off for the birth or adoption of a child or for military service in time of war or national emergency is not considered a break in service.

DETERMINING YOUR PAYMENT

Most employers use one of three ways to determine your monthly pension benefit.

- *Flat benefit formula plans* pay a flat dollar amount each month at retirement. The more years you worked at a company, the higher the monthly payment. Such plans are typically offered to hourly and unionized workers whose benefits are specified in collective bargaining agreements.

- *Career-average formula plans* average the income you earned over your entire career at a company to determine your monthly payment. In some cases, you receive a percentage of your pay for every year you participated in the pension plan. Other companies average your yearly salary for as long as you took part in the pension plan. Your benefit is then determined by a specified percentage of your career-average pay multiplied by the number of years you worked at the company.

- *Final-pay formula plans,* which generally produce the highest monthly payments, average your income for your last few years (typically five) at a company, when you probably earned your peak salary. Once you retire, you receive a payment based on a percentage of these average earnings multiplied by the number of years you worked at the firm.

Both career-average and final-pay formula plans are usually offered to professionals in nonunionized situations, though some unions manage to obtain these more favorable calculation methods through bargaining agreements.

Your retirement benefit is determined not only by one of these formulas but also by your age when you retire. In general, the later you retire, the higher your monthly payment. If you bow out at age 55, you will receive a much smaller payout than you would at age 65 because the company figures you will collect that payment for a much longer time. In some cases, when a company encourages workers to retire early (before age 65), it offers credit for a few extra years of service that you have not actually worked. For example, if you are 58 years old, the company might give you pension benefits as if you were age 62 to induce you to retire. On the other hand, if you work beyond age 65, you may qualify for a deferred retirement benefit, which can be more than the payment that 65-year-olds receive. But no matter when you retire, your plan must begin your benefits by age 70½, and you must pay income tax on those payments every year.

A series of Congressional laws and IRS rules limit the amount that a pension plan can pay you in any year. When the maximum was first defined in the 1970s, it was 100 percent of your average pay for your three highest earning years, up to $75,000. That maximum has been raised to about $115,000, though the amount moves upward each year. To prevent the top executives in a company from grabbing most of the pension benefits, a complex series of rules limits pension payments to those earning the highest salaries. This prevents a plan from becoming top-heavy and discriminating against lower-paid workers.

How You Get Paid

While you have no say as an employee about how much your company puts into the pension plan, how the funds are invested or the formula used to pay benefits, you do have options on how you receive the money at retirement. Normally, you must decide between an *annuity,* which pays a specific monthly sum for a particular period of time, and a *lump sum*—all the cash at once.

Annuity Options

Annuities offer many payment options. In general, the longer you obligate the company to pay benefits, the smaller your monthly check. Your regular stipend will be based on whether you think you'll live for a short or a long time. Following are the usual options you will be offered:

Ten-year term certain annuity. If you think you will live ten years or less after retirement, choose an annuity that will pay you or your heirs for only ten years. This option provides the highest monthly benefit. However, if you live more than ten years, you're out of luck (at least as far as the company's obligation goes). This is a very risky strategy—unless you are in very poor health when you retire—because the average life expectancy today is well into a person's 80s, or more than 20 years from the usual retirement age of 65.

Life annuity with ten-year term certain. This annuity will pay a fixed monthly amount for the rest of your life. However, if you die before the annuity has paid you benefits for ten years, your beneficiary (usually your spouse) will receive your payments only for the remainder of the original ten years. This form of annuity pays less than the ten-year term certain. It also is significantly riskier for your spouse, who would not receive payments after ten years from the date of your retirement, assuming that you have died. If you select this option, make sure that your spouse has enough other sources of income to fall back on to cover the shortfall.

Life annuity. This plan would cut your monthly payout from the ten-year term certain significantly but would assure you of an income for life. After you die, your beneficiary receives no payments.

Joint and survivor annuity. If you are married or if someone depends on your income, you may want to select this option, which pays a fixed amount until both you and your spouse or dependent die. When you die, your spouse or dependent receives *qualified joint and survivor annuity* (QJSA) payments until he or she dies. These payments are usually less than the amount you received, but by law they cannot be less than 50 percent of your payment. Because both you and your spouse or dependent may live a long time, the joint and survivor plan offers the lowest monthly payment of those options discussed here. However, it is also the safest plan because it ensures that your spouse or dependent will receive a monthly income after you are gone.

If you are married and want to receive your benefits on the life annuity option or assign your survivor benefit to someone other than your spouse, you must obtain written spousal consent confirming that your spouse knows what he or she is relinquishing and that he or she does so willingly. (If you are asked to sign such a consent form, don't—unless you fully understand the financial impact of the alternate election and are so wealthy you can't envision ever needing the money.)

THE LUMP-SUM OPTION

If your company offers the option and you feel you are a savvy investor, you might take your pension in a *lump sum* instead of an annuity. With a lump sum, you receive your entire plan benefit in one check. After the check has cleared, you usually have no more rights under the pension plan. Most people roll this lump sum within 60 days into a tax-deferred account like an individual retirement account (IRA) or a Keogh account so that capital gains, dividends and interest continue to compound tax deferred until you begin withdrawing the money. Make sure that the lump sum is transferred directly from your company's pension fund to your IRA trustee at a bank, brokerage or mutual fund. If you get your hands on that check for even a second, you might have to pay a 20 percent withholding tax. If you do not roll over the money into a tax-deferred account, you will owe enormous income taxes on the entire amount in the year you receive it. To make matters even worse, you must pay a 10 percent penalty if you draw on a lump-sum distribution before you reach age 59½.

Taking a lump sum may sound enticing, but it can be tricky from both an investment and a tax point of view. On the investment front, you must make sure that you can produce the regular income you need by investing the lump sum wisely. If you have little investment experience, you may fall prey to investment opportunities that promise big returns and no risk but deliver big losses, high risks and obscene brokerage commissions. With your limited experience, even if you invest the money wisely, the capital may run out a few years later. Therefore, you cannot count on the monthly income that an annuity would guarantee. On the other hand, if you are an experienced investor, you may be able to earn a much higher return than a pension fund manager can. However, be sure that you have enough discipline to resist spending the principal because that, of course, reduces the amount of money you have to invest for income.

On the tax front, many complex rules govern lump-sum distributions. You should understand these rules before you choose this payment option. For example, if you take a lump-sum distribution after age 59½, you might elect *five-year forward averaging*. With this averaging method, the amount of your pension is taxed as though it were received over a five-year period, and the tax is computed separately from other income. This will greatly reduce the tax bite on your lump sum. Limits on how much of a lump sum you can apply to this rule and many other rules make it necessary to consult your employee benefits department or a good tax lawyer before you opt for this payment plan.

If you become permanently disabled before you retire, many plans will allow you to qualify for full pension benefits. The amount you receive depends on your age and how long you worked at the company. Some plans offer a flat, monthly amount until you reach retirement age, when you will receive your normal retirement benefit. More generous plans offer full retirement benefits from the time you are officially declared disabled. If you are covered by a long-term disability insurance plan, pension payments normally will not begin until disability plan payments lapse.

If you die before you reach retirement age, your spouse will receive a portion of your pension benefit. The plan usually begins payment in the year you would have received the benefit. This is known as a *qualified preretirement survivor annuity* (QPSA).

PROTECTION AGAINST PENSION PLAN DEFAULT

From the 1920s to 1974, pension plans proliferated without a comprehensive set of rules protecting pensioners. Companies could go bankrupt, and employees who had counted on their pensions would be left in the lurch. In 1974, Congress passed the landmark *Employee Retirement Income Security Act* (ERISA), which has become the governing legislation for pension plans. ERISA instituted a set of strict guidelines requiring companies offering pension plans to contribute enough each year to pay for the annual cost of the plans. Generally, this amount covers at least the benefits that participants earned that year. If a company cannot make its required payment because of extremely bad business conditions, it can apply for a waiver from the IRS for that year, though benefit obligations continue to accrue at the regular rate. In addition, if a pension fund suffers a sharp loss of value because of poor investment performance, the company must make up the difference so that promised benefits are paid.

When a company goes bankrupt with an underfunded pension plan, a government agency—the *Pension Benefit Guaranty Corporation* (PBGC), established as part of ERISA—comes to the rescue of employees. The PBGC is an insurance fund, similar to the Federal Deposit Insurance Corporation (FDIC) for bank depositors, which collects premiums from pension plans to cover defaults. The PBGC covers only private-company defined benefit pension plans, not plans sponsored by federal, state or local governments, nonprofit groups or professional associations, such as those plans for doctors and lawyers.

If you are a pensioner of a failed company, the PBGC will assume responsibility for paying your monthly benefit. The PBGC guarantees *basic benefits,* including the monthly pension check, some early retirement and disability benefits and some benefits for survivors of deceased beneficiaries. The agency does *not* cover other retirement benefits, such as health and welfare plans.

The PBGC guarantees benefits up to a maximum yearly amount, which is adjusted every year in line with changes in the Social Security contribution and benefit base. For a plan terminating in 1998, the maximum stood at $2,880 per month, or $34,568 per year. Don't expect great generosity from the PBGC, however. The benefit will never be more than you would have received if your plan had not defaulted.

Some plans guarantee steady increases in benefits, such as regular cost-of-living adjustments. If your plan contains such a provision when it defaults, you may or may not receive those increases. If your plan has enough assets to pay them, you will get the additional payments. If the plan has only enough money to pay part of the increases, you will get what the plan can afford. But chances are that a defaulted plan won't have enough money to follow through on a promise of increased benefits. In that case, the PBGC may make up part of the difference. If a cost-of-living promise was made in the five years before the plan defaulted, the agency will cover either 20 percent of the increase or $20 per month, whichever is larger. If the promise was made more than five years before the plan defaulted, the PBGC will cover the increase in full.

A company does not have to file for bankruptcy to terminate its pension plan. In recent years, many companies with existing defined benefit plans have opted to convert to defined contribution plans. In this case, the PBGC requires your company to prove that its current pension plan has enough money to pay all pension benefits to which retired and existing employees are entitled. If the PBGC is satisfied that this is the case, a *standard termination* will take place. Usually, the employer will use the pension fund assets to buy an annuity from an insurance company that promises to make the required payments to pensioners (at which point the PBGC no longer provides protection). You may be offered a lump-sum amount from your pension plan instead of a monthly annuity payment when this happens. Normally, you should roll any lump sum into an IRA within 60 days so that the money continues to grow tax deferred until you draw on it. Take the lump sum only if you feel confident enough that you can invest the money and generate a higher level of monthly income than the annuity would pay.

Some companies terminate their pension plans because they are in such poor financial condition that their pension costs threaten to sink them. In these cases, the PBGC permits what is known as *distress terminations.* The agency takes over as trustee of the funds and makes up the difference between what the plans can afford to pay and the minimum guaranteed benefit. If the entire value of your accrued benefits in a plan is $3,500 or less, the PBGC will usually pay you the amount in a lump sum.

If your pension plan is about to terminate under either standard or distress conditions, the plan must send you a *Notice of Intent to Terminate* letter. Soon after that missive, you will get another letter called a *Notice of Plan Benefits,* which describes the pension benefit you will receive. Though you may not be happy to receive these letters, at least you know that the PBGC stands behind your pension plan. Therefore, unlike the days before ERISA, you have no reason to panic.

A good defined benefit pension plan will never make you wealthy, but it can build a firm foundation for your retirement. Knowing that you will receive a certain amount of monthly income should give you at least a minimal sense of financial security. It's the least you deserve after spending so many years working productively for your company.

Defined Contribution Pension Plans

Unlike a good defined benefit plan, a properly invested defined contribution plan allows you to accumulate an enormous amount of capital to enjoy at retirement. And unlike a benefit plan, a contribution plan gives you plenty of choices and responsibility. For example, you must decide how much of your salary to contribute and how to invest the money among several options. If your selections prove profitable, you can end up with far more money at retirement than you ever dreamed possible. However, if you invest poorly, you must live with the consequences of a retirement not as financially secure as it could have been.

Several types of defined contribution plans exist. In some cases, an employer contributes to its plan each year based on the firm's profitability. The better the firm does, the bigger its contribution to your account. If the firm loses money one year, it may contribute nothing. In other cases, an employer provides a plan but makes no contributions. Contributions must be made totally by employees on a voluntary basis. Most plans provide some mix of the two, with employers matching employee contributions to a greater or lesser extent. When you reach retirement, you can either roll over the accumulated funds contributed by both you and your employer or convert the assets into an annuity to be paid out over the rest of your life.

The main types of defined contribution plans follow.

Employee stock ownership plan. Commonly called an ESOP, such a plan allows you, as an employee, to share in the profits of your company. The firm's and your contributions are invested in company stock, which gives you and other employees more incentive to work diligently and help the company prosper. Another version on an ESOP is a leveraged ESOP, where the plan borrows millions of dollars to buy most or all of the company's stock and, in effect, places the company in the employees' hands. The loan is generally paid off over time by company contributions to the plan. Participate in an ESOP only if you believe your company has a solid long-term future. Because ESOP funds are not diversified, you could take a big loss if the company falters.

Money-purchase pension plan. With a money purchase plan, your employer is obligated to contribute a set amount of your salary to the plan each year, no matter whether profits are up or down. When you retire from the company, your monthly benefit payment is based on the amount that has accumulated in the plan.

Profit-sharing plan. Such a plan requires that your company contribute a certain percentage of your salary to the plan each year, depending on the firm's profits. This may amount to as much as 15 percent to 20 percent of your income in an extremely profitable year or as little as nothing if the company lost money or earned anemic profits. However, earnings are not required for the company to contribute. The board of directors can decide to contribute to the profit-sharing plan because, for example, the employees endured a tough year and the board wants to reward employee loyalty. Profit-sharing plan assets can be invested in company stock, widely diversified stock, bond and money-market funds, or real estate or insurance programs.

Salary reduction plan. A salary reduction plan allows employees to defer a certain percentage of their salary—usually up to 10 percent—to a tax-deferred account and invest the money in stocks, bonds, money-market funds and guaranteed investment contracts (GICs, similar to long-term CDs). When offered to employees of a corporation, the plan is called a *401(k)*. When offered to workers at a nonprofit organization like a school, hospital, church or social welfare agency, it is known as a *403(b)* plan. These extremely popular programs, also known as CODAs *(cash-or-deferred arrangements),* allow you to contribute pretax dollars to a plan. In other words, the money you invest is taken off the top of your salary, and the amount of income reported to the IRS on your W-2 form is reduced by that amount. You pay taxes on these assets only years later when you withdraw money from the plan—presumably in retirement when you are subject to lower tax rates.

This pretax feature makes salary reduction plans far superior to other defined contribution plans, which are funded with dollars remaining after you have paid federal, state, local and Social Security taxes. Some salary reduction plans even let you make additional, voluntary contributions to your 401(k) plan on top of the money withheld from your salary. You are currently limited to a total contribution of about $10,000 a year, however. (That limit moves up a bit each year in line with inflation.)

In addition to the benefit of pretax funding, most companies match to some degree your salary reduction plan contributions, either in cash or in company stock, making the deal even sweeter. The most generous companies match your contributions dollar for dollar, giving you a 100 percent return before the money is even invested. Many others match your contributions at 50 percent.

According to IRS rules, you can withdraw funds from your salary reduction account only in the case of a well-defined financial hardship. This means that you must have an immediate and heavy need for funds for a major medical expense, to purchase a home as a primary residence, to avoid eviction from your apartment or foreclosure on your mortgage, or for post-secondary education expenses. You must prove not only that you have these expenses but also that you have no other resources to pay them. The government tries to make it difficult for you to get at your salary reduction money because it wants you to have the assets available when you retire. However, most plans allow you to borrow against your plan's assets at a reasonable interest rate, so it makes little sense to withdraw the assets unless it is an emergency and you see no way to pay back a loan.

Stock bonus plan. Such a plan is similar to a profit-sharing plan in that bonuses are given at the board's discretion when the company's profits are high. When you retire under a stock bonus plan, however, your benefits are paid in stock rather than cash.

Thrift savings plan. With a thrift savings plan, you—as an employee—can contribute a certain percentage of your salary (up to about 10 percent) on an after-tax basis to the plan. The money can be invested in stocks, bonds, money-market funds, GICs or company stock. The corporation may or may not match your contributions, depending on how company profits fare and how much the firm wants to promote the plan. Usually, the company's matching funds must remain in an investment they require, such as company stock or a GIC. The company is under no obligation to contribute or match your investment. In some cases, employers will match your contributions up to a certain level—say, 6 percent of your salary—after which your funds will not be matched.

Participating in a defined contribution plan holds several advantages.

- It is fairly painless to contribute because the money is deducted automatically from your paycheck. When you never see the money, doing without it is easier.

- You automatically dollar cost average because you invest the same dollar amount every paycheck. Those dollars buy more shares when prices are down and fewer shares when prices are up, giving you—over time—an overall lower cost of shares.

- You pay no commissions because your employer absorbs all costs of buying stock and administering the program. If you choose to have your money invested in mutual funds, you will pay a slight annual management fee of about 1 percent of your assets. Nevertheless, that small fee is worthwhile because your money will be managed by a top money manager, who will probably achieve better returns than you could produce on your own.

- Any company match of your contributions boosts your return dramatically. If your company matches every dollar you contribute to a salary reduction plan with $.50, for example, you are already far ahead most investors. What other investment pays an immediate tax-deferred 50 percent return?

- Many plans offer several investment options, allowing you to tailor the portfolio to your needs and risk tolerance. You can also transfer money among stocks, bonds and GICs, sometimes as frequently as daily but at least once a year. (This is discussed in more detail later in this chapter.)

- You can save a tremendous amount of money through pretax contributions and the tax-deferred accumulation of funds in a defined contribution plan.

- Defined contribution plans can be sources of inexpensive loans. Most companies allow you to borrow against the value of your plan, often at an interest rate of one percentage point more than the prime rate. Paying back the loan is also easy because it is accomplished through payroll deduction over as long as five years.

Under IRS rules, you cannot invest more than 25 percent of your salary or $30,000, whichever is less, in any combination of these defined contribution plans. After all, you need money to live on, and the IRS wants to limit the amount of money you can shelter from taxes through employee benefit plans. The maximum amount of compensation you can use to calculate contributions is $160,000 in 1997 (the amount is adjusted upwards each year slightly.)

If defined contribution plans are so wonderful, why doesn't everyone participate in them? Unfortunately, many people don't understand the power of these plans, and some are afraid to take responsibility for making investment decisions. If you're offered one of these plans, seize the opportunity to invest.

VESTING RULES

The vesting rules for defined contribution pension plans are quite different from those for defined benefit plans. With a traditional pension plan, it can take five to ten years of service at a company before you are entitled to retirement benefits. With a defined contribution plan, the amount of cash you invest is immediately vested, and you cannot lose it if you leave the company. Tax lawyers call your contribution *nonforfeitable.*

You may lose some or all of the company's matching contributions if you leave the company, however. Rules vary widely by company, but usually a company's matching funds become vested only after a specified period. For example, you might have to wait two or three years before each year's matching funds are yours to keep. In other companies, your benefits might become fully vested if you stay at the firm at least seven years. This delay is intended to deter you, as a valued employee, from leaving the corporation soon after you sign on. No matter how long you have worked at a company, however, you become fully vested when you reach normal retirement age.

CURRENT TAX SAVINGS

As mentioned earlier, the defined contribution plan that not only generates tax-deferred retirement funds but also lowers your current tax bill is the salary reduction plan, which takes the form of a 401(k) plan at a corporation or a 403(b) plan at a nonprofit institution. Because your contributions to this plan come off the top of every paycheck, you avoid paying federal, state and local income taxes on the money. That, in itself, is a big boost, which is magnified when you add in any matching funds your company contributes.

The following simple example, provided by the employee benefits consulting firm of Hewitt Associates, compares the investment that a salary reduction plan offers to the investment that you can amass on your own after taxes.

Assume that you earn $40,000 a year and contribute 6 percent of your salary to the plan ($2,400). Your company matches $.30 on the dollar. Plan savings versus personal savings would accumulate as illustrated in Figure 16.1.

This example, in fact, understates the advantage of salary reduction plans because the tax savings would be much greater if you include all state and local income taxes you also would avoid. In addition, earnings on your after-tax investment of

Figure 16.1
Tax Savings from a Salary Reduction Plan

	With a Salary Reduction Plan	On Your Own
Annual pay	$40,000	$40,000
Minus pretax investment	– 2,400	– 0
Taxable pay	$37,600	$40,000
Minus federal income tax (based on 28% tax bracket)	– 9,021	– 9,693
Take-home pay	$28,579	$30,307
Minus after-tax investment	– 0	– 2,400
Take-home pay (including investment)	$28,579	$27,907
Taxes saved ($28,579 – $27,907)	$ 672	$ 0
Plus company match (at 30% of $2,400)	+ 720	0
TOTAL SAVINGS	**$ 1,392**	**$ 0**

Source: Reprinted by permission of Hewitt Associates, Lincolnshire, Illinois.

$2,400 would be taxed every year in the future, while your salary reduction plan balance would grow tax deferred until you withdraw the money at retirement.

THE BOOST FROM TAX DEFERRAL

When you combine the advantages of tax-deferred compounded savings and matching company contributions, the results can dramatically outperform the savings you could accumulate on your own with after-tax dollars. The example in Figure 16.2, prepared by the benefits consulting firm of Greenwich Associates in Greenwich, Connecticut, assumes the following:

- You begin contributing to a salary reduction plan at age 25, when you earn an annual salary of $25,000. Every year, your salary rises by 4 percent to keep pace with inflation.

- You contribute 6 percent of your salary to the plan each year, and your employer matches you at $.50 on the dollar.

- You invest half the money in stocks and half in bonds, achieving a long-term average 9 percent rate of return.

- You would have paid a 30 percent federal income tax rate on your savings outside the plan.

- You retire at age 65.

Scenario 1 indicates that you would have amassed $1,315,944 if you received a company match of 50 percent and paid no taxes along the way. Scenario 3 demonstrates that even without the employer match, you still would have accumulated $877,296 because of the tax-deferred compounding of your contributions. Scenario 2 shows that if you received an employer match of 50 percent but paid taxes every year, you would have ended up with $709,167. Scenario 4 indicates that if you saved exactly the same amount of money and earned the same return over the 40 years but received no employer match and enjoyed no tax shelter, you would have accumulated only $472,778.

The growth analysis example demonstrates that with a company match and tax deferral, you would have ended up with nearly three times the money you would have accumulated outside a salary reduction plan. If even one of several factors were altered—such as assuming a higher tax rate, a higher rate of investment return or a more generous company match—the differential would have been much higher.

THE BENEFITS OF AN EARLY START

The best way to maximize your assets in a salary reduction or another defined contribution plan is to begin contributing as early as possible. The longer money compounds, the more funds you will have at retirement. To illustrate this point dramatically, the employee benefits consulting firm of Kwasha Lipton in Fort Lee,

Figure 16.2
Salary Reduction Plan Growth under Four Different Scenarios

Account Balance

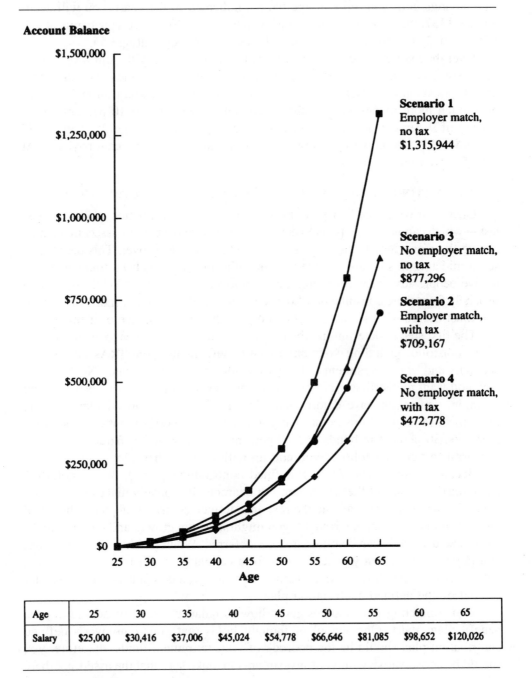

Age	25	30	35	40	45	50	55	60	65
Salary	$25,000	$30,416	$37,006	$45,024	$54,778	$66,646	$81,085	$98,652	$120,026

Source: Greenwich Associates, Greenwich, Connecticut. Used with permission.

New Jersey, compiled the chart in Figure 16.3. Kwasha Lipton assumed that you save $1,000 a year, starting at age 25, 35, 45 and 55, and earn 9 percent a year on your savings until you retire at age 65. As indicated in the chart, you will accumulate $337,882 if you begin saving at age 25, $136,308 if you begin at 35, $51,160 if you begin at 45 and only $15,193 if you begin at age 55.

Over the long run, it can also pay to be more aggressive with your investments because each percentage point of higher return can mean thousands of dollars extra in your pocket at retirement. In the chart in Figure 16.4, Kwasha Lipton illustrates how much more money you would accumulate if you earned 10 percent a year instead of 9 percent. For example, if you begin investing at age 25, you would amass $104,711 more with a 10 percent return than with a 9 percent payback. At age 55, you would earn $744 more.

ALLOCATING YOUR ASSETS IN A DEFINED CONTRIBUTION PLAN

Once you've decided to participate in a defined contribution plan, the next task—which can be difficult—is to determine how to allocate your assets in the plan among the many investment options presented by your employer. This decision is so intimidating to so many people that an entire industry has been founded solely to give people advice on allocating their employee plan benefits. While you might seek help from these consultants, who often charge $100 an hour or more, ultimately, you must decide what is best for you and how that might change over time.

The first step in determining the proper mix of investments is to examine your entire portfolio, including your employee benefit plans, your IRAs and Keogh accounts and your investment holdings outside of employee plans. Next, decide how you want to distribute your assets among broad categories of investment. For example, you might have determined, after reading the financial planning and investment sections of this book, that you need to keep 60 percent of your assets in stocks, 30 percent in bonds and 10 percent in cash vehicles. Your next task is to rearrange your portfolio so you end up with roughly that allocation.

Because your assets within a defined contribution plan grow tax deferred, make maximum use of the tax shelter. For example, it probably makes more sense to buy bonds, which pay taxable interest, in a defined contribution plan, where that interest compounds tax deferred. Or you might invest in growth and income stocks so taxable dividends can be reinvested tax deferred. When you buy growth stocks, you pay tax only when you sell shares for a capital gain. Therefore, if you hold onto stocks that pay little or no dividends for years, you do not need the tax shelter offered by the defined contribution plan.

Two competing philosophies about how to balance assets inside and outside benefit plans exist. One school of thought holds that your employer's defined contribution plan should be the bedrock of your retirement funds; therefore, you should be conservative with your investments to make sure that the assets are there when you need them. Advisers in this camp recommend keeping to blue chip stock

Figure 16.3
Amount of Money Available for Retirement

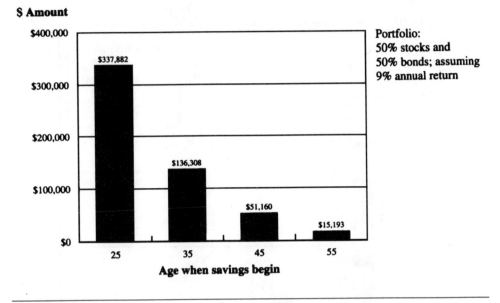

Portfolio:
50% stocks and
50% bonds; assuming
9% annual return

Source: Reprinted by permission of Kwasha Lipton, Fort Lee, New Jersey.

funds, balanced funds that own both stocks and bonds, and fixed-rate GICs. Most higher risk investing should take place outside your benefit plans, where you can use capital losses to offset capital gains.

Adherents to the other philosophy hold the opposite view. They say that a salary reduction plan is the perfect vehicle to achieve maximum capital gains over time. Particularly if you begin investing at an early age, your chances of earning high returns from aggressive growth stocks are quite high. As the charts from Kwasha Lipton illustrate, the higher your return and the younger you start, the larger your retirement fund grows. Once you retire, you can invest conservatively and convert your assets from growth stocks into income-producing bonds.

Before you decide where you stand in this debate, factor in your tolerance for risk. Refer back to the results of the risk analysis you completed in Chapter 1. If you found that you have some ability (emotionally, that is) to withstand the ups and downs of the stock market, invest more of your money in growth stocks, particularly if you are fairly young. If you are frightened by the possibility of any capital loss, scale back the portion of your assets going into stocks. However, do not eliminate stocks from your portfolio altogether; if you do so, you cut out your best chance for long-term growth. Typically, most people keep too much of their money in bonds or GICs, which—while they are safe—offer limited growth potential.

Figure 16.4
Impact of Additional 1 Percent Portfolio Return

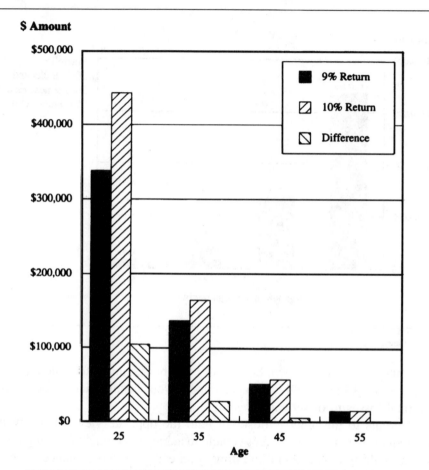

Age when savings begin	25	35	45	55
9% Return	$337,882	$136,308	$51,160	$15,193
10% Return	442,593	164,494	57,275	15,937
Difference	104,711	28,186	6,115	744

Original Portfolio: 50% stocks and 50% bonds
Second Portfolio: 75% stocks and 25% bonds

Source: Reprinted by permission of Kwasha Lipton, Fort Lee, New Jersey.

Another asset in which people invest too much of their money is their own company's stock. Even if you believe your company is a wonderful place to work and has a great future, take advantage of the diversification options your benefit plans offer. When you tie up too much of your entire net worth in one company, you expose yourself to great danger if anything negative happens to the firm. You already have made a big commitment to your firm by choosing it as your employer. Take the opportunity your company gives you to branch out by investing in stock funds that may own shares in hundreds of companies.

Following are some rules of thumb regarding asset allocation that you can modify according to your risk tolerance level and where you stand between the two schools of thought just described.

- In your 20s and 30s, keep 70 percent of your money in aggressive growth or blue chip stock funds and 30 percent in bonds, GICs or money funds (see Figure 16.5).

- In your 40s, allocate about 50 percent of your money to stocks and 50 percent to bonds, GICs and money funds (see Figure 16.6).

- In your 50s, scale back a bit more, keeping 30 percent in stocks and 70 percent in bonds, GICs and money funds (see Figure 16.7).

- By the time you retire in your 60s, have about 20 percent of your money in stocks and 80 percent in various fixed-income instruments. Do not make the mistake of transferring all your money into bonds and GICs at this time, however, because you still need some capital growth to stay ahead of inflation. You can get this growth only from stocks (see Figure 16.8).

These suggestions only broadly outline a strategy to maximize your defined contribution assets throughout your career. The precise allocation of assets at any particular time depends on interest rates, stock and bond prices and the outlook for the economy. For example, if interest rates are falling, you might want to keep more of your money in stocks, which are helped by falling rates, and less of your money in GICs and money funds, which pay lower returns as rates drop. On the other hand, if interest rates begin rising, you might want to pull some money out of stocks and invest it in GICs and money funds. The general strategy remains consistent, however. Take more risk with your money when you are young and able to bounce back from temporary downswings in the stock market. As you near retirement, scale back your growth stocks in favor of more stable income-producing assets.

By the time you reach retirement age, you have a more pleasant decision to make: how you should receive all the benefits you accumulated throughout your career.

Figure 16.5
Asset Allocation for the 20s and 30s Age Group

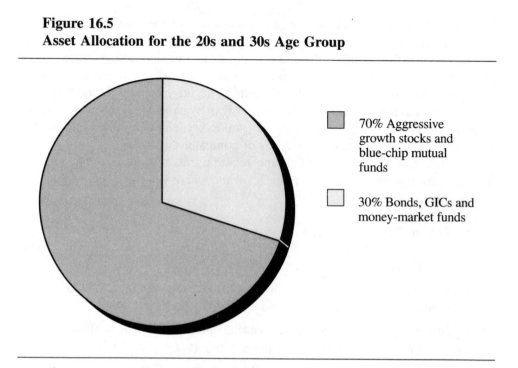

70% Aggressive
growth stocks and
blue-chip mutual
funds

30% Bonds, GICs and
money-market funds

Figure 16.6
Asset Allocation for the 40s Age Group

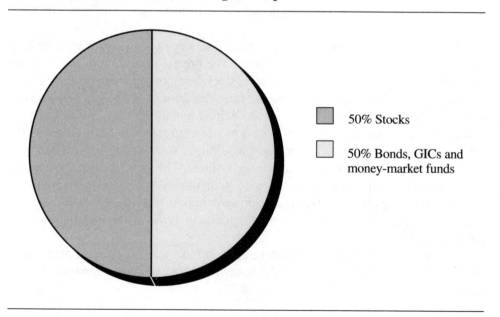

50% Stocks

50% Bonds, GICs and
money-market funds

Figure 16.7
Asset Allocation for the 50s Age Group

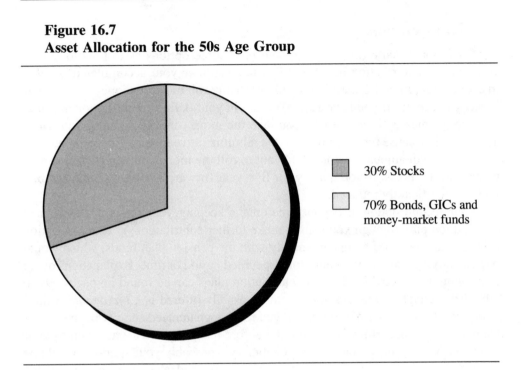

30% Stocks

70% Bonds, GICs and
money-market funds

Figure 16.8
Asset Allocation for the Retirement Years

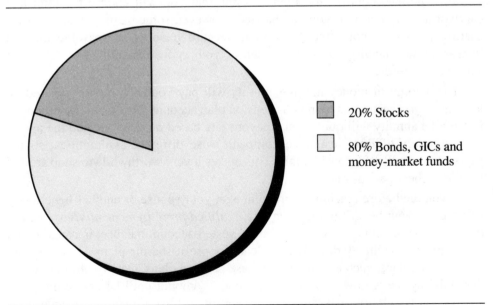

20% Stocks

80% Bonds, GICs and
money-market funds

Payout Options

Once you reach retirement age, you have three options as to how to collect your defined contribution benefits. First, you can take your accumulated benefits in a lump sum, in which case you would probably roll over the money into an IRA or Keogh account. If you have $5,000 or less in your defined contribution account, most companies will require that you take the money in a lump sum, (known as a *cash-out*), because they do not want the administrative hassle of keeping records for such a small amount. If you decide not to roll the money into an IRA, you may be hit hard by taxes. If you qualify for five-year forward averaging, your tax bite will be significantly reduced.

Your second option at payout time entails keeping your funds in the defined contribution plan (though you cannot make further contributions). Your last option is buying an insurance company annuity with the pension plan funds, which would pay you a certain monthly amount for a specified period of time. Explanations of the basic annuities offered by defined contribution plans can be found on pages 697 to 698 of this chapter. One additional annuity usually offered is a *life annuity with a cash refund feature*. With this annuity, you receive guaranteed annuity payments for the rest of your life. However, if you die before receiving at least as much as your employer paid for the annuity, your beneficiary—probably your spouse—would be entitled to the difference between the money you had already received and the amount the company paid for the annuity. Monthly payments under this type of plan are lower than those under a straight life annuity with no guarantees.

Most defined contribution plans assume that you will choose the joint and survivor annuity option if you are married. However, some plans—such as profit-sharing plans—do not offer this option because benefits are payable only in lump-sum, not annuity, form. Nevertheless, your spouse is entitled to that lump sum when you die.

The amount of money that the annuity will pay you each month is based on how much you accumulated in your pension plan account. The insurance company issuing the annuity will quote you a payout rate based on your age and the age of your spouse. Different insurance companies use different assumptions, so the payout terms will vary considerably. This makes it very worthwhile to shop around for the highest payout rate.

If you die before reaching retirement age, your spouse or another beneficiary will receive your benefit in the form of a *qualified preretirement survivor annuity* (QPSA). That amount, which is the entire vested account balance, is usually paid as a lump sum within 90 days of your death for profit-sharing plans. Other defined contribution plans, such as money-purchase pension plans, usually offer annuities that will pay the widow or widower a monthly amount until he or she dies.

As you weigh your payout options, keep in mind your overall financial plan. Whether you come to a conclusion on your own or with help from a financial adviser, determine which form of pension plan distribution will best complement your Social Security payments and returns on other investments. You will have to live with the consequences of your pension plan payout option for many years to come. Spend a good amount of time and effort making sure that you choose what's best for you.

Retirement Plans for Employees of Small Companies and the Self-Employed

The fact that you do not work for a major corporation that offers defined benefit and defined contribution plans does not mean that you can't have a retirement savings plan of your own. If you run or work for a small business or if you are self-employed, you have three options: the *simplified employee pension plan* (SEP), the savings incentive match plan for employees (SIMPLE), or the *Keogh plan.* All three of these programs offer some of the same tax advantages as defined contribution plans, including tax-deferred accumulation of investment earnings until retirement. They also offer similar investment and payout options. A few special rules apply to each, however.

Simplified Employee Pension (SEP) Plans

A simplified employee pension plan, as the name implies, is a simpler, small-company version of the defined contribution plan offered by larger employers. The paperwork, recordkeeping and reporting are also simpler with SEPs than with defined contribution plans. For example, a SEP does not have to be filed with the Department of Labor or the IRS, as the plans of larger companies must. Only firms with 25 or fewer employees can offer SEPs although at least half of the employees must sign up for the plan to make it effective.

Companies that offer SEPs set up an IRA for each eligible employee. This is why these plans are often called SEP-IRAs. As an employee, you become eligible if you have worked at a firm for at least three of the past five years and have earned at least $400 during the year. (This amount moves up with inflation each year.) The account can be funded by you, your employer or a combination of the two. In many cases, the employer matches employee contributions to some extent.

IRS rules limit the amount of total contributions to a SEP to $30,000 in one year. Of that, the employer's contribution is limited to 13.0435 percent of his eligible earnings. The maximum amount of compensation that can be taken into account for this formula is $160,000. For employees, contributions are limited to 15 percent of their wages, up to a $160,000 maximum. Just as with a defined contribution plan, the money you invest in a SEP can be taken off the top of your salary and therefore escapes federal, state and local taxes. Thus, this salary reduction feature gives you a current tax benefit in the year you contribute. If you also participate in a 401(k) or 403(b) plan, the amount you can contribute to the SEP is reduced somewhat.

Whatever you or your firm contributes to the SEP is immediately vested, meaning that you can roll it over into another retirement plan if you leave the company. As with all other qualified retirement plans, you suffer a 10 percent penalty if you withdraw money from the plan before you reach age 59½, and you must begin taking out money once you've turned age 70½. Unlike you can under many other defined contribution plans, you cannot borrow against your SEP account balance.

If your employer offers a SEP, take advantage of the opportunity to cut your taxes and build up funds for retirement. If your firm does not yet sponsor a SEP, try to convince the company head to start one. It's not expensive and involves far less paperwork than your employer might think.

SIMPLE PLANS

Small employers may want to set up what is known as a SIMPLE Plan for their employees. SIMPLE stands for Savings Incentive Match Plan for Employees. They also are known as SIMPLE IRAs. These plans, which are similar to 401(k) plans, are allowed for companies with no more than 100 employees earning at least $5,000 a year. If a company offers the SIMPLE plan, it cannot offer other qualified retirement plans to its workers. The most that workers can contribute to a SIMPLE plan is $6,000 a year. A major advantage of these contributions is that they are made on a pretax basis, so workers avoid federal and state income tax withholding on that part of their salaries. The employer can match his employee's contributions up to 3 percent of their salaries, or contribute 2 percent of the wages for all eligible workers, even if some workers choose not to contribute to the plan. If the employer decides to make the 2 percent contribution, it is capped at a salary of $160,000, or a contribution of $3,200. All matching contributions are deductible business expenses for the employer. Though your employer may pick a financial institution such as a bank or mutual fund to be the custodian of the SIMPLE plan, you have the right to choose your own financial institution and have your contributions transferred to it. The other rules surrounding SIMPLE plans—such as how the money can be invested and how money can be withdrawn—are the same as those applying to 401(k) plans.

KEOGH PLANS

If you are self-employed on a full-time basis, or even if you earn extra income through freelance work, you can set up a Keogh retirement plan, also known as HR 10 plans. These plans are named after Eugene J. Keogh, the Congressional representative from New York who first sponsored the idea in 1962. Keogh plans allow entrepreneurs to set aside money for retirement in the same manner as employees do at large corporations.

Current rules allow you to invest as much as $30,000 a year in a Keogh. You can only contribute a maximum of 13.0435 percent of income up to $160,000 for each plan year for yourself as the employer, and 15 percent of salary up to $160,000 a year for employees if you have set up a profit-sharing Keogh plan. If you have established a money-purchase Keogh, which requires the employer to make fixed contributions each year without regard to the business's profits, you can contribute up to 20 percent of net earnings for the employer and 25 percent of wages for employees, up to the $160,000 salary limit. You must deposit the money by December 31 of each tax year. While these contributions must be made with after-tax dollars (in contrast to the pretax dollars of a salary reduction plan), you can deduct your Keogh contributions on your tax return. That makes such plans even more attractive. You not only get all the benefits of tax deferral on the earnings of the investments in the Keogh, but you also save on taxes in the year you contribute.

As with all other retirement plans, you must pay a 10 percent penalty if you withdraw money before you reach age 59½, and you must start withdrawals at age 70½. You can also take the money in a lump sum, which would force you to pay huge taxes in the year you do so; roll the money into an IRA; or buy an annuity, which would pay you regular income for the rest of your life. If you choose an annuity payout, you would pay taxes on the income over the many years you received it.

A Keogh plan is designed as a tool to build up a retirement fund. If you are the only participant in the plan, you are not allowed to borrow against it.

You can invest the proceeds of your Keogh in individual stocks and bonds, mutual funds, bank certificates of deposit (CDs) or insurance company products, including annuities. Be sure to balance the types of investments in your Keogh with the investments in your nonretirement accounts. For example, if you have invested most of your nonretirement money in conservative bonds and bank CDs, allocate more of your Keogh money to stocks and stock mutual funds, which offer more long-term growth potential.

If you are eligible for a Keogh and haven't already established one, do so. Any bank, brokerage firm or insurance company would be glad to help you with the paperwork to open the account. You don't have to wait for your company to offer you a retirement savings plan.

Individual Retirement Accounts (IRAs)

Even if you have a defined benefit, a defined contribution, a SEP or a Keogh plan, you can still open an IRA. The rules about whether or not your contribution is tax deductible are complex, but even if you can't deduct your contribution, your earnings will grow tax deferred inside the IRA account. Even better is the Roth IRA, in which earnings compound completely tax-free as long as you keep the assets in the account for at least five years.

Whenever you invest money in an IRA, it must come from earned income, whether that means wages or freelance income; you cannot deposit unearned income you receive from bond interest or stock dividends. You can contribute until April 15 following the end of the tax year. (For example, you can make your 1998 contribution up to April 15, 1999.)

No matter what your level of income, you and your spouse can deduct up to $4,000 a year in IRA contributions if you are not what the IRS terms an *active participant* in an employer-sponsored retirement plan. That means that you cannot work full time or part time for a company that offers a defined benefit or defined contribution plan, even if you do not participate in the plan. If you are working, you can invest up to $2,000 and your spouse can contribute up to $2,000 in a spousal IRA, whether or not the spouse works.

However, if your income falls under certain limits, you can deduct your IRA contributions even if you are an active participant in a company-sponsored pension plan. If you earn less than $30,000 as a single person or $50,000 as a married couple filing jointly, you can deduct your full IRA contribution of up to $2,000 per person. These limits are scheduled to climb to $50,000 for a single by the year 2005 and $80,000 for a couple by the year 2007. If, as a single, you report an adjusted gross income (AGI) between $30,000 and $40,000, the amount you can deduct is phased out by $1 for each $5 of income above $30,000 (the ceiling for full deductibility). For example, if you earn $35,000, you can deduct $1,000 toward an IRA contribution. The $40,000 limit is scheduled to climb gradually to $60,000 by the year 2005. The same phase-out rule applies to married couples earning between $50,000 and $60,000 a year. Therefore, a couple earning $55,000 qualifies for a $1,000 deduction based on their income over $50,000. This limit is scheduled to rise gradually from $60,000 to $100,000 in the year 2007. If you earn over the limit ($60,000 for singles in 2005 and $100,000 for couples in 2007), your IRA contributions are not deductible.

If you qualify to deduct some or all of your IRA contributions, take advantage of this option if you can afford to do it. A deductible IRA is one of the few tax breaks remaining, and it can be a powerful way to accumulate money for retirement. Even better than the traditional IRA is the Roth IRA, created by the Taxpayer Relief Act of 1997. Though your contributions are never tax deductible, all earnings grow tax-free as long as you keep assets in the account for five years or longer. For a more detailed description of the rules surrounding Roth IRAs and the pros and cons of using them, consult page 640 in Chapter 14 on retirement.

Health Care Benefits

While retirement savings programs are critical for your long-term financial needs, health coverage has a greater impact on you now, particularly if you need frequent medical attention. Years ago, companies provided medical benefits so lavish that you hardly had to worry about what ailed you because you had an unlimited choice of doctors and no caps on how much could be spent to bring you back to peak condition. How medical coverage has changed!

Today, a plethora of complex options exists, each one costing far more in premiums, deductibles, co-payments, out-of-pocket expenses and paperwork than those of years past. And health care costs will only continue to rise, meaning more complications and expense for recipients of health care benefits.

Having medical coverage is crucial because the cost of health care is so exorbitant today that even a minor procedure can take a major bite out of your budget. Serious surgery and extended recovery can cost tens of thousands of dollars and wipe you out financially if you are uninsured. Even preventive care and maintenance drugs can be expensive, though they are cost-effective because they prevent slight health problems from escalating into major ones. Because medical costs have risen so sharply in recent years, medical insurance premiums paid by employers have also skyrocketed, forcing companies to either cut back on coverage or boost the contributions employees make toward that insurance.

Two basic kinds of health coverage exist: traditional *fee-for-service plans* and *prepaid plans* such as health maintenance organizations (HMOs). With traditional plans, you pay a fee for the services provided by a doctor or another health care professional and then are reimbursed by an insurance company. Under prepaid plans, an employer pays an insurance company a fixed fee for each employee, who can use the HMO as much as he or she needs without paying for each visit.

When an employer offers a health plan, it usually covers all employees, as well as their spouses and children. Until recently, the premiums have been paid by the employer, though increasingly employees are required to contribute at least part of the premium, usually through automatic payroll deduction. Employers with 50 or fewer employees and the self-employed can take advantage of medical savings accounts (MSAs), which allow employees to put aside money out of their paychecks on a pretax basis to be used to pay health expenses or health insurance premiums. Employees are eligible to participate in these plans if they are only covered under a high-deductible health plan. For more information on whether an MSA makes sense for you or your company, you can call the Employers Council on Flexible Compensation at 202-842-3232.

How Fee-for-Service Plans Work

Traditional fee-for-service plans buy insurance either through a commercial health insurance company, such as Blue Cross and Blue Shield, or through a program of self-insurance. If your company contracts with a health insurer, you submit all bills directly to the insurance company by mail, then are reimbursed within a few weeks, according to the provisions of the plan. The insurance company pays you back for each procedure or drug prescription based on either a fixed schedule of fees or what is known as *usual, customary and reasonable charges.* Under the latter, if your doctor charges more than the insurance company considers reasonable, you must pay the amount the company deems excessive.

At the beginning of each year, you must satisfy a deductible before the insurance company begins to reimburse your expenses. For example, one insurance company plan might impose a $100 deductible. This means that you would not receive cash back for your first $100 in medical claims. In many cases today, the deductible is not one fixed amount for all employees; it is calculated as a percentage of each worker's annual salary.

Even after you've met the deductible, most insurers will not reimburse you for your total bill. They impose a *coinsurance provision.* Typically, an insurer will compensate you for 80 percent of a doctor's charges, and you must cover the other 20 percent. That 20 percent is known as your *co-payment.* It is imposed not only to reduce the insurance company's expenditures but also to provide an incentive for you to keep your medical bills in check.

Most traditional health insurance plans set a limit, known as the *out-of-pocket maximum,* on how much your co-payments can total in a year. The insurance company keeps track of how much you spend, and after you hit the out-of-pocket maximum, the insurer will pay 100 percent of your medical bills. This maximum is designed to protect you from financial hardship brought on by a series of large medical bills. While many companies set a dollar-amount limit—like $1,000 a year—for all employees, others calculate the out-of-pocket maximum as a percentage of each worker's salary.

In addition to setting deductibles and out-of-pocket maximums, most plans limit the amount of money that the health insurance company can pay you. Some companies place a ceiling on the cost of a single hospital stay, while others cap the amount you can be paid in your lifetime. Usually, these caps are set quite high, such as $1 million over a lifetime, but you should still know at what point your insurance company will no longer cover your bills.

If your company self-insures, you may still have to submit your bills to a commercial insurance company for reimbursement. In this case, the insurance company acts as a claims processor and assumes no risk, as it does when issuing a health insurance policy. Sometimes employers buy stop-loss coverage from an insurance company. This coverage kicks in after an employee's costs soar beyond a predetermined maximum due to some catastrophic illness. From your point of view, however, coverage by a self-insured employer is similar to coverage by a commercial insurance firm.

Blue Cross and Blue Shield plans cover your hospital expenses. Blue Cross pays for charges from the hospital itself, such as room, board and drugs, based on a preset fee schedule. Blue Shield pays doctors, surgeons and other specialists who serve you in the hospital. If you are hospitalized away from your hometown, your charges will be covered by Blue Cross and Blue Shield, although they may pay only up to the amount they would pay for the same procedures in your hometown. You may have to pay any amount over that limit if you get sick in a high-cost area.

In addition to your basic health coverage, most employers provide major medical insurance, which is designed to protect against catastrophic claims. This insurance sometimes covers procedures that basic plans do not, or it might set higher limits for the same services. Major medical plans usually pay for hospital care, intensive nursing care, prescription drugs you take at home and special medical equipment or devices. Like regular medical coverage, however, major medical plans also impose deductibles and coinsurance requirements.

Most medical plans do not cover dental or vision care; therefore, these are usually provided separately, with their own premiums, deductibles and co-payments. The amount of coverage can vary significantly, allowing only a certain number of teeth cleanings, x-rays or vision tests each year. Depending on the condition of your teeth and eyes, these policies may meet your needs, or you may need to supplement them with additional dental and vision coverage.

Other increasingly popular benefits are various types of *discount prescription drug plans.* To cut down on the cost of drugs purchased by employees, companies enroll in drug plans offered by commercial insurance companies, Blue Cross and Blue Shield, labor unions, HMOs and mail-order drug services. Some employers pay the entire cost of these plans, while others require workers to contribute at least part of the cost through regular payroll deduction.

Under such discount drug plans, you can purchase up to 100 doses of a prescription drug per month or as much as a 34-day supply, whichever is more. Some plans impose a co-payment of 20 percent of the cost of the drugs; however, usually no maximum amount is set on the purchase of a drug. Some drug plans allow you to fill your prescriptions at any pharmacy, then submit the bills for reimbursement. Other plans restrict you to pharmacies that have agreed to accept fixed prices for drugs. In these cases, the drug plans pay the pharmacies directly.

Your company also might offer a mail-order drug plan, in which case your prescriptions are dispensed to your firm, which then mails the drugs to your home. Typically, these plans distribute maintenance drugs such as antibiotics or insulin rather than drugs needed in emergency situations. Because these mail-order operations deal in such large quantities of drugs, they receive special discounts of 20 percent to 40 percent from drugmakers, which they pass on to you.

The final form of drug plan that your company might offer issues a prescription card, which can be used to receive discounts on drugs at pharmacies that have joined a large network.

WHEN YOU LEAVE YOUR COMPANY

Your company is required by law to continue your fee-for-service health insurance coverage if you either quit or lose your job for any reason other than gross misconduct. Under the *Consolidated Omnibus Budget Reconciliation Act of 1985* (COBRA), you—as a laid-off worker—must have access to the same level of coverage for 18 months after you leave a company. If you are covered by COBRA, you have to pay premiums, but you pay them at the lower, advantageous group rate. Protection under COBRA applies even if you are hired by another company with an inferior health plan. When the 18 months expire, the company must offer you the opportunity to convert your group coverage into an individual policy, although this policy will be far more expensive than the group policy. Under the Health Insurance Portability and Accountability Act (HIPAA) of 1997, you also may have rights to continue to be covered by your company's health care policies. For more information on your rights under this law, contact your company's employee benefits office.

Many company medical plans will continue your coverage when you retire. Your benefits usually remain the same after retirement although, in many cases, you must pay more of the premiums and higher co-payments than you did when you worked for the company. If you qualify for Medicare, your employer's health insurance or even your Medigap policy kicks in only after Medicare has paid its share. Therefore, your primary health coverage shifts from your private plan to Medicare although it is certainly helpful to use your private plan as a backup when Medicare limits what it will pay.

PREPAID PLANS: ALTERNATIVE HEALTH INSURANCE

As costs of traditional fee-for-service plans rose, employers and insurance companies groped for an alternative health insurance system that would contain price increases. They arrived at two solutions: Establish a prepaid medical plan in which companies could pay a fixed monthly fee per employee, or organize a system of health care facilities and professionals willing to negotiate predetermined fee schedules. The two most common variants on these plans are *health maintenance organizations* (HMOs) and *preferred provider organizations* (PPOs), respectively.

How HMOs Work

When your company contracts with an HMO, it agrees to pay a fixed monthly fee for each worker. In return, you can visit an HMO facility as often as you like. HMOs emphasize preventive care because it is far less expensive to treat you when your symptoms just emerge than when you develop a full-blown illness. HMOs have another powerful financial incentive to head off expensive medical procedures: They receive the same fee from employers no matter how much or how little they treat employees. An HMO with healthy members profits; one that defers treatment until illnesses become severe loses money. So far, the incentive has worked. HMO members check into the hospital far less frequently than patients in the fee-for-service system.

The typical HMO provides nearly every medical service you might need. This includes both general practice and specialty physicians, full hospital treatment, mental health care, treatment for drug or alcohol addiction, radiology, psychiatric care, lab work and home health care. Some HMOs offer even more services, such as eye care, dentistry, prescription drugs and physical therapy.

HMOs come in several forms. Usually, they provide comprehensive health services at several central facilities. If you have a problem that the facility can't handle, it will either bring in a specialist to treat you or send you to the specialist. Another form of HMO is an *individual practice association* (IPA). Under this plan, doctors work in their own private practice offices but see HMO patients under a contract that predetermines fees.

Before you sign up for an HMO, visit the facility or the doctors who are part of the network to get a feel for the quality of care provided. Talk to workers at your company who have had experience with the HMO, or talk to patients as you tour the facility. Some HMOs are run wonderfully and have excellent reputations; others are known for long waiting lists and rushed, inexperienced doctors. Once you enroll in an HMO, you give up your ability to choose your doctor, which may or may not be important to you. Therefore, you should have a good feeling about the HMO before you agree to let it cover all your health care needs.

How PPOs Work

Unlike companies with HMOs, employers offering PPOs do not prepay a fixed fee for the health coverage of their employees. Neither do PPOs provide centralized health care facilities. Instead, they assemble a network of affiliated doctors, hospitals and other health care operations that offer medical services to a large group of employees at predetermined rates.

Under a PPO, you can visit any doctor you want, and you are reimbursed to some extent for that visit by your health insurance company. However, you receive a more generous reimbursement if you use one of the preferred providers within the network. Some PPOs cover more services for physicians in the network than for those outside the system. In other cases, the percentage of your bill that is reimbursed is higher and the deductibles are lower for PPO doctors than for independent physicians. For example, you might have a $100 deductible if you see a doctor who is part of the PPO and a $300 deductible for an unaffiliated doctor. Or your insurance company might pay 80 percent of your charges for a PPO provider, while it reimburses you only 60 percent for an unaffiliated physician. With this payment system, both your employer and the insurance company try to provide powerful financial incentives to take your business to PPO doctors, who offer lower rates than independent operators.

In some cases, employers require that you use the doctors in the insurance network. This is called an *exclusive provider organization* (EPO). If you use a doctor outside the prescribed list, you will not be reimbursed. This style of PPO is the exception, however.

Employees often favor PPOs over HMOs because PPOs provide more choice of doctors. If you insist on going to a doctor you have known and trusted for years, you can see him or her under a PPO although you will be reimbursed less than if you visit a doctor in the PPO. For many people, however, that freedom of choice is worth the extra money. Other people prefer the broad range of services offered by HMOs because they pay no bills when they walk out the door. Whatever health insurance system you ultimately choose, weigh both the convenience and quality of service provided, as well as the financial impact of your decision.

Flexible Spending Accounts (FSAs)

Despite rising health insurance costs, most companies offer at least one bit of good news: *flexible spending accounts* (FSAs). If your firm offers an FSA, you can pay for increasing insurance premiums, deductibles and co-payments with pretax dollars instead of expensive after-tax dollars. In addition, you can use the FSA to pay for dependent and child care expenses.

A typical FSA works as follows: At the beginning of each year, you tell your company how much you want to set aside (up to $5,000) to fund the FSA for that year. That amount is then deducted off the top of your paycheck and invested in an FSA. This money therefore escapes federal, state and local income taxes, as well as Social Security levies. In some cases, your employer will also contribute to your FSA. Over the next year, you will incur medical expenses that are not fully covered by your health insurance. These include deductibles, co-payments and premiums. In addition, you might incur medical expenses that are never covered by your insurance, such as orthodontia, routine physical exams, elective surgery and vision care. You might also pay child care expenses, either to a babysitter or to a child care center. (FSAs can also be used to care for an elderly person—such as a parent—living in your home.) You simply submit these medical and child care bills to your company or an outside administrator, which reimburses you out of the FSA fund within a few weeks.

Be careful when you determine how much money to invest in an FSA. You receive only one opportunity a year to set the amount unless a major change occurs in your family situation, such as the birth of a child or a marriage. Also, FSAs are a use-it-or-lose-it proposition. If you do not claim the money in the FSA by the end of the year, you forfeit it forever. Therefore, look at how much you paid out of pocket last year as a guide to figuring the coming year's FSA contribution. Be a bit conservative in estimating how much of your medical expenses will not be covered by your regular health insurance in the coming year. It's better to end the year having too many unreimbursed expenses to submit to your FSA rather than too few. The worksheet in Figure 16.9 will help you determine how much to set aside in your health care FSA.

To determine how much an FSA could save you in taxes, multiply your combined federal, state and local tax brackets by your total unreimbursed medical expenses. (You can get a rough idea of your combined tax bracket by dividing the

Figure 16.9   FSA Funding Worksheet

	$ Amount
Annual Deductible for Medical Plan	$ _____
Annual Deductible for Dental Plan	_____
Co-payment for Medical Plan (the portion of expenses not covered)	_____
Co-payment for Dental Plan	_____
Elective Surgery (cosmetic surgery, hair transplants, sterilization, major dental bills)	_____
Hearing Care (testing and hearing aids)	_____
Orthodontia	_____
Psychotherapy (the portion of expenses not covered by your medical plan)	_____
Routine Physical Exams	_____
Vision Care (testing and eyeglasses)	_____
TOTAL UNREIMBURSED MEDICAL EXPENSES	$ _____

amount of taxes withheld from your paycheck by your gross salary.) For instance, if you have $1,000 in uncovered medical expenses and your total tax bracket is 40 percent, you will save $400 in taxes by signing up for an FSA.

Dependent care expenses should be a bit easier to forecast because your child care or elder care worker receives a regular rate of pay. Your employee must be in this country legally and paid on the books because you must submit his or her Social Security number as part of your FSA application. If you employ someone without a Social Security number, your FSA will not reimburse you. FSA money can also be used to reimburse child care expenses at a day care center whether the center is run by your company or another organization. The simple worksheet in Figure 16.10 will help you estimate your annual dependent care expenses.

In the same manner that you figured your tax savings for a health care FSA, multiply your combined federal, state and local income tax brackets by your total dependent care expenses to calculate your tax savings. For example, if you have $3,500 in expenses and a combined tax bracket of 40 percent, you would save $1,400 in taxes with an FSA.

Figure 16.10   Dependent Care Expenses Worksheet

	$ Amount
Day Care Center Costs	$
Babysitter or Eldersitter Costs	
Taxes Paid for Babysitter or Eldersitter (such as Social Security taxes)	
TOTAL UNREIMBURSED DEPENDENT CARE EXPENSES	$

If your company offers an FSA and you have unreimbursed medical and dependent care expenses, sign up for the plan. The example in Figure 16.11, prepared by the benefits consulting firm of Hewitt Associates, illustrates just how much money you could save by funding an FSA. The example assumes that you are married with two children; report $45,000 a year in earnings on a joint tax return; and deposit $1,000 in the health care FSA and $3,500 in the dependent care FSA.

Figure 16.11
Amount Saved by Funding an FSA

	Using the FSA	*Not Using the FSA*
Income	$45,000	$45,000
Minus FSA deposits	− 4,500	− 0
Taxable income	$40,500	$45,000
Minus federal taxes (28% Tax bracket)	− 6,833	− 7,853
Take-home pay	$33,667	$37,147
Minus after-tax expenses	− 0	− 4,500
Spendable pay	$33,667	$32,647
Tax savings ("Using the FSA" minus not "Using the FSA")	$ 1,020	$ 0

Source: Reprinted by permission of Hewitt Associates, Lincolnshire, Illinois.

This example calculates only the federal income taxes you would save. In fact, you would also sidestep state and local taxes. If you pay high state and local taxes, that can add up to significant additional savings.

Clearly, you should take advantage of an FSA if you can. If your company does not yet offer one, talk to your benefits officer or, even better, the chief executive. Such plans are usually adopted when employees clamor for them.

Dependent Care Benefits

In addition to FSAs for reimbursement of child or elder care, many companies offer other valuable dependent care benefits. The following are just a few of the innovative programs that some employers sponsor:

- *Companies sometimes offer child care centers at or near your place of employment.* These centers can be run either by your company or by a day care firm that specializes in operating such centers. Because these centers are quite expensive to run, they are not free to employees' children. However, you might pay rates reduced from those of a commercial day care center. Other advantages of these centers are that you can always pop in to see your children during your lunch break, you are at hand if a problem occurs and it is easy to pick your children up when you go home. Some employers, rather than supporting a full child care center of their own, contribute to a community center, thereby reserving places at that facility for their employees' children.

- *Some employers offer referral services that help you learn about child care options in your area.* Several employers in a community might join together to sponsor such a hot-line to help employees cope with the strains of finding high-quality child care. Some services even offer child care workers who will arrive at your home within hours of your call if, for example, your child gets sick and you cannot find a babysitter.

- *Flextime allows you to work hours that accommodate your child care responsibilities.* From your employer's point of view, what counts is that the necessary work gets done, not that you work certain hours. In some cases, this arrangement might entail permitting you to work part time and still retain full-time benefits. In other cases, one job may be split between two employees who both have children for whom they must care. This arrangement is usually called *job sharing,* and it can be difficult, although not impossible, to establish.

- *According to the Family and Medical Leave Act (FMLA) of 1993, parental leave must be granted to covered employees for a maximum of 12 weeks for a new child whether it is natural, adopted or in foster care.* Many companies already granted maternity and paternity leave for their employees. The FMLA expanded these rights to include almost all employees of firms with 50 or more workers and employees who have worked for 1,250 hours in the 12 months preceding the leave. Usually, you are not paid when you take parental leave, though you must be guaranteed your current job or an equivalent position. In addition, employers are required by the act to maintain health insurance coverage during the leave. Some employers grant this guarantee if you return within one month; others extend the promise for as long as a year.

- *According to the FMLA, leave must also be granted to employees with serious health conditions that prevent them from performing their job and to employees who need time to care for a family member such as a spouse, child or parent.*

- *Adoption assistance is also becoming increasingly available from many companies.* Some firms donate cash of up to $2,000 to help cover the myriad costs of adopting a child. Others grant paid or unpaid leave for several weeks.

Employee Assistance Programs (EAPs)

An increasingly common benefit that many companies provide on top of health and dependent care plans is the *employee assistance program* (EAP). Such confidential plans are designed to help employees cope with the many stresses and strains of modern life. Some of the areas EAPs cover include the following:

- *Drug, alcohol or other substance abuse.*

- *Mental health and emotional issues.* EAPs often offer advice from psychologists, which can be helpful after a death in the family or the breakup of a relationship.

- *Disabilities either you or a family member suffers.* EAP counselors can help you find specialized care providers to help you or your loved one overcome the disability.

- *Marital and family problems.* EAPs often offer sessions with marriage counselors and help with the stresses of finding good child care or dealing with an elderly parent whose health is failing.

- *Financial problems caused by excessive debt or spending sprees.* EAP counselors are usually not financial planners, but they can refer you to appropriate experts.

- *Legal problems.* EAP counselors are not lawyers, but they can help determine whether you need a lawyer and, if so, how to find a good one.

Employers who offer such progressive EAPs realize that a normally productive employee can be dragged down by any of these problems and that it is cost effective to offer help in that time of turmoil. If your employer is one of the enlightened few, take advantage of the services if you need them.

Education Benefits

As the increasingly competitive workplace makes it more and more important for employees to sharpen their skills, many companies offer incentives for workers to return to school. Part of your education may be formal training classes held at your company for employees learning to operate a new piece of equipment, for example. In addition, some companies pay most or all of the tuition at outside schools for classes directly related to your ability to keep or enhance your job. Many companies also reimburse most or all of your tuition if you can show that courses relate to a direction your career might take in the future. Finally, many firms also reimburse you in part for courses unrelated to your job. Typically, you will receive 50 percent of the tuition for unrelated courses and even memberships at health clubs.

Different companies set varying requirements for tuition reimbursement. Some firms insist only that you pass the course; others reimburse you according to your grade (100 percent for an A, 80 percent for a B, etc.). In some cases, employers pay the school directly; in other cases, you must put out your own money, and your firm will reimburse you at the end of the term, when you prove that you completed the course satisfactorily.

If you receive education assistance, it is not considered taxable income unless your tuition bills exceed $5,250 per year. If you spend your own money on books, lab fees, tutors, travel or other extras, you can take a personal deduction on your tax return if your employer does not reimburse you for those costs.

Other forms of education assistance that employers provide are cash awards, scholarships, loans and grants. Your company might pay for you to attend business school, for example, and also grant you paid or unpaid leave to complete the program. Many companies also offer scholarship programs for the children of employees, as well as various contests that offer thousands of dollars toward college tuition.

Legal Services Benefits

Employers increasingly offer access to simple legal services at substantial discounts from what you might pay on your own. Companies sign up with one of the many group plans available from nationwide law firms, and employees are able to consult with lawyers either in person or over the telephone for a small fee or, in some cases, at no charge.

Some of the legal work these plans are designed to handle include the following:

- Drawing up or reviewing wills, leases, sales agreements and other documents, including adoption papers and name change requests.

- Representing you in a civil or criminal trial, usually involving minor infractions of the law such as the loss of a driver's license or a misdemeanor.

- Helping resolve landlord-tenant disputes.

- Enforcing domestic disputes over child support payments or visitation rights. These lawyers can also represent you in divorce or separation proceedings.

- Helping collect benefits due from Social Security, the Department of Veterans Affairs (VA) or another agency.

While employers offering legal services plans want to help you, they do not want huge legal bills. Therefore, they normally cap the amount of a lawyer's time you can consume or the dollar value of services. If you use legal services provided through your employer's plan, you do not pay income taxes on the benefits you receive.

Company-Sponsored Insurance Programs

Most companies offer several forms of insurance protection to their employees. Companies buy coverage at group rates, which are significantly cheaper than you could buy on your own. The three most common forms of insurance are term life, survivor income and disability.

Most employers provide life insurance for their active employees at little or no cost. This coverage is designed to help survivors of deceased employees cope with the potentially devastating loss of income that can occur when someone dies. When you receive a policy for such coverage, make sure to designate a beneficiary. Normally, employees who are married name their spouse as primary beneficiary and their children as secondary beneficiaries. If you do not name a beneficiary, the death benefit goes into your estate to be distributed by the estate's trustee.

TERM LIFE INSURANCE

Companies offer group life insurance, usually at a far better price than you could obtain by purchasing individual life insurance. When companies employ hundreds or even thousands, the chances of death claims are relatively small; therefore, insurance companies give them favorable rates. Each contract is based on the makeup of a company's work force and its experience with death claims.

The only kind of insurance that companies buy is *term insurance,* which pays only a death benefit if an employee dies. Unlike whole or variable life insurance, term insurance provides no cash value buildup or savings component. Term contracts usually run for a year at a time, at which point they are normally renewed. This is why these policies are called *annual renewable term.*

When a company offers group life insurance, usually all full-time employees of the firm are covered by the policy. Some policies cover specific groups of employees who do not necessarily work together, such as those belonging to a particular union. The amount of term insurance provided for each employee varies. It is usually calculated as a percentage of the worker's salary, up to twice his or her annual gross pay. Therefore, a worker making $30,000 a year would be insured for $60,000. Other companies cover all employees for the same dollar amount, such as $50,000, no matter what their salary.

In the vast majority of cases, employers pick up the entire cost of the insurance premiums. When employees must chip in, they pay a flat amount per month, based on a formula. For example, you might pay $.50 per $1,000 of coverage. So, if you are covered for $50,000, you would have to pay $25 a month, or $300 a year.

According to IRS regulations, any group life insurance coverage up to $50,000 is not considered taxable income to you, the employee. Any amount exceeding $50,000, which is called *supplemental coverage,* is considered taxable. Usually, companies require that you contribute some or all of the premiums on coverage of more than $50,000.

Even if you must pay a small amount, supplemental coverage is worthwhile. Because your employer buys at a low group rate, you get a good price. And the convenience of paying the premiums out of your paycheck also makes the policy a good deal. Hopefully, your family members will never collect the death benefit, but if they do, they will be glad that you obtained all the coverage you could.

Once you leave a company, your group life insurance is normally canceled, though some firms allow you to continue coverage at a reduced level if you pay some or all of the premiums. By the time your reach your 60s and 70s, however, the premiums on term insurance can be extremely high because your chance of dying is much greater than it was when you were in your 20s and 30s.

In addition to group life policies, most companies offer accidental death and dismemberment insurance, which covers you while you are at work or are traveling on company business. You or your beneficiary will receive payment if an accident either kills you or causes you to lose a hand, a foot, an eye or so on.

SURVIVOR INCOME INSURANCE

Another form of life insurance protection offered by most companies is the survivor income plan. Such policies pay a regular monthly income to your surviving dependents, who count on the income generated. Benefits are based on a percentage of your salary, with a spouse receiving up to 30 percent of your pay and children receiving an additional 20 percent. If you have young children, the plan may provide income for as long as 20 years, depending on their needs. If your spouse remarries and is financially able to survive without the payments, usually the cash is discontinued. Such plans are designed to supplement the Social Security survivor benefits to which your spouse and children may be entitled. While most companies pay the entire premium for survivor income plans, others require that you contribute at least part of the premium through payroll deduction. As with regular life insurance coverage, all survivor income coverage up to $50,000 is tax free to you, the employee. You must pay taxes on any amount exceeding $50,000, however.

DISABILITY INSURANCE

If you have a serious accident or are otherwise injured while not on the job, your medical bills will probably be covered by your employer's disability income insurance plan. Unlike workers' compensation plans, which pay only if you are injured on the job, disability programs pay a regular income if you are hurt outside your employment hours. *Workers' comp* is a program run by your state labor department to cover medical costs and to replace lost wages. *Disability* coverage is a private insurance program designed to pay for short-term and long-term illnesses.

You can qualify for two kinds of disability payment plans if you are badly injured. Short-term plans sometimes replace your income for up to a year (52 weeks) although half a year (26 weeks) is more common. You qualify for short-term disability if your injury makes it impossible for you to perform your normal job functions. Before you begin collecting disability, however, you must prove that your injury is serious. Once you do so, you must wait at least a week for your first check. For that week or so, you may receive your full salary under your company's sick leave policy. Once the disability checks start, you can count on getting up to about two-thirds (67 percent) of your salary. (Your employer wants you to have an incentive to come back to work, so it won't pay 100 percent of your regular income.)

If you still are not able to work after 26 to 52 weeks of short-term disability, you may transfer to long-term disability coverage. To qualify, you must be incapable of performing not only your prior job but also any other job that you have the experience and training to perform. Long-term disability payments, when combined with Social Security disability payments, can amount to as much as 80 percent of your former salary. Most long-term disability plans will pay the agreed-upon amount for a specific number of years (usually at least ten) or until you reach age 65, when Social Security and your employer's pension plan kick in.

While the costs of short-term disability plans are usually paid completely by employers, long-term disability plan costs are typically shared between employers and employees. An LTD line on your paycheck stub indicates how much you pay toward long-term disability insurance premiums.

Most employees pay little attention to disability insurance coverage—until they have an accident or suffer some other disabling misfortune and need the insurance money to survive. If you are offered a chance to buy long-term disability coverage through your employer, grab it. Such coverage is inexpensive, and if you ever need it, the plan could be an enormous help in getting you through a difficult time. This is one insurance coverage on which you should not skimp.

The whole field of employee benefits can be complex and confusing. As you can see, however, it is extremely worthwhile to delve into that information on employee benefits packages that you are handed when you start work at a new company. By taking full advantage of your employer's retirement, health, dependent care, employee assistance, education, legal and insurance programs, you will be better able to improve your financial well-being and realize your financial goals than if you lock that thick benefits book in a drawer, unread and little understood.

Resources

BOOKS

Employee Benefits, by Burton Beam, Jr., and John McFadden (Dearborn Financial Publishing, 155 N. Wacker Dr., Chicago, IL 60606; 312-836-4400; 800-322-8621; www.dearborn.com). Comprehensive explanation of employee benefits, updated to incorporate the Health Insurance Portability and Accountability Act and the implications of the latest tax laws.

Fundamentals of Employee Benefits Programs (Employee Benefit Research Institute, 2121 K St., N.W., Suite 600, Washington, DC 20037-1893; 202-659-0670; www.ebri.org). A comprehensive overview of all major employee benefits programs, including Social Security, pension plans, salary reduction plans, profit-sharing plans, employee stock ownership plans, SEPs, IRAs, health insurance, dental insurance, drug prescription plans, group life insurance, disability insurance, education assistance, FSAs, Medical Savings Accounts (MSAs) and temporary leave programs.

Looking out for #2: A Married Couple's Guide to Understanding Your Benefit Choices at Retirement from a Defined Benefit Plan (Item #4432) (Internal Revenue Service, Department of the Treasury, Consumer Information Center, Pueblo, CO 81009; 719-948-3334; www.pueblo.gsa.gov). A helpful booklet prepared by the IRS. Explains the basics of defined benefit pension plans.

Looking out for #2: A Married Couple's Guide to Understanding Your Benefit Choices at Retirement from a Defined Contribution Plan (Item #4442) (Internal Revenue Service, Department of the Treasury, Consumer Information Center, Pueblo, CO 81009; 719-948-3334; www.pueblo.gsa.gov). Another helpful booklet prepared by the IRS. Explains the basics of defined contribution plans, including 401(k) plans, employee stock ownership plans, stock bonus plans and thrift savings plans.

TRADE ASSOCIATIONS

American Association of Health Plans (1129 20th St., N.W., Suite 600, Washington, DC 20036; 202-778-3200; www.aahp.org). A group of employers, insurance companies and others in the health care industry concerned with the implementation of quality managed health care employee benefits programs.

American Prepaid Legal Services Institute (541 Fairbanks Ct., Chicago, IL 60611; 312-988-5751; www.abanet.org/legalserv/APIhome.html). Dedicated to studying and promoting the use of prepaid legal services—in some cases, as an employee benefit.

Catalyst (120 Wall St., New York, NY 10005; 212-514-7600). Nonprofit advocacy group working with business and professional organizations to further the advancement of women in business. They do research on such issues as child care, adoption and women's career advancement.

Employee Assistance Professionals Association (2101 Wilson Blvd., Suite 500, Arlington, VA 22201-3062; 703-522-6272; www.eap-association.com). Promotes employee assistance programs as a basic employee benefit.

Employee Benefit Research Institute (2121 K St., N.W., Suite 600, Washington, DC 20037; 202-659-0670; www.ebri.org). EBRI is a private, nonprofit, nonpartisan public policy research organization. Its mission is to contribute to, encourage and enhance the development of sound employee benefit programs and sound public policy through objective research and education. EBRI is a member-based organization of small and large private corporations, nonprofit organizations, employee benefits consulting firms and unions. Offers the following publications: *EBRI Issue Briefs, EBRI Pension Investment Report, EBRI Washington Bulletin* and *EBRI Notes*. Also publishes *The EBRI Data Book on Employee Benefits*.

Employers Council on Flexible Compensation (927 15th St., N.W., Suite 1000, Washington, DC 20005; 202-659-4300; www.ecfc.org). A group of companies that study and promote the use of flexible spending accounts (FSAs), medical savings accounts (MSAs) and other cafeteria-style employee benefit offerings. For more information on setting up a medical savings account for small companies or by self-employed people, call 202-842-3232.

ESOP Association (1726 M St., N.W., Suite 501, Washington, DC 20036; 202-293-2971; www.theesop-emplowner.org). An association of companies offering ESOPs that promotes wider use of the plans. Offers several publications, including the brochures "It's Your ESOP, It's For All of Us" and "ESOP: The Concept" as well as the books *How the ESOP Really Works, Valuing ESOP Shares* and *ESOP Administration Handbook*.

International Foundation of Employee Benefit Plans, Inc. (P.O. Box 69, 18700 W. Bluemound Rd., Brookfield, WI 53008-0069; 414-786-6700; 888-334-3327; www.ifebp.org). An educational association for those in the employee benefits field. Programs and services include seminars and conferences, books and periodicals, an information center, research surveys, and the Certified Employee Benefit Specialist (CEBS) program. Offers publications for a nominal fee, including "Financial Planning for a Secure Retirement," "Your Pension and Your Spouse: The Joint and Survivor Dilemma," "Selecting Investments for Your Retirement Account" and "The Mid-Career Planner."

National Center for Employee Ownership (1201 Martin Luther King Jr. Way, Oakland, CA 94612; 510-272-9461; www.nceo.org). Dedicated to the growth of employee ownership benefit plans, such as ESOPs. Offers several publications, including *Selling to an ESOP*, a book for owners of privately held businesses selling their businesses to an ESOP; "The Rights of ESOP Participants," an excerpt from the *Journal of Employee Ownership Law and Finance;* and "The Charitable ESOP," a booklet explaining how ESOPs and charitable gift combinations work.

National Institute for Working and Learning (1875 Connecticut Ave., N.W., Suite 900, Washington, DC 20009-1202; 202-884-8186; www.aed.org). An Institute of the Academy for Educational Development seeks to bring work, education, government and community sectors together around the shared goal of working collaboratively to improve education-work relationships in the interest of individuals and society. Three areas of concentration define the Institute's activities: successful youth transition, worklife education and adult literacy, and productive aging. The Institute accomplishes its mission in each of these areas through research, program documentation and evaluation, policy analysis, technical assistance and training, and information networking.

Pension Rights Center (918 16th St., N.W., Suite 704, Washington, DC 20006; 202-296-3778). Educates the public about pension issues. For a nominal fee, will send publications titled *Can You Count on Getting a Pension?; The Pension Plan Almost Nobody Knows About: SEPS;* and *Your Pension Rights at Divorce.* Offers a lawyer referral service for pension-related problems.

Profit Sharing/401(k) Council of America (10 S. Riverside, Suite 1610, Chicago, IL 60606; 312-441-8550; www.psca.org). Devoted to explaining and promoting the use of profit-sharing and 401(k) plans. Council members are companies offering profit-sharing and 401(k) plans to employees. The Council produces a monthly magazine called *Profit Sharing* and a newsletter called *Profit Sharing.*

Profit Sharing/401(k) Research Foundation (10 S. Riverside, Suite 1610, Chicago, IL 60606; 312-441-8550; www.psca.org). Specializes in studying employee benefits such as profit-sharing and 401(k) plans.

Workers' Compensation Research Institute (101 Main St., Cambridge, MA 02142; 617-494-1240). Researches workers' compensation issues and how they affect employers and employees.

Federal Government Regulators

Internal Revenue Service, Employee Plans (1111 Constitution Ave., N.W., Washington, DC 20224; 202-622-8300; www.irs.ustreas.gov). Sets the complex rules on funding pension plans, vesting and compliance with tax forms.

Labor Department, Pension and Welfare Benefits Administration (200 Constitution Ave., N.W., Washington, DC 20210-0999; 202-219-8840; www.dol.gov). Sets rules for and oversees all employee benefit programs. Can explain your rights under federal law.

Pension Benefit Guaranty Corporation (1200 K St. N.W., Washington, DC 20005-4026; 202-326-4000; www.pbgc.gov). Insures corporate defined benefit pension plans to make certain that covered pensioners receive the money due them. Offers two free publications: *Your Guaranteed Pension* and *Your Pension: Things You Should Know about Your Pension Plan.*

17

Finding Financial
Advisers Who
Are Right for You

As you can see by the amount of material this book covers, the world of personal finance is quite complex. Unless you work in the financial services field, do not expect to be an expert in all—or, for that matter, any—of the many financial arenas. Learning the fundamentals in each is challenging enough. Keeping up with the latest developments is truly a full-time job and therefore unrealistic for most people. You have your own profession, so don't feel guilty if you don't know the most recent tax law changes, the hottest stocks, the most popular insurance policies or the latest financial planning strategies.

Some aspects of your financial life, like buying or selling real estate, choosing a life insurance policy or writing a will, you will confront infrequently during your lifetime. Other areas, such as filing taxes or creating a comprehensive financial plan, you need to do only once a year. And some aspects of your financial picture, such as investing or banking, demand your continuous attention. In general, the less frequently you deal with an area of finance, the less you should expect yourself to know and the more you may have to rely on professionals.

That's why it makes sense to hire an expert whose job it is to know the details of his or her financial field. If you find a qualified financial adviser, any fees or commissions can pay for themselves many times over if the adviser's recommendations are wise. Good counsel not only can make you money—for example, a broker might suggest a stock or mutual fund that appreciates sharply—it can also prevent you from losing money. A will written by a good lawyer or an insurance plan assembled by a top-rate insurance agent can protect you from estate taxes and financial turmoil if you die much sooner than you expect. A knowledgeable accountant can save you thousands of dollars in taxes by helping you conduct your financial affairs in a way that minimizes the government's tax bite.

On the other hand, an unqualified adviser who sees you as a cash cow to be milked for fees and commissions can do far more damage to your finances than you might do yourself. If the financial adviser sounds like he or she is interested in your welfare but, in fact, is more concerned about lining his or her own pockets, you could be asking for trouble by dealing with the adviser.

One of the biggest questions I hear constantly from people who call radio and television shows on which I appear and at seminars I lead is: "Who can I trust to give me good financial advice?" It is an excellent question because, clearly, plenty of sharks will take your money if you are not wary. However, the fear of being cheated so paralyzes people that they trust no one—and therefore never take advantage of the many trustworthy financial experts.

This chapter will help you separate the knowledgeable advisers from the charlatans by providing specific questions to ask most varieties of advisers (for example, financial planners, attorneys and real estate brokers). It's impossible to guarantee that an adviser you've selected, even when you use the guidelines provided here, will not cheat you or give bad advice. But if you follow the steps outlined in this chapter, the chances of turning your finances over to an incompetent adviser will be greatly reduced.

First, a few general tips will help you separate the good from the bad advisers in any financial arena.

- *Think carefully about what kinds of experts you should hire.* Your financial situation must be complicated enough or you must have enough money at stake to make an adviser's fees worthwhile. If you think that you need help, determine what you already know and what you need to know. Hire someone to aid you only in the areas about which you're uncertain.

- *Take advice only from those qualified to give it.* This might sound obvious, but, very often, people act on stock tips from their lawyer, obtain recommendations about insurance policies from their accountant or solicit tax advice from their stockbroker. Listen to someone because he or she is a true expert in a particular field, not because the person happens to have an opinion, well-founded or not.

- *Don't hire the first candidate you find.* Just as you usually tour many homes before you purchase one, you should interview several advisers before settling on the best one for you. After all, you will tell this person all of the most intimate details of your financial life; therefore, you want to feel comfortable with him or her. Collect five to ten names before you narrow the list to your final choice.

- *Arrange meetings with at least three advisers before you settle on one.* Though this takes time, it allows you to gauge the chemistry between you, your spouse and an adviser. If the adviser is good, he or she should spend much time asking you about your financial needs and goals and how comfortable you are with different levels of risk. He or she should also listen carefully to what you say and not belittle you for asking unsophisticated questions or being unwilling to take risk. Avoid advisers who seem interested mostly in your money and assets; their thoughts have turned to how much money they can make off you.

- *Ask for references from friends, relatives and business colleagues.* While such references do not guarantee you an honest adviser, it is unlikely that people will recommend someone who cheated them out of their life savings.

- *Check out any adviser you are considering seriously with the local professional group with which he or she should be affiliated, or call your state's attorney general's office.* For example, a certified public accountant (CPA) should be a member of the local American Institute of Certified Public Accountants (AICPA), and it is best if a financial planner has a Certified Financial Planner (CFP) designation from the Certified Financial Planner Board of Standards. The names and addresses of all such groups, plus a list of the attorney general's offices in all 50 states, appear in the "Resources" section at the end of this chapter. If you learn that several complaints or lawsuits have been filed against an adviser, look for another.

- *Choose someone you can meet face to face.* Even though most of your business may be conducted over the phone or through the mail, it is reassuring if you can meet your adviser in person at least occasionally. The biggest problems arise when people work with faceless advisers hundreds or thousands of miles away. Often, these people, as smooth as they may sound on the phone, operate a makeshift business designed to pressure people into buying stocks, real estate, gold or another asset at inflated prices. By the time people figure out they have been swindled, the crooks have closed up shop and moved on to find other victims under another company name.

- *Demand references from the adviser you have tentatively chosen.* He or she should not hesitate to provide you with the names and phone numbers of three current clients. Of course, expect these referrals to be pleased with the adviser. Nevertheless, you can get a sense of the service he or she offers if you ask how well the adviser handles their accounts and whether the adviser has been responsive when called on in a pinch. Also, ask the clients whether the adviser ever did or said anything that displeased them. Such referrals should weigh more in your decision than casual references from people who vaguely recall that the adviser has a good reputation.

- *Ask the adviser what professional degrees or credentials he or she has earned.* Some fields, such as accounting and law, demand intense training exams and continuing education to qualify, respectively, as a CPA or Juris

Doctorate (J.D.). Other fields, such as financial planning, award licenses such as the CFP only after educational criteria are fulfilled and a certification exam is passed. Licensees must also commit to a code of ethics and a continuing education requirement. By narrowing your search to advisers who have earned professional designations, you certainly avoid outright frauds, though you cannot be assured that your adviser is totally competent. Some credentials may sound impressive but have little meaning. For example, all it takes to become a Registered Investment Adviser (RIA) with the Securities and Exchange Commission (SEC) is to file a certain form and pay a fee. The SEC imposes no education or competency requirements because it is chronically short-staffed and without the personnel to oversee the RIA's competence.

- *Do not hire friends or relatives as your financial advisers.* It can be dangerous to entangle your interpersonal relationships with your business dealings, particularly your personal finances. Even though Cousin Ed may be a perfectly competent attorney or stockbroker, family strains can be amplified if something goes wrong. You have plenty of qualified nonrelatives from whom to choose.

- *Understand clearly how the adviser gets paid.* Some advisers work only for fees—flat fees, hourly fees or fees based on a percentage of your assets. Other advisers work only for commissions, which they earn when you take their advice and buy the products they sell. Certain professionals mix the two by charging a lower fee than a fee-only adviser levies and collecting a commission as well. The method of compensation is important because it can sway an adviser to recommend a course of action that earns him or her larger fees by collecting commissions on products handled or produced by their company but that may not be in your best interest. By knowing the adviser's incentives, you can guard against self-serving advice.

- *Even after you've hired an adviser, stay involved in your financial affairs.* As much as you might like to hand over all responsibility for your financial planning, insurance, taxes and investments to the experts, you ask for trouble if you disengage yourself completely. Time after time, state regulators tell the tale of people who turned over all their papers to a seemingly reputable financial adviser only to be cleaned out before they ever knew what happened. Remember the very first line in this book: *No one will ever care about your personal financial situation as much as you do.*

While all of these suggestions will help you choose an honest and competent financial professional, the following qualities should tip you off to trouble:

- Your adviser brags about how well he or she does and ostentatiously displays fancy clothing, jewelry and cars.

- Your adviser rushes you into decisions without making sure that you understand the details. Sometimes, he or she does not explain an investment or a tax strategy so you can make sense of it—maybe because the adviser doesn't understand it well. In other cases, the adviser purposefully tries to confuse you about how an investment works to hide the fact that he or she will earn huge commissions if you take the advice.

- Your adviser promises high returns at no or low risk. In this case, the question is: If it's so easy to make big money with no risk, why isn't he or she doing it instead of telling you about it? Usually, promises of high returns mean guarantees of lavish fees for the adviser and low yields for you. As any respected adviser will admit, the only way to achieve high returns over time is to take above-average risks.

- Your adviser pressures you to act quickly, telling you that he or she offers a limited-time opportunity that will never come your way again. Putting time pressure on clients to act is the oldest method around to get their money. If an investment is that good today, it will still be around tomorrow—and weeks and months from now. Enter into an investment because it makes sense, not because you are rushing to beat a deadline, real or artificial.

The best way to work with a financial adviser once you've chosen one is to develop written guidelines and expectations. If you each have a copy of your proposal, which spells out what you expect to accomplish and how you expect to pay, it will be difficult for either you or the adviser to later claim a misunderstanding.

With these general principles in mind, let's look at the specific ways you can find a financial professional in eight areas of specialty: accounting and tax preparation; banking; financial planning; insurance; law; money management; real estate; and stocks.

Tax Preparers

The person who helps prepare your income tax return can save you a great deal of money if you establish a good yearlong working relationship. However, the best way to prepare for filing your tax return is to understand the tax implications of all major financial moves you make.

For example, if you currently rent a place to live, you might ask your tax preparer whether the interest deductions generated by taking out a mortgage on a home would cut your taxes enough to make it worthwhile to assume monthly mortgage payments greater than your rent. Or you might inquire whether you have your company withholding too much or too little from your paycheck. These kinds of decisions will have a major impact on whether you approach the tax-filing season confident about how much you will owe or dreading news from your preparer that you must come up with thousands of dollars by April 15 to keep the federal government happy.

Though Congress often talks about simplifying the tax code, it seems to get only more complicated. Try to keep up with the basics of tax planning, but find a preparer who immerses himself or herself in the details of the tax code and who can determine how changes in the law affect you. For example, when a Supreme Court decision or an IRS ruling narrows the definition of a deductible home office, the ideal preparer would notify you of the change if he or she knows that you have claimed a home office deduction for several years. The preparer should advise you whether the new ruling limits or ends your deduction and inform you of any business practice you can change to qualify for a deduction under the new rules. When Congress changes the rules in response to a Supreme Court decision, as they did in the case of home offices in the Taxpayer Relief Act of 1997, your tax specialist should keep you informed of this change.

Many levels of tax preparation advice exist, from the free and simple variety to the most complex and expensive kind. The level of tax advice that is appropriate for you depends on the money you earn, the number of deductions and credits you claim and whether you take the standard deduction or itemize. You will want to line up your tax preparer months ahead of the tax season; if you wait until February through April, you probably will not be able to hire the person or firm you want. Following is a rundown of available tax advisers, starting with the simplest and ending with the most specialized.

INTERNAL REVENUE SERVICE

While the IRS will not actually fill out your return, it will help you do so free of charge. All IRS offices conduct tax preparation clinics, distribute free publications and answer tax questions over the phone. (A list of IRS phone numbers and publications appears in Chapter 13's "Resources" section.) Some of the people giving guidance are participating in the *Volunteer Income Tax Assistance* (VITA) program, which trains people to answer tax questions, particularly for low-income or disabled taxpayers. Don't count on getting personal attention from the IRS, though, because their offices and phone lines are swamped during tax season.

The IRS sponsors several programs designed to help physically or mentally handicapped people, as well as non-English-speaking citizens, prepare their tax returns. If you are age 60 or older, you can also participate in the cooperative arrangement between the IRS and the *American Association of Retired Persons* (AARP), which holds tax preparation clinics across the country during tax season. The tax counselors who work in this program also make housecalls and visit nursing homes to help people file their returns. Volunteers are specially trained in the tax laws that affect the elderly.

Unfortunately, the IRS does not hold its agents responsible for inaccurate information, given either in person or over the phone. Several tests conducted by

Money magazine and others have shown varying rates of IRS error over the years, but IRS advisers always make some mistakes. Therefore, you might take the return you have completed with IRS help to a professional preparer to see whether he or she can spot any glaring mistake that might have been based on IRS advice.

LOCAL TAX PREPARERS

Around tax time, individuals with various levels of training advertise themselves as tax preparation specialists. Be especially wary if such people guarantee a tax refund to anyone who retains them. They usually deliver on this promise by taking aggressive tax preparation risks that may trigger an audit. No law bans these people from helping you fill out your tax return, though they are not certified by the state or IRS. The quality of tax advice you receive varies widely according to the knowledge of the preparer, but you have little assurance that he or she does a good job. Interview such a tax preparer carefully, and ask to see written testimonials or other references. The preparer may turn out to be totally competent and professional. Then again, he or she may not, and it may be hard to find the preparer after April 15 when your audit notice arrives in the mail.

NATIONAL TAX PREPARATION CHAINS

Large companies with offices across the country, like H&R Block and Jackson Hewitt, offer several advantages. They are convenient to use because they offer thousands of locations from which to choose, and they help you on a first-come, first-served basis. Because they process millions of tax returns, they can quote you a bargain price if your taxes are relatively simple. The chains also make it easy to file electronically, which can speed a refund to you. In fact, if you use a chain to send your return by computer, it will usually grant you an instant refund. This refund is actually a loan that is paid back when your refund arrives from the IRS in a few weeks. Though instant refunds supply immediate money, you pay a high price because the interest rate charged on such short-term loans can be astronomically high—more than 20 percent or 30 percent at an annual rate.

The people who work in national tax chains must pass a 75-hour tax course given by the companies that covers most common tax situations they will encounter. During tax season, the national chains are typically overwhelmed with demand and may hire inexperienced people preparing returns for the first time. These workers see the job as a way to earn extra money during tax season, not as a career. Because each preparer is paid by the number of returns he or she files plus a commission, the incentive is to complete as many as possible and not fuss over details. Don't expect to establish a long-term relationship with the person filling out your tax forms.

If your situation is more complex, you might consider using the national chains' higher level services, usually called *executive tax services*. You must make an appointment to see an executive service worker, and fees can be double or triple what you would pay at a walk-in tax preparation center. If you like the person assigned to you, you can develop a relationship and come back to him or her year after year.

Most national chains will have a preparer accompany you to an IRS audit for no extra charge. Technically, the preparer is not your legal representative and need not answer auditor's questions or plead your case. In fact, many of them know the auditors and do speak up in your defense in their role as witness.

ACCREDITED TAX PREPARERS^{SM} (ATP) OR ACCREDITED TAX ADVISORS^{SM} (ATA)

These professionals are qualified to prepare tax returns, based on their successful completion of the College for Financial Planning's Accredited Tax Preparer Program. Not only can tax advisers prepare returns; they can provide even more sophisticated advice on many areas of the tax code. The more complex your case, the higher your fees will be. Both preparers and advisers who have earned these designations have passed an exam administered by the Accreditation Council for Accountancy and Taxation (ACAT, 1010 N. Fairfax St., Alexandria, VA 22314; 703-549-6400; 800-966-6679; www.acatcredential.org). Call for a free directory of names and accredited preparers and advisers near you.

ENROLLED AGENTS

Little known and underutilized, enrolled agents are tax experts who worked for the IRS at least five years as auditors or who have passed a strenuous two-day test of federal tax law. To remain enrolled agents, they must complete annually 24 hours of college-level continuing education courses in tax regulations and accounting methods.

Enrolled agents are experts in all areas of tax preparation, yet they are not all certified as CPAs. This means that they are significantly less expensive on both an hourly and a per-return basis. Some enrolled agents specialize in a few areas of the tax law, so determine an agent's specialty before you hire him or her. If you like the enrolled agent who fills out your return, you can go back to him or her year after year because these agents usually build a clientele.

Enrolled agents work either independently or as part of a CPA or tax law firm. To locate a qualified enrolled agent near you, contact the National Association of Enrolled Agents (200 Orchard Ridge Dr., Suite 302, Gaithersburg, MD 20878; 301-212-9608; 800-424-4339; www.naea.org). The NAEA will send you a list of four agents in your area.

CERTIFIED PUBLIC ACCOUNTANTS (CPAs)

To be licensed and accredited, CPAs must have earned at least a bachelor's degree and have passed a stringent uniform national examination that is administered on a state level. They must also meet several requirements for continuing education to show that they keep current on the latest changes in tax laws. CPAs specialize in accounting issues, which may or may not include tax preparation. Therefore, before you hire a CPA, make sure that he or she is experienced in handling tax returns. Also, gauge the professional chemistry between you and the CPA. You will need to develop a good working relationship as you discuss tax issues over the years.

You might choose a CPA rather than another tax preparer under various circumstances. You will probably need a CPA if your tax situation is complex. For example, you may run a small business or be self-employed. Or you may earn a high salary and claim many deductions. If a major change in your family situation has occurred in the last year, such as marriage, divorce, death, career change or retirement, a CPA's advice may be worthwhile. Most good CPAs not only prepare your return; they also help you plan your taxes throughout the year. For instance, they might run through a tax projection exercise sometime in the fall to see whether you can take steps before the year ends to lighten your tax burden.

CPAs can be in business for themselves, or they can work for CPA firms that specialize in accounting and consulting work for corporations. Usually, it is best to avoid dealing with a CPA from such a firm because they do not specialize in individual returns. They fill out tax forms mostly as a favor to the top executives of the companies they audit and for which they do accounting work. If you're not one of those top executives, your return probably will be handled by a junior CPA—who gets his or her on-the-job training by filling out your return.

A qualified CPA should be a member of the AICPA, as well as the state society. AICPA members are governed by a strict code of ethics, and their firms must undergo a quality review once every three years. The CPA also should be licensed to practice in your state. Before you make your final decision, check with the state board of accountancy to see whether complaints have been filed against him or her or, even worse, disciplinary or licensing action has been taken.

Of course, this higher level of expertise and tax planning does not come free. CPAs charge more than any other tax preparer, either on an hourly basis or as a flat fee per return. If a CPA charges by the hour, ask the CPA to estimate how many hours he or she might need to complete your return. If the CPA quotes a flat fee, find out what other services he or she includes in the fee, such as offering tax planning advice or attending an audit, if necessary. (CPAs will always represent you at an audit, though they normally charge for the time it takes to prepare for and attend the audit session.) If your tax situation is complex enough, a good CPA who knows the tax rules inside out can easily pay for himself or herself by suggesting strategies that result in significant tax savings.

Any reputable CPA will have you sign a *letter of engagement* that states what the CPA will do for you and what he or she will charge. One way to minimize CPA fees is to provide accurate records and fill out as completely as possible the tax organizer that he or she will give you. The worst thing you can do is dump a box of receipts and unopened bank and brokerage statements on a CPA's desk and say, "You figure it all out." You will be charged premium rates for the many hours the CPA or his or her staff devotes to organizing your records.

Before you hire a CPA, ask how many tax returns he or she prepares each year. Usually, a good CPA cannot fill out more than 300 to 350 returns without skimping on quality or farming out a great deal of the work to assistants. Also, ask what percentage of the CPA's clients had to file an extension last year. If more than 15 percent to 20 percent filed late, the CPA probably is taking on more clients than he or she can handle.

You can find a CPA through the national AICPA or your state society or through references from lawyers, bankers, investment advisers or other prominent financial professionals in your town.

TAX ATTORNEYS

Lawyers who specialize in taxation usually do not prepare tax returns. Instead, they offer advice to your CPA or enrolled agent on tricky or controversial areas of tax law. Tax lawyers generally specialize in one area of tax law, such as estate planning, divorce or small business taxation. A tax attorney can be worthwhile if you become embroiled in a serious dispute with the IRS that may have to be resolved in Tax Court. Clearly, this level of sophisticated advice can be extremely expensive; tax lawyers charge as much as several hundred dollars per hour. If they win your case, however, their lofty fees, which may be deductible, can be a smart investment.

Paying hundreds or even thousands of dollars to have your tax return prepared does not guarantee that you will pay the lowest amount of tax possible. For several years, *Money* magazine has been running a tax test in which about 50 preparers fill out a hypothetical family's return. Each year, the tax due varies by several thousand dollars, as do the fees charged. Unfortunately, no correlation normally exists between the tax and the fee. Some expensive CPAs conclude that the family owes thousands of dollars in taxes, while other less costly preparers say that the family must pay only hundreds—or even that the family is due a refund. The same lack of consistency holds true for enrolled agents and representatives of national tax preparation chains.

No matter whether your tax preparer gives simple or in-depth advice, whether you pay nothing or thousands of dollars, *you* are ultimately responsible for your tax return. Be honest with your preparer because he or she is not liable if the IRS determines that you hid income or fabricated deductions. Even if you deal truthfully with your tax preparer and he or she tries to deceive the government, the IRS will impose penalties that can amount to hundreds or even thousands of dollars on both you and your preparer. The IRS reasons that though you may not understand everything your preparer does in filling out your return, you should, at least, have some idea that your preparer has stretched the facts before the IRS calls it to your attention.

Bankers

In the days before brokerage firms, mutual funds, insurance companies and other financial service companies invaded their turf, banks were seen as the main source of good financial advice in most towns. Your friendly banker would not only help you get a loan; he or she would guide you to the highest yielding certificates of deposit (CDs) and money-market accounts and even offer some basic financial planning.

The intense competition for your investment dollars and financial planning business long ago destroyed the bank's local monopoly. Today, most consumers see banks as transaction-oriented institutions. You use the bank to get cash, to make deposits to savings accounts and CDs, to obtain checking accounts for paying bills and to assume a variety of loans, from overdraft protection to mortgages.

However, banks are catching up with their competition quickly. Banks have seen the future and realize that if they can't fight the competition successfully, they may as well join it. Most larger institutions now offer a full family of name-brand mutual funds, as well as a discount brokerage operation to buy and sell individual stocks. Some banks sell annuities from major life insurance companies. Many banks offer rudimentary financial planning services as well.

Bank employees who sell these more complex products are a different breed from traditional tellers and platform officers. To offer a mutual fund or an annuity, the employee must pass certain tests and be licensed to sell securities. Some banks pay their investment consultants by the commissions they generate, as do regular full-service brokers. Other banks pay these specialists a flat salary, hoping to convince customers that the salespeople are not under pressure to sell. In many cases, however, this new breed of banker has been recruited from the brokerage business and brings the same aggressive salesmanship for which brokers are known.

If a bank offers a full line of banking, investment, insurance and financial planning products and services, you might give it a try. It is certainly convenient to funnel most or all of your financial transactions through one institution, which can give you a complete monthly statement of where you stand. Many banks today also offer an automated telephone system or a home banking connection that can tell you how much your funds are worth, what checks have cleared, when your CD matures, how much interest you must pay on your loan and so forth.

Whether you can find a properly qualified financial adviser at a bank is questionable. Many bankers have not had the training to understand or explain complex investment products that can fluctuate in value sharply. Bankers often think more about the safety of their depositors' money than about earning higher returns by taking more risk. Still, you may find a young banker who has received enough training, either inside or outside the bank, to help you plan your finances and choose investments. When you interview such a person, find out their background, and learn whether they plan to work at the bank for a while. You don't want to develop a relationship with someone who sees his or her bank job as a stepping stone to a more lucrative career as a stock broker, for instance.

THE TRUST DEPARTMENT ALTERNATIVE

Banks offer a much higher level of service in their trust department—which you will never encounter if you merely walk into a branch. The trust department typically caters to wealthier customers with assets of at least $100,000 but usually $300,000 or more. Trust officers and their assistants are usually far more experienced and qualified to deal with your financial needs than are bankers. They offer in-depth financial and estate planning, tax preparation, insurance advice and investment expertise.

Most banks employ a chief investment officer to invest bank-sponsored pools of money collected from trust customers. In general, these funds tend to be invested extremely conservatively because wealthy people are more concerned about capital preservation and income generation than about capital growth. Usually, trust departments offer several different pools, similar to mutual funds, which offer investment objectives such as growth, growth and income, balanced (part stocks and part bonds), taxable income and tax-free income. Like mutual funds, bank-managed trust funds offer a broad range of performance. Before you commit to a particular bank, ask how their funds' returns compare to other bank pools with the same investment objective over the last year, three years and five years.

Trust departments tend to base fees on the total dollar value of your account. For example, they might charge between 1 percent and 2 percent of the value of your assets each year. For that fee, you receive high-quality advice on many financial matters, as well as a comprehensive bank account that tracks your securities, checking accounts, savings accounts and loans. As a trust customer, you are considered a valued bank client; therefore, you tend to pay lower interest rates on loans and earn higher yields on CDs and money-market accounts than the average customer. Also, many trust departments will not nick you with per-check fees on your checking accounts, and they might throw in other perks like no-fee traveler's checks and free financial seminars.

A trust department, as its name implies, also can act as trustee to help settle an estate or manage a portfolio for a minor. When drafting a will, you might appoint a bank trust department as the trustee of your children's bank and securities account. When you die, your assets would go into a trust for your children that the conservative trust department would manage. This set-up is probably much better than giving all the money to your children with no strings attached at age 18, when they might be tempted to spend the cash on a sports car or something else you might consider unwise.

As with any other financial adviser, arrange a face-to-face interview to get a sense of the experience and personality of the trust officer with whom you will work if you commit to a bank. You want someone with the proper background for your situation and someone who shares your philosophy of risk. If you find a well-qualified banker, he or she can be a tremendous asset in maximizing your financial opportunities.

Financial Planners

In the best of all worlds, the financial planner you hire would be a jack-of-all-financial-trades. He or she would know everything about budgeting, investments, taxes, insurance, credit, real estate, employee benefits, estate planning, retirement, college financing, career advancement and every other aspect of your financial life. He or she would help you assess where you stand now, what you want to accomplish and how you can attain your goals. He or she would be personable and a good listener. He or she would maintain objectivity so as not to recommend an investment just because he or she gets a commission on it.

Do such paragons of virtue exist? Indeed they do, but to find one, you must weed out the incompetent and self-serving neophytes from the experienced professionals who can help you obtain your financial goals.

Before you begin interviewing candidates, though, assess your situation to determine whether you need a financial planner. If you need only one financial service, like tax return preparation or auto insurance, it is probably not cost effective to pay the fees that a planner charges. On the other hand, if you need an overall strategy that ties together the many aspects of your complex financial picture—past, present and future—a planner's services may be invaluable. For example, if you have specific long-term goals, such as saving enough to buy your first home, starting a business, funding your children's college education or building a retirement nest egg, a financial planner can start you on the right path. Even if you don't have a major financial goal, possessing a well-designed financial plan can guide you to live within your income, maintain a good credit record, spend more wisely and generally feel confident about your financial future.

FINANCIAL PLANNER DESIGNATIONS

Once you've determined that you need a financial planner, look into the different professionals who label themselves as such. Anyone can call himself or herself a planner; no federal, state or local laws require certain qualifications, such as those imposed upon other professionals, including accountants and lawyers. However, several associations and organizations grant credentials that signify a planner's level of education. Some of the most commonly recognized designations follow.

Certified Financial Planner (CFP). This designation is earned by people who have been licensed by the Certified Financial Planner Board of Standards (CFP Board). All licencees have completed financial planning courses through a CFP-Board-registered college or university. These people must complete a ten-hour two-day comprehensive exam to prove their expertise in financial planning, insurance, investing, taxes, retirement planning, employee benefits, estate planning and risk management. The test is difficult and requires the test taker to apply his or her financial planning knowledge to three case studies and multiple choice questions. In addition to having passed the tests, a CFP licensee must possess a certain amount of work experience in the financial services industry, have a defined amount of college education, abide by a strict code of ethics and fulfill continuing education requirements.

Chartered Financial Analyst (CFA). This designation is earned by those who pass a series of three exams administered by the Association for Investment Management and Research (AIMR) of Charlottesville, Virginia. CFA charterholders must demonstrate their expertise in investment valuation and management, asset valuation, portfolio management and industry ethics. CFAs must have a bachelor's degree, adhere to the AIMR Code of Ethics, have at least three years of work experience and a high level of professional conduct. Many CFAs also have branched out into full-service financial planning. The best time to seek a CFA is when you have a great amount of money to invest and you need the guidance of an investment professional.

Chartered Financial Consultant (ChFC). The ChFC designation is conferred by the American College in Bryn Mawr, Pennsylvania. The ChFC curriculum covers a broad range of financial planning issues. Many ChFC's have particular expertise in life insurance matters. To earn the designation, the financial planner must pass ten college-level courses on all major topics of personal finance and business planning, possess industry experience and adhere to strict ethical standards. To maintain the designation, they must obtain continuing education credits.

Personal Financial Specialist (PFS). The PFS is awarded only to people who are already CPAs. To retain their license, they are required to renew their license annually and complete at least 30 hours of continuing education credits every two years. Within the AICPA, those with a PFS concentrate on financial planning. They must be members in good standing of the AICPA, possess at least three years of personal financial planning experience and demonstrate special expertise by passing a comprehensive financial planning exam. To keep their PFS status, they must be reaccredited every three years, a process that includes continuing education and an extensive peer review.

INTERVIEWING A FINANCIAL PLANNER

If you limit your search to financial planners who have earned one or more of these six designations, you will have plenty of qualified planners from whom to choose. As with any financial professional you consider hiring, arrange a face-to-face interview, where you can get a sense of the planner's personality and areas of expertise. The Financial Adviser Disclosure Form in Figure 17.1 will help you gather and evaluate information about the planners you interview.

Following are a few sample questions you should ask prospective financial planners:

- *What services do you provide?* Most planners will help you assemble a comprehensive plan, while others specialize in particular areas of finance. The services you should expect include cash management and budgeting; education funding; estate planning; investment review and planning; life, health and property/casualty insurance review; retirement planning; goal and objective setting; and tax planning. Ask about each service specifically.

- *Will you show me a sample financial plan you have done?* Without revealing confidential information or client names, the planner should be glad to show you the kind of plan you can expect when the data-gathering and planning process is complete.

- *What type of clientele do you serve?* Some planners specialize by income category, age or professional group. If you are nearing retirement, do not hire a planner whose clients are mostly young entrepreneurs. If you are a dentist, you might look for a planning firm that specializes in serving dentists or other medical professionals.

- *Who will I deal with on a day-to-day basis?* In larger planning firms, you might see the chief planner only at the beginning and end of the planning process and work with his or her associates in the meantime. If that is the case, meet the staff with whom you will be working, and ask about their qualifications.

- *Do you have access to other professionals if our planning process takes us into areas in which you are not an expert?* A good planner has a network of top accountants, lawyers, insurance specialists and investment pros to fall back on if he or she has questions.

- *Do you just give financial advice, or do you also execute the advice by selling financial products?* The great fault line in the financial planning industry lies between these two types of professionals.

- *Will your advice include specific product recommendations, or will you suggest only generic product categories?* Most planners will name a particular stock or mutual fund, for example. Others will advise that you keep 50 percent of your assets in stocks, 30 percent in bonds and 20 percent in cash, leaving you to determine which stocks, bonds and cash instruments are appropriate.

- *Will you spend the time to explain your rationale for recommending a specific product and how it suits my goals, my tolerance for risk and my circumstances? How do you plan to monitor a recommended mutual fund or insurance product once I've bought it?* You should feel comfortable that the planner will make the effort to ensure that you understand the strategy and products he or she recommends.

- *How will you follow up after you've delivered the plan to ensure that it is implemented?* A good planner makes sure that you don't just file away the comprehensive plan and never put it into action. Not only should the plan be implemented; it also should be reviewed and revised as conditions in your life, tax laws or the investment environment shifts.

- *How do you get compensated?* Some planners charge for the advice they give. Others collect commissions from the sale of products they recommend. And still others charge both a planning fee and a sales charge. (These styles are discussed further below.) However your planner gets paid, make sure that you receive a written estimate of any fees you must pay.

- *Are there any potential conflicts of interest in the investments you recommend?* A planner must inform you, for example, if he or she or the planner's firm earns fees as a general partner in a limited partnership that the planner touts. He or she must also tell you if the planner receives some form of payment (commonly known as a *referral fee*) when he or she refers you to another firm, such as a law or an accounting firm.

- *Will you have direct access to my money?* Some planners want *discretionary control* of their clients' funds, which allows the planners to invest as they see fit. Be extremely careful about agreeing to this arrangement, which is fraught with potential for fraud and malfeasance. If you do agree to it, make sure that the planner is bonded. This insurance will cover you in case he or she runs off with your money.

- *What professional licenses and designations have you earned?* Besides looking on his or her walls for diplomas, inquire whether the planner holds a CFA, CFP, ChFC, CPA or a PFS. Determine whether the planner is licensed to sell securities, which include stocks, bonds, partnerships and mutual funds. If the planner wants to sell disability, life and property/casualty insurance, as well as fixed or variable annuities, he or she needs a license to sell insurance products. Also find out the planner's educational background. If he or she started out as a lawyer, an insurance agent, an accountant or some other specialist, it will most likely affect the advice the planner gives.

- *Is he or she registered as an investment adviser with the Securities and Exchange Commission or your state?* All planners who provide investment advice should be registered with either the SEC or your state. If registered with the SEC, the planner is required to show you Part Two of his or her Form ADV or a brochure containing the same information. Disclosure requirements for state-registered advisers vary, so check with your state's securities department to find out what's required in your state. The North American Securities Administrators Association (NASAA) can provide you with more information about these requirements at 888-846-2722.

- *Have you ever been cited by a professional or governmental organization for disciplinary reasons?* Even if the planner says that he or she has never been in such trouble, you can check with the state attorney general's office, the state securities office and the state societies of financial planning organizations. (See the "Resources" section at the end of this chapter for more information on these offices.)

How Financial Planners Get Paid

The question of how a financial planner gets paid is a particularly important one as you establish a relationship with your planner. You do not want to be plagued by a nagging fear that your planner recommends products for the commissions they generate rather than for their appropriateness to your situation. In theory, financial planners have an ethical obligation to hold your financial interests above their own, but the incentive structure can make that philosophy difficult to execute. Planners are compensated in four basic ways:

Commission only. Such planners offer free consultation and profit only when you buy a product, such as a mutual fund, an annuity or a life insurance policy. In some cases, the commissions are explicit—for example, a 4 percent front-end load on a mutual fund. In other cases, the fees are lumped into the general expenses of the product, as with life insurance, so you won't know how much your planner makes unless you ask him or her. Because a planner who works on commission collects only if you buy, remain aware of his or her incentives as you consider the planner's advice. When you interview such a planner, ask him or her approximately what percentage of his or her firm's commission revenue comes from annuities, coins and other tangibles, insurance products, limited partnerships, mutual funds and stocks and bonds. The planner's answers will give you a sense of the kind of advice his firm usually gives.

Fees are paid not only in the form of up-front cash but also as ongoing charges that apply as long as you hold an investment. For example, mutual funds often levy *12b(1) fees,* which are annual charges of about 1 percent of your assets designed to reward brokers and financial planners for keeping clients in a fund, and insurance companies pay planners trailing fees for each year a client pays the premiums on an insurance policy.

In other cases, you must pay a fee if you sell a product before a particular amount of time has elapsed. If you want to cash in an annuity or insurance policy early, you must pay surrender charges of 7 percent or so of your investment, part of which reimburses the insurer for the commissions it has paid your planner. If you sell certain mutual funds within four years of buying them, you must remit a

Figure 17.1
Financial Adviser Disclosure Form

IAFP Financial Adviser Disclosure Form
Consumers who contact the IAFP for an adviser in their area and receive your name, will receive a compilation of the information you provide on and with this form

1. General Information

Name _____ Phone: _____-_____-_____,ext. _____

Title _____ Fax: _____-_____-_____

Company _____

Address _____

City, State, Zip _____

If your prospect market is based in a different zip code than the one listed above, please indicate your market area zip codes here (maximum of 5)
_____
We recommend that you do not use this option unless the zip code indicated above is outside your market area.

2. General Overview of your Business
Please attach a separate sheet *to convey any special message to the consumer - typical clients and services you provide, specialty areas, civic activities, personal information or anything else you would like the consumer to know about you and your practice* **(limited to 200 words) This section must be typed. See example adviser sheet for ideas.**

3. Experience
I have been offering financial advice to clients since 19_____. Other relevant experience includes:
(Limited to 50 words)**This section must be typed - you may attach a separate sheet if you wish.**

4. Financial Services Provided (check all that apply)

Comprehensive financial planning	Retirement planning
Investment & asset management	Banking and/or trust management
Tax preparation	Cash management & budgeting
Insurance	Stock and Bond Brokerage
Charitable Giving	Employee Benefits and Qualified Retirement Planning for
Elder and Long-Term Care Planning	Businesses
Funding Education	Work with Owners of Closely-Held Businesses
Estate planning	Other

5. Regulatory Registration & Compliance
At my last reporting to regulators, I had assets under management in the amount of $_____.
Check the most appropriate description of your status:
- ☐ I am or my firm is registered with the SEC as an investment adviser.
- ☐ I am or my firm is registered with the following state(s) as an investment adviser:
_____

I am excluded from registering as an investment adviser with the SEC or any state because:
- ☐ providing investment advice is incidental to my practice of accounting and/or law.
- ☐ I am employed by a bank.
- ☐ Providing investment advice is incidental to my business as a broker dealer.
Other _____

Source: Provided with permission by the International Association for Financial Planning (5775 Glenridge Dr., NE, Suite B-300, Atlanta, GA 30328-5364).

Figure 17.1
(continued)

6. Licenses, Certifications, Education & Affiliations

A. Securities Licenses	B. Broker-Dealer Affiliation:

A. Securities Licenses
- Stocks and Bonds
- Mutual funds
- Limited partnerships

C. Insurance Licenses
- Life insurance
- Health/Disability insurance
- Property/casualty
- Fixed annuities
- Variable annuities

D. Education   **Area of Study**   **University**   **Year Received**
- Bachelors _____
- Masters _____
- Doctorate _____

E. Other Licenses & Designations and Year Received

Certified Financial Planner (CFP) year: _____	Chartered Financial Analyst (CFA) year: _____
Chartered Financial Consultant (ChFC) year: ____	Certified Trust & Financial Advisor (CTFA) year: _____
Chartered Life Underwriter (CLU) year: _____	Enrolled Agent (EA) year: _____
Certified Public Accountant (CPA) year: _____	Admitted to Bar State(s): _____ year: _____
Personal Financial Specialist (PFS) year: _	Other year:

7. Charges to Clients for Services (check all that may apply)

Adviser Controlled Charges	Charges Not Set By Adviser
Fee for financial planning (initial, hourly, and/or retainer)	Commissions and/or loads for investment products purchased
Fee based on percentage of assets managed percentage ranges:	Trail fees on mutual funds or insurance products
	Redemption fees on mutual funds or insurance products
(_____% - _____%)	Commissions on insurance products purchased
	Account fees (such as for IRA accounts)
Other	Other

8. Compensation (check all that apply)

I work on a fee only basis

When requested, I will work with clients on a fee only basis

When requested, I will inform clients of the dollar amount of fees (commissions or loads) they will pay on the purchase of any product.

My clients' interests come first. I will recommend products based on what is in their best interest and not based on which one would give me more earnings.

When appropriate, I may refer my clients to other, related professionals for services they are better able to provide than I.

      I sometimes receive referral or other fees from these professionals.

      I do not receive referral or other fees from these professionals.

My firm does not, nor does any affiliate or member of my firm, act as a general partner, participate in or receive compensation as a general partner from investments that I recommend.

9. Miscellaneous (check all that apply)

To maintain my licenses and/or designations, I am required to earn _____ continuing education credits every _____ (period).

I will provide prospective clients with references.

I have been cited by a professional or regulator governing body for disciplinary reasons. (If this box is checked, please attach more information.)

I will provide a free initial consultation to prospective clients so that we may determine if their needs and my practice are well-matched.

INTERNATIONAL ASSOCIATION
FOR FINANCIAL PLANNING

back-end load, which allows the fund company to recover the up-front sales load it paid your planner. Such back-end loads usually are applied on a sliding scale, so you pay 4 percent if you sell during the first year, 3 percent the second year, 2 percent the third year and 1 percent the fourth year. After that, you will not be charged a back-end fee.

Many commission-motivated planners also win prizes of merchandise or free travel if their sales of a particular product reach a target level. And *soft-dollar arrangements* award planners with noncash goods and services, such as computer software, investment research or magazine subscriptions, if their sales hit certain goals.

Though your planner might not like your questioning his or her cash payment and other perks, it is your right to know whether the products you buy generate direct fees and indirect benefits for the planner. By knowing the full extent of your planner's compensation, you will be better able to decide whether his or her advice is objective or self-serving.

Fee only. Some professional planners assess your financial situation for a fee, set in advance, based on time spent with you, a flat dollar amount or a percentage of your income or assets. Usually, such planners offer a no-cost, no-obligation initial consultation to explore your financial needs. They provide advice on how to imple-ment their recommendations, but they do not collect a dime from commissions if you take their suggestions. The advantage of this arrangement, of course, is that the planner has no vested interest in having you buy one product over another because he or she does not stand to gain personally from any specific recommendation. These planners therefore suggest no-load mutual funds or low-load life insurance policies that you probably would never hear about from a commission-oriented planner. The largest association of fee-only planners is the National Association of Personal Financial Advisors (NAPFA) in Buffalo Grove, Illinois, which will supply a list of fee-only planners near you if you call the association at 800-366-2732. You also can ask for references of fee-only planners from the International Association for Fi-nancial Planning's Adviser Referral Program at 888-806-7526 or at their Web site at www.iafp.org. The IAFP will send you two brochures explaining the financial planning process and how to select a financial adviser, an interview sheet to guide you through the selection process, and detailed background information on five advisers that will match the criteria you specify.

Fee and commission. The majority of financial planners charge some sort of fee for providing a basic plan but make most of their income from commissions on the products they recommend. In some cases, such planners are actually captives of one company, so they recommend only its product line. Other such planners are independent and therefore recommend the mutual funds or insurance policies of any company with which they affiliate. However, because your planner earns most of his or her living by selling something to you, consider any advice warily, and try to determine a way to accomplish the same goals with lower priced products.

A variation on this form of compensation is called *fee offset,* meaning that any commission revenue your planner earns from selling you products reduces his or her fee for planning. If you buy so many products that your entire fee is covered, you deserve a refund of the fee you paid for your basic plan.

Salary. Many banks, credit unions, savings and loans and other organizations that offer financial planning provide the service through a salaried planner. While these planners do not have as strong an incentive to sell products as do commission-oriented planners, they still steer you toward products offered by the financial institution, on which the institution earns a sales fee. If most of the salaried planner's clients execute his or her advice outside the bank or other financial institution, the planner probably will not keep his or her job for very long.

From these descriptions, a fee-only planner probably sounds best; however, this alternative also has several drawbacks. First, not many fee-only planners exist. Second, because these planners make their living only from fees, you typically need enough cash and assets to justify their fees. Depending on the planner, that may mean as much as $100,000 or more. Third, you must take the initiative to follow up on a fee-only planner's advice. This means contacting other financial service companies, such as insurance or mutual fund firms. Therefore, don't dismiss commission-only, fee and commission, and salaried planners. Many of them are truly helpful professionals, and the commissions or salaries they earn by selling products may help keep the cost of their services within your reach. Just remember, when such a planner makes recommendations, be as fully informed as possible about his or her background and incentives as you decide how much of the advice to implement.

Insurance Agents

The idea of seeking out a life insurance agent might sound ironic because so many people spend time avoiding life insurance salespeople. However, taking the initiative to find a reliable agent with a good reputation makes more sense than waiting for a phone call from someone "dialing for dollars" off a phone list provided by an insurance company. If you locate a good specialist, he or she can help you determine your insurance needs and find a reasonably priced policy to satisfy you.

People tend to avoid life insurance agents for several reasons. First, the subject of death and how to prepare for it is distasteful to most people. Second, the money you pay for life insurance premiums comes out of your pocket now, and you may not see benefits from it for years—if ever. Your premium dollars buy a promise from the insurance company to pay a death benefit to your family if you die. If you reach retirement age, you can tap the policy's cash value in a variety of ways to supplement your income. Either way, you give up present consumption for long-term intangible benefits, which is not a trade-off most people relish. Finally, insurance is complex and accompanied by a lexicon of terms, charts and graphs that can be intimidating. It's no wonder that insurance buying is not most people's favorite activity. Despite these roadblocks, however, you probably need life insurance, so you should find an agent who can assist you.

To locate a good agent, start by calling the local office of an insurance company with a good reputation, or ask friends, relatives and business associates for names of agents with whom they have had good experiences.

Once you've got a few names, ask an agent you're interested in how long he or she has been in the business and what his or her qualifications are. Inquire whether the agent sells policies for only one company, in which case he or she is an *exclusive* or a *captive agent,* or whether the agent sells policies for many companies, in which case he or she is an *independent agent.* Either an exclusive or independent agent can offer you the best deal, depending on your situation and what the agent has to sell. Captive agents tend to earn lower commissions than independent agents, and captives usually know their company's insurance policy's provisions better than independents because they sell only one brand. On the other hand, independent agents, in theory, provide you with more options because they offer competing policies from several firms. What you may not know is that they show you the policies that earn them the highest commissions.

INTERVIEWING INSURANCE AGENTS

The first task of a qualified agent is to help you assess your need for insurance. You can use the insurance worksheets in Chapter 11 to give you a start. Some of the questions the agent should ask you include the following:

- What is your current income?
- How much are your assets worth?
- What kind of investment portfolio have you assembled?
- Are you married, and do you have children?
- How long have you been at your company, and do you anticipate staying there a long time?
- Do you have group insurance coverage through your company, and if so, how much?
- How much money would your spouse need to replace your income and maintain his or her standard of living if you were to die unexpectedly?
- How much money can you afford on a monthly or an annual basis for insurance premiums?

If the agent does not ask these kinds of questions, he or she has no way to determine your insurance needs. Therefore, if an agent starts your meeting with an intense sales pitch about how much his or her policy can earn for you or how inexpensive it is, move on to your next candidate. A policy's returns and price are incidental to the main purpose of insurance, which is to protect your family from losing a source of income if you die.

Once the agent has evaluated your needs, he or she should propose several insurance programs tailored to your budget and desire for protection. Insurance policies come in many varieties, with endless combinations of premiums, cash values and coverages. Because many ways to reach the same goal exist, your agent should demonstrate several approaches.

When the agent explains these alternatives, he or she will usually use *policy illustrations,* which are columns of numbers that project what your life insurance could be worth in 5, 10, 20 and 30 years, under certain conditions. Be skeptical of these illustrations because the underlying assumptions may not hold true. For example, a policy might project how dramatically your cash value will grow if you earn 10 percent a year for the life of the policy. But if interest rates drop, you might not earn anywhere near 10 percent, and the pie-in-the-sky figures at the bottom of the columns of numbers will never be reached. The agent should also point out the column illustrating the guaranteed minimum return, which usually is about 4 percent. What you actually earn will probably lie somewhere between that bare-bones minimum and the optimistic projection.

To keep policy illustrations from misleading customers, the National Association of Insurance Commissioners (NAIC) adopted the Life Insurance Illustrations Model Regulation, which has been adopted by many states. Under this law, illustrations must clearly depict which rates of return are guaranteed and which are not. In addition, agents must make sure that you understand that the nonguaranteed elements of the policy are subject to change and can be higher or lower than what is illustrated. Illustrations must include a column that shows a rate of return between what is currently being paid by the company and what would be paid if the nonguaranteed rates were midway between the current and guaranteed rates. Finally, the illustrations must be signed by you and the agent, assuring you that the numbers have been properly explained.

As you listen to the agent's pitch, remain aware of his or her financial incentives. *Agents earn far more by selling new policies than they do by providing service to existing policyholders.* For example, an agent might earn from 30 percent to as much as 125 percent of your first-year premium when you buy a new policy. The only way to find out how much the agent earns on the policy he or she proposes is to ask. The agent may not like the question and refuse to answer, but it is worth trying to find out how much of your first-year premium goes to the agent and how much ends up with the insurer.

After a policy has been in force for a year, the agent may receive between 2 percent and 10 percent annually as long as you continue to pay your premiums. Therefore, the agent has an incentive to make sure that you maintain the policy. An insurance agent's worst nightmare is a policyholder who lets his or her policy lapse or replaces his or her policy with another company's product. These actions discontinue the agent's continuous stream of commission dollars from policies in force.

The agent should continue to earn his or her fees by touching base with you at least once a year to find out whether your situation has changed. For example, your insurance policies need to be updated when you have a child or when you get married or divorced. The agent also should be available to help you maximize the benefits of your policy and handle any administrative problems. For instance, a good agent guides you in shifting the allocation of assets within a variable insurance policy if the assets you chose several years ago are no longer performing well. In addition, the agent should be able to cut through any red tape if your insurance premium check gets lost at headquarters or if you encounter other administrative mix-ups. Of course, if you die, your beneficiaries should know who your agent is. He or she will make sure that the death benefit check is issued and will probably deliver it to the survivors in person.

Life Insurance Agent Designations

Because each insurance company sets its prices uniformly, you can't get a better price by playing one agent off against another, as you can with car dealers. Therefore, you might as well hire the best qualified agent.

You have several ways to make sure that you select a qualified life insurance professional. Each state requires that each agent pass standard tests and take continuing education courses to obtain a license to sell insurance in that state. Beyond this bare minimum, however, several professional designations indicate a higher level of professional and ethical standards. Following are the credentials you are likely to encounter:

Certified Financial Planner (CFP). The CFP, a designation licensed by the Certified Financial Planner Board of Standards (CFP Board) in Denver, covers the entire spectrum of financial planning issues, including insurance. CFPs must complete a ten-hour two-day comprehensive exam to prove their expertise in financial planning, insurance, investing, taxes, retirement planning, employee benefits, estate planning and risk management. The test is difficult and requires the test taker to apply his or her financial planning knowledge to three case studies and multiple choice questions. In addition to having passed the tests, a CFP licensee must possess a certain amount of work experience in the financial services industry, have a defined amount of college education, abide by a strict code of ethics and fulfill continuing education requirements.

Chartered Financial Consultant (ChFC). The ChFC designation is conferred by the American College in Bryn Mawr, Pennsylvania. The ChFC curriculum covers a broad range of financial planning issues, but many ChFC's have particular expertise in life insurance matters. To earn the designation, the financial planner must pass ten college-level courses on all major topics of personal finance and business planning, possess industry experience and adhere to strict ethical standards. To maintain the designation, they must obtain continuing education credits.

Chartered Life Underwriter (CLU). Awarded by the American College in Bryn Mawr, Pennsylvania, the CLU is the top credential for life insurance agents. It may take an agent up to five years to earn a CLU designation, which is granted only after he or she passes ten rigorous courses, possesses industry experience and commits to a strict ethical code. To maintain a CLU, agents must obtain continuing education credits.

In addition to watching for these designations, you can ask your agent whether he or she is a member of the National Association of Life Underwriters (NALU), which is the umbrella group for agents. NALU imposes certain professional and ethical standards on its members.

As a general rule, the best life insurance agents tend to work for the highest quality insurance companies. (See Chapter 11, "All about Insurance," for information about how to find top-rated companies.) These companies are in the strongest financial condition, offer the most competitively priced policies and usually pay their agents lower percentage commissions than other insurance companies. That doesn't bother top agents, however, because the companies' policies usually are easier to sell in larger quantities to more sophisticated clients. The lower quality the insurance company, the more it has to pay agents to peddle its policies and, in general, the less coverage you receive as a policyholder.

While most life insurance salespeople work for insurance companies, a relatively new breed of experts works for insurance buyers. These *insurance advisers* (or *brokers*) often analyze policy proposals more objectively than agents and give you their honest advice with no conflict of interest. For this advice, insurance advisers earn a fee, which is determined in advance and based on the complexity of your situation. You may pay as little as $500 for a simple evaluation and recommendation of a policy worth $50,000 to $100,000, or you may pay as much as $10,000 for a complicated case requiring millions of dollars in coverage. Life insurance advisers not only recommend policies; they can help you obtain coverage at wholesale rates or through no-load or low-load insurance companies. The easiest way to find a qualified adviser is to contact the Life Insurance Advisers Association (800-521-4578).

However you find someone to help you buy life insurance, don't put off the task. Insurance is the kind of product that you don't miss until you need it. If you postpone meeting with an agent or adviser, you might never obtain the coverage you require. And if a sudden accident or disease takes your life, your family may suffer from your procrastination.

Lawyers

You may think you will never need a lawyer's services—and you may be right. But chances are that sometime during your life, you will require reliable legal advice. When you do need a lawyer, you should know how to find one that specializes in your kind of problem because attorneys often practice in only one or two areas of the law. You also should understand the different ways that lawyers get paid; legal bills can quickly get out of hand if you don't realize how your attorney charges. Nevertheless, if you retain a qualified lawyer to help you prevent trouble or resolve a problem, he or she can be well worth the fees.

When you run into legal trouble, determine whether you can handle the problem yourself or whether you need the special training that an attorney offers. Assess whether the problem is so complex that it might end up in court or whether it is simple enough that it can be settled more quickly and inexpensively outside of court. Ask yourself whether the problem involves a sufficient amount of money, property or time to warrant a lawyer's attention or whether bringing in a lawyer constitutes overkill. Finally, analyze whether complex papers must be prepared and filed to defend your rights or whether such papers are superfluous.

ALTERNATIVES TO RETAINING A LAWYER

Even if it looks like your problem is serious enough to hire a lawyer, look into the following alternatives before retaining an attorney:

Small claims court. Here, you can resolve claims up from a few hundred dollars to thousands of dollars by representing yourself at minimal cost and at informal proceedings. Almost every local community has some kind of small claims court.

Arbitration. Through this process, which is far quicker and less expensive than a court proceeding, an impartial arbitrator resolves your dispute with a binding decision. The *arbitrator* is usually a lawyer or businessperson with expertise in the question at hand. When you agree to have the problem arbitrated, you and the other party set the ground rules and the scope of the monetary damages that can be awarded. The hearing is not only quick; it is private, unlike a public court hearing. Some of the most common disputes resolved through arbitration include those between homeowners and home contractors, between labor and management, between insurance companies and claimants and between stockbrokers and their customers. For more information on arbitration, contact the American Arbitration Association (AAA)—see the "Resources" section at the end of this chapter) or your local Better Business Bureau (BBB), which may offer arbitration services.

Mediation. With mediation, a neutral third party is hired to try to help you and your adversary resolve the dispute. The mediator may offer suggestions to help the process along, but ultimately, you and your opposition must agree on the terms of the settlement. Like arbitration, mediation is quick, private, informal, inexpensive and often successful. The AAA and BBB also have information on mediation.

Consumer protection agencies. Whether on the federal, state or local level, consumer protection agencies may be able to help you resolve the problem at little or no cost if they think your concern presents a danger to many citizens who need to be protected. A list of each state attorney general appears in the "Resources" section at the end of this chapter. Those offices can direct you to other consumer protection agencies in your city or state.

Do-it-yourself legal guidebooks and software. Such resources may help you resolve the problem yourself. For instance, the American Bar Association's (ABA's) book *Family Legal Guide* (800-285-2221) might answer many basic questions about your legal rights. Another source of help is HALT, an Organization of Americans for Legal Reform (1612 K St., N.W., Suite 510, Washington DC 20006; 202-887-8255; 888-367-4258), which offers an extensive list of self-help legal publications. In addition, many of the books and software published by Nolo Press (950 Parker St., Berkeley, CA 94710; 510-549-1976; 800-992-6656; www.nolo.com) can be informative if you want to draft your own will, set up a trust, handle your own divorce, enforce child support claims, file bankruptcy or write simple contracts. As a backup, you may want to have an attorney look over what you have done.

Private counselors. Various independent advisers may be able to resolve the dispute. For example, marriage or family counselors may help resolve problems that could lead to divorce. A priest, a rabbi or another clergyperson may be able to mediate a dispute with a neighbor or fellow congregant. And a credit counselor may be able to negotiate with creditors.

Media hot-lines. Hot-lines run by local newspapers or TV stations may be able to draw attention to the problem if it makes a good story. However, such hot-lines publicize only a small number of cases that the public brings them, and you probably won't receive help if your case is not dramatic enough to interest readers or viewers.

TYPES OF LAWYERS

If your problem cannot be solved by any of these means or is too complex for all these alternatives, it's time to shop for a lawyer. Your first step is to identify the kind of lawyer best able to help you.

All lawyers must pass a state bar examination as well as a character and fitness review in order to receive a law license to practice law from the Supreme Court in the states where they practice. Some lawyers work on their own in solo practices, while others join small or large law firms, many of which specialize in certain kinds of law. Following are just a few of the legal specialists available:

- *Business lawyers* set up corporations and partnerships; write contracts; complete mergers, acquisitions and dispositions of businesses; and handle other corporate matters.

- *Consumer lawyers* resolve problems between their clients and stores or consumer product companies.

- *Criminal lawyers* defend those accused of crimes.

- *Estate planning lawyers* write wills, set up trusts, serve as the executors of estates, deal with probate court and handle other related matters.

- *Governmental lawyers* help their clients comply with federal, state and local regulations and dispute governmental rulings that affect them unfairly.

- *Immigration lawyers* help their clients attain naturalization and citizenship papers and help them avoid deportation.

- *Intellectual property lawyers* help their clients obtain a copyright, trademark or patent if they invent or create something that needs protection from theft. They also negotiate contracts with publishers, record companies and film studios.

- *Labor lawyers* specialize in cases of age, sex and race discrimination, workplace safety, union organizing and other employment issues.

- *Marital lawyers* handle divorce, annulment, separation, child custody and child support issues.

- *Personal injury lawyers* represent those who have been hurt, either intentionally or negligently, by a product or car or in any other way. These attorneys may also specialize in workers' compensation claims of those injured on the job.

- *Real estate lawyers* handle real estate contracts, mortgage applications and closings, disputes with real estate brokers and home contractors and other real-estate-related issues.

- *Tax lawyers* help their clients interpret the tax code when they have particularly complex tax questions. These lawyers will not fill out your tax return, however.

FINDING A LAWYER

Once you have determined which type of lawyer specializes in your problem, you have several ways to locate a good attorney. Many law firms pitch their services in advertisements on television, on the radio, in newspapers and even on billboards. But, as with most other professions, you will probably uncover a knowledgeable lawyer by asking friends, relatives or business associates for recommendations. You can also query other financial professionals you deal with, such as your financial planner, banker, insurance agent or even your company's legal department personnel. It would be best if the people you ask have experienced a problem similar to yours that the recommended lawyer dealt with successfully.

Your city, state, county or local bar association offers a free lawyer referral service that lists lawyers by their area of specialty. (A list of these services appears in the "Resources" section at the end of this chapter.) Each referral service assembles its list a little differently. Some include any attorney who is a member of the bar and wants to be listed. Other services charge lawyers a fee or require a particular amount of experience before they will add an attorney to their lists. When you use one of these services, ask what screening procedures it employs.

Lawyers also advertise in the *Yellow Pages* these days, and they usually list the area of the law in which they concentrate. The *Martindale-Hubbell Law Directory* (see the "Resources" section), available in most public libraries, provides a complete roster of lawyers and their backgrounds, listed by location and area of interest. If you live or work near a law school, call the dean's office for recommendations of professors or graduates in the local area who may be experts in your legal dilemma.

In addition, you might be able to line up a qualified attorney through public institutions. For example, the government-supported Legal Aid Society may be able to help if your income is low enough and it handles your kind of case. If you are charged with a crime and cannot afford a lawyer, you have a constitutional right to a free court-appointed attorney from the public defender's office. The state attorney general's office may be able to provide enough legal guidance to help you fill out government forms and handle other simple legal matters.

Also, walk-in legal clinics, which advertise heavily on television and radio, may be ideal for routine legal matters, such as simple wills, bankruptcies, divorces and traffic offenses. Finally, you can subscribe to a prepaid legal services plan, or your employer may make such a plan available to you. These plans provide legal advice over the phone or in person, up to certain time and financial limits.

INTERVIEWING LAWYERS

Once you have found a lawyer who is qualified and willing to help you with your problem, set up an initial consultation, which might be free or may require a small fee of about $25. Before you attend this meeting, write down all the points you want to make and all the questions you want answered, and bring copies of all important documents the lawyer will need. Following are a few general questions you can ask the lawyer as you get acquainted:

- *Will you work on my case personally, or will assistants, law clerks or paralegals do most of the work?*

- *If you do not have the expertise to handle this case, do you work with other lawyers who can help?*

- *What are the potential outcomes of my case?* No good lawyer should guarantee that you will win; otherwise, exactly half would be wrong. Have your lawyer give you a frank assessment of the strengths and weaknesses of your case so you can realistically gauge your chances of winning. Ask your lawyer whether he or she thinks that your case will go to trial or might be settled out of court. Inquire whether an appeal is possible if you lose.

- *How do you work with clients?* Make sure that your lawyer will consult you regarding all decisions that affect your case and will explain everything in terms you can understand. Also, determine whether you will be given copies of all relevant papers filed in the case for your own records.

- *If I am dissatisfied with your work, how will you resolve my complaints?* Agree in advance how to negotiate a resolution of any dispute, whether through an organized dispute resolution center, a small claims court or the local bar association.

- *How will you get paid?* Lawyers receive payment in many ways; therefore, know exactly how your attorney will be compensated before the meter starts running.

How Lawyers Get Paid

The most common methods of paying lawyers follow:

- *Flat fees* are paid for a straightforward task that is predictable in the skills and amount of time it will require. This might apply to composing a deed or conducting a title search, for instance.

- *Hourly fees* are typical if it is not clear in advance how many hours your lawyer must spend on the case. Fees can start as low as $25 an hour and escalate to $500 an hour or even more, depending on the level of expertise required and the size of the law firm. The more experienced the lawyer and the larger the firm, the higher the hourly rate. Hourly fees for courtroom time are usually higher than charges for time spent in the library or office. Usually, lawyers keep a careful log of the time they spend on your case, broken down in tenths or quarters of an hour. Out-of-pocket expenses for copies, faxes, postage, messenger services, long-distance phone calls and court fees are usually added to the hourly fees. When they take the case, some lawyers will limit the amount you can be charged.

- A *retainer* is a fixed amount of money paid to a lawyer on a regular basis that ensures the lawyer will be available whenever you need him or her. Retainers are used most often by companies or individuals needing constant legal service. A retainer is like a down payment because if you use a lawyer heavily, you will still be charged for his or her time. A retainer agreement should stipulate the approximate number of hours covered.

- A *referral fee* is paid if your lawyer refers your case to another lawyer who is more of an expert in your problem. If both your lawyer and the lawyer to whom he or she refers the case work on it, both are entitled to a fee. But if your lawyer turns the case over to the expert entirely, your lawyer should receive no further payment. You must be informed of the agreement between the two lawyers, however, and make sure that each is paid an amount proportionate to the work he or she has done.

- *Percentage fees* are based on the management or disposition of assets. For example, a lawyer sometimes earns a percentage of the assets probated in a will or the value of a house sold at a closing. Under such an arrangement, you know exactly how much your lawyer will be paid because it is based on a fixed percentage of the assets involved. However, that fee may or may not reflect the amount of work the lawyer does in the case. If a closing is routine and the home costs several hundred thousand dollars, for example, the percentage fee your lawyer suggests may be unfair to you. In that case, press for a lower percentage or an hourly fee schedule.

- A *contingent fee* is paid to a lawyer who wins your case. If you cannot afford to pay any of the fees listed above but your lawyer thinks you have a good chance of winning a lawsuit for a significant amount of money, he or she may take your case on a contingent basis. Most often, this style of payment applies to personal injury cases involving negligence. If you win, the lawyer receives a certain percentage—ranging from 25 percent to 50 percent—of the winnings. Many states limit the maximum fee. Often, a lawyer takes home a third of the money awarded you. Some lawyers propose a *sliding scale arrangement,* where their percentage rises if the trial lasts a long time or is appealed. Other sliding scales call for a *declining percentage* as the dollar amount of the judgment increases.

    If you lose the case, the lawyer receives nothing for his or her efforts. However, you may have to pay *court costs,* such as filing fees and the like, so don't believe a contingent fee lawyer who says, "You will never have to pay a penny to try this case." In fact, make sure that your agreement with the lawyer clearly states whether such expenses are to be deducted before or after the contingency fee is calculated.

SMART STRATEGIES FOR WORKING WITH YOUR LAWYER

Once you have chosen a lawyer and agreed on a payment method, get an agreement in writing. You will protect both yourself and your lawyer by putting on paper what the lawyer has agreed to do, how he or she will charge, how expenses will be covered, what kind of itemized bills you will receive and how any disputes will be settled. Also, try to obtain a written estimate of how much the lawyer thinks your case will cost. You might have him or her give you high and low estimates of the total fees, depending on how much time is involved and the complexity of the case. If you finally find a lawyer you like and trust but cannot pay his or her fees in a lump sum, ask whether the lawyer offers a *payment plan.* Many even take credit cards.

However you decide to pay your lawyer, you can save money by taking the following steps:

- *Be organized.* Think about and write down what you want to discuss with your lawyer before you meet with or talk to him or her. Collect all relevant facts, dates, phone numbers and documents ahead of time so you do not search while the meter is running.

- *Be quick.* Limit your conversations to your case so you can minimize the time your lawyer spends on the case.

- *Keep your lawyer informed.* It costs more money to withhold important information from your lawyer than it does to tell him or her everything you know about the case. If circumstances change, tell your lawyer right away. This might affect your lawyer's strategies and save time that he or she might have spent pursuing another course of action.

- *Stay on top of the case.* Do not delay your problem's resolution because you have not paid attention to your responsibilities or followed up on your lawyer's advice.

As is true of other professionals, a good lawyer can be well worth his or her fees. A lawyer who writes a contract that protects you bypasses the possibility of many future problems by persuading all parties to agree up front. If you are already in trouble, a lawyer can defend you or argue your case in court so that your grievance can be heard and, hopefully, won. By using the selection process outlined above, you should minimize any problems with lawyers and maximize your results.

Money Managers

If you don't have the time or knowledge to invest your capital, you might need a personal money manager. When you buy shares in a mutual fund, in effect, you hire a money manager. However, you will probably never meet the manager of your mutual fund, and your money is combined with millions of dollars of other investors' money. Retaining your own money manager differs from opening a mutual fund account in several other ways:

- *Individual money managers offer more personal service and recordkeeping.*

- *Money manager fees are generally more than mutual fund fees.* Managers may charge as much as 2 percent a year versus 1 percent or less for mutual funds.

- *The required minimum initial investment imposed by money managers is much higher than it is for mutual funds.* While most mutual funds require only about $1,000 to start, money managers usually insist on $100,000 to $1 million before they will take you as a client.

Because money managers charge higher fees and impose larger minimums, why would you want to hire one? Usually, the answer is performance. Many money managers provide far better long-term results to clients than do mutual funds. In addition, you often can meet with your money manager to discuss how he or she allocates your assets.

The main job of a money manager is to choose the stocks and bonds he or she thinks best achieve your financial goals. Your money manager will not consult with you on a day-to-day basis as he or she buys and sells securities. You must develop enough trust in the manager's abilities to let the manager trade as he or she sees fit. If you are young and looking for long-term capital growth, the money manager will usually assemble a portfolio of stocks. If you are retired, he or she will buy bonds and high-yielding stocks, providing you with stable income.

Money Managers and Brokers

While money managers decide which securities to buy, they usually execute their trades through a stock broker seeking the best execution. That could be a broker with whom you already do business or a broker that normally works with the money manager. Because money managers generally handle several accounts worth millions of dollars, brokers offer them discounts on regular retail commission rates. These discounts could total as much as 50 percent, depending on a manager's volume of trades.

To protect you against the possibility that a money manager will run off with your money, your assets should be held by a separate custodian such as a bank or brokerage firm, not by the money manager directly. You do not have to restrict yourself to a money manager in or near your hometown. One of the chief advantages of selecting a skilled money manager is that you can have access to superior stock- and bond-choosing skills, no matter where the manager is located. The manager should agree to send you regular statements, usually quarterly, explaining where your money is invested and what returns it has been earning.

The money management business has grown to immense proportions in recent years. Thousands of money managers are registered with the SEC. And each one would probably tell you that he or she has found the best method to provide high returns with minimal risk. Most of them would also boast that their track record consistently beats the Standard & Poor's (S&P) 500 Index or some other well-known performance benchmark. The truth is that every year, more than half of all money managers underperform the S&P 500 and that many of them take higher risks and provide lower returns than advertised.

Checking Their Record

Before you commit to any money manager, check into his or her background and track record. Every legitimate fund manager must register as an investment adviser with the SEC. Once the manager registers, he or she may use the initials RIA. However, don't be too impressed by that designation; it entails only filing an ADV form and paying a fee. The short-staffed SEC rarely audits money managers. When you interview a money manager, ask for a copy of his or her ADV form, particularly Part II, which describes the manager's education, experience, fee structure and investment style and results. The form should also reveal any trouble the manager has had with the SEC or any other government agency.

While obtaining an ADV form is a good start, investigate the money manager further. Ask him or her to give you the names of three or four satisfied clients. The manager should have no qualms in doing so. Then, ask the clients whether they have earned the returns the manager claims and whether recordkeeping has been maintained professionally. (Tell the manager you want to look at a few quarterly client statements. See whether they look easy to understand as well as comprehensive and whether the manager's performance matches the figures he or she advertises.) Also, inquire of the clients how well the money manager handles their questions and concerns.

In addition, look closely at the manager's performance record. Most compare their returns to the S&P 500 performance on a year-by-year basis and also over the last five and ten years if they have been in business that long. If this evaluation is too difficult or time-consuming for you, you may want to hire an investment management consultant who specializes in screening money managers on clients' behalf. (See the section later in this chapter on finding and using these consultants.)

Do not expect your manager to outperform the S&P 500 or any other index every year because few manage that feat. Nevertheless, hire a manager only if he or she can beat the index over a longer period of time, preferably at least five years. If you choose someone on a hot streak for the last year or two, you might be buying in just as he or she is cooling off. Ideally, settle on a stock fund manager who has provided at least a 10 percent to 15 percent long-term gain or a bond manager providing an 8 percent to 10 percent average annual return. Also, most managers who quote their returns to clients should include the effect of all fees and brokerage commissions. If such charges are not included, the manager is trying to inflate his or her actual performance figures.

Finally, it is probably best if you hire a manager who has been in business at least five years, and preferably ten, so he or she has had experience in both bull and bear markets. The money manager also should have accumulated a significant pool of assets—at least $10 million and probably more than $50 million—to show that he or she has kept many clients satisfied.

EVALUATE THE FEES

If you are satisfied with the money manager's record, look at his or her fee structure. Usually, a manager will levy a fee based on an annual percentage of your account's value. The fee may range from 1 percent to 2 percent of your account balance. Obviously, as your account grows, so does the manager's fee; therefore, he or she has a strong incentive to provide superior returns. Most managers will give you a discount if you invest far more than the minimum they require. For instance, if a manager charges a 2 percent fee on $100,000, he or she may assess a 1 percent fee if you invest $1 million.

Most money manager fees include brokerage commissions, so you do not have to pay higher fees if they are frequent traders. Usually, a manager investing mostly in bonds charges a lower fee than a stock manager because bonds are easier to select and buy and are traded less frequently than stocks. Certain money management firms will nick you with another round of fees, commonly called *reporting* or *administrative charges.* This is usually some flat amount, such as $100 a year, to cover the printing and mailing of quarterly reports and tax statements.

Many brokerage and other financial firms offer what are known as *wrap accounts* as a way for investors to have access to top money managers. The total fee on a wrap account, which includes money management services and brokerage commissions, should never exceed 3 percent of the value of your portfolio. Currently, most managers charge between 1.5 and 2 percent. Wrap accounts usually have lower minimums than direct accounts with money managers—some brokerage firms let you in for as little as $25,000 or $50,000. Brokerage firms monitor the performance of the money managers and research other managers with different investment styles so that you receive superior performance.

INVESTMENT STYLES

Once you are satisfied that the manager is honest, possesses a good record and charges reasonable fees, examine his or her style of investment. First, determine how aggressive or conservative the manager is—and how daring you want him or her to be. Keep in mind that the greater the risks a manager takes, the higher your returns should be in the long term. Three broad categories of investment objectives exist, and several styles within each category achieve those objectives.

Growth. Growth accounts are designed to produce long-term capital appreciation, usually by buying particular types of stocks. Some of the most common growth investment techniques include the following:

- *Aggressive growth investing,* in which managers buy stocks of companies with rapidly growing earnings. Some managers concentrate on large growth companies with sales of $500 million to several billion dollars, while others specialize in small companies with sales of less than $500 million.

- *Value investing,* in which managers buy stocks with low price-earnings (PE) ratios that are shunned by most investors. By purchasing such stocks inexpensively, they hope to reap big gains when a stock recovers and investors bid up its share price.

- *Cash-flow investing,* in which managers buy stocks that generate a great deal of cash from their operations, which can be used to buy back stock or reinvest in the business. Managers like to buy such stocks at the lowest price-cash flow ratios possible.

- *Asset investing,* in which managers buy shares of companies selling for less than the true worth of the companies' assets. Those assets may include real estate, brand names, copyrights or anything else of value. The stocks' prices will tend to rise as the asset values are realized. This might happen when the assets are sold at market prices or when the assets earn a higher return. In some cases, these undervalued companies might be taken over by a raider or another company that hopes it can better use the assets.

- *Sector rotation investing,* in which managers move money from one industry to another to take advantage of changes in the economy and investor sentiment. For example, a manager might buy *stable demand stocks,* such as food, drugs and utilities, if the economy is heading into a recession because those stocks tend to outperform others when demand is weak. As the economy emerges from the recession, the manager might transfer funds to more economically sensitive *cyclical stocks,* such as cars, paper, chemical and steel producers, where profits would rise faster as the economy rebounds. Sector rotation works extremely well in hindsight but is often hard to execute; it is difficult to identify the sectors that are growing hot and cold.

- *Market timing,* in which managers forecast when stock and bond prices will rise and fall. Based on those predictions, the managers try to buy before prices rise and sell before they fall, keeping clients' money in cash instruments while they wait out the market declines. Sounds easy? Market timers use many elaborate computer models to determine which way prices will go at a particular time. However, it is still a very unreliable art because news events and human behavior are not as predictable as computer models would have you believe.

Fixed-income money management. Such investment accounts are designed to yield some capital appreciation and a regular stream of income from various types of bonds. A fixed-income account is appropriate if you want a properly diversified portfolio or if you are retired and living off the income from your investments. Some of the different styles of fixed-income management include the following:

- *Government securities investing,* in which managers buy Treasury bonds and government-backed securities like Ginnie Maes. Government securities are the most conservative form of bond; therefore, they usually offer the lowest yields. However, managers can augment returns by purchasing government securities with different maturities to take advantage of interest rate trends. Some government-oriented managers also buy bonds of foreign governments, which can pay higher yields but present currency risks.

- *Corporate securities investing,* in which managers buy everything from corporate bonds of AAA-rated blue chip companies to junk bonds in or near default. Some corporate securities managers specialize in convertible bonds, which combine high income with stock-like appreciation potential. Clearly, corporate bonds present more risk than government bonds, but they offer higher reward potential. For instance, the monthly or quarterly income from corporate securities tends to be higher than that of government bonds.

- *Tax-free, fixed-income securities investing,* in which managers assemble a portfolio of municipal bonds that produce regular income, free from income taxes. Some money managers also tailor portfolios to people living in a particular state or city so the income is double- or triple-tax free.

Balanced accounts. These accounts, managed by financial professionals who tend to be conservative, mix stocks and bonds to provide both growth potential and income. Balanced accounts tend to yield lower returns than do both growth and fixed-income accounts. However, they take far less risk because bond holdings cushion any decline in the stock portion of the portfolio.

In deciding how to allocate your money among these styles of investment, remember the investment pyramid of risk in Chapter 1. Growth managers sit at the top of the pyramid; balanced managers, in the middle; and fixed-income managers, at the bottom. Your best choice, if you can afford it, is to place some money with each style of manager to create a well-diversified portfolio.

INVESTMENT MANAGEMENT CONSULTANTS

If the whole process of choosing a money manager seems difficult and time consuming, you have another option: an *investment management consultant.* This relatively new breed of investment adviser does not select stocks or bonds; he or she hires money managers to select stocks and bonds and evaluate the managers' performance based on the client's guidelines.

Investment consulting has become extremely popular among clients, brokers and money managers. From your point of view, the consultant constantly monitors many money managers possessing different investment styles and may recommend that you transfer assets from one manager to another if the manager's performance slips. The consultant, often associated with a brokerage firm, also performs all necessary recordkeeping and sends you statements quarterly.

From the broker's point of view, he or she has no liability for recommending losing investments. The broker, if acting as a consultant, removes himself or herself from the dangerous business of selling individual stocks, bonds or mutual funds. If the money manager fails, the broker will advise you to fire him or her. In addition, the broker continues to earn annual consulting fees no matter which manager handles your money, as long as the broker keeps your account.

From the money manager's viewpoint, dealing with consultants frees the manager to concentrate on choosing stocks and bonds, rather than marketing his or her investment services. If the money manager builds a good track record, consultants will beat a path to his or her door and flood the manager with new money. In addition, consultants must handle all client problems.

A good investment management consultant will help you determine what kind of money manager best suits your needs. He or she will ask you to fill out a questionnaire listing your assets, liabilities and investing experience. The consultant should then take you through an exercise that defines your risk tolerance and financial goals. (You will be well prepared for this process if you have completed the financial planning worksheets in Chapter 1.) The consultant will then explain different money management styles and recommend several money managers who have superior records in each style.

The best consultants maintain databases that track hundreds of money managers. The consultants monitor not only investment performance but also personnel changes, investment styles and methods of stock- and bond-choosing. Because consultants are in constant contact with managers, they should also know whether a particular manager's back-office service—e.g., accounting, recordkeeping, client statements, etc.—is of consistently high quality. Often, a money manager with a hot record will be overwhelmed by new money. His or her staff may then have trouble keeping up with the business, and clients' account statements may show errors.

Good consultants favor money managers with strong long-term performance records so you will not have to shift your portfolio every few months or every year among the hottest managers. The consultants can also examine objectively money managers' claims. By selecting a certain time period, managers can distort their records to make themselves look good. Some money managers conveniently drop losing stocks from their portfolios at reporting time or the end of a quarter to enhance their records. Qualified consultants should be able to see through such ruses.

Finally, the consultant should design a portfolio using several managers; therefore, if one performs badly, you will not lose all your money. After your portfolio has been established, the consultant should monitor the managers closely to ensure that they do what they promised to do and deliver the expected results. The consultant should also stay in touch with your current situation so he or she can shift your money accordingly—to income-oriented managers as you near retirement, for example.

Consultants usually work under a wrap-fee arrangement. If they charge a 3 percent annual fee, for instance, the consultant might get 1 percent of it and the money manager, 2 percent. The money manager usually places his or her stock and bond trades through the consultant's brokerage firm, which generates commissions for the brokerage.

When choosing a consultant, watch for potential conflicts of interest. For example, if a money manager pays a finder's fee to a consultant, that arrangement must be disclosed in the manager's ADV form filed with the SEC. Also, determine how much of a consultant's clients' assets rest with one money manager. If he or she has placed too many customers with one manager, it may be difficult for the consultant to pull out if the manager's performance declines. The only way to uncover such potential conflicts of interest is to question the consultant before you hire him or her.

You can locate a qualified investment management consultant through most major brokerage firms. To locate a Certified Investment Management Analyst, contact the Investment Management Consultants Association (IMCA, 9101 E. Kenyon Ave., Suite 3000, Denver, CO 80237; 303-770-3377; 800-599-9462 www.imca.org). Members of IMCA must meet high standards of ethical behavior and follow certain rules regarding disclosure and reporting of investment results to clients.

If you find an honest consultant, he or she can provide a sensible long-term strategy that will hopefully provide you with high returns at relatively low risk by placing your assets with top money managers. However, make sure to monitor the consultant. Just because he or she watches the money managers doesn't mean that you should not watch the consultant.

Real Estate Brokers

Buying or selling a home is probably the most important financial transaction you will ever make. It is therefore crucial that you learn to use the services of a real estate broker to your maximum advantage.

SELLING ON YOUR OWN

Before you hire a real estate agent to sell your home, you might try saving commission costs by selling it on your own. Some people give it a shot, at least for a month or so. If you are selling in a hot market, you may be able to find a buyer easily, saving yourself thousands of dollars.

The first step in selling your home is to decide on a price. You can get a feel for prices in your area by looking at ads and listings for similar homes in your neighborhood. You can also gather real estate agents' opinions about what your home should bring. Agents will prepare a *competitive market analysis* (CMA), sizing up how your home compares to others available in the neighborhood. You may also want to hire a professional appraiser. If you sell without a broker, you can lower your price a bit because the sales proceeds will not have to cover an agent's commission costs.

Once you settle on a realistic price, market your home aggressively. Start by getting your home and property in top condition. Paint, clean, cut the grass, remove excess furniture from the rooms and even place fresh flowers strategically around your home. Prepare a one-page description of your home's amenities, and attach a photo and floor plan to help buyers remember your home after they have looked at many.

In several newspapers targeting your market area, place an ad detailing what makes your property unique. Also, state at the end of the ad that the home is for sale by owner, a tip-off to potential buyers that they may be able to get a good price because no brokers receive commissions. On your front lawn, place a large for-sale-by-owner sign that lists your name and phone number. You may even want to hold an open house on weekends, which will attract browsers as well as serious potential buyers.

If you are committed to selling the home on your own, you must show it to whoever wants to see it whenever he or she wants. That means keeping your home neat at all times and being available whenever a buyer wants to drop in to take a look. Don't count on any weekend trips until you find a buyer.

If you do attract a buyer with whom you agree on price, judge whether he or she is financially able to buy your home or qualify for a mortgage. One way to test this is to demand a deposit, sometimes known as *earnest money,* which may or may not be refundable, depending on the conditions you set. Once you are satisfied with the buyer, have a real estate lawyer draw up the sales contract and make sure that all the closing details are handled correctly.

USING A BROKER

If, instead of selling quickly, your home languishes on the market, it is probably time to call in a real estate *agent* or *broker.* Agents have earned a state real estate license allowing them to sell real estate. Brokers are also licensed, but they may own a real estate company and are responsible for the actions of the agents working for them. There are state-by-state regional differences in the status of brokers. For brevity's sake, the following text uses the terms interchangeably.

Brokers and agents perform many services for their fee. First, an agent sizes up your property and estimates what price it might bring. The agent also prequalifies buyers to make sure that they can afford your home. In addition, the agent handles all negotiations between seller and buyer and advises the seller on strategies to obtain the highest price possible without scaring away the buyer. The agent can also arrange to bring in inspectors or appraisers if the buyer requests them. Also, the agent might direct the buyer to sources of mortgage financing once the seller and buyer have agreed on a price. Finally, the agent can make sure that the sale closes on schedule.

Before you commit to a particular agent, interview several in your community. Ask friends, relatives and business associates for recommendations of top brokers. Notice which agencies have the most for-sale signs in your neighborhood and also which homes sell the fastest. Attend a few open houses sponsored by different agencies to see how well they are run. Request the names of satisfied clients from any broker you are considering; call to ask those clients whether they would sell their home through that agent again.

Once you narrow your search to a few agents, give each a tour of your home, and ask him or her for a CMA—a frank appraisal of what price you might get in the current market. Each broker will then make a *listing presentation.* This is basically a sales pitch from the agency to convince you that it knows the local market well and will be able to sell your home for a higher price than any other agency. The broker should tell you how many similar homes the agency currently lists and how many sales it has completed in the last two or three months. Also, ask how many listings expired or were canceled recently because the agency was unable to locate a buyer.

Other questions you should ask each potential broker include the following:

- *How long have you worked in this neighborhood?*

- *Are you licensed to sell real estate in this state?* For safety's sake, you might even ask to see the agent's license, which proves he or she passed the state real estate examination.

- *Are you a member of the National Association of REALTORS® (NAR)?* NAR requires members to follow a strict code of ethics and provides ongoing training to improve its members' professionalism. If you have any complaints about your REALTOR®, bring your problem to NAR's local Board of REALTORS®.

- *Is this your full-time or part-time job?* Many agents sell real estate as a sideline and therefore cannot put as much effort into selling your home as a full-time pro.

- *What is your marketing plan to sell my home?* A good agent should be able to tell you specifically what he or she will do and how long it should take to attract qualified buyers.

- *What services does your company offer?* For example, the agency might participate in a computerized *multiple-listing service* (MLS), which can offer your home to a wide audience of potential buyers. Also, the agency should place television or newspaper ads to help sell properties. And make sure that if your agent is not available for whatever reason, the agency will supply someone else to show your home if a buyer wants to see it.

In making your final decision on a broker, also consider whether the broker works for a small local agency or for a large national company like Century 21 or Coldwell Banker. A local company may have more connections and expertise in selling homes in your neighborhood. However, a national firm may have tie-ins to relocation services, which provide names of potential buyers moving to your town. Some larger firms also arrange mortgage financing options. These can make it easier for a buyer to afford your home.

THE LISTING AGREEMENT

Once you choose a broker, carefully examine the listing agreement. The contract specifies the asking price of the home, what personal property—such as appliances—are included in the asking price, what services the broker will provide, how much you will pay the broker if the home sells and when the contract expires. Most contracts extend 90 or 180 days, though you should retain the right to cancel the contract at any time (with some notice) if your broker does little to sell your home. Usually, the agreement stipulates that your home will be listed with an MLS. That means any real estate agent using the MLS can show your home to prospective buyers.

Some brokers would rather show your home on an exclusive basis, meaning that no other broker is allowed to sell the listing for a specified amount of time—usually three months. Brokers with exclusive contracts should be motivated to work particularly diligently on your behalf because they will keep the entire commission. Unless you have an exceptional broker, however, such exclusive contracts usually do not work to your advantage.

Brokers will propose several types of contracts in selling your property.

- An *exclusive right to sell* means that the broker gets his or her commission no matter who sells the home. Therefore, the broker gets paid even if you find the buyer yourself.

- An *exclusive agency agreement* stipulates that the listing real estate broker collects a commission if any broker arranges the sale. If you find a buyer on your own, you do not pay the commission.

- An *open listing arrangement* allows any broker who sells the property to receive a commission. No broker has an exclusive right to the percentage. Clearly, brokers are less motivated to sell your home under this arrangement than an exclusive listing agreement.

- A *net listing* is an agreement between a broker and a homeowner in which the broker guarantees a certain net sales price to the homeowner. The price is usually a bit below the real market value of the home. The broker pays the homeowner in cash and keeps any difference between the net price and the actual selling price. Net listings are illegal in many states and usually should be avoided.

Once you agree with a buyer on a price, have a real estate attorney draw up a sales contract. Your agent can help make sure that the contract lists all necessary details. For example, the contract should include the sales price, an exact description of the home and the property included in the sale, and all requirements for title searches, insurance, deeds and real estate taxes. The contract should also specify a date for the *closing* (also known as escrow, transfer of title, passing papers, etc.) and by which the buyer must secure financing and a date when the buyer can move into the home.

COMMISSIONS

In return for advising you on a strategy to sell your home, finding a buyer and bringing the deal to completion, most real estate agents receive a commission of between 5 percent and 7 percent of the sales price. Other brokers will work for a flat fee instead of a percentage. In either case, a broker receives not one dime until your home is sold; therefore, he or she has a strong incentive to get the job done as quickly as possible.

Commission percentages are negotiable, however, and may be less if the home is expensive or competition among agents is fierce. You can negotiate a lower commission in various ways. For example, the agent might agree to a lower percentage if he or she provides less service, such as placing fewer newspaper ads or holding fewer open houses. Or you may stipulate that the broker will receive a certain commission if he or she sells your home within a specified number of days (usually 60) and that the percentage will fall if it takes longer.

To afford the commission, which often amounts to thousands of dollars, you probably will try to figure the fee into the selling price of your home. In some cases, if you and a buyer have difficulty agreeing on a price, an agent will cut his or her commission to close the deal. Agents do this very reluctantly, but they figure it is better to receive a smaller piece of a done deal than a higher percentage of nothing.

Your agent does not keep the entire commission. He or she splits it with the agency and, if another broker found the buyer, with the cooperating broker.

IF YOU'RE BUYING

For the most part, real estate agents represent sellers of homes. Nevertheless, they can help buyers identify properties, and they can serve as intermediaries during negotiations over sales contracts. Inform an agent what size home you need, what amenities you desire, what location you are interested in and roughly what you can afford. The agent will then look through the listings and show you what he or she thinks might be a good match. The broker will always accompany you to the home and try to make it look as good as possible. (Remember, the broker works for the seller.) If you are unfamiliar with the neighborhood, the agent can tell you about local real estate tax rates, as well as schools, cultural activities, churches, transportation, shopping, hospitals and the like. Take this information with a grain of salt because, obviously, the agent has a vested interest in making the neighborhood look as idyllic as possible. If you are dissatisfied with one broker, for whatever reason, take your business to another. As a buyer, you are under no obligation to any particular broker.

Constantly remind yourself, however, that the agent works for the seller, so the incentive is to get you to pay as high a price as possible—which will please the seller and fatten the agent's commission. Do not expect the broker to tell you what bid the seller will accept, even if the broker knows what that price is, because it would breach the broker's fiduciary responsibility. Also, be discreet in telling the broker how high you will go in making an offer for a home because the broker will tell the seller.

Another alternative is to hire a broker who works for you, the buyer. The *buyer's broker* often possesses in-depth knowledge of the local market. In addition, he or she can make sure that you receive full disclosure from a seller regarding any problems in a home before you purchase it. In some states, all sellers must provide a full written disclosure of any problems. You can use this disclosure as evidence in a lawsuit if a problem worsens after you buy. Based on his or her expertise, the buyer's broker can also help negotiate the lowest price. For example, he or she can point out what is wrong with a home and use that as a bargaining chip to help lower the price. Buyer's brokers usually share in the commission, get paid on an hourly fee basis, or earn a set fee if they locate a home that you end up purchasing. Some work for a percentage—usually about 3 percent—of the purchase price. Make sure, however, that the broker works only for you. It is a blatant conflict of interest to collect fees from both the buyer and the seller. To find a qualified buyer's broker, call the Buyer's Homefinding Network at 800-893-0864.

It is not necessary to buy through either a buyer's or a seller's agent. You can purchase directly from a seller who advertises in the newspaper or posts a sign on the front lawn. However, before you try this approach, learn as much as you can about the local real estate market. You might pay too much if you don't know what comparable properties have sold for recently. Also, you will not have access to the range of properties currently on the market.

Whether you sell or purchase a home, you will probably deal with a real estate agent at some point in the transaction. You must understand the ground rules well to make sure that your rights are protected and that you obtain the best deal possible.

Stockbrokers

If you need advice about which individual stocks, bonds or mutual funds can help you achieve your financial goals, you might find it useful to retain a full-service stockbroker. An experienced broker can steer you to securities that you probably never would hear about on your own—and recommend when to sell these securities and move on to others. On the other hand, a newcomer to the field who specializes in "cold calling" potential customers to pitch the hot stock of the day could do serious damage to your net worth. The key to selecting a stockbroker is to separate the truly helpful professional from the out-to-make-a-buck salesperson.

Because the key benefit of working with a full-service broker is the advice he or she gives, *investigate carefully any broker you consider hiring.* As with other professionals, the best way to locate a qualified broker is to ask friends, relatives or business associates for referrals. If that method doesn't uncover a satisfactory professional, visit the branch office of a nearby brokerage house, and ask to see the branch manager. Explain your situation and investing needs, and describe approximately how much money you have to invest. If the branch manager values you as a customer, he or she will refer you to a broker whose experience matches your situation. For example, if you are young and looking to build capital with aggressive growth stocks and funds, the manager should not recommend a broker who specializes in retirement portfolios. If you merely walk in the brokerage house and don't ask the branch manager for a referral, you will be assigned to the broker of the day—someone who handles off-the-street referrals. You may be lucky and get an experienced pro; most likely, you will be assigned to a novice who is still learning the ropes.

Interview at least three brokers before you choose one. Ask each broker whether he or she has dealt with clients in situations similar to yours. If so, ask for their names, and call them to see what they say about the broker. Also, ask the broker how long he or she has been in the business and whether the broker specializes in one investment type. Some brokers may be able to get you in on a new stock issue, for example, while others know the options market well. Many brokers recommend only mutual funds; others act as investment management consultants. Some brokers consider themselves "stock jockeys" and follow the daily stream of developments affecting companies. Others see themselves as financial planners, concerned more about the overall financial needs of their clients. The broker you choose should offer a specialty that matches your level of experience and the amount of money you have to invest. Most of all, however, the broker should be a good listener. You should feel that he or she genuinely understands your concerns, that the broker is trustworthy and that he or she will not push you into products that you might not understand or that are not appropriate for your situation.

Finally, check the broker's record with your state securities department. (A list of all 50 appears in the "Resources" section at the end of Chapter 3, "Picking Winning Stocks.") State regulators have teamed up with the National Association of Securities Dealers (NASD) to create the *Central Registration Depository* (CRD), a computerized database tracking each broker's work history for the past decade. It lists the broker's employment record and any information about fraud, bankruptcies, arbitration judgments or any other violations of securities laws. Your state securities department will send you free of charge the record of any broker.

NATIONAL VERSUS REGIONAL FIRMS

Generally, two kinds of full-service brokerage houses exist. National firms, such as Merrill Lynch, Smith Barney Shearson, Dean Witter, Prudential Securities and PaineWebber, are commonly known as *wirehouses.* Their research analysts track almost every stock imaginable, and their brokers are equipped with the latest technology that can call up any research or data on any security instantly and sell the widest array of financial products and services. However, not only do these firms sell products; they also create them. For instance, a Merrill Lynch broker sells Merrill mutual funds, limited partnerships, unit investment trusts (UITs) and new stock and bond issues underwritten by Merrill, as well as products created by independent firms.

The other type of full-service brokerage firm, called a *regional firm,* specializes in a region of the country, and its analysts tend to focus on stocks in that region. Regional brokers may therefore discover local companies with good long-term potential long before the national firms hear about them. While some regional firms create their own products, many of them sell funds, partnerships and UITs sponsored by independent companies that pay commissions. (Therefore, don't expect a regional broker to recommend a no-load fund.) Firms such as A. G. Edwards in St. Louis, BT Alex. Brown in Baltimore, Advest in Hartford, Piper Jaffray in Minneapolis, and Wheat First Butcher Singer in Richmond sell mutual funds from fund companies not affiliated with the wirehouses.

The best broker, whether he or she works for a wirehouse or a regional firm, does his or her own research in addition to screening the research performed by the firm's analysts. Such a broker might follow the progress of local companies with promise, or the broker might specialize in one industry, like oil or health care. A broker who thinks for himself or herself is much more useful than a salesperson who merely parrots back the firm's research, whether the broker agrees with it or not.

BROKERS' SERVICES

Both national and regional full-service firms offer *asset management accounts,* where your stocks, bonds and mutual funds are held. All dividends and interest received are automatically swept into a money-market mutual fund until you decide where to reinvest the money. Most asset management accounts let you write checks, and they offer a credit card. The accounts also allow you to buy securities or borrow for other reasons on margin and to sell short. Your broker will hold all your securities in *street name*—the name of the brokerage firm—making it easy for the brokerage to transfer ownership when you decide to sell. In case the brokerage goes bankrupt, the federal Securities Investor Protection Corporation (SIPC) insures your brokerage account for up to $500,000 in securities and $100,000 in cash. Many firms now impose an annual charge of $50 to $100 for keeping an asset management account, which can be steep if you do not trade actively and use few of the services the account offers. Some firms add another layer of fees to cover the postage and handling incurred whenever you execute a trade.

In addition to the accounts offered by a brokerage firm, you want your broker to be responsive to your questions. Because brokers are paid based on the commissions they generate, you will receive far more attention if you trade actively than if you buy only one or two stocks or mutual funds each year. Don't expect to hold long conversations with your broker about housekeeping details on your account, such as mistakes or questions about your account statement. Usually, the broker employs an assistant to handle such matters. Do, however, expect your broker to call you with investment ideas and to tell you when a stock or fund you own looks vulnerable to decline. A good broker will also admit a mistake and suggest when to cut your losses on a poor investment the broker recommended.

COMMISSIONS AND FEES

In return for advice and service, you must pay retail commissions to national or regional full-service brokers. The less often you trade and the lower your volume of trading, the higher your commissions per share. If you buy just a few shares of a low-priced stock, for example, you might pay a commission of up to $.40 or $.50 a share, or as much as 5 percent of the money you invest. On the other hand, if you buy several hundred shares of a high-priced stock, you may pay as little as $.10 a share, or less than 1 percent of the purchase price. If you become a regular customer, you can demand discounts. Usually, a broker is glad to grant these reductions in order to keep your business.

Brokers also charge some kind of commission on mutual funds, though you may not have to pay it up front. The traditional commission—or *load,* as it is called—is 5 percent off the top. So, for every $100 you invest, $95 goes to the fund. Some brokers, instead of charging up front, take a *back-end load*—a fee you must pay if you sell the fund within the first few years of owning it. For example, a back-end-loaded fund might hit you for a 4 percent fee if you sell it in the first year; 3 percent, in the second; 2 percent, in the third; and 1 percent, in the fourth. Starting in the fifth year, you would incur no sales charge if you sell the fund. Fund companies use this technique because the broker receives his or her commission up front, and the company needs to recover that money from you if you withdraw from the fund before it can recoup the commission through annual management fees.

For individual bonds, brokers usually do not charge an explicit commission. Instead, they buy the bond at one price and sell it to you at a higher price. The difference between the brokers' price and yours is known as the *spread,* and it acts as the commission. As with stocks, the size of the spread is determined by the amount of money you invest. The more bonds you buy, the smaller the spread. For example, if you buy just one bond, you might pay a 5 percent spread; if you purchase ten bonds, you might pay a 1 percent or 2 percent spread.

Other products, such as UITs, limited partnerships, annuities, life insurance, options and new stock and bond issues, all charge different commissions. Usually, the broker keeps between 35 percent and 45 percent of the fee, with the rest going to the brokerage firm. In general, the more complicated a product, the harder it is to sell, and the higher the commission.

In addition to up-front commissions, brokers receive ongoing fees for your continued participation in a product like a mutual fund, a limited partnership or an annuity. Though you don't have to write a check for it, each year, you pay a management fee to the fund, partnership or annuity company, part of which goes to the broker. The fee is automatically deducted from your account balance and may amount to as much as 1 percent of your principal.

In the end, be aware of all these commissions and fees before you buy anything from a broker. Remember, transactions generate fees. In the most blatant cases, brokers will *churn* clients' accounts—meaning that they trade excessively just to generate commissions, not because such transactions are in your best interest. If you don't pay attention to what your broker charges you, you may be vulnerable to paying excess fees, which can take a big bite out of your capital.

The Discount Broker Alternative

One sure way to cut your commission expenses is to work with a discount broker. Unlike full-service brokers, discounters generally do not offer advice about what to buy or sell. They merely execute your orders at much lower fees than full-service firms. Discount firms do not have to maintain a staff of expensive research analysts to provide buy, sell and hold recommendations, and they pass those savings on to you. Some discounters will assign you a regular broker if you trade actively enough. In most firms, though, you will not develop a relationship with an individual broker, as you do in a full-service firm—which may or may not be an advantage. If you choose a winning stock, you take all the credit. However, if you pick a loser, you have no one else to blame.

Three kinds of discount brokers exist: *full service, deep discount* and *electronic.* The three largest full-service discounters—Charles Schwab based in San Francisco, Fidelity Investments in Boston and Quick & Reilly in New York City (owned by Fleet Financial Bank)—offer almost every service that you can get from a national full-service firm like Merrill Lynch—except advice from the firms' analysts. Full-service discount firms offer SIPC insurance, walk-in offices across the country, comprehensive asset management accounts, individual retirement accounts (IRAs), Keogh accounts, computer software and Web sites to execute trades and follow news and stock prices, automatic telephone systems to place orders, and hundreds of mutual funds, many with no or low loads. Full-service discounters also will show you independent research on companies in which you are interested, from sources such as Value Line or Standard & Poor's. All full-service discounters offer elaborate Web sites allowing you to research stocks, bonds, mutual funds, options and other investments, as well as track economic news that will affect your holdings. Some firms will assemble research reports from many sources, showing you, for example, how many analysts from full-commission brokerage houses recommend buying, selling or holding a particular stock and why. However, the discount broker will not make its own recommendation on the stock. In addition, you can call them 24 hours a day, 7 days a week to place orders. Yet the commissions they charge can be anywhere from 20 percent to 60 percent lower than national full-service brokerage house charges, depending on the size of your trades. Most discount brokers will give you a further discount if you trade online instead of speaking to a live broker.

Deep-discount firms charge even less but offer fewer services. Some of these firms—such as Jack White in San Diego, JB Oxford & Co. in Beverly Hills, Brown & Company in Boston, Waterhouse Securities in New York and about 100 others—may execute a trade for as much as 90 percent less than what Merrill Lynch or PaineWebber charges or 50 percent less than what Schwab or Fidelity charges. Deep discounters do not have offices across the country, and they do almost all of their business with customers over the phone. They can buy or sell the full range of securities, including stocks, bonds, options, futures and often mutual funds, in both regular and IRA and Keogh accounts. Several deep discounters also offer stock-price quotes and automatic ordering systems over the telephone. Deep discount firms are designed for active investors who know what they're doing. However, if you just want to sell some stock you inherited from your grandmother, you might as well do it through a deep discounter because you will pay the lowest commission possible.

The third kind of discount broker is totally electronic. These brokers operate through their Web sites and because they have much lower expenses can pass the savings on to their customers in the form of even lower commissions. Firms such as Ameritrade (www.ameritrade.com), Datek Online (www.datek.com), Discover Brokerage Direct (www.discoverbrokerage.com), DLJ Direct (www.DLJdirect.com), E*Trade Securities (www.etrade.com) and Wall Street Electronica (www.wallstreete.com) are designed for knowledgeable traders who like to buy and sell stocks, bonds, options and mutual funds on their own at the lowest price possible. You can open an account online. All of these online brokers offer real-time price quotes, account information, research links and technical support.

Discount brokers use two methods in quoting commissions. *Share brokers* charge on a per-share basis. They might charge a flat $.03 per share, for example, no matter whether you trade 100 or 10,000 shares. *Value brokers* charge according to the value of your trade. The more money involved, the lower your per-share costs. You can calculate in advance whether your commissions will be less with a share or a value broker, depending on whether you trade many shares at a low price or few shares at a high price. Some firms mix the two systems and base commissions on both the number of shares traded and the value of the trade. All discount brokers set a minimum fee per trade, which ranges from $8 to about $40.

When seeking the lowest commissions, call several firms to determine what you will pay to execute a particular trade. (A list of discount brokers appears in the "Resources" section at the end of this chapter.) The most comprehensive survey of discount brokers' fees and services is undertaken annually by Mercer, Inc. (379 W. Broadway, Suite 400, New York, NY 10012; 212-334-6212; 800-582-9854). Mercer found that for several trades averaging about $8,000 each, full-service brokers charged an average of about $179; full-service discounters, $100; and deep discounters, only $18.

Following is a sample of the commissions you would be charged for particular trades at several discount brokers, compared to a standard full-service broker, as described in the Mercer survey and provided as an excerpt with permission of Mercer, Inc. As you can see, the fee varies widely, depending on the number of shares traded, the price per share and the brokerage firm.

Trade: 1,000 shares at $1 a share

> Full-service broker: $142
> Ameritrade: $18
> JB Oxford & Co.: $23
> Wall Street Equities: $24

Trade: 1,000 shares at $5 a share

> Full-service broker: $212
> Tradewell Discount Investing: $27
> Brown & Company: $29
> Regal Investor Services: $29

Trade: 500 shares at $10 a share

> Full-service broker: $223
> Wall Street Equities: $24
> Tradewell Discount Investing: $27
> Pacific Brokerage Services: $29

Trade: 200 shares at $30 a share

> Full-service broker: $149
> Aufhauser & Company: $27
> Brown & Company: $29
> Kennedy, Cabot & Company: $33

Trade: 100 shares at $50 a share

> Full-service broker: $103
> Empire Financial: $28
> Scottsdale Securities: $31
> National Discount Brokers: $33

Trade: 500 shares at $40 a share

> Full-service broker: $382
> Freedom Investments: $28

Regal Investor Services: $29
CompuTEL Securities: $30

Whether you use a full-service, discount or electronic broker, finding a firm that offers good advice and reliable service will make your financial affairs much easier to manage. In fact, many people maintain accounts at both full-service and discount brokerages. They execute investment recommendations from their full-service broker at his or her firm and buy or sell stocks that they hear about independently at the discounter. With all the sophisticated services offered by brokers today, you have no reason to go it alone in the investment world.

Resources

Books

Investors Beware! How To Protect Your Money from Wall Street's Dirty Tricks, by John Lawrence Allen (John Wiley & Sons Inc., 1 Wiley Dr., Somerset, NJ 08875; 800-225-5945; www.wiley.com). Discusses how to protect yourself against bad financial advice from brokers, explains how brokerage houses work and gives warning signs of fraudulent brokers.

Martindale-Hubbell Law Directory (Martindale-Hubbell, 630 Central Ave., New Providence, NJ 07974; 908-464-6800; 800-526-4902; www.martindalehubbell.com). A complete listing of U.S. and international lawyers by state and specialty.

The Prudent Investor: The Definitive Guide to Professional Investment Management, by James P. Owen (McGraw-Hill, Shoppenhangers Rd., Maidenhead, Berkshire, FL6 2QL England; 441-628-23432 or 800-722-4726; www.mcgraw-hill.com.uk). Guides you in hiring someone to manage your investments.

Using a Lawyer . . . What To Do if Things Go Wrong, by Kay Ostberg (HALT, 1612 K St., N.W., Suite 510, Washington, DC 20006; 202-887-8255; www.halt.org). A complete guide to shopping for and working with a lawyer. Provides sample fee agreements and a state-by-state list of lawyer grievance committees.

Trade Associations

Accreditation Council for Accountancy and Taxation (ACAT, 1010 N. Fairfax St., Alexandria, VA 22314; 703-549-6400; 800-966-6679; www.acatcredential.org). Accredits specialists in accounting and taxation who serve the financial needs of individuals and small businesses. ACAT also oversees the examinations and standards for Accredited Tax Preparers and Accredited Tax Advisors. The organization will send you a free directory of their members.

American Arbitration Association (335 Madison Ave., 10th Floor, New York, NY 10013; 212-484-4000; 800-778-7879; www.adr.org). Will supply you with an arbitrator if you need to settle a dispute with a financial adviser. Has branches in most states. Offers the following free brochures: "Commercial Arbitration Rules"; "Commercial Mediation Rules"; "Facts about the American Arbitration Association"; "Resolving Your Disputes"; and "Securities Arbitration Rules."

American Bar Association (750 N. Lake Shore Dr., Chicago, IL 60611; 312-988-5000; www.abanet.org). The main trade association for U.S. lawyers. Offers the following publications: *The American Lawyer: When and How To Use One; Dealing with Debt: Your Guide to Bankruptcy and Other Options; Getting and Keeping Credit: Your Guide to Credit Cards and Credit Records; Guide to Consumer Law: Buying, Selling, Contracts and Guarantees; Guide to Family Law; Guide to Home Ownership; Guide to Wills and Estates; Guide to Workplace Law; Landlords & Tenants: Your Guide to the Law; Handbook on Courtroom Procedures; Law and the Courts; Legal Guide for Older Americans: The Law Every American Over 50 Needs to Know;* and *A Life in the Law.* Also offers a massive but simply written book covering all aspects of the law titled *Family Legal Guide.*

American Institute of Certified Public Accountants (1211 Avenue of the Americas, New York, NY 10036-8775; 212-596-6200; 800-862-4272; www.aicpa.org). Represents and maintains standards for CPAs. Can help you find a tax-oriented accountant or an accountant who provides financial planning services. Also licenses Personal Financial Specialists (PFS), who are accountants concentrating on financial planning. For a list of PFS members nationally, call 888-999-9256. Will send a free copy of the following brochures: "Do I Need Personal Financial Planning?"; "Find Out What You're Worth with Your Own Personal Financial Statement"; "Getting Started Financially"; "Guide To Finding a Personal Financial Planner"; "How To Choose and Use a CPA"; "Invest in Your Future: Choose a Personal Financial Specialist"; "Keeping Financial Records"; "Planning for the Future: Your Social Security Benefits"; "Retirement Planning: Achieving Financial Security for Your Future"; "Saving for College: Easing the Financial Burden"; and "Understanding and Using CPA Services."

American Society of CLU & ChFC (270 S. Bryn Mawr Ave., Bryn Mawr, PA 19010-2195; 610-526-2500; 888-243-2258; www.asclu.org). The association of insurance and financial services professionals holding the Chartered Life Underwriters (CLU) and Chartered Financial Consultants (ChFC) designations. Will refer you to an insurance agent or a financial consultant in your area. Will also send a free copy of "How To Select a Qualified Financial Consultant" and "Financial Planning for a New Millenium."

Association for Investment Management and Research (5 Boar's Head Lane, P.O. Box 3668, Charlottesville, VA 22903; 804-980-3668; 800-247-8132; www.aimr.org). Confers the Chartered Financial Analyst (CFA) designation on those who have passed a series of examinations relating to investment management. The CFA course teaches investment valuation and management, asset valuation and portfolio management. To receive a CFA, you must have graduated from college, abide by a strict code of ethics and have a minimum of three years of work experience in the investment field. CFAs tend to be portfolio managers for institutions, like mutual funds, insurance companies and high-net-worth individuals, and industry analysts at brokerage firms. The Association offers a free investor fact sheet titled "Selecting an Investment Adviser," and a brochure titled "Chartered Financial Analyst," which describes the qualifications for a CFA charterholder.

Certified Financial Planner Board of Standards (1700 Broadway, Suite 2100, Denver, CO 80290; 303-830-7500; 888-237-6275; www.cfp-board.org). Administers CFP examinations and licenses individuals to use the CFP designation. Planners using the CFP designation must maintain certain standards of conduct and meet continuing education requirements. You can contact the CFP Board to check if a planner is certified, if they have been disciplined by the Board, or to lodge a complaint. For referrals to financial planners in your area, contact the International Association for Financial Planning or the Institute of Certified Financial Planners.

Chartered Property Casualty Underwriters (CPCU) Society (720 Providence Rd., Malvern, PA 19355-0709; 610-644-2100; 800-932-2728; www.cpcusociety.org). The Society is a professional association for agents selling property and casualty insurance and risk management services. The American Institute for CPCU develops the program that confers the CPCU designation for members. Those who have earned the CPCU must follow a code of ethics and meet continuing education requirements. The Society publishes several newsletters about developments in the property-casualty field, including *CPCU Journal* and *CPCU News.* The Society will send you a directory of qualified property-casualty insurance experts in your area. The Society's Web site also contains an agent/broker locator section that allows consumers to find a CPCU professional by specialty or geographic location.

Consumer Federation of America (1424 16th St., N.W., Suite 604, Washington, DC 20036; 202-387-6121). Consumer-oriented group has done several studies on the financial advice industry. They offer such publications as "How Big a Problem is the Financial Planner 'Name Game'" and "Investment Adviser Regulation: Deficient Oversight."

Council of Better Business Bureaus (4200 Wilson Blvd., Suite 800, Arlington, VA 22203-1838; 703-276-0100; www.bbb.org). An excellent source of information about many consumer matters, including choosing a financial adviser. Offers the following publications: *How To Be an Informed Investor: Protect Your Money from Schemes, Scams and Frauds; Tips on Financial Planners;* and *Tips on Tax Preparers.* The BBB also has an extensive list of publications on almost every area of concern to consumers. Their publication list is available on their Web site and is divided into these categories: Advertising Issues; Alternative Dispute Resolution; Automobile; Business and Professional Services; Charity and Philanthropy; Computer and Online Services; Consumer and Business Alerts; Consumer Goods and Services; Family; Health, Beauty and Fitness; Home; Marketplace Ethics; Money and Investments; Telemarketing; and Travel.

The Institute of Certified Financial Planners (3801 E. Florida Ave., Suite 708, Denver, CO 80210; 303-759-4900; 800-282-7526; www.icfp.org). Represents financial planners who have passed the CFP examination. Will refer you to three planners in your area. Publishes a magazine titled *The Journal of Financial Planning*. Will also send free copies of the following: "The CFP Professional"; "Q and A About Financial Planning"; and "Selecting a Qualified Financial Planning Professional: Twelve Questions To Consider." On the Institute's Web site is a publication titled "Your Children's College Bill: How To Figure It . . . How To Pay for It."

Institute of Business and Finance (7911 Herschel Ave., Suite 201, La Jolla, CA 92037-4413; 800-848-2029; 619-454-4073; www.icfs.com/icfs). Organization granting the Certified Fund Specialist (CFS) designation. The Institute sponsors a 60-hour self-study course about mutual funds, including modern portfolio theory, how to select mutual funds, dollar cost averaging and staying invested, withdrawing funds and picking annuities. CFS designees also are required to take continuing education courses every year. Certified Fund Specialists are skilled at helping you assemble a mutual fund portfolio that is appropriate for your needs. The Institute also sponsors several other board-certified designations in other areas of personal finance, including a BCE for estate planning, a BCS for securities, a BCI for insurance, a BCT for income taxes, a BCM for mutual funds and a BCF for financial planning.

International Association for Financial Planning (IAFP, 5775 Glenridge Dr., N.E., Suite B-300, Atlanta, GA 30328-5364; 800-945-IAFP; www.iafp.org). Represents financial planners and financial services companies offering products and services to financial planners. Will refer you to member planners in your area. Will also send a free copy of their brochure "Consumer Guide to Comprehensive Financial Planning" and the Financial Adviser Disclosure Form. You also can ask for references of financial planners from the International Association for Financial Planning's Adviser Referral Program at 888-806-7526 or at their Web site. The IAFP will send you two brochures explaining the financial planning process and how to select a financial adviser, an interview sheet to guide you through the selection process, and detailed background information on five advisers that will match the criteria you specify.

Investment Counsel Association of America (1050 17th St., Suite 725, Washington, DC 20036; 202-293-4222; www.icaa.org). Professional organization of independent investment counsel firms that manage the assets of individuals, pension plans, trusts and nonprofit institutions, such as foundations. Offers a free membership directory for those looking for an investment counselor.

Investment Management Consultants Association (9101 E. Kenyon Ave., Suite 3000, Denver, CO 80237-8015; 303-770-3377; www.imca.org). The professional group for consultants who find and monitor the performance of money managers on behalf of individual and institutional investors. Will send a free list of certified investment management analysts in your area. Offers the following publications for a nominal charge: "The Consultant's Performance Standards"; "Investment Policy and the Asset Allocation Process"; "Manager Search and Selection"; "Performance Measurement and Evaluation"; and "Why an Investment Management Consultant?"

Life and Health Insurance Foundation for Education (1922 F St., N.W., Washington, DC 20006-4387; 202-331-2170; 888-543-3777; www.life-line.org). A not-for-profit education foundation committed to better educating the public about life, health and disability insurance, and the value-added role of the agent. Offers a free brochure called "Why Life? Because You Care."

National Association of Enrolled Agents (200 Orchard Ridge Dr., Suite 302, Gaithersburg, MD 20878; 301-212-9608; 800-424-4339; www.naea.org). A group of enrolled agents—former IRS employees who offer tax advice and preparation services. Will send names of four enrolled agents in your area.

National Association of Life Underwriters (NALU, 1922 F St., N.W., Washington, DC 20006-4387; 202-331-6000; www.agents-online.org). The trade association of health and life insurance agents and brokers. Educates the public about insurance and how to work with insurance agents and brokers. Offers the following free publications when you call 202-331-6086: "Annuities: Building Your Retirement Nest Egg"; "Life Insurance: Choosing Your Best Buy"; "Long Term Care Insurance: Is It in Your Future?"; and "Medigap Insurance: Supplementing Your Medicare Coverage."

National Association of Personal Financial Advisors (NAPFA, 355 W. Dundee Rd., Suite 200, Buffalo Grove, IL 60089; 847-537-7722; 800-366-2732; www.napfa. org). Represents financial planners who work for fees only and collect no commissions from the sale of products. Will refer you to fee-only planners in your state. Will also send free brochures titled "Financial Planner Interview: How To Choose a Financial Planner"; and "Why Select a Fee-Only Financial Advisor."

National Association of REALTORS® (NAR, 430 N. Michigan Ave., Chicago, IL 60611; 312-329-8200; 800-874-6500; www.realtor.com). The trade group for real estate agents. Can help you find a qualified real estate broker or agent in your area. Offers the following consumer-oriented publications for a small fee: *Buying a Home? Working with a REALTOR®; If You Are Thinking Investment, Think Real Estate; Selling or Buying a Home . . . It Pays To Work with a REALTOR®; Selling Your Home? Work with a REALTOR®; Sixteen Essentials for Greater Profits; Speed the Sale of Your Home; Sell It for Every Dollar It's Worth!;* and *Your American Dream Home: The Complete Guide To Buying or Selling Your Home.* The NAR Web site features an extensive bookstore listing books on real estate arranged by subject. Some of the subjects covered include: mortgages, real estate study guides, general real estate books, home inspections, home appraisals, home improvement and real estate dictionaries. The NAR Web site also helps consumers find a home, locate a REALTOR®, access mortgage information, use a movers toolkit and browse in a real estate library.

National Fraud Exchange (12020 Sunrise Valley Dr., Suite 360, Reston, VA 20191; 703-620-6262; 800-894-2031). Provides a comprehensive background check on financial professionals. NAFEX is a national database containing information on individuals and companies that are or have been subject to certain criminal, civil or administrative actions in the real estate, banking, securities, commodities and financial service industries. The records in NAFEX are obtained directly from a wide range of sources, including federal and state government agencies, stock exchanges, self-regulatory agencies and others. You can use NAFEX for due diligence or background checks when making any type of business or investment decision.

National Institute of Dispute Resolution (1726 M St., N.W., Suite 500, Washington, DC 20036; 202-466-4764; www.nidr.org). A research and information center specializing in alternative dispute resolution techniques. Publishes a directory of organizations in the field. Also publishes the "Conflict Educational Catalog" aimed at schools and "Spectrum on Adult Mediation" aimed at adults.

North American Securities Administrators Association (10 G St., N.E., Suite 710, Washington, DC 20002; 202-737-0900; 888-846-2722; www.nasaa.org). Represents state securities enforcement agencies. Responsible for investor protection. Can help you check out a stockbroker's work record. Offers several free pamphlets on avoiding scams, including blind pool offerings, dirt pile gold swindles, penny stock fraud and unsuitable investments. Also offers a book titled *How to be an Informed Investor: Protect Your Money from Schemes, Scams and Frauds.* NASAA has released a ten-point investor bill of rights to help investors guard against becoming a victim of securities fraud and abuse. NASAA's Web site is packed with information about frauds and schemes. It is organized into these categories: Affinity Fraud; Blind Pool Investment Offerings; Bogus "IRA Approved" Investment Schemes; Bulletin for Older Investors; Cold Calling Alert; Commodity Investments; Cyberspace Fraud and the Small Investor; "Field of Schemes"; Get-Rich-Quick Self-Employment Scams; How Older Americans Can Avoid Investment Fraud and Abuse; How To Protect Your Money From Theft by Dishonest Investment Advisers; How To Spot a Con Artist; How To Spot and Avoid "Boiler Room" Scams; "Information Superhighway" Scams; International Investment Fraud; Investment Basics: Prodigy Q+A; Investor Bill of Rights; Mutual Funds; Phone Hucksters Target Investors in Stock; Questions for Informed Investors; Who's Who in the Financial Planner and Investment Adviser Field.

Society of Professionals in Dispute Resolution (1621 Connecticut Ave., N.W., Suite 400, Washington, DC 20009; 202-783-7277; www.spidr.org). A group of people interested in alternative dispute resolution techniques, such as mediation and arbitration, which avoid expensive lawsuits.

FEDERAL GOVERNMENT REGULATOR

Federal Trade Commission (6th St. and Pennsylvania Ave. N.W., Washington, DC 20580; 202-326-2222; 202-326-3128 [consumer response center]; www.ftc.gov). Offers many helpful brochures, including "Facts about Financial Planners" and "How to Talk to and Select Lawyers, Financial Planners, Tax Preparers and Real Estate Brokers." The FTC's Web site features ConsumerLine, which is a service of the Office of Consumer and Business Education of the Bureau of Consumer Protection. It lists FTC publications, Consumer Alerts, Education Campaigns, the Consumer's Resource Handbook and allows you to lodge fraud complaints.

DISCOUNT BROKERAGE FIRMS

The following list of discount brokers is presented courtesy of Mercer, Inc. (379 W. Broadway, Suite 400, New York, NY 10012; 212-334-6212; 800-582-9854). Mercer conducts an annual comprehensive survey of commissions charged by and services offered by all discount brokerage firms. This survey is for sale to the public.

Accutrade Inc. (4211 S. 102nd St., Omaha, NE 68127; 402-330-7605; 800-228-3011; www.accutrade.com)

The Advisors Group Corp. (51 Louisiana Ave., N.W., Washington, DC 20001; 202-783-0759; 800-777-1500 [national])

American Express Financial Direct (733 Marquette Ave., Minneapolis, MN 55402; 612-671-9055; 800-658-4677; www.americanexpress.com/direct/)

Ameritrade (4211 S. 102 St., Omaha, NE 68127; 402-331-2744; 800-454-9272; www.ameritrade.com)

Andrew Peck Associates (111 Pavonia Ave., Jersey City, NJ 07310; 201-217-9500; 800-221-5873; www.thehost.com//peck/)

Arnold Securities, Inc. (830 2nd Ave. S., Minneapolis, MN 55402; 612-339-7040; 800-292-4135 [Minnesota]; 800-328-4076 [national])

Aufhauser & Company (53 Wall St., 5th Floor, New York, NY 10005-2887; 800-368-3668; www.aufhauser.com)

Baker & Company (1940 E. 6th St., Cleveland, OH 44114; 216-696-0167; 800-362-2008 [Ohio]; 800-321-1640 [national]; www.bakernyse.com)

Barry Murphy & Company, Inc. (77 Summer St., Boston, MA 02110; 617-426-1770; 800-221-2111)

Berlind Securities (1 N. Broadway, White Plains, NY 10601; 914-761-6665)

Bidwell & Company (209 S.W. Oak St., Portland, OR 97204; 503-790-9000; 800-547-6337; www.bidwell.com)

Brown & Company (20 Winthrop Square, Boston, MA 02110-1236; 617-426-8241; 800-225-6707; www.brownco.com)

Bruno, Stolze & Company (Manchester/270 Office Center, 12444 Powerscourt Dr., Suite 230, St. Louis, MO 63131-3660; 314-821-1990; 800-899-6878)

Bull & Bear Securities Inc. (11 Hanover Square, New York, NY 10005; 212-742-1300; 800-262-5800; www.bullbear.com)

Burke, Christensen & Lewis (303 W. Madison St., Chicago, IL 60606; 800-621-0392; www.bclnet.com)

Charles Schwab (101 Montgomery St., San Francisco, CA 94104; 415-627-7000; 212-938-0407; 800-435-4000; www.schwab.com)

CompuTEL Securities, a division of Thomas F. White & Co. (1 Second St., 5th Floor, San Francisco, CA 94105; 800-432-0327; www.rapidtrade.com)

Consolidated Financial Investments, Inc. (287 N. Lindbergh, Suite 201, St. Louis, MO 63141; 314-991-4030; 800-292-6637)

Cutter & Company Brokerage, Inc. (130 E. Jefferson, 2nd Floor, Kirkwood, MO 63122; 314-965-6337; 800-218-4625; www.stocktrader.com)

Datek Online (100 Wood Ave. S., Iselin, NJ 08830-2716; 732-744-2835; 888-463-2835; www.datek.com)

Discover Brokerage Direct (333 Market St., 25th Floor, San Francisco, CA 94105; 415-597-6829; 800-688-6896 [national]; 800-688-3462 [California]; www.discover brokerage.com)

DLJDirect (One Pershing Plaza, Jersey City, NJ 07399; 201-413-2771; 800-825-5723; www.DLJdirect.com)

Downstate Discount Brokers (259 Indian Rocks Rd. North, Belleair Bluffs, FL 34640; 813-586-3541; 800-780-3543)

E*Trade Securities, Inc. (4 Embarcadero Place, 2400 Geng Rd., Palo Alto, CA 94303; 800-786-2575; www.etrade.com)

Empire Financial (220 Crown Oak Centre, Longwood, FL 32779; 407-260-0084; 800-900-8101; www.lowfees.com)

Fidelity Investments (161 Devonshire St., Boston, MA 02110; 617-737-6075; 800-544-8666; www.fidelity.com)

First Union Brokerage Services (301 S. College St., 5th Floor, Charlotte, NC 28288-1167; 704-383-0915; 800-326-4434; www.firstunion.com)

Fleet Brokerage Securities (67 Wall St., 9th Floor, New York, NY 10005; 212-806-2888; 800-221-8210; www.fleet.com)

Freedom Investments (555 Madison Ave., New York, NY 10022; 212-248-1818; 800-221-1660 [national]; 800-427-9503 [New York State]; www.tradeflash.com)

Freeman Welwood & Company (1501 Fourth Ave. Suite 1700, Seattle, WA 98101; 206-382-5353; 800-729-7585)

Investors National Corporation (1300 N. State St., Bellingham, WA 98225; 360-734-1266; 800-728-1266; www.saturna.com)

Jack White & Company (91919 Town Centre Dr., Suite 220, San Diego, CA 92122; 619-587-2000; 800-233-3411; http://pawws.com.jwc)

JB Oxford & Company (665 Wilshire Blvd., 3rd Floor, Beverly Hills, CA 90212; 310-275-7745; 800-500-5007; www.jboxford.com)

J.D. Siebert & Company, Inc. (20 W. 9th St., Cincinnati, OH 45202; 513-241-8888; 800-247-3396 [National]; 800-224-9100 [State])

John Finn & Company, Inc. (205 Dixie Terminal Building, Cincinnati, OH 45202; 513-579-0066; 800-743-7059)

Kashner Davidson Securities Corporation (77 S. Palm Ave., Sarasota, FL 34236; 941-951-2626; 800-678-2626)

Kennedy Cabot & Company, Inc. (9470 Wilshire Blvd., Beverly Hills, CA 90212; 310-550-0711; 800-252-2045 [California]; 800-252-0090 [national])

Levitt & Levitt (135 S. LaSalle St., Suite 1945, Chicago, IL 60603-4303; 312-263-8500; 800-671-8505; www.levitt-levitt.com)

Marquette de Bary Company, Inc. (477 Madison Ave., New York, NY 10022; 212-644-5300; 800-221-3305; www.debary.com)

Marsh Block & Company (50 Broad St., New York, NY 10004; 212-292-7000; 800-729-9099)

Max Ule (26 Broadway, Suite 200, New York, NY 10004; 212-809-1160; 800-223-6642; www.maxule.com)

Midwest Discount Brokers, Inc. (5945 Mission Gorge Rd., San Diego, CA 92160; 619-562-1131; www.mdbi.com)

Mongerson & Company (135 S. LaSalle St., Suite 2145, Chicago, IL 60603; 312-263-3100; 800-621-2627)

Muriel Siebert & Company (885 Third Ave., 17th Floor, New York, NY 10022-4802; 212-644-2400; 800-872-0711; www.siebert.com)

National Discount Brokers (7 Hanover Square, 4th Floor, New York, NY 10004; 212-248-2310; 800-888-3999; www.nbd.com)

Olde Discount Stockbrokers (751 Griswold St., Detroit, MI 48226; 313-961-6666; 800-823-5400; www.olde.com)

Pacific Brokerage Services, Inc. (5757 Wilshire Blvd., Suite 3, Los Angeles, CA 90036; 213-939-1101; 800-421-8395; www.tradepbs.com)

Peremel & Company, Inc. (Woodhome Business Center, 1829 Reisterstown Rd., Suite 120, Baltimore, MD 21208; 410-486-4700; 800-666-1440)

Prestige Status, Inc. (271-603 Grand Central Pkwy., Floral Park, NY 11005; 718-229-4500; 800-782-8871)

Principal Financial Securities (2 N. LaSalle St., Chicago, IL 60602-3702; 312-444-2110; 800-621-4480 [national]; 800-642-3105 [Illinois])

PT Discount Brokerage (11 S. LaSalle St., 15th Floor, Chicago, IL 60603; 800-248-5008; www.ptdiscount.com)

Quick & Reilly, Inc. (26 Broadway, 11th Floor, New York, NY 10004; 212-747-1200; 800-672-7220 [national]; www.quick-reilly.com)

Recom Securities, Inc. (619 Marquette Ave., Minneapolis, MN 55402; 612-339-5566; 800-328-8600)

R.F. Lafferty & Company (50 Broad St., New York, NY 10004; 212-293-9000; 800-488-0090)

Regal Discount Securities (209 W. Jackson Blvd., 4th Floor, Chicago, IL 60606; 312-554-2240; 800-786-9000; www.regaldiscount.com)

Rodecker & Company (4000 Town Center, Southfield, MI 48075; 810-358-2282; 800-676-1848)

R.J. Forbes Group (150 Broad Hollow Rd., Melville, NY 11747; 516-549-7000; 800-488-0090; www.rjforbes.com)

Russo Securities (128 Sand Ln., Staten Island, NY 10305; 718-448-2900; 800-451-7877)

Savoy Discount Brokerage (823 3rd Ave., Suite 206, Seattle, WA 98104-1617; 800-961-1500; www.savoystocks.com)

S.C. Costa Company, Inc. (320 S. Boston Ave., W. Lobby, Tulsa, OK 74103; 918-481-7090)

Scottsdale Securities, Inc. (12855 Flushing Meadow Dr., St. Louis, MO 63131-0759; 314-965-1555; 800-619-7283; www.discountbroker.com)

Seaport Securities Corporation (19 Rector St., 32nd Floor, New York, NY 10006; 212-482-8689; 800-732-7678)

Shearman Ralston, Inc. (17 Battery Pl., Suite 604, New York, NY 10004; 212-248-1160; 800-221-4242)

Shochet Securities, Inc, (2351 Hallandale Beach Blvd., Hallandale, FL 33009; 954-454-0304; 800-940-4567 [Florida]); 800-327-1536 [national]

Spectrum Securities, Inc. (21800 Burbank Blvd., Suite 100, Woodland Hills, CA 91367; 818-715-1776; 800-400-1776)

State Discount Brokers, Inc. (27600 Chagrin Blvd., Cleveland, OH 44122; 216-765-8500; 800-222-5520; www.state-discount.com)

St. Louis Discount Securities, Inc. (200 S. Hanley, Lobby Suite 103, Clayton, MO 63105; 314-721-7400; 800-726-7401; 800-421-6563 [Missouri])

Sterling Investment Securities (135 S. LaSalle St., Suite 2100, Chicago, IL 60603; 312-236-0676; 800-782-1522)

StockCross (One Washington Mall, Boston, MA 02108; 617-367-5700; 800-392-6104 [Massachusetts]; 800-225-6196 [national])

Stock Mart (12655 Beatrice St., Los Angeles, CA 90066; 310-577-7460; 800-421-6563)

Summit Discount Brokerage (305 Route 17 S., Paramus, NJ 07652; 201-262-8400; 800-631-1635)

Sunlogic Securities, Inc. (5333 Thornton Ave., Newark, CA 94560; 800-556-4600; www.sunlogic.com)

T. Rowe Price Discount Brokerage, Inc. (100 E. Pratt St., Baltimore, MD 21202; 410-547-2308; 800-225-7720; www.troweprice.com)

Tradewell Discount Investing (25 Broadway, 7th Floor, New York, NY 10004; 212-514-4000; 800-289-7355; www.tradewell.com)

Tradex Brokerage Service, Inc. (20 Vesey St., Suite 800, New York, NY 10007; 212-233-2000; 800-522-3000)

Tuttle Securities Corporation (307 S. Townsend St., Syracuse, NY 13202; 315-422-2515; 800-962-5489)

USAA Brokerage Services (9800 Fredericksburg Rd., San Antonio, TX; 210-456-7215; 800-531-8343)

The Vanguard Group (Vanguard Financial Center, Valley Forge, PA 19482; 800-992-8327; www.vanguard.com)

Voss & Company (6225 Brandon Ave., Suite 120, Springfield, VA 22150; 703-569-9300; 800-426-8106)

W.J. Gallagher & Company (2920 Garfield, Suite 303, Missoula, MT 59801; 406-721-1777; 800-935-6633)

Wall Street Access (17 Battery Pl., New York, NY 10004; 212-709-9518; 800-925-5781; www.wsaccess.com)

Wall Street Discount Corporation (100 Wall St., New York, NY 10005; 212-747-5100; 800-221-7990; www.wsdc.com)

Wall Street Equities (40 Exchange Pl., New York, NY 10005; 212-425-4768; 800-447-8625 [national]; 800-499-9144 [New York State])

Wall Street Electronica (247 E. 28th St., Suite 11A, New York, NY 10016; 212-213-8743; 800-925-5783; www.wallstreete.com)

Washington Discount Brokerage (100 Wall St., New York, NY 10005; 212-425-0228; 800-843-9601)

Waterhouse Securities (100 Wall St., New York, NY 10005; 212-344-7500; 800-934-4430 [brokerage]; www.waterhouse.com)

Wilshire Capital Management (120 Broadway, Suite 960, New York, NY 10271; 212-433-6490; 800-926-9991; www.wilshirecm.com)

Wisconsin Discount Securities Corporation (7161 N. Port Washington Rd., Milwaukee, WI 53217; 414-352-5050; 800-537-0239)

York Securities, Inc. (160 Broadway, East Building, 7th Floor, New York, NY 10038; 212-349-9700; 800-221-3154)

Young, Stovall and Company (9627 S. Dixie Hwy., Suite 101, Miami, FL 33156; 305-666-2511; 800-433-5132)

Your Discount Broker (855 S. Federal Hwy., Miami, FL 33156; 305-666-2511; 800-433-5132)

Ziegler Thrift Trading, Inc. (733 Marquette Ave., Suite 106, Minneapolis, MN 55402-2340; 612-333-4206; www.ziegler-thrift.com)

FULL-SERVICE BROKERAGE FIRMS

The following is a list of the largest full-service brokerage firms in the United States. Brokers affiliated with these firms will give you investment advice, whereas discount brokers merely execute trades. In return for the advice, you pay higher commission rates. This list includes both national wirehouse firms and firms specializing in regional stocks.

Adams, Harkness & Hill, Inc. (Sixty State St., Suite 1200, Boston, MA 02109-1803; 617-371-3900)

Advest Group, Inc. (90 State House Square, Hartford, CT 06103; 203-509-1000; 800-243-8115 [Connecticut])

Allmerica Investments, Inc. (440 Lincoln St., Worcester, MA 01653; 800-818-1844)

Ameritas Investment Corp. (5900 O St., 4th Floor, Lincoln, NE 68510; 402-466-4565)

Anderson & Strudwick, Inc. (1108 E. Main St., Richmond, VA 23219; 804-643-2400)

Arnhold and S. Bleichroeder, Inc. (1345 Avenue of the Americas, New York, NY 10105-4300; 212-698-3000)

Arthurs, Lestrange & Company Incorporated (Two Gateway Center, Pittsburgh, PA 15222; 412-566-6800; 800-800-7079)

Robert W. Baird & Company, Inc. (777 E. Wisconsin Ave., Milwaukee, WI 53202; 414-765-3500; 800-792-2473)

Banc One Securities Corporation (733 Greencrest Dr., Westerville, OH 43081; 614-248-5119; 800-274-5115)

George K. Baum & Company (Twelve Wyandotte Plaza, 120 W. 12th St., Kansas City, MO 64105; 816-474-1100)

The Bear Stearns Companies, Inc. (245 Park Ave., New York, NY 10167; 212-272-2000)

Sanford C. Bernstein & Company, Inc. (767 5th Ave., New York, NY 10153; 212-486-5800)

Berthel, Fisher & Company Financial Services, Inc. (100 2nd St. SE, Cedar Rapids, IA 52401; 319-365-2506; 800-356-5234)

William Blair & Company LLC (222 W. Adams St., Chicago, IL 60606; 312-236-1600)

Boenning & Scattergood, Inc. (Four Falls Corporate Center, Suite 212, West Conshohocken, PA 19428; 610-832-1212)

J.C. Bradford & Co. LLC (330 Commerce St., Nashville, TN 37201; 615-748-9000)

Branch, Cabell & Co. (919 E. Main St., Suite 1700, Richmond, VA 23219; 804-225-1400; 800-627-2624)

Brean Murray & Co., Inc. (570 Lexington Ave., New York, NY 10022; 212-702-6500)

BT Alex. Brown Inc. (One Bankers Trust Plaza, New York, NY 10167; 212-250-2500)

Butler, Wick & Company Inc. (City Centre One, Suite 700, Youngstown, OH 44503; 330-744-4351)

Calvert Distributors, Inc. (4550 Montgomery Ave., Suite 1000N, Bethesda, MD 20814; 301-951-4800)

Carty & Company (6263 Poplar Ave., Suite 800, Memphis, TN 38119; 901-767-8940)

CIBC Wood Gundy Securities Corp. (425 Lexington Ave., New York, NY; 212-856-4000)

Citicorp Investment Services (One Court Square, 24th Floor, Long Island City, NY 11120; 212-559-1000)

Citicorp Securities, Inc. (399 Park Ave., 2nd Floor, New York, NY 10043; 212-559-1000)

Cowen & Company (Financial Square, New York, NY 10005; 212-495-6000)

Credit Suisse First Boston (11 Madison Ave., New York, NY 10010-3629; 212-325-2000)

Crowell, Weedon & Co. (One Wilshire Blvd., Los Angeles, CA 90017; 213-620-1850)

Cruttenden Roth Inc. (18301 Von Karman, Suite 100, Irvine, CA 92612; 714-757-5700)

Daiwa Securities America Inc. (32 Old Slip, One Financial Square, New York, NY 10005; 212-612-7000)

Dakin Securities Corporation (505 Sansome St., 8th Floor, San Francisco, CA 94111; 415-981-2114)

Davenport & Company LLC (901 E. Cary St., 11th Floor, Richmond, VA 23219; 804-780-2000)

D.A. Davidson & Company, Inc. (Davidson Building, 8 3rd St., North, Great Falls, MT 59401; 406-727-4200)

Dean Witter Reynolds Inc. (Two World Trade Center, New York, NY 10048; 212-392-2222)

Deutsche Morgan Grenfell/C.J. Lawrence Inc. (31 W. 52nd St., New York, NY 10019; 212-469-5000)

Dominick & Dominick, Inc. (Financial Square, 32 Old Slip, 34th Floor, New York, NY 10005; 212-558-8800)

Donaldson, Lufkin & Jenrette, Inc. (277 Park Ave., New York, NY 10172; 212-892-3000)

A.G. Edwards & Sons, Inc. (1 N. Jefferson, St. Louis, MO 63103; 314-955-3000)

Equitable Securities Corporation (800 Nashville City Center, 511 Union St., Nashville, TN 37219-1743; 615-780-9300)

Fahnestock & Company, Inc. (110 Wall St., New York, NY 10005; 212-668-8000)

Ferris, Baker Watts, Inc. (1720 Eye St., N.W., Washington, DC 20006; 202-429-3500)

Financial Network Investment Corporation (2780 Skypark Dr., Suite 300, Torrance, CA 90505; 310-326-3100)

First Albany Corporation (30 S. Pearl St., Albany, NY 12207; 518-447-8500)

First Equity Corporation of Florida (1400 Miami Center, 201 S. Biscayne Blvd., Miami, FL 33131; 305-379-0731)

First Investors Corporation (95 Wall St., New York, NY 10005; 212-858-8000)

First Manhattan Company (437 Madison Ave., New York, NY 10022; 212-756-3300)

First Marathon Inc. (2 First Canadian Pl., Suite 3200, Toronto, Ontario M5X 1J9 Canada; 416-869-3707)

First Union Brokerage Services, Inc. (201 S. College St., 4th Floor, Charlotte, NC 28288-1167; 704-374-6927; 800-326-4434)

Folger Nolan Fleming Douglas, Inc. (725 15th St., N.W., Washington, DC 20005; 202-783-5252)

Furman Selz LLC (230 Park Ave., New York, NY 10169; 212-309-8200)

GKN Securities Corporation (61 Broadway, 12th Floor, New York, NY 10006; 212-509-3800)

The Goldman Sachs Group, LP (85 Broad St., New York, NY 10004; 212-902-1000)

Greenwich Capital Markets, Inc. (600 Steamboat Rd., Greenwich, CT 06830; 203-625-2700)

Gruntal Financial LLC (14 Wall St., New York, NY 10005; 212-267-8800)

Hambrecht & Quist LLC (One Bush St., San Francisco, CA 94104; 415-439-3000)

Harris-Nesbitt Thomson Securities Inc. (115 S. LaSalle St., 20th Floor, Chicago, IL 60603; 312-461-6220)

Hazlett, Burt & Watson, Inc. (1300 Chapline St., Wheeling, WV 26003; 304-233-3312)

Hefren-Tillotson, Inc. (308 7th Ave., Pittsburgh, PA 15222; 412-434-0990)

Heidtke & Company, Inc. (SunTrust Bank Building, 19th Floor, 201 4th Ave. N., Nashville, TN 37219; 615-254-1603)

Herzog Heine Geduld, Inc. (26 Broadway, Suite 200, 2nd Floor, New York, NY 10004; 212-908-4000)

Hibernia Investment Securities, Inc. (313 Carondelet, 6th Floor, New Orleans, LA 70130; 504-533-5259)

J.J.B. Hilliard, W.L. Lyons, Inc. (Hilliard Lyons Center, 501 S. 4th Ave., Louisville, KY 40232-2760; 502-588-8400)

William R. Hough & Co. (100 2nd Ave. S., Suite 800, St. Petersburg, FL 33701; 813-895-8880)

Howe Barnes Investments, Inc. (135 S. LaSalle St., Suite 1500, Chicago, IL 60603; 312-655-3000)

HSBC Securities, Inc. (140 Broadway, New York, NY 10005-1101; 212-825-6780)

Wayne Hummer Investments LLC (300 S. Wacker Dr., Suite 1500, Chicago, IL 60606; 312-431-1700)

ING Baring (U.S.) Securities, Inc. (667 Madison Ave., New York, NY 10021; 212-409-7700)

Ingalls & Snyder LLC (61 Broadway, New York, NY 10006; 212-269-7800; 800-221-2598)

Interra Financial Inc. (Dain Bosworth Plaza, 60 S. 6th St., Minneapolis, MN 55402-4402; 612-371-7750)

Interstate/Johnson Lane Corporation (Interstate Tower, 121 W. Trade St., Charlotte, NC 28202; 704-379-9000)

Janney Montgomery Scott Incorporated (1801 Market St., Philadelphia, PA 19103; 215-665-6000; 800-526-6397)

Johnston, Lemon & Company, Inc. (1101 Vermont Ave., N.W., Suite 800, Washington, DC 20005; 202-842-5500; 800-424-5158)

Edward Jones (12555 Manchester Rd., St. Louis, MO 63131; 314-515-2000)

Keefe, Bruyette & Woods, Inc. (Two World Trade Center, Suite 8566, New York, NY 10048; 212-323-8300)

C.L. King & Associates, Inc. (9 Elk St., Albany, NY 12207; 518-431-3500)

John G. Kinnard & Company (920 2nd Ave. S., Minneapolis, MN 55402; 612-370-2700)

Kirkpatrick Pettis (10250 Regency Circle, Suite 400, Omaha, NE 68114; 402-397-5777)

Ladenberg Thalmann & Co., Inc. (590 Madison Ave. New York, NY 10022; 212-409-2000)

Emmett A. Larkin Company, Inc. (100 Bush St., 10th Floor, San Francisco, CA 94104; 415-986-2332)

Lazard Fréres & Co. LLC (30 Rockefeller Plaza, New York, NY 10020; 212-632-6000)

Lebenthal & Co., Inc. (120 Broadway, 12th Floor, New York, NY 10271-0005; 212-748-5500)

Legg Mason Wood Walker, Inc. (Legg Mason Tower, 111 S. Calvert St., Baltimore, MD 21202; 410-539-3400)

Levesque Beaubien Geoffrion Inc. (1155 Metcalfe St., 5th Floor, Montreal, Quebec H3B 4S9 Canada; 514-879-2222)

Lombard Securities, Inc. (300 E. Lombard St., Suite 920, Baltimore, MD 21202; 410-783-1600)

Mabon Securities Inc. (One Liberty Plaza, 65 Broadway, 31st Floor, New York, NY 10006; 212-346-5000)

McDonald & Company Securities, Inc. (800 Superior Ave., Suite 2100, Cleveland, OH 44114; 216-443-2300; 800-553-2240)

Merrill Lynch & Company, Inc. (World Financial Center, 250 Vesey St., North Tower, New York, NY 10281; 212-449-1000)

Mesirow Financial Holdings, Inc. (350 N. Clark St., Chicago, IL 60610; 312-595-6000)

H. J. Meyers & Co., Inc. (1895 Mt. Hope Ave., Rochester, NY 14620; 716-256-4700; 800-678-4852)

Morgan Keegan, Inc. (Morgan Keegan Tower, 50 Front St., Memphis, TN 38103; 901-524-4100)

J.P. Morgan Securities, Incorporated (60 Wall St., New York, NY 10260; 212-483-2323)

Morgan Stanley Dean Witter (1585 Broadway, New York, NY 10036; 212-761-3000)

Murphey Favre, Inc. (1201 3rd Ave., Suite 780, Seattle, WA 98101; 206-461-8900; 800-548-7011)

Nat City Investments, Inc. (1965 E. 6th St., Suite 800, Cleveland, OH 44114; 216-575-9590)

Nathan & Lewis Securities, Inc. (1140 Avenue of the Americas, 4th Floor, New York, NY 10036; 212-354-8800; 800-873-7702)

Neuberger & Berman, LLC (605 3rd Ave., New York, NY 10158; 212-476-9000)

Nikko Securities Co. International, Inc. (200 Liberty St., New York, NY 10281; 212-416-5400)

Nomura Securities International, Inc. (2 World Financial Center, Building B, New York, NY 10281-1198; 212-667-9300)

David A. Noyes & Co. (208 S. LaSalle St., Suite 610, Chicago, IL 60604; 312-782-0400)

Nutmeg Securities, Ltd. (495 Post Rd. E., Westport, CT 06880; 203-226-1857)

Offerman & Company (600 Highway 169 S., Suite 1100, Interchange Tower, Minneapolis, MN 55426-1200; 612-541-8900)

Ohio Company (155 E. Broad St., Columbus, OH 43215; 614-464-6811)

Oppenheimer & Company, Inc. (World Financial Center, Oppenheimer Tower, New York, NY 10281; 212-667-7000; 800-999-6726)

PaineWebber Group, Inc. (1285 Avenue of the Americas, New York, NY 10019; 212-713-2000; 800-221-3260)

Paribas Corporation (787 Seventh Ave., New York, NY 10019; 212-841-3000)

Parker/Hunter, Inc. (600 Grant St., Suite 3100, Pittsburgh, PA 15219; 412-562-8000; 800-441-1514)

Piper Jaffray Companies Inc. (Piper Jaffray Tower, 222 S. 9th St., Minneapolis, MN 55402; 612-342-6000)

Podesta & Company (135 S. LaSalle St., Suite 2145, Chicago, IL 60603; 312-889-0133; 800-229-0008)

Principal Financial Securities, Inc. (1445 Ross Ave., Suite 2300, Dallas, TX 75202; 214-880-9000; 800-336-1780)

Prudential Securities Incorporated (One Seaport Plaza, New York, NY 10292; 212-214-1000)

Ragen MacKenzie Incorporated (999 3rd Ave., Suite 4300, Seattle, WA 98104; 206-343-5000; 800-456-4457 [Washington]; 800-456-4503 [national])

Raymond James Financial, Inc. (880 Carillon Pkwy., St. Petersburg, FL 33716; 813-573-3800)

Rhodes Securities, Inc. (306 W. 7th St., Suite 505, Fort Worth, TX 76102; 817-334-0455)

Richards, Merrill & Peterson, Inc. (One Skywalk, U.S. Bank Building, 422 W. Riverside, Spokane, WA 99201; 509-624-3174; 800-572-5296)

Robertson, Stephens & Company LLC (555 California St., Suite 2600, San Francisco, CA 94104; 415-781-9700)

Robinson & Robinson, Inc. (1337 Hamilton St., Allentown, PA 18102; 610-435-3518)

Robinson-Humphrey Company, Inc. (Atlanta Financial Center, 3333 Peachtree Rd., N.E., Atlanta, GA 30326; 404-266-6000)

Rodecker & Company, Investment Brokers, Inc. (4000 Town Center Suite, Suite 101, Southfield, MI 48075; 810-358-2282)

Rodman & Renshaw, Inc. (Two World Financial Center, Tower B, 30th Floor, New York, NY 10281; 212-416-7000)

Roney & Co. (1 Griswold St., Detroit, MI 48226; 313-963-6700)

Rothschild Inc. (1251 Avenue of the Americas, New York, NY 10020; 212-403-3500)

Royal Alliance Associates, Inc. (733 3rd Ave., 4th Floor, New York, NY 10017; 212-551-5100; 800-821-5100)

Salomon Smith Barney, Inc. (388 Greenwich St., New York, NY 10013; 212-816-6000)

SBC Warburg Dillon Read Inc. (222 Broadway, New York, NY 10038; 212-335-1000)

Scott & Stringfellow, Inc. (Mutual Building, 909 E. Main St., Richmond, VA 23219; 804-643-1811; 800-552-7757; 800-446-7075)

Securities Corporation of Iowa (200 Second Ave. S.E., Cedar Rapid, IA 52401; 319-366-7801)

The Seidler Companies Inc. (515 S. Figueroa St., Suite 600, Los Angeles, CA 90071; 213-624-4232; 800-421-8070)

Smith Barney Shearson, Inc. (1345 Avenue of the Americas, 21st Floor, New York, NY 10105; 212-399-6000)

Smith, Moore & Co. (400 Locust St., St. Louis, MO 63102; 314-421-5225)

Southwest Securities Group, Inc. (1201 Elm St., Suite 3500, Dallas, TX 75270; 214-651-1800)

Spear, Leeds & Kellogg (120 Broadway, New York, NY 10271; 212-433-7000)

Spelman & Company, Inc. (2355 Northside Dr., Suite 200, San Diego, CA 92108-2707; 619-584-7050)

Stephens Inc. (111 Center St., Little Rock, AK 72201; 501-374-4361)

Stifel, Nicolaus & Company, Inc. (500 N. Broadway, St. Louis, MO 63102; 314-342-2000)

Sutro & Company, Inc. (201 California St., 3rd Floor, San Francisco, CA 94111; 415-445-8500)

Traub and Company, Inc. (320 N. Meridian St., Suite 300, Indianapolis, IN 46204; 317-639-5474; 800-875-1036)

Trubee, Collins & Company, Inc. (1350 One M&T Plaza, Buffalo, NY 14203; 716-849-1401; 800-836-4050)

Tucker Anthony, Inc. (1 Beacon St., Boston, MA 02108; 617-725-2000; 800-225-6713)

UBS Securities LLC (299 Park Ave., New York, NY 10171; 212-821-4000)

Unterberg Harris (10 E. 50th St., 22nd Floor, New York, NY 10022; 212-572-8000)

UVest Corporation, Inc. (128 S. Tryon St., Suite 1340, Charlotte, NC 28202; 704-375-0484; 800-277-7700)

Vanguard Capital (4660 LaJolla Village Dr., Suite 100, San Diego, CA 92122; 619-455-5070; 800-743-5070)

Van Kampen American Capital Distributors, Inc. (One Parkview Plaza, Oakbrook Terrace, IL 60181; 708-684-6000; 800-225-2222)

H.C. Wainwright & Company, Inc. (One Boston Place, 31st Floor, Boston, MA 02108; 617-227-3100; 800-727-7176)

Wedbush Morgan Securities (1000 Wilshire Blvd., Los Angeles, CA 90017; 213-688-8000)

H.G. Wellington & Company, Inc. (14 Wall St., Suite 1702, New York, NY 10005; 212-732-6800; 800-221-3553)

Wheat First Butcher Singer (901 E. Byrd St., Richmond, VA 23219; 804-649-2311; 800-627-8625)

The Ziegler Companies, Inc. (215 N. Main St., West Bend, WI 53095; 414-334-5521; 800-558-1776)

RATING SERVICE

Weiss Research, Inc. (4176 Burns Rd., Palm Beach Gardens, FL 33410; 561-627-3300; 800-289-9222; www.weissratings.com). Rates the safety of thousands of banks, savings and loans, insurance companies and brokerage firms. Safety ratings range from A (excellent) to F (failed or in the process of failing). Offers a booklet titled

How To Get Safety Information from Your Financial Institution, which includes pre-printed postcards you can send to banks or savings and loans asking about bad loans, levels of shareholders' equity, loan loss reserves and other measures of financial stability; to brokerage firms asking about levels of net capital; and to insurance companies asking about holdings of junk bonds and nonperforming mortgages. Weiss also publishes a newsletter called *Safe Money Report* and several books rating various financial institutions, including *The Weiss Ratings Guide to Life, Health and Annuity Insurers; The Weiss Ratings Guide to Property & Casualty Insurers;* and *Weiss Ratings Guide to Banks and Thrifts.*

State Attorney General Offices

Following is a list of each state's attorney general. The attorney general has broad powers and is considered the "people's lawyer" on many issues. The attorney general's responsibilities include the following: representing clients in civil and criminal lawsuits; challenging or defending legislative or administrative actions; representing state agencies; enforcing antitrust laws; enforcing air and water pollution and hazardous waste laws; enforcing the provisions of charitable trusts; and intervening in public utility cases. If you do not know where to turn to satisfy a complaint, start with the attorney general's office in your state.

Alabama: 11 S. Union St., Montgomery 36130; 334-242-7300

Alaska: Diamond Courthouse, P.O. Box 110300, Juneau 99811-0300; 907-465-3600

Arizona: 1275 W. Washington, Phoenix 85007; 602-542-4266

Arkansas: 200 Catlett-Prien Building, 323 Center St., Little Rock 72201-2610; 501-682-2007

California: 1300 I St., Sacramento 95814; 916-324-5437

Colorado: 1525 Sherman St., Denver 80203-1525; 303-866-3611

Connecticut: 55 Elm St., Hartford 06141-0120; 860-566-2026

Delaware: 820 N. French St., 7th and 8th Floors, Wilmington 19801; 302-577-3838

District of Columbia: Office of the Corporation Counsel, 441 4th St., N.W., Suite 1060N, Washington 20001; 202-727-6248

Florida: State Capitol Building, PL 01, Tallahassee 32399-1050; 904-487-1963

Georgia: 40 Capitol Square, S.W., Atlanta 30334-1300; 404-656-4585

Hawaii: 425 Queen St., Honolulu 96813; 808-586-1282

Idaho: P.O. Box 83720, Statehouse, Boise 83720-0010; 208-334-2400

Illinois: State of Illinois Center, 100 W. Randolph St., 11th Floor, Chicago 60601; 312-814-3000

Indiana: Indiana State Government Center South Building, 402 W. Washington St., 5th Floor, Indianapolis 46204; 317-233-4386

Iowa: Hoover State Office Building, 2nd Floor, Des Moines 50319; 515-281-5164

Kansas: 301 W. 10th St., Topeka 66612-1597; 913-296-2215

Kentucky: State Capitol, Frankfort 40601; 502-564-7600

Louisiana: Department of Justice, P.O. Box 94095, Baton Rouge 70804-9005; 504-342-7013

Maine: State House, Station 6, Augusta 04333; 207-626-8800

Maryland: 200 St. Paul Pl., Baltimore 21202-2202; 410-576-6300

Massachusetts: 1 Ashburton Pl., Boston 02108-1698; 617-727-2200

Michigan: Law Building, 525 W. Ottawa St., Lansing 48909-0212; 517-373-1110

Minnesota: 102 State Capitol, St. Paul 55155; 612-296-6196

Mississippi: Carroll Gartin Justice Building, P.O. Box 220, Jackson 39205-0220; 601-359-3692

Missouri: P.O. Box 899, 207 W. High St., Jefferson City 65102; 573-751-3321

Montana: Justice Building, 215 N. Sanders St., 3rd Floor, Helena 59620-1401; 406-444-2026

Nebraska: 2115 State Capitol, P.O. Box 98920, Lincoln 68509-8920; 402-471-2682

Nevada: Heroes Memorial Building, Capitol Complex, 198 S. Carson St., Carson City 89710; 702-687-4170

New Hampshire: 25 Capitol St., Concord 03301-6397; 603-271-3658

New Jersey: Office of the Attorney General, Department of Law & Public Safety, CN080, 25 Market St., Trenton 08625; 609-292-4925

New Mexico: Bataan Memorial Building, P.O. Drawer 1508, Santa Fe 87504-1508; 505-827-6000

New York: The Capitol, Albany 12224; 518-474-7330

North Carolina: P.O. Box 629, 2 E. Morgan St., Raleigh 27602-0629; 919-733-3377

North Dakota: State Capitol, 600 E. Boulevard Ave., Bismarck 58505; 701-328-2210

Ohio: 30 E. Broad St., 17th Floor, Columbus 43266-0410; 614-466-3376

Oklahoma: State Capitol Building, 2300 N. Lincoln Blvd., Suite 112, Oklahoma City 73105; 405-521-3921

Oregon: 1162 Court St. Northeast, Salem 97310; 503-378-6002

Pennsylvania: Strawberry Square, 16th Floor, Harrisburg 17120; 717-787-3391

Rhode Island: 150 S. Main St., Providence 02903; 401-274-4400

South Carolina: Rembert C. Dennis Building, P.O. Box 11549, Columbia 29211-1549; 803-734-3970

South Dakota: 500 E. Capitol, Pierre 57501-5070; 605-773-3215

Tennessee: 500 Charlotte Ave., Nashville 37243-0497; 615-741-6474

Texas: Capitol Station, P.O. Box 12548, Austin 78711-2548; 512-463-2191

Utah: 236 State Capitol, Salt Lake City 84114-0810; 801-538-1326

Vermont: 109 State St., 2nd Floor, Montpelier 05609-1001; 802-828-3171

Virginia: 900 E. Main St., Richmond 23219; 804-786-2071

Washington: 1125 Washington St., S.E., P.O. Box 40100, Olympia 98504-0100; 360-753-6200

West Virginia: State Capitol, Room 26, E. Wing, Charleston 25305-0220; 304-558-2021

Wisconsin: 114 E. State Capitol, P.O. Box 7857, Madison 53707-7857; 608-266-1221

Wyoming: 123 Capitol Building, Cheyenne 82002; 307-777-7841

STATE BAR ASSOCIATIONS

The following state bar associations can refer you to a lawyer specializing in your area of need. They can also help you with dispute resolution alternatives, such as arbitration and mediation. In addition, if you have a complaint against a lawyer, you can contact the bar association's disciplinary bodies. The first telephone number listed for each entry is the bar association's main number. The telephone number following the letters "LRS" is for the local *Lawyer Referral Service,* which can refer you to a lawyer specializing in your legal question. In most cases, the LRS number covers the entire state; for states having more than one referral service, the telephone numbers are provided with the cities. If you live in a city other than the LRS city, you can call the state bar association, which will refer you to the closest attorney who specializes in your problem. You also can get a list of Lawyer Referral Services on the American Bar Association's Web site at www.abanet.org.

Alabama: 415 Dexter Ave., Montgomery 36104; 334-269-1515; LRS: 334-269-1515; 800-392-5660

Alaska: 510 L St., Suite 602, Anchorage 99501; 907-272-7469; LRS: 907-272-0352; 800-770-9999

Arizona: 111 West Monroe, Suite 1800, Phoenix 85003-1742; 602-252-4804; LRS: 602-257-4434 (Phoenix); 520-623-6159 (Tucson)

Arkansas: 400 W. Markham, Little Rock 72201; 501-375-4605; LRS: 501-375-4605; 800-482-9406

California: 26500 W. Agoura Rd., Suite 517, Calabasas, CA 91302; 888-733-3752; LRS: 510-893-8683 (Alameda County); 310-553-4022 (Beverly Hills); 818-843-0931 (Burbank); 916-891-6808 (Butte County); 510-825-5700 (Contra Costa County); 818-331-6377 (Covina County); 619-588-1936 (El Cajon); 209-264-0137 (Fresno County); 818-956-1633 (Glendale); 707-445-2652 (Humboldt County); 805-325-3340 (Kern County); 562-432-5913 (Long Beach County); 213-243-1525 (Los Angeles); 415-453-5505 (Marin County); 707-463-0131 (Mendocino County); 209-383-3886 (Merced County); 408-375-9889 (Monterey County); 916-272-6064 (Nevada County); 760-758-4755 (Northern San Diego County); 562-868-6787 (Norwalk); 714-772-8244 (Orange County); 818-795-5702 (Pasadena); 916-823-1094 (Placer County); 909-695-2501 (Riverside County); 916-444-2333 (Sacramento County); 909-388-0550 (San Bernadino County); 619-295-1654 (San Diego County); 415-989-1616 (San Francisco); 818-966-5530 (San Gabriel Valley); 209-943-2920 (San Joaquin County); 415-369-4230 (San Mateo County); 805-962-8191 (Santa Barbara County); 415-326-8322 (Santa Clara County); 408-425-4755 (Santa Cruz County); 310-451-5633 (Santa Monica); 707-552-7530 (Solano County); 707-546-5297 (Sonoma County); 310-320-9350 (South Bay-Torrance); 209-577-1121 (Stanislaus County); 209-732-2513 (Tulare County); 818-340-4529 (Ventura County)

Colorado: 1900 Grant St., Suite 950, Denver 80203; 303-860-1112; LRS: 719-636-1532 (Colorado Springs); 303-831-8000 (Denver); 303-226-1122 (Ft. Collins)

Connecticut: Connecticut Bar Association, 101 Corporate Pl., Rocky Hill 06067-1894; 203-721-0025; LRS: 203-335-4116 (Fairfield); 860-525-6052, (Hartford); 203-562-5750 (New Haven); 860-889-9384 (New London); 203-753-1938 (Waterbury)

Delaware: 1201 Orange St., Suite 1100, Wilmington 19801; 302-658-5279; LRS: 302-658-5278; 800-773-0606

District of Columbia: 1250 H St., N.W., 6th Floor, Washington 20005; 202-737-4700; HelpLine: 202-626-3499; 202-296-7845

Florida: Florida Bar, 650 Apalachee Pkwy., Tallahassee 32399; 850-561-5600; LRS: 904-561-5600; 800-342-8011; 407-242-1551 (Brevard County); 954-764-8040 (Broward County); 941-775-3939 (Collier County); 813-221-7780 (Hillsborough County); 904-399-5780 (Jacksoville); 407-422-4537 (Orange County); 561-687-3266 (Palm Beach County); 813-848-7433 (Pasco County); 813-461-4880 (Pinnellas County); 813-686-8215 (Polk County); 904-434-6009 (Santa Rosa County); 407-834-0530 (Seminole County); 813-821-5450 (South Pinellas County)

Georgia: 800 The Hurt Building, 50 Hurt Plaza, Atlanta 30303; 404-527-8700; LRS: 404-521-0777

Hawaii: P.O. Box 26, Honolulu 96810; 808-537-1868; LRS: 808-537-9140

Idaho: P.O. Box 895, Boise 83701-0895; LRS: 208-334-4500

Illinois: Illinois Bar Center, Springfield 62701; 217-525-1760; LRS: 217-525-5297

Indiana: 230 E. Ohio St., 4th Floor, Indianapolis 46204; 317-639-5465; LRS: 317-269-2222

Iowa: 521 E. Locust, Suite 300, Des Moines 50309-1939; 515-243-3179; LRS: 515-280-7429; 800-532-1108

Kansas: P.O. Box 1037, Topeka 66601-1037; 785-234-5696; LRS: 913-233-4322

Kentucky: 514 W. Main St., Frankfort 40601-1883; 502-564-3795; LRS: 502-583-1576; 800-899-4529; 606-225-8644 (Lexington); 606-781-1300 (Highland Heights)

Louisiana: 601 St. Charles Ave., New Orleans 70130; 504-566-1600; 504-344-9926 (Baton Rouge); 318-237-4700 (Lafayette); 318-436-3308 (Lake Charles); 504-561-8828 (New Orleans); 318-222-0720 (Shreveport)

Maine: 124 State St., Augusta 04332; 207-622-7523; LRS: 207-622-1460

Maryland: 520 W. Fayette St., Baltimore 21201; 410-685-7878; LRS: 800-303-9978 (Charles); 800-649-1090 (Frederick); 410-280-6950 (Annapolis); 410-539-3112 (Baltimore); 410-465-2721 (Howard County); 800-649-1090 and 410-857-1451 (Frederick County); 301-279-9100 (Montgomery County); 301-952-1440 (Prince George's County)

Massachusetts: 20 West St., Boston 02111; 617-338-0500; LRS: 617-654-0400; 800-392-6164 (instate); 617-338-2625 (TDD); 617-742-0625 and 800-552-7046 (Boston); 508-990-1303 and 800-647-5151 (Bristol County); 508-741-7888 (Essex County); 413-732-4648 (Hampden County); 413-586-8729 (Hampshire County); 617-494-4150 (Middlesex County); 508-752-1311 or 800-622-9700 (Worchester County)

Michigan: 306 Townsend St., Lansing 48933; 517-372-3310; LRS: 800-968-0738; 313-996-3229 (Ann Arbor); 313-961-3545 (Detroit); 810-232-6000 (Genesee County); 616-454-9493 (Grand Rapids); 626-384-8257 (Kalamazoo); 517-482-8816 (Lansing); 810-468-8300 (Macomb County); 248-338-2100 (Oakland County); 517-362-4441 (Tawas City); 616-922-4713 (Traverse City)

Minnesota: 514 Nicollet Mall, Suite 300, Minneapolis 55402; 612-333-1183; LRS: 612-333-1183; 800-292-4152 (instate); 612-339-8777 (Minneapolis); 612-224-1775 (St. Paul); 612-351-7172 (Washington County)

Mississippi: P.O. Box 2168, Jackson 39225; 601-948-4471; LRS: 601-948-5488; 800-682-6423 (instate)

Missouri: 326 Monroe St., Jefferson City 65101; 573-636-3635; LRS: 573-635-4128; 816-221-9472 (Kansas City); 417-831-2783 (Springfield); 314-621-6681 (St. Louis)

Montana: P.O. Box 577, Helena 59624; 406-442-7660; LRS: 406-449-6577

Nebraska: 635 S. 14th St., Lincoln 68508; 402-475-7091; LRS: 402-341-4104 (Omaha); 800-742-3005

Nevada: 1325 Airmotive Way, Suite 140, Reno 89502; 702-329-4100; 800-789-5747 (instate); LRS: 702-382-0504 (Las Vegas)

New Hampshire: 112 Pleasant St., Concord 03301; 603-224-6942; LRS: 603-224-3333; 800-639-5290 (instate)

New Jersey: CN973 Richard Hughes Justice Complex, Trenton 08625; 609-984-7783; LRS: 201-906-8444; 800-367-0089; 609-345-3444 (Atlantic City); 201-488-0044 (Bergen County); 609-261-4862 (Burlington County); 609-964-4520 (Camden); 609-463-0313 (Cape May); 609-692-6207 (Cumberland County); 973-622-6207 (Essex County); 609-848-4589 (Gloucester County); 908-735-2611 (Hunterdon County); 609-585-6200 (Mercer County); 732-828-0053 (Middlesex County); 732-431-5544 (Monmouth County); 201-267-5882 (Morris County); 201-278-9223 (Passaic County); 908-685-2323 (Somerset County); 201-267-5882 (Sussex County); 908-353-4715 (Union County); 201-267-5882 (Warren County)

New Mexico: P.O. Box 25883, Albuquerque 87125; 505-243-2615; LRS: 505-848-3777 (instate); 800-357-0777

New York: One Elk St., Albany 12207; 518-463-3200; LRS: 518-463-3200; 800-342-3661; 212-626-7373 (New York City); 518-445-7691 (Albany County); 607-723-6331 (Broome County); 718-293-5600 (Bronx County); 607-734-9687 (Chemung County); 914-473-7941 (Dutchess County); 716-852-3100 (Erie County); 718-624-0843 (Kings County); 716-546-2130 (Monroe County); 516-747-4832 (Nassau County); 716-284-4101 (Niagara County); 315-471-2690 (Onondaga County); 914-294-8222 (Orange County); 914-225-4904 (Putnam County); 718-291-4500 (Queens County); 718-442-4500 (Richmond County); 914-634-2149 (Rockland County); 516-234-5577 (Suffolk County); 518-792-9239 (Warren County); 914-761-5151 (Westchester County)

North Carolina: P.O. Box 25908, Raleigh 27611; 919-828-4620; LRS: 919-677-8574; 800-662-7660; 704-375-0120 (Charlotte)

North Dakota: P.O. Box 2136, Bismarck 58502; 701-255-1404; LRS: 701-255-1406; 800-932-8880

Ohio: P.O. Box 16562, Columbus 43216; 614-487-2050; LRS: 330-253-5038 (Akron); 513-381-8359 (Cincinnati); 216-696-3532 (Cleveland); 614-221-0754 (Columbus); 937-222-6102 (Dayton); 419-242-2000 (Toledo); 513-896-6671 (Butler County); 330-746-2737 (Columbia County); 216-621-2414 (Cuyahoga County); 614-385-4456 (Hocking County); 440-352-6044 (Lake County); 440-323-8416 (Lorrain County); 330-296-6357 (Portage County); 330-453-0686 (Stark County); 330-675-2415 (Trumbull County); 216-262-6198 (Wayne County)

Oklahoma: P.O. Box 53036, Oklahoma City 73152; 405-524-2365; LRS: 918-584-5243 (Tulsa)

Oregon: 5200 S.W. Meadows Rd., Lake Oswego 97035; 503-620-0222; LRS: 503-684-3763; 800-452-7636

Pennsylvania: P.O. Box 186, Harrisburg 17108; 717-238-6715; LRS: 717-238-6715; 215-238-6333 (Philadelphia); 412-261-0158 (Pittsburgh)

Puerto Rico: P.O. Box 1900, San Juan 00903; 809-721-3358

Rhode Island: 115 Cedar St., Providence 02903; 401-421-5740; LRS: 401-421-7799

South Carolina: P.O. Box 608, Columbia 29202; 803-799-6653; LRS: 803-799-7100; 800-868-2284

South Dakota: 222 E. Capitol, Pierre 57501; 605-224-7554; LRS: 605-224-7554; 800-952-2333

Tennessee: 3622 West End Ave., Nashville 37205; 615-383-7421; LRS: 423-266-5950 (Chattanooga); 423-522-7501 (Knoxville); 901-529-8800 (Memphis); 615-242-6546 (Nashville); 615-741-3234 (Board of Law Commissioners); 615-741-3096 (CLE Commission); 615-361-7500 or 800-486-5714 (Board of Professional Responsibility)

Texas: 1414 Colorado, Austin 78711; 512-463-1463; LRS: 512-463-1474; 800-252-9690; 214-220-7444 (Dallas); 713-237-9429; 800-289-4577 (Houston); 512-227-1853 (San Antonio); 915-532-7052 (El Paso); 409-835-8438 (Orange County); 817-336-4101 (Tarrant County); 512-472-8303 (Travis County)

Utah: 645 S. 200 E., Salt Lake City 84111; 801-531-9077; LRS: 801-531-9077; 800-698-9077

Vermont: P.O. Box 100, Montpelier 05601; 802-223-2020; LRS: 802-223-2020; 800-639-7036

Virginia: 707 E. Main St., Suite 1500, Richmond 23219-2803; 804-775-0500; LRS: 804-775-0808; 800-552-7977; 703-548-1105 (Alexandria); 703-358-3390 (Arlington); 703-246-3780 (Fairfax); 757-623-0132 (Norfolk); 540-982-2345 (Roanoke)

Washington: 500 Westin Building, 2001 6th Ave., Seattle 98121-2599; 206-623-2766; LRS: 206-623-2551 (Seattle); 509-456-3655 (Spokane); 253-383-3432 (Tacoma/Pierce County); 360-748-0430 (Chehalis)

West Virginia: 2006 Kanawha Blvd. E., Charleston 25311; 304-558-2456; LRS: 304-558-7991

Wisconsin: P.O. Box 7158, Madison 53707-7158; 608-257-3838; LRS: 608-257-4666; 414-274-6768 (Milwaukee); 800-362-9082 (instate)

Wyoming: P.O. Box 109, Cheyenne 82003; 307-632-9061; LRS: 307-632-9061

18

Smart Money
Strategies for Every
Age and Situation

The first 17 chapters of this book explained almost everything you need to know about all aspects of your personal finances. Only one element remains: how to apply all this advice to your current situation. Depending on your age and family status, some strategies are more appropriate than others. This final chapter offers some guidelines to help you tailor the book's general principles of personal finance to your specific situation. As you move through life, this chapter will help you reevaluate your money strategies.

While this chapter provides rules of thumb appropriate for every age and situation, filter the advice to take into account your unique circumstances. For example, it is much easier to invest, buy a home and purchase insurance if you earn a high salary. Or, depending on your risk tolerance, you may feel more or less comfortable taking the amount of investment risk described here for different ages and situations. Similarly, the opportunities to participate in various employee benefit programs will vary greatly depending on whether you work for a large company offering many choices, you are self-employed or you work for a small firm providing few benefits.

The following sections offer tips about each area of personal finance as you progress through the life cycle. They first cover each age grouping, separated into youth (20s and 30s), middle age (40s and 50s) and retirement years (60s and older). The next sections offer advice for the four most common marital statuses—single, married, divorced or widowed. For every age and situation, the chapter offers advice for each area of personal finance, as defined by and in the order of the chapters in this book.

Your 20s and 30s—Establishing Your Financial Foundation

The transition from school to the work force can be both exhilarating and frustrating. Once you land a job after graduation, you may feel the thrill of financial independence from your parents for the first time. Yet your starting salary may be far too low to purchase your first home or even rent your own apartment. In addition, you may be loaded with debts accumulated to pay for your education. As you progress through your 30s, your career should become more firmly established, your income and assets should grow and you should gain total financial independence from your parents. While in your youth, you can do plenty to establish good financial habits. In fact, there's no better time to start!

GIVING YOURSELF A FINANCIAL CHECKUP

As you work through the exercises in Chapter 1, "Giving Yourself a Financial Checkup," don't feel discouraged if you haven't yet built up much in income or assets or if your expenses seem out of control. Establishing your financial independence is expensive. Don't expect substantial income until you have several years of job experience, perhaps by your late 20s or early 30s. Asset accumulation will follow.

Your 20s and 30s are a great time to establish solid financial habits. For example, set up an efficient recordkeeping system, track your cash flow carefully and create a budget you can follow. Even if you still rely on your parents for financial help, balance your income and expenses without regard to parental support. Prioritize short-, medium- and long-term goals. You have most of your life ahead of you, and the sooner you determine what you want to accomplish first, the greater the chance you have of realizing your dreams. Don't expect to meet all your goals at once; saving for a down payment on a home, for example, may be a higher priority than buying a car or having a child.

In assessing your risk tolerance, realize that while you may not yet have a great deal of money, you do have a great deal of time for your investments to grow. At this age, you have a lifetime to bounce back if a risky investment fails. In addition, if you can tolerate more risk, your investments will have a long time to appreciate significantly. Most people in their 20s and 30s are apt to be too conservative with their money. Instead, they should take more risk in hopes of higher long-term returns.

Investing. Start to assemble a portfolio of stocks, bonds and mutual funds as early as you can afford to save. Chapters 2 through 7 provide explanations of the various ways to build your portfolio. Aim to set aside as much as 10 percent of your after-tax income. If you don't have much capital, mutual funds probably make more sense than individual stocks or bonds. Funds require minimum initial investments of only $250 to $1,000 and offer diversification. One easy way to invest in funds is to enroll in an automatic investment program in which a mutual fund group deducts a set amount, such as $100 a month, from your checking account and deposits it in whatever fund you choose. Several fund groups even waive their minimum initial investments if you commit to an automatic investing plan.

Favor stock funds over bond funds because stock funds have much more growth potential over the long haul than bond funds. You might allocate 70 to 80 percent of your savings to equity funds, with a high proportion of that money in aggressive growth, growth and international funds, which will probably provide the highest long-term returns. Bonds pay regular income, but that is probably not as important in this stage of life as growth of capital. Unless you have a great deal of extra money and time to learn, avoid speculating in futures, options, gold and collectibles while in your 20s and 30s.

Also, establish a good relationship with a bank. If you can build up enough money in checking and savings accounts to meet minimum requirements, you can save hundreds of dollars in monthly account and per-check fees. In addition, keep an emergency reserve fund in a bank or money-market mutual fund of at least three months' living expenses in case you get laid off, suffer a medical emergency, have a large car repair bill or incur some other unforeseen expense.

Real estate. The move from a rented house or apartment to home ownership is almost every young person's dream. However, it takes a disciplined savings program to assemble the down payment of 5 to 10 percent of a home's value, as well as closing costs of several thousand dollars. And once you have scraped together the down payment, the costs of carrying a mortgage may take a huge bite out of your budget—28 to 36 percent of your gross income. Over time, if your income rises and the mortgage costs remain the same, that percentage should fall. To minimize mortgage costs, look into all the mortgage alternatives described in Chapter 8, "Inside Real Estate." For example, you will make much lower monthly payments on an adjustable-rate mortgage than you will on a fixed loan. You might also investigate the loan programs sponsored by state housing agencies that make homes affordable for first-time home buyers. These programs often demand lower down payments and offer mortgage rates of 1 or 2 percentage points below the current market rates.

If you cannot afford a home, spend as little as possible on rent because you receive nothing in return for the money other than housing for that month. By keeping your rent low, you can invest any excess earnings in a savings or mutual fund account, which will build up your capital over time.

Credit. Get off to a good start by establishing credit with several lenders and paying your loans punctually. Remember, credit reporting agencies track how well or poorly you repay your debts. The time to establish a good credit record is early in your career. If necessary, have your parents cosign a loan or credit card application so you qualify; then, as soon as possible, take over the payments until you qualify for the loan on your own record.

Resist the great temptation to buy more than your income can support. You may want a new car, better furniture, a state-of-the-art stereo and lots more, but you will only ruin your credit record if you go on a spending binge, then are unable to pay your bills. Instead, be disciplined in your use of credit, and try to pay off one major purchase before you take on the next. One easy way to save money is to apply for the credit cards with the lowest interest rates and annual fees. A listing of such cards is available from the CardTrack and other credit card services described in Chapter 9, "You and Your Credit—Managing It Wisely."

If you have outstanding loans that financed college or other education, you will have to devote a good amount of your income to paying them off. If you pay a particularly high interest rate on your student loans, look into consolidating them under one lower rate loan. The Student Loan Marketing Association (Sallie Mae) offers such a consolidation loan through its SMART Loan Account. For more information, call 800-524-9100. To some extent, the amount of money you devote to repaying education loans will limit the amount of additional credit you can qualify for and should assume.

Though you should be careful in taking on credit, it is not sinful to borrow when you are in your 20s and 30s. Because you are establishing a household, you need to buy many things that will last for years. Therefore, expect to take on some debt—just don't let it overwhelm you.

Cars. Depending on whether you are single or married, with or without children, buy a less expensive car while you are young. Unless you love cars or spend much time commuting, try to limit your auto outlays so you have money left over for more important priorities. Work through the buy-versus-lease exercise in Chapter 10, "Getting the Most for Your Money When Buying a Car," to determine the least expensive way to finance your vehicle. Because your car needs will probably change if you get married, have children or move, it might be worth leasing and trading in the car several years from now for a model that suits your new circumstances. As you move through your 30s and have children, you will need a larger, more expensive car.

Insurance. You will need all five types of insurance: car, disability, health, homeowner's (or renter's) and life.

Your *car insurance* rates will probably be higher than they will in later years because people in their 20s tend to drive less responsibly and therefore have more accidents than their elders. To keep your rates as low as possible, drive carefully. If you have no accidents, your rates should fall by the time you reach your 30s.

Disability insurance is vital when you are in your 20s and 30s. If you are seriously injured, you may suffer several decades of lost wages. It is therefore crucial that you obtain adequate disability protection.

Health insurance is also important even though you probably are vital and healthy at this age. Before you get your first permanent, full-time job, continue coverage under your parents' policy, which is usually possible until you turn 23.

After that, consider taking out a short-term comprehensive policy. As you search for your first job or look to switch employers, scrutinize the health plan that a company offers to learn how much both you and the company pay. Also, ask whether the health plan offers alternatives such as health maintenance organizations (HMOs) or preferred provider organizations (PPOs). As you move into your 30s, you might switch your insurance coverage from a traditional policy to an HMO if you must cover a spouse and children. If your employer provides no health insurance or you are self-employed, look into obtaining coverage through some group that you already belong to or may be able to join. Even though you are young and probably in good health, insurance premiums can be extremely high and take a huge bite out of your budget.

Homeowner's insurance is a must if you own a home. Read through the descriptions of the various kinds of protection in Chapter 11, "All about Insurance," and make sure that you have enough. For your first home, you may not need much coverage because you probably do not have many possessions. However, make sure to update the policy as the value of your home and belongings increases over the years. If you rent, look into *renter's insurance* to protect the value of your possessions. Depending on the value of what you own and the chances of loss or damage, decide whether renter's insurance is worthwhile.

Life insurance is necessary if you support someone financially, such as a spouse or child. If you are young and single, however, you have little or no need for protection because no one depends on your income. One advantage in buying *term life* insurance when you are in your 20s and 30s is that the premiums are far less expensive than they will be as you move into your 40s and 50s. Insurance companies figure that the younger you are, the less chance you have of dying. If you need only the death benefit protection, buy the least expensive term policy you can find through one of the services listed in Chapter 11. Cash-value policies such as *whole life, variable life* and *universal life* offer two other advantages to buying while you are young: First, you can lock in the premium at a considerably lower annual cost than you can if you wait until your 40s or 50s. Also, the longer your money compounds tax deferred in an insurance policy or *annuity,* the more it will grow by the time you retire. Despite these financial advantages, most young people do not place life insurance at the top of their list of priorities, and with good reason.

Education. Because you only recently completed your own schooling and still may be paying off college loans, it might seem unthinkable to start saving for your children's college costs. But, as explained in Chapter 12, "How To Finance a College Education," the earlier you start, the less you must save each month, and the less you will have to borrow when your children start school.

Taxes. If you have just started a career, you probably don't earn enough income to catapult you into the top tax brackets. Therefore, you probably don't qualify for many deductions or credits. Most likely, you will take the standard deduction and not itemize your return. Once you earn more, buy a home, have children and start investing, you may find it worthwhile to itemize. The more money you make, the more often that the tax reduction strategies detailed in Chapter 13, "The Basics of Tax Planning," will apply.

Retirement. Though it may seem eons into the future, retirement will be upon you sooner than you think. You would be wise to start a retirement savings program as soon as you have established yourself at your first permanent, full-time job. The earlier you start saving, the more you will accumulate by retirement. For example, if you make $25,000 annually and begin saving $125 a month when you are age 25, and if you earn an average 8 percent rate of return, you will amass $288,647 by age 60. If everything in this example remains the same except that you begin your retirement savings at age 35, you will end up with $119,671. And if you procrastinate until age 45, you will build up only $43,543. Clearly, you should begin saving as early as possible. Chapter 14, "Retirement—How To Get There from Here," explains your retirement savings options.

Estate planning. It is always a good idea to have a will so that your assets can be distributed according to your wishes when you die. If you are married and own a home, a will and an estate plan become even more important. However, you needn't worry about elaborate estate planning unless your assets total more than $625,000 (rising by law to $1 million in 2006). If you have children, estate planning establishes guardianship and often sets up trusts to pass assets to the children over time. Chapter 15, "Estate Planning—Keeping Your Assets in the Family," discusses estate planning techniques that you can adapt to your situation.

Employee benefits. By participating in all your employer's benefits programs as soon as you start your job or qualify for the programs, you can get off to a solid start in laying your financial foundation. In addition to weighing all the other factors that go into your acceptance of a particular position, look into potential employers' benefits packages carefully when evaluating job offers, and accept the position that provides the most lucrative benefits. Once on the job, enroll in every available retirement savings program, such as profit-sharing and salary reduction plans. The earlier you begin participating, the more the company's matching contributions will total, and the larger your retirement nest egg will grow. Within the plans, allocate most of your money to growth vehicles such as stocks. Remember, you can borrow against your retirement savings if necessary, so don't consider the money totally out of reach until retirement. See Chapter 16, "Making the Most of Your Employee Benefits," for more details.

Also, investigate the health insurance options your company offers to determine which plan will cost you the least in premiums and offer you the broadest coverage. Sign up for a flexible spending account (FSA) if your company offers one and if you think that you will have enough out-of-pocket health care or day care costs that will not be covered by your regular insurance plan.

If you are self-employed or work for a small company that offers no retirement plan, fund an individual retirement account (IRA), a Keogh or another qualified plan. Within these plans, invest most of your assets in growth stocks or mutual funds, which offer maximum growth potential.

Your 40s and 50s—The Peak Earning Years of Middle Age

When you enter your peak earning years, you may join what many call the sandwich generation. At the same time that you support your children, perhaps paying their college tuition bills, your financial and other responsibilities for your parents may grow as well if they are still alive and have not saved enough to live comfortably in retirement. Meanwhile, you have your own expenses to worry about, as well as a need to save for retirement. Many middle-agers short-change themselves by disbursing their assets among their children and parents. The only solution to this dilemma is careful planning and tracking of your personal finances so you can set targets and monitor your progress toward them. If you delay this budgeting process, your retirement years inevitably will suffer.

GIVING YOURSELF A FINANCIAL CHECKUP

By the time you reach your 40s and 50s, your income should be substantially higher than it was in your 20s and 30s, and you should have accumulated a considerable pool of assets. All this should be reflected in a sizeable net worth. You probably have accomplished many of the short- and medium-term goals you set when you were younger, though you have new goals to meet. Some of your long-term goals, such as saving for retirement, traveling extensively or starting a business, may still lie ahead of you. Working through the cash flow and budgeting exercises in Chapter 1 is as important as ever because you should have more sources of income, as well as more expenses. When you assess your risk tolerance, you may find that you have mellowed a bit since your youth. If you have built up a substantial pool of assets, you may be more interested in preserving that capital than in making it grow. On the other hand, if you have not invested much, you will have to become even more of a risk taker to earn the high returns you need to finance a comfortable retirement.

Investing. If you have already established a substantial portfolio of stocks and equity mutual funds, you might begin to scale back the risk level of your holdings as you move through your 40s and 50s. See Chapters 2 through 7 for more information on investing. If 70 percent of your portfolio consisted of aggressive growth or growth stocks when you were in your 20s and 30s, 30 to 50 percent is more appropriate now. You can allocate the rest of your capital to more conservative growth and income investments, such as equity-income, balanced and convertible mutual funds. Also, increase your bond holdings to about 50 to 70 percent of your portfolio over time, and reinvest the dividends if you don't need the income the bonds generate. If you are in the top tax bracket, consider investing your money in municipal bonds rather than taxable Treasuries or corporates. If you have excess risk capital that you can afford to lose, you might dabble in more speculative arenas, such as options, futures, gold, collectibles and limited partnerships, but move cautiously.

If you have not saved or invested over the years, do so immediately. Aim to set aside at least 10 percent of your after-tax income—as much as 15 percent, if possible. If your employer offers a salary reduction plan and you have not yet enrolled, do so to the maximum extent possible, particularly if the company matches your contribution. By not saving over the past 20 or more years, you have forgone a tremendous opportunity for which you must now compensate. Your goal is to create a large enough pool of capital to generate the income you need to live well in retirement, which is now only 10 to 25 years away. If you can amass $100,000, that will create an income stream of $5,000 a year if you earn a 5 percent return and $10,000 a year if you manage 10 percent.

Your banking relationships should be well established by now, and you should be maintaining checking, savings and certificate of deposit (CD) balances high enough to avoid account fees and per-check charges. If you keep money in several banks, consolidate it in one institution to minimize fees. Make sure that your account is insured by the Federal Deposit Insurance Corporation (FDIC).

Real estate. If you haven't already purchased a home, you should have saved enough to make a down payment, and your income should be high enough to maintain a mortgage. Owning real estate is often appealing to those in their 40s and 50s because the deductions from mortgage interest and property taxes produce significant tax savings. Chapter 8 on real estate offers guidance on what size mortgage you would qualify for and the best kind of mortgage to obtain, depending on your financial situation.

If you rent, use any cash that would normally be applied to home ownership costs to build up your stock, bond and mutual fund portfolio. You do not generate home ownership tax deductions, but renting may give you the excess cash to fund your retirement.

If you already own a home, you may be in a position to invest in rental real estate, which—if it generates positive cash flow—can provide a regular source of income in retirement.

Credit. If you have paid your bills on time over the last few years, you should have established a solid credit record that allows you to borrow as much as you need. However, if you have consistently fallen behind in your payments or have defaulted on a loan, your poor credit record will hinder you from borrowing.

While in your 40s and 50s, borrow less than you did in your 20s and 30s, when you established your first home. Your biggest loans, other than a mortgage, will probably be to finance your children's college education. Instead of taking on a loan to buy a new car, consider leasing. If you run into a cash squeeze, you might need to borrow against your employee benefits plans or life insurance policies.

As you move into your late 50s, pay off far more debt than you take on. Aim to pay off most or all your debt—except, perhaps, your mortgage—by the time you retire. If you remain heavily in debt at this stage of life, reexamine your budget, and cut back on spending to bring expenses in line with income. Chapter 9 can give you more details on credit.

Cars. While in your 40s and 50s, you probably need a larger, more luxurious car than you owned when you were younger. You may need two or even three cars, depending on how many drivers are living at home. This may be because you have children in the house who tote much paraphernalia when they attend football practice or music lessons. Also, as you age, you often value comfort over flashiness.

As far as financing your car, work through the buy-versus-lease analysis in Chapter 10 on cars to determine the better option. You may find it more advantageous to lease a car and invest your excess capital in stocks, bonds and mutual funds rather than tie up a lot of money in a car certain to depreciate in value.

Insurance. You will need all five types of insurance: car, disability, health, homeowner's and life.

If you have been a careful driver, your *car insurance* rates should be much lower than you paid in your daredevil days. However, the value of your car may be greater if you have a larger, more luxurious vehicle, so increase your coverage appropriately. Review the standard methods of reducing your premium, such as installing a passive restraint system and antitheft devices, as well as the other suggestions in Chapter 11 on insurance.

Disability protection is also important because you could lose years of income if you are injured or become sick on the job. You are protecting a substantial income at this age, so don't skimp on the coverage.

Clearly, it is critical to have adequate *health insurance.* As you age, medical problems tend to increase, and you will therefore probably make more frequent claims. Insurers realize this too and increase their premiums to account for their greater risk. If you are covered through your employer, you might have to pay larger deductibles and co-payments if the policy is based on your rising salary. If the premiums, deductibles and co-payments become too expensive, look into a health maintenance organization (HMO) or preferred provider organization (PPO) as a way of capping your out-of-pocket health care costs. Whatever you do, don't let your health insurance coverage lapse; you expose yourself to potentially catastrophic medical bills.

If you own your home and have *homeowner's insurance,* make sure that your policy is up to date. Over the years, you have probably acquired many possessions, and you want to make sure that your policy will pay to replace them if your home is burglarized, hit by a natural disaster or otherwise harmed. If you own valuable artwork, computers, jewelry or other items, you might purchase special riders to cover them. It's easy to renew your homeowner's policy year after year without updating it. Now is the time to ensure that you are well protected.

At this age, *life insurance* coverage is worthwhile if a spouse or children depend on your income. As you move through your 40s and 50s, *term insurance* premiums become more and more expensive until they are often unaffordable in your late 50s. Cash-value policies such as *whole life, variable life* and *universal life* allow you to lock in a premium rate or, at least, have some choice in the size of your premium. The earlier you sign up for such a plan, the lower your premium. If you start a cash-value policy in your mid-to-late 50s, you probably will not have enough time to accumulate significant cash values because such policies are loaded with front-end costs, such as sales commissions. As your children become self-supporting, you might reduce your insurance coverage a bit, as long as your spouse could live on the reduced death benefit. Keep enough insurance to cover funeral expenses, taxes and some ready cash for your spouse.

At this age, you might also look into *annuities.* You can use these as tax-deferred savings vehicles funded by regular contributions. Or you may want to use a lump sum from your employer's benefits plans to buy an immediate annuity, which will establish an income stream starting at age 59½. Chapter 11 explains the various types of annuities and payout options.

Education. Your children probably will enter college while you are in your 40s and 50s. If you haven't saved over the past years, you will have to borrow a huge sum from many sources and go through the difficult process of applying for financial aid and grants. Chapter 12 on financing college can give you tips on where to begin. If you have a few years before your oldest child's freshman year, save as much as you can as soon as possible. The more you reduce the amount of money you must borrow when your children enter school, the more capital you will accumulate for your own goals, such as retirement.

Taxes. As you enter your peak earning years, your tax obligations will probably rise. It is therefore more important than ever to maximize all the legal tax reduction strategies discussed in Chapter 13 on tax planning. For example, if your company offers a salary reduction plan and a flexible spending account (FSA) for medical and dependent care expenses, take full advantage of them. If you are not eligible for a pension, contribute to a deductible individual retirement account (IRA). If you are self-employed, fund a Keogh account with as much money as you can afford. Invest in tax-sheltered vehicles such as municipal bonds and municipal bond funds, annuities and life insurance. If your calculations show that it is advantageous, buy a home, and use the mortgage to generate interest deductions. If you already own a home and have built up a substantial amount of equity, convert your nondeductible consumer loans to deductible home-equity debt. Remember that if you sell your principal residence in which you have lived for at least two of the past five years, you will not have to pay capital gains tax as long as your profit is less than $500,000 for a married couple filing jointly or $250,000 for a single. If you want to downsize to a smaller home or apartment, you are under no obligation to reinvest the proceeds. You may want to rent and invest the proceeds of your home sale in income-producing stocks, bonds and mutual funds. Maximize deductions by bunching them in one year. And, finally, set up trusts to pass on your assets to your children with a minimal amount of estate taxes.

Retirement. You still have time to plan for and fund your retirement, but that time is dwindling. If you have short-changed your retirement fund for seemingly more urgent needs, such as your children's education, start to set aside money for yourself, and increase that amount as much as possible over the years. Remember, the earlier you begin to save, the more time that interest has to compound. Project your income and expenses in the worksheets in Chapter 14 on retirement planning. Contact the Social Security Administration to make sure that it has correctly recorded your earnings. Review the retirement plans your employer offers so you understand what benefits they provide. If you have access to a defined contribution plan like a 401(k), 403(b) or 457 salary reduction plan, contribute as much as possible, and take full advantage of any employer match. As you move through your 50s, be prepared for an early-retirement offer from your employer, whether or not you want to receive one. Think about your employment alternatives ahead of time so you do not make your decision to accept or reject the offer under duress. Also, start thinking about where you might want to live in retirement and what activities you want to pursue.

Estate planning. The more assets you accumulate through your 40s and 50s, the more important estate planning becomes. Once your family's assets exceed $625,000 (rising to $1 million in 2006), you might need to transfer the ownership of some assets to your spouse so you can both take advantage of the unified tax credit. If your assets exceed $1.25 million (rising to $2 million in 2006), you might need to set up a trust for your children and other beneficiaries. Also, make sure that you have a valid will, and update it regularly to account for changes in your family situation and tax laws. Many people unwisely postpone estate planning until their late 50s or even until they are retired. Consult a good estate planning attorney when you are younger, or use self-help books or software to establish a solid estate plan. Consult Chapter 15 to help you identify your estate planning needs and goals.

Employee benefits. If you have worked for your employer for several years, you should be familiar with all your benefits by now. If you're not, study your benefits manual to determine whether your employer offers any benefit that you are not taking full advantage of. If you have any questions, visit your employer's benefits office. In addition, Chapter 16 explains the various types of benefit plans that might be available to you. Enroll in all savings and profit-sharing plans and FSAs, and fund them to the maximum amount possible. If you need to borrow against your retirement plan assets, do so, but repay the loan before you retire. Select the form of health insurance coverage that best meets your needs, whether it be a traditional reimbursement system, an HMO or a PPO. If you choose a traditional plan, consider opting for a higher deductible if you can afford it. This option will lower your premiums considerably. Inquire about subsidized college education loans for your children. Make sure that you understand any life or disability insurance provided by your employer. If you don't have enough coverage, ask your benefits department whether you can purchase more through payroll deduction. Avail yourself of any other benefits, such as employee assistance programs, job retraining or financial planning. Because your 40s and 50s are your peak earning years and your employee benefits are usually tied to your salary, they are worth the most to you during this time. Take full advantage of them.

Your 60s and Up—The Retired Years

If you have planned for retirement most of your working life, the transition into retirement starting in your 60s should be relatively smooth. Ideally, you will have accumulated enough capital through a combination of employee benefits plans and personal investments to produce enough income to live comfortably. You will have developed enough hobbies and other interests aside from your job that you will not feel at a loss about what to do with all the free time that retirement offers. And you will have given thought to your retirement housing options and done some estate planning.

Few people actually get around to mapping out all these aspects of their retirement ahead of time. However, don't think of retirement as lasting a few short years before you die, as earlier generations did. Today, the average life expectancy for someone in good health who retires in his or her early 60s is at least 20 years, and many retirees live into their 90s or even 100s. Therefore, you have many golden years for which to plan. As you enter your preretirement and retirement years, evaluate each aspect of your personal finances so you can enjoy an active and stimulating retirement.

Giving Yourself a Financial Checkup

As you make the transition from the working years into retirement, complete the worksheets in Chapter 1 to assess your current net worth and cash flow. Hopefully, you will have amassed a significant amount of assets and paid off most, if not all, of your debts. You should be operating with much positive cash flow because many of the expenses of your earlier years, such as college tuition and buying everything from baby clothes to furniture, no longer apply. Meanwhile, once you retire, you should receive income from Social Security, your company's defined benefit and/or defined contribution pension plan, your investments and your annuities. On the other hand, if your living expenses exceed your income, use Chapter 1's budgeting exercise to find ways to reduce your expenses, as well as increase your income.

Be sure to complete the Recordkeeping Worksheet so your family knows the location of all records and can locate all financial advisers when you die. By now, you will have built up a lifetime of contacts, and it could be extremely time consuming for your loved ones to reconstruct the family's financial life without this information.

As you redefine your financial goals, consider how many of your past goals you have accomplished. It may give you a great sense of satisfaction to remember that the most important goals of your youth—to buy a home, to put your children through college or to travel extensively, for example—were met. Or the exercise may remind you of what you hoped to accomplish but never got around to during your working life. In reprioritizing your goals for your retirement years, you might aim to achieve some of these unsatisfied goals, if they still apply.

In reassessing your risk tolerance, you will probably find that you have grown much more risk averse than ever. That is appropriate. As you move into retirement, capital preservation takes priority over capital growth.

As you move through your 60s into your 70s and 80s, give yourself a complete financial checkup every few years. The exercise will keep you up to date with your financial situation.

Investing. Once you stop bringing home a salary, you might be tempted to convert your investment portfolio from a broad mix of stocks, bonds and cash instruments to solely income-oriented bonds. That could be the worst investment move you'll ever make. If you live for another 20 or 30 years, not only will your portfolio have to provide you with current income; it must also protect you against inflation. Someone who retired in the 1950s might have felt totally secure putting all his or her money in long-term bonds yielding about 3 percent. But over the next few decades, the purchasing power of the money would have been devalued considerably by rampaging inflation. Therefore, if you lock yourself into current yields by buying only bonds, your capital will not grow as it most likely will if you own stocks.

So the best investing strategy in retirement is to assemble a conservative mix of stocks, bonds and cash vehicles that produces enough income to live on but also grows in value over time. This might mean keeping about 80 percent of your assets in cash instruments, like money-market funds, and fixed-income assets, such as Treasury, high-quality corporate, junk and municipal bonds, mortgage-backed securities and the mutual funds that hold these assets. In assessing which bond fund is best, scrutinize expense ratios; the greater a fund's expenses, the less your yield. Bond funds should have expense ratios of 1.3 percent or less, and preferably less than 1 percent of their assets—a figure you can determine by looking at the cover of the prospectus or asking a fund representative. Also, consider closed-end bond funds, which can offer very attractive yields, particularly if they sell at a discount. Depending on whether yields make it profitable, some of this fixed-income money could be invested in certificates of deposit (CDs).

Invest the remaining 20 percent of your money in stocks or stock mutual funds, which provide an inflation hedge. Most of these stocks and funds should be high yielding so they give you current income, as well as growth. To find safe, high-yielding stocks, search such industries as electric, gas, water and telephone utilities, banking, oil and insurance. If you would like to have a bit of fun, invest a small portion of your portfolio—perhaps 10 percent—in more speculative growth stocks. Be prepared to lose some or all of this money, and don't invest cash you can't afford to part with. For a more diversified portfolio, buy mutual funds holding mostly high-yielding stocks. Types of funds you might want in your portfolio that offer growth potential and current income include total return, balanced, flexible, equity-income, growth and income, and convertible funds. You can buy such funds in either open-end or closed-end form. For more details, consult Chapter 4 on mutual funds.

As the value of your portfolio changes over time, keep a proper mix of income and growth components. For example, if the stock market rises sharply, your equity portion may rise significantly beyond 20 percent. Thus, you might consider selling some of the stocks and reinvesting the money in bonds, which will produce more income. If stock prices fall, you might buy stocks at bargain prices with some of the income from your bonds. See Chapters 2 thru 7 for more details.

Real estate. By the time you retire, your children probably will have left your home, and you might have more space than you need. Some retirees sell their home and move into a smaller rented apartment or a retirement community, either in the state where they have been living or in a more benign climate. If you sell your home, reinvest the proceeds in income-producing stocks and bonds. Remember, you can avoid all capital gains taxes on the sale of your home as long as your profit is less than $500,000 for a married couple filing jointly or $250,000 for a single and as long as it has been your primary residence for two of the past five years. If you remain in your home, pay off your mortgage, if possible; you do not want to expend your income on monthly debt. You might take out a reverse mortgage, in which the bank sends you a monthly check until you die. The amount is based on the value of your home, your age and life expectancy, and the interest rate on the mortgage. For more about such mortgages, see Chapter 8 on real estate.

Also, consider various forms of real estate as income producers. Rental real estate—as long as the rent is higher than your operating costs—can be attractive though you may not want the headaches of being a landlord. You can also earn significant income without management hassles by buying into real estate investment trusts (REITs), real estate mutual funds or income-oriented real estate limited partnerships, all discussed in more detail in Chapter 8.

Credit. Try to minimize debt as much as possible in your retirement years. Because you no longer have a salary to produce income for debt payments, debt is particularly burdensome when you are retired. Use debt for the convenience of arranging large purchases, such as a new car or extensive travel. Before you take on such an obligation, however, make sure that you have the income to pay off the debt quickly. One of the worst situations a retiree can face is to struggle to pay off large balances on credit cards that charge double-digit, nondeductible interest rates.

By your retirement years, you will have established an extensive credit record. For more information on credit records, see Chapter 9 on maintaining good credit. If you have handled debt responsibly and paid your bills on time, you will probably receive continuous offers of credit cards and unsecured lines of personal credit. Accept these offers only if you need to borrow for a specific large purchase. Otherwise, having these credit lines may tempt you to assume debt unnecessarily. On the other hand, if you have established a poor credit record, littered with overdue bills and default judgments, you will have a hard time obtaining credit. The Equal Credit Opportunity Act specifies that you cannot be denied credit because of your age, but lenders certainly can turn you down if your income is too low or you have a poor credit history.

Cars. As long as you can drive safely, keep your car. You might want to trade up to a more luxurious model that offers conveniences that make it easier to drive as you get older. For example, you may opt for a car with a large electronic instrument panel display that is easy to read or a windshield heating system that makes it easy to scrape ice and snow off your car after a snowstorm.

You must go through the process of deciding whether to buy or lease your car, just as you did when you were younger. To help you make the decision, complete the worksheets in Chapter 10 on buying a car. If you buy a car, you spend your capital, which will no longer be available to produce income. If you lease, you do not have to make a large down payment, and your costs might be lower than for an auto loan, depending on the terms of and interest rate on the loan. A lease therefore may cost you less each month and allow you to keep more of your capital invested in income-producing stocks, bonds and mutual funds. Those who plan to keep their car only three to five years should seriously consider leasing.

Insurance. Your needs for the five types of insurance—car, disability, health, homeowner's and life—differ significantly in retirement from your insurance needs during your working years.

Car insurance is mandatory in most states. If you have a superior driving record and file few claims, your premiums now should be much lower than you paid when you were younger. Many insurers offer mature driver discounts of about 10 percent off your premium. On the other hand, if you have been a reckless driver and have been rejected by many insurance companies, you probably find coverage expensive and difficult to obtain now. Depending on the condition of your car, you may be able to lower your premium by reducing the amount of collision damage coverage you carry. Don't cut back on basic comprehensive liability coverage, though; a massive lawsuit could wipe out your retirement nest egg if you get into an accident.

Disability insurance, because it is designed to replace lost wages if you are injured on the job, is not necessary once you retire. If you have been receiving disability payments, they may cease once you reach age 65 or qualify for Social Security, which also pays disability benefits. Some disability policies offer a life-extension rider that will pay you benefits for the rest of your life if you are permanently disabled before age 60. Such riders are quite expensive and usually not worthwhile.

Health insurance is extremely important in your retirement years because, as you age, you will probably need more medical care. The best health coverage is probably that provided by the company from which you retired even though you must pay the full premiums. You might find a good health maintenance organization (HMO) or preferred provider organization (PPO) that provides good care and controls your health costs. In addition, sign up for both Part A and Part B of Medicare after evaluating the various plans described in Chapter 11 on insurance. You will also need a Medigap policy on top of Medicare, also described in Chapter 11. If your income is low enough, you can also qualify for Medicaid. If you are a veteran, you may be able to obtain medical care through the Department of Veterans Affairs (VA). If you anticipate needing a nursing home or medical care in your own residence, look into the many long-term-care policies offered by insurance companies. The younger you buy such a policy, the less expensive your premiums will be. If you purchase the policy right before you need the benefits, it will be prohibitively expensive.

Homeowner's insurance continues to be necessary if you still own your home. Work through the Household Inventory Worksheet in Chapter 11 to document all the possessions you have accumulated over the years, and make sure that you have enough coverage to replace essential items if they are damaged, lost or stolen. If you have acquired valuable property, such as jewelry, computers or artwork, you might buy a rider to cover them adequately. If you sell your home and move into an apartment or a condominium, buy enough insurance to replace your possessions, if necessary.

Life insurance can be very useful for retirees. If you have funded a cash-value policy—such as *whole life, variable life* or *universal life*—for many years, you probably have built up considerable cash value. Either you can let that cash value continue to accumulate tax deferred, or you can tap that asset by converting it into an annuity that pays monthly income for the rest of your life or for the rest of both your life and your spouse's life. If you have *term insurance,* the premiums are now probably so high that it makes little sense to continue coverage. The main reason for life insurance is to replace your salary for your spouse and children if you die during your working years. When you no longer produce a salary, the need for coverage disappears.

The life insurance product often appropriate in retirement is an *annuity.* You can either transfer a lump sum from a pension plan payout into an annuity or buy one with your accumulated investment capital. Whatever the funds' source, several payout options exist and are described in great detail in Chapter 11. The longer you obligate the insurance company to pay benefits, the lower your monthly check.

Education. By the time you retire, your children should either have graduated college or be nearing graduation. You may be paying off education loans for years to come if you did not save enough for their education while they were still young. See Chapter 12 for ways to fund college. Once your children establish themselves and earn a regular income, ask them to help pay off the loans if they are financially able to do so.

If you have grandchildren, you may want to start a college fund for them. You can give up to $10,000 per child annually free of gift tax, which should be placed in a Uniform Gifts to Minors Act (UGMA) account in the grandchild's name. If the child is younger than ten years of age, invest the money in growth-oriented investments, such as growth-stock mutual funds. As the child approaches college age, invest the capital in more conservative assets, such as growth and income stock mutual funds and bonds.

Taxes. In theory, you should pay less taxes once you retire because your lack of salary places you in a lower tax bracket. This old rule of thumb is not necessarily valid today. Your combined income from pensions, Social Security, individual retirement accounts (IRAs), Keogh plans, annuities and investments may place you in or near the top tax bracket. To minimize the tax bite, receive your retirement income in a way that will stretch out your tax liability for as many years as possible. Chapter 13 shows you tax planning strategies. For example, unless you absolutely need the capital to live on, do not take distributions from your IRA or Keogh until you reach age 70½. This strategy allows the maximum amount of time for your assets to accumulate tax deferred. If you withdraw funds from an insurance contract, first take out your original principal, which is not taxable, then receive distributions from investment earnings, which are subject to taxation. If you are in the top tax bracket, you may want to sell investments producing taxable income, such as Treasury or corporate bonds, and buy municipal bonds paying tax-free income. If you live in a high-tax state, buy bonds issued by that state to sidestep both federal and state taxes.

Take full advantage of the many provisions in the tax code aimed at senior citizens. If you are age 65 or older, the following provisions apply:

- You must file a return only if you report a gross income of $7,800 or more for a single person, or $13,800 for a married couple filing jointly.

- If you do not itemize, you qualify for a higher standard deduction of as much as $1,000.

- You may qualify for a tax credit if you do not receive Social Security or railroad retirement benefits.

- All income you receive from Social Security is tax free if your provisional income is $44,000 or less and you are married, filing jointly, or if your income is $34,000 or less and you file singly, as the head of a household or as a widow or widower.

- If your income is between $32,001 and $44,000 as a married couple filing jointly, or between $25,001 and $34,000 filing singly, you are taxed on as much as 50 percent of your Social Security benefits. If your provisional income is $44,000 or more and you are married, filing jointly, or if your provisional income is $34,000 or more and you file singly, you will have to pay income tax on up to 85 percent of your benefits.

- If you move into a continuing-care or life-care community, the portion of your monthly fees allocated to health care services is deductible as an itemized medical expense.

Retirement. If you have planned for retirement most of your working life, now is the time to reap the rewards of your efforts. On the financial front, you should know how much income you will receive from your pension, IRA, Keogh, salary reduction plan, annuities, Social Security and investment portfolio. To help you review these retirement planning strategies, see Chapter 14. You should also have an estimate of your living expenses in retirement. Once you have been retired for a few months, redo your budget so you can realistically balance your expenses with your income. If you have not planned for retirement, you have a lot of catching up to do. You have run out of time to save and invest money from your salary; therefore, you must draw up a realistic budget based on the assets you have, the income those assets can generate and your expenses.

On the nonfinancial front, plan how to use your time so you feel productive and busy. This may involve developing a hobby, going back to school, traveling, volunteering or spending more time with your children and grandchildren. Your retirement can be the best or worst time of your life, depending on how you spend your time.

Estate planning. If you have accumulated assets worth more than $625,000 (rising to $1 million in 2006, and $1.3 million for farmers and small business owners), you need to execute a detailed estate plan, which may involve establishing trusts. Even if you do not have that much money, you need a will to instruct the probate court how to distribute your assets. To avoid probate, look into establishing a *living trust,* which you control while you are alive but that can curb estate taxes and complications for your heirs when you die.

To guard against the possibility that you may become mentally or physically incapacitated, execute a *living will, durable power of attorney* or *health care power of attorney,* which allows your spouse, children, doctor or close friend to make vital medical decisions if you are incapable of doing so.

Also, plan your funeral, and make arrangements for burial, cremation, donation to science or whichever method you choose to dispose of your remains.

For a more detailed explanation of estate planning, consult Chapter 15.

Employee benefits. Once you retire, you lose your active employee benefits, but you can start to collect on the pension funds you have accumulated for years. When you leave the payroll, you no longer are covered by your employer's group term life insurance. Neither do you qualify for education or employee assistance programs. And your employer no longer covers your health insurance premiums.

Some benefits, though, may continue into retirement; make sure that you know which ones they are. For example, try to obtain continued medical coverage. You will have to pay the full premium, but your company's retiree health plan probably offers far better rates than you could get on your own.

Determine when it is most advantageous to retire. The later you stop working, the greater your monthly Social Security and defined benefit pension checks. Your benefits counselor can calculate your monthly pension check at different retirement ages. If you receive an early-retirement offer, your company may add a few years to your actual years of service to allow you to qualify for a more generous pension.

You will be offered several options for the payout of the accumulated value in your defined contribution plan. For example, you may take the money in a lump sum and roll it into your IRA or buy an annuity with it. Or you may leave the money with the company and withdraw cash regularly. Consult an employee benefits counselor or a financial planner when making such decisions. Chapter 16 describes employee benefit options and plans in more detail.

When You're Single

If you are single, you probably fall into one of two camps. Either you have chosen to remain single because you like the lifestyle, and you never plan to marry (a committed single) or you are currently single but hope to marry someday (a temporary single). Couples who live together represent a compromise between the lifestyles: Both people are legally single, but their financial lives are closely intertwined, like a married pair's. The best financial strategies for you depend heavily on which kind of single you are.

Being single means that you must worry only about yourself, at least for the immediate future. In the long term, temporary singles may have responsibility for a spouse and, perhaps, children. And committed singles may have to support elderly parents. Singles who live together often feel some sense of responsibility for each other even though they may not be legally liable. The personal finance discussions that follow touch on all three single lifestyles.

GIVING YOURSELF A FINANCIAL CHECKUP

No matter what your age or family situation, you need to work through the exercises in Chapter 1 to evaluate where you stand financially, where you want to go and how you plan to get there. Because you are the only one who benefits by creating a personal budget, performing a cash flow analysis, setting financial goals and assessing risk tolerance, don't expect someone else to nudge you into action. You have no one to clear your decisions with, so completing these worksheets should be much easier for you than for someone who must hash them out with a spouse. For example, the spending priorities you set in your budget may seem illogical to another person, but they can be just right for you. When you evaluate your risk tolerance, your investment choices affect only you. So, if you buy a high-flying stock that crashes, only your portfolio is adversely affected; you must justify your gamble to no one. Singles can take a bit more risk in search of higher returns than investors financially responsible for others can.

Investing. Before you invest too much in stocks, bonds and mutual funds, establish an emergency reserve fund consisting of at least three months'—and preferably six months'—salary. Because you have no one else to rely on if you get sick or have an unexpectedly large car repair bill, you must be prepared to fund these contingencies on your own.

With your rainy-day fund well established, enroll in every investment program your employer offers. This might include a *salary reduction* or *profit-sharing plan* to which you can contribute on either a pretax or an after-tax basis through payroll deduction. At a minimum, contribute enough to take advantage of any employer match. In your younger years, invest aggressively because you need growth of capital to fund your retirement. If you eventually marry and have children, you will still need to build capital for retirement. As you approach retirement, allocate your assets more conservatively so you preserve enough capital to produce the income you need for the rest of your life.

Finally, set up an investment account separate from your employer's in which you accumulate stocks, bonds, mutual funds and cash instruments. The only way to build up a substantial portfolio is to experiment and learn by trial and error. Reread Chapters 2 through 8 for the investment background you need to get started. The earlier you begin funding this account, the greater your assets will be at retirement. If you ultimately marry, your portfolio will surely help fund your new household.

If you live with your partner, avoid mingling your investment assets. A joint account requires that you agree on an investment strategy and share tax obligations. If you break up, the process of determining which partner contributed how much to each investment can be excruciatingly difficult and may result in legal wrangling.

Real estate. Singles who live alone need less space than families and therefore can save money on renting or buying real estate. Unless you earn a significant salary, you will also have less income to allocate to rent or a mortgage. Thus, while you are single and young, save money by limiting your spending on real estate. One way to cut expenses is to share your apartment with one or more roommates. As you age and your income rises, you might feel that it is time to buy your own place.

If you are a committed single, buy a home or an apartment in which you are comfortable, as long as you don't stretch your budget too much to do so. Lenders don't want you to spend more than 28 percent of your monthly income on mortgage payments. When you own your own home, you benefit from mortgage interest deductions and probably have a greater sense of permanence in your life than if you continue to rent.

If you are a temporary single, it is unwise to buy a home or an apartment because your future mate might not like the property, the area or even the state. If you have to sell your home in a weak market, you might take a loss, particularly once you count closing costs, which can total several thousand dollars. Therefore, if marriage is likely within three to five years, wait and buy real estate with your spouse.

Be extremely careful if you purchase real estate with someone you have been living with outside of marriage. Have a lawyer draw up a *cohabitation agreement* that specifies who is responsible for how much of the mortgage and maintenance payments and who gets what if you break up or if one of you wants to sell his or her share of the property. If you and your partner have a dispute over who owns what, the person named on the deed or who proves that he or she holds title probably will retain rights to the property. For more information on buying real estate, see Chapter 8.

Credit. Your spending and debt management habits are the keys to building a solid credit rating. Because you are responsible only for yourself, you have no one else to blame if you fall behind on your bills or default on your loans. On the other hand, with total control, if you handle debt adroitly, you will be rewarded with the ability to borrow whatever you need whenever you want.

The temptation to take on many credit cards, spend recklessly and assume a great deal of debt is often strong when you are single because you might feel that no one is watching. In fact, you *are* monitored—by the credit bureaus that receive reports on how promptly you pay your bills. If you apply for a loan, the potential lender checks this record before granting your request. To contain uncontrolled spending, consolidate several credit card accounts into one or two, and pay at least the monthly minimum due, if not the entire balance.

When you wed, you bring your credit record into the marriage. If your record is filled with black marks from credit grantors, it will hurt your ability to qualify for credit cards, mortgages and other loans when you apply jointly with your spouse. Therefore, even though you are single now, your present debt habits will affect you and your spouse, for better or for worse, in the future.

If you live with someone, keep your credit lives separate. If you open a joint credit card account, for example, you are both liable for any charges. So, if your partner buys something you disapprove of and then doesn't pay the bill, you must either pay it or have your credit record sullied. For more information on establishing and maintaining good credit, see Chapter 9 on credit.

Cars. As a single, you can probably get by with a smaller, less expensive car. However, many singles see a car as the ultimate expression of their personality, so they buy a fancier model than is practical. It's up to you, but realize that the money you spend on a snazzy convertible is no longer available to fund other needs or to invest for your retirement.

Committed singles should feel more comfortable about buying a car than singles who may someday marry. If you plan to live alone for life, get the car you want, and hold onto it. On the other hand, if you hope to marry, your spouse might have different ideas about the ideal car. If you have children, your transportation needs will change even more. Therefore, depending on the terms of a lease and prevailing interest rates on auto loans, it might make more sense for a committed single to buy a car and a temporary single to lease.

If you live with someone, it is dangerous to buy or lease a car jointly. Both of you are liable for car payments, and if one doesn't pay, the other must. If you split up, you might battle over who keeps the car. You can avoid many problems if only one of you buys or leases the car in his or her name. Chapter 10 offers more details on buying versus leasing cars.

Insurance. Your priorities for buying the five types of insurance—car, disability, health, homeowner's and life—as a single differ from those of a married couple. Your highest insurance priority should be disability coverage because you will need to replace your income if you are injured on the job. Your employer probably provides some *disability* coverage, but often it is not enough. Look into a supplemental policy that will pay 60 to 70 percent of your salary if you become incapacitated. Make sure that the policy is guaranteed renewable and locks in a premium until age 65. With such a supplemental policy, the insurance company cannot discontinue coverage, even if you make several claims. You might also be eligible for payments under Social Security's disability program. For more details on disability and other kinds of insurance, see Chapter 11 on insurance.

Singles' needs for *auto insurance* do not vary much from those of married couples. The amount of collision coverage you carry depends on the value of your car more than on your marital status. Make sure to obtain adequate comprehensive and liability coverage to protect your assets against lawsuits. Some insurance companies charge singles more than married people on the premise that singles are out and about in their car more than married people, who drive carefully to protect their spouse and children. You might overcome this disadvantage if you maintain a clean driving record.

Adequate *health insurance* is extremely important for singles. Because you depend on only one income, you are more vulnerable to a severe financial reversal if you suffer an expensive medical treatment that goes unreimbursed. You probably have health coverage provided by your employer; however, you might have to pay an ever-rising share of the premiums. A less expensive alternative that may provide satisfactory medical care is a *health maintenance organization* (HMO) or *preferred provider organization* (PPO) plan offered through your employer. If you cannot obtain health coverage from your job, you might find the cost of an individual health insurance policy prohibitive. See whether you can enroll in an HMO, a PPO or another managed care plan during one of its open enrollment periods. Otherwise, you might have to buy coverage from your local Blue Cross/ Blue Shield carrier during their open enrollment.

If you own your home or apartment, *homeowner's insurance* will protect you against liability suits and loss or damage to your possessions. If you have particularly valuable jewelry, artwork or electronic equipment, consider adding riders to cover these possessions if they are damaged or stolen. Single renters also should consider buying *renter's insurance* to replace their possessions and defend against liability lawsuits.

Life insurance should not be a priority for you if you are single. Because life insurance is designed to replace your income upon your death for someone who depends on it, you have no need for coverage if you support no one but yourself. This is particularly true for the committed single; a *term insurance* policy would be a total waste of money. If you are a single who plans to marry and have children someday, you have one reason to buy a *whole life* policy now: You lock in a premium rate for life when you buy the policy, and the younger you are, the cheaper the premium. So, if you buy a whole life policy when you are 25 years old and still single, then marry at age 35, you will already have some of the coverage you need locked in at an age-25 premium level.

For singles living together outside of marriage, life insurance might make sense because the surviving partner may depend on the income generated by their mate. You must make sure to designate your mate as the beneficiary of the policy, however, because your family members may object if your mate, not your family members, receives the death benefit.

For a tax-deferred retirement savings vehicle, consider an *annuity.* You can buy either a fixed annuity, which pays a specified rate of interest each year, or a variable annuity, which gives you far more growth potential because it offers the ability to move your assets between stock, bond and money-market funds within a tax-deferred insurance contract. By the time you retire, you might have amassed a large amount of assets, which you can then convert into a monthly stream of income for the rest of your life.

Education. If you've recently graduated from college, you will probably have to repay education loans for years. This can take quite a bite out of your monthly budget. Try to accelerate repayment of your loans if you earn a good income or receive a windfall from an inheritance or lottery winnings, for example. If you are a committed single without children, you will never have to worry about funding college tuition. Invest the extra money in your retirement fund. Even temporary singles should not save for college until they marry and have children. Read Chapter 12 for more information on college financing.

Taxes. Unmarried singles have two options in filing their tax status: single or head of household. Single status is usually more costly than head-of-household status because you move into higher tax brackets at lower levels of income. For example, in 1998 the 28 percent tax bracket begins at $24,651 for single filers and

$33,051 for head-of-household filers. To qualify as a head of household, you must be unmarried, maintain a household for more than half the year for a child or dependent relative, and pay more than half the cost of that household. Become familiar with the many IRS tax code provisions for taxpayers filing singly and as heads of household. For instance, in 1998 your personal exemption begins to be phased out when your adjusted gross income exceeds $121,200 as a single or $151,500 as a head of household.

The tax code also establishes numerous rules governing the self-employed single, including provisions regarding the payment of self-employment Social Security taxes and regulations governing contributions to Keogh, SEP and SIMPLE accounts. For more detail on these matters and other tax considerations, consult Chapter 13 on tax planning.

Retirement. If singles don't save for their own retirement, who will? You will receive some income from Social Security and your defined benefit pension if you have one; other than that, you're on your own. Take advantage of the fact that you have no one else to support financially, and stash away cash in your retirement plans as soon as you can afford to do so. The earlier you start, the more money you will have to live on in retirement. Participate in any defined contribution plan your employer offers. At a minimum, contribute enough to take advantage of any company matching funds. However, if you can afford it, have the maximum allowable contribution deducted from your paycheck. Not only will you amass a larger retirement fund; you will cut this year's taxes if you make contributions on a pretax basis.

If you are not be eligible for any pension plan, open an individual retirement account (IRA), and make tax-deductible contributions every year. If you run your own business or produce self-employment income through freelance activities, you can also fund a Keogh and deduct your contributions. Your money grows tax deferred inside both an IRA and a Keogh. This gives these vehicles a tremendous edge over regular accounts, on which you pay taxes on income or capital gains each year.

As you near retirement, plan which activities or hobbies you will pursue to keep your mind and body active. Loneliness can be a major problem among single retirees, so anticipate how to avoid it; consider travel, volunteer work, counseling or a new hobby. Also, look into retirement housing options. You may want to stay in the home or apartment you now occupy. Or you might be happy living in a continuing-care community that provides independence while offering easy access to medical care and the opportunity to make friends. For more on these and other retirement options, consult Chapter 14 on retirement.

Estate planning. With no spouse or children to inherit your assets, you do not have an urgent need for complex estate planning. Nevertheless, if you want to contribute your assets to a close friend, his or her children or your favorite charity, consult an estate-planning attorney. You might set up a *trust* in which you place assets that provide you income for the rest of your life. When you die, the assets in the trust are passed on to the beneficiary. To allocate any of your possessions to a particular person, include a set of detailed instructions in your will. If you do no estate planning, the government will take a huge portion of your estate in taxes and distribute your assets in a way you might not choose.

If you live with someone outside of marriage, a *will* becomes even more critical. Both you and your partner should write wills distributing all your possessions to each other. Otherwise, your assets will go to your next of kin or to whomever the probate court judge names. Because your will may be contested by potential beneficiaries of your assets, it is important to have it drawn up by a qualified estate planning lawyer and witnessed properly. You may also want to place assets in a living trust so that when you die, they pass immediately from you to your housemate outside of probate court. A good lawyer will advise you on the wisdom of this strategy, based on your circumstances.

For more on these and other estate planning strategies, see Chapter 15 on estate planning.

Employee benefits. Because you are the only person to benefit from your employee perks, learn about all the benefits your employer offers, and take maximum advantage of them. If you don't look into these benefit plans, no one else will do it for you. Determine which health insurance plan will cost you the least and give you the broadest coverage. Sign up for a *flexible spending account* (FSA), which will reimburse you for medical bills not covered by your regular health insurance. Avail yourself of education or employee assistance programs if you need them. Participate in any retirement savings program your company offers. By the time you retire, you should be able to roll over a significant lump sum from your savings programs into your IRA to fund years of comfortable retirement living. For more on how to get the most from your employer, reread Chapter 16 on employee benefits.

When You're Married

Three types of married couples exist: those with children, those currently without children but hoping to have them someday and those who anticipate never having children. The state of marriage itself affects many financial decisions; when you add children, even more financial planning is necessary. Raising and educating children costs tens of thousands of dollars, for which you need to budget. In addition, you must decide what kind of home and car you need, how much insurance will adequately cover you and your possessions and which estate planning techniques are most appropriate for passing on your assets to your children. The following discussion of various personal finance issues covers all three types of married couples.

GIVING YOURSELF A FINANCIAL CHECKUP

It is vital that each married couple assess their financial situation whether they are just newlyweds or have celebrated their golden anniversary. In some marriages, the husband takes the lead in family financial matters; in others, the wife takes charge. While one spouse may dominate the financial responsibilities, it is important that his or her mate plays an active role in setting priorities and making financial decisions.

Begin your financial checkup by completing with your spouse the worksheets in Chapter 1.

- Compiling your net worth will give you a chance to add up all the assets and liabilities you have accumulated at this point in your marriage.

- Writing down where you keep all your important documents, what financial advisers you consult and how to contact your relatives will help in an emergency.

- Setting financial goals will test your ability to compromise because you must prioritize those things that are more and less important to both of you in the short, medium and long term.

- Completing a cash flow statement will give you an accurate picture of your spending habits and update you on how much income you and your spouse earn.

- Creating a monthly budget will help you put your priorities into practice as you allocate your income among competing spending priorities.

- Assessing your risk tolerance will determine whether you and your spouse agree on how much investment uncertainty you should accept to earn higher returns on your assets. In most marriages, one spouse is dedicated to capital preservation, while the other is more willing to take risks.

Once you have completed these exercises, discuss what you have learned about your financial situation and your attitudes toward your personal finances. Don't expect to agree about everything all—or even most—of the time. Nevertheless, listen to your partner's point of view, and take it into account when you decide on a final course of action.

Not only is making important financial decisions jointly good for the longevity of your marriage; it also allows both partners to understand their current financial affairs. Quite frequently, a husband who has taken care of the family finances by himself for decades dies suddenly, leaving his widow without a clue about their investments, insurance, estate plans and every other financial matter. Unscrupulous insurance salespeople, brokers and financial planners often try to capitalize on such a widow's naivete. Also, such a widow's confusion and lack of knowledge about her financial situation may cause her to panic and make hasty decisions or be indecisive when she needs to take action to protect her future financially.

If you have children, involve them in your family's finances as much as possible as they grow older. Giving youngsters the opportunity to handle money responsibly helps them get a head start in life. Of course, discuss only those money subjects that a child is able to comprehend at different ages. Following are a few general age guidelines for talking money with your children.

- *From the time they speak coherently to the time they enter preschool,* explain what money is and how it works. When you buy items at the grocery store, have them hand the cashier the money so they grasp the concept of receiving goods in exchange for cash. Give your children a dollar or two, and explain how much things cost so they must choose the item they want most among several potential purchases.

- *From preschool to first grade,* give your children a weekly allowance in exchange for behaving well or doing certain chores, such as picking up the toys in their playroom. However, make it clear that such behavior is expected and need not be compensated.

- *From second grade through junior high school,* boost your children's weekly allowance in return for additional and more responsible chores. For example, your older child may babysit your younger child. Or your children might mow the lawn, shovel the snow or paint the house. Some parents pay a certain dollar amount for high grades in school, though this can put a great deal of pressure on your youngsters. As your children grow older, encourage them to save some of their money in either a bank or a mutual fund account. To give them extra incentive to do so, match their deposit dollar for dollar. This will teach them about investing and promote the saving habit early.

- *From high school through college,* make your children fully aware of your family's financial situation. Encourage them to participate in important financial discussions, and give them a family credit card so they learn to use credit responsibly. Help your children obtain jobs in the summer or even during the school year that will expose them to a profession they are interested in pursuing. Involve them in all discussions about how their college education will be financed, including how much they might work during college to qualify for various forms of financial aid.

- *By the time your children graduate from college,* they should have had years of exposure to money management so they can use credit, open a bank account, make investments, buy a car and accomplish other common financial transactions on their own. If you did not introduce them to personal finance as they grew up, their transition to independence could be much more difficult.

You also might tap into the tremendous number of resources on the Internet to teach your children about money. Many brokerage firms and mutual funds devote part of their Web sites to educating kids about money issues. Another area to check out is the Investing Forum for Children under "Sage" on America Online. You and your children can learn in what is known as the "Kidz Korner" about stocks, mutual funds, banking and saving, among other topics. There are bulletin boards where your kids can post questions, broken down into young investors, age 14 and under, and age 15 and over categories. Some other child-oriented financial sites include: Kids' Money Web Resources (www.pages.prodigy.com/kidsmoney); Kid's Club (www.Isttech.com/kidsclb/); Money KaZAM (www.finitycorp.com/). Another site, sponsored by the Mutual Fund Education Alliance and called All About Investing for Children (www.mfea.com/childfeatr/), links you to the sites of many of the Alliance's mutual fund members and explains UGMA accounts, college savings strategies and funds designed for young investors.

Investing. One of the most difficult habits for couples to establish is regular investment. Begin such a program with the defined contribution, salary reduction or profit-sharing plan offered by your and your spouse's employers. Enroll as soon as you are eligible, and deposit as much money out of your paycheck as possible. Not only do these plans allow you to amass a sizeable, tax-deferred retirement fund; they also cut your current tax bill if you are allowed to contribute pretax dollars.

Also, deposit a certain amount of your earnings in a joint savings and investment account aside from the one your employer offers. Start by building your emergency cash reserve to at least three months'—and, preferably, six months'—salary. You never know when you might need this money to cover unexpected medical bills, travel or breakdowns of major appliances. For more information on cash instruments, see Chapter 2.

In the years when you have no children, strive to save 10 to 20 percent of your gross income. While you are young, invest most of the money in growth-oriented vehicles, such as growth stocks or aggressive growth and international stock mutual funds. You can also enroll in one of the approximately 1,000 dividend reinvestment plans (DRIPs) described in Chapter 3 on stocks. Or you can set up an automatic investment program with almost any mutual fund. The fund debits your bank account for whatever amount you specify, whether it be $50 or $5,000, on a biweekly, monthly or quarterly basis.

By accumulating a substantial pool of capital when you have fewer financial obligations, you will be better able to afford the expenses of raising and educating your children when they arrive. Unfortunately, many couples believe that they have little reason to save until they have children, so they spend lavishly in their childless years.

Once you have children, financing their education often becomes a top-priority investment goal. The earlier you start saving money and the more aggressively you invest it, the more chance you have of paying for college without extreme financial strain. You might try saving with one of the many child-oriented mutual funds, such as the no-load Stein Roe Young Investor Fund (800-403-5437), which only requires a $100 minimum initial investment in the Wealth Builder plan and provides a great deal of literature teaching children about money in general and investing in particular. Another example is First Start Growth, sponsored by USAA (800-531-0553). It has a minimum initial investment of $250, with subsequent investments of $20. It also provides newsletters, games and other kid-friendly literature. If you wait until your children become teenagers, you will have to come up with far more money, and you probably will not be able to cover college expenses. This may mean that you and your children will assume thousands of dollars in college debt.

You also might look into some of the mutual funds that are specifically aimed at building a college fund for children. For example, the American Century Twentieth Century Giftrust Investors Fund (800-345-2021) is designed to invest aggressively in a child's name inside a trust and have the capital stay in the fund for at least ten years, at which time it can be used to fund college education. Another such fund is the Royce GiftShares Fund (800-221-4268), which similarly is set up as a trust for a child and is designed to provide long-term capital growth. If the parents want, they can have the Royce Fund pay college expenses directly out of the fund.

If you do not plan to have children, concentrate on making large purchases, such as a home or car, and building your retirement fund. Invest aggressively in your younger years, then become more conservative as you move toward retirement. Most important, set up a disciplined investment program so you do not spend your excess cash frivolously. See Chapters 2 thru 8 for more information.

Real estate. The decision to rent or buy a place to live is a major one for any couple. Not only is buying a home or an apartment a major financial commitment; it also plants your roots in a particular community and leads you to adopt a certain lifestyle. You and your spouse must agree on the kind of housing you want, where you want it and how much of your income you will devote to it. Reread Chapter 8 on real estate to help you assess your short-term and long-term housing needs. If you have no children now but expect to within a few years, consider getting a home large enough to accommodate them, if you can afford it. If you do not plan to have children, you will look for different amenities in the home of your dreams than will a couple with children. For example, you won't need a playroom, but you might want an elegant dining room.

If you and your spouse agree to purchase a home and assemble enough money for a down payment, you must then shop for a mortgage. You can qualify for a much larger loan if you and your spouse earn two incomes rather than one. Assume the mortgage—and therefore own the home—jointly, at least at first. Later, when you are more concerned with estate planning, you might transfer the property into the name of only one spouse to make maximum use of the $625,000 (rising to $1 million in 2006) exemption from estate taxes.

Before you apply for a mortgage, discuss with your spouse the pros and cons of a *fixed-rate* versus a *variable-rate* mortgage. The fixed-rate loan costs much more on a monthly basis, at least in the first few years, but it provides you with the security that your rate will never rise. On the other hand, the variable-rate loan saves money up front, but it exposes you to the risk of higher interest rates in the future. You and your spouse should weigh the financial advantages of the variable-rate loan against the emotional security of the fixed-rate loan until you agree on which is the better mortgage.

If you are financially able to do so, consider purchasing *rental real estate* as well. If one spouse has the time, knowledge and desire to manage the property, you eliminate the cost of hiring a leasing or managing agent. You have two strategies when looking for rental real estate. You can buy an inexpensive property that needs work and raise the rents considerably, once it is repaired, to cover the cost of your improvements. Or you can purchase an apartment or a home in good condition and profit by charging rent higher than your operating costs.

In addition to the potential for profit, you may also qualify for a tax break. See page 555 in Chapter 13 for the details. You can deduct up to $25,000 in losses generated by the property against regular income, as long as your *adjusted gross income* (AGI) is less than $100,000. If your AGI falls between $100,000 and $149,999, you receive a partial write-off. You cannot deduct losses if your AGI is $150,000 or more. Assign the job of landlord to one spouse, however, so both of you are not bothered by the nagging details of managing the property.

Credit. You and your spouse may have different attitudes toward debt. One of you may abhor the idea of borrowing money, while the other may have grown up in a family accustomed to charging even life's basic necessities. Discuss your attitudes about debt, and come to an agreement about how much debt is appropriate for your income and lifestyle.

Though a couple's finances may be intertwined, each spouse's credit records are maintained separately by credit reporting bureaus if the spouse has established credit in his or her own name. Therefore, it is important that both husband and wife take out credit cards and other loans in their own names and repay these loans responsibly. Many a widow is shocked to discover that she cannot qualify for credit when her husband dies because she never established a credit history in her own name. Read Chapter 9 for more information on establishing a credit record.

Once you establish credit, devise a strategy to manage it wisely. Set a limit on the total amount of your income devoted to debt service. While you are young, this may be up to 20 percent; over time, reduce it to 10 percent or less. If you have several credit cards or lines of personal credit, consolidate them into one or two accounts offering the lowest interest rates and annual fees.

If you bring significant debt into your marriage, such as numerous college loans, assume primary responsibility for paying off those loans. The faster you dispose of the debts, the better it is for your marriage.

When you consider taking out loans against the value of your assets, make such decisions jointly. This applies to home-equity, margin and life insurance loans, as well as to borrowing against your retirement plan assets at work. The more you share responsibility for credit decisions with your spouse, the easier it will be for the surviving spouse to carry on when one of you dies.

Cars. The kind of car you buy depends on whether you plan to have children. If you do not think you will, you can forgo a station wagon or mini-van in favor of a more luxurious sedan or sports car. However, if you already have children or expect to soon, look into a more spacious car with the durability to withstand the punishment of tots.

Once you choose a car, decide whether to buy or lease it. If you are childless now but anticipate having children in the next several years, leasing might make more sense because you can turn in your car and buy or lease another that better suits your new family status. If you already have children, leasing might be preferable if you plan to trade your car for another in three to five years, when your child has grown up and takes up more space in the car. On the other hand, if you find a car that will serve you at least five—and possibly ten—years, consider buying it. Also base your buy-versus-lease decision on the terms of the lease, the cost of the car, the interest rate on the loan and other financial factors. Remember, any interest you pay on the car loan is no longer tax deductible. For more on evaluating buying versus leasing, reread Chapter 10 on buying a car.

Insurance. Married couples need all five types of insurance—car, disability, health, homeowner's and life—whether they have children or not. However, the amount of coverage often depends on the existence of children.

Your *auto insurance* contract is more a function of the kind of car you own than the number of children you have. Make sure that you possess adequate comprehensive and liability protection to defend your family's assets against a lawsuit. Retain enough collision coverage to pay for the complete repair of your car in case of an accident.

Disability insurance is critical to protect your spouse and family against a major loss of income if you get injured or ill on the job. Your employer may offer some disability coverage, but look into buying a supplemental policy that would generate between 60 and 70 percent of your salary. If both spouses work, each should have adequate disability protection. Under some circumstances, Social Security will also pay disability benefits.

Health insurance protects your family against the high costs of medical care. If you receive health insurance through your employer, you probably have to pay part of the premium for family coverage, but it is far less expensive to buy insurance in this manner than on your own. If your employer offers the option, look into *health maintenance organizations* (HMOs) or *preferred provider organizations* (PPOs) in your area. These plans should emphasize preventive care and employ a knowledgeable staff of pediatric generalists and specialists if you have children. If your company does not offer health insurance, see whether you can join an HMO, a PPO or another managed care plan during an open enrollment period. If you can't, you will probably have to sign up with Blue Cross/Blue Shield during their open enrollment period, where family rates may be extremely expensive.

If your company offers flexible spending accounts (FSAs) for health and dependent care, take advantage of them. When you enroll in a health care FSA, you must set aside a certain amount of money at the beginning of each year, which will be deducted from your paycheck on a pretax basis. You then use these funds to pay your out-of-pocket expenses, such as unreimbursed deductibles, co-payments, and medical procedures or devices not covered by your primary health insurance. The dependent care FSA works the same way, except that the money reimburses you for child care or the care of elderly parents who live with you. Because the money you siphon into FSAs sidesteps federal, state, local and Social Security taxes, you save significantly using these plans.

Homeowner's insurance protects you against liability claims and damage to or loss of your possessions if you own a home or an apartment. When you marry, you merge possessions from two households, giving you more objects to insure. Children require a whole new roster of items, from bassinets and cribs when they are infants to computers and electronic gadgetry when they are teenagers. Keep your homeowner's policy up to date as you purchase valuable new items.

Life insurance protects your spouse and children against the possibility of your unexpected death and the resulting loss of income. If your spouse also produces income, you need insurance policies for both of you. Add children to the equation, and your need for life insurance grows even greater. If your spouse stays home to care for the children, insurance coverage helps the surviving spouse pay for day care. To calculate exactly how much insurance coverage you require, consult the Survivor's Worksheet in Chapter 11 on insurance.

Once you determine the optimal amount of coverage, decide whether to buy *term insurance* or a form of *cash value insurance,* such as whole life, variable life or universal life. If you are young and earn limited income, term coverage is less expensive but pays off only if you die. As you get older, you might convert some of that term insurance into a cash value policy, which allows you to build a tax-deferred savings reserve.

Insurance experts argue the merits of both term and cash value policies. Term is certainly cheaper, and if you systematically invest the difference between the term premium and a cash value premium, you will probably come out ahead with the term. However, if you are not a disciplined saver, you might find that the cash value policy provides a form of forced savings, which might come in handy when you retire. If you accumulate a considerable amount of cash value and no longer need the death benefit, you can convert the savings into an annuity, which will pay you monthly income for the rest of your life.

You and your spouse might also consider an *annuity* as a tax-deferred retirement savings vehicle. You can either contribute to an annuity during your working years or roll over a lump sum at retirement into an annuity. A fixed annuity pays the same rate for a specified period of time, such as one or three years. A variable annuity allows you to transfer your money among stock, bond and money-market accounts. It is riskier but often yields higher returns. When you withdraw funds from an annuity, you have several payout options, as described in Chapter 11 on insurance. One of the most popular options for a married couple is the *joint and survivor payout plan,* which pays monthly income for the rest of your and your spouse's lives.

Education. Start a college savings program once you have your first child. As soon as he or she is born, set up a *Uniform Gifts to Minors Act* (UGMA) account, and deposit money regularly to help defray those frightening tuition bills that will start in 18 years. As long as your child is younger than age 14, his or her account can generate up to $700 of income per year without taxation. Income from $700 to $1,400 is taxed at the child's tax rate. Income exceeding $1,400 is taxed at the parent's tax rate, which is usually higher than the child's.

For at least the first ten years of the child's life, invest the college funds aggressively in growth stocks or growth-stock mutual funds, which have the best chance of appreciating sharply. As the first tuition bill draws nearer, become more and more conservative with the money so ideally, the day your child starts school, you have all the cash you need in a money-market fund.

In addition to traditional investing techniques, you may want to investigate some of the newer alternatives, such as baccalaureate bonds, prepaid tuition plans and College Savings CDs, which are discussed in more detail in Chapter 12 on financing a college education. The longer you delay your savings and investment program, the more difficult it will be to fund your child's education, and the more you might have to rely on loans. Chapter 12 describes the many types of loans and grants available today, as well as the arduous process of applying for them. Most financial aid is awarded to families who need it, as determined by strict criteria. You are far better off saving for college while your child is young than you are enduring the financial aid process and saddling yourself and your child with huge loans that will take years to repay.

Taxes. The tax code offers married couples many advantages. For example, married couples filing jointly move into higher tax brackets at higher levels of income than do singles. For instance, in the 1997 tax year, married couples filing jointly move from the 15 percent to the 28 percent tax bracket at an income of $41,200, while singles are bumped up to the higher bracket at $24,650 and a couple filing separately each is thrown into the higher bracket at $20,600.

Most couples save money if they file a joint return. However, it could be more profitable to file separately if both spouses earn significant taxable income and generate substantial deductions. The IRS says that you must file separately if you and your spouse have different tax-reporting fiscal years, if one spouse is a nonresident alien or if either spouse is claimed as a dependent on someone else's return.

For each of your children, you can claim an exemption that lowers your tax bill. Each exemption provided the equivalent of a $2,650 deduction in 1997. However, those exemptions are phased out if your income is high enough. If you filed jointly for 1997, you start to lose the value of personal exemptions when you report an AGI exceeding $181,800. Your exemptions are completely phased out if your AGI is more than $304,300.

The tax law establishes other rules for couples. For example, if one spouse does not work, the other can still contribute up to $2,000 in a spousal *individual retirement account* (IRA), on top of $2,000 to a regular IRA. For more on tax-planning strategies for married couples, consult Chapter 13.

Retirement. If you and your spouse are in good health, you probably will live well into your 70s, 80s or even 90s. To calculate how much you might need to live comfortably in retirement, complete the worksheets in Chapter 14 on retirement. They will give you some idea of how much money you should set aside each month to accumulate the capital you will need in your later years.

Start saving as early as possible to fund those decades when you will earn no salary. If both you and your spouse are offered a defined contribution plan through your employers, enroll and have as much deducted from your paychecks as is allowed. At a minimum, contribute the most that your employers will match in cash or stock.

In addition to contributing to employer-sponsored savings programs, build your regular joint savings and investment portfolios as much as possible. Set aside a certain amount—preferably 10 to 20 percent—of your incomes, and invest for long-term growth in stocks, bonds and mutual funds.

While you can count on Social Security to provide some income at retirement, don't expect it to cover a significant portion of your living expenses. The combination of your pensions, personal investments and Social Security will provide the income you need for many years of leisure.

Determining how to finance your later years is only part of your retirement considerations. Discuss with your spouse and children where you might want to live and what kinds of activities you might want to pursue in retirement. If you take up a hobby or get involved in civic, political or religious activities to a limited extent while you are still working, you can establish which interests you want to develop further when you retire. Your spouse may want to join you in certain pursuits, such as travel, but expect him or her to participate in other activities in which you have no interest.

Estate planning. Married couples should plan their estates whether or not they have children. If a couple has no will, many state laws say that all the assets of one spouse automatically transfer to the surviving spouse when the first one dies. Some states have different laws of intestate succession that do not make such a transfer automatic. Under federal estate law, however, there is an unlimited marital deduction, so no estate taxes are due when assets pass from one spouse to the other. However, the estate of the surviving spouse will be taxed heavily when he or she dies if none of the assets has been gifted away or no estate planning has been done. If you have children, one of various kinds of trusts may be appropriate. You also need a *will* to designate a guardian to raise your underage children if both you and your spouse die unexpectedly. If you have no children, make provisions to pass your assets to whomever you please, whether it be your next of kin, a close friend or your favorite charity. Chapter 15 on estate planning describes many kinds of trusts and estate-planning strategies in greater detail.

Also, make provisions for the funeral and burial of both you and your spouse. As distasteful as this subject may be, it is far better to handle it objectively in advance than in the midst of your or your surviving spouse's grief.

Employee benefits. One of your family's greatest assets can be the employee benefits you earn as part of your compensation. Your health, term life and disability insurance, retirement savings plans, profit-sharing programs, college education loans, savings bond payroll deduction plans and other benefits can provide a solid financial foundation for your family that would be prohibitively expensive to duplicate on your own.

Coordinate your employee benefits with those of your spouse. For instance, your mate's company may offer an excellent health insurance policy but a limited retirement savings plan, while your firm may provide a mediocre health plan but a generous savings plan. In this case, use your spouse's health policy as the primary insurer, and deposit the maximum possible in your savings plan. Many companies offer cafeteria-style plans that allow you to mix and match benefits according to your needs. If both you and your spouse have such flexibility, you may be able to create a combined set of benefits far superior to those you could obtain on your own.

Discuss your benefits package with your spouse so he or she understands the main provisions of the plans in case you die unexpectedly. The material explaining your company's benefits package can be quite thick and complex, but it is worth reading, at least to learn the basics of how your insurance and savings programs function. Understanding both your and your spouse's benefits packages also helps you plan in the event that one spouse loses his or her job and the family must rely on the remaining benefits. Chapter 16 covers employee benefits in greater detail.

When You're Divorced or Widowed

The emotional trauma of losing a spouse through either death or divorce can be life shattering. But the financial consequences might be even more devastating.

Widows are frequently ill-prepared to handle the many complex aspects of personal finance when their husbands die. The same may hold true for widowers if their wives took charge of the finances; however, it is often husbands who never share information about the family's finances. If, as a widow, you are in such a situation, you must scramble to reassemble your financial foundation. So much needs to be done when you are least able to cope. You must collect on life insurance policies; establish your own credit identity; work with estate lawyers, trustees and probate courts; and assess your investment portfolio, among other things. These overwhelming circumstances can make you particularly vulnerable to misleading or self-serving advice from financial product salespeople presenting themselves as objective financial planners.

Men or women going through a divorce, no matter what their age, suffer some of the same problems as widows and widowers, as well as problems unique to their situation. The process of disassembling a marriage, particularly one in which there are children to consider and many valuable possessions to divide, is not only emotionally wrenching but also expensive and legally complex. Once the divorce is complete, each person must go on with his or her life and deal with numerous complicated personal finance issues. In many cases, one of the partners, usually the woman, has considerably less income to live on after the divorce. This increases the financial pressure on her even more. No one goes into a marriage expecting divorce, but if it happens to you, the following sections could prove to be of great help as you adjust to your new financial reality.

Giving Yourself a Financial Checkup

Whenever you undergo a major change in your family situation, whether it be the death of a spouse or a divorce, it is important to take stock of where you stand financially.

Widowed. As a widow or widower, you will inherit some or all of your spouse's assets, depending on the provisions in his or her will and the estate planning you have done. This will dramatically change your net worth statement, as well as your cash flow and budgeting worksheets found in Chapter 1. If you receive a life insurance settlement, your assets will rise by the amount of the death benefit. However, if your spouse received payments from an annuity with a term certain payout option, annuity payments will cease. Redo your net worth, cash flow and budgeting statements to account for your changed circumstances.

Your recordkeeping worksheet is particularly useful when your spouse dies because it lists the telephone numbers and addresses of all the professional advisers and family members you should contact immediately. If you haven't yet completed this worksheet, do so.

Also, prioritize your financial goals. Without your spouse to consider, you may have different priorities. For instance, you might want to move to another home.

Now that you are alone, assess your risk tolerance as a guide to reallocating your investment portfolio. You might find that you are more willing to take risk than was your spouse, or perhaps you are more conservative. Whatever the case, know where you stand on the risk spectrum before you make any investment moves.

Divorced. Those going through a divorce should follow the same steps as widows in reassessing their financial situation. Once the marriage ends, revise your net worth, cash flow and budget worksheets from Chapter 1. You may now have expenses, such as alimony and child support, that you did not have to account for previously. Or you may bring in dramatically less income after the divorce, so you must adjust your spending accordingly.

It's also time to redo the Recordkeeping Worksheet and eliminate the professional contacts your spouse used. You might have to find new financial planners, accountants, doctors and other professionals. And you will probably have far less contact with your ex-spouse's family.

After the divorce, reset your financial goals. For example, you may have been saving money to buy a home but now find that goal no longer attainable. Instead, your highest priority may be to pay off bills or build your emergency reserve fund.

Finally, reassess your risk tolerance. You may find that because of the divorce, you have become more conservative in your investment outlook. Or you might feel more able to take risk now that you are not restrained by your former spouse. Whatever the case, evaluate your risk profile before making any investment moves.

Investing.

Widowed. Depending on the age you are widowed and the amount of assets you inherit, you will probably want to invest conservatively and stress income over growth of capital. The largest pot of money you will have to invest will be the death benefit of your spouse's life insurance policy, assuming that he or she was covered. Because this capital is designed to replace your spouse's income, it should be invested in income-producing securities, such as utility stocks; Treasury, municipal or corporate bonds; or mutual funds holding such stocks and bonds. Stock mutual funds that are conservative and produce a steady stream of income include equity-income, growth and income, convertible, balanced and flexible funds. All bond funds (except zero-coupon funds) pay regular income, though you will probably want to concentrate on government, corporate, municipal and international bond funds.

Nevertheless, do not invest all of your inherited capital in income-oriented funds. Assuming that you will live a long time, you should have some percentage—perhaps as much as 25 percent—of your portfolio in growth-oriented stocks and stock mutual funds. As the value of such funds increases over time, your assets will be protected against inflation.

You still will need an emergency cash reserve to pay bills and meet unexpected expenses. This might amount to 5 to 10 percent of the value of your portfolio. As you calculate the optimal allocation of your assets among stocks, bonds and cash, keep your risk tolerance in mind. Do not take substantial risk with your money if it makes you uncomfortable. On the other hand, don't invest your money so conservatively that it does not grow fast enough to keep up with inflation or your expenses. Read Chapters 2 through 7 for more information on cash instruments and investing.

Divorced. Divorcees frequently have little money left over to invest if the breakup was bitter and protracted. If you are a divorcee who ends up with few assets, establish a disciplined savings program to get you back on your feet. Set aside each month a regular amount of money, whether it be $10 or $100, in a bank account or mutual fund so you can build a capital base. If you are a divorcee who ends up with some assets, also establish a regular savings program, though you might be able to create a larger and more diversified portfolio than a less fortunate divorcee. If you are young, invest more aggressively in a growth-oriented stock or mutual fund. If you are elderly, keep the money in income-producing vehicles, such as bonds, bond funds or certificates of deposit (CDs). For more information, read Chapters 2 through 7 on cash instruments and various investment vehicles.

Real estate.

Widowed. Widows and widowers tend to stay in the homes they shared with their spouses, for both emotional and financial reasons. If you own a home or an apartment, it is costly and disruptive to sell it and move to a smaller place when your spouse dies. One way to remain in your home and still receive income from the property is to assume a reverse mortgage, which is discussed in more detail in Chapter 8 on real estate. The size of the monthly check you receive from the bank depends on the amount of equity you have in the home, your age and life expectancy, the loan's interest rate and other terms of the deal.

For apartment and house renters, it may be necessary to move to a less expensive place if your income falls so sharply when your spouse dies that you no longer can afford the rent. If possible, while your spouse is still alive, determine whether you would have enough income to stay in your residence if he or she died. If you decide that you would have to move, buy a life insurance policy on your spouse that would provide enough capital to let you stay.

If you want to assume a mortgage to buy a home, you might have difficulty doing so as a widow unless you can show the bank that you have enough assets and income to qualify for the loan. Many widows who depended on their husband's earnings all their lives find that they cannot qualify for loans once their husbands die. By the time you reach your 70s and 80s, you might look into alternative housing options, such as continuing-care communities, which offer independence, as well as easy access to medical care and help around the house.

Divorced. In a divorce, real estate becomes a major point of contention. One spouse must move out of the home, which disrupts his or her life significantly. Major battles in divorce court are fought over which spouse stays and which one goes. If you are the spouse who is forced to move, rent a house or an apartment to re-establish your home. Over time, if your income is high enough, you may be able to buy a home. To qualify for a mortgage, you must prove that you can cover the payments with only your own income and assets. For more information on buying a home, see Chapter 8 on real estate.

Credit. One of the biggest problems facing widows, widowers and divorcees is that they often have not established their own credit histories and records of earnings, which lenders use to assess their ability to repay debts. Chapter 9 discusses credit in detail.

Widowed. Before you are widowed, you might never consider the need to establish your own credit identity. By the time your spouse dies, it is too late to accumulate a history. This is why it is critical for both husband and wife to take out credit cards and other loans in their separate names in their younger years. Each spouse should pay some household bills from his or her own checking account.

Divorced. The same advice holds true if you are divorced. You probably never expected to part ways with your spouse, but if you relied totally on your mate's credit and earnings history during your marriage, you are likely experiencing difficulty now that the marriage has ended. Therefore, each partner should make sure that he or she establishes a separate credit identity, which will see the spouse through in case of a divorce. After a breakup, your income may fall, and it will be more important than ever to have access to credit to tide you over until you are back on your feet financially. Under the Equal Credit Opportunity Act (ECOA), lenders may not discriminate against you because you are divorced, but that doesn't mean they cannot reject your application if you have no credit history or independent sources of income.

If you have trouble finding a bank that will grant you an open-end line of credit, you might establish your creditworthiness by assuming a secured credit line. In this case, you deposit a certain amount of money, such as $500, and thereby receive a $500 credit line. Over time, as you pay your bills responsibly, you may qualify for an unsecured credit line.

If you get into serious trouble with lenders as a widow, widower or divorcee, contact your local chapter of the National Foundation for Consumer Credit (800-388-CCCS). NFCC credit counselors can intervene with lenders on your behalf and help you work out a reasonable repayment schedule.

Cars. The kind of car you drive does not depend on whether you are widowed or divorced. It should be bought or leased based on your transportation needs. Chapter 10 on buying a car discusses the buying-versus-leasing issue.

Widowed. Once you are widowed, you will probably not need as large a car as you did when you drove with your spouse. Nevertheless, it makes little sense to trade in your car for a smaller one unless the car payments become unaffordable. (If you both had cars, you may want to sell one.) If you want to trade in your existing car for a new one, you may have trouble leasing or qualifying for an auto loan if you have not established a credit record and an income stream of your own. Such leases and loans are granted based on a strong credit history and record of steady income. If your spouse was the only one to create such a history, your credit request may be denied. As discussed earlier, you can avoid this problem by establishing your own solid credit history while your spouse is still alive.

Divorced. In a divorce, when only one car exists, one spouse will lose the use of that vehicle. If you're the unlucky one, you will have to buy or lease a car of your own, which may be difficult if your income has been reduced. Therefore, finance an inexpensive, basic model that will get you where you need to go without many frills. You also should make sure to establish a separate credit identity from your spouse during your marriage. Without a solid credit history and record of regular earnings, your application for a car lease or loan will probably be denied. If you are the spouse who keeps the car, reregister and reinsure it in your own name.

Insurance. If you are widowed or divorced, you will probably need all five major types of insurance—car, disability, health, homeowner's and life—depending on your situation. Chapter 11 discusses all five types of insurance in great detail.

Widowed. As long as you own a car, you should have *auto insurance.* If you are widowed, make sure that the auto insurance policy is in your name, not your spouse's. If the policy was purchased in your spouse's name, transfer it to yours. You will need to maintain the standard auto insurance coverages—comprehensive, liability, uninsured motorist and collision. If you own an old car of little value, reduce the collision coverage. To cut your premium costs, qualify for as many discounts as possible. Some of the most common discounts are given for installing antitheft devices and passive restraints like air bags and automatic seat belts; passing a driver education course; and promising to drive fewer than a specific number of miles each year, as set by the insurance company. Many insurers also offer discounts to those older than age 50 who have good driving records.

Disability insurance may be very important to you if you become widowed. If your spouse is disabled and receives disability payments, those payments will probably stop when he or she dies, depriving you of a regular source of income. Your spouse might also receive Social Security disability payments. When he or she dies, these benefits will be changed to survivors benefits once you provide the Social Security Administration with a valid death certificate. Once you turn 65, the disability payments will be converted into Social Security retirement benefits. The Social Security Administration has established many complex rules regarding the amount of disability benefits that widows and widowers receive, depending on their situation and age. For more details, call the Social Security Administration (800-772-1213; www.ssa.gov). To gain an overview of Social Security benefits for widows and widowers, request the brochure, "When You Get Social Security Disability Benefits . . . What You Need To Know."

Disability insurance is vital for widows and widowers who still work. Because you are the only person supporting yourself and any dependent children, you need to be protected in case you become seriously injured or ill. The best way to purchase disability insurance is through your employer though you can also buy it from most life insurance companies. Follow the advice in Chapter 11 on insurance when deciding which kind of policy to buy.

Having access to good *health insurance* is also crucial for widows and widowers. Depending on your spouse's employer's policy, your health insurance premiums may or may not be paid by the employer when your spouse dies. However, under the *Congressional Omnibus Budget Reconciliation Act* (COBRA), you and your dependent children must be permitted to continue group coverage for three years after your spouse dies at the same price your spouse's employer would have paid for coverage, plus a small fee for administration. While you gain the advantage of group rates, you still have to pay the health insurance premium, which you might not have had to do when your spouse was alive. If you cannot obtain coverage through your spouse's employer, try to sign on with a managed care program, a *health maintenance organization* (HMO) or a *preferred provider organization* (PPO) during one of their open enrollment periods. If you can't secure coverage with such an organization, you might have to buy an individual policy through Blue Cross/Blue Shield during their one of open enrollment periods, which can be extremely expensive.

Widows and widowers who are homeowners should carry adequate *homeowner's insurance.* Doing so will probably mean continuing with your existing policy. Make sure that your name, not that of your deceased spouse, is on the policy. Once you have recovered from the emotional trauma of losing your mate, evaluate your homeowner's policy to determine whether it requires updating. The policy may insure possessions that you no longer own, or it may not cover valuables that you have acquired recently. An easy way to tote the worth of your possessions is to take a household inventory using the Household Inventory Worksheet in Chapter 11 on insurance.

Life insurance pays off when you are widowed. The premise behind any kind of life insurance, whether it is a *term* or a *cash-value policy,* is that the surviving spouse will need the insurance proceeds to replace the insured spouse's income. Remember, collect the proceeds on individual policies that covered your spouse, as well as term policies provided by his or her employer.

When you receive the insurance proceeds, invest the money extremely carefully because it must support you for the rest of your life. You may receive the proceeds in a lump sum, in installments for the remainder of your life or in payments for a specific number of years. If you take the lump sum, do not rush into any investment even though you may find several financial advisers eager to tell you how to invest the money in return for fees and commissions. Diversify among several investments, some providing high income and others offering more growth potential. The younger you are when you become widowed, the longer you will live on the insurance money. If you are widowed in your 60s, invest about a third of your portfolio in high-quality stocks or stock mutual funds, which will provide capital growth, as well as current income. Invest the remaining two-thirds in fixed-income instruments, such as CDs, bonds and bond mutual funds, to provide the highest current income with the least risk.

If you have little investment experience, consider buying an *annuity* with the insurance proceeds. This annuity could pay you a fixed monthly amount for the rest of your life so you would not have to worry about investing the money. Compare several insurance companies' payout policies before you settle on an annuity. You can do so easily by consulting a publication such as *Annuity & Life Insurance Shopper* (800-872-6684).

If you are a widow or widower who works and supports children, you also should maintain life insurance. If you died, the insurance proceeds could go either directly to the children or to a trust on the children's behalf. Your dependent children would need the insurance proceeds to support themselves until they finish their education and become self-supporting. Whether you purchase *term* or *cash-value insurance* depends on your age, how high a premium you can afford and whether you need the forced savings and tax shelter provided by a cash-value policy. For widows in their 60s or older, both term and cash-value policies would be extremely expensive, however.

Divorced.   The same advice that applies to widows and widowers holds true for divorcees. Make sure that the *auto insurance* policy is in your name if you receive a car as part of the divorce settlement. Obtain all the standard coverages, and apply for as many discounts as you qualify for. The insurance company cannot discriminate against you by raising your rates or canceling your policy because you are divorced.

If you divorce a disabled spouse, you will no longer receive part of his or her *disability payments.* However, if you work, it is important to purchase adequate disability coverage because you will most likely support yourself. Even if you receive alimony, you probably cannot live comfortably on that money. If you get seriously injured or ill, you will need the income that a disability policy provides. Purchase a policy that is guaranteed renewable and offers an appropriate elimination period—the time you must wait before you begin receiving payments. If payments are delayed three months, for example, make sure that you have accumulated enough emergency savings to tide you over until the checks start flowing. The most inexpensive way to buy disability insurance is through your employer, though you can also buy it from most major life insurance companies.

Divorcees, because they sever most relations with their former spouses, should not expect to have access to their ex-spouses' *health insurance* programs. Divorcees do, however, have rights to receive health insurance coverage under COBRA for 36 months. Try to line up health insurance through your own employer or through any group of which you are a member, such as a trade association. Buying health insurance individually can be extremely expensive and probably is unaffordable if your income has been slashed by your divorce. When negotiating the divorce settlement, try to obtain some provision from your former spouse to pay for health insurance, at least for a transitional period of a year or two.

If you receive your home or apartment as part of the divorce settlement, follow the procedure for *homeowner's insurance* described for widows and widowers. First, remove your ex-spouse's name from the insurance policy. Because your ex-spouse will have carted off many possessions from your home, take a fresh household inventory to assess whether you have adequate insurance coverage. See the Household Inventory Worksheet from Chapter 11. If you rent, purchase a *renter's policy* to cover the replacement cost of your possessions.

Divorcees should re-evaluate their *life insurance* needs. In many cases, only one spouse in a marriage, usually the husband, is covered by a policy aside from that provided by an employer. After a divorce, he probably will remove his ex-wife as the policy's beneficiary. Any children of the marriage will likely remain as beneficiaries, however. If you are a divorced woman with custody of the children, whether or not you work, purchase an insurance policy on your life. If you were to die while your children were young, they would need the life insurance proceeds to get them through school and on the road to self-sufficiency. For pure insurance protection, buy a *term policy*. To build cash value that you might use in retirement, purchase a *cash-value policy,* such as whole, variable or universal life. If your budget is tight, however, you will probably be able to afford only a term policy.

Education.

Widowed. Widows with children may find the task of financing the children's college education overwhelming. It might seem difficult enough to meet current expenses on a reduced income, never mind the tens of thousands of dollars that public or private schools cost. You have two solutions to this dilemma: Increase your savings, or qualify for more loans. If you are widowed when your children are young, you have enough time to start a college savings plan. The more and earlier you save, the easier it will be to pay tuition bills. The best way to start is to enroll in an *automatic investment program,* such as one offered by a mutual fund, or in a *payroll deduction savings bond plan.* You may also want to buy shares in a solid company paying a high dividend, such as a utility, and enroll in the *dividend reinvestment plan* (DRIP), which will compound your principal over time effortlessly and at no cost.

You face a different situation if you become widowed when your children are near college age or already enrolled at a university. Without much accumulated savings, you will have to rely on the many grants, loans and scholarships described in Chapter 12 on how to finance college. With lower income brought on by your status as a widow or widower, you will likely be considered more in financial need than other families and thereby qualify for more generous grants and loans. Nevertheless, you and your children can be burdened by years of interest payments if you take on too many loans. Apply for as many grants as you can find because grant money need not be repaid.

Divorced. If you are a divorcee, with custody of the children, you may be in a situation similar to that of a widow or widower with children. Depending on the terms of the divorce settlement, your ex-spouse may pay part or all of your children's college expenses as part of child support obligations. If your ex-spouse is not able or willing to put the children through school, you will have to fund their education yourself. If your children are young, you have time to build a portfolio by enrolling in an *automatic investment program.* For children near or at college age, you will probably have to rely more on the financial aid and loans outlined in Chapter 12 on financing college. If your income level has dropped significantly because of the divorce, you should be able to qualify for more grants, scholarships and loans.

Taxes.

Widowed. Several rules in the tax code are specially designed for widows and widowers. For tax purposes, a widow or widower is considered unmarried and therefore usually must file his or her return as a single person. If you were widowed in the last two years, however, you may submit a return using the married-filing-jointly status (usually more advantageous than single status) if you meet the following four conditions:

- You continue to maintain a primary home for a dependent child, and you provide at least half of the living costs of that child.
- You are entitled to claim that child as a dependent.
- You could have filed a joint return in the year your spouse died.
- You have not remarried by January 1 of the following tax year. For example, in filing your 1999 tax return, you can use married status if you do not remarry before January 1, 2000.

As the surviving spouse of a marriage that filed jointly, you inherit all the tax liabilities of your marriage. If you have executed proper estate and life insurance planning, your deceased spouse's estate should possess enough assets to pay estate taxes. However, if the estate does not provide enough capital, you must pay the taxes, which could be extremely burdensome, particularly in your time of grief.

If you find it to your advantage, file as head of household once you are widowed. To do so, you must support a dependent child with at least half of his or her living expenses. Your spouse must have died in a year prior to the current tax year. And you must have filed jointly in the year your spouse died. Widows or widowers younger than age 65 who support children on an income of $9,550 or less need not file a tax return. Widows or widowers age 65 and older who support children need not file a return if their income is $10,350 or less.

When your spouse dies, you probably will have to file several tax returns: a *federal estate tax return,* a *state inheritance tax return* in states that impose inheritance taxes and your *personal federal* and *state income tax returns.* You must file an estate tax return if your spouse leaves an estate worth more than $625,000 (rising to $1 million in 2006). Working with an accountant and filing all of these returns are probably the chores you least want to undertake after losing your spouse. However, the returns must be filed according to federal and state rules if you want to avoid penalties.

If you are a widow whose spouse had taken care of most of the family's financial affairs, in general, and taxes, in particular, reread Chapter 13 on the basics of tax planning to learn more about the tax code. After you become more aware of the tax consequences of your actions, you can plan accordingly.

Divorced. Divorcees also face a new tax situation after the divorce becomes final. During the negotiations over terms of the divorce, tax issues must be considered carefully by both spouses, their attorneys and their accountants. Some of the most important issues to be resolved include who will pay alimony and child support and in what amounts, how property will be distributed, who will receive the exemptions for dependent children and how assets from qualified retirement plans such as pensions, 401(k)s and Keoghs will be distributed. Certain IRS rules apply specifically to divorce. For example, transfers of property between a divorcing couple are considered tax-free exchanges as long as they take place within one year of the final divorce decree.

If your divorce decree becomes final in the current tax year, you cannot file your tax return jointly with your ex-spouse. You must pay tax rates of a single individual, which are higher than rates for married couples. However, if you support a child with more than half of his or her living expenses, you can file as a head of household, which is less expensive than filing as a single.

The ex-spouse who makes alimony payments as part of a divorce settlement qualifies for an alimony deduction on his or her return, as long as he or she provides the Social Security number of the ex-spouse receiving the alimony. You can claim this deduction on your Form 1040 even if you do not itemize your return.

The ex-spouse receiving alimony must pay income taxes on it. Taxable alimony is reported on your Form 1040. If applicable, list your ex-spouse's Social Security number on your tax return.

If you are an ex-spouse who left most financial matters, including tax planning and preparation, up to your partner when married, you need to develop an awareness of the tax code. Become familiar with all the deductions, credits, exemptions and other benefits to which you may be entitled by rereading Chapter 13 on the basics of tax planning. You also must learn how to file your own return or at least prepare your own records and find a tax preparer whom you trust.

Retirement.

Widowed. If you are a young widow or widower, retirement planning might seem like your least important priority. And, for the short term, it is because you must first adjust both emotionally and financially to life without your spouse.

However, after this period ends, plan seriously for your retirement years. Complete the worksheets in Chapter 14 on retirement to estimate how much money you will need to live comfortably in retirement and how much you must save each month to collect enough capital to fulfill that goal. Calculate what you might receive from Social Security in the future, counting both retirement and survivors benefits. You can obtain these numbers from the Social Security Administration (800-772-1213; www.ssa.gov).

Next, set up your savings regimen using one of the many *automatic investment programs* offered by mutual funds, banks, stockbrokers and insurance companies. If your employer gives you the opportunity to contribute to a *tax-deferred retirement plan,* such as a salary reduction or profit-sharing plan, take full advantage of the offer. In plans where your employer matches your contributions, invest at least the maximum that is matched. Also, establish a Keogh account if you produce self-employment income, or fund an individual retirement account (IRA) whether or not your contribution is deductible.

If you are widowed while already retired, you confront a different financial situation. If you receive regular income from an annuity, those payments will continue until you die, as long as you and your spouse chose the joint and survivor payout option. However, if your spouse selected the life annuity or term certain option, the annuity payments may stop either right away or within a few years. This is why it is so important to choose an annuity payout option carefully. (For more details, see Chapter 11 on insurance.)

Depending on your age, your spouse's earnings record and whether you have children, you might be eligible for Social Security benefits. You will receive survivors benefits if you are younger than age 60 and support children younger than 16 years old. However, if you are younger than 60 years old but have no children, you will not receive Social Security benefits. Nevertheless, register your spouse's death with the Social Security Administration by supplying a copy of your marriage certificate and the death certificate. You will then be eligible for a funeral expense payment of $225.

Widows and widowers between age 60 and 65 are eligible for survivors benefits from Social Security benefits. However, your monthly check will be less than if you begin receiving benefits at age 65. If your spouse was married to someone else for at least ten years and then divorced, the former spouse is also entitled to receive Social Security benefits on your spouse's earnings record, as long as the ex-spouse did not remarry. At age 65, you are eligible to sign up for Medicare Part A, which covers hospital charges, and Part B, which reimburses doctors' bills and other nonhospital costs.

If your spouse was an armed forces veteran, you might qualify for an additional pension benefit. You may also be eligible to receive reimbursement of burial and funeral expenses from both federal and state veterans programs, as long as you file a claim within two years of your spouse's death.

Beyond the financial aspects of retirement, you must make many decisions about the kind of lifestyle you want. You may find that the home you shared with your spouse for so many years is too large and expensive to maintain. In that case, investigate continuing-care communities or other housing options described in Chapter 14. One of the biggest problems for widows and widowers is loneliness, so choose a community in which you can make friends. You also should plan to pursue hobbies, political causes, social activities, educational opportunities and travel in retirement. Though you may not enjoy participating in these activities as much as you would have with your spouse, make the most of your retirement years.

Divorced. Divorcees should also plan for their retirement. If you divorce at a young age, take the same steps as a young widow. Complete the worksheets in Chapter 14 on retirement to project how much money you will need to retire, and set up a savings program to meet your goal. Enroll in all employer-sponsored retirement savings plans, and set aside as much of your salary as you can afford. Set up your own *Keogh plan* if you earn self-employment income, as well as an *individual retirement account* (IRA). As a divorcee, you need to take these steps even more urgently than a widow or widower because you cannot count on receiving benefits from your ex-spouse's employer-sponsored pension plans, his or her Keogh or any other source that you could tap as a widow or widower. In many cases, retirement plan benefits are considered a marital asset and are divided as part of a divorce settlement. How much of your ex-spouse's benefit assets you receive, if any, depend on many factors, including the competence of your lawyer and which judge handles your case.

You will receive no Social Security benefits based on your former spouse's work record unless you meet several conditions:

- Your marriage must have lasted at least ten years.
- You must be at least 62 years old and unmarried.
- Your ex-spouse must also be at least 62 years old. However, if you have been divorced for at least two years, you can receive benefits even if your ex-spouse is not retired.

Don't feel guilty that the benefits you receive as a divorcee will reduce the benefits of your ex-spouse's current mate. The amount of benefits a divorced spouse receives *has no effect* on what the current spouse gets. To find out how much you deserve in divorcee Social Security benefits, call the Social Security Administration (800-772-1213; www.ssa.gov). Even if you meet the criteria, don't expect the payments to be generous. You certainly will not be able to live comfortably on these benefits alone.

If you do not qualify for Social Security benefits, your total retirement income must come from your own resources. This includes your savings and investment portfolio, IRA and Keogh plans, defined benefit or defined contribution plans sponsored by your employer and annuities. Because many divorcees have not built up all or even some of these assets, they may live a meager retirement existence. This is why it is important to set up your own savings plans during your marriage and, if you have not done so, to start investing soon after your divorce.

As a retired divorcee, you must make certain lifestyle decisions. Depending on what you can afford, you might move into a continuing-care or another retirement community that offers quality health care and social activities. To combat loneliness, engage in various activities, such as hobbies, education, travel and political causes. Because you are no longer married, you cannot rely on your spouse to provide for you, either financially or socially. You must take charge if you are to enjoy your retirement years.

Estate Planning.

Widowed. Once you are widowed, the estate plan you have assembled should kick into action. That's assuming you have done some estate planning. If you have neglected this vital area of your financial life, it will be that much more difficult to re-establish your financial foundation after your spouse's death.

If your spouse is terminally ill, you still have time to write a *will* and set up trusts. The will should spell out who is to inherit which assets and who will serve as executor of your estate. Working with a knowledgeable financial planner or estate planning lawyer, divide your assets between yourself and your spouse to minimize estate taxes. Each person can pass up to $625,000 (rising to $1 million in 2006) worth of assets to beneficiaries free of estate tax. Therefore, balance the ownership of your assets so that both you and your spouse have roughly $625,000 (rising to $1 million in 2006) or less. If your assets exceed $625,000 (rising to $1 million in 2006), establish trusts in your will to pass assets to your children or other people you care about. The will should also appoint a guardian for your children if they are minors. In addition, include in your will a *power of attorney,* which gives someone you trust—like a family friend or lawyer—the right to make important health or financial decisions if you are incapacitated. You might also sign a *living will,* giving a trusted person the right to make decisions about whether you should be kept alive through extreme life-saving measures or allowed to die if you are unable to make those decisions yourself. Keep the will, power of attorney and living will up to date by reviewing it every few years.

If you planned your estate while your mate was alive, you may inherit some assets at his or her death. However, if your assets are significant enough, they might be funneled into a trust, which will pay you income for the rest of your life. The principal in the trust will pass directly to your children or other beneficiaries when you die, thereby avoiding estate taxes. The many kinds of trusts are discussed in Chapter 15 on estate planning. One of the most common trusts used today is the *living trust,* which allows you to sidestep probate court. You move all your assets into the trust while you are living by retitling the ownership certificates. When you die, those assets pass directly to your heirs.

Divorced. Once your divorce is final, you are likely to be cut out of your ex-spouse's will. Make sure that this will is invalidated and destroyed so you can write a new one for yourself. All the assets that you receive from your divorce settlement should be taken out of joint name and placed in yours alone. If those assets total more than $625,000 (rising to $1 million in 2006), you may want to set up trusts through your will to avoid estate taxes. You also need a will to tell a probate court how you want your assets distributed. For more details, consult Chapter 15 on estate planning. To avoid probate court, you may want to write a living trust, which will pass your assets directly to your heirs when you die. You also should name a guardian in your will if you have underage children.

If you remarry after your divorce, estate planning can become extremely complex, especially if your new spouse brings children to the marriage. You might want some of your assets to go to the children from your first marriage, while your new spouse might want assets to go to the children of his or her previous marriage. This may require setting up several trusts to accommodate the needs of a blended family.

Employee Benefits.

Widowed. Your spouse's employer may be an important source of financial support when you are widowed. If the employee benefits department has not yet been notified of your spouse's demise, write a letter informing the department of his or her date of death and Social Security number. Request information about the benefits you should expect to receive and what steps you must take to begin the payments. Chapter 16 explains employee benefits in greater depth.

In most companies, employees are covered by term life insurance amounting to at least one year's salary or, in many cases, double one year's wages. Therefore, if your spouse earned $50,000 annually, you might be eligible for a death benefit of $100,000. In addition to term life insurance, many companies offer an *accidental death benefit policy,* which pays you a lump sum if your spouse dies while traveling on company business.

Many employers also provide a *survivor income plan.* Such a policy pays a regular monthly income to widows or widowers and their dependents who counted on the income generated by the spouse before he or she died. Benefits are based on a percentage of the worker's salary, with a spouse getting up to 30 percent of the employee's pay and children receiving an additional 20 percent. For young children, the plan may pay benefits for as long as 20 years, depending on their needs. However, if you remarry and are financially able to survive without the payments, they usually cease. Survivor income plans are designed to supplement Social Security survivors benefits.

Depending on the employer's benefits plan, you may be eligible to receive pension benefits based on defined benefit and defined contribution plans if your spouse was vested at the time of his or her death. Your spouse may have worked at several companies and become vested in many pension plans during his or her working life, so contact all past employers, as well as the current employer, to receive pension payments. You must choose between receiving the value of a pension in a lump sum or as an annuity in monthly installments for the rest of your life. If you feel able to invest the money wisely, take the lump sum and invest in a diversified portfolio of stocks, bonds and mutual funds that will provide steady income, as well as growth potential. However, if you have little confidence in your investing ability, opt for the annuity, which will relieve you of the responsibility of investing the money and which will ensure stable income for life.

You and your family also are eligible to continue coverage under your spouse's health insurance plan for three years at the same price the employer would have paid, plus a small administrative fee. This continuation is guaranteed under the federal *Congressional Omnibus Budget Reconciliation Act* (COBRA). You will have to pay premiums, which you might not have had to pay when your spouse was alive; however, you will receive group insurance rates. These will be far lower than you could qualify for as an individual.

When an employee has left the payroll, most companies do not offer survivors the rest of the companies' benefits. Therefore, do not expect to participate in flexible spending accounts (FSAs) for dependent or health care expenses, educational scholarships, employee assistance programs, legal services or disability insurance.

Divorced. When you are divorced, do not expect many perks from your ex-spouse's employee benefits package. Your former mate probably removed your name as beneficiary of his or her life insurance policy, and you would not be eligible to receive survivor's income payments unless your divorce decree contains a specific clause stipulating such payments. You also will not receive pension payments once you or your ex-spouse retires. However, you may try to claim part of your ex-spouse's defined contribution plan assets as part of your divorce settlement. You might receive title to some of those assets. More and more states have been granting pension rights to divorcees.

The *Congressional Omnibus Budget Reconciliation Act* (COBRA) guarantees the right to continue health insurance under your ex-spouse's policy for up to three years. Furthermore, your dependent children must continue to be covered under your ex-spouse's health insurance policy, and the premiums must be paid under the same terms as before the divorce. Thus, you will be able to take advantage of group health insurance rates for three years, and your children will be covered at no cost to you. Once the children are no longer minors, they will not be covered by your ex-spouse's policy.

Coverage under COBRA is not automatic, however. You must tell your ex-spouse's employer within 60 days of the date you are notified of your rights that you plan to continue the health insurance policy. If you receive no such notification from the insurance company within a few weeks after the divorce is finalized, inquire further. If you let this 60-day period elapse, you lose your COBRA rights.

If you are divorced and still working, study your employee benefits even more carefully than before, and maximize whatever options your employer provides.

This means you should participate in retirement savings plans, health and disability insurance plans and educational scholarship programs. Chapter 16 explains employee benefit options in detail. Your employer also may offer employee assistance programs, which might help you overcome the emotional and financial turmoil of your divorce. Perhaps you relied on your spouse to look after your employee benefits while you were married. After the divorce, you are responsible for making the most of the benefits that your employer offers.

Conclusion

The lessons in *Everyone's Money Book* can be applied to your particular circumstances, no matter what your age or family situation. I have given you the information you need to take charge of every aspect of your personal finances, both in the 18 chapters of this book and in the "Resources" section at the end of each chapter. Now is your chance to put all of this information into action!

Resources

BOOKS

Child Custody: Building Parenting Agreements That Work, by Mimi Lyster (Nolo Press, 950 Parker St., Berkeley, CA 94710; 510-549-1976; 800-992-6656; www.nolo. com). Step-by-step methods for overcoming obstacles and putting together parenting agreements that everyone—particularly the children—can live with. Has worksheets and fill-in-the-blank custody agreements.

Divorce and Money: How To Make the Best Financial Decisions During Divorce, by Violet Woodhouse and Victoria Felton-Collins (Nolo Press, 950 Parker St., Berkeley, CA 94710; 510-549-1976; 800-992-6656; www.nolo.com). A step-by-step guide to dividing such major assets as family businesses, homes, investments and pensions in a way that is fair to both spouses involved in a divorce. Provides information on setting alimony and child support. Includes worksheets, charts, formulas and tables to figure out settlements.

The Divorce Decisions Workbook: A Planning and Action Guide, by Marjorie L. Engel (McGraw-Hill, Order Dept., 860 Taylor Station Rd., Blacklick, OH 43004; 800-722-4726; www.mcgraw-hill.com). Covers the four key decision areas involved in a divorce: financial, legal, practical and emotional. Provides worksheets for each.

The Dollars and Sense of Divorce, by Judith Briles, Edwin Schilling and Carol Ann Wilson (Dearborn Financial Publishing, 155 N. Wacker Dr., Chicago, IL 60606; 312-836-4400; 800-322-8621; www.dearborn.com). Explains what you need to know if you are contemplating divorce. Describes how to start the process, choose an attorney, gather documents and maintain emotional balance. Helps parents deal with child custody issues. Teaches you to navigate the divorce system successfully.

The Financial Power of Attorney Workbook: Who Will Handle Your Finances If You Can't?, by Shae Irving (Nolo Press, 950 Parker St., Berkeley, CA 94710; 510-549-1976; 800-992-6656; www.nolo.com). Provides step-by-step instructions showing people how they can give another person the legal authority to handle their financial matters if they are unable to do so for themselves. Includes all necessary power of attorney forms and a floppy disk with the forms on it.

The Living Together Kit, by Toni Ihara and Ralph Warner (Nolo Press, 950 Parker St., Berkeley, CA 94710; 510-549-1976; 800-992-6656; www.nolo.com). Provides a written agreement covering the ownership of property, particularly real estate, wills and parenthood for unmarried people living together. Offers sample agreements, forms and instructions for most situations such couples will face.

Love, Marriage & Money: Understanding and Achieving Financial Compatibility Before—and After—You Say "I Do," by Gail Liberman and Alan Lavine (Dearborn Financial Publishing, 155 N. Wacker Dr., Chicago, IL 60606; 312-836-4400; 800-322-8621; www.dearborn.com). Explains how to integrate financial considerations into a successful marriage. Describes money rules during dating, buying wedding rings, joint versus separate bank accounts, prenuptial agreements, buying homes together and the finances of having children.

On Your Own: A Widow's Passage to Emotional and Financial Well-Being, by Alexandra Armstrong and Mary R. Donahue (Dearborn Financial Publishing, 155 N. Wacker Dr., Chicago, IL 60606; 312-836-4400; 800-322-8621; www.dearborn.com). Covers the financial and emotional needs of widows.

Your Wealthbuilding Years: Financial Planning for 18- to 38-Year-Olds, by Adriane G. Berg (Random House, 400 Hahn Rd., Westminster, MD 21157; 800-733-3000; www.randomhouse.com). A practical guide aimed at young people wanting to get their finances organized.

PAMPHLET

Staying Independent: Planning for Financial Independence in Later Life (Consumer Information Center, Pueblo, CO 81009; 719-948-3334; www.pueblo.gov). An inexpensive brochure produced by IDS, a financial services company that helps you plan for your later years. Covers budgeting and deciding whether to relocate or stay in your current home.

TRADE ASSOCIATIONS

American Academy of Matrimonial Lawyers (150 N. Michigan Ave., Suite 2040, Chicago, IL 60601; 312-263-6477; www.aaml.org). A group of lawyers specializing in matrimonial issues, such as divorce and child custody. Will refer you to a qualified lawyer near your home if you have matrimonial legal problems.

Association for Children for Enforcement of Support (2260 Upton Ave., Toledo, OH 43606; 419-472-6609; 800-537-7072; www.childsupport/aces.org). Educates divorced parents on how to locate ex-spouses who are delinquent in their child support payments and explains how to collect the money due. Offers a book and videotape, *How To Collect Child Support,* by Executive Director Geraldine Jensen.

National Child Support Enforcement Association (Hall of States, 444 N. Capitol St., N.W., Suite 414, Washington, DC 20001; 202-624-8180; www.ncsea.org). A group of professionals in the child support field. Can locate a professional to help you collect delinquent child support.

National Displaced Homemakers' Network (1625 K St., N.W., Suite 300, Washington, DC 20006; 202-467-6346). Provides support and education for homemakers who are divorced or widowed.

Stepfamily Association of America (650 J St., Suite 205, Lincoln, NE 68508-1834; 402-477-7837; 800-735-0329; www.stepfam.org). Provides education and support for stepfamilies and works to create a more positive image for stepfamilies. Supports local chapters across the country. Publishes a newsletter called *Stepfamilies* that sometimes deals with the financial issues facing divorced and remarried couples. Will send for a nominal charge a copy of its *Catalog of Resources,* which lists 60 books on topics of interest to stepfamilies, such as joint custody and second marriages.

Women Work! (1625 K St., N.W., Suite 300, Washington, DC 20006; 202-467-6346; 800-235-2732; www.womenwork.org). Provides support and education for homemakers who are divorced and widowed. Offers publications, including "Domestic Violence, Employment and Self-Sufficiency" and "Substance Abuse, Job Training and Self-Sufficiency." Also publishes a newsletter called *Network News.*

FEDERAL GOVERNMENT REGULATORS

Administration for Children and Families, Office of Child Support Enforcement (370 L-Enfant Promenade, S.W., Washington, DC 20447; 202-401-9373; www.acf.dhhs.gov). Helps locate parents who do not make their required child support payments. Has access to the employment and income records of such scofflaw parents who neglect their duties to their children. Offers a book titled *Giving Hope and Support to America's Children: A Handbook on Child Support Enforcement.*

Appendix
The *Money* Magazine
Small Investor Index

For years, large institutional investors have used a variety of indexes—including the Dow Jones Industrial Average and the Standard & Poor's 500 Index—to benchmark their performances. But until *Money* magazine created its Small Investor Index in 1988, you, the small investor, had no equivalent to determine how you were doing against other individual investors.

I was very much involved in creating the index in the first place, and I wrote a weekly "Small Investor Index" column that appeared in hundreds of newspapers for several years. The Index continues to appear in *Money* magazine every month in the Wall Street department. I used to talk about the index on "NBC News at Sunrise" program each Tuesday morning, though lately I comment on many other topics, including the economy and the outlook for stocks, bonds and other investments.

The *Money* Magazine Small Investor Index quite simply combines all the major investments discussed in Chapters 2 through 8 into one portfolio. It allows you to determine how each element is performing and what return the typical investor's overall portfolio is achieving. Following are the ten elements that compose the index:

Stocks have three components: (1) New York Stock Exchange listed stocks; (2) American Stock Exchange and Nasdaq stocks; and (3) stock mutual funds. The mutual funds category includes all types of stock funds, including aggressive growth, growth, growth and income, equity-income and balanced.

Bonds have three components: (4) taxable bonds, which include government, U.S. savings, corporate and foreign bonds; (5) municipal bonds; and (6) bond mutual funds, which include national and single-state municipal, government, mortgage-backed, corporate, foreign and junk bond funds.

Cash has two components: (7) certificates of deposit (CDs), which include CDs of all maturities at banks and savings and loans; and (8) money funds, which include money-market mutual funds, bank money-market deposit accounts, passbook savings accounts and NOW checking accounts.

Two other components complete the Money Magazine Small Investor Index: (9) gold, which includes gold coins and bars, gold-mining shares and gold mutual funds; and (10) real estate, which includes real estate investment trusts (REITs) and real estate limited partnerships (RELPs). Individual homes and rental real estate are excluded because they are impossible to value on a weekly uniform national basis.

The *Money* Magazine Small Investor Index compiles the most recent individual investor holdings in each of the ten categories and computes the latest weekly total return (price change plus dividends and interest) for each. The index then weights those returns by the amount of money individuals hold in the assets. So the more of an asset people hold, the more important it becomes in determining the index's return. For example, if Americans hold 40 percent of their typical portfolio in cash, the weekly return from cash gets a 40 percent weighting in the index.

To determine the dollar amount of the average individual's portfolio, *Money* takes the total assets represented by the ten categories—which amounts to trillions of dollars—and divides it by the Census Department's latest figures for the U.S. adult population older than age 21. In recent years, this calculation has resulted in an average portfolio between $40,000 and $80,000 per individual investor. Most individuals have far less than that amount, and many have more, but this represents the national average for all investors.

The tables and chart shown in Figure Appendix.1 report several pieces of information that can help your investment planning. The table titled "Latest changes for each asset" recounts how much each of the ten assets rose or fell since the beginning of the year, in the latest week and in the last 52 weeks. At the beginning of each year, the index is recalibrated to 100 so you can tell at any point in the year how the overall index is doing and how each of the ten components is faring year to date. If the index or one of the components stands at 110, for example, this means that it is up 10 percent so far this year. If it stands at 90, it is down 10 percent.

The other table, titled "Where average small investors have their money now," reports how investors move their capital from one asset to another. The percentages shown compare the latest week with the same week a year ago. In this case, you can see that the amount of money allocated to CDs has fallen, while the flow into equity and bond funds has risen sharply.

The chart illustrates what has happened to the Small Investor Index over the last 52 weeks. By scanning the graph, you can tell immediately whether the trend generally has been up or down. The text that accompanies the tables and graph discusses where small investors like you have been moving their money lately and whether the strategies are sound.

Figure Appendix.1
The *Money* Magazine Small Investor Index

The Money Small Investor Index

Small Investors Pile Into Europe

AUGUST 9—Sensing opportunity in Europe's latest currency crisis, U.S. small investors are continuing to pour millions of dollars into mutual funds that invest abroad, according to data gathered for MONEY magazine's Small Investor Index.

Last week, as Europe's finance ministers dramatically loosened the ties between most continental currencies and the German mark, U.S. investors directed $966 million to international stock and bond funds, accelerating a year-long trend. They were quickly rewarded: International stock funds jumped 2.4 percent for the week, and global bond funds climbed 1 percent.

Analysts attribute the flood of cash partly to small investors' expectation that European interest rates will fall in the aftermath of the currency turmoil. After a similar exchange-rate upheaval last September, Britain's finance minister allowed the value of the pound to fall. The result: British interest rates declined, lifting stock and bond prices.

Gary Kreps, head of fixed-income investing for G.T. Global, predicts that rates will drop across the continent this time. "Countries like France and the United Kingdom have hit 30-year inflation lows, and yet interest rates are still high," he says. "As they come down, bond and equity prices will move higher."

Small investors seem to have got the message. Mutual fund giant Fidelity, for example, reports that its 10 international funds averaged 250 new accounts a day in July, up from 50 a day in March; the funds took in a net $210 million in July, vs. $37 million in March.

Last week, the Small Investor Index, which tracks the typical individual's holdings, rose $35 to a record $46,911. Stocks gained $20, while bonds returned $29. A sell-off in gold cost small investors $21.

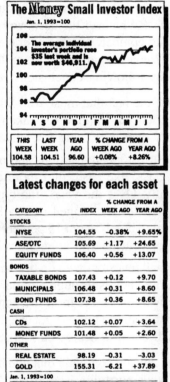

The Money Small Investor Index
Jan. 1, 1993=100

The average individual investor's portfolio rose $35 last week and is now worth $46,911.

THIS WEEK	LAST WEEK	YEAR AGO	% CHANGE FROM A	
			WEEK AGO	YEAR AGO
104.58	104.51	96.60	+0.06%	+8.26%

Latest changes for each asset

CATEGORY	INDEX	% CHANGE FROM A	
		WEEK AGO	YEAR AGO
STOCKS			
NYSE	104.55	−0.38%	+9.65%
ASE/OTC	105.69	+1.17	+24.65
EQUITY FUNDS	106.40	+0.56	+13.07
BONDS			
TAXABLE BONDS	107.43	+0.12	+9.70
MUNICIPALS	106.48	+0.31	+8.60
BOND FUNDS	107.38	+0.36	+8.65
CASH			
CDs	102.12	+0.07	+3.64
MONEY FUNDS	101.48	+0.05	+2.60
OTHER			
REAL ESTATE	98.19	−0.31	−3.03
GOLD	155.31	−6.21	+37.89

Jan. 1, 1993=100

Sources: *Bank Rate Monitor,* the Federal Reserve, Investment Company Institute, Lehman Bros., Lipper Analytical Services, Merrill Lynch, *Money Fund Report,* Morgan Stanley Capital International, National Association of Real Estate Investment Trusts, Prudential Asset Management, Standard & Poor's, Robert Stanger & Co., World Gold Council

Where average small investors have their money now					
	Current	Year Ago		Current	Year Ago
NYSE	21.34%	21.48%	Bond funds	7.54%	6.46%
ASE/OTC	6.74	6.78	CDs	13.38	15.97
Equity funds	7.89	5.86	Money funds	24.46	24.54
Taxable bonds	9.77	9.82	Real estate	0.87	0.80
Municipals	7.31	7.75	Gold	0.70	0.54

Source: *Money* Small Investor Index, August 9, 1993.

You have several ways to use the Small Investor Index as a benchmark. On the performance side, compare the returns you earn on stocks, bonds, cash, gold and real estate, both individually and as a group, with the average investor's returns. Over the long term, the typical portfolio has yielded about 9 to 10 percent a year, which is quite good considering that most people keep between 30 and 40 percent of their money in extremely safe cash instruments.

You can also use the index to compare your allocation of assets with the current division of assets among the ten asset categories. You might find that you are more conservative than the average investor, with more of your money in cash instruments, or you may discover that you are more aggressive, with more of your money in stocks. Whatever the case, you will be better able to assess the amount of risk you take compared to the average U.S. individual investor.

Because *Money* has covered the small investor's portfolio for several years, it has come to the following conclusions:

- Despite the fact that most Wall Street brokers find small investors to be an inexperienced, gullible lot, taken en masse, their portfolios perform admirably over time, with a relatively low amount of risk.

- Small investors are cautious and move their money from one conservative asset class, like cash, into more aggressive ones, like stocks and bonds, gradually. Over the years, the typical individual's portfolio allocation to cash vehicles has ranged from a low of about 30 percent to a high of 45 percent; to bonds, from 15 percent to 25 percent; to stocks, from 28 percent to 55 percent; and to gold and real estate, from 1 percent to 2 percent.

- The small investors who do best are those who consistently put money into stocks and bonds through a dollar-cost-averaging program. The losers are those who try to get in at the bottom of a market and get out at the top. Invariably, market timers get caught up in the enthusiasm of a rising market and sell out in a depressed market, when they should do the opposite.

No longer can you complain that you have no benchmark for comparison when you evaluate your portfolio. The *Money* Magazine Small Investor Index is your ticket to a better understanding of how you rate as an investor.

Index